ROLLING STONE
ROCK
ALMANAC

THE CHRONICLES OF ROCK & ROLL

ROLLING STONE
ROCK
ALMANAC

THE CHRONICLES OF ROCK & ROLL

By the Editors of Rolling Stone
Foreword by Peter Wolf

A ROLLING STONE PRESS BOOK

COLLIER BOOKS
Macmillan Publishing Company
New York

COLLIER MACMILLAN PUBLISHERS
London

ACKNOWLEDGMENTS

The editors of Rolling Stone Press would like to thank the following people, whose help, cooperation and knowledge were essential to the creation of this book.

We would like to thank Philip Bashe, Ken Braun, Wayne King and Michael Shore for researching, compiling and writing the individual entries. Michael Shore also wrote the book's introduction and the essays that precede each year. Steve Futterman and Holly George provided additional research and chart information.

For help in preparing the manuscript, we thank Janis Bultman of Rolling Stone Press and her staff: Betsy Aidem, Renee Belisle, Kaija Berzins, George Hagen and Patti Munter.

The writers and editors wish to acknowledge the New York Public Library for the Performing Arts and the Port Washington Public Library for their help in obtaining rare periodicals. We also thank the countless performers, publicists, managers, writers and collectors who answered questions and provided assistance. And we would like to especially thank Peter Wolf and Michael Ochs for their contributions to this book.

We thank our editors: Patrick Filley at Macmillan for his support and encouragement, and Patty Romanowski, Sarah Lazin and Jann S. Wenner at Rolling Stone Press.

Vintage Photographs Courtesy The Michael Ochs Archives

Macmillan Publishing Company
866 Third Avenue, New York, N.Y. 10022
Collier Macmillan Canada, Inc.

Library of Congress Cataloging in Publication Data
Main entry under title:

The Rolling Stone rock almanac.

   "A Rolling Stone Press Book."
   Includes indexes.
   1. Rock music—Dictionaries.   2. Rock music—Bio-bibliography.   I. Rolling stone.
ML102.R6R66   1983   784.5'4'009   83-16178
ISBN 0-02-081320-1

First Collier Books Edition 1983

10 9 8 7 6 5 4 3 2 1

Printed in the United States of America

The Rolling Stone Rock Almanac is also published in a hardcover edition by Macmillan Publishing Company.

"Such a Night," by Lincoln Chase © 1954 Shelby Singleton Music Inc.

"Work With Me Annie," by Hank Ballard © 1954 Armo Music Publishing Co., renewed and assigned to Ft. Knox Music Co.

"Speedo," by Navarro. (No publishing information.)

CONTENTS

FOREWORD

When I was growing up in New York, every Saturday I would take the subway down to Times Square, to a wonderful record store right outside the subway station under the old Times Square Building. The store was very small, narrow and always crowded. And on special days, singing groups would perform live radio broadcasts. My friends and I would gather on the subway steps outside and trade records, magazines, photos and any information about rock & roll—the music we loved and so very much needed.

In those days, newspapers ran lots of articles about this new music. They were generally all against it. Some articles dealt with the idea that rock & roll was "the devil's music," others claimed it was the cause of juvenile delinquency. They even went so far as to print the results of so-called scientific tests in which laboratory animals were driven mad after being exposed to this new sound. Television comedians would make fun of it and portray rock performers and their fans as some pathetic joke, a trend that was bound to pass in time—the sooner the better, as far as they were concerned.

But they were all so very wrong, and yet how could they understand? Rock & roll wasn't made for Mom and Pop. It was born out of the poverty of the South and the ghettos of the North. It moved into the garages and basements of suburbia, to the beaches of California and even crossed oceans. It had its own codes; its own language; its own style of dress, hair and, of course, dance. It was, and still is today, a music that at its best challenges, defies and never stops searching.

This book is about rock & roll—the people and events, the origins and history of a music that is still very much alive today. It's the story of the music that shook the world.

Peter Wolf

Boston, 1983

PREFACE

The Rolling Stone Rock Almanac is a chronological history of rock & roll as it happened. Beginning with January 1954, the *Almanac* presents day-by-day accounts of rock & roll's development, with each year introduced by an overview essay. Each month also includes charts listing the Number One U.S. pop and R&B singles and pop LPs, and the Number One British pop singles and LPs.

We began our work on this book by researching all the available sources including newspapers, periodicals, books, fan magazines, trade publications, press releases, press files, records, liner notes, televised and broadcast interviews, and films. Though we sought corroboration among our best sources, we anticipate future revisions and welcome all comments, suggestions, additional information, and corrections. These should be addressed to Rolling Stone Press, 745 Fifth Avenue, New York, New York 10151.

Through our research, we noted several irregularities in the documentation and wish to call attention to them here. One of the biggest obstacles to finding correct information on record release dates, especially in the Fifties, was that many of the companies have gone out of business or have destroyed their files. We documented the first dates that a record was reviewed in the trades; in most cases the actual release preceded or followed that date by less than a week. Our intention is to give the reader some idea of what other records were being released simultaneously. As for the record charts themselves, the American chart positions are all from *Billboard*'s Hot 100 chart or the equivalent, the Top LPs chart or its equivalent, and the R&B chart or its equivalent. Over the years, *Billboard* has published numerous charts; in the Fifties, for example, there were separate charts for retail sales, airplay, and jukebox play. Our Number One singles are taken from a chart that used the averages from the other three charts. After August 10, 1958, the Number One single is the top-charting single on *Billboard*'s Hot 100 chart. In addition, *Billboard* also published an R&B chart, which initially provided information on the so-called "race records." Over the years, the R&B and pop charts have at times been strikingly similar and at others highly divergent. The R&B charts are really the "other half" of the pop charts for several reasons, the most important being that many of rock & roll's most important stars—James Brown, among others—never had a Number One pop hit despite having had perhaps so many as a dozen R&B Number Ones. In addition, during certain periods, R&B records actually outsell similarly ranked pop singles and although they may never cross over as successfully to the pop chart, their influence on the pop hits is almost without exception more pronounced than pop's influence on R&B. For reasons unknown—but perhaps because for a time the songs on both the pop and R&B charts were similar—*Billboard* discontinued the R&B chart in late November 1963 only to resume it again in January 1965. As with the early pop charts, there have been several other charts (disco, black airplay), and the R&B chart has been renamed a few times (soul, currently black). Although

Rhythm & Blues may seem a misnomer, we have continued to label this chart R&B to avoid confusion. Unlike the singles charts, which were published weekly, the LP chart appearances were erratic and confusing. Suffice to say, it wasn't until 1963 that *Billboard* inaugurated a Top LPs chart. Previous to that there were several charts including, for a time, one for stereo and another for monaural releases. Charts that did appear sometimes did so only once a month; in these cases we have simply repeated a title for each of the subsequent weeks. That chart, however, was based solely on sales, but given the facts that LP sales represented only a fraction of all record sales for many years and that in one year as few as four titles could hit Number One (1955), it is virtually impossible that any other album could have "slipped" in to the top position for just a week or two and not have been documented. All U.S. record positions were taken from *Billboard* magazine and Joel Whitburn's Record Research. Record Research currently publishes a wide array of chart books and supplements, including the pop, R&B, and country singles and LP charts as well as other chart information. These books and supplements are available from Record Research, Inc., P.O. Box 206, Menomonee Falls, Wisconsin 53051

British chart positions from 1954 through 1960 are from *Record Mirror,* one of Britain's first music-trade papers. From 1960 on, they are from *New Musical Express,* a weekly general-readership music publication. Because of irregularities in publishing schedules and the constant discrepancy between the publication dates of American and British sources, all Almanac charts are labeled "week ending" and dated seven days apart. In most instances the chart position listed derives from a chart published three or fewer days before the date on the chart. Leap years, holidays, and other abberations (double year-end issues that include December's last two weeks) have thus been converted and in the case of double issues, we have assumed that the same title was ranked at Number One for both weeks.

All other dates are self-explanatory. Keep in mind, however, that there are what seem to be discrepancies between dates given by American and British publications. After a lot of research, we discovered that these discrepancies most often involved events that occurred either a few hours before or after midnight and were the result of the 5-hour time difference between London and New York. We have used the U.S. date throughout.

Gold and platinum dates and figures are based on information from the Recording Industry Association of America (R.I.A.A.), the organization that certifies these awards. All information regarding the Grammy Awards is taken from materials published by the National Academy of Recording Arts and Sciences, the organization that presents the Grammy.

Patricia Romanowski, Editor

INTRODUCTION

What is rock & roll?

There are as many answers to that question as there are rock performers, rock styles, rock fans and rock critics—and there are more than enough of each to go around. Rock & roll has only been with us a comparatively short time—barely thirty years. Yet during its turbulent history, rock & roll has produced thousands of performers, millions of records and many millions of fans. It's evolved from a naive aberration to a self-conscious revolution to an established entertainment institution. Despite that, it stands apart from all other entertainment institutions and cultural forms. Rock & roll was the first, and remains the only, form of popular culture that by its nature questions, challenges and directly changes social convention. And through it all, still retains, remakes and rekindles its revolutionary impulse. There's nothing else like it: it is both music and message, attitude and politics, escapist and confrontational, and it touches and is touched by just about every other kind of popular, semipopular and even obscure form of culture there is.

Rock & roll, perhaps above all else, is an ongoing series of paradoxical, contradictory reactions. It is the embodiment of the dialectic at the root of American civilization: good versus evil, restraint versus urgency, decorum versus passion, repression versus liberation, convention versus rebellion. Rock is a metaphor for America's own variegated, volatile melting pot; it's a mirror, showing us where and how we are and what we're up to.

Rock is also something of a mirror of the American experience, with its dialectical polarities of ideal and reality. The American ideal is high-minded—a new country and a new frontier to be conquered by individualistic ingenuity and willfulness. The reality is frequently less inspiring. Rock established itself as an international phenomenon, just as America, once it had conquered its own geographical boundaries, set its sights on the world. But rock & roll could only have come from America; Elvis Presley and especially Jerry Lee Lewis were the embodiment of classic American archetypes: Elvis, the outlaw-as-hero; Jerry Lee, the man torn and driven by the sacred-profane dialectic. If it weren't for the American melting pot and its ideal-reality contradictions—and especially if it weren't for the addition of that crucial ingredient to the melting pot, the importation of African slaves to the "land of the free" less than a hundred years after American won its independence—there could not have been rock & roll.

Black Africans brought something new and different to an America made up of Old World expatriates: something exotic and non-Western, something both fearsome and attractive. All Americans were, in a sense, rootless, or at least *uprooted* and transplanted, but America's frontier, can-do spirit superseded residual feelings of alienation. But it was something else again for the antebellum black slaves: they, too, were uprooted and transplanted, but they were generally reviled by the inhabitants of their new homeland. Before the Civil War, Southern plantation owners banned the use of native African instruments. The slaves preserved their tradition through the secret use of essentials: the voice, the drum and the body. Even after the Civil War, of course, the lot of Afro-Americans hardly improved. But they preserved some of their culture—and inevitably that merged with the dominant white culture to form a new culture. Over time, and by degree, both pure and diluted forms of Afro-American expression found their ways to white audiences. There were the medicine and tent shows and the minstrel shows. The latter—the more adulterated, white-sanctioned form—became an instant sensation with whites in America and around the civilized Western world. Soon, whites were donning blackface make-up to do their own versions of minstrelsy—perhaps the first example of establishment co-optation of a culture and entertainment medium too pure (i.e., dangerous) in its original manifestation.

As time went by, such phenomena continued: white and black cultures continued to evolve in a series of overlapping, parallel developments, one influencing the other and so on. Thus was set the pattern of growth that rock & roll itself would follow. Early in the twentieth century came the seminal developments of ragtime, blues and jazz. Ragtime added black vitality to traditional Euroclassical forms, and it showed white America for the first time that blacks, such as Scott Joplin, possessed as much refined "talent" in the acceptable sense as whites.

Ragtime, however, arrived just before the crucial cusp of modern history, where technology and culture and art combined to cross-pollinate ever more furiously. Jazz was the first popular music form spread far and wide through the new recording technology, and it demonstrated the vivid ways in which Afro-Americans redefined and revivified popular music. The blacks "jazzed it up," and though subsequent history makes us dismiss early doo-wacka-doo jazz as quaint and corny, it must be remembered that at the time jazz was a scandal. It was dirty, raunchy, exciting dance music, and it sounded crazy and dangerous to most whites. But the jazz-age babies—white American youth—took right to it, despite what their parents said. Or maybe *because* of what their parents said. There it was: youth rebelling against adult convention in search of the kind of enjoyment and release that could only come from black-rooted music.

Jazz continued to follow the pattern that rock & roll would repeat: from scandalous beginnings it grew to be accepted and created by whites as well as blacks; it became an entertainment institution, but managed to retain some of its power to challenge established ideology and provide both release and a means of cultural identification for that great American archetype, the outsider, the outlaw, and the rebel. Remember the hipster cults and Beatnik romanticists of the bebop era. But also remember the swing era, when a more homogenized form of jazz spoke to and for *everyone,* the same way certain styles of rock & roll would.

While jazz was beginning, another Afro-American musical form that had already been around some time was coming into its own: the blues. Blues, too, was a revolution. Musically, it was based around the idea of "blue notes," which were essentially regular, acceptable notes played in a deliberately rough, imprecise way that made them new notes. It was by playing blue notes, and by applying African rhythmic directness and vitality to them, that such jazz musicians as Louis Armstrong and Coleman Hawkins were able to reshape, reclaim and revolutionize the sound and feeling of American music.

But beyond the blue notes, blues music itself was dark and foreboding. Its form precisely fit its content, for blues was the first and purest musical expression of Afro-American alienation, the nigh-existential torment of being persecuted strangers in a strange land, of being nearly homeless in a homeland away from home. Blues didn't present an outright challenge to the established order of things. Rather, it served as both commentary on and release from a seemingly intolerable situation. The blues was an outsider-culture speaking to and about itself—again, just like rock & roll would be. As the late great bluesman Muddy Waters once sang, "The blues had a baby, and they called it rock & roll."

The term of gestation was comparatively long—at least thirty years, dating from the first blues recordings to the first explosion of rock & roll, and much longer than that considering that blues was around long before it got recorded. The influence of blues on pop led to jazz. Blues and Dixieland jazz influenced white country music to form one of the first mutant-fusion hybrids, Western Swing, which would go on to influence country-boogie and, subsequently, rockabilly. Ragtime, meanwhile, had led, through James P. Johnson and Fats Waller and others, to stride piano, which led to boogie-woogie, which influenced jazz and pop and country. Southern bluesmen moved to the big cities up north, and urban blues were born. They became electric blues and merged with the horn-section legacy of swing big bands to produce rhythm & blues.

By the Fifties, the recording industry and the music scene on the whole had fermented dozens of black and white popular and semipopular genres. It was possible for the arbiters of sanctioned taste to make sure that blues and R&B and the like were kept in their places. So, we had pop records, which it was okay for anyone to buy; and we had other records—jazz, blues, R&B, etc.—that it was *not* okay for a white kid to buy, even though white kids may have liked black music when they heard it. *Especially* because of that attraction, black music was still considered dangerous in its unadulterated form. The pop music that prevailed was innocuous, coy and squeaky-clean, primly and properly dressed.

But it did *not* reflect what the growing mass of American youth felt. The shadow of the A-bomb had been cast; for the first time, a generation was growing up with the full knowledge that life as they knew it could end in seconds. Adult American culture responded by providing escapism. The country seemed to be sleepwalking; or maybe it was a big luxury car cruising down the road to somewhere-nowhere on automatic pilot. Rock & roll simply *had* to happen when it did, the way it did.

The rock & roll eruption was immediately presaged by a big jump in the sales of black R&B to the young, white record-buying public. Then came the first outbreak—Elvis Presley, Little Richard, Chuck Berry, Jerry Lee Lewis, the Coasters, *et al.* Rock & roll was essentially little more than exuberant, nonsensical kidding around. But what was revolutionary about "Hound Dog" and "Tutti Frutti" and "Maybellene" and "Whole Lotta Shakin'" and "Yakety Yak" was precisely that spirit of crazed abandonment and the raucous sound that went with it. They were loud, irreverent, celebratory snorts in the face of the pop establishment's domesticated, wistful sanctity.

More than that, rock & roll was revolutionary in another way. By the Fifties, the music industry had developed a strictly and rigidly demarcated system to delineate genres and audiences: there was pop, there was rhythm & blues (originally called "race records") and there was a country & western (originally "hillbilly music")—and never the twain should meet, commercially speaking. Nor *did* they meet until rock & roll came along. Rock & roll records were the first to simultaneously top the pop, R&B and C&W charts. Not only was rock & roll changing the way music sounded and felt, but the way it was bought and sold as well.

The Beats had made similar waves just before the rise of rock & roll, but they were a fringe movement, a bohemian cult. No matter how ahead of their time the Beats were, with their romanticized identification with and adoption of black subcultural style, they were too radically adventurous and self-consciously intellectual to be the mass phenomenon that rock & roll would be. Where the Beats, with their poetry and bebop, were cerebral, nearly high-brow, and rather elitist, rock & roll was not only gloriously nonsensical, but physical, down-to-earth, *people's* music.

And rock & roll sold—a fact even anti-rock & roll segments of the American establishment could not overlook. Commercial exploitation—and the attendant potential to remake youth culture into an acceptable adult image and sell it back to the kids—proved effective. Thus, in near-instant response to the first rock & roll explosion, came the innocuous, adult-groomed teen idols. Because the rock & roll audience was not yet nearly self-conscious enough to notice or care about the difference, it made the teen idols stars, too. But it still kept buying the real, dangerous thing as well. And the real, dangerous thing kept coming.

And so, here was another crucial dialectic that has always been at the root of rock & roll as a socioeconomic as well as sociocultural phenomenon: ideology versus commercialism, pure expression versus adulterated exploitation. Right at the dawn of rock & roll, there was Sam Phillips, dreaming of Elvis Presley and declaring, "If I could just find a white man with the Negro sound and the Negro feel, I could make a billion dollars." There you have it in a nutshell. Later on, in the mid-Sixties, Elvis' manager, Col. Tom Parker, reflected, "When I first met Elvis, he had a million dollars' worth of talent. Now he has a million dollars."

By that time, rock & roll had moved on with the times, and Elvis had all but ceased to be a vital rock & roll force. But Elvis *had* promoted the crucial musical Americanization of the free world, and the seeds he sowed began to sprout. It was the time of the Beatles and the British Invasion—

further proof that the American ideals and realities embodied in rock & roll resonated around the world, and that rock was now an international phenomenon and was here to stay. But there was also proof that big business hovered like a specter over every rock & roll development. Take, for example, the first American music-industry trade-magazine ad for the Rolling Stones, who were at that time (1964) considered the nastiest and most dangerous rock band in the world. The ad read, in part: "They're young! They're rebels! They're outrageous! *They sell!*" (emphasis ours). Again, rebellion as a commodity.

As time passed, rock & roll became *rock*—a world unto itself that still spoke to the world at large, with an audience vast and variegated enough to support a welter of semipopular styles, movements and performers, from vanguard bohemian cults to superstars. Rock became important; it was seen and heard as poetry and politics. And the rock audience became a serious, self-consciously antiestablishment counterculture. In the politically turbulent Sixties, rock frequently anticipated and sparked social change as often as it mirrored it.

But as rock grew in size and scope, those old social-dialectical battle lines increasingly were drawn *within* the rock world, too. The music and its culture became divided and divisive—between revolutionaries and teenyboppers, the serious and the facetious, psychedelia and bubble-gum, and so on. The music took on pretensions to art, while there arose a cadre of articulate rock fans, the rock critics, who wrote in rock-culture journals and derided arty pretension in music while defending the unself-consciousness of early rock & roll and those artists that the critics saw as still preserving roots-rock's folkish, utilitarian tenets. Yet, paradoxically, these same critics introduced academic pretension to rock culture. And, as often as not, the music the critics hated sold better than the music the critics hailed.

Not so ironically, as rock became institutionalized, its audience became conservative and reactionary. Now it was merely a matter of which style would win the latest fashion-and-music war. Thus, the "Disco Sucks" movement. Thus, the spectacle of punk rock, which negated itself almost at its inception, only to eventually filter into the mainstream as denatured new wave and to spawn the fringe-cult of post-punk "hard-core" rock. And thus, Neil Young's eulogy for punk, as the Seventies became the Eighties: "It's better to burn out than to fade away." No wonder that few, if any, bothered to posit the option that maybe it's better to stick around and fight.

Whereas in 1958 Danny and the Juniors sang that "Rock and roll is here to stay, it will never die," twenty years later the Who were singing "Rock is dead—long live rock!" Indeed, the music does live on—as myth and as reality. Rock's iconography and sensibility have drawn from all aspects of culture, and rock in turn has touched all aspects of culture, from theater to film to television, from poetry to literature to journalism, from the Old World to the Third World. Rock never really dies—it just remakes itself, rises from its ashes and rekindles its fire, over and over again. Even when it seems little more than a fashion statement, some segments of rock remain on the cutting edge. Rock may have fed a corpulent entertainment institution, but it still keeps on sprouting movements within itself that challenge the established order. And because rock is big business with high media exposure and accessibility to millions, those impulses eventually enter the cultural mainstream, one way or another.

The history of rock's impulse-and-assimilation, cat-and-mouse game is a tangled one. The *Rolling Stone Rock & Roll Almanac* is an attempt to make serious sense of all those changes and contradictions, on a day-by-day, week-by-week, month-by-month, year-by-year, decade-by-decade, era-by-era—and yes, even trend-by-trend—basis. By including relevant and significant world-news events as well as rock history itself, it's possible to see how seriously rock & roll was taken by authorities (the public outcries, the censorship, the ridicule) and how seriously it *wasn't* taken (the way Buddy Holly's career was completely overlooked in reports of his death). And it can be seen how seriously the music was taken by both its partisans and its foes. The speed and intensity of the changes in the music and its audience—the ways it was co-opted and the ways it fought back, the ways it assimilated and was assimilated, the widening of its horizons and the narrowing of rock's various audience segments—can all be precisely gauged. It's now possible to relive rock history as it happened—or to learn about it anew.   Michael Shore

ROLLING STONE

ROCK
ALMANAC

THE CHRONICLES OF ROCK & ROLL

1954

*I*t's often been said that the only people who call the Fifties fabulous are those who were born too late to have lived through them. Nostalgia and ignorance tend to erase those things better left forgotten and to romanticize what is left.

This was the Eisenhower era, a period when a strange mixture of post-World War II pride and paranoia combined to turn America from a frontier continent full of go-getter philanthropy for world liberty into a conservative, reactionary nation of the proverbial men in gray flannel suits. Burgeoning consumerism could scarcely conceal the fear and suspicion stewing beneath America's optimistic facade. After all, this was also the time of McCarthyism, the Cold War and the generally accepted belief that one could survive an atom-bomb explosion by falling to the ground and covering one's head with a coat.

However, the growing consumerism kept the record industry, among others, moving full steam ahead. Technological advances changed how people listened to music. The stepped-up use of the lightweight 45 rpm disc (introduced in 1949) rendered the 78 rpm disc obsolete; the twelve-inch long-play disc surpassed the ten-inch extended-play disc in the classical and "mood music" fields. And in 1953, record sales hit an all-time high of $205 million. With the introduction this year of "high fidelity," a new quality standard for monaural recordings, record sales would go even higher.

But what was *on* most of those records was another matter entirely. Culturally, the heady, swinging sophistication of previous decades had given way to a self-conscious, neutered coyness. Romantic love was depicted in music and film as a rarified, abstract concept, and any references to sex were strictly forbidden. This year, the most popular song in America was John Turner's "Oh, My Papa," a sentimental ode to filial love and respect. It became a Number One hit for Eddie Fisher, who, though a typically well-groomed, inoffensive, *adult* crooner, was also young and handsome and sang romantic songs and thus was an idol of teenage girls. When he performed in New York, one concert review was headlined EDDIE FISHER *Rocks* KIDS AT CARNEGIE (emphasis ours).

It now seems absurd to think of Eddie Fisher and the word *rock* in the same phrase. Dull as such musical fare may seem to us now, however, earlier generations were as enthusiastic about it as later generations would be about their own music. Indeed, the screams Eddie Fisher inspired at Carnegie Hall probably were somewhat analogous to the effects rock concerts would soon have on young audiences.

And there is the rub, for beneath America's seemingly moribund exterior, something was brewing—something that would deliver what young audiences may have been too repressed by convention to realize they wanted and needed: a less adulterated brand of excitement and, yes, even sex, in the form of rock & roll. In 1954, the fastest-growing segment of the record business, for the first time ever, was rhythm & blues, the postwar hybrid of blues and big-band horns (formerly referred to as "race records") by "colored" or "Negro" musicians. And the people buying those records were white teenagers. What are often considered the first rock & roll records—Bill Haley and the Comets' "Rock around the Clock" and the Chords' "Sh-Boom"—entered the pop chart this year. In June, Elvis Presley made his first recordings.

The postwar baby boom was beginning to flower, and sweeping changes it would bring appeared as mere fleeting aberrations. For example, the Midnighters' sexually explicit "Work with Me, Annie" provoked controversy over, and the banning of, countless "off-color" R&B and pop songs, but to little or no avail. They sold thousands of copies anyway. Cleveland disc jockey Alan Freed, the man credited with having coined the term *rock & roll,* attracted a sell-out throng of 10,000 to the first rock & roll dance concert he'd held outside his home base in Newark, New Jersey. And the U.S. Senate Subcommittee on Juvenile Delinquency opened hearings to determine the effects on America's youth of rock & roll music, films and television shows. At the time, rock & roll seemed a threat, but certainly one that authorities and interested parties believed they could control and ultimately banish from the American scene.

Though it may not have been obvious back then, the battle lines for a cultural revolution were being drawn.

JANUARY

4 A young truck driver named **Elvis Presley** records a ten-inch acetate demo at the Memphis Recording Service, an open-to-the-public side business run by Sun Records owner **Sam Phillips**. The two songs Presley records are "Casual Love Affair" and "I'll Never Stand in Your Way." It's Presley's second trip to the Recording Service, and the first time he meets Phillips, his future producer. The previous summer he recorded another demo, "My Happiness" and "That's When Your Heartaches Begin," only one copy of which now exists.

7 Chicago Blues legend **Muddy Waters** records "I'm Your Hoochie-Coochie Man" for Chess Records. By March, the record will become Waters' fifth consecutive R&B Top Ten hit since his chart debut in 1951 with "Louisiana Blues."

18 In what *Billboard* later terms "a move to capture the Negro market for potential advertisers," New York City radio station WMGM signs **Noble Sissle**, the so-called Mayor of Harlem, as a Monday-through-Saturday disc jockey. Sissle, an actor and composer, is best known for collaborating with composer **Eubie Blake** on "I'm Just Wild about Harry," "Love Will Find a Way," the Broadway musical *Shuffle Along* and another musical, *Chocolate Dandies*.

23 New York City radio station WNBC announces plans to abandon its "longhair [i.e., classical] all-night record show in favor of a new pop platter program." This format change puts WNBC in direct competition with New York's preeminent pop station, WNEW.

30 Rhythm & blues singer **Big Joe Turner's** fifth R&B hit, "TV Mama," hits #9. A native of Kansas City, Missouri, Turner is one of the top vocalists of his day and is often billed as "The Boss of the Blues."

FEBRUARY

6 After raising the price of LPs two weeks earlier, RCA Victor cuts the price by nearly two dollars to a low $3.99. The price reduction is just one of several maneuvers made by record companies to bolster sales of LPs in a market long dominated by 78 rpm singles.

10 *The Glenn Miller Story,* starring **Jimmy Stewart** as the Big Band orchestra leader, premieres in New York City. The movie's soundtrack, featuring **Glenn Miller**, will become one of the year's best-selling LPs.

13 Blues guitarist and singer **Guitar Slim (Eddie Jones)** has his only chart hit, "The Things That I Used to Do" (#1 R&B). Jones, only one of three performers known as Guitar Slim (the other two, **Alexander Seward** and **Norman Green**, preceded him by two decades), worked with

New Orleans pianist **Huey "Piano" Smith** in the Forties.

26 Republican Representative **Ruth Thompson** of Michigan proposes a bill in the U.S. House of Representatives that would ban mailing or transporting any "obscene, lewd, lascivious or filthy" phonograph disc or "other article capable of producing sound." The bill calls for convicted offenders to pay fines up to $5,000, be imprisoned for up to five years, or both. ◆

WEEK ENDING JANUARY 2		
U.S. #1 POP 45	"Oh, My Papa"	Eddie Fisher
U.S. #1 POP LP	*"Glenn Miller Story"*	Glenn Miller & Orch.
U.S. #1 R&B 45	"Money, Honey"	The Drifters
U.K. #1 POP 45		

WEEK ENDING JANUARY 9		
U.S. #1 POP 45	"Oh, My Papa"	Eddie Fisher
U.S. #1 POP LP	*"Glenn Miller Story"*	Glenn Miller & Orch.
U.S. #1 R&B 45	"Money, Honey"	The Drifters
U.K. #1 POP 45		

WEEK ENDING JANUARY 16		
U.S. #1 POP 45	"Oh, My Papa"	Eddie Fisher
U.S. #1 POP LP	*"Glenn Miller Story"*	Glenn Miller & Orch.
U.S. #1 R&B 45	"Money, Honey"	The Drifters
U.K. #1 POP 45		

WEEK ENDING JANUARY 23		
U.S. #1 POP 45	"Oh, My Papa"	Eddie Fisher
U.S. #1 POP LP	*"Glenn Miller Story"*	Glenn Miller & Orch.
U.S. #1 R&B 45	"I'll Be True"	Faye Adams
U.K. #1 POP 45		

WEEK ENDING JANUARY 30		
U.S. #1 POP 45	"Oh, My Papa"	Eddie Fisher
U.S. #1 POP LP	*"Glenn Miller Story"*	Glenn Miller & Orch.
U.S. #1 R&B 45	"The Things That I Used to Do"	Guitar Slim
U.K. #1 POP 45		

WEEK ENDING FEBRUARY 6		
U.S. #1 POP 45	"Oh, My Papa"	Eddie Fisher
U.S. #1 POP LP	*"Glenn Miller Story"*	Glenn Miller & Orch.
U.S. #1 R&B 45	"The Things That I Used to Do"	Guitar Slim
U.K. #1 POP 45		

WEEK ENDING FEBRUARY 13		
U.S. #1 POP 45	"Oh, My Papa"	Eddie Fisher
U.S. #1 POP LP	*"Glenn Miller Story"*	Glenn Miller & Orch.
U.S. #1 R&B 45	"The Things That I Used to Do"	Guitar Slim
U.K. #1 POP 45		

WEEK ENDING FEBRUARY 20		
U.S. #1 POP 45	"Secret Love"	Doris Day
U.S. #1 POP LP	*"Glenn Miller Story"*	Glenn Miller & Orch.
U.S. #1 R&B 45	"The Things That I Used to Do"	Guitar Slim
U.K. #1 POP 45		

WEEK ENDING FEBRUARY 27		
U.S. #1 POP 45	"Secret Love"	Doris Day
U.S. #1 POP LP	*"Glenn Miller Story"*	Glenn Miller & Orch.
U.S. #1 R&B 45	"The Things That I Used to Do"	Guitar Slim
U.K. #1 POP 45		

MARCH

3 **The Drifters'** second R&B hit, "Such a Night," goes to #5. The group's debut single, "Money, Honey," hit the R&B Number One spot four months earlier. Though both records become best sellers, neither ever enters the pop chart. Like many R&B hits of the day, "Such a Night" is also recorded, or covered, by a white performer. In this case, top pop balladeer **Johnnie Ray** records the song for Columbia, but within a month of its April 1954 release, it is banned in the U.S. for being too sexually suggestive. The offensive lines: "Just the thought of your kiss sets me afire/I reminisce and I'm filled with desire."

10 **The Clovers'** tenth R&B hit single, "Lovey Dovey," goes to #2. Their previous R&B hits included three Number Ones—"Don't You Know I Love You" (1951), "Fool, Fool, Fool" (1951) and "Ting-a-Ling" (1952)—as well as half a dozen others in the Top Ten.

20 *Billboard* reports that Decca, Columbia and MGM, following the lead of RCA Victor, Capitol, London and other labels, are introducing records that will be designated "high fidelity," the industry's state of the art in recorded sound.

24 Blind blues singer **Ray Charles'** third R&B hit, "It Should've Been Me," peaks at #7. Charles' two earlier hits were "Baby Let Me Hold Your Hand" in 1951 and "Kiss Me Baby" in 1952.

31 **The Crows'** sole chart entry, "Gee," hits #6 on the R&B charts. Also this week, New Orleans pianist and singer **Fats Domino's** tenth R&B hit, "You Done Me Wrong," peaks at #10 but stays on the charts only one week. Domino, who is one of R&B's greatest stars, has had earlier hits, including: "The Fat Man" and "Every Night about This Time" (1950), "Rockin' Chair" (1951), "Goin' Home," "How Long" (1952), "Goin' to the River," "Please Don't Leave Me," "Rose Mary" and "Something's Wrong" (1953).

APRIL

12 **Bill Haley and the Comets** record two

songs, "Thirteen Women" and "(We're Gonna) Rock around the Clock," for Decca Records at the Pythian Temple Studio in New York City. The latter song eventually becomes Haley's biggest hit and the first rock & roll tune to be featured in a movie, when it's used during the opening and closing credits of *Blackboard Jungle* in 1956. The session is produced by **Milt Gabler**.

14 **The Midnighters** have their first hit since changing their name from the **Royals** with the sexually explicit—and later quite controversial—"Work with Me, Annie." The first single of the so-called Annie trilogy, "Work with Me, Annie" was written by lead singer **Hank Ballard** and featured the straightforward lines "Annie please don't cheat/Give me all my meat."

21 **The Spaniels,** a black vocal group from Gary, Indiana, have a second R&B Top Ten hit with "Goodnite, Sweetheart, Goodnite," released on Vee Jay Records, the label their manager founded to record them.

28 **Big Joe Turner's** "Shake, Rattle and Roll" hits #2 on the R&B chart. Yet another sexually suggestive song, it is significantly cleaned up by **Bill Haley,** whose group has a hit with it later the same year. Haley explains his change in lyrics: "We steer completely clear of anything suggestive!"

30 The Music Performance Trust Fund re-

ports to the Recording Industry Association of America (RIAA) that record sales in 1953 reached an all-time high of $205 million. The market is divided among 78 rpm discs (which account for fifty-two percent of all sales), 45 rpm discs (twenty-eight percent) and the relatively new category, LPs (twenty percent).

The Metropolitan Disc Jockey Club and Association of Broadcasters is officially launched at a New York City press party at the Hotel Theresa. The Association of New York-Area Rhythm and Blues Disc Jockeys announces that its primary objective is to discourage the playing of records that could be considered either racially derogatory or in bad taste. ◆

WEEK ENDING MARCH 3		
U.S. #1 POP 45	"Make Love to Me"	Jo Stafford
U.S. #1 POP LP	*"Glenn Miller Story"*	Glenn Miller & Orch.
U.S. #1 R&B 45	"The Things That I Used to Do"	Guitar Slim
U.K. #1 POP 45		

WEEK ENDING MARCH 10		
U.S. #1 POP 45	"Secret Love"	Doris Day
U.S. #1 POP LP	*"Glenn Miller Story"*	Glenn Miller & Orch.
U.S. #1 R&B 45	"The Things That I Used to Do"	Guitar Slim
U.K. #1 POP 45		

WEEK ENDING MARCH 17		
U.S. #1 POP 45	"Make Love to Me"	Jo Stafford
U.S. #1 POP LP	*"Glenn Miller Story"*	Glenn Miller & Orch.
U.S. #1 R&B 45	"You'll Never Walk Alone"	Roy Hamilton
U.K. #1 POP 45		

WEEK ENDING MARCH 24		
U.S. #1 POP 45	"Make Love to Me"	Jo Stafford
U.S. #1 POP LP	*"Glenn Miller Story"*	Glenn Miller & Orch.
U.S. #1 R&B 45	"You'll Never Walk Alone"	Roy Hamilton
U.K. #1 POP 45		

WEEK ENDING MARCH 31		
U.S. #1 POP 45	"Wanted"	Perry Como
U.S. #1 POP LP	*"Glenn Miller Story"*	Glenn Miller & Orch.
U.S. #1 R&B 45	"You'll Never Walk Alone"	Roy Hamilton
U.K. #1 POP 45		

WEEK ENDING APRIL 7		
U.S. #1 POP 45	"Wanted"	Perry Como
U.S. #1 POP LP	*"Glenn Miller Story"*	Glenn Miller & Orch.
U.S. #1 R&B 45	"You'll Never Walk Alone"	Roy Hamilton
U.K. #1 POP 45		

WEEK ENDING APRIL 14		
U.S. #1 POP 45	"Wanted"	Perry Como
U.S. #1 POP LP	*"Glenn Miller Story"*	Glenn Miller & Orch.
U.S. #1 R&B 45	"You'll Never Walk Alone"	Roy Hamilton
U.K. #1 POP 45		

WEEK ENDING APRIL 21		
U.S. #1 POP 45	"Wanted"	Perry Como
U.S. #1 POP LP	*"Glenn Miller Story"*	Glenn Miller & Orch.
U.S. #1 R&B 45	"You'll Never Walk Alone"	Roy Hamilton
U.K. #1 POP 45		

WEEK ENDING APRIL 28		
U.S. #1 POP 45	"Wanted"	Perry Como
U.S. #1 POP LP	*"Glenn Miller Story"*	Glenn Miller & Orch.
U.S. #1 R&B 45	"You'll Never Walk Alone"	Roy Hamilton
U.K. #1 POP 45		

MAY

1 **Alan "Moondog" Freed**, the most famous disc jockey in rock and the man who popularized the term *rock & roll*, conducts his first dance outside his home base of Cleveland, Ohio. The show, which is held at the Newark (New Jersey) Armory, draws a crowd of more than 10,000. The Moondog Coronation Ball features the **Clovers**, the **Buddy Johnson Orchestra**, **Nolan Lewis**, **Muddy Waters**, **Charles Brown**, the **Harptones** and others. Tickets go for two dollars at the door, $1.50 advance sales. Because of overcrowding, thousands are turned away.

8 After airing **Johnnie Ray**'s cover of the **Drifters**' "Such a Night" and receiving what its spokesperson terms "a raft of complaints from listeners," the British Broadcasting Company (BBC) blacklists the record because it is "too suggestive."

15 *Billboard* reports Americans bought 30 million country & western recordings in 1953, accounting for more than thirteen percent of all record sales. The most popular artists are **Hank Williams**, **Jean Shepard**, **Carl Smith**, **Jim Reeves**, **Hank Snow**, **Webb Pierce** and **Eddy Arnold**.

19 Modern classical composer **Charles Ives**, winner of a Pulitzer Prize in 1947 for his third symphony, dies at age seventy-nine at his New York City home. Ives' work will prove influential on other musicians, including Seventies avant-rocker **Don Van Vliet** (a.k.a. **Captain Beefheart**).

22 **Robert Zimmerman** celebrates his bar mitzvah in Minnesota.

26 The second annual National Hillbilly Music Festival and Jimmie Rodgers Memorial Day is observed in Rodgers' hometown, Meridian, Mississippi. Net proceeds total more than $8,000.

30 "Jukebox Jury," a sixty-minute-long Sunday evening show, debuts on the CBS radio network as a summer replacement for "The Jack Benny Show" and "Amos 'n' Andy." The show, which features popular music, will later appear on television as well.

JUNE

5 Major record labels will supply radio station disc jockeys with 45 rpm rather than popular 78 rpm singles be-

ginning next month, *Billboard* reports. Although 45 rpm discs have been available since 1949, the industry has never adopted the small disc as the standard for singles. The change, which is cited as a "money-saving move," will prove to be the subject of great debate and controversy over the next few months.

17 The British music magazine *Record Mirror* publishes its first issue. The magazine is one of the first popular music publications aimed at a general readership.

23 The **Chords**' "Sh-Boom" enters the charts. It will become one of the few original R&B recordings to surpass its white cover version (by the **Crew-Cuts**) in sales. ◆

WEEK	ENDING	MAY 5
U.S. #1 POP 45	"Wanted"	Perry Como
U.S. #1 POP LP	*"Glenn Miller Story"*	Glenn Miller & Orch.
U.S. #1 R&B 45	"You'll Never Walk Alone"	Roy Hamilton
U.K. #1 POP 45		

WEEK	ENDING	MAY 12
U.S. #1 POP 45	"Wanted"	Perry Como
U.S. #1 POP LP	*"Glenn Miller Story"*	Glenn Miller & Orch.
U.S. #1 R&B 45	"Work with Me, Annie"	Hank Ballard & the Midnighters
U.K. #1 POP 45		

WEEK	ENDING	MAY 19
U.S. #1 POP 45	"Wanted"	Perry Como
U.S. #1 POP LP	*"Glenn Miller Story"*	Glenn Miller & Orch.
U.S. #1 R&B 45	"Work with Me, Annie"	Hank Ballard & the Midnighters
U.K. #1 POP 45		

WEEK	ENDING	MAY 26
U.S. #1 POP 45	"Little Things Mean Alot"	Kitty Kallen
U.S. #1 POP LP	*"Glenn Miller Story"*	Glenn Miller & Orch.
U.S. #1 R&B 45	"Work with Me, Annie"	Hank Ballard & the Midnighters
U.K. #1 POP 45		

WEEK	ENDING	JUNE 2
U.S. #1 POP 45	"Little Things Mean Alot"	Kitty Kallen
U.S. #1 POP LP	*"Glenn Miller Story"*	Glenn Miller & Orch.
U.S. #1 R&B 45	"Work with Me, Annie"	Hank Ballard & the Midnighters
U.K. #1 POP 45		

WEEK	ENDING	JUNE 9
U.S. #1 POP 45	"Little Things Mean Alot"	Kitty Kallen
U.S. #1 POP LP	*"Glenn Miller Story"*	Glenn Miller & Orch.
U.S. #1 R&B 45	"Work with Me, Annie"	Hank Ballard & the Midnighters
U.K. #1 POP 45		

WEEK	ENDING	JUNE 16
U.S. #1 POP 45	"Little Things Mean Alot"	Kitty Kallen
U.S. #1 POP LP	*"Glenn Miller Story"*	Glenn Miller & Orch.
U.S. #1 R&B 45	"Work with Me, Annie"	Hank Ballard & the Midnighters
U.K. #1 POP 45		

WEEK	ENDING	JUNE 23
U.S. #1 POP 45	"Little Things Mean Alot"	Kitty Kallen
U.S. #1 POP LP	*"Glenn Miller Story"*	Glenn Miller & Orch.
U.S. #1 R&B 45	"Work with Me, Annie"	Hank Ballard & the Midnighters
U.K. #1 POP 45		

WEEK	ENDING	JUNE 30
U.S. #1 POP 45	"Little Things Mean Alot"	Kitty Kallen
U.S. #1 POP LP	*"Glenn Miller Story"*	Glenn Miller & Orch.
U.S. #1 R&B 45	"Honey Love"	Clyde McPhatter & the Drifters
U.K. #1 POP 45		

JULY

5 **Bill Haley and the Comets** finally reach the pop Top Ten with their cover of **Big Joe Turner**'s R&B hit "Shake, Rattle and Roll." Their previous single, "Rock around the Clock," flopped the first time out, although it eventually would become the group's biggest hit. Their first big hit was "Crazy Man Crazy" in 1953.

6 **Elvis Presley**, with **Bill Black** and **Scotty Moore**, records his first single at Sun Records in Memphis. The single's A side, "That's All Right," is an **Arthur "Big Boy" Crudup** song originally recorded earlier that year. The B side, a country blues song entitled "Blue Moon of Kentucky," was a hit by country star **Bill Monroe** in 1946.

7 Two versions of "Sh-Boom" are in the pop Top Ten: The original by the **Chords** is at #9, and the cover version by a white group, the **Crew-Cuts**, is at #5. On the R&B chart, the Chords' version is #4, and the Crew-Cuts are nowhere in sight.

Memphis disc jockey **Dewey Phillips** (no relation to Sam) premieres **Elvis Presley**'s "That's All Right" on his "Red, Hot and Blue" program on WHBQ just after 9:30 p.m. Later that evening, Presley is interviewed on the air by Phillips.

10 Cleveland disc jockey **Alan Freed** is expected to start work at New York City's WINS in September, *Billboard* reports. Freed's move to New York City will later be seen as a crucial step in the widespread popularization of R&B and rock & roll music.

15 The **Treniers**, a black vocal group, record "Say Hey (the Willie Mays Song)" for Columbia Records' Okeh subsidiary in New York City. The song, which also features the voice of New York Giants center fielder **Willie Mays** himself, is recorded under the direction of twenty-one-year-old **Quincy Jones**.

19 Sun Records officially releases **Elvis Presley**'s debut single, "That's All Right," backed with "Blue Moon of Kentucky."

28 **Ruth Brown**'s eighth R&B hit, "Oh What a Dream I Had Last Night," enters the R&B charts. Although Brown, along with **LaVern Baker**, is one of the most popular female R&B singers of the decade, her hits will never crack the pop Top Twenty.

30 The **Midnighters** record "Annie Had a

Baby," the second in the controversial Annie trilogy. Like its predecessor, the single will become a top R&B hit.

AUGUST

6 Gale's Rhythm & Blues Show, a road tour featuring the **Drifters**, the **Spaniels**, **Roy Hamilton** and others, opens in Cleveland, Ohio.

7 *Billboard* reviews **Elvis Presley**'s debut single, "That's All Right," backed with "Blue Moon of Kentucky," in its "Review Spotlight on Talent" in the country & western section. The reviewer calls Presley "a strong new talent."

In response to a 45 rpm shortage, *Billboard* reports that some radio stations are receiving promotional copies of new singles in the form of shellac, test-pressing 78s.

10 **Elvis Presley** makes an unannounced appearance at the Overton Park Shell in Memphis, Tennessee.

14 The popularity of an African folk song, "Skokiaan," is noted in *Billboard.* Both the **Ray Anthony** and **Ralph Marterle** orchestras have covered the song, as have the **Four Lads**. The original version was recorded by Rhodesia's **Bulawayo Orchestra**.

19 Twenty-four hundred fans jam Hollywood's Savoy Ballroom to see **B. B. King**, **Johnny Otis**, the **Platters** and other top R&B acts.

28 **Elvis Presley**'s "Blue Moon of Kentucky" enters the country & western Territorial Best Sellers chart for the week ending August 18, for Memphis, at #3. The following week, the single's A side, "That's All Right," enters at #4.

29 **Louis Jordan**, one of the foremost R&B musicians and composers of the postwar era, kicks off a four-month tour of one-nighters with a show in El Paso, Texas. ◆

WEEK ENDING JULY 7		
U.S. #1 POP 45	"Little Things Mean Alot"	Kitty Kallen
U.S. #1 POP LP	*"Glenn Miller Story"*	Glenn Miller & Orch.
U.S. #1 R&B 45	"Honey Love"	Clyde McPhatter & the Drifters
U.K. #1 POP 45		

WEEK ENDING JULY 14		
U.S. #1 POP 45	"Little Things Mean Alot"	Kitty Kallen
U.S. #1 POP LP	*"Glenn Miller Story"*	Glenn Miller & Orch.
U.S. #1 R&B 45	"Honey Love"	Clyde McPhatter & the Drifters
U.K. #1 POP 45		

WEEK ENDING JULY 21		
U.S. #1 POP 45	"Little Things Mean Alot"	Kitty Kallen
U.S. #1 POP LP	*"Glenn Miller Story"*	Glenn Miller & Orch.
U.S. #1 R&B 45	"Honey Love"	Clyde McPhatter & the Drifters
U.K. #1 POP 45		

WEEK ENDING JULY 28		
U.S. #1 POP 45	"Sh-Boom"	The Crew-Cuts
U.S. #1 POP LP	*"Glenn Miller Story"*	Glenn Miller & Orch.
U.S. #1 R&B 45	"Honey Love"	Clyde McPhatter & the Drifters
U.K. #1 POP 45		

WEEK ENDING AUGUST 4		
U.S. #1 POP 45	"Sh-Boom"	The Crew-Cuts
U.S. #1 POP LP	*"Glenn Miller Story"*	Glenn Miller & Orch.
U.S. #1 R&B 45	"Honey Love"	Clyde McPhatter & the Drifters
U.K. #1 POP 45		

WEEK ENDING AUGUST 11		
U.S. #1 POP 45	"Sh-Boom"	The Crew-Cuts
U.S. #1 POP LP	*The Student Prince*	Mario Lanza
U.S. #1 R&B 45	"Honey Love"	Clyde McPhatter & the Drifters
U.K. #1 POP 45		

WEEK ENDING AUGUST 18		
U.S. #1 POP 45	"Sh-Boom"	The Crew-Cuts
U.S. #1 POP LP	*The Student Prince*	Mario Lanza
U.S. #1 R&B 45	"Honey Love"	Clyde McPhatter & the Drifters
U.K. #1 POP 45		

WEEK ENDING AUGUST 25		
U.S. #1 POP 45	"Sh-Boom"	The Crew-Cuts
U.S. #1 POP LP	*The Student Prince*	Mario Lanza
U.S. #1 R&B 45	"What a Dream"	Ruth Brown
U.K. #1 POP 45		

SEPTEMBER

9 **Elvis Presley** performs at the grand opening of Katz's Drug Store in his hometown, Memphis, Tennessee.

Alan Freed begins work as a disc jockey at radio station WINS in New York City.

11 A survey of the National Ballroom Operators Association reveals that business is down fifty-four percent compared to the first half of 1953. Musicians and ballroom operators complain that "record hop" dances, which are cheaper and treat audiences to the most popular recorded versions of the tunes, account for the drop in attendance.

"Blue Moon of Kentucky" hits Number One on the country & western Territorial Best Sellers chart for Memphis. "That's All Right" is at #7.

18 There is a trend toward syndicated R&B disc jockey shows, *Billboard* notes, citing the success of **Alan Freed** at New York City's WINS, KVD-LA's **Hunter Hancock** and others. "No one knows why R&B dee-jays have been successful with syndicated shows when so many pop dee-jays have failed to make much of an impression." In the same issue, another article states: "Youngsters, the backbone of the pop record business, appear to want R&B music so much that they search it out in stores and jukeboxes."

25 **Stan Freberg**, a comedian whose parody disc "Sh-Boom" has been played on CBS's "Jukebox Jury" is quoted in *Billboard* as saying, "I hope this puts an end to R&B." Los Angeles R&B disc jockey **Hunter Hancock** replies, "It'll take more than Freberg to stop R&B."

Sun Records releases **Elvis Presley**'s second single, a cover of **Wynonie Harris**' 1947 R&B hit, "Good Rockin' Tonight," backed with "I Don't Care If the Sun Don't Shine." On the same day, Presley makes his first —and last—appearance at the Grand Ole Opry. After his performance, during which he sings "Blue Moon of Kentucky," the Opry's talent coordinator, **James Denny**, advises Presley to go back to driving trucks. The following year, *Billboard* magazine will name Denny its Man of the Year.

OCTOBER

1 The **Penguins**' "Earth Angel," written by Jesse Belvin about his girlfriend and later considered one of the classic singles of the doo-wop era, is released on Dootone Records. By year's end, it makes R&B Number One but is the group's only chart entry.

2 *Billboard* publishes an editorial in which it protests the recent spate of "obscene," "offensive" and "off-color" R&B records.

6 Soul singer **Dinah Washington**'s fifteenth R&B Top Fifteen hit, "I Don't Hurt Anymore," enters the charts. Her earlier hits, dating back to 1949, include the Number One "Baby Get Lost."

After five weeks, **Elvis Presley**'s "That's All Right" drops off the Memphis charts; "Blue Moon of Kentucky," in its sixth week on the chart, drops only to #6.

9 The controversy over sexually explicit lyrics continues. **George A. Miller**, president of the Music Operators of America, a jukebox operators association, decries off-color R&B records and the jukebox operators who program them into machines.

16 **Elvis Presley** makes his first of many appearances on "The Louisiana Hayride" and sings his current hits "That's All Right" and "Blue Moon of Kentucky."

20 R&B singer **LaVern Baker** records "Tweedle Dee" in New York City for Atlantic Records; the session is produced by label co-owners **Jerry Wexler** and **Ahmet Ertegun**.

Elvis Presley's third single, "Good Rockin' Tonight," enters the Memphis charts at #5.

27 Blues singer and guitarist **B. B. King**'s seventh R&B hit, "You Upset Me Baby," enters the charts. His first two R&B hits, "Three O'Clock Blues" (1951) and "You Know I Love You" (1952) both went to Number One.

30 According to *Billboard*, the **Midnighters**' "Work with Me, Annie" and "Annie Had a Baby," along with the **Drifters**' "Honey Love," are but three of the R&B records Memphis radio station WDIA banned after instituting a program to screen all records for "offensive" lyrics. ◆

WEEK ENDING SEPTEMBER 1		
U.S. #1 POP 45	"Sh-Boom"	The Crew-Cuts
U.S. #1 POP LP	*The Student Prince*	Mario Lanza
U.S. #1 R&B 45	"What a Dream"	Ruth Brown
U.K. #1 POP 45		

WEEK ENDING SEPTEMBER 8		
U.S. #1 POP 45	"Sh-Boom"	The Crew-Cuts
U.S. #1 POP LP	*The Student Prince*	Mario Lanza
U.S. #1 R&B 45	"What a Dream"	Ruth Brown
U.K. #1 POP 45		

WEEK ENDING SEPTEMBER 15		
U.S. #1 POP 45	"Hey, There"	Rosemary Clooney
U.S. #1 POP LP	*The Student Prince*	Mario Lanza
U.S. #1 R&B 45	"Annie Had a Baby"	Hank Ballard & the Midnighters
U.K. #1 POP 45		

WEEK ENDING SEPTEMBER 22		
U.S. #1 POP 45	"Hey, There"	Rosemary Clooney
U.S. #1 POP LP	*The Student Prince*	Mario Lanza
U.S. #1 R&B 45	"Annie Had a Baby"	Hank Ballard & the Midnighters
U.K. #1 POP 45		

WEEK ENDING SEPTEMBER 29		
U.S. #1 POP 45	"Hey, There"	Rosemary Clooney
U.S. #1 POP LP	*The Student Prince*	Mario Lanza
U.S. #1 R&B 45	"What a Dream"	Ruth Brown
U.K. #1 POP 45		

WEEK ENDING OCTOBER 6		
U.S. #1 POP 45	"Hey, There"	Rosemary Clooney
U.S. #1 POP LP	*The Student Prince*	Mario Lanza
U.S. #1 R&B 45	"Hurts Me to My Heart"	Faye Adams
U.K. #1 POP 45		

WEEK ENDING OCTOBER 13		
U.S. #1 POP 45	"Hey, There"	Rosemary Clooney
U.S. #1 POP LP	*The Student Prince*	Mario Lanza
U.S. #1 R&B 45	"Hurts Me to My Heart"	Faye Adams
U.K. #1 POP 45		

WEEK ENDING OCTOBER 20		
U.S. #1 POP 45	"Hey, There"	Rosemary Clooney
U.S. #1 POP LP	*Music, Martinis and Memories*	Jackie Gleason & Orchestra
U.S. #1 R&B 45	"Hurts Me to My Heart"	Faye Adams
U.K. #1 POP 45		

WEEK ENDING OCTOBER 27		
U.S. #1 POP 45	"Hey, There"	Rosemary Clooney
U.S. #1 POP LP	*Music, Martinis and Memories*	Jackie Gleason & Orchestra
U.S. #1 R&B 45	"Hurts Me to My Heart"	Faye Adams
U.K. #1 POP 45		

NOVEMBER

5 Jazz trumpeter **Oran "Hot Lips" Page**, a leader in the Kansas City jazz movement, dies in New York City of a heart attack at age forty-six.

13 A *Billboard* disc jockey poll finds that DJs play forty-two percent pop, eleven percent country & western and five percent R&B. The most-played artists are **Perry Como** and **Patti Page**; favorite singers include **Frank Sinatra** and **Doris Day**; the favorite record is Sinatra's "Young at Heart." The favorite R&B record is **Bill Haley**'s version of **Big Joe Turner**'s "Shake, Rattle and Roll."

18 ABC radio and television blacklists **Rosemary Clooney**'s hit "Mambo Italiano" because of what it considers "offensive lyrics." Clooney's label, Columbia, counters with a statement in which it quotes an NYU professor of romance languages and a Catholic priest, both of whom claim that the Italian lyrics are "in no way offensive or vulgar."

20 The local bartenders union in Hammond, Indiana, has requested that WJOB disc jockey **Len Ellis** stop playing country singer **Ferlin Huskey**'s "The Drunken Driver." The song, which relates the story of a car crash in which a drunken driver kills two children, is hurting business, the union says.

After more than two decades in the music business, singing cowboy **Gene Autry** makes his first appearance at the Grand Ole Opry.

24 **Lowell Fulson**'s "Reconsider Baby" enters the R&B charts; it later peaks at #3. Fulson would have only one more R&B Top Ten hit (in 1966, with "Tramp"); he had had an R&B Number One hit in 1950, with "Blue Shadows."

Disc jockey **Alan Freed** is enjoined by a New York State Supreme Court for using the nickname "Moondog" or any variation thereof on his radio show. The injunction is granted to a blind New York City street singer named **Louis "Moondog" Hardin** whose uncopyrighted "Moondog Symphony" became the theme song for Freed's "Moondog Matinee" show back in 1951. Freed complies and renames his show, currently heard on New York's WINS but soon to be syndicated nationwide, "The Rock and Roll Show."

30 **Nat "King" Cole** opens the first of six nights at Harlem's Apollo Theater in New York.

DECEMBER

1 **Fred Rose**, who, with **Roy Acuff**, founded **Acuff-Rose Publications**, the leading publisher of country & western music, dies of a heart attack in Nashville at age fifty-seven.

3 A benefit concert to aid crippled black children is held at Memphis's Ellis Au-

ditorium. Among the performers are **Muddy Waters**, **Little Walter**, **Big John Greer** and **Rufus Thomas**.

7 Country star **Marty Robbins** records his version of **Arthur Crudup**'s "That's All Right." The song, which was a groundbreaking hit single for **Elvis Presley** six months earlier, flops for Robbins.

8 The **Drifters**' version of the biggest-selling record in the world, "White Christmas," makes its first appearance on the R&B chart. This year it will peak at #2; next year, at #3. It will also appear on the pop charts in 1955, 1960 and 1962.

11 *Billboard* predicts that 78 rpm discs "may fade into oblivion" because of the popularity of the smaller 45s.

24 R&B vocalist **Johnny Ace** (b. John Marshall Alexander, Jr.) dies of a self-inflicted gunshot wound that he reportedly sustained while playing Russian roulette backstage at Houston's Civic Auditorium. He was twenty-five and, at the time of his death, one of the most popular R&B singers of his day. Indeed, earlier the same year, *Cashbox* named him "the most programmed artist of the year." In February 1955, his "Pledging My Love" will begin a nine-week run as the Number One R&B hit. His earlier hits included "Cross My Heart," "Please Forgive Me," "Yes Baby," "The Clock" and "Never Let Me Go." ◆

WEEK ENDING NOVEMBER 3		
U.S. #1 POP 45	"Hey, There"	Rosemary Clooney
U.S. #1 POP LP	*The Student Prince*	Mario Lanza
U.S. #1 R&B 45	"Hurts Me to My Heart"	Faye Adams
U.K. #1 POP 45		

WEEK ENDING NOVEMBER 10		
U.S. #1 POP 45	"I Need You Now"	Eddie Fisher
U.S. #1 POP LP	*The Student Prince*	Mario Lanza
U.S. #1 R&B 45	"Mambo Baby"	Ruth Brown
U.K. #1 POP 45		

WEEK ENDING NOVEMBER 17		
U.S. #1 POP 45	"I Need You Now"	Eddie Fisher
U.S. #1 POP LP	*The Student Prince*	Mario Lanza
U.S. #1 R&B 45	"Hearts of Stone"	The Charms
U.K. #1 POP 45		

WEEK ENDING NOVEMBER 24		
U.S. #1 POP 45	"Mr. Sandman"	The Chordettes
U.S. #1 POP LP	*The Student Prince*	Mario Lanza
U.S. #1 R&B 45	"Hearts of Stone"	The Charms
U.K. #1 POP 45		

WEEK ENDING DECEMBER 1		
U.S. #1 POP 45	"Mr. Sandman"	The Chordettes
U.S. #1 POP LP	*The Student Prince*	Mario Lanza
U.S. #1 R&B 45	"Hearts of Stone"	The Charms
U.K. #1 POP 45		

WEEK ENDING DECEMBER 8		
U.S. #1 POP 45	"Mr. Sandman"	The Chordettes
U.S. #1 POP LP	*The Student Prince*	Mario Lanza
U.S. #1 R&B 45	"Hearts of Stone"	The Charms
U.K. #1 POP 45		

WEEK ENDING DECEMBER 15		
U.S. #1 POP 45	"Mr. Sandman"	The Chordettes
U.S. #1 POP LP	*The Student Prince*	Mario Lanza
U.S. #1 R&B 45	"Hearts of Stone"	The Charms
U.K. #1 POP 45		

WEEK ENDING DECEMBER 22		
U.S. #1 POP 45	"Mr. Sandman"	The Chordettes
U.S. #1 POP LP	*The Student Prince*	Mario Lanza
U.S. #1 R&B 45	"Hearts of Stone"	The Charms
U.K. #1 POP 45		

1955

Regardless of how dramatic last year's events seemed in terms of their ultimate impact on rock & roll, they had little effect on pop music. Although insouciant R&B and nascent rock & roll were beginning to make their mark, Fifties pop was still Fifties pop. The most popular songs of the year were "Little Things Mean a Lot," "Yellow Rose of Texas," "Love Is a Many Splendored Thing"—and one rock & roll song, "Sh-Boom."

But by then, the concept of "most popular song" was beginning to become outmoded, based as it was in the Tin Pan Alley era when singers were viewed as song sellers more than artists in their own right. The music trade magazines ran weekly sheet-music charts, and individual songs were recorded by any number of singers. Because few singers wrote their own material, they depended on publishers to provide songs. Of course, publishers welcomed competing versions of a song since, theoretically, they would earn more money on royalties. So, it made perfect sense for *Billboard* to favorably review Elvis Presley's "Milkcow Blues Boogie" by commenting, "The guy sells all the way." What most people didn't yet realize was that rock & roll was not about selling and reselling the same old standards.

By 1955, even pop music was inadvertently acknowledging the growing prominence of R&B and rock & roll by covering not just pop hits, but any R&B hit in sight, often with predictably greater sales than the black originals. Georgia Gibbs' "Dance with Me, Henry," a cleaned-up remake of Etta James' "Roll with Me, Henry," which was an answer to the Midnighters' controversial "Work with Me, Annie," far outsold the original, as did Pat Boone's version of Fats Domino's "Ain't That a Shame" and Gale Storm's version of Smiley Lewis' "I Hear You Knockin'." At one point, R&B singer LaVern Baker unsuccessfully petitioned Congress to ban the "note-for-note copying" of R&B originals, and some radio stations enacted policies banning the playing of duplicate covers of R&B songs.

Meanwhile, Pat Boone emerged, a harbinger of the soon-to-flourish "teen idol" phenomenon, in which clean-cut young white singers temporarily revived the pop crooner style to displace less inhibited types like Elvis Presley. But the prominence of more acceptable types like Boone still wasn't enough. By now, people began to suspect that rock & roll was more than a passing fad, and thus perceived it as that much more dangerous. Editorials in Catholic periodicals in Boston and Chicago protesting "off-color" R&B records prompted the formation of record-censorship boards in those cities; Bridgeport and New Haven, Connecticut, banned rock & roll dances altogether. BMI (Broadcast Music, Inc.), which licenses songs and recordings for public performance and broadcast, announced a spring offensive against "vulgar and offensive lyrics in R&B and popular songs." Elvis Presley provoked his first riot at a Jacksonville, Florida, concert, and in this, the year that Perry Como and Patti Page topped WNEW-New York radio's listener popularity poll, Elvis was rejected by Arthur Godfrey's "Talent Scouts" TV show (on which Pat Boone came in first place).

In the midst of all the outcry, major department-store chains like J. C. Penny installed record departments in their stores for the first time. Chuck Berry, Bo Diddley, Little Richard and Carl Perkins released their first records. Rock & roll package tours proliferated around the country. And when Bill Haley's "Rock around the Clock" entered the British pop chart, rock & roll started becoming America's biggest cultural export.

And finally, on May 17, what may have been the first pro-rock & roll demonstration took place at Princeton University in New Jersey, when one student began blaring "Rock around the Clock" out of his dorm window. Other students followed suit, and at midnight dozens of students paraded across the campus chanting the song. But things weren't as revolutionary as we might like to believe. It all ended when the college dean awoke, came out and told all the kids to go back to sleep. They did.

JANUARY

1 RCA Victor announces "Operation TNT," an effort to spur record sales. RCA drops the list price on LPs from $5.95 to $3.98, EPs from $4.95 to $2.98, 45 EPs from $1.58 $1.49 to and 45 singles from $1.16 to eighty-nine cents. Other major labels soon follow suit.

Billboard lists the top five hits of 1954: "Little Things Mean a Lot," "Wanted," "Sh-Boom," "Oh, My Papa" and "Hey There."

5 LaVern Baker's "Tweedle Dee" enters the R&B chart. It will later peak at #4 and become the first of Baker's thirteen R&B Top Twenty hits.

8 On his twentieth birthday, **Elvis Presley** releases his third single, "Milkcow Blues Boogie," backed with "You're a Heartbreaker."

12 Blues singer **Etta James**' "Wallflower," her first R&B hit, is released on Modern Records.

14 Disc jockey **Alan Freed** begins his first New York area Rock and Roll Ball, a two-night affair to be held at the Saint Nicholas Arena in Harlem. Both shows at the 6,000-seat arena are sold out far in advance, grossing $24,000. Among the acts scheduled to perform: **Big Joe Turner**, the **Clovers**, **Fats Domino**, the **Moonglows**, the **Drifters** and the **Harptones**.

15 "Music with an R&B beat is no longer regarded as a passing phase by major recording firms," reports *Billboard.* The magazine notes that **Perry Como**, the **Crew-Cuts**, the **Hutton Sisters** and **Bill Darnell** and **Rosemary Clooney** have each recorded cover versions of **Gene and Eunice**'s #7 R&B hit "Ko Ko Mo." The success of the Crew Cuts' cover of the **Chords**' "Sh-Boom" is cited as a main factor in pop artists' interest in R&B covers.

26 **Bill Haley and the Comets**' "Dim Dim the Lights" enters the R&B chart. It will later hit #10 R&B, #11 pop.

28 The Top Ten R&B Show, starring the **Clovers**, **Faye Adams**, **Fats Domino**, **Joe Turner**, the **Moonglows**, **Amos Milburn**, **Charlie and Ray**, the **Paul Williams Orchestra**, and the **Bill Doggett Trio** kicks off its tour of forty-two one-nighters in New York City. The package tour plans to hit every area of the country except the West Coast.

FEBRUARY

2 **Petula Clark**'s first hit, "Majorca," debuts on the British chart. Although the single is the first of a string of Top Twenty hits in the U.K. and Europe, it will be a decade before Clark places a hit in the U.S. charts.

5 WNEW radio in New York City announces the results of its annual music popularity poll. The winners are **Perry Como**, **Patti Page**, the **Crew-Cuts** and **Ray Anthony**.

9 **Etta James**' "The Wallflower" enters the R&B chart; it will eventually hit #2.

19 A Dot Records advertisement in *Billboard* introduces "A GREAT NEW VOICE—PAT BOONE" singing "Tra-La-La" and "Two Hearts," the latter of which hits #16 in April and becomes the first of Boone's thirty-eight Top Forty hits over the next seven years.

20 Released today are **Big Joe Turner**'s "Flip, Flop and Fly," **Wynonie Harris**' "Good Mambo Tonight" and **Jimmy Reed**'s "You Don't Have to Go Boogie in the Park."

23 **Jimmy Reed**'s debut release, "You Don't Have to Go," enters the R&B charts; it later goes to #9 and becomes the first of thirteen R&B Top Twenty hits Reed will have over the next six years.

26 For the first time since their introduction in 1949, 45 rpm discs are outselling the old standard, the 78, *Billboard* reports. Another change in the industry is also noted. On some New York City jukeboxes it now costs ten cents instead of five cents to play a record.

LaVern Baker appeals to Congress, in a letter to Michigan

Representative Charles Diggs, Jr., to revise the Copyright Act of 1909 so that recording artists can be protected against "note-for-note copying" of previously recorded R&B tunes and arrangements by white (i.e., pop) artists and arrangers. Baker's R&B hit "Tweedle Dee" was covered by **Georgia Gibbs** *and* **Vicki Young**, both of these versions—at least theoretically—have deprived the original artists of the royalties they might have received if there had been no competing version. ♦

WEEK ENDING JANUARY 5		
U.S. #1 POP 45	"Mr. Sandman"	The Chordettes
U.S. #1 POP LP	*The Student Prince*	Mario Lanza
U.S. #1 R&B 45	"Hearts of Stone"	The Charms
U.K. #1 POP 45	"Finger of Suspicion"	Dickie Valentine

WEEK ENDING JANUARY 12		
U.S. #1 POP 45	"Let Me Go, Lover"	Joan Weber
U.S. #1 POP LP	*The Student Prince*	Mario Lanza
U.S. #1 R&B 45	"Hearts of Stone"	The Charms
U.K. #1 POP 45	"Mambo Italiano"	Rosemary Clooney

WEEK ENDING JANUARY 19		
U.S. #1 POP 45	"Let Me Go, Lover"	Joan Weber
U.S. #1 POP LP	*The Student Prince*	Mario Lanza
U.S. #1 R&B 45	"Earth Angel"	The Penguins
U.K. #1 POP 45	"Mambo Italiano"	Rosemary Clooney

WEEK ENDING JANUARY 26		
U.S. #1 POP 45	"Hearts of Stone"	Fontane Sisters
U.S. #1 POP LP	*The Student Prince*	Mario Lanza
U.S. #1 R&B 45	"Earth Angel"	The Penguins
U.K. #1 POP 45	"I Need You Now"	Eddie Fisher

WEEK ENDING FEBRUARY 2		
U.S. #1 POP 45	"Sincerely"	The McGuire Sisters
U.S. #1 POP LP	*The Student Prince*	Mario Lanza
U.S. #1 R&B 45	"Earth Angel"	The Penguins
U.K. #1 POP 45	"I Need You Now"	Eddie Fisher

WEEK ENDING FEBRUARY 9		
U.S. #1 POP 45	"Sincerely"	The McGuire Sisters
U.S. #1 POP LP	*The Student Prince*	Mario Lanza
U.S. #1 R&B 45	"Pledging My Love"	Johnny Ace
U.K. #1 POP 45	"Softly, Softly"	Ruby Murray

WEEK ENDING FEBRUARY 16		
U.S. #1 POP 45	"Sincerely"	The McGuire Sisters
U.S. #1 POP LP	*The Student Prince*	Mario Lanza
U.S. #1 R&B 45	"Pledging My Love"	Johnny Ace
U.K. #1 POP 45	"Softly, Softly"	Ruby Murray

WEEK ENDING FEBRUARY 23		
U.S. #1 POP 45	"Sincerely"	The McGuire Sisters
U.S. #1 POP LP	*Music, Martinis and Memories*	Jackie Gleason & Orchestra
U.S. #1 R&B 45	"Pledging My Love"	Johnny Ace
U.K. #1 POP 45	"Softly, Softly"	Ruby Murray

MARCH

5 In the wake of the ever growing controversy over so-called off-color or offensive R&B records, BMI, the largest organization of music publishers, announces plans to tighten controls on objectionable lyrics. BMI never granted clearance to nearly a dozen singles, some of which—like **Big Joe Turner**'s "Shake, Rattle and Roll"—became major hits.

Elvis Presley makes his television debut on the regionally telecast "The Louisiana Hayride."

10 Atlantic Records vice-presidents **Ahmet Ertegun** and **Jerry Wexler** present **Ruth Brown** with a gold record to commemorate the more than 5 million records she's sold since her debut on Atlantic. The award is given at New York's Apollo Theater.

12 Jazz saxophonist **Charlie "Bird" Parker** dies in New York City of heart failure at age thirty-four. The virtual inventor of the be-bop form played his last gig a week before at the New York City jazz club Birdland, which was named for him.

16 **Roy Hamilton**'s "Unchained Melody" is released by Epic Records. The song eventually reaches #6

and is later recorded by several other singers, including, in 1965, the **Righteous Brothers**.

21 Blues shouter **Big Maybelle** records "Whole Lotta Shakin' Goin' On" for Columbia Records' Okeh subsidiary in New York City. The session guitarist is **Mickey Baker**, later of **Mickey and Sylvia** fame.

22 Disc jockey **Alan Freed** joins the staff of Coral Records as an A&R (artists and repertoire) man for R&B. Freed's two-year contract also calls for him to work with Coral's parent company, Decca, as a producer.

26 Pop covers of R&B hit songs are now dominating the pop chart despite what *Billboard* describes as the "scarcely veiled antagonism of many pop publishers and A&R men toward R&B material."

APRIL

1 **Elvis Presley**'s fourth single, a cover of **Arthur Gunter**'s "Baby, Let's Play House," backed with "I'm Left, You're Right, She's Gone," is released. Later this month, Presley, along with **Bill Black** and **Scotty Moore**, goes to New York City to audition for "Arthur Godfrey's Talent Scouts," as has **Pat Boone**. Pres-

ley is rejected; Boone later wins first place.

8 New York City WINS disc jockey **Alan Freed**'s Rock and Roll Easter Jubilee opens a one-week run at Brooklyn's Paramount Theater. Despite the fact that the show opens on Good Friday, the 4,400-seat theater is over half full. The performers include the **Moonglows**, the **Penguins** and **LaVern Baker**.

Johnnie Ray's first U.K. hit, "If You Believe," debuts on the British charts.

12 "Your Hit Parade," a nationally broadcast radio program featuring the hit records of the day, celebrates its twentieth anniversary.

15 The **Crew-Cuts**' cover of the **Penguins**' 1954 Number One R&B hit "Earth Angel" begins a twenty-week run on the British charts.

17 **Fats Domino**'s "Ain't That a Shame," which *Billboard* erroneously lists for months as "Ain't *It* a Shame," is released on Commodore Records.

27 **Georgia Gibbs**' cover of R&B singer **Etta James**' "Dance with Me, Henry" (originally entitled "Roll with Me, Henry") and thus, like many sexually explicit R&B tunes, deemed objectionable by radio programmers) peaks on the *Billboard* charts at #2; it will stay on the chart for the next four and a half months.

28 **Alan Freed** and Coral Records mutually agree to invalidate an earlier agreement that made Freed a Coral A&R man and producer. Freed claims he lacks time to carry out those responsibilities but that he may work in those capacities on a freelance basis for Coral and other labels.

30 Rockabilly singer **Charlie Feathers** releases his debut single, "Peepin' Eyes," backed with "I've Been Deceived," on Flip Records. Though *Billboard*'s review calls Feathers "a major country talent," Feathers' career is never as successful as those of rockabillies **Carl Perkins**, **Johnny Cash** or **Elvis Presley**. ◆

WEEK ENDING MARCH 2		
U.S. #1 POP 45	"Sincerely"	The McGuire Sisters
U.S. #1 POP LP	*The Student Prince*	Mario Lanza
U.S. #1 R&B 45	"Pledging My Love"	Johnny Ace
U.K. #1 POP 45	"Give Me Your Word"	Tennessee Ernie Ford
WEEK ENDING MARCH 9		
U.S. #1 POP 45	"Sincerely"	The McGuire Sisters
U.S. #1 POP LP	*The Student Prince*	Mario Lanza
U.S. #1 R&B 45	"Pledging My Love"	Johnny Ace
U.K. #1 POP 45	"Give Me Your Word"	Tennessee Ernie Ford
WEEK ENDING MARCH 16		
U.S. #1 POP 45	"The Ballad of Davy Crockett"	Bill Hayes
U.S. #1 POP LP	*The Student Prince*	Mario Lanza
U.S. #1 R&B 45	"Pledging My Love"	Johnny Ace
U.K. #1 POP 45	"Give Me Your Word"	Tennessee Ernie Ford
WEEK ENDING MARCH 23		
U.S. #1 POP 45	"The Ballad of Davy Crockett"	Bill Hayes
U.S. #1 POP LP	*The Student Prince*	Mario Lanza
U.S. #1 R&B 45	"Pledging My Love"	Johnny Ace
U.K. #1 POP 45	"Give Me Your Word"	Tennessee Ernie Ford
WEEK ENDING MARCH 30		
U.S. #1 POP 45	"The Ballad of Davy Crockett"	Bill Hayes
U.S. #1 POP LP	*The Student Prince*	Mario Lanza
U.S. #1 R&B 45	"Pledging My Love"	Johnny Ace
U.K. #1 POP 45	"Give Me Your Word"	Tennessee Ernie Ford

WEEK ENDING APRIL 6		
U.S. #1 POP 45	"The Ballad of Davy Crockett"	Bill Hayes
U.S. #1 POP LP	*The Student Prince*	Mario Lanza
U.S. #1 R&B 45	"Pledging My Love"	Johnny Ace
U.K. #1 POP 45	"Give Me Your Word"	Tennessee Ernie Ford
WEEK ENDING APRIL 13		
U.S. #1 POP 45	"The Ballad of Davy Crockett"	Bill Hayes
U.S. #1 POP LP	*The Student Prince*	Mario Lanza
U.S. #1 R&B 45	"My Babe"	Little Walter
U.K. #1 POP 45	"Give Me Your Word"	Tennessee Ernie Ford
WEEK ENDING APRIL 20		
U.S. #1 POP 45	"Cherry Pink & Apple Blossom"	Perez Prado
U.S. #1 POP LP	*The Student Prince*	Mario Lanza
U.S. #1 R&B 45	"My Babe"	Little Walter
U.K. #1 POP 45	"Cherry Pink & Apple Blossom"	Perez Prado
WEEK ENDING APRIL 27		
U.S. #1 POP 45	"Cherry Pink & Apple Blossom"	Perez Prado
U.S. #1 POP LP	*The Student Prince*	Mario Lanza
U.S. #1 R&B 45	"My Babe"	Little Walter
U.K. #1 POP 45	"Cherry Pink & Apple Blossom"	Perez Prado

MAY

12 The Gale Agency's Big R&B Show of 1955 kicks off a six-week tour of one-nighters in Omaha, Nebraska. The revue includes **Roy Hamilton**, the **Drifters**, **Willie Mabon** and **LaVern Baker**.

13 Elvis Presley's performance at Jacksonville, Florida, is the first Presley show at which a riot ensues.

14 Bo Diddley's "Bo Diddley," backed with "I'm a Man," debuts on the R&B chart; it will later hit #2 making it the Chicago singer/guitarist's most successful record. The A side introduces what will become known as the Bo Diddley beat.

Perez Prado's "Cherry Pink and Apple Blossom White" sells over a million records, more than 280,000 of which were sold overseas. Prado, a native of Cuba, is known as "El Rey de Mambo," or the Mambo King, but only four of his singles hit in the U.S.: "Patricia" (1958), "Guaglione" (1958) and "Patricia Twist" (1962).

22 Police in Bridgeport, Connecticut, cancel a dance scheduled to be held at the Ritz ballroom and headlined by **Fats Domino**. The authorities say the cancellation resulted when they found that "rock & roll dances might be featured" and justify their action by referring to "a recent near-riot at the New Haven Arena,"

where rock & roll dances were featured.

25 The **Nutmegs**, a Connecticut group who named themselves after their home state's tree, have their first, last and only hit when "Story Untold" enters the R&B chart.

28 "The Ballad of Davy Crockett" is the most popular song in the United States. *Billboard* refers to the tune as a "disc entity" and reports that if one adds up the sales of the many available versions—including those by **Bill Hayes**, **Tennessee Ernie Ford**, **Burl Ives**, **Steve Allen**, the **Walter Schumann Voices**, the **Sons of the Pioneers**, **Rusty Draper** and the original television series soundtrack version by **Fess Parker**—more than 18 million copies have been purchased in six months.

JUNE

26 Decca Records announces that **Bill Haley and the Comets** have sold more than three million records in thirteen months.

"Rock around the Clock" and "Shake, Rattle and Roll" each have sold over a million copies, while "Dim, Dim the Lights" and "Mambo Rock" each have sold about 500,000.

29 Count Basie's "Every Day" enters the R&B chart. With his use of riffing, of loose, stripped-down arrangements and hard-hitting, four-to-the-bar rhythms, pianist and bandleader Basie has been an important—though mostly unrecognized—influence on rock & roll.

Bill Haley and the Comets' "Rock around the Clock" becomes the first rock & roll song

to hit Number One on the American pop chart. While rock & roll, called by one name or another, has been around since at least the early Forties, it has been dismissed or repressed as "race music"—not suitable, with its primitive rhythms, raw emotion and sexual suggestiveness, for "civilized" white audiences. Haley, a white former country & western singer, changes all that: His may be slightly tamer than the music made by his black contemporaries, but it serves notice to the nation that rock & roll is not black music or white music but American music. ◆

WEEK ENDING MAY 4		
U.S. #1 POP 45	"Cherry Pink & Apple Blossom"	Perez Prado
U.S. #1 POP LP	*The Student Prince*	Mario Lanza
U.S. #1 R&B 45	"My Babe"	Little Walter
U.K. #1 POP 45	"Stranger in Paradise"	Tony Bennett

WEEK ENDING MAY 11		
U.S. #1 POP 45	"Cherry Pink & Apple Blossom"	Perez Prado
U.S. #1 POP LP	*The Student Prince*	Mario Lanza
U.S. #1 R&B 45	"Unchained Melody"	Roy Hamilton
U.K. #1 POP 45	"Stranger in Paradise"	Tony Bennett

WEEK ENDING MAY 18		
U.S. #1 POP 45	"Cherry Pink & Apple Blossom"	Perez Prado
U.S. #1 POP LP	*Crazy Otto*	Crazy Otto
U.S. #1 R&B 45	"Unchained Melody"	Roy Hamilton
U.K. #1 POP 45	"Cherry Pink & Apple Blossom"	Eddie Calvert

WEEK ENDING MAY 25		
U.S. #1 POP 45	"Unchained Melody"	Les Baxter
U.S. #1 POP LP	*Crazy Otto*	Crazy Otto
U.S. #1 R&B 45	"Unchained Melody"	Roy Hamilton
U.K. #1 POP 45	"Cherry Pink & Apple Blossom"	Eddie Calvert

WEEK ENDING JUNE 1		
U.S. #1 POP 45	"Unchained Melody"	Les Baxter
U.S. #1 POP LP	*Starring Sammy Davis, Jr.*	Sammy Davis, Jr.
U.S. #1 R&B 45	"Ain't That a Shame"	Fats Domino
U.K. #1 POP 45	"Cherry Pink & Apple Blossom"	Eddie Calvert

WEEK ENDING JUNE 8		
U.S. #1 POP 45	"Unchained Melody"	Les Baxter
U.S. #1 POP LP	*Starring Sammy Davis, Jr.*	Sammy Davis, Jr.
U.S. #1 R&B 45	"Ain't That a Shame"	Fats Domino
U.K. #1 POP 45	"Unchained Melody"	Jimmy Young

WEEK ENDING JUNE 15		
U.S. #1 POP 45	"Unchained Melody"	Les Baxter
U.S. #1 POP LP	*Starring Sammy Davis, Jr.*	Sammy Davis, Jr.
U.S. #1 R&B 45	"Ain't That a Shame"	Fats Domino
U.K. #1 POP 45	"Unchained Melody"	Jimmy Young

WEEK ENDING JUNE 22		
U.S. #1 POP 45	"Unchained Melody"	Les Baxter
U.S. #1 POP LP	*Starring Sammy Davis, Jr.*	Sammy Davis, Jr.
U.S. #1 R&B 45	"Ain't That a Shame"	Fats Domino
U.K. #1 POP 45	"Cherry Pink & Apple Blossom"	Eddie Calvert

WEEK ENDING JUNE 29		
U.S. #1 POP 45	"Rock around the Clock"	Bill Haley & the Comets
U.S. #1 POP LP	*Starring Sammy Davis, Jr.*	Sammy Davis, Jr.
U.S. #1 R&B 45	"Ain't That a Shame"	Fats Domino
U.K. #1 POP 45	"Unchained Melody"	Jimmy Young

JULY

6 "Baby, Let's Play House" becomes **Elvis Presley**'s first single to place on the national charts and hits #10 on the country & western charts.

Pat Boone's cover of **Fats Domino**'s "Ain't That a Shame" debuts on the U.S. pop chart at #14. Meanwhile, Domino's original version has hit Number One on the R&B chart.

15 American country yodeler **Slim Whitman**'s "Rosemarie" debuts on the British charts. Two weeks later it will begin its eleven-week run at the Number One spot, thus becoming one of the longest-running chart-toppers in British history. Whitman (born Otis Dewey) will also become the first country performer to play the London Palladium.

16 *Billboard* notes the boom in the popularity of R&B, citing the presence of R&B stars like **Sammy Davis, Jr.**, **Sarah Vaughan** and **LaVern Baker** on the pop charts. In a related story, the magazine attributes the "good health" of R&B to covers by pop artists, like **Eddie Fisher**'s cover of **Johnnie Ray**'s "Song of a Dreamer," **Patti Page**'s covers of **Nappy Brown**'s "Piddily Patter Patter" and **Ruth Brown**'s "Oh What a Dream I Had Last Night" and **Bill Haley**'s cover of **Big Joe Turner**'s "Shake, Rattle and Roll."

23 An advertisement for Chess Records announces the release of **Chuck Berry**'s "Maybellene" (which *Billboard* reviews and declares "fine jockey and juke wax"), "Mannish Boy" by **Muddy Waters** and "Do Me Right" by **Lowell Fulson**.

25 The **Collins Kids**, Larry, 10, and Lorrie, 13, sign to Columbia. A rockabilly act, the brother-and-sister duo will have several country hits, including "Mercy," "Whistle Bait" and "Boppin' Baby" but never enter the pop chart. Larry will later write **Helen Reddy**'s 1973 Number One pop hit, "Delta Dawn."

27 **Chuck Berry**'s first hit record, "Maybellene," enters the R&B chart.

Billboard claims that only two singing stars can be considered guaranteed hitmakers these days: **Nat "King" Cole** and country star **Webb Pierce**.

CBS-TV announces the production of a jazz version of Gilbert and Sullivan's *The Mikado*, starring **Lena Horne**, **Louis Armstrong** and **Eartha Kitt**.

AUGUST

3 **Bill Haley** files suit against **Dave Miller** of Essex Records, asking for a court injunction that would bar Miller from issuing recordings Haley made while under contract to Essex. The suit describes those recordings as "of inferior quality to said plaintiff's current releases."

10 Two weeks after its R&B Top Ten debut, **Chuck Berry**'s "Maybellene" enters the pop chart at #23.

13 In response to the unprecedented number of pop hits that are remakes of other, especially R&B, hits, Savoy Records announces that persons wishing to record "cover" versions of songs must obtain permission from the copyright office.

19 New York City's WINS radio announces that henceforth, it will not play "copy" recordings—covers that closely copy the arrangements or vocal phrasings of previously issued records. In a list circulated to its disc jockeys, the station management states that they must play **Fats Domino**'s "Ain't That a Shame" (not **Pat Boone**'s), **LaVern Baker**'s "Tweedle Dee" (not **Georgia Gibbs**') and **Chuck Berry**'s "Maybellene" (not **Johnny Long**'s). The policy does not apply to remakes in which the arrangements or phrasing are sufficiently different from the original recording as to amount to a reinterpretation.

20 Harlem's Apollo Theater presents—on one bill—**Big Joe Turner**, **Bo Diddley**, the **Five Keys**, the

Hearts, the **Spaniels** and other top R&B acts.

31 A London judge fines **Sidney Adams Turner** three pounds, ten shillings for "creating an abominable noise." Turner's crime: After threatening his neighbors, saying "I will drive you mad," he proceeded to play **Bill Haley and the Comets**' "Shake, Rattle and Roll" at top volume continuously from 2:00 p.m. until 4:30 p.m.

Smiley Lewis' "I Hear You Knockin'" debuts on the R&B chart. It later peaks at #2. ◆

WEEK ENDING JULY 6		
U.S. #1 POP 45	"Rock around the Clock"	Bill Haley & the Comets
U.S. #1 POP LP	*Starring Sammy Davis, Jr.*	Sammy Davis, Jr.
U.S. #1 R&B 45	"Ain't That a Shame"	Fats Domino
U.K. #1 POP 45	"Unchained Melody"	Jimmy Young

WEEK ENDING JULY 13		
U.S. #1 POP 45	"Rock around the Clock"	Bill Haley & the Comets
U.S. #1 POP LP	*Lonesome Echo*	Jackie Gleason
U.S. #1 R&B 45	"Ain't That a Shame"	Fats Domino
U.K. #1 POP 45	"Dreamboat"	Alma Cogan

WEEK ENDING JULY 20		
U.S. #1 POP 45	"Rock around the Clock"	Bill Haley & the Comets
U.S. #1 POP LP	*Lonesome Echo*	Jackie Gleason
U.S. #1 R&B 45	"Ain't That a Shame"	Fats Domino
U.K. #1 POP 45	"Dreamboat"	Alma Cogan

WEEK ENDING JULY 27		
U.S. #1 POP 45	"Rock around the Clock"	Bill Haley & the Comets
U.S. #1 POP LP	*Love Me or Leave Me*	Doris Day
U.S. #1 R&B 45	"Ain't That a Shame"	Fats Domino
U.K. #1 POP 45	"Rosemarie"	Slim Whitman

WEEK ENDING AUGUST 3		
U.S. #1 POP 45	"Rock around the Clock"	Bill Haley & the Comets
U.S. #1 POP LP	*Love Me or Leave Me*	Doris Day
U.S. #1 R&B 45	"Ain't That a Shame"	Fats Domino
U.K. #1 POP 45	"Rosemarie"	Slim Whitman

WEEK ENDING AUGUST 10		
U.S. #1 POP 45	"Rock around the Clock"	Bill Haley & the Comets
U.S. #1 POP LP	*Love Me or Leave Me*	Doris Day
U.S. #1 R&B 45	"Ain't That a Shame"	Fats Domino
U.K. #1 POP 45	"Rosemarie"	Slim Whitman

WEEK ENDING AUGUST 17		
U.S. #1 POP 45	"Rock around the Clock"	Bill Haley & the Comets
U.S. #1 POP LP	*Love Me or Leave Me*	Doris Day
U.S. #1 R&B 45	"Maybellene"	Chuck Berry
U.K. #1 POP 45	"Rosemarie"	Slim Whitman

WEEK ENDING AUGUST 24		
U.S. #1 POP 45	"Yellow Rose of Texas"	Mitch Miller
U.S. #1 POP LP	*Love Me or Leave Me*	Doris Day
U.S. #1 R&B 45	"Maybellene"	Chuck Berry
U.K. #1 POP 45	"Rosemarie"	Slim Whitman

WEEK ENDING AUGUST 31		
U.S. #1 POP 45	"Yellow Rose of Texas"	Mitch Miller
U.S. #1 POP LP	*Love Me or Leave Me*	Doris Day
U.S. #1 R&B 45	"Maybellene"	Chuck Berry
U.K. #1 POP 45	"Rosemarie"	Slim Whitman

SEPTEMBER

3 **Bill Haley and the Comets** turn down their first invitation to tour outside the U.S. because of fear of flying. The Australian offer guaranteed the group $2,000 a day for fifteen dates, but it wasn't enough to get them on a plane.

Billboard reports that independent record manufacturers are continuing to expand at an unprecedented rate, despite publicized marketing efforts on the part of majors to check the growth of independents. The latter grossed $20 million in 1954, with the larger labels—**Modern, Chess, Savoy, Peacock, Jubilee, Aladdin** and **Specialty**—leading in sales.

9 The J. P. Seeburg Corporation introduces its Dual Music System Jukebox, the first ever equipped to handle a hundred singles and two-song-per-side EPs, thus bringing the total number of selections to three hundred. Unlike jukeboxes that follow, this one plays only the A side of a record.

10 **Big Maybelle**'s "One Monkey Don't Stop No Show," backed with "Whole Lotta Shakin' Goin' On," is released on Okeh.

17 Capitol Records releases a **Les Paul** single, "Magic Melody, Part Two," that it claims is the shortest song ever released: It consists of only two notes. Paul decided to make the recording after Capitol had received complaints from disc jockeys about Paul's "Magic Melody." It seems that "Magic Melody" ended with the familiar "shave and a haircut, two bits" musical phrase—minus the last two notes—the "two bits," which "Magic Melody, Part Two" supplies.

21 The **Platters**' first million-selling single, "Only You (and You Alone)" enters the pop charts at #24. The song hits Number One on the R&B chart, where it made its debut ten weeks before. "Only You" later becomes the first record to sell more than a million copies in France (on the Barclay label).

28 The **Coasters**, still going by the name the **Robins**, record "Smokey Joe's Cafe" and "Riot in Cell Block Number Nine," both written and produced by **Jerry Leiber and Mike Stoller** and engineered by **Bunny Robyn** at Master Recorders, Los Angeles. The single is released on Leiber and Stoller's Spark label but later is included on the Coasters' first Atlantic album.

OCTOBER

5 **Elvis Presley**'s "I Forgot to Remember to Forget Her" hits #2 on the Memphis charts. The Number One song is **Johnny Cash**'s "Cry, Cry, Cry."

12 **Gale Storm**'s cover of **Smiley Lewis**' #2 R&B hit from a few months earlier, "I Hear You Knockin'," is released by Dot.

Sonny Boy Williamson's "Don't Start Me Talkin'" debuts on the R&B charts, where it later peaks at #7.

14 Nineteen-year-old **Buddy Holly** and his sidemen, **Larry Welborn** and **Bob Montgomery**, open a concert in Lubbock, Texas (Holly's hometown), for **Bill Haley and the Comets**. Nashville talent agent **Eddie Crandall** is in the audience; in upcoming weeks, he will arrange for Holly to make his first demo recordings for Decca Records in Nashville.

15 **Elvis Presley** plays Lubbock, Texas' Cotton Club. His opening act is **Buddy** (Holly) and **Bob** (Montgomery). A thirteen-year-old **Mac Davis** is in the audience.

ABC-TV premieres a new hour-long, every-fourth Saturday night series, "Grand Ole Opry," live from Nashville's Ryman Auditorium, the home of the Opry since 1942. The show's first guest stars are **Les Paul and Mary Ford**.

28 Several R&B artists, including **Little Willie John, Champion Jack Dupree, Little George Smith** and **Otis Williams** (formerly of the **Charms**), play the first date on a three-month-long tour of one-nighters at Harlem's Apollo Theater.

Johnnie Ray's "Song of the Dreamer" debuts on the British chart; it will become his fifth British chart entry and third single to chart in October alone.

Little Willie John's first chart hit, "All around the World," debuts on the R&B chart.

29 **Little Richard**'s "Tutti Frutti," backed with "I'm Just a Lonely Boy," is reviewed by *Billboard*: " . . . cleverly styled novelty with nonsense words, rapid-fire delivery."

R&B and soul singer **Joe Tex**'s debut, "Davy, You Upset My Home" (an "answer" record to the concurrent Davy Crockett trend), backed with "Come in This House," is released by King Records. ◆

WEEK	ENDING	SEPTEMBER	7
U.S. #1 POP 45	"Yellow Rose of Texas"		Mitch Miller
U.S. #1 POP LP	*Love Me or Leave Me*		Doris Day
U.S. #1 R&B 45	"Maybellene"		Chuck Berry
U.K. #1 POP 45	"Rosemarie"		Slim Whitman

WEEK	ENDING	SEPTEMBER	14
U.S. #1 POP 45	"Yellow Rose of Texas"		Mitch Miller
U.S. #1 POP LP	*Love Me or Leave Me*		Doris Day
U.S. #1 R&B 45	"Maybellene"		Chuck Berry
U.K. #1 POP 45	"Rosemarie"		Slim Whitman

WEEK	ENDING	SEPTEMBER	21
U.S. #1 POP 45	"Yellow Rose of Texas"		Mitch Miller
U.S. #1 POP LP	*Love Me or Leave Me*		Doris Day
U.S. #1 R&B 45	"Maybellene"		Chuck Berry
U.K. #1 POP 45	"Rosemarie"		Slim Whitman

WEEK	ENDING	SEPTEMBER	28
U.S. #1 POP 45	"Love Is a Many Spendored . . ."		Four Aces
U.S. #1 POP LP	*Love Me or Leave Me*		Doris Day
U.S. #1 R&B 45	"Maybellene"		Chuck Berry
U.K. #1 POP 45	"Rosemarie"		Slim Whitman

WEEK	ENDING	OCTOBER	5
U.S. #1 POP 45	"Yellow Rose of Texas"		Mitch Miller
U.S. #1 POP LP	*Love Me or Leave Me*		Doris Day
U.S. #1 R&B 45	"Maybellene"		Chuck Berry
U.K. #1 POP 45	"Man from Laramie"		Jimmy Young

WEEK	ENDING	OCTOBER	12
U.S. #1 POP 45	"Love Is a Many Spendored"		Four Aces
U.S. #1 POP LP	*Love Me or Leave Me*		Doris Day
U.S. #1 R&B 45	"Maybellene"		Chuck Berry
U.K. #1 POP 45	"Man from Laramie"		Jimmy Young

WEEK	ENDING	OCTOBER	19
U.S. #1 POP 45	"Autumn Leaves"		Roger Williams
U.S. #1 POP LP	*Love Me or Leave Me*		Doris Day
U.S. #1 R&B 45	"Only You"		The Platters
U.K. #1 POP 45	"Man from Laramie"		Jimmy Young

WEEK	ENDING	OCTOBER	26
U.S. #1 POP 45	"Autumn Leaves"		Roger Williams
U.S. #1 POP LP	*Love Me or Leave Me*		Doris Day
U.S. #1 R&B 45	"Only You"		The Platters
U.K. #1 POP 45	"Man from Laramie"		Jimmy Young

NOVEMBER

12 *Billboard* publishes the results of its annual disc jockey poll. The most played R&B single is **Johnny Ace**'s posthumous hit, "Pledging My Love," most promising R&B artist is **Chuck Berry** and the favorite R&B artist is **Fats Domino**. In the pop category, rock & roll, despite all the year's breakthroughs, is barely present. **Elvis Presley** is voted the most promising country & western artist.

14 A reissue of **Bill Haley and the Comets**' "Rock around the Clock" debuts, again, on the U.K. chart. This is only the second of the song's five chart appearances. Others follow in 1956, 1968 and 1974.

20 New York City disc jockey **Tommy "Dr. Jive" Smalls** appears on **Ed Sullivan**'s television show, where he acts as emcee for a fifteen-minute segment featuring **LaVern Baker**, **Bo Diddley**, the **Five Keys** and **Willis "Gator Tail" Jackson**. During rehearsals, Diddley refuses Sullivan's request that he play "Sixteen Tons." Nonetheless, Diddley, who claims not to know the tune, is coached and provided cue cards during rehearsals. But come show time, Diddley performs his own "Bo Diddley." Sullivan's reaction: "more surprised than pleased."

22 RCA Victor makes its best investment ever: A&R man **Steve Sholes** signs **Elvis Presley** to the label. The deal, which is made final at New York City's Warwick Hotel, involves $40,000—a then-unprecedented sum—which was divided between Sun Records ($25,000 for Presley's contract) and Hi-Lo Music ($15,000 for Presley's song publishing). In addition, Elvis himself got $5,000. Sun Records owner **Sam Phillips** invests his $25,000 in the Holiday Inn hotel chain, Presley buys himself a new Cadillac, and, within twenty years, RCA sells half a billion Elvis records.

23 The **Cadillacs**' "Speedoo" enters the charts. The song's title is the nickname of the vocal group's lead singer, **Earl Carroll**. The line "Everybody calls me Speedoo, but my real name is Mr. Earl" is revived two decades later by **Paul Simon** in "Was a Sunny Day."

DECEMBER

3 **Ernest Kador**—who later renames himself **Ernie K-Doe**—releases "Eternity," backed with "Do, Baby, Do," on Specialty Records.

5 At the BMI Annual Awards Dinner in New York City, R&B songs win an unprecedented eleven (out of twenty-three) awards. Among the feted songs are "Maybellene," "I Hear You Knockin'," "Pledging My Love," "Sincerely," "Earth Angel," "Dance with Me, Henry" and "Only You."

15 Sun Records releases **Johnny Cash**'s "Folsom Prison Blues." Cash, who has never served time in prison (although he will spend a night in jail in 1963), was inspired to write the song after seeing the movie *Inside the Walls of Folsom Prison*. Cash's live recording in Folsom Prison in 1968 will be one of his most popular albums.

17 With "Only You" at #2, the **Platters**' "The Great Pretender" enters the R&B chart at #13.

Tennessee Ernie Ford's "Sixteen Tons" tops both the pop and country & western charts.

19 **Carl Perkins** records what will be his biggest (#2) pop hit, "Blue Suede Shoes," at Sun Studios in Memphis.

23 New York City is the location of two big-budget rock & roll shows, each extending seven days (23 through 27) over the Christmas holidays. One, at the Brooklyn Paramount, is conducted by WWRL's **Dr. Jive (Tommy Smalls)**, grosses $85,000 and stars **Ruth Brown** and **Clyde McPhatter**. The second show, with WINS' **Alan Freed** as host, is held at Manhattan's Academy

THE CADILLACS

of Music, grosses over $100,000 and is headlined by **Count Basie**, **Boyd Bennett**, **LaVern Baker**, the **Cadillacs** and others.

26 **Bill Haley and the Comets**' "See You Later, Alligator" is released by Decca Records. Peaking at #6 on the pop chart and #14 on the R&B chart, it will be Haley's biggest hit since "Rock around the Clock."

28 **Drifters** lead singer **Clyde McPhatter**'s first solo hit, "Seven Days," enters the R&B chart. It will later peak at #3 and go on to #44 on the pop chart in 1956.

31 "Unchained Melody" is named the Number One top tune of 1955 based on *Billboard's* Honor Roll of Hits, a chart that takes into consideration dealer sales, disc jockey favorites and jukebox play. ◆

WEEK ENDING NOVEMBER 2		
U.S. #1 POP 45	"Autumn Leaves"	Roger Williams
U.S. #1 POP LP	*Love Me or Leave Me*	Doris Day
U.S. #1 R&B 45	"Only You"	The Platters
U.K. #1 POP 45	"Hernando's Hideaway"	The Johnston Brothers

WEEK ENDING NOVEMBER 9		
U.S. #1 POP 45	"Love Is a Many Spendored . . ."	Four Aces
U.S. #1 POP LP	*Love Me or Leave Me*	Doris Day
U.S. #1 R&B 45	"Only You"	The Platters
U.K. #1 POP 45	"Hernando's Hideaway"	The Johnston Brothers

WEEK ENDING NOVEMBER 16		
U.S. #1 POP 45	"Love Is a Many Spendored . . ."	Four Aces
U.S. #1 POP LP	*Love Me or Leave Me*	Doris Day
U.S. #1 R&B 45	"Only You"	The Platters
U.K. #1 POP 45	"Rock around the Clock"	Bill Haley & the Comets

WEEK ENDING NOVEMBER 23		
U.S. #1 POP 45	"Sixteen Tons"	Tennessee Ernie Ford
U.S. #1 POP LP	*Love Me or Leave Me*	Doris Day
U.S. #1 R&B 45	"Only You"	The Platters
U.K. #1 POP 45	"Rock around the Clock"	Bill Haley & the Comets

WEEK ENDING NOVEMBER 30		
U.S. #1 POP 45	"Sixteen Tons"	Tennessee Ernie Ford
U.S. #1 POP LP	*Love Me or Leave Me*	Doris Day
U.S. #1 R&B 45	"Only You"	The Platters
U.K. #1 POP 45	"Rock around the Clock"	Bill Haley & the Comets

WEEK ENDING DECEMBER 7		
U.S. #1 POP 45	"Sixteen Tons"	Tennessee Ernie Ford
U.S. #1 POP LP	*Love Me or Leave Me*	Doris Day
U.S. #1 R&B 45	"Hands Off"	Jay McShaun
U.K. #1 POP 45	"Christmas Alphabet"	Dickie Valentine

WEEK ENDING DECEMBER 14		
U.S. #1 POP 45	"Sixteen Tons"	Tennessee Ernie Ford
U.S. #1 POP LP	*Love Me or Leave Me*	Doris Day
U.S. #1 R&B 45	"Hands Off"	Jay McShaun
U.K. #1 POP 45	"Christmas Alphabet"	Dickie Valentine

WEEK ENDING DECEMBER 21		
U.S. #1 POP 45	"Sixteen Tons"	Tennessee Ernie Ford
U.S. #1 POP LP	*Oklahoma!*	soundtrack
U.S. #1 R&B 45	"Hands Off"	Jay McShaun
U.K. #1 POP 45	"Christmas Alphabet"	Dickie Valentine

WEEK ENDING DECEMBER 28		
U.S. #1 POP 45	"Sixteen Tons"	Tennessee Ernie Ford
U.S. #1 POP LP	*Oklahoma!*	soundtrack
U.S. #1 R&B 45	"The Great Pretender"	The Platters
U.K. #1 POP 45	"Christmas Alphabet"	Dickie Valentine

1956

This was the year when it all broke wide open, thanks mainly to Elvis Presley. Elvis seemed to be everywhere. He was all over the charts, be they pop, R&B or country & western. Though Carl Perkins' "Blue Suede Shoes" was actually the first C&W tune to enter the R&B chart, it was Elvis' first RCA Victor release, "Heartbreak Hotel," that topped the pop, R&B and C&W charts simultaneously. This crossover trend would continue throughout the year, with records by Elvis and others signaling a cross-fertilization of previously demarcated and segregated genres. Rock & roll was the all-American hybrid, and here was the proof.

This year, Elvis made his first national television appearances. He played his first American concert above the Mason-Dixon line (in Dayton, Ohio, in May). He made his first appearance in Las Vegas, opening for comic Shecky Greene and Freddie Martin's Orchestra (Elvis was canceled after one week). Earlier in the year, Ed Sullivan announced that he would never allow Elvis on his TV show, but by the end of the year, Sullivan had reneged and Elvis had appeared on his show three times, each time drawing phenomenal ratings. Elvis became a sensation outside America as well, topping British and European charts. In Canada, he sold more records at a faster clip than anyone ever had before.

Elvis was fast becoming rock & roll's first great star. And, not surprisingly, his music, his personality, his style—even his background—became fair game for critics of all types. While some criticisms were colorful—a TV critic described Elvis' gyrations as "the mating dance of an aborigine"—others were unfair, even demeaning. *Life* magazine, for example, not only derisively termed Elvis "a howling hillbilly," but when quoting him, transcribed his words phonetically so that *I* became *Ah.* Then there was outright censorship: for his third appearance on the "Ed Sullivan Show," Sullivan had his cameramen shoot Elvis from the waist up. Steve Allen went so far as to dress Elvis in tails and have him sing "Hound Dog" to a real live bassett hound. One imagines Allen having a laugh, but certainly not the last: the next day teenagers picketed his studio, carrying placards that read, WE WANT THE *Real* ELVIS.

Of course, the attacks on rock & roll in general grew as well. Dance concerts continued to be banned, newspapers ran anti-rock & roll editorials, often quoting psychiatrists like the one who described the music as a "disease." Shortly after the first national rock & roll radio shows began broadcasting, television journalist Eric Sevareid conducted a radio panel discussion on rock & roll's effect on American youth, featuring two psychiatrists, rock & roll DJ Alan Freed and one of rock & roll's most outspoken opponents, Columbia Records executive and recording artist Mitch Miller. And the North Alabama White Citizens Council declared that rock & roll music was a nefarious racial plot.

But it was all for naught. Bill Haley's *Rock around the Clock* became the first rock & roll album to enter the pop LP chart. In September, RCA announced that Elvis accounted for sixty percent of the company's production, and had already sold over 10 million records worldwide. For the first time, original R&B recordings were consistently outselling their white pop cover versions. Meanwhile, rock & roll began spreading like wildfire around the world—especially in England where the new sounds would inspire a generation of musicians who would change rock & roll's future. Bill Haley's movie *Rock around the Clock* sparked teen riots at U.K. showings. London's first rock & roll club, Studio 51, opened. The first British rock & roll discs were recorded by Johnny "King of Zing" Brandon and Elvis-clone Tommy Steele.

By the end of the year, RCA had marketed a line of phonographs autographed by Elvis Presley. They sold like hotcakes. Rock & roll was big money.

JANUARY

11 The **Coasters**, formerly the **Robins**, record their first sides under their new name. The songs, "Down in Mexico" and "Turtle Dovin'," are written and produced by Jerry Leiber and Mike Stoller and engineered by Bunny Robyn in Hollywood, California.

18 **Little Richard** enters the pop chart at #26 with "Tutti Frutti" (currently on the R&B chart). His original edges out covers by **Pat Boone** and **Elvis Presley**. The Top Fifteen pop album chart, dominated as usual by records like *Jackie Gleason Plays Music for Lovers Only, Jackie Gleason Plays Music to Make You Misty* and *Jackie Gleason Plays Romantic Jazz,* lists its first rock & roll entry, **Bill Haley and the Comets'** *Rock around the Clock,* at #12.

26 **Buddy Holly's** first recording session for Decca is held in Nashville.

27 Probably the most star-studded R&B package tour to date gets under way in Pittsburgh, Pennsylvania. Promoted by impresario **Irvin Feld**, the show features **Bill Haley and the Comets**, the **Platters**, **LaVern Baker**, **Shirley and Lee**, **Red Prysock**, the **Drifters**, **Joe Turner**, the **Five Keys**, **Bo Diddley**, **Roy Hamilton** and the **Turbans**. The ten-date tour through the South will conclude in Washington, D.C. on February 5.

RCA releases its first new **Elvis Presley** material: "Heartbreak Hotel," backed with "I Was the One."

28 **Elvis Presley** makes his national television debut on "The Dorsey Brothers Stage Show" on CBS.

30 Seventeen thousand country music fans ignore a four-inch snowstorm in Denver, Colorado, to attend a Coliseum concert featuring **Webb Pierce**, **Red Foley**, the **Foggy River Boys**, **Ray Price**, **Floyd Cramer**, **Roy Hill**, the **Echo Valley Boys** and others.

Jerry Lee Lewis plays piano for rockabilly singer **Billy Lee Riley's** Sun Studio session. They record "Red Hot," which will become Riley's most successful record. Earlier, Riley and his group, the **Little Green Men**, had a local hit with "Flying Saucers Rock 'n' Roll," one of the most unusual rockabilly songs ever recorded.

FEBRUARY

1 The Rock and Roll Ice Revue, billed "the hottest production ever staged on ice," opens at the Roxy Theater in New York City.

2 Atlantic Records signs the **Coasters**, made up of former **Robins** **Carl Gardner** and **Bobby Nunn**, along with **Billy Guy** and **Leon Hughes**, and rushes to release their first record, "Down in Mexico," backed with "Turtle Dovin'," both written by new

Atlantic writers Leiber and Stoller.

8 **Frankie Lymon and the Teenagers'** "Why Do Fools Fall in Love" and the **Teen Queens'** "Eddie, My Love" enter the R&B chart.

12 Crypt-kicker Screamin' Jay Hawkins records "I Put a Spell on You" for Okeh Records in New York City.

13 **Alan Freed** signs with Coral Records for the second time. He is to compile and promote four dance and party album sets his first year.

16 The American Guild of Variety Artists' national administrative secretary, **Jackie Bright**, declares at a press conference in New York that "DJs who put on record dances are putting musicians out of work." He threatens to forbid guild members to cooperate with disc jockeys.

22 *Billboard* reviews **James Brown's** debut record, "Please, Please, Please": "A dynamic, religious fervor runs through the pleading solo here. Brown and the Famous Flames group let off plenty of steam."

24 Police in Cleveland, Ohio, invoke a 1931 ordinance barring people under eighteen years of age from danc-

ing in public unless accompanied by an adult.

25 Disc jockeys from fifteen cities meet in New York City to form the National Rhythm and Blues Disc Jockey Association of America to combat offensive song lyrics and payola, the practice whereby artists "pay" disc jockeys to play their records.

27 **Little Richard's** first Number One R&B hit, "Slippin' and Slidin'," backed with "Long Tall Sally," is released on Specialty.

29 **Elvis Presley's** "Heartbreak Hotel" enters the pop chart at #22; **Carl Perkins'** "Blue Suede Shoes" enters at #28. ◆

WEEK ENDING JANUARY 4

U.S. #1 POP 45	"Memories Are Made of This"	Dean Martin
U.S. #1 POP LP	*Oklahoma!*	soundtrack
U.S. #1 R&B 45	"The Great Pretender"	The Platters
U.K. #1 POP 45	"Rock around the Clock"	Bill Haley & the Comets

WEEK ENDING JANUARY 11

U.S. #1 POP 45	"Memories Are Made of This"	Dean Martin
U.S. #1 POP LP	*Oklahoma!*	soundtrack
U.S. #1 R&B 45	"The Great Pretender"	The Platters
U.K. #1 POP 45	"Rock around the Clock"	Bill Haley & the Comets

WEEK ENDING JANUARY 18

U.S. #1 POP 45	"Memories Are Made of This"	Dean Martin
U.S. #1 POP LP	*Oklahoma!*	soundtrack
U.S. #1 R&B 45	"The Great Pretender"	The Platters
U.K. #1 POP 45	"Sixteen Tons"	Tennessee Ernie Ford

WEEK ENDING JANUARY 25

U.S. #1 POP 45	"Memories Are Made of This"	Dean Martin
U.S. #1 POP LP	*Oklahoma!*	soundtrack
U.S. #1 R&B 45	"The Great Pretender"	The Platters
U.K. #1 POP 45	"Sixteen Tons"	Tennessee Ernie Ford

WEEK ENDING FEBRUARY 1

U.S. #1 POP 45	"Memories Are Made of This"	Dean Martin
U.S. #1 POP LP	*Oklahoma!*	soundtrack
U.S. #1 R&B 45	"The Great Pretender"	The Platters
U.K. #1 POP 45	"Sixteen Tons"	Tennessee Ernie Ford

WEEK ENDING FEBRUARY 8

U.S. #1 POP 45	"Memories Are Made of This"	Dean Martin
U.S. #1 POP LP	*Oklahoma!*	soundtrack
U.S. #1 R&B 45	"The Great Pretender"	The Platters
U.K. #1 POP 45	"Sixteen Tons"	Tennessee Ernie Ford

WEEK ENDING FEBRUARY 15

U.S. #1 POP 45	"Rock and Roll Waltz"	Kay Starr
U.S. #1 POP LP	*Oklahoma!*	soundtrack
U.S. #1 R&B 45	"The Great Pretender"	The Platters
U.K. #1 POP 45	"Memories Are Made of This"	Dean Martin

WEEK ENDING FEBRUARY 22

U.S. #1 POP 45	"Rock and Roll Waltz"	Kay Starr
U.S. #1 POP LP	*Oklahoma!*	soundtrack
U.S. #1 R&B 45	"The Great Pretender"	The Platters
U.K. #1 POP 45	"Memories Are Made of This"	Dean Martin

WEEK ENDING FEBRUARY 29

U.S. #1 POP 45	"Rock and Roll Waltz"	Kay Starr
U.S. #1 POP LP	*Oklahoma!*	soundtrack
U.S. #1 R&B 45	"The Great Pretender"	The Platters
U.K. #1 POP 45	"Memories Are Made of This"	Dean Martin

MARCH

7 **Carl Perkins**' "Blue Suede Shoes" enters the R&B chart. It is the first time a C&W artist has made the R&B chart.

15 **Colonel Tom Parker** becomes **Elvis Presley**'s manager. Parker's previous show-business experience included managing country stars **Hank Snow, Gene Autry** and **Eddy Arnold** and, earlier, founding the Great Parker Pony Circus and Colonel Tom Parker and His Dancing Turkeys. Parker would manage Presley all his life and after his death.

22 **Carl Perkins** is injured in a car accident near Wilmington, Delaware, en route to New York to perform on the Ed Sullivan show. Perkins is forced to spend several months in the hospital, a career setback from which he never completely recovers.

25 By the end of **Alan Freed**'s three-day Rock 'n' Roll Show at the Stage Theater in Hartford, Connecticut, police have arrested eleven teenagers and revoked the theater's license to operate. The incident prompts Hartford Institute of Living psychiatrist **Dr. Francis J. Braceland** to testify at license hearings that rock & roll is "a communicable disease, with music appealing to adolescent insecurity and driving teenagers to do outlandish things. . . . It's cannibalistic and tribalistic." In response to Braceland, swing-era bandleader **Sammy Kaye**, in an open letter denounces those remarks as "thoughtless and in bad taste."

31 In a rally in Birmingham, Alabama, **Asa Carter**, executive secretary of the North Alabama White Citizen's Council, charges that rock & roll was introduced to white teenagers by the National Association for the Advancement of Colored People and other pro-integration forces. He initiates a campaign to pressure radio stations to bar what he terms "immoral" music.

APRIL

3 **Elvis Presley** makes the first of two appearances on "The Milton Berle Show." Presley sings "Heartbreak Hotel," "Money, Honey" and "Blue Suede Shoes," and earns $5,000. It is estimated that one out of every four Americans sees his performance.

6 Paramount Pictures signs **Elvis Presley** to a three-picture deal only five days after he makes his first screen test in Hollywood.

7 The CBS Radio Network premieres the first regularly scheduled national broadcast rock & roll show, "Rock 'n' Roll Dance Party," with **Alan Freed** as host.

10 **Nat "King" Cole** is attacked and severely beaten by a group of racial segregationists while singing onstage at the Municipal Hall in Birmingham, Alabama. Two days later, **Bob Raiford**, a disc jockey for WBT in Charlotte, North Carolina, is summarily fired for "taking an unauthorized stand on a controversial issue." Raiford's "stand" consisted of denouncing on the air the racially motivated attack.

11 The man who later will be known as Soul Brother Number One, **James Brown**, has his first chart entry when "Please, Please, Please" debuts on the R&B chart.

15 **Alan Freed**, Columbia Records A&R director **Mitch Miller**, two psychiatrists and two teenage rock & roll fans discuss rock & roll on **Eric Sevareid**'s CBS television talk show. Freed, addressing "Mom and Dad," argues that stories of rock & roll-incited riots are "grossly exaggerated."

16 One week after CBS unveiled the first national rock & roll show, ABC airs its own: "Rhythm on Parade," which is broadcast live from the Flame Show Bar in Detroit, with host **Willie Bryant**.

23 **Elvis Presley**, accompanied by **Bill Black** and **Scotty Moore**, makes his Las Vegas debut at the New Frontier Hotel, where he is the opening act for the **Freddie Martin Orchestra** and comedian **Shecky Greene**. The two-week run is canceled after only one week because of poor reception. Presley will not play Las Vegas again for almost thirteen years. ◆

WEEK ENDING MARCH 7		
U.S. #1 POP 45	"The Poor People of Paris"	Les Baxter
U.S. #1 POP LP	*Oklahoma!*	soundtrack
U.S. #1 R&B 45	"Why Do Fools Fall in Love"	Frankie Lymon & the Teenagers
U.K. #1 POP 45	"Memories Are Made of This"	Dean Martin

WEEK ENDING MARCH 14		
U.S. #1 POP 45	"Rock and Roll Waltz"	Kay Starr
U.S. #1 POP LP	*Belafonte*	Harry Belafonte
U.S. #1 R&B 45	"Why Do Fools Fall in Love"	Frankie Lymon & the Teenagers
U.K. #1 POP 45	"It's Almost Tomorrow"	Dream Weavers

WEEK ENDING MARCH 21		
U.S. #1 POP 45	"The Poor People of Paris"	Les Baxter
U.S. #1 POP LP	*Belafonte*	Harry Belafonte
U.S. #1 R&B 45	"Why Do Fools Fall in Love"	Frankie Lymon & the Teenagers
U.K. #1 POP 45	"It's Almost Tomorrow"	Dream Weavers

WEEK ENDING MARCH 28		
U.S. #1 POP 45	"The Poor People of Paris"	Les Baxter
U.S. #1 POP LP	*Belafonte*	Harry Belafonte
U.S. #1 R&B 45	"Why Do Fools Fall in Love"	Frankie Lymon & the Teenagers
U.K. #1 POP 45	"Rock and Roll Waltz"	Kay Starr

WEEK ENDING APRIL 4		
U.S. #1 POP 45	"The Poor People of Paris"	Les Baxter
U.S. #1 POP LP	*Belafonte*	Harry Belafonte
U.S. #1 R&B 45	"Why Do Fools Fall in Love"	Frankie Lymon & the Teenagers
U.K. #1 POP 45	"It's Almost Tomorrow"	Dream Weavers

WEEK ENDING APRIL 11		
U.S. #1 POP 45	"The Poor People of Paris"	Les Baxter
U.S. #1 POP LP	*Belafonte*	Harry Belafonte
U.S. #1 R&B 45	"Long Tall Sally"	Little Richard
U.K. #1 POP 45	"The Poor People of Paris"	Winifred Attwell

WEEK ENDING APRIL 18		
U.S. #1 POP 45	"The Poor People of Paris"	Les Baxter
U.S. #1 POP LP	*Belafonte*	Harry Belafonte
U.S. #1 R&B 45	"Long Tall Sally"	Little Richard
U.K. #1 POP 45	"The Poor People of Paris"	Winifred Attwell

WEEK ENDING APRIL 25		
U.S. #1 POP 45	"Heartbreak Hotel"	Elvis Presley
U.S. #1 POP LP	*Elvis Presley*	Elvis Presley
U.S. #1 R&B 45	"Long Tall Sally"	Little Richard
U.K. #1 POP 45	"The Poor People of Paris"	Winifred Attwell

MAY

2 For the first time in *Billboard* history, five records appear in both the pop *and* the R&B Top Ten. The five hits are **Elvis Presley**'s "Heartbreak Hotel" (#1 pop, #6 R&B), **Carl Perkins**' "Blue Suede Shoes" (#4 pop, #3 R&B), **Little Richard**'s "Long Tall Sally (#9 pop, #1 R&B), the **Platters**' "Magic Touch" (#10 pop, #7 R&B) and **Frankie Lymon and the Teenagers**' "Why Do Fools Fall in Love" (#7 pop, #4 R&B). Presley's and Perkins' singles are also in the country & western Top Ten, #1 and #2 respectively.

5 Rock & Roll pioneer **Johnny Burnette** and **Rock and Roll Trio** (which includes his older brother **Dorsey** on bass and their friend **Paul Burlison** on guitar) record their first single, "Tear It Up."

14 Mercury Records releases *The Platters,* the million-selling vocal group's first album. Although in the next several years it will sell over 50,000 copies, it contains none of their three recent hits.

19 **Lonnie Donegan**, one of England's biggest stars and the leader of the skiffle craze, makes his U.S. debut on NBC-TV's "Perry Como Show"

before beginning a one-month tour. "The Rock Island Line" is Donegan's best-known tune, but his highest charting U.S. single would be the nonsensical "Does Your Chewing Gum Lose Its Flavor (on the Bedpost Overnight)" in 1961.

30 *Time* magazine, in an article entitled "Teener's Hero," explains **Elvis Presley**'s mystique. After a drawn-out description of his singing style ("His diction is poor"), the writer hits upon Presley's appeal: "his movements suggest, in a word, sex."

JUNE

5 **Elvis Presley** makes his second appearance on "The Milton Berle Show." Berle presents Presley with two *Billboard* Triple Crown awards for "Heartbreak Hotel," which is currently Number One on the pop, R&B and country & western charts for sales, disc jockey and jukebox play. Within days, however, television critics across the country begin attacking Presley and, most of all, his hip-swiveling dancing style, which one describes as "the mating dance of an aborigine." An unidentified disc jockey predicts that the young star may "end up as 'Pelvis Presley' in a circus sideshow."

6 **Gene Vincent and the Blue Caps**' first—and biggest—hit, "Be-Bop-a-Lula," is

released. In April, Vincent, who cowrote the song with a friend, went to Los Angeles, won first prize in a talent contest and signed to Capitol Records. "Be-Bop-a-Lula" will eventually sell over 1 million copies.

23 The **Cadets**' only hit, a cover of the **Jayhawks**' "Stranded in the Jungle," is released by Modern. Soon after, the Los Angeles-based vocal quartet disbands. **Will Jones** joins the **Coasters**, and **Aaron Collins** (brother of **Teen Queens Betty** and **Rosie**, whose "Eddie My Love" was an R&B hit in February) helps found the **Flares**. Their big hit will be "Foot Stomping, Part I" in 1961.

26 "I guess it's okay, man. At least it has a beat," **Benny Goodman** says of rock & roll in a *Look* magazine article entitled "The Great Rock 'n' Roll Controversy." The writer's conclusion reads: "Going to a rock 'n' roll show is like attending the rites of some obscure tribe whose means of communication are incomprehensible." ◆

WEEK ENDING MAY 2		
U.S. #1 POP 45	"Heartbreak Hotel"	Elvis Presley
U.S. #1 POP LP	*Elvis Presley*	Elvis Presley
U.S. #1 R&B 45	"Long Tall Sally"	Little Richard
U.K. #1 POP 45	"No Other Love"	Ronnie Hilton

WEEK ENDING MAY 9		
U.S. #1 POP 45	"Hot Diggity"	Perry Como
U.S. #1 POP LP	*Elvis Presley*	Elvis Presley
U.S. #1 R&B 45	"Long Tall Sally"	Little Richard
U.K. #1 POP 45	"No Other Love"	Ronnie Hilton

WEEK ENDING MAY 16		
U.S. #1 POP 45	"Heartbreak Hotel"	Elvis Presley
U.S. #1 POP LP	*Elvis Presley*	Elvis Presley
U.S. #1 R&B 45	"Long Tall Sally"	Little Richard
U.K. #1 POP 45	"No Other Love"	Ronnie Hilton

WEEK ENDING MAY 23		
U.S. #1 POP 45	"Heartbreak Hotel"	Elvis Presley
U.S. #1 POP LP	*Elvis Presley*	Elvis Presley
U.S. #1 R&B 45	"I'm in Love Again/Blue Heaven"	Fats Domino
U.K. #1 POP 45	"No Other Love"	Ronnie Hilton

WEEK ENDING MAY 30		
U.S. #1 POP 45	"Heartbreak Hotel"	Elvis Presley
U.S. #1 POP LP	*Elvis Presley*	Elvis Presley
U.S. #1 R&B 45	"I'm in Love Again/Blue Heaven"	Fats Domino
U.K. #1 POP 45	"No Other Love"	Ronnie Hilton

WEEK ENDING JUNE 6		
U.S. #1 POP 45	"Heartbreak Hotel"	Elvis Presley
U.S. #1 POP LP	*Elvis Presley*	Elvis Presley
U.S. #1 R&B 45	"I'm in Love Again/Blue Heaven"	Fats Domino
U.K. #1 POP 45	"No Other Love"	Ronnie Hilton

WEEK ENDING JUNE 13		
U.S. #1 POP 45	"Wayward Wind"	Gogi Grant
U.S. #1 POP LP	*Elvis Presley*	Elvis Presley
U.S. #1 R&B 45	"I'm in Love Again/Blue Heaven"	Fats Domino
U.K. #1 POP 45	"I'll Be Home"	Pat Boone

WEEK ENDING JUNE 20		
U.S. #1 POP 45	"Wayward Wind"	Gogi Grant
U.S. #1 POP LP	*Elvis Presley*	Elvis Presley
U.S. #1 R&B 45	"I'm in Love Again/Blue Heaven"	Fats Domino
U.K. #1 POP 45	"I'll Be Home"	Pat Boone

WEEK ENDING JUNE 27		
U.S. #1 POP 45	"Wayward Wind"	Gogi Grant
U.S. #1 POP LP	*Elvis Presley*	Elvis Presley
U.S. #1 R&B 45	"I'm in Love Again/Blue Heaven"	Fats Domino
U.K. #1 POP 45	"I'll Be Home"	Pat Boone

JULY

1 **Elvis Presley** appears on "The Steve Allen Show." Host **Steve Allen** instructs Presley *not* to dance and has him sing "Hound Dog" to a real basset hound while wearing tails. The following day, teenagers picket NBC with signs reading: WE WANT THE REAL ELVIS.

2 **Elvis Presley** records "Hound Dog," "Don't Be Cruel" and "Any Way You Want Me" for RCA in New York City. This is the first recording session to feature the **Jordanaires**, a vocal harmony quartet. The group, which includes **Gordon Stoker**, **Hoyt Hawkins**, **Neal Matthews** and **Hugh Jarrett**, formed eight years before in Springfield, Missouri.

5 Jazz singer **Billie Holiday**'s autobiography, *Lady Sings the Blues*, is published by Doubleday in New York City. More than sixteen years later, the book, in which Holiday recounts her career and her problems with drug addiction, serves as the basis for a movie of the same name, starring **Diana Ross**.

14 Columbia reactivates its "race record" label, Okeh, as an R&B label. Among the R&B stars who record for Okeh are **Smiley Lewis**, the **Marquees** and a Teenagers-style vocal group called the **Schoolboys**. In its previous incarnation, the label included **Big Maybelle** and **Johnnie Ray** on its roster.

It's correct, but it's not right: A trade ad for **Bo Diddley**'s "Who Do You Love" reads "Whom Do You Love."

21 *Billboard* calls **Elvis Presley** "the most controversial entertainer since Liberace." The article also notes that **Ed Sullivan**, who once vowed that Presley would never appear on his show, has just signed the singer for three appearances.

28 Blues singer **Big Walter**'s "Pack Fair and Square" is released on Peacock. Sixteen years later, the song is covered by the **J. Geils Band**.

31 A committee forms in Hollywood to help combat the unfavorable press rhythm & blues music is getting. The founders include L.A. R&B disc jockey **Hunter Hancock**, promoter **Hal Zeiger**, **Art Rupe** of Specialty Records and R&B band leader **Johnny Otis**.

AUGUST

2 In an article entitled "Elvis Presley . . . He Can't Be . . . But He Is," *Look* magazine reports that **Elvis Presley**'s records have grossed over $6 million dollars and that the singer receives over 3,000 fan letters a week.

14 A Washington, D.C., disc jockey named **Bob Rickman** forms the Society for the Prevention of Cruelty to Elvis Presley. National press coverage of the young singing idol has been largely critical and derisive, as evidenced in the dozens of headlines that refer to Presley as a hillbilly.

18 On the same day that **Elvis Presley**'s rendition of "Hound Dog" enters the R&B chart at #11, Peacock Records rereleases **Big Mama Thornton**'s original version. That version was Thornton's only chart hit and an R&B Number One in 1953.

Little Willie John's original version of "Fever" enters the pop chart at #24. The song, which will later be a smash for the **McCoys** and **Peggy Lee**, was a Number One R&B in the spring.

22 The **Five Satins**' doo-wop classic "In the Still of the Night" (featuring lead vocalist **Freddie Parris**) debuts on the R&B chart. It will eventually sell over 15 million copies.

24 London's first rock & roll club, Studio 51, opens. The first act to perform there is **Rory Blackwell's Rock 'N' Rollers**.

25 The **Coney Island Kids**' "We Want a Rock & Roll President" is released on Josie Records. Among their nominees for the nation's top position are **Bo Diddley**, **Elvis Presley**, **Bill Haley** and **Pat Boone**.

28 **Alan Freed**'s second-annual ten-day Rock & Roll Show opens at the Brooklyn Paramount Theater. Among the performers are **Fats Domino** and **Frankie Lymon and the Teenagers**. ◆

WEEK ENDING JULY 4		
U.S. #1 POP 45	"Wayward Wind"	Gogi Grant
U.S. #1 POP LP	*My Fair Lady*	original cast
U.S. #1 R&B 45	"I'm in Love Again/Blue Heaven"	Fats Domino
U.K. #1 POP 45	"I'll Be Home"	Pat Boone

WEEK ENDING JULY 11		
U.S. #1 POP 45	"Wayward Wind"	Gogi Grant
U.S. #1 POP LP	*My Fair Lady*	original cast
U.S. #1 R&B 45	"Fever"	Little Willie John
U.K. #1 POP 45	"I'll Be Home"	Pat Boone

WEEK ENDING JULY 18		
U.S. #1 POP 45	"I Want You, Need You"	Elvis Presley
U.S. #1 POP LP	*My Fair Lady*	original cast
U.S. #1 R&B 45	"Fever"	Little Willie John
U.K. #1 POP 45	"Why Do Fools Fall in Love"	Frankie Lymon & the Teenagers

WEEK ENDING JULY 25		
U.S. #1 POP 45	"My Prayer"	The Platters
U.S. #1 POP LP	*My Fair Lady*	original cast
U.S. #1 R&B 45	"Rip It Up"	Little Richard
U.K. #1 POP 45	"Why Do Fools Fall in Love"	Frankie Lymon & the Teenagers

WEEK ENDING AUGUST 1		
U.S. #1 POP 45	"My Prayer"	The Platters
U.S. #1 POP LP	*My Fair Lady*	original cast
U.S. #1 R&B 45	"Rip It Up"	Little Richard
U.K. #1 POP 45	"Why Do Fools Fall In Love"	Frankie Lymon & the Teenagers

WEEK ENDING AUGUST 8		
U.S. #1 POP 45	"Hound Dog"/"Don't Be Cruel"	Elvis Presley
U.S. #1 POP LP	*My Fair Lady*	original cast
U.S. #1 R&B 45	"Keep It Up"	Little Richard
U.K. #1 POP 45	"Que Sera, Sera"	Doris Day

WEEK ENDING AUGUST 15		
U.S. #1 POP 45	"Hound Dog"/"Don't Be Cruel"	Elvis Presley
U.S. #1 POP LP	*My Fair Lady*	original cast
U.S. #1 R&B 45	"Honky Tonk (Parts I and II)"	Bill Doggett
U.K. #1 POP 45	"Que Sera, Sera"	Doris Day

WEEK ENDING AUGUST 22		
U.S. #1 POP 45	"Hound Dog"/"Don't Be Cruel"	Elvis Presley
U.S. #1 POP LP	*My Fair Lady*	original cast
U.S. #1 R&B 45	"Honky Tonk (Parts I and II)"	Bill Doggett
U.K. #1 POP 45	"Que Sera, Sera"	Doris Day

WEEK ENDING AUGUST 29		
U.S. #1 POP 45	"Hound Dog"/"Don't Be Cruel"	Elvis Presley
U.S. #1 POP LP	*Calypso*	Harry Belafonte
U.S. #1 R&B 45	"Honky Tonk (Parts I and II)"	Bill Doggett
U.K. #1 POP 45	"Que Sera, Sera"	Doris Day

SEPTEMBER

1 But don't you be nobody's fool: **Elvis Presley** buys his mother a pink Cadillac.

Veteran song publisher **Howie Richmond** founds Roulette Records in New York City. The first release, "King of Nothin'," by **Bernie Knoe** is hardly a hit, but the label will later come to the fore as a leader in doo-wop, and in the middle and late Sixties, in bubblegum and American pop rock.

9 **Elvis Presley** makes his first of three appearances on the Ed Sullivan show. He sings "Love Me Tender," "Hound Dog," "Don't Be Cruel" and "Ready Teddy."

10 Record dealers across the country are swamped with requests for copies of **Elvis Presley**'s "Love Me Tender." The song, which is the title theme from his upcoming movie, has not yet been released.

22 In a cover article headlined ROCK 'N' ROLL IN DISFAVOR, *Billboard* reports, "With new experiences to their credit, such as calling riot squads and with scars such as damaged seats, some arena and auditorium operators have turned thumbs down on any more rock 'n' roll. Some nix the whole idea. Some prohibit dancing but not all concerts. Some just hire extra cops and let 'em go. . . ."

26 **Fats Domino**'s "Blueberry Hill" enters the pop chart, where it will reach #4, making it his biggest pop success. An R&B hitmaker since 1950, the singer/pianist from New Orleans will eventually sell 65 million records and earn over 15 gold discs.

This day is proclaimed **Elvis Presley** Day in Presley's hometown, Tupelo, Mississippi.

28 Singer **Alis Lesley**, one of the first women rockers to be billed "the Female Presley," debuts in a Hollywood rock show that also includes **Gene Vincent** and the **Coasters**. Little is known of Lesley, but like all of the so-called female Presleys, she soon fades from view.

29 So far, RCA Victor has received over 856,327 advance orders for **Elvis Presley**'s "Love Me Tender."

OCTOBER

6 *Billboard* reports that major Hollywood studios are diving into the rock &

roll film market: Twentieth Century-Fox with *Do Re Mi*, starring **Fats Domino**, **Jayne Mansfield** and **Little Richard**, and another project titled *Cool It, Baby*; and Paramount's *Lonesome Cowboy*, to star **Elvis Presley**. (The latter film is never made.)

20 **Elvis Presley**'s "Love Me Tender" becomes the first song ever to enter the pop chart at #2. It also enters the country & western chart (#9), the R&B chart (#10) and the Top One Hundred (#12).

27 R&B singer **Clarence Henry**'s "Ain't Got No Home" is released on Argo Rec-

ords. It's Henry's first hit and, because he sings like a frog on it, he will earn the nickname "Frogman."

28 **Elvis Presley** makes his second appearance on Ed Sullivan's show and sings "Don't Be Cruel," "Love Me Tender," "Hound Dog" and "Love Me." ◆

WEEK	ENDING SEPTEMBER 5	
U.S. #1 POP 45	"Hound Dog"/"Don't Be Cruel"	Elvis Presley
U.S. #1 POP LP	Calypso	Harry Belafonte
U.S. #1 R&B 45	"Honky Tonk (Parts I and II)"	Bill Doggett
U.K. #1 POP 45	"Que Sera, Sera"	Doris Day

WEEK	ENDING SEPTEMBER 12	
U.S. #1 POP 45	"Don't Be Cruel"/"Hound Dog"	Elvis Presley
U.S. #1 POP LP	Calypso	Harry Belafonte
U.S. #1 R&B 45	"Honky Tonk (Parts I and II)"	Bill Doggett
U.K. #1 POP 45	"Que Sera, Sera"	Doris Day

WEEK	ENDING SEPTEMBER 19	
U.S. #1 POP 45	"Don't Be Cruel"/"Hound Dog"	Elvis Presley
U.S. #1 POP LP	Calypso	Harry Belafonte
U.S. #1 R&B 45	"Honky Tonk (Parts I and II)"	Bill Doggett
U.K. #1 POP 45	"Lay Down Your Arms"	Anne Shelton

WEEK	ENDING SEPTEMBER 26	
U.S. #1 POP 45	"Don't Be Cruel"/"Hound Dog"	Elvis Presley
U.S. #1 POP LP	The King and I	original cast
U.S. #1 R&B 45	"Honky Tonk (Parts I and II)"	Bill Doggett
U.K. #1 POP 45	"Lay Down Your Arms"	Anne Shelton

WEEK	ENDING OCTOBER 3	
U.S. #1 POP 45	"Don't Be Cruel"/"Hound Dog"	Elvis Presley
U.S. #1 POP LP	The Eddie Duchin Story	soundtrack
U.S. #1 R&B 45	"Honky Tonk (Parts I and II)"	Bill Doggett
U.K. #1 POP 45	"Lay Down Your Arms"	Anne Shelton

WEEK	ENDING OCTOBER 10	
U.S. #1 POP 45	"Don't Be Cruel"/"Hound Dog"	Elvis Presley
U.S. #1 POP LP	Calypso	Harry Belafonte
U.S. #1 R&B 45	"Honky Tonk (Parts I and II)"	Bill Doggett
U.K. #1 POP 45	"Lay Down Your Arms"	Anne Shelton

WEEK	ENDING OCTOBER 17	
U.S. #1 POP 45	"Don't Be Cruel"/"Hound Dog"	Elvis Presley
U.S. #1 POP LP	Calypso	Harry Belafonte
U.S. #1 R&B 45	"Honky Tonk (Parts I and II)"	Bill Doggett
U.K. #1 POP 45	"Woman in Love"	Frankie Laine

WEEK	ENDING OCTOBER 24	
U.S. #1 POP 45	"Love Me Tender"	Elvis Presley
U.S. #1 POP LP	Calypso	Harry Belafonte
U.S. #1 R&B 45	"Honky Tonk (Parts I and II)"	Bill Doggett
U.K. #1 POP 45	"Woman in Love"	Frankie Laine

WEEK	ENDING OCTOBER 31	
U.S. #1 POP 45	"Love Me Tender"	Elvis Presley
U.S. #1 POP LP	Calypso	Harry Belafonte
U.S. #1 R&B 45	"Honky Tonk (Parts I and II)"	Bill Doggett
U.K. #1 POP 45	"Woman in Love"	Frankie Laine

NOVEMBER

10 The results of *Billboard*'s ninth annual nationwide DJ poll reveal that among America's record-spinners, the favorite record is "Moonglow and Theme from *Picnic*" by **Morris Stoloff** ("The Great Pretender" is fourteenth, "Don't Be Cruel," seventeenth); the most played record is **Kay Starr**'s "Rock & Roll Waltz" ("The Great Pretender" is third, "Heartbreak Hotel," fifth, "Don't Be Cruel," seventh, "Hound Dog," nineteenth, "Blue Suede Shoes," twentieth); the favorite male vocalist is **Frank Sinatra** (**Elvis Presley** doesn't even make the list); the most played male vocalist is **Elvis Presley** (**Fats Domino** is ninth); the favorite LP is Sinatra's *Songs for Swinging Lovers* (*Elvis Presley* is seventeenth, *The Platters*, fifteenth); Elvis is the most played C&W artist; **George Jones**, most promising C&W artist; **Fats Domino** is the favorite R&B artist, with Elvis fiftieth in both categories.

Entering the British pop charts are "Rock with the Caveman," by British Elvis-clone **Tommy Steele** at #13, and **Gene Vincent and his Blue Caps**' "Blue Jean Bop" at #19.

16 **Elvis Presley**'s film debut, *Love Me Tender*, opens in New York City. Despite mixed critical reaction, it grosses nearly $4 million in just two months.

17 WINS-New York disc jockey **Alan Freed** announces that he will star in another rock & roll film—he's already appearing in *Don't Knock the Rock* and *Rock around the Clock*—*Rock, Rock, Rock*, to premiere in New York City December 5. Freed owns ten percent of the film outright and has arranged for the release of DJ-only promotional albums of the film's soundtrack, featuring **Chuck Berry**, the **Flamingos**, **Johnny Burnette**'s **Rock & Roll Trio**, **Frankie Lymon and the Teenagers**, **LaVern Baker** and others.

18 **Fats Domino** appears on the Ed Sullivan show singing his hit "Blueberry Hill."

26 Famed swing-era band leader and trombonist **Tommy Dorsey** is found dead, the result of an accident, in his Greenwich, Connecticut, home. In addition to bringing **Frank Sinatra** to prominence in his swing orchestra, Tommy, with his brother Jimmy, conducted the "Dorsey Brothers Stage Show," the first nationally broadcast TV show to feature Elvis Presley.

DECEMBER

4 Four Sun Records stars—**Elvis Presley**, **Carl Perkins**, **Jerry Lee Lewis** and **Johnny Cash**—record as what will later be known as the Million Dollar Quartet. Recordings from the impromptu session won't be released for twenty-five years.

Jerry Lee Lewis, whose first release for Sun Records, "Crazy Arms," backed with "End of the Road," did not succeed, plays piano for **Carl Perkins** during a session. They record "Your True Love" and "Matchbox," a remake of **Blind Lemon Jefferson**'s "Matchbox Blues."

8 *Billboard* reports that **Elvis Presley** is setting new sales records in Canada, where a hit record usually might make 100,000 sales, and where "Hound Dog," backed with "Don't Be Cruel," has already sold over 225,000 copies and "Love Me Tender" has sold over 135,000 copies in sixteen weeks. The article also reports that Presley has sparked a boom in overall record sales, and in the sale of guitars, in Canada.

22 **Elvis Presley** had the most charting records in 1956, with seventeen, *Billboard* reports. **Pat Boone** is next, with five, followed by **Fats Domino**, **Little Richard** and the **Platters** with three each. Another article notes that, while more money than ever has been spent on records in 1956, record-buyers are more unpredictable in their tastes than ever before.

26 **Fats Domino**'s "Blue Monday" enters the pop chart, eventually to peak at #9. On the R&B chart, it will reach Number One. **Mickey and Sylvia** make their pop chart debut with "Love Is Strange," which will peak there at #13 while reaching #2 on the R&B chart. It will be the biggest hit for this duo, who both sing and play guitar, but **Sylvia Robinson** will return to the charts in 1973 with "Pillow Talk," a #3 pop hit and a Number One R&B hit. A businesswoman as well as musician, she will go on to found such record companies as All-Platinum and Sugarhill. ◆

WEEK ENDING NOVEMBER 7		
U.S. #1 POP 45	"Love Me Tender"	Elvis Presley
U.S. #1 POP LP	*Calypso*	Harry Belafonte
U.S. #1 R&B 45	"Honky Tonk (Parts I and II)"	Bill Doggett
U.K. #1 POP 45	"Woman in Love"	Frankie Laine
WEEK ENDING NOVEMBER 14		
U.S. #1 POP 45	"Love Me Tender"	Elvis Presley
U.S. #1 POP LP	*Calypso*	Harry Belafonte
U.S. #1 R&B 45	"Blueberry Hill"	Fats Domino
U.K. #1 POP 45	"Just Walking in the Rain"	Johnnie Ray
WEEK ENDING NOVEMBER 21		
U.S. #1 POP 45	"Love Me Tender"	Elvis Presley
U.S. #1 POP LP	*Calypso*	Harry Belafonte
U.S. #1 R&B 45	"Honky Tonk (Parts I and II)"	Bill Doggett
U.K. #1 POP 45	"Just Walking in the Rain"	Johnnie Ray
WEEK ENDING NOVEMBER 28		
U.S. #1 POP 45	"Singing the Blues"	Guy Mitchell
U.S. #1 POP LP	*Elvis*	Elvis Presley
U.S. #1 R&B 45	"Blueberry Hill"	Fats Domino
U.K. #1 POP 45	"Just Walking in the Rain"	Johnnie Ray

WEEK ENDING DECEMBER 5		
U.S. #1 POP 45	"Singing the Blues"	Guy Mitchell
U.S. #1 POP LP	*Elvis*	Elvis Presley
U.S. #1 R&B 45	"Blueberry Hill"	Fats Domino
U.K. #1 POP 45	"Just Walking in the Rain"	Johnnie Ray
WEEK ENDING DECEMBER 12		
U.S. #1 POP 45	"Singing the Blues"	Guy Mitchell
U.S. #1 POP LP	*Elvis*	Elvis Presley
U.S. #1 R&B 45	"Blueberry Hill"	Fats Domino
U.K. #1 POP 45	"Just Walking in the Rain"	Johnnie Ray
WEEK ENDING DECEMBER 19		
U.S. #1 POP 45	"Singing the Blues"	Guy Mitchell
U.S. #1 POP LP	*Elvis*	Elvis Presley
U.S. #1 R&B 45	"Blueberry Hill"	Fats Domino
U.K. #1 POP 45	"Just Walking in the Rain"	Johnnie Ray
WEEK ENDING DECEMBER 26		
U.S. #1 POP 45	"Singing the Blues"	Guy Mitchell
U.S. #1 POP LP	*Elvis*	Elvis Presley
U.S. #1 R&B 45	"Blueberry Hill"	Fats Domino
U.K. #1 POP 45	"Just Walking in the Rain"	Johnnie Ray

1957

In the wake of last year's rock & roll eruption, this year the music industry tried to make sense, not to mention dollars, out of rock & roll. A January *Billboard* cover story warned that the trade had to revise or abandon the old boundary lines. Indeed, categories like pop, rhythm & blues and country & western *were* becoming more and more abstract as time passed, and the old boundary lines *had* been abandoned by the youth audience. It was now up to the industry to catch up with the cultural revolution.

By the winter of 1957, the top two songs on the pop, R&B and C&W charts were identical: Elvis Presley's "All Shook Up" and the Everly Brothers' "Wake Up Little Susie." The #3 through #6 songs on the pop and R&B charts were also the same: Sam Cooke's "You Send Me" (generically and R&B song), the Rays' "Silhouettes" (what the trades called a "rocka-ballad"—a slow doo-wop tune with a big beat), Ricky Nelson's "Be-Bop Baby" (teen-idol rockabilly pop) and Jimmie Rodgers' "Honeycomb" (country pop). Shortly thereafter, Jerry Lee Lewis' second smash hit, "Great Balls of Fire," reached #2 on the pop chart, #3 on the R&B chart and Number One on the C&W chart. But was "Great Balls of Fire" a pop song (even though it *was* popular)? Was it R&B? Was it country? Actually, it was all and none of the above at the same time—it was out of control, it was rock & roll: sexy, threatening, powerful.

There were still protests against and bannings of rock & roll records and dances. Elvis Presley's Christmas album stirred up a particularly vehement controversy; one disc jockey was fired for violating his station's ban on playing Elvis' version of "White Christmas," and the station owner who fired him explained, "Playing Presley's version of that song is like having a stripper give my kids Christmas gifts."

But by this time, rock & roll TV shows, in the form of DJ-hosted record hops, began to take over the airwaves, beginning with the first national broadcast of the Philadelphia-based "American Bandstand" in August. Britain had its first rock & roll TV show as well this year with "Cool for Cats." In April, DJ Alan Freed—one of the men most often vilified as a popularizer of rock & roll—proved that rock & roll had a social conscience by hosting a forty-eight-hour radio telethon for the National Arthritis and Rheumatism Foundation. One month later, he had a nationwide rock & roll TV show. In July, NBC-TV's "Studio One Summer Theater" presented a satire on the rock & roll world, "The Hit," written by one Romeo Muller.

By the end of the year, even as dogged an opponent of rock & roll as Mitch Miller would answer a DJ's question about the connection between rock & roll and juvenile delinquency by saying, "There is not a piece of music written or recorded that can do to a child what the home has not already done." (Apparently, Mitch had listened hard to the psychiatrist with whom he appeared on Eric Sevareid's radio rock & roll panel discussion in 1956.) At roughly the same time, a *Billboard* article described the media's recent speculation on the imminent demise of rock & roll as "so much wishful thinking."

JANUARY

1 "Cool for Cats," a British rock & roll television show, premieres on BBC.

4 **Louis Jordan** and his **Tympany Five** record **Jimmie Cox**'s "Nobody Knows You When You Are Down and Out."

Fats Domino records "I'm Walkin'" in New Orleans. With him for the session are producer **Dave Bartholomew**, tenor saxophonists **Lee Allen** and **Herb Hardesty**, guitarist **Walter Nelson**, bassist **Frank Fields** and drummer **Earl Palmer**. The single will reach #4 on the pop chart and Number One on the R&B chart in April.

Former heavyweight boxing champ **Joe Louis** appears on "The Steve Allen Show" to introduce singer **Solomon Burke**, who performs Louis' "You Can Run, but You Can't Hide."

6 **Elvis Presley** makes his last appearance on the Ed Sullivan show in New York City. Over twenty minutes are devoted to him, and he sings seven numbers—"Hound Dog," "Don't Be Cruel," "Love Me Tender," "Heartbreak Hotel," "Peace in the Valley," "Too Much" and "When My Blue Moon Turns to Gold Again."

8 **Bill Haley**, who previously rejected an invitation to tour Australia because some of his **Comets** were averse to flying, begins a two-week tour down under (with new Comets) in Newcastle. Sharing the bill are **LaVern Baker** and **Joe Turner**.

On his twenty-second birthday, **Elvis Presley** takes the army preinduction exam in Memphis and passes.

10 The **Crew-Cuts**, an all-Canadian group, make their U.S. debut, appearing live on CBS-TV's "Dorsey Brothers Stage Show," out of Cleveland, Ohio.

16 **Elvis Presley**'s "Too Much" enters the pop chart. It will become the first of four charttoppers for Presley this year.

The Cavern Club opens in a former wine cellar on Mathew Street in Liverpool, England, presenting jazz and skiffle bands. The club will earn its landmark status in 1961 and 1962 when the **Beatles** are its house band.

23 On tour in Australia, **Bill Haley and the Comets** attend the world premiere of *Don't Knock the Rock*, in which Haley and his band make cameo appearances.

FEBRUARY

2 **Fats Domino** sings "Blueberry Hill" and "Blue Monday" on Perry Como's television show.

6 The **Del-Vikings**' first and biggest hit, "Come Go with Me," debuts on the pop chart. In four weeks, it peaks at #5 while on the R&B chart, it hits #3.

12 The **Coasters** record "Young Blood," written and produced by **Jerry Leiber** and **Mike Stoller**.

13 Elvis lookalike **Tommy Sands** makes his first appearance on the pop chart with "Teen-age Crush," which will hit #3, by far the highest position of his short-lived career.

15 Impresario **Irvin Feld** premieres his Greatest Shows of 1957, in Pittsburgh. The bill includes **Chuck Berry**, **Clyde McPhatter**, **LaVern Baker**, **Fats Domino**, **Bill Doggett**, the **Five Keys**, the **Moonglows**, the **Five Satins**, **Eddie Conley and the Dimples**, **Charles Brown**, **Ann Cole**, the **Schoolboys** and the **Paul Williams Band**. Before it closes May 5, the tour will go through every region of the United States, including some—such as the northern Rocky Mountain states—which have never witnessed live rock & roll.

22 In a small club in Blytheville, Arkansas,

Jerry Lee Lewis plays "Whole Lotta Shakin' Goin' On." Although Lewis did not write the song—**Roy Hall** and **Dave Williams** were the authors—it has been a favorite of his since he first heard it over a year ago. This is the first time Lewis adds his own words to replace those he has forgotten.

Columbia Pictures' *Don't Knock the Rock* is given its American premiere at the Paramount Theater in New York City. **Alan Freed**, playing himself, defends rock & roll against charges of lasciviousness, delinquency and violence, and **Little Richard**, the **Platters**, **Fats Domino**, **Gene Vincent** and **Bill Haley and the Comets** testify as witnesses for both sides.

25 **Buddy Holly and the Crickets** record "That'll Be the Day" in their first session with producer **Norman Petty** at his Clovis, New Mexico, studio. Despite Petty's doubts about the song's hit potential, it proves to be Holly's biggest, rising to #2 on the pop chart and #3 on the R&B chart. ◆

WEEK ENDING JANUARY 2		
U.S. #1 POP 45	"Singing the Blues"	Guy Mitchell
U.S. #1 POP LP	*Calypso*	Harry Belafonte
U.S. #1 R&B 45	"Blueberry Hill"	Fats Domino
U.K. #1 POP 45	"Singing the Blues"	Guy Mitchell

WEEK ENDING JANUARY 9		
U.S. #1 POP 45	"Singing the Blues"	Guy Mitchell
U.S. #1 POP LP	*Calypso*	Harry Belafonte
U.S. #1 R&B 45	"Blueberry Hill"	Fats Domino
U.K. #1 POP 45	"Singing the Blues"	Tommy Steele

WEEK ENDING JANUARY 16		
U.S. #1 POP 45	"Singing the Blues"	Guy Mitchell
U.S. #1 POP LP	*Calypso*	Harry Belafonte
U.S. #1 R&B 45	"Blue Monday"	Fats Domino
U.K. #1 POP 45	"Singing the Blues"	Guy Mitchell

WEEK ENDING JANUARY 23		
U.S. #1 POP 45	"Young Love"	Sonny James
U.S. #1 POP LP	*Calypso*	Harry Belafonte
U.S. #1 R&B 45	"Blue Monday"	Fats Domino
U.K. #1 POP 45	"Garden of Eden"	Frankie Vaughan

WEEK ENDING JANUARY 30		
U.S. #1 POP 45	"Young Love"	Sonny James
U.S. #1 POP LP	*Calypso*	Harry Belafonte
U.S. #1 R&B 45	"Blue Monday"	Fats Domino
U.K. #1 POP 45	"Garden of Eden"	Frankie Vaughan

WEEK ENDING FEBRUARY 6		
U.S. #1 POP 45	"Young Love"	Sonny James
U.S. #1 POP LP	*Calypso*	Harry Belafonte
U.S. #1 R&B 45	"Blue Monday"	Fats Domino
U.K. #1 POP 45	"Garden of Eden"	Frankie Vaughan

WEEK ENDING FEBRUARY 13		
U.S. #1 POP 45	"Young Love"	Sonny James
U.S. #1 POP LP	*Calypso*	Harry Belafonte
U.S. #1 R&B 45	"Blue Monday"	Fats Domino
U.K. #1 POP 45	"Garden of Eden"	Frankie Vaughan

WEEK ENDING FEBRUARY 20		
U.S. #1 POP 45	"Young Love"	Sonny James
U.S. #1 POP LP	*Calypso*	Harry Belafonte
U.S. #1 R&B 45	"Blue Monday"	Fats Domino
U.K. #1 POP 45	"Young Love"	Tab Hunter

WEEK ENDING FEBRUARY 27		
U.S. #1 POP 45	"Young Love"	Sonny James
U.S. #1 POP LP	*Calypso*	Harry Belafonte
U.S. #1 R&B 45	"Blue Monday"	Fats Domino
U.K. #1 POP 45	"Young Love"	Tab Hunter

MARCH

1 Chess Records of Chicago releases **Muddy Waters**' "I Got My Mojo Working," backed with "Rock Me," and **Chuck Berry**'s "School Day," backed with "Deep Feeling." **Harry Belafonte**'s "Banana Boat Song (Day-O)" debuts on the British chart, where it will rise to #3. The folk song from Trinidad sparks a British calypso craze.

3 **Samuel Cardinal Strich**, head of the Catholic archdiocese of Chicago (the largest in the world), bans rock & roll from Catholic schools and "recreations" in his district, decrying its "tribal rhythms" and "encouragement to behave in a hedonistic manner." Chicago record retailers report no drop in sales of hedonism-encouraging records.

6 The doo-wop quartet the **Diamonds** make their pop chart debut with "Little Darlin'," their biggest hit. It will reach #2 on the pop chart and #3 on the R&B chart.

18 **Bill Haley and the Comets** return from an eleven-week tour of Australia, Europe and the British Isles, on which he played for half a million fans.

31 **Johnny Cash**, **Carl Perkins**, **Jerry Lee Lewis**, **Onie Wheeler** and **Glen Douglas** open a tour of the South in Little Rock, Arkansas.

APRIL

1 **Frankie Lymon and the Teenagers** open a twelve-week tour of Europe with a concert at the Palladium in London, England.

Cadence Records releases the **Everly Brothers**' "Bye Bye Love." Written by Nashville songwriter **Boudleaux Bryant**, the song has been rejected by thirty acts before the Everly Brothers record it as their second release and first for Cadence. (Their debut record, "The Sun Keeps Shining," was a flop for Columbia.) "Bye Bye Love" will go to #2 on the pop chart, Number One on the country & western chart and #5 on the rhythm & blues chart, and Don and Phil Everly, sons of C&W duo **Ike and Margaret Everly**, will have introduced the high, clean close harmonies of country singing to rock & roll.

12 **Alan Freed**'s Rock and Roll Easter Jubilee opens for a ten-day run at the Brooklyn Paramount in New York. The bill reflects the growing interest in country music among New York rock & roll fans: **Charlie Gracie**, **Jim Bowen** and **Buddy Knox** star, along with the **Cleftones**, **Bob Davies and the Rhythm Jesters**, the **Harptones**, **El Boy**, the **Rosebuds**, **Anita Ellis** and **Bo Diddley**.

18 Army reserve Lieutenant **Buddy Knox**, whose "Party Doll" was recently Number One, is called up for six months of active duty. Roulette Records' A&R team, **Hugo Peretti** and **Luigi Creatore**, rushes him into the studio to cut over twenty sides to ensure that his career does not stall while he's in uniform.

24 Verve Records releases **Ricky Nelson**'s first record, "Teenager's Romance,"

with his cover of **Fats Domino**'s "I'm Walkin'" on the flip side. The sixteen-year-old Nelson is already well known to millions of Americans from his appearances on television's popular "Adventures of Ozzie and Harriet," which stars his parents. His record will sell almost 60,000 copies within three days.   ◆

WEEK ENDING MARCH 6		
U.S. #1 POP 45	"Young Love"	Sonny James
U.S. #1 POP LP	*Calypso*	Harry Belafonte
U.S. #1 R&B 45	"Blue Monday"	Fats Domino
U.K. #1 POP 45	"Young Love"	Tab Hunter

WEEK ENDING MARCH 13		
U.S. #1 POP 45	"Young Love"	Sonny James
U.S. #1 POP LP	*Calypso*	Harry Belafonte
U.S. #1 R&B 45	"I'm Walkin'"	Fats Domino
U.K. #1 POP 45	"Young Love"	Tab Hunter

WEEK ENDING MARCH 20		
U.S. #1 POP 45	"Party Doll"	Buddy Knox
U.S. #1 POP LP	*Calypso*	Harry Belafonte
U.S. #1 R&B 45	"I'm Walkin'"	Fats Domino
U.K. #1 POP 45	"Young Love"	Tab Hunter

WEEK ENDING MARCH 27		
U.S. #1 POP 45	"Butterball"	Charlie Gracie
U.S. #1 POP LP	*Calypso*	Harry Belafonte
U.S. #1 R&B 45	"I'm Walkin'"	Fats Domino
U.K. #1 POP 45	"Young Love"	Tab Hunter

WEEK ENDING APRIL 3		
U.S. #1 POP 45	"Butterfly"	Andy Williams
U.S. #1 POP LP	*Calypso*	Harry Belafonte
U.S. #1 R&B 45	"I'm Walkin'"	Fats Domino
U.K. #1 POP 45	"Young Love"	Tab Hunter

WEEK ENDING APRIL 10		
U.S. #1 POP 45	"Butterfly"	Andy Williams
U.S. #1 POP LP	*Calypso*	Harry Belafonte
U.S. #1 R&B 45	"I'm Walkin'"	Fats Domino
U.K. #1 POP 45	"Cumberland Gap"	Lonnie Donegan

WEEK ENDING APRIL 17		
U.S. #1 POP 45	"All Shook Up"	Elvis Presley
U.S. #1 POP LP	*Calypso*	Harry Belafonte
U.S. #1 R&B 45	"I'm Walkin'"	Fats Domino
U.K. #1 POP 45	"Cumberland Gap"	Lonnie Donegan

WEEK ENDING APRIL 24		
U.S. #1 POP 45	"All Shook Up"	Elvis Presley
U.S. #1 POP LP	*Calypso*	Harry Belafonte
U.S. #1 R&B 45	"All Shook Up"	Elvis Presley
U.K. #1 POP 45	"Cumberland Gap"	Lonnie Donegan

MAY

2 **Elvis Presley** records "Jailhouse Rock," the Leiber and Stoller song that will inspire Presley's choreographical debut, the convicts' dance in the MGM movie *Jailhouse Rock.*

4 **Alan Freed** premieres his half-hour "Alan Freed Show" on ABC-TV. His first guests include **Guy Mitchell**, the **Del-Vikings, Screamin' Jay Hawkins**, the **Clovers, June Valli, Martha Carson** and, naturally, the **Alan Freed Rock & Roll Orchestra**, featuring **Sam the Man Taylor, Big Al Sears, Panama Francis** and **Freddie Mitchell**.

15 Mercury Records signs the **Del-Vikings**, whose "Come Go with Me" was a hit for the small, independent label Dot.

27 Brunswick Records releases the **Crickets'** (with lead singer **Buddy Holly**) first record and only charttopper, "That'll Be the Day," backed with "I'm Looking for Someone to Love." Although Holly's recording career will last less than two years, it will be filled with more true classics of rock & roll than all but a few special artists create in careers that last ten times as long.

Mercury Records releases *Swinging Guitars,* an album by **Jorgen Ingmann**. The LP contains Ingmann's rockabilly instrumental hit, "Apache," whose reverberating lead guitar will be emulated by future guitarists, from **Duane Eddy** to **Hank Marvin** of the **Shadows**, to **Matthew Ashman** of **Bow Wow Wow**.

Despite its lowly origins as kitchen jam session music, played on washboard drums and washtub basses, skiffle rises to the heights of the British record industry. Four skiffle songs are in the U.K. Top Twenty, led by **Lonnie Donegan**'s "Cumberland Gap." Meanwhile, in Liverpool, sixteen-year-old **John Lennon** leads a skiffle band named the **Quarrymen**; "Cumberland Gap" is one of their specialties.

JUNE

3 RCA Victor releases a single, "Butter Fingers," backed with "Fingertips," by **Cool Dip** (born **Kuldip Singh**), a rockabilly singer from India.

Teenage Records releases "Angels Cried," backed with "The Cow Jumped over the Moon," the **Isley Brothers'** first record. It begins a string of flops broken by "Twist and Shout" in 1962.

5 "Suzie Q," a **Dale Hawkins** recording, debuts on the pop chart. It will peak at #29, only to return eleven years later when it reaches #11 with **Creedence Clearwater Revival**'s version.

10 Jacksonville, Florida, schoolteacher **Mae Axton**, who, with **Tommy Durden**, wrote "Heartbreak Hotel," reveals to *Billboard* that she allows her students to listen to **Elvis Presley** records in class when their minds stray from their studies. "You'd be surprised how enthusiastic they become," she says.

12 **Jerry Lee Lewis'** "Whole Lotta Shakin' Goin' On" enters the national country & western chart, by the next week it will have made its debut on the national pop chart as well.

19 **Jerry Lee Lewis** makes his first appearance on the national pop chart with "Whole Lotta Shakin'." His first release, a cover of **Ray Price**'s country & western hit, "Crazy Arms," was moderately popular in Memphis, where he had recorded it for Sun Records. But his second release, made at the Sun studios in one impromptu take, is pure rock & roll, and it shakes a whole lotta the nation, reaching Number One on the C&W chart, Number One on the R&B chart and #3 on the pop chart.

20 Coral Records, with whom **Buddy Holly** has a solo contract (the **Crickets** are signed to Brunswick), releases "Words of Love," backed with "Mailman, Bring Me No Blues," credited to Holly alone. The single will have none of the success of the Crickets' "That'll Be the Day," but the A side will be revived six years later by the **Beatles**.

21 Imperial Records releases **Chris Kenner**'s debut record, "Nothing Will Keep Me Away from You," backed with "Sick and Tired." It will go mostly unnoticed outside of New Orleans, where Kenner is a respected songwriter. Recognition will accrue to Kenner in the Sixties, when his "I Like It Like That" and "Land of 1000 Dances" become well known. ♦

WEEK ENDING MAY 1		
U.S. #1 POP 45	"All Shook Up"	Elvis Presley
U.S. #1 POP LP	*Calypso*	Harry Belafonte
U.S. #1 R&B 45	"All Shook Up"	Elvis Presley
U.K. #1 POP 45	"Cumberland Gap"	Lonnie Donegan

WEEK ENDING MAY 8		
U.S. #1 POP 45	"All Shook Up"	Elvis Presley
U.S. #1 POP LP	*Calypso*	Harry Belafonte
U.S. #1 R&B 45	"All Shook Up"	Elvis Presley
U.K. #1 POP 45	"Cumberland Gap"	Lonnie Donegan

WEEK ENDING MAY 15		
U.S. #1 POP 45	"All Shook Up"	Elvis Presley
U.S. #1 POP LP	*Love Is the Thing*	Nat "King" Cole
U.S. #1 R&B 45	"School Day"	Chuck Berry
U.K. #1 POP 45	"Rock-a-Billy"	Guy Mitchell

WEEK ENDING MAY 22		
U.S. #1 POP 45	"Love Letters in the Sand"	Pat Boone
U.S. #1 POP LP	*Love Is the Thing*	Nat "King" Cole
U.S. #1 R&B 45	"Searchin' "/"Young Blood"	The Coasters
U.K. #1 POP 45	"Butterfly"	Andy Williams

WEEK ENDING MAY 29		
U.S. #1 POP 45	"Love Letters in the Sand"	Pat Boone
U.S. #1 POP LP	*Love Is the Thing*	Nat "King" Cole
U.S. #1 R&B 45	"Searchin' "/"Young Blood"	The Coasters
U.K. #1 POP 45	"Yes, Tonight Josephine"	Johnnie Ray

WEEK ENDING JUNE 7		
U.S. #1 POP 45	"Love Letters in the Sand"	Pat Boone
U.S. #1 POP LP	*Love Is the Thing*	Nat "King" Cole
U.S. #1 R&B 45	"Searchin' "/"Young Blood"	The Coasters
U.K. #1 POP 45	"Yes, Tonight Josephine"	Johnnie Ray

WEEK ENDING JUNE 14		
U.S. #1 POP 45	"Love Letters in the Sand"	Pat Boone
U.S. #1 POP LP	*Love Is the Thing*	Nat "King" Cole
U.S. #1 R&B 45	"Searchin' "/"Young Blood"	The Coasters
U.K. #1 POP 45	"Yes, Tonight Josephine"	Johnnie Ray

WEEK ENDING JUNE 21		
U.S. #1 POP 45	"Love Letters in the Sand"	Pat Boone
U.S. #1 POP LP	*Love Is the Thing*	Nat "King" Cole
U.S. #1 R&B 45	"Searchin' "/"Young Blood"	The Coasters
U.K. #1 POP 45	"Puttin' on the Style"	Lonnie Donegan

WEEK ENDING JUNE 28		
U.S. #1 POP 45	"Teddy Bear"/"Loving You"	Elvis Presley
U.S. #1 POP LP	*Love Is the Thing*	Nat "King" Cole
U.S. #1 R&B 45	"Searchin' "/"Young Blood"	The Coasters
U.K. #1 POP 45	"Puttin' on the Style"	Lonnie Donegan

JULY

1 " 'Good music' may be making a comeback on the best-seller charts," *Billboard* announces in a front-page article, "but rock & roll discs continue to dominate the pop market."

3 Atlantic Records releases a package of similarly designed, eponymously titled albums by **Ray Charles**, **Big Joe Turner**, **LaVern Baker**, **Ruth Brown**, **Clyde McPhatter and the Drifters** and **Ivory Joe Hunter**.

5 Excello Records releases **Slim Harpo's** "I'm a King Bee." The sexually suggestive rhythm & blues song never makes it as a hit, but in later years, the **Rolling Stones** and **Jimi Hendrix**, among others, record their own versions.

6 **John Lennon** meets **Paul McCartney** at a church picnic in the Liverpool suburb of Woolton, where John's skiffle band, the **Quarrymen**, is playing. In the church basement between sets, fourteen-year-old McCartney teaches sixteen-year-old Lennon to play and sing **Eddie Cochran's** "Twenty Flight Rock" and **Gene Vincent's** "Be-Bop-a-Lula."

12 **Alan Freed** kicks off a thirteen-week rock & roll show on ABC-TV, with guests **Frankie Lymon**, the **Everly Brothers**, **Buddy Knox**, **Connie Francis**, Ferlin **Huskey**, **Billy Williams** and others. The show airs every Friday night from ten to 10:30, Eastern time.

24 The **Coasters** record "Idol with the Golden Head," written and produced by **Jerry Leiber** and **Mike Stoller**.

27 The **Bobbettes'** first release and only Top Forty single, "Mr. Lee," enters the pop chart. The song is about the trio's high-school principal. Three years and zero hits later, they will record a follow-up tune, "I Shot Mr. Lee."

28 **Jerry Lee Lewis** makes his television debut on "The Steve Allen Show" and is booked for two more appearances with Allen, the first on August 11 and the second sometime in September. He is also scheduled to perform in **Alan Freed's** rock & roll shows at the Paramount in Brooklyn, New York, August 28 through September 8.

A *Billboard* "Spotlight Review" reports that the **Crickets'** "That'll Be the Day" has been on the market for a while without attracting much attention but has suddenly started to move. (In two months it will reach the top of the pop chart.)

AUGUST

4 The **Everly Brothers** make their second appearance on the Ed Sullivan show and introduce their forthcoming release, "Wake Up Little Susie."

5 "American Bandstand" makes its national debut on ABC-TV. "Bandstand" originated in 1952 as a local hit parade show in Philadelphia. **Dick Clark** assumed the role of host in 1956. The national show, aired Saturday mornings at eleven, Eastern time, will prove to be rock & roll's most enduring television program, still showing no signs of closing down in 1983. Clark's first guests are the **Chordettes**.

8 Imperial Records releases **Fats Domino's** first album, *This Is Fats,* which contains some past and future hits.

11 Just nine days after his appearance on "The Big Beat," **Jerry Lee Lewis** returns to the program. He again closes the show with "Whole Lotta Shakin' Goin' On." By the end of the month, the single will top both the country & western and the R&B charts. Later next month, Lewis records his second smash hit, "Great Balls of Fire."

15 Decca Records issues an early, previously unreleased recording of "That'll Be the Day," made by **Buddy Holly** without the **Crickets** when Decca had an option on his contract. It is only now, when the Crickets' version of the song is moving up the charts, that Decca releases any Holly material.

This brings to three the number of labels representing the singer, the others being Brunswick, to whom the Crickets (including Holly) are contracted, and Coral, which has a solo deal with the singer/guitarist.

24 Entering the R&B chart, **Jerry Lee Lewis'** "Whole Lotta Shakin' Goin' On" is now on all three major charts. It has already reached Number One on the C&W chart; in September it will hit Number One on the R&B chart and #3 on the pop chart. ◆

WEEK ENDING JULY 6		
U.S. #1 POP 45	"Teddy Bear"/"Loving You"	Elvis Presley
U.S. #1 POP LP	*Love Is the Thing*	Nat "King" Cole
U.S. #1 R&B 45	"Searchin' "/"Young Blood"	The Coasters
U.K. #1 POP 45	"All Shook Up"	Elvis Presley

WEEK ENDING JULY 13		
U.S. #1 POP 45	"Teddy Bear"/"Loving You"	Elvis Presley
U.S. #1 POP LP	*Around the World Eighty Days*	soundtrack
U.S. #1 R&B 45	"Searchin' "/"Young Blood"	The Coasters
U.K. #1 POP 45	"All Shook Up"	Elvis Presley

WEEK ENDING JULY 20		
U.S. #1 POP 45	"Teddy Bear"/"Loving You"	Elvis Presley
U.S. #1 POP LP	*Loving You*	Elvis Presley
U.S. #1 R&B 45	"Searchin' "/"Young Blood"	The Coasters
U.K. #1 POP 45	"All Shook Up"	Elvis Presley

WEEK ENDING JULY 27		
U.S. #1 POP 45	"Teddy Bear"/"Loving You"	Elvis Presley
U.S. #1 POP LP	*Loving You*	Elvis Presley
U.S. #1 R&B 45	"Searchin' "/"Young Blood"	The Coasters
U.K. #1 POP 45	"All Shook Up"	Elvis Presley

WEEK ENDING AUGUST 3		
U.S. #1 POP 45	"Teddy Bear"/"Loving You"	Elvis Presley
U.S. #1 POP LP	*Loving You*	Elvis Presley
U.S. #1 R&B 45	"Searchin' "/"Young Blood"	The Coasters
U.K. #1 POP 45	"All Shook Up"	Elvis Presley

WEEK ENDING AUGUST 10		
U.S. #1 POP 45	"Teddy Bear"/"Loving You"	Elvis Presley
U.S. #1 POP LP	*Loving You*	Elvis Presley
U.S. #1 R&B 45	"Searchin' "/"Young Blood"	The Coasters
U.K. #1 POP 45	"All Shook Up"	Elvis Presley

WEEK ENDING AUGUST 17		
U.S. #1 POP 45	"Tammy"	Debbie Reynolds
U.S. #1 POP LP	*Loving You*	Elvis Presley
U.S. #1 R&B 45	"Searchin' "/"Young Blood"	The Coasters
U.K. #1 POP 45	"All Shook Up"	Elvis Presley

WEEK ENDING AUGUST 24		
U.S. #1 POP 45	"Tammy"	Debbie Reynolds
U.S. #1 POP LP	*Loving You*	Elvis Presley
U.S. #1 R&B 45	"Teddy Bear"/"Loving You"	Elvis Presley
U.K. #1 POP 45	"All Shook Up"	Elvis Presley

WEEK ENDING AUGUST 31		
U.S. #1 POP 45	"Diana"	Paul Anka
U.S. #1 POP LP	*Loving You*	Elvis Presley
U.S. #1 R&B 45	"Whole Lotta Shakin' Goin' On"	Jerry Lee Lewis
U.K. #1 POP 45	"Diana"	Paul Anka

SEPTEMBER

4 WJZ-TV in Baltimore, Maryland, premieres "The **Buddy Deane** Bandstand," a rock & roll television disc-jockey show airing from three to five every afternoon except Sunday. Viewer response is overwhelming: when Deane invites his fans to phone the station to speak to their favorite stars, local phone lines are swamped, and phone company officials must ask Deane to desist. Twenty-five years later, film clips from the Deane program will be included in the **Ramones'** "Rock & Roll Radio" video.

8 Brunswick Records releases **Jackie Wilson's** first solo record, "Reet Petite," a song written in part by **Berry Gordy, Jr.** The record fails to attract much notice, and it will be another year before Wilson, formerly a member of **Billy Ward's Dominoes** (he replaced **Clyde McPhatter** in 1953), will find his mass audience with "Lonely Teardrops."

18 CBS-TV premieres "The Big Record," a record-hop-style show. The host is **Patti Page,** and her guests are **Sal Mineo, Billy Ward and the Dominoes** and Tony Bennett.

20 Songwriting and production duo **Jerry Leiber** and **Mike Stoller** ("Hound Dog," "Searchin'," "Jailhouse Rock") are contracted by RCA Victor to serve as independent producers and artist and repertoire (A&R) directors.

They will work with **Elvis Presley, Jaye P. Morgan, Lena Horne** and **Julius LaRosa,** among others, and continue to work with other companies, notably Atlantic, whose **Coasters** were Leiber and Stoller's discovery.

23 "Violent riots led by leather-jacketed motorcycle gangs" are reported at the Copenhagen, Denmark, premiere of *Rock around the Clock.* A far tamer reaction greets English Elvis clone **Tommy Steele,** in Copenhagen to promote his movie, *Young Man with a Guitar.*

24 **Alan Freed** tells his story in *Mister Rock and Roll,* premiering at Freed's favorite theater, the Paramount, New York City. The cameos make this movie worth the ticket: **Chuck Berry, Little Richard, Clyde McPhatter, Brook Benton, Frankie Lymon and the Teenagers** and the **Moonglows.**

25 Roulette Records releases **Frankie Lymon's** first solo disc, "My Girl." Without the **Teenagers,** it seems, his career is virtually over: he has no more hits.

OCTOBER

2 Specialty Records releases "Bony Maronie," backed with "You Bug Me, Baby," **Larry Williams'** followup to his summer pop and R&B Top Five hit, "Short Fat Fannie." "Bony Maronie" will peak at #14 on the pop chart and #9 on the R&B chart.

7 RCA Victor has already received half-a-million advance orders for **Elvis Presley's** Christmas album, of which only 200,000 copies have been pressed.

12 After a Sydney, Australia, concert, **Little Richard** announces his intention to give up rock & roll. "If you want to live for the Lord," he says, "you can't rock & roll, too. God doesn't like it." When his saxophonist, **Clifford Burks,** dares Richard to prove his "faith in God," Little Richard tosses four diamond rings, valued at $8,000, into Sydney's Hunter River. The next day, he flies to Los Angeles to be baptized a Seventh Day Adventist and "to prepare for the end of the world," as he puts it.

16 Keen Records releases **Sam Cooke's** "You Send Me," backed with "Summertime." The single will be the former gospel singer's biggest hit, eventually selling 2.5 million copies.

29 **Buddy Holly and the Crickets'** "Oh Boy," backed with "Not Fade Away," is released by Brunswick Records. The A side peaks in December at #10 on the pop chart; the B side will become one of Holly's most covered songs. ◆

WEEK ENDING SEPTEMBER 7		
U.S. #1 POP 45	"Tammy"	Debbie Reynolds
U.S. #1 POP LP	*Loving You*	Elvis Presley
U.S. #1 R&B 45	"Whole Lotta Shakin' Goin' On"	Jerry Lee Lewis
U.K. #1 POP 45	"Diana"	Paul Anka

WEEK ENDING SEPTEMBER 14		
U.S. #1 POP 45	"That'll Be the Day"	The Crickets
U.S. #1 POP LP	*Loving You*	Elvis Presley
U.S. #1 R&B 45	"Diana"	Paul Anka
U.K. #1 POP 45	"Diana"	Paul Anka

WEEK ENDING SEPTEMBER 21		
U.S. #1 POP 45	"Honeycomb"	Jimmie Rodgers
U.S. #1 POP LP	*Loving You*	Elvis Presley
U.S. #1 R&B 45	"Diana"	Paul Anka
U.K. #1 POP 45	"Diana"	Paul Anka

WEEK ENDING SEPTEMBER 28		
U.S. #1 POP 45	"Honeycomb"	Jimmie Rodgers
U.S. #1 POP LP	*Loving You*	Elvis Presley
U.S. #1 R&B 45	"Diana"	Paul Anka
U.K. #1 POP 45	"Diana"	Paul Anka

WEEK ENDING OCTOBER 5		
U.S. #1 POP 45	"Wake Up Little Susie"	The Everly Brothers
U.S. #1 POP LP	*Around the World Eighty Days*	soundtrack
U.S. #1 R&B 45	"Honeycomb"	Jimmie Rodgers
U.K. #1 POP 45	"Diana"	Paul Anka

WEEK ENDING OCTOBER 12		
U.S. #1 POP 45	"Jailhouse Rock"/"Treat Me Nice"	Elvis Presley
U.S. #1 POP LP	*Around the World Eighty Days*	soundtrack
U.S. #1 R&B 45	"Jailhouse Rock"/"Treat Me Nice"	Elvis Presley
U.K. #1 POP 45	"Diana"	Paul Anka

WEEK ENDING OCTOBER 19		
U.S. #1 POP 45	"Jailhouse Rock"/"Treat Me Nice"	Elvis Presley
U.S. #1 POP LP	*Around the World Eighty Days*	soundtrack
U.S. #1 R&B 45	"Jailhouse Rock"/"Treat Me Nice"	Elvis Presley
U.K. #1 POP 45	"Diana"	Paul Anka

WEEK ENDING OCTOBER 26		
U.S. #1 POP 45	"Jailhouse Rock"/"Treat Me Nice"	Elvis Presley
U.S. #1 POP LP	*Around the World Eighty Days*	soundtrack
U.S. #1 R&B 45	"Jailhouse Rock"/"Treat Me Nice"	Elvis Presley
U.K. #1 POP 45	"Diana"	Paul Anka

NOVEMBER

3 Sun Records releases **Jerry Lee Lewis'** "Great Balls of Fire," backed with "You Win Again." "Great Balls of Fire" is an **Otis Blackwell** and **Jack Hammer** composition, will become Lewis' biggest hit, reaching #2 on the pop chart, #3 on the R&B chart and Number One on the C&W chart.

Danny and the Juniors' "At the Hop" is released by ABC-Paramount. The Philadelphia vocal quartet's best-known song previously was issued on the small independent Singular label, in which form it sold 7,000 copies locally.

4 The top six songs on the pop and R&B charts are identical: **Elvis Presley's** "Jailhouse Rock," the **Everly Brothers'** "Wake Up Little Susie," **Sam Cooke's** "You Send Me," the **Rays'** "Silhouettes," **Rickie Nelson's** "Be-Bop Baby" and **Jimmie Rodgers'** "Honeycomb." "Jailhouse Rock" and "Wake Up Little Susie" are also Number One and #2, respectively, on the C&W chart.

12 *Jamboree*, the first movie in which **Jerry Lee Lewis** appears, previews in Hollywood. Among the other performers featured in the film are **Fats Domino** (with whom Lewis shares top billing), **Carl Perkins**, **Frankie Avalon**, **Slim Whitman** and **Connie Francis**.

19 Chicago's WCFL is picketed by the local chapter of the **Elvis Presley** Fan Club when it bans Presley's records from its playlists. The radio station is unmoved.

25 Rock & roll acts are turning away from the "increasingly disappointing grosses" of big package shows, *Billboard* reports, in favor of smaller-scale, DJ-sponsored "teen record hops," at which performers appear for smaller guarantees but bigger percentages of the gate.

Gene Vincent and the Blue Caps appear on the Ed Sullivan show, playing "Lotta Lovin'" and "Dance to the Bop." It's their first national television appearance.

DECEMBER

1 **Ed Sullivan** presents three rock & roll acts—each making its national television debut—on his Sunday evening show: **Buddy Holly and the Crickets**, playing "That'll Be the Day," **Sam Cooke**, singing "You Send Me," and the **Rays**, performing their hit "Silhouettes."

4 Prompted by reports that many radio stations have banned *Elvis' Christmas Album* because of the averred impropriety of "the Pelvis" singing religious songs, DJ **Allen Brooks** of CKWS, Kingston, Ontario, plays the album and invites listeners to call in their opinions. Of 800 callers, including several clergymen, all but fifty-six approve of Presley's sacred music—and those who disapprove add that they wouldn't listen to Presley under *any* circumstances.

6 Mercury Records releases the **Diamonds'** cover of the **Chuck Willis** dance tune "The Stroll." It will peak at #7 on the R&B chart, #8 on the pop chart and spark a fad for the dance of that name.

11 **Jerry Lee Lewis** secretly weds his third wife, third cousin **Myra Gale Brown**, in Hernando, Tennessee.

12 The controversy over *Elvis' Christmas Album* rages on: DJ **Al Priddy** of KEX, Portland, Oregon, is fired for violating the radio station's ban against playing Presley's rendition of "White Christmas."

15 **Sammy Davis, Jr.**, initiates a Westinghouse syndicated radio talk show with a "round-table" discussion of rock & roll; his guests are Columbia Records executive **Mitch Miller** and MGM Records president **Arnold Maxim**. When Davis and Miller blast

rock & roll as "the comic books of music," Maxim takes an opposing viewpoint and says, "I don't see any end to rock & roll in the near future." To which Davis replies, "I might commit suicide." A week later, Davis still will be alive—and releasing a cover of the rockabilly standard "I'm Comin' Home."

17 **Bobby Helms'** "Jingle Bell Rock" enters the pop chart for the first time. It will reenter in December 1958, 1960, 1961 and 1962. ♦

WEEK ENDING NOVEMBER 2		
U.S. #1 POP 45	"Jailhouse Rock"/"Treat Me Nice"	Elvis Presley
U.S. #1 POP LP	*Around the World Eighty Days*	soundtrack
U.S. #1 R&B 45	"Jailhouse Rock"/"Treat Me Nice"	Elvis Presley
U.K. #1 POP 45	"That'll Be the Day"	The Crickets

WEEK ENDING NOVEMBER 9		
U.S. #1 POP 45	"Jailhouse Rock"/"Treat Me Nice"	Elvis Presley
U.S. #1 POP LP	*My Fair Lady*	original Broadway cast
U.S. #1 R&B 45	"Jailhouse Rock"/"Treat Me Nice"	Elvis Presley
U.K. #1 POP 45	"That'll Be the Day"	The Crickets

WEEK ENDING NOVEMBER 16		
U.S. #1 POP 45	"Jailhouse Rock"/"Treat Me Nice"	Elvis Presley
U.S. #1 POP LP	*Around the World Eighty Days*	soundtrack
U.S. #1 R&B 45	"You Send Me"	Sam Cooke
U.K. #1 POP 45	"That'll Be the Day"	The Crickets

WEEK ENDING NOVEMBER 23		
U.S. #1 POP 45	"You Send Me"	Sam Cooke
U.S. #1 POP LP	*Around the World Eighty Days*	soundtrack
U.S. #1 R&B 45	"You Send Me"	Sam Cooke
U.K. #1 POP 45	"Mary's Boy Child"	Harry Belafonte

WEEK ENDING NOVEMBER 30		
U.S. #1 POP 45	"You Send Me"	Sam Cooke
U.S. #1 POP LP	*Around the World Eighty Days*	soundtrack
U.S. #1 R&B 45	"You Send Me"	Sam Cooke
U.K. #1 POP 45	"Mary's Boy Child"	Harry Belafonte

WEEK ENDING DECEMBER 7		
U.S. #1 POP 45	"Jailhouse Rock"	Elvis Presley
U.S. #1 POP LP	*Elvis' Christmas Album*	Elvis Presley
U.S. #1 R&B 45	"You Send Me"	Sam Cooke
U.K. #1 POP 45	"Mary's Boy Child"	Harry Belafonte

WEEK ENDING DECEMBER 14		
U.S. #1 POP 45	"April Love"	Pat Boone
U.S. #1 POP LP	*Elvis' Christmas Album*	Elvis Presley
U.S. #1 R&B 45	"You Send Me"	Sam Cooke
U.K. #1 POP 45	"Mary's Boy Child"	Harry Belafonte

WEEK ENDING DECEMBER 21		
U.S. #1 POP 45	"April Love"	Pat Boone
U.S. #1 POP LP	*Elvis' Christmas Album*	Elvis Presley
U.S. #1 R&B 45	"You Send Me"	Sam Cooke
U.K. #1 POP 45	"Mary's Boy Child"	Harry Belafonte

WEEK ENDING DECEMBER 28		
U.S. #1 POP 45	"At the Hop"	Danny & the Juniors
U.S. #1 POP LP	*Elvis' Christmas Album*	Elvis Presley
U.S. #1 R&B 45	"At the Hop"	Danny & the Juniors
U.K. #1 POP 45	"Mary's Boy Child"	Harry Belafonte

1958

The rock & roll business was still booming—as was the outcry against it. Early in the year, many radio stations around the country began holding "record-breaking weeks," during which they destroyed rock & roll records on the air. Many other stations adopted the Top Forty format, with its restricted playlist of popular tunes. Although this format was widely accepted by the mid-Sixties, it initially provoked great controversy: scores of disc jockeys quit such stations, some protesting that the format interfered with their on-air personalities, others that the playlist was too predictable and rigid, still others that the format promoted rock & roll too heavily, or not heavily enough. Results from a January survey by the Gilbert Youth Research Organization claimed that rock & roll was not as popular with youth as it was last year. And a program of "typical American DJ shows" that toured army bases overseas found rock & roll music and DJs conspicuously absent. The reason: both a senator and an anti-rock & roll DJ claimed that the presence of rock & roll on such a tour would injure international relations by touching off teen riots in Europe, thus "giving the Russians a real story for their propaganda machine."

Although rock & roll had proven its profit potential, anti-rock & roll campaigns within the media continued. In one, NBC's spot-sales advertising department shipped an advertising-programming guide album to radio stations around the country. It featured DJ Al Ross of Washington, D.C., station WRC introducing various rock & roll hits: "Well, let's see what garbage—er, rock & roll music we have here. This one's by the Coasters, four fugitives from the hog-calling seminar, and they've come up with an ear-caressing little dandy called 'Yakety Yak'. . . . This next little gem features one of the rocking immortals, a real talent by the name of Buddy Holly." After spinning Holly's "Rave On," Ross continued: "What'd he say? What? That was Buddy Holly with mood music for stealing hubcaps. 'Rave On,' it's called. You know, for a few seconds there, it did." The disc heavily promoted RCA star Perry Como as the kind of singer who attracted more affluent listeners, but it judiciously failed to attack—or even mention—RCA's biggest seller, Elvis Presley. And ABC-Paramount had such teen idols as Paul Anka and George Hamilton IV (other teen idols who emerged this year included Frankie Avalon and Tommy Sands) record a single titled "The Teen Commandments," with such lyrics as "Stop and think before you drink" and "Be humble enough to obey—you'll be giving orders yourself some day."

Billboard inaugurated its Hot 100 chart this year, officially recognizing the irrelevance of such "abstract boundaries" as pop, R&B and C&W. Independent labels from all over kept popping up with such one-hit wonders as the Silhouettes ("Get a Job") and the Sparkletones ("Black Slacks"). "American Bandstand" became the hottest show on daytime TV (Dick Clark, the host of "Bandstand," even got his own Saturday night show), and hundreds of other such shows debuted all over the country. Stereo records and phonographs, tapes and tape recorders were introduced, and they sold well. The Platters even received gold medallions from the Pope.

But there was still one potent weapon that threatened to stop rock & roll dead in its tracks: the sheer weight of adult morality and patriotic obligation, which even rock & roll had not yet been able to vanquish. Jerry Lee Lewis married his fourteen-year-old third cousin and was too ingenuous to lie about it; the resultant outcry nearly ended his career. And Elvis Presley was drafted into the army, an event that was expected to have ended his career as well.

J A N U A R Y

6 Gibson patents its "Flying V" electric guitar. The design will become a favorite of many rock guitarists and the trademark instrument of bluesman **Albert King**.

20 St. Louis radio station KWK finishes its "Record Breaking Week." By executive order of station management, all rock & roll music has been banned from KWK's airwaves; during "Record Breaking Week," KWK disc jockeys gave every rock & roll record in the station library a "farewell spin" before smashing it to pieces on mike. KWK station manager **Robert Convey** calls the action "a simple weeding out of undesirable music."

23 Brunswick Records releases the **Crickets'** "Maybe Baby" backed with "Tell Me How"; the next day, Coral Records releases **Buddy Holly**'s "I'm Gonna Love You Too" backed with "Listen to Me." In three days, Holly and the Crickets will appear on Ed Sullivan's show.

25 Elvis Presley's "Jailhouse Rock" becomes the first single ever to enter the U.K. pop chart at Number One.

27 Little Richard enrolls in Oakwood College, a Huntsville, Alabama, school for blacks run by the Seventh Day Adventist Church. In an announcement, Little Richard explains that, while flying over the Philippines on tour, the wing of his plane caught fire, and his prayers that the flames go out were answered; and that he had dreamed that "the world was burning up, the sky melting from the heat." As a result, he is giving up rock & roll so that he can serve God.

Entering the pop chart are **Frankie Avalon**'s "De De Dinah" at #38, **Paul Anka**'s "You Are My Destiny" at #45 and **Elvis Presley**'s "Don't" backed with "I Beg of You" at #25.

28 Jerry Lee Lewis and Ronald J. Hargrave copyright "High School Confidential," the title theme song to the second movie in which Lewis appeared.

29 Challenge Records releases "Tequila" backed with "Train to Nowhere" by the **Champs**, an instrumental group that includes **Jim Seals** and **Dash Crofts**, later to become **Seals and Crofts**. The A side will reach Number One in mid-March.

F E B R U A R Y

9 The January report of the American Research Bureau cites **Dick Clark**'s "American Bandstand" as the top-ranked daytime television program, drawing an average of 8,400,000 viewers per day.

12 Argo Records releases the **Monotones'** doo-wop classic, "Book of Love" backed with "You Never." Rising to the Top Five on both the pop and R&B charts, "Book of Love" will be the only success for the vocal sextet from Newark, New Jersey, who built their song on the jingle from a Pepsodent toothpaste commercial.

14 Rock the Casbah 1958: CBS television newsman **Walter Cronkite** reports that the government of Iran has banned rock & roll on the grounds that it is against the concepts of Islam and also a hazard to health. Iranian doctors have advised that the "extreme gyrations" of rock & roll dances are injurious to the hips.

15 Jerry Lee Lewis performs "Great Balls of Fire" and his latest release, "Breathless," on "American Bandstand." Later today "The Dick Clark Show," a new Saturday night rock & roll television program hosted by **Dick Clark** of "American Bandstand," premieres on ABC-TV. The half-hour show features appearances by **Jerry Lee Lewis, Pat Boone, Connie Francis,** Chuck Willis, the **Royal Teens** and **Johnnie Ray**.

19 Motown releases the **Miracles'** first record, "Got a Job," an "answer song" to the **Silhouettes'** "Get a Job." The song is written by Miracle **William "Smokey" Robinson**, Motown president **Berry Gordy, Jr.** and **Tyrone Carlo**.

Carl Perkins, whose "Blue Suede Shoes" was one of the biggest hits of 1957, leaves Sun Records to become Columbia's first rockabilly artist. Two weeks later, Columbia releases Perkins' first single for his new label, "Pink Pedal Pushers" backed with "Jive after Five."

21 *Sing, Boy, Sing*, Twentieth Century-Fox's movie about a Southern boy faced with the dilemma of furthering his career as a rockabilly singer or returning home to enter the ministry, premieres at the Mayfair Theater, New York City. **Tommy Sands** stars. ◆

WEEK ENDING JANUARY 4		
U.S. #1 POP 45	"At the Hop"	Danny & the Juniors
U.S. #1 POP LP	*Elvis' Christmas Album*	Elvis Presley
U.S. #1 R&B 45	"At the Hop"	Danny & the Juniors
U.K. #1 POP 45	"Mary's Boy Child"	Harry Belafonte
WEEK ENDING JANUARY 11		
U.S. #1 POP 45	"At the Hop"	Danny & the Juniors
U.S. #1 POP LP	*Elvis' Christmas Album*	Elvis Presley
U.S. #1 R&B 45	"At the Hop"	Danny & the Juniors
U.K. #1 POP 45	"Mary's Boy Child"	Harry Belafonte
WEEK ENDING JANUARY 18		
U.S. #1 POP 45	"At the Hop"	Danny & the Juniors
U.S. #1 POP LP	*Ricky*	Ricky Nelson
U.S. #1 R&B 45	"At the Hop"	Danny & the Juniors
U.K. #1 POP 45	"Great Balls of Fire"	Jerry Lee Lewis
WEEK ENDING JANUARY 25		
U.S. #1 POP 45	"At the Hop"	Danny & the Juniors
U.S. #1 POP LP	*My Fair Lady*	original cast
U.S. #1 R&B 45	"At the Hop"	Danny & the Juniors
U.K. #1 POP 45	"Jailhouse Rock"	Elvis Presley

WEEK ENDING FEBRUARY 1		
U.S. #1 POP 45	"At the Hop"	Danny & the Juniors
U.S. #1 POP LP	*Come Fly with Me*	Frank Sinatra
U.S. #1 R&B 45	"Get a Job"	The Silhouettes
U.K. #1 POP 45	"Jailhouse Rock"	Elvis Presley
WEEK ENDING FEBRUARY 8		
U.S. #1 POP 45	"At the Hop"	Danny & the Juniors
U.S. #1 POP LP	*Come Fly with Me*	Frank Sinatra
U.S. #1 R&B 45	"Get a Job"	The Silhouettes
U.K. #1 POP 45	"Jailhouse Rock"	Elvis Presley
WEEK ENDING FEBRUARY 15		
U.S. #1 POP 45	"Sugartime"	The McGuire Sisters
U.S. #1 POP LP	*Come Fly with Me*	Frank Sinatra
U.S. #1 R&B 45	"Get a Job"	The Silhouettes
U.K. #1 POP 45	"The Story of My Life"	Michael Holliday
WEEK ENDING FEBRUARY 22		
U.S. #1 POP 45	"Sugartime"	The McGuire Sisters
U.S. #1 POP LP	*Come Fly with Me*	Frank Sinatra
U.S. #1 R&B 45	"Get a Job"	The Silhouettes
U.K. #1 POP 45	"The Story of My Life"	Michael Holliday

MARCH

9 As the three-day First Annual Pop Disc Jockey Convention in Kansas City, Missouri, comes to an end, the most outspoken message delivered to radio station owners, managers and program directors is that disc jockeys are opposed to the Top Forty format, which they see as "restrictive," "dull," "unimaginative" and designed to "de-activate them as personalities by confining their duties to impersonal intros to the same top-selling records every station plays."

12 Jazz singer **Billie Holiday**, who had pled guilty to a narcotics-possession charge in 1956, is given a year's probation by a Philadelphia court.

19 Cadence Records releases **Link Wray**'s pioneering instrumental, "Rumble." With its slow tempo, thick riffs and distorted guitar, the recording will much later be called "the first heavy-metal song," and Wray will be credited with inventing guitar fuzztone. The story goes that Wray, piqued by his malfunctioning amplifier, punched a hole in the speaker and discovered that he liked the dirty, distorted sound it produced.

Big Records releases "Our Song," the first record by a teenage duo from Queens, New York, who go by the names **Tom and Jerry**. The pair will become famous in the Sixties under their real names—**Paul Simon and Art Garfunkel**.

22 Hank Williams, Jr. makes his stage debut in Swainsboro, Georgia. He is the eight-year-old son of the late country singer (who died on New Year's Day in 1953) and his wife, **Audrey Williams**, also a singing star.

24 Elvis Presley, age twenty-three, is inducted into the army in Memphis. Over the next two years, his serial number— 53310761—will become perhaps the most famous in history.

28 William Christopher "W. C." Handy, composer of such blues standards as "St. Louis Blues," "Memphis Blues" and "Beale Street Blues," dies at age eighty-four of natural causes in New York City.

APRIL

2 Veteran disc jockeys **Gene Norman** and **Dick Haynes** quit KLAC, Los Angeles, in protest over format. "It would be inconceivable for me to desert my fifteen-year standards by resorting to a Top Forty format," says Norman.

5 Irvin Feld's Greatest Show of Stars opens its eighty-day North American tour in Norfolk, Virginia. Headlining are **Sam Cooke**, the **Silhouettes**, the **Royal Teens**, the **Everly Brothers**, **Jimmy Reed** and **Clyde McPhatter**. On March 17, when the tour heads into Canada for a week, the bill is expanded with the addition of **Paul Anka**, **Roy Hamilton**, **LaVern Baker**, **Frankie Avalon**, the **Crescendos**, the **Story Sisters**, the **Monotones** and others. The tour is expected to gross over $1 million.

9 Bill Haley and the Comets open their first tour of South America in Buenos Aires, Argentina. The month-long junket will take them to Sao Paulo, Montevideo and Rio de Janeiro, Brazil.

10 Chuck Willis dies from a perforated stomach ulcer at Hugh Spalding Hospital, Atlanta, Georgia, at age thirty. Only two weeks before, the singer and songwriter released his most successful single, "Hang Up My Rock & Roll Shoes" backed with "What Am I Living For." An R&B hitmaker since 1952, Willis had only recently gained a large pop following with songs like "C.C. Rider" and "Betty and Dupree." Many of his songs were recorded by **Patti Page**, the **Clovers**, the **Five Keys** and the **Cadillacs**.

24 The Bronx-based Laurie Records debuts with **Dion and the Belmonts**' first single, "I Wonder Why" backed with "Teen Angel." The Belmonts, whose "Runaround Sue" and "The Wanderer" will

be huge hits in the early Sixties, are named after Belmont Avenue in the Fordham Road section of the Bronx.

31 ABC-Paramount releases **Carole King**'s first record, "The Right Girl" backed with "Goin' Wild." While King's recording career will take low priority and receive little recognition until the early Seventies, she and her husband, **Gerry Goffin**, will write some of the biggest pop hits of the late Fifties and early Sixties, including **Bobby Vee**'s "Take Good Care of My Baby," the **Drifters**' "Up on the Roof" and the **Shirelles**' "Will You Love Me Tomorrow." ◆

WEEK ENDING MARCH 1		
U.S. #1 POP 45	"Sugartime"	The McGuire Sisters
U.S. #1 POP LP	*Come Fly with Me*	Frank Sinatra
U.S. #1 R&B 45	"Sweet Little Sixteen"	Chuck Berry
U.K. #1 POP 45	"Magic Moments"	Perry Como

WEEK ENDING MARCH 8		
U.S. #1 POP 45	"Catch a Falling Star"	Perry Como
U.S. #1 POP LP	*The Music Man*	original cast
U.S. #1 R&B 45	"Sweet Little Sixteen"	Chuck Berry
U.K. #1 POP 45	"Magic Moments"	Perry Como

WEEK ENDING MARCH 15		
U.S. #1 POP 45	"Tequila"	The Champs
U.S. #1 POP LP	*The Music Man*	original cast
U.S. #1 R&B 45	"Sweet Little Sixteen"	Chuck Berry
U.K. #1 POP 45	"Magic Moments"	Perry Como

WEEK ENDING MARCH 22		
U.S. #1 POP 45	"Tequila"	The Champs
U.S. #1 POP LP	*The Music Man*	original cast
U.S. #1 R&B 45	"Tequila"	The Champs
U.K. #1 POP 45	"Magic Moments"	Perry Como

WEEK ENDING MARCH 29		
U.S. #1 POP 45	"Tequila"	The Champs
U.S. #1 POP LP	*My Fair Lady*	original cast
U.S. #1 R&B 45	"Tequila"	The Champs
U.K. #1 POP 45	"Magic Moments"	Perry Como

WEEK ENDING APRIL 5		
U.S. #1 POP 45	"Tequila"	The Champs
U.S. #1 POP LP	*My Fair Lady*	original cast
U.S. #1 R&B 45	"Tequila"	The Champs
U.K. #1 POP 45	"Magic Moments"	Perry Como

WEEK ENDING APRIL 12		
U.S. #1 POP 45	"He's Got the Whole World"	Laurie London
U.S. #1 POP LP	*The Music Man*	original cast
U.S. #1 R&B 45	"Tequila"	The Champs
U.K. #1 POP 45	"Magic Moments"	Perry Como

WEEK ENDING APRIL 19		
U.S. #1 POP 45	"He's Got the Whole World"	Laurie London
U.S. #1 POP LP	*The Music Man*	original cast
U.S. #1 R&B 45	"Twilight Time"	The Platters
U.K. #1 POP 45	"Magic Moments"	Perry Como

WEEK ENDING APRIL 26		
U.S. #1 POP 45	"Witch Doctor"	David Seville
U.S. #1 POP LP	*The Music Man*	original cast
U.S. #1 R&B 45	"Twilight Time"	The Platters
U.K. #1 POP 45	"Whole Lotta Woman"	Marvin Rainwater

MAY

3 Outside the Boston Arena, following a rock & roll show hosted by **Alan Freed**, teenagers allegedly attack policemen with stones and bottles. Several policemen and teenagers reportedly are injured, and the press terms the incident a "riot." Over the next several days, authorities will also claim that stabbings, looting, rapes and narcotics were involved, although no arrests are made. Police blame Freed for the riot, saying that it was his remark during the show—"The police don't want you to have any fun here"—that incited the violence. Freed counters that the police had been hostile toward both him and the audience, that the audience had been well-behaved during the show, and that the incident afterward had nothing to do with the show.

9 One day after **Alan Freed** is indicted for inciting unlawful destruction of property in Boston on May 3, he quits his job at New York's WINS, citing what he sees as the station's failure to "stand behind my policies and principles."

16 One week after resigning from WINS, **Alan Freed** signs with WABC New York, where he will work in both radio and television. Earlier today, Freed is arraigned by a Suffolk County, Massachusetts, grand jury on charges of inciting the May 3 "riot."

22 **Jerry Lee Lewis** arrives at London's Heathrow Airport to begin his first British tour. He is accompanied by his fourteen-year-old wife (and third cousin), **Myra**, and several members of his family. Although he has been advised by his managers not to reveal his marriage to the press, he answers all questions truthfully. The public's shock over Lewis' marriage marks the beginning of the controversy that will eventually ruin his career.

26 Just four days after his arrival, **Jerry Lee Lewis** plays the third—and last—show of what was to have been a thirty-seven-date tour. This morning, the *London Evening Star* runs an editorial in which it calls Lewis "an undesirable alien" and calls for his immediate deportation. That night, Lewis is booed from the

stage. Tomorrow, he will return to America after his tour is canceled.

JUNE

1 **Jimmie Rodgers** appears on "The Ed Sullivan Show"; **John Wayne** and **Frank Shuster** are the guest hosts.

9 **Jerry Lee Lewis**, with the help of his producer, **Sam Phillips**, takes out a full-page ad in *Billboard*. In the ad, written as an open letter, Lewis says, "This whole thing started because I tried and did tell the truth," and goes on to explain the circumstances of his second divorce. Lewis closes saying, "I hope that if I am washed up as an entertainer it won't be because of this bad publicity, because I can cry and wish all I want to, but I can't control the press or the sensationalism that these people will go to, to get a scandal started to sell papers." Just five days earlier, Lewis had rewed his third wife—and third cousin—**Myra**, but when filling out his application for a wedding license, he had falsely stated that there was no relationship between the two.

11 **Jerry Lee Lewis** appears at New York City's Cafe de Paris. Although it is only the first of two scheduled shows, Lewis returns home the following day. Not only had the press again been openly hostile toward Lewis, but the show had not even sold out.

13 **Frank Zappa** graduates from Antelope Val-

ley High School in Lancaster, California.

15 The **Platters** sing "Twilight Time" on "The Ed Sullivan Show." Several weeks earlier, while on tour in Italy, the group was granted an "unprecedented" audience with **Pope Pius XII**, who gave each of the members a gold medal.

Also today, the pop music show "Oh Boy" debuts on British TV.

21 Entering the pop Top Thirty today: **Elvis Presley**'s "Hard Headed Woman" and **Bobby Darin**'s "Splish Splash," both tied at #20 ("Hard Headed Woman" also hits #17 R&B), and **Dion and the Belmonts**' "I Wonder Why" at #28. ◆

WEEK ENDING MAY 3		
U.S. #1 POP 45	"Witch Doctor"	David Seville
U.S. #1 POP LP	*The Music Man*	original cast
U.S. #1 R&B 45	"Twilight Time"	The Platters
U.K. #1 POP 45	"Whole Lotta Woman"	Marvin Rainwater

WEEK ENDING MAY 10		
U.S. #1 POP 45	"All I Have to Do Is Dream"	The Everly Brothers
U.S. #1 POP LP	*The Music Man*	original cast
U.S. #1 R&B 45	"All I Have to Do Is Dream"	The Everly Brothers
U.K. #1 POP 45	"Whole Lotta Woman"	Marvin Rainwater

WEEK ENDING MAY 17		
U.S. #1 POP 45	"All I Have to Do Is Dream"	The Everly Brothers
U.S. #1 POP LP	*The Music Man*	original cast
U.S. #1 R&B 45	"All I Have to Do Is Dream"	The Everly Brothers
U.K. #1 POP 45	"Who's Sorry Now?"	Connie Francis

WEEK ENDING MAY 24		
U.S. #1 POP 45	"All I Have to Do Is Dream"	The Everly Brothers
U.S. #1 POP LP	*The Music Man*	original cast
U.S. #1 R&B 45	"All I Have to Do Is Dream"	The Everly Brothers
U.K. #1 POP 45	"Who's Sorry Now?"	Connie Francis

WEEK ENDING MAY 31		
U.S. #1 POP 45	"All I Have to Do Is Dream"	The Everly Brothers
U.S. #1 POP LP	*Johnny's Greatest Hits*	Johnny Mathis
U.S. #1 R&B 45	"All I Have to Do Is Dream"	The Everly Brothers
U.K. #1 POP 45	"Who's Sorry Now?"	Connie Francis

WEEK ENDING JUNE 7		
U.S. #1 POP 45	"The Purple People Eater"	Sheb Wooley
U.S. #1 POP LP	*Johnny's Greatest Hits*	Johnny Mathis
U.S. #1 R&B 45	"All I Have to Do Is Dream"	The Everly Brothers
U.K. #1 POP 45	"Who's Sorry Now?"	Connie Francis

WEEK ENDING JUNE 14		
U.S. #1 POP 45	"The Purple People Eater"	Sheb Wooley
U.S. #1 POP LP	*The Music Man*	original cast
U.S. #1 R&B 45	"Yakety Yak"	The Coasters
U.K. #1 POP 45	"Who's Sorry Now?"	Connie Francis

WEEK ENDING JUNE 21		
U.S. #1 POP 45	"The Purple People Eater"	Sheb Wooley
U.S. #1 POP LP	*The Music Man*	original cast
U.S. #1 R&B 45	"Yakety Yak"	The Coasters
U.K. #1 POP 45	"Who's Sorry Now?"	Connie Francis

WEEK ENDING JUNE 28		
U.S. #1 POP 45	"The Purple People Eater"	Sheb Wooley
U.S. #1 POP LP	*Johnny's Greatest Hits*	Johnny Mathis
U.S. #1 R&B 45	"Yakety Yak"	The Coasters
U.K. #1 POP 45	"On the Street Where You Live"	Vic Damone

JULY

1 **Alan Freed**'s TV show "The Big Beat" debuts on New York's WABC-TV, from five p.m. to six p.m., Monday through Friday. Guests on the first show include the **Four Lads** (who make a hasty retreat from the studio after lip-syncing their hit "Enchanted Island," when Freed suggests they dance with some of the bobbysoxers in the audience) and **Chuck Berry**, who lip-syncs "Johnny B. Goode" and holds a question-and-answer session with the audience.

5 **Ray Charles** appears at the Newport Jazz Festival, much to the indignation of jazz snobs, who consider Charles practically a rock & roller. A recording of the set will be released by Atlantic Records in 1973.

9 Following in the footsteps of **Carl Perkins**, ex-Sun Records artist **Johnny Cash** signs with Columbia Records.

Minneapolis-based Catholic youth magazine *Contacts* launches a campaign for "clean lyrics in pop songs," listing as no-no's such tunes as **Elvis Presley**'s "Wear Your Ring around My Neck" (it promotes "going steady") and starting a national contest to write "good, wholesome lyrics."

15 During Senate hearings on the music industry, American Guild of Authors and Composers counsel **John Schulman** plays the **Coasters**' "Yakety Yak," citing it as an offender in the alleged "cheapening of American music" by rock & roll, against which Schulman seeks legislation. The hearings had resulted from suits between the two biggest music-licensing organizations, ASCAP and BMI.

21 Pittsburgh radio station WAMP drops "all rock & roll discs and other raucous tunes in the so-called Top Forty charts." It's part of an anti-Top Forty backlash that also includes WZIP in Cincinnati and KSEL in Lubbock, Texas, **Buddy Holly**'s hometown.

28 *Billboard* reports on a just-issued claim by the Esso Gas Research Center that "tuning in rock & roll music on a car radio can cost a motorist money," because the rhythm can cause a driver to unconsciously jiggle the gas pedal, thus wasting fuel.

AUGUST

4 *Billboard* inaugurates its "Hot 100" record chart, a combined popularity chart and barometer of the movement of potential hits.

14 **Elvis Presley**'s mother, **Gladys**, dies of a heart attack due to liver complications in Memphis at age forty-two.

Seminal folk-blues singer/songwriter/guitarist **Big Bill Broonzy** dies after a long illness at age sixty-five, while on the way to a hospital from his Chicago home.

18 The Mutual Broadcasting System switches its twenty-one-hours-per-week disc-programming service for affiliates from "Top Fifty" to "Pop Fifty"—eliminating not all rock & roll tunes but, in the words of music director **Phil Lampkin**, "that which is distorted, monotonous, noisy music and/or has suggestive or borderline salacious lyrics." Lampkin adds that "most good rock & roll tunes are released on reputable major labels, whereas nearly all the undesirable ones are by one-shot companies . . . the major labels, by the way, are in full accord with our policies."

29 **Alan Freed**'s Big Beat Show opens at Brooklyn's Fox Theater, instead of his usual venue, the Paramount, because the latter's management felt the memory of the "riot" following Freed's Boston concert in May was "still too fresh in the public's mind." On opening night of the week-long series of shows, Freed goes onstage and tells the sellout crowd, "My critics once said four years ago that rock & roll wouldn't last more than six months. Here I am today, and we'll be here in four more years." The opening night show grosses a Brooklyn record of $200,000. Performers include **Frankie Avalon**, **Jimmy Clanton**, **Bobby Freeman**, the **Elegants**, the **Danleers**, **Bill Haley and the Comets** and **Chuck Berry**.

George Harrison joins **John Lennon** and **Paul McCartney** in Liverpool band the **Quarrymen**. ◆

WEEK ENDING JULY 5		
U.S. #1 POP 45	"The Purple People Eater"	Sheb Wooley
U.S. #1 POP LP	*The Music Man*	original cast
U.S. #1 R&B 45	"Yakety Yak"	The Coasters
U.K. #1 POP 45	"On the Street Where You Live"	Vic Damone

WEEK ENDING JULY 12		
U.S. #1 POP 45	"Hard Headed Woman"	Elvis Presley
U.S. #1 POP LP	*Gigi*	soundtrack
U.S. #1 R&B 45	"Yakety Yak"	The Coasters
U.K. #1 POP 45	"All I Have to Do Is Dream"	The Everly Brothers

WEEK ENDING JULY 19		
U.S. #1 POP 45	"Hard Headed Woman"	Elvis Presley
U.S. #1 POP LP	*Gigi*	soundtrack
U.S. #1 R&B 45	"Yakety Yak"	The Coasters
U.K. #1 POP 45	"All I Have to Do Is Dream"	The Everly Brothers

WEEK ENDING JULY 26		
U.S. #1 POP 45	"Poor Little Fool"	Ricky Nelson
U.S. #1 POP LP	*Gigi*	soundtrack
U.S. #1 R&B 45	"Yakety Yak"	The Coasters
U.K. #1 POP 45	"All I Have to Do Is Dream"	The Everly Brothers

WEEK ENDING AUGUST 2		
U.S. #1 POP 45	"Poor Little Fool"	Ricky Nelson
U.S. #1 POP LP	*Como's Golden Records*	Perry Como
U.S. #1 R&B 45	"Patricia"	Perez Prado
U.K. #1 POP 45	"All I Have to Do Is Dream"	The Everly Brothers

WEEK ENDING AUGUST 9		
U.S. #1 POP 45	"Volare"	Domenico Modugno
U.S. #1 POP LP	*Tchaikovsky's Piano Concerto*	Van Cliburn
U.S. #1 R&B 45	"Patricia"	Perez Prado
U.K. #1 POP 45	"All I Have to Do Is Dream"	The Everly Brothers

WEEK ENDING AUGUST 16		
U.S. #1 POP 45	"Bird Dog"	The Everly Brothers
U.S. #1 POP LP	*Tchaikovsky's Piano Concerto*	Van Cliburn
U.S. #1 R&B 45	"Just a Dream"	Jimmy Clanton
U.K. #1 POP 45	"All I Have to Do Is Dream"	The Everly Brothers

WEEK ENDING AUGUST 23		
U.S. #1 POP 45	"Volare"	Domenico Modugno
U.S. #1 POP LP	*Tchaikovsky's Piano Concerto*	Van Cliburn
U.S. #1 R&B 45	"Little Star"	The Elegants
U.K. #1 POP 45	"When"	The Kalin Twins

WEEK ENDING AUGUST 30		
U.S. #1 POP 45	"Volare"	Domenico Modugno
U.S. #1 POP LP	*Tchaikovsky's Piano Concerto*	Van Cliburn
U.S. #1 R&B 45	"Little Star"	The Elegants
U.K. #1 POP 45	"When"	The Kalin Twins

SEPTEMBER

8 Philadelphia teen idol **Paul Anka** launches a month-long tour of the Orient in Tokyo.

Billboard reports that **Dick Clark** has signed an album deal with ABC-Paramount Records. His first LP will consist of instrumental versions of contemporary hits by the **Bandstanders**, with the album titled *Dance with Dick Clark*.

19 **Elvis Presley** leaves a Brooklyn naval base to sail to Germany, where he'll join his army unit.

27 Entering the pop chart: **Fabian**'s "Got the Feeling" at #62, **Bo Diddley**'s "Say Man" at #71 and the **Isley Brothers**' "Shout" at #82.

28 The **Teddy Bears**' "To Know Him Is to Love Him," composed and arranged by eighteen-year-old **Phil Spec-** tor, is released on Dore Records. The title is taken from the inscription on Spector's father's tombstone. The song will reach Number One by the end of the year.

29 The **Big Bopper**'s "Chantilly Lace" enters the pop chart at #27; the **Moonglows**' "10 Commandments of Love" enters the pop chart at #41. "Chantilly Lace" enters the R&B chart at #14, and **Chuck Berry**'s "Carol" enters the R&B chart at #16.

OCTOBER

6 A *Billboard* story claims that "payola, that under-the-turntable device whereby record companies win plugs and influence disc jockeys, is fast growing into a monster that may yet destroy its creators. According to key record execs, jockey payola is so widespread that it's no longer possible to measure its effectiveness." The article goes on to note that "one West Coast sta-

tion, which instigated an official pay-for-plays policy a few months ago, recently dropped the idea when they discovered the paid plugs were ruining their programming structure." There is no mention, however, of **Alan Freed**, whose career will shortly be destroyed by payola scandal.

Conway Twitty's "It's Only Make Believe" enters the pop chart at #47. It will eventually reach Number One in both America and Britain.

13 A *Billboard* featurette on the **Teddy Bears** notes that member "18-year-old **Phil Spector**, who wrote and arranged their hit 'To Know Him Is to Love Him,' is studying to be a court reporter."

Federal Records releases **James** **Brown**'s "Try Me" backed with "Tell Me What I Did Wrong." It will be his first pop success (reaching #48) and first R&B Number One.

20 Roulette Records releases the **Playmates**' "Beep Beep." Its success will surpass that of the vocal trio's first hit, "Jo-Ann," peaking at #4 on the pop chart in December.

21 In what will be his last studio session, **Buddy Holly** records "True Love Ways," "It Doesn't Matter Anymore," "Moondreams" and "Raining in My Heart" with the **Crickets** in New York City. ◆

WEEK ENDING SEPTEMBER 6		
U.S. #1 POP 45	"Volare"	Domenico Modugno
U.S. #1 POP LP	*South Pacific*	soundtrack
U.S. #1 R&B 45	"Little Star"	The Elegants
U.K. #1 POP 45	"When"	The Kalin Twins
WEEK ENDING SEPTEMBER 13		
U.S. #1 POP 45	"Volare"	Domenico Modugno
U.S. #1 POP LP	*Tchaikovsky's Piano Concerto*	Van Cliburn
U.S. #1 R&B 45	"Little Star"	The Elegants
U.K. #1 POP 45	"When"	The Kalin Twins
WEEK ENDING SEPTEMBER 20		
U.S. #1 POP 45	"It's All in the Game"	Tommy Edwards
U.S. #1 POP LP	*Tchaikovsky's Piano Concerto*	Van Cliburn
U.S. #1 R&B 45	"It's All in the Game"	Tommy Edwards
U.K. #1 POP 45	"When"	The Kalin Twins
WEEK ENDING SEPTEMBER 27		
U.S. #1 POP 45	"It's All in the Game"	Tommy Edwards
U.S. #1 POP LP	*Sing Along with Mitch*	Mitch Miller
U.S. #1 R&B 45	"It's All in the Game"	Tommy Edwards
U.K. #1 POP 45	"Carolina Moon"/"Stupid Cupid"	Connie Francis

WEEK ENDING OCTOBER 4		
U.S. #1 POP 45	"It's All in the Game"	Tommy Edwards
U.S. #1 POP LP	*Only the Lonely*	Frank Sinatra
U.S. #1 R&B 45	"It's All in the Game"	Tommy Edwards
U.K. #1 POP 45	"Carolina Moon"/"Stupid Cupid"	Connie Francis
WEEK ENDING OCTOBER 11		
U.S. #1 POP 45	"It's All in the Game"	Tommy Edwards
U.S. #1 POP LP	*Only the Lonely*	Frank Sinatra
U.S. #1 R&B 45	"Rockin' Robin"	Bobby Day
U.K. #1 POP 45	"Carolina Moon"/"Stupid Cupid"	Connie Francis
WEEK ENDING OCTOBER 18		
U.S. #1 POP 45	"It's All in the Game"	Tommy Edwards
U.S. #1 POP LP	*Only the Lonely*	Frank Sinatra
U.S. #1 R&B 45	"Topsy II"	Cozy Cole
U.K. #1 POP 45	"Carolina Moon"/"Stupid Cupid"	Connie Francis
WEEK ENDING OCTOBER 25		
U.S. #1 POP 45	"It's All in the Game"	Tommy Edwards
U.S. #1 POP LP	*Only the Lonely*	Frank Sinatra
U.S. #1 R&B 45	"Topsy II"	Cozy Cole
U.K. #1 POP 45	"Carolina Moon"/"Stupid Cupid"	Connie Francis

N O V E M B E R

10 A *Billboard* article notes **Dick Clark's** "phenomenal" rapport with his teenage audience and that advertisers see him as "one of the hottest merchandising and promotional properties on TV." The article also notes that Beechnut gum's sales have gone up 100 percent since the company became an "American Bandstand" sponsor.

Sam Cooke suffers minor eye injuries in an auto accident near Marion, Arkansas, that claims the life of his chauffeur, **Edward Cunningham**, and also injures singer **Lou Rawls** of the **Pilgrim Travelers Quartet**, who are on tour with Cooke.

11 **Hank Ballard and the Midnighters** record the original "The Twist" in King Studios, Cincinnati, Ohio.

17 **Alan Freed's** trial for allegedly inciting a riot after a Boston rock & roll show on May 3, 1958, scheduled to begin today, is postponed until January 5, 1959, due to investigations into a related charge of violating Massachusetts anti-anarchy laws.

Eddie Cochran's "Summertime Blues" enters the U.K. pop chart at #20; **Fats Domino's** "Whole Lotta Loving" enters the U.S. pop chart at #81.

24 In Britain's music weekly *Melody Maker*, British orchestra leader **Vic Lewis** blasts rock & roll as "pop rot from the jungle of American entertainment . . . . It's time we stop these insults to teenagers—they deserve a better deal. Are the stars of the future to be drawn exclusively from the ranks of these three-chord guitar bashers and bawlers of gibberish?"

30 Coed Records releases the **Crests'** "16 Candles." It will be the **Johnny Maestro**-led group's biggest hit, reaching #2 on the pop chart and #4 on the R&B chart in January.

D E C E M B E R

15 In its year-end survey, *Billboard* rates the top pop tune of 1958 as **Domenico Modugno's** "Volare," the top R&B tune as **Chuck Willis'** "Hang Up My Rock & Roll

Shoes," the best-selling LP as the original cast album of *My Fair Lady* and the best-selling EP as **Elvis Presley's** *Jailhouse Rock*.

22 **Bobby Helms'** "Jingle Bell Rock," last year's Christmas hit, reappears in time for Santa Claus. It will return again for Christmas 1960, 1961 and 1962. Helms' first hits, "Fraulein" and "My Special Angel," made the Top Forty and Top Ten, respectively, in 1957.

25 **Alan Freed's** Christmas Rock & Roll Spectacular opens a ten-day run at the Loew's State Theater in Manhattan with seventeen acts, including **Bo Diddley, Chuck Berry, Eddie Cochran,** the **Moonglows, Jackie Wilson, Frankie Avalon** and the **Everly Brothers. Johnnie Ray**, not a typical rock & roll show attraction, tops the bill the first five nights of the run, but it's Bo Diddley who steals the show.

The Everly Brothers headline the last five nights of the run.

26 **Johnny Cash** tops a country & western bill also including **Tex Ritter** and the **Sons of the Pioneers**, opening at the Showboat Hotel in Las Vegas. ◆

WEEK	ENDING NOVEMBER 1	
U.S. #1 POP 45	"It's Only Make Believe"	Conway Twitty
U.S. #1 POP LP	*Only the Lonely*	Frank Sinatra
U.S. #1 R&B 45	"Topsy II"	Cozy Cole
U.K. #1 POP 45	"Carolina Moon"/"Stupid Cupid"	Connie Francis

WEEK	ENDING NOVEMBER 8	
U.S. #1 POP 45	"Tom Dooley"	Kingston Trio
U.S. #1 POP LP	*South Pacific*	soundtrack
U.S. #1 R&B 45	"Topsy II"	Cozy Cole
U.K. #1 POP 45	"It's All in the Game"	Tommy Edwards

WEEK	ENDING NOVEMBER 15	
U.S. #1 POP 45	"It's Only Make Believe"	Conway Twitty
U.S. #1 POP LP	*The Kingston Trio*	The Kingston Trio
U.S. #1 R&B 45	"Topsy II"	Cozy Cole
U.K. #1 POP 45	"It's All in the Game"	Tommy Edwards

WEEK	ENDING NOVEMBER 22	
U.S. #1 POP 45	"To Know Him Is to Love Him"	The Teddy Bears
U.S. #1 POP LP	*Sing Along with Mitch*	Mitch Miller
U.S. #1 R&B 45	"Topsy II"	Cozy Cole
U.K. #1 POP 45	"It's All in the Game"	Tommy Edwards

WEEK	ENDING NOVEMBER 29	
U.S. #1 POP 45	"To Know Him Is to Love Him"	The Teddy Bears
U.S. #1 POP LP	*Sing Along with Mitch*	Mitch Miller
U.S. #1 R&B 45	"A Lover's Question"	Clyde McPhatter
U.K. #1 POP 45	"Hoots Mon"	Lord Rockingham's XI

WEEK	ENDING DECEMBER 6	
U.S. #1 POP 45	"To Know Him Is to Love Him"	The Teddy Bears
U.S. #1 POP LP	*Sing Along with Mitch*	Mitch Miller
U.S. #1 R&B 45	"Lonely Teardrops"	Jackie Wilson
U.K. #1 POP 45	"Hoot Mon"	Lord Rockingham's XI

WEEK	ENDING DECEMBER 13	
U.S. #1 POP 45	"The Chipmunk Song"	David Seville & the Chipmunks
U.S. #1 POP LP	*Sing Along with Mitch*	Mitch Miller
U.S. #1 R&B 45	"Lonely Teardrops"	Jackie Wilson
U.K. #1 POP 45	"Hoot Mon"	Lord Rockingham's XI

WEEK	ENDING DECEMBER 20	
U.S. #1 POP 45	"The Chipmunk Song"	David Seville & the Chipmunks
U.S. #1 POP LP	*Christmas Sing Along*	Mitch Miller
U.S. #1 R&B 45	"Lonely Teardrops"	Jackie Wilson
U.K. #1 POP 45	"It's Only Make Believe"	Conway Twitty

WEEK	ENDING DECEMBER 27	
U.S. #1 POP 45	"The Chipmunk Song"	David Seville & the Chipmunks
U.S. #1 POP LP	*Christmas Sing Along*	Mitch Miller
U.S. #1 R&B 45	"Lonely Teardrops"	Jackie Wilson
U.K. #1 POP 45	"It's Only Make Believe"	Conway Twitty

1959

The Year the Music Died. The day (commemorated in 1971 by Don McLean's "American Pie") was February 3rd, when a tour plane carrying Buddy Holly, Ritchie Valens and J. P. "Big Bopper" Richardson crashed in a Clear Lake, Iowa, cornfield, killing all three. Though Valens ("La Bamba," "Come On, Let's Go") and the Big Bopper ("Chantilly Lace") had each made their immortal contributions to rock & roll, it was Holly's death that would prove most epochal.

At the time, few seemed to realize the full weight and scope of Holly's achievements. The *Billboard* report on the tragic crash didn't even carry any details about the careers of the three deceased; instead it played up the fact that the tour promoters had resourcefully booked some teen idols to take their places. And though a 1973 film, *American Graffiti,* set in 1962, would have one character say, "Rock & roll's been going downhill ever since Buddy Holly died," that was more revisionist, wishful thinking than anything else. Few really mourned Holly's loss until much later, when history had proven the true worth of his brief but brilliant career. But aside from creating a host of influential and inimitable rock & roll classics, Holly was, as Dave Marsh noted in his introduction to John Goldrosen's *The Buddy Holly Story,* "a prophetic figure . . . the first to involve himself in all phases of his work—performing, writing, production, guitar playing, arrangements." Indeed, Holly stood in direct contrast not only to the established tradition of pop singers as mere sellers of songs, but also to such seminal white rock & rollers as Elvis Presley and Jerry Lee Lewis—neither of whom composed his own material.

Later in the year, rock & roll's public image suffered another crucial blow: Chuck Berry, rock & roll's first and arguably greatest poet, was convicted under the Mann Act of transporting a minor across state lines for immoral purposes. Berry had picked up an Apache prostitute in Mexico and brought her to the amusement park named after him in St. Louis, where she was to work as a hat-check girl in Berry's Club Ballroom; when he fired her, she went to the police. Though she admitted she was a prostitute, and though the first of Berry's two protracted trials was so blatantly racist it was declared a mistrial, Berry was still found guilty in 1962 and would serve two years in prison.

With four of its greatest performers out of action—Presley continued to be a presence via records released in his absence—"real" rock & roll music began to take a back seat to divergent forms of pop music which were influenced by rock & roll and which, in turn, would influence rock & roll. This was the year that rock & roll began spawning semipopular subgenres. The first to flourish was teen-idol music. Frankie Avalon's biggest hit, "Venus," was released only days before Buddy Holly's death.

As if all this weren't enough, late in 1959 Alan Freed lost his radio and TV jobs when the federal government stepped up its investigation into disc-jockey payola. Like the Chuck Berry case, it was another hard, legal bombshell to reinforce the attitudinal sea-change signaled by the popularity of the teen idols. A bad year, indeed.

JANUARY

5 Coral Records releases what will be **Buddy Holly**'s last record before his death, "It Doesn't Matter Anymore" backed with "Raining in My Heart." "It Doesn't Matter Anymore"—one of the few songs Holly recorded that was not his composition (**Paul Anka** wrote it for him)—peaked at #13 two months after the Clear Lake tragedy.

19 The ARB TV ratings for December 1958 list **Dick Clark**'s "American Bandstand" as the country's most popular daytime show.

A *Billboard* article on the general easing of TV and radio censorship of pop songs notes one exception—and it's an instrumental: **Link Wray**'s hit "Rumble" is still considered unplayable by some authorities because its title connotes teengang violence (the accuracy of this suspicion was later confirmed when Wray revealed that the title came from an incident where the **Wraymen** had to play the instrumental onstage in order to distract participants in a gang "rumble"). When Wray and his Wraymen recently appeared on "American Bandstand" to perform "Rumble," **Dick Clark** was forbidden to mention the title, so he simply said, "and now, here's Link Wray" as an introduction.

21 The **Kingston Trio**, one of the foremost groups behind the current folk music revival in America, re-

ceive their first gold record for "Tom Dooley." The song is a Southern folk song that originated in the years just after the Civil War.

22 Alone with an automatic guitar and tape recorder in his New York City apartment, **Buddy Holly** makes his last recordings. The songs taped this day, or in the preceding couple of weeks, are "Peggy Sue Got Married," "Crying, Waiting, Hoping," "That's What They Say," "What to Do," "Learning the Game" and "That Makes It Tough." The recordings will be overdubbed posthumously and released by Coral Records.

26 **Larry Williams**' "Bad Boy" backed with "She Said 'Yeah!' " is released on Specialty Records; **Roy Orbison**'s "Almost 18" backed with "Jolie" is released on RCA Records.

FEBRUARY

2 **Buddy Holly**, **Ritchie Valens** and the **Big Bopper** make their last onstage appearances during the GAC Winter Show tour, at the Surf Ballroom in Clear Lake, Iowa.

Entering the pop chart: the **Coasters**' "Charlie Brown" at #69, and **Link Wray and his Wraymen**'s "Rawhide" at #98. **Ricky Nelson**'s LP *Ricky Sings Again* enters the album chart at #24.

Frankie Avalon's "Venus" is released on Chancellor Records. It will become the teen idol's greatest hit.

3 **Buddy Holly**, **Ritchie Valens** and the **Big Bopper** are killed when their GAC Winter Show tour plane crashes in the Iowa countryside. *Billboard*'s item on the tragedy gives no details on the crash, nor on the careers of the three late rock & roll stars; instead, under the headline TRAGEDY FAILS TO HALT GAC WINTER TOUR, it notes that the show went on the night of the crash, with the **Crickets**, **Dion and the Belmonts** and **Frankie Sardo** performing; that the next day **Frankie Avalon** and **Jimmy Clanton** are booked to perform, but that the day after *that*, Avalon comes down with pneumonia, leaving **Fabian** and **Paul Anka** to finish out the tour as headliners.

7 New Orleans blues and R&B guitarist/singer **Eddie "Guitar Slim" Jones** dies of pneumonia in New York City at age thirty-three. His best-

known song was "The Things That I Used to Do," and his wildly electrified guitar style influences **Jimi Hendrix**, among others.

9 **Irvin Feld**, rock & roll package-tour promoter (who runs the GAC Winter Show, among others), reports to *Billboard* that "after a long, hard pull in 1958"—a bad year for rock & roll package tours—"the rock & roll package-show business is looking up, with the best advance sales since the spring of '57." Feld's current Biggest Show of Stars package, set to open a seven-week tour March 29 in Richmond, Virginia, includes performers such as **Bo Diddley**, **Clyde McPhatter**, the **Coasters**, **Lloyd Price**, **Little Anthony and the Imperials** and others.

23 Three weeks after their deaths, **Buddy Holly**'s "It Don't Matter Anymore" enters the Hot 100 at #82, and the **Big Bopper**'s LP *Chantilly Lace* is released on Mercury Records. ◆

WEEK	ENDING	JANUARY 4
U.S. #1 POP 45	"The Chipmunk Song"	David Seville & the Chipmunks
U.S. #1 POP LP	*Sing Along with Mitch*	Mitch Miller
U.S. #1 R&B 45	"Lonely Teardrops"	Jackie Wilson
U.K. #1 POP 45	"It's Only Make Believe"	Conway Twitty

WEEK	ENDING	JANUARY 11
U.S. #1 POP 45	"Smoke Gets in Your Eyes"	The Platters
U.S. #1 POP LP	*Sing Along with Mitch*	Mitch Miller
U.S. #1 R&B 45	"Lonely Teardrops"	Jackie Wilson
U.K. #1 POP 45	"It's Only Make Believe"	Conway Twitty

WEEK	ENDING	JANUARY 18
U.S. #1 POP 45	"Smoke Gets in Your Eyes"	The Platters
U.S. #1 POP LP	*Sing Along with Mitch*	Mitch Miller
U.S. #1 R&B 45	"Lonely Teardrops"	Jackie Wilson
U.K. #1 POP 45	"It's Only Make Believe"	Conway Twitty

WEEK	ENDING	JANUARY 25
U.S. #1 POP 45	"Smoke Gets in Your Eyes"	The Platters
U.S. #1 POP LP	*Flower Drum Song*	original cast
U.S. #1 R&B 45	"Try Me"	James Brown
U.K. #1 POP 45	"One Night"/"I Got Stung"	Elvis Presley

WEEK	ENDING	FEBRUARY 1
U.S. #1 POP 45	"Stagger Lee"	Lloyd Price
U.S. #1 POP LP	*Flower Drum Song*	original cast
U.S. #1 R&B 45	"Stagger Lee"	Lloyd Price
U.K. #1 POP 45	"I Got Stung"/"One Night"	Elvis Presley

WEEK	ENDING	FEBRUARY 8
U.S. #1 POP 45	"Stagger Lee"	Lloyd Price
U.S. #1 POP LP	*Peter Gunn*	Henry Mancini
U.S. #1 R&B 45	"Stagger Lee"	Lloyd Price
U.K. #1 POP 45	"I Got Stung"/"One Night"	Elvis Presley

WEEK	ENDING	FEBRUARY 15
U.S. #1 POP 45	"Stagger Lee"	Lloyd Price
U.S. #1 POP LP	*Peter Gunn*	Henry Mancini
U.S. #1 R&B 45	"Stagger Lee"	Lloyd Price
U.K. #1 POP 45	"Smoke Gets in Your Eyes"	The Platters

WEEK	ENDING	FEBRUARY 22
U.S. #1 POP 45	"Venus"	Frankie Avalon
U.S. #1 POP LP	*Peter Gunn*	Henry Mancini
U.S. #1 R&B 45	"It's Just a Matter of Time"	Brook Benton
U.K. #1 POP 45	"Smoke Gets in Your Eyes"	The Platters

MARCH

10 **Elvis Presley**'s "I Need Your Love Tonight" backed with "A Fool Such as I" is released on RCA Records. The next day, based on advance orders for the disc totalling nearly 1 million, RCA ships a gold record for the platter to Elvis, who is stationed in Germany.

15 Saxophonist **Lester Young**, a jazz giant, dies at age forty-nine of a heart attack in New York City.

16 Plans are announced for the first American rock & roll package tour to hit Europe. Performers will include **Bobby Darin**, **Conway Twitty**, **Duane Eddy**, **Dale Hawkins**, the **Poni Tails**, with British star **Cliff Richard** as guest for some British dates. The tour will kick off April 22 in London.

19 Representative **Torbert McDonald** (D-Massachusetts) introduces congressional legislation to limit special postage rates on recordings to only those with "educational or cultural value," and lashes out at "postal rates which subsidize rock & roll, jazz and hillbilly musicians—that is, subsidizing musical illiterates by designating *all* phonograph records as educational material."

24 The re-formed **Drifters**' "There Goes My Baby" is released on Atlantic Records. Not only is it the group's first disc with new lead singer **Ben E. King** replacing the departed **Clyde McPhatter**, but it sports innovative and ultimately influential (on such early Sixties producers as **Phil Spector**) orchestral production by **Jerry Leiber** and **Mike Stoller**.

30 *Billboard* reports that a professor at Orange County Community College in Middletown, New York, recently based some psychology exam questions on the **Coasters**' class-clown anthem, "Charlie Brown," i.e., "Is Charlie Brown a 'conformist or a nonconformist?' Can you differentiate between his life-space and his environment?"

APRIL

6 In what *Billboard* terms "the most unlike-

ly meeting of the minds this year," **Mitch Miller**—Columbia Records A&R chief, producer, arranger, recording artist and noted rock & roll adversary—announces that he is negotiating a series of freelance production deals with **Jerry Leiber** and **Mike Stoller**, noted producer/arranger team and coauthors of such hit rock & roll tunes as "Hound Dog," "Charlie Brown" and "K. C. Lovin'," upon which the just-released versions of "Kansas City" are based. The article also notes that Columbia's singles sales have fallen off recently, and concludes that "what Columbia needs is some good, swinging rock & roll records."

13 **Chuck Berry**'s "Little Queenie" enters the Hot 100 at #99, followed by **Wilbert Harrison**'s "Kansas City" at #100.

20 **Dolly Parton**'s first record, "Puppy Love,"

is released on Gold Band Records. *Billboard*'s capsule review notes, "She sounds about twelve years old." Dolly is thirteen.

22 **Alan Freed** premieres what will be his last rock & roll movie, *Go, Johnny, Go.* As always, the music makes up for any shortcomings in the plot: included are performances by **Chuck Berry**, **Ritchie Valens**, **Jackie Wilson**, **Eddie Cochran**, the **Cadillacs**, the **Flamingos**, **Harvey Fuqua** and **Jo Ann Campbell**.

24 "Your Hit Parade," the Saturday night pop music show that has aired regularly on the radio since April 20, 1935, and more recently on television, is given its last broadcast. ◆

WEEK ENDING MARCH 1

U.S. #1 POP 45	"Venus"	Frankie Avalon
U.S. #1 POP LP	*Peter Gunn*	Henry Mancini
U.S. #1 R&B 45	"It's Just a Matter of Time"	Brook Benton
U.K. #1 POP 45	"Smoke Gets in Your Eyes"	The Platters

WEEK ENDING MARCH 8

U.S. #1 POP 45	"Venus"	Frankie Avalon
U.S. #1 POP LP	*Peter Gunn*	Henry Mancini
U.S. #1 R&B 45	"It's Just a Matter of Time"	Brook Benton
U.K. #1 POP 45	"Smoke Gets in Your Eyes"	The Platters

WEEK ENDING MARCH 15

U.S. #1 POP 45	"Venus"	Frankie Avalon
U.S. #1 POP LP	*Peter Gunn*	Henry Mancini
U.S. #1 R&B 45	"It's Just a Matter of Time"	Brook Benton
U.K. #1 POP 45	"Smoke Gets in Your Eyes"	The Platters

WEEK ENDING MARCH 22

U.S. #1 POP 45	"Venus"	Frankie Avalon
U.S. #1 POP LP	*Peter Gunn*	Henry Mancini
U.S. #1 R&B 45	"It's Just a Matter of Time"	Brook Benton
U.K. #1 POP 45	"Smoke Gets in Your Eyes"	The Platters

WEEK ENDING MARCH 29

U.S. #1 POP 45	"Come Softly to Me"	The Fleetwoods
U.S. #1 POP LP	*Peter Gunn*	Henry Mancini
U.S. #1 R&B 45	"It's Just a Matter of Time"	Brook Benton
U.K. #1 POP 45	"Side Saddle"	Russ Conway

WEEK ENDING APRIL 5

U.S. #1 POP 45	"Come Softly to Me"	The Fleetwoods
U.S. #1 POP LP	*Peter Gunn*	Henry Mancini
U.S. #1 R&B 45	"It's Just a Matter of Time"	Brook Benton
U.K. #1 POP 45	"Side Saddle"	Russ Conway

WEEK ENDING APRIL 12

U.S. #1 POP 45	"Come Softly to Me"	The Fleetwoods
U.S. #1 POP LP	*Peter Gunn*	Henry Mancini
U.S. #1 R&B 45	"It's Just a Matter of Time"	Brook Benton
U.K. #1 POP 45	"Side Saddle"	Russ Conway

WEEK ENDING APRIL 19

U.S. #1 POP 45	"Come Softly to Me"	The Fleetwoods
U.S. #1 POP LP	*Peter Gunn*	Henry Mancini
U.S. #1 R&B 45	"It's Just a Matter of Time"	Brook Benton
U.K. #1 POP 45	"It Doesn't Matter Anymore"	Buddy Holly

WEEK ENDING APRIL 26

U.S. #1 POP 45	"Come Softly to Me"	The Fleetwoods
U.S. #1 POP LP	*Gigi*	soundtrack
U.S. #1 R&B 45	"It's Just a Matter of Time"	Brook Benton
U.K. #1 POP 45	"It Doesn't Matter Anymore"	Buddy Holly

MAY

4   **Dick Clark** announces the first motion-picture project of his recently formed production company Drexel Films Corp. It'll be called *Harrison High*, based on a novel by twenty-two-year-old **John Farris**. According to Drexel Executive VP **Chuck Reeves**, it "will place a special emphasis on the lives of decent teenagers who make up the vast majority of today's young adult population." Reportedly, **Fabian** and **Bobby Darin** are up for the lead role. Clark himself will portray a high-school teacher in the film.

Two more versions of the song "Kansas City" enter the Hot 100—by **Hank Ballard and the Midnighters** and **Rocky Olson**, at #73 and #98 respectively. **Neil Sedaka**'s "I Go Ape" enters the U.K. pop chart at #11.

The winners of the first annual Grammy Awards, given by the recently formed National Academy of Recording Arts and Sciences, are announced. **Domenico Modugno**'s "Volare" wins Record of the Year; **Henry Mancini**'s *Peter Gunn* is Album of the Year; the **Champs**' "Tequila" is best R&B Performance; and the **Kingston Trio**'s "Tom Dooley" is Best C&W Performance of the Year. Most awards won go to **Ross "David Seville" Bagdasa-rian**, whose "The Chipmunk Song" wins for Best Recording for Children, Best Comedy Performance and Best Engineered Record.

29   One of rock's first outdoor festivals takes place—typically—in the rain at the Herndon Stadium in Atlanta, Georgia. The bill features **Ray Charles**, **B. B. King**, **Ruth Brown**, **Jimmy Reed**, the **Drifters** and others. The festival draws more than 9,000 spectators.

JUNE

1   Some teenagers are saving money on buying records by taping singles off of Top Forty radio shows, claims *Billboard*. It also mentions that there are fewer million-selling records than in past years, and many more bombs, but attributes this phenomenon to the exigencies of an overcrowded market.

Entering the Hot 100 this week are: the **Flamingos**' "I Only Have Eyes for You" at #60, **Sam Cooke**'s "Only Sixteen" at #71, **Ronnie Hawkins**' "40 Days" at #84 and the **Drifters**' "There Goes My Baby" at #98.

5   **Bob Zimmerman** graduates from Hibbing High School in Hibbing, Minnesota. Known to his classmates as a "greaser" because of his long sideburns, his leather jacket, his Harley-Davidson and his love for rock & roll, the eighteen year old soon leaves Hibbing and his malcontent image for the ways of a serious student at the University of Minnesota in Minneapolis, where he begins performing in campus coffee houses under the name **Bob Dylan**.

12   Chess/Checker releases **Chuck Berry**'s *Chuck Berry on Top* LP and **Bo Diddley**'s *Go Go Bo Diddley* LP.

22   Entering the Hot 100 are **Chuck Berry**'s "Back in the U.S.A." at #56 and the **Platters**' "Remember When?" at #68. Entering the U.K. pop chart are the **Everly Brothers**' "Poor Jenny" at #17, **Duane Eddy**'s "Peter Gunn" at #19 and **Lloyd Price**'s "Personality" at #20.

29   **Dick Clark** announces that he is teaming up with veteran rock & roll package-tour promoter **Irvin Feld**, forming Clark-Feld Productions, to stage a series of Dick Clark Caravans. Clark will not appear on the tours themselves, but will personally select all talent, attend rehearsals, et cetera. Clark says that there will be four Dick Clark Caravans each year, with the first touring the East Coast from September 18 to November 8. Feld says he estimates that over $1 million will be invested in talent for the tours. ◆

WEEK ENDING MAY 3		
U.S. #1 POP 45	"The Happy Organ"	Dave "Baby" Cortez
U.S. #1 POP LP	*Gigi*	soundtrack
U.S. #1 R&B 45	"Kansas City"	Wilbert Harrison
U.K. #1 POP 45	*"I Need Your Love Tonight"*	Elvis Presley

WEEK ENDING MAY 10		
U.S. #1 POP 45	"Kansas City"	Wilbert Harrison
U.S. #1 POP LP	*Gigi*	soundtrack
U.S. #1 R&B 45	"Kansas City"	Wilbert Harrison
U.K. #1 POP 45	*"I Need Your Love Tonight"*	Elvis Presley

WEEK ENDING MAY 17		
U.S. #1 POP 45	"Kansas City"	Wilbert Harrison
U.S. #1 POP LP	*Gigi*	soundtrack
U.S. #1 R&B 45	"Kansas City"	Wilbert Harrison
U.K. #1 POP 45	*"I Need Your Love Tonight"*	Elvis Presley

WEEK ENDING MAY 24		
U.S. #1 POP 45	"The Battle of New Orleans"	Johnny Horton
U.S. #1 POP LP	*Gigi*	soundtrack
U.S. #1 R&B 45	"Kansas City"	Wilbert Harrison
U.K. #1 POP 45	*"I Need Your Love Tonight"*	Elvis Presley

WEEK ENDING MAY 31		
U.S. #1 POP 45	"The Battle of New Orleans"	Johnny Horton
U.S. #1 POP LP	*Gigi*	soundtrack
U.S. #1 R&B 45	"Kansas City"	Wilbert Harrison
U.K. #1 POP 45	*"I Need Your Love Tonight"*	Elvis Presley

WEEK ENDING JUNE 7		
U.S. #1 POP 45	"The Battle of New Orleans"	Johnny Horton
U.S. #1 POP LP	*Gigi*	soundtrack
U.S. #1 R&B 45	"Kansas City"	Wilbert Harrison
U.K. #1 POP 45	*"I Need Your Love Tonight"*	Elvis Presley

WEEK ENDING JUNE 14		
U.S. #1 POP 45	"The Battle of New Orleans"	Johnny Horton
U.S. #1 POP LP	*Exotica, Vol I*	Martin Denny
U.S. #1 R&B 45	"Kansas City"	Wilbert Harrison
U.K. #1 POP 45	*"I Need Your Love Tonight"*	Elvis Presley

WEEK ENDING JUNE 21		
U.S. #1 POP 45	"The Battle of New Orleans"	Johnny Horton
U.S. #1 POP LP	*Exotica, Vol I*	Martin Denny
U.S. #1 R&B 45	"Personality"	Lloyd Price
U.K. #1 POP 45	"Roulette"	Russ Conway

WEEK ENDING JUNE 28		
U.S. #1 POP 45	"The Battle of New Orleans"	Johnny Horton
U.S. #1 POP LP	*Exotica, Vol I*	Martin Denny
U.S. #1 R&B 45	"Personality"	Lloyd Price
U.K. #1 POP 45	"Roulette"	Russ Conway

JULY

11 **Joan Baez** makes her first recording, a duet with **Bob Gibson**, recorded live at the Newport Folk Festival.

12 Entering the pop chart: **Elvis Presley**'s "A Big Hunk o' Love" at #43, **Ricky Nelson**'s "Sweeter than You" at #53, **Ray Charles**' "What'd I Say" at #82 and **Bo Diddley**'s "Crackin' Up" at #98.

16 The **Coasters** record "Poison Ivy" at Atlantic Recording Studios, New York City. It's written and produced by **Jerry Leiber** and **Mike Stoller** and engineered by **Tom Dowd**.

17 Jazz singer **Billie Holiday** dies from a liver ailment in a New York City hospital shortly after being arrested on her deathbed for a small quantity of heroin found in her room; she is forty-four. Holiday, whose recordings in the late Thirties and early Forties had a tremendous impact on jazz vocalists and instrumentalists alike, has, in the past several years, barely had a career: illness, numerous arrests, a prison term, loss of her New York City cabaret license and loss of self-confidence made her live and recorded performances rare and painful.

19 Entering the pop chart: **Elvis Presley**'s "My Wish Came True" at #39, the **Eternals**' "Rockin' in the Jungle" at #95, the **Shirelles**' "De-dicated to the One I Love" at #96 and **Ritchie Valens**' "Little Girl" at #97.

AUGUST

6 ABC-Paramount acquires British teen-idol **Cliff Richard**'s hit "Livin' Doll" for U.S. release.

10 **Tony Williams, David Lynch, Alex Hodge** and **Paul Robi**—the male members of the vocal quintet the **Platters**—are arrested in a room at the Sheraton Gibston Hotel in Cincinnati, where the group has just completed a three-day engagement. Detectives, acting on a tip from a hotel employee, discover the four black men with four nineteen-year-old women—three whites, one black—all in various stages of undress. The men are charged with aiding and abetting prostitution, lewdness and assignation, and the women with prostitution, lewdness and assignation. In December, all eight will be acquitted, but in the meantime, the scandal—which many in the music business charge is fueled by rac-

ism—will almost destroy the Platters' career.

24 ROCK AND ROLL AIN'T READY FOR OL' ROCKIN' CHAIR YET declares a *Billboard* headline. The story reports that, though rock & roll seemed to be losing popularity a year ago, it's clear that the record-buying public still likes **Elvis Presley, Fats Domino** and **Lloyd Price,** and eagerly accepts such newcomers as the **Everly Brothers,** the **Drifters, Ricky Nelson** and **Brook Benton,** and that rock & roll records still fill fifty percent of the Hot 100 chart.

30 **Bobby Darin**'s "Mack the Knife" enters the

pop chart. With this English version of **Kurt Weill** and **Bertolt Brecht**'s "Moritat" from *The Three-Penny Opera,* Darin leaves behind the rock & roll stylings of his earlier hits, "Splish Splash" and "Dream Lover," adopting **Frank Sinatra**'s suave, finger-snapping showbiz style. "Mack the Knife" will become Darin's all-time biggest hit. ◆

WEEK ENDING JULY 5		
U.S. #1 POP 45	"Lonely Boy"	Paul Anka
U.S. #1 POP LP	*Exotica, Vol. I*	Martin Denny
U.S. #1 R&B 45	"Personality"	Lloyd Price
U.K. #1 POP 45	"Dream Lover"	Bobby Darin

WEEK ENDING JULY 12		
U.S. #1 POP 45	"Lonely Boy"	Paul Anka
U.S. #1 POP LP	*Exotica, Vol. I*	Martin Denny
U.S. #1 R&B 45	"Personality"	Lloyd Price
U.K. #1 POP 45	"Dream Lover"	Bobby Darin

WEEK ENDING JULY 19		
U.S. #1 POP 45	"Lonely Boy"	Paul Anka
U.S. #1 POP LP	*Film Encores*	Mantovani
U.S. #1 R&B 45	"There Goes My Baby"	The Drifters
U.K. #1 POP 45	"Dream Lover"	Bobby Darin

WEEK ENDING JULY 26		
U.S. #1 POP 45	"Lonely Boy"	Paul Anka
U.S. #1 POP LP	*The Kingston Trio at Large*	The Kingston Trio
U.S. #1 R&B 45	"There Goes My Baby"	The Drifters
U.K. #1 POP 45	"Dream Lover"	Bobby Darin

WEEK ENDING AUGUST 2		
U.S. #1 POP 45	"Lonely Boy"	Paul Anka
U.S. #1 POP LP	*The Kingston Trio at Large*	The Kingston Trio
U.S. #1 R&B 45	"What'd I Say"	Ray Charles
U.K. #1 POP 45	"Livin' Doll"	Cliff Richard

WEEK ENDING AUGUST 9		
U.S. #1 POP 45	"Lonely Boy"	Paul Anka
U.S. #1 POP LP	*The Kingston Trio at Large*	The Kingston Trio
U.S. #1 R&B 45	"What'd I Say"	Ray Charles
U.K. #1 POP 45	"Livin' Doll"	Cliff Richard

WEEK ENDING AUGUST 16		
U.S. #1 POP 45	"A Big Hunk o' Love"	Elvis Presley
U.S. #1 POP LP	*The Kingston Trio at Large*	The Kingston Trio
U.S. #1 R&B 45	"Thank You Pretty Baby"	Brook Benton
U.K. #1 POP 45	"Livin' Doll"	Cliff Richard

WEEK ENDING AUGUST 23		
U.S. #1 POP 45	"A Big Hunk o' Love"	Elvis Presley
U.S. #1 POP LP	*The Kingston Trio at Large*	The Kingston Trio
U.S. #1 R&B 45	"Thank You Pretty Baby"	Brook Benton
U.K. #1 POP 45	"Livin' Doll"	Cliff Richard

WEEK ENDING AUGUST 30		
U.S. #1 POP 45	"The Three Bells"	The Browns
U.S. #1 POP LP	*The Kingston Trio at Large*	The Kingston Trio
U.S. #1 R&B 45	"Thank You Pretty Baby"	Brook Benton
U.K. #1 POP 45	"Only Sixteen"	Craig Douglas

SEPTEMBER

4 In the wake of the stabbing deaths of two teenagers by a seventeen year old and other similar incidents of violence in New York City, WCBS radio in New York bans all versions of the **Brecht-Weill** song "Mack the Knife"—the song that's currently a chart-climbing hit for **Bobby Darin**.

6 Entering the pop chart: **Frankie Avalon**'s "Just Ask Your Heart" at #65, **Paul Anka**'s "Put Your Head on My Shoulder" at #67, **Eddie Cochran**'s "Somethin' Else" at #68, **Connie Francis**' "You're Gonna Hear from Me" at #69 and **Bobby Vee and the Shadows**' (not to be confused with the British guitar-based instrumental **Shadows** who back **Cliff Richard**) "Suzy Baby" at #87.

7 **Dick Clark**'s Michigan State Fair stage show, winding up a four-day stand, attracts 15,000 spectators—the most in the fair's 110-year history—with acts such as **Frankie Avalon** and **Annette Funicello**, **LaVern Baker**, **Freddie Cannon**, the **Coasters**, **Duane Eddy**, **Jan and Dean**, **Lou Rawls**, **Bobby Rydell**, **Santo and Johnny**, **Skip and Flip** and others.

22 Atlantic Records releases the **Drifters**' "Dance with Me" backed with "True Love, True Love."

OCTOBER

9 At age twenty-two, **Bobby Darin** becomes the youngest performer ever to headline at the Sands Hotel's Copa Room in Las Vegas (the previous record-holder, **Johnny Mathis**, did it at age twenty-

three). Darin is a hit with the crowd.

12 **Neil Sedaka**'s "Oh! Carol" enters the pop chart at #73. The song was written by Sedaka for his friend and Brill Building songwriting colleague **Carole King**, who would later go on to have a highly successful singing career of her own. Sedaka's "Oh! Carol" will spend eighteen weeks on the pop chart, eventually reaching #9.

19 **Tommy Facenda**'s "High School, U.S.A." enters the pop chart at #97. One of the more novel novelty discs of all time, it is released in dozens of different versions, mentioning different high schools for different cities.

25 WMCA New York disc jockey **Scott Muni** emcees a charity rock & roll dance at the New York Coliseum in Manhattan. The 6,500 attending the sold-out show see performers like **Clyde McPhatter**, **Roy Hamilton** and the **Four Lads**.

26 The **Everly Brothers** announce that they are thinking of leaving their record label, Cadence, and are talking with RCA and Warner Bros. Records. ◆

WEEK ENDING SEPTEMBER 5

U.S. #1 POP 45	"The Three Bells"	The Browns
U.S. #1 POP LP	*The Kingston Trio at Large*	The Kingston Trio
U.S. #1 R&B 45	"Thank You Pretty Baby"	Brook Benton
U.K. #1 POP 45	"Only Sixteen"	Craig Douglas

WEEK ENDING SEPTEMBER 12

U.S. #1 POP 45	"The Three Bells"	The Browns
U.S. #1 POP LP	*The Kingston Trio at Large*	The Kingston Trio
U.S. #1 R&B 45	"I'm Gonna Get Married"	Lloyd Price
U.K. #1 POP 45	"Only Sixteen"	Craig Douglas

WEEK ENDING SEPTEMBER 19

U.S. #1 POP 45	"The Three Bells"	The Browns
U.S. #1 POP LP	*The Kingston Trio at Large*	The Kingston Trio
U.S. #1 R&B 45	"I'm Gonna Get Married"	Lloyd Price
U.K. #1 POP 45	"Only Sixteen"	Craig Douglas

WEEK ENDING SEPTEMBER 26

U.S. #1 POP 45	"Sleep Walk"	Santo and Johnny
U.S. #1 POP LP	*The Kingston Trio at Large*	The Kingston Trio
U.S. #1 R&B 45	"I Want to Walk You Home"	Fats Domino
U.K. #1 POP 45	"Only Sixteen"	Craig Douglas

WEEK ENDING OCTOBER 4

U.S. #1 POP 45	"Sleep Walk"	Santo and Johnny
U.S. #1 POP LP	*The Kingston Trio at Large*	The Kingston Trio
U.S. #1 R&B 45	"I'm Gonna Get Married"	Lloyd Price
U.K. #1 POP 45	"Only Sixteen"	Craig Douglas

WEEK ENDING OCTOBER 11

U.S. #1 POP 45	"Mack the Knife"	Bobby Darin
U.S. #1 POP LP	*The Kingston Trio at Large*	The Kingston Trio
U.S. #1 R&B 45	"Sea of Love"	Phil Phillips
U.K. #1 POP 45	"Only Sixteen"	Craig Douglas

WEEK ENDING OCTOBER 18

U.S. #1 POP 45	"Mack the Knife"	Bobby Darin
U.S. #1 POP LP	*The Kingston Trio at Large*	The Kingston Trio
U.S. #1 R&B 45	"You Better Know It"	Jackie Wilson
U.K. #1 POP 45	"Travellin' Light"	Cliff Richard

WEEK ENDING OCTOBER 25

U.S. #1 POP 45	"Mack the Knife"	Bobby Darin
U.S. #1 POP LP	*The Kingston Trio at Large*	The Kingston Trio
U.S. #1 R&B 45	"Poison Ivy"	The Coasters
U.K. #1 POP 45	"Travellin' Light"	Cliff Richard

NOVEMBER

1 The **Spacemen**'s "The Clouds" enters the R&B chart at #24. Their only chart entry ever, it will eventually become an R&B Number One and will remain on the R&B chart for eighteen weeks.

9 RCA A&R execs **Hugo and Luigi** offer a guarantee of $100,000 to **Sam Cooke** in an effort to lure him to RCA when his Keen Records contract expires.

Today marks the beginning of what *Billboard* terms "one of the most frantic weeks in the history of the music business," as the government's probe into disc jockey payola steps up.

20 **Alan Freed**, refusing to vouch that he never accepted payola, is fired from his position at WABC television in New York. Eight days later, he will also be fired from WNEW-TV New York.

21 **Alan Freed** is fired by WABC radio in New York City after refusing to sign an affidavit stating that he never took payola.

23 RCA Records emphatically denies that **Elvis Presley** will change his style when he leaves the army. "It just ain't true," one spokesman remarks.

29 **Jackie Wilson**'s "Talk That Talk" enters the R&B chart at #28. It will eventually rise to #3 and will remain on the R&B chart for eighteen weeks.

Bobby Darin is the winner of the 1959 Grammy Awards for the Record of the Year—"Mack the Knife"—and the Best New Artist of the Year. **Frank Sinatra**'s *Come Dance with Me* is the Album of the Year.

30 *Billboard* reports that the payola scandal "will substantially damage the careers of at least twenty-five DJs." **Alan Freed** is quoted as saying that his career has gone "down the drain."

DECEMBER

10 The four male members of the **Platters** are acquitted of charges of aiding and abetting prostitution, lewdness and assignation stemming from their August 10 arrest in Cincinnati. Municipal Court judge **Gilbert Bettman**, in handing down the decision, tells the black singers: "You have lost an opportunity to be an example to your people.... You have taken that which can be the core of reproductive life and turned it into a socially abhorrent, tawdry indulgence in lust.... For these transgressions you will be accountable in that highest court before which you must in

the end stand final judgment." Also acquitted are the four women—three white and one black—arrested with the four Platters.

14 *Billboard* reports that in the wake of the government's payola investigations, the pay-for-play phenomenon has all but ceased in Philadelphia, to name one major American city. "You can't even buy the disc jockeys lunch," complains one disgruntled Philadelphia record distributor.

A report by the Ohio State University Research Center states that though rock & roll is the overwhelming favorite of fourteen-to-eighteen-year-olds, more adults aged nineteen to seventy list it as their least favorite form of music.

15 The **Everly Brothers** record "Let It Be Me" in New York City—the first time they've recorded outside of

Nashville and the first time they've recorded with strings.

25 **Richard Starkey** receives his first drum set for Christmas. The eighteen-year-old Liverpudlian, who—as the **Beatles**' **Ringo Starr**—will become one of the most famous rock & roll drummers in the world, is currently working as an apprentice engineer. ◆

WEEK ENDING NOVEMBER 1		
U.S. #1 POP 45	"Mack the Knife"	Bobby Darin
U.S. #1 POP LP	*The Kingston Trio at Large*	The Kingston Trio
U.S. #1 R&B 45	"Poison Ivy"	The Coasters
U.K. #1 POP 45	"Travellin' Light"	Cliff Richard

WEEK ENDING NOVEMBER 8		
U.S. #1 POP 45	"Mack the Knife"	Bobby Darin
U.S. #1 POP LP	*Heavenly*	Johnny Mathis
U.S. #1 R&B 45	"Poison Ivy"	The Coasters
U.K. #1 POP 45	"Travellin' Light"	Cliff Richard

WEEK ENDING NOVEMBER 15		
U.S. #1 POP 45	"Mr. Blue"	The Fleetwoods
U.S. #1 POP LP	*Heavenly*	Johnny Mathis
U.S. #1 R&B 45	"So Many Ways"	Brook Benton
U.K. #1 POP 45	"Travellin' Light"	Cliff Richard

WEEK ENDING NOVEMBER 22		
U.S. #1 POP 45	"Mack the Knife"	Bobby Darin
U.S. #1 POP LP	*Heavenly*	Johnny Mathis
U.S. #1 R&B 45	"Don't You Know"	Della Reese
U.K. #1 POP 45	"Travellin' Light"	Cliff Richard

WEEK ENDING NOVEMBER 29		
U.S. #1 POP 45	"Mack the Knife"	Bobby Darin
U.S. #1 POP LP	*Heavenly*	Johnny Mathis
U.S. #1 R&B 45	"Don't You Know"	Della Reese
U.K. #1 POP 45	"Travellin' Light"	Cliff Richard

WEEK ENDING DECEMBER 6		
U.S. #1 POP 45	"Mack the Knife"	Bobby Darin
U.S. #1 POP LP	*Heavenly*	Johnny Mathis
U.S. #1 R&B 45	"The Clouds"	The Spacemen
U.K. #1 POP 45	"What Do You Want?"	Adam Faith

WEEK ENDING DECEMBER 13		
U.S. #1 POP 45	"Heartaches by the Number"	Guy Mitchell
U.S. #1 POP LP	*Here We Go Again*	The Kingston Trio
U.S. #1 R&B 45	"So Many Ways"	Brook Benton
U.K. #1 POP 45	"What Do You Want?"	Adam Faith

WEEK ENDING DECEMBER 20		
U.S. #1 POP 45	"Heartaches by the Number"	Guy Mitchell
U.S. #1 POP LP	*Here We Go Again*	The Kingston Trio
U.S. #1 R&B 45	"So Many Ways"	Brook Benton
U.K. #1 POP 45	"What Do You Want?"	Adam Faith

WEEK ENDING DECEMBER 27		
U.S. #1 POP 45	"Why"	Frankie Avalon
U.S. #1 POP LP	*Here We Go Again*	The Kingston Trio
U.S. #1 R&B 45	"The Clouds"	The Spacemen
U.K. #1 POP 45	"What Do You Want?"	Adam Faith

1960

As one of the most tumultuous decades of the twentieth century got under way, America's establishment held its breath in the hope that rock & roll really was dead and buried. In February, the House of Representatives officially opened its payola hearings, but by that time the hearings themselves were a mere formality. A host of rock & roll disc jockeys had either quit or been fired from their jobs already; *Billboard* had begun reporting last winter that in cities like Philadelphia, record distributors were complaining that they couldn't even buy DJs lunch.

While the payola investigations were not without justification—payola *did* exist, and some disc jockeys did get writers' credit, and thus royalties, for songs they did not compose—the hearings themselves revealed the extent to which a legal and commercial clean-up operation sought to exorcise demon rock & roll. New York representative Emanuel Celler of the payola investigating subcommittee blamed the play-for-pay phenomenon for "the popularity of this cacophonous music called rock & roll . . . especially among teenagers"—as if the musical end of things had nothing to do with it. Furthermore, payola subcommittee chairman Oren Harris told Dick Clark, *after* Clark had divested himself of interests in thirty-three businesses and admitted his own part in payola, "You're not the inventor of this system, or even its architect. You're a product of it. Obviously, you're a fine young man."

A week after the payola hearings opened, Elvis Presley garnered his first gold record, for his 1956 debut album, *Elvis.* By March, he was back home, out of the army, to receive it a few weeks later. Elvis then took a train from Memphis to Miami, Florida, making numerous whistle stops along the way to greet throngs of adoring fans, with the only sour note being an egg-throwing incident in Hollywood, Florida. In Miami, he taped a Timex TV variety special with such arbiters of gray-flannel cool as Frank Sinatra, Dean Martin and Sammy Davis, Jr. Though he would continue to make great pop records, and even a rock & roll record now and again, Elvis had been assimilated; his army term was as much a cultural turning point as the untimely death of Buddy Holly. And then, this year, Eddie Cochran died, too.

But all was not lost for rock & roll. Despite the paranoia brought about by the payola scandal, the power of rock & roll and rhythm & blues could not be denied. On June 6, *Billboard* reported on the DJ-promoted resurgence of such R&B artists as James Brown, Jimmy Reed, Hank Ballard, Etta James and LaVern Baker on the singles charts. And what the kids wanted, they began hearing in a greater and greater variety of subgenres: Motown released its first records; the Ventures kicked off the surf-instrumental genre; the Silver Beatles and Gerry and the Pacemakers played their first live concerts, laying the groundwork for British rock and all *its* attendant subgenres; and in the summer, *Billboard* reported on the new movement of "folkniks," who had "the ability to play guitar or bongos, sing a bit, and to have attended—or appear to have attended—college, preferably in the Ivy League." If they only knew!

JANUARY

9 **Emile Ford and the Checkmates**, a British group of Bahamian immigrants, becomes the first homeland black act to top the British charts when "What Do You Want to Make Those Eyes at Me For?" hits Number One. It will be the only such success for Ford.

10 **Bill Black's Combo** reaches Number One on the R&B chart with an instrumental, "Smokie, Part 2." Black, a native of Memphis, Tennessee, began his career as a session bassist at Sun Studios and, in that role, backed **Elvis Presley** on his Sun sides. Black's bass technique, which bridged R&B and C&W, was integral to the Presley sound, and Presley kept Black with him—both for studio and stage dates—when he left Sun for RCA. Black formed his own band in 1959 and signed with Memphis' Hi Records; "Smokie, Part 2" is his first hit (it makes #17 on the pop chart), to be followed by "White Silver Sand" (#1 R&B, #9 pop) later in the year. The Bill Black Combo will be a model for such future Memphis instrumental groups as the **Mar-Keys** and **Booker T. and the MGs.**

24 **Johnny Preston** hits Number One on the American pop chart with "Running Bear," a song written by a fellow Texan, the late **J. P. Richardson** (alias the **Big Bopper**), who also provided the track's "oom pah pah" backing. "Running Bear," Preston's first hit, will also reach Number One on the British pop chart and #3 on the American R&B chart.

"Baby (You've Got What It Takes)" by **Brook Benton** and **Dinah Washington** enters the R&B chart, fast on its way to Number One. The duet is the first for Benton—a former gospel singer whose soul ballads took him to the top of the R&B chart three times in 1959—and Washington, the grand dame of black pop in the Fifties. A second duet, "A Rockin' Good Way," will return the two to Number One in June.

31 **Jimmy Jones'** "Handy Man" enters the R&B chart, soon to reach #3. The song, written and produced by **Otis Blackwell**, is the first solo hit for the former lead singer for the **Sparks of Rhythm**, the **Pretenders** and the **Savoys**; **James Taylor** will make it a #4 pop hit in 1977.

FEBRUARY

6 **Jesse Belvin**, an important figure in West Coast R&B during the Fifties, dies in an automobile accident in Los Angeles at age twenty. Belvin had his first R&B hit, "Dream Girl," as half of **Jesse and Marvin** in 1953. On his own, he had hits with "Goodnight My Love" in 1956 and with "Funny" and "Guess Who" in 1959. He also sang as a member of such doo-wop groups as the **Cliques**, the **Sharptones**, **Three Dots and a Dash**, and the **Sheiks**. He made his biggest impact, however, as the co-author of "Earth Angel," the **Penguins'** doo-wop classic of 1954.

7 **Barrett Strong's** "Money" enters the pop chart, where it will peak at #23; on the R&B chart it will go to #2. The record was released on Detroit's Anna label, which is owned by **Gwen Gordy**—**Berry Gordy, Jr.**'s sister. Encouraged by its success, Berry Gordy begins his own label, Tamla, and his first release is a reissue of "Money." The song will endure: between 1963 and 1979 it will be covered by the **Beatles**, the **Kingsmen**, **Jr. Walker and the All Stars** and the **Flying Lizards**.

8 The House of Representatives Special Subcommittee on Legislative Oversight opens hearings on disc jockey "payola," with disc jockeys from Boston and Cleveland testifying.

12 **Pat Boone** receives a gold LP for *Pat's Great Hits*. The album includes Boone's whitewashed covers of Little Richard's "Tutti Frutti" and "Long Tall Sally," but for the most part focuses on his more recent Tin Pan Alley tunes, such as "Love Letters in the Sand" and "April Love," the title theme from one of Boone's movies.

17 **Elvis Presley** receives his first gold album, for *Elvis*. The LP includes "Rip It Up," "Old Shep," "When My Blue Moon Turns to Gold Again," "Paralyzed" and "Ready Teddy."

28 **B. B. King's** "Sweet Sixteen" peaks at #2 on the R&B chart—the Memphis bluesman's biggest hit since the early Fifties, when he introduced the sophistication of jazz soloing to the earthiness of the blues with records like "3 O'clock Blues," "You Know I Love You," "Please Love Me" and "You Upset Me, Baby." "Sweet Sixteen" will not appear on the pop chart until it's reissued in 1972. ◆

WEEK ENDING JANUARY 3		
U.S. #1 POP 45	"Why"	Frankie Avalon
U.S. #1 POP LP	*Here We Go Again*	The Kingston Trio
U.S. #1 R&B 45	"The Clouds"	The Spacemen
U.K. #1 POP 45	"What Do You Want . . .?"	Adam Faith

WEEK ENDING JANUARY 10		
U.S. #1 POP 45	"El Paso"	Marty Robbins
U.S. #1 POP LP	*Here We Go Again*	The Kingston Trio
U.S. #1 R&B 45	"The Clouds"	The Spacemen
U.K. #1 POP 45	"What Do You Want . . .?"	Emile Ford

WEEK ENDING JANUARY 17		
U.S. #1 POP 45	"El Paso"	Marty Robbins
U.S. #1 POP LP	*Here We Go Again*	The Kingston Trio
U.S. #1 R&B 45	"The Clouds"	Bill Black's Combo
U.K. #1 POP 45	"What Do You Want . . .?"	Emile Ford

WEEK ENDING JANUARY 24		
U.S. #1 POP 45	"Running Bear"	Johnny Preston
U.S. #1 POP LP	*Here We Go Again*	The Kingston Trio
U.S. #1 R&B 45	"Smokie, Part 2"	Bill Black's Combo
U.K. #1 POP 45	"What Do You Want . . .?"	Emile Ford

WEEK ENDING JANUARY 31		
U.S. #1 POP 45	"Running Bear"	Johnny Preston
U.S. #1 POP LP	*Here We Go Again*	The Kingston Trio
U.S. #1 R&B 45	"Smokie, Part 2"	Bill Black's Combo
U.K. #1 POP 45	"Starry Eyed"	Michael Holliday

WEEK ENDING FEBRUARY 7		
U.S. #1 POP 45	"Running Bear"	Johnny Preston
U.S. #1 POP LP	*Here We Go Again*	The Kingston Trio
U.S. #1 R&B 45	"Smokie, Part 2"	Bill Black's Combo
U.K. #1 POP 45	"Why"	Anthony Newley

WEEK ENDING FEBRUARY 14		
U.S. #1 POP 45	"Teen Angel"	Mark Dinning
U.S. #1 POP LP	*The Sound of Music*	original cast
U.S. #1 R&B 45	"Smokie, Part 2"	Bill Black's Combo
U.K. #1 POP 45	"Why"	Anthony Newley

WEEK ENDING FEBRUARY 21		
U.S. #1 POP 45	"Teen Angel"	Mark Dinning
U.S. #1 POP LP	*The Sound of Music*	original cast
U.S. #1 R&B 45	"Baby (You Got What It Takes)"	B. Benton & D. Washington
U.K. #1 POP 45	"Why"	Anthony Newley

WEEK ENDING FEBRUARY 28		
U.S. #1 POP 45	"Theme from *A Summer Place*"	Percy Faith
U.S. #1 POP LP	*The Sound of Music*	original cast
U.S. #1 R&B 45	"Baby (You Got What It Takes)"	B. Benton & D. Washington
U.K. #1 POP 45	"Why"	Anthony Newley

MARCH

4 It is revealed, in connection with the current Congressional investigation into payola, that Federal Communications Chairman **John Doerfer** took a six-day trip to Florida courtesy of Storer Broadcasting.

5 **Elvis Presley** is released from the army. Two days earlier, he left Germany and arrived at McGuire Air Force Base in New Jersey. Earlier this year, Presley had been promoted to sergeant.

10 The British music weekly *Record Retailer* (later known as *Music Week*) publishes the first U.K. LP chart. *The Explosive Freddy Cannon* is the first Number One LP in the U.K.

14 **Sam Cooke** kicks off his first tour of the West Indies with a concert in Montego Bay, Jamaica. In the next two weeks, Cooke will set attendance records everywhere he appears. His influence on Jamaican singers will be manifested in a couple of years when **Jimmy Cliff**, **Bob Marley**, **Owen Gray** and others begin making records. Cooke will return to the West Indies twice before his death in 1964.

28 Two antipayola bills are introduced in Congress by Representative Emanuel Celler of New York. He blames payola for "the cacophonous music called rock & roll" and claims that rock & roll would never have achieved popularity, "especially among teenagers," if not for the push provided by payola. His bills propose penalties of $1,000 and one year in jail for those found guilty of either giving or receiving payola.

30 Representative **Thomas O'Neill** (of Massachusetts) wants the Federal Communications Commission to investigate all stations whose employees are involved in payola, and report the results to Congress. O'Neill is convinced that the "captive audience" of American youth must be safeguarded from the demoralizing effects of payola and rock & roll, "a type of sensuous music unfit for impressionable minds."

APRIL

1 In Miami's Fountainbleu Hotel, **Frank Sinatra**, **Sammy Davis, Jr.**, **Dean Martin**, **Mitch Miller** and **Elvis Presley** tape Sinatra's Timex Special for ABC-TV, to be aired May 12. Presley, accompanied by his manager, **Colonel Tom Parker**, arrived in Miami on a train from Memphis—making a series of "whistle stops" along the way to greet throngs of adoring fans.

2 The National Association of Record Merchants (NARM) presents its first annual awards in Las Vegas. **Elvis Presley** is named best-selling male artist, **Connie Francis** best-selling female artist.

3 The **Everly Brothers**, later named by the **Beatles** and **Rolling Stone** Keith **Richards** as prime influences, make their British concert debut, kicking off their first U.K. tour in London.

4 *Billboard* reports that RCA Victor Records will release all pop singles simultaneously in mono and stereo—the first record company to do so. **Elvis Presley**'s first post-army single, "Stuck on You," is RCA's first mono-stereo release.

17 **Eddie Cochran** dies in a hospital in Bath, England, from severe brain injuries sustained in a car crash near Chippenham, Wiltshire, early that morning. Also injured in the crash were **Gene Vincent**—who was on the ten-week tour of England with Cochran—and Cochran's girlfriend, Sharon Sheeley, an American songwriter. Cochran's last released single before his death was "Three Steps to Heaven."

20 **Elvis Presley**'s return to Hollywood to film *G.I. Blues* is greeted by tremendous fanfare. Coverage of his arrival is the top story in all local media—it even makes page one of the local newspapers.

21 **Dick Clark**, described as "the single most influential person" in the pop music business, testifies before the Congressional committee investigating payola. He admits that he had a financial interest in twenty-seven percent of the records he played on "American Bandstand" in a twenty-eight-month period, but emerges from the hearings relatively untainted. "You're not the inventor of the system or even its architect," chairman **Oren Harris** tells him. "You're a product of it. Obviously, you're a fine young man." Harris himself will soon be incriminated in a conflict-of-interests scandal. ◆

WEEK ENDING MARCH 6		
U.S. #1 POP 45	"Theme from *A Summer Place*"	Percy Faith
U.S. #1 POP LP	*The Sound of Music*	original cast
U.S. #1 R&B 45	"Baby (You Got What It Takes)"	B. Benton & D. Washington
U.K. #1 POP 45	"Poor Me"	Adam Faith

WEEK ENDING MARCH 13		
U.S. #1 POP 45	"Theme from *A Summer Place*"	Percy Faith
U.S. #1 POP LP	*The Sound of Music*	original cast
U.S. #1 R&B 45	"Baby (You Got What It Takes)"	B. Benton & D. Washington
U.K. #1 POP 45	"Poor Me"	Adam Faith

WEEK ENDING MARCH 20		
U.S. #1 POP 45	"Theme from *A Summer Place*"	Percy Faith
U.S. #1 POP LP	*The Sound of Music*	original cast
U.S. #1 R&B 45	"Baby (You Got What It Takes)"	B. Benton & D. Washington
U.K. #1 POP 45	"Running Bear"	Johnny Preston

WEEK ENDING MARCH 27		
U.S. #1 POP 45	"Theme from *A Summer Place*"	Percy Faith
U.S. #1 POP LP	*The Sound of Music*	original cast
U.S. #1 R&B 45	"Baby (You Got What It Takes)"	B. Benton & D. Washington
U.K. #1 POP 45	"My Old Man's a Dustman"	Lonnie Donegan

WEEK ENDING APRIL 4		
U.S. #1 POP 45	"Theme from *A Summer Place*"	Percy Faith
U.S. #1 POP LP	*The Sound of Music*	original cast
U.S. #1 R&B 45	"Baby (You Got What It Takes)"	B. Benton & D. Washington
U.K. #1 POP 45	"My Old Man's a Dustman"	Lonnie Donegan

WEEK ENDING APRIL 11		
U.S. #1 POP 45	"Theme from *A Summer Place*"	Percy Faith
U.S. #1 POP LP	*The Sound of Music*	original cast
U.S. #1 R&B 45	"Baby (You Got What It Takes)"	B. Benton & D. Washington
U.K. #1 POP 45	"My Old Man's a Dustman"	Lonnie Donegan

WEEK ENDING APRIL 18		
U.S. #1 POP 45	"Theme from *A Summer Place*"	Percy Faith
U.S. #1 POP LP	*The Sound of Music*	original cast
U.S. #1 R&B 45	"Fannie Mae"	Buster Brown
U.K. #1 POP 45	"My Old Man's a Dustman"	Lonnie Donegan

WEEK ENDING APRIL 25		
U.S. #1 POP 45	"Theme from *A Summer Place*"	Percy Faith
U.S. #1 POP LP	*The Sound of Music*	original cast
U.S. #1 R&B 45	"White Silver Sands"	Bill Black's Combo
U.K. #1 POP 45	"Do You Mind?"	Anthony Newley

MAY

2 In the wake of the payola scandal, *Billboard* reports that many radio stations across the country are adopting a "better music" format and banning rock & roll from their airwaves. WNTA, Newark, announces its new "Golden Sound" format, which excludes all rock & roll music entirely.

Former **Drifters** lead singer **Ben E. King**, at one time known as **Benny Nelson**, signs a solo recording contract with Atco Records.

12 **Frank Sinatra**'s "Timex Spectacular" is broadcast on ABC-TV. Sinatra and **Elvis Presley** trade hits, Elvis singing "Witchcraft" and Sinatra crooning "Love Me Tender." *Billboard*'s review states that "Presley needs a lot of coaching on how to stand and how to talk." The trade weekly also notes that Sinatra's daughter **Nancy** "displayed great poise, charm, a pleasant singing voice and an ability to dance."

16 *Billboard* reports that **Berry Gordy, Jr.**, Detroit songwriter and publisher, is preparing his own record label, after successfully producing many hit singles.

20 DJ **Alan Freed** is indicted, along with seven others, for receiving $30,650 in payola from six record companies. Two years later, he receives a suspended sentence and a $300 fine. At the time of his arrest, Freed had just joined radio station KDAY in Los Angeles, whose program director, **Mel Leeds**, is also arrested. Freed pleads not guilty to the payola charges, and a trial date of September 19 is set.

21 Teen idol **Fabian** is on the West Coast filming *High Times* with **Bing Crosby** and *Go North* with **John Wayne**.

JUNE

5 "Alley-Oop" by the **Hollywood Argyles** enters the pop chart, heading for Number One. The rock & roll novelty song was written by **Dallas Frazier** and produced, in this version, by **Kim Fowley**, who gave us **Bumble B. and the Stingers**, the **Innocents** and **Skip and Flip**, and who will later introduce the **Rivingtons**, **Paul Revere and the Raiders** and the **Runaways**.

6 **Platters** lead singer **Tony Williams** leaves the vocal quintet to embark on a solo career. He has already released several solo records in the past two years, while continuing to record and appear with the Platters; his solo career will prove, however, to be unsuccessful. The Platters, on the other hand, will continue to make hits through 1967, with **Sonny Turner** taking Williams' place.

The **Silver Beatles** and the **Pacemakers** share the bill at the Grosvenor Ballroom, Wallasey, England.

19 "The **Kingston Trio** Show," to be aired six days a week at various times, debuts on CBS radio. The five-minute show is sponsored by the soft drink Seven-Up.

24 The second annual Newport Folk Festival opens its three days with emcee **Studs Terkel** presiding. Performers include **Joan Baez**, **John Lee Hooker**, **Lester Flatt and Earl Scruggs**, the **Weavers**, **Mahalia Jackson** and many others. ◆

WEEK ENDING MAY 1		
U.S. #1 POP 45	"Stuck on You"	Elvis Presley
U.S. #1 POP LP	*The Sound of Music*	original cast
U.S. #1 R&B 45	"White Silver Sands"	Bill Black's Combo
U.K. #1 POP 45	"Cathy's Clown"	The Everly Brothers

WEEK ENDING MAY 8		
U.S. #1 POP 45	"Stuck on You"	Elvis Presley
U.S. #1 POP LP	*Sold Out*	The Kingston Trio
U.S. #1 R&B 45	"White Silver Sands"	Bill Black's Combo
U.K. #1 POP 45	"Cathy's Clown"	The Everly Brothers

WEEK ENDING MAY 15		
U.S. #1 POP 45	"Stuck on You"	Elvis Presley
U.S. #1 POP LP	"Theme from *A Summer Place*"	Billy Vaughn
U.S. #1 R&B 45	"Doggin' Around"	Jackie Wilson
U.K. #1 POP 45	"Cathy's Clown"	The Everly Brothers

WEEK ENDING MAY 22		
U.S. #1 POP 45	"Stuck on You"	Elvis Presley
U.S. #1 POP LP	*Sold Out*	The Kingston Trio
U.S. #1 R&B 45	"Doggin' Around"	Jackie Wilson
U.K. #1 POP 45	"Cathy's Clown"	The Everly Brothers

WEEK ENDING MAY 29		
U.S. #1 POP 45	"Cathy's Clown"	The Everly Brothers
U.S. #1 POP LP	*Sold Out*	The Kingston Trio
U.S. #1 R&B 45	"Doggin' Around"	Jackie Wilson
U.K. #1 POP 45	"Cathy's Clown"	The Everly Brothers

WEEK ENDING JUNE 7		
U.S. #1 POP 45	"Cathy's Clown"	The Everly Brothers
U.S. #1 POP LP	*Sold Out*	The Kingston Trio
U.S. #1 R&B 45	"Cathy's Clown"	The Everly Brothers
U.K. #1 POP 45	"Cathy's Clown"	The Everly Brothers

WEEK ENDING JUNE 14		
U.S. #1 POP 45	"Cathy's Clown"	The Everly Brothers
U.S. #1 POP LP	*Sold Out*	The Kingston Trio
U.S. #1 R&B 45	"A Rockin' Good Way"	D. Washington & B. Benton
U.K. #1 POP 45	"Cathy's Clown"	The Everly Brothers

WEEK ENDING JUNE 21		
U.S. #1 POP 45	"Cathy's Clown"	The Everly Brothers
U.S. #1 POP LP	*Sold Out*	The Kingston Trio
U.S. #1 R&B 45	"A Rockin' Good Way"	D. Washington & B. Benton
U.K. #1 POP 45	"Good Timin' "	Jimmy Jones

WEEK ENDING JUNE 28		
U.S. #1 POP 45	"Cathy's Clown"	The Everly Brothers
U.S. #1 POP LP	*Sold Out*	The Kingston Trio
U.S. #1 R&B 45	"A Rockin' Good Way"	D. Washington & B. Benton
U.K. #1 POP 45	"Good Timin' "	Jimmy Jones

JULY

3 **Ray Charles'** first release on the ABC-Paramount label, "Sticks and Stones," enters the R&B and pop charts, where it will peak at #2 and #40 respectively. Charles made his reputation as the preeminent R&B vocalist of the late Fifties with such records as "I've Got a Woman," "Hallelujah I Love Her So," "What'd I Say" and other hits on the Atlantic label; with ABC, he will branch out into other styles—most successfully country & western and Tin Pan Alley—with such hits as "I Can't Stop Loving You," "You Don't Know Me" and "You Are My Sunshine."

17 **Lloyd Price's** "Question" enters the R&B chart, where it will peak at #5, his last R&B Top Ten single; on the pop chart, where it will peak at #19, it will be his last pop Top Twenty single. Price has been a leading figure in New Orleans rock & roll since 1952, when he recorded the classic "Lawdy Miss Clawdy."

Jackie Wilson's "A Woman, a Lover, a Friend" enters the R&B chart, where it will become the Detroit soul singer's fourth Number One single in two years.

24 The **Ventures'** "Walk, Don't Run" enters the pop chart and, with its rolling beat and tremelo-heavy lead guitar, introduces the instrumental "surf sound" to rock & roll. "Walk, Don't Run" will peak at #2, and with followups like "Perfidia" and "Walk, Don't Run '64," the Ventures will exert considerable influence on American rock & roll until the British Invasion renders their sound outmoded. In 1969, however, they will return to the pop charts with their recording of the "Hawaii Five-O" television show theme song.

Duane Eddy reaches #4 on the pop chart with "Because They're Young," the title song from a movie starring **Dick Clark** and **Tuesday Weld.** It is the Rebel Rouser's biggest hit.

AUGUST

1 **Aretha Franklin** records her first pop sides: "Right Now," "Today I Sing the Blues," "Love Is the Only Thing" and "Over the Rainbow." The New York City ses-

sions are produced by **John Hammond** for Columbia Records. Franklin, the daughter of the Reverend C. L. Franklin, turned eighteen just five months ago and had recorded her first gospel songs when she was fourteen.

Billboard reports the findings of a *Seventeen* magazine survey: the average teenage girl listens to the radio two hours and thirteen minutes a day and plays records two hours and twelve minutes a day.

3 **Mickey (Baker)** and **Sylvia (Robinson)** reunite and return to the recording studio at the bidding of RCA A&R executives **Hugo (Peretti)** and **Luigi (Creatore).** Their last big hit, prior to splitting up and each going solo in 1958, was "Love Is Strange."

7 **Ike and Tina Turner's** first single, "A Fool in Love," enters the R&B chart, soon to enter the pop chart; it will peak at #2 R&B and #27 pop, eventually selling a million copies. It is twenty-one-year-old Tina's recording debut, but husband Ike has been making records since 1951, when he led the **Kings of Rhythm** on "Rocket 88," one of the seminal rock & roll recordings; he has also been involved, as an A&R man and producer, in recordings by **B. B. King**, **Howlin' Wolf** and **Bobby Bland.**

8 According to *Billboard,* English Decca Records has scrapped 25,000 copies of **Ray Peterson's** "Tell Laura I Love Her"—a song re-

counting the last thoughts of a teenager dying from a car crash—because it feels the song is "too tasteless and vulgar for the English sensibility."

17 The **Beatles** begin what would become a three-month engagement at the Indra Club in Hamburg, Germany—their first appearance outside England.

20 Teen hitmaker **Connie Francis** begins working on her acting debut, as filming for MGM's *Where the Boys Are* begins in Ft. Lauderdale, Florida.

21 British teen idol **Cliff Richard's** "Please Don't Tease" is knocked out of the Number One spot on the U.K. pop chart by "Apache" by his backing band the **Shadows** (the song was originally recorded by **Jorgen Ingmann**). ◆

WEEK ENDING JULY 3		
U.S. #1 POP 45	"Everybody's Somebody's Fool"	Connie Francis
U.S. #1 POP LP	*Sold Out*	The Kingston Trio
U.S. #1 R&B 45	"A Rockin' Good Way"	D. Washington & B. Benton
U.K. #1 POP 45	"Good Timin'"	Jimmy Jones

WEEK ENDING JULY 10		
U.S. #1 POP 45	"Everybody's Somebody's Fool"	Connie Francis
U.S. #1 POP LP	*Sold Out*	The Kingston Trio
U.S. #1 R&B 45	"There's Something on Your Mind"	Bobby Marchan
U.K. #1 POP 45	"Good Timin'"	Jimmy Jones

WEEK ENDING JULY 17		
U.S. #1 POP 45	"Alley-Oop"	The Hollywood Argyles
U.S. #1 POP LP	*Sold Out*	The Kingston Trio
U.S. #1 R&B 45	"A Rockin' Good Way"	D. Washington & B. Benton
U.K. #1 POP 45	"Good Timin'"	Jimmy Jones

WEEK ENDING JULY 24		
U.S. #1 POP 45	"I'm Sorry"	Brenda Lee
U.S. #1 POP LP	*Button-Down Mind*	Bob Newhart
U.S. #1 R&B 45	"This Bitter Earth"	Dinah Washington
U.K. #1 POP 45	"Please Don't Tease"	Cliff Richard

WEEK ENDING JULY 31		
U.S. #1 POP 45	"I'm Sorry"	Brenda Lee
U.S. #1 POP LP	*Button-Down Mind*	Bob Newhart
U.S. #1 R&B 45	"A Woman, a Lover, a Friend"	Jackie Wilson
U.K. #1 POP 45	"Please Don't Tease"	Cliff Richard

WEEK ENDING AUGUST 7		
U.S. #1 POP 45	"I'm Sorry"	Brenda Lee
U.S. #1 POP LP	*Button-Down Mind*	Bob Newhart
U.S. #1 R&B 45	"A Woman, a Lover, a Friend"	Jackie Wilson
U.K. #1 POP 45	"Please Don't Tease"	Cliff Richard

WEEK ENDING AUGUST 14		
U.S. #1 POP 45	"Yellow Polka Dot Bikini"	Brian Hyland
U.S. #1 POP LP	*Button-Down Mind*	Bob Newhart
U.S. #1 R&B 45	"A Woman, a Lover, a Friend"	Jackie Wilson
U.K. #1 POP 45	"Please Don't Tease"	Cliff Richard

WEEK ENDING AUGUST 21		
U.S. #1 POP 45	"It's Now or Never"	Elvis Presley
U.S. #1 POP LP	*Button-Down Mind*	Bob Newhart
U.S. #1 R&B 45	"A Woman, a Lover, a Friend"	Jackie Wilson
U.K. #1 POP 45	"Apache"	The Shadows

WEEK ENDING AUGUST 28		
U.S. #1 POP 45	"It's Now or Never"	Elvis Presley
U.S. #1 POP LP	*Button-Down Mind*	Bob Newhart
U.S. #1 R&B 45	"Kiddio"	Brook Benton
U.K. #1 POP 45	"Apache"	The Shadows

SEPTEMBER

4 The **Flamingos**' "Mio Amore" enters the R&B chart, where it will peak at #27. It will be the doo-wop quintet's last hit until 1966, when they will return to the R&B Top Thirty with "The Boogaloo Party." The Flamingos, who formed in Chicago in 1952, are best known for "I Only Have Eyes for You."

11 **Jimmy Charles**' "A Million to One" enters the R&B chart. Peaking at #8 R&B and #5 pop, it will be the singer's only hit.

25 **Sam Cooke**'s "Chain Gang" peaks at #2 on the R&B chart and the pop chart simultaneously. It is the great soul singer's biggest hit since "You Send Me" in 1957 and his first major hit since signing with RCA earlier this year. "Chain Gang," along with "Wonderful World" (which charted in June), signals a resurgence in Cooke's career—one that will bear fruit with "Cupid," "Twistin' the Night Away," "Bring It on Home to Me," "Having a Party" and seven other Top Twenty hits before his death in December 1964.

OCTOBER

2 "Stay" by **Maurice Williams and the Zodiacs**, enters the R&B chart, where it will peak at #3. On the pop chart, it will go to Number One and popularize the "beach sound" of the South Carolina shore resorts. The Zodiacs, originally known as the **Gladiolas**, made their first record, "Little Darlin'," in 1957; it failed to make any impact on the R&B or pop markets, but a cover version by the **Diamonds** was a huge hit in America and Britain later that year. "Stay" will return to the charts in 1978 in a live version by **Jackson Browne**.

11 **Aretha Franklin** makes her New York City pop stage debut, singing blues and pop standards at the Village Vanguard.

16 **Floyd Cramer**'s "Last Date" enters the pop chart. Peaking at #2 pop, #3 R&B and #11 C&W, it will be the first and biggest hit for the Nashville pianist, whose work behind **Chet Atkins**, **Jim Reeves** and **Elvis Presley**, among others, will help to define "the Nashville Sound."

17 *Billboard* reports that **Dion and the Belmonts** have "ankled one another's scene"—that is, they're splitting up.

27 **Ben E. King**, the **Drifters**' former lead singer, records his first solo sides, "Spanish Harlem" and "Stand by Me," at Atlantic Records' New York City studios, **Jerry Leiber** and **Mike Stoller** producing with **Phil Spector** assisting. "Spanish Harlem" (cowritten by Spector and Leiber), released first, will peak at #15 on the R&B chart and #10 on the pop chart in January 1961; "Stand by Me" will go to Number One on the R&B chart and #4 on the pop chart. King's only other big hit will be "Don't Play That Song" in 1962. ♦

WEEK ENDING SEPTEMBER 4		
U.S. #1 POP 45	"It's Now or Never"	Elvis Presley
U.S. #1 POP LP	*Button-Down Mind*	Bob Newhart
U.S. #1 R&B 45	"Kiddio"	Brook Benton
U.K. #1 POP 45	"Apache"	The Shadows

WEEK ENDING SEPTEMBER 11		
U.S. #1 POP 45	"It's Now or Never"	Elvis Presley
U.S. #1 POP LP	*Button-Down Mind*	Bob Newhart
U.S. #1 R&B 45	"Kiddio"	Brook Benton
U.K. #1 POP 45	"Apache"	The Shadows

WEEK ENDING SEPTEMBER 18		
U.S. #1 POP 45	"It's Now or Never"	Elvis Presley
U.S. #1 POP LP	*String Along*	The Kingston Trio
U.S. #1 R&B 45	"Kiddio"	Brook Benton
U.K. #1 POP 45	"Apache"	The Shadows

WEEK ENDING SEPTEMBER 25		
U.S. #1 POP 45	"The Twist"	Chubby Checker
U.S. #1 POP LP	*String Along*	The Kingston Trio
U.S. #1 R&B 45	"Kiddio"	Brook Benton
U.K. #1 POP 45	"Apache"	The Shadows

WEEK ENDING OCTOBER 2		
U.S. #1 POP 45	"Mind of Its Own"	Connie Francis
U.S. #1 POP LP	*String Along*	The Kingston Trio
U.S. #1 R&B 45	"Kiddio"	Brook Benton
U.K. #1 POP 45	"Tell Laura I Love Her"	Ricky Valance

WEEK ENDING OCTOBER 9		
U.S. #1 POP 45	"Mr. Custer"	Larry Verne
U.S. #1 POP LP	*String Along*	The Kingston Trio
U.S. #1 R&B 45	"Kiddio"	Brook Benton
U.K. #1 POP 45	"Only the Lonely"	Roy Orbison

WEEK ENDING OCTOBER 16		
U.S. #1 POP 45	"Mr. Custer"	Larry Verne
U.S. #1 POP LP	*String Along*	The Kingston Trio
U.S. #1 R&B 45	"Kiddio"	Brook Benton
U.K. #1 POP 45	"Only the Lonely"	Roy Orbison

WEEK ENDING OCTOBER 23		
U.S. #1 POP 45	"Save the Last Dance for Me"	The Drifters
U.S. #1 POP LP	*Nice and Easy*	Frank Sinatra
U.S. #1 R&B 45	"Kiddio"	Brook Benton
U.K. #1 POP 45	"Only the Lonely"	Roy Orbison

WEEK ENDING OCTOBER 30		
U.S. #1 POP 45	"I Want to Be Wanted"	Brenda Lee
U.S. #1 POP LP	*Button-Down Mind*	Bob Newhart
U.S. #1 R&B 45	"Save the Last Dance for Me"	The Drifters
U.K. #1 POP 45	"It's Now or Never"	Elvis Presley

NOVEMBER

5 **Johnny Horton**, who had a Number One hit with "Battle of New Orleans," is killed in a Texas automobile accident at age thirty-three. Ironically, Horton had just played his last show, at the Skyline in Austin, Texas—where **Hank Williams** had played his last concert as well. Horton's widow, **Billy Joe**, was also Hank Williams' widow.

7 **Alvin Pleasant (A.P.) Carter**, founder and leader of the seminal country-gospel **Carter Family Singers**, dies at age sixty-two in Kingsport, Tennessee.

10 **Gregg Allman** receives a guitar for his thirteenth birthday. He and his fourteen-year-old brother, **Duane**, will learn to play the instrument by listening to blues records, and in a year will form their first group, the **Kings**, in Daytona Beach, Florida. The two will lead several more groups, including the **Allman Joys** and **Hourglass**, before forming the **Allman Brothers Band** in 1969—by which time Gregg will have lain down the guitar to take up the organ.

14 *Billboard* reports that **Elvis Presley**'s "It's Now or Never" has become the fastest-selling single in British history. In its first week of British release, it sold 780,000 copies.

21 **Ray Charles** has four hits in the Hot 100: "Georgia on My Mind" at #5, "Ruby" at #61, "Hard Hearted Hannah" at #66 and "Come Rain or Come Shine" (used as the theme song of the 1983 film *King of Comedy*) at #95.

"Twang"-guitarist **Duane Eddy** and producer **Lee Hazlewood** have parted company after three successful years, *Billboard* reports. Hazlewood, a former Phoenix, Arizona, disc jockey, has had almost as much to do with creating Eddy's distinctive sound as the guitarist himself: he and Eddy cowrote most of Eddy's material, including the hits "Rebel Rouser," "Forty Miles of Bad Road" and "Because They're Young," and it was Hazlewood who suggested that the guitarist play his leads on the bass instead of the treble strings and who applied the essential reverb. Eddy, henceforth producing himself, will be unable to repeat the success he had with Hazlewood; Hazlewood will devote himself to operating his Phoenix recording studio.

DECEMBER

5 *Billboard* reports that five "answer records" to **Elvis Presley**'s "Are You Lonesome Tonight?" have been released. Four of them are versions of the same song—"Yes, I'm Lonesome Tonight"; the other is the standard "Oh How I Miss You Tonight."

WNTA-Newark DJ **Clay Cole** will host the Christmas Rock & Roll Show at Brooklyn's Paramount Theater, *Billboard* reports. Cole replaces **Alan Freed**. The 1959 Christmas Rock & Roll Show had been canceled due to Freed's involvement in the payola scandals. The show, running from December 23 to January 1, will feature **Chubby Checker, Bobby Rydell, Neil Sedaka,** the **Drifters, Little Anthony, Bobby Vee,** the **Skyliners, Dion, Bo Diddley, Johnny Burnette, Dante and the Evergreens** and others.

24 The Philadelphia Orphan's Court raises **Chubby Checker**'s weekly allowance from $150 to $200. The nineteen-year-old singer (born **Ernest Evans**) has already put three songs—"The Class," "The Twist" and "The Hucklebuck"—in the pop Top Forty.

25 **Mary Wells** makes her debut on the R&B chart with "Bye Bye Baby," her first—and one of Motown's first—releases. The record will make the R&B Top Ten and the pop Top Fifty. In the next five years, the

seventeen-year-old native of Detroit, who was signed to Motown when she walked into an audition uninvited, in hopes of selling a song, will provide that label with eleven pop Top Forty hits, including "The One Who Really Loves You," "You Beat Me to the Punch," "Two Lovers" and "My Guy."

27 The **Beatles**, following their extended stay in Hamburg, Germany, play a "Welcome Home" concert in Liverpool. The group will return to Hamburg three times for engagements lasting a month or more. ◆

WEEK ENDING NOVEMBER 6		
U.S. #1 POP 45	"Save the Last Dance for Me"	The Drifters
U.S. #1 POP LP	*Button-Down Mind*	Bob Newhart
U.S. #1 R&B 45	"Let's Go, Let's Go, Let's Go"	Hank Ballard
U.K. #1 POP 45	"It's Now or Never"	Elvis Presley

WEEK ENDING NOVEMBER 13		
U.S. #1 POP 45	"Save the Last Dance for Me"	The Drifters
U.S. #1 POP LP	*Button-Down Mind*	Bob Newhart
U.S. #1 R&B 45	"He Will Break Your Heart"	Jerry Butler
U.K. #1 POP 45	"It's Now or Never"	Elvis Presley

WEEK ENDING NOVEMBER 20		
U.S. #1 POP 45	"Georgia on My Mind"	Ray Charles
U.S. #1 POP LP	*Button-Down Mind*	Bob Newhart
U.S. #1 R&B 45	"Let's Go, Let's Go, Let's Go"	Hank Ballard
U.K. #1 POP 45	"It's Now or Never"	Elvis Presley

WEEK ENDING NOVEMBER 27		
U.S. #1 POP 45	"Stay"	M. Williams & the Zodiacs
U.S. #1 POP LP	*Button-Down Mind*	Bob Newhart
U.S. #1 R&B 45	"He Will Break Your Heart"	Jerry Butler
U.K. #1 POP 45	"It's Now or Never"	Elvis Presley

WEEK ENDING DECEMBER 4		
U.S. #1 POP 45	"Are You Lonesome Tonight?"	Elvis Presley
U.S. #1 POP LP	*G.I. Blues*	Elvis Presley
U.S. #1 R&B 45	"Let's Go, Let's Go, Let's Go"	Hank Ballard
U.K. #1 POP 45	"It's Now or Never"	Elvis Presley

WEEK ENDING DECEMBER 11		
U.S. #1 POP 45	"Are You Lonesome Tonight?"	Elvis Presley
U.S. #1 POP LP	*Button-Down Mind*	Bob Newhart
U.S. #1 R&B 45	"He Will Break Your Heart"	Jerry Butler
U.K. #1 POP 45	"It's Now or Never"	Elvis Presley

WEEK ENDING DECEMBER 18		
U.S. #1 POP 45	"Are You Lonesome Tonight?"	Elvis Presley
U.S. #1 POP LP	*G.I. Blues*	Elvis Presley
U.S. #1 R&B 45	"He Will Break Your Heart"	Jerry Butler
U.K. #1 POP 45	"It's Now or Never"	Elvis Presley

WEEK ENDING DECEMBER 25		
U.S. #1 POP 45	"Are You Lonesome Tonight?"	Elvis Presley
U.S. #1 POP LP	*G.I. Blues*	Elvis Presley
U.S. #1 R&B 45	"He Will Break Your Heart"	Jerry Butler
U.K. #1 POP 45	"Poetry in Motion"	Johnny Tillotson

1961

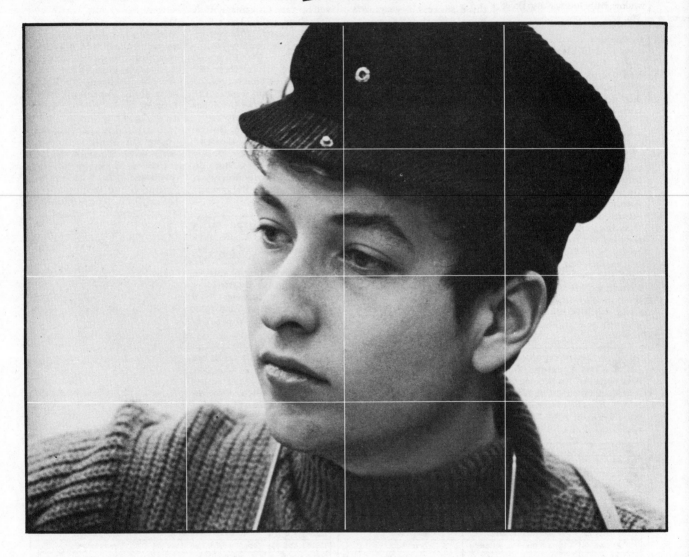

*T*he "dance craze" phenomenon started this year with the Twist, which became such a sensation that it even won adult sanction, with Twist lessons on New York TV stations, the album *Twistin' in High Society* by Lester Lanin, the favorite bandleader of the White House, and a report in *Billboard* that New York's Peppermint Lounge had become "a haven for Twist dancers of all walks of life, from the leather-jacket crowd right up to the carriage and Cadillac trade."

Meanwhile, Bob Dylan played his first concerts. Within a few months, he was receiving ecstatic press notices in the *New York Times*. The *Times* coverage signaled the beginning of the inevitable maturation of rock & roll into "rock." Though it may have been revolutionary by virtue of its brash inhibition and vitality, rock & roll was also quite often callow, nonsensical, fun-oriented—a light-hearted, rather than deliberately serious, form of subversion. But with the folk boom, and especially with the emergence of Dylan, a strain of popular music would become intensely serious, relevant and topical. As the children of the baby boom grew, pockets of bohemia evolved into a radical *zeitgeist,* and folk music would come to decisively influence rock—and not only in terms of the folk-rock genre, either. Dylan would become the first youth-culture performer to be canonized as a poet—an honor that one could argue should have gone to Chuck Berry years before. There was no turning back, and folk would go on to become *self-consciously* serious and relevant.

A different kind of self-consciousness surfaced when Phil Spector kicked off his own record label in October. With an unprecedented, acute awareness of the ways that studio technology could be marshaled to both mirror and mythologize the world of America's teenagers, Spector and his wall-of-sound created what Spector himself—fully conscious of what he was doing—termed "little symphonies for the kids." Bohemian *zeitgeists?* Self-conscious topicality? Symphonic myth-making? The times, they indeed were a-changing.

JANUARY

4 Atlantic Records releases **Carla Thomas'** "Gee Whiz (Look at His Eyes)." Reaching #10 on the pop chart and #5 on the R&B chart, it will be the first and biggest hit for the daughter of Memphis disc jockey **Rufus Thomas** (who will himself have a #10 hit with "Walking the Dog" in 1963).

30 **Jerry Leiber** and **Mike Stoller** announce they are in the process of forming their own independent production company to make records for other companies. Leiber and Stoller Enterprises will include departments of talent management, music writing and publishing, recording and engineering and will leave record manufacturing, distributing and promoting to client companies. Among the major companies that will contract Leiber and Stoller are Atlantic and RCA Victor.

Two doo-wop hits of the mid-Fifties—the **Five Satins'** "In the Still of the Night" and the **Mello-Kings'** "Tonight, Tonight"—reappear on the pop chart.

FEBRUARY

4 **Johnny Burnette** is rushed to Cedars of Lebanon Hospital in Hollywood for an emergency appendectomy. The Nashville rocker, whose "You're Sixteen" is in the Top Forty, is forced to cancel $10,000 worth of engagements in Hollywood and postpone a twenty-eight-date tour of the British Isles that was to begin in three days.

5 Two mainstays of Sixties pop make their debuts—**Mary Wells** with "Bye Bye Baby" and **Gene Pitney** with "(I Wanna) Love My Life Away." Motown's reigning teen queen, Wells will have nine Top Forty hits in the next five years before handing her crown to **Diana Ross.** Pitney's sixteen Top Forty hits in the coming decade will find him singing everything from flat-out rockers to country ballads to Italian arias.

12 The **Miracles'** "Shop Around" becomes Motown Records' first million-seller. In the following decade, Miracles hits will account for six of Motown's million-sellers.

13 **Frank Sinatra** unveils his own label, Reprise Records, with a new single, "The Second Time Around" backed with "Tina." Despite Sinatra's often disparaging remarks about rock & roll over the years, Reprise will come to represent the **Beach Boys,** the **Jimi Hendrix Experience, Neil Young, Joni Mitchell, Randy Newman,** the **Kinks** and **Captain Beefheart,** among others.

14 In Chicago, the **Platters** file suit against Mercury Records, charging breach of contract. The decision stems from Mercury's refusal to accept some recordings on which **Tony Williams** does not sing lead. The Platters and their manager, **Buck Ram,** claim that the contract does not stipulate who must sing lead and that, in fact, others in the group have always sung lead on about one in every four Platters recordings. Meanwhile, Williams, **Paul Robi** and **Zola Taylor** have each recorded solo records for other labels.

24 Le Palais des Sports, Paris, is the site of the First French International Rock & Roll Festival. The headliners are **Bobby Rydell,** representing the U.S.A., **Little Tony** of Italy, **Emile Ford** of Great Britain, and French stars **Johnny Halliday, Frankie Jordan** and **Les Chausettes Noires.** ◆

WEEK ENDING JANUARY 1		
U.S. #1 POP 45	"Are You Lonesome Tonight?"	Elvis Presley
U.S. #1 POP LP	*G.I. Blues*	Elvis Presley
U.S. #1 R&B 45	"He Will Break Your Heart"	Jerry Butler
U.K. #1 POP 45	"Poetry in Motion"	Johnny Tillotson

WEEK ENDING JANUARY 8		
U.S. #1 POP 45	"Are You Lonesome Tonight?"	Elvis Presley
U.S. #1 POP LP	*G.I. Blues*	Elvis Presley
U.S. #1 R&B 45	"He Will Break Your Heart"	Jerry Butler
U.K. #1 POP 45	"Poetry in Motion"	Johnny Tillotson

WEEK ENDING JANUARY 15		
U.S. #1 POP 45	"Wonderland by Night"	Bert Kaempfert
U.S. #1 POP LP	*Button-Down Mind Strikes Back*	Bob Newhart
U.S. #1 R&B 45	"He Will Break Your Heart"	Jerry Butler
U.K. #1 POP 45	"Poetry in Motion"	Johnny Tillotson

WEEK ENDING JANUARY 22		
U.S. #1 POP 45	"Wonderland by Night"	Bert Kaempfert
U.S. #1 POP LP	*Wonderland by Night*	Bert Kaempfert
U.S. #1 R&B 45	"Shop Around"	The Miracles
U.K. #1 POP 45	"Poetry in Motion"	Johnny Tillotson

WEEK ENDING JANUARY 29		
U.S. #1 POP 45	"Wonderland by Night"	Bert Kaempfert
U.S. #1 POP LP	*Wonderland by Night*	Bert Kaempfert
U.S. #1 R&B 45	"Shop Around"	The Miracles
U.K. #1 POP 45	"Are You Lonesome Tonight?"	Elvis Presley

WEEK ENDING FEBRUARY 5		
U.S. #1 POP 45	"Will You Love Me Tomorrow"	The Shirelles
U.S. #1 POP LP	*Exodus*	soundtrack
U.S. #1 R&B 45	"Shop Around"	The Miracles
U.K. #1 POP 45	"Are You Lonesome Tonight?"	Elvis Presley

WEEK ENDING FEBRUARY 12		
U.S. #1 POP 45	"Will You Love Me Tomorrow"	The Shirelles
U.S. #1 POP LP	*Wonderland by Night*	Bert Kaempfert
U.S. #1 R&B 45	"Shop Around"	The Miracles
U.K. #1 POP 45	"Are You Lonesome Tonight?"	Elvis Presley

WEEK ENDING FEBRUARY 19		
U.S. #1 POP 45	"Calcutta"	Lawrence Welk
U.S. #1 POP LP	*Wonderland by Night*	Bert Kaempfert
U.S. #1 R&B 45	"Shop Around"	The Miracles
U.K. #1 POP 45	"Are You Lonesome Tonight?"	Elvis Presley

WEEK ENDING FEBRUARY 26		
U.S. #1 POP 45	"Calcutta"	Lawrence Welk
U.S. #1 POP LP	*Exodus*	soundtrack
U.S. #1 R&B 45	"Shop Around"	The Miracles
U.K. #1 POP 45	"Are You Lonesome Tonight?"	Elvis Presley

MARCH

10 Twenty-two-year-old songwriter **Jeff Barry**, whose "Tell Laura I Love Her" was a Top Ten hit for **Ray Peterson** in 1960, signs an exclusive writing and recording contract with Trinity Music. After marrying **Ellie Greenwich** in 1962, Barry will work for **Phil Spector** and then **Shadow Morton**, and Barry and Greenwich will write "Da Doo Ron Ron" and "Then He Kissed Me" for the **Crystals**, "Be My Baby" for the **Ronettes**, "Chapel of Love" for the **Dixie Cups**, "Do Wah Diddy Diddy" for **Manfred Mann**, "Leader of the Pack" for the **Shangri-Las**, "River Deep, Mountain High" for **Ike and Tina Turner**, "Hanky Panky" for **Tommy James and the Shondells** and "Cherry Cherry" for **Neil Diamond**.

17 "Five Star Jubilee" premieres on NBC-TV at eight p.m. The country music show takes it name from the five stars who will rotate as hosts of the weekly program: **Snooky Lanson**, **Tex Ritter**, **Rex Allen**, **Carl Smith** and **Jimmy Wakely**.

20 Disc jockey **Peter Tripp**, recently fired from WMGM, New York City, and hired by KYA, San Francisco, goes on trial before a Special Sessions Court in New York City on thirty-nine counts of commercial bribery—payola. In May, the court will find Tripp guilty.

25 **Elvis Presley** performs his last live show for eight years at Block Arena in Pearl Harbor, Hawaii. The show, a benefit for the U.S.S. *Arizona*, raised $62,000 for the U.S.S. *Arizona* memorial fund. For the next eight years, fans must be content with seeing him only on the movie screen.

26 **Gene McDaniels'** "One Hundred Pounds of Clay," his first and biggest hit, enters the pop chart. It will peak at #3.

Elvis Presley sets a British chart first: Number One with three consecutive releases: "It's Now or Never," "Are You Lonesome Tonight" and "Wooden Heart."

31 Instant Records releases **Chris Kenner's** "I Like It like That" backed with "I Like It like That, Part Two." It will be Kenner's only hit recording outside of his hometown, New Orleans, although **Wilson Pickett** will do very well with Kenner's "Land of 1000 Dances" in 1966.

APRIL

2 **Paul Revere and the Raiders** make their national pop chart debut with "Like, Long Hair"—a curiously prescient song for a group that will later (around 1965) become known for their Revolutionary War-era ponytails.

Irvin Feld's Biggest Show of Stars 1961 premieres in Philadelphia. The featured acts, who will tour most parts of the U.S.A and some parts of Canada, include **Fats Domino**, **Chubby Checker**, the **Shirelles**, the **Drifters**, the **Shells**, **Bo Diddley**, **Ben E. King**, **Chuck Jackson** and the **Paul Williams Band**.

11 **Bob Dylan** makes his New York City stage debut at Gerde's Folk City, a small Greenwich Village club, opening for bluesman **John Lee Hooker**. The nineteen-year-old Dylan, who arrived in New York less than three months before, performs "The House of the Rising Sun," "Song to Woody" (which he had written for Woody Guthrie) and a few other numbers.

12 The winners of the Third Annual Grammy Awards are announced. For the first time, rock & roll is noticeably absent. The big winner is **Ray Charles**, who wins Best Vocal Performance, Male, Best Performance by a Pop Single Artist for "Georgia on My Mind," Best Vocal Performance (Album), Male, for *The Genius of Ray Charles* and Best R&B Performance for "Let the Good Times Roll."

22 The First Annual Country Music Festival gets under way at the 13,000-seat Coliseum in Jacksonville, Florida. The attractions include **Webb Pierce**, **Faron Young**, **Porter Wagoner**, **Lester Flatt**

and **Earl Scruggs**, **Patsy Cline**, the **Louvin Brothers**, **Mel Tillis**, **George Hamilton IV** and the **Foggy Mountain Boys**.

Johnny Burnette, recovered from his appendicitis in February, embarks on a one-week tour of Australia and New Zealand.

24 **Bob Dylan** makes his recording debut, playing harmonica on the title track of **Harry Belafonte's** *Midnight Special* album, for which he is paid fifty dollars. ◆

WEEK ENDING MARCH 5		
U.S. #1 POP 45	"Pony Time"	Chubby Checker
U.S. #1 POP LP	*Exodus*	soundtrack
U.S. #1 R&B 45	"Shop Around"	The Miracles
U.K. #1 POP 45	"Walk Right Back"	The Everly Brothers

WEEK ENDING MARCH 12		
U.S. #1 POP 45	"Pony Time"	Chubby Checker
U.S. #1 POP LP	*Calcutta*	Lawrence Welk
U.S. #1 R&B 45	"Pony Time"	Chubby Checker
U.K. #1 POP 45	"Walk Right Back"	The Everly Brothers

WEEK ENDING MARCH 19		
U.S. #1 POP 45	"Pony Time"	Chubby Checker
U.S. #1 POP LP	*Calcutta*	Lawrence Welk
U.S. #1 R&B 45	"Pony Time"	Chubby Checker
U.K. #1 POP 45	"Walk Right Back"	The Everly Brothers

WEEK ENDING MARCH 26		
U.S. #1 POP 45	"Surrender"	Elvis Presley
U.S. #1 POP LP	*Calcutta*	Lawrence Welk
U.S. #1 R&B 45	"Pony Time"	Chubby Checker
U.K. #1 POP 45	"Wooden Heart"	Elvis Presley

WEEK ENDING APRIL 2		
U.S. #1 POP 45	"Surrender"	Elvis Presley
U.S. #1 POP LP	*Calcutta*	Lawrence Welk
U.S. #1 R&B 45	"I Pity the Fool"	Bobby Bland
U.K. #1 POP 45	"Wooden Heart"	Elvis Presley

WEEK ENDING APRIL 9		
U.S. #1 POP 45	"Blue Moon"	The Marcels
U.S. #1 POP LP	*G.I. Blues*	Elvis Presley
U.S. #1 R&B 45	"Blue Moon"	The Marcels
U.K. #1 POP 45	"Are You Sure?"	The Allisons

WEEK ENDING APRIL 16		
U.S. #1 POP 45	"Blue Moon"	The Marcels
U.S. #1 POP LP	*Calcutta*	Lawrence Welk
U.S. #1 R&B 45	"Blue Moon"	The Marcels
U.K. #1 POP 45	"Wooden Heart"	Elvis Presley

WEEK ENDING APRIL 23		
U.S. #1 POP 45	"Blue Moon"	The Marcels
U.S. #1 POP LP	*Calcutta*	Lawrence Welk
U.S. #1 R&B 45	"One Mint Julep"	Ray Charles
U.K. #1 POP 45	"Wooden Heart"	Elvis Presley

WEEK ENDING APRIL 30		
U.S. #1 POP 45	"Runaway"	Del Shannon
U.S. #1 POP LP	*Calcutta*	Lawrence Welk
U.S. #1 R&B 45	"Mother-in-Law"	Ernie K-Doe
U.K. #1 POP 45	"You're Driving Me Crazy"	The Temperance Seven

MAY

7 **Tony Orlando** makes his chart debut with "Halfway to Paradise," which will peak at #39. After a second Top Forty single—"Bless You"—in 1961, Orlando will not be heard from until 1970, when he reappears leading a trio, **Dawn**.

11 Soviet bandleader and musicologist **Alexander Utyosov**, writing in the East Berlin *Freie Walt*, contends that "what some people now call 'Dixieland' music was played for many years in Odessa in our Socialist Motherland before it was called to life in New Orleans."

19 The **Everly Brothers** launch their own record label, Calliope, intending "to discover and develop new talent." Their own recordings will continue to be issued exclusively by Warner Bros.

21 "Every Beat of My Heart" enters the Hot 100 in two versions—one on the Fury label by **Gladys Knight**, the other on the Vee Jay label by the **Pips**. They are not the same recording, but are rendered by the same act, victims of a contract dispute. The Vee Jay single will be the more successful, rising to #6 on the pop chart and Number One on the R&B chart. Gladys Knight and the Pips, whose first hits these are, will eventually sign to Motown's soul label.

31 **Chuck Berry** opens Berry Park, an outdoor amusement park in Wentzville, Missouri, about twenty miles outside of St. Louis. The thirty-acre complex includes a miniature golf course, a swimming pool, a Ferris wheel and other rides, a children's zoo, a ballroom and a picnic grove with barbecue pits.

JUNE

2 In Hackensack, New Jersey, two men are sentenced to prison for a year and a day, and a third man is given a suspended sentence in the first successful conviction of record bootleggers.

8 **Elvis Presley**'s seventh film, *Wild in the Country*, premieres in Memphis. The screenplay was written by **Clifford Odets** and the film was originally released without any of Elvis' singing. However, the movie got such negative reviews—from both critics and fans—that it was re-edited and several songs were added, including the title theme song, "I Slipped, I Stumbled, I Fell" and

"In My Way." Elvis' costars in this tale of a poor juvenile delinquent (Elvis) and the women who try to change his life are **Tuesday Weld** and **Hope Lange**.

12 **Frankie Avalon** begins a fifteen-day tour of South America in Buenos Aires, Argentina.

14 Country singer **Patsy Cline** sustains serious head injuries and a fractured and dislocated right hip in a car crash near Madison, Tennessee, that kills one passenger in another car.

25 **Alan Freed**, now at radio station KDAY, Los Angeles, premieres his latest tour of outdoor arenas with a show at the Hollywood Bowl. The bill features the **Shirelles**,

Brenda Lee, **Bobby Vee**, **Etta James**, **Gene McDaniels**, the **Ventures**, **Clarence "Frogman" Henry**, the **Fleetwoods**, **Kathy Young and the Innocents** and **Jerry Lee Lewis**. Freed's trial on payola charges, originally scheduled to begin June 15, has been postponed until October.

The **Spinners** make their national chart debut with "That's What Girls Are Made For," which will peak at #3 on the R&B chart and at #27 on the pop chart. It will be another ten years before the Spinners, under the direction of songwriter and producer **Thom Bell**, will become consistent hitmakers. ◆

WEEK ENDING MAY 7		
U.S. #1 POP 45	"Runaway"	Del Shannon
U.S. #1 POP LP	*Calcutta*	Lawrence Welk
U.S. #1 R&B 45	"Mother-in-Law"	Ernie K-Doe
U.K. #1 POP 45	"Blue Moon"	The Marcels

WEEK ENDING MAY 14		
U.S. #1 POP 45	"Runaway"	Del Shannon
U.S. #1 POP LP	*Calcutta*	Lawrence Welk
U.S. #1 R&B 45	"Mother-in-Law"	Ernie K-Doe
U.K. #1 POP 45	"Blue Moon"	The Marcels

WEEK ENDING MAY 21		
U.S. #1 POP 45	"Runaway"	Del Shannon
U.S. #1 POP LP	*G.I. Blues*	Elvis Presley
U.S. #1 R&B 45	"Mother-in-Law"	Ernie K-Doe
U.K. #1 POP 45	"Runaway"	Del Shannon

WEEK ENDING MAY 28		
U.S. #1 POP 45	"Mother-in-Law"	Ernie K-Doe
U.S. #1 POP LP	*G.I. Blues*	Elvis Presley
U.S. #1 R&B 45	"Mother-in-Law"	Ernie K-Doe
U.K. #1 POP 45	"Surrender"	Elvis Presley

WEEK ENDING JUNE 4		
U.S. #1 POP 45	"Travelin' Man"	Ricky Nelson
U.S. #1 POP LP	*G.I. Blues*	Elvis Presley
U.S. #1 R&B 45	"Stand by Me"	Ben E. King
U.K. #1 POP 45	"Surrender"	Elvis Presley

WEEK ENDING JUNE 11		
U.S. #1 POP 45	"Running Scared"	Roy Orbison
U.S. #1 POP LP	*Camelot*	original cast
U.S. #1 R&B 45	"Stand by Me"	Ben E. King
U.K. #1 POP 45	"Surrender"	Elvis Presley

WEEK ENDING JUNE 18		
U.S. #1 POP 45	"Travelin' Man"	Ricky Nelson
U.S. #1 POP LP	*Camelot*	original cast
U.S. #1 R&B 45	"Stand by Me"	Ben E. King
U.K. #1 POP 45	"Surrender"	Elvis Presley

WEEK ENDING JUNE 25		
U.S. #1 POP 45	"Moody River"	Pat Boone
U.S. #1 POP LP	*Camelot*	original cast
U.S. #1 R&B 45	"Stand by Me"	Ben E. King
U.K. #1 POP 45	"Runaway"	Del Shannon

JULY

6 The first issue of *Mersey Beat*, the fan magazine and newspaper of the Liverpool, England, rock scene is published. This issue contains an article by a local musician, **John Lennon**, entitled "Being a Short Diversion on the Dubious Origins of Beatles."

10 The **Mar-Keys**, a Memphis-based instrumental group featuring guitarist **Steve Cropper** and bassist **Donald "Duck" Dunn**—both future members of **Booker T. and the MGs**—enter the Hot 100 with the instrumental "Last Night."

12 **Pat Boone** begins a ten-day tour of South Africa at the Ice Drome in Durban. Upon his return to California, he will begin filming *State Fair*.

14 According to a *Billboard* story, the teenage dance craze the Twist is now catching on with adults—in Philadelphia, at least, where dance-club contests have prodded parents into Twisting as avidly as their adolescent offspring.

17 The **Supremes'** debut single, "Buttered Popcorn" backed with "Who's Loving You," is released on Motown Records. Though it will fail to make the chart, the vocal trio will go on to become one of the most consistently successful hitmaking groups of the Sixties. The Supremes—at this time consisting of **Diana Ross**, **Mary Wilson** and **Florence Ballard**—began their singing career earlier this year as the **Primettes**, playing warm-ups in Detroit nightclubs for the male quartet the **Primes**, who would soon become the **Temptations**, another successful Motown vocal group.

29 **Dick Clark** premieres his summer stage show, The Dick Clark Caravan of Stars, at the Steel Pier in Atlantic City, New Jersey. By the time the caravan comes to a rest in Detroit on September 4, **Chubby Checker**, **Freddy Cannon**, the **Shirelles**, **Duane Eddy and the Rebels**, **Bobby Rydell**, **Dodie Stevens**, **Gary "U.S." Bonds**, **Johnny and the Hurricanes**, **Chuck Jackson**,

Mike Clifford and **Fabian** will have appeared on its bill.

AUGUST

2 The **Beatles** begin their engagement as regular headliners at Liverpool's Cavern Club, where they will perform some 300 times over the next two years.

24 Atlantic Records releases its first **Solomon Burke** single, "Just out of Reach (of My Two Empty Arms)," which will go to #7 on the R&B chart and #24 on the pop chart. Burke has been singing professionally since he was nine years old, when he was the star of the Philadelphia gospel stage. He was host of his own gospel radio show, "Solomon's Temple," as a teenager and became known on the national gospel circuit as "the Wonder Boy Preacher." He recorded pop and R&B material as well as gospel for the Apollo and Singular labels in the late Fifties, but had no hits until "Just out of Reach (of My Two Empty Arms)."

28 Tamla Records (a Motown label) releases the **Marvelettes'** debut single, "Please Mr. Postman." The all-girl vocal quintet led by **Gladys Horton** was formed at Inkster High School in Detroit and came to the attention of Tamla's Berry Gordy, Jr. after winning a school talent contest. "Please Mr. Postman," a million-seller, will be the group's biggest hit. ♦

WEEK ENDING JULY 2		
U.S. #1 POP 45	"Quarter to Three"	Gary "U.S." Bonds
U.S. #1 POP LP	*Camelot*	original cast
U.S. #1 R&B 45	"Every Beat of My Heart"	The Pips
U.K. #1 POP 45	"Runaway"	Del Shannon

WEEK ENDING JULY 9		
U.S. #1 POP 45	"Quarter to Three"	Gary "U.S." Bonds
U.S. #1 POP LP	*Camelot*	original cast
U.S. #1 R&B 45	"Tossin' and Turnin'"	Bobby Lewis
U.K. #1 POP 45	"Runaway"	Del Shannon

WEEK ENDING JULY 16		
U.S. #1 POP 45	"Tossin' and Turnin'"	Bobby Lewis
U.S. #1 POP LP	*Camelot*	original cast
U.S. #1 R&B 45	"Tossin' and Turnin'"	Bobby Lewis
U.K. #1 POP 45	"Runaway"	Del Shannon

WEEK ENDING JULY 23		
U.S. #1 POP 45	"Tossin' and Turnin'"	Bobby Lewis
U.S. #1 POP LP	*Stars for a Summer Night*	various artists
U.S. #1 R&B 45	"Tossin' and Turnin'"	Bobby Lewis
U.K. #1 POP 45	"Temptation"	The Everly Brothers

WEEK ENDING JULY 30		
U.S. #1 POP 45	"Tossin' and Turnin'"	Bobby Lewis
U.S. #1 POP LP	*Stars for a Summer Night*	various artists
U.S. #1 R&B 45	"Tossin' and Turnin'"	Bobby Lewis
U.K. #1 POP 45	"Temptation"	The Everly Brothers

WEEK ENDING AUGUST 7		
U.S. #1 POP 45	"Tossin' and Turnin'"	Bobby Lewis
U.S. #1 POP LP	*Stars for a Summer Night*	various artists
U.S. #1 R&B 45	"Tossin' and Turnin'"	Bobby Lewis
U.K. #1 POP 45	"Well I Ask You"	Eden Kane

WEEK ENDING AUGUST 14		
U.S. #1 POP 45	"Tossin' and Turnin'"	Bobby Lewis
U.S. #1 POP LP	*Stars for a Summer Night*	various artists
U.S. #1 R&B 45	"Tossin' and Turnin'"	Bobby Lewis
U.K. #1 POP 45	"You Don't Know"	Helen Shapiro

WEEK ENDING AUGUST 21		
U.S. #1 POP 45	"Tossin' and Turnin'"	Bobby Lewis
U.S. #1 POP LP	*Stars for a Summer Night*	various artists
U.S. #1 R&B 45	"Tossin' and Turnin'"	Bobby Lewis
U.K. #1 POP 45	"Johnny Remember Me"	John Leyton

WEEK ENDING AUGUST 28		
U.S. #1 POP 45	"Tossin' and Turnin'"	Bobby Lewis
U.S. #1 POP LP	*Something for Everybody*	Elvis Presley
U.S. #1 R&B 45	"Tossin' and Turnin'"	Bobby Lewis
U.K. #1 POP 45	"Johnny Remember Me"	John Leyton

SEPTEMBER

4 The **Marvelettes**' first hit, "Please Mr. Postman," enters the Hot 100 at #95. It will eventually go on to top both the pop and R&B charts and will be covered by the **Beatles** and the **Carpenters.**

26 **Bob Dylan** begins a two-week engagement as the opening act for the **Greenbriar Boys** at Gerde's Folk City in New York's Greenwich Village.

29 *New York Times* music critic **Robert Shelton** sees **Bob Dylan** open at Gerde's Folk City, New York City, for the **Greenbriar Boys.** His review of the Greenbriar Boys' show describes Dylan as "a cross between a choir boy and a beatnik" and "bursting at the seams with talent." It is Dylan's first press notice.

30 **Bob Dylan** plays harmonica on three cuts recorded for his friend **Caroline Hester**'s first Columbia album. The session is produced by **John Hammond**, whose early production credits include **Bessie Smith, Count Basie, Billie Holiday, Pete Seeger** and **Aretha Franklin.** Hammond is so impressed by Dylan that he immediately signs him to a Columbia Records contract and arranges for a solo recording session in October.

OCTOBER

2 Vanguard Records releases the album

Volume Two and single "Banks of the Ohio" backed with "Old Blue," by twenty-year-old folksinger **Joan Baez.** Baez made a striking debut at the 1959 Newport Folk Festival and has been a favorite on the Greenwich Village folk scene ever since because of the crystalline clarity and purity of her soprano voice. Born in New York City of mixed English, Scottish and Spanish parentage, Baez will go on to become one of the most popular and outspoken protest singers of the Sixties.

21 **Bob Dylan** records his first album, *Bob Dylan,* for Columbia Records. The session, produced by **John Hammond**, presents the twenty-year-old singer accompanied by his guitar and harmonica only. The recording is finished in one day and production costs are $400. Filling out his income-tax form, Dylan gives his name as Blind Boy Grunt.

23 Minit Records releases "I Cried My Last Tear" by New Orleans R&B singer **Ernie K-Doe** (né Ernest Kador), but his only big hit will be the novelty song "Mother-in-Law," which made Number One earlier this year. "I Cried My Last Tear" will rise as high as #69 in the pop chart, and K-Doe will have two more minor hits in the next several months.

With his first single, "Who Put the Bomp?," still riding high on the charts, **Barry Mann**'s "Little Miss U.S.A." backed with "Find Another Fool," is released on ABC-Paramount Records. It will fail to make the chart, though

Mann will have a few more hits as a recording artist and will go on to pen some classic pop songs as part of a Brill Building team with **Cynthia Weill.** Among their many hits: the **Crystals**' "Uptown" and "He's Sure the Boy I Love," the **Paris Sisters**' "I Love How You Love Me," the **Righteous Brothers**' "You've Lost That Lovin' Feeling," the **Animals**' "We Gotta Get outta This Place" and **Paul Revere and the Raiders**' "Kicks."

30 **Phil Spector**'s Philles label—destined to become one of the most successful and influential labels of the Sixties—releases its first record, the **Crystals**' "Oh, Yeah, Maybe Baby" backed with "There's No Other (like My Baby)." The B side will go on to reach #20 on the pop chart and will eventually sell over 1 million copies worldwide.   ◆

WEEK ENDING SEPTEMBER 4		
U.S. #1 POP 45	"Wooden Heart"	Joe Dowell
U.S. #1 POP LP	*Something for Everybody*	Elvis Presley
U.S. #1 R&B 45	"Tossin' and Turnin'"	Bobby Lewis
U.K. #1 POP 45	"Johnny Remember Me"	John Leyton

WEEK ENDING SEPTEMBER 11		
U.S. #1 POP 45	"Michael"	The Highwaymen
U.S. #1 POP LP	*Something for Everybody*	Elvis Presley
U.S. #1 R&B 45	"Tossin' and Turnin'"	Bobby Lewis
U.K. #1 POP 45	"You Don't Know"	Helen Shapiro

WEEK ENDING SEPTEMBER 18		
U.S. #1 POP 45	"Michael"	The Highwaymen
U.S. #1 POP LP	*Judy at Carnegie Hall*	Judy Garland
U.S. #1 R&B 45	"My True Story"	The Jive Five
U.K. #1 POP 45	"Johnny Remember Me"	John Leyton

WEEK ENDING SEPTEMBER 25		
U.S. #1 POP 45	"Take Good Care of My Baby"	Bobby Vee
U.S. #1 POP LP	*Judy at Carnegie Hall*	Judy Garland
U.S. #1 R&B 45	"My True Story"	The Jive Five
U.K. #1 POP 45	"Johnny Remember Me"	John Leyton

WEEK ENDING OCTOBER 1		
U.S. #1 POP 45	"Take Good Care of My Baby"	Bobby Vee
U.S. #1 POP LP	*Judy at Carnegie Hall*	Judy Garland
U.S. #1 R&B 45	"My True Story"	The Jive Five
U.K. #1 POP 45	"Johnny Remember Me"	John Leyton

WEEK ENDING OCTOBER 8		
U.S. #1 POP 45	"Take Good Care of My Baby"	Bobby Vee
U.S. #1 POP LP	*Judy at Carnegie Hall*	Judy Garland
U.S. #1 R&B 45	"Hit the Road Jack"	Ray Charles
U.K. #1 POP 45	"Johnny Remember Me"	John Leyton

WEEK ENDING OCTOBER 15		
U.S. #1 POP 45	"Hit the Road Jack"	Ray Charles
U.S. #1 POP LP	*Judy at Carnegie Hall*	Judy Garland
U.S. #1 R&B 45	"Hit the Road Jack"	Ray Charles
U.K. #1 POP 45	"Michael"	The Highwaymen

WEEK ENDING OCTOBER 22		
U.S. #1 POP 45	"Hit the Road Jack"	Ray Charles
U.S. #1 POP LP	*Judy at Carnegie Hall*	Judy Garland
U.S. #1 R&B 45	"Hit the Road Jack"	Ray Charles
U.K. #1 POP 45	"Walkin' Back to Happiness"	Helen Shapiro

WEEK ENDING OCTOBER 29		
U.S. #1 POP 45	"Runaround Sue"	Dion and the Belmonts
U.S. #1 POP LP	*Judy at Carnegie Hall*	Judy Garland
U.S. #1 R&B 45	"Hit the Road Jack"	Ray Charles
U.K. #1 POP 45	"Walkin' Back to Happiness"	Helen Shapiro

NOVEMBER

3 **Jimmie Rodgers** (1897–1933) is unanimously elected the first member of the Country Music Hall of Fame in Nashville. Rodgers, known as "The Singing Brakeman," was famous throughout the United States during the Depression years for such songs as "Mule Skinner Blues," "Hobo Bill's Last Ride" and "Waitin' for a Train."

4 **Bob Dylan** makes his concert-hall debut at the Carnegie Chapter Hall in New York City. Fifty people—most of them Dylan's friends—pay two dollars apiece to attend, and Dylan earns twenty dollars for the night.

6 Minit Records releases the rock & roll anthem "It Will Stand" by the **Showmen**, whose lead singer, **General Johnson**, will resurface in early 1970 as the distinctively scatting and hiccuping lead voice on **Chairmen of the Board**'s soul hit "Give Me Just a Little More Time."

9 **Brian Epstein**, the manager of several record shops in Liverpool, pays a noontime visit to the Cavern Club to see the **Beatles**, whom he heard about from a teenaged customer looking for their record "My Bonnie." Impressed by the Beatles' performance, he introduces himself to **George Harrison** and **Paul McCartney** (who informs him that "My Bonnie" is **Tony Sheridan**'s record—the Beatles merely provided his backup). By the end of the month, Epstein will have persuaded the Beatles that he should be their manager, and on January 24, 1962, a contract will be signed. Epstein will manage the Beatles until his death in August 1967.

20 *Billboard* reports on the global Twist Craze: WOR-TV in New York has shot a series of one- and five-minute "Twist Lessons" with **Chubby Checker**, to be shown hourly every day; Checker has also been signed for a British-American film production, *It's Trad Dad;* **Joey Dee and the Starliters**, whose album *Doin' the Twist at the Peppermint Lounge* is released this week on Roulette, have been signed for the Paramount film *Hey, Let's Twist;* **Dion** has been signed to star in Columbia's *Twist around the Clock;* and in France, there are forty-five different "Twist" records on the market, with versions of "The Twist" by **Johnny Halliday** and **Richard Anthony** sharing the Number One spot on the French pop chart.

DECEMBER

4 **Gene Chandler**'s "Duke of Earl" is released on Vee Jay Records. This novel throwback to the doo-wop era will become Chandler's biggest hit, reaching Number One and selling over 1 million copies worldwide. Though Chandler will go on to have many other, less substantial hits, the biggest of which will be 1970's "Groovy Situation" (which will reach #12 on the pop chart), he will never lose his "Duke of Earl" renown. Chandler would go on to produce the hit single "Backfield in Motion" by **Mel and Tim** in 1969 and found two record labels, Mr. Chan, in the early Seventies, and ChiSound, of which he will become vice-president in 1979.

8 "Surfin'," the **Beach Boys**' first recording, is released by Candix Records, a small, Los Angeles-based company. The song was written by **Brian Wilson** and his cousin **Mike Love**, and recorded with Brian's brothers, **Carl** and **Dennis**, and their friend **Alan Jardine**—Carl playing acoustic guitar, Al on double bass, and Brian keeping time on a garbage can.

18 **Chubby Checker**'s "The Twist" has now been on the Hot 100 chart for twenty-three consecutive weeks—longer than any other disc on the chart.

24 "The Lion Sleeps Tonight" becomes the first African song to hit Number One on the American pop chart. The American version, by the **Tokens**, is a translation of a South African folk song known variously as "Mbube" and "Wimoweh" and has been recorded previously by the **Weavers** and **Miriam Makeba**; in 1972, a version by **Robert John**

will peak at #3, and in 1976, **David Bowie** will record the song.

31 Appearing at the **Ritchie Valens** Memorial Concert at the Long Beach (California) Municipal Auditorium, the **Beach Boys** play their first show under that name. Prior to this, they have called themselves the **Pendletones** and **Carl and the Passions.** ♦

WEEK ENDING NOVEMBER 5		
U.S. #1 POP 45	"Runaround Sue"	Dion and the Belmonts
U.S. #1 POP LP	*Judy at Carnegie Hall*	Judy Garland
U.S. #1 R&B 45	"Hit the Road Jack"	Ray Charles
U.K. #1 POP 45	"Walkin' Back to Happiness"	Helen Shapiro

WEEK ENDING NOVEMBER 12		
U.S. #1 POP 45	"Big Bad John"	Jimmy Dean
U.S. #1 POP LP	*Judy at Carnegie Hall*	Judy Garland
U.S. #1 R&B 45	"Ya Ya"	Lee Dorsey
U.K. #1 POP 45	"Walkin' Back to Happiness"	Helen Shapiro

WEEK ENDING NOVEMBER 19		
U.S. #1 POP 45	"Big Bad John"	Jimmy Dean
U.S. #1 POP LP	*Judy at Carnegie Hall*	Judy Garland
U.S. #1 R&B 45	"Please Mr. Postman"	The Marvelettes
U.K. #1 POP 45	"His Latest Flame"	Elvis Presley

WEEK ENDING NOVEMBER 26		
U.S. #1 POP 45	"Big Bad John"	Jimmy Dean
U.S. #1 POP LP	*Judy at Carnegie Hall*	Judy Garland
U.S. #1 R&B 45	"Please Mr. Postman"	The Marvelettes
U.K. #1 POP 45	"His Latest Flame"	Elvis Presley

WEEK ENDING DECEMBER 3		
U.S. #1 POP 45	"Big Bad John"	Jimmy Dean
U.S. #1 POP LP	*Judy at Carnegie Hall*	Judy Garland
U.S. #1 R&B 45	"Please Mr. Postman"	The Marvelettes
U.K. #1 POP 45	"His Latest Flame"	Elvis Presley

WEEK ENDING DECEMBER 10		
U.S. #1 POP 45	"Big Bad John"	Jimmy Dean
U.S. #1 POP LP	*Judy at Carnegie Hall*	Judy Garland
U.S. #1 R&B 45	"Please Mr. Postman"	The Marvelettes
U.K. #1 POP 45	"Take Good Care of My Baby"	Bobby Vee

WEEK ENDING DECEMBER 17		
U.S. #1 POP 45	"Please Mr. Postman"	The Marvelettes
U.S. #1 POP LP	*Blue Hawaii*	Elvis Presley
U.S. #1 R&B 45	"Please Mr. Postman"	The Marvelettes
U.K. #1 POP 45	"Tower of Strength"	Frankie Vaughan

WEEK ENDING DECEMBER 24		
U.S. #1 POP 45	"The Lion Sleeps Tonight"	The Tokens
U.S. #1 POP LP	*Blue Hawaii*	Elvis Presley
U.S. #1 R&B 45	"Please Mr. Postman"	The Marvelettes
U.K. #1 POP 45	"Tower of Strength"	Frankie Vaughan

WEEK ENDING DECEMBER 31		
U.S. #1 POP 45	"The Lion Sleeps Tonight"	The Tokens
U.S. #1 POP LP	*Blue Hawaii*	Elvis Presley
U.S. #1 R&B 45	"Please Mr. Postman"	The Marvelettes
U.K. #1 POP 45	"Tower of Strength"	Frankie Vaughan

1962

*C*oventional wisdom holds that 1962 was one of those limbo years—between the first great death of rock & roll and its first great rebirth with the British Invasion—during which virtually nothing of significance happened. The conventional wisdom, however, is wrong.

The year's first Number One hit was a carry-over from the end of 1961, the Tokens' "The Lion Sleeps Tonight"—a fusion of doo-wop and African folk song. The year's last Number One hit was the Tornadoes' "Telstar"—a classic of naive pop futurism complete with surf-rock beat, protosynthesizer melody and space-age sound effects. Aside from being the memorable products of one-hit wonders, both records were typical of the period's anything-might-hit, scattershot eclecticism. It was a time when a seminal rock & roller like Fats Domino could appear on the same episode of "The Ed Sullivan Show" as teel idol Tommy Sands, when a lot of gimmicks (like Bobby "Boris" Pickett's "Monster Mash") and dance-craze capitalizations (like "The Peppermint Twist") were run high up the flagpole. There were not undisputed rock & roll pacesetters, only an ever-expanding field of young-turk contenders.

The folk boom continued, though it would still be a few more years before it would have a strong impact on rock music. Bob Dylan's second album, *The Freewheelin' Bob Dylan,* outsold his debut album four times over in its first week of release, and featured such future classics as "Blowin' in the Wind" and "Masters of War."

On the R&B front, the Platters embarked on a European tour that took them behind the Iron Curtain. Motown began racking up hits, including its first million-seller, the Miracles' "You've Really Got a Hold on Me," and put the first of its package tours—featuring Marvin Gaye, Mary Wells, the Supremes, Little Stevie Wonder and the Miracles—on the road. James Brown continued to perfect the stage act that made him known as the "Hardest Working Man in Show Business," and recorded the legendary *Live at the Apollo* album, which set sales records for R&B LPs. And in England, the Beatles finally got a recording contract, while the Rolling Stones played their first local shows.

Then there was the most glorious musical chapter of these limbo years, the girl groups and Phil Spector, whose smash hits "Uptown" and "He's a Rebel" by the Crystals saw the girl-group sound evolve from pure epic teen-dream romance into something more socially, even politically, conscious. On October 6, 1962, at age twenty-one, Phil Spector—the first man to make rock & roll music into art—bought out his partners at Philles Records and became the youngest record-label chief in history. He was already a millionaire. In these limbo years, when rock & roll's initial impetus seemed almost to have petered out, Phil Spector—the first record-company executive young enough to listen to, enjoy and *feel* the music he was producing (well, since Sam Phillips, at least)—was beating the establishment at its own game and making immortal rock & roll music in the process.

JANUARY

1 The **Beatles** perform their first audition for a major record company, Decca, in London. They run through fifteen songs—mostly standards, only three **Lennon-McCartney** originals—for Decca's **Mike Smith**, who hears **Brian Poole and the Tremeloes** audition the same day. Decca ends up signing the Tremeloes, but not the Beatles.

13 The **Beach Boys'** "Surfin'" is getting airplay in Los Angeles and enters *Billboard*'s Bubbling under the Hot 100 chart at #118.

21 Singer **Jackie Wilson**, whose most recent hit is "My Heart Belongs to Only You," appears on "The Ed Sullivan Show."

24 Teenage twist star **Danny Peppermint**—who had earlier released a version of "The Peppermint Twist" different from, but competing with, the version by **Joey Dee and the Starliters**—is nearly killed when he touches a microphone stand at the Thunderbird Hotel in Las Vegas and is electrocuted. He is rushed to a nearby hospital, where he recovers.

25 **Sam Cooke**'s "Twistin' the Night Away," later covered by **Rod Stewart**, is released on RCA Records. It will eventually hit #9 in the pop chart.

26 **Bishop Burke** of the Buffalo, New York, Catholic Diocese bans the Twist. It cannot be danced, sung about or listened to in any Catholic school, parish or youth organization event. Later in the year, the Twist will be banned from community center dances in Tampa, Florida, as well.

27 **Elvis Presley** receives his twenty-ninth gold record for "Can't Help Falling in Love," just weeks after receiving one for the soundtrack to his seventh movie, *Blue Hawaii*.

29 Warner Bros. Records signs the folk trio **Peter, Paul and Mary** (respective surnames **Yarrow**, **Stookey** and **Travers**), already favorites on the Greenwich Village folk scene in New York. The trio will go on to have big hits with their smoothly harmonized versions of such **Bob Dylan** songs as "Blowin' in the Wind" and "Don't Think Twice, It's Alright," as well as "If I Had a Hammer," "Puff, the Magic Dragon" and "Leavin' on a Jet Plane."

FEBRUARY

10 The instrumental "Soul Twist" is released on Enjoy Records. The record features saxophonist **King Curtis**, who provided the raunchy, honking tenor sax breaks in such **Coasters** classics as "Charlie Brown" and "Yakety Yak." The record will eventually reach #17 on the pop chart.

17 **Adam Young**, Chairman of the Radio Trade Practices Committee, has proposed that all pop lyrics be screened by the National Association of Broadcasters Code Committee, according to *Billboard*. Young stated that there is a need for such a measure "due to the proliferation of songs dealing with raw sex and violence beamed directly and singularly at children and teenagers."

28 New York City's top rock & roll radio station, WINS, switches its music format from rock & roll to "pretty music" and changes its call letters back to its original ones, WHN. A station spokesman claims that top rock DJ **Murray the K** will program his shows according to the new format. Several months later, the station will once more move back to rock & roll Top Forty programming. ◆

WEEK ENDING JANUARY 6		
U.S. #1 POP 45	"The Lion Sleeps Tonight"	The Tokens
U.S. #1 POP LP	*Blue Hawaii*	Elvis Presley
U.S. #1 R&B 45	"Unchain My Heart"	Ray Charles
U.K. #1 POP 45	"Moon River"	Danny Williams

WEEK ENDING JANUARY 13		
U.S. #1 POP 45	"The Twist"	Chubby Checker
U.S. #1 POP LP	*Blue Hawaii*	Elvis Presley
U.S. #1 R&B 45	"Unchain My Heart"	Ray Charles
U.K. #1 POP 45	"Moon River"	Danny Williams

WEEK ENDING JANUARY 20		
U.S. #1 POP 45	"The Twist"	Chubby Checker
U.S. #1 POP LP	*Blue Hawaii*	Elvis Presley
U.S. #1 R&B 45	"I Know"	Barbara George
U.K. #1 POP 45	"The Young Ones"	Cliff Richard

WEEK ENDING JANUARY 27		
U.S. #1 POP 45	"Peppermint Twist"	Joey Dee and the Starliters
U.S. #1 POP LP	*Blue Hawaii*	Elvis Presley
U.S. #1 R&B 45	"I Know"	Barbara George
U.K. #1 POP 45	"The Young Ones"	Cliff Richard

WEEK ENDING FEBRUARY 3		
U.S. #1 POP 45	"Peppermint Twist"	Joey Dee and the Starliters
U.S. #1 POP LP	*Blue Hawaii*	Elvis Presley
U.S. #1 R&B 45	"I Know"	Barbara George
U.K. #1 POP 45	"The Young Ones"	Cliff Richard

WEEK ENDING FEBRUARY 10		
U.S. #1 POP 45	"Peppermint Twist"	Joey Dee and the Starliters
U.S. #1 POP LP	*Blue Hawaii*	Elvis Presley
U.S. #1 R&B 45	"I Know"	Barbara George
U.K. #1 POP 45	"The Young Ones"	Cliff Richard

WEEK ENDING FEBRUARY 17		
U.S. #1 POP 45	"Duke of Earl"	Gene Chandler
U.S. #1 POP LP	*Blue Hawaii*	Elvis Presley
U.S. #1 R&B 45	"Duke of Earl"	Gene Chandler
U.K. #1 POP 45	"The Young Ones"	Cliff Richard

WEEK ENDING FEBRUARY 24		
U.S. #1 POP 45	"Duke of Earl"	Gene Chandler
U.S. #1 POP LP	*Blue Hawaii*	Elvis Presley
U.S. #1 R&B 45	"Duke of Earl"	Gene Chandler
U.K. #1 POP 45	"The Young Ones"	Cliff Richard

MARCH

8 The **Beatles** make their television debut, appearing on the BBC program "Teenager's Turn" to play Roy Orbison's "Dream Baby."

17 The **Shirelles'** "Soldier Boy" is released on Scepter Records. The song would become the girl group's biggest hit, reaching Number One, selling over 1 million copies and earning a gold record.

Billboard reports that **Ray Charles** has started his own label, Tangerine Records, following a trend recently started among top recording artists, such as **Sam Cooke** with SAR Records and the **Everly Brothers** with Calliope Records.

Blues Incorporated, possibly the first white blues band in either the U.K. or the U.S., plays its first gig at the Ealing Club in London. The band includes guitarist **Alexis Korner**, drummer **Charlie Watts**, pianist **Dave Stevens**, saxophonist **Dick Heckstall-Smith**, bassist **Andy Hoogenboom** and **Cyril Davies** on harmonica. **Jack Bruce** will take over on bass when the band plays the Marquee Club in two weeks, and before long **Mick Jagger** will become the band's vocalist.

18 **Gary "U.S." Bonds** appears on "The Ed Sullivan Show" to perform his latest hit, "Twist, Twist, Señora."

24 The **Crystals'** "Uptown" is released on **Phil Spector's** Philles label. Like the girl group's first record, "There's No Other (Like My Baby)," "Uptown" would eventually sell over 1 million copies. The Crystals will become the first and arguably the most important girl group in establishing Spector's recording empire.

29 **Gene Chandler** receives a gold record for the biggest hit of his career, "Duke of Earl."

APRIL

7 **Mick Jagger**, **Keith Richards** and **Dick Taylor** meet **Brian Jones** (alias **Elmo Lewis**) at the Ealing Club, a London hangout for blues devotees.

James Brown's predominantly instrumental "Night Train," based on an earlier instrumental hit by ex-**Count Basie** saxophonist **Jimmy Forrest**, is released on King Records. It will reach #35 on the pop chart and #11 on the R&B chart.

10 **Stuart Sutcliffe**, an original member of the **Beatles**, dies at age twenty-two of cerebral paralysis caused by a brain hemorrhage, in Hamburg, Germany. Sutcliffe met **John Lennon** in 1959 when the two were art-school classmates in Liverpool: Sutcliffe introduced Lennon to modern art and literature; Lennon introduced Sutcliffe to rock & roll. He joined the Beatles that year, buying a bass guitar with money earned by selling a painting (**Paul McCartney** was rhythm guitarist at the time), and he dropped out of art school—in spite of his promise as a painter—to accompany the band to Hamburg in 1960. He left the band in mid-1961 to resume painting and because his headaches made the late nights on the stages of Hamburg beer halls painful, but by then he had given the Beatles the look that would soon charm the world: their shaggy, brushed-forward hairstyles.

to England, nearly four years after he'd left the country in disgrace following the publicity about his marriage to **Myra**. His first performance, at Newcastle, is greeted with enthusiasm by fans. ◆

12 Columbia Records tapes **Bob Dylan's** concert at Town Hall, New York City, eventually releasing the recording of "Tomorrow Is a Long Time" made this evening.

28 The National Association of Record Merchandisers (NARM) announces that **Elvis Presley** is the best-selling male vocalist of 1961, and **Connie Francis** the best-selling female vocalist. The best-selling vocal group is **Mitch Miller and the Gang.**

29 Just five days after his son **Steve Allen** drowns in his home swimming pool, **Jerry Lee Lewis** returns

WEEK ENDING MARCH 3		
U.S. #1 POP 45	"Duke of Earl"	Gene Chandler
U.S. #1 POP LP	*Blue Hawaii*	Elvis Presley
U.S. #1 R&B 45	"Duke of Earl"	Gene Chandler
U.K. #1 POP 45	"Let's Twist Again"	Chubby Checker

WEEK ENDING MARCH 10		
U.S. #1 POP 45	"Hey! Baby"	Bruce Channel
U.S. #1 POP LP	*Blue Hawaii*	Elvis Presley
U.S. #1 R&B 45	"Duke of Earl"	Gene Chandler
U.K. #1 POP 45	"Let's Twist Again"	Chubby Checker

WEEK ENDING MARCH 17		
U.S. #1 POP 45	"Hey! Baby"	Bruce Channel
U.S. #1 POP LP	*Blue Hawaii*	Elvis Presley
U.S. #1 R&B 45	"Duke of Earl"	Gene Chandler
U.K. #1 POP 45	"March of the Siamese Children"	Kenny Ball

WEEK ENDING MARCH 24		
U.S. #1 POP 45	"Hey! Baby"	Bruce Channel
U.S. #1 POP LP	*Blue Hawaii*	Elvis Presley
U.S. #1 R&B 45	"Twistin' the Night Away"	Sam Cooke
U.K. #1 POP 45	"March of the Siamese Children"	Kenny Ball

WEEK ENDING MARCH 31		
U.S. #1 POP 45	"Don't Break the Heart. . . ."	Connie Francis
U.S. #1 POP LP	*Blue Hawaii*	Elvis Presley
U.S. #1 R&B 45	"Twistin' the Night Away"	Sam Cooke
U.K. #1 POP 45	"Wonderful Land"	The Shadows

WEEK ENDING APRIL 7		
U.S. #1 POP 45	"Johnny Angel"	Shelley Fabares
U.S. #1 POP LP	*Blue Hawaii*	Elvis Presley
U.S. #1 R&B 45	"Twistin' the Night Away"	Sam Cooke
U.K. #1 POP 45	"Wonderful Land"	The Shadows

WEEK ENDING APRIL 14		
U.S. #1 POP 45	"Johnny Angel"	Shelley Fabares
U.S. #1 POP LP	*Blue Hawaii*	Elvis Presley
U.S. #1 R&B 45	"Soul Twist"	King Curtis
U.K. #1 POP 45	"Wonderful Land"	The Shadows

WEEK ENDING APRIL 21		
U.S. #1 POP 45	"Good Luck Charm"	Elvis Presley
U.S. #1 POP LP	*Blue Hawaii*	Elvis Presley
U.S. #1 R&B 45	"Soul Twist"	King Curtis
U.K. #1 POP 45	"Wonderful Land"	The Shadows

WEEK ENDING APRIL 28		
U.S. #1 POP 45	"Good Luck Charm"	Elvis Presley
U.S. #1 POP LP	*Blue Hawaii*	Elvis Presley
U.S. #1 R&B 45	"Mashed Potato Time"	Dee Dee Sharp
U.K. #1 POP 45	"Wonderful Land"	The Shadows

MAY

5 **Cliff Richard** receives a British gold record for the title song from his first movie, *The Young Ones.*

12 *Billboard* reports that 1961's most-played jukebox disc was country star (and future TV-show host) **Jimmy Dean**'s "Big Bad John," followed—by one vote—by **Chubby Checker**'s "The Twist."

26 The **Isley Brothers'** "Twist and Shout" is released on Wand Records. It will rise up to #17 on the pop chart, and will be covered in two years by the **Beatles**, whose version will go to #2 in 1964.

27 *The Freewheelin' Bob Dylan,* his second album, is released by Columbia Records. With such songs as "Blowin' in the Wind," "Masters of War," "A Hard Rain's A-Gonna Fall" and "Don't Think Twice, It's Alright," the album seals **Dylan**'s reputation as a writer.

Its initial sales of 200,000 copies surpass by four times those of his first album. In 1963, **Peter, Paul and Mary** will make Top Ten hits of "Blowin' in the Wind" and "Don't Think Twice."

JUNE

2 Island Records releases its first single, **Owen Gray**'s "Twist Baby." Founded only weeks before in London by a Jamaican, **Chris Blackwell**, the company is intended primarily to be a distributor of West Indian records to the West Indian population in Great Britain. By the late Sixties, however, Island will be better known for its British acts than its West Indian ones; its roster will include **Traffic, Free, Spooky Tooth, Fairport Convention, Jethro Tull, King Crimson, Emerson, Lake and Palmer** and **Cat Stevens**. In the Seventies, with the popularity of Jamaican reggae increasing worldwide, Island will again become known as a maverick label, promoting such acts as **Bob Marley and the Wailers, Toots and the Maytals, Burning Spear, Grace Jones, Black Uhuru** and **Marianne Faithfull**.

6 The **Beatles**, following an unsuccessful audition for Decca Records, audition for EMI producer **George Martin** at EMI's Parlophone Studios in London. Martin will be the Beatles' arranger and producer through 1969.

8 *The New Musical Express,* Great Britain's leading pop music periodical,

initiates an LP best-seller chart. **Elvis Presley**'s *Blue Hawaii* soundtrack is its first Number One.

23 British vocal group the **Springfields**—which includes **Dusty Springfield**, who would later go on to become a singing star in her own right—release their debut single, "Silver Threads and Golden Needles," on Philips Records. The group will record one more minor hit, "Dear Hearts and Gentle People," before disbanding. ◆

WEEK ENDING MAY 5		
U.S. #1 POP 45	"Soldier Boy"	The Shirelles
U.S. #1 POP LP	*West Side Story*	soundtrack
U.S. #1 R&B 45	"Mashed Potato Time"	Dee Dee Sharp
U.K. #1 POP 45	"Wonderful Land"	The Shadows

WEEK ENDING MAY 12		
U.S. #1 POP 45	"Soldier Boy"	The Shirelles
U.S. #1 POP LP	*West Side Story*	soundtrack
U.S. #1 R&B 45	"Mashed Potato Time"	Dee Dee Sharp
U.K. #1 POP 45	"Wonderful Land"	The Shadows

WEEK ENDING MAY 19		
U.S. #1 POP 45	"Soldier Boy"	The Shirelles
U.S. #1 POP LP	*West Side Story*	soundtrack
U.S. #1 R&B 45	"Mashed Potato Time"	Dee Dee Sharp
U.K. #1 POP 45	"Wonderful Land"	The Shadows

WEEK ENDING MAY 26		
U.S. #1 POP 45	"Stranger on the Shore"	W. Acker Bilk
U.S. #1 POP LP	*West Side Story*	soundtrack
U.S. #1 R&B 45	"I Can't Stop Loving You"	Ray Charles
U.K. #1 POP 45	"Good Luck Charm"	Elvis Presley

WEEK ENDING JUNE 2		
U.S. #1 POP 45	"I Can't Stop Loving You"	Ray Charles
U.S. #1 POP LP	*West Side Story*	soundtrack
U.S. #1 R&B 45	"I Can't Stop Loving You"	Ray Charles
U.K. #1 POP 45	"Good Luck Charm"	Elvis Presley

WEEK ENDING JUNE 9		
U.S. #1 POP 45	"I Can't Stop Loving You"	Ray Charles
U.S. #1 POP LP	*West Side Story*	soundtrack
U.S. #1 R&B 45	"I Can't Stop Loving You"	Ray Charles
U.K. #1 POP 45	"Good Luck Charm"	Elvis Presley

WEEK ENDING JUNE 16		
U.S. #1 POP 45	"I Can't Stop Loving You"	Ray Charles
U.S. #1 POP LP	*West Side Story*	soundtrack
U.S. #1 R&B 45	"I Can't Stop Loving You"	Ray Charles
U.K. #1 POP 45	"Good Luck Charm"	Elvis Presley

WEEK ENDING JUNE 23		
U.S. #1 POP 45	"I Can't Stop Loving You"	Ray Charles
U.S. #1 POP LP	*Modern Sounds in Country. . . .*	Ray Charles
U.S. #1 R&B 45	"I Can't Stop Loving You"	Ray Charles
U.K. #1 POP 45	"Good Luck Charm"	Elvis Presley

WEEK ENDING JUNE 30		
U.S. #1 POP 45	"I Can't Stop Loving You"	Ray Charles
U.S. #1 POP LP	*Modern Sounds in Country. . . .*	Ray Charles
U.S. #1 R&B 45	"I Can't Stop Loving You"	Ray Charles
U.K. #1 POP 45	"Come Outside"	Mike Sarne

JULY

12 The **Rolling Stones** make their performing debut at the Marquee Club in London. The group, according to a handbill publicizing the event, is composed of vocalist **Mick Jagger**, guitarists **Keith Richards** and **Elmo Lewis**, bassist **Dick Taylor**, pianist **Stu** and drummer **Mick Avery**. Future **Kinks** drummer Avory's name is misspelled. Stu is **Ian Stewart**, who will remain the Stone's unofficial pianist. Dick Taylor will soon leave the group to form the **Pretty Things**. Elmo Lewis is actually **Brian Jones**.

23 The American communications satellite Telstar makes its very first transatlantic television transmission, thus inspiring British record producer **Joe Meek** to compose the instrumental "Telstar." Recorded later this week by a group called the **Tornadoes**, the song will become a Number One smash.

28 **Tommy Roe**'s "Sheila," the first of his many pop hits, enters the Hot 100 at #93. It will reach Number One by September 1. Roe had written the song for his local Atlanta band the **Satins** in 1959, and had first recorded it in 1960 for Judd Records, unsuccessfully.

29 **Bob Dylan** makes his radio broadcast debut on New York City's WRVR-FM, performing on the station's hootenanny special.

AUGUST

11 **Booker T. and the MGs'** instrumental classic "Green Onions" is released on Stax Records. It will eventually hit #3 on the pop chart. The band contains ex-members of yet another popular Stax instrumental combo, the **Mar-Keys**, in guitarist **Steve Cropper** and bassist **Donald "Duck" Dunn**, both of whom will later join the **Blues Brothers'** backing band.

18 **Ringo Starr** makes his first appearance as a member of the **Beatles** at a Cavern Club gig in Liverpool. The former drummer for **Rory Storme and the Hurricanes** replaces original drummer **Pete Best**, whom manager **Brian Epstein** asked to leave two days ago on the urging of producer **George Martin**, who believes Starr to be the better drummer. Best, reportedly the most popular Beatle with the group's hometown fans, will join **Lee Curtis and the All Stars** before embarking on a semisuccessful career as a game-show guest.

23 **John Lennon** marries **Cynthia Powell** at the Mount Pleasant Registry Office in Liverpool. With only **Paul** and **George** in attendance, the Lennons were wed in what they hoped would be a secret civil ceremony—John was the first married Beatle. However, John, being a local celebrity, was spotted leaving the registry office. Initially, the couple denied that they were married, but later admitted it. Their son Julian was born on April 8, 1963.

25 The **Four Seasons'** "Sherry" enters the Hot 100 at #91. The song, the debut recording by the quartet with the higher-than-high falsetto voices that was previously known as the **Four Lovers**, will reach Number One on the pop chart within a month. "Sherry" was cowritten by the band's producer, **Bob Crewe**, and the most recent addition to the Four Seasons, **Bob Gaudio**, who had been specially recruited from the **Royal Teens** (of "Short Shorts" fame) by Crewe. ◆

WEEK ENDING JULY 7		
U.S. #1 POP 45	"The Stripper"	Dave Rose and His Orchestra
U.S. #1 POP LP	*Modern Sounds in Country. . . .*	Ray Charles
U.S. #1 R&B 45	"I Can't Stop Loving You"	Ray Charles
U.K. #1 POP 45	"Good Luck Charm"	Elvis Presley

WEEK ENDING JULY 14		
U.S. #1 POP 45	"Roses Are Red"	Bobby Vinton
U.S. #1 POP LP	*Modern Sounds in Country. . . .*	Ray Charles
U.S. #1 R&B 45	"I Can't Stop Loving You"	Ray Charles
U.K. #1 POP 45	"I Can't Stop Loving You"	Ray Charles

WEEK ENDING JULY 21		
U.S. #1 POP 45	"Roses Are Red"	Bobby Vinton
U.S. #1 POP LP	*Modern Sounds in Country. . . .*	Ray Charles
U.S. #1 R&B 45	"I Can't Stop Loving You"	Ray Charles
U.K. #1 POP 45	"I Can't Stop Loving You"	Ray Charles

WEEK ENDING JULY 28		
U.S. #1 POP 45	"Roses Are Red"	Bobby Vinton
U.S. #1 POP LP	*Modern Sounds in Country. . . .*	Ray Charles
U.S. #1 R&B 45	"I Can't Stop Loving You"	Ray Charles
U.K. #1 POP 45	"I Remember You"	Frank Ifield

WEEK ENDING AUGUST 4		
U.S. #1 POP 45	"Roses Are Red"	Bobby Vinton
U.S. #1 POP LP	*Modern Sounds in Country. . . .*	Ray Charles
U.S. #1 R&B 45	"You'll Lose a Good Thing"	Barbara Lynn
U.K. #1 POP 45	"I Remember You"	Frank Ifield

WEEK ENDING AUGUST 11		
U.S. #1 POP 45	"Breaking Up Is Hard to Do"	Neil Sedaka
U.S. #1 POP LP	*Modern Sounds in Country. . . .*	Ray Charles
U.S. #1 R&B 45	"Wolverton Mountain"	Claude King
U.K. #1 POP 45	"I Remember You"	Frank Ifield

WEEK ENDING AUGUST 18		
U.S. #1 POP 45	"Breaking Up Is Hard to Do"	Neil Sedaka
U.S. #1 POP LP	*Modern Sounds in Country. . . .*	Ray Charles
U.S. #1 R&B 45	"You'll Lose a Good Thing"	Barbara Lynn
U.K. #1 POP 45	"I Remember You"	Frank Ifield

WEEK ENDING AUGUST 25		
U.S. #1 POP 45	"The Loco-Motion"	Little Eva
U.S. #1 POP LP	*Modern Sounds in Country. . . .*	Ray Charles
U.S. #1 R&B 45	"The Loco-Motion"	Little Eva
U.K. #1 POP 45	"I Remember You"	Frank Ifield

SEPTEMBER

8 The novelty rock song "Monster Mash" by **Bobby "Boris" Pickett and the Crypt-Kickers** enters the Hot 100 at #85. A tongue-in-cheek ode to such movie monsters as Dracula and Frankenstein set to a rock & roll beat, the song will remain on the chart for fourteen weeks, reaching Number One on October 20, and staying atop for two weeks. The song will be re-released in the summer of 1970, but will only go as high as #91. In the summer of 1973, however, it reaches #10. Pickett would have two more novelty hits with "Monster's Holiday" (#30 in December 1962) and "Graduation Day" (#88 in June 1963).

11 Seven days after beginning their first recording sessions, the **Beatles** cut two **Lennon-McCartney** originals, "Love Me Do" and "P.S. I Love You," at EMI's St. John's Wood Studio in London. At producer **George Martin**'s insistence, session drummer **Andy White** sits in on the chance that the Beatles' new drummer, **Ringo Starr**, doesn't work out. (He does.) The day's work yields the Beatles' first hit single.

15 **Brian Epstein** brings the **Beatles** to the London offices of *The Daily Mirror* for an interview with **Peter Jones**, who concludes they are "a nothing group."

OCTOBER

5 "Love Me Do" backed with "P.S. I Love You," the **Beatles'** first single, is released in the U.K. on the Parlophone label, and is given its first radio play that evening on the EMI-owned Radio Luxembourg. It will peak at #17 on the U.K. chart in December.

10 BBC, the British radio and television network, bans **Bobby "Boris" Pickett**'s huge American hit, "Monster Mash." Although the song is neither obscene nor particularly controversial—it's about a horror-movie-star record hop—"Monster Mash," like many other songs, is banned under a catch-all regulation that prohibits the broadcasting of anything deemed "offensive."

12 **Little Richard** headlines a concert at New

Brighton Tower, Liverpool; one opening act is the **Beatles**. The once peerless rocker and the soon-to-be-peerless rockers reportedly get along famously.

16 Motown Records launches a two-month package tour of the U.S. in Washington, D.C. The bill features the **Miracles**, **Mary Wells**, the **Supremes**, **Marvin Gaye** and **Little Stevie Wonder**, "the twelve year old who plays piano, drums, organ, banjo, harmonica and sings too." The tour will conclude with a four-night stand at the Apollo Theater in New York City.

21 Top British rock star **Cliff Richard** appears on "The Ed Sullivan Show." Though Richard's singles regularly hit the U.K. Top Ten, his popularity in America would remain marginal until the late Seventies.

23 Twelve-year-old **Steveland Morris Judkins**, renamed **Little Stevie Wonder**, records his first single, "Thank You for Loving Me All the Way," for Motown Records. Blind from birth but proficient on piano, organ, drums and harmonica and an ebullient gospel-styled singer, Wonder is billed as "The Twelve-Year-Old Genius"—an attempt to identify him with **Ray Charles**. Although "Thank You for Loving Me" is unsuccessful, within a year Wonder will have a chart-breaker with "Fingertips, Pt. 1," and will go on to become one of the most important pop musicians of the Sixties, Seventies and Eighties.

24 **James Brown** records *Live at the Apollo, Volume I* at the landmark theater in Harlem, New York City. The album will sell over a million copies—an unprecedented feat for an R&B album—and will later earn a reputation for being one of the finest concert albums ever made. ◆

WEEK ENDING SEPTEMBER 1		
U.S. #1 POP 45	"Sheila"	Tommy Roe
U.S. #1 POP LP	*Modern Sounds in Country . . .*	Ray Charles
U.S. #1 R&B 45	"The Loco-Motion"	Little Eva
U.K. #1 POP 45	"I Remember You"	Frank Ifield

WEEK ENDING SEPTEMBER 8		
U.S. #1 POP 45	"Sheila"	Tommy Roe
U.S. #1 POP LP	*Modern Sounds in Country . . .*	Ray Charles
U.S. #1 R&B 45	"The Loco-Motion"	Little Eva
U.K. #1 POP 45	"I Remember You"	Frank Ifield

WEEK ENDING SEPTEMBER 15		
U.S. #1 POP 45	"Sherry"	The Four Seasons
U.S. #1 POP LP	*Modern Sounds in Country . . .*	Ray Charles
U.S. #1 R&B 45	"Green Onions"	Booker T. and the MG's
U.K. #1 POP 45	"I Remember You"	Frank Ifield

WEEK ENDING SEPTEMBER 22		
U.S. #1 POP 45	"Sherry"	The Four Seasons
U.S. #1 POP LP	*Modern Sounds in Country . . .*	Ray Charles
U.S. #1 R&B 45	"You Beat Me to the Punch"	Mary Wells
U.K. #1 POP 45	"She's Not You"	Elvis Presley

WEEK ENDING SEPTEMBER 29		
U.S. #1 POP 45	"Sherry"	The Four Seasons
U.S. #1 POP LP	*West Side Story*	soundtrack
U.S. #1 R&B 45	"Green Onions"	Booker T. and the MG's
U.K. #1 POP 45	"She's Not You"	Elvis Presley

WEEK ENDING OCTOBER 6		
U.S. #1 POP 45	"Sherry"	The Four Seasons
U.S. #1 POP LP	*West Side Story*	soundtrack
U.S. #1 R&B 45	"Sherry"	The Four Seasons
U.K. #1 POP 45	"She's Not You"	Elvis Presley

WEEK ENDING OCTOBER 13		
U.S. #1 POP 45	"Sherry"	The Four Seasons
U.S. #1 POP LP	*West Side Story*	soundtrack
U.S. #1 R&B 45	"Green Onions"	Booker T. & the MG's
U.K. #1 POP 45	"Telstar"	The Tornadoes

WEEK ENDING OCTOBER 20		
U.S. #1 POP 45	"Monster Mash"	Bobby (Boris) Pickett
U.S. #1 POP LP	*Peter, Paul and Mary*	Peter, Paul and Mary
U.S. #1 R&B 45	"Do You Love Me?"	The Contours
U.K. #1 POP 45	"Telstar"	The Tornadoes

WEEK ENDING OCTOBER 27		
U.S. #1 POP 45	"Monster Mash"	Bobby (Boris) Pickett
U.S. #1 POP LP	*Peter, Paul and Mary*	Peter, Paul and Mary
U.S. #1 R&B 45	"Green Onions"	Booker T. and the MG's
U.K. #1 POP 45	"Telstar"	Tornadoes

NOVEMBER

1 The **Beatles** open a two-week engagement at their old stomping ground, the Star Club in Hamburg, Germany. A recording made on a small, portable tape recorder one evening will be pressed and issued as Lingasong Records' *Live! At the Star Club in Hamburg, Germany, 1962* in 1977. That album will present the Beatles playing such later-recorded numbers as "Roll Over Beethoven," "Kansas City," "Mr. Moonlight," "Matchbox," "Long Tall Sally" and "Everybody's Trying to Be My Baby," as well as such classics as "Be-Bop-a-Lula," "Hippy Hippy Shake" and "Red Sails at Sunset."

9 Motown Records releases the **Miracles'** "You've Really Got a Hold on Me," which will eventually reach #8 on the pop chart in early 1963 and will later be covered by the **Beatles, Gayle McCormick** and **Eddie Money.** This song marks the first production by Miracles lead singer/songwriter **William "Smokey" Robinson,** who would later go on to produce some of Motown's finest moments, such as the **Miracles'** "Tracks of My Tears" and "Mickey's Monkey," and the **Four Tops'** "My Girl."

20 The **Four Seasons'** "Big Girls Don't Cry" is released on Vee Jay Records. It eventually reaches Number One on the pop chart, as does their first—and current—hit, "Sherry." Both songs feature lead singer **Frankie Valli's** falsetto.

DECEMBER

8 After three months, **Alan Freed** leaves Miami's WQAM in order to appear at his payola trial in New York, which begins December 10. On December 22, Freed testifies that on September 29, 1958, he received $2,000 from Cognat Distributors in exchange for a promise to play their records on his New York radio show, and that on February 16, 1958, he'd worked a similar deal with Superior Record Sales Company for $700. Freed pleads guilty to payola charges and is fined $300 and given six months probation.

19 **Berry Gordy, Jr.,** brings the Tamla-Motown Rock & Roll Show to New York City's Apollo Theater for a ten-day run. The show features the **Supremes,** the **Miracles, Marvin Gaye, Mary Wells** and the **Contours.**

22 The **Rebels'** instrumental "Wild Weekend," covered in the seventies by **Roxy Music** saxophonist **Andy Mackay,** is released on Swan Records. It will reach #8 on the pop chart.

The **Tornadoes'** "Telstar" becomes the first record by a British group to top the American pop chart. The song was inspired by the launching of the Telstar commu-satellite in July. It is the only significant American hit for the organ-dominated instrumental group,

although such follow-up recordings as "Globe Trotter," "Robot" and "The Ice Cream Man" make the British Top Twenty in the coming year.

30 Pop singer **Brenda Lee** is slightly injured when she runs into her burning Nashville home to rescue her poodle, Cee Cee. But it is too late for Cee Cee: the pet, who has toured the world with Lee, has succumbed to smoke inhalation. The home is destroyed by fire. ◆

WEEK ENDING NOVEMBER 3		
U.S. #1 POP 45	"He's a Rebel"	The Crystals
U.S. #1 POP LP	*Peter, Paul and Mary*	Peter, Paul and Mary
U.S. #1 R&B 45	"Do You Love Me?"	The Contours
U.K. #1 POP 45	"Telstar"	The Tornadoes

WEEK ENDING NOVEMBER 10		
U.S. #1 POP 45	"He's a Rebel"	The Crystals
U.S. #1 POP LP	*Peter, Paul and Mary*	Peter, Paul and Mary
U.S. #1 R&B 45	"Do You Love Me?"	The Contours
U.K. #1 POP 45	"Telstar"	The Tornadoes

WEEK ENDING NOVEMBER 17		
U.S. #1 POP 45	"Big Girls Don't Cry"	The Four Seasons
U.S. #1 POP LP	*Peter, Paul and Mary*	Peter, Paul and Mary
U.S. #1 R&B 45	"Big Girls Don't Cry"	The Four Seasons
U.K. #1 POP 45	"Lovesick Blues"	Frank Ifield

WEEK ENDING NOVEMBER 24		
U.S. #1 POP 45	"Big Girls Don't Cry"	The Four Seasons
U.S. #1 POP LP	*Peter, Paul and Mary*	Peter, Paul and Mary
U.S. #1 R&B 45	"Big Girls Don't Cry"	The Four Seasons
U.K. #1 POP 45	"Lovesick Blues"	Frank Ifield

WEEK ENDING DECEMBER 1		
U.S. #1 POP 45	"Big Girls Don't Cry"	The Four Seasons
U.S. #1 POP LP	*My Son, the Folk Singer*	Allan Sherman
U.S. #1 R&B 45	"Big Girls Don't Cry"	The Four Seasons
U.K. #1 POP 45	"Lovesick Blues"	Frank Ifield

WEEK ENDING DECEMBER 8		
U.S. #1 POP 45	"Big Girls Don't Cry"	The Four Seasons
U.S. #1 POP LP	*My Son, the Folk Singer*	Allan Sherman
U.S. #1 R&B 45	"Release Me"	"Little Esther" Phillips
U.K. #1 POP 45	"Lovesick Blues"	Frank Ifield

WEEK ENDING DECEMBER 15		
U.S. #1 POP 45	"Big Girls Don't Cry"	The Four Seasons
U.S. #1 POP LP	*The First Family*	Vaughan Meader
U.S. #1 R&B 45	"You Are My Sunshine"	Ray Charles
U.K. #1 POP 45	"Lovesick Blues"	Frank Ifield

WEEK ENDING DECEMBER 22		
U.S. #1 POP 45	"Telstar"	The Tornadoes
U.S. #1 POP LP	*The First Family*	Vaughan Meader
U.S. #1 R&B 45	"Release Me"	"Little Esther" Phillips
U.K. #1 POP 45	"Return to Sender"	Elvis Presley

WEEK ENDING DECEMBER 29		
U.S. #1 POP 45	"Telstar"	The Tornadoes
U.S. #1 POP LP	*The First Family*	Vaughan Meader
U.S. #1 R&B 45	"You Are My Sunshine"	Ray Charles
U.K. #1 POP 45	"Return to Sender"	Elvis Presley

1963

The last year before the Beatles blitzed America and redefined pop and rock music. Although Motown, Phil Spector and the Beach Boys were still making good, often great, rock & roll hits, there were also the schlocky novelties like "Sukiyaki" and "Hey Paula." The album charts were still frequently dominated by Andy Williams and Frank Fontaine—another bit of pop tradition the Beatles would help to change forever. There weren't really any movements, only trends—like the hot-rod-song trend kicked off by the Beach Boys' "Little Deuce Coupe." Their record company, Capitol, sent disc jockeys and record retailers a glossary of hot-rod terms. Ironically, the hot-rod trend displaced the surf-anthem trend the Beach Boys themselves had fostered—and which, a year before, had caused Capitol to send out a glossary of surfing terms to music-business song pushers.

But there was one movement—in the sense that movements run deeper, more seriously and politically than mere fads. It was the folk movement, again. In March, folksingers gathered to protest ABC-TV's banning of Pete Seeger and the Weavers from the first network folk-music show, "Hootenanny," because of their "radical" political beliefs. Who knew then that soon the term *radical* would lose its quotation marks? After he performed at Town Hall, *Billboard* raved that Bob Dylan was "the stuff of which legends are made." A month later, Dylan walked off "The Ed Sullivan Show," again, due to censorship, this time of his song "Talkin' John Birch Society Blues." A few months later, Dylan made his sensational debut at the Newport Folk Festival. A few months after *that*, the hootenanny craze spread across the country. Phil Ochs—one of the most recalcitrantly radical of the folkies—could be found serenading customers at a New Jersey shopping center. By year's end, Peter, Paul and Mary had introduced the mass pop audience to Dylan's "Blowin' in the Wind" and "Don't Think Twice, It's Alright."

Meanwhile, across the ocean, the Beatles had become a sensation, the Rolling Stones landed a recording contract after a long stand at London's Crawdaddy Club. But despite their phenomenal rise in Britain, the Beatles failed to excite American record executives, and Capitol Records, the U.S. sister company of the Beatles' EMI Records label, refused to release "Please Please Me" and "From Me to You." It was left to tiny independent Swan Records to release the U. S. debut, "She Loves You." Due to several industry vagaries, mainly Swan's microscopic promotional budget, it wasn't a hit—yet. But shortly after the Beatles capped off the year with two first-places in the *New Musical Express* popularity poll, a Royal Command Performance and the honor of being called "the greatest composers since Beethoven" by London's *Sunday Times,* Capitol released "I Want to Hold Your Hand" just before 1963 became 1964—just before things began to change, forever.

JANUARY

1 The **Beatles** begin a five-day tour of Scotland to promote their first record, "Love Me Do."

2 Duke Records of Houston releases **Bobby "Blue" Bland**'s "That's the Way Love Is," his second R&B Number One and third Top Forty single.

5 "As it stands today, there's virtually no difference between rock & roll, pop and rhythm & blues," **Leonard Chess**, cofounder of Chess Records, tells *Billboard*. "The music has completely overlapped."

7 Gary "U.S." Bonds files a $100,000 suit against **Chubby Checker**, charging that Checker "stole" Bonds' "Quarter to Three" and turned it into "Dancin' Party," "a flagrant imitation," Bonds claims, "made to deceive and confuse the public and unlawfully capitalize on the popularity of 'Quarter to Three.'" The suit will be settled out of court.

11 The Whiskey-A-Go-Go opens its doors on Sunset Boulevard in Los Angeles, the first rock club in that city. In the next decade or more, the Whisky will be a popular meeting place for the record industry and a good place to be seen if getting into the industry is one's objective. The **Doors**, among others, will get their start there.

12 **Bob Dylan** records a radio play, "Madhouse on Castle Street," for the BBC in London. For a $1,000 fee, he portrays a hobo and sings "Blowin' in the Wind" and "Swan on the River" (an original composition he will never put on wax).

Parlophone releases "Please Please Me" backed with "Ask Me Why," the **Beatles**' second British single. Within two months, it will hit #2 on the U.K. chart, yet it will not appear on the U.S. chart for another year.

The **Cascades**, a vocal quintet from San Diego, California, make their chart debut with "Rhythm of the Rain." Their biggest hit, it will go to #3 on the pop chart and #7 on the R&B chart.

FEBRUARY

2 **Helen Shapiro**—who catapulted to fame throughout the U.K. two years ago with such hits as "Don't Treat Me Like a Child" when she was fourteen years old—opens a tour of England at the Gaumont Theater in Bradford. Her support act is the **Beatles**, on their first tour of their home country.

9 **Ruby and the Romantics**' "Our Day Will Come" enters the pop chart. The debut release for this Akron, Ohio, group (a male quartet called the **Supremes** until joined by **Ruby Nash**), it will hit Number One on both the pop and the R&B charts in

March, making it the group's biggest hit, followed by "My Summer Love" and "Hey There Lonely Boy."

Doo-wop group **Shep and the Limelites** enter the Hot 100 for the last time with "Remember Baby," which enters the chart at #91 and drops out next week. Their biggest hit (they had six Hot 100 entries in all) was "Daddy's Home," which reached #2 in early 1961.

11 The **Beatles** record "I Saw Her Standing There," "Boys," "Do You Want to Know a Secret," "There's a Place," "Twist and Shout" and other songs for their first British album, *Please Please Me* (to be released on March 22), at EMI's Abbey Road studios in London.

16 British band the **Tornadoes**, who hit Number One a few months ago with the space-surf instrumental "Telstar," enter the Hot 100 for the second and last time with another instrumental, "Ridin' the Wind," which will peak at #63 in its five weeks on the chart.

23 Motown singer **Mary Wells'** "Laughing Boy" becomes her sixth Hot 100 entry. The song will peak at #15 in its nine weeks on the chart.

The **Chiffons**' "He's So Fine" enters the pop chart on its way to Number One. It is the second pop chart appearance for this female vocal quartet from the Bronx, New York, and their biggest (it went to Number One on the R&B chart as well), fol-

lowed by "One Fine Day" (#5 pop, #6 R&B in June 1963). "He's So Fine," written by the Chiffons' manager, **Ronald Mack**, will return to the news when in 1976 a court finds **George Harrison** guilty of "unknowingly plagiarizing the song in his 'My Sweet Lord.'"

25 Vee Jay Records, the small Chicago-based label, releases the first **Beatles** record in the U.S.A., "Please Please Me" backed with "Ask Me Why." In spite of "Please Please Me" being a smash hit in England, virtually no one notices it in America (perhaps because Vee Jay credits the record to "The Beattles"). ◆

WEEK ENDING JANUARY 5		
U.S. #1 POP 45	"Telstar"	The Tornadoes
U.S. #1 POP LP	*The First Family*	Vaughan Meader
U.S. #1 R&B 45	"Release Me"	"Little Esther" Phillips
U.K. #1 POP 45	"The Next Time"/"Bachelor Boy"	Cliff Richard

WEEK ENDING JANUARY 12		
U.S. #1 POP 45	"Go Away Little Girl"	Steve Lawrence
U.S. #1 POP LP	*The First Family*	Vaughan Meader
U.S. #1 R&B 45	"You Are My Sunshine"	Ray Charles
U.K. #1 POP 45	"The Next Time"/"Bachelor Boy"	Cliff Richard

WEEK ENDING JANUARY 19		
U.S. #1 POP 45	"Go Away Little Girl"	Steve Lawrence
U.S. #1 POP LP	*The First Family*	Vaughan Meader
U.S. #1 R&B 45	"Two Lovers"	Mary Wells
U.K. #1 POP 45	"The Next Time"/"Bachelor Boy"	Cliff Richard

WEEK ENDING JANUARY 26		
U.S. #1 POP 45	"Walk Right In"	The Rooftop Singers
U.S. #1 POP LP	*The First Family*	Vaughan Meader
U.S. #1 R&B 45	"Two Lovers"	Mary Wells
U.K. #1 POP 45	"Dance On"	The Shadows

WEEK ENDING FEBRUARY 2		
U.S. #1 POP 45	"Walk Right In"	The Rooftop Singers
U.S. #1 POP LP	*The First Family*	Vaughan Meader
U.S. #1 R&B 45	"Two Lovers"	Mary Wells
U.K. #1 POP 45	"Diamonds"	Jet Harris and Tony Meehan

WEEK ENDING FEBRUARY 9		
U.S. #1 POP 45	"Hey Paula"	Paul and Paula
U.S. #1 POP LP	*The First Family*	Vaughan Meader
U.S. #1 R&B 45	"Two Lovers"	Mary Wells
U.K. #1 POP 45	"Diamonds"	Jet Harris and Tony Meehan

WEEK ENDING FEBRUARY 16		
U.S. #1 POP 45	"Hey Paula"	Paul and Paula
U.S. #1 POP LP	*The First Family*	Vaughan Meader
U.S. #1 R&B 45	"You've Really Got a Hold on Me"	The Miracles
U.K. #1 POP 45	"Diamonds"	Jet Harris and Tony Meehan

WEEK ENDING FEBRUARY 23		
U.S. #1 POP 45	"Hey Paula"	Paul and Paula
U.S. #1 POP LP	*The First Family*	Vaughan Meader
U.S. #1 R&B 45	"Hey Paula"	Paul and Paula
U.K. #1 POP 45	"Wayward Wind"	Frank Ifield

MARCH

2 **Chubby Checker** hosts "The Limbo Party" at San Francisco's Cow Palace. His special guests include **Marvin Gaye**, **Lou Christie**, the **Four Seasons**, **Paul and Paula**, **Dick and Dee Dee**, the **Crystals** and **Herb Alpert and the Tijuana Brass**.

5 **Patsy Cline**, the country singer who won crossover popularity with such pop Top Twenty hits as "Walkin' after Midnight," "I Fall to Pieces" and "Crazy," is killed in a single-engine plane crash near Camden, Tennessee. Also killed are country stars **Cowboy Copas** and **Hawkshaw Hawkins**. The musicians were en route to Nashville from St. Louis, where they had performed at a benefit concert for the widow of DJ **Cactus Jack Call**, recently killed in a car crash.

19 Fifty folksingers convene at the Village Gate, a music club in New York City's Greenwich Village, to plan action to be taken against the ABC-TV show "Hootenanny," which has black-listed **Pete Seeger** and the **Weavers** from appearing on the folk-music program because of their leftist politics. **Joan Baez** has already refused to appear on "Hootenanny."

22 EMI-Parlophone releases the **Beatles'** first album, *Please Please Me,* in the U.K. Within three weeks it will hit Number One on the British album chart.

23 **Otis Redding** makes its R&B chart debut with "These Arms of Mine," which will peak at #20. Redding has recorded previously with **Otis and the Shooters**, **Johnny Jenkins and the Pinetoppers** and as a soloist, with only minor success. He was employed as Jenkins' chauffeur when **Jim Steward** of Memphis' Stax Records agreed to let him fill up a few minutes of studio time at the end of a Pinetoppers' session. Redding recorded "These Arms of Mine," his own composition, and thus was introduced as one of the most important and influential voices in soul music.

Jackie Wilson's "Baby Workout" enters the R&B chart, where it will be his fifth Number One. On the pop chart it will peak at #5, making it his second biggest hit (after 1960's "Night").

APRIL

6 **Martha and the Vandellas** make their chart debut with "Come and Get These Memories," which will peak at #6 on the R&B chart and #29 on the pop chart. The Motown female vocal trio led by **Martha Reeves** first recorded as backup singers on several Marvin Gaye records; their group name was derived from *vandal,* for it was said that they stole the limelight from Gaye. Martha and the Vandellas will establish themselves as a mainstay of Sixties pop with such hits as "Heat Wave," "Dancing in the Streets" and "Jimmy Mack."

In spite of a boycott of the program by many of America's most important and popular folksingers, ABC-TV premieres its folk music show "Hootenanny." Taped before student audiences on college campuses around the country, the show is the first of its kind on television. The boycott was initiated when ABC announced that it would not allow performers associated with "radical causes" to appear on its program.

ABC-Paramount announces that it has signed **Fats Domino** away from Imperial Records, for whom he has sold around 60 million records since 1950. ABC will be considerably less fortunate with Domino than Imperial: he will make only a couple of moderate hits for the Nashville-based label.

11 Parlophone releases "From Me to You" backed with "Thank You Girl." The **Beatles'** third single, it will be their first to hit Number One in Britain. Neither side will be released in America until a year later, when Vee Jay will pair "From Me to You" (#41) with "Please Please Me" (#3), and "Thank You Girl" (#35) with "Do You Want to Know a Secret" (#2).

12 **Bob Dylan** performs his first major solo concert at Town Hall in New York City. *Billboard's* review is typical of public reaction to the concert: "Dylan . . . is the stuff of which legends are made. . . . His talent will be around for a long, long time."

14 **Cliff Richard and the Shadows** appear on "The Ed Sullivan Show," performing their current U.K. Number One, "Summer Holiday."

28 **Andrew Loog Oldham**, a nineteen-year-old music-business publicist and former associate of **Brian Epstein**, catches a gig by the **Rolling Stones** at London's Crawdaddy Club, where owner **Giorgio Gomelsky** (future manager for the **Yardbirds** and the **Brian Auger Trinity**, among others) has engaged them regularly. The following day, Oldham will sign the Stones to their first management contract. ◆

WEEK ENDING MARCH 2		
U.S. #1 POP 45	"Walk Like a Man"	The Four Seasons
U.S. #1 POP LP	*The First Family*	Vaughan Meader
U.S. #1 R&B 45	"Hey Paula"	Paul and Paula
U.K. #1 POP 45	"Wayward Wind"	Frank Ifield

WEEK ENDING MARCH 9		
U.S. #1 POP 45	"Walk Like a Man"	The Four Seasons
U.S. #1 POP LP	*The First Family*	Vaughan Meader
U.S. #1 R&B 45	"That's the Way Love Is"	Bobby Bland
U.K. #1 POP 45	"Wayward Wind"	Frank Ifield

WEEK ENDING MARCH 16		
U.S. #1 POP 45	"Walk Like a Man"	The Four Seasons
U.S. #1 POP LP	*Songs I Sing on the Gleason Show*	Frank Fontaine
U.S. #1 R&B 45	"That's the Way Love Is"	Bobby Bland
U.K. #1 POP 45	"Summer Holiday"	Cliff Richard

WEEK ENDING MARCH 23		
U.S. #1 POP 45	"Our Day Will Come"	Ruby and the Romantics
U.S. #1 POP LP	*Songs I Sing on the Gleason Show*	Frank Fontaine
U.S. #1 R&B 45	"Our Day Will Come"	Ruby and the Romantics
U.K. #1 POP 45	"Summer Holiday"	Cliff Richard

WEEK ENDING MARCH 30		
U.S. #1 POP 45	"He's So Fine"	The Chiffons
U.S. #1 POP LP	*Songs I Sing on the Gleason Show*	Frank Fontaine
U.S. #1 R&B 45	"Our Day Will Come"	Ruby and the Romantics
U.K. #1 POP 45	"Foot Tapper"	The Shadows

WEEK ENDING APRIL 6		
U.S. #1 POP 45	"He's So Fine"	The Chiffons
U.S. #1 POP LP	*Songs I Sing on the Gleason Show*	Frank Fontaine
U.S. #1 R&B 45	"He's So Fine"	The Chiffons
U.K. #1 POP 45	"How Do You Do It?"	Gerry and the Pacemakers

WEEK ENDING APRIL 13		
U.S. #1 POP 45	"He's So Fine"	The Chiffons
U.S. #1 POP LP	*Songs I Sing on the Gleason Show*	Frank Fontaine
U.S. #1 R&B 45	"He's So Fine"	The Chiffons
U.K. #1 POP 45	"How Do You Do It?"	Gerry and the Pacemakers

WEEK ENDING APRIL 20		
U.S. #1 POP 45	"He's So Fine"	The Chiffons
U.S. #1 POP LP	*West Side Story*	soundtrack
U.S. #1 R&B 45	"He's So Fine"	The Chiffons
U.K. #1 POP 45	"How Do You Do It?"	Gerry and the Pacemakers

WEEK ENDING APRIL 27		
U.S. #1 POP 45	"I Will Follow Him"	Little Peggy March
U.S. #1 POP LP	*West Side Story*	soundtrack
U.S. #1 R&B 45	"He's So Fine"	The Chiffons
U.K. #1 POP 45	"From Me to You"	The Beatles

MAY

10 At the Olympic Sound Studios in London, the **Rolling Stones**, still a sextet (with pianist **Ian Stewart**), record **Chuck Berry**'s "Come On" and **Willie Dixon**'s "I Want to Be Loved" for their first single. It is not their first recording session (they recorded a demo tape with their friend, engineer **Glyn Johns**, in January), but they are novices, and it is the first time their producer, **Andrew Loog Oldham**, has been in a studio.

12 **Bob Dylan** walks out of dress rehearsals for "The Ed Sullivan Show" when CBS censors tell him he cannot perform his "Talking John Birch Society Blues." On being informed that the song—which mocks the segregationalist and militarist organization—may be libelous, Dylan refuses to appear on the show.

15 The winners of the fifth annual Grammy Awards (for 1962) are announced. Record of the Year is **Tony Bennett**'s "I Left My Heart in San Francisco." **Peter, Paul and Mary**'s "If I Had a Hammer" wins both Best Performance by a Vocal Group and Best Folk Recording. **Bent Fabric**'s "Alley Cat" wins Best Rock & Roll Recording. Best Rhythm & Blues Recording is **Ray Charles**' "I Can't Stop Loving You."

17 The first Monterey Folk Festival gets under way in Monterey, California. High-lights of the three-day festival include performances by **Joan Baez**, **Bob Dylan**, **Pete Seeger**, the **Weavers**, **Peter, Paul and Mary** and **Mance Lipscomb**.

18 The **Beatles** kick off their first headlining tour with a concert at the Grenada Theatre in Slough, England.

21 **Little Stevie Wonder**, who turned thirteen eight days before, records his second album, *The Twelve-Year-Old Genius*, live at a Detroit ballroom. One selection from the album, "Fingertips, Part Two," will become Wonder's first hit, topping both the R&B and the pop charts.

24 **Elmore James** suffers a fatal heart attack in Chicago at age forty-five. The Mississippi-born bluesman, who spent most of his professional life in Chicago, was probably the most influential electric blues guitarist of all time, and his musical progeny include **Brian Jones** and **Keith Richards** of the **Rolling Stones**, **Peter Green** and **Jeremy Spencer** of **Fleetwood Mac**, **Johnny Winter** and **Eric Clapton**.

JUNE

4 Pye Records releases the **Searchers**' debut single, their cover of the **Drifters**' "Sweets for My Sweet," which will hit Number One on the U.K. chart in August, bringing yet another Merseyside group to nationwide popularity.

7 Decca Records of London releases "Come On" backed with "I Want to Be Loved," the **Rolling Stones**' first record. That evening, the group makes its television debut, appearing on "Thank Your Lucky Stars" to play "Come On," a **Chuck Berry** number. The single will peak at #21 on the British chart.

8 "Easier Said Than Done" enters the pop chart, destined to hit Number One on both the pop and the R&B charts. The record is by a group of five Marine Corps officers (four men and a woman) called the **Essex**, who recorded "Easier Said Than Done" for Roulette Records while on leave.

15 "Sukiyaki" by **Kyu Sakamoto**, hits Number One on the pop American chart—the first Japanese song ever to do so. Sakamoto has been a singing star in Japan for five years, with fifteen hit singles and half as many hit albums to his credit. "Sukiyaki," under its original title, "Ue O Mui Te Aruko," was a huge Japanese hit before Capitol Records released it in the U.S., changing the title to one of the few Japanese words Americans would recognize. In spite of the record's success, it will prove to be Sakamoto's only U.S. hit.

29 **Del Shannon**'s "From Me to You" enters the Hot 100—the first song written by **John Lennon** and **Paul McCartney** to do so. Shannon had met the **Beatles** on a recent British tour, where they gave him the tune. Shannon's version will peak at #77 in its four weeks on the chart.

Beach Boy Brian Wilson and his father, **Murray**, have formed their own record production company, *Billboard* reports. The Sea of Tunes Production Company was created to supply readymade recordings of surf music to "any legitimate record company," using both Sea of Tunes artists and repertoire and those belonging to client companies. ◆

WEEK ENDING MAY 4		
U.S. #1 POP 45	"I Will Follow Him"	Little Peggy March
U.S. #1 POP LP	*Days of Wine and Roses*	Andy Williams
U.S. #1 R&B 45	"Baby Workout"	Jackie Wilson
U.K. #1 POP 45	"From Me to You"	The Beatles

WEEK ENDING MAY 11		
U.S. #1 POP 45	"I Will Follow Him"	Little Peggy March
U.S. #1 POP LP	*Days of Wine and Roses*	Andy Williams
U.S. #1 R&B 45	"Baby Workout"	Jackie Wilson
U.K. #1 POP 45	"From Me to You"	The Beatles

WEEK ENDING MAY 18		
U.S. #1 POP 45	"If You Wanna Be Happy"	Jimmy Soul
U.S. #1 POP LP	*Days of Wine and Roses*	Andy Williams
U.S. #1 R&B 45	"Baby Workout"	Jackie Wilson
U.K. #1 POP 45	"From Me to You"	The Beatles

WEEK ENDING MAY 25		
U.S. #1 POP 45	"If You Wanna Be Happy"	Jimmy Soul
U.S. #1 POP LP	*Days of Wine and Roses*	Andy Williams
U.S. #1 R&B 45	"I Will Follow Him"	Little Peggy March
U.K. #1 POP 45	"From Me to You"	The Beatles

WEEK ENDING JUNE 1		
U.S. #1 POP 45	"It's My Party"	Lesley Gore
U.S. #1 POP LP	*Days of Wine and Roses*	Andy Williams
U.S. #1 R&B 45	"If You Wanna Be Happy"	Jimmy Soul
U.K. #1 POP 45	"Do You Want to Know a Secret"	Billy J. Kramer and the Dakotas

WEEK ENDING JUNE 8		
U.S. #1 POP 45	"It's My Party"	Lesley Gore
U.S. #1 POP LP	*Days of Wine and Roses*	Andy Williams
U.S. #1 R&B 45	"Another Saturday Night"	Sam Cooke
U.K. #1 POP 45	"Do You Want to Know a Secret"	Billy J. Kramer and the Dakotas

WEEK ENDING JUNE 15		
U.S. #1 POP 45	"Sukiyaki"	Kyu Sakamoto
U.S. #1 POP LP	*Days of Wine and Roses*	Andy Williams
U.S. #1 R&B 45	"It's My Party"	Lesley Gore
U.K. #1 POP 45	"I Like It"	Gerry and the Pacemakers

WEEK ENDING JUNE 22		
U.S. #1 POP 45	"Sukiyaki"	Kyu Sakamoto
U.S. #1 POP LP	*Days of Wine and Roses*	Andy Williams
U.S. #1 R&B 45	"It's My Party"	Lesley Gore
U.K. #1 POP 45	"I Like It"	Gerry and the Pacemakers

WEEK ENDING JUNE 29		
U.S. #1 POP 45	"Sukiyaki"	Kyu Sakamoto
U.S. #1 POP LP	*Days of Wine and Roses*	Andy Williams
U.S. #1 R&B 45	"It's My Party"	Lesley Gore
U.K. #1 POP 45	"I Like It"	Gerry and the Pacemakers

JULY

1 The **Beatles** record "She Loves You" and "I'll Get You" at EMI's Abbey Road studios in London. Released on a Parlophone single on August 23, "She Loves You" will be the Beatles' second British Number One.

6 Because of their "wildly enthusiastic and loyal" teenage fans, the New York Mets hire several rock & roll acts, including **Chubby Checker** and **Dee Dee Sharp**, to perform before a game with the Pittsburgh Pirates at the Polo Grounds in New York. The Met office explains, "We're making it a Saturday-night show. It's the kind of thing that would seem to appeal to our type of fan."

The **Four Seasons** enter the Hot 100 for the seventh time, with "Candy Girl," which will go as high as #3 in its thirteen weeks on the chart.

26 Motown Records releases the **Miracles'** "Mickey's Monkey." Written and produced by Motown's ace team of **Brian Holland**, **Lamont Dozier** and **Eddie Holland**, "Mickey's Monkey" will peak at #3 on the R&B chart and #8 on the pop chart—the Miracles' third big hit—and help to popularize a new dance, the Monkey, also celebrated in **Major Lance**'s "Monkey Time" (#4 R&B, #8 pop in August).

27 The **Supremes** enter the Hot 100 for the third time with "A Breath-Taking Guy," which will peak at #75 in its seven weeks on the chart. Their next release, "When the Lovelight Starts Shining through His Eyes," will become their biggest hit yet, reaching #23 late this year. The Supremes, of course, will go on to become one of Motown's most successful pop-soul vocal groups.

29 After a four-year hiatus, the Newport Folk Festival reopens in Newport, Rhode Island. This year's festival is notable for the young urban folksingers—"Woody's Children," as **Pete Seeger** calls them (referring to their inspiration, **Woody Guthrie**)—who attract the most attention in the next three days: **Joan Baez**, **Phil Ochs**, **Tom Paxton**, **Ramblin' Jack Elliott**, **Peter, Paul and Mary** and, most especially, **Bob Dylan**, making his Newport debut.

AUGUST

3 The **Beatles** play their last gig at the Cavern, the club where **Brian Epstein** first saw them. On the same day, the Beatles make their first appearance on an American chart when "From Me to You" shows up at #125 on *Billboard*'s Top Two Hundred.

7 *Beach Party,* the original beach movie, premieres. **Frankie Avalon** and ex-Mouseketeer **Annette Funicello** star; **Dick Dale and His Del-Tones** provide the surf beat.

9 "Ready Steady Go," the British Broadcasting Corporation's rock & roll television show, makes its first broadcast.

11 The First Annual Richmond Jazz and Blues Festival opens in Richmond, England. The day's biggest noise is provided by the **Rolling Stones**.

24 **Little Stevie Wonder** is the first artist to make the Number One position on the pop singles chart, the pop albums chart and the R&B singles chart all at one time. In fact, no one before him has made the pop-singles and the pop-albums charts simultaneously, let alone the R&B singles chart too. Wonder's wonders are *The Twelve-Year-Old-Genius* and one selection from that live album, "Fingertips, Part Two."

28 In Washington, D.C., 200,000 black and white demonstrators join the March on Washington to rally for civil rights. **Martin Luther King, Jr.**, delivers his "I Have a Dream" address on the steps of the Lincoln Memorial, and **Mahalia Jackson**, **Joan Baez**, **Bob Dylan**, **Odetta**, **Peter, Paul and Mary** and other prominent musician/activists lead songs of the civil-rights movement.

29 As the hootenanny craze spreads from college campuses to the rest of America, even shopping centers are holding their own "hoots." On this summer day, **Phil Ochs**—who will later become notorious for ascerbic social commentaries like "Small Circle of Friends," "Love Me, I'm a Liberal" and "Draft-Dodger Rag"—serenades the shoppers at New Jersey's Garden State Plaza.   ◆

WEEK	ENDING	JULY 6
U.S. #1 POP 45	"Easier Said Than Done"	The Essex
U.S. #1 POP LP	*Days of Wine and Roses*	Andy Williams
U.S. #1 R&B 45	"Hello Stranger"	Barbara Lewis
U.K. #1 POP 45	"I Like It"	Gerry and the Pacemakers

WEEK	ENDING	JULY 13
U.S. #1 POP 45	"Easier Said Than Done"	The Essex
U.S. #1 POP LP	*Days of Wine and Roses*	Andy Williams
U.S. #1 R&B 45	"Hello Stranger"	Barbara Lewis
U.K. #1 POP 45	"I'm Confessin'"	Frank Ifield

WEEK	ENDING	JULY 20
U.S. #1 POP 45	"Surf City"	Jan and Dean
U.S. #1 POP LP	*Days of Wine and Roses*	Andy Williams
U.S. #1 R&B 45	"Easier Said Than Done"	The Essex
U.K. #1 POP 45	"I'm Confessin'"	Frank Ifield

WEEK	ENDING	JULY 27
U.S. #1 POP 45	"Surf City"	Jan and Dean
U.S. #1 POP LP	*Days of Wine and Roses*	Andy Williams
U.S. #1 R&B 45	"Easier Said Than Done"	The Essex
U.K. #1 POP 45	"I'm Confessin'"	Frank Ifield

WEEK	ENDING	AUGUST 3
U.S. #1 POP 45	"So Much in Love"	The Tymes
U.S. #1 POP LP	*Days of Wine and Roses*	Andy Williams
U.S. #1 R&B 45	"Fingertips, Part Two"	Stevie Wonder
U.K. #1 POP 45	"Sweets for My Sweet"	The Searchers

WEEK	ENDING	AUGUST 10
U.S. #1 POP 45	"Fingertips, Part Two"	Stevie Wonder
U.S. #1 POP LP	*Days of Wine and Roses*	Andy Williams
U.S. #1 R&B 45	"Fingertips, Part Two"	Stevie Wonder
U.K. #1 POP 45	"Sweets for My Sweet"	The Searchers

WEEK	ENDING	AUGUST 17
U.S. #1 POP 45	"Fingertips, Part Two"	Stevie Wonder
U.S. #1 POP LP	*Days of Wine and Roses*	Andy Williams
U.S. #1 R&B 45	"Fingertips, Part Two"	Stevie Wonder
U.K. #1 POP 45	"Sweets for My Sweet"	The Searchers

WEEK	ENDING	AUGUST 24
U.S. #1 POP 45	"Fingertips, Part Two"	Stevie Wonder
U.S. #1 POP LP	*Little Stevie Wonder*	Stevie Wonder
U.S. #1 R&B 45	"Fingertips, Part Two"	Stevie Wonder
U.K. #1 POP 45	"Bad to Me"	Billy J. Kramer and the Dakotas

WEEK	ENDING	AUGUST 31
U.S. #1 POP 45	"My Boyfriend's Back"	The Angels
U.S. #1 POP LP	*My Son, the Nut*	Allan Sherman
U.S. #1 R&B 45	"Fingertips, Part Two"	Stevie Wonder
U.K. #1 POP 45	"Bad to Me"	Billy J. Kramer and the Dakotas

SEPTEMBER

6 Jerry Lee Lewis' contract with Sun Records expires. Within the month, he will sign with Smash, a Nashville-based division of Mercury.

14 Bowing to pressure from folksingers boycotting television's "Hootenanny" program ABC-TV invites **Pete Seeger** to appear on the show, but only if he will sign an oath of loyalty to the United States. Seeger refuses, and ABC will extend its ban on the outspoken leftist musician.

16 The **Beatles**' "She Loves You" backed with "I'll Get You" is released in the U.S. on the small, independent, New York-based Swan label, as Capitol Records—EMI's American affiliate—has refused it, just as it refused "Please Please Me" and "From Me to You." Currently Number One in Britain, "She Loves You" will be ignored in America until early 1964, when it bounds to Number One here too.

21 **Jimmy Gilmer and the Fireballs**' "Sugar Shack" enters the Hot 100, where it will stay for fifteen weeks, peaking at Number One for five weeks starting October 12. On November 29 it will win a gold record. Gilmer will leave after two more minor hits; the **Fireballs** will hit with "Bottle of Wine," #9 in 1967.

27 Parlophone releases **Cilla Black**'s first single, "Love of the Loved," a song written for her by **John Lennon** and **Paul McCartney**. **Brian Epstein** discovered the nineteen-year-old **Priscilla White** at the Cavern Club in Liverpool, where she worked as a coat checker and occasionally sang between band sets. After changing her name and signing her to a management contract, Epstein masterminded a career for her, one which will lead to eleven U.K. Top Ten hits in the next ten years and, in the Seventies, her own television show.

29 The **Everly Brothers** embark on a tour of the British Isles. Supporting the bill are **Bo Diddley** and the **Rolling Stones**—the latter making their first tour of their homeland. As of October 5, **Little Richard** will be joining the bill.

OCTOBER

11 The **Springfields**, who have had five British Top Forty hits in the past three years ("Come on Home" is currently #6 on the U.K. chart), give their first concert at the London Palladium. The trio, made up of **Tom** and **Mary O'Brien** and **Mike Pickworth**, is splitting up to allow Mary to pursue a solo career. Under her stage name, **Dusty Springfield**, she has already sent a solo single, "I Only Want to Be with You," to #4 on the U.K. chart; it will later hit #12 in the U.S. In the remainder of the Sixties, Dusty Springfield will have British and American hits with "I Just Don't Know What to Do with Myself," "Wishin' and Hopin'," "You Don't Have to Say You Love Me," "I Close My Eyes (And Count to Ten)" and "Son of a Preacher Man."

12 Hot-rodding songs are the latest teen fad, observes *Billboard*, replacing surfing songs. Foremost among the souped-up records is "Little Deuce Coupe" (#15 on the pop chart) by that quintessential surf-song group, the **Beach Boys**. Capitol Records (the Beach Boys' label), is supplying DJs and record retailers with a dictionary of hot-rod terms similar to the dictionary of surfing terms the label offered last year.

13 The **Beatles** appear on BBC's "Sunday Night at the London Palladium." Thousands of fans jam the streets adjacent to the theater; hundreds "battle" with police as they attempt to gain admittance to the rehearsal: It is the first full-scale demonstration of Beatlemania. The Beatles' television performance is seen by 15 million British viewers.

24 The **Beatles** embark on their first tour outside of Great Britain—six dates in Sweden, where the newspapers describe their haircuts as "Hamlet-style." The group from Liverpool discovers that Beatlemania extends beyond the shores of Britannia.

27 **Peter, Paul and Mary**, the folksinging trio who, along with **Joan Baez**, have introduced songwriters like **Bob Dylan** to mainstream audiences, hold the top two

positions on the pop album chart with *In the Wind*—which features Dylan's "Blowin' in the Wind" and "Don't Think Twice, It's Alright"—and *Peter, Paul and Mary*, their 1962 debut.

29 ABC Publications unveils the premiere issue of *Hootenanny*, a magazine for folk-music fans, based on the ABC-TV show of the same name. ◆

WEEK ENDING SEPTEMBER 7		
U.S. #1 POP 45	"My Boyfriend's Back"	The Angels
U.S. #1 POP LP	My Son, the Nut	Allan Sherman
U.S. #1 R&B 45	"Heat Wave"	Martha and the Vandellas
U.K. #1 POP 45	"She Loves You"	The Beatles

WEEK ENDING SEPTEMBER 14		
U.S. #1 POP 45	"My Boyfriend's Back"	The Angels
U.S. #1 POP LP	My Son, the Nut	Allan Sherman
U.S. #1 R&B 45	"Heat Wave"	Martha and the Vandellas
U.K. #1 POP 45	"She Loves You"	The Beatles

WEEK ENDING SEPTEMBER 21		
U.S. #1 POP 45	"Blue Velvet"	Bobby Vinton
U.S. #1 POP LP	My Son, the Nut	Allan Sherman
U.S. #1 R&B 45	"Heat Wave"	Martha and the Vandellas
U.K. #1 POP 45	"She Loves You"	The Beatles

WEEK ENDING SEPTEMBER 28		
U.S. #1 POP 45	"Blue Velvet"	Bobby Vinton
U.S. #1 POP LP	My Son, the Nut	Allan Sherman
U.S. #1 R&B 45	"Heat Wave"	Martha and the Vandellas
U.K. #1 POP 45	"She Loves You"	The Beatles

WEEK ENDING OCTOBER 5		
U.S. #1 POP 45	"Blue Velvet"	Bobby Vinton
U.S. #1 POP LP	My Son, the Nut	Allan Sherman
U.S. #1 R&B 45	"Heat Wave"	Martha and the Vandellas
U.K. #1 POP 45	"Do You Love Me?"	Brian Poole and the Tremeloes

WEEK ENDING OCTOBER 12		
U.S. #1 POP 45	"Sugar Shack"	Jimmy Gilmer and the Fireballs
U.S. #1 POP LP	My Son, the Nut	Allan Sherman
U.S. #1 R&B 45	"Cry Baby"	Garnet Mimms & the Enchanters
U.K. #1 POP 45	"Do You Love Me?"	Brian Poole and the Tremeloes

WEEK ENDING OCTOBER 19		
U.S. #1 POP 45	"Sugar Shack"	Jimmy Gilmer and the Fireballs
U.S. #1 POP LP	My Son, the Nut	Allan Sherman
U.S. #1 R&B 45	"Part-Time Love"	Little Johnny Taylor
U.K. #1 POP 45	"Do You Love Me?"	Brian Poole and the Tremeloes

WEEK ENDING OCTOBER 26		
U.S. #1 POP 45	"Sugar Shack"	Jimmy Gilmer and the Fireballs
U.S. #1 POP LP	Peter, Paul and Mary	Peter, Paul and Mary
U.S. #1 R&B 45	"Cry Baby"	Garnet Mimms & the Enchanters
U.K. #1 POP 45	"You'll Never Walk Alone"	Gerry and the Pacemakers

NOVEMBER

1 Playing a concert at the Odeon Theatre in Cheltenham, England, the **Beatles** begin their second headlining tour of England and find that since their first, in May, the country has gone mad. Everywhere they go on the thirty-five-city tour, fans have lined up for two days, sometimes more, for tickets.

2 After complaining, to no avail, that the go-go dancers surrounding him on stage are distracting him, **Dion** walks off stage during a live taping of his performance for the British television show "Ready, Steady, Go" in London.

4 The **Beatles** appear at the Royal Command Performances at the Prince of Wales Theatre in London before a glittering audience that includes the **Queen Mother**, **Princess Margaret** and **Lord Snowden**. "Will people in the cheaper seats clap your hands?" bids **John Lennon**. "All the rest of you, if you'll just rattle your jewelry." The British press will report the next morning that "The Royal Box was stomping."

8 **Dick Clark**'s traveling Caravan of Stars opens its Fall 1963 tour in Teaneck, New Jersey. The bill features **Bobby Vee**, **Brian Hyland**, the **Ronettes**, Little **Eva** and the **Dovells**, among others.

29 The **Beatles**' fifth British single, "I Want to Hold Your Hand" backed with "This Boy," is released by Parlophone Records. Advance orders exceed 700,000, and within three days the record will have sold 1 million copies, making it their second million-seller.

30 Thanks to the interest in American R&B sparked by such British bands as the **Rolling Stones**, the **Yardbirds** and the **Alan Price Combo**, some of the originators of that sound are enjoying revived popularity in Britain: **Chuck Berry** and **Bo Diddley** each have two albums in the U.K. Top Twenty—Berry's *On Stage* and *Chuck Berry*, and Diddley's *Bo Diddley* and *Bo Diddley Is a Gunslinger*.

DECEMBER

14 **Dinah Washington** dies of an overdose of sleeping pills at age thirty-nine in Detroit. Born **Ruth Jones** in Tuscaloosa, Alabama, Washington was a church pianist before she began singing jazz with **Lionel Hampton**'s band. From the late Forties through the Fifties and into the Sixties, she sang a wide variety of material, from blues to country to pop, in a rich, elegant voice. She had numerous R&B and pop hits, most notably "What a Diff'rence a Day Makes," "Unforgettable," "September in the Rain" and, with **Brook Benton**, "Baby (You've Got What It Takes)" and "A Rockin' Good Way."

26 Capitol Records, the EMI-affiliated company that has rejected American rights to every **Beatles** record offered it so far, finally rush-releases "I Want to Hold Your Hand" backed with "I Saw Her Standing There." Within five weeks, it will be the Number One single in the U.S.

27 The music critics of the *London Times* names **John Lennon** and **Paul McCartney** as "The Outstanding Composers of 1963." Two days later, the *Sunday Times'* music critic **Richard Buckle** proclaims the same two songwriters "the greatest composers since Beethoven."

29 The **Weavers**, America's preeminent folk music group, give their farewell concert at Orchestra Hall in Chicago. The vocal quartet was formed in 1949 by **Pete Seeger**, **Ronnie Gilbert**, **Lee Hays** and **Fred Hellerman**. They immediately made a nationwide impact with recordings of **Leadbelly**'s "Goodnight Irene" and the American folk song "On Top of Old Smokey." Blacklisted for their outspoken political views during the McCarthy years, they broke up in 1952 but reunited in 1955 and went on to popularize such songs as "Rock Island Line," "Kisses Sweeter Than Wine," "Wimoweh" and "Guantanamera." Seeger left the

group to pursue a solo career in 1958; he was replaced, in succession, by **Erik Darling**, **Frank Hamilton** and **Bernie Krause**. In 1981, shortly before Hay's death, the original Weavers—whose influence on such folk groups as the **Kingston Trio**, **Peter, Paul and Mary**, even the **Byrds**, has been profound—will join together one last time for a triumphant concert at Carnegie Hall in New York City.

20 *New Musical Express'* Twelfth International Popularity Poll lists British acts at the top of most categories for the first time. The Number One male singer is **Cliff Richard**, the Number One group is the **Beatles**. The Record of the Year is "She Loves You" by the Beatles. ◆

WEEK ENDING NOVEMBER 2		
U.S. #1 POP 45	"Sugar Shack"	Jimmy Gilmer and the Fireballs
U.S. #1 POP LP	*In the Wind*	Peter, Paul and Mary
U.S. #1 R&B 45	"Cry Baby"	Garnett Mimms & the Enchanters
U.K. #1 POP 45	"You'll Never Walk Alone"	Gerry and the Pacemakers

WEEK ENDING NOVEMBER 9		
U.S. #1 POP 45	"Sugar Shack"	Jimmy Gilmer and the Fireballs
U.S. #1 POP LP	*In the Wind*	Peter, Paul and Mary
U.S. #1 R&B 45	"It's All Right"	The Impressions
U.K. #1 POP 45	"You'll Never Walk Alone"	Gerry and the Pacemakers

WEEK ENDING NOVEMBER 16		
U.S. #1 POP 45	"Deep Purple"	Nino Tempo and April Stevens
U.S. #1 POP LP	*In the Wind*	Peter, Paul and Mary
U.S. #1 R&B 45	"It's All Right"	The Impressions
U.K. #1 POP 45	"You'll Never Walk Alone"	Gerry and the Pacemakers

WEEK ENDING NOVEMBER 23		
U.S. #1 POP 45	"I'm Leaving It Up to You"	Dale and Grace
U.S. #1 POP LP	*In the Wind*	Peter, Paul and Mary
U.S. #1 R&B 45	"Sugar Shack"	Jimmy Gilmer and the Fireballs
U.K. #1 POP 45	"You'll Never Walk Alone"	Gerry and the Pacemakers

WEEK ENDING NOVEMBER 30		
U.S. #1 POP 45	"I'm Leaving It Up to You"	Dale and Grace
U.S. #1 POP LP	*In the Wind*	Peter, Paul and Mary
U.S. #1 R&B 45	"Sugar Shack"	Jimmy Gilmer and the Fireballs
U.K. #1 POP 45	"She Loves You"	The Beatles

WEEK ENDING DECEMBER 7		
U.S. #1 POP 45	"Dominique"	The Singing Nun
U.S. #1 POP LP	*The Singing Nun*	The Singing Nun
U.S. #1 R&B 45	"Sugar Shack"	Jimmy Gilmer and the Fireballs
U.K. #1 POP 45	"I Want to Hold Your Hand"	The Beatles

WEEK ENDING DECEMBER 14		
U.S. #1 POP 45	"Dominique"	The Singing Nun
U.S. #1 POP LP	*The Singing Nun*	The Singing Nun
U.S. #1 R&B 45	"Sugar Shack"	Jimmy Gilmer and the Fireballs
U.K. #1 POP 45	"I Want to Hold Your Hand"	The Beatles

WEEK ENDING DECEMBER 21		
U.S. #1 POP 45	"Dominique"	The Singing Nun
U.S. #1 POP LP	*The Singing Nun*	The Singing Nun
U.S. #1 R&B 45	"Sugar Shack"	Jimmy Gilmer and the Fireballs
U.K. #1 POP 45	"I Want to Hold Your Hand"	The Beatles

WEEK ENDING DECEMBER 28		
U.S. #1 POP 45	"Dominique"	The Singing Nun
U.S. #1 POP LP	*The Singing Nun*	The Singing Nun
U.S. #1 R&B 45	"Sugar Shack"	Jimmy Gilmer and the Fireballs
U.K. #1 POP 45	"I Want to Hold Your Hand"	The Beatles

1964

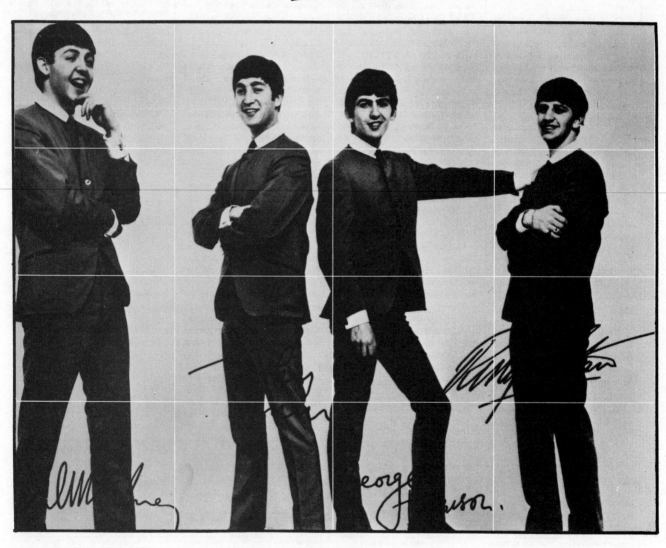

The year of rock & roll's first gigantic renaissance: Beatlemania and the British Invasion. Beatlemania had begun in Britain the year before around February 1963, when Vee Jay Records released the first American Beatles disc, "Please Please Me." It failed to chart, as did Vee Jay's *Introducing the Beatles* in July. So why, then, did Beatlemania break out in America as it did, virtually overnight, at the beginning of 1964?

In the intervening years, we've become so inured to the Beatles' lasting greatness that to look back and wonder why seems almost ludicrous. There are several theories. The Beatles might have filled a cultural-social gap that nobody had realized even existed. John F. Kennedy, America's youngest, most popular and exciting president, had been assassinated in November 1963, and the civil-rights movement prompted a national reevaluation of priorities. For the time being at least, the compulsive topicality of the folk movement was *too* serious, depressing even, in the wake of the shattering of the New Frontier's dreams. And apparently, the classic rock & roll that *was* being made by Phil Spector, Motown and the Beach Boys just wasn't enough.

Into this void came the Beatles. It was important that they were British: if, as it seems now, our pop salvation *had* to come from abroad, what better place than England? Over there, rock & roll held a curious place in the lives of young Britishers like the Beatles. They, like most of America's youth, grew up with and through the whole of rock & roll history, but the British—locked into a class-ruled society much more rigid and gray than America's—must have seen rock & roll's promise of liberation as something desperately crucial, a kind of fun treated much more seriously than American kids could conceive. Yet it sounded anything *but* serious. The Beatles made rock & roll music with a mixture of earnestness and ebullience, innocence and abandon, and it sounded like perfect, classic teenage rock & roll noise. We could not know that they had a whole lot more to offer.

Musically, the Beatles were the first group to embody just about all of rock's stylistic eclecticism: in their sound were Chuck Berry and Little Richard, Elvis and rockabilly, vocal harmonies from doo-wop to the Everly Brothers and the Beach Boys, the yearning romance of Buddy Holly and the Phil Spector-Brill Building girl-group pop. Because of all this, the Beatles became the first rock *group* to achieve the kind of status previously reserved for such solo performer-icons as Elvis Presley. They did what Buddy Holly had died too soon to do: ensured that from then on, rock performers could be independent, self-contained artistic entities, composing and performing their own music.

After them came the British Invasion, carrying to America's shores the nasty white-Negroisms of the Rolling Stones and the Animals, the ephemeral trash-thrash of the Dave Clark Five and the Swinging Blue Jeans, the equally ephemeral sweetness-and-light of Herman's Hermits, the jangly proto-Byrds folk-rock of the Searchers, the somber romanticism of Gerry and the Pacemakers . . . and more, much more. Not to mention the Who, the Kinks and the Yardbirds.

Perhaps the best testament of what the Beatles meant to America's youth at the time—and perhaps the best answer to the question "why?"—was provided by the *New York Times,* which reviewed the Beatles' Carnegie Hall performance by crediting the screaming 3,000-strong audience with giving the performance, and the Beatles for supplying the accompaniment. The *Times* probably didn't realize just how close to home it had hit.

1 The BBC broadcasts the first "Top of the Pops" TV rock show. The show features the top rock acts of the day.

3 "The Jack Paar Show" features a clip of the **Beatles**, taken from a concert in Bournemouth, England.

4 *Billboard* gives the **Beatles**' "I Want to Hold Your Hand" a spotlight review: "This is the hot British group that has struck gold overseas. Side A is a driving rocker with surf-on-the-Thames sound and strong vocal work from the group."

In a trade survey, record company executives predict that 1964 will be "the hottest year yet" for the American record industry. Meanwhile, the British Board of Trade announces that Britain's "record boom" reached a new high in October 1963, making 1963 the British record industry's "Golden Year."

6 The **Rolling Stones** begin their first headlining British tour in Harrow. The **Ronettes** are the opening act.

7 Harmonica player **Cyril Davies**, a pioneer

of the early Sixties British blues movement that eventually spawned such bands as the **Rolling Stones**, dies in London of leukemia at age thirty-two. Davies had begun his musical career playing blues and jazz with another British blues-rock pioneer, **Alexis Korner**, in the mid-Fifties. The two formed **Blues Incorporated** in 1961; the band gave such musicians as **Charlie Watts**, **Ginger Baker**, **Jack Bruce** and **Long John Baldry** their first professional jobs. In 1962, Davies left Blues Incorporated to form his own R&B All-Stars and scored one minor hit single, "Country Line Special" backed with "Chicago Calling."

15 Vee Jay Records brings suit against Capitol and Swan Records in New York over manufacturing and distribution rights to **Beatles** recordings.

In Chicago, Capitol Records is granted an injuction restraining Vee Jay Records from further manufacturing, distributing, advertising or otherwise disposing of recordings by the **Beatles**. Vee Jay had released the Beatles' "Please Please Me," *Introducing the Beatles* and *The Beatles and Frank Ifield*; Swan had released "She Loves You"; and Capitol had released "I

Want to Hold Your Hand" and will soon release *Meet the Beatles*.

17 Vee Jay Records files a motion in New York Supreme Court against Capitol Records and Swan Records, seeking an injuction restraining Capitol and Swan from manufacturing, distributing, advertising or otherwise disposing of recordings by the **Beatles**.

18 The **Beatles**' "I Want to Hold Your Hand" enters the Hot 100 at #45, just ten days after its release, making it

the fastest-breaking and the fastest-selling single in Capitol Records history. "I Want to Hold Your Hand" had gone gold in just ten days. This same day, *Billboard* gives a spotlight review to the **Dave Clark Five**'s "Glad All Over": "Here's a rocking, romping group vocal effect much akin to the Liverpool sound and the **Beatles** school. Solid beat and echo quality make it a strong possibility."

20 The album *Meet the Beatles* is released in the U.S. on Capitol Records. It's the British group's U.S. debut LP.

23 The **Rolling Stones** fly back to the U.K. upon completion of their first U.S. tour.

25 Producer **Phil Spector** appears as a panelist on the British rate-a-record TV show "Juke Box Jury."

27 The **Rolling Stones** appear as judges on the British rate-a-record TV show "Juke Box Jury." Their somewhat impolite behavior on the show causes a furor in the British press. ♦

WEEK ENDING JANUARY 4

U.S. #1 POP 45	"There! I've Said It Again"	Bobby Vinton
U.S. #1 POP LP	*The Singing Nun*	The Singing Nun
U.S. #1 R&B 45	—	—
U.K. #1 POP 45	"I Want to Hold Your Hand"	The Beatles

WEEK ENDING JANUARY 11

U.S. #1 POP 45	"There! I've Said It Again"	Bobby Vinton
U.S. #1 POP LP	*The Singing Nun*	The Singing Nun
U.S. #1 R&B 45	—	—
U.K. #1 POP 45	"I Want to Hold Your Hand"	The Beatles

WEEK ENDING JANUARY 18

U.S. #1 POP 45	"There! I've Said It Again"	Bobby Vinton
U.S. #1 POP LP	*The Singing Nun*	The Singing Nun
U.S. #1 R&B 45	—	—
U.K. #1 POP 45	"Glad All Over"	The Dave Clark Five

WEEK ENDING JANUARY 25

U.S. #1 POP 45	"There! I've Said It Again"	Bobby Vinton
U.S. #1 POP LP	*The Singing Nun*	The Singing Nun
U.S. #1 R&B 45	—	—
U.K. #1 POP 45	"Glad All Over"	The Dave Clark Five

1 Cameo-Parkway Records releases the **Swans**' "The Boy with the Beatle Hair," and Capitol releases **Donna Lynn**'s "My Boyfriend Got a Beatle Haircut."

Billboard reports that Elektra Records has signed folksinger **Phil Ochs**, already a favorite on New York's Greenwich Village scene, where he was discovered by Elektra A&R man **Paul Rothchild** (who would later go on to produce the **Doors**' records for the label).

Indiana governor **Matthew Welsh** declares that the song "Louie Louie" by the **Kingsmen** (currently #6 on the Hot 100) is "pornographic" and asks that the Indiana Broadcasters Association ban the disc. Although radio stations claim that it is impossible to accurately discern the lyrics from "the unintelligible rendition as performed by the Kingsmen," Governor Welsh claims his "ears tingled" when he heard the song, sent to him by a Frankfort, Indiana, high-school student.

7 The **Beatles** arrive at New York's Kennedy Airport for their first appearance on "The Ed Sullivan Show." They are greeted by thousands of screaming fans in what is the first demonstration of Beatlemania in America.

8 **Martha and the Vandellas**' "Live Wire" enters the Hot 100 at #98. It will remain on the charts for seven weeks, eventually taking the Motown vocal group as high as #42.

Max Firetag, publisher of "Louie Louie" as recorded by the **Kingsmen** for Wand Records, denies Indiana governor **Matthew Welsh**'s claim that the song is "pornographic" and offers $1,000 to anyone who can find anything "suggestive" in the song's lyrics.

The **Temptations**' "The Way You Do the Things You Do" is released on Motown. The **Beach Boys**' "Fun, Fun, Fun" is released on Capitol. The album *Beatlemania in the USA!* by the **Liverpools** is released on Wyngate Records.

11 The **Beatles** play their first American concert for a general (not television) audience at the outdoor Washington Coliseum in Washington, D.C. That evening they attend a masked ball as guests of the British ambassador to the United States, **Sir David Ormsby-Gore, Lord Harlech**. The British prime minister, **Sir Alec Douglas-Home**, was to have attended the ball, but postpones his arrival in Washington so as not to be upstaged by the Beatles.

12 The **Beatles** play two concerts at New York City's Carnegie Hall. *The New York Times'* review of the second performance credits the 3,000 fans in the audience as giving the concert and the Beatles as merely their accompanists.

15 A *Billboard* story headlined "U.S. ROCKS & REELS FROM BEATLES INVASION—BEATLES BEGIN NEW BRITISH ARTIST PUSH" goes on to report that "Great Britain hasn't been as influential in American affairs since 1775. The sensational impact of the **Beatles** on England's former colonies has had the explosive effect of sending major and independent firms here scrambling for more and more British product." Among those British acts being signed are: **Gerry and the Pacemakers**, the **Dave Clark Five**, **Cliff Richard**, the **Shadows**, the **Searchers**, **Billy J. Kramer and the Dakotas**, the **Fourmost**, the **Swinging Blue Jeans**, **Kathy Kirby**, **Dusty Springfield**, the **Caravelles**, **Frank Ifield**, and **Freddie and the Dreamers**. Not yet signed, but hot in England, are the **Rolling Stones**, the **Hollies** and the **Merseybeats**. Meanwhile, *Billboard*, for the first time in its history, lists one act—the **Beatles**—with five songs in the Hot 100 (all climbing on the chart): "I Want to Hold Your Hand," "I Saw Her Standing There," "She Loves You," "Please Please Me" and "My Bonnie." The Beatles also have three albums on the Top LPs chart: *Meet the Beatles* (at Number One), *Introducing the Beatles* and *With the Beatles*.

Sam Cooke, who normally tours eight months per year, announces that he will cut down his performances to two months per year in order to concentrate on songwriting and on building his record labels, Sar and Derby.

29 **Betty Everett**'s "The Shoop Shoop Song (It's in His Kiss)" enters the pop chart, where it will peak at #6—the biggest hit for the soul singer who introduced "You're No Good" last year. ◆

WEEK ENDING FEBRUARY 1

U.S. #1 POP 45	"I Want to Hold Your Hand"	The Beatles
U.S. #1 POP LP	*The Singing Nun*	The Singing Nun
U.S. #1 R&B 45	—	—
U.K. #1 POP 45	"Needles and Pins"	The Searchers

WEEK ENDING FEBRUARY 8

U.S. #1 POP 45	"I Want to Hold Your Hand"	The Beatles
U.S. #1 POP LP	*The Singing Nun*	The Singing Nun
U.S. #1 R&B 45	—	—
U.K. #1 POP 45	"Needles and Pins"	The Searchers

WEEK ENDING FEBRUARY 15

U.S. #1 POP 45	"I Want to Hold Your Hand"	The Beatles
U.S. #1 POP LP	*Meet the Beatles*	The Beatles
U.S. #1 R&B 45	—	—
U.K. #1 POP 45	"Needles and Pins"	The Searchers

WEEK ENDING FEBRUARY 22

U.S. #1 POP 45	"I Want to Hold Your Hand"	The Beatles
U.S. #1 POP LP	*Meet the Beatles*	The Beatles
U.S. #1 R&B 45	—	—
U.K. #1 POP 45	"Anyone Who Had a Heart"	Cilla Black

WEEK ENDING FEBRUARY 29

U.S. #1 POP 45	"I Want to Hold Your Hand"	The Beatles
U.S. #1 POP LP	*Meet the Beatles*	The Beatles
U.S. #1 R&B 45	—	—
U.K. #1 POP 45	"Anyone Who Had a Heart"	Cilla Black

2 The **Beatles'** "Twist and Shout" backed with "There's a Place" is released in the U.S. on Tollie Records, the fourth label to release Beatles product here.

The **Beatles** begin work on their first feature-length film, *A Hard Day's Night,* in London with director **Richard Lester.**

7 The **Beatles'** "I Want to Hold Your Hand" and "She Loves You" are "neck and neck," according to *Billboard,* in the race for the Number One spot on the singles chart. The former, on Capitol, has an edge over the latter, on Swan, due to Capitol's superior distribution.

Columbia Records is suddenly inundated with requests for heavyweight boxing champ **Cassius Clay's** album, *I Am the Greatest,* released in September 1963 but now in great demand after Clay's defeat of **Sonny Liston** on February 25. Columbia expects to sell 500,000 copies. Says Clay: "I'm better and prettier than **Chubby Checker.**"

11 **Elvis Presley's** fourteenth movie, *Kissin' Cousins,* is released by Metro-Goldwyn-Mayer. The movie, in which Presley plays a double role, features the songs "Kissin' Cousins" and "Once Is Enough."

13 *Cash Box* lists four **Beatles** singles in the top four positions on its chart: "She Loves You," "I Want to Hold Your Hand," "Please Please Me" and "Twist and Shout." So far *Meet the Beatles* has sold over 3½ million copies in the U.S.—the most in recording history to date.

14 *Billboard* reports that **Beatles** records have claimed sixty percent of the singles market.

16 Capitol releases the **Beatles'** "Can't Buy Me Love" backed with "You Can't Do That." Capitol has already reported advance orders for the single of over 1½ million. By now, advance orders for the **Beatles'** "Can't Buy Me Love" have topped the 2 million mark in the U.S.

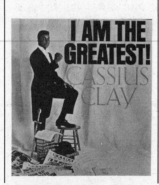

Alan Freed is charged with income-tax evasion, the grand jury indictment stemming from the earlier payola investigation that ruined the career of the ex-DJ who helped put rock & roll on the map.

21 For the first time in British recording history, all Top Ten singles in the U.K. are by British acts.

25 For the first time in its twelve-year history, Britain's *New Musical Express* has every position in its Top Ten pop chart occupied by a British artist or band.

26 Ex-**Beatles** drummer **Pete Best** flies to the U.S. for an appearance on the TV show "I've Got a Secret" (he does not sing "Do You Want to Know a Secret").

27 The British Invasion spreads around the world: **Beatles** occupy the top six positions in the Australian pop chart.

28 Madame Tussaud's Wax Museum in London announces that the **Beatles** will be cast in wax—the first pop stars to be so honored.

Britain's first "pirate radio station," Radio Caroline, begins broadcasting from a barge at the mouth of the River Thames.

30 The British press reports on the first riotous clash between the mods and the rockers, in Clacton, England. The mods and the rockers are two different youth factions, each differentiated by its own distinctive style of dress, hair, musical taste, etcetera. The mods wear natty suits and ties, **Beatle**-ish hair cuts and are big fans of contemporary bands like the **Who**; the rockers are somewhat related to Britain's Fifties fans, the Teddy Boys, and are something like stylized Fifties "greasers," dressing in leather and riding big motorcycles, as opposed to the mods' little scooters. The late-Seventies film *Quadrophenia,* based on the Who's album of the same name, semifictionalized this era, centering on the constant and often very violent clashes between the mods and the rockers. ◆

WEEK ENDING MARCH 7

U.S. #1 POP 45	"I Want to Hold Your Hand"	The Beatles
U.S. #1 POP LP	*Meet the Beatles*	The Beatles
U.S. #1 R&B 45	—	—
U.K. #1 POP 45	"Anyone Who Had a Heart"	Cilla Black

WEEK ENDING MARCH 14

U.S. #1 POP 45	"I Want to Hold Your Hand"	The Beatles
U.S. #1 POP LP	*Meet the Beatles*	The Beatles
U.S. #1 R&B 45	—	—
U.K. #1 POP 45	"Anyone Who Had a Heart"	Cilla Black

WEEK ENDING MARCH 21

U.S. #1 POP 45	"She Loves You"	The Beatles
U.S. #1 POP LP	*Meet the Beatles*	The Beatles
U.S. #1 R&B 45	—	—
U.K. #1 POP 45	"Little Children"	Billy J. Kramer and the Dakotas

WEEK ENDING MARCH 28

U.S. #1 POP 45	"She Loves You"	The Beatles
U.S. #1 POP LP	*Meet the Beatles*	The Beatles
U.S. #1 R&B 45	—	—
U.K. #1 POP 45	"Can't Buy Me Love"	The Beatles

3 **Bob Dylan** makes his first entry into the British pop chart with "The Times They Are A-Changin'."

4 Girl group the **Ronettes**, produced by **Phil Spector** for his Philles label, enter the Hot 100 with "(The Best Part of) Breakin' Up." Their third hit (after "Be My Baby" and "Baby I Love You" in 1963), it will reach #39.

The **Impressions'** "I'm So Proud" enters the Hot 100, where it will remain for eleven weeks, eventually reaching as high as #14. One of the most consistently successful vocal groups in soul music in the Sixties—especially one *not* on the Motown label (the Impressions record for ABC-Paramount)—the Impressions had once featured singer **Jerry Butler**, who left them in 1958 to pursue a successful solo career. They are now led by singer, guitarist and composer **Curtis Mayfield**, who will leave for his own solo career in 1970.

One-time **Impressions** lead singer **Jerry Butler** enters the Hot 100 with "Giving Up on Love," which will reach #56.

Motown vocal group the **Contours**, whose biggest hit was 1962's "Do You Love Me?," enter the Hot 100 with another dance-craze song (à la "Do You Love Me?" and "Can You Jerk Like Me?," to be released later this year), "Can You Do It?," which will reach #41.

Motown singer **Mary Wells'** biggest hit, "My Guy," enters the Hot 100. The song, written and produced for Wells by **Smokey Robinson** of the **Miracles**, will remain on the chart for fifteen weeks and reach Number One, where it will remain for two weeks.

The **Beatles** hold the top five positions on *Billboard's* Hot 100 with, in order from Number One to #5, "Can't Buy Me Love," "Twist and Shout," "She Loves You," "I Want to Hold Your Hand" and "Please Please Me."

Billboard reports that "just about everyone is tired of the **Beatles**. Disc jockeys are tired of playing the hit group, the writers of trade and consumer publications are tired of writing about them, and the manufacturers of product other than Beatles records are tired of hearing about them. Everyone's tired of the Beatles—except the listening and buying public."

Beechwood Music, a subsidiary of Capitol Records, wins copyright and royalties on the song "Surfin' Bird" by the **Trashmen**

on Garrett Records. The copyright court had earlier found that "Surfin' Bird" was copied from the Beechwood songs "Papa Oom Mow Mow" and "The Bird Is the Word" by the **Rivingtons**.

5 The **Searchers** appear on "The Ed Sullivan Show," becoming the first British Invasion group to appear on the show after the **Beatles**.

9 Capitol and Vee Jay settle their feud over the rights to recordings by the **Beatles** out of court. Capitol wins.

11 **Martha and the Vandellas'** "In My Lonely Room" enters the Hot 100 at #96. It will eventually reach #44.

17 The **Rolling Stones'** debut album, *The Roll-ing Stones,* is released in the U.K. on Decca Records. It will later be released in the U.S. on London Records as *England's Newest Hitmakers.*

25 **Dionne Warwick's** "Walk On By" enters the Hot 100. Her fifth and, to date, biggest hit, it will eventually reach #6 and will remain on the chart for thirteen weeks. This is the second of Warwick's hits to be composed by the songwriting team of **Burt Bacharach** and **Hal David**; the first, "Anyone Who Had a Heart," had reached #8 earlier this year. (**Cilla Black's** version was Number One in the U.K.) Later Warwick hits by Bacharach-David would include "A House Is Not a Home" later this year; "Message to Michael" and "I Just Don't Know What to Do with Myself" in 1966 (the latter would later be covered by **Dusty Springfield** and **Elvis Costello**); "Alfie" and "I Say a Little Prayer" in 1967; "Do You Know the Way to San Jose," "Always Something There to Remind Me" and "Promises, Promises" in 1968; and "This Girl's in Love with You" and "I'll Never Fall in Love Again" in 1969.

Peter and Gordon reach Number One on the U.K. pop chart with "World without Love," a song composed by **Paul McCartney** of the **Beatles**. The duo would also have a couple of more hits before **Gordon Waller** would try an unsuccessful solo career. **Peter Asher**, whose sister **Jane** becomes **Paul McCartney's** girlfriend, would go on to become a staff producer for the Beatles' Apple Records in the late Sixties, then would move to Los Angeles, where he would become a prime mover of the L.A. country-pop scene as manager-producer of **James Taylor** and **Linda Ronstadt**.

26 The **Rolling Stones** perform in London at the *New Musical Express* poll winners' show. ◆

WEEK ENDING APRIL 4		
U.S. #1 POP 45	"Can't Buy Me Love"	The Beatles
U.S. #1 POP LP	*Meet the Beatles*	The Beatles
U.S. #1 R&B 45	—	—
U.K. #1 POP 45	"Can't Buy Me Love"	The Beatles

WEEK ENDING APRIL 11		
U.S. #1 POP 45	"Can't Buy Me Love"	The Beatles
U.S. #1 POP LP	*Meet the Beatles*	The Beatles
U.S. #1 R&B 45	—	—
U.K. #1 POP 45	"Can't Buy Me Love"	The Beatles

WEEK ENDING APRIL 18		
U.S. #1 POP 45	"Can't Buy Me Love"	The Beatles
U.S. #1 POP LP	*Meet the Beatles*	The Beatles
U.S. #1 R&B 45	—	—
U.K. #1 POP 45	"Can't Buy Me Love"	The Beatles

WEEK ENDING APRIL 25		
U.S. #1 POP 45	"Can't Buy Me Love"	The Beatles
U.S. #1 POP LP	*Meet the Beatles*	The Beatles
U.S. #1 R&B 45	—	—
U.K. #1 POP 45	"World without Love"	Peter & Gordon

2 *The Beatles' Second Album* reaches Number One on the U.S. LP chart in its second week of release—the first album ever to reach the top of the chart that quickly.

4 The **Moody Blues** are formed in Birmingham, England, by **Denny Laine**, **Mike Pinder**, **Ray Thomas**, **Clint Warwick** and **Graeme Edge**. Their second single, "Go Now," will reach Number One in the U.K. and #10 in the U.S. in early 1965, but its R&B flavor will become atypical of the band's subsequent output, which, with its emphasis on symphonic structure and Mellotron string sections, will be an important and influential precursor to British art rock and classical rock.

12 Winners of the sixth annual Grammy Awards (for 1963) are announced. Record of the Year is **Henry Mancini**'s "The Days of Wine and Roses," which also wins Song of the Year. Album of the Year is *The Barbra Streisand Album*. Best Performance by a Vocal Group goes to **Peter, Paul and Mary** for the second consecutive year for "Blowin' in the Wind," which also wins them Best Folk Recording for the second year in a row. Best Instrumental Arrangement goes to **Quincy Jones**' "I Can't Stop Loving You" (as recorded by **Count Basie's Orchestra**). Best Rock & Roll Recording is **Nino Tempo and April Stevens**' "Deep Purple." Best Rhythm and Blues Recording is **Ray Charles**' "Busted." Best Gospel Recording is "Dominique" by the **Singing Nun**. Best Comedy Performance is **Allan Sherman**'s "Hello Mudduh, Hello Faddah."

British pirate radio station Radio Atlanta begins broadcasting from a ship anchored off the coast of England in the North Sea. It will later join forces with England's pioneer pirate radio station, Radio Caroline.

14 A *Billboard* article notes that "London Records is preparing a giant promotion on behalf of the **Rolling Stones**, hot British group which has scored so strongly in Britain with its smash single 'Not Fade Away' and album *The Rolling Stones*." The same issue carries a full-page ad from London Records that reads: "WATCH OUT USA . . . HERE THEY ARE! THE ROLLING STONES! THEY'RE GREAT! THEY'RE OUTRAGEOUS! THEY'RE REBELS! THEY SELL! THEY'RE ENGLAND'S HOTTEST— BUT HOTTEST—GROUP!"

The "blue beat" dance craze has taken hold in Cleveland and Detroit in the wake of **Millie Small**'s chart-climbing hit "My Boy Lollipop." According to *Billboard*, the song that is based on Jamaican prereggae ska music, is a smash in Britain. Within one week, Atlantic Records president **Ahmet Ertegun** and engineer **Tom Dowd** will fly to Jamaica and return with forty newly recorded sides by ska acts like the **Blues Busters**, the **Charmers**, **Stranger Cole**, the **Maytals** and others.

23 **Millie Small**'s "My Boy Lollipop," already a hit in the U.K., enters the Hot 100 in the U.S. It will remain on the chart for twelve weeks, eventually reaching #2, becoming the first—and one of the only—ska-inflected song to enter the U.S. chart. The song's success will spark anticipation of a ska trend, which will never really take off in America.

27 Flamboyant British R&B singer **Screaming Lord Sutch** launches his own pirate radio station, Radio Sutch. Sutch, one of the most colorful and publicity-conscious figures in the history of British rock, wore long hair before it was fashionable; occasionally employed such musicians as **Jimmy Page**, **Jeff Beck**, **Nicky Hopkins** and **Ritchie Blackmore** in his backing band, the **Savages**, and stole his name and stage act—including a grand entrance in a coffin for his only real hit, "Hands of Jack the Ripper"—from American R&B star **Screamin' Jay Hawkins**.

29 Britain's *Daily Mirror* says of the **Rolling Stones**: "Everything seems to be against them on the surface. They are called the ugliest group in Britain. They are not looked on very kindly by most parents or by adults in general. They are even used to the type of article that asks big brother if he would let his sister go out with one of them."

30 The Jamaican government, in cooperation with Atlantic Records, announces that it will send six dancers to demonstrate the ska at New Jersey's Palisades Amusement Park in June. The Jamaican government will later send artists like **Jimmy Cliff** and **Byron Lee and the Dragonnaires** to the New York World's Fair in the summer of 1964.

The **Dave Clark Five**, a British Invasion group who have already had two Top Ten hits with "Glad All Over" and "Bits and Pieces," perform at Carnegie Hall in New York. The following night they will appear on "The Ed Sullivan Show." ◆

WEEK ENDING MAY 2

U.S. #1 POP 45	"Can't Buy Me Love"	The Beatles
U.S. #1 POP LP	*The Beatles' Second Album*	The Beatles
U.S. #1 R&B 45	—	—
U.K. #1 POP 45	"World without Love"	Peter & Gordon

WEEK ENDING MAY 9

U.S. #1 POP 45	"Hello, Dolly!"	Louis Armstrong
U.S. #1 POP LP	*The Beatles' Second Album*	The Beatles
U.S. #1 R&B 45	—	—
U.K. #1 POP 45	"Don't Throw Your Love Away"	The Searchers

WEEK ENDING MAY 16

U.S. #1 POP 45	"My Guy"	Mary Wells
U.S. #1 POP LP	*The Beatles' Second Album*	The Beatles
U.S. #1 R&B 45	—	—
U.K. #1 POP 45	"Don't Throw Your Love Away"	The Searchers

WEEK ENDING MAY 23

U.S. #1 POP 45	"My Guy"	Mary Wells
U.S. #1 POP LP	*The Beatles' Second Album*	The Beatles
U.S. #1 R&B 45	—	—
U.K. #1 POP 45	"Juliet"	The Four Pennies

WEEK ENDING MAY 30

U.S. #1 POP 45	"Love Me Do"	The Beatles
U.S. #1 POP LP	*The Beatles' Second Album*	The Beatles
U.S. #1 R&B 45	—	—
U.K. #1 POP 45	"You're My World"	Cilla Black

1 The **Rolling Stones** land at JFK International Airport in New York for their first U.S. tour, which begins the next day at the Manning Bowl, a high-school football stadium in Lynn, Massachusetts, a suburb of Boston. Local garage band **Barry and the Remains** open this show. Later in the tour, they will be supported by **Bobby Vee**, the **Chiffons**, **Bobby Goldsboro** and **Bobby Comstock**.

2 Of the **Rolling Stones**, who've arrived in New York City to begin their first American tour, the Associated Press says: "They are dirtier and streakier and more dissheveled than the **Beatles**, and in some places, they are more popular than the Beatles."

3 The **Beatles** embark on a world tour, leaving behind drummer **Ringo Starr**, who has collapsed from exhaustion. He will rejoin the group June 12 in Australia. In the meantime, deputy drummer **Jimmy Nicol** fills in.

The **Rolling Stones** make their American TV debut on "The Hollywood Palace," with **Dean Martin** hosting.

5 Vocalion Records in England releases "Liza Jane," the debut record by **David Jones and the King Bees**. Jones will become famous in the Seventies under a new name (conceived to avoid confusion with future **Monkee Davy Jones**)—**David Bowie**.

6 Music Publishers Holding Company in New York announces that it has contracted folksinger **Bob Dylan** to publish a songbook for harmonica.

A full-page ad taken out in six music trades by anonymous advertisers "in the public interest" reads, "Watch the **Rolling Stones** crush the **Beatles**!"

10 The **Rolling Stones** realize a dream as they record in Chicago's Chess Recording Studio. Blues giants **Willie Dixon** and **Muddy Waters** and original rock & roller **Chuck Berry**—Chess artists all—drop by. Each of the band members is a big American blues and R&B fan; in fact, as a teenager, **Mick Jagger** frequently wrote away to Chess to order records that were not available in England.

Capitol Records releases the single "A Hard Day's Night" by the **Beatles**, and the album of the same name.

13 Police battalions are called in Cleveland to

quiet some 3,000 "shrieking Beatles fans," when girls arrive early to challenge others who'd been waiting in line all night for tickets to the **Beatles**' Cleveland concert on September 15. The sponsor of the concert, radio station WHK, had sent 5,000 letters to Cleveland girls selected by computer for first choice of seats.

15 Peter and Gordon arrive in the U.S. for their first stateside tour. Four days later, they will perform at the New York World's Fair.

20 "Mixed Up, Shook Up Girl," by obscure soul vocal group **Patty and the Emblems** (on Herald Records), enters the Hot 100. It will eventually reach #37 and will be covered in a hit version in the late Seventies by New York band **Mink DeVille**.

The **Rolling Stones**' "Not Fade Away" is released in the U.S. on London Records.

Billboard reports that Atlantic Records is beginning to promote a ska dance craze in the U.S. The label has signed **Bryon Lee** and has made a deal with Arthur Murray Dance Studios to help promote "the Jamaican dance."

24 **Sam Cooke** begins a two-week engagement at New York's Copacabana Club. A seventy-foot billboard announcing the engagement is erected in New York City's Times Square.

27 The **Drifters**' last Top Ten hit, "Under the Boardwalk," enters the Hot 100. It will reach #4 and will be covered by the **Rolling Stones**.

Billboard gives the **Rolling Stones** LP *England's Newest Hitmakers* a pop spotlight review: "This, the latest of the British invaders, is the toughest sounding. . . ." In the singles spotlight reviews, the Stones' "Tell Me" is described as "Neanderthal music at its best. A crude beat and the rockiest sound around." ◆

WEEK ENDING JUNE 6

U.S. #1 POP 45	"Chapel of Love"	The Dixie Cups
U.S. #1 POP LP	*Hello, Dolly!*	original cast
U.S. #1 R&B 45	—	—
U.K. #1 POP 45	"You're My World"	Cilla Black

WEEK ENDING JUNE 13

U.S. #1 POP 45	"Chapel of Love"	The Dixie Cups
U.S. #1 POP LP	*Hello, Dolly!*	Louis Armstrong
U.S. #1 R&B 45	—	—
U.K. #1 POP 45	"You're My World"	Cilla Black

WEEK ENDING JUNE 20

U.S. #1 POP 45	"Chapel of Love"	The Dixie Cups
U.S. #1 POP LP	*Hello, Dolly!*	Louis Armstrong
U.S. #1 R&B 45	—	—
U.K. #1 POP 45	"You're My World"	Cilla Black

WEEK ENDING JUNE 27

U.S. #1 POP 45	"A World without Love"	Peter and Gordon
U.S. #1 POP LP	*Hello, Dolly!*	Louis Armstrong
U.S. #1 R&B 45	—	—
U.K. #1 POP 45	"It's Over"	Ray Orbison

1 United Artists rushes advance copies of the soundtrack to the upcoming first **Beatles** film, *A Hard Day's Night,* to radio stations, in order to beat out Capitol, who plan to release an album consisting of the seven songs featured in the film.

4 *Billboard* reports that **Brian Epstein** claims that the **Beatles'** upcoming U.S. tour (August 19 to September 20) is a complete sell-out. **Rolling Stones** tour agent **Eric Easton** reports that his band netted $100,000 on their recent U.S. tour.

6 The **Beatles'** first film, *A Hard Day's Night,* premieres in London at the Pavillion Theater at 9 p.m. At 9 a.m., huge mobs of fans had begun to gather outside the theater, with 200 policemen summoned to control the crowd. Among those attending the premiere are **Princess Margaret** and the **Earl of Snowden.** Tickets are priced at forty-two dollars, with proceeds going to the Variety Clubs of Great Britain. In the U.K., the film's soundtrack album has already sold 1½ million copies in nine days—reportedly the fastest-selling LP in British recording history. The Beatles themselves do not see the film until four days later.

10 *Off the Beatle Track,* an album of instrumental versions of **Beatles** songs produced by **George Martin,** is released on Capitol Records. The same day, the single "A Hard Day's Night" and album of the same name are released, in the U.K. on Parlophone. The album was released in the U.S. in late June.

11 The **Supremes,** destined to become Motown's most successful recording artists, enter the Hot 100 with "Where Did Our Love Go?" It will remain on the chart for fourteen weeks and will reach Number One, beginning an incredible string of smash hits that will see them chalk up five more Number One hits within the next year and a half.

Bobby Freeman's last big hit (his first was 1958's "Do You Wanna Dance"), "C'mon and Swim," enters the Hot 100. It will reach #5.

12 The **Beatles'** *A Hard Day's Night* enters the LP chart at #12. Due to album sales, the film will make enough money for United Artists to cover the costs of making it, even before the film opens in the U.S. — a first in the entertainment industry. Capitol claims the LP, which has sold over 1 million copies in four days, is the fastest seller in history.

17 Britain's *New Musical Express* reports that **Frank Sinatra, Bing Crosby, Sammy Davis, Jr.,** and **Dean Martin,** calling themselves the Bumblers, have recorded a **Beatles** parody disc.

18 New Orleans-based female vocal trio the **Dixie Cups,** who hit Number One earlier this year with "Chapel of Love," enter the Hot 100 with their second hit, "People Say," which will remain on the chart for nine weeks and will eventually reach #12.

Memphis gospel-soul singer **Solomon Burke** enters the Hot 100 with "Everybody Needs Somebody to Love," which will eventually reach #58 and later will be covered by **Wilson Pickett** and the **Rolling Stones.**

20 **Beatles** records released this week include: the singles "And I Love Her" backed with "If I Fell," and "I'll Cry Instead" backed with "I'm Happy Just to Dance with You," and the album *Something New.*

24 Fans overreact to a **Rolling Stones** concert in Blackpool, England (the town, incidentally, where **Jethro Tull** would be formed some five years later), and cause a riot.

25 *Billboard* reports that England's hottest new group is a band from Newcastle, the **Animals,** whose debut single, "The House of the Rising Sun," (produced by **Mickie Most**) had entered the U.K. chart at #16, jumped to #3 the following week and then to Number One. To promote the band in the U.S., MGM Records sends boxes of animal crackers wrapped with special promo materials to DJs.

31 Country music singing star **Jim Reeves** dies when a single-engine plane flying him from Arkansas to Nashville crashes in thick fog. He was forty-one years old. One of the first country singers to cross over into the pop market, Reeves had a Number One pop hit in 1953 with "Mexican Joe," and his biggest hit was 1959's "He'll Have to Go." He was voted into the Country Music Hall of Fame in 1967. His hits continued after his death: "It's Nothin' to Me" made the C&W Top Twenty in 1977. Intriguingly, Reeves was also a very popular artist in, of all places, Africa. Nigerian juju star **King Sunny Adé** in 1983 attributed his own use of exotic pedal steel guitar effects to his love of Jim Reeves records.

A **Rolling Stones** concert in Belfast, Northern Ireland, provokes another riot—but this time, the show must be stopped after only twelve minutes. ◆

WEEK ENDING JULY 4

U.S. #1 POP 45	"I Get Around"	The Beach Boys
U.S. #1 POP LP	*Hello, Dolly!*	Louis Armstrong
U.S. #1 R&B 45	—	—
U.K. #1 POP 45	"It's Over"	Roy Orbison

WEEK ENDING JULY 11

U.S. #1 POP 45	"I Get Around"	The Beach Boys
U.S. #1 POP LP	*Hello, Dolly!*	Louis Armstrong
U.S. #1 R&B 45	—	—
U.K. #1 POP 45	"It's Over"	Roy Orbison

WEEK ENDING JULY 18

U.S. #1 POP 45	"Rag Doll"	The Four Seasons
U.S. #1 POP LP	*Hello, Dolly!*	original cast
U.S. #1 R&B 45	—	—
U.K. #1 POP 45	"It's Over"	Roy Orbison
U.K. #1 POP LP	*A Hard Day's Night*	The Beatles

WEEK ENDING JULY 25

U.S. #1 POP 45	"Rag Doll"	The Four Seasons
U.S. #1 POP LP	*A Hard Day's Night*	The Beatles
U.S. #1 R&B 45	—	—
U.K. #1 POP 45	"The House of the Rising Sun"	The Animals
U.K. #1 POP LP	*A Hard Day's Night*	The Beatles

1 Early rockabilly star **Johnny Burnette**, who as a leader of the **Rock & Roll Trio** recorded seminal versions of the classics "Train Kept A-Rollin'" and "You're Sixteen," is killed in a boating accident on California's Clear Lake. He was thirty years old.

The harmonica is making a big comeback, says *Billboard,* as a popular instrument, due to its use by such recording artists as **Stevie Wonder**, the **Rolling Stones**, the **Beatles** and **Bob Dylan**.

7 *Time* magazine headlines its review of the **Beatles** movie *A Hard Day's Night* as BEATLES BLOW IT, and advises readers to "avoid this film at all costs." *Life* magazine's review of the film, on the other hand, notes "some **Marx Brothers** surrealism." One week later, a Los Angeles *Herald-Examiner* review will term the Beatles' performance in the film "amusing and engaging," and the *Los Angeles Times* compares the Beatles to Mack Sennett and the Marx Brothers, a comparison also evoked on August 16 by Bosley Crowther in the *New York Times.*

8 The **Rolling Stones** again cause a riot at one of their concerts — this one in the Hague, Netherlands.

Billboard spotlights a new record by the **Young World Singers** called "Ringo for President." Starr's reaction to his "nomination": "I don't believe I will have the time."

RCA Victor Records reports that Japan is rated the third largest record market in the world, after the U.S. and the U.K.

Eric Burdon, lead singer of the **Animals**, tells *Billboard* that it was the band's fans who first called it "The Animals," back when it was officially known as the **Alan Price Combo**. "The name," explains Burdon, "was probably an association with the kind of music we play, earthy and gutty. It's sort of an animal sound, and on stage we can be pretty wild."

12 **Millie Small**, "The Queen of Bluebeat," performs on "Millie Small Day" at the New York World's Fair, singing her hit "My Boy Lollipop."

15 *Billboard* reports that MGM Studios has signed British Invasion group the **Dave Clark Five** to a film contract. They will go on to star in *Having a Wild Weekend,* directed by **John** *(Deliverance)* **Boorman**.

17 The **Kinks'** classic "You Really Got Me" is released in the U.K. on Pye Records. The song will later be covered fourteen years later by American heavy-metal band **Van Halen**.

19 The **Beatles'** first U.S. tour opens at the Cow Palace in San Francisco. Other acts on the bill include the **Righteous Brothers**, **Jackie DeShannon**, the **Exciters** and **Bill Black's Combo**.

22 Liberty Records reports that the album *The Chipmunks Sing the Beatles* is selling 25,000 copies a day.

24 "As Tears Go By," composed by **Mick Jagger** and **Keith Richards** of the **Rolling Stones** and sung by **Marianne Faithfull**, is released on London Records in the U.K. It will go on to make the British Top Ten and the American Top Forty, establishing her first, brief singing career. She will later become Jagger's girlfriend, then will fall victim to drug addiction, from which she will return in the late Seventies to renew her solo career—and the dulcet tones of the early Faithfull would be replaced by a rougher growl.

28 The **Beatles** play the first of two successive nights at New York's Forest Hills Tennis Stadium. The 15,000 fans at each show demonstrate their affections by showering the band with jellybeans and by screaming so loudly throughout the shows that it's nearly impossible to hear the music.

29 *Billboard* reports that guitar sales in the U.S. and the U.K. have, in the wake of the British Invasion, hit their highest sales peak since 1957, when the emergence of **Elvis Presley** had sparked an earlier sales boom. ◆

WEEK ENDING AUGUST 1

U.S. #1 POP 45	"A Hard Day's Night"	The Beatles
U.S. #1 POP LP	*A Hard Day's Night*	The Beatles
U.S. #1 R&B 45	—	—
U.K. #1 POP 45	"A Hard Day's Night"	The Beatles
U.K. #1 POP LP	*A Hard Day's Night*	The Beatles

WEEK ENDING AUGUST 8

U.S. #1 POP 45	"A Hard Day's Night"	The Beatles
U.S. #1 POP LP	*A Hard Day's Night*	The Beatles
U.S. #1 R&B 45	—	—
U.K. #1 POP 45	"A Hard Day's Night"	The Beatles
U.K. #1 POP LP	*A Hard Day's Night*	The Beatles

WEEK ENDING AUGUST 15

U.S. #1 POP 45	"Everybody Loves Somebody"	Dean Martin
U.S. #1 POP LP	*A Hard Day's Night*	The Beatles
U.S. #1 R&B 45	—	—
U.K. #1 POP 45	"A Hard Day's Night"	The Beatles
U.K. #1 POP LP	*A Hard Day's Night*	The Beatles

WEEK ENDING AUGUST 22

U.S. #1 POP 45	"Where Did Our Love Go?"	The Supremes
U.S. #1 POP LP	*A Hard Day's Night*	The Beatles
U.S. #1 R&B 45	—	—
U.K. #1 POP 45	"A Hard Day's Night"	The Beatles
U.K. #1 POP LP	*A Hard Day's Night*	The Beatles

WEEK ENDING AUGUST 29

U.S. #1 POP 45	"Where Did Our Love Go?"	The Supremes
U.S. #1 POP LP	*A Hard Day's Night*	The Beatles
U.S. #1 R&B 45	—	—
U.K. #1 POP 45	"Do Wah Diddy Diddy"	Manfred Mann
U.K. #1 POP LP	*A Hard Day's Night*	The Beatles

4 The **Animals** make their U.S. performing debut at the Brooklyn Paramount Theater, famous for **Alan Freed**'s rock & roll spectaculars of the late Fifties, which reopens for the group's ten-night stand after being closed down for several years. Other acts appearing with the Animals during the ten days include **Jan and Dean, Bobby Rydell, Del Shannon, Chuck Berry**, the **Dixie Cups, Dee Dee Sharp, Elkie Brooks** and others.

5 **Jerry Butler** and **Betty Everett**'s "Let It Be Me"—one of their two hits as a duo (the other would be "Smile" in December of this year), though each would have long-lasting and successful solo careers—enters the Hot 100. It will remain there for thirteen weeks, eventually reaching #5. The song was written by the Nashville songwriting couple **Beaudleaux and Felice Bryant**, who supplied the **Everly Brothers** with many of their early hits. It was a hit for the Everlys in 1960 and would be a hit for **Glen Campbell** and **Bobbie Gentry** in 1969.

Billboard reports that **President Johnson** has invited the **Four Seasons** to perform at the upcoming Democratic National Convention.

"Mercy, Mercy" by **Don Covay and the Goodtimers** enters the Hot 100. It will eventually reach #35 and will be the biggest hit for Memphis soul singer and composer Covay under his own name in the Sixties. In 1968, Covay's song "Chain of Fools" will become a smash hit in a version sung by **Aretha Franklin**, and will win her a Grammy for Best Rhythm and Blues Performance.

10 **Rod Stewart** records his first single, "Good Morning, Little Schoolgirl," the blues standard by **Willie Dixon**, with **John Paul Jones** on bass. Stewart will go on to sing with the **Jeff Beck Group** and the **Faces**, and will also have a long and successful solo career; Jones will go on to become a member of **Led Zeppelin**.

11 Beatle **George Harrison** forms his own song publishing company, Harrisongs.

12 The **Temptations'** "Girl (Why You Wanna Make Me Blue)" enters the Hot 100. It will eventually reach #26.

13 New York DJ **Murray the K** hosts the conclusion of the ten-day rock & roll extravaganza at Brooklyn's Fox Theater, held to compete with the **Animals'** ten-day run at Brooklyn's Paramount Theater. Acts on the Fox bill include **Marvin Gaye**, the **Miracles**, the **Supremes, Martha and the Vandellas**, the **Contours**, the **Temptations**, the **Searchers, Jay and the Americans**, the **Dovells, Little Anthony and the Imperials**, the **Newbeats**, the **Shangri-Las** and the **Ronettes**. Both shows have tickets priced at $2.50. The Fox show outdraws the concurrent Paramount show.

15 The **Beatles**, performing at Cleveland's Public Auditorium on their U.S. tour, are ordered off the stage for fifteen minutes by police inspector **Carl Baer** of the Cleveland Juvenile Bureau, so that the screaming crowd can calm down.

16 "Shindig!" premieres on ABC-TV. The brainchild of British pop-TV-show producer **Jack Good**, "Shindig!" was inspired by the success of British Invasion groups on the "The Ed Sullivan Show." "Shindig!" features not only a stream of British and American rock and pop performers, but its own cast of go-go dancers and a house band, the **Shindogs**. The first "Shindig!" show features **Sam Cooke**, the **Everly Brothers, Bobby Sherman** and the **Righteous Brothers**. Within a few months, it spawns an imitator, NBC-TV's "Hullabaloo."

19 The **Miracles'** "That's What Love Is Made Of" enters the Hot 100. It will remain on the chart for six weeks and will reach #35.

Marvin Gaye's "Baby Don't You Do It" enters the Hot 100 at #95. It will remain on the chart for nine weeks, eventually reaching #27.

20 The **Beatles**, who finish their U.S. tour this day with a charity show in Brooklyn, make another appearance on "The Ed Sullivan Show."

25 **Brian Epstein**, **Beatles** manager, turns down a £3,500,000 offer from a group of American businessmen to buy out his management contract with the group.

26 According to a *Billboard* market survey, "the teenbeat factor" is up eighteen percent over 1963's record-sales study rate, accounting for forty-five of the top 150 best-selling LPs.

The **Drifters'** "I've Got Sand in My Shoes" enters the Hot 100. It will remain on the chart for seven weeks and will reach #33.

27 California surf-rock band the **Beach Boys** make their first appearance on "The Ed Sullivan Show." ◆

WEEK ENDING SEPTEMBER 5

U.S. #1 POP 45	"The House of the Rising Sun"	The Animals
U.S. #1 POP LP	*A Hard Day's Night*	The Beatles
U.S. #1 R&B 45	—	—
U.K. #1 POP 45	"Do Wah Diddy Diddy"	Manfred Mann
U.K. #1 POP LP	*A Hard Day's Night*	The Beatles

WEEK ENDING SEPTEMBER 12

U.S. #1 POP 45	"The House of the Rising Sun"	The Animals
U.S. #1 POP LP	*A Hard Day's Night*	The Beatles
U.S. #1 R&B 45	—	—
U.K. #1 POP 45	"Have I the Right"	The Honeycombs
U.K. #1 POP LP	*A Hard Day's Night*	The Beatles

WEEK ENDING SEPTEMBER 19

U.S. #1 POP 45	"The House of the Rising Sun"	The Animals
U.S. #1 POP LP	*A Hard Day's Night*	The Beatles
U.S. #1 R&B 45	—	—
U.K. #1 POP 45	"Have I the Right"	The Honeycombs
U.K. #1 POP LP	*A Hard Day's Night*	The Beatles

WEEK ENDING SEPTEMBER 26

U.S. #1 POP 45	"Oh, Pretty Woman"	Roy Orbison
U.S. #1 POP LP	*A Hard Day's Night*	The Beatles
U.S. #1 R&B 45	—	—
U.K. #1 POP 45	"You Really Got Me"	The Kinks
U.K. #1 POP LP	*A Hard Day's Night*	The Beatles

1 Vee Jay Records, capitalizing on material it owns recorded by its two best-selling groups, releases the album *The Beatles Vs. The Four Seasons*. Despite the awesome combined sales might of the two groups involved, the album—consisting of previously released material—will only stay on the LP chart three weeks, reaching only as high as #142 on October 10.

3 The **Supremes**' "Baby Love" enters the Hot 100. It will remain on the chart for thirteen weeks, becoming their second Number One release in a row.

7 The **Beatles** appear on an episode of "Shindig!" taped on location in London. They perform "I'm a Loser," "Kansas City" and "Boys." Also appearing on this show are such British acts as **Sandie Shaw**, **Cilla Black** and **Tommy Quickly**.

9 The **Rolling Stones** announce the cancellation of a planned South African tour due to an anti-apartheid embargo by the British Musicians' Union.

10 "Jump Back" by flamboyant Memphis R&B singer and dance-craze booster **Rufus Thomas** (of "Walkin' the Dog," "Funky Chicken" and "Funky Penguin" fame) enters the Hot 100. It will remain on the chart for seven weeks, eventually reaching #49.

14 In secret, **Rolling Stones**' drummer **Charlie Watts** weds **Shirley Ann Arnold**.

15 Flamboyant British rock singer **Screaming Lord Sutch** places himself on the ballot for election to the British House of Parliament.

17 The **Velvelettes**' "Needle in a Haystack," on Motown's V.I.P. subsidiary, enters the Hot 100. It will remain on the chart for eight weeks, eventually reaching #45. The girl group's only other hit will be "He Was Really Saying Something," which will reach #64 in early 1965, and will be covered by British girl group **Bananarama** in 1982.

18 The **Animals**' first U.K. tour as headliners opens in Manchester, England, with **Carl Perkins**, **Gene Vincent**, **Tommy Tucker** and the **Nashville Teens** as support acts. The two-month tour was prompted by the success of the Animals' single "The House of the Rising Sun," which sold 500,000 copies in the U.K. in two weeks.

24 "Little Marie," one of **Chuck Berry**'s last hits before his early Seventies comeback with his only Number One hit ever, the obscene novelty song "My Ding-a-Ling," enters the Hot 100. It will remain on the charts for six weeks and will reach #54.

R&B singer **Maxine Brown**'s last Top Forty hit, "Oh No Not My Baby," enters the Hot 100. It will remain on the chart for thirteen weeks, and will eventually reach #24. The song will later be covered by both **Manfred Mann** and **Merry Clayton**. Brown's other big hits were "All in My Mind" and "Funny" in 1961.

Dionne Warwick's "Reach Out for Me" enters the Hot 100, where it will stay for eight weeks, eventually reaching #20. It's her third Top Forty hit of the year, the others being "Walk On By" and "You'll Never Get to Heaven."

25 The British music industry awards the **Beatles** five Ivor Novello Awards for 1963: most outstanding contribution to music; "She Loves You," most-broadcast song and best-selling record; "I Want to Hold Your Hand," second best-selling record; and "All My Loving," second most outstanding song.

30 Roy Orbison's "Oh, Pretty Woman" becomes a gold record. His ninth and last Top Ten single, the song had entered the Hot 100 August 29, 1964. The song would remain on the chart a total of fifteen weeks.

31 **Mary Wells**' second and last hit of 1964, "Ain't It the Truth," enters the Hot 100, where it will stay for eight weeks and will eventually reach #45. Her "My Guy" had gone to Number One earlier in the year.

Bob Dylan performs at Philharmonic Hall—now known as Avery Fisher Hall—in New York City. ◆

WEEK ENDING OCTOBER 3

U.S. #1 POP 45	"Oh, Pretty Woman"	Roy Orbison
U.S. #1 POP LP	*A Hard Day's Night*	The Beatles
U.S. #1 R&B 45	—	—
U.K. #1 POP 45	"I'm into Something Good"	Herman's Hermits
U.K. #1 POP LP	*A Hard Day's Night*	The Beatles

WEEK ENDING OCTOBER 10

U.S. #1 POP 45	"Oh, Pretty Woman"	Roy Orbison
U.S. #1 POP LP	*A Hard Day's Night*	The Beatles
U.S. #1 R&B 45	—	—
U.K. #1 POP 45	"Oh, Pretty Woman"	Roy Orbison
U.K. #1 POP LP	*A Hard Day's Night*	The Beatles

WEEK ENDING OCTOBER 17

U.S. #1 POP 45	"Do Wah Diddy Diddy"	Manfred Mann
U.S. #1 POP LP	*A Hard Day's Night*	The Beatles
U.S. #1 R&B 45	—	—
U.K. #1 POP 45	"Oh, Pretty Woman"	Roy Orbison
U.K. #1 POP LP	*A Hard Day's Night*	The Beatles

WEEK ENDING OCTOBER 24

U.S. #1 POP 45	"Do Wah Diddy Diddy"	Manfred Mann
U.S. #1 POP LP	*A Hard Day's Night*	The Beatles
U.S. #1 R&B 45	—	—
U.K. #1 POP 45	"Always Something There to Remind Me"	Sandie Shaw
U.K. #1 POP LP	*A Hard Day's Night*	The Beatles

WEEK ENDING OCTOBER 31

U.S. #1 POP 45	"Baby Love"	The Supremes
U.S. #1 POP LP	*People*	Barbra Streisand
U.S. #1 R&B 45	—	—
U.K. #1 POP 45	"Always Something There to Remind Me"	Sandie Shaw
U.K. #1 POP LP	*A Hard Day's Night*	The Beatles

1 The **Dave Clark Five** appear on "The Ed Sullivan Show" singing their hit "Glad All Over." Sullivan compares them favorably to the **Rolling Stones**, saying that unlike the latter, the DC5 are "nice, neat boys."

2 Almost four years to the day after **Johnny Horton's** death in an auto accident, his *Greatest Hits* album goes gold. Most of Horton's hits were based on historical incidents and related bits of Americana, prime examples being "The Battle of New Orleans" (Number One, 1959), "Johnny Reb" (#54, 1959), "Sink the Bismarck" (#3, 1960), "Johnny Freedom" (#69, 1960) and "North to Alaska" (#4, 1960, and later covered by **NRBQ**).

7 The **Marvelettes'** "Too Many Fish in the Sea" enters the Hot 100, where it will eventually reach #25. It will also go to #15 on the R&B chart.

The **Beach Boys'** "Dance, Dance, Dance" enters the Hot 100, where it will remain for eleven weeks, eventually reaching #8. It is their seventh and last chart entry this year, and the fourth to make the Top Twenty.

14 The **Drifters'** last Top Twenty hit, "Saturday Night at the Movies," enters the Hot 100, where it will remain for nine weeks, eventually reaching #18.

The **Supremes'** "Come See about Me" enters the Hot 100, where it will remain for fourteen weeks, eventually becoming their third release in a row to reach Number One.

R&B singer **Chuck Jackson**, one-time lead vocalist of doo-wop group the **Del-Vikings** (of "Come Go with Me" fame), enters the Hot 100 with his version of the **Skyliners'** 1959 hit "Since I Don't Have You," which will stay on the chart for eight weeks, eventually reaching #47. Jackson will go on to have a few more Top 100 hits on his own and in duets with **Maxine Brown**.

18 The **Supremes** appear on "Shindig!" singing "Baby Love" and "Come See about Me," and the **Righteous Brothers** appear on the same show performing "Little Latin Lupe Lu."

21 Motown's **Marvin Gaye** enters the Hot 100 for the fourth and last time this year with "How Sweet It Is (To Be Loved by You)," which will remain on the chart for fourteen weeks, eventually reaching #6. The song will later become a hit in a version by pop-folk singer/songwriter **James Taylor** in the mid Seventies.

23 The **Rolling Stones** show up late for the BBC radio shows "Top Gear" and "Saturday Club" and are banned by the BBC.

Beatles records released this week include the album *The Beatles Story* on Capitol, and the single "I Feel Fine" backed with "She's a Woman" on Capitol.

24 Manx Radio, Britain's first land-based commerical radio station, begins broadcasting from a moveable "caravan" studio.

27 **Mick Jagger** of the **Rolling Stones** is fined £16 for driving offenses in Tottenhall, England.

The **Beatles'** single "I Feel Fine" and album *Beatles for Sale* are released in the U.K. on Capitol Records.

28 "Leader of the Pack" by girl trio the **Shangri-Las** reaches Number One on the U.S. pop chart. The song, a tragic love song to the leader of a motorcycle gang, becomes a fondly remembered piece of pop culture for its melodramatic production and story line, which incorporates motorcycle rev-up and crashing sounds at appropriate moments.

The **Four Tops'** second hit, "Without the One You Love" (the first was "Baby I Need Your Loving," which had entered the chart August 15, 1964, and eventually reached #11), enters the Hot 100. It will remain there for five weeks, eventually reaching #43. They will, of course, go on to become one of Motown's more successful male vocal groups, with a total of six Top Ten records.

"The Price," by Memphis gospel-soul singer **Solomon Burke**, enters the Hot 100, where it will remain for five weeks, eventually reaching #57.

Soul singer **Betty Everett** enters the Hot 100 for the fourth time in her career with "Getting Mighty Crowded," which will remain on the chart for six weeks, eventually reaching #65. The song was written by **Van McCoy**, at the time a house composer/arranger for Everett's label, Vee Jay; he would go on to become a prime mover of the disco movement in the Seventies with such hits as "The Hustle." "Getting Mighty Crowded" would be covered by **Elvis Costello** in the late Seventies. ♦

WEEK ENDING NOVEMBER 7

U.S. #1 POP 45	"Baby Love"	The Supremes
U.S. #1 POP LP	*People*	Barbra Streisand
U.S. #1 R&B 45	—	—
U.K. #1 POP 45	"Always Something There to Remind Me"	Sandie Shaw
U.K. #1 POP LP	*A Hard Day's Night*	The Beatles

WEEK ENDING NOVEMBER 14

U.S. #1 POP 45	"Baby Love"	The Supremes
U.S. #1 POP LP	*People*	Barbra Streisand
U.S. #1 R&B 45	—	—
U.K. #1 POP 45	"Oh, Pretty Woman"	Roy Orbison
U.K. #1 POP LP	*A Hard Day's Night*	The Beatles

WEEK ENDING NOVEMBER 21

U.S. #1 POP 45	"Baby Love"	The Supremes
U.S. #1 POP LP	*People*	Barbra Streisand
U.S. #1 R&B 45	—	—
U.K. #1 POP 45	"Baby Love"	The Supremes
U.K. #1 POP LP	*A Hard Day's Night*	The Beatles

WEEK ENDING NOVEMBER 28

U.S. #1 POP 45	"Leader of the Pack"	The Shangri-Las
U.S. #1 POP LP	*People*	Barbra Streisand
U.S. #1 R&B 45	—	—
U.K. #1 POP 45	"Baby Love"	The Supremes
U.K. #1 POP LP	*A Hard Day's Night*	The Beatles

4 The **Beatles** Fan Club in England announces that its current membership now totals 65,000.

5 Motown girl group **Martha and the Vandellas** enter the Hot 100 for the fourth time this year with "Wild One," which will remain on the chart for seven weeks, eventually reaching #34.

11 **Sam Cooke**, one of the most popular and influential R&B singers of his generation, dies under violent and mysterious circumstances in Los Angeles. According to court testimony, Cooke—at the time married to his high-school sweetheart, **Barbara Campbell**—picked up a twenty-two-year-old woman named **Elisa Boyer** at a party this night. He promised her a ride home, but instead took her to a Los Angeles motel. Boyer claimed that Cooke forced her into the motel room and began ripping her clothes off. Boyer managed to escape, with Cooke's clothes, while he was in the bathroom. She claimed Cooke pursued her, dressed only in a sports coat and shoes. While she called police from a nearby phone booth, Cooke began pounding on the door of the office of the motel's manager, fifty-five-year-old **Bertha Franklin**, demanding to know Boyer's whereabouts. Cooke allegedly broke the door open, assaulted Franklin, who shot him three times, and kept coming at Franklin, who then beat Cooke with a stick. By the time police arrive, Cooke is dead.

12 Capitol's "documentary" album *The Beatles Story* enters the U.S. LP chart at #97. It will rise to #7 and will go gold on December 31, 1964.

The **Miracles** enter the Hot 100

for the fourth time this year with "Come On, Do the Jerk," which will remain on the chart for eight weeks, eventually reaching #50. One week later, another Motown-associated record based on the Jerk dance craze, the **Contours**' "Can You Jerk Like Me?," will enter the Hot 100, where it will remain for seven weeks, eventually reaching #47.

18 Funeral services are held in Chicago for **Sam Cooke**. Hundreds of distraught fans break the glass doors of, and cause other damage to, the A. R. Leak Funeral Home, where Cooke's body is on display in a glass-covered coffin. Among Cooke's big hits were "Cupid," "You Send Me," "Bring It On Home to Me," "Chain Gang," "Twistin' the Night Away," "Having a Party" (later covered by **Southside Johnny and the Asbury Jukes**) and "Wonderful World" (later covered by **Art Garfunkel**).

19 "Downtown," the first U.S. hit by British pop singer **Petula Clark**, enters the Hot 100, where it will remain for fifteen weeks. It will hit

Number One January 23, 1965, and will stay atop the charts for two weeks. Clark will go on to have five more Top Ten hits in the Sixties, including "I Know a Place" (#3, 1965), "My Love" (#1, 1965), "I Couldn't Live without Your Love" (#9, 1966), "This Is My Song" (#3, 1967) and "Don't Sleep in the Subway" (#5, 1967). "Downtown" would be covered in the late Seventies by the **B-52's**.

"Hold What You've Got," the first hit record by Memphis soul singer **Joe Tex**, enters the Hot 100, where it will remain for eleven weeks, reaching #5 — the highest position Tex will hit on the charts until 1972, when "I Gotcha" will hit #2.

23 The **Beach Boys** make their first appearance on "Shindig!," singing "Little Saint Nick," "Dance, Dance, Dance," "Johnny B. Goode" and "Monster Mash."

24 The **Beatles**' series of Christmas concerts opens at London's Hammersmith Odeon.

25 George Harrison's girlfriend **Patti Boyd** is attacked by female Beatle fans at one of the **Beatles**' Christmas shows in London. It seems the fans were resentful of Patti's place in George Harrison's life.

31 The **Beatles**' single "I Feel Fine" and album *Beatles '65* are certified gold. ◆

WEEK ENDING DECEMBER 5

U.S. #1 POP 45	"Ringo"	Lorne Greene
U.S. #1 POP LP	*The Beach Boys' Concert*	The Beach Boys
U.S. #1 R&B 45	—	—
U.K. #1 POP 45	"Little Red Rooster"	The Rolling Stones
U.K. #1 POP LP	*A Hard Day's Night*	The Beatles

WEEK ENDING DECEMBER 12

U.S. #1 POP 45	"Mr. Lonely"	Bobby Vinton
U.S. #1 POP LP	*The Beach Boys' Concert*	The Beach Boys
U.S. #1 R&B 45	—	—
U.K. #1 POP 45	"I Feel Fine"	The Beatles
U.K. #1 POP LP	*Beatles for Sale*	The Beatles

WEEK ENDING DECEMBER 19

U.S. #1 POP 45	"Come See about Me"	The Supremes
U.S. #1 POP LP	*The Beach Boys' Concert*	The Beach Boys
U.S. #1 R&B 45	—	—
U.K. #1 POP 45	"I Feel Fine"	The Beatles
U.K. #1 POP LP	*Beatles for Sale*	The Beatles

WEEK ENDING DECEMBER 26

U.S. #1 POP 45	"I Feel Fine"	The Beatles
U.S. #1 POP LP	*The Beach Boys' Concert*	The Beach Boys
U.S. #1 R&B 45	—	—
U.K. #1 POP 45	"I Feel Fine"	The Beatles
U.K. #1 POP LP	*Beatles for Sale*	The Beatles

1965

The Beatles, and their British Invasion counterparts, kept coming and coming. And this year, America began responding. As testament to rock & roll's growing stature, American kids could watch the latest British and American salvos in the rock wars every week on two network-TV rock shows, "Shindig!" and "Hullabaloo."

The Byrds, obviously influenced by British bands like the Searchers, hit big with their jangly, sweetly harmonized version of Bob Dylan's "Mr. Tambourine Man." This inspired Dylan to "go electric" himself—first in the studio in June by recording the withering, epochal "Like a Rolling Stone"; then onstage in July with his controversial appearance at the Newport Folk Festival, where he razed the barriers between folk and rock. "Like a Rolling Stone" was not only classic rock & roll, it was a benediction of sorts: the folk movement, in the form of its biggest star, had wielded its influence decisively on rock & roll.

The Lovin' Spoonful, on the other hand, emerged with a lighter, cuter, poppier—more Beatlesque, one might say—brand of folk-rock in "Do You Believe in Magic," the title of which served as an apt rhetorical statement of what rock & roll helped put in the air, what an entire generation of youth was sensing.

In San Francisco, another kind of magic began weaving its spell, as Ken Kesey and his Merry Pranksters reinvented the Beatnik myth, staged the first acid tests and got psychedelia off the ground. America's first and most important localized rock scene took shape with the emergence of the Charlatans, the Jefferson Airplane, the Great Society, the Grateful Dead, the first Fillmore shows and the first dance-concert-happenings by the Family Dog.

But the most widespread reaction to the British Invasion in America was garage rock, an unselfconscious celebration of fun that had been presaged last year by the Kingsmen's hit "Louie Louie." Garage rock's roots actually went back to 1961, when Paul Revere and the Raiders entered the charts with "Like, Long Hair." By 1965, the Raiders were just one of many rough-edged, energetic, relatively untutored regional bands bashing out their crude, ragged-but-right versions of British rock or American R&B or whatever struck their fancies as an appropriate expression of being a modern American teenager. Most were obscure one-shot outfits who'd make their one claim to fame and never be heard from again. Many of them wore Beatles-style haircuts and formed Beatles-style lineups. Fittingly, one of 1965's last great garage-rock hits, the Knickerbockers' "Lies," was a stunningly accurate impersonation of the Beatles. But there was also the Strangeloves' "I Want Candy"—not just a timely revival of the Bo Diddley beat, but the first rock & roll use of virtually uncut African polyrhythms (though the Tokens' "The Lion Sleeps Tonight" had beat them to Afro-pop fusion). And the Sir Douglas Quintet's "She's about a Mover," the Gentrys' "Keep on Dancing," Sam the Sham and the Pharaohs' "Wooly Bully" and the Castaways' "Liar Liar" evolved a whole subgenre based on the now-classic sound of Farfisa and Vox compact electronic organs, first introduced by the Animals on "The House of the Rising Sun."

In 1965, there were two other crucial attitudes that completed the *zeitgeist* of a world of youth infested by the magic of rock & roll, the music that could set them free: alienation from an adult world and a growing sense of generational bonding with other youths. The wearing of long hair, first seen as a joke with the arrival of the Beatles, became a serious issue. Even garage rock produced a comment on it: Boston garage rockers the Barbarians' "Are You a Boy or Are You a Girl?" But it was two British bands who made the anthemic statements about those two crucial attitudes: the Rolling Stones with "(I Can't Get No) Satisfaction" and the Who with "My Generation."

By the end of the year, even the relentlessly cheery and innocent Beatles had gotten serious with *Rubber Soul.* When they topped the charts with "Yesterday," even adults took notice.

1 England's *New Musical Express* reports that the U.S. government, for undisclosed reasons, has denied working visas to British rock bands. This means the cancellation of tours by groups like the **Nashville Teens**, the **Zombies** and the **Hullabaloos**, who are already in New York with DJ **Murray the K** of New York's WMCA.

Them, a rock band from Belfast, Northern Ireland, enters the *New Musical Express* chart with their first hit, a version of blues standard "Baby Please Don't Go." In the *NME* profile, guitarist **Bobby Harrison** is named as Them's leader, rather than singer **Van Morrison**, who is now generally considered to have been the band's driving force.

4 Fender Guitars is sold to CBS for $13 million. **Leo Fender**, founder of Fender Guitars, was a pioneer in the development of the solid-body electric guitar, developing the original Fender, the Broadcaster (later the Telecaster) in the late Forties. Fender guitars, along with Gibson's, are a favorite brand among rock & rollers, the most popular models being the Telecaster (the signature instrument of **Steve Cropper**, **James Burton**, **Roy Buchanan** and others), the Stratocaster (most famously associated with **Jimi Hendrix**) and the Jazz-master and Jaguar, popularized by surf-rock bands like the **Ventures**. Fender's Precision and Jazz basses have also become industry standards.

12 "Hullabaloo" premieres on NBC-TV. Featured acts include host **Jack Jones**, the **New Christy Minstrels**, comedian **Woody Allen**, actress **Joey Heatherton**, and a segment from London in which **Brian Epstein** presents the **Zombies** and **Gerry and the Pacemakers**.

15 In a *New Musical Express* interview, New York DJ **Murray the K**—also known as the "Fifth Beatle" for his constant PR campaigns on their behalf—states that "outside of the **Beatles**, British bands can't carry a show by themselves."

17 **Rolling Stones** drummer **Charlie Watts'** book, *Ode to a High Flying Bird*, a tribute to bebop jazz saxophone giant **Charlie "Yardbird" Parker**, is published in London by Beat Publications. At a press conference on the same day before the Stones leave for an Australian tour with **Roy Orbison**, Watts is asked who Parker is. His reply: "I think he plays for the **Yardbirds**."

The **Rolling Stones** record "The Last Time" (their first **Jagger-Richards**-composed A side) and "Play with Fire" at RCA's Hollywood Studios in Los Angeles, with **Dave Hassinger** engineering and **Phil Spector** playing acoustic guitar on "Play with Fire."

20 **Alan Freed**—who, as a disc jockey in the mid- to late-Fifties, played as big a role as any one person in helping promote the rise of rock & roll and rhythm & blues, then saw his career shattered by the

payola scandals—dies of uremia in Palm Springs, California.

The **Rolling Stones** and the **Kinks** make their first appearance on ABC-TV's "Shindig!" Also appearing on this night's show are the **Dave Clark Five**, **Petula Clark**, **Gerry and the Pacemakers**, **Bobby Vee** and **Bobby Sherman**.

21 The **Animals** cancel a show scheduled for New York's Apollo Theater after the U.S. Immigration Department, continuing its crackdown on British bands, forces the band to leave the theater. Their only New York appearance is on "The Ed Sullivan Show," where—ironically enough—they perform "Don't Let Me Be Misunderstood," which is officially released in the U.K. a week later.

The **Rolling Stones** and **Roy Orbison** arrive in Sydney, Australia, to begin a tour of Down Under.

28 The **Who** make their first appearance on the British TV rock show "Ready Steady Go!" With the studio audience packed with mods by **Who** managers **Kit Lambert** and **Pete Stamp**, the Who go over big.

29 During a concert in London, pop-rock singer **P. J. Proby** splits his trousers onstage, thus significantly increasing his "naughty" reputation. On February 1, he is banned by Britain's ABC theater chain for his new habit of purposely splitting his trousers onstage for dramatic effect. ◆

WEEK ENDING JANUARY 2

U.S. #1 POP 45	"I Feel Fine"	The Beatles
U.S. #1 POP LP	*Roustabout*	Elvis Presley
U.K. #1 POP 45	"I Feel Fine"	The Beatles
U.K. #1 POP LP	*Beatles for Sale*	The Beatles

WEEK ENDING JANUARY 9

U.S. #1 POP 45	"I Feel Fine"	The Beatles
U.S. #1 POP LP	*Beatles '65*	The Beatles
U.K. #1 POP 45	"I Feel Fine"	The Beatles
U.K. #1 POP LP	*Beatles for Sale*	The Beatles

WEEK ENDING JANUARY 16

U.S. #1 POP 45	"Come See about Me"	The Supremes
U.S. #1 POP LP	*Beatles '65*	The Beatles
U.K. #1 POP 45	"I Feel Fine"	The Beatles
U.K. #1 POP LP	*Beatles for Sale*	The Beatles

WEEK ENDING JANUARY 23

U.S. #1 POP 45	"Downtown"	Petula Clark
U.S. #1 POP LP	*Beatles '65*	The Beatles
U.K. #1 POP 45	"I Feel Fine"	The Beatles
U.K. #1 POP LP	*The Rolling Stones No. 2*	The Rolling Stones

WEEK ENDING JANUARY 30

U.S. #1 POP 45	"Downtown"	Petula Clark
U.S. #1 POP LP	*Beatles '65*	The Beatles
U.S. #1 R&B 45	"My Girl"	The Temptations
U.K. #1 POP 45	"Yeh, Yeh"	Georgie Fame
U.K. #1 POP LP	*The Rolling Stones No. 2*	The Rolling Stones

5 **Screaming Jay Hawkins** begins his first British tour. He tells the *NME*, "I want to meet this guy **Screaming Lord Sutch**"—referring to the British rock singer who took both his name and flamboyant stage act from Hawkins.

7 At London's University College Hospital, **Beatle George Harrison** has his tonsils removed. The operation, which does not affect his singing voice, takes place just a few weeks after a dentist friend of his had surreptitiously introduced George and **John Lennon** to LSD.

8 **P. J. Proby**, scheduled for an appearance on "Shindig!," is banned by ABC-TV as a result of his British trouser-splitting incidents.

11 **Beatles** drummer **Ringo Starr** marries **Maureen Cox** in London, with **John Lennon**, his wife **Cynthia** and **George Harrison** attending. **Paul McCartney** is away on vacation in Tunisia.

12 *NME* reports that **Donovan** has been signed by Pye Records. The psychedelic folkie will go on to score many hits in the U.K. and the U.S., including "Sunshine Superman," "First There Is a Mountain," "Atlantis," "Mellow Yellow" and "Hurdy Gurdy Man"."

NME reports that the **Beatles** will appear in a film version of **Richard Condon**'s novel *A Talent for Loving,* a western about a 1,400-mile horse race. This never happens.

13 Motown group **Jr. Walker and the All Stars** enter both the pop and R&B charts for the first time with "Shotgun," which establishes the band's trademark hard-driving "roadhouse" R&B sound, featuring the vocals and sax of leader Walker. The song will go on to reach Number One on the R&B chart and #4 on the pop chart. The group will go on to have big hits with "(I'm a) Road Runner" (#20, 1966), a version of **Marvin Gaye**'s "How Sweet It Is (To Be Loved by You)" (#18, 1966), "What Does It Take (to Win Your Love)" (#4, 1969) and a version of the **Guess Who**'s "These Eyes" (#16, 1969).

20 The **Supremes** enter the pop and R&B charts with "Stop! In the Name of Love," which will reach #2 on the R&B chart, and Number One on the pop chart—their fourth consecutive release to hit Number One on the Hot 100, continuing a winning streak that began in July 1964 with "Where Did Our Love Go?"

21 The **Rolling Stones'** third single, "Not Fade Away" (a cover version of an early **Buddy Holly** hit), is released on London Records. It will become their first Top Ten single.

24 **P. J. Proby** is banned from televised appearances in Britain by the BBC.

25 The **Rolling Stones'** "The Last Time" backed with "Play with Fire" is released in the U.K. on London Records. This same day, the Stones perform the song on the British TV rock show "Ready Steady Go!"

26 London guitarist **Jimmy Page**—already a busy and sought-after session-man, and who has played on singles by the **Kinks**—releases his first, and one of his only, solo singles, "She Just Satisfies," on Fontana Records. Page will go on to join the **Yardbirds** and become a founding member of **Led Zeppelin**.

27 **P. J. Proby**'s latest record, "I Apologize," enters the U.K. pop chart despite being banned from most media exposure. ◆

WEEK ENDING FEBRUARY 7

U.S. #1 POP 45	"You've Lost That Lovin' Feelin'"	The Righteous Brothers
U.S. #1 POP LP	*Beatles '65*	The Beatles
U.S. #1 R&B 45	"My Girl"	The Temptations
U.K. #1 POP 45	"Go Now"	The Moody Blues
U.K. #1 POP LP	*The Rolling Stones No. 2*	The Rolling Stones

WEEK ENDING FEBRUARY 14

U.S. #1 POP 45	"You've Lost That Lovin' Feelin'"	The Righteous Brothers
U.S. #1 POP LP	*Beatles '65*	The Beatles
U.S. #1 R&B 45	"My Girl"	The Temptations
U.K. #1 POP 45	"Go Now"	The Moody Blues
U.K. #1 POP LP	*The Rolling Stones No. 2*	The Rolling Stones

WEEK ENDING FEBRUARY 21

U.S. #1 POP 45	"This Diamond Ring"	Gary Lewis and the Playboys
U.S. #1 POP LP	*Beatles '65*	The Beatles
U.S. #1 R&B 45	"My Girl"	The Temptations
U.K. #1 POP 45	"You've Lost That Lovin' Feelin'"	The Righteous Brothers
U.K. #1 POP LP	*The Rolling Stones No. 2*	The Rolling Stones

WEEK ENDING FEBRUARY 28

U.S. #1 POP 45	"This Diamond Ring"	Gary Lewis and the Playboys
U.S. #1 POP LP	*Beatles '65*	The Beatles
U.S. #1 R&B 45	"My Girl"	The Temptations
U.K. #1 POP 45	"Tired of Waiting for You"	The Kinks
U.K. #1 POP LP	*The Rolling Stones No. 2*	The Rolling Stones

1 **Petula Clark**'s "Downtown," the British pop singer's first U.S. hit, is awarded a gold record.

3 Motown Records releases the **Miracles'** "Ooo Baby Baby," written and produced by the group's leader, **William "Smokey" Robinson**. The song will eventually rise to #13 on the Hot 100.

The **Rolling Stones** appear on ABC-TV's "Shindig!" performing "Suzie Q." Also appearing: **Freddie and the Dreamers** (singing "If You Gotta Make a Fool of Somebody"), **Little Eva** (singing "The Loco-motion") and **Jay and the Americans** (singing "Come a Little Bit Closer").

5 The **Yardbirds'** "For Your Love" is released on EMI/Columbia records in the U.K. The song will become a Top Ten hit in both the U.K. and the U.S.

The **Rolling Stones** begin another British tour, supported by the **Hollies**, **Goldie and the Gingerbreads** (Goldie being **Genya Ravan**), the **Checkmates** and the **Konrads**.

British Parlophone Records releases the single "I Pity the Fool" backed with "Take My Tip" by the **Manish Boys**, whose members include one **David Jones**, who is later known as **David Bowie**.

6 The **Rolling Stones** record tracks for the LP *Got Live If You Want It* in Liverpool; the next day, more tracks are recorded at their Manchester concert.

Memphis gospel and soul singer **Solomon Burke** enters the pop and R&B charts with the single that will be his biggest hit on both charts, "Got to Get You off My Mind," which will peak at pop #22 and be an R&B Number One.

13 **Freddie and the Dreamers'** "I'm Telling You Now" enters the Hot 100, where it will stay for eleven weeks, eventually climbing to Number One for two weeks starting April 10. It will be the biggest hit of the British Invasion band's brief career.

The **Kinks'** "Tired of Waiting for You" becomes their third

Hot 100 entry. It will remain on the chart for eleven weeks, eventually reaching #6.

18 **Rolling Stones** Mick Jagger, Keith Richards and Bill Wyman are arrested for "insulting behavior" in London. The "insulting behavior" turns out to be urinating on the wall of the Francis Garage, a gas station where the band members had sought use of the men's room; when the owner refused that permission, they initiated their insulting behavior. The incident occurs after the Stones' British tour had concluded earlier in the day with a concert in Romford.

20 British Invasion band **Wayne Fontana and the Mindbenders** enter the Hot 100 for the first time with "Game of Love," which will stay on the chart for eleven weeks, reaching Number One (where it will remain for one week) in late April, knocking fellow Merseybeat band **Freddie and the Dreamers'** "I'm Telling You Now" out of the top spot. Fontana and the Mindbenders will enter the Hot 100 only once more, with "It's Just a Little Bit Too Late" in June 1965, which will reach #45.

Petula Clark's "I Know a Place" enters the Hot 100. It will stay on the chart for twelve weeks, eventually hitting #3.

24 On the first date of their Scandanavian tour, **Rolling Stones** bassist **Bill Wyman** is knocked unconscious by an electrical shock from a microphone stand in Odense, Denmark.

26 *NME* announces guitarist Eric Clapton's replacement in the **Yardbirds**: **Jeff Beck**. Clapton had quit the band in protest over the commerciality of such songs as "For Your Love" and "Heart Full of Soul" (both composed by **Graham Gouldman**, who would later join **10cc**). Beck will go on to become a guitar hero of stature comparable to Clapton, and will lead a succession of Jeff Beck groups playing hard, flashy rock before the guitarist moves off in a jazz-fusion direction in the mid-Seventies.

27 Though he has yet to split his trousers this evening, **P. J. Proby** is ordered off the stage at the Hereford Municipal Ballroom in England.

Little Milton's "We're Gonna Make It" enters the pop and R&B charts on its way to pop #25 and R&B Number One, proving that the blues haven't been forgotten. Little Milton, a Memphis blues guitarist and singer, made his first recordings for Sun Records with **Ike Turner**'s band in the early Fifties. "We're Gonna Make It" will be his biggest hit. ◆

WEEK ENDING MARCH 7

U.S. #1 POP 45	"My Girl"	The Temptations
U.S. #1 POP LP	*Beatles '65*	The Beatles
U.S. #1 R&B 45	"My Girl"	The Temptations
U.K. #1 POP 45	"I'll Never Find Another You"	The Seekers
U.K. #1 POP LP	*The Rolling Stones No. 2*	The Rolling Stones

WEEK ENDING MARCH 14

U.S. #1 POP 45	"Eight Days a Week"	The Beatles
U.S. #1 POP LP	*Mary Poppins*	soundtrack
U.S. #1 R&B 45	"Shotgun"	Jr. Walker and the All Stars
U.K. #1 POP 45	"I'll Never Find Another You"	The Seekers
U.K. #1 POP LP	*The Rolling Stones No. 2*	The Rolling Stones

WEEK ENDING MARCH 21

U.S. #1 POP 45	"Eight Days a Week"	The Beatles
U.S. #1 POP LP	*Goldfinger*	soundtrack
U.S. #1 R&B 45	"Shotgun"	Jr. Walker and the All Stars
U.K. #1 POP 45	"It's Not Unusual"	Tom Jones
U.K. #1 POP LP	*The Rolling Stones No. 2*	The Rolling Stones

WEEK ENDING MARCH 28

U.S. #1 POP 45	"Stop! In the Name of Love"	The Supremes
U.S. #1 POP LP	*Goldfinger*	soundtrack
U.S. #1 R&B 45	"Shotgun"	Jr. Walker and the All Stars
U.K. #1 POP 45	"The Last Time"	The Rolling Stones
U.K. #1 POP LP	*The Rolling Stones No. 2*	The Rolling Stones

3 "She's about a Mover" by the **Sir Douglas Quintet** enters the Hot 100, where it will remain for twelve weeks, eventually reaching #13. This is the first hit record for the Tex-Mex garage-rock band led by **Doug Sahm**, which would hit again with "The Rains Came" (#31, 1966), "Mendocino" (#27, 1969) and "Dynamite Woman" (#83, 1969). The band has remained together in one form or another to the present day. Aside from vocalist, guitarist and fiddler Sahm, the band's sole constant has been Vox organ-pumper **Augie Meyer**.

The **Temptations**, one of Motown's most successful male vocal groups, enter the Hot 100 for the fifth time with "It's Growing," which will remain on the chart for nine weeks, eventually reaching #18.

9 The **Rolling Stones** make their first live appearance on British TV's "Ready Steady Go!"

10 British Invasion band **Freddie and the Dreamers** hit Number One in

the U.S. with "I'm Telling You Now." Their only other hit, the dance song "Do the Freddie"—included on their album of the same name, with a cover depicting the steps to the awkward dance that never really became a craze—would hit #18 on the pop chart within several weeks.

11 Both the **Beatles** and the **Rolling Stones** perform at the *New Musical Express'* poll winners' concert. The concert is held in London's Wembley Empire Pool. In addition to the Beatles and Stones, performing in the three-and-a-half-hour show are the **Moody Blues**, **Freddie and the Dreamers**, **Herman's Hermits**, the **Seekers**, **Georgie Fame and His Blue**

Flames, **Wayne Fontana and the Mindbenders**, **Cilla Black**, **Donovan**, **Them**, **Tom Jones**, the **Searchers**, **Dusty Springfield**, the **Animals**, and the **Kinks**.

13 Winners of the seventh annual Grammy Awards (for 1964) are announced. Record of the Year is "The Girl from Ipanema" by **Stan Getz** and **Astrud Gilberto**. Album of the Year is *Getz/Gilberto* by Stan Getz and **Joao Gilberto**. Song of the Year is "Hello, Dolly!" by **Jerry Herman**. Best Performance by a Vocal Group is the **Beatles'** "A Hard Day's Night." Best Rock & Roll Recording is **Petula Clark's** "Downtown." The Beatles are voted Best New Artist(s) of 1964.

14 **Millie Small** appears on ABC-TV's "Shindig!" performing her ska smash "My Boy Lollipop." Also appearing on the show are **Jerry Lee Lewis** (performing "I Believe in You") and **Neil Sedaka** (singing "Breaking Up Is Hard to Do").

16 The **Hollies** open their first U.S. tour at the Brooklyn Paramount Theater in

New York. The English group has had only one very minor success in America, their Hot 100 cover of **Doris Troy's** "Just One Look."

19 The film *The T.A.M.I.* (T.A.M.I. standing for Teen-Age Music International) *Show*—featuring **James Brown**, the **Rolling Stones**, the **Supremes**, the **Beach Boys**, the **Four Tops**, **Marvin Gaye** and **Smokey Robinson and the Miracles**—opens in London under the title *Teenage Command Performance*. The film, partially financed by Phil Spector, will become one of the most popular documentaries of the rock era.

21 The **Beach Boys** appear on ABC-TV's "Shindig!" performing their current hit, "Do You Wanna Dance?"

23 The **Rolling Stones** begin their third North American tour with a show at the Forum in Montreal.

29 **Gerry and the Pacemakers** perform at the Brooklyn Fox Theater in New York, kicking off a month-long tour of the U.S.

30 The **Kinks** begin their first headlining U.K. tour, with the **Yardbirds** and **Goldie and the Gingerbreads** providing support.

Bob Dylan's British tour—which will be filmed by **D. A. Pennebaker** for the movie *Don't Look Back*—begins in Sheffield, with the **Band** (minus drummer **Levon Helm**, replaced for the tour by **Mickey Jones**) backing him up. ◆

WEEK ENDING APRIL 4

U.S. #1 POP 45	"Stop! In the Name of Love"	The Supremes
U.S. #1 POP LP	*Goldfinger*	soundtrack
U.S. #1 R&B 45	"Got to Get You off My Mind"	Solomon Burke
U.K. #1 POP 45	"For Your Love"	The Yardbirds
U.K. #1 POP LP	*The Rolling Stones No. 2*	The Rolling Stones

WEEK ENDING APRIL 11

U.S. #1 POP 45	"I'm Telling You Now"	Freddie and the Dreamers
U.S. #1 POP LP	*Goldfinger*	soundtrack
U.S. #1 R&B 45	"Got to Get You off My Mind"	Solomon Burke
U.K. #1 POP 45	"Ticket to Ride"	The Beatles
U.K. #1 POP LP	*Rolling Stones No. 2*	The Rolling Stones

WEEK ENDING APRIL 18

U.S. #1 POP 45	"I'm Telling You Now"	Freddie and the Dreamers
U.S. #1 POP LP	*Goldfinger*	soundtrack
U.S. #1 R&B 45	"Got to Get You off My Mind"	Solomon Burke
U.K. #1 POP 45	"Ticket to Ride"	The Beatles
U.K. #1 POP LP	*Beatles for Sale*	The Beatles

WEEK ENDING APRIL 25

U.S. #1 POP 45	"Game of Love"	Wayne Fontana and the Mindbenders
U.S. #1 POP LP	*Goldfinger*	soundtrack
U.S. #1 R&B 45	"Got to Get You off My Mind"	Solomon Burke
U.K. #1 POP 45	"Ticket to Ride"	The Beatles
U.K. #1 POP LP	*Beatles for Sale*	The Beatles

1 British Invasion group **Herman's Hermits** reach Number One on the U.S. pop chart with "Mrs. Brown, You've Got a Lovely Daughter."

6 In their Clearwater, Florida, hotel room, two members of the **Rolling Stones** begin work on a song that will become a rock & roll anthem. **Keith Richards**, who has just gotten a Gibson "fuzz box" (guitar distortion device) on this day and has been trying it out, wakes up in the middle of the night to bang on **Mick Jagger**'s hotel-room door: Richards has come up with a fuzz-tone guitar riff that he can't get out of his head. He plays it for Jagger, who likes it. The riff will become the foundation for "(I Can't Get No) Satisfaction."

9 Bob Dylan plays the first of two nights at London's Royal Albert Hall, concluding his celebrated tour of Europe, where he has been received more as a pop star—a teen idol—than as a writer and singer of protest songs. Both Royal Albert Hall concerts sold out within four hours of tickets going on sale. In the audience this first night are the **Beatles** and **Donovan**, who spend the evening with Dylan after the show.

12 The **Rolling Stones** begin two days of recording at Chess Studios in Chicago. Here they record the original tracks for "(I Can't Get No) Satisfaction," which they work on again two days later at RCA's Hollywood studios in Los Angeles, where they also record tracks for the album *Out of Our Heads*.

15 The **Byrds** enter the Hot 100 for the first of many times, with an electric version of **Bob Dylan**'s "Mr. Tambourine Man," which will peak at Number One in its thirteen weeks on the chart—and its success will inspire Dylan himself to "go electric." This seminal L.A. country-rock band will hit again with such Dylan tunes as "All I Really Want to Do" (#40, later this year), "My Back Pages" (#30, 1967) and "You Ain't Goin' Nowhere" (#74, 1968). They will hit Number One for the second and last time later this year with "Turn! Turn! Turn!," the lyrics of which are taken from the Biblical book of Ecclesiastes. The tune was written by **Pete Seeger**.

────────

Barbara Mason's "Yes I'm Ready" enters the Hot 100 a week after entering the R&B chart. The song will peak at #5 on the pop chart and #2 on the R&B chart. It is Mason's first pop hit, and will be followed by "Sad, Sad Girl" (#27, later this year) and several minor hits through 1972.

16 The **Rolling Stones** appear with **Chuck Berry** on the television show "Hollywood A-Go-Go." The Stones, trying to drive off in a limousine after the show, are attacked by a mob of fans.

────────

The **Beach Boys** appear on "The Ed Sullivan Show" performing their latest hit, "Help Me, Rhonda."

21 The **Who**'s second single, "Anyway, Anyhow, Anywhere" backed with "Anytime You Want Me," is released on Decca Records in the U.K., and the band debuts it the same evening on British TV's "Ready Steady Go!," which later adopts "Anyway, Anyhow, Anywhere" as its theme song.

25 Blues giant **Sonny Boy Williamson**, born Aleck "Rice" Miller on December 5, 1899, dies in his sleep of natural causes in his Helena, Arkansas, home. Actually the second blues harmonica great to play under the name Sonny Boy Williamson (the first, **John Lee "Sonny Boy" Williamson**, died in 1948 as the result of skull fractures suffered in a fight), he wrote and recorded such classics as "Eyesight to the Blind" (covered by the **Who** on *Tommy*), "One Way Out" (covered by the **Allman Brothers** Band on *Eat a Peach*) and "Take Your Hand Out of My Pocket" (covered by **Van Morrison** on *It's Too Late to Stop Now*).

────────

Kinks guitarist **Dave Davies** is knocked unconscious when he careens into drummer **Mick Avory**'s cymbal during a London concert; the Kinks cancel the remainder of their U.K. tour.

26 Bob Dylan enters St. Mary's Hospital in Paddington, England, with a viral infection.

────────

The **Rolling Stones** appear on "Shindig!" along with **Jackie DeShannon, Sonny and Cher** and **Jimmy Rodgers**. ◆

WEEK ENDING MAY 2

U.S. #1 POP 45	"Mrs. Brown, You've Got a Lovely Daughter"	Herman's Hermits
U.S. #1 POP LP	*Goldfinger*	soundtrack
U.S. #1 R&B 45	"We're Gonna Make It"	Little Milton
U.K. #1 POP 45	"Ticket to Ride"	The Beatles
U.K. #1 POP LP	*Beatles for Sale*	The Beatles

WEEK ENDING MAY 9

U.S. #1 POP 45	"Mrs. Brown, You've Got a Lovely Daughter"	Herman's Hermits
U.S. #1 POP LP	*Goldfinger*	soundtrack
U.S. #1 R&B 45	"We're Gonna Make It"	Little Milton
U.K. #1 POP 45	"Ticket to Ride"	The Beatles
U.K. #1 POP LP	*The Freewheelin' Bob Dylan*	Bob Dylan

WEEK ENDING MAY 16

U.S. #1 POP 45	"Mrs. Brown, You've Got a Lovely Daughter"	Herman's Hermits
U.S. #1 POP LP	*Goldfinger*	soundtrack
U.S. #1 R&B 45	"We're Gonna Make It"	Little Milton
U.K. #1 POP 45	"Where Are You Now?"	Jackie Trent
U.K. #1 POP LP	*Bringing It All Back Home*	Bob Dylan

WEEK ENDING MAY 23

U.S. #1 POP 45	"Ticket to Ride"	The Beatles
U.S. #1 POP LP	*Goldfinger*	soundtrack
U.S. #1 R&B 45	"I'll Be Doggone"	Marvin Gaye
U.K. #1 POP 45	"Long Live Love"	Sandie Shaw
U.K. #1 POP LP	*Bringing It All Back Home*	Bob Dylan

WEEK ENDING MAY 30

U.S. #1 POP 45	"Help Me, Rhonda"	The Beach Boys
U.S. #1 POP LP	*Goldfinger*	soundtrack
U.S. #1 R&B 45	"Back in My Arms Again"	The Supremes
U.K. #1 POP 45	"Long Live Love"	Sandie Shaw
U.K. #1 POP LP	*Bringing It All Back Home*	Bob Dylan

4 The **Rolling Stones'** "(I Can't Get No) Satisfaction" enters the American pop chart, where—in spite of being banned by numerous radio stations because of its supposedly suggestive lyrics—it will become the Stones' first U.S. Number One. It will also make the R&B Top Twenty.

11 The **Rolling Stones** EP *Got Live If You Want It*—a live recording on which the screaming of the audience almost completely drowns out the music—is released in the U.K.

12 In London, it is announced that all four members of the **Beatles** will receive MBE (Member of the Most Excellent Order of the British Empire) awards from **Queen Elizabeth**. The announcement sparks some controversy, as several previous MBE recipients turn their medals in. The award ceremony will take place October 26, 1965, at Buckingham Palace. **John Lennon** will return his MBE in November 1969, protesting Britain's supporting U.S. involvement in Vietnam and the poor showing of his current single, "Cold Turkey."

14 The album *Beatles VI* is released in the U.S. on Capitol Records. The album includes such songs as "Eight Days a Week," "Every Little Thing" (later covered by **Yes**), "Words of Love" and "Yes It Is."

15 **Bob Dylan** records "Like a Rolling Stone" at Columbia Studio A in New York City. This is Dylan's first "electric" recording, featuring himself and **Mike Bloomfield** on electric guitars and **Al Kooper** on organ (it was the first time Kooper, normally a pianist, ever played an organ, but Dylan liked the squeezed sound he got out of his studio Hammond). It was also the last time **Tom Wilson** would produce a Dylan session. "Like a Rolling Stone" would eventually reach #2 on the pop chart, and served pointed notice to Dylan's old folk audience that he was moving decisively on to the wider horizons of rock & roll.

16 British Invasion band **Herman's Hermits** win their first gold record, for "Mrs. Brown, You've Got a Lovely Daughter," which had been Number One on the pop chart for three weeks in May.

17 The **Kinks** arrive in New York City to begin their first American tour. The English quartet has already had American Top Ten hits with "You Really Got Me," "All Day and All of the Night" and "Tired of Waiting for You."

19 New Orleans R&B singer **Lee Dorsey** enters the R&B chart with his third hit, "Ride Your Pony." The song will reach #7 on the R&B chart and #28 on the pop chart. It will be covered in 1982 by New York garage-rock band the **Fleshtones**. Dorsey's first and biggest hit was the nonsense ditty "Ya Ya," which made Number One R&B and #7 pop in 1961. Though he would continue to have hits through the Sixties, his last big hit would be "Working in a Coal Mine," which would hit #5 R&B and #8 pop in 1966, and would be covered in 1981 by **Devo**.

21 The **Charlatans** play their first show at the Red Dog Saloon in Virginia City, Nevada, The band, consisting of **Mike Wilhelm** (guitar), **Mike Ferguson** (keyboards), **Richard Olson** (bass), **Dan Hicks** (drums) and **George Hunter** (vocals), is the very first "San Francisco" rock band, although founder Hunter, a draftsman and artist, originally conceived them as more of a visual statement than a musical group. Their penchant for western regalia—buckskin fringe, cowboy boots and hats, bandanas—and Victoriana visually defined the Haight-Ashbury ethos that would soon flower in San Francisco. Nevertheless, the Charlatans develop a repertoire of modernized Americana—electrified country and folk songs—and within a few months will return to Haight-Ashbury. For better or worse, the Charlatans were always too quixotic to ever actually make a serious recording, so there is virtually no documented evidence of their sound.

23 Motown Records releases "The Tracks of My Tears" by **Smokey Robinson and the Miracles**. The song will be a hit for Linda Ronstadt in 1976.

26 The **Strangeloves'** garage-rock classic "I Want Candy"—which integrates a **Bo Diddley** beat with the band's imitations of African Masai tribal percussion patterns—enters the Hot 100, where it will peak at #11 in its ten weeks on the chart. The song will become a hit in 1982 for British band **Bow Wow Wow**. The Strangeloves will go on to have two more hits "Cara-Lin," and "Night Time," before fading into obscurity.

Memphis soul singer **Joe Tex** enters the Hot 100 for the sixth time, with "One Monkey Don't Stop No Show," which will reach as high as #65 in its four weeks on the chart. The song will be covered in 1971 by female soul vocal trio **Honeycone**, whose version will reach #15 on the chart. ◆

W E E K   E N D I N G   J U N E   6

U.S. #1 POP 45	"Help Me, Rhonda"	The Beach Boys
U.S. #1 POP LP	*Goldfinger*	soundtrack
U.S. #1 R&B 45	"I Can't Help Myself"	The Four Tops
U.K. #1 POP 45	"Piece of Love"	The Everly Brothers
U.K. #1 POP LP	*Bringing It All Back Home*	Bob Dylan

W E E K   E N D I N G   J U N E   1 3

U.S. #1 POP 45	"Back in My Arms Again"	The Supremes
U.S. #1 POP LP	*Goldfinger*	soundtrack
U.S. #1 R&B 45	"I Can't Help Myself"	The Four Tops
U.K. #1 POP 45	"Crying in the Chapel"	Elvis Presley
U.K. #1 POP LP	*Bringing It All Back Home*	Bob Dylan

W E E K   E N D I N G   J U N E   2 0

U.S. #1 POP 45	"I Can't Help Myself"	The Four Tops
U.S. #1 POP LP	*Goldfinger*	soundtrack
U.S. #1 R&B 45	"I Can't Help Myself"	The Four Tops
U.K. #1 POP 45	"Crying in the Chapel"	Elvis Presley
U.K. #1 POP LP	*The Sound of Music*	soundtrack

W E E K   E N D I N G   J U N E   2 7

U.S. #1 POP 45	"Mr. Tambourine Man"	The Byrds
U.S. #1 POP LP	*Goldfinger*	soundtrack
U.S. #1 R&B 45	"I Can't Help Myself"	The Four Tops
U.K. #1 POP 45	"I'm Alive"	The Hollies
U.K. #1 POP LP	*Bringing It All Back Home*	Bob Dylan

10 **Sonny and Cher** make their chart debut with "I Got You Babe." The couple met two years ago at a **Ronettes** recording session on which **Sonny Bono** was working under **Phil Spector**, and **Cher Sarkasian LaPier** was singing backing vocals. They were married in 1964. "I Got You Babe," written, arranged and produced by Bono, will bring Sonny and Cher pop stardom.

17 **James Brown**'s "Papa's Got a Brand New Bag" enters the R&B and the pop charts. It will hit R&B Number One—Brown's first single to do so since "Try Me" in 1958—and reach pop #8—Brown's first to break the pop Top Ten. In the next ten years, Brown will have fifteen more R&B Number Ones and five more pop Top Tens (but no Number Ones), earning the indefatigable singer/dancer such epithets as "The Hardest-working Man in Show Business," "Soul Brother Number One," "Mr. Dynamite," "The Godfather of Soul" and "Minister of the New, New Superheavy Funk."

20 Columbia Records releases **Bob Dylan**'s

"Like a Rolling Stone" and opens the floodgates. Peaking at #2 on the U.S. pop chart and #4 on the U.K. chart, it will be Dylan's biggest hit ever, and as his first "electric" song, it will necessitate a new way of listening to electric music.

———

Kama Sutra Records releases "Do You Believe in Magic" by Greenwich Village-based folk-pop band the **Lovin' Spoonful**, whose members include **John Sebastian**, **Zal Yanovsky** (both previously together in the jugband the **Mugwumps**, which also included **Cass Elliot** and **Denny Doherty**, later of the **Mamas and the Papas**), **Steve Boone** and **Joe Butler**. "Do You Believe in Magic," the band's first record,

will reach #9 on the pop chart, and will remain in the chart for thirteen weeks.

———

21 Appearing this evening on "Shindig!": **Gary Lewis and the Playboys** singing "This Diamond Ring," the **Sir Douglas Quintet** performing "She's about a Mover" and **Gene Pitney** singing country star George Jones' hit "The Race Is On."

22 **Rolling Stones** Mick Jagger, Keith Richards and **Bill Wyman** appear in a London court and are found guilty of "insulting behavior" for the incident earlier this year in which they urinated against the wall of a London gas station. They are fined five pounds each.

25 **Bob Dylan** performs at the Newport Folk Festival, unveiling his electric music for the first time onstage. After three songs—"Like a Rolling Stone," "Maggie's Farm" and "It Takes a Lot to Laugh, It Takes a Train to Cry"—he is booed offstage by the crowd of angered folk purists. He returns for an acoustic encore, playing "It's All Over Now, Baby Blue" (which folk magazine *Sing Out!* will later describe as "fearfully appropriate") and "Mr. Tambourine Man."

29 The **Beatles** film *Help!* premieres at London's Pavillion Theater. The film's debut attracts a sell-out crowd of Beatlemaniacs and receives bemused reactions from the press. ◆

WEEK ENDING JULY 4

U.S. #1 POP 45	"I Can't Help Myself"	The Four Tops
U.S. #1 POP LP	*Goldfinger*	soundtrack
U.S. #1 R&B 45	"I Can't Help Myself"	The Four Tops
U.K. #1 POP 45	"I'm Alive"	The Hollies
U.K. #1 POP LP	*Bringing It All Back Home*	Bob Dylan

WEEK ENDING JULY 11

U.S. #1 POP 45	"(I Can't Get No) Satisfaction"	The Rolling Stones
U.S. #1 POP LP	*Beatles VI*	The Beatles
U.S. #1 R&B 45	"I Can't Help Myself"	The Four Tops
U.K. #1 POP 45	"Mr. Tambourine Man"	The Byrds
U.K. #1 POP LP	*Bringing It All Back Home*	Bob Dylan

WEEK ENDING JULY 18

U.S. #1 POP 45	"(I Can't Get No) Satisfaction"	The Rolling Stones
U.S. #1 POP LP	*Beatles VI*	The Beatles
U.S. #1 R&B 45	"I Can't Help Myself"	The Four Tops
U.K. #1 POP 45	"Mr. Tambourine Man"	The Byrds
U.K. #1 POP LP	*The Sound of Music*	soundtrack

WEEK ENDING JULY 25

U.S. #1 POP 45	"(I Can't Get No) Satisfaction"	The Rolling Stones
U.S. #1 POP LP	*Beatles VI*	The Beatles
U.S. #1 R&B 45	"I Can't Help Myself"	The Four Tops
U.K. #1 POP 45	"Help!"	The Beatles
U.K. #1 POP LP	*The Sound of Music*	soundtrack

6 The **Who**, the **Yardbirds** and others perform at England's Richmond Jazz and Blues Festival.

The **Small Faces'** debut single, "Whatcha Gonna Do about It," is released in the U.K. on Decca Records. The band will go on to have a few more hits, such as the innovative "Itchykoo Park" (the first recorded use of "phase shifter" electronic effects) and will become a favorite of Britain's mod audience before breaking up, with leader **Steve Marriott** going on to form **Humble Pie**, and the rest of the band reforming with singer **Rod Stewart** and guitarist **Ron Wood** as the **Faces**.

13 The **Jefferson Airplane**—consisting of **Marty Balin**, **Signe Toly Anderson**, **Paul Kantner**, **Jorma Kaukonen**, **Jack Casady**

and **Skip Spence**—makes its stage debut at the Matrix Club in San Francisco, playing mostly electrified blues and folk covers, plus a few originals. Later this year, they will become the first San Francisco rock group to sign a major recording contract.

15 The **Beatles** perform before 56,000 screaming fans at Shea Stadium in New York—the largest single crowd to see a rock & roll concert to date.

21 **Joe Simon** makes his chart debut with "Let's Do It Over." The country-styled soul singer has made several unsuccessful records before, but "Let's Do It Over," which will reach #13 on the R&B chart, will be followed by such hits as "The Chokin' Kind" in 1969, "Drowning in the Sea of Love" and "Power of Love" in 1972,

and "Get Down, Get Down (Get on the Floor)" in 1975.

The **Rolling Stones** album *Out of Our Heads*—which includes such classics as "Satisfaction," "Play with Fire" and "The Last Time"—reaches Number One on the U.S. album chart.

23 Hundreds of British fans of the **Rolling Stones**, waiting for the band to arrive for a TV taping at the

BBC's Manchester Studios, are hosed down by police.

27 **Elvis Presley** plays host to the **Beatles** at his Beverly Hills home, a mansion he has rented to live in while filming in Hollywood. The visit lasts four hours.

Bob Dylan's album *Highway 61 Revisited*—his second electric album, featuring "Like a Rolling Stone," "Ballad of a Thin Man" (with its famous refrain "There's something happening here but you don't know what it is, do you, Mr. Jones?") and "Just like Tom Thumb's Blues"—is released by Columbia Records.

Bob Dylan performs at the Forest Hills Tennis Stadium in Queens, New York, with a band that includes guitarist **Robbie Robertson** and drummer **Levon Helm** of the Hawks. After Dylan's appearance with electric guitar and band at the Newport Folk Festival in July, the audience is prepared for his new sound: some are prepared to embrace this union of visionary writing and rock & roll, others are prepared to heckle and boo. This time Dylan holds the stage. Next time, the sight and sound of Dylan with an electric guitar will seem natural.

28 **Joe Tex**'s "I Want To (Do Everything for You)" enters the R&B and pop charts, where it will hit Number One and #23, respectively. The Texan soul singer's first hit, "Hold What You've Got," went to #2 on the R&B chart and #5 on the pop chart last year; he will follow "I Want To" with another R&B Number One (pop #29) single, "A Sweet Woman like You," in December.

The **Rolling Stones** announce that they will be comanaged by **Andrew Loog Oldham**, their first manager, and **Allen Klein**, whom they met three days ago. They also sign a five-year recording contract with Decca Records. ◆

WEEK ENDING AUGUST 1		
U.S. #1 POP 45	"(I Can't Get No) Satisfaction"	The Rolling Stones
U.S. #1 POP LP	*Beatles VI*	The Beatles
U.S. #1 R&B 45	"I Can't Help Myself"	The Four Tops
U.K. #1 POP 45	"Help!"	The Beatles
U.K. #1 POP LP	*The Sound of Music*	soundtrack

WEEK ENDING AUGUST 8		
U.S. #1 POP 45	"I'm Henry VIII, I Am"	Herman's Hermits
U.S. #1 POP LP	*Beatles VI*	The Beatles
U.S. #1 R&B 45	"In the Midnight Hour"	Wilson Pickett
U.K. #1 POP 45	"Help!"	The Beatles
U.K. #1 POP LP	*Help!*	The Beatles

WEEK ENDING AUGUST 15		
U.S. #1 POP 45	"I Got You Babe"	Sonny and Cher
U.S. #1 POP LP	*Beatles VI*	The Beatles
U.S. #1 R&B 45	"Papa's Got a Brand New Bag"	James Brown
U.K. #1 POP 45	"Help!"	The Beatles
U.K. #1 POP LP	*Help!*	The Beatles

WEEK ENDING AUGUST 22		
U.S. #1 POP 45	"I Got You Babe"	Sonny and Cher
U.S. #1 POP LP	*Out of Our Heads*	The Rolling Stones
U.S. #1 R&B 45	"Papa's Got a Brand New Bag"	James Brown
U.K. #1 POP 45	"I Got You Babe"	Sonny and Cher
U.K. #1 POP LP	*Help!*	The Beatles

WEEK ENDING AUGUST 29		
U.S. #1 POP 45	"I Got You Babe"	Sonny and Cher
U.S. #1 POP LP	*Out of Our Heads*	The Rolling Stones
U.S. #1 R&B 45	"Papa's Got a Brand New Bag"	James Brown
U.K. #1 POP 45	"(I Can't Get No) Satisfaction"	The Rolling Stones
U.K. #1 POP LP	*Help!*	The Beatles

1 Rockabilly singer **Sleepy LaBeef** records "Shame, Shame, Shame" and **Chuck Berry**'s "You Can't Catch Me" for Columbia Records.

James Brown appears on "Shindig!" performing "Papa's Got a Brand New Bag." Also appearing on the show are **Booker T. and the MGs** performing "Bootleg."

2 The **Rolling Stones** appear on the British pop TV show "Ready Steady Go!" with **Mick Jagger** and **Andrew Loog Oldham** performing a parody of Sonny and Cher's "I Got You Babe."

3 The **Rolling Stones** perform in Dublin, Ireland, and film *Charlie Is My Darling.*

4 The **Who** have their equipment van stolen outside the Battersea Dog's Home in England while they are inside the Home buying a guard dog.

5 The **Rolling Stones** fly to Los Angeles to record "Get Off My Cloud" and other songs.

11 The **Gentrys**' "Keep on Dancing," a garage-rock classic, enters the Hot 100, where it will stay for thirteen weeks, eventually reaching #4. The group, generally considered one-hit wonders, like most mid-Sixties garage-rock bands, actually stayed together through the early Seventies, racking up five more hits, though none of them were as big as "Keep on Dancing."

12 The **Beatles**' "Yesterday" is released in the U.S. on Capitol Records. They also appear this evening on "The Ed Sullivan Show," in a segment

taped before a live audience in August.

16 The **Rolling Stones** help open the second season of "Shindig!," performing "(I Can't Get No) Satisfaction." The **Kinks**, the **Byrds** and the **Everly Brothers** also appear on the show.

22 The **Who** begin a short tour of Scandinavia in Copenhagen; **Roger Daltrey** punches out **Keith Moon**, and is all but thrown out of the band.

San Francisco rock group the **Great Society**, featuring singer **Grace Slick**, makes its stage debut at the Coffee Gallery in North Beach, California.

23 The **Yardbirds** (featuring lead guitarist **Jeff Beck**) appear on "Shindig!" performing "Heart Full of Soul." Also appearing are the **Pretty Things**, **Jerry Lee Lewis** and **Raquel Welch** singing "Dancing in the Street."

25 "The Beatles," a half-hour Saturday morning cartoon show featuring genuine **Beatles** songs but *not* their real voices, premieres on ABC-TV. The show will run through September 7, 1969.

Len Barry's "1–2–3" enters both the pop and R&B charts. The song, produced by **Leon Huff** (who, with **Kenny Gamble** would become the famed Gamble-Huff Philadelphia soul production team), will peak at #2 on the pop chart and #11 on the R&B chart. Barry had started as a Philadelphia teen idol in the late Fifties, and from 1961 to 1963 sang lead vocals with the **Dovells**, who had big hits with "Bristol Stomp" and "You Can't Sit Down." Barry would go on to have four more minor hits before fading to the supper-club circuit after 1966.

30 The **Hollies**, the **Dave Clark Five**, **Donovan** and the **Turtles** appear on "Shindig!" ◆

WEEK ENDING SEPTEMBER 5

U.S. #1 POP 45	"Help!"	The Beatles
U.S. #1 POP LP	*Out of Our Heads*	The Rolling Stones
U.S. #1 R&B 45	"Papa's Got a Brand New Bag"	James Brown
U.K. #1 POP 45	"(I Can't Get No) Satisfaction"	The Rolling Stones
U.K. #1 POP LP	*Help!*	The Beatles

WEEK ENDING SEPTEMBER 12

U.S. #1 POP 45	"Help!"	The Beatles
U.S. #1 POP LP	*Help!*	The Beatles
U.S. #1 R&B 45	"Papa's Got a Brand New Bag"	James Brown
U.K. #1 POP 45	"(I Can't Get No) Satisfaction"	The Rolling Stones
U.K. #1 POP LP	*Help!*	The Beatles

WEEK ENDING SEPTEMBER 19

U.S. #1 POP 45	"Help!"	The Beatles
U.S. #1 POP LP	*Help!*	The Beatles
U.S. #1 R&B 45	"Papa's Got a Brand New Bag"	James Brown
U.K. #1 POP 45	"Tears"	Ken Dodd
U.K. #1 POP LP	*Help!*	The Beatles

WEEK ENDING SEPTEMBER 26

U.S. #1 POP 45	"Eve of Destruction"	Barry McGuire
U.S. #1 POP LP	*Help!*	The Beatles
U.S. #1 R&B 45	"Papa's Got a Brand New Bag"	James Brown
U.K. #1 POP 45	"Tears"	Ken Dodd
U.K. #1 POP LP	*Help!*	The Beatles

2 The **Who** make their American TV debut on "Shindig!" performing "I Can't Explain." Also on the show are the **Four Tops** singing "I Can't Help Myself," and **Gerry and the Pacemakers** singing "Ferry Cross the Mersey."

Soul singer **Fontella Bass'** "Rescue Me," already climbing the R&B chart, enters the Hot 100 pop chart, where it will remain for thirteen weeks, reaching as high as #4. It will reach Number One on the R&B chart at the end of this month. This is the first solo hit for Bass, who had had minor hits with **Bobby McClure** ("Don't Mess Up a Good Thing" and "You'll Miss Me," both in 1965). She will go on to have three more pop hits, the biggest of which, "Recovery," will reach #37 at the end of this year. Bass will go on to marry trumpeter **Lester Bowie**

of the noted avant-garde jazz group the **Art Ensemble of Chicago**, with whom she will sing on the album *Les Stances à Sophie* in the early Seventies. In the early Eighties, she would join Bowie's gospel unit, **From the Root to the Source**.

Motown soul singer **Kim Weston**'s "Take Me in Your Arms (Rock Me a Little While)" enters the Hot 100, where it will remain for eight weeks, reaching as high as #50. It is the biggest of her four hits, the first having been "Love Me All the Way" (#88, 1963) and the others including "Helpless" (#56, 1966) and "I Got What You Need" (#99, 1967).

9 The **Miracles'** "My Girl Has Gone" enters the Hot 100, where it will go as high as #14 in ten weeks. It is the Motown vocal group's twentieth pop chart entry.

Marvin Gaye's "Ain't That Peculiar" becomes his twelfth entry into the Hot 100. The song will stay on the chart for twelve weeks, reaching as high as #8; it also reaches Number One on the R&B chart. The song will reach #85 on the pop chart when covered by the all-female rock band **Fanny** in 1972.

10 The **Supremes** make the first of many ap-

pearances on "The Ed Sullivan Show."

16 The **Family Dog**, San Francisco's concert-organizing commune, presents its first show at San Francisco's Longshoreman's Hall. The concert, titled "A Tribute to Dr. Strange" (referring to the Marvel comic-book character), features the **Great Society**, the **Jefferson Airplane** and the **Charlatans**.

21 **Bill Black**—upright bassist on **Elvis Presley**'s original Sun Records sessions, a member of Presley's backup band through the Fifties and leader of his own **Bill Black's Combo**, a popular and influential instrumental rock combo—dies at age thirty-nine in his hometown of Memphis following surgery for a brain tumor.

The **Kingsmen** appear on "Shindig!" performing "Louie Louie," along with the **Dave Clark Five** (performing "Having a Wild Weekend" from their movie of the same title) and guest hostess **Hedy Lamarr**.

22 The **Rolling Stones'** "Get Off My Cloud" is released in the U.K. Less than two weeks later it hits Number One on the U.K. pop chart.

23 The **Temptations** enter the Hot 100 for the seventh time with "My Baby," which will reach #13 in eight weeks on the chart. The single's flip side, "Don't Look Back," will reach #83 on the pop chart in December.

30 The **Supremes'** "I Hear a Symphony" enters the Hot 100, where in ten weeks on the chart it will become the Motown girl group's sixth Number One record out of the last seven releases (the group's prior release, "Nothing but Heartaches," peaked at #11 three months ago). It would be their last Number One hit until "You Can't Hurry Love" in August 1966.

31 **Annabella Lwin**, who will become lead singer of British Afro-punk band **Bow Wow Wow** some fourteen years later, is born in Burma. ◆

WEEK ENDING OCTOBER 3

U.S. #1 POP 45	"Hang On Sloopy"	The McCoys
U.S. #1 POP LP	*Help!*	The Beatles
U.S. #1 R&B 45	"Papa's Got a Brand New Bag"	James Brown
U.K. #1 POP 45	"Tears"	Ken Dodd
U.K. #1 POP LP	*Help!*	The Beatles

WEEK ENDING OCTOBER 10

U.S. #1 POP 45	"Yesterday"	The Beatles
U.S. #1 POP LP	*Help!*	The Beatles
U.S. #1 R&B 45	"I Want To (Do Everything for You)"	Joe Tex
U.K. #1 POP 45	"Tears"	Ken Dodd
U.K. #1 POP LP	*Help!*	The Beatles

WEEK ENDING OCTOBER 17

U.S. #1 POP 45	"Yesterday"	The Beatles
U.S. #1 POP LP	*Help!*	The Beatles
U.S. #1 R&B 45	"I Want To (Do Everything for You)"	Joe Tex
U.K. #1 POP 45	"Tears"	Ken Dodd
U.K. #1 POP LP	*Help!*	The Beatles

WEEK ENDING OCTOBER 24

U.S. #1 POP 45	"Yesterday"	The Beatles
U.S. #1 POP LP	*Help!*	The Beatles
U.S. #1 R&B 45	"I Want To (Do Everything for You)"	Joe Tex
U.K. #1 POP 45	"Tears"	Ken Dodd
U.K. #1 POP LP	*The Sound of Music*	soundtrack

WEEK ENDING OCTOBER 31

U.S. #1 POP 45	"Yesterday"	The Beatles
U.S. #1 POP LP	*Help!*	The Beatles
U.S. #1 R&B 45	"Rescue Me"	Fontella Bass
U.K. #1 POP 45	"Get Off My Cloud"	The Rolling Stones
U.K. #1 POP LP	*The Sound of Music*	soundtrack

5 Decca Records releases the **Who**'s anthemic "My Generation." The **Pete Townshend** song will be the English group's biggest British hit, reaching #2, but it will get no higher than #74 in the U.S.

6 **Bill Graham**, who will become one of rock's most powerful entrepreneurs, produces his first rock concert at the Fillmore Auditorium in San Francisco's Fillmore, a black ghetto. The show, a benefit for San Francisco's Mime Troupe (a free street-theater commune), features the **Grateful Dead**, **Jefferson Airplane** and the **Charlatans**.

The **Rolling Stones** (performing "Good Times" and "Have Mercy"), the **Strangeloves** (performing "I Want Candy") and **Fontella Bass** (singing "Rescue Me") appear on "Shindig!"

On the night of New York City's famous blackout, **Bob Dylan**, the **Band**'s **Robbie Robertson** and Dylan friend **Bob Neuwirth** jam with **Brian Jones** of the **Rolling Stones** in his suite at the New York Hilton.

13 **James Brown**'s "I Got You (I Feel Good)" enters both the pop and R&B charts. The song will reach Number One R&B and #3 pop, and will become one of the Godfather of Soul's most enduring and most readily identifiable classics.

Memphis soul singer/songwriter **Don Covay**, who had begun his career in the late Fifties as a **Little Richard** protégé called "Pretty Boy," enters the Hot 100 for the last time in the Sixties with "See Saw." The song will reach #44 on the pop chart and #5 on the R&B chart, and will be a #14 pop hit for **Aretha Franklin** in 1968.

15 The **Rolling Stones** make their debut on NBC-TV's "Hullabaloo" TV rock show, performing "Get Off My Cloud."

19 At the Glad Rags Ball in London, the **Who**'s lead singer, **Roger Daltrey**, storms offstage in the midst of a set plagued with PA problems. Rumors of a Who breakup spread quickly through London, with most of them naming **Boz Bur-**

rell (later of **King Crimson** and **Bad Company**) as Daltrey's possible replacement.

20 **Little Richard** enters the R&B chart for the first time since 1958 with "I Don't Know What You've Got but It's Got Me." The song will reach #12 on the R&B chart and #92 on the Hot 100. In July 1964, Little Richard had entered the Hot 100 for the first time since 1958 with "Bama Lama Bama Loo," which reached #82.

22 Tamla-Motown Records releases **Stevie Wonder**'s "Uptight (Everything's Alright)." Peaking at Number One on the R&B chart and #3 on the pop chart, it will

be the fifteen-year-old Wonder's biggest hit since "Fingertips, Part Two" in 1963.

Bob Dylan marries **Sara Lowndes**, a former model and a divorcée with a daughter, in a Nassau County (Long Island), New York, civil ceremony attended only by a few close friends. Four days later, Dylan will embark on a world tour, his first with the **Band** (or the **Hawks**, as they are still named). Not until February will Dylan acknowledge his marriage to the public.

27 Novelist **Ken Kesey** (*One Flew over the Cuckoo's Nest, Sometimes a Great Notion*) and his band of **Merry Pranksters** (the gang of LSD experimenters that includes archetypal beatnik **Neal Cassady**) hold their first public acid test at San Francisco's Longshoreman's Hall. The order of the day is to imbibe "electric kool-aid" (fruit juice spiked with LSD), wander around, space out on the light show, groove on the **Grateful Dead**'s free-form "prankster music," maybe talk into one of the dozens of microphones set up throughout the hall. Kesey and the Merry Pranksters, as much as anyone else, will introduce psychedelia into the public consciousness. Their exploits will be described in **Tom Wolfe**'s book *The Electric Kool-Aid Acid Test*.

30 The Colorado State government, on the occasion of the **Rolling Stones**' concert in Denver, declares this day to be Rolling Stones Day. ◆

WEEK ENDING NOVEMBER 7

U.S. #1 POP 45	"Get Off My Cloud"	The Rolling Stones
U.S. #1 POP LP	*Help!*	The Beatles
U.S. #1 R&B 45	"Rescue Me"	Fontella Bass
U.K. #1 POP 45	"Get Off My Cloud"	The Rolling Stones
U.K. #1 POP LP	*The Sound of Music*	soundtrack

WEEK ENDING NOVEMBER 14

U.S. #1 POP 45	"Get Off My Cloud"	The Rolling Stones
U.S. #1 POP LP	*The Sound of Music*	soundtrack
U.S. #1 R&B 45	"Rescue Me"	Fontella Bass
U.K. #1 POP 45	"Get Off My Cloud"	The Rolling Stones
U.K. #1 POP LP	*The Sound of Music*	soundtrack

WEEK ENDING NOVEMBER 21

U.S. #1 POP 45	"I Hear a Symphony"	The Supremes
U.S. #1 POP LP	*The Sound of Music*	soundtrack
U.S. #1 R&B 45	"Rescue Me"	Fontella Bass
U.K. #1 POP 45	"Get Off My Cloud"	Rolling Stones
U.K. #1 POP LP	*The Sound of Music*	soundtrack

WEEK ENDING NOVEMBER 28

U.S. #1 POP 45	"I Hear a Symphony"	The Supremes
U.S. #1 POP LP	*Whipped Cream and Other Delights*	Herb Alpert and the Tijuana Brass
U.S. #1 R&B 45	"Ain't That Peculiar"	Marvin Gaye
U.K. #1 POP 45	"1–2–3"	Len Barry
U.K. #1 POP LP	*The Sound of Music*	soundtrack

4 With the British Invasion and "Swinging London" at the peak of their powers, the **Kinks** enter the Hot 100 with a song that sets them apart from every other contemporary British band—"A Well Respected Man," a caustically analytical tune that marks the beginning of band leader **Ray Davies**' sociological examinations of the British way of life. The song will peak at #13 in its fourteen weeks on the chart.

The **Knickerbockers** enter the Hot 100 with their first of only three hits, the garage-rock classic "Lies," which will peak at #20 in its thirteen weeks on the chart. Their other two hits would be "One Track Mind" (#46, 1966) and "High on Love" (#94, 1966).

Rolling Stones guitarist **Keith Richards** is knocked unconscious by an ungrounded microphone during a concert in Sacramento, California. He recovers in seven minutes, and the concert continues.

On the first of two "Shindig!" shows taped at the Richmond-on-Thames Jazz Festival, the **Animals** perform "We Gotta Get Out of This Place," the **Moody Blues** perform "I Go Crazy" and **Georgie Fame and His Blue Flames** perform "Monkey Around." Five days later, part two will feature **Manfred Mann** ("If You Gotta Go, Go Now"), the **Yardbirds** ("For Your Love") and the **Who** ("Anyway, Anyhow, Anywhere," "Shout and Shimmy"). Also taped is a performance by **Brian Auger**'s Steampacket, with **Julie Driscoll**, **Rod Stewart** and **Long John Baldry** on vocals.

6 Motown Records releases **Smokey Robinson and the Miracles**' "Going to a Go-Go," later covered by the **Rolling Stones**. The Miracles' version will reach #11 on the pop chart.

The **Rolling Stones** enter RCA's Hollywood Studios in Los Angeles to record "19th Nervous Breakdown," "Mother's Little Helper" and other tracks.

11 **Ray Charles**' "Crying Time" enters the Hot 100, where it will stay for fifteen weeks, reaching as high as #6. It is his forty-fifth chart entry.

18 The **Beatles** enter the Hot 100—yet again—with both sides of their latest single, "We Can Work It Out" and "Day Tripper." The former will remain on the chart for twelve weeks, eventually reaching Number One; the latter will go as high as #5 in its ten weeks on the chart. "We Can Work It Out" will also be a hit for **Stevie Wonder** in 1971; "Day Tripper" will chart for **Ramsey Lewis** and the **Vontastics** in 1966.

Stevie Wonder's "Uptight (Everything's Alright)" enters the Hot 100, where it will stay for fourteen weeks, peaking at #3—Wonder's first Top Ten pop hit since his first hit, "Fingertips," which hit Number One in 1963. "Uptight (Everything's Alright" will also be a hit in versions by **Nancy Wilson** and the **Jazz Crusaders** (later known simply as the Crusaders) in 1966.

24 The **Beatles** earn yet another gold record, for the album *Rubber Soul*, just two-and-a-half weeks after its release. The disc, which includes "I've Just Seen a Face," "Norwegian Wood" (one of the first uses of the Indian sitar in rock), "Girl," "Michelle," "In My Life" and "You Won't See Me," will come to be seen by many critics as an important turning point in the Beatles' career, marking their progression to a more serious brand of pop music.

25 **Lou Christie**'s biggest hit, "Lightning Strikes," enters the Hot 100, where it will remain for fifteen weeks, eventually giving Christie his only Number One hit. His other big hits include "Two Faces Have I" (#6, 1963) and "I'm Gonna Make You Mine" (#10, 1969). In the early Eighties, while German new-wave cult figure **Klaus Nomi** was performing a neo-operatic-disco version of "Lightning Strikes" in New York clubs, Christie attempted an ill-fated, rap-oriented comeback.

New York band the **Young Rascals**, later to be known simply as the **Rascals**, enter the Hot 100 for the first of many times with "I Ain't Gonna Eat Out My Heart Anymore," which will peak at #52 in its nine weeks on the chart. Their next hit, "Good Lovin'," will hit Number One in early 1966, becoming the first of their three Number Ones and their five Top Ten hits.

The **Rolling Stones** enter the Hot 100 for the tenth time with "As Tears Go By," which will peak at #6 in its nine weeks on the chart. The song had originally been a hit for **Marianne Faithfull** in late 1964; **Mick Jagger** of the Stones had written the song for her before she became his girlfriend.

The **Dave Clark Five** hit Number One on the U.S. pop chart with "Over and Over." Despite eight Top Ten records in their career, this is their only Number One hit.

30 The **Who** perform "Daddy Rolling Stone" on "Shindig!" Also featured on the show are **Gerry and the Pacemakers**, the **Kinks**, the **Hollies**, **Manfred Mann** and **Georgie Fame**. ◆

WEEK ENDING DECEMBER 5

U.S. #1 POP 45	"Turn! Turn! Turn!"	The Byrds
U.S. #1 POP LP	*Whipped Cream and Other Delights*	Herb Alpert and the Tijuana Brass
U.S. #1 R&B 45	"I Got You (I Feel Good)"	James Brown
U.K. #1 POP 45	"Day Tripper"/"We Can Work It Out"	The Beatles
U.K. #1 POP LP	*Rubber Soul*	The Beatles

WEEK ENDING DECEMBER 12

U.S. #1 POP 45	"Turn! Turn! Turn!"	The Byrds
U.S. #1 POP LP	*Whipped Cream and Other Delights*	Herb Alpert and the Tijuana Brass
U.S. #1 R&B 45	"I Got You (I Feel Good)"	James Brown
U.K. #1 POP 45	"Day Tripper"/"We Can Work It Out"	The Beatles
U.K. #1 POP LP	*Rubber Soul*	The Beatles

WEEK ENDING DECEMBER 19

U.S. #1 POP 45	"Turn! Turn! Turn!"	The Byrds
U.S. #1 POP LP	*Whipped Cream and Other Delights*	Herb Alpert and the Tijuana Brass
U.S. #1 R&B 45	"I Got You (I Feel Good)"	James Brown
U.K. #1 POP 45	"Day Tripper"/"We Can Work It Out"	The Beatles
U.K. #1 POP LP	*Rubber Soul*	The Beatles

WEEK ENDING DECEMBER 26

U.S. #1 POP 45	"Over and Over"	The Dave Clark Five
U.S. #1 POP LP	*Whipped Cream and Other Delights*	Herb Alpert and the Tijuana Brass
U.S. #1 R&B 45	"I Got You (I Feel Good)"	James Brown
U.K. #1 POP 45	"Day Tripper"/"We Can Work It Out"	The Beatles
U.K. #1 POP LP	*Rubber Soul*	The Beatles

1966

By far the most sensational rock-related event of the year was John Lennon's statement in March to a British tabloid that he felt the Beatles had become more popular than Jesus Christ. A gigantic, worldwide anti-Beatles backlash developed. In July, there were the first public burnings of Beatles records. In August, the Beatles were frequently pelted with debris by outraged fans at shows on their U.S. tour. Late in the month, John Lennon appeared at a press conference and flouted everyone's expectations of a public apology by instead announcing his approval of American draft dodgers. A few days later, Lennon did make his public apology for the Jesus remark, but the earlier press conference stood as a fine example of how far rock had come in terms of sociopolitical import and relevancy. After all, here was a rock & roll star giving a press conference; a rock & roll star who had, perhaps unwittingly, attacked institutionalized religion and who endorsed political subversion.

This was also the year that psychedelia flowered. In January, the Psychedelic Shop opened in San Francisco's hippie center, the Haight-Ashbury district. By the summer, Beatle George Harrison and Rolling Stone Brian Jones were reportedly studying the classical Indian instrument the sitar, which Harrison introduced into rock on "Norwegian Wood" on last year's *Rubber Soul,* and which Jones put to brilliant use on this year's Stones hit "Paint It Black." Psychedelia was responsible for this growing fascination with exotic Eastern mysticism, which was part and parcel of the whole hippie ethos, encompassing more than just music, which was now being consciously used as a weapon in what was becoming a cultural war between the young generation and the old establishment. By October, the Vietnam War escalated. While the U.S. government was declaring LSD illegal, Britain got its own psychedelic underground going with the UFO Club and bands like Pink Floyd and Soft Machine. And then there was the emergence in London of Jimi Hendrix—a product of psychedelia, no doubt, but much more than a psychedelic rocker.

The proof of just how serious rock and its audience had become arrived this year in February, with the publication of the first issue of the first "rock culture" or "youth culture" magazine, *Crawdaddy.* By the end of the year, Britain had its own counterpart in *International Times.* Things weren't all *that* serious everywhere, though. Television produced such rock-derived novelty hits as the theme from "Batman" by both bandleader Neal Hefti and surf rockers the Marketts, and the Alka-Seltzer jingle tune "No Matter What Shape Your Stomach's In" by the T-Bones. Film and TV executives tried, and succeeded in, foisting on the public four blatant prefabricated Beatles clones, the Monkees. And the Beach Boys spent more money than anyone ever had in producing one single, "Good Vibrations"—an intricate ode to that simple sensation of feelin' groovy.

But in 1966, there were two important harbingers of things to come that—though they may not have seemed and may, in fact, not have *been*, all that serious at the time—would later have serious ramifications: Cream was formed, and thus was born the phenomenon whereby a large portion of the rock audience demands formal and technical virtuosity from rock instrumentalists; and the Rolling Stones—of course—committed what may have been rock's first self-conscious flirtation with decadence and perversion by releasing their single "Have You Seen Your Mother, Baby (Standing in the Shadow?)" in a sleeve featuring the band dressed in drag.

1 The **Beach Boys** enter the Hot 100 for the twenty-third time with "Barbara Ann," previously a hit for the **Regents** in 1961. The Beach Boys' version will hang in the charts for eleven weeks, peaking at #2. It inaugurates a hit-filled year for the California surf-rock group, who will go on to have four more hits, three of them—"Sloop John B," "Wouldn't It Be Nice" and "Good Vibrations"—making the Top Ten. The other, "God Only Knows," will make the Top Forty.

Motown girl group the **Marvelettes** enter the Hot 100 for the fifth time with "Don't Mess with Bill," which will become one of their biggest hits, peaking at #7 in its twelve weeks on the chart.

3 The **Beatles** appear on "Hullabaloo," performing "Day Tripper" and "We Can Work It Out" on videotape.

6 Two days before it begins a three-week reign in the Number One spot, the **Beatles'** "We Can Work It Out" is awarded a gold record. It had entered the chart on December 18, 1965, and will remain in the Hot 100 a total of twelve weeks.

8 The final episode of "Shindig!," featuring the **Kinks** ("I Gotta Move") and the **Who** ("I Can't Explain"), is broadcast on ABC-TV. The show had premiered in September 1964 and from 1965 had aired twice weekly, on Thursday and Saturday evenings.

Motown vocalist **Tammi Terrell** enters the Hot 100 for the first time with "I Can't Believe You Love Me," which will peak at #72 in five weeks on the chart. She will go on to have two more minor hits, and will find greater success in a duo with Motown's **Marvin Gaye**, with whom she will record such hits as "Ain't No Mountain High Enough," "Your Precious Love" and "Ain't Nothing like the Real Thing." She will die of a brain tumor at age twenty-four on March 16, 1970.

11 British Invasion band **Herman's Hermits** receive a gold record for the album *The Best of Herman's Hermits*.

14 Britain's Parlophone Records releases the single "Can't Help Thinking about Me" backed with "And I Say to Myself" by **David Bowie and the Lower Third**. Bowie (ne Jones) had only recently changed his name to avoid confusion between himself and young theater star **Davy Jones**, later of the **Monkees**.

15 Motown's most successful female vocal group, the **Supremes**, enter the Hot 100 for the thirteenth time with "My World Is Empty without You," which in eleven weeks on the chart will peak at #5—one of their few releases of this period that fails to reach Number One.

The **Rolling Stones** receive their third gold record for the album *December's Children*, which features such songs as "Get Off My Cloud," "Route 66," "As Tears Go By" and "I'm Free." Their other gold records were for "(I Can't Get No) Satisfaction" on July 19, 1965, and the album *Out of Our Heads* on October 12, 1965.

20 **Bill Graham** helps **Ken Kesey** and his **Merry Pranksters** stage a three-day Trips Festival, a sort of extended acid test that Kesey himself terms "the graduation from the acid tests," at San Francisco's Longshoreman's Hall.

21 Beatle George Harrison marries his longtime girlfriend, fashion model **Patti Boyd**. The two had met on the set of the Beatles' first movie, *A Hard Day's Night*. She would leave Harrison in the mid-Seventies to take up with their neighbor **Eric Clapton**, who would write the song "Layla" about her, and whom she would marry in May 1979.

22 **Frank Sinatra**'s daughter **Nancy** enters the Hot 100 for the second time with what will become her biggest hit, the defiant "These Boots Are Made for Walkin'." In fourteen weeks on the chart, the song will hit Number One for one week on February 26 and will inspire one U.S. tire manufacturer to advertise a model called the Wide Boot, the commercials for which feature the song's descending guitar riff.

29 Folk singer **Joan Baez** wins three gold records this day—for the albums *Joan Baez, Joan Baez, Vol. 2* and *Joan Baez in Concert*. ◆

WEEK ENDING JANUARY 1

U.S. #1 POP 45	"Sounds of Silence"	Simon and Garfunkel
U.S. #1 POP LP	*Whipped Cream and Other Delights*	Herb Alpert and the Tijuana Brass
U.S. #1 R&B 45	"I Got You (I Feel Good)"	James Brown
U.K. #1 POP 45	"Day Tripper"/"We Can Work It Out"	The Beatles
U.K. #1 POP LP	*Rubber Soul*	The Beatles

WEEK ENDING JANUARY 8

U.S. #1 POP 45	"We Can Work It Out"	The Beatles
U.S. #1 POP LP	*Rubber Soul*	The Beatles
U.S. #1 R&B 45	"A Sweet Woman Like You"	Joe Tex
U.K. #1 POP 45	"Keep on Running"	The Spencer Davis Group
U.K. #1 POP LP	*Rubber Soul*	The Beatles

WEEK ENDING JANUARY 15

U.S. #1 POP 45	"We Can Work It Out"	The Beatles
U.S. #1 POP LP	*Rubber Soul*	The Beatles
U.S. #1 R&B 45	"I Got You (I Feel Good)"	James Brown
U.K. #1 POP 45	"Keep on Running"	The Spencer Davis Group
U.K. #1 POP LP	*Rubber Soul*	The Beatles

WEEK ENDING JANUARY 22

U.S. #1 POP 45	"Sounds of Silence"	Simon and Garfunkel
U.S. #1 POP LP	*Rubber Soul*	The Beatles
U.S. #1 R&B 45	"Uptight (Everything's Alright)"	Stevie Wonder
U.K. #1 POP 45	"Keep on Running"	The Spencer Davis Group
U.K. #1 POP LP	*Rubber Soul*	The Beatles

WEEK ENDING JANUARY 29

U.S. #1 POP 45	"We Can Work It Out"	The Beatles
U.S. #1 POP LP	*Rubber Soul*	The Beatles
U.S. #1 R&B 45	"Up Tight (Everything's Alright)"	Stevie Wonder
U.K. #1 POP 45	"Michelle"	The Overlanders
U.K. #1 POP LP	*Rubber Soul*	The Beatles

5 Surf-rockers the **Marketts** enter the Hot 100 for the fifth and last time with "Batman Theme," which reaches #17 in nine weeks on the chart. Their biggest hit was 1963's "Out of Limits," which hit #3.

Sergeant Barry Sadler's "The Ballad of the Green Berets," a patriotic novelty song in which gung-ho ex-Green Beret Sadler recites an ode to "fighting men . . . of America's best" over a march rhythm, enters the lower reaches of the pop chart. It will quickly skyrocket to Number One, remain in the pop chart for thirteen weeks and go gold, as will Sadler's album, *Ballads of the Green Berets*. The latter includes such tunes as "Letter from Vietnam," "Trooper's Lament," "Saigon" and "The A Team," the latter of which will become Sadler's second and last hit (it would reach #28 in April). "The Ballad of the Green Berets" was inspired by **Robin Moore**'s book *The Green Berets*, and Moore cowrote the hit with Sadler. Sadler will not be heard from again until December 1978, when he will be involved in a Nashville shooting incident that leaves songwriter **Lee Bellamy** dead at age fifty-one. In 1981, Sadler will be involved in another shooting, in Memphis, but this time the victim—a one-time business partner of Sadler's—will survive. In fact, Sadler will justify his innocent plea by explaining, "I'm a Green Beret—if I'd shot him, he'd be dead."

7 The first issue of the rock-culture magazine *Crawdaddy* is published in New York City by **Paul Williams** (not to be confused with the singer/songwriter of the same name), who will edit the magazine for its first few years. *Crawdaddy* would go on to gain a sizable audience and much critical respect before changing its name to *Feature* and running aground in 1979.

The **Beach Boys** album *Summer Days* goes gold—their sixth album to do so. The others are *Beach Boys Today, Surfer Girl, Surfin' USA, Beach Boys in Concert* and *All Summer Long,* all of which went gold in 1965.

12 The **McCoys** enter the Hot 100 for the third time with "Up and Down," which will peak at #46 in its six weeks on the chart. Their first and biggest hit, "Hang On Sloopy," reached Number One in October 1965. They will have six more minor hits. Their members include guitarist **Rick Derringer** (ne Zehringer), who will go on to gain fame on his own and work as a collaborator with blues-rock guitarist **Johnny Winter**.

The **Rolling Stones** fly to New York to tape an appearance on "The Ed Sullivan Show," which is aired the next evening.

14 The *New York Times* reports on the **Moppets,** an all-girl rock band formed by four Mount Holyoke College students, and notes other groups at other women's schools.

Simon and Garfunkel receive their first gold record for "Sounds of Silence," which had hit Number One on the pop chart on January 1 of this year.

15 Nat "King" Cole dies of complications following surgery for lung cancer at age forty-six in Santa Monica, California.

17 **Sergeant Barry Sadler** receives two gold-record awards on this day—for the single "The Ballad of the Green Berets," which will not hit Number One on the pop chart until March 5 (it will stay atop the charts for five weeks), and the album *Ballads of the Green Berets.*

19 *Billboard* reports that the **Rolling Stones,** following their tour of Australia and New Zealand, will fly to Los Angeles to record nine songs for their planned film, *Back, Behind and In Front.*

The **Outsiders'** first and biggest hit, "Time Won't Let Me," enters the Hot 100, where in fifteen weeks on the chart it will peak at #5. The band will have three more minor hits this year— "Girl in Love," "Respectable" and "Help Me Girl"—before fading into obscurity.

25 Nancy Sinatra receives her first gold record for "These Boots Are Made for Walkin'." She will share a gold record with her father **Frank** in 1967 for "Somethin' Stupid."

26 The **Temptations'** "Get Ready" enters the Hot 100. It will peak at #29 in its seven weeks on the pop chart and will hit Number One on the R&B chart. The song will be covered by **Rare Earth** in 1970, and their version will go to #4.

Boston garage-rock band the **Barbarians** hit the chart for the second and last time with "Moulty," a bizarre tribute to the band's drummer, who has one artificial hand. The song peaks at #90 in its four weeks on the chart, but will later be immortalized on the *Nuggets* garage-rock anthology released in the Seventies. The band's previous chart entry, "Are You a Boy or Are You a Girl?," hit #55 in October 1965.

28 CBS Labs develops a metal disc that reproduces motion pictures through a television set.

Liverpool's Cavern Club, where the **Beatles** had first risen to fame, closes. ◆

WEEK ENDING FEBRUARY 5

U.S. #1 POP 45	"My Love"	Petula Clark
U.S. #1 POP LP	*Rubber Soul*	The Beatles
U.S. #1 R&B 45	"Uptight (Everything's Alright)"	Stevie Wonder
U.K. #1 POP 45	"These Boots Are Made for Walkin'"	Nancy Sinatra
U.K. #1 POP LP	*Rubber Soul*	The Beatles

WEEK ENDING FEBRUARY 12

U.S. #1 POP 45	"My Love"	Petula Clark
U.S. #1 POP LP	*Rubber Soul*	The Beatles
U.S. #1 R&B 45	"Uptight (Everything's Alright)"	Stevie Wonder
U.K. #1 POP 45	"Keep on Running"	The Spencer Davis Group
U.K. #1 POP LP	*Rubber Soul*	The Beatles

WEEK ENDING FEBRUARY 19

U.S. #1 POP 45	"Lightnin' Strikes"	Lou Christie
U.S. #1 POP LP	*Rubber Soul*	The Beatles
U.S. #1 R&B 45	"Uptight (Everything's Alright)"	Stevie Wonder
U.K. #1 POP 45	"Keep on Running"	The Spencer Davis Group
U.K. #1 POP LP	*Rubber Soul*	The Beatles

WEEK ENDING FEBRUARY 26

U.S. #1 POP 45	"These Boots Are Made for Walkin'"	Nancy Sinatra
U.S. #1 POP LP	*Rubber Soul*	The Beatles
U.S. #1 R&B 45	"Baby, Scratch My Back"	Slim Harpo
U.K. #1 POP 45	"19th Nervous Breakdown"	The Rolling Stones
U.K. #1 POP LP	*The Sound of Music*	soundtrack

1 In Liverpool, over 100 youths barricade themselves inside the recently closed Cavern Club, where the **Beatles** began their rise to fame. They protest the club's closing due to bankruptcy and keep the police out of the club.

The New York State Supreme Court dismisses a suit by the East Meadow Community Concerts Association to enjoin a New York school from canceling a **Pete Seeger** concert.

3 In Los Angeles, singer-guitarists **Neil Young, Stephen Stills** and **Richie Furay** form seminal West Coast country-rock band **Buffalo Springfield** with bassist **Bruce Palmer** and drummer **Dewey Martin**. Stills, who had worked in New York with Furay and the **Au Go Go Singers**, had met Young while the latter was a solo folk singer in his native Canada. The day before, a story goes, Stills and Furay were caught in an L.A. traffic jam when they spotted a hearse with Ontario license plates and guessed that Young was in it. He was. With him was fellow Canadian and bassist Palmer. Buffalo Springfield's self-titled debut album, released a year later, would yield the band's only big hit single, Stills' ominous protest song "For What It's Worth," which would reach #7 on the pop chart. Buffalo Springfield also contained the seeds of such country-rock bands as **Crosby, Stills, Nash and Young** and **Poco**.

The **Rolling Stones** enter RCA's Hollywood Studios in Los Angeles to record tracks for the album *Aftermath*.

4 The London newspaper *The Evening Standard* publishes an interview with **Beatle John Lennon** in which he remarks, "Christianity will go. It will vanish and shrink. I needn't argue about that, I'm right and will be proved right. We're more popular than Jesus Christ right now." This quote will touch off a storm of international protest and will result in a world-wide series of Beatles records burnings.

The **Who**'s self-produced "Substitute" is released on **Robert Stigwood**'s Reaction label, violating their production contract with **Shel Talmy** and their recording contract with Decca. The resultant uproar prevents the Who from releasing any more material for almost six months.

6 British **Beatles**' fans give British Prime Minister **Harold Wilson** a petition with 5,000 signatures, asking that Liverpool's Cavern Club be reopened.

7 The **Shadows of Knight**—a Chicago garage-rock band managed by **Terry Knight** (hence their name), who would go on to manage **Grand Funk Railroad**—enter the Top Ten with their biggest hit, "Gloria" (previously recorded by **Van Morrison and Them** and later covered by **Patti Smith**), which will reach #10.

12 The self-titled debut album by Los Angeles band **Love** is released on Elektra Records. The album contains Love's version of the **Burt Bacharach-Hal David** song "My Little Red Book," originally recorded by **Manfred Mann**; Love's version will become one of their few hit singles, reaching #52 on the pop chart within a month. Love, led by singer/guitarists **Arthur Lee** and **Bryan McLean**, would become a critically respected, though never extremely popular, progressive-pop band; they would be reformed several times by the eccentric Lee before breaking up for good in 1974.

15 Winners of the eighth annual Grammy Awards for 1965 are announced. Record of the Year is "A Taste of Honey" by **Herb Alpert and the Tijuana Brass**. Album of the Year is **Frank Sinatra**'s *September of My Years*. Song of the Year is "The Shadow of Your Smile" by **Paul Francis Webster** and **Johnny Mandel**. Best Small Group Jazz Instrumental is **Ramsey Lewis**' "The 'In' Crowd." Best New Artist of 1965 is **Tom Jones**. Best Contemporary (Rock and Roll) Vocal Performance (Female) is **Petula Clark**'s "I Know a Place." Best Contemporary (Rock and Roll) Vocal Performance (Male) is **Roger Miller**'s "King of the Road," which also wins Best Country and Western Single, Best Country and Western Vocal Performance (Male) and Best Country and Western Song; Miller's *Return of Roger Miller* wins Best Country and Western Album. Best Rhythm and Blues Recording is **James Brown**'s "Papa's Got a Brand New Bag." Best Contemporary (Rock and Roll) Group Performance is the **Statler Brothers**' "Flowers on the Wall."

24 The New York State Assembly passes a bill making it a misdemeanor to sell unauthorized copies of records or tapes; such records are commonly known as bootlegs.

28 New York City Parks Commissioner **Thomas Hoving** describes plans for rock & roll dance concerts to be held in Central Park.

30 At the **Rolling Stones**' concert at the Olympia in Paris, 85 audience members are arrested after the crowd's heated reaction to the Stones gets out of hand. ◆

WEEK ENDING MARCH 5

U.S. #1 POP 45	"The Ballad of the Green Berets"	Sgt. Barry Sadler
U.S. #1 POP LP	*Going Places*	Herb Alpert and the Tijuana Brass
U.S. #1 R&B 45	"Baby, Scratch My Back"	Slim Harpo
U.K. #1 POP 45	"I Can't Let Go"	The Hollies
U.K. #1 POP LP	*The Sound of Music*	soundtrack

WEEK ENDING MARCH 12

U.S. #1 POP 45	"The Ballad of the Green Berets"	Sgt. Barry Sadler
U.S. #1 POP LP	*Ballads of the Green Berets*	Sgt. Barry Sadler
U.S. #1 R&B 45	"634-5789"	Wilson Pickett
U.K. #1 POP 45	"The Sun Ain't Gonna Shine Anymore"	The Walker Brothers
U.K. #1 POP LP	*The Sound of Music*	soundtrack

WEEK ENDING MARCH 19

U.S. #1 POP 45	"The Ballad of the Green Berets"	Sgt. Barry Sadler
U.S. #1 POP LP	*Ballads of the Green Berets*	Sgt. Barry Sadler
U.S. #1 R&B 45	"634-5789"	Wilson Pickett
U.K. #1 POP 45	"The Sun Ain't Gonna Shine Anymore"	The Walker Brothers
U.K. #1 POP LP	*The Sound of Music*	soundtrack

WEEK ENDING MARCH 26

U.S. #1 POP 45	"The Ballad of the Green Berets"	Sgt. Barry Sadler
U.S. #1 POP LP	*Ballads of the Green Berets*	Sgt. Barry Sadler
U.S. #1 R&B 45	"634-5789"	Wilson Pickett
U.K. #1 POP 45	"The Sun Ain't Gonna Shine Anymore"	The Walker Brothers
U.K. #1 POP LP	*The Sound of Music*	soundtrack

1 Britain's Pye Records releases **David Bowie**'s first solo single: "Do Anything You Say" backed with "Good Morning Girl." Bowie has previously recorded as **David Jones and the Lower Third.**

3 Folk singer **Peter Tork** opens a solo engagement at Hollywood's most prestigious folk club, the Troubadour. Tork, a former member of **the Phoenix Singers**, has already auditioned for a role in NBC-TV's "The Monkees," which will premiere in September, with Tork as one of its four stars.

11 NBC broadcasts the final episode of "Hullabaloo," which features **Paul Anka, the Cyrkle, Lesley Gore** and **Peter and Gordon.** The show had premiered in January 1965,
a year after ABC had introduced "Shindig!"

12 **Jan Berry**, half of the hitmaking surf-rock vocal duo **Jan and Dean** (**Dean Torrence** being the other half), runs his Corvette into a parked truck on Los Angeles' Whittier Boulevard. Berry suffers total physical paralysis for over a year, as well as extensive brain damage that makes it nearly impossible, despite a few unsuccessful attempts, to return to performing. The duo will try one big comeback at a 1973 Surfer's Stomp festival in Los Angeles, but the comeback becomes a fiasco. Their last hit before the accident was "Batman," which reached #66 on the pop chart; their last big hit was "Popsicle," which reached #21 in July; and their final hit would be "Fiddle Around," which would reach #93 in September.

15 Decca Records releases the **Rolling Stones'** *Aftermath* in Britain. Featuring "Mother's Little Helper," "Under My Thumb," "Goin' Home," "Lady Jane," "Out of Time" and other gems of the Stones' repertoire, it is the first album comprised entirely of **Mick Jagger-Keith Richards** originals. In two weeks, it will hit Number One for a nine-week stay at that position on the U.K. album chart. In the U.S., *Aftermath* will reach #2.

22 "Wild Thing" by British band the **Troggs** is released in the U.S. on both the Atco and Fontana labels (Fontana being their British label). The group, led by **Reg Presley**, had taken their name from the word "troglodyte." The song will reach Number One in June, will later be covered by **Jimi Hendrix**, among others (including imitators of U.S. senators Robert Kennedy and Everett Dirksen) and becomes both a garage-punk anthem and an important precursor to heavy-metal rock.

23 New York City radio station WOR, anticipating the Federal Communications Commission's imminent ruling regarding duplication of AM and FM programming, announces that it will open an FM outlet that, in contrast to talk-oriented WOR-AM, will feature music.

26 *The New York Times* reports that R&B immortal **Ray Charles** will undergo hospital tests in Boston to determine whether or not he has abstained from narcotic drugs.

29 New York City Parks Commissioner **Thomas Hoving** announces a series of concerts to be held in the summer in Central Park's Wollman Rink. The concerts, featuring rock, pop, folk, jazz and ethnic music, will be underwritten by Rheingold Beer.

30 Folk singer/songwriter/ author **Richard Fariña**—at the time married to folksinger **Mimi Fariña, Joan Baez'** younger sister—dies in a motorcycle accident in California, following the party celebrating the publication of his underground novel *Been Down So Long It Looks Up to Me.* Fariña, an outspoken political performer who had backed revolutionary causes in his native Cuba as well as Ireland, was twenty-nine years old, and had written such songs as "Pack Up Your Troubles" and "Hard Lovin' Loser." The book will be published again in 1983. ◆

WEEK ENDING APRIL 2

U.S. #1 POP 45	"The Ballad of the Green Berets"	Sgt. Barry Sadler
U.S. #1 POP LP	*Ballads of the Green Berets*	Sgt. Barry Sadler
U.S. #1 R&B 45	"634–5789"	Wilson Pickett
U.K. #1 POP 45	"The Sun Ain't Gonna Shine Anymore"	The Walker Brothers
U.K. #1 POP LP	*The Sound of Music*	soundtrack

WEEK ENDING APRIL 9

U.S. #1 POP 45	"(You're My) Soul and Inspiration"	The Righteous Brothers
U.S. #1 POP LP	*Ballads of the Green Berets*	Sgt. Barry Sadler
U.S. #1 R&B 45	"634–5789"	Wilson Pickett
U.K. #1 POP 45	"The Sun Ain't Gonna Shine Anymore"	The Walker Brothers
U.K. #1 POP LP	*The Sound of Music*	soundtrack

WEEK ENDING APRIL 16

U.S. #1 POP 45	"(You're My) Soul and Inspiration"	The Righteous Brothers
U.S. #1 POP LP	*Ballads of the Green Berets*	Sgt. Barry Sadler
U.S. #1 R&B 45	"634–5789"	Wilson Pickett
U.K. #1 POP 45	"Somebody Help Me"	The Spencer Davis Group
U.K. #1 POP LP	*The Sound of Music*	soundtrack

WEEK ENDING APRIL 23

U.S. #1 POP 45	"(You're My) Soul and Inspiration"	The Righteous Brothers
U.S. #1 POP LP	*Ballads of the Green Berets*	Sgt. Barry Sadler
U.S. #1 R&B 45	"634–5789"	Wilson Pickett
U.K. #1 POP 45	"You Don't Have to Say You Love Me"	Dusty Springfield
U.K. #1 POP LP	*The Sound of Music*	soundtrack

WEEK ENDING APRIL 30

U.S. #1 POP 45	"Good Lovin'"	The Young Rascals
U.S. #1 POP LP	*Ballads of the Green Berets*	Sgt. Barry Sadler
U.S. #1 R&B 45	"Get Ready"	The Temptations
U.K. #1 POP 45	"You Don't Have to Say You Love Me"	Dusty Springfield
U.K. #1 POP LP	*Aftermath*	The Rolling Stones

1 The **Beatles**, the **Rolling Stones** and the **Who** perform at the *New Musical Express'* poll winners' show in London. This will be the last live U.K. performance by the Beatles.

7 **Simon and Garfunkel**'s "I Am a Rock" enters the Hot 100—the folk-pop duo's third chart entry. In its eleven weeks on the chart, it will peak at #3.

Del Shannon, who had big hits in 1961 with "Runaway" and "Hats Off to Larry," enters the Hot 100 for the sixteenth and last time with "The Big Hurt," which in its two weeks on the chart will peak at #94. Little will be heard from Shannon again until 1981, when he has a Top Forty hit with "Sea of Love," produced by **Tom Petty**.

10 **Rolling Stones** manager/producer **Andrew Loog Oldham** announces that his clients will receive $1 million dollars to appear in *Only Lovers Left Alive*, a film based on **Dave Willis**' novel about the violent conquest of Britain by rebellious youth (fictitious, of course). The film, like the Stones' recently aborted *Back, Behind and In Front*, will never be completed.

13 Decca Records in the U.K. and London Records in the U.S. release the **Rolling Stones'** "Paint It Black" backed with "Long Long While." "Paint It Black," one of the first rock records to use a sitar, will hit Number One in both countries.

14 Seminal garage-rock band the **Kingsmen**—who had left an indelible mark on rock history with their first hit, "Louie Louie," which reached #2 on the pop chart in 1963—enter the Hot 100 for the ninth and last time with a rereleased "Louie Louie," which remains on the chart for only two weeks, going only as high as #97. It will, however, incite some controversy over its unintelligible, but assumed obscene lyrics.

Bob Dylan and the **Hawks**, after touring Australia, Scandinavia and now the British Isles, give a concert in Liverpool. The live recording of "Just like Tom Thumb's Blues" made here will be released as the B side of the single "I Want You."

20 **Pete Townshend** and **Roger Daltrey** of the **Who**, tired of waiting for the tardy **John Entwistle** and **Keith Moon**, go onstage at the Ricky Tick Club in Windsor, England, and play a set with the bassist and drummer of the local band that opened the show. When Moon and Entwistle arrive midway through the set, Townshend hits Moon on the head with his guitar and Moon promptly quits the band—for a week.

21 The **Kinks'** "Dedicated Follower of Fashion"—which, like their earlier "A Well Respected Man," displays band leader **Ray Davies'** droll, ironic sociological analysis of the British way of life—enters the Hot 100, where it will remain for six weeks, peaking at #36.

British singer **Dusty Springfield**'s "You Don't Have to Say You Love Me" enters the Hot 100, where in thirteen weeks on the chart it will become her biggest hit, reaching #4.

22 Sixteen-year-old **Bruce Springsteen** and his first band, the **Castilles**, record their first and only record, "That's What You Get" backed with "Baby I," in Bricktown, New Jersey. It will never be released.

26 **Bob Dylan** and the **Hawks** rock & roll at the Royal Albert Hall in London. In attendance are the **Rolling Stones** (coming straight from a taping of "Paint It Black" for BBC-TV's "Top of the Pops"), members of the **Beatles** and other aristocrats of British rock. The concert is surreptitiously recorded, later to be heard on various bootleg albums that substantiate claims made for the concert—that it is one of the high-water marks of live rock & roll.

28 Soul singer **Wilson Pickett**'s "Ninety-Nine and a Half (Won't Do)" enters the Hot 100, where in eight weeks on the chart it will peak at #53. Pickett's next release, "Land of 1000 Dances," will be one of his biggest hits, reaching #6 in August of this year.

Ike and Tina Turner's "River Deep, Mountain High" enters the Hot 100, where it will stay for only four weeks, reaching as high as #88, though it was a massive hit in the U.K. The record's producer, **Phil Spector**, considers the song the high point of his legendary production career, and is so embittered by its failure to hit in America that he would go into seclusion for two years.

The **Temptations'** "Ain't Too Proud to Beg" enters the Hot 100, where it will stay for thirteen weeks, peaking at #13. It will later be covered by the **Rolling Stones** on their album *It's Only Rock 'N' Roll*, and will be a hit for them as well. ◆

WEEK ENDING MAY 7

U.S. #1 POP 45	"Monday, Monday"	The Mamas and the Papas
U.S. #1 POP LP	*Ballads of the Green Berets*	Sgt. Barry Sadler
U.S. #1 R&B 45	"When a Man Loves a Woman"	Percy Sledge
U.K. #1 POP 45	"Pretty Flamingo"	Manfred Mann
U.K. #1 POP LP	*Aftermath*	The Rolling Stones

WEEK ENDING MAY 14

U.S. #1 POP 45	"Monday, Monday"	The Mamas and the Papas
U.S. #1 POP LP	*Ballads of the Green Berets*	Sgt. Barry Sadler
U.S. #1 R&B 45	"When a Man Loves a Woman"	Percy Sledge
U.K. #1 POP 45	"Pretty Flamingo"	Manfred Mann
U.K. #1 POP LP	*Aftermath*	The Rolling Stones

WEEK ENDING MAY 21

U.S. #1 POP 45	"Monday, Monday"	The Mamas and the Papas
U.S. #1 POP LP	*If You Can Believe Your Eyes and Ears*	The Mamas and the Papas
U.S. #1 R&B 45	"When a Man Loves a Woman"	Percy Sledge
U.K. #1 POP 45	"Pretty Flamingo"	Manfred Mann
U.K. #1 POP LP	*Aftermath*	The Rolling Stones

WEEK ENDING MAY 28

U.S. #1 POP 45	"When a Man Loves a Woman"	Percy Sledge
U.S. #1 POP LP	*What Now My Love*	Herb Alpert and the Tijuana Brass
U.S. #1 R&B 45	"When a Man Loves a Woman"	Percy Sledge
U.K. #1 POP 45	"Paint It Black"	The Rolling Stones
U.K. #1 POP LP	*Aftermath*	The Rolling Stones

5 *The New York Times* reports on the success of WJRZ, the first radio station in the New York City area to broadcast only country music.

Films made by the **Beatles** to accompany their recordings of "Paperback Writer" and "Rain" are shown on "The Ed Sullivan Show." The films, like the songs, find the Beatles experimenting far beyond the usual parameters of pop performance.

7 Roy Orbison's wife **Claudette** (for whom he'd written a song of the same name with which the **Everly Brothers** had a hit in the late Fifties) is killed in a motorcycle accident, which he witnesses. This was the first of two personal tragedies that would set back Orbison's career; in September 1968, two of his three children would perish in a fire that would consume his Nashville home.

10 The **Beatles'** "Rain"— their first song to use the reversed-tape effect that would later figure prominently in the "Paul McCartney Is Dead" controversy—is released on Capitol Records.

11 **Janis Joplin** sings onstage with **Big Brother and the Holding Company** for the first time at San Francisco's Avalon Ballroom. Joplin, who has only recently arrived in California from her home in Port Arthur, Texas, is twenty-three.

In announcements on various European radio stations, **Who** lead singer **Roger Daltrey** is reportedly dead. Actually, it was Who guitarist **Pete Townshend** who had suffered minor injuries in a car accident a few days earlier; European radio stations got wind of the accident and reported the misinformation.

15 The **Beatles'** album *Yesterday and Today* is released by Capitol Records in its controversial "butcher" sleeve—a cover photo of the Beatles smiling amid a bunch of bloodied, decapitated baby dolls. The original photo would quickly become the object of controversy, and Capitol would soon withdraw it from circulation, replacing it with a more conventional cover and turning the "butcher" original into a valuable collector's item. Through the years, Beatlemaniacs have maintained that Capitol pasted the new cover over the first pressings with the offending original, and that owners could discover if they own a copy of the sought-after "butcher" cover simply by steaming the second cover off.

17 British guitarist **Peter Greenbaum**, using his stage name **Peter Green**, joins **John Mayall's Bluesbreakers**. Green would go on to become a founding member of **Fleetwood Mac**, as well as one of Britain's most respected electric guitarists.

20 *The New York Times* reports that **George Harrison** of the **Beatles** and **Brian Jones** of the **Rolling Stones** have taken up the sitar, an ancient, traditional Indian stringed instrument that produces a buzzing, droning sound. In the same article, Indian sitar master **Ravi Shankar** comments on the sitar fad in Great Britain. The sitar fad is an outgrowth of the psychedelic-era fascination with exotic Eastern cultures and mysticism. Brian Jones used the sitar in an inspired rock & roll style on the Stones' "Paint It Black." Subsequently, the sitar would become so big that the Danelectro Guitar Company would introduce a six-string electric sitar (the traditional sitar has twenty-one strings and is acoustic) that would become popular with many bands, including the **Turtles** and, later, **Yes** (whose guitarist, **Steve Howe**, used it on the album *Close to the Edge*).

21 The **Rolling Stones**, preparing for a tour of the U.S., sue fourteen New York City hotels that have banned the group from their premises. The ban hurts the group's reputation, the suit claims, and amounts to "discrimination on account of national origin," a violation of New York State civil-rights laws.

23 The **Rolling Stones** depart London for their third tour of America only two weeks after **Mick Jagger** was hospitalized after collapsing from exhaustion at the conclusion of whirlwind tours of Australia and Europe.

25 The **Beach Boys** headline a "Summer Spectacular" concert at the Hollywood Bowl. Also appearing are the **Byrds**, the **Lovin' Spoonful**, **Chad and Jeremy**, the **Outsiders**, **Percy Sledge**, the **Sir Douglas Quintet**, the **Leaves**, **Love** and **Captain Beefheart and His Magic Band**.

29 The **Beatles** perform in Tokyo, Japan, before a sold-out crowd of screaming fans. Five hundred police are called to keep the crowd in control. ◆

WEEK ENDING JUNE 4

U.S. #1 POP 45	"When a Man Loves a Woman"	Percy Sledge
U.S. #1 POP LP	*What Now My Love*	Herb Alpert and the Tijuana Brass
U.S. #1 R&B 45	"It's a Man's Man's Man's World"	James Brown
U.K. #1 POP 45	"Strangers in the Night"	Frank Sinatra
U.K. #1 POP LP	*Aftermath*	The Rolling Stones

WEEK ENDING JUNE 11

U.S. #1 POP 45	"Paint It Black"	The Rolling Stones
U.S. #1 POP LP	*What Now My Love*	Herb Alpert and the Tijuana Brass
U.S. #1 R&B 45	"It's a Man's Man's Man's World"	James Brown
U.K. #1 POP 45	"Strangers in the Night"	Frank Sinatra
U.K. #1 POP LP	*Aftermath*	The Rolling Stones

WEEK ENDING JUNE 18

U.S. #1 POP 45	"Paint It Black"	The Rolling Stones
U.S. #1 POP LP	*What Now My Love*	Herb Alpert and the Tijuana Brass
U.S. #1 R&B 45	"Hold On! I'm Comin'"	Sam and Dave
U.K. #1 POP 45	"Strangers in the Night"	Frank Sinatra
U.K. #1 POP LP	*Aftermath*	The Rolling Stones

WEEK ENDING JUNE 25

U.S. #1 POP 45	"Paperback Writer"	The Beatles
U.S. #1 POP LP	*What Now My Love*	Herb Alpert and the Tijuana Brass
U.S. #1 R&B 45	"Ain't Too Proud to Beg"	The Temptations
U.K. #1 POP 45	"Paperback Writer"	The Beatles
U.K. #1 POP LP	*Aftermath*	The Rolling Stones

4 The **Beatles** perform in Manila, Philippines, and are mobbed by fans and police at the local airport after a mix-up with local authorities regarding their no-show at the presidential palace.

6 During a show at Syracuse, New York's War Memorial Hall, the **Rolling Stones** allegedly drag an American flag along the floor of the stage.

The New York Times reports that the **Beatles** were booed recently at a Manila, Philippines, airport after they failed to make a private appearance before Philippines President **Marcos** and his wife and 300 Filipino children. The Beatles claim they were not told of the engagement, and Marcos makes a statement regretting the airport inci-

dent. From Manila, the Beatles fly to New Delhi, India.

8 Following a Syracuse, New York, concert during which they allegedly dragged an American flag across the stage, the **Rolling Stones** are accused by local authorities of desecrating the American flag.

15 Soul singer **Percy Sledge**'s first and biggest hit, "When a Man Loves a Woman"—which hit Number One for two weeks starting May 28—earns him his first and only gold record. Sledge would go on to have twelve more hits, including "Take Time to Know Her," which would reach #11 in mid-1968.

16 In London, three musicians—ex-**John Mayall Bluesbreaker** and **Yardbird Eric Clapton** (guitar), and ex-

Graham Bond Organisation members **Jack Bruce** (bass) and **Ginger Baker** (drums)—form the band **Cream**, who would go on to become one of the most popular and influential rock groups of the Sixties. According to Clapton, Cream was originally planned as a blues trio—"Buddy Guy with a rhythm section," in his words. However, Cream would become best known as pioneers of extended blues-based group improvisations. They would have hit singles with "Sunshine of Your Love," "Strange Brew," "White Room," "Crossroads," "I'm So Glad," "I Feel Free" and "Badge," and would release such top-selling albums as *Fresh Cream, Disraeli Gears, Wheels of Fire* and *Goodbye*. Cream would ultimately come to be regarded as rock's first supergroup—predating Clapton and Baker's next band, **Blind Faith**, the first band to actually be cal-

led a supergroup upon its inception.

18 **Bobby Fuller**, leader of the **Bobby Fuller Four**, a Texas rock band, is found dead in his car in Los Angeles; no conclusive cause of death is ever established. The Bobby Fuller Four had hits in 1966 with "I Fought the Law" (written by **Sonny Curtis**, a member of **Buddy Holly**'s **Crickets**) and Buddy Holly's "Love's Made a Fool of You."

23 **Stevie Wonder**'s version of **Bob Dylan**'s "Blowin' in the Wind"—previously a hit for folk trio **Peter, Paul and Mary**—enters the Hot 100. It will remain on the chart for ten weeks, reaching as high as #9.

24 *The New York Times* reports that British Prime Minister **Harold Wilson** was present at the recent reopenings of the Cavern Club in Liverpool. The club had closed due to bankruptcy, but thousands of **Beatles** fans signed a petition requesting Wilson to have the club reopened.

25 The **Rolling Stones** perform their last American concert with **Brian Jones**, in San Francisco.

29 **Bob Dylan** crashes his Triumph 55 motorcycle while riding near Woodstock, New York. He is rushed to Middletown Hospital with several broken vertebrae in his neck, a concussion and lacerations of the face and scalp. He remains in serious condition for a week and is confined to bed, suffering mild amnesia, minor paralysis and internal injuries for a month. Rampant rumors have it that he is in a coma, has become a vegetable, will never perform again, is dodging the draft, has died, or has merely lost his mind due to drug use.

30 New York City radio station WOR announces that WOR-FM will soon go on the air with a rock & roll music format—but minus four disc jockeys, including **Murray the K**, because of labor disputes with the American Federation of Television and Radio Artists. ◆

WEEK ENDING JULY 2

U.S. #1 POP 45	"Strangers in the Night"	Frank Sinatra
U.S. #1 POP LP	*What Now My Love*	Herb Alpert and the Tijuana Brass
U.S. #1 R&B 45	"Ain't Too Proud to Beg"	The Temptations
U.K. #1 POP 45	"Paperback Writer"	The Beatles
U.K. #1 POP LP	*The Sound of Music*	soundtrack

WEEK ENDING JULY 9

U.S. #1 POP 45	"Paperback Writer"	The Beatles
U.S. #1 POP LP	*What Now My Love*	Herb Alpert and the Tijuana Brass
U.S. #1 R&B 45	"Ain't Too Proud to Beg"	The Temptations
U.K. #1 POP 45	"Sunny Afternoon"	The Kinks
U.K. #1 POP LP	*The Sound of Music*	soundtrack

WEEK ENDING JULY 16

U.S. #1 POP 45	"Hanky Panky"	Tommy James and the Shondells
U.S. #1 POP LP	*Strangers in the Night*	Frank Sinatra
U.S. #1 R&B 45	"Ain't Too Proud to Beg"	The Temptations
U.K. #1 POP 45	"Sunny Afternoon"	The Kinks
U.K. #1 POP LP	*The Sound of Music*	soundtrack

WEEK ENDING JULY 23

U.S. #1 POP 45	"Hanky Panky"	Tommy James and the Shondells
U.S. #1 POP LP	*Strangers in the Night*	Frank Sinatra
U.S. #1 R&B 45	"Let's Go Get Stoned"	Ray Charles
U.K. #1 POP 45	"Out of Time"	Chris Farlowe
U.K. #1 POP LP	*The Sound of Music*	soundtrack

WEEK ENDING JULY 30

U.S. #1 POP 45	"Wild Thing"	The Troggs
U.S. #1 POP LP	*Yesterday and Today*	The Beatles
U.S. #1 R&B 45	"Let's Go Get Stoned"	Ray Charles
U.K. #1 POP 45	"Out of Time"	Chris Farlowe
U.K. #1 POP LP	*The Sound of Music*	soundtrack

3 In Los Angeles for concert appearances, the **Rolling Stones** record "Have You Seen Your Mother, Baby (Standing in the Shadow)?" with pianist **Jack Nitzsche** and engineer **Dave Hassinger** at RCA's Hollywood Studios. When the single, backed with "Who's Driving Your Plane," is released on September 23, almost as much controversy is generated by the picture on the sleeve as by the crashing wave of sound from the grooves: The photograph shows the five Rolling Stones dressed in drag and lolling around on New York City's Park Avenue.

4 The day after the South African government had banned the playing of any and all **Beatles** records in response to **John Lennon**'s statement that the band was now more popular than Jesus Christ, a ban on the broadcast of any and all Beatles records on America's radio stations goes into effect on most of the country's radio stations.

5 The **Beatles** album *Revolver* is released in the U.K. by Capitol Records. Seen by many critics as an important transitional album between *Rubber Soul* and *Sgt. Pepper's Lonely Hearts Club Band*, the album would yield such hit singles as "Yellow Submarine" and "Eleanor Rigby," as well as containing "Got to Get You into My Life," later covered by **Earth, Wind and Fire**. The U.S. version of the album, which differs slightly in the song selection, is released four days later.

New York State's antipiracy bill, barring unauthorized reproduction of phonograph records and requiring record companies to print their names and addresses on album jackets, is signed into law.

8 An advertisement for the album *LSD* appears in *The New York Times*. It's a recording of people under the influence of the drug.

11 The controversy over **John Lennon**'s remark about the **Beatles** being more popular than Jesus Christ continues: Stock in the band's label, Capitol, drops sharply on the New York Stock Exchange, and the city fathers of Memphis re-

quest the cancelation of an upcoming Beatles concert there.

12 The **Beatles** begin their final American tour, at Chicago's International Amphitheater. Earlier in the day, the Beatles had held a local news conference at which **John Lennon** publicly apologized for his remark about the band being more popular than Jesus Christ.

14 According to an item in *The New York Times* that the Roman newspaper *Observatore Romano* has accepted **Beatle John Lennon**'s apology for his remark that the group is more popular than Jesus Christ; London's *Catholic Herald* has called Len-

non's remark "arrogant," but has also admitted that, as Lennon himself recently asserted, it's still probably true.

17 At a Toronto press conference, **John Lennon** of the **Beatles** expresses his admiration for American draft dodgers.

20 Despite the protests of city fathers over their scheduled concert appearance in Memphis, the **Beatles** perform there anyway. Firecrackers, fruit and other debris are hurled at the group by fans outraged at **John Lennon**'s recent remarks.

22 *The New York Times* announces that **Jerry Lee Lewis** has been signed by producer **Jack Good** to play Iago in *Catch My Soul*, a rock version of Shakespeare's *Othello*.

23 The **Beatles** arrive in New York City for their Shea Stadium concert. Two young ladies, fans of the group, threaten to jump from the twenty-second floor of the Americana Hotel unless they see the group. The police arrive soon to rescue them. Three days later, the girls will be charged with disorderly conduct and paroled to the New York Youth Bureau.

29 The **Beatles** perform their last public concert, at San Francisco's Candlestick Park. The concert is filmed by Beatles press officer **Tony Barrow**, though the film is never released. ◆

WEEK ENDING AUGUST 6

U.S. #1 POP 45	"Wild Thing"	The Troggs
U.S. #1 POP LP	*Yesterday and Today*	The Beatles
U.S. #1 R&B 45	"Let's Go Get Stoned"	Ray Charles
U.K. #1 POP 45	"A Girl like You"	The Troggs
U.K. #1 POP LP	*The Sound of Music*	soundtrack

WEEK ENDING AUGUST 13

U.S. #1 POP 45	"Summer in the City"	The Lovin' Spoonful
U.S. #1 POP LP	*Yesterday and Today*	The Beatles
U.S. #1 R&B 45	"Let's Go Get Stoned"	Ray Charles
U.K. #1 POP 45	"A Girl like You"	The Troggs
U.K. #1 POP LP	*Revolver*	The Beatles

WEEK ENDING AUGUST 20

U.S. #1 POP 45	"Summer in the City"	The Lovin' Spoonful
U.S. #1 POP LP	*Yesterday and Today*	The Beatles
U.S. #1 R&B 45	"Let's Go Get Stoned"	Ray Charles
U.K. #1 POP 45	"Yellow Submarine"/"Eleanor Rigby"	The Beatles
U.K. #1 POP LP	*Revolver*	The Beatles

WEEK ENDING AUGUST 27

U.S. #1 POP 45	"Summer in the City"	The Lovin' Spoonful
U.S. #1 POP LP	*Yesterday and Today*	The Beatles
U.S. #1 R&B 45	"Blowin' in the Wind"	Stevie Wonder
U.K. #1 POP 45	"Yellow Submarine"/"Eleanor Rigby"	The Beatles
U.K. #1 POP LP	*Revolver*	The Beatles

3 The **Four Tops**' "Reach Out I'll Be There" enters the Hot 100, where it will hit Number One on October 15.

?(Question Mark) and the Mysterians' "96 Tears," considered by many fans and critics to be *the* classic garage-rock song, enters the Hot 100, where it will peak at Number One for one week starting October 29. The song's repetitive, staccato one-finger Vox organ melody will become one of rock's most recognizable and best-remembered signature sounds, and will go on to influence much of the new-wave rock of the Seventies. "96 Tears" will be covered by **Big Maybelle** in 1967 and by **Garland Jeffreys** in 1981. ? and the Mysterians are a group of Mexican-Americans from Saginaw, Michigan; the immortal organ riff on "96 Tears" is played by **Frank Rodriguez**; the mysterious ?, who always wears sunglasses and never gives his real name, will later reveal himself as **Rudy Martinez** when he attempts a brief and ill-fated comeback in the early Eighties, fronting what would sound like a heavy-metal bar band. "96 Tears" will not be

? and the Mysterians' only hit—they will score again with "I Need Somebody" (#22 later this year), "Can't Get Enough of You, Baby" (#56, 1967) and "Girl (You Captivate Me)" (#98, 1967)—just their biggest.

9 *Life* magazine's cover story: "New Experience That Bombards the Senses: LSD Art." In the same issue, an ad for Coty lipsticks asks the question: "If Mother Nature is so smart, why weren't we born with gold lips." The proliferation of psychedelic art bears out the statement of a leading LSD expert that this is the "year of turning on without drugs." "We try to vaporize the mind," says one psychedelic artist, "by bombarding the senses."

11 The **Rolling Stones** appear on "The Ed Sullivan Show." Guitarist **Brian Jones** performs despite the cast on his right hand, which was broken in a fall in Tangier.

12 The TV show "The Monkees"—depicting the zany antics of a lovable, long-haired rock band obviously modeled after the **Beatles**

and their film *A Hard Day's Night*—premieres on NBC-TV. The **Monkees**—**Davy Jones**, **Mike Nesmith**, **Peter Tork** and **Mickey Dolenz**—were formed expressly for the TV show, and were chosen more for their telegenic qualities than their musical abilities. In fact, at the beginning of their career, they sang but did not play any instruments on their recordings. Their records and TV show became tremendous successes. The show remained on the air through 1969. Two days ago, their debut single, "Last Train to Clarksville," entered the Hot 100, where it would peak at Number One for a week starting November 5. The Monkees will go on to have two more Number One hits ("I'm a Be-

liever" in early 1967—later covered by ex-**Soft Machine** drummer/vocalist **Robert Wyatt**—and "Daydream Believer" in late 1967), three more Top Ten hits and four other Top Forty hits. Most of these songs were written by the songwriting team of **Tommy Boyce** and **Bobby Hart**. Eventually, however, the **Monkees** would get to play their own instruments and even record some of their original compositions.

16 Member of Parliament **Tom Driberg** asks Britain's House of Commons to officially "deplore" the action of a magistrate who'd earlier called the **Rolling Stones** "complete morons...who wear filthy clothes."

19 The **Lovin' Spoonful**'s fifth hit single and first Number One pop hit, "Summer in the City"—which hit the top of the chart a month ago—wins the New York-based folk-pop band a gold record, their first.

20 **George Harrison** of the **Beatles** goes to India for his first visit with spiritual guru **Maharishi Mahesh Yogi**.

21 **Jimi Hendrix** and his manager, ex-**Animals** bassist **Chas Chandler**, arrive in London from New York, where Chandler had discovered Hendrix working in Greenwich Village go-go clubs and convinced him that Britain would be more receptive than America to his flamboyant interpretation of the blues. During the transatlantic flight, Hendrix changes the spelling of his first name from Jimmy to **Jimi**.

22 On the same day that their single "Have You Seen Your Mother, Baby?" is released in the U.K. on London Records, the **Rolling Stones** begin a British tour at London's Royal Albert Hall. Accompanied by the **Ike and Tina Turner Revue** and the **Yardbirds**, it will be the Stones' last British tour for more than four years. ◆

WEEK ENDING SEPTEMBER 3

U.S. #1 POP 45	"Sunshine Superman"	Donovan
U.S. #1 POP LP	*Yesterday and Today*	The Beatles
U.S. #1 R&B 45	"You Can't Hurry Love"	The Supremes
U.K. #1 POP 45	"Yellow Submarine"/"Eleanor Rigby"	The Beatles
U.K. #1 POP LP	*Revolver*	The Beatles

WEEK ENDING SEPTEMBER 10

U.S. #1 POP 45	"You Can't Hurry Love"	The Supremes
U.S. #1 POP LP	*Revolver*	The Beatles
U.S. #1 R&B 45	"You Can't Hurry Love"	The Supremes
U.K. #1 POP 45	"Yellow Submarine"/"Eleanor Rigby"	The Beatles
U.K. #1 POP LP	*Revolver*	The Beatles

WEEK ENDING SEPTEMBER 17

U.S. #1 POP 45	"You Can't Hurry Love"	The Supremes
U.S. #1 POP LP	*Revolver*	The Beatles
U.S. #1 R&B 45	"Land of 1,000 Dances"	Wilson Pickett
U.K. #1 POP 45	"All or Nothing"	The Small Faces
U.K. #1 POP LP	*Revolver*	The Beatles

WEEK ENDING SEPTEMBER 24

U.S. #1 POP 45	"Cherish"	The Association
U.S. #1 POP LP	*Revolver*	The Beatles
U.S. #1 R&B 45	"Beauty Is Only Skin Deep"	The Temptations
U.K. #1 POP 45	"Distant Drums"	Jim Reeves
U.K. #1 POP LP	*Revolver*	The Beatles

7 Veteran New Orleans R&B singer **Smiley Lewis**, born **Overton Amos Lemons** on July 5, 1920, dies of stomach cancer in New Orleans. A guitarist as well as a singer, Lewis had big R&B hits with "The Bells Are Ringing" in 1952 and "I Hear You Knocking" in 1955, but is generally considered to have been vastly overlooked by the populace. His "One Night" was later covered by **Elvis Presley**, who had a big hit with it; "I Hear You Knocking" was successfully covered by **Gale Storm** in the Fifties and Britisher **Dave Edmunds** in the early Seventies.

Early British rocker **Johnny Kidd** is killed in a car accident in Lancashire, England. Kidd, born **Frederick Heath** in London December 23, 1939, led the **Pirates**, arguably the first truly raunchy band in British rock history. Their biggest hit was 1960's "Shakin' All Over."

8 The U.S government officially declares the psychedelic drug LSD, also known as acid, to be a dangerous and illegal substance.

9 **John Lennon** meets **Yoko Ono** for the first time at the Indica Gallery in London's West End, where Ono is giving an exhibition of her avant-garde art. Ono supposedly does not know who her visitor is; she tells him that for five shillings he can hammer a nail into one of the participatory exhibits, even though the show has not opened yet. "Well," says Lennon (as he will later recount the meeting), "I'll give you an imaginary five shillings and hammer an imaginary nail in." Lennon: "And that's when we really met."

Concluding a tour of Great Britain at London's Royal Albert Hall, the **Rolling Stones** record their first live album, *Got Live If You Want It,* a disc notable chiefly for the din of the audience, which all but drowns out the band. A live EP with the same title was released earlier in Britain only.

14 Singer **Grace Slick** makes her first appearance with the **Jefferson Airplane** at the Fillmore West in San Francisco. She replaces **Signe Toly Anderson**, who has left the band to have a baby.

15 **Pink Floyd** and **Soft Machine** perform at the launching party for the new British-based youth-culture paper *International Times.*

18 The **Jimi Hendrix Experience** plays its debut concert for an audience of 14,500 at Paris' Olympia Theatre, opening a show for French pop star **Johnny Halliday**. On returning to London to play club dates, Hendrix will be instantly embraced by London's rock aristocracy—**Brian Jones**, **Eric Clapton**, **John Mayall**, **Pete Townshend**, **Jeff Beck** and others—as the latest rage. The British press will characterize Hendrix as "the wild man of pop" and a "Mau Mau."

19 The **Yardbirds** arrive in New York for their first American tour, with **Jeff Beck** and **Jimmy Page** on lead guitars. This configuration would break up after playing two dates of the tour. With Beck's departure, Jimmy Page would take over the lead guitar, while rhythm guitarist **Chris Dreja** would switch to bass.

21 The **Who**—done up in pop-art costumes and items of disguise, and equipped with smoke bombs, flash powder and other stage devices of their "Theatre of the Absurd" (as manager **Kit Lambert** sees it)—appear on British television's "Ready Steady Go!" performing the material from their rush-released EP, *Ready Steady Who!*: "Batman Theme," the **Regents**' "Barbara Ann," **Ronny and the Daytonas**' "Bucket 'T' " and **Pete Townshend** originals "Circles" and "Disguises."

22 The **Beach Boys** release their classic single "Good Vibrations" on Capitol Records. The song, featuring inspired use of the sci-fi movie sound-effects instrument the theremin, is the most expensive production for a single up to this time.

28 The British Musicians Union announces its opposition to the British government's recently announced plans to form a Popular Music Authority to broadcast continuous pop music over the BBC's radio waves; the union says its members will take part in no live broadcasts and will make no more records until the idea is dropped.

29 Memphis' Beale Street, immortalized by seminal blues songwriter **W.C. Handy** in "Beale Street Blues," is made a national landmark as "the home of the blues." ♦

WEEK ENDING OCTOBER 1

U.S. #1 POP 45	"Cherish"	The Association
U.S. #1 POP LP	*Revolver*	The Beatles
U.S. #1 R&B 45	"Beauty Is Only Skin Deep"	The Temptations
U.K. #1 POP 45	"Distant Drums"	Jim Reeves
U.K. #1 POP LP	*The Sound of Music*	soundtrack

WEEK ENDING OCTOBER 8

U.S. #1 POP 45	"Cherish"	The Association
U.S. #1 POP LP	*Revolver*	The Beatles
U.S. #1 R&B 45	"Beauty Is Only Skin Deep"	The Temptations
U.K. #1 POP 45	"Distant Drums"	Jim Reeves
U.K. #1 POP LP	*The Sound of Music*	soundtrack

WEEK ENDING OCTOBER 15

U.S. #1 POP 45	"Reach Out I'll Be There"	The Four Tops
U.S. #1 POP LP	*Revolver*	The Beatles
U.S. #1 R&B 45	"Beauty Is Only Skin Deep"	The Temptations
U.K. #1 POP 45	"Distant Drums"	Jim Reeves
U.K. #1 POP LP	*The Sound of Music*	soundtrack

WEEK ENDING OCTOBER 22

U.S. #1 POP 45	"Reach Out I'll Be There"	The Four Tops
U.S. #1 POP LP	*Supremes A'Go-Go*	The Supremes
U.S. #1 R&B 45	"Beauty Is Only Skin Deep"	The Temptations
U.K. #1 POP 45	"Distant Drums"	Jim Reeves
U.K. #1 POP LP	*The Sound of Music*	soundtrack

WEEK ENDING OCTOBER 29

U.S. #1 POP 45	"96 Tears"	? and the Mysterians
U.S. #1 POP LP	*Supremes A' Go-Go*	The Supremes
U.S. #1 R&B 45	"Reach Out I'll Be There"	The Four Tops
U.K. #1 POP 45	"Reach Out I'll Be There"	The Four Tops
U.K. #1 POP LP	*The Sound of Music*	soundtrack

1 Three **Elvis Presley** albums are certified gold this day: his 1956 debut album, *Elvis Presley, Elvis' Golden Records, Vol. 2* and *Elvis' Golden Records, Vol. 3.*

2 Bluesman **Mississippi John Hurt** dies of a heart attack at age seventy-three in Grenada, Mississippi. Among the singer/guitarist's best-known songs were "Coffee Blues," "Chicken" and "Beulah Land."

9 On this day, as rumor and morbid speculation arising from the "Paul Is Dead" hoax of 1969 will date it, **Paul McCartney** is fatally decapitated in a car crash somewhere in England and is replaced in the **Beatles** by a lookalike, one William Campbell—or is it Billy Shears?

19 The **Supremes'** "You Keep Me Hangin' On" hits Number One on the pop chart, and will hit the same position on the R&B chart a week later. It is the Motown female trio's eighth pop Number One and third R&B chart-topper. The **Vanilla Fudge**'s slowed-down, "heavier" cover of the Holland-Dozier-Holland composition will make the pop Top Ten in 1968.

23 **Elvis Presley**'s twenty-second film, *Spinout,* premieres in Los Angeles. The movie, another box-office success and critical disaster for Elvis, also stars **Shelley Fabares** (of "The Donna Reed Show" and "Johnny Angel" fame) and **Deborah Walley** (star of many of the *Gidget* films).

25 The **Jimi Hendrix Experience** (Hendrix, drummer **Mitch Mitchell** and bassist **Noel Redding**) makes its London performing debut at the Bag o' Nails Club.

26 The **Temptations'** "(I Know) I'm Losing You" enters the R&B chart, where it will become the Motown group's fourth consecutive Number One. On the pop chart, it will peak at #8, the Temps' eighth Top Forty single. The **Norman Whitfield-Brian Holland** song will return to the pop Top Forty in versions by **Rare Earth** in 1970 and **Rod Stewart** in 1971.

British band the **Yardbirds** enter the Hot 100 with their last Top Forty hit, "Happenings Ten Years Time Ago," which in nine weeks on the chart will peak at #30. They will have three more minor hits—"Little Games" (#51), "Ha Ha Said the Clown" (#45) and "Ten Little Indians" (#96)—in 1967 before breaking up the following year.

———

Soul singer **Wilson Pickett** enters the Hot 100 with "Mustang Sally," which in nine weeks on the chart will peak at #23. It will hit #6 on the R&B chart. "Mustang Sally," along with Pickett's first big hit, "In the Midnight Hour" (which hit #21 in late 1965 and will later be covered by the **Mirettes**,

Roxy Music and reggae band **Ras Michael and the Sons of Negus**), will become staples of the repertoires of bar bands across America.

28 Several gold records are certified this day. The **Righteous Brothers** get one for their album *Soul and Inspiration,* which features the title single, a Number One hit in April 1966 and their first gold record. Incredibly, according to Recording Industry Association of America records, the Righteous Brothers never received a gold record for their biggest hit, 1964's "You've Lost That Lovin' Feelin'," which was on the chart for sixteen weeks and hit Number One in early 1965, a discrepancy probably due to the reluctance of certain record labels to be audited for gold-record statistics; "You've Lost That Lovin' Feelin' " was on **Phil Spector**'s Philles label, while "Soul and Inspiration" was the Righteous Brothers' first hit for Verve Records. The **Monkees** earn their third gold record for "I'm a Believer," which will hit Number One for seven weeks starting December 31, 1966 (their other gold records were for "Last Train to Clarksville" and their debut album, *The Monkees*). And a gold record goes to the **New Vaudeville Band,** a British studio aggregation, for their Twenties-style novelty song (complete with **Rudy Vallee**-style megaphone vocals), "Winchester Cathedral," which will hit Number One for three weeks beginning on December 3. They will have only one more hit, "Peek-a-Boo" (not to be confused with **Devo**'s 1982 hit), which will peak at #72 in early 1967. ◆

WEEK ENDING NOVEMBER 5

U.S. #1 POP 45	"Last Train to Clarksville"	The Monkees
U.S. #1 POP LP	*Doctor Zhivago*	soundtrack
U.S. #1 R&B 45	"Reach Out I'll be There"	The Four Tops
U.K. #1 POP 45	"Reach Out I'll Be There"	The Four Tops
U.K. #1 POP LP	*The Sound of Music*	soundtrack

WEEK ENDING NOVEMBER 12

U.S. #1 POP 45	"Poor Side of Town"	Johnny Rivers
U.S. #1 POP LP	*Doctor Zhivago*	soundtrack
U.S. #1 R&B 45	"Love Is a Hurtin' Thing"	Lou Rawls
U.K. #1 POP 45	"Love Is a Hurtin' Thing"	Lou Rawls
U.K. #1 POP LP	*The Sound of Music*	soundtrack

WEEK ENDING NOVEMBER 19

U.S. #1 POP 45	"You Keep Me Hangin' On"	The Supremes
U.S. #1 POP LP	*The Monkees*	The Monkees
U.S. #1 R&B 45	"Knock on Wood"	Eddie Floyd
U.K. #1 POP 45	"Good Vibrations"	The Beach Boys
U.K. #1 POP LP	*The Sound of Music*	soundtrack

WEEK ENDING NOVEMBER 26

U.S. #1 POP 45	"You Keep Me Hangin' On"	The Supremes
U.S. #1 POP LP	*The Monkees*	The Monkees
U.S. #1 R&B 45	"You Keep Me Hangin' On"	The Supremes
U.K. #1 POP 45	"Good Vibrations"	The Beach Boys
U.K. #1 POP LP	*The Sound of Music*	soundtrack

1 California folk-pop vocal group the **Mamas and the Papas** earn their fourth gold record for their second album, *Cass, John, Michelle & Denny.* Prior gold records were for the singles "California Dreamin'" and "Monday, Monday" and their debut album, *If You Can Believe Your Eyes and Ears.*

3 Two songs by Memphis soul singer **Otis Redding**, "Fa-Fa-Fa-Fa-Fa" and "Try a Little Tenderness," enter the Hot 100, where they will peak at #29 and #25 respectively. "Fa-Fa-Fa-Fa-Fa" has already risen to #12 on the R&B chart; "Try a Little Tenderness" will enter the R&B chart in one week and will rise to #4. "Try a Little Tenderness" will also be covered by **Three Dog Night**, whose version will hit #29 in 1969.

Motown soul singer **Jimmy Ruffin**, whose brother **David** sings with the **Temptations**, enters the Hot 100 for the second time with "I've Passed This Way Before," which in its eleven weeks on the chart will peak at #17; it will go as high as #10 on the R&B chart. His biggest hit was his first, "What Becomes of the Broken Hearted," which hit #6 on the R&B chart and #7 on the pop chart in August.

Paul Revere and the Raiders enter the Hot 100 with their seventh hit, "Good Thing," which will reach #4 in its fourteen weeks on the chart. This matched the chart performance of their biggest hit to date, "Kicks," the anti-drug song composed by **Barry Mann** and **Cynthia Weil**, which hit #4 earlier this year. The group's first hit was "Like, Long Hair" in

1961. They will go on to have sixteen more chart entries, the biggest being "Indian Reservation," which will hit Number One in 1971. The band's lead singer, **Mark Lindsay**, will embark on a successful solo career in 1969.

16 Polydor Records releases the **Jimi Hendrix Experience**'s debut single, "Hey Joe" backed with "Stone Free." "Hey Joe," an old **Billy Roberts** song, in Hendrix' repertoire for years, will peak at #6 on the U.K. chart; it will not be released as a single in the U.S., but will be included on the Experience's first album, *Are You Experienced?*, in 1967.

17 The **Four Tops**' "Standing in the Shadows of Love" enters the Hot 100. In its ten weeks on the chart, it will peak at #6. It will also reach #2 on the R&B chart.

21 The **Beach Boys** receive three gold-record citations, for the single "Good Vibrations," which hit Number One eleven days ago, and the albums *Little Deuce Coup* and *Shut Down, Vol. 2.*

23 BBC-TV broadcasts "Ready Steady Go!" for the last time after more than three years in which the weekly show was Britain's most popular pop-music television program. The special guests for the farewell show are the **Who**.

Pink Floyd perform at the opening of a London club called the Night Tripper, which will soon change its name to the UFO Club and become the center of London's psychedelic underground.

24 **Tommy James and the Shondells** record "I Think We're Alone Now," which will become a huge "bubblegum" hit and will later be covered by **Lene Lovich** in 1980. James' version will peak at #4 in its seventeen weeks on the chart, and is one of the band's seven Top Ten hits, the others including their first hit (and first of two Number Ones) "Hanky Panky" (earlier this year), "Mirage" (mid-1967), "Mony Mony" (#3, early 1968), "Crimson and Clover" (Number One, early 1969), "Sweet Cherry Wine" (#7, early 1969) and "Crystal Blue Persuasion" (#2, mid-1969).

Sam the Sham and the Pharaohs, one of America's best-loved garage-rock bands—as much for leader Sam's goatee and ever-present fez as for their nonsensical good-time rock & roll—enter the Hot 100 with one of their last hits, "How Do You Catch a Girl," which will peak at #27 in its eight weeks on the chart. Their first hit, the classic "Wooly Bully," hit #2 in mid-1965, and their other big hits include "Li'l Red Riding Hood" (#2, mid-1966) and "The Hair on My Chinny Chin Chin" (#22, two months ago). They will have two more hits in 1967, "Oh That's Good, No That's Bad" (#54) and "Black Sheep" (#68). ◆

WEEK ENDING DECEMBER 3

U.S. #1 POP 45	"Winchester Cathedral"	The New Vaudeville Band
U.S. #1 POP LP	*The Monkees*	The Monkees
U.S. #1 R&B 45	"You Keep Me Hangin' On"	The Supremes
U.K. #1 POP 45	"Green Green Grass of Home"	Tom Jones
U.K. #1 POP LP	*The Sound of Music*	soundtrack

WEEK ENDING DECEMBER 10

U.S. #1 POP 45	"Good Vibrations"	The Beach Boys
U.S. #1 POP LP	*The Monkees*	The Monkees
U.S. #1 R&B 45	"You Keep Me Hangin' On"	The Supremes
U.K. #1 POP 45	"Green Green Grass of Home"	Tom Jones
U.K. #1 POP LP	*The Sound of Music*	soundtrack

WEEK ENDING DECEMBER 17

U.S. #1 POP 45	"Winchester Cathedral"	The New Vaudeville Band
U.S. #1 POP LP	*The Monkees*	The Monkees
U.S. #1 R&B 45	"You Keep Me Hangin' On"	The Supremes
U.K. #1 POP 45	"Green Green Grass of Home"	Tom Jones
U.K. #1 POP LP	*The Sound of Music*	soundtrack

WEEK ENDING DECEMBER 24

U.S. #1 POP 45	"Winchester Cathedral"	The New Vaudeville Band
U.S. #1 POP LP	*The Monkees*	The Monkees
U.S. #1 R&B 45	"(I Know) I'm Losing You"	The Temptations
U.K. #1 POP 45	"Green Green Grass of Home"	Tom Jones
U.K. #1 POP LP	*The Sound of Music*	soundtrack

WEEK ENDING DECEMBER 31

U.S. #1 POP 45	"I'm a Believer"	The Monkees
U.S. #1 POP LP	*The Monkees*	The Monkees
U.S. #1 R&B 45	"(I Know) I'm Losing You"	The Temptations
U.K. #1 POP 45	"Green Green Grass of Home"	Tom Jones
U.K. #1 POP LP	*The Sound of Music*	soundtrack

1967

Rock music was becoming more than mere entertainment, more than a generation's mouthpiece. It was now a symbol, a communal rallying point, a flag to be waved and a weapon to be fired in the escalating war that raged across the so-called generation gap. The political commitment of rock and rock-associated performers took on new heights: Joan Baez, censored by Japanese TV in January, was arrested along with 123 others in October for blocking the entrance to the Oakland Armed Forces Induction Center as a protest against the Vietnam War. In July, the Beatles signed an ad in British newspapers urging the legalization of marijuana.

Rock and its audience were growing in terms of both awareness and sheer number; rock's power and influence took it into heretofore unthinkable places. The Rolling Stones performed behind the Iron Curtain. CBS-TV ran a prime-time special on "the rock revolution" (classical-music conductor Leonard Bernstein hosted it), and two months later, the Beatles commanded a worldwide TV hookup to deliver the musical message "All You Need Is Love." A writer for *Time* magazine reviewed the Doors as though he were writing about an arty foreign film. Pink Floyd performed, and then *discussed* its performance, at London's Institute of Contemporary Art.

This self-conscious artiness, which had been manifested on occasion in the past, became the year's dominant musical trend. The Beatles introduced avant-garde *musique concrète* techniques to rock with "Strawberry Fields Forever" and, a few months later, released *Sgt. Pepper's Lonely Hearts Club Band,* the first "art rock" or concept album. It was quickly followed by classical rock, another art-rock offshoot, in Procol Harum's Bach-based "A Whiter Shade of Pale." And Traffic, arguably the first pop-rock band to infuse jazz into its sound, was formed.

How could rock, a music rooted in such simple, people's-music genres as folk, blues and R&B, have so quickly taken on pretensions to art? Nobody was sure, and most people were just too excited by these rarefied aesthetic heights to care. They were also excited by the continuing evidence of the power of rock and its audience. The first rock festivals—the Human Be-In in January, the Fantasy Faire and Magic Mountain Music Fest in June, quickly followed by the first *big* rock fest, Monterey Pop—took place. The biggest and what would be the longest-lasting rock-culture magazine, *Rolling Stone,* published its first issue. With Tom Donahue launching "progressive, underground" FM radio at San Francisco's KMPX in April, the youth-oriented rock audience had their own radio, too.

The generational war evolved into a game of cat-and-mouse between the revolutionaries and what was then called the establishment. There were drug busts and obscenity busts of rock performers, but the establishment's biggest and strongest weapon was the co-optation of rock's revolutionary impulse—something that couldn't have been possible without the marketing possibilities created by the sheer size and scope of the rock audience. For instance, both the debut album by the Grateful Dead and Scott McKenzie's innocuous tribute to Haight-Ashbury and the hippies, "San Francisco (Be Sure to Wear Flowers in Your Hair)," were released on the same day in May. It was a sign of the times that the former stiffed and the latter became a huge hit. The "poppification" of rock's radical impulses continued in October as *Hair* opened off-Broadway. Jimi Hendrix made his first U.S. appearances—opening for the Monkees—and was booed off the stage.

While the establishment—against which rock was supposed to be rebelling—became more adept at selling its own sanctioned versions of rock back to the audience, the audience itself had grown to such a massive size that it would soon begin to fragment. It would become art rockers versus roots purists, radicals versus teenyboppers, progressive FM versus Bill Drake's AM formats, and so on. And it was all happening too quickly for anyone to notice.

1 Country-music star **Moon Mullican** dies at age fifty-eight of natural causes at his Tennessee home. Though he never had any pop hits, Mullican's two-fingered "hillbilly boogie" piano style made him arguably the first white boogie-woogie pianist and a definite influence on the pounding piano style of **Jerry Lee Lewis**.

14 The *New Musical Express* reports that psychedelic folk singer **Donovan** has been commissioned to write incidental music for a production of Shakespeare's *As You Like It*, produced by London's National Theatre and starring **Laurence Olivier**. *NME* also reports that at a recent solo performance at London's Royal Albert Hall, Donovan was accompanied by a ballerina for his twelve-minute ballet "Golden Apples."

The **Dave Clark Five** has started its own film company, Big Five Films, to make low-budget features and documentaries, according to the *New Musical Express*. The company's first production, *The Dave Clark Five*, will be sold to an American theater chain.

The first Human Be-In and Gathering of the Tribes—a forerunner of the rock festival—is held in San Francisco's Golden Gate Park. Twenty thousand people, including **Ken Kesey**, **Allen Ginsberg**, **Tim Leary** and **Jerry Rubin**, tune in to the good vibes coming from the **Grateful Dead**, the **Jefferson Airplane**, **Quicksilver Messenger Service** and **Dizzy Gillespie**.

15 The **Rolling Stones** appear on "The Ed Sullivan Show" performing their latest hit, "Let's Spend the Night Together." Singer Mick Jagger, asked by Sullivan to change the song's lyrics, instead slurs his way through the title chorus, leading some to believe he'd sung "Let's spend some time together," though he would always assert that he'd "just sung mumble."

16 **Pink Floyd** perform at London's Institute of Contemporary Art and discuss their performance with the audience after the show.

17 The Tea Party, Boston's first rock venue, opens. It's also the East Coast's first big rock ballroom and the second-biggest rock ballroom in the country after San Francisco's Avalon Ballroom.

19 The *New York Times* reports that 100 French musicians have appealed to the French Roman Catholic Episcopate to bar the playing of jazz and avant-garde music at Catholic church services, claiming that the use of vernacular in the mass is disturbing due to the lack of "singable" religious music in French. The music critic for the Paris newspaper *La Monde* has attacked the group in print.

20 The **Monkees**' eponymous TV series premieres in England on BBC-TV. Already a hit in the U.S., the series will make the group stars in the U.K.

21 Japanese and American press stories claim that political statements made by folk singer **Joan Baez** during a recent Tokyo TV appearance were softened by an interpreter under pressure from CIA agent **"H. Cooper."** The U.S. Embassy denies the charge of censorship. The next day, the Japanese interpreter will deny that he was under any CIA pressure. On February 24, Baez will state that she knew her remarks were inaccurately translated on Tokyo TV.

22 The **Rolling Stones** appear on the British TV show "Sunday Night at the London Palladium," but refuse to stand on the show's revolving stage for the grand finale—an action construed in the British press as "an insult to show-business tradition."

24 **John Sinclair**, leader of the White Panther Party, manager of the **MC5** and originator of the slogan "Rock & roll, dope, and fucking in the streets," is arrested along with fifty-seven other persons at his Artists' and Writers' Workshop in Detroit and is charged with possession of two joints. Sinclair will eventually be convicted and sentenced to nine and a half years in prison.

Cat Stevens' debut album, *Cats and Dogs,* is released in the U.K. on Deram Records. Within a few years, Stevens will become an enormously popular folk-pop singer/songwriter, through such early Seventies albums as *Tea for the Tillerman* and *Teaser and the Firecat* and such hit singles as "Wild World," "Moonshadow," "Morning Has Broken" and "Peace Train."

Rolling Stone Mick Jagger gives his reaction to the sensational stage show of London's latest rage, **Jimi Hendrix**: "Most sexual thing I've seen in a long time!"

31 A New York State Supreme Court dismisses a suit brought by school officials from Yorktown (New York) Heights High School that sought to bar folk singer **Pete Seeger** from performing there. According to press accounts, the plaintiffs feared that Seeger's presence might incite the students to riot. The concert, originally scheduled for the day before yesterday, is held on February 3. Over fifty policemen are on hand for the event; there are no disturbances. ◆

WEEK ENDING JANUARY 7

U.S. #1 POP 45	"I'm a Believer"	The Monkees
U.S. #1 POP LP	*The Monkees*	The Monkees
U.S. #1 R&B 45	"(I Know) I'm Losing You"	The Temptations
U.K. #1 POP 45	"Green Green Grass of Home"	Tom Jones
U.K. #1 POP LP	*The Sound of Music*	soundtrack

WEEK ENDING JANUARY 14

U.S. #1 POP 45	"I'm a Believer"	The Monkees
U.S. #1 POP LP	*The Monkees*	The Monkees
U.S. #1 R&B 45	"Tell It Like It Is"	Aaron Neville
U.K. #1 POP 45	"I'm a Believer"	The Monkees
U.K. #1 POP LP	*The Sound of Music*	soundtrack

WEEK ENDING JANUARY 21

U.S. #1 POP 45	"I'm a Believer"	The Monkees
U.S. #1 POP LP	*The Monkees*	The Monkees
U.S. #1 R&B 45	"Tell It Like It Is"	Aaron Neville
U.K. #1 POP 45	"I'm a Believer"	The Monkees
U.K. #1 POP LP	*The Sound of Music*	soundtrack

WEEK ENDING JANUARY 28

U.S. #1 POP 45	"I'm a Believer"	The Monkees
U.S. #1 POP LP	*The Monkees*	The Monkees
U.S. #1 R&B 45	"Tell It Like It Is"	Aaron Neville
U.K. #1 POP 45	"I'm a Believer"	The Monkees
U.K. #1 POP LP	*The Sound of Music*	soundtrack

3 **Joe Meek**, early British pop and rock producer, fatally shoots himself in the head. Meek had produced British hits in the Fifties for **Lonnie Donegan** ("Cumberland Gap"), **John Leyton** ("Johnny Remember Me," a futuristic arrangement that highlighted Meek's prowess at the mixing board) and **Mike Berry** ("Tribute to Buddy Holly"). But his biggest hit was "Telstar," which he wrote. Recorded by a group of his sessionmen under the name the **Tornadoes**, the instrumental—a surf-rock-style piece featuring the early electronic keyboard synthesizer the Clavioline—became a Number One hit in both the U.K. and the U.S. in 1962. Meek had a few more minor hits with other groups in the early Sixties, but after the Merseybeat explosion, he fell upon the hard times in the mid-Sixties that prompted his suicide.

5 POP STARS AND DRUGS—FACTS THAT WILL SHOCK YOU headlines a story in the Sunday edition of the British tabloid *News of the World.* The story reports on LSD parties given by the **Moody Blues** and attended by **Pete Townshend**, **Ginger Baker** and other rock stars; quotes **Mick Jagger** admitting to having used LSD; and claims that Jagger took benzedrine tablets and displayed a quantity of hashish while in the reporter's company. That afternoon, as a guest on BBC-TV's "Eammon Andrews Show," Jagger announces that his lawyers will file a writ of libel against *News of the World,* for—as it will be revealed later—the *News* reporter has overheard **Brian Jones** talking about drugs in a London disco and mistaken him for Jagger. Jagger's suit, filed February 7, will set off a feud between *News of the World* and the Stones that will lead to a police raid on **Keith Richards**' home five days later.

7 **Barry**, **Robin** and **Maurice Gibb**—known as the **Bee Gees**—return to their native England after nine years in Australia. Pop stars in Australia with their own weekly television show and a Number One single, the Bee Gees are now ready to become pop stars in England—a feat accomplished in three months with their first U.K. Top Ten single, "New York Mining Disaster 1941."

12 Fifteen policemen, operating on a tip from *News of the World* informants and armed with a search warrent obtained under the British Dangerous Drugs Act, raid **Keith Richards**' country home, Redlands, in West Wittering, Sussex, England. The police find "various substances of a suspicious nature," but arrest no one until May 10, when Richards and **Mick Jagger** will be arraigned on drug charges.

13 The **Beatles**' new single—"Penny Lane" backed with "Strawberry Fields Forever"—is released in the U.S. four days before its British release. The Beatles' first record since

Revolver in August 1966 and their last before *Sgt. Pepper's Lonely Hearts Club Band* in June this year, it indicates their direction toward electronically produced or manipulated sounds. It will hit Number One in the U.S. and #2 in the U.K.

23 Jamaican ska singer and producer **Prince Buster**'s "Al Capone" becomes the first Jamaican record to enter the U.K. pop chart. (**Millie Small**'s "My Boy Lollipop," which had earlier kicked off the ska boom, was recorded in London.) The song will later be covered under the title "Gangsters" by British "two-tone" ska-rock band the **Specials** in the late Seventies.

24 The **Bee Gees** sign a management contract with **Robert Stigwood**. Stigwood would manage the group through the Seventies.

27 In London, **Pink Floyd** record their first single, "Arnold Layne," which will go on to top the British charts but will not become a hit in America. ◆

WEEK ENDING FEBRUARY 4

U.S. #1 POP 45	"I'm a Believer"	The Monkees
U.S. #1 POP LP	*The Monkees*	The Monkees
U.S. #1 R&B 45	"Tell It Like It Is"	Aaron Neville
U.K. #1 POP 45	"I'm a Believer"	The Monkees
U.K. #1 POP LP	*The Monkees*	The Monkees

WEEK ENDING FEBRUARY 11

U.S. #1 POP 45	"I'm a Believer"	The Monkees
U.S. #1 POP LP	*More of the Monkees*	The Monkees
U.S. #1 R&B 45	"Are You Lonely for Me"	Freddy Scott
U.K. #1 POP 45	"This Is My Song"	Petula Clark
U.K. #1 POP LP	*The Monkees*	The Monkees

WEEK ENDING FEBRUARY 18

U.S. #1 POP 45	"Kind of a Drag"	The Buckinghams
U.S. #1 POP LP	*More of the Monkees*	The Monkees
U.S. #1 R&B 45	"Are You Lonely for Me"	Freddy Scott
U.K. #1 POP 45	"This Is My Song"	Petula Clark
U.K. #1 POP LP	*The Monkees*	The Monkees

WEEK ENDING FEBRUARY 25

U.S. #1 POP 45	"Kind of a Drag"	The Buckinghams
U.S. #1 POP LP	*More of the Monkees*	The Monkees
U.S. #1 R&B 45	"Are You Lonely for Me"	Freddy Scott
U.K. #1 POP 45	"Release Me"	Englebert Humperdinck
U.K. #1 POP LP	*The Monkees*	The Monkees

2 Winners of the ninth annual Grammy Awards (for 1966) are announced. Record of the Year is **Frank Sinatra**'s "Strangers in the Night." *Sinatra, a Man and His Music* wins Album of the Year. Song of the Year is **John Lennon** and **Paul McCartney**'s "Michelle." McCartney also wins Best Contemporary (Rock and Roll) Solo Vocal Performance (Male or Female) for the **Beatles**' "Eleanor Rigby." Best Contemporary (Rock and Roll) Group Performance goes to the **Mamas and the Papas** for "Monday, Monday." Best Contemporary (Rock and Roll) Recording is the **New Vaudeville Band**'s "Winchester Cathedral." **Ray Charles**' "Crying Time" wins both Best Rhythm and Blues Recording and Best Rhythm and Blues Solo Vocal Performance. Best Instrumental Theme is **Neal Hefti**'s "Batman Theme" (covered by the **Kinks** on *The Live Kinks*). The Beatles' *Revolver* wins **Klaus Voormann** the award for Best Album Cover, Graphic Arts.

3 In Ottawa, Ontario, Canada, British band the **Animals** refuse to play a scheduled concert unless they are paid in advance. Over 3,000 youths in the audience for the show riot; causing $5,000 worth of damage.

The new **Jeff Beck Group**—featuring **Rod Stewart**, bassist **Ron Wood** and drummer **Aynsley Dunbar**—makes its stage debut in London ("disastrously," according to later press reports).

4 The *New Musical Express* reports that the **Spencer Davis Group**'s manager, **Chris Blackwell**, has announced that **Stevie Winwood** (who sings and plays guitar and keyboards with the Spencer Davis Group) and his brother **Muff** (bass) will leave the band after an April 2 show in Liverpool. Stevie, age eighteen, had been with the band since he was fourteen. He will go on to cofound **Traffic**.

5 The *New York Times* reports that the East German press has assailed the popularity of the civil-rights hymn "We Shall Overcome," introduced there by folk singer **Pete Seeger**. The Communist

Party of East Germany and other groups have called for the creation of East Germany's own "fighting songs."

18 The *New Musical Express* reports that **Stevie Winwood**, about to depart the **Spencer Davis Group**, has already formed a new band with singer/drummer **Jim Capaldi**, saxophonist **Chris Wood** and singer/guitarist **Dave Mason**. The band plans to move in with Winwood in his country cottage to spend six months composing new material. The band, as yet unnamed, will become **Traffic**, one of Britain's most critically and commerically successful electric-progressive pop bands. Brother Muff will go on to become a successful producer.

25 The **Who** make their American stage debut at the first of a week-long five-shows-a-day stand as a low-billed act in **Murray the K**'s Easter rock & roll extravaganza. Ranking stars in England, the Who are virtually unknown in the U.S. Also today, the so-called British supergroup **Cream** arrive in New York City to begin their first American tour. The band—**Eric Clapton**, **Ginger Baker** and **Jack Bruce**—will make their U.S. debut at the Easter show. Like the Who, Cream are relatively unknown here, and it won't be until next May that they score even a minor hit single, with "Anyone for Tennis," which peaks at #64.

Jefferson Airplane's *Surrealistic Pillow* and the **Doors**' self-titled debut album both enter the *Billboard* album charts.

27 Fans at a **Rolling Stones** concert in Halsingborg, Sweden, throw bottles, chairs and fireworks on stage, prompting police to move in with batons and dogs, the Stones to flee the theater. Five days later, in Vienna, Austria, 154 fans will be arrested when a similar riot breaks out at the Stones' concert there. Violence will also mar Stones appearances in Zurich, Switzerland, on April 15, when **Mick Jagger** will be thrown to the floor by an overzealous fan.

In London, the British music industry awards **Beatles John Lennon** and **Paul McCartney** an Ivor Novello Award for writing the most-performed song of 1966 in Great Britain—"Michelle."

31 **Jimi Hendrix**, performing with the **Experience** at Finsbury Park, London, sets his guitar afire on stage for the first time. The pyrotechnics will become the ballyhooed climax of his biggest shows for the next two years. ◆

WEEK ENDING MARCH 4

U.S. #1 POP 45	"Ruby Tuesday"	The Rolling Stones
U.S. #1 POP LP	*More of the Monkees*	The Monkees
U.S. #1 R&B 45	"Love Is Here and Now You're Gone"	The Supremes
U.K. #1 POP 45	"Release Me"	Englebert Humperdinck
U.K. #1 POP LP	*The Monkees*	The Monkees

WEEK ENDING MARCH 11

U.S. #1 POP 45	"Love Is Here and Now You're Gone"	The Supremes
U.S. #1 POP LP	*More of the Monkees*	The Monkees
U.S. #1 R&B 45	"I Never Loved a Man (the Way I Love You)"	Aretha Franklin
U.K. #1 POP 45	"Release Me"	Englebert Humperdinck
U.K. #1 POP LP	*The Monkees*	The Monkees

WEEK ENDING MARCH 18

U.S. #1 POP 45	"Penny Lane"	The Beatles
U.S. #1 POP LP	*More of the Monkees*	The Monkees
U.S. #1 R&B 45	"I Never Loved a Man (the Way I Love You)"	Aretha Franklin
U.K. #1 POP 45	"Release Me"	Englebert Humperdinck
U.K. #1 POP LP	*The Monkees*	The Monkees

WEEK ENDING MARCH 25

U.S. #1 POP 45	"Happy Together"	The Turtles
U.S. #1 POP LP	*More of the Monkees*	The Monkees
U.S. #1 R&B 45	"I Never Loved a Man (the Way I Love You)"	Aretha Franklin
U.K. #1 POP 45	"Release Me"	Englebert Humperdinck
U.K. #1 POP LP	*The Sound of Music*	soundtrack

7 Veteran San Francisco disc jockey **Tom "Big Daddy" Donahue** inaugurates "progressive FM radio" on San Francisco's KMPX. "Progressive," or "underground" radio avoided the incessant patter, hyperkinetic pacing and general "bubblegum" orientation of Top Forty AM radio, evolving instead an open-ended "free-form" approach to programming that favored low-key, genuinely hip disc jockeys playing album cuts, regardless of their length or sales statistics. "Progressive FM" radio would become a dominant force within a few years, before gradually rigidifying in the Seventies into "album-oriented radio."

13 The **Rolling Stones** perform their first concert behind the Iron Curtain at the Palace of Culture in Warsaw, Poland. Police with batons and tear gas bombs are required to subdue 2,000 fans hoping to get into the sold-out concert hall.

Catch My Soul closes after grossing over half a million dollars. **Jerry Lee Lewis**, who had portrayed the villain Iago in this modernized version of Shakespeare's *Othello,* received the best reviews. Although Lewis played it straight for the most part, on occasion he did bring something of a new approach to the part, as when he once ad-libbed "Great balls of fire! My friend Roderigo!" in Act V.

14 With a promotional slogan announcing "The Most Significant Talent Since the Beatles," Polydor Records releases the **Bee Gees'** first made-in-England record, "New York Mining Disaster 1941" backed with "I Can't See Nobody." The single will reach #10 in Britain and #14 in America.

Deram Records releases **David Bowie**'s "The Laughing Gnome" to almost utter failure. Re-released in 1973, however, it reaches #12 on the U.K. chart.

15 Decca Records releases the **Who**'s "Happy Jack" in the U.S. Thanks to the English band's first American concerts in March, "Happy Jack" will peak at #24, making it the Who's first record to crack the Top Seventy.

19 "Somethin' Stupid" by **Frank and Nancy Sinatra** is gold certified. The single is the only collaboration between this father and daughter to meet with any success. Individually, though, each has had a few hits.

Jerry Lee Lewis records "What's Made Milwaukee Famous (Has Made a Loser Out of Me)," which will hit #2 on the country chart by the end of July.

26 CBS-TV broadcasts "Inside Pop—The Rock Revolution," hosted by New York Philharmonic Orchestra conductor **Leonard Bernstein**. Among Bernstein's guests is sixteen-year-old **Janis Ian**, who sings her "Society's Child." At the time of the song's release a year before, it had been banned by some radio stations because of its subject—an interracial love affair—and ignored by most. But following Ian's television appearance, the song bolts to the Top Twenty.

28 "This Diamond Ring," by **Gary Lewis and the Playboys**, is certified gold. It will be the only gold record for Lewis (the son of comedian **Jerry Lewis**), but his collaborations with arranger **Leon Russell** will result in ten more Top Twenty hits, including "Count Me In," "Everybody Loves a Clown" and "She's Just My Style."

British pop singer **Petula Clark**, whose current hit is "This Is My Song," performs at the White House Press Correspondents' dinner.

29 Bluesman **J. B. Lenoir** dies of a heart attack at age thirty-eight in Urbana, Illinois, following an auto accident there. Lenoir may be most familiar to rock fans as one of the favorites of British blues revivalist **John Mayall**. Lenoir's best-known songs include "Eisenhower Blues" and "Vietnam Blues."

The *New York Times* reports that a Munich court has ruled that "beat band music" (rock & roll to you) is subject to taxation as entertainment, and that it is not comparable to concert music presented to "passive listeners." Tax authorities had submitted test results from a recent "pop beat show" registering the band's sound level at 117 decibels, and the audience's sound level at 105 decibels. ◆

WEEK ENDING APRIL 2

U.S. #1 POP 45	"Happy Together"	The Turtles
U.S. #1 POP LP	*More of the Monkees*	The Monkees
U.S. #1 R&B 45	"I Never Loved a Man (the Way I Love You)"	Aretha Franklin
U.K. #1 POP 45	"Release Me"	Englebert Humperdinck
U.K. #1 POP LP	*The Monkees*	The Monkees

WEEK ENDING APRIL 9

U.S. #1 POP 45	"Happy Together"	The Turtles
U.S. #1 POP LP	*More of the Monkees*	The Monkees
U.S. #1 R&B 45	"I Never Loved a Man (the Way I Love You)"	Aretha Franklin
U.K. #1 POP 45	"Somethin' Stupid"	Frank and Nancy Sinatra
U.K. #1 POP LP	*The Sound of Music*	soundtrack

WEEK ENDING APRIL 16

U.S. #1 POP 45	"Somethin' Stupid"	Frank and Nancy Sinatra
U.S. #1 POP LP	*More of the Monkees*	The Monkees
U.S. #1 R&B 45	"I Never Loved a Man (the Way I Love You)"	Aretha Franklin
U.K. #1 POP 45	"Puppet on a String"	Sandie Shaw
U.K. #1 POP LP	*The Sound of Music*	soundtrack

WEEK ENDING APRIL 23

U.S. #1 POP 45	"Somethin' Stupid"	Frank and Nancy Sinatra
U.S. #1 POP LP	*More of the Monkees*	The Monkees
U.S. #1 R&B 45	"I Never Loved a Man (the Way I Love You)"	Aretha Franklin
U.K. #1 POP 45	"Puppet on a String"	Sandie Shaw
U.K. #1 POP LP	*More of the Monkees*	The Monkees

WEEK ENDING APRIL 30

U.S. #1 POP 45	"Somethin' Stupid"	Frank and Nancy Sinatra
U.S. #1 POP LP	*More of the Monkees*	The Monkees
U.S. #1 R&B 45	"I Never Loved a Man (the Way I Love You)"	Aretha Franklin
U.K. #1 POP 45	"Puppet on a String"	Sandie Shaw
U.K. #1 POP LP	*The Sound of Music*	soundtrack

1 **Elvis Presley** marries **Priscilla Beaulieu**, daughter of a U.S. army colonel, in Las Vegas. Presley had met Priscilla when he was stationed in Germany. Upon his return to the States, the two had corresponded, and Presley eventually convinced her parents to allow her to move to Memphis and live at Graceland. At the time she moved to Memphis, Priscilla was sixteen. Presley agreed that he would oversee her education. She lived with his father **Vernon** and stepmother, **Dee**, in a house behind Graceland.

2 Capitol Records announces that one of the most cryptic periods in the **Beach Boys**' career has come to a close, as they've abandoned the *Smile* album project. Brainchild of Beach Boys leader **Brian Wilson**, *Smile*, which he took over a year to compose and to produce with collaborator **Van Dyke Parks**, became more of a Brian Wilson obsession than anything else. Reportedly, with *Smile*, Wilson hoped to do battle for supremacy of the pop arena with the **Beatles**; but when the latter released *Sgt. Pepper's Lonely Hearts Club Band* before *Smile* was completed, Wilson became convinced that *Smile* would forever be seen as "second best" and aborted the project. Wilson would then take a few of the *Smile* songs, integrate them with new material and put together the *Smiley Smile* album, released later this year.

3 The *New York Times* reports on a "Cosmic Love In" held at New York City's Village Theater, which would soon become the Fillmore East.

4 The **Turtles** receive their first of two gold singles, for their recent pop Number One hit, "Happy Together." Their second gold single will come with "She'd Rather Be with Me."

6 **Keith Moon**, in an interview in *Melody Maker*, offers this advice to his legions of drummer-admirers: "To get your playing more forceful, hit the drums harder."

Scott McKenzie's "San Francisco (Be Sure to Wear Flowers in Your Hair)" enters the Hot 100, and the **Grateful Dead**'s self-titled debut LP enters the album chart.

7 According to the *New York Times,* Soviet youths openly defied police a week ago and danced the twist in Moscow's Red Square during May Day celebrations.

10 At the very hour that, in a West Sussex court, **Mick Jagger** is formally charged with illegal possession of pep pills and **Keith Richards** with permitting cannabis to be smoked on his premises on February 12, police arrest Jagger and Richards' fellow Rolling Stone **Brian Jones** in his London apartment and charge him with unlawful possession of drugs. Jagger and Richards are jailed overnight and released on £100 bail pending their June 27 trial. Jones is remanded on £250 bail pending his October 31 trial.

13 The **Bee Gees** enter the U.K. pop chart for the first time with "New York Mining Disaster 1941." The trio, brothers **Barry, Robin and Maurice Gibb**, had begun releasing singles as far back as 1962 and even hosted a weekly television show in Australia. Their first big hit had been "Spicks and Specks," a U.K. Number One earlier this year.

17 *Don't Look Back,* D. A. Pennebaker's film documentary on **Bob Dylan**'s 1965 British tour, premieres at the Presidio Theater in San Francisco. Dylan will later denounce the film and file a court injunction to bar its being shown.

20 **Jimi Hendrix** signs his first American record contract with Reprise Records. He and his band, the **Jimi Hendrix Experience**, have already released records on the Polydor and Track labels in Britain (the latter owned by **Who** manager **Kit Lambert**).

Only one week after surrendering the top of the R&B chart to **Martha and the Vandellas**, **Aretha Franklin** retakes it with a new single, "Respect," which will also hit Number One on the pop chart. "Respect" was written and originally recorded by **Otis Redding**, who will later say that he prefers Franklin's rendition to his own.

27 **Otis Redding**'s band, the **Bar-Kays**, enters the R&B chart with "Soul Finger," an instrumental that will peak at #3 R&B and #17 pop, making it their biggest hit without their famous vocalist. Six months later, four members of the brass-dominated band will die in the plane crash that kills Redding.

Two of America's biggest record labels, Columbia and RCA Victor, announce that they will raise the list price of monaural albums by $1 on June 1—the first such price increase in mono LPs since 1953. The two companies cite the exigencies of mono production costs in a stereo world. ◆

WEEK ENDING MAY 7

U.S. #1 POP 45	"Somethin' Stupid"	Frank and Nancy Sinatra
U.S. #1 POP LP	*More of the Monkees*	The Monkees
U.S. #1 R&B 45	"I Never Loved a Man (the Way I Love You)"	Aretha Franklin
U.K. #1 POP 45	"Puppet on a String"	Sandie Shaw
U.K. #1 POP LP	*The Sound of Music*	soundtrack

WEEK ENDING MAY 14

U.S. #1 POP 45	"The Happening"	The Supremes
U.S. #1 POP LP	*More of the Monkees*	The Monkees
U.S. #1 R&B 45	"Jimmy Mack"	Martha and the Vandellas
U.K. #1 POP 45	"Silence Is Golden"	The Tremeloes
U.K. #1 POP LP	*The Sound of Music*	soundtrack

WEEK ENDING MAY 21

U.S. #1 POP 45	"Groovin'"	The Young Rascals
U.S. #1 POP LP	*More of the Monkees*	The Monkees
U.S. #1 R&B 45	"Respect"	Aretha Franklin
U.K. #1 POP 45	"Silence Is Golden"	The Tremeloes
U.K. #1 POP LP	*The Sound of Music*	soundtrack

WEEK ENDING MAY 28

U.S. #1 POP 45	"Groovin'"	The Young Rascals
U.S. #1 POP LP	*More of the Monkees*	The Monkees
U.S. #1 R&B 45	"Respect"	Aretha Franklin
U.K. #1 POP 45	"Silence Is Golden"	The Tremeloes
U.K. #1 POP LP	*The Sound of Music*	soundtrack

1 The **Beatles**' album *Sgt. Pepper's Lonely Hearts Club Band* is released in the U.K. on Capitol/EMI Records. The album, aside from becoming yet another best-seller for the group, will also come to be seen as something of an epochal album—the beginning of self-conscious "art rock." The record is released in the U.S. two days later.

3 **Marvin Gaye** and **Tammi Terrell** make their duo debut on the R&B chart with "Ain't No Mountain High Enough." Gaye, of course, has been making hits for Tamla-Motown Records since 1962; Terrell—a former medical student—had been making solo records for only a year. With "Ain't No Mountain High Enough," a **Nickolas Ashford-Valerie Simpson** composition later covered by **Diana Ross**, Gaye and Terrell become Motown's leading couple. Their first collaboration will reach #3 on the R&B chart and #19 on the pop chart, to be followed more successfully by such hits as "Your Precious Love," "Ain't Nothing Like the Real Thing" and "You're All I Need to Get By."

The **Doors**' first single, "Light My Fire," enters the pop chart, where in two months it will hit Number One, launching this Los Angeles band into national popularity.

10 Fifteen thousand people gather in Mt. Tamalpais, California, for the two-day Fantasy Faire and Magic Mountain Music Fest, where the performers include the **Jefferson Airplane**, the **Doors**, the **Byrds**, **Smokey Robinson**, **Country Joe and the Fish** and **Dionne Warwick**. In spite of its relatively small size, it is notable as the first Sixties-style rock festival and as a successful nonprofit event.

In Woodstock, New York, **Bob Dylan** and the **Band** begin recording the long-unreleased sessions that will eventually see the light of day as an album titled *The Basement Tapes*, by which name the sessions had long been unofficially known.

15 Guitarist **Peter Green** leaves **John Mayall**'s **Bluesbreakers** to become a founding member of British blues-rock band **Fleetwood Mac**.

16 The Monterey Pop Festival begins in Monterey, California. In the next three days, 50,000 people witness the first major American appearances of the **Who**, **Jimi Hendrix** and **Janis Joplin**, the introduction of **Otis Redding**, **Ravi Shankar** and **Hugh Masekela** to rock audiences, and performances by the **Grateful Dead**, the **Jefferson Airplane**, the **Byrds**, the **Association**, the **Electric Flag**, the **Paul Butterfield Blues Band**, **Canned Heat**, **Laura Nyro**, **Booker T. and the MGs**, the **Mamas and the Papas**, **Buffalo Springfield**, the **Blues Project**, **Country Joe and the Fish** and **Quicksilver Messenger Service**. **John Phillips** and **Lou Adler** are the organizers, **Paul McCartney** a talent consultant and **Brian Jones** one of the emcees. **D. A. Pennebaker** films the event for his documentary, *Monterey Pop*, and the age of the rock festival dawns.

22 The drug-possession trial of **Rolling Stones**

Mick Jagger and **Keith Richards** opens in London.

23 **Arthur Conley** receives a gold record for "Sweet Soul Music," his first hit. The song—a rewrite of Sam Cooke's "Yeah Man"—is a tribute to the current soul music explosion and names **Otis Redding** (Conley's mentor), **James Brown**, **Wilson Pickett**, **Lou Rawls** and **Sam and Dave**. "Sweet Soul Music" did equally well (#2) on both the pop and R&B charts in May.

24 **Procol Harum**'s first single, "A Whiter Shade of Pale," enters the American pop chart, where it will peak at #5; it is already Number One in the U.K. Vocalist and pianist **Gary Brooker** and lyricist **Keith Reid** formed this English group expressly to record this song, soon to be famous for its Dylan-esque, surrealist lyrics and its organ part based on a Bach cantata.

25 Over an international television hookup connected to most of the free world, the **Beatles** perform "All You Need Is Love" in a TV studio packed with people holding up signs carrying the song title in various languages. Among those in the studio are **Mick Jagger** and **Brian Jones** of the **Rolling Stones**, as well as Jagger's girlfriend **Marianne Faithfull**.

29 **Keith Richards** is found guilty of allowing his property to be used for the smoking of cannabis at his Redlands home on February 12, and is sentenced to one year in jail and is fined £500. **Mick Jagger** is found guilty of illegal possession of pep pills on the same occasion, and is sentenced to three months in jail and is fined £300. ◆

WEEK ENDING JUNE 5

U.S. #1 POP 45	"Respect"	Aretha Franklin
U.S. #1 POP LP	*More of the Monkees*	The Monkees
U.S. #1 R&B 45	"Respect"	Aretha Franklin
U.K. #1 POP 45	"Silence Is Golden"	The Tremeloes
U.K. #1 POP LP	*Sgt. Pepper's Lonely Hearts Club Band*	The Beatles

WEEK ENDING JUNE 12

U.S. #1 POP 45	"Respect"	Aretha Franklin
U.S. #1 POP LP	*More of the Monkees*	The Monkees
U.S. #1 R&B 45	"Respect"	Aretha Franklin
U.K. #1 POP 45	"A Whiter Shade of Pale"	Procol Harum
U.K. #1 POP LP	*Sgt. Pepper's Lonely Hearts Club Band*	The Beatles

WEEK ENDING JUNE 19

U.S. #1 POP 45	"Respect"	Aretha Franklin
U.S. #1 POP LP	*Sounds Like*	Herb Alpert and the Tijuana Brass
U.S. #1 R&B 45	"Respect"	Aretha Franklin
U.K. #1 POP 45	"A Whiter Shade of Pale"	Procol Harum
U.K. #1 POP LP	*Sgt. Pepper's Lonely Hearts Club Band*	The Beatles

WEEK ENDING JUNE 26

U.S. #1 POP 45	"Respect"	Aretha Franklin
U.S. #1 POP LP	*Headquarters*	The Monkees
U.S. #1 R&B 45	"Respect"	Aretha Franklin
U.K. #1 POP 45	"A Whiter Shade of Pale"	Procol Harum
U.K. #1 POP LP	*Sgt. Pepper's Lonely Hearts Club Band*	The Beatles

1 After almost ten years together, the **Parliaments** make both their pop and R&B chart debuts with "(I Wanna) Testify," which will reach #20 pop and #3 R&B. Following this initial success, the Parliaments, under the leadership of vocalist, songwriter and producer **George Clinton**, will modify their name to Parliament and expand their ranks to include an instrumental section, **Funkadelic**, which will also make its own Clinton-directed records. In the Seventies, **Parliament-Funkadelic** and other permutations such as **Bootsy's Rubber Band**, the **Brides of Funkenstein**, the **Horny Horns** and **Parlet**, will epitomize the street-smart spaced-out jumble of rhythm & blues and acid rock called funk. Their slogan: "Funk for its own sake."

Following **Mick Jagger**'s conviction on drug charges, the venerable *London Times* declares itself sympathetic to Jagger. A lengthy editorial by **W. E. Rees-Mogg** concludes: "It should be the particular quality of British justice to ensure that Mr. Jagger is treated exactly the same as anyone else, no better and no worse. There must remain a suspicion in this case that Mr. Jagger received a more severe sentence than would have been thought proper for any purely anonymous young man."

7 The **Lovin' Spoonful** may now be suffering from ill repute because of **Steve Boone** and **Zal Yanofsky**'s drug bust (in which they incriminated some of San Francisco's best-connected drug suppliers), but fans remember their "good time music" of 1965 and 1966—such hits as "Do You Believe In Magic," "Daydream," "Did You Ever Have to Make Up Your Mind" and "Summer in the City"—and assure that *The Best of the Lovin' Spoonful* is certified gold.

11 One day after leaving the **New Christy Minstrels**, singer **Kenny Rogers** forms his own band, the **First Edition**, who will go on to have hits with such pop tunes as the mildly psychedelic "Just Dropped in (to See What Condition My Condition Was In)," the countryish "Ruby (Don't Take Your Love to Town)" and the soul-inflected "Something's Burning." Rogers himself will go on to become a hugely successful country-pop star in the Seventies with such million-selling hits as "The Gambler," "Lucille" and "Lady." By 1981, Rogers will own a $14-million mansion.

14 The **Who** begin their first full-scale American tour—as the opening act for **Herman's Hermits**.

17 The **Monkees** perform at Forest Hills Stadium in New York. The **Jimi Hendrix Experience** opens the show.

20 **Jerry Lee Lewis** returns to England, the scene of his May 1958 downfall, and finds that there are a few English rock & rollers willing to forgive and forget and who never deserted him. His shows are well attended and generally receive favorable reviews.

24 The **Jefferson Airplane**'s second album, *Surrealistic Pillow*, propelled by their recent Top Ten hits, "Somebody to Love" and "White Rabbit," is certified gold.

25 The **Beatles** and other prominent British rock bands urge the British government to legalize the use of marijuana, in an advertisement in the *London Times* signed by all four Beatles.

At the annual music-teachers symposium Music in American Society, delegate **W. H. Cornog** urges that the music of the **Beatles**, the **Rolling Stones** and similar bands be listened to intently to provide clues to what today's youth are thinking and feeling.

28 Also at the annual music-teachers symposium Music in America Society, **Paul Williams**, the nineteen-year-old editor of rock-culture magazine *Crawdaddy*, tells music teachers how to reach the young music students of America.

31 A London Appeals Court throws out **Keith Richards**' drug conviction of a month earlier, describing the evidence against him as "flimsy," and reduces **Mick Jagger**'s sentence on a related conviction from three months imprisonment to conditional discharge with probation. Chief Justice **Lord Parker** admonishes Jagger to remember his responsibilities as a pop idol. ♦

WEEK ENDING JULY 3

U.S. #1 POP 45	"Windy"	The Association
U.S. #1 POP LP	*Sgt. Pepper's Lonely Hearts Club Band*	The Beatles
U.S. #1 R&B 45	"Respect"	Aretha Franklin
U.K. #1 POP 45	"A Whiter Shade of Pale"	Procol Harum
U.K. #1 POP LP	*Sgt. Pepper's Lonely Hearts Club Band*	The Beatles

WEEK ENDING JULY 10

U.S. #1 POP 45	"Windy"	The Association
U.S. #1 POP LP	*Sgt. Pepper's Lonely Hearts Club Band*	The Beatles
U.S. #1 R&B 45	"Respect"	Aretha Franklin
U.K. #1 POP 45	"A Whiter Shade of Pale"	Procol Harum
U.K. #1 POP LP	*Sgt. Pepper's Lonely Hearts Club Band*	The Beatles

WEEK ENDING JULY 17

U.S. #1 POP 45	"Windy"	The Association
U.S. #1 POP LP	*Sgt. Pepper's Lonely Hearts Club Band*	The Beatles
U.S. #1 R&B 45	"I Was Made to Love Her"	Stevie Wonder
U.K. #1 POP 45	"All You Need Is Love"	The Beatles
U.K. #1 POP LP	*Sgt. Pepper's Lonely Hearts Club Band*	The Beatles

WEEK ENDING JULY 24

U.S. #1 POP 45	"Windy"	The Association
U.S. #1 POP LP	*Sgt. Pepper's Lonely Hearts Club Band*	The Beatles
U.S. #1 R&B 45	"Make Me Yours"	Bettye Swan
U.K. #1 POP 45	"All You Need Is Love"	The Beatles
U.K. #1 POP LP	*Sgt. Pepper's Lonely Hearts Club Band*	The Beatles

WEEK ENDING JULY 31

U.S. #1 POP 45	"Light My Fire"	The Doors
U.S. #1 POP LP	*Sgt. Pepper's Lonely Hearts Club Band*	The Beatles
U.S. #1 R&B 45	"Baby I Love You"	Aretha Franklin
U.K. #1 POP 45	"All You Need Is Love"	The Beatles
U.K. #1 POP LP	*Sgt. Pepper's Lonely Hearts Club Band*	The Beatles

5 **Pink Floyd**'s first album, *The Piper at the Gates of Dawn,* is released in the U.K. on EMI Records. Unlike the band's prior minor-hit U.K. singles, "Arnold Layne" and "See Emily Play"—both short, concise, bizarre psychedelic-pop excursions composed by leader **Syd Barrett**—the album focuses on such extended space-travel epics as "Interstellar Overdrive," which is highlighted by **Richard Wright**'s exotic Farfisa organ work. It is this album, more than the previous singles, that helps establish Pink Floyd's psychedelic reputation around the world.

9 While performing at the Sunbury Jazz and Blues Festival in England, **Jerry Lee Lewis** drives the audience to such a frenzy that festival officials halt his show and ask Lewis to leave the stage.

12 **Fleetwood Mac**—the British blues-rock band formed by ex-**John Mayall** sidemen **Peter Green**, **John McVie** and **Mick Fleetwood** with guitarist **Jeremy Spencer**—makes its stage debut at the London National Jazz & Blues Festival.

13 The Daughters of the American Revolution refuse to allow folk singer **Joan Baez** to perform at Constitution Hall in Washington, D.C., because of her opposition to the Vietnam War. Two days later, Baez gives her scheduled concert in an outdoor theater near the Washington Monument.

15 The British government's anti-pirate radio legislation goes into effect. As of this time, the only private radio station still broadcasting is the original pirate radio station, Radio Caroline, operating from a boat anchored outside Britain's three-mile limit. The new anti-pirate radio legislation is not enforced on the Isle of Man—much to the relief of the Man House of Keys, which a few days earlier had appealed to the Commonwealth prime ministers *not* to enact the legislation because Radio Caroline had been broadcasting free commercials for tourism on the Isle of Man.

20 The *New York Times* reports on a new noise-reduction system for album and tape recording developed by technicians **R.** and **D. W. Dolby**. Elektra Records' new subsidiary, Checkmate Records, will be the first record label to use the new Dolby process in its recordings.

24 **Patti Harrison**, having heard that the **Maharishi Mahesh Yogi** was due in London this day to give a lecture at the Park Lane Hilton Hotel before retiring to a "life of silence," convinces her husband **George** and the rest of the **Beatles** to attend the lecture this evening. They do. After the lecture they send a note to the Maharishi, who until this time was unaware of their presence, requesting a private audience. In their meeting, the Beatles offer themselves to the Maharishi as his disciples. The Maharishi accepts, and invites them to attend an indoctrination course for "spiritual regeneration" he would give two days later at University College in Bangor, North Wales. The Beatles go to the lecture, accompanied by **Rolling Stone Mick Jagger** and his girlfriend **Marianne Faithfull**. The Beatles invite their manager, **Brian Epstein**, to come along, but he tells them he has other plans for the

weekend and may join them later in the ten-day course. It is the first trip of any kind the Beatles have made without Epstein's company. **John Lennon** would later compare the experience to "going somewhere without your trousers." Lennon's wife, **Cynthia**, also misses the train ride to North Wales—she was held back at the station by a policeman who thought she was one of the horde of fans there to see the Beatles off.

26 With journalists swarming over University College to see the **Beatles** and the **Maharishi Mahesh Yogi**, the Maharishi agrees to give a press conference. The Beatles, seated next to the Maharishi, give such strong and sincere responses to the press' sarcastic questions that the Maharishi's other disciples break into spontaneous applause. The Beatles also announce that they have given up drugs. **Paul McCartney** explains: "It was an experience we went through. We don't need it anymore. We're finding different ways to get there."

27 At University College in Bangor, North Wales, **Paul McCartney** receives a phone call telling him that **Beatles** manager **Brian Epstein** has been found dead, locked in the bedroom of his London apartment. A week later, a coroner's inquest into his death reveals that Epstein died of an overdose of the sleeping pill Carbitrol. The death is ruled accidental due to "incautious self-overdoses" of the drug, which Epstein had apparently been taking in increasing dosages over a period of time. The Beatles, shocked at the news of the tragedy, are told by the **Maharishi Mahesh Yogi** that Epstein's death, being in the realm of the physical world, is "not important." ◆

WEEK ENDING AUGUST 7

U.S. #1 POP 45	"Light My Fire"	The Doors
U.S. #1 POP LP	*Sgt. Pepper's Lonely Hearts Club Band*	The Beatles
U.S. #1 R&B 45	"Baby I Love You"	Aretha Franklin
U.K. #1 POP 45	"All You Need Is Love"	The Beatles
U.K. #1 POP LP	*Sgt. Pepper's Lonely Hearts Club Band*	The Beatles

WEEK ENDING AUGUST 14

U.S. #1 POP 45	"Light My Fire"	The Doors
U.S. #1 POP LP	*Sgt. Pepper's Lonely Hearts Club Band*	The Beatles
U.S. #1 R&B 45	"Baby I Love You"	Aretha Franklin
U.K. #1 POP 45	"San Francisco (Be Sure to Wear Flowers in Your Hair)"	Scott McKenzie
U.K. #1 POP LP	*Sgt. Pepper's Lonely Hearts Club Band*	The Beatles

WEEK ENDING AUGUST 21

U.S. #1 POP 45	"All You Need Is Love"	The Beatles
U.S. #1 POP LP	*Sgt. Pepper's Lonely Hearts Club Band*	The Beatles
U.S. #1 R&B 45	"Baby I Love You"	Aretha Franklin
U.K. #1 POP 45	"San Francisco (Be Sure to Wear Flowers in Your Hair)"	Scott McKenzie
U.K. #1 POP LP	*Sgt. Pepper's Lonely Hearts Club Band*	The Beatles

WEEK ENDING AUGUST 28

U.S. #1 POP 45	"Ode to Billie Joe"	Bobbie Gentry
U.S. #1 POP LP	*Sgt. Pepper's Lonely Hearts Club Band*	The Beatles
U.S. #1 R&B 45	"Baby I Love You"	Aretha Franklin
U.K. #1 POP 45	"San Francisco (Be Sure to Wear Flowers in Your Hair)"	Scott McKenzie
U.K. #1 POP LP	*Sgt. Pepper's Lonely Hearts Club Band*	The Beatles

1 Guitarist/vocalist **Boz Scaggs** joins San Francisco blues-rock outfit the **Steve Miller Band**. It's actually a reunion of two old friends and colleagues: Scaggs had first met Miller at high school in Dallas, Texas, and had joined Miller's high school band, the **Marksmen**; he then went with Miller to the University of Wisconsin and played in Miller's band, the **Ardells**, there. Scaggs would remain with the Steve Miller Band for two albums, *Children of the Future* and *Sailor,* before embarking on a solo career in 1969.

3 Folk singer **Woody Guthrie** dies of Huntington's Chorea at age fifty-two in a Queens, New York, hospital. An incalculably influential figure in the history of folk music, Guthrie began writing and singing his songs—celebrations of rural Americana, protests against injustices—in the thirties. Among his most famous songs are "This Land Is Your Land," "This Train Is Bound for Glory," "So Long, It's Been Good to Know You," "Reuben James," "Pastures of Plenty" and "Roll On, Columbia." His autobiography, *Bound for Glory,* was published in 1943, and will be made into a film (**David Carradine** starring as Guthrie) in 1977. Guthrie was a strong influence on another folk giant, **Pete Seeger** (the two sang together in the **Almanac Singers** in the forties); folk singer **Ramblin' Jack Elliott** dedicated himself to carrying on Guthrie's legacy; and Guthrie's tireless political commitment and dry, ironic "talking blues" style were decisive inspirations and influences for **Bob Dylan**. Guthrie's son **Arlo** will have a successful folk-singing career of his own. Woody Guthrie entered the hospital in 1952, suffering the debilitating hereditary disease Huntington's Chorea. Ironically, his rise to greatest fame occured as he lay dying a slow and agonizing death. In the early sixties, Dylan—among many others—paid him frequent hospital visits. Following his death, several tribute concerts will be staged around the country, most of them featuring such folk giants as Seeger, **Odetta**, Elliott, **Joan Baez** and, in some cases, Dylan.

4 Over 1,000 youths gather in Woodstock, New York, for the Sound Out Festival of rock, folk, jazz and blues.

6 In the British press, the British government takes out advertisements explaining its recent enacting of legislation outlawing pirate radio. The prime reason cited by the government is the interference with ship-to-shore radio frequencies caused by pirate radio stations broadcasting from boats anchored off Britain's coast.

11 The **Beatles** postpone a planned journey to India to study with the mystic guru **Maharishi Mahesh Yogi** in order to complete a one-hour TV special for the BBC.

A *New York Times* article notes that American record companies are increasingly using younger producers and younger independent companies more attuned to the teenage market.

The **Beatles**' "Magical Mystery Tour" bus begins cruising the English countryside, carrying the band and assorted other actors and friends, all involved in making the short film *Magical Mystery Tour,* songs from which will later be released on an album of the same name. The bus and the costumes of its riders are highly psychedelic.

17 The **Doors** perform "Light My Fire" and "People Are Strange" on "The Ed Sullivan Show." Prior to the show, Sullivan had asked Doors singer **Jim Morrison** to change or omit the line "Girl we couldn't get much higher" in "Light My Fire," but Morrison sings it that way anyway.

29 Motown's Soul label releases **Gladys Knight and the Pips**' "I Heard It through the Grapevine." It will reach #2 on the pop chart and Number One on the R&B chart.

30 On TV's "The David Frost Show," **Beatles John Lennon** and **Paul McCartney** espouse the **Maharishi Mahesh Yogi**'s doctrines of Transcendental Meditation. ◆

WEEK ENDING SEPTEMBER 2

U.S. #1 POP 45	"Ode to Billie Joe"	Bobbie Gentry
U.S. #1 POP LP	*Sgt. Pepper's Lonely Hearts Club Band*	The Beatles
U.S. #1 R&B 45	"Baby I Love You"	Aretha Franklin
U.K. #1 POP 45	"San Francisco (Be Sure to Wear Flowers in Your Hair)"	Scott McKenzie
U.K. #1 POP LP	*Sgt. Pepper's Lonely Hearts Club Band*	The Beatles

WEEK ENDING SEPTEMBER 9

U.S. #1 POP 45	"Ode to Billie Joe"	Bobbie Gentry
U.S. #1 POP LP	*Sgt. Pepper's Lonely Hearts Club Band*	The Beatles
U.S. #1 R&B 45	"Cold Sweat"	James Brown
U.K. #1 POP 45	"The Last Waltz"	Englebert Humperdinck
U.K. #1 POP LP	*Sgt. Pepper's Lonely Hearts Club Band*	The Beatles

WEEK ENDING SEPTEMBER 16

U.S. #1 POP 45	"Ode to Billie Joe"	Bobbie Gentry
U.S. #1 POP LP	*Sgt. Pepper's Lonely Hearts Club Band*	The Beatles
U.S. #1 R&B 45	"Cold Sweat"	James Brown
U.K. #1 POP 45	"The Last Waltz"	Englebert Humperdinck
U.K. #1 POP LP	*Sgt. Pepper's Lonely Hearts Club Band*	The Beatles

WEEK ENDING SEPTEMBER 23

U.S. #1 POP 45	"The Letter"	The Box Tops
U.S. #1 POP LP	*Sgt. Pepper's Lonely Hearts Club Band*	The Beatles
U.S. #1 R&B 45	"Cold Sweat"	James Brown
U.K. #1 POP 45	"The Last Waltz"	Englebert Humperdinck
U.K. #1 POP LP	*Sgt. Pepper's Lonely Hearts Club Band*	The Beatles

WEEK ENDING SEPTEMBER 30

U.S. #1 POP 45	"The Letter"	The Box Tops
U.S. #1 POP LP	*Sgt. Pepper's Lonely Hearts Club Band*	The Beatles
U.S. #1 R&B 45	"Funky Broadway"	Wilson Pickett
U.K. #1 POP 45	"The Last Waltz"	Englebert Humperdinck
U.K. #1 POP LP	*Sgt. Pepper's Lonely Hearts Club Band*	The Beatles

1 Hoping to take advantage of the British government's recent ban on pirate radio stations, the BBC airs Radio One, a new broadcasting service modeled on American rock & roll radio.

A *New York Times* article discussing American youth's increasing fascination with non-Western musics and cultures sees this trend as a symbol of youth's moral, aesthetic and psychological revolution.

Pink Floyd arrive in New York to begin their first American tour.

2 All six members of the **Grateful Dead** are busted by California narcotics agents for possession of marijuana at their 710 Ashbury Street house in San Francisco. After six hours in jail, they are released on bail.

7 South African émigré singer **Miriam Makeba** makes her pop and R&B chart debut with "Pata Pata," which will peak at #12 pop and #7 R&B. Makeba—who came to America under the auspices of Harry Belafonte in 1960 and was married to South African trumpeter **Hugh Masekela** ("Grazing in the Grass") before returning to Africa as the wife of American black nationalist **Stokely Carmichael**—sings this dance song in English and in her native Xhosa language.

Cass Elliot of the **Mamas and the Papas** is jailed overnight in London after a dispute over a hotel bill.

The **Beatles** reject an offer of $1 million to play a concert at Shea Stadium in New York from promoter **Sid Bernstein**—who had originally brought them to Shea Stadium in August 1965.

9 An ominous harbinger of format radio: **Murray the K** is fired from New York City's WOR-FM because of his "inability to live with direction"—that direction coming from programming consultant and format-radio pioneer **Bill Drake**, who has already redirected West Coast stations with his on-the-air contests and other gimmicks. Upon hearing of Murray Kaufman's fate, fellow WOR DJ **Bill "Rosco" Mercer** quits on the air.

14 Track Records and its American affiliate, Decca, release the **Who**'s "I Can See for Miles." In the U.K., where the single will peak at #12, it will be a moderate success by the Who's standards; in the U.S., where it will reach #9, it will be the group's all-time biggest hit until 1982.

16 **Joan Baez** and 123 other antidraft demonstrators are arrested for blocking the entrance to the Oakland, California, Armed Forces Induction Center. Baez and other demonstration organizers are jailed for ten days.

18 *How I Won the War*, Richard Lester's antiwar black comedy starring **John Lennon**, is given its world premiere at London's Pavillion Theatre. Lennon cut his long hair and traveled to Germany and Spain in September 1966 to play the part of Private Gripweed. A photograph of Lennon as Gripweed will grace the front page of *Rolling Stone*'s first edition next month.

19 Tamla-Motown releases **Smokey Robin-**

son and the Miracles' "I Second That Emotion." The single, written and produced by Robinson and **Al Cleveland**, will reach #4 on the pop chart and Number One on the R&B chart, making it their biggest hit since "Shop Around" in 1960.

22 In an interview with the *New York Times*, Indian sitar master **Ravi Shankar**, currently teaching a sitar course at City University of New York, admits that he is disturbed by the adulation he receives from hippies.

29 *Hair*, advertised as "The American Tribal Love-Rock Musical," opens off-Broadway at the Public Theater in New York's East Village. The youth-culture–oriented musical will eventually move to Broadway for a hugely successful run; the play's original cast recording album will become a big seller, spawning such hit singles as "Aquarius" and "Let the Sunshine In" (both sung in a hit medley by the Fifth Dimension) and "Good Morning Starshine" (a hit version by Oliver). The play will also be made into a film in 1978.

30 **Brian Jones**, in a London Magistrates Court on drug-possession charges arising from his March arrest, pleads guilty of possessing cannabis and not guilty of possessing cocaine and methedrine. The court accepts both pleas and remands him to Wormwood Scrubs Prison until sentencing the following day. He will be sentenced to nine months imprisonment and released on bail pending an appeal. ◆

WEEK ENDING OCTOBER 7

U.S. #1 POP 45	"The Letter"	The Box Tops
U.S. #1 POP LP	*Sgt. Pepper's Lonely Hearts Club Band*	The Beatles
U.S. #1 R&B 45	"(Your Love Keeps Lifting Me) Higher and Higher"	Jackie Wilson
U.K. #1 POP 45	"The Last Waltz"	Engelbert Humperdinck
U.K. #1 POP LP	*Sgt. Pepper's Lonely Hearts Club Band*	The Beatles

WEEK ENDING OCTOBER 14

U.S. #1 POP 45	"The Letter"	The Box Tops
U.S. #1 POP LP	*Ode to Billie Joe*	Bobbie Gentry
U.S. #1 R&B 45	"Soul Man"	Sam and Dave
U.K. #1 POP 45	"The Last Waltz"	Engelbert Humperdinck
U.K. #1 POP LP	*Sgt. Pepper's Lonely Hearts Club Band*	The Beatles

WEEK ENDING OCTOBER 21

U.S. #1 POP 45	"To Sir with Love"	Lulu
U.S. #1 POP LP	*Ode to Billie Joe*	Bobbie Gentry
U.S. #1 R&B 45	"Soul Man"	Sam and Dave
U.K. #1 POP 45	"Massachusetts"	The Bee Gees
U.K. #1 POP LP	*The Sound of Music*	soundtrack

WEEK ENDING OCTOBER 28

U.S. #1 POP 45	"To Sir with Love"	Lulu
U.S. #1 POP LP	*Diana Ross and the Supremes' Greatest Hits*	Diana Ross and the Supremes
U.S. #1 R&B 45	"Soul Man"	Sam and Dave
U.K. #1 POP 45	"Massachusetts"	The Bee Gees
U.K. #1 POP LP	*The Sound of Music*	soundtrack

1 British band **Family** plays its first live concert. The band will go on to attract a sizable cult following for its hard-to-classify blend of rock, blues and jazz. The band is led by the distinctively throaty vocals of **Roger Chapman**, but two other members, both bassists, will go on to greater glory: **Rick Grech**, who will join **Blind Faith**; and his replacement, **John Wetton**, who will go on to **King Crimson**, **Roxy Music**, **U.K.** and **Asia**.

2 The five members of the **Move** and their manager, **Tony Secunda**, appear in a London court for hearings on a suit filed against them by British Prime Minister **Harold Wilson**. The subject of the suit is a picture postcard the Move used to promote their single "Flowers in the Rain." It depicts the prime minister nude in bed. The court will later decide in Wilson's favor, fine the Move and confiscate all remaining copies of the offending postcard.

4 A *New York Times* article describes the new electric six-string sitar introduced by Danelectro Guitar Company, which is being used by many rock bands.

9 In a move later to be described by both parties as arising from conflicting egos, **Roger McGuinn** expels **David Crosby** from the **Byrds**. Crosby's replacement is **Gene Clark**, an original member of the group returning after a two-year absence. For the next year, Crosby will do little besides sail the yacht bought with money from his ouster settlement, but in December 1968, he will join ex-**Buffalo Springfield** member **Stephen Stills** and ex-**Hollie Graham Nash** to form **Crosby, Stills and Nash**.

The first issue of rock-culture magazine *Rolling Stone*, which includes a free "roach clip" (a device with which to hold the butt-end, or "roach," of a marijuana cigarette), is published in San Francisco.

10 The two-night, 9 p.m. to 9 a.m. "Paris Love-In" begins in Paris, France, featuring concerts by the **Spencer Davis Group**, **Soft Machine**, **Dandelions's Chariot**, **Keith West and Tomorrow** and other European bands.

12 **Jerry Lee Lewis** records "To Make Love Sweeter for You." It will become his second country Number One, his first since "Great Balls of Fire" almost ten years before.

17 **Davy Jones** of the **Monkees** opens a Greenwich Village, New York, boutique, Zilch I.

20 *Time*, reviewing the **Doors'** second album, *Strange Days,* reports that the Doors' music "takes its listeners not only past such familiar landmarks of the youth odyssey as alienation and sex, but into symbolic realms of the unconscious—eerie night worlds filled with throbbing rhythms, shivery metallic tones, unsettling images." No wonder the album is soon to hit #3 on the national chart.

The **Beach Boys'** *Smiley Smile* album—featuring the song "Vegetables," produced by **Paul McCartney** and the **Beach Boys**—is released in the U.K. on Capitol Records and in the U.S. on the band's own Brothers label. The album fails to make the Top Forty in either country, and the single will not chart at all, demonstrating the Beach Boys' dwindling popularity and sending leader **Brian Wilson** further into his reclusiveness.

21 Decca Records releases the **Who's** album *The Who Sell Out,* with its hilarious cover depicting the band's members endorsing such "products" as "Odorono" deodorant. The record is one of the first examples of what will come to be known as the "concept album," purporting to depict a typical day of AM-radio programming, and includes the classic "I Can See for Miles" and the pre-*Tommy* mini-opera "Rael."

23 *Rolling Stone* quotes San Francisco's veteran disc jockey **Tom Donahue**: "Top Forty radio, as we know it today and have known it for the last ten years, is dead, and its rotting corpse is stinking up the airwaves."

27 Capitol Records releases the **Beatles'** *Magical Mystery Tour* album in the U.S. One side contains songs from the Beatles film of the same name ("I Am the Walrus," "Fool on the Hill," etc.), and the other side contains singles previously unavailable on a long-player ("Penny Lane," "Strawberry Fields Forever," "Hello Goodbye," etc.). On December 8, EMI will release a double-EP containing only the songs from the film. Both the American LP and the British EP will be big sellers; the film, however, will be a commercial and critical failure. ◆

WEEK ENDING NOVEMBER 4

U.S. #1 POP 45	"To Sir with Love"	Lulu
U.S. #1 POP LP	*Diana Ross and the Supremes' Greatest Hits*	Diana Ross and the Supremes
U.S. #1 R&B 45	"Soul Man"	Sam and Dave
U.K. #1 POP 45	"Massachusetts"	The Bee Gees
U.K. #1 POP LP	*The Sound of Music*	soundtrack

WEEK ENDING NOVEMBER 11

U.S. #1 POP 45	"To Sir with Love"	Lulu
U.S. #1 POP LP	*Diana Ross and the Supremes' Greatest Hits*	Diana Ross and the Supremes
U.S. #1 R&B 45	"Soul Man"	Sam and Dave
U.K. #1 POP 45	"Baby, Now That I've Found You"	The Foundations
U.K. #1 POP LP	*The Sound of Music*	soundtrack

WEEK ENDING NOVEMBER 18

U.S. #1 POP 45	"To Sir with Love"	Lulu
U.S. #1 POP LP	*Diana Ross and the Supremes' Greatest Hits*	Diana Ross and the Supremes
U.S. #1 R&B 45	"Soul Man"	Sam and Dave
U.K. #1 POP 45	"Baby, Now That I've Found You"	The Foundations
U.K. #1 POP LP	*The Sound of Music*	soundtrack

WEEK ENDING NOVEMBER 25

U.S. #1 POP 45	"Incense and Peppermints"	Strawberry Alarm Clock
U.S. #1 POP LP	*Diana Ross and the Supremes' Greatest Hits*	Diana Ross and the Supremes
U.S. #1 R&B 45	"Soul Man"	Sam and Dave
U.K. #1 POP 45	"Baby, Now That I've Found You"	The Foundations
U.K. #1 POP LP	*The Sound of Music*	soundtrack

2 **Jimmie Rodgers**—the son of country-music star **Hank Snow**, who named him after the original country singer **Jimmie Rodgers**, "The Singing Brakeman"—is found in his car with a fractured skull after a serious accident. Rodgers had had three big hits in 1958 in a country-pop vein: "Kisses Sweeter than Wine," "Oh Oh, I'm Falling in Love Again" and the Number One hit "Honeycomb." He would recover from the auto accident, but his career would be over.

9 **Jim Morrison** is arrested onstage in New Haven, Connecticut. Backstage before the **Doors'** concert in New Haven, Morrison had mouthed off to a policeman, who responded by macing the singer. Later, during the concert, while singing "Back Door Man," Morrison delivered a tirade about the incident, which prompted police to turn on the house lights, pull Morrison offstage and charge him with breach of peace and resisting arrest.

10 The **Steve Miller Blues Band**, an unrecorded San Francisco group via Texas and Chicago, signs with Capitol Records for an unprecedented $750,000, and in so doing drops the "Blues" from its name.

Otis Redding, one of the giants of soul music, is killed when his tour plane crashes into a Wisconsin lake. He was twenty-six years old, and had written and sung such R&B pop hits as "Try a Little Tenderness," "I Can't Turn You Loose," "Fa-Fa-Fa-Fa-Fa," "I've Been Loving You Too Long," "Mr. Pitiful," "Respect" and "Shout Bamalama." However, his biggest hit, "(Sittin' on) The Dock of the Bay," will not be released until after his death, when it will become his only Number One on either the pop or R&B charts. Also killed in the crash are members of Redding's tour band, the **Bar-Kays**: **Jimmy King**, **Ron Caldwell**, **Phalm Jones** and **Carl Cunningham**.

12 A London Appeals Court commutes **Brian Jones'** nine-month prison sentence for possession of cannabis after hearing testimony from three psychiatrists that Jones is "an extremely frightened young man" and could not stand nine months in prison.

14 **Dick Clark** announces that he is making a film about hippies—*The Love Children*, which stars **Jack Nicholson**, **Dean Stockwell** and **Susan Strasberg** and features the music of the **Strawberry Alarm Clock** and the **Seeds**.

"I've always been identified with kids," the thirty-eight-year-old Clark tells *Rolling Stone*.

20 The First Czechoslovak National Festival of Rock Music opens for two days in Prague. Featured among the performing bands is the **Primitives**, who will later be known as the **Plastic People of the Universe**.

In Blackpool, England, two recently departed members of the **John Evan Blues Band**—vocalist **Ian Anderson** and bassist **Glenn Cornick**—form **Jethro Tull**, naming their band after the eighteenth-century inventor of a number of farm implements. Evan will later rejoin them as Jethro Tull's keyboard player.

21 The **Rolling Stones** album *Their Satanic Majesties Request* is released by London Records in the U.S.

26 The **Beatles'** self-directed film *Magical Mystery Tour* premieres on BBC-TV. Audiences are mystified, critics either disappointed or contemptuous, and the Beatles suffer their first flop.

29 Singer, guitarist and songwriter **Dave Mason** quits **Traffic**, one of Britain's most popular and successful rock bands. Mason will embark on a successful solo career, interrupting it briefly to rejoin a reformed version of Traffic in 1971.

31 **Bert Berns**, veteran songwriter, arranger, producer and record-label chief, dies of a heart attack in New York City at age thirty-eight. At the time of his death, Berns was president of Web 4 Music, which owned labels like Bang and Shout. Born Bert Russell and sometimes known by the pseudonym Russell Byrd, Berns cowrote such hits as "Twist and Shout", "Cry to Me", "Hang On Sloopy", "Piece of My Heart," "Here Comes the Night," and "Brown Eyed Girl". ◆

WEEK ENDING DECEMBER 2

U.S. #1 POP 45	"Daydream Believer"	The Monkees
U.S. #1 POP LP	*Pisces, Aquarius, Capricorn and Jones, Ltd.*	The Monkees
U.S. #1 R&B 45	"I Heard It through the Grapevine"	Gladys Knight & the Pips
U.K. #1 POP 45	"Let the Heartaches Begin"	Long John Baldry
U.K. #1 POP LP	*The Sound of Music*	soundtrack

WEEK ENDING DECEMBER 9

U.S. #1 POP 45	"Daydream Believer"	The Monkees
U.S. #1 POP LP	*Pisces, Aquarius, Capricorn and Jones, Ltd.*	The Monkees
U.S. #1 R&B 45	"I Heard It through the Grapevine"	Gladys Knight and the Pips
U.K. #1 POP 45	"Hello Goodbye"	The Beatles
U.K. #1 POP LP	*The Sound of Music*	soundtrack

WEEK ENDING DECEMBER 16

U.S. #1 POP 45	"Daydream Believer"	The Monkees
U.S. #1 POP LP	*Pisces, Aquarius, Capricorn and Jones, Ltd.*	The Monkees
U.S. #1 R&B 45	"I Heard It through the Grapevine"	Gladys Knight and the Pips
U.K. #1 POP 45	"Hello Goodbye"	The Beatles
U.K. #1 POP LP	*The Sound of Music*	soundtrack

WEEK ENDING DECEMBER 23

U.S. #1 POP 45	"Daydream Believer"	The Monkees
U.S. #1 POP LP	*Pisces, Aquarius, Capricorn and Jones, Ltd.*	The Monkees
U.S. #1 R&B 45	"I Heard It through the Grapevine"	Gladys Knight and the Pips
U.K. #1 POP 45	"Hello Goodbye"	The Beatles
U.K. #1 POP LP	*The Sound of Music*	soundtrack

WEEK ENDING DECEMBER 30

U.S. #1 POP 45	"Hello Goodbye"	The Beatles
U.S. #1 POP LP	*Pisces, Aquarius, Capricorn and Jones, Ltd.*	The Monkees
U.S. #1 R&B 45	"I Heard It through the Grapevine"	Gladys Knight and the Pips
U.K. #1 POP 45	"Hello Goodbye"	The Beatles
U.K. #1 POP LP	*The Sound of Music*	soundtrack

1968

In January of this year, *Billboard* reported that an unprecedented $1 billion had been spent on records the previous year—most of it on rock music. And confirming the growing seriousness of rock and its audience, *Billboard* also reported that for the first time in music-industry history, albums outsold singles. This did not mean the death of singles as a pop-rock medium, for the rock audience was now massive enough to accommodate scads of semipopular subgenres. One of them was bubblegum—a manufactured facsimile of the innocent exuberance of garage rock preened by studio expertise. It took off this year with the emergence and chart popularity of the 1910 Fruitgum Company and the Ohio Express. Another rapidly emerging, but enduring subgenre was heavy metal, which began to come of age this year via Cream (despite the mid-year news of their impending dissolution), Iron Butterfly and Led Zeppelin. Yet another was British progressive rock, sired by the art rock of the Beatles and the classical rock of Procol Harum. Fittingly, the opening band at Cream's November farewell concert in London was Yes, who would go on to become kings of progressive rock; another British band, the Nice—featuring keyboardist Keith Emerson, a future progressive-rock lord with Emerson, Lake and Palmer—made plenty of waves, too.

Rock and rock-associated music hadn't forgotten their political commitments, though. In February, folksinger Pete Seeger was finally allowed to sing the complete "Waist Deep in the Big Muddy" on TV, on the Smothers Brothers show, but many local stations cut to commercials to censor the song's last, anti-Vietnam War verse. In September, the Rolling Stones proved that rock & roll could still be dangerous when their "Street Fighting Man" was banned from broadcast by many cities across America that feared it would provoke, well, fighting in the streets. And—one month after Diana Ross got a standing ovation from Britain's Royal Family by interrupting a Supremes command performance to make a plea for interracial understanding—Grace Slick of the Jefferson Airplane appeared on the Smothers Brothers show wearing blackface makeup; at the conclusion of the Airplane's "Crown of Creation," she raised her black-gloved, clenched fist.

But rock & roll was still being co-opted, or openly fought, by the establishment. Staffers at the country's first progressive FM station, San Francisco's KMPX, went on strike to protest loss of programming control and hassles over the length of their hair. Progressive FM's nemesis and opposite, Bill Drake's AM formats (which last year caused the firing of veteran rock DJ and one-time "Fifth Beatle" Murray the K from New York's WOR), spread faster than underground FM could. The second Monterey Pop Festival was canceled due to local community pressure and alleged financial misdealings; local citizenry also brought about the dawn of the end of an era when they forced the Family Dog to leave the Avalon Ballroom in San Francisco. And within days of the opening of the first Family Dog-style multimedia environmental rock ballroom, L.A.'s Kaleidoscope, *Hair* began its successful Broadway run.

Meanwhile, rock hadn't forgotten Eastern mysticism; it had simply renounced it, as the Beatles declared their dalliance with the Maharishi "a public mistake" and the guru's much-ballyhooed tour with the Beach Boys turned into a resounding flop.

This same callow faddishness had much deeper and uglier ramifications when it came to the rock culture's antiestablishment politics. The Yippies, for example, embodied everything wrong about the radical counterculture—they were politically half-baked and expedient, they were irresponsible—yet they managed to attract followers and to command center stage in the media.

The ugliness of the Yippies culminated in the violence at August's Democratic National Convention in Chicago. Sure, the Chicago police were overly brutal in their treatment of the young protesters, but the Yippies were just as wrong in the shabby way they "organized" the demonstrations. As the world reeled, it seemed youth could have all been singing to themselves the refrain of Bob Dylan's 1966 classic "Ballad of a Thin Man": "There's something here but you don't know what it is, do you, Mr. Jones?"

1 Americans spent an unprecedented sum of more than $1 billion on phonograph records in 1967, according to *Billboard*. And for the first time, album sales (192 million units) surpassed singles sales (187 million).

5 *Bob Dylan's Greatest Hits* is certified gold nine months after its release. The album package includes an award-winning poster by graphic artist/designer **Milton Glaser**.

6 Television producer and "American Bandstand" host **Dick Clark** premieres his latest TV series, "Happening '68." The prime-time show, featuring popular rock acts, runs through September 1969.

7 San Francisco's KMPX-FM, one of America's pioneering "underground" radio stations (free-form programming, playing album cuts, etc.), holds a "grass ballot" vote among its listeners, and among those elected are **Bob Dylan** (president), **Paul Butterfield** (vice president), **George Har-**

rison (U.N. ambassador), **Jefferson Airplane** (secretary of transportation), the **Grateful Dead** (attorney general) and its blues harpist, **Pigpen** (secretary of agriculture), **Joan Baez** (secretary of state), the **Mothers of Invention** (secretary of labor), Zen advocate **Alan Watts** (secretary of health, education and welfare) and LSD king **Owsley Stanley** (secretary of commerce).

10 **Aretha Franklin** earns her fourth gold single with "Chain of Fools." The record goes on to win the 1968 Grammy Award for Best Rhythm & Blues Performance by a Female.

11 The *Daily Mirror* of London reports that **Jimi Hendrix** has moved into the London townhouse where **George Frederick Handel** is believed to have composed *Water Music* and the *Messiah* over 200 years earlier. Hendrix assures the *Mirror* that he, too, will compose in the Handel house and "not let the tradition down."

12 *Strange Days*, the **Doors'** second album,

goes gold. The album's highlights include "People Are Strange," "Love Me Two Times," "Moonlight Drive" and "When the Music's Over."

13 Dr. **K. C. Pollock** of the University of Florida audio lab reports that his tests have found that the noise generated at rock & roll concerts is harmful to teenage ears.

20 Despite his much-rumored falling-out with the New York-Cambridge folk singer circle, **Bob Dylan** joins Pete Seeger, Judy Col-

lins, Arlo Guthrie, Odetta, Richie Havens, Ramblin' Jack Elliott and the Band in commemorating the late **Woody Guthrie** at a Carnegie Hall benefit concert. This is Dylan's first public appearance since his motorcycle accident two years earlier.

New Musical Express reports that **Rolling Stones** drummer **Charlie Watts** has moved into a "centuries old" English countryside manor that was reputedly used as a hunting lodge by the first archbishop of Canterbury.

27 The **Bee Gees** make their U.S. debut with two concerts at the Anaheim Convention Center in California, collecting $50,000 and immediately returning home to England without appearing elsewhere in the States.

29 Rolling Stone **Mick Jagger** is reportedly in Los Angeles to seek out artists, engineers and others to work for the Stones' new record label, to be called Mother Earth. Stones drummer **Charlie Watts**, who, before joining the group, had worked in an advertising agency, is to design the logo. The label is never realized.

31 John Fred and His Playboy Band's "Judy in Disguise (with Glasses)" and the **American Breed**'s "Bend Me, Shape Me" are certified gold. Neither group came even close to selling that many records with any other release.

WEEK ENDING JANUARY 6

U.S. #1 POP 45	"Hello Goodbye"	The Beatles
U.S. #1 POP LP	*Magical Mystery Tour*	The Beatles
U.S. #1 R&B 45	"I Heard It through the Grapevine"	Gladys Knight and the Pips
U.K. #1 POP 45	"Hello Goodbye"	The Beatles
U.K. #1 POP LP	*Sgt. Pepper's Lonely Hearts Club Band*	The Beatles

WEEK ENDING JANUARY 13

U.S. #1 POP 45	"Hello Goodbye"	The Beatles
U.S. #1 POP LP	*Magical Mystery Tour*	The Beatles
U.S. #1 R&B 45	"I Second That Emotion"	Smokey Robinson and the Miracles
U.K. #1 POP 45	"Hello Goodbye"	The Beatles
U.K. #1 POP LP	*Sgt. Pepper's Lonely Hearts Club Band*	The Beatles

WEEK ENDING JANUARY 20

U.S. #1 POP 45	"Judy in Disguise (with Glasses)"	John Fred and His Playboy Band
U.S. #1 POP LP	*Magical Mystery Tour*	The Beatles
U.S. #1 R&B 45	"Chain of Fools"	Aretha Franklin
U.K. #1 POP 45	"The Ballad of Bonnie and Clyde"	Georgie Fame
U.K. #1 POP LP	*Val Doonican Rocks, but Gently*	Val Doonican

WEEK ENDING JANUARY 27

U.S. #1 POP 45	"Judy in Disguise (with Glasses)"	John Fred and His Playboy Band
U.S. #1 POP LP	*Magical Mystery Tour*	The Beatles
U.S. #1 R&B 45	"Chain of Fools"	Aretha Franklin
U.K. #1 POP 45	"Everlasting Love"	Love Affair
U.K. #1 POP LP	*Sound of Music*	soundtrack

♦

1 Nine months after marrying **Elvis Presley**, **Priscilla Beaulieu Presley** gives birth to Elvis' only child and sole heir, **Lisa Marie**, at the Baptist Memorial Hospital in Memphis.

Universal International Studios offers the **Doors** $500,000 to star in a feature film. The band also announces plans for an ABC-TV special, a "humor book" by the whole group and a book of lyrics and poetry by singer **Jim Morrison**. Only the last project ever comes to fruition.

3 **Paul McCartney** records "Lady Madonna" at EMI's Abbey Road studios. Although the recording is credited to the Beatles, all parts, save McCartney's, are played by anonymous session musicians instead of the other three Beatles.

10 The **Beatles** close Beatles U.S.A., their American fan club and business office, and fire their American press agents, severing all American business connections; they also withdraw from the late **Brian Epstein**'s NEMS Enterprises and turn all business affairs over to their newly formed record company, Apple.

12 **Jimi Hendrix** returns home to Seattle, Washington, where he plays for the students of Garfield High (from which he dropped out) and receives a key to the city from the mayor.

14 **Frank Zappa and the Mothers of Invention** announce work on two films: *Uncle Meat,* a "surrealistic documentary on the group," and a monster movie to be made in Japan, "where," Zappa opines, "they do the best monster work."

15 **Little Walter Jacobs**, the premier Chicago blues harmonica player and **Muddy Waters**' invaluable sideman, as well as a bandleader in his own right, dies of coronary thrombosis after being stabbed in a Chicago street fight. Jacobs was thirty-eight years old.

16 **George** and **Patti Harrison** and **John** and **Cynthia Lennon** fly to India for two months of transcendental meditation study with the **Maharishi Mahesh Yogi**.

Ringo and **Maureen Starr**, **Paul McCartney**, **Jane Asher**, **Mia Farrow** and **Donovan** join them three days later, but the Starrs return to England before two weeks are over, complaining about the spicy food. Later this month, the Maharishi will give a press conference at New York's Plaza Hotel to announce an upcoming tour with the **Beach Boys**, organized by Beach Boy and Transcendental Meditator **Mike Love**. In response to the question of how can there be peace in this world when so many suffer from poverty? the Maharishi will reply, "People are in poverty because they lack intelligence and are lazy. Transcendental Meditation will teach them the virtues of selflessness and give them the energy not to be poor."

Elvis Presley's fourth gospel album, *How Great Thou Art,* is certified gold. The album includes Presley's 1965 #3 hit, "Crying in the Chapel."

18 Guitarist **Dave Gilmour** joins Pink Floyd, replacing founder **Syd Barrett**, who checks into a psychiatric hospital before going into seclusion.

21 McGraw-Hill, Inc. outbids eight other American publishers and pays $150,000 for the U.S. rights to **Hunter Davies**' authorized biography of the **Beatles**.

22 **Genesis**, a group formed as a songwriters' cooperative by three English schoolboys, **Peter Gabriel**, **Tony Banks** and **Mike Rutherford**, release its first single, "The Silent Sun."

24 CBS-TV permits **Pete Seeger** to sing all six verses of his "Waist Deep in the Big Muddy" on "The Smothers Brothers Comedy Hour," although some local affiliates around the country cut to commercials rather than air the last, outspokenly antiwar verse. The song was censored from a **Smothers Brothers** show the previous September because it was interpreted by some to be critical of President Johnson's Vietnam policy. "Maybe the song helped to do some good," Seeger would later reflect. "President Johnson decided not to run again a month after I finally got it on the air."

28 **Frankie Lymon**, who, with the **Teenagers** had a Number One hit with "Why Do Fools Fall in Love?" when he was thirteen, is found dead of a heroin overdose at age twenty-five in his mother's New York City apartment.

29 The 1967 Grammy Awards are announced. "Up, Up and Away" is the big winner: Record of the Year (as recorded by the **Fifth Dimension**), Song of the Year (to writer **Jim Webb**), Best Performance by a Vocal Group of Two to Six Persons (the Fifth Dimension), Best Performance by a Chorus of Seven or More Persons (the **Johnny Mann Singers**), Best Contemporary Single (the Fifth Dimension's version) and Best Contemporary Group Performance, Vocal or Instrumental (the Fifth Dimension again). **The Beatles'** *Sgt. Pepper's Lonely Hearts Club Band* is named Album of the Year, Best Contemporary Album, Best Engineered Record and Best Album Cover, Graphic Arts. ◆

WEEK ENDING FEBRUARY 3

U.S. #1 POP 45	"Green Tambourine"	The Lemon Pipers
U.S. #1 POP LP	*Magical Mystery Tour*	The Beatles
U.S. #1 R&B 45	"Chain of Fools"	Aretha Franklin
U.K. #1 POP 45	"Everlasting Love"	Love Affair
U.K. #1 POP LP	*Greatest Hits*	The Supremes

WEEK ENDING FEBRUARY 10

U.S. #1 POP 45	"Love Is Blue"	Paul Mauriat
U.S. #1 POP LP	*Magical Mystery Tour*	The Beatles
U.S. #1 R&B 45	"Chain of Fools"	Aretha Franklin
U.K. #1 POP 45	"Everlasting Love"	Love Affair
U.K. #1 POP LP	*Greatest Hits*	The Supremes

WEEK ENDING FEBRUARY 17

U.S. #1 POP 45	"Love Is Blue"	Paul Mauriat
U.S. #1 POP LP	*Magical Mystery Tour*	The Beatles
U.S. #1 R&B 45	"I Wish It Would Rain"	The Temptations
U.K. #1 POP 45	"Mighty Quinn"	Manfred Mann
U.K. #1 POP LP	*Greatest Hits*	The Supremes

WEEK ENDING FEBRUARY 24

U.S. #1 POP 45	"Love Is Blue"	Paul Mauriat
U.S. #1 POP LP	*Magical Mystery Tour*	The Beatles
U.S. #1 R&B 45	"I Wish It Would Rain"	The Temptations
U.K. #1 POP 45	"Mighty Quinn"	Manfred Mann
U.K. #1 POP LP	*Greatest Hits*	The Supremes

5 Sales of "Simon Says," the **1910 Fruitgum Company**'s pop hit based on a children's game, pass the million mark, thus harkening the arrival of the short-lived but immensely successful "bubblegum" craze.

8 **Bill Graham**, owner of the Fillmore, San Francisco's legendary rock ballroom, opens the Fillmore East in an abandoned movie theater on Second Avenue and Sixth Street in New York City. The opening-night bill features **Albert King**, **Tim Buckley** and **Big Brother and the Holding Company**, performing for a capacity throng in the 3,000-seat theater.

9 The members of eight rock & roll performers and/or bands are included in the 1968 edition of *Who's Who in America*, the first to be included since **Elvis Presley** and the **Beatles**. They are the **Rolling Stones**, the **Grateful Dead**, the **Jefferson Airplane**, **Country Joe and the Fish**, **Donovan**, the **Doors**, the **Monkees** and the **Mamas and the Papas**.

11 "(Sittin' on) The Dock of the Bay" earns **Otis Redding** his only gold record—three months after his death.

15 The Diocese of Rome announces that it deplores but will not prohibit "rock & roll masses" at the Church of San Lessio Falconieri.

17 The **Bee Gees** make their American TV debut on "The Ed Sullivan Show," singing "To Love Somebody" and their current Top Twenty hit, "Words."

18 At three a.m., the staff of San Francisco's "progressive" rock station, KMPX-FM, walks out on strike, citing a lack of control over programming and "hassles over the whole long-hair riff." Performers like the **Rolling Stones**, **John Mayall**, the **Grateful Dead**, the **Jefferson Airplane** and **Joan Baez** request that the station, and affiliate KPPC-FM in Pasadena, not play their music so long as the station is run by strikebreakers. At a block party held the night of the walkout, the Grateful Dead's **Jerry Garcia** jams with **Traffic**.

19 **Bob Dylan**'s *John Wesley Harding* and the **Jimi Hendrix Experience**'s debut LP, *Are You Experienced?*, are both certified gold.

20 Two days after the KMPX-FM staff walks out, supporters hold a strikers' benefit at the Avalon Ballroom. Among the performers are the **Grateful Dead**.

Eric Clapton and three members of the **Buffalo Springfield**—**Neil Young**, **Richie Furay** and **Jim Messina**—are arrested in Los Angeles for "being at a place where it is suspected marijuana is being used," a misdemeanor for which Clapton will later be found innocent, the others paying small fines. The bust comes just after Young announced he was leaving the Springfield to go solo.

27 **Little Willie John** dies of a heart attack in Walla Walla Penitentiary, Washington, at age thirty-one. Born William J. Woods, he had been a teenage R&B singer in the gospel-influenced mold of James Brown, Sam Cooke and Jackie Wilson before being imprisoned for killing a man in a street fight in 1961.

Grapefruit, an English pop band managed by **John Lennon**, makes its stage debut at the Royal Albert Hall, London. Despite this auspicious start, the group returns to obscurity within a few months.

The **Bee Gees** perform at the Royal Albert Hall, backed by a sixty-seven-piece orchestra, the fifty-piece Royal Airforce Band and a large choir. ◆

WEEK ENDING MARCH 2

U.S. #1 POP 45	"Love Is Blue"	Paul Mauriat
U.S. #1 POP LP	*Blooming Hits*	Paul Mauriat and His Orchestra
U.S. #1 R&B 45	"I Wish It Would Rain"	The Temptations
U.K. #1 POP 45	"Cinderella Rockefella"	Esther and Abi Ofarim
U.K. #1 POP LP	*Greatest Hits*	The Supremes

WEEK ENDING MARCH 9

U.S. #1 POP 45	"Love Is Blue"	Paul Mauriat
U.S. #1 POP LP	*Blooming Hits*	Paul Mauriat and His Orchestra
U.S. #1 R&B 45	"We're a Winner"	The Impressions
U.K. #1 POP 45	"Cinderella Rockafella"	Esther and Abi Ofarim
U.K. #1 POP LP	*Greatest Hits*	The Supremes

WEEK ENDING MARCH 16

U.S. #1 POP 45	"(Sittin' on) The Dock of the Bay"	Otis Redding
U.S. #1 POP LP	*Blooming Hits*	Paul Mauriat and His Orchestra
U.S. #1 R&B 45	"(Sittin' on) The Dock of the Bay"	Otis Redding
U.K. #1 POP 45	"Cinderella Rockafella"	Esther and Abi Ofarim
U.K. #1 POP LP	*John Wesley Harding*	Bob Dylan

WEEK ENDING MARCH 23

U.S. #1 POP 45	"(Sittin' on) The Dock of the Bay"	Otis Redding
U.S. #1 POP LP	*Blooming Hits*	Paul Mauriat and His Orchestra
U.S. #1 R&B 45	"(Sittin' on) The Dock of the Bay"	Otis Redding
U.K. #1 POP 45	"Cinderella Rockafella"	Esther and Abi Ofarim
U.K. #1 POP LP	*John Wesley Harding*	Bob Dylan

WEEK ENDING MARCH 30

U.S. #1 POP 45	"(Sittin' on) The Dock of the Bay"	Otis Redding
U.S. #1 POP LP	*Blooming Hits*	Paul Mauriat and His Orchestra
U.S. #1 R&B 45	"(Sittin' on) The Dock of the Bay"	Otis Redding
U.K. #1 POP 45	"Lady Madonna"	The Beatles
U.K. #1 POP LP	*John Wesley Harding*	Bob Dylan

1 **Dick Clark** appears at an outdoor San Francisco concert by the **Siegel-Schwall Band** to promote his new hippie film, *Psyche-Out,* previously titled *The Love Children.* "It's a fairly honest film," says Clark of the movie, which stars **Jack Nicholson** and **Dean Stockwell,** "and if I had to compare it to any other film, it'd be *Hell's Angels on Wheels.*"

4 **Martin Luther King, Jr.,** is shot and killed on the balcony of a Memphis hotel. Riots break out in thirty American cities, leaving thirty-nine dead. In Washington, D. C., **James Brown** goes on national television to urge restraint and constructive channeling of anger—an act for which he is officially commended by Vice President **Hubert Humphrey.** In New York, **Jimi Hendrix, B. B. King** and **Buddy Guy** gather in a club to play blues all night, and in closing the show, take a collection for King's Southern Christian Leadership Conference, to which Hendrix personally donates $5,000.

6 **Steve Miller,** on tour in England, writes a *Rolling Stone* column decrying the British rock scene as "more an industry than a scene . . . : It's at a low, lifeless point . . . The only good bands I've seen are **Traffic, Marmalade** and **Procol Harum** . . . I've seen bands doing queer bits in their underwear to get attention."

MGM Records launches its "Bosstown Sound" promotion campaign. The hype—generally regarded as one of the glaring failures of the pop music industry—seeks to create a Boston rock scene à la the San Francisco or London scenes and focuses on the **Ultimate Spinach** and the **Beacon Street Union,** neither of which is ever heard from again.

Apple Corps Ltd., the **Beatles'** new record company and management and publishing firm, opens offices at 95 Wigmore Street, London.

Pink Floyd announces that founder **Syd Barrett** has officially left the group. Barrett, suffering from psychiatric disorders compounded by drug use, retires to seclusion in his mother's house and later releases two solo albums.

10 *Rolling Stone* reports that **Mickey Hart** has joined the **Grateful Dead** at the invitation of Dead drummer Bill Kreutzmann, who'd been studying with Hart; the **Byrds** expand to a quartet again with the addition of **Gram Parsons; Nick Gravenites** and **Barry Goldberg** leave the **Electric Flag,** soon to be followed by **Mike Bloomfield.**

12 **Frank Zappa and the Mothers of Invention** perform at the National Academy of Recording Arts and Sciences Dinner in New York City. Zappa derides the audience and declares the event "a load of pompous hokum . . . All year long you people have manufactured this crap, now for one night your're gonna have to listen to it!" Zappa later remarks, "We played the ugliest shit we could . . . That's what they expected us to play."

Life runs a piece on the **Doors** entitled "Wicked Go the Doors." **Jim Morrison,** reports writer **Fred Powledge,** "is twenty-four years old, out of U.C.L.A., and he appears—in public and on his records—to be moody, tempermental, enchanted in the mind and extremely stoned on something."

19 **John Lennon, George Harrison** and their wives leave the **Maharishi Mahesh Yogi's** ashram in Rishikesh, India, two weeks before their study is completed. **Ringo Starr** and **Paul McCartney** have already left. Later, all four Beatles will renounce their association with the Maharishi.

20 Future heavy-metal heavyweights **Deep Purple,** composed of **Jon Lord, Ritchie Blackmore, Ian Paice, Rod Evans** and **Nick Semper,** give their concert debut in Tastrup, Denmark.

25 The **Beatles** refuse to perform for the **Queen of England** at a British Olympic Appeal Fund show. **Ringo Starr** explains, "Our decision would be the same no matter what the cause. We don't do benefits."

28 After six months at the off-Broadway New York Shakespeare Festival Theater, *Hair* opens at the Biltmore Theater, New York, and thus is the first "rock musical" to play on the Great White Way. The show, which features songs about drugs and draft-card burning and a controversial nude scene, goes on to give 1,729 performances on Broadway, tours the United States, is produced in more than eight countries and is made into a movie in 1979.

30 Los Angeles' first so-called total environment mixed-media rock ballroom, the Kaleidoscope, opens on Sunset Strip, with the **Jefferson Airplane, Canned Heat** and **Fever Tree** playing the premier bill.

31 Founder **Al Kooper** and saxophonist **Randy Brecker** leave **Blood, Sweat and Tears** after recording the octet's first album. ◆

WEEK ENDING APRIL 6

U.S. #1 POP 45	"(Sittin' on) The Dock of the Bay"	Otis Redding
U.S. #1 POP LP	*The Graduate* (soundtrack)	Simon and Garfunkel
U.S. #1 R&B 45	"(Sweet, Sweet Baby) Since You've Been Gone"	Aretha Franklin
U.K. #1 POP 45	"Lady Madonna"	The Beatles
U.K. #1 POP LP	*John Wesley Harding*	Bob Dylan

WEEK ENDING APRIL 13

U.S. #1 POP 45	"Honey"	Bobby Goldsboro
U.S. #1 POP LP	*The Graduate* (soundtrack)	Simon and Garfunkel
U.S. #1 R&B 45	"(Sweet, Sweet Baby) Since You've Been Gone"	Aretha Franklin
U.K. #1 POP 45	"Congratulations"	Cliff Richard
U.K. #1 POP LP	*John Wesley Harding*	Bob Dylan

WEEK ENDING APRIL 20

U.S. #1 POP 45	"Honey"	Bobby Goldsboro
U.S. #1 POP LP	*The Graduate* (soundtrack)	Simon and Garfunkel
U.S. #1 R&B 45	"(Sweet, Sweet Baby) Since You've Been Gone"	Aretha Franklin
U.K. #1 POP 45	"What a Wonderful World"	Louis Armstrong
U.K. #1 POP LP	*John Wesley Harding*	Bob Dylan

WEEK ENDING APRIL 27

U.S. #1 POP 45	"Honey"	Bobby Goldsboro
U.S. #1 POP LP	*The Graduate* (soundtrack)	Simon and Garfunkel
U.S. #1 R&B 45	"I Got the Feelin'"	James Brown
U.K. #1 POP 45	"What a Wonderful World"	Louis Armstrong
U.K. #1 POP LP	*John Wesley Harding*	Bob Dylan

2 The **Box Tops**' "Cry like a Baby" becomes the Memphis "blue-eyed soul" groups' second gold single.

3 The **Beach Boys** open a seventeen-date U.S. tour with a concert in New York. The second half of the show is given over to the **Maharishi Mahesh Yogi**, who lectures the audience on "spiritual regeneration." But so negative is the audience response, that more than half of the tour's dates are canceled.

4 Welsh singer **Mary Hopkin**, who turned eighteen only the day before, appears on the British TV show "Opportunity Knocks," where she is spotted by star model **Twiggy**, who recommends her to **Paul McCartney**. McCartney will sign her to Apple Records and produce her best-selling single "Those Were the Days."

5 After months of internal dissension, **Buffalo Springfield** play their final concert in Long Beach, California.

7 One hundred fifty riot police storm the stage at the Rome Pop Festival when the **Move** set off explosives as part of their act. No actual damage is done, and only a few minor injuries result from the police action.

11 *The Birds, the Bees and the Monkees,* which was certified gold upon its release in April, enters the LP chart at #80. In one week, propelled by its singles, "Daydream Believer" and "Valleri," it will jump to #3.

Jerry Rubin announces the formation of the Youth International Party and its plans for a massive demonstration at the Democratic National Convention in Chicago in August. A *Rolling Stone* cover story by **Jann Wenner** accuses the Yippies and Rubin of "recklessness and a thorough lack of moral compunction . . . This looks like a shuck . . . Apparently Rubin didn't hear **Bob Dylan** when he sang, 'Don't follow leaders, read the parking meters.' "

12 The **Rolling Stones** perform at the *New Musical Express* Pollwinners Concert in London—their first appearance in almost two years.

Jimi Hendrix is arrested for possession of hashish and heroin as he crosses the Canadian border for a concert in Toronto. He claims that the drugs were planted, and he is later exonerated.

18 Two dozen people are hospitalized near the site of the Northern California Folk-Rock Festival in Santa Clara, California, after they take mysterious pills given out by people calling themselves Hog Man and Hog Woman. The latter at one point leaps onstage, grabs the mike and shouts, "We're all on Hog!" urging everyone to take the pills.

The Turtles' Greatest Hits

passes the six-month mark on the album chart. The collection, certified gold on April 12, contains the **Turtles**' seven Top Forty entries ("Happy Together," "She'd Rather Be with Me," etc.), as well as favorite cuts from their two previous albums.

20 **Pete Townshend** marries **Karen Astley**, daughter of British composer and producer **Edwin Astley**.

21 Rolling Stone **Brian Jones** is arrested a second time for possession of cannabis in his London apartment.

Ten weeks after walking out on KMPX-FM, San Francisco's striking DJs find work on San Francisco's KSAN-FM, formerly a classical station.

22 **Cream** earns its first gold record with its second album, *Disraeli Gears,* which includes such hard-rock standards-to-be as "Sunshine of Your Love," "Strange Brew" and "Tales of Brave Ulysses."

Texan R&B group **Archie Bell and the Drells** are awarded their only gold record with the mostly instrumental dance hit "Tighten Up."

25 Abandoning their experiments with psychedelia, the **Rolling Stones** return to straight rock & roll, releasing "Jumpin' Jack Flash," a single later included on several greatest-hits collections but not on a regular-release album.

The 1968 Monterey International Pop Festival is canceled because of pressure from the local government and citizenry. In the wake of the cancellation, $52,000 is discovered missing from the previous festival's profits, and the festival's bookkeeper, **Mrs. Sandra Beebe**, is nowhere to be found. ◆

WEEK ENDING MAY 4

U.S. #1 POP 45	"Honey"	Bobby Goldsboro
U.S. #1 POP LP	*The Graduate* (soundtrack)	Simon and Garfunkel
U.S. #1 R&B 45	"I Got the Feelin' "	James Brown
U.K. #1 POP 45	"What a Wonderful World"	Louis Armstrong
U.K. #1 POP LP	*This Is Soul*	various artists

WEEK ENDING MAY 11

U.S. #1 POP 45	"Honey"	Bobby Goldsboro
U.S. #1 POP LP	*The Graduate* (soundtrack)	Simon and Garfunkel
U.S. #1 R&B 45	"Cowboys to Girls"	The Intruders
U.K. #1 POP 45	"What a Wonderful World"	Louis Armstrong
U.K. #1 POP LP	*This Is Soul*	various artists

WEEK ENDING MAY 18

U.S. #1 POP 45	"Tighten Up"	Archie Bell and the Drells
U.S. #1 POP LP	*The Graduate* (soundtrack)	Simon and Garfunkel
U.S. #1 R&B 45	"Tighten Up"	Archie Bell and the Drells
U.K. #1 POP 45	"Young Girl"	Gary Puckett and the Union Gap
U.K. #1 POP LP	*This Is Soul*	various artists

WEEK ENDING MAY 25

U.S. #1 POP 45	"Tighten Up"	Archie Bell and the Drells
U.S. #1 POP LP	*Bookends*	Simon and Garfunkel
U.S. #1 R&B 45	"Tighten Up"	Archie Bell and the Drells
U.K. #1 POP 45	"Young Girl"	Gary Puckett and the Union Gap
U.K. #1 POP LP	*This Is Soul*	various artists

1 Six months after quitting **Traffic**, guitarist and songwriter **Dave Mason** rejoins the English group.

5 Senator **Robert F. Kennedy** is shot in the Ambassador Hotel, Los Angeles, minutes after delivering his victory speech on winning the California Democratic party presidential primary. He dies early the next morning. His assassin, **Sirhan Sirhan**, is arrested at the scene of the shooting. Rock & roll will commemorate the tragedy in the **Rolling Stones**' "Sympathy for the Devil," recorded June 6 ("I shouted out, 'Who killed the Kennedys . . .'") and **Crosby, Stills and Nash**'s "Long Time Gone," which **David Crosby** writes that night.

8 Buddah Records books New York's Carnegie Hall for a promotional concert at which the entire Buddah roster—eight groups, including the **1910 Fruitgum Company**, the **Ohio Express**, the **Lemon Pipers** and other leading purveyors of bubblegum pop—combines to form the forty-six-strong **Kasenetz-Katz Singing Orchestral Circus**, which follows up its Carnegie Hall triumph with a hit single, "Quick Joey Small."

10 *Sovetskaya Rossiya*, a Soviet newspaper, denounces actor/musician **Viktor Vystosky** for singing "slangy and dirty songs about banal things and low morals" and for starting a fad for decadent Western guitar music.

At the two-day Zurich Rock Festival in Switzerland, police search for drugs, and club the audience and performers (**Jimi Hendrix**, **Traffic**, **Eric Burdon**

and the Animals and others) alike.

15 The **Beatles** renounce the **Maharishi Mahesh Yogi** as "a public mistake" at a New York City press conference. Later, on "The Tonight Show," guest host **Joe Garagiola** watches, bemused, as actress **Tallulah Bankhead** refers to **John Lennon** and **Paul McCartney** as "you kids" and wonders aloud, "How can one tell the boys from the girls?"

Wes Montgomery, the jazz guitar giant who found pop market success with his recordings of "Windy," "A Day in the Life" and "Georgia on My Mind," dies of a heart attack at age forty-five in his Indianapolis home.

16 The Fillmore West holds a benefit concert for the landmark San Francisco music club the Matrix. The evening's entertainment is provided by **Big Brother and the Holding Company**, the **Steve Miller Band** and **Santana**.

17 The **Ohio Express** nets its first gold single with "Yummy, Yummy, Yummy." The song is one of a string of bubblegum hits including "Chewy, Chewy," "Simon Says" (the **1910 Fruitgum Company**) and "Gimme Gimme Good Lovin'" (**Crazy Elephant**), all on Buddah Records.

21 The Museum of Modern Art in New York City presents a rock concert by **Earth Opera**, a Boston folk-rock band, as part of its Jazz in the Garden series.

22 The **Jeff Beck Group** makes its U.S. debut at the Fillmore East in New York City. Lead singer **Rod Stewart** is afflicted with such a case of stage fright that he hides behind speaker cabinets at the back of the stage through the first song.

27 **Elvis Presley** begins taping his first television special, "Elvis," at the NBC studios in Burbank, California. The show's success is later seen as the beginning of his comeback.

28 The **Rascals** win their third gold single (and first since shortening their name from the **Young Rascals**) with "Beautiful Morning."

29 The free rock concert in London's Hyde Park—a popular, regular event for several summers to come—is initiated by **Pink Floyd**. The **Rolling Stones** and **Blind Faith** are among the acts that follow Pink Floyd's example. ♦

WEEK ENDING JUNE 1

U.S. #1 POP 45	"Mrs. Robinson"	Simon and Garfunkel
U.S. #1 POP LP	*Bookends*	Simon and Garfunkel
U.S. #1 R&B 45	"Shoo-be-doo-be-doo-da-day"	Stevie Wonder
U.K. #1 POP 45	"Young Girl"	Gary Puckett and the Union Gap
U.K. #1 POP LP	*This Is Soul*	various artists

WEEK ENDING JUNE 8

U.S. #1 POP 45	"Mrs. Robinson"	Simon and Garfunkel
U.S. #1 POP LP	*Bookends*	Simon and Garfunkel
U.S. #1 R&B 45	"Ain't Nothing like the Real Thing"	Marvin Gaye and Tammi Terrell
U.K. #1 POP 45	"Young Girl"	Gary Puckett and the Union Gap
U.K. #1 POP LP	*This Is Soul*	various artists

WEEK ENDING JUNE 15

U.S. #1 POP 45	"Mrs. Robinson"	Simon and Garfunkel
U.S. #1 POP LP	*The Graduate* (soundtrack)	Simon and Garfunkel
U.S. #1 R&B 45	"Think"	Aretha Franklin
U.K. #1 POP 45	"Young Girl"	Gary Puckett and the Union Gap
U.K. #1 POP LP	*This Is Soul*	various artists

WEEK ENDING JUNE 22

U.S. #1 POP 45	"This Guy's in Love with You"	Herb Alpert
U.S. #1 POP LP	*The Graduate* (soundtrack)	Simon and Garfunkel
U.S. #1 R&B 45	"Think"	Aretha Franklin
U.K. #1 POP 45	"Jumpin' Jack Flash"	The Rolling Stones
U.K. #1 POP LP	*This Is Soul*	various artists

WEEK ENDING JUNE 29

U.S. #1 POP 45	"This Guy's in Love with You"	Herb Alpert
U.S. #1 POP LP	*Bookends*	Simon and Garfunkel
U.S. #1 R&B 45	"Think"	Aretha Franklin
U.K. #1 POP 45	"Jumpin' Jack Flash"	The Rolling Stones
U.K. #1 POP LP	*This Is Soul*	various artists

5 **Bill Graham** moves his San Francisco rock concert operation from the original Fillmore Theater to the Carousel Ballroom in San Francisco, renaming the latter the Fillmore West to complement Graham's recently opened Fillmore East in New York City. Graham cites the Carousel's larger seating capacity (roughly 4,000, compared to the old Fillmore's 1,500) and safer, more accessible location (the old Fillmore was located in San Francisco's black ghetto, where the harassment of Fillmore patrons had become more pronounced in the wake of the assassination of Martin Luther King, Jr.). The Carousel has been operated since February 14, 1968, by Headstone Productions, which financed its operations with well-attended dance concerts featuring the **Jefferson Airplane** and the **Grateful Dead**.

7 Three years after **Eric Clapton** left the pioneering British blues guitar band and eighteen months after **Jeff Beck**'s departure, the **Yardbirds** finally break up, leaving guitarist **Jimmy Page** to fulfill upcoming concert obligations. He forms a group called the **New Yardbirds**, but in response to a remark attributed to **Keith Moon**—"It'll probably go over like a lead zeppelin" (as in lead balloon)—regarding the group's initial reception, Page changes the name to **Led Zeppelin**.

9 The **Temptations** appear at the Valley Forge Music Fair in Pennsylvania without baritone **David Ruffin**. Ruffin, it turns out, has been fired by Motown Records because of his desire to change the Temps' image from "the suits, ties and patent shoes" and "go into a deep soul bag"—a direction that the group ends up following later when producer **Norman Whitfield** steps in. Ruffin's place in the quintet is taken by **Dennis Edwards**, formerly of the **Contours**, and Motown rehires Ruffin as a solo artist.

Scattered violence breaks out at a city-sponsored concert in Boston's South End, headlined by **Smokey Robinson and the Miracles**. Poor amplification is cited as a contributing cause.

10 Guitarist and vocalist **Eric Clapton** announces the breakup of **Cream** because of "a loss of direction." Three days later, the band's manager, **Robert Stigwood**, makes it official, adding that the group will play one more "farewell tour" in the autumn.

The British "classical rock" band the **Nice**, which features future progressive-rock keyboard star **Keith Emerson**, stomps and burns an American flag during its performance of "First Amendment," a song based on **Leonard Bernstein**'s "America" (from *West Side Story*). The Nice are banned from ever again appearing at Royal Albert Hall, where the offense was committed.

17 The **Beatles**' feature-length animated movie *Yellow Submarine*, directed by **George Dunning** and animated by **Heinz Edelman**, premieres at the Pavillion in London. **John Lennon**, **Paul McCartney** and **George Harrison** attend the event and witness what will be the last big public outburst of Beatlemania (as in riots) during the group's lifespan.

Tim Hardin, author of "If I Were a Carpenter" and many other contemporary folk music standards, performs to a sold-out house including the **Beatles**, the **Rolling Stones** and **Donovan**, at London's Royal Albert Hall. The balance of his U.K. tour must be canceled, however, when doctors discover that Hardin has contracted pleurisy, a lung disease.

18 South African emigré trumpeter **Hugh Masekela** claims his only gold record, with an instrumental single, "Grazin' in the Grass" (later given a hit vocal treatment by the **Friends of Distinction**).

20 Iron Butterfly's *In-a-Gadda-da-Vida*, featuring its now-famous seventeen-minute title track, which in turn contains one of the longest drum solos in the history of rock, debuts on the American chart.

25 **Big Brother and the Holding Company** release their most critically and commercially successful album, *Cheap Thrills*, which includes the classic **Janis Joplin** performances of "Piece of My Heart," "Combination of the Two," "Summertime" and "Ball and Chain" and features the cover art of "underground" cartoonist **R. Crumb**.

26 The new **Rolling Stones** album, *Beggar's Banquet*, fails to come out on its scheduled release date because the Stones' U.S. label, London, refuses to distribute the album with its cover photograph of a graffiti-scrawled lavatory wall.

29 The **Byrds** embark on their tour of South Africa without singer and guitarist **Gram Parsons**, who refuses to set foot in the nation where apartheid—the legal separation of black and white citizens—is official policy. Parsons announces that he will form a new "Southern soul group playing country and gospel oriented music with a steel guitar." Thus the **Flying Burrito Brothers** are born. ◆

WEEK ENDING JULY 6

U.S. #1 POP 45	"This Guy's in Love with You"	Herb Alpert
U.S. #1 POP LP	Bookends	Simon and Garfunkel
U.S. #1 R&B 45	"I Could Never Love Another (after Loving You)"	The Temptations
U.K. #1 POP 45	"Baby Come Back"	The Equals
U.K. #1 POP LP	Ogden's Nut Gone Flake	The Small Faces

WEEK ENDING JULY 13

U.S. #1 POP 45	"This Guy's in Love with You"	Herb Alpert
U.S. #1 POP LP	Bookends	Simon and Garfunkel
U.S. #1 R&B 45	"Grazin' in the Grass"	Hugh Masekela
U.K. #1 POP 45	"Baby Come Back"	The Equals
U.K. #1 POP LP	Ogden's Nut Gone Flake	The Small Faces

WEEK ENDING JULY 20

U.S. #1 POP 45	"Grazin' in the Grass"	Hugh Masekela
U.S. #1 POP LP	Bookends	Simon and Garfunkel
U.S. #1 R&B 45	"Grazin' in the Grass"	Hugh Masekela
U.K. #1 POP 45	"Baby Come Back"	The Equals
U.K. #1 POP LP	Ogden's Nut Gone Flake	The Small Faces

WEEK ENDING JULY 27

U.S. #1 POP 45	"Grazin' in the Grass"	Hugh Masekela
U.S. #1 POP LP	The Beat of the Brass	Herb Alpert and the Tijuana Brass
U.S. #1 R&B 45	"Grazin' in the Grass"	Hugh Masekela
U.K. #1 POP 45	"Mony Mony"	Tommy James and the Shondells
U.K. #1 POP LP	Ogden's Nut Gone Flake	The Small Faces

4 The two-day Newport Pop Festival gets under way in Costa Mesa, California. One hundred thousand people turn out for **Sonny and Cher**, **Steppenwolf**, the **Chambers Brothers**, **Tiny Tim**, the **James Cotton Blues Band**, **Canned Heat**, **Country Joe and the Fish**, the **Electric Flag**, the **Paul Butterfield Blues Band**, the **Jefferson Airplane**, the **Grateful Dead**, **Iron Butterfly**, **Blue Cheer**, **Eric Burdon and the Animals**, the **Byrds**, the **Quicksilver Messenger Service** and other acts.

6 The **Doors'** third album, *Waiting for the Sun*, brings them their third gold LP. The fold-out Unipac cover includes the complete text of Jim Morrison's poem, "The Celebration of the Lizard-King," which the Doors perform only in concert, though the LP includes an excerpt from it, "Not Touch the Earth." The complete "Celebration" is later recorded for *Absolutely Live*.

10 *Music from Big Pink*, the debut album by a group who'd worked as **Bob Dylan** sidemen called the **Band**, enters the American chart. The title refers to the house in Woodstock, New York, in whose basement the album was recorded.

14 In an article entitled "Lyrics of Pop Songs Are Getting New Emphasis," the *New York Times* notes the confluence of modern poetry and pop music, quoting song lyrics by **Bob Dylan**, **Paul Simon**, **Leonard Cohen**, **Laura Nyro**, **Rod McKuen** and others. The article finds that most literary critics dismiss pop song lyrics as "doggerel, simplistically banal," and concludes that pop song-writing "attracts those who are house painters with words rather than fine artists."

16 **Ray Charles'** *A Man and His Soul* is certified gold. After recording albums of jazz, pop and country & western music, Charles has returned to the style he virtually invented—gospel-rooted soul.

17 McGraw-Hill rushes **Hunter Davies'** authorized biography of the **Beatles** to bookstores ahead of schedule to prevent loss of sales to **Julian Fast**'s unauthorized *The Beatles: Real Story*. Fast admits having never met Lennon, McCartney, Harrison or Starr.

20 Dr. **David M. Lipscomb**, director of the University of Tennessee's audio lab, reports that a guinea pig subjected over a three-month period to eighty-eight hours of rock music recorded at a Knoxville discotheque at 120 decibels suffered acute damage to the inner ears. **Steve Paul**, owner of the Scene, a New York disco, tells the *New York Times*, "Should a major increase in guinea pig attendance occur at the Scene, we'll certainly bear their comfort in mind."

22 **Cynthia Powell Lennon** sues **John Lennon** for divorce on the grounds of adultery after returning from a vacation to find **Yoko Ono** living in the Lennon's London home.

23 **Aretha Franklin**'s *Lady Soul* is awarded a gold LP, while the **Rascals'** "People Got to Be Free" wins a gold 45.

24 *Billboard* and England's *New Musical Express* report rumors predicting that lead singer **Diana Ross** will soon leave the **Supremes**.

Joe McDonald, **Barry Felton** and **David Cohen** of **Country Joe and the Fish**, in Chicago to perform for demonstrators outside the Democratic National Convention, are assaulted in an elevator by three Vietnam veterans who taunt them, "Don't you like America?"

26 Apple Corps releases its first product: five singles, including the **Beatles'** "Hey Jude" backed with "Revolution," which is destined to be the group's biggest hit.

"Harper Valley P.T.A.," **Jeannie C. Riley**'s country-pop crossover hit about small-town hypocrisy, is certified gold.

28 The **Doors'** "Hello, I Love You" is a million-seller. The song, which has none of the sinister quality of their first million-seller, "Light My Fire," marks the group's successful move into a more mainstream rock sound.

31 **Fleetwood Mac** announces the addition of eighteen-year-old **Danny Kirwan**, who brings the British blues band's lead guitar lineup to three (**Peter Green** and **Jeremy Spencer** are the others). ♦

WEEK ENDING AUGUST 3

U.S. #1 POP 45	"Hello, I Love You"	The Doors
U.S. #1 POP LP	*The Beat of the Brass*	Herb Alpert and the Tijuana Brass
U.S. #1 R&B 45	"Grazin' in the Grass"	Hugh Masekela
U.K. #1 POP 45	"Mony Mony"	Tommy James and the Shondells
U.K. #1 POP LP	*Bookends*	Simon and Garfunkel

WEEK ENDING AUGUST 10

U.S. #1 POP 45	"Hello, I Love You"	The Doors
U.S. #1 POP LP	*Wheels of Fire*	Cream
U.S. #1 R&B 45	"Stay in My Corner"	The Dells
U.K. #1 POP 45	"Mony Mony"	Tommy James and the Shondells
U.K. #1 POP LP	*Delilah*	Tom Jones

WEEK ENDING AUGUST 17

U.S. #1 POP 45	"People Got to Be Free"	The Rascals
U.S. #1 POP LP	*Wheels of Fire*	Cream
U.S. #1 R&B 45	"Stay in My Corner"	The Dells
U.K. #1 POP 45	"Mony Mony"	Tommy James and the Shondells
U.K. #1 POP LP	*Bookends*	Simon and Garfunkel

WEEK ENDING AUGUST 24

U.S. #1 POP 45	"People Got to Be Free"	The Rascals
U.S. #1 POP LP	*Wheels of Fire*	Cream
U.S. #1 R&B 45	"Stay in My Corner"	The Dells
U.K. #1 POP 45	"Help Yourself"	Tom Jones
U.K. #1 POP LP	*Bookends*	Simon and Garfunkel

WEEK ENDING AUGUST 31

U.S. #1 POP 45	"People Got to Be Free"	The Rascals
U.S. #1 POP LP	*Wheels of Fire*	Cream
U.S. #1 R&B 45	"You're All I Need to Get By"	Marvin Gaye and Tammi Terrell
U.K. #1 POP 45	"Help Yourself"	Tom Jones
U.K. #1 POP LP	*Bookends*	Simon and Garfunkel

2 The three-day Sky River Rock Festival and Lighter than Air Fair draws successfully to a conclusion in Sultan, Washington. The nonprofit event attracted 15,000 celebrants to see and hear **Country Joe and the Fish**, the **Grateful Dead**, **It's a Beautiful Day**, **Santana**, **Muddy Waters**, the **James Cotton Blues Band**, **"Big Mama" Willie Mae Thornton**, **Ramblin' Jack Elliott**, the **New Lost City Ramblers**, **Dino Valenti**, the **Youngbloods**, **Mark Spoelstra** and other acts.

4 The **Rolling Stones'** latest single, "Street Fighting Man," is banned in Chicago and other American cities where authorities fear it might "incite riots and other forms of public disorder."

In a speech to the seventy-sixth Annual Conference of the American Psychological Association, semanticist, academician and California legislator **S. I. Hayakawa** attributes the anti-materialism, drug experimenting, social alienation and radical politics of American youth to "an overdue negative reaction to television's message that material possessions are everything, that this headache remedy, this luxurious carpeting, this new model Camaro will bring all kinds of happiness."

Currently riding the charts with "People Got to Be Free," the **Rascals** add two LPs to their collection of gold discs: their two-year-old debut, *The Young Rascals,* and their recently released greatest hits collection, *Time Peace.*

5 Herbert Khaury, better known as **Tiny Tim**, sues Bouquet Records for $1 million in damages when the record label releases early recordings of Khaury without his permission.

11 Arriving in London for a tour of the U.K., **Sly and the Family Stone** bassist **Larry Graham** is arrested for possession of cannabis. As a result, the BBC cancels a scheduled television appearance by the group, and a London hotel refuses to honor band members' reservations. A week later, the band returns to the U.S., having given no concerts abroad.

13 For the first time, the Waldorf-Astoria Hotel on New York's Park Avenue engages a rock group—the **Savages**—to perform between shows in the Empire Room. "In our efforts to keep the Empire Room in tune with the times," the management states. "We feel that our regular customers will accept this change."

14 In an interview published in *Rolling Stone,* **Pete Townshend** outlines his plans to write a rock opera about a boy who is deaf, dumb and blind.

Forty overseas officials of the United States Information Agency are required to attend a Washington, D.C. concert by **Blood, Sweat and Tears** as part of a USIA program to acquaint its overseas staff with cultural developments in the homeland.

Don Kirshner, the mastermind behind "The Monkees," premieres his latest youth-market show on CBS-TV—"The Archies Show," a Saturday-morning cartoon series about a high school rock band, based on the popular *Archie* comic-book series.

15 "Soul!," a television weekly variety program aimed at black audiences, premieres on NBC. The opening-night show features **Lou Rawls**, **Martha Reeves and the Vandellas** and comedian **Red Foxx**.

17 The **Fifth Dimension** pick up their second gold disc with their rendition of **Laura Nyro's** "Stoned Soul Picnic."

19 **Steppenwolf** earns its first gold disc with a single, "Born to Be Wild," later to be featured in the soundtrack of the youth-cult film *Easy Rider.* A phrase from the song, "heavy-metal thunder," is purportedly the source of the term *heavy metal,* although the term previously appeared in a novel by **William Burroughs**, *Naked Lunch.*

20 The **1910 Fruitgum Company's** "1, 2, 3, Red Light"—like the group's "Simon Says," inspired by a children's game—repeats the earlier hit's success by earning $1 million for Buddah Records, the self-proclaimed (and widely acknowledged) home of bubblegum music.

28 Manager **Albert Grossman** announces that **Janis Joplin** will leave **Big Brother and the Holding Company** in November after fulfilling current obligations. Joplin explains that she and the band "weren't growing together anymore."   ♦

WEEK ENDING SEPTEMBER 7

U.S. #1 POP 45	"People Got to Be Free"	The Rascals
U.S. #1 POP LP	*Waiting for the Sun*	The Doors
U.S. #1 R&B 45	"You're All I Need to Get By"	Marvin Gaye and Tammi Terrell
U.K. #1 POP 45	"I've Got to Get a Message to You"	The Bee Gees
U.K. #1 POP LP	*Bookends*	Simon and Garfunkel

WEEK ENDING SEPTEMBER 14

U.S. #1 POP 45	"People Got to Be Free"	The Rascals
U.S. #1 POP LP	*Waiting for the Sun*	The Doors
U.S. #1 R&B 45	"You're All I Need to Get By"	Marvin Gaye and Tammi Terrell
U.K. #1 POP 45	"Hey Jude"	The Beatles
U.K. #1 POP LP	*Greatest Hits*	The Hollies

WEEK ENDING SEPTEMBER 21

U.S. #1 POP 45	"Harper Valley P.T.A."	Jeannie C. Riley
U.S. #1 POP LP	*Waiting for the Sun*	The Doors
U.S. #1 R&B 45	"You're All I Need to Get By"	Marvin Gaye and Tammi Terrell
U.K. #1 POP 45	"Hey Jude"	The Beatles
U.K. #1 POP LP	*Greatest Hits*	The Hollies

WEEK ENDING SEPTEMBER 28

U.S. #1 POP 45	"Hey Jude"	The Beatles
U.S. #1 POP LP	*Time Peace*	The Rascals
U.S. #1 R&B 45	"You're All I Need to Get By"	Marvin Gaye and Tammi Terrell
U.K. #1 POP 45	"Hey Jude"	The Beatles
U.K. #1 POP LP	*Greatest Hits*	The Hollies

2 Motown Records and its publishing affiliate, Jobete Music, files a $4-million suit against songwriters and producers **Edward Holland**, **Lamont Dozier** and **Brian Holland**, the team responsible for many of Motown's biggest hits. Motown charges that Holland-Dozier-Holland have not written any new songs or produced any new recordings since late 1967—a breach of contract.

5 The **Who**, the **Small Faces**, the **Crazy World of Arthur Brown** and **Joe Cocker** kick off a package tour of Britain with a concert in London.

Cream begins its farewell tour of the U.S. with a concert in Oakland, California.

6 *The Doors Are Open,* a documentary film about the **Doors**, is aired on British television.

8 **Cass Elliot** debuts as a solo act at Caesar's Palace, Las Vegas, but cancels her two-week engagement when opening night proves to be a fiasco; she has tonsilitis

and her band has not rehearsed sufficiently. Meanwhile, Dunhill Records is suing her former colleagues in the **Mamas and the Papas** for $200,000, charging that **John Phillips**, **Denny Doherty** and **Michele Phillips** have not met contractual obligations since disbanding the group.

11 **Aretha Franklin** adds gold single number seven, her recording of **Burt Bacharach** and **Hal David**'s "I Say a Little Prayer," to her collection.

12 **John Sebastian** leaves the **Lovin' Spoonful** to begin his solo career, following **Zal Yanovsky**, who left the group at the end of 1967.

14 **Frank Weber**, millionaire and former manager of the **Kingston Trio**, is arrested in San Francisco along with five others when 400 pounds of marijuana are found in their possession.

17 **Jose Feliciano**, the blind Hispanic singer-guitarist, issues his controversial, bluesy rendition of "The Star-Spangled Banner" on RCA

Records. He first perfomed it at a 1968 World Series game between the Detroit Tigers and the St. Louis Cardinals. Baseball fans in the stands booed Feliciano's performance.

18 **Led Zeppelin** plays its first U.K. date at London's Marquee Club. The seminal heavy-metal band made its world debut on tour in Scandinavia at the beginning of the month.

John Lennon and **Yoko Ono** are arrested and charged with possession of marijuana during

a raid on **Ringo Starr**'s London apartment, where the two are staying.

19 At the invitation of **Small Faces** singer/guitarist **Steve Marriott**, singer/guitarist **Peter Frampton** of the **Herd** joins the Small Faces during a performance in London, thus setting the stage for **Humble Pie**, the band Marriott and Frampton leave their respective groups to form.

21 Nashville's top Country Music Awards go to **Jeannie C. Riley**'s "Harper Valley P.T.A." for best song and to *Johnny Cash at Folsom Prison* for best album.

22 A revolutionary street gang called the **Motherfuckers** attempts to "liberate" the Fillmore East in New York City, charging that owner **Bill Graham** has "sucked the blood of the community and made himself rich off of rock," which belongs to the people." Graham counters: "Nobody wanted to liberate this place a year ago when it was a rat-infested dump. You can go liberate the opera house."

26 Legendary disc jockey **Murray the K** returns to WMCA, the New York City radio station where he began his broadcasting career in the early Fifties.

31 The **MC5**, whose radical politics will later get them in trouble with both the law and their record company, record their incendiary first album, *Kick Out the Jams,* live at the Grande Ballroom in Detroit. ◆

WEEK ENDING OCTOBER 5

U.S. #1 POP 45	"Hey Jude"	The Beatles
U.S. #1 POP LP	*Waiting for the Sun*	The Doors
U.S. #1 R&B 45	"Say It Loud—I'm Black and I'm Proud"	James Brown
U.K. #1 POP 45	"Those Were the Days"	Mary Hopkin
U.K. #1 POP LP	*Greatest Hits*	The Hollies

WEEK ENDING OCTOBER 12

U.S. #1 POP 45	"Hey Jude"	The Beatles
U.S. #1 POP LP	*Cheap Thrills*	Big Brother and the Holding Company
U.S. #1 R&B 45	"Say It Loud—I'm Black and I'm Proud"	James Brown
U.K. #1 POP 45	"Those Were the Days"	Mary Hopkin
U.K. #1 POP LP	*Greatest Hits*	The Hollies

WEEK ENDING OCTOBER 19

U.S. #1 POP 45	"Hey Jude"	The Beatles
U.S. #1 POP LP	*Cheap Thrills*	Big Brother and the Holding Company
U.S. #1 R&B 45	"Say It Loud—I'm Black and I'm Proud"	James Brown
U.K. #1 POP 45	"Those Were the Days"	Mary Hopkin
U.K. #1 POP LP	*Greatest Hits*	The Hollies

WEEK ENDING OCTOBER 26

U.S. #1 POP 45	"Hey Jude"	The Beatles
U.S. #1 POP LP	*Cheap Thrills*	Big Brother and the Holding Company
U.S. #1 R&B 45	"Say It Loud—I'm Black and I'm Proud"	James Brown
U.K. #1 POP 45	"Those Were the Days"	Mary Hopkin
U.K. #1 POP LP	*Greatest Hits*	The Hollies

1 **George Harrison** becomes the first Beatle to issue a solo album when he releases *Wonderwall Music,* the soundtrack to the film *Wonderwall,* on Apple.

Former **Count Basie Orchestra** vocalist **O. C. Smith** wins the only gold record of his career with "Little Green Apples," which also wins two 1968 Grammy Awards.

2 The four-day Czechoslovakian International Beat Festival, to be headlined by the **Soul Men** from Bratislava, is canceled by Soviet invasion authorities.

Appearing at Madison Square Garden, New York, on its farewell tour of the U.S., **Cream** is awarded a platinum disc marking sales of over $2 million of its double album *Wheels of Fire,* by their American record company, Atco. (The Recording Industry Association of America is still seven years away from awarding platinum discs.)

8 **Cynthia Powell Lennon** is granted a divorce from her husband of six years, **John Lennon,** in a London court. John is absent from court. He is attending **Yoko Ono** (the woman named in Cynthia's charge of adultery) in a hospital, where it is feared she might suffer a miscarriage (she indeed miscarries on November 21).

9 "Rock & roll music contributes to both the usage of drugs and the high VD rate among enlisted men in the army today," a U.S. Army captain tells *Rolling Stone.*

13 Rolling Stone **Brian Jones** purchases Cotchford Farms in Sussex, England, where **A. A. Milne** wrote *Winnie the Pooh.* There are statues of *Pooh* characters on the grounds.

15 Memphis soul singer **Johnnie Taylor,** who replaced **Sam Cooke** in the **Soul Stirrers** before starting his solo career, earns his first gold record with "Who's Making Love."

18 The **Jimi Hendrix Experience**'s third album, *Electric Ladyland,* earns the group its third gold LP. "Crosstown Traffic," a version of **Bob Dylan's** "All along the Watchtower" and "Voodoo Chile" are the two-record set's highlights.

Glen Campbell, a former session musician for **Frank Sinatra, Nat "King" Cole** and the **Beach Boys,** earns a gold disc for his recording of "Wichita Lineman."

19 **Diana Ross,** onstage with the **Supremes** at the Royal Command Variety Performance in London, interupts the show with a plea for interracial understanding. The audience, which includes members of the royal family, applauds for two minutes.

22 The **Beatles** release their long-awaited double album, simply entitled *The Beatles* but better known as "The White Album." Among the set's twenty-nine songs is **Ringo Starr's** first songwriting contribution to the band's repertoire, "Don't Pass Me By," which, as a single, hits Number One in Scandinavia.

23 Beginning of the end of an era: *Rolling Stone* reports that San Francisco's **Family Dog** has lost its license to operate out of the Avalon Ballroom, site of marathon dance concerts featuring the **Grateful Dead,** the **Jefferson Airplane, Moby Grape, Quicksilver Messenger Service** and other psychedelic luminaries. Neighbors of the Avalon complained to authorities that the Family Dog frequently ran shows past its two a.m. limit, also about the ill effects of "all those hippie kids" on the neighborhood.

26 **Cream** gives its last concert at the Royal Albert Hall, London. "God save the Cream," chants the crowd. The event is documented in **Tony Palmer's** film *Goodbye Cream.*

27 **Steppenwolf's** eponymous first album, which includes its biggest hits, "Born to Be Wild" and "Magic Carpet Ride," is certified gold.

29 **John Lennon,** the first Beatle to be tried on drug charges, is convicted of possession of cannabis (marijuana) and fined £150 ($360.) in London. The court accepts his explanation that he no longer uses marijuana and that the amount found in his possession was an old, forgotten stash. **Yoko Ono,** who was arrested with Lennon on October 18, is cleared of charges. ◆

WEEK ENDING NOVEMBER 2

U.S. #1 POP 45	"Hey Jude"	The Beatles
U.S. #1 POP LP	*Cheap Thrills*	Big Brother and the Holding Company
U.S. #1 R&B 45	"Say It Loud—I'm Black and I'm Proud"	James Brown
U.K. #1 POP 45	"Those Were the Days"	Mary Hopkin
U.K. #1 POP LP	*Greatest Hits*	The Hollies

WEEK ENDING NOVEMBER 9

U.S. #1 POP 45	"Hey Jude"	The Beatles
U.S. #1 POP LP	*Cheap Thrills*	Big Brother and the Holding Company
U.S. #1 R&B 45	"Say It Loud—I'm Black and I'm Proud"	James Brown
U.K. #1 POP 45	"With a Little Help from My Friends"	Joe Cocker
U.K. #1 POP LP	*Greatest Hits*	The Hollies

WEEK ENDING NOVEMBER 16

U.S. #1 POP 45	"Hey Jude"	The Beatles
U.S. #1 POP LP	*Electric Ladyland*	The Jimi Hendrix Experience
U.S. #1 R&B 45	"Hey Western Union Man"	Jerry Butler
U.K. #1 POP 45	"The Good, the Bad and the Ugly"	Hugo Montenegro
U.K. #1 POP LP	*Greatest Hits*	The Hollies

WEEK ENDING NOVEMBER 23

U.S. #1 POP 45	"Hey Jude"	The Beatles
U.S. #1 POP LP	*Electric Ladyland*	The Jimi Hendrix Experience
U.S. #1 R&B 45	"Who's Making Love"	Johnnie Taylor
U.K. #1 POP 45	"Eloise"	Barry Ryan
U.K. #1 POP LP	*Greatest Hits*	The Hollies

WEEK ENDING NOVEMBER 30

U.S. #1 POP 45	"Love Child"	Diana Ross and the Supremes
U.S. #1 POP LP	*Cheap Thrills*	Big Brother and the Holding Company
U.S. #1 R&B 45	"Who's Making Love"	Johnnie Taylor
U.K. #1 POP 45	"Eloise"	Barry Ryan
U.K. #1 POP LP	*The Beatles*	The Beatles

3 Elvis Presley's NBC-TV special, "Elvis," sponsored by the Singer Sewing Machine Company, is aired. The special also contains videotape of a live performance given earlier at NBC's Burbank studios—his first appearance before a live audience since 1961. "Elvis" constitutes the King's first big step toward his successful comeback.

Three singles strike gold: the O'Kaysions' "Girl Watcher," the Grass Roots' "Midnight Confession" and the Crazy World of Arthur Brown's "Fire." Among the gold albums awarded this day are Aretha Franklin's *Aretha Now,* Iron Butterfly's *In-a-Gadda-da-Vida* and Cream's 1967 debut, *Fresh Cream.*

4 The *New York Times* quotes Soviet music critic A. Martinosa saying that the Beatles "have become rich idols of the Philistines."

The Chambers Brothers net their only gold record with their album *The Time Has Come,* which contains the hit single "Time Has Come Today."

5 Five months after its originally scheduled release date, the Rolling Stones unveil *Beggar's Banquet* in an uncontroversial white cover designed to resemble a formal invitation. A London party to celebrate the record's release lives up to the album title when a custard pie fight breaks out.

6 James Taylor's self-titled debut album is released in Britain on Apple. Most attention focuses on the contributions of Paul McCartney and George Harrison.

Aides to President-elect Richard Nixon send out 66,000 letters, signed by Nixon, to potential administrative office holders. Among the recipients is the king of rock himself, Elvis Presley.

7 Eric Burdon announces that he will disband the Animals after a December 22 concert at Newcastle City Hall (Newcastle being the Animals' hometown) and will move to California to embark on a film-acting career.

8 Graham Nash quits the Hollies, which he cofounded in 1962, announcing that he intends to form a trio with ex-Byrd David Crosby and ex-Buffalo Springfield Steve Stills.

12 The Rolling Stones convene in a London film studio with John Lennon, Yoko Ono, Eric Clapton, the Who, Jethro Tull, Mitch Mitchell, Marianne Faithfull, Taj Mahal, Mia Farrow and a company of clowns and acrobats to film their "Rolling Stones Rock & Roll Circus," which is never given a public showing.

15 Grace Slick, performing with the Jefferson Airplane on "The Smothers Brothers Comedy Hour," appears in blackface and raises a black-leather-gloved fist in the black power salute at the conclusion of "Crown of Creation." The incident is one of several contributing to the show's cancellation the following year.

18 At a Christmas party entitled "An Alchemical Wedding" at the Underground club in London, John Lennon and Yoko Ono appear—sort of. They're both onstage, all right, but they aren't visible—they're crawling around inside a large, white bag. This is the beginning of what Yoko terms *bag-ism;* by remaining hidden, she claims, the meaning of their message will not be confused by physical appearances. Both the audience and the press fail to get whatever message they may have intended.

21 Janis Joplin is the only act not from Memphis to appear at the Second Annual Stax/Volt Yuletide Thing, in Memphis; the rest of the bill is filled by Booker T. and the MGs, the Staple Singers, Albert King, the Bar-Kays, Rufus and Carla Thomas, Johnnie Taylor, Eddie Floyd and other citizens of "Soulsville, U.S.A."

22 In an article in the *New York Times,* New York Philharmonic Orchestra conductor Leonard Bernstein expresses his enthusiasm for the New York Rock & Roll Ensemble, a group whose repertoire includes both rock and classical music.

28 The Miami Pop Festival—the first big rock festival held on the East Coast, gets under way in Hallendale, Florida. Tickets sell for six dollars and seven dollars, and 100,000 people attend the three-day event featuring Jose Feliciano, Terry Reid, Procol Harum, Buffy Sainte-Marie, Country Joe and the Fish, Three Dog Night, Chuck Berry, the McCoys, Booker T. and the MGs, Fleetwood Mac, Pacific Gas and Electric, Steppenwolf, Marvin Gaye, the Grateful Dead, Hugh Masekela, Flatt and Scruggs, the Paul Butterfield Blues Band, Joni Mitchell, the James Cotton Blues Band, Richie Havens, the Box Tops, Iron Butterfly, the Turtles, Canned Heat, the Grass Roots, Junior Walker and the All Stars, Sweetwater, Joe Tex, Ian and Sylvia and the Charles Lloyd Quartet. ◆

WEEK ENDING DECEMBER 7

U.S. #1 POP 45	"Love Child"	Diana Ross and the Supremes
U.S. #1 POP LP	*Cheap Thrills*	Big Brother and the Holding Company
U.S. #1 R&B 45	"Who's Making Love"	Johnnie Taylor
U.K. #1 POP 45	"Lily the Pink"	The Scaffold
U.K. #1 POP LP	*The Beatles*	The Beatles

WEEK ENDING DECEMBER 14

U.S. #1 POP 45	"I Heard It through the Grapevine"	Marvin Gaye
U.S. #1 POP LP	*Cheap Thrills*	Big Brother and the Holding Company
U.S. #1 R&B 45	"I Heard It through the Grapevine"	Marvin Gaye
U.K. #1 POP 45	"Lily the Pink"	The Scaffold
U.K. #1 POP LP	*The Beatles*	The Beatles

WEEK ENDING DECEMBER 21

U.S. #1 POP 45	"I Heard It through the Grapevine"	Marvin Gaye
U.S. #1 POP LP	*Wichita Lineman*	Glen Campbell
U.S. #1 R&B 45	"I Heard It through the Grapevine"	Marvin Gaye
U.K. #1 POP 45	"Lily the Pink"	The Scaffold
U.K. #1 POP LP	*The Beatles*	The Beatles

WEEK ENDING DECEMBER 28

U.S. #1 POP 45	"I Heard It through the Grapevine"	Marvin Gaye
U.S. #1 POP LP	*The Beatles*	The Beatles
U.S. #1 R&B 45	"I Heard It through the Grapevine"	Marvin Gaye
U.K. #1 POP 45	"Lily the Pink"	The Scaffold
U.K. #1 POP LP	*Sound of Music*	soundtrack

1969

As this decade, fraught with so many grand-scale and rapid-fire changes, hurtled to a close, it seemed as though the very pace of life itself was accelerating. So much was going on, it was impossible to tell what was really happening.

With the rock audience more communal and commercial than ever before, 1969 became the year of the rock festival. Festivals—where thousands of fans gathered to see what usually amounted to at least a dozen acts—were a way of not only coming together, but of demonstrating the actual size, scope and strength of the rock-culture community. This was also the year of violence at rock festivals: over half the major rock festivals held in America this year were marred by outbreaks of violence, by police brutality, by gate-crashers causing riots, or by people "freaking out" on bad drugs they'd taken, sometimes unwittingly.

But it was really the year of Woodstock—the biggest and best of them all, as more than 400,000 gathered to see a galaxy of rock's biggest stars. There was virtually no violence; and if bad drugs were going around, there were announcements made about it. The feeling on the scene was so beatific that when thousands arrived without tickets, the promoters (wisely) declared it a free festival, and there was none of the typical gate-crashing furor.

There was one disquieting incident at Woodstock, a particularly telling one that most of the audience was either too blissed-out or too far from the stage to notice. During the Who's performance, Yippie Abbie Hoffman leapt onstage uninvited, ostensibly to deliver a typical antiestablishment rant; Pete Townshend, who'd been unwittingly slipped a dose of LSD, freaked out and literally threw Hoffman off the stage. And there it all was: questionable, opportunistic politics impinging on music and communal celebration; psychic overload and violence due to drugs unknowingly ingested. It was a paradigm, a sign of the times.

Then there was Altamont—the last major rock festival of the year, of the decade, and in some senses, the death knell for the rock festival as a phenomenon. The ugliness of the Hell's Angels killing a fan, the circumstances that could lead anyone to hire them as "security" in the first place are hard to grasp. Though the young rock generation would still hold onto some kind of hope in the magic of the music that could set them free, it would not be long before Altamont would come to be seen as the symbol of the death of the "Woodstock Nation" that had only been envisioned a few months before.

3 Police at New Jersey's Newark Airport confiscate 30,000 copies of **John Lennon** and **Yoko Ono**'s *Two Virgins* album, declaring its cover photo of the nude John and Yoko "pornographic." In Chicago, vice squad officers close down a record shop for displaying the cover.

4 Kasenetz-Katz Associates, the production-publishing-management firm responsible for "bubblegum" music giants like the **1910 Fruitgum Company** and the **Ohio Express**, has reported an eighty-five percent sales increase from 1967 to 1968, according to *Billboard*. The firm's independent production company, Super K Productions, accounts for twenty-five charting singles in 1968—including six gold records—for gross retail sales of $25 million. This same day, Buddah Records releases three Super K-produced albums: the 1910 Fruitgum Company's *Goody Goody Gum Drops*, the Ohio Express' *Chewy Chewy* and *Kasenetz-Katz Super Circus*, which combines members of the 1910 Fruitgum Company, the Ohio Express, the

Music Explosion, **Professor Morrison's Lollipop** and the **Shadows of Knight**.

7 *Look* magazine, in a special issue devoted to relations between blacks and whites, features an article on **Jimi Hendrix** entitled "Jimi Hendrix Socks It to the White Cats." Illustrated with a photograph of the black musician lounging beside a swimming pool surrounded by bikini-clad white women, the story informs readers that "For the volatile hard-core—the fourteen-to-nineteen bag—Jimi is not so much the Experience as a menace to public health. Plugged in and zonked, he only has to step across the stage (which he does like a high-strutting chicken going after a kernel of corn) to turn on their high-pitched passion."

Bubblegum band the **Ohio Express** is awarded a gold record for sales over 1 million of their single "Chewy Chewy," their second to couch sexual metaphors in a song about eating.

11 Album-cover nudity hits the bubblegum

genre as Buddah Records Vice President and General Manager **Neil Bogart** designs a cover featuring a photo of six nude women for the bubblegum greatest-hits LP *The Naked Truth*. Bogart claims the nudes on the cover depict "what life is really all about," and represent "the freedom of expression common to music today and the new attitude toward living."

13 **Elvis Presley** records in Memphis for the first time since his early days with Sun Records; the session eventually produces his eighteenth Number One hit single, "Suspicious Minds."

18 Albums released this week include the **Beatles**' *Yellow Submarine* on Apple Records; **Tommy James and the Shondells**' *Crimson and Clover* on Roulette; **Creedence Clearwater Revival**'s *Bayou Country* on Fantasy; and the self-titled LP by "jazz-rock" band **Blood, Sweat and Tears** on Columbia. Singles released this week include **James Brown**'s "Give It Up or Turn It Loose" on King; **Cream**'s "Crossroads" on Atco; the **1910 Fruitgum Company**'s "Indian

Giver" on Buddah; and **Tiny Tim**'s version of **Jerry Lee Lewis**' 1957 hit "Great Balls of Fire" on Reprise.

24 **Jethro Tull** plays its first U.S. concert in New York City. The band, already popular with critics and audiences in England, opens for heavy-metal supergroup **Led Zeppelin**.

25 Union County, New Jersey, bans the sale of "the **Beatles** album *Two Virgins* [*sic*]"; police seize 22,300 album covers and 3,300 records at Bestway Products, Mountainside, New Jersey; in Cleveland, the chief prosecutor declares the cover photo "obscene," thereby making any Ohio merchandiser who carries the record liable for prosecution of a felony.

29 "The Bosstown Sound" hype reaches *Newsweek*, which reports on such Boston phenomena as the **Ultimate Spinach**, **Earth Opera** and **Phluph**, and the clubs where these bands may be experienced—the Psychedelic Supermarket, the Catacombs and the Boston Tea Party. The article quotes one **Peter Wolf** of the **Hallucinations** (later of the **J. Geils Band**): "Kids wandered around Boston for years saying, 'Something's got to happen in this town,' but nothing happened and they left. Now I get calls saying, 'We're coming back to Boston. Something's happening there.'"

30 The **Beatles** make their last-ever public appearance as a group, performing on the roof of Apple Studios at 30 Saville Row, London. The show, filmed for the subsequent movie *Let It Be*, is stopped when police arrive after neighbors complain about the noise.

31 **Meher Baba**, spiritual avatar to **Pete Townshend**, **Ronnie Lane** and a small number of other rock stars, dies at age seventy-four. The Indian mystic had not uttered a word for forty-three years because, his followers explain, the right way to live had been taught by God's previous representatives on earth, and there was nothing more that needed to be said. ◆

WEEK ENDING JANUARY 4

U.S. #1 POP 45	"I Heard It through the Grapevine"	Marvin Gaye
U.S. #1 POP LP	*The Beatles*	The Beatles
U.S. #1 R&B 45	"I Heard It through the Grapevine"	Marvin Gaye
U.K. #1 POP 45	"Lily the Pink"	The Scaffold
U.K. #1 POP LP	*The Beatles*	The Beatles

WEEK ENDING JANUARY 11

U.S. #1 POP 45	"I Heard It through the Grapevine"	Marvin Gaye
U.S. #1 POP LP	*The Beatles*	The Beatles
U.S. #1 R&B 45	"I Heard It through the Grapevine"	Marvin Gaye
U.K. #1 POP 45	"Ob-La-Di, Ob-La-Da"	The Beatles
U.K. #1 POP LP	*The Beatles*	The Beatles

WEEK ENDING JANUARY 18

U.S. #1 POP 45	"I Heard It through the Grapevine"	Marvin Gaye
U.S. #1 POP LP	*The Beatles*	The Beatles
U.S. #1 R&B 45	"I Heard It through the Grapevine"	Marvin Gaye
U.K. #1 POP 45	"Ob-La-Di, Ob-La-Da"	The Beatles
U.K. #1 POP LP	*The Beatles*	The Beatles

WEEK ENDING JANUARY 25

U.S. #1 POP 45	"I Heard It through the Grapevine"	Marvin Gaye
U.S. #1 POP LP	*The Beatles*	The Beatles
U.S. #1 R&B 45	"I Heard It through the Grapevine"	Marvin Gaye
U.K. #1 POP 45	"Albatross"	Fleetwood Mac
U.K. #1 POP LP	*The Beatles*	The Beatles

3 John Lennon, George Harrison and Ringo Starr hire Allen Klein as Beatles business manager. Paul McCartney dissents.

4 Columbia Records signs Johnny Winter to a five-year, $300,000 contract—an unprecedented deal for a new artist. The Texan albino blues guitarist and singer came to national attention through a *Rolling Stone* article in 1968. New York club owner Steve Paul arranged for Winter and his band to come to New York and negotiated the contract with Columbia.

5 The Beatles' *Yellow Submarine* album, the soundtrack to the animated film of that name, is awarded a gold record. The album contains only four previously unreleased Beatles songs: George Harrison's "It's All Too Much" and "Only a Northern Song," and John Lennon and Paul McCartney's "Hey Bulldog" and "All Together Now."

8 Ex-Cream guitarist Eric Clapton and drummer Ginger Baker and ex-Traffic keyboardist and singer Stevie Winwood announce they are forming a new band and auditioning for a bassist; with the addition of ex-Family bassist Rick Grech, the band will become the "supergroup" Blind Faith.

9 The Beatles appoint the law firm of Eastman and Eastman to the position of Apple Records legal counsel. The Eastmans, Lee and John, are Paul McCartney's future father-in-law and brother-in-law, respectively. The arrangement, however, proves short-lived.

10 The New York Rock & Roll Ensemble performs in concert with the New

York Philharmonic Orchestra at Avery Fisher Hall in New York City.

12 The South Vietnamese government bans the antiwar songs of singer/songwriter Trinh Cong Son, who admits he's influenced by Bob Dylan and Joan Baez.

Steppenwolf's album *The Second* wins a gold record for sales of $1 million.

13 The Doors' single "Touch Me" and Sly and the Family Stone's single "Everyday People" win gold records.

17 Bob Dylan and Johnny Cash begin recording together at Columbia Studios in Nashville. The only song ever released from the sessions will be "Girl from the North Country," which will appear on Dylan's *Nashville Skyline* LP. Dylan and Cash will also perform the song later that year on "The Johnny Cash Show."

18 Pop stars Lulu (Marie McDonald Laurie) and Bee Gee Maurice Gibb are wed at St. James' Church, Ger-

rard's Cross, Buchs, England. Maurice's twin brother and fellow Bee Gee, Robin, is best man. Three thousand uninvited guests turn out for the affair.

20 *Goodbye Cream*, a film of Cream's November 26, 1968, farewell concert at London's Royal Albert Hall, opens in Baltimore to small crowds and very negative critical response because of poor sound quality and incomprehensibly "arty" editing. When it also opens poorly in New York a week later, promoter Ron Delsener terms the film "a real bomb."

The film *Candy* premieres, featuring Ringo Starr in his first nonmusical role.

22 Tyrannosaurus Rex embarks on a tour of England with a concert at the Free Trade Hall in Manchester. Opening the group's show is David Bowie—performing not a musical act, but a silent one-man mime telling the story of a young Tibetan Buddhist monk. Bowie has recently studied mime and Buddhism.

24 The Jimi Hendrix Experience plays its last British concert at London's Royal Albert Hall before breaking up. ◆

WEEK ENDING FEBRUARY 1

U.S. #1 POP 45	"Crimson and Clover"	Tommy James and the Shondells
U.S. #1 POP LP	*The Beatles*	The Beatles
U.S. #1 R&B 45	"Can I Change My Mind"	Tyrone Davis
U.K. #1 POP 45	"Albatross"	Fleetwood Mac
U.K. #1 POP LP	*The Best of the Seekers*	The Seekers

WEEK ENDING FEBRUARY 8

U.S. #1 POP 45	"Crimson and Clover"	Tommy James and the Shondells
U.S. #1 POP LP	*TCB*	Diana Ross and the Supremes with the Temptations
U.S. #1 R&B 45	"Can I Change My Mind"	Tyrone Davis
U.K. #1 POP 45	"Albatross"	Fleetwood Mac
U.K. #1 POP LP	*Diana Ross and the Supremes Join the Temptations*	The Supremes and the Temptations

WEEK ENDING FEBRUARY 15

U.S. #1 POP 45	"Everyday People"	Sly and the Family Stone
U.S. #1 POP LP	*The Beatles*	The Beatles
U.S. #1 R&B 45	"Can I Change My Mind"	Tyrone Davis
U.K. #1 POP 45	"Blackberry Way"	The Move
U.K. #1 POP LP	*Diana Ross and the Supremes Join the Temptations*	The Supremes and the Temptations

WEEK ENDING FEBRUARY 22

U.S. #1 POP 45	"Everyday People"	Sly and the Family Stone
U.S. #1 POP LP	*The Beatles*	The Beatles
U.S. #1 R&B 45	"Everyday People"	Sly and the Family Stone
U.K. #1 POP 45	"Half as Nice"	Amen Corner
U.K. #1 POP LP	*Diana Ross and the Supremes Join the Temptations*	The Supremes and the Temptations

1 At Miami's Dinner Key Auditorium, **Jim Morrison** of the **Doors** is arrested for allegedly exposing his penis during the show. Several weeks later, after the event has become a *cause célèbre* in the media, Morrison is officially charged with lewd and lascivious behavior (a felony carrying a maximum three-year sentence), indecent exposure, open profanity and public drunkenness. All Doors concerts over the next five months are canceled. On April 3, Morrison surrenders to the FBI in Los Angeles and is charged with interstate flight to avoid prosecution on his Miami charges. Over a year later, on the day before sentencing, Morrison is found asleep on a woman's porch in Los Angeles and is charged with public drunkenness. Morrison is found guilty in August 1970 of indecent exposure and profanity. His sentence, totaling eight months hard labor and a $500 fine, is on appeal when Morrison dies in Paris in 1971.

7 The **Who** release "Pinball Wizard" in the U.K. It is the first selection the public hears from the rock opera *Tommy*.

Tommy Roe's single "Dizzy" wins a gold record for sales over 1 million.

8 England's current "face," **Peter Frampton**, announces he will leave his band, the **Herd**, within a month. Rumors that he will start a new band with ex-**Small Faces** leader **Steve Marriott** proved accurate on April 26, 1969, when the formation of **Humble Pie** is announced.

9 "The Smothers Brothers' Comedy Hour," which featured such rock bands as the **Beatles**, the **Who**, the **Jefferson Airplane** and the **Doors**, is canceled by CBS-TV in the wake of controversy over the on-air censorship of guest star **Joan Baez**.

12 The Eleventh Annual Grammy Winners (1968) are announced. **Simon and Garfunkel**'s "Mrs. Robinson" is named Record of the Year. **Jose Feliciano**, whose "Light My Fire" wins Best Contemporary Pop Vocal Performance, Male, is named Best New Artist of 1968.

Paul McCartney weds American photographer **Linda Eastman** in the Marylebone Register's Office, London. McCartney's only brother, Mike McGear, is best man. No other **Beatles** are present.

13 **George Harrison** and wife **Patti** are arrested in London on charges of marijuana possession after police find 120 joints in their apartment. Harrison calls it a frame-up timed to coincide with **Paul McCartney**'s wedding, but on March 31, both will plead guilty and be fined £250.

16 A *New York Times* article detailing the growth of the U.S. recording industry cites retail album volume at $1.39 billion and retail tape volume at $247 million for 1968. The figures are linked to the surge in sales of "contemporary sounds" to the under-twenty-five age group.

22 Two days after they are married in a private ceremony in Gibraltar, **John Lennon** and **Yoko Ono** begin their first "bed-in for peace" in the presidential suite of the Amsterdam Hilton.

23 Thirty thousand people, including **Jackie Gleason**, **Kate Smith**, the **Lettermen** and **Anita Bryant**, appear at the Rally for Decency in Miami, organized by Catholic teen groups in the wake of **Jim Morrison**'s indecent exposure bust there. Announcements publicizing the rally warn that "longhairs and weird dressers" will be refused admittance. Four days later, **President Richard M. Nixon** sends a letter of congratulation and appreciation to the organizers of the rally.

26 The *Eye* has had it. The *Eye,* the Hearst Corporation's youth culture magazine, folds after a year in operation. Falling "far short of profitable," Hearst had brought in *Cosmopolitan*'s Helen Gurley Brown to stoke things up. Brown's assessment of the *Eye* was: "Take my word for it, it's a lousy book."

28 In London, **Ringo Starr** says the Beatles will make no more public appearances; **John Lennon** counters that there will be several in 1969.   ◆

WEEK ENDING MARCH 1

U.S. #1 POP 45	"Everyday People"	Sly and the Family Stone
U.S. #1 POP LP	*The Beatles*	The Beatles
U.S. #1 R&B 45	"Everyday People"	Sly and the Family Stone
U.K. #1 POP 45	"Where Do You Go to (My Lovely)"	Peter Sarstedt
U.K. #1 POP LP	*Diana Ross and the Supremes Join the Temptations*	The Supremes and the Temptations

WEEK ENDING MARCH 8

U.S. #1 POP 45	"Everyday People"	Sly and the Family Stone
U.S. #1 POP LP	*Wichita Lineman*	Glen Campbell
U.S. #1 R&B 45	"Give It Up or Turn It Loose"	James Brown
U.K. #1 POP 45	"Where Do You Go to (My Lovely)"	Peter Sarstedt
U.K. #1 POP LP	*Diana Ross and the Supremes Join the Temptations*	The Supremes and the Temptations

WEEK ENDING MARCH 15

U.S. #1 POP 45	"Dizzy"	Tommy Roe
U.S. #1 POP LP	*Wichita Lineman*	Glen Campbell
U.S. #1 R&B 45	"Give It Up or Turn It Loose"	James Brown
U.K. #1 POP 45	"Where Do You Go to (My Lovely)"	Peter Sarstedt
U.K. #1 POP LP	*Diana Ross and the Supremes Join the Temptations*	The Supremes and the Temptations

WEEK ENDING MARCH 22

U.S. #1 POP 45	"Dizzy"	Tommy Roe
U.S. #1 POP LP	*Wichita Lineman*	Glen Campbell
U.S. #1 R&B 45	"Run Away Child Running Wild"	The Temptations
U.K. #1 POP 45	"Where Do You Go to (My Lovely)"	Peter Sarstedt
U.K. #1 POP LP	*Goodbye*	Cream

WEEK ENDING MARCH 29

U.S. #1 POP 45	"Dizzy"	Tommy Roe
U.S. #1 POP LP	*Blood, Sweat and Tears*	Blood, Sweat and Tears
U.S. #1 R&B 45	"Run Away Child Running Wild"	The Temptations
U.K. #1 POP 45	"I Heard It through the Grapevine"	Marvin Gaye
U.K. #1 POP LP	*Goodbye*	Cream

1 The **Beach Boys** announce that they are suing their record label, Capitol, for $2,041,446.64 in royalties and producer's fees for **Brian Wilson**. The band also announces that it will start its own label, Brother Records, which ultimately will be distributed by Warner/Reprise.

5 **Tammy Wynette**, **George Jones**, **Loretta Lynn**, **Conway Twitty** and others perform at the First International Festival of Country & Western Music, at the Empire Pool in Wembley, England.

6 **Ike and Tina Turner**, **Procol Harum**, **John Mayall** and others appear at the first—and last—Palm Springs Pop Festival and San Andreas Boogie in Palm Springs, California. The festival site—a drive-in theater parking lot—holds under 15,000 people, but over 25,000 vacationing students and other young people arrive in the tiny resort town. Police helicopters arrive to disperse the crowd and the crowd riots, wreaking havoc on a nearby gas station. The gas station owner fires his rifle into the crowd, seriously wounding a sixteen-year-old boy and a twenty-year-old woman.

Peter Quaife, bassist with the **Kinks** since 1962, when they were called the **Ravens**, leaves the group. He is replaced by **John Dalton**.

10 **Tom "Big Daddy" Donahue** resigns his posts as Operations Manager and deejay at San Francisco's KSAN-FM, just one year after he and his associates had walked out on strike from KMPX-FM, the San Francisco station Donahue transformed from a foreign-language station to America's first album-cut-oriented radio station. Donahue's departure is amicable.

15 Philadelphia's biggest and most popular rock ballroom, the Electric Factory, is ordered closed by a local judge on the grounds that it is "a public nuisance…and provides a gathering point for dealers in illicit drugs." The American Civil Liberties Union, and just about every newspaper, TV and radio station in Philadelphia, rallies to the cause. Earlier in the month, Police Commissioner **Frank Rizzo**, running for mayor, bragged that he would "turn this joint into a parking lot."

16 Detroit's revolutionary rockers the MC5 are kicked off Elektra Records in the wake of controversy over their Elektra debut album's underground anthem "Kick Out the Jams," which contains the refrain "Kick out the jams, motherfuckers!" The band consented to rerecord "Kick Out the Jams," substituting "brothers and sisters" for the offending expletive, but then went around plastering stores that refused to stock their album with Elektra stationery upon which they'd scrawled "Fuck You!"

17 The **Band** plays its first concert as an independent group (that is, not backing **Ronnie Hawkins** as the **Hawks** or **Bob Dylan** as the **Band**) at San Francisco's Winterland, opening a national tour to promote its first album, *Music from Big Pink*.

20 The L. A. Free Festival in Venice, California, ends in violence before it really

starts, with many injured and 117 arrested. The trouble began when police chased one youth through the crowd on the beach. When they handcuffed him, the crowd began chanting "Pig, pig, pig!" A riot ensued. None of the bands scheduled to play appeared.

22 The **Who** give the first complete live performance of their "rock opera" *Tommy* at a concert in Dolton, England. This much-anticipated debut was unannounced; the Who officially premiered *Tommy* for the British press two weeks later in a show at Ronnie Scott's club in London.

23 Los Angeles folk-blues club the Ash Grove burns down. Such performers as **Canned Heat**, **Taj Mahal** and the **Chambers Brothers** got their starts there.

24 Blues giant **Muddy Waters** records his *Fathers and Sons* album live in Chicago with **Paul Butterfield** and **Mike Bloomfield**, among others.

26 Baltimore's Rally for Decency—set up by **Michael Levesque** of the Miami Teens for Decency—erupts into a race riot, because the organizers promised an appearance by **James Brown**, who doesn't show. Other rallies are staged in Enterprise, Alabama (with Governor **George Wallace** making an appearance), and in Columbus, Ohio, with Levesque flown in at the cities' expense to organize the events.

30 The **Fifth Dimension** are awarded a gold single for "Aquarius/Let the Sunshine In," a medley from the hit rock musical *Hair*. ♦

WEEK ENDING APRIL 5

U.S. #1 POP 45	"Dizzy"	Tommy Roe
U.S. #1 POP LP	*Wichita Lineman*	Glen Campbell
U.S. #1 R&B 45	"Only the Strong Survive"	Jerry Butler
U.K. #1 POP 45	"I Heard It through the Grapevine"	Marvin Gaye
U.K. #1 POP LP	*Goodbye*	Cream

WEEK ENDING APRIL 12

U.S. #1 POP 45	"Aquarius/Let the Sunshine In"	The Fifth Dimension
U.S. #1 POP LP	*Blood, Sweat and Tears*	Blood, Sweat and Tears
U.S. #1 R&B 45	"Only the Strong Survive"	Jerry Butler
U.K. #1 POP 45	"The Israelites"	Desmond Dekker
U.K. #1 POP LP	*Goodbye*	Cream

WEEK ENDING APRIL 19

U.S. #1 POP 45	"Aquarius/Let the Sunshine In"	The Fifth Dimension
U.S. #1 POP LP	*Blood, Sweat and Tears*	Blood, Sweat and Tears
U.S. #1 R&B 45	"It's Your Thing"	The Isley Brothers
U.K. #1 POP 45	"The Israelites"	Desmond Dekker
U.K. #1 POP LP	*Goodbye*	Cream

WEEK ENDING APRIL 26

U.S. #1 POP 45	"Aquarius/Let the Sunshine In"	The Fifth Dimension
U.S. #1 POP LP	*Hair*	original cast
U.S. #1 R&B 45	"It's Your Thing"	The Isley Brothers
U.K. #1 POP 45	"The Israelites"	Desmond Dekker
U.K. #1 POP LP	*Goodbye*	Cream

3 **Jimi Hendrix** is arrested at Toronto International Airport for possession of narcotics and is subsequently released on $10,000 bail.

4 **Richard Tapper**, twenty-two-year-old drummer for Los Angeles rock band **TIME** (Trust In Men Everywhere) is critically wounded when two gunmen jump him and shoot him three times in the midsection as he is on his way to a jam session at the L.A. club Thee Experience.

7 The battle for control of the **Beatles'** Northern Songs goes on. Late last month, the Beatles made a $5.1 million counteroffer to Northern Songs stockholders in an attempt to thwart Associated TV's bid to win control of the company. Today, representatives of Warner Bros.-Seven Arts are expected in London to discuss the purchase of fifteen percent of the company.

14 **Jeanne "Genie the Taylor" Franklin** dies in a London car crash that also claims Fairport Convention drummer **Martin Lamble**. Genie the Taylor had begun designing rock stars' clothes in 1965, and her clients included the **Lovin' Spoonful**, the **Jefferson Airplane**, the **Turtles**, **Donovan**, the **Mamas and the Papas**, **Jimi Hendrix**, **Tiny Tim**, the **Rascals** and **Eric Burdon and the Animals**, among many others. She was a cousin of folk singer **Phil Ochs**. Ex-**Cream** bassist **Jack Bruce** later dedicated his solo LP *Songs for a Tailor* to her.

16 **John Lennon**, declared "an inadmissible immigrant to the U.S.," seeks a visa to visit America. Ten days earlier, Lennon's "standing visa" was revoked by the U.S. Embassy in London because of his November 1968 drug conviction.

Jefferson Airplane bassist **Jack Casady** is arrested for possession of marijuana at the Royal Orleans Hotel in New Orleans and receives a two-and-a-half-year suspended sentence.

The **Who's** Pete Townshend spends a night in a New York City jail after being charged with assault: plainclothes policeman **Daniel Mulhearn** ran onstage at the Fillmore East to grab the microphone to alert the audience that a grocery store next door to the theater was on fire; Townshend, thinking he was just an audience member, kicked him off the stage. The audience, refusing to believe that the theater is in serious danger of burning down, doesn't leave the Fillmore until Townshend is finally dragged off the stage.

17 Marauding bands of motorcyclists disrupt the Aldergrove Beach Rock Festival in British Columbia, Canada, by cutting guy wires holding lighting scaffolds over the stage (the lights crash to the stage, narrowly missing a band that is playing), gang-raping women and trying to raid the stage. Canadian Mounted Police finally chase the bikers out; the festival concludes peacefully. More than 27,000 people were there to see the **New Vaudeville Band**, **Guitar Shorty** and others.

The *New Musical Express* announces that, for the first time ever, album production and sales outpaced production and sales of singles in Great Britain, in 1968.

Associated TV fails in its bid to take over **Beatles** music company Northern Songs' offer for all shares, expiring with only forty-seven percent of stock committed.

19 The **Beatles'** single "Get Back" is awarded a gold record for sales over 1 million; within a week it will hit Number One in the U.S.

21 The **Beatles** officially announce the appointment of New York City accountant **Allen Klein** and his firm, ABKCO, to handle their financial dealings. Klein had earlier represented the **Rolling Stones** and **Donovan** in a similar capacity.

John Lennon and **Yoko Ono** begin a ten-day "bed-in" in Montreal's Queen Elizabeth Hotel.

28 **Rolling Stone** Mick **Jagger** and girlfriend **Marianne Faithfull** are arrested in their London home on charges of possession of marijuana.

31 *Rolling Stone* reports that **Frank Zappa** has become a lecturer on the college circuit, speaking at NYC's New School, UCLA, Villanova and the University of South Carolina. For speaking on such subjects as "Pigs, Ponies and Rock & Roll," Zappa is paid $1,500. ◆

WEEK ENDING MAY 3

U.S. #1 POP 45	"Aquarius/Let the Sunshine In"	The Fifth Dimension
U.S. #1 POP LP	*Hair*	original cast
U.S. #1 R&B 45	"It's Your Thing"	The Isley Brothers
U.K. #1 POP 45	"Get Back"	The Beatles
U.K. #1 POP LP	*Goodbye*	Cream

WEEK ENDING MAY 10

U.S. #1 POP 45	"Aquarius/Let the Sunshine In"	The Fifth Dimension
U.S. #1 POP LP	*Hair*	original cast
U.S. #1 R&B 45	"It's Your Thing"	The Isley Brothers
U.K. #1 POP 45	"Get Back"	The Beatles
U.K. #1 POP LP	*On the Threshold of a Dream*	The Moody Blues

WEEK ENDING MAY 17

U.S. #1 POP 45	"Aquarius/Let the Sunshine In"	The Fifth Dimension
U.S. #1 POP LP	*Hair*	original cast
U.S. #1 R&B 45	"Chokin' Kind"	Joe Simon
U.K. #1 POP 45	"Get Back"	The Beatles
U.K. #1 POP LP	*On the Threshold of a Dream*	The Moody Blues

WEEK ENDING MAY 24

U.S. #1 POP 45	"Get Back"	The Beatles
U.S. #1 POP LP	*Hair*	original cast
U.S. #1 R&B 45	"Chokin' Kind"	Joe Simon
U.K. #1 POP 45	"Get Back"	The Beatles
U.K. #1 POP LP	*Nashville Skyline*	Bob Dylan

WEEK ENDING MAY 31

U.S. #1 POP 45	"Get Back"	The Beatles
U.S. #1 POP LP	*Hair*	original cast
U.S. #1 R&B 45	"Chokin' Kind"	Joe Simon
U.K. #1 POP 45	"Get Back"	The Beatles
U.K. #1 POP LP	*Nashville Skyline*	Bob Dylan

5 *Feast of Friends*, a forty-minute documentary film on the **Doors** made by the band and its friends, premieres at the Los Angeles Cinematheque 16, along with **Andy Warhol**'s *I a Man* and poetry readings by **Michael McClure** and **Jim Morrison**, in a benefit for **Norman Mailer**'s New York mayorality bid. At the same time, politicians in both St. Louis and Honolulu force the cancellation of upcoming Doors concerts.

6 **Rod Stewart**, vocalist for the **Jeff Beck Group**, signs a solo recording contract with Mercury Records.

7 The **Who**'s *Tommy* enters the *Billboard* chart at #96. It reaches #7 on July 26, making it the Who's first American Top Ten album, before slipping back. By April 4, 1970, it has disappeared from the Top 200. With the success of the Who's follow-up album, *Live at Leeds*, however, *Tommy* makes a dramatic reappearance, bulleting to #4 on September 19, 1970, well over a year after its release. It leaves the chart a

second time on October 23, 1971, and returns yet again for a sixteen-week stay on April 12, 1975, after the *Tommy* movie is released.

Blind Faith debuts with a free concert in London's Hyde Park. There are 120,000 in attendance, including **Mick Jagger**, **Mick Fleetwood**, **Donovan**, **Chas Chandler**, **Mitch Mitchell** and **Noel Redding** of the **Jimi Hendrix Experience**, **Jim Capaldi** and **Chris Wood** of **Traffic**, **Terry Hicks** of the **Hollies**, and **Mike Hogg** of **Manfred Mann**. **Richie Havens** opens the show.

9 **Brian Jones** announces his departure from the **Rolling Stones**: "I want to play my kind of music, which is no longer the Stones' music. The music Mick and Keith have been writing is at a tangent, so far as my own taste is concerned." "We'd known for a few months that Brian wasn't keen on it," says **Mick Jagger**. Jones' replacement is ex-**John Mayall** guitarist **Mick Taylor**, who had been rehearsing occasionally with the Stones for the last few months.

San Francisco band **Moby Grape** has officially disbanded, nearly a year after guitarist **Alex "Skip" Spence** departed. Over the succeeding months, bassist/vocalist **Bob Mosley** and guitarist **Peter Lewis** also departed; the remnants of the original band entered a protracted legal wrangle with ex-manager **Matthew Katz** over ownership of the name Moby Grape. Later, Katz and a band of unknown Seattle musicians become Moby Grape.

11 **David Bowie**'s single "Space Oddity" is released to coincide with the first lunar landing.

13 Soul Bowl '69, promoted as "the biggest soul music festival ever," begins at the Houston Astrodome. Performers include **Aretha Franklin**, **Ray Charles**, the **Reverend James Cleveland**, **Sam and Dave**, the **Staple Singers** and many more.

20 The three-day Newport '69 rock festival begins in Northridge, California's Devonshire Downs. One hundred fifty thousand persons attend;

performers include **Jimi Hendrix**, **Joe Cocker**, **Ike and Tina Turner**, **Creedence Clearwater Revival**, **Steppenwolf**, **Jethro Tull**, the **Rascals**, the **Byrds**, **Johnny Winter** and **Booker T. and the MGs**. Newport '69 is the first large-scale rock festival of the year.

22 Toronto's first rock festival, where 50,000 people see shows by **Steppenwolf**, the **Band**, **Procol Harum**, **Chuck Berry** and **Blood, Sweat and Tears**, is a success: there is no violence.

24 Jamaican reggae singer **Max Romeo**, arriving in England for a tour, finds that he's been banned by Mecca Ballrooms, one of Britain's largest chain of theaters, because of the "controversial" lyrics of his hit single "Dream"—also known as "Wet Dream."

27 The Denver Pop Festival opens at Mile High Stadium, with over 50,000 in attendance to see and hear **Jimi Hendrix**, **Johnny Winter**, **Joe Cocker**, **Creedence Clearwater Revival**, the **Mothers of Invention**, **Tim Buckley**, **Poco**, **Iron Butterfly** and **Big Mama Thornton**. Violence erupts in the audience, and police move in with clubs and tear gas. On the festival's last day, June 29, the **Jimi Hendrix Experience** plays its last concert.

28 **Jimi Hendrix** announces a new bassist, his old army buddy **Billy Cox**, and a new approach: "A sky church sort of thing . . . I want to get the whole **Buddy Miles** group and call them the Freedom Express . . ." Hendrix adds that **Noel Redding** and **Mitch Mitchell** aren't necessarily out of his band. Nonetheless the name Jimi Hendrix Experience will no longer be used, and Redding has already formed his own band, **Fat Mattress**.

29 **Shorty Long**, the Detroit soul singer who recorded the original version of "Devil with a Blue Dress On" (later made famous by **Mitch Ryder and the Detroit Wheels**), drowns at age twenty-nine when his boat capsizes off Sandwich Island, Ontario, Canada. Long's hits included "Function at the Junction" and "Here Comes the Judge."   ◆

WEEK ENDING JUNE 7

U.S. #1 POP 45	"Get Back"	The Beatles
U.S. #1 POP LP	*Hair*	original cast
U.S. #1 R&B 45	"Too Busy Thinking about My Baby"	Marvin Gaye
U.K. #1 POP 45	"Dizzy"	Tommy Roe
U.K. #1 POP LP	*Nashville Skyline*	Bob Dylan

WEEK ENDING JUNE 14

U.S. #1 POP 45	"Get Back"	The Beatles
U.S. #1 POP LP	*Hair*	original cast
U.S. #1 R&B 45	"Too Busy Thinking about My Baby"	Marvin Gaye
U.K. #1 POP 45	"Dizzy"	Tommy Roe
U.K. #1 POP LP	*Nashville Skyline*	Bob Dylan

WEEK ENDING JUNE 21

U.S. #1 POP 45	"Get Back"	The Beatles
U.S. #1 POP LP	*Hair*	original cast
U.S. #1 R&B 45	"Too Busy Thinking about My Baby"	Marvin Gaye
U.K. #1 POP 45	"The Ballad of John and Yoko"	The Beatles
U.K. #1 POP LP	*My Way*	Frank Sinatra

WEEK ENDING JUNE 28

U.S. #1 POP 45	"Love Theme from *Romeo & Juliet*"	Henry Mancini and Orchestra
U.S. #1 POP LP	*Hair*	original cast
U.S. #1 R&B 45	"Too Busy Thinking about My Baby"	Marvin Gaye
U.K. #1 POP 45	"The Ballad of John and Yoko"	The Beatles
U.K. #1 POP LP	*My Way*	Frank Sinatra

1 **Sam Phillips** sells Sun Records, the Memphis label he founded and which released the first recordings by **Elvis Presley, Johnny Cash, Bobby "Blue" Bland, Ike Turner, Junior Parker, Conway Twitty, Jerry Lee Lewis, Roy Orbison, Carl Perkins, Charlie Rich** and **James Cotton,** to Nashville record mogul **Shelby Singleton,** for an undisclosed sum.

3 Ex-Rolling Stones guitarist **Brian Jones** is found dead at the bottom of the swimming pool at his Cotchford Farm, Hartfield, England, home. Rumors of murder and suicide run rampant, but the official coroner's report, while citing high levels of alcohol and barbiturates in Jones' blood, attributes his drowning death to "misadventure."

The Newport Jazz Festival opens in Newport, Rhode Island. For the first—and last—time, rock performers appear at a major, established jazz festival: **Jeff Beck, Led Zeppelin, Jethro Tull, Ten Years After, James Brown,** and **Sly and the Family Stone.** Seventy-eight thousand attend the four-day fest.

4 The Atlanta Pop Festival opens for two days of music by **Delaney and Bonnie, Ten Wheel Drive, Creedence Clearwater Revival, Canned Heat, Johnny Winter, Paul Butterfield, Joe Cocker, Led Zeppelin, Janis Joplin,** and **Blood, Sweat and Tears.** The festival draws 140,000 and concludes without any incidents of violence.

5 The **Rolling Stones** give a free concert for 250,000 fans in London's Hyde Park. The event was planned several weeks before to introduce new guitarist **Mick Taylor,** but with **Brian Jones'** death on July 3, the concert becomes a tribute to the late Stone. **Mick Jagger** eulogizes Jones by reading Shelley's "Adonais," a poem written to commemorate the death of the poet Keats.

8 In what authorities later rule an attempted suicide, **Marianne Faithfull** takes an overdose of barbiturates on the Australian movie set of *Ned Kelly,* in which she and her boyfriend **Mick Jagger** are to star. Faithfull is dropped from the cast; two days later she enters a hospital for treatment of heroin addiction.

12 New York rock impresario **Steve Paul** closes his club, the Scene, in order to devote more time to his management interests, which include **Johnny Winter.** The Scene gave many big-name rock bands early starts, and was the site of jam sessions between the likes of **Frank Zappa** and the **Monkees, Jimi Hendrix** and the **Doors, Jimmy Page** and **Jeff Beck, Janis Joplin** and **Eric Burdon,** and even **Tiny Tim** and the **Doors.**

Half of the Top Forty AM stations in the country ban the new **Beatles** single, "The Ballad of John and Yoko." According to *Rolling Stone,* stations consider the refrain "Christ, you know it ain't easy . . ." "offensive" and "sacrilegious."

Blind Faith makes its U.S. debut at Madison Square Garden in New York City.

14 **Bob Dylan** makes a surprise appearance with the **Band** at the Mississippi River Rock Festival in Edwardsville, Missouri. Dylan, in cowboy garb, performs three numbers, including the country standard "In the Pines" and an encore of "Slippin' and Slidin'."

20 **Roy Hamilton,** the baritone-voiced balladeer who had hits with "You'll Never Walk Alone" (1954), "Unchained Melody" (1955) and "You Can Have Her" (1961), dies of a stroke at age forty.

22 **Aretha Franklin** is arrested on charges of disorderly conduct after creating a disturbance in a Detroit parking lot.

23 **James Brown** walks out of the Los Angeles mayor's office when Mayor **Sam Yorty** fails to show up at ten a.m., as promised, to give Brown a proclamation for James Brown Day, in honor of Soul Brother Number One's concert at the Forum that day.

25 The three-day Seattle Pop Festival opens in Woodenville, Washington, with 70,000 attending to see performances by **Chuck Berry, Bo Diddley,** the **Doors, Led Zeppelin, Vanilla Fudge,** the **Byrds, Chicago Transit Authority** and others.

Neil Young makes his first in-concert appearance with **Crosby, Stills and Nash** at New York City's Fillmore East.

31 A Moscow police official reports that thousands of Moscow telephone booths have been rendered inoperable because of thieves who've stolen phone parts to convert their acoustic guitars to electric; an article in a local youth publication detailed the technique.

Elvis Presley opens in Las Vegas. The shows are taped for the *From Memphis to Vegas* album. His four-week run at the Las Vegas International Hotel (now the Las Vegas Hilton) nets Presley over $1 million. ◆

WEEK ENDING JULY 5

U.S. #1 POP 45	"Love Theme from *Romeo & Juliet*"	Henry Mancini and Orchestra
U.S. #1 POP LP	*Hair*	original cast
U.S. #1 R&B 45	"Too Busy Thinking about My Baby"	Marvin Gaye
U.K. #1 POP 45	"Something in the Air"	Thunderclap Newman
U.K. #1 POP LP	*This Is Tom Jones*	Tom Jones

WEEK ENDING JULY 12

U.S. #1 POP 45	"In the Year 2525"	Zager and Evans
U.S. #1 POP LP	*Hair*	original cast
U.S. #1 R&B 45	"Too Busy Thinking about My Baby"	Marvin Gaye
U.K. #1 POP 45	"Something in the Air"	Thunderclap Newman
U.K. #1 POP LP	*This Is Tom Jones*	Tom Jones

WEEK ENDING JULY 19

U.S. #1 POP 45	"In the Year 2525"	Zager and Evans
U.S. #1 POP LP	*Hair*	original cast
U.S. #1 R&B 45	"What Does It Take to Win Your Love"	Jr. Walker and the All Stars
U.K. #1 POP 45	"In the Ghetto"	Elvis Presley
U.K. #1 POP LP	*This Is Tom Jones*	Tom Jones

WEEK ENDING JULY 26

U.S. #1 POP 45	"In the Year 2525"	Zager and Evans
U.S. #1 POP LP	*Blood, Sweat and Tears*	Blood, Sweat and Tears
U.S. #1 R&B 45	"What Does It Take to Win Your Love"	Jr. Walker and the All Stars
U.K. #1 POP 45	"Honky Tonk Women"	The Rolling Stones
U.K. #1 POP LP	*This Is Tom Jones*	Tom Jones

1 The three-day Atlantic City Pop Festival opens in Atlantic City, New Jersey—the first pop festival in the New York-Philadelphia area. Over 110,000 come to see the **Jefferson Airplane**, **Creedence Clearwater Revival**, **B. B. King**, the **Byrds**, **Procol Harum**, **Iron Butterfly**, **Dr. John**, **Janis Joplin**, **Little Richard**, **Santana**, **Joe Cocker** and others.

2 The Moose Lodge of Hibbing, Minnesota, hosts the tenth-year reunion of the 1959 Hibbing High School graduating class. **Bob Dylan** shows up unexpectedly with his wife, Sara, and leaves after an hour when a drunk tries to pick a fight with him.

3 Beach Boy **Carl Wilson** is indicted by a federal court in Los Angeles for failure to report for civilian duty in lieu of serving two years in the army. Wilson, in fact, reported to L.A. County Hospital at his appointed date, but to conduct music classes for handicapped patients rather than to act as "an institutional helper."

4 **Bill Graham**, concert promoter and owner of the Fillmores East and West, announces that he's "through with San Francisco" as of December 31, when new owners take over the Fillmore West.

15 The Woodstock Music and Art Fair opens for three days on **Max Yasgur's** farm in Bethel, New York. Over 400,000 people show up, most without tickets, prompting the organizers to declare the festival open and free. Performances by **Jimi Hendrix**, **Santana**, **Sly and the Family Stone**, **Joan Baez**, the **Who**, the **Grateful Dead**, **Janis Joplin**, **Joe Cocker**, the **Jefferson Airplane**, **Ten Years After**, **Canned Heat**, **Country Joe and the Fish**, **Ravi Shankar**, the **Paul Butterfield Blues Band**, **Crosby, Stills, Nash and Young**, and many other acts contribute to the legend, but above all it is the happy, peaceful masses who make Woodstock a unique event. Despite rampant drug use, inadequate food and sanitation, three deaths, two births and four miscarriages, the three days inspire utopian visions of the Woodstock Nation.

17 During the **Who's** performance at Woodstock, **Pete Townshend** knocks Yippie **Abbie Hoffman** offstage. Hoffman ran onstage during "Tommy" to offer propaganda to the crowd; Townshend later says he was unwittingly slipped a dose of LSD, which no doubt fueled his anger at Hoffman's abrupt interruption.

19 With no rehearsals and virtually no instruction, pioneering jazz trumpeter **Miles Davis** leads what he calls "the best damn rock & roll band in the world" in recording his epochal jazz-rock fusion double album, *Bitches Brew*, in New York. The band includes **John McLaughlin**, **Chick Corea**, **Wayne Shorter**, **Joe Zawinul**, **Jack De Johnette** and seven other future fusionists.

20 **Frank Zappa**, "tired of playing for people who clap for all the wrong reasons," disbands the **Mothers of Invention** immediately following an eight-day Canadian tour.

30 The three-day Texas International Pop Festival opens at Dallas International Motor Speedway in Lewisville, Texas, with 120,000 attending and performers including homecomers **Janis Joplin** and **Johnny Winter**, as well as **Canned Heat**, **Chicago Transit Authority**, **Santana**, **Led Zeppelin**, **Grand Funk Railroad**, **Sly and the Family Stone** and **B. B. King**. Police report many drug-related incidents, the worst being the case of a three-year-old boy in serious condition with an LSD overdose, purportedly caused when he drank some orange juice in which his parents had dissolved some acid.

The Second Annual Sky River Rock Festival opens for two days near Seattle, Washington, with 25,000 there to see **Big Mama Thornton**, **Country Joe and the Fish**, **Quicksilver Messenger Service** and the **Steve Miller Band**, among others.

31 The two-day New Orleans Pop Festival opens in Prairieville, Louisiana, with 25,000 attendees and performers, including **Janis Joplin**, the **Jefferson Airplane**, the **Grateful Dead**, the **Who**, **Santana**, **It's a Beautiful Day**, **Country Joe and the Fish**, and **Chicago Transit Authority**.

Bob Dylan makes his first paid appearance, at England's Isle of Wight Pop Festival, since his motorcycle accident three years before. He is backed by the **Band** and receives £38,000 cash for a one-hour show. ◆

WEEK ENDING AUGUST 2

U.S. #1 POP 45	"In the Year 2525"	Zager and Evans
U.S. #1 POP LP	*Blood, Sweat and Tears*	Blood, Sweat and Tears
U.S. #1 R&B 45	"Mother Popcorn"	James Brown
U.K. #1 POP 45	"Honky Tonk Women"	The Rolling Stones
U.K. #1 POP LP	*Flaming Star*	Elvis Presley

WEEK ENDING AUGUST 9

U.S. #1 POP 45	"In the Year 2525"	Zager and Evans
U.S. #1 POP LP	*Blood, Sweat and Tears*	Blood, Sweat and Tears
U.S. #1 R&B 45	"Mother Popcorn"	James Brown
U.K. #1 POP 45	"Honky Tonk Women"	The Rolling Stones
U.K. #1 POP LP	*Stand Up*	Jethro Tull

WEEK ENDING AUGUST 16

U.S. #1 POP 45	"In the Year 2525"	Zager and Evans
U.S. #1 POP LP	*Blood, Sweat and Tears*	Blood, Sweat and Tears
U.S. #1 R&B 45	"Choice of Colors"	The Impressions
U.K. #1 POP 45	"Honky Tonk Women"	The Rolling Stones
U.K. #1 POP LP	*Stand Up*	Jethro Tull

WEEK ENDING AUGUST 23

U.S. #1 POP 45	"Honky Tonk Women"	The Rolling Stones
U.S. #1 POP LP	*At San Quentin*	Johnny Cash
U.S. #1 R&B 45	"Share Your Love with Me"	Aretha Franklin
U.K. #1 POP 45	"Honky Tonk Women"	The Rolling Stones
U.K. #1 POP LP	*Stand Up*	Jethro Tull

WEEK ENDING AUGUST 30

U.S. #1 POP 45	"Honky Tonk Women"	The Rolling Stones
U.S. #1 POP LP	*At San Quentin*	Johnny Cash
U.S. #1 R&B 45	"Share Your Love with Me"	Aretha Franklin
U.K. #1 POP 45	"In the Year 2525"	Zager and Evans
U.K. #1 POP LP	*Stand Up*	Jethro Tull

4 The **Youngbloods** do *not* appear on "The Tonight Show" as scheduled. As **Johnny Carson** puts it in his monologue, "They complained about the set, the lighting, the sound, the show—everything. So we wiped their noses, told them they'd been in show business a day and a half and sent them home." Youngblood **Banana** retorts, "We weren't treated like guests so much as niggers."

5 Bluesman **Josh White**, author of "Ball and Chain Blues" (popularized by **Janis Joplin** as "Ball and Chain") and a favorite of the early Sixties Greenwich Village folk scene, dies during open heart surgery in a Manhasset (Long Island), New York hospital at age fifty-four.

6 **James Brown** announces, after a show at the Memphis Mid-South Coliseum, his retirement from live performance after July 4, 1970. "I'm tired, man," says the hardest-working man in show business. "My brain seems to get much heavier." Meanwhile, Brown fights a paternity suit filed in Sacramento, California, by a one-time president of the local James Brown Fan Club.

13 **John Lennon** and **Yoko Ono's Plastic Ono Band**—made up of guitarist **Eric Clapton**, session bassist and **Beatle**-buddy **Klaus Voormann** (who designed the *Revolver* cover) and drummer **Alan White** (later with **Yes**)—makes a surprise live debut at the Rock 'n' Roll Revival Concert in Toronto, Canada. Also performing at the concert are **Chuck Berry**, **Bo Diddley**, **Jerry Lee Lewis**, **Gene Vincent**, **Little Richard**, **Alice Cooper**, **Chicago**, the **Doors**, **Screaming Lord Sutch** and others. "I can't remember when I had such a good time," says Lennon after the show.

14 Seattle's Roman Catholic archdiocese runs a two-page ad in the *Seattle Post-Intelligencer* calling for criminal prosecution against "rock festivals and their drug-sex-rock-squalor culture." The ad is accompanied by photos from the recent Sky River Rock Festival and Lighter than Air Fair, held near Seattle, with portions of the photos showing nudity and drug use blacked out.

15 **Ed Sullivan** releases a rock & roll record, "The Sulli-Gulli," backed by the **Ed Sullivan Singers** and **Orchestra**.

Deep Purple, with new vocalist **Ian Gillan** and bassist **Roger Glover**, perform keyboardist **Jon Lord's** "Concerto for Rock Band and Orchestra" with the Royal Philharmonic Orchestra at London's Royal Albert Hall.

16 In Britain, Philips Records pulls **Jane Birkin** and **Serge Gainsbourg's** hit single "Je T'aime . . . Moi Non Plus" off the market because of charges of "salaciousness." Within days, the record is reissued on the Major Minor label and continues to climb the U.K. chart, hitting #2 on September 24 and remaining in the Top Thirty for thirteen weeks.

20 Associated TV spends a million pounds to gain control of the **Beatles'** music publishing company, Northern Songs.

22 A new weekly prime-time rock-oriented show, "The Music Scene," debuts on ABC. In its one-year run, the forty-five-minute show, conducted by comedian **David Steinberg**, features such stars as **James Brown**, **Crosby, Stills, Nash and Young**, **Janis Joplin**, **Sly and the Family Stone**, **Stevie Wonder**, **Isaac Hayes**, **Tom Jones** and **Cass Elliot**.

The Illinois University newspaper *The Northern Star* runs an article under the headline CLUES HINT AT BEATLE DEATH, citing the *Sgt. Pepper* album cover and the line "I buried Paul" (actually "I'm very bored," **John Lennon** would later claim) in the fade-out of "Strawberry Fields Forever," kicking off one of the hypes of the decade: the Paul (McCartney) Is Dead controversy. Within weeks, **Paul McCartney** will inform journalists from his Scotland farm that reports of his demise are premature.

26 The **Beatles** release their thirteenth album in the U.K.—and last made together as a group—*Abbey Road*. It's released a week later in the U.S. **John Lennon** shrugs it off as "a reasonably good album, but nothing special." Within a month, the LP begins an eleven-week run in the Number One spot. *Abbey Road*'s cover photo further fuels the Paul Is Dead controversy, as some observers note that Paul's appearance—he's dressed all in black and is barefoot—is markedly different from the rest of the Beatles.

The original Fillmore Auditorium in San Francisco, vacated a year earlier by longtime owner-operator **Bill Graham**, reopens as a rock dance hall with the **Flamin' Groovies** and other bands.

30 David Crosby's girlfriend, **Christine Gail Hinton**, is killed in a head-on auto accident north of San Francisco, the same day the *Crosby, Stills and Nash* album goes gold. ◆

WEEK ENDING SEPTEMBER 6

U.S. #1 POP 45	"Honky Tonk Women"	The Rolling Stones
U.S. #1 POP LP	*At San Quentin*	Johnny Cash
U.S. #1 R&B 45	"Share Your Love with Me"	Aretha Franklin
U.K. #1 POP 45	"In the Year 2525"	Zager and Evans
U.K. #1 POP LP	*Stand Up*	Jethro Tull

WEEK ENDING SEPTEMBER 13

U.S. #1 POP 45	"Honky Tonk Women"	The Rolling Stones
U.S. #1 POP LP	*At San Quentin*	Johnny Cash
U.S. #1 R&B 45	"Share Your Love with Me"	Aretha Franklin
U.K. #1 POP 45	"In the Year 2525"	Zager and Evans
U.K. #1 POP LP	*Stand Up*	Jethro Tull

WEEK ENDING SEPTEMBER 20

U.S. #1 POP 45	"Sugar, Sugar"	The Archies
U.S. #1 POP LP	*Blind Faith*	Blind Faith
U.S. #1 R&B 45	"Share Your Love with Me"	Aretha Franklin
U.K. #1 POP 45	"Bad Moon Rising"	Creedence Clearwater Revival
U.K. #1 POP LP	*At San Quentin*	Johnny Cash

WEEK ENDING SEPTEMBER 27

U.S. #1 POP 45	"Sugar, Sugar"	The Archies
U.S. #1 POP LP	*Blind Faith*	Blind Faith
U.S. #1 R&B 45	"Oh What a Night"	The Dells
U.K. #1 POP 45	"Bad Moon Rising"	Creedence Clearwater Revival
U.K. #1 POP LP	*At San Quentin*	Johnny Cash

1 A portent of Seventies "progressive" radio programming: Denver's KMYR-FM drops its pop format in favor of comedy and top instrumental arrangements of contemporary hits. The station's programming pioneers call it "Pzazz-95."

3 Legendary bluesman **Nehemiah "Skip" James** dies of cancer in Philadelphia at age sixty-seven. His best-known song was "I'm So Glad," which **Cream** covered in 1967.

5 **Dianne Linkletter**, daughter of TV personality Art Linkletter and an aspiring actress, leaps to her death from her West Hollywood apartment. Linkletter claims his daughter was under the influence of LSD at the time of her apparent suicide. "It isn't suicide," he protests, "it's murder."

6 For the first time in **Beatles** history, a **George Harrison** song gets the A side of a 45. "Something" backed with Lennon and McCartney's "Come Together" will reach Number One next month.

11 **Grand Funk Railroad**'s debut LP, *On Time*, enters the chart at #65, much to the chagrin of rock critics, who launch an all-out verbal assault on the band. Within the year, Grand Funk will be among the best-selling acts in rock history.

12 A mysterious phone caller urges **Russ Gibb**, DJ at Detroit underground radio station WKNR, to listen to the **Beatles**' "Revolution Number Nine" played *backward*. Gibb does so, and listeners think they hear a voice saying, "Turn me on, dead man." Thus the Paul Is Dead craze approaches **Orson Welles**' "War of the Worlds" radio broadcast as a great media hoax.

14 The **Jimi Hendrix Experience**'s *Smash Hits* is certified gold. The set includes such songs as "Stone Free" and "Red House," which have hitherto been available only as singles, plus favorite cuts from Hendrix's first three albums—"Purple Haze," "Crosstown Traffic" and more.

15 Hundreds of thousands of protesters turn out in U.S. cities to march against the Vietnam War. World Peace Day is declared such a success (even by former Vice President **Hubert Humphrey**) that two more moratoriums are held on November 14 and 15.

16 **Leonard Chess**, who, with his brother **Phil**, founded Chess Records in 1948, dies of a heart attack in Chicago at age fifty-two. He recorded scores of influential blues and R&B artists, including **Muddy Waters**, **Howlin' Wolf**, **Willie Dixon**, **Otis Spann**, **Bo Diddley**, **Chuck Berry** and the **Rolling Stones**.

17 **Led Zeppelin**, British blues-rock heir-apparent to **Cream**, begins its third U.S. tour at New York's Carnegie Hall. It also releases its *Led Zeppelin II* LP, destined to become the heavy-metal Bible.

The **Kinks** launch their first U.S. tour in four years. "It wasn't that we didn't want to come back," leader **Ray Davies** apologizes, adding that the band encountered permit problems with the American Federation of Musicians because of its frequent boozing and fisticuffs onstage.

18 Fifties rock returns when promoter **Richard Nader** stages the first of many Rock & Roll Revival concerts at New York's Felt Forum. On the bill are **Bill Haley** (who receives an eight-and-a-half minute standing ovation), **Chuck Berry**, the **Platters**, the **Coasters**, **Jimmy Clanton**, the **Shirelles** and a new group of Fifties revialists called **Sha Na Na**.

20 The **Who** open a six-night stand at New York's Fillmore East, with the two-hour-plus show centered on *Tommy*.

Further signs of discord among the **Beatles**: **John Lennon** releases his second solo single, "Cold Turkey," again under the band name **Plastic Ono Band**. The song, which deals explicitly with drug abuse, was rejected by the group, so Lennon put it out himself. It reaches no higher than #30 on the U.S. chart and #13 on the U.K. chart. When Lennon returns his Member of the Order of the British Empire (MBE) medal to the Queen later in the year, he wryly cites the 45's poor chart showing as one of his grievances.

23 **King Crimson** makes its American debut at Goddard College in Plainfield, Vermont. Band leader and guitarist **Robert Fripp** notes that "the audience appeared to be a peace-and-love crowd, sitting dreamily in lotus positions, probably expecting psychedelic folk or some such. After our first number, there was no applause, just dead silence. I looked up. The audience looked as if it had been squashed by a steamroller."

Bob Dylan's *Great White Wonder* bootleg album sells like hotcakes in the U.S. and Canada, at prices ranging from $6.50 to twenty dollars. Columbia Records, which has Dylan under exclusive contract, announces it will pursue court action to stop the bootleg's sales; Dylan refuses to comment. ◆

WEEK ENDING OCTOBER 4

U.S. #1 POP 45	"Sugar, Sugar"	The Archies
U.S. #1 POP LP	*Green River*	Creedence Clearwater Revival
U.S. #1 R&B 45	"I Can't Get Next to You"	The Temptations
U.K. #1 POP 45	"Bad Moon Rising"	Creedence Clearwater Revival
U.K. #1 POP LP	*Abbey Road*	The Beatles

WEEK ENDING OCTOBER 11

U.S. #1 POP 45	"Sugar, Sugar"	The Archies
U.S. #1 POP LP	*Green River*	Creedence Clearwater Revival
U.S. #1 R&B 45	"I Can't Get Next to You"	The Temptations
U.K. #1 POP 45	"I'll Never Fall in Love Again"	Bobbie Gentry
U.K. #1 POP LP	*Abbey Road*	The Beatles

WEEK ENDING OCTOBER 18

U.S. #1 POP 45	"I Can't Get Next to You"	The Temptations
U.S. #1 POP LP	*Green River*	Creedence Clearwater Revival
U.S. #1 R&B 45	"I Can't Get Next to You"	The Temptations
U.K. #1 POP 45	"I'll Never Fall in Love Again"	Bobbie Gentry
U.K. #1 POP LP	*Abbey Road*	The Beatles

WEEK ENDING OCTOBER 25

U.S. #1 POP 45	"I Can't Get Next to You"	The Temptations
U.S. #1 POP LP	*Green River*	Creedence Clearwater Revival
U.S. #1 R&B 45	"I Can't Get Next to You"	The Temptations
U.K. #1 POP 45	"I'll Never Fall in Love Again"	Bobbie Gentry
U.K. #1 POP LP	*Abbey Road*	The Beatles

1 The *New York Times* reports on the Paul Is Dead rumor sweeping the world. The *Times* gives it no credence but cites such compelling evidence as the hand that appears over **Beatle Paul McCartney**'s head on the cover of *Sgt. Pepper's Lonely Hearts Club Band*—an ancient Indian symbol of death.

7 The **Rolling Stones** open their first American tour in three years in Denver, Colorado. In those three years, the Stones have been the almost-constant hero-villains of public controversy over their drug busts, censorship battles and reportedly unconventional sex lives. The tour is already a media event.

8 On the second date of their U.S. tour, the **Rolling Stones** break the Los Angeles concert gross record held by the **Beatles** since 1966, when they grossed £100,000; the Stones gross £108,000 and add an extra date to their L.A. Forum Stand stand and a fourth date to their upcoming stand at New York City's Madison Square Garden.

11 **Jim Morrison** of the **Doors** is jailed for "interfering with the flight of an intercontinental aircraft and public drunkenness." Morrison and friend **Tom Baker** were en route from Los Angeles to Phoenix, Arizona, to see the **Rolling Stones**, when Morrison pestered a flight attendant, drawing a charge that carries a $10,000 fine and a possible ten-year jail sentence. Eventually the flight attendant, whose testimony is essential to the case, withdraws her accusation and all charges are dropped.

14 Three hundred thousand antiwar demonstrators assemble in Washington, D.C., and 150,000 assemble in San Francisco for a two-day National Moratorium to call attention to widespread opposition to U.S. policy in Vietnam. The **Plastic Ono Band**'s "Give Peace a Chance" is adopted as the unofficial Moratorium anthem.

15 **Janis Joplin** is arrested in Tampa, Florida, on charges of using "vulgar and indecent language" at her concert. According to witnesses, the incident began when a policeman with a bullhorn ordered people in the audience to sit down, and Joplin responded, "Don't fuck with those people! Hey, Mister, what're you so uptight about? Did you buy a five-dollar ticket?" When police backstage instructed Joplin to tell the audience to take their seats, she replied, "I'm not telling them shit." After being arrested in her dressing room, Joplin is released on $504 bond. All charges are eventually dropped.

The Star Club in Hamburg, Germany, where the **Beatles** played their first major engagements beginning in December 1960 and through 1962, announces that it will close before the end of the month. Rock & roll bands, the management explains, have become too expensive to book.

22 Singer **Sandy Denny** and guitarist **Tyger Hutchings** leave the seminal British folk-rock group, **Fairport Convention**, to begin solo careers. Coming less than a year after founder/singer/guitarist **Ian Matthews**' departure, the latest development leaves guitarist **Richard Thompson** to carry the lead vocals.

24 The **Rolling Stones'** *Let It Bleed*, which contains the original versions of "You Can't Always Get What You Want" and "Honky Tonk Women" (in an acoustic rendition titled "Country Honk") and the concert show-stopper "Midnight Rambler" but no hit singles, is certified gold.

25 **John Lennon** returns his MBE to **Queen Elizabeth**, citing British involvement in the Nigeria-Biafra war, political support of the U.S. position in Vietnam and the poor reception given the **Plastic Ono Band**'s "Cold Turkey." The other three Beatles keep their MBEs, which they received in October 1965.

27 The **Rolling Stones** open their four-night stand at New York City's Madison Square Garden, where the first two shows are recorded for their live album *Get Yer Ya-Ya's Out*.

30 **David Bowie**, **Dusty Springfield**, **Grapefruit**, the **Graham Bond Organisation** and other acts perform at the Save Rave '69 benefit concert to aid the youth culture magazine, *Rave*, in London. ◆

WEEK ENDING NOVEMBER 1

U.S. #1 POP 45	"Suspicious Minds"	Elvis Presley
U.S. #1 POP LP	*Abbey Road*	The Beatles
U.S. #1 R&B 45	"I Can't Get Next to You"	The Temptations
U.K. #1 POP 45	"Sugar, Sugar"	The Archies
U.K. #1 POP LP	*Abbey Road*	The Beatles

WEEK ENDING NOVEMBER 8

U.S. #1 POP 45	"Wedding Bell Blues"	The Fifth Dimension
U.S. #1 POP LP	*Abbey Road*	The Beatles
U.S. #1 R&B 45	"Baby, I'm for Real"	The Originals
U.K. #1 POP 45	"Sugar, Sugar"	The Archies
U.K. #1 POP LP	*Abbey Road*	The Beatles

WEEK ENDING NOVEMBER 15

U.S. #1 POP 45	"Wedding Bell Blues"	The Fifth Dimension
U.S. #1 POP LP	*Abbey Road*	The Beatles
U.S. #1 R&B 45	"Baby, I'm for Real"	The Originals
U.K. #1 POP 45	"Oh Well"	Fleetwood Mac
U.K. #1 POP LP	*Abbey Road*	The Beatles

WEEK ENDING NOVEMBER 22

U.S. #1 POP 45	"Wedding Bell Blues"	The Fifth Dimension
U.S. #1 POP LP	*Abbey Road*	The Beatles
U.S. #1 R&B 45	"Baby, I'm for Real"	The Originals
U.K. #1 POP 45	"Sugar, Sugar"	The Archies
U.K. #1 POP LP	*Abbey Road*	The Beatles

WEEK ENDING NOVEMBER 29

U.S. #1 POP 45	"Come Together"/"Something"	The Beatles
U.S. #1 POP LP	*Abbey Road*	The Beatles
U.S. #1 R&B 45	"Baby, I'm for Real"	The Originals
U.K. #1 POP 45	"Sugar, Sugar"	The Archies
U.K. #1 POP LP	*Abbey Road*	The Beatles

1 **"Magic Sam" Maghett**, the Chicago bluesman best known for his 1964 recording of "High Heel Sneakers," dies after suffering a heart attack in Chicago at age thirty-two.

4 President **Richard M. Nixon**, Vice-President **Spiro T. Agnew** and forty U.S. governors embark on a magical mystery fact-finding mission to discover the causes of the generation gap. They view films of "simulated acid trips" and listen to hours of "antiestablishment rock music."

Santana's eponymous debut album, **Janis Joplin**'s *I Got Dem Ol' Kozmic Blues Again, Mama* and **Sly and the Family Stone**'s *Stand!* are certified gold. All three acts had appeared at Woodstock in August.

6 The **Rolling Stones** play a free "thank-you" concert for 300,000 fans at the Altamont Speedway in Livermore, California. Among the performing guests are the **Jefferson Airplane**, **Santana**, **Crosby, Stills, Nash and Young** and the **Flying Burrito Brothers**. The hastily organized event rapidly degenerates into a disaster that marks the beginning of the end of the rock festival phenomenon and shatters the utopian dreams of the Woodstock Nation. The chilly day of catastrophic overcrowding, drug overdoses and violence climaxes while the Stones are onstage in the fatal stabbing of spectator **Meredith Hunter** by Hell's Angels, who were appointed security guards for the event. The incident is captured on film by the **Maysles Brothers** and later seen by millions in their feature-length documentary *Gimme Shelter*.

8 Testifying at his trial for possession of hashish and heroin in the Toronto Supreme Court, **Jimi Hendrix** claims that he has smoked pot four times and hashish five times, taken LSD five times and sniffed cocaine twice, and that he has now "outgrown" drugs. After eight hours of deliberations, the jury finds him not guilty.

12 Two Memphis musicians are awarded gold albums: **Elvis Presley** for *From Memphis to Las Vegas* (his fourteenth gold album), and **Isaac Hayes** for *Hot Buttered Soul* (his first gold).

15 **John Lennon** and **Yoko Ono's Plastic Ono Band**—with guest musicians **George Harrison**, **Delaney and Bonnie Bramlett**, **Jim Price**, **Bobby Keys**, **Jim Gordon**, **Klaus Voormann**, **Keith Moon**, **Billy Preston**, **Alan White** and **Legs Larry Smith**—performs its U.K. debut at the Lyceum in London. The War Is Over concert lasts forty minutes and includes only two songs, "Cold Turkey" and "Don't Worry Kyoko." The same day, John and Yoko's "War Is Over!/If You Want It" billboards go up in twelve major cities around the world, including New York, London and Hollywood.

17 **Chicago**'s first album, *Chicago Transit Authority*, is certified gold. The two-record set contains the hits "25 or 6 to 4" and "Does Anybody Really Know What Time It Is?"

21 A *New York Times* article estimates that the youth audience in America accounts for seventy-five percent of the $1 billion spent annually on recorded music. The same issue contains one of **John Lennon** and **Yoko Ono's** full-page "War Is Over" ads.

Ginger Baker's thirteen-piece **Air Force**, which features **Steve Winwood** (Traffic, Blind Faith), **Rick Grech** (Family, Blind Faith, Traffic), **Chris Wood** (Traffic), **Denny Laine** (Moody Blues, Wings) and British blues patriarch **Graham Bond**, debuts in Amsterdam.

22 **John Lennon** and **Yoko Ono** meet for one hour with Canadian Prime Minister **Pierre Trudeau** in Ottawa. Earlier in the day, they met with Canadian Minister of Health **John Munro** to discuss drug abuse.

24 *The Buddy Holly Story*, an album commemorating the tenth anniversary of the pioneering rocker's death, is certified gold. One week later, "That'll Be the Day," probably **Buddy Holly's** best-loved song, is certified a gold single.

29 The **Bonzo Dog Band**, the British group that skipped over the line between rock & roll and comedy, perform at the Lyceum in London, augmented by drummers **Keith Moon** and **Aynsley Dunbar**, and announce before the concert's finale that they will disband after playing dates scheduled in January and February. Founder **Viv Stanshall** has already begun work on a solo album, aided by **Paul McCartney**, **Pete Townshend**, **Eric Clapton** and **Keith Moon**.

31 At a New Year's Eve concert at the Fillmore East, New York City, **Jimi Hendrix** introduces his new all-black, **Band of Gypsys**—bassist **Billy Cox** and drummer **Buddy Miles**. The concert is recorded for the live album *Band of Gypsys*. ◆

WEEK ENDING DECEMBER 6

U.S. #1 POP 45	"Na Na Hey Hey Kiss Him Goodbye"	Steam
U.S. #1 POP LP	*Abbey Road*	The Beatles
U.S. #1 R&B 45	"Baby, I'm for Real"	The Originals
U.K. #1 POP 45	"Yester-Me, Yester-You, Yesterday"	Stevie Wonder
U.K. #1 POP LP	*Abbey Road*	The Beatles

WEEK ENDING DECEMBER 13

U.S. #1 POP 45	"Na Na Hey Hey Kiss Him Goodbye"	Steam
U.S. #1 POP LP	*Abbey Road*	The Beatles
U.S. #1 R&B 45	"Someday We'll Be Together"	Diana Ross and the Supremes
U.K. #1 POP 45	"Ruby, Don't Take Your Love to Town"	Kenny Rogers and the First Edition
U.K. #1 POP LP	*Abbey Road*	The Beatles

WEEK ENDING DECEMBER 20

U.S. #1 POP 45	"Leaving on a Jet Plane"	Peter, Paul and Mary
U.S. #1 POP LP	*Abbey Road*	The Beatles
U.S. #1 R&B 45	"Someday We'll Be Together"	Diana Ross and the Supremes
U.K. #1 POP 45	"Two Little Boys"	Rolf Harris
U.K. #1 POP LP	*Abbey Road*	The Beatles

WEEK ENDING DECEMBER 27

U.S. #1 POP 45	"Someday We'll Be Together"	Diana Ross and the Supremes
U.S. #1 POP LP	*Led Zeppelin II*	Led Zeppelin
U.S. #1 R&B 45	"Someday We'll Be Together"	Diana Ross and the Supremes
U.K. #1 POP 45	"Two Little Boys"	Rolf Harris
U.K. #1 POP LP	*Abbey Road*	The Beatles

1970

*E*arly in the new decade, there was already evidence to confirm that rock was now more a part of institutionalized, established culture than a force against it. In January, the Who became the first rock band to play at many of Europe's most venerable opera houses (in June they became the first rock band to play New York's Metropolitan Opera House), as they toured their rock opera *Tommy.* In February, *Look* magazine took the line "I read the news today, oh boy" from the Beatles' "A Day in the Life" as a title for its look back at the Sixties. In April, the Beatles' Yellow Submarine was adopted as a religious symbol by various American Christian youth groups.

But there was much worse than that in 1970. Though the ramifications of what had happened at Altamont may not have fully sunken in yet, John Lennon had his finger on the pulse in January when he recorded "Instant Karma!"—and though the comeuppence from the bad karma that had been infecting rock's utopian-radical thrust may not have been instant, it was quick enough in coming. In March, the sensational court case of tribal-hippie-guru and murderer Charles Manson opened, revealing the inspiration Manson claimed from the Beatles' "White Album." That same month, a New York City group calling itself Revolutionary Force 9 after another "White Album" song claimed credit for some local terrorist bombings.

There continued to be rock festivals in the wake of Altamont, but most of them fell flat. The fiascos of the Powder Ridge Festival (which never happened but still drew thousands), the "Canadian Woodstock" (only a few thousand fans and one band bothered to show) and the Ann Arbor Blues and Jazz Festival (where promoters passed the hat through the crowd to try to recoup their deficit) were typical—as was Britain's Isle of Wight Pop Festival, where cops disguised as hippies arrested 120 audience members for drugs, the crowd caused thousands of dollars worth of damage to the site, and one fan leapt onstage during Joni Mitchell's set to declare, "This is just a hippie concentration camp!" Instant karma, indeed.

Perhaps worst of all was the second great wave of rock star deaths that claimed Jimi Hendrix in September and Janis Joplin in October. It was a tragic trilogy that would be completed next year by Jim Morrison. And if that weren't bad enough, 1970 also saw the death of a rock band—that of the Beatles. If anything could make a generation stop and think and take stock of itself, it was this.

Meanwhile, the music and culture continued to surge ahead. In June, the Grateful Dead officially marked the end of psychedelia with *Workingman's Dead.* In August, there was the first performance by one of the first progressive-rock supergroups, Emerson, Lake and Palmer. In September, *Melody Maker* announced that for the first time in eight years the Beatles had been displaced as Britain's most popular band—by heavy-metal supergroup Led Zeppelin.

Rock and youth culture could still make some headlines—witness the running feud between Vice President Agnew and FCC Commissioner Nicholas Johnson—but even something like the heinous tragedies at Kent State and Jackson State could only inspire a momentary rallying call and, later, one good rock protest song in Crosby, Stills, Nash and Young's "Ohio." By now, rock was moving away from *making* headlines and toward becoming so much grist for the headline writer's mill.

3 The **Beatles** record what will be their last song together, "I Me Mine." A decade later it becomes the title of **George Harrison**'s autobiography.

One year after **Peter Tork**'s departure from the teen-idol band, lead singer **Davy Jones** announces he, too, is leaving the **Monkees**.

7 **Max Yasgur**, on whose upstate New York farm the August, 1969 Woodstock Festival was held, is sued for $35,000 in property damages by neighboring farmers.

16 **John Lennon**'s London Art Gallery exhibit of erotic lithographs, Bag One, is closed by Scotland Yard, and eight prints are confiscated as evidence of pornography.

The **Who** begins its first tour of Europe in four years, with a performance of its "rock opera," *Tommy,* at the Theatre Champs Elysees in Paris—the first pop concert ever given at that establishment. From there the band goes on to the Royal Danish Opera House in Copenhagen, the Cologne Opera House, the Hamburg Opera House and the German Opera House, Berlin.

17 Chicago R&B singer **Billy Stewart** and three of his band members are killed when their car goes out of control and plummets off a bridge over the River Neuse in North Carolina. Stewart, who also played piano, was best known for his 1966 hit version of **George Gershwin**'s "Summertime," replete with his typical yodeling, hiccuping, scatting vocal style. He was thirty-two years old.

The **Doors**' two-night stand at the Felt Forum in New York is recorded for their forthcoming album, *Absolutely Live.* Several other shows around the country will also be recorded for the album.

23 Folk singer **Judy Collins** is denied permission by the court to sing as part of her testimony at the trial of the Chicago Seven; others denied the same privilege are **Pete Seeger, Phil Ochs, Arlo Guthrie** and **Country Joe McDonald**.

24 **James "Shep" Shephard**, onetime doo-wopper with the **Heartbeats** and the **Limeliters**, is found beaten to death and robbed in his car on New York's Long Island Expressway.

Robert Moog introduces his "Mini-Moog" synthesizer, suitable for concert stages, available for about $2,000. Soon the American Federation of Musicians will consider a ban on the Mini-Moog, fearing that its ability to simulate acoustic instruments could put musicians out of business.

It's announced that **John Lennon** and **Yoko Ono** have shaven their heads to commemorate the start of Year One for Peace.

26 **John Lennon** and **Phil Spector** write and record "Instant Karma," which is released in early February.

Australia's first rock festival, the Ourimbah Rock Festival, is attended by 11,000 people over the weekend; there are only twenty-six arrests.

28 The Vietnam Moratorium Committee holds a seven-hour benefit concert at Madison Square Garden and sets a new attendance record for nonsporting event gate receipts, bringing in $143,000. Donating their services to the cause are promoter **Sid Bernstein**, the Fillmore East stage crew and performers **Jimi Hendrix**, the **Rascals, Blood, Sweat and Tears, Peter, Paul and Mary, Judy Collins, Richie Havens**, the **Voices of East Harlem, Dave Brubeck, McHenry Boatwright, Harry Belafonte, Mother Earth** and the cast of *Hair*.

31 England's biggest reggae stars—**Desmond Dekker, Jimmy Cliff, Max Romeo**, the **Upsetters**, the **Pioneers** and **Harry J's All-Stars**—kick off a package tour of England at London's Royal Albert Hall.

Bluesman **Slim Harpo**, whose "I'm a King Bee" was covered by the **Rolling Stones** on record and **Captain Beefheart** in concert, dies of a heart attack at age forty-six in Baton Rouge, Louisiana. ◆

WEEK ENDING JANUARY 3

U.S. #1 POP 45	"Raindrops Keep Falling on My Head"	B. J. Thomas
U.S. #1 POP LP	Abbey Road	The Beatles
U.S. #1 R&B 45	"Someday We'll Be Together"	Diana Ross and the Supremes
U.K. #1 POP 45	"Two Little Boys"	Rolf Harris
U.K. #1 POP LP	Abbey Road	The Beatles

WEEK ENDING JANUARY 10

U.S. #1 POP 45	"Raindrops Keep Falling on My Head"	B. J. Thomas
U.S. #1 POP LP	Abbey Road	The Beatles
U.S. #1 R&B 45	"I Want You Back"	The Jackson 5
U.K. #1 POP 45	"Two Little Boys"	Rolf Harris
U.K. #1 POP LP	Abbey Road	The Beatles

WEEK ENDING JANUARY 17

U.S. #1 POP 45	"Raindrops Keep Falling on My Head"	B. J. Thomas
U.S. #1 POP LP	Led Zeppelin II	Led Zeppelin
U.S. #1 R&B 45	"I Want You Back"	The Jackson 5
U.K. #1 POP 45	"Two Little Boys"	Rolf Harris
U.K. #1 POP LP	Abbey Road	The Beatles

WEEK ENDING JANUARY 24

U.S. #1 POP 45	"Raindrops Keep Falling on My Head"	B. J. Thomas
U.S. #1 POP LP	Abbey Road	The Beatles
U.S. #1 R&B 45	"I Want You Back"	The Jackson 5
U.K. #1 POP 45	"Two Little Boys"	Rolf Harris
U.K. #1 POP LP	Abbey Road	The Beatles

WEEK ENDING JANUARY 31

U.S. #1 POP 45	"I Want You Back"	The Jackson 5
U.S. #1 POP LP	Led Zeppelin II	Led Zeppelin
U.S. #1 R&B 45	"I Want You Back"	The Jackson 5
U.K. #1 POP 45	"Reflections of My Life"	Marmalade
U.K. #1 POP LP	Abbey Road	The Beatles

2 *Look* magazine uses the opening line of the **Beatles'** "A Day in the Life"—"I read the news today oh boy"—to headline its look back at the Sixties. The line was also used as the title of a regular music-news column in the magazine *Jazz & Pop*.

6 **John Lennon's** "Instant Karma" backed with **Yoko Ono's** "Who Has Seen the Wind?" is released in the U.K. on Apple Records.

7 **Johnny Cash's** album *Hello, I'm Johnny Cash* goes gold. Cash's label, Columbia, also reports that his LPs *At Folsom Prison* and *At San Quentin* have sold over 2 million copies each, and that his LP *Greatest Hits* has sold over a million copies.

9 **Simon and Garfunkel's** album *Bridge over Troubled Water* and **Sly and the Family Stone's** single "Thank You (Faletinme Be Mice Elf Agin)" both go gold, as does the LP *Bobby Sherman* the next day.

11 The film *The Magic Christian,* featuring **Ringo Starr,** premieres in New York City. The film's soundtrack album—featuring **Badfinger's** "Come and Get It," written and produced by **Paul McCartney**—is released on Apple the same day.

In a letter to the Federal Communications Commission, **Judy Collins** protests that her critical remarks about the Chicago Seven trial were censored by ABC-TV on a prime-time news program.

14 According to a *Billboard* headline, the Recording Industry Association of America is MOUNTING TOTAL WAR AGAINST TAPE PIRATING of prerecorded music.

The **Who** tape a concert at Leeds University in Leeds, England, for their forthcoming album, *Live at Leeds.* The set features early, pre-*Tommy* material—"My Generation," "Substitute," "Magic Bus"—and classic rockers "Young Man Blues," "Summertime Blues" and "Shakin' All Over."

15 The Daughters of the American Revolution impose a ban against rock concerts at their Washington, D.C. auditorium, Constitution Hall, after **Sly and the Family Stone** arrive five hours late for their Constitution Hall gig and the disquieted audience (eighteen of whom are arrested) inflict $1,000 worth of damage on the building.

17 **Joni Mitchell** announces her retirement from live performances after her show at London's Royal Albert Hall. Like many such announcements, it is premature: Within the year she is on the boards again.

18 **Yoko Ono** celebrates her thirty-seventh birthday. To mark the occasion, **John Lennon** throws a party at the London offices of Apple Records.

20 **John Lennon's** "Instant Karma" backed with **Yoko Ono's** "Who Has Seen the Wind?" is released in the U.S. on Apple Records. The following day, it enters the U.K. pop chart, where it will remain for six weeks, rising as high as #5.

21 **Simon and Garfunkel's** album *Bridge over Troubled Water* enters the U. K. chart at Number One and stays there for nearly forty weeks; it remains in the Top Ten for 126 weeks. The title single goes gold on February 27.

23 The **Doors'** album *Morrison Hotel* goes gold, becoming the band's fifth gold album in a row.

26 The **Beatles'** album *Hey Jude,* consisting of singles previously unavailable on album, is released in the U.S. on Apple Records.

28 **Led Zeppelin** performs in Copenhagen under the pseudonym the **Nobs** because of a threat of suit by **Eva von Zeppelin**, a relative of the airship designer **Ferdinand**, if the band plays under the name Zeppelin in Denmark. ◆

WEEK ENDING FEBRUARY 7

U.S. #1 POP 45	"Venus"	Shocking Blue
U.S. #1 POP LP	*Led Zeppelin II*	Led Zeppelin
U.S. #1 R&B 45	"Thank You (Falettinme Be Mice Elf Agin)"	Sly and the Family Stone
U.K. #1 POP 45	"Love Grows"	Edison Lighthouse
U.K. #1 POP LP	*Led Zeppelin II*	Led Zeppelin

WEEK ENDING FEBRUARY 14

U.S. #1 POP 45	"Thank You (Falettinme Be Mice Elf Agin)"	Sly and the Family Stone
U.S. #1 POP LP	*Led Zeppelin II*	Led Zeppelin
U.S. #1 R&B 45	"Thank You (Falettinme Be Mice Elf Agin)"	Sly and the Family Stone
U.K. #1 POP 45	"Love Grows"	Edison Lighthouse
U.K. #1 POP LP	*Led Zeppelin II*	Led Zeppelin

WEEK ENDING FEBRUARY 21

U.S. #1 POP 45	"Thank You (Falettinme Be Mice Elf Agin)"	Sly and the Family Stone
U.S. #1 POP LP	*Led Zeppelin II*	Led Zeppelin
U.S. #1 R&B 45	"Thank You (Falettinme Be Mice Elf Agin)"	Sly and the Family Stone
U.K. #1 POP 45	"Love Grows"	Edison Lighthouse
U.K. #1 POP LP	*Bridge over Troubled Water*	Simon and Garfunkel

WEEK ENDING FEBRUARY 28

U.S. #1 POP 45	"Bridge over Troubled Water"	Simon and Garfunkel
U.S. #1 POP LP	*Led Zeppelin II*	Led Zeppelin
U.S. #1 R&B 45	"Thank You (Falettinme Be Mice Elf Agin)"	Sly and the Family Stone
U.K. #1 POP 45	"I Want You Back"	The Jackson 5
U.K. #1 POP LP	*Bridge over Troubled Water*	Simon and Garfunkel

6 The **Beatles'** album *Hey Jude,* goes gold.

Charles Manson releases an album, *Lie,* to finance his defense in the Tate-LaBianca murder case. The album cover is a mock-up of the *Life* magazine cover photo of Manson, with the *F* taken out of *Life.*

8 **Diana Ross** opens an eleven-date cabaret engagement in Framingham, Massachusetts, her first outing as a solo performer.

11 The 1969 Grammy Award winners are announced. The **Fifth Dimension's** "Aquarius/Let the Sun-

shine In" is Record of the Year. *Blood, Sweat and Tears,* by the band of the same name, is Album of the Year. **Joe South's** "Games People Play" is Song of the Year. **Crosby, Stills and Nash** are named Best New Artist. The Annotator's award goes to Johnny Cash for his liner notes to Bob Dylan's *Nashville Skyline.* The Best Spoken Word Recording is "We Love You, Call Collect" by **Art Linkletter and Dianne.**

13 A group calling itself "Revolutionary Force 9" takes credit for three bombings in New York City. The *New York Times* notes a "possible connection to the **Beatles** song 'Revolution 9.'"

16 **Tammi Terrell,** best known for her duets with **Marvin Gaye**—"Ain't No Mountain High Enough," "Your Precious Love," "Ain't Nothin' like the Real Thing" and others—dies at Graduate Hospital in Philadelphia after undergoing six brain tumor operations in eighteen months. Doctors first discovered Terrell's brain tumor after she collapsed in Gaye's arms onstage in 1967. She was 24.

Sandy Denny makes her first solo appearance since leaving British folk-rockers **Fairport Convention,** at Birmingham Town Hall in England.

18 **Country Joe McDonald** is convicted for obscenity and fined $500 for leading a crowd in his Fish Cheer ("Gimme an F...U...C...K!") at a Worcester, Massachusetts, concert.

British label Immediate Records (whose roster included the

Small Faces), founded by former **Rolling Stones** manager **Andrew Loog Oldham,** goes out of business.

20 **David Bowie** marries American-born model **Angela Barnett** in Bromley, England. Angela, fresh out of Swiss finishing school, first met Bowie at a press reception for **King Crimson's** *In the Court of the Crimson King* in London in 1969. She will shortly give birth to their son, **Zowie,** and subsequently, the entire Bowie family (with David in ankle-length dress) would pose for some publicity shots.

21 The re-formed **Faces,** with new singer **Rod Stewart,** release their debut LP, *First Step.*

22 The Electric Circus, a rock club in New York City's East Village, is damaged by a bomb explosion. Police will be unable to provide an explanation.

25 **Crosby, Stills, Nash and Young's** first and only studio album, *Déjà Vu,* goes gold. The LP yielded hit singles in "Woodstock" and "Teach Your Children."

26 **Peter Yarrow** of Peter, Paul and Mary, whose album, *Peter, Paul and Mommy,* is the latest Grammy Award-winner for Best Recording for Children, pleads guilty to "taking immoral liberties" with a fourteen-year-old girl in Washington, D.C. ◆

WEEK ENDING MARCH 7

U.S. #1 POP 45	"Bridge over Troubled Water"	Simon and Garfunkel
U.S. #1 POP LP	*Bridge over Troubled Water*	Simon and Garfunkel
U.S. #1 R&B 45	"Thank You (Falettinme Be Mice Elf Agin)"	Sly and the Family Stone
U.K. #1 POP 45	"Wanderin' Star"	Lee Marvin
U.K. #1 POP LP	*Bridge over Troubled Water*	Simon and Garfunkel

WEEK ENDING MARCH 14

U.S. #1 POP 45	"Bridge over Troubled Water"	Simon and Garfunkel
U.S. #1 POP LP	*Bridge over Troubled Water*	Simon and Garfunkel
U.S. #1 R&B 45	"Rainy Night in Georgia"	Brook Benton
U.K. #1 POP 45	"Wanderin' Star"	Lee Marvin
U.K. #1 POP LP	*Bridge over Troubled Water*	Simon and Garfunkel

WEEK ENDING MARCH 21

U.S. #1 POP 45	"Bridge over Troubled Water"	Simon and Garfunkel
U.S. #1 POP LP	*Bridge over Troubled Water*	Simon and Garfunkel
U.S. #1 R&B 45	"Call Me"	Aretha Franklin
U.K. #1 POP 45	"Wanderin' Star"	Lee Marvin
U.K. #1 POP LP	*Bridge over Troubled Water*	Simon and Garfunkel

WEEK ENDING MARCH 28

U.S. #1 POP 45	"Bridge over Troubled Water"	Simon and Garfunkel
U.S. #1 POP LP	*Bridge over Troubled Water*	Simon and Garfunkel
U.S. #1 R&B 45	"Call Me"	Aretha Franklin
U.K. #1 POP 45	"Wanderin' Star"	Lee Marvin
U.K. #1 POP LP	*Bridge over Troubled Water*	Simon and Garfunkel

2 The London Magistrate's Court hears arguments on **John Lennon**'s indecency summons for his exhibition of erotic lithographs in January.

Donovan's *A Gift from a Flower to a Garden* and **Bobby Sherman**'s "Easy Come, Easy Go" both go gold.

5 A *New York Times* article defends rock music as "the most popular of creative arts today."

10 At a concert in Boston, **Doors** singer **Jim Morrison** asks the audience if "anyone wants to see my genitals," just after a brief power failure.

11 **Paul McCartney** announces a "temporary break with the **Beatles**," citing "personal differences" and adding that he will no longer record with **John Lennon**; his move is linked to disapproval of **Yoko Ono** and of Beatles financial adviser **Allen Klein**.

Peter Green, founding member and guitarist with **Fleetwood Mac**, announces he will leave the band on May 25 to devote himself to "what God would have me do."

Nice organist **Keith Emerson** and ex-**King Crimson** bassist-vocalist **Greg Lake** are reportedly auditioning drummers for a new trio in London. With the addition of ex-**Atomic Rooster** drummer **Carl Palmer**, of course, they'll become art-rock supergroup **Emerson, Lake and Palmer**.

13 **Led Zeppelin**'s "Whole Lotta Love" and the album *Chicago Transit Authority* both go gold.

15 **George Goldner**, New York City music entrepreneur, dies at age fifty-two. A longtime backer of doo-wop who released the **Flamingos**' classic "I Only Have Eyes for You," Goldner cofounded the Red Bird Record label (**Shangri-Las**, **Dixie Cups**) with producers **Phil Spector** and **Shadow Morton** and songwriters **Jerry Leiber** and **Mike Stoller**. He had previously co-founded Roulette Records.

17 **Johnny Cash** performs at the White House at the invitation of President **Richard M. Nixon** but refuses to oblige the president by singing "Welfare Cadillac" or "Okie from Muskogee," which are not his songs; he does, however, comply with an executive request for his Number One hit, "A Boy Named Sue."

Paul McCartney releases his first solo album, *McCartney,* further fueling rumors of an imminent **Beatles** breakup.

18 The Reverend **Daniel Berrigan** is hailed at the America Is Hard to Find Rock Festival at Cornell University in Ithaca, New York. The festival ends April 19 with a rock Mass.

20 The *New York Times* reports that Catholic and Protestant youth groups have adopted the Yellow Submarine as a religious symbol.

21 Blues guitarist **Earl Hooker** dies of tuberculosis in Chicago at age forty. Aside from playing on many Fifties and Sixties Chicago blues sessions, he also made the LP *Hooker & Steve* with **Steve Miller**.

23 **Norman Greenbaum**'s single "Spirit in the Sky" goes gold. His only other claim to fame is the cult novelty tune "The Eggplant That Ate Chicago," which he recorded in the late Sixties as **Dr. West's Medicine Show and Junk Band**.

24 Invited by **Tricia Nixon**, daughter of the president, to a White House tea party for alumni of Finch College, **Grace Slick** of the **Jefferson Airplane** shows up with "escort" **Abbie Hoffman**. Hoffman, on trial for conspiring to riot at the 1968 Democratic National Convention in Chicago, is turned away at the gate, and Slick leaves with him, without having either met Ms. Nixon or introducing her to tea laced with LSD, as she suggested she might do.

25 After playing a concert in Raleigh, North Carolina, where men in the crowd taunted the interracial band with racial insults, **Pacific Gas and Electric** is shot at as its van leaves the club. Four bullets hit the vehicle, but no one is hurt.

Chicago blues piano giant **Otis Spann**, a longtime member of **Muddy Waters**' band, dies of cancer in Chicago at age forty. Among his best-known tunes were "Bertha," "Off the Hook" and "Two Bugs and a Roach."

27 A May Day Rock Festival planned at Southern Illinois University in Carbondale, Illinois, is threatened by suits from the state of Illiniois and S. I. U. Illinois State Attorney **R. E. Richman** and architect/author/philosopher **Buckminster Fuller** urge hospitality for the festival.

29 **George Harrison** says the **Beatles** will reunite eventually and announces plans for his first post-Beatles solo LP. ◆

WEEK ENDING APRIL 4

U.S. #1 POP 45	"Bridge over Troubled Water"	Simon and Garfunkel
U.S. #1 POP LP	*Bridge over Troubled Water*	Simon and Garfunkel
U.S. #1 R&B 45	"ABC"	The Jackson 5
U.K. #1 POP 45	"Bridge over Troubled Water"	Simon and Garfunkel
U.K. #1 POP LP	*Bridge over Troubled Water*	Simon and Garfunkel

WEEK ENDING APRIL 11

U.S. #1 POP 45	"Let It Be"	The Beatles
U.S. #1 POP LP	*Bridge over Troubled Water*	Simon and Garfunkel
U.S. #1 R&B 45	"ABC"	The Jackson 5
U.K. #1 POP 45	*"Bridge over Troubled Water"*	Simon and Garfunkel
U.K. #1 POP LP	*Bridge over Troubled Water*	Simon and Garfunkel

WEEK ENDING APRIL 18

U.S. #1 POP 45	"Let It Be"	The Beatles
U.S. #1 POP LP	*Bridge over Troubled Water*	Simon and Garfunkel
U.S. #1 R&B 45	"ABC"	The Jackson 5
U.K. #1 POP 45	"Bridge over Troubled Water"	Simon and Garfunkel
U.K. #1 POP LP	*Bridge over Troubled Water*	Simon and Garfunkel

WEEK ENDING APRIL 25

U.S. #1 POP 45	"ABC"	The Jackson 5
U.S. #1 POP LP	*Bridge over Troubled Water*	Simon and Garfunkel
U.S. #1 R&B 45	"ABC"	The Jackson 5
U.K. #1 POP 45	"Spirit in the Sky"	Norman Greenbaum
U.K. #1 POP LP	*Bridge over Troubled Water*	Simon and Garfunkel

4 Four students at Kent State University in Kent, Ohio, are killed and eleven are wounded by National Guard troops at a campus demonstration protesting the escalation of the Vietnam War to include Cambodia. It is only the most dramatic event in a month of widespread campus unrest and increasingly agitated antiwar sentiments throughout the U. S. By May 7, more than 400 colleges and universities have closed down as a result of student boycotts. Police and National Guardsmen are dispatched to many campuses to "control" demonstrations. On May 14, two students are killed by police at Jackson State University in Jackson, Mississippi. The Kent State incident inspires **Neil Young** to compose "Ohio," which will become a hit for **Crosby, Stills, Nash and Young**.

Gold records go to the *Midnight Cowboy* soundtrack album, **Frijid Pink**'s heavy-metal remake of "The House of the Rising Sun," and R&B singer **Tyrone Davis**' "Turn Back the Hands of Time."

11 The triple-album *Woodstock* soundtrack is released on Cotillion Records. The document of the epochal rock festival will go gold within two weeks.

"Give Me Just a Little More Time" by the **Chairmen of the Board** goes gold. This is the first hit for Invictus Records, the label begun by Motown songwriting team **Holland-Dozier-Holland** in the wake of their controversial split from Motown. The Chairmen of the Board include **General Johnson**, who, as a member of the **Showmen**, wrote their classic 1961 rock anthem, "It Will Stand."

13 The *New York Times'* random survey of underground rock radio stations finds that much of the underground radio audience uses it for background music "to get stoned by," and reports that TV personality **Art Linkletter**, whose daughter **Dianne** leaped to her death allegedly while on LSD, is the most articulate foe of underground radio and the rock subculture in general.

16 Jefferson Airplane singer **Marty Balin** is busted for marijuana possession and for contributing to the delinquency of minors in Bloomington, Minnesota. Balin, arrested along with Airplane soundman **Gary O'Dell** and friend **Terry Cost**, is surprised in his hotel room by police at 5:30 a.m. The cops were tipped

off by neighbors who complained of noise from a party at the hotel. They found Balin and friends with several girls aged twelve to seventeen. Balin is sentenced to one year's hard labor and a $100 fine; his appeal is slated for August 3. He ends up paying only the fine.

23 *New Musical Express* reports that the **Beatles**' *Let It Be* has set a new record for initial U. S. sales, with 3.7 million advance orders (representing $26 million retail gross). The album goes gold within days of its release.

The **Grateful Dead** plays its first British concert at the Hollywood Rock Festival. The Dead's four-hour set is preceded by a performance by **Mungo Jerry**, playing its big hit "In the Summertime."

30 Columbia Records announces plans to re-release 160 tracks by seminal blues singer **Bessie Smith** on five double-album sets over the next year, aiming the project at the youth market created by the blues revival.

Toronto's "total environment" multiroom rock club, the Electric Circus—which contains "the Womb Room," where you can crawl into a hole in the wall and "the Meditation Room," with a computerized sound-and-light setup—is closed because of a simple lack of business, attributed mainly to the club's excessively high prices. In September, it is put up for auction. There are no takers. ◆

WEEK ENDING MAY 2

U.S. #1 POP 45	"ABC"	The Jackson 5
U.S. #1 POP LP	*Bridge over Troubled Water*	Simon and Garfunkel
U.S. #1 R&B 45	"Turn Back the Hands of Time"	Tyrone Davis
U.K. #1 POP 45	"Spirit in the Sky"	Norman Greenbaum
U.K. #1 POP LP	*Bridge over Troubled Water*	Simon and Garfunkel

WEEK ENDING MAY 9

U.S. #1 POP 45	"American Woman"	The Guess Who
U.S. #1 POP LP	*Bridge over Troubled Water*	Simon and Garfunkel
U.S. #1 R&B 45	"Turn Back the Hands of Time"	Tyrone Davis
U.K. #1 POP 45	"Back Home"	England World Cup Squad
U.K. #1 POP LP	*Bridge over Troubled Water*	Simon and Garfunkel

WEEK ENDING MAY 16

U.S. #1 POP 45	"American Woman"	The Guess Who
U.S. #1 POP LP	*Déjà Vu*	Crosby, Stills, Nash and Young
U.S. #1 R&B 45	"Love on a Two-Way Street"	The Moments
U.K. #1 POP 45	"Back Home"	England World Cup Squad
U.K. #1 POP LP	*Bridge over Troubled Water*	Simon and Garfunkel

WEEK ENDING MAY 23

U.S. #1 POP 45	"American Woman"	The Guess Who
U.S. #1 POP LP	*McCartney*	Paul McCartney
U.S. #1 R&B 45	"Love on a Two-Way Street"	The Moments
U.K. #1 POP 45	"Back Home"	England World Cup Squad
U.K. #1 POP LP	*Bridge over Troubled Water*	Simon and Garfunkel

WEEK ENDING MAY 30

U.S. #1 POP 45	"Everything Is Beautiful"	Ray Stevens
U.S. #1 POP LP	*McCartney*	Paul McCartney
U.S. #1 R&B 45	"Love on a Two-Way Street"	The Moments
U.K. #1 POP 45	"Question"	The Moody Blues
U.K. #1 POP LP	*Bridge over Troubled Water*	Simon and Garfunkel

3 **Jimi Hendrix**'s live album *Band of Gypsys*, featuring his new **Billy Cox–Buddy Miles** rhythm section, goes gold.

Kinks singer **Ray Davies** makes the 6,000-mile round trip from New York to London and back again, interrupting the band's U.S. tour, in order to rerecord one word on the band's new single, "Lola." Davies changes "Coca-Cola"—a trademark that would have violated the BBC's advertising ban—to "cherry cola."

8 The **Who** play the alleged "final performance" of their rock opera, *Tommy*, at New York's Metropolitan Opera House. This and the previous night's performance are the only times a pop group has appeared at the Met.

9 **Bob Dylan** receives an honorary doctorate of music degree from Princeton University.

11 A U.S. tour planned by **Ginger Baker's Air Force** is canceled because of "the political climate," though slow ticket sales may have something to do with it as well.

12 Berlin Philharmonic Orchestra conductor **Herbert von Karajan** offers himself as a guinea pig for tests investigating the effect of drugs in performing and listening to music.

13 With their *Let It Be* album at Number One, the **Beatles** have their last Number One single in the U.S., "The Long and Winding Road."

Christine Perfect McVie releases a self-titled solo LP on the Blue Horizon label and announces that she will give up music in order to be simply Mrs. John McVie.

14 **Derek and the Dominos** make their U.K. live debut with **Dave Mason** replacing **Duane Allman** on guitar.

The **Grateful Dead** release *Workingman's Dead*, a mellow, country-flavored departure from their previous psychedelic output.

Grand Funk Railroad spends $100,000 for a block-long billboard in New York's Times Square to advertise its latest record, *Closer to Home*.

Blood, Sweat and Tears embarks on a tour of Yugoslavia, Rumania and Poland—the first tour by a Western rock band of Soviet-bloc countries

16 **Woodstock Ventures**, sponsors of the Woodstock Festival of August 1969, announces that it lost more than $1.2 million on the festival, which it hopes to recoup from sales of the *Woodstock* album, receipts from the documentary film *Woodstock*, which opened a month before, and Woodstock-related memorabilia.

21 **Pete Townshend**'s inopportune use of the British slang term *bomb* draws police and FBI scrutiny at the Memphis International Airport. Townshend was overheard remarking, "*Tommy* seems to be going down a bomb," meaning it was a hit. Officials heard only "bomb" and panicked.

23 Twist king **Chubby Checker** and three others are arrested at Niagara Falls after marijuana, hashish and unidentified drug capsules are found in Checker's car.

25 KRLA-FM in Pasadena, California, drops its long-running series of ten-minute daily comedy routines by the **Credibility Gap**, a hip satirical outfit, explaining that "Humor is no longer funny in today's society."

27 The Schaefer Music Festival opens its first season in New York's Central Park, with **Ray Charles** performing; later this summer the **Guess Who**, **Delaney and Bonnie**, **Mountain** and others will appear at the festival. ◆

WEEK ENDING JUNE 6

U.S. #1 POP 45	"Everything Is Beautiful"	Ray Stevens
U.S. #1 POP LP	*McCartney*	Paul McCartney
U.S. #1 R&B 45	"Love on a Two-Way Street"	The Moments
U.K. #1 POP 45	"Yellow River"	Christie
U.K. #1 POP LP	*Let It Be*	The Beatles

WEEK ENDING JUNE 13

U.S. #1 POP 45	"The Long and Winding Road"	The Beatles
U.S. #1 POP LP	*Let It Be*	The Beatles
U.S. #1 R&B 45	"Love on a Two-Way Street	The Moments
U.K. #1 POP 45	"In the Summertime"	Mungo Jerry
U.K. #1 POP LP	*Let It Be*	The Beatles

WEEK ENDING JUNE 20

U.S. #1 POP 45	"The Long and Winding Road"	The Beatles
U.S. #1 POP LP	*Let It Be*	The Beatles
U.S. #1 R&B 45	"The Love You Save"	The Jackson 5
U.K. #1 POP 45	"In the Summertime"	Mungo Jerry
U.K. #1 POP LP	*Let It Be*	The Beatles

WEEK ENDING JUNE 27

U.S. #1 POP 45	"The Love You Save"	The Jackson 5
U.S. #1 POP LP	*Let It Be*	The Beatles
U.S. #1 R&B 45	"The Love You Save"	The Jackson 5
U.K. #1 POP 45	"In the Summertime"	Mungo Jerry
U.K. #1 POP LP	*Bridge over Troubled Water*	Simon and Garfunkel

1 The "American Top Forty" syndicated AM radio show, hosted by **Casey Casem**, debuts in Boston, Philadelphia, Detroit, St. Louis, San Antonio, San Francisco, San Bernardino, San Diego, Albany, Minneapolis and Honolulu.

3 The three-day Atlanta Pop Festival opens at Middle Georgia Raceway in Byron, Georgia. The crowd of 200,000 sees and hears **Jimi Hendrix** (playing his version of the "Star-Spangled Banner" on July 4), **B. B. King**, **John Sebastian**, **Mountain**, **Procol Harum**, **Jethro Tull**, **Poco**, **Johnny Winter**, the **Allman Brothers Band** and many others. As the festival ends, local doctors beg federal and state authorities to declare the festival a health disaster area because of an "out-of-control drug situation." Earlier, the festival promoters threw open the gates after thousands of youths outside pressed for free entry. Two days after the festival, Georgia Governor **Lester Maddox** announces he will seek legislation banning rock festivals in the state.

4 The FBI, in cooperation with special investigators from the Recording Industry Association of America and the National Association of Merchandizers, opens an investigation into counterfeit record rings in twelve states, as sales of bootlegs proliferate, cutting legitimate album sales.

8 The **Everly Brothers** are hosts of their own ABC-TV variety show, which runs through September 16, 1970.

10 After a "tense flirtation" with rock acts in 1969, the Newport Jazz Festival reverts to its traditional all-jazz format.

12 South Dakota judge **S. K. Hicks**, who claims to be the inspiration for Johnny Cash's hit single "A Boy Named Sue," receives autographed records and photos from Cash.

Janis Joplin plays her first gig with the new **Full Tilt Boogie Band** in Louisville, Kentucky.

14 Brave New World Productions announces that some proceeds of its three-day Randall's Island Rock Festival, scheduled to open July 17 on Randall's Island, New York, will go to "community groups" like the Young Lords and the White Panther Party.

17 The mayor of Love Valley, North Carolina, hails the Love Valley Rock Festival scheduled to start there the next day, saying, "I'm the first mayor to sanction one of these things . . . I don't think the kids will let me down." However, Mayor Barker fails to get the audience to pray and sing the national anthem with him, one youth is wounded by a shotgun blast in a scuffle with a sheriff, and one youth dies of heat stroke. The **Allman Brothers**, among others, perform.

18 The Randall's Island Rock Festival's gates are crashed and all comers are admitted free; more than 30,000 people end up seeing performances by **Jimi Hendrix**, **Grand Funk Railroad**, **Little Richard**, **Elephant's Memory**, **Steppenwolf**, **Jethro Tull** and others. Afterward, the festival's producers call it a financial disaster, allegedly because of those "community groups" who had threatened to call it a free festival if they weren't guaranteed some proceeds.

23 Bowing to pressure from local government and citizens, a New Haven, Connecticut, district court rules that the Powder Ridge Rock Festival, scheduled for July 30 through August 1 at the Powder Ridge Ski Resort in Middlefield, Connecticut, would create a public nuisance and can't be held. However, over 18,000 tickets have already been sold at twenty dollars apiece. Over the next few days, performers like **Janis Joplin**, **Chuck Berry**, **Led Zeppelin** and **Sly and the Family Stone** are informed of a ban on their appearance at the festival site. Though state police post signs along the routes to the site that there will be no festival, crowds keep coming anyway.

29 The **Rolling Stones**, whose contract with Britain's Decca Records has just expired, and who've been discussing forming their own record company for some time, inform their business manager, **Allen Klein**, that "neither he nor ABKCO Industries have any authority to negotiate recording contracts on their behalf in the future." Klein took over the Stones' management and publishing on August 28, 1965.

30 Over 30,000 people have showed up at the Powder Ridge Rock Festival site, even though police barricaded all roads leading to the festival site for up to 2 miles. All utilities on the site are cut off, but the kids party anyway. The festival's promoters are nowhere to be found. On July 31, **Melanie** and two local rock bands play, temporarily checking a slow exodus from the area. Doctors report over 800 bad drug reactions among the audience. The Powder Ridge promoters later tried to stage followup concerts at Yankee Stadium in New York and Robert F. Kennedy Stadium in Washington, D.C., to no avail. ◆

WEEK ENDING JULY 4

U.S. #1 POP 45	"The Love You Save"	The Jackson 5
U.S. #1 POP LP	Let It Be	The Beatles
U.S. #1 R&B 45	"The Love You Save"	The Jackson 5
U.K. #1 POP 45	"In the Summertime"	Mungo Jerry
U.K. #1 POP LP	Bridge over Troubled Water	Simon and Garfunkel

WEEK ENDING JULY 11

U.S. #1 POP 45	"Mama Told Me Not to Come"	Three Dog Night
U.S. #1 POP LP	Woodstock	various artists
U.S. #1 R&B 45	"The Love You Save"	The Jackson 5
U.K. #1 POP 45	"All Right Now"	Free
U.K. #1 POP LP	Bridge over Troubled Water	Simon and Garfunkel

WEEK ENDING JULY 18

U.S. #1 POP 45	"Mama Told Me Not to Come"	Three Dog Night
U.S. #1 POP LP	Woodstock	various artists
U.S. #1 R&B 45	"The Love You Save"	The Jackson 5
U.K. #1 POP 45	"All Right Now"	Free
U.K. #1 POP LP	Let It Be	The Beatles

WEEK ENDING JULY 25

U.S. #1 POP 45	"(They Long to Be) Close to You"	The Carpenters
U.S. #1 POP LP	Woodstock	various artists
U.S. #1 R&B 45	"The Love You Save"	The Jackson 5
U.K. #1 POP 45	"All Right Now"	Free
U.K. #1 POP LP	Bridge over Troubled Water	Simon and Garfunkel

4 The Medicine Ball Caravan, featuring the **Grateful Dead** and hippiescene people like **Wavy Gravy (Hugh Romney)** of the Hog Farm, becomes rock's first and last movable festival as it leaves San Francisco on a cross-country trek, pulling seven tie-dyed tepees along with it. The caravan will eventually reach the United Kingdom, document itself with an album, and its own rock band, **Stoneground**, will emerge from it.

Canadian Woodstock, Quebec's first rock festival, ends disastrously: only 10,000 people show up, and only one of twelve scheduled performers appears.

6 On the twenty-fifth anniversary of America's dropping of the atom bomb in Hiroshima, 20,000 people paying from $5.50 to $8.50 apiece gather at New York's Shea Stadium for an antiwar rock festival that lasts twelve hours and includes performances by **John Sebastian, Janis Joplin, Paul Simon, Paul Butterfield, Steppenwolf, Johnny Winter** and the cast of *Hair.* The attendance is well below expectations, and a similar concert planned for the same day in Philadelphia never comes off at all because of legal hassles concerning the concert's length and the rental fee for JFK Stadium.

8 Thousands of American youths are refused entry to Canada for the Strawberry Fields Rock Festival in Mosport, Ontario, on grounds that they "failed to produce adequate monies to support themselves" ("a fairly routine action," says an Ottawa immigration official). Over 8,000 Americans make it there anyway.

Bessie Smith, "Empress of Blues" and prime inspiration for **Janis Joplin** and countless other blues singers, finally gets a stone for her grave in Philadelphia's Mount Lawn Cemetery. Smith died during a tour on September 26, 1937, in Clarksdale, Mississippi, bleeding to death after she was refused admittance to a whites-only hospital for treatment of injuries she sustained in an auto accident. She was buried in an unmarked grave in Mount Lawn. Her tombstone, which Joplin paid for, bears an epitaph written by John Hammond, an executive of her label, CBS Records: THE GREATEST BLUES SINGER IN THE WORLD WILL NEVER STOP SINGING.

11 The Ann Arbor Blues and Jazz Festival in Michigan opens with performances by **John Lee Hooker** and **Big Mama Thornton**, as well as unscheduled appearances by **Johnny Winter** and **Buddy Guy**. The festival's producers pass collection baskets through the audience, hoping to alleviate their estimated $20,000 deficit.

12 **Bob Dylan, Joan Baez, Arlo Guthrie, Ramblin' Jack Elliott** and others appear at a **Woody Guthrie** memorial concert held at California's Hollywood Bowl.

15 ESP Disk, the adventurous avant-garde jazz label that printed liner notes in Esperanto, buys exclusive manufacturing and distribution rights to recordings by **Charles Manson**, currently on trial in the Tate, LaBianca murder case.

17 **Christine Perfect McVie** joins **Fleetwood Mac**, the band co-founded by her husband, John McVie, two months after announcing she would retire from performing.

22 **Elvis Presley** announces the six-date itinerary of his first tour since 1958, to start in Phoenix, Arizona, on September 9 and to end September 14 in Mobile, Alabama.

25 British singer and pianist **Elton John** makes his first U.S. appearance at Los Angeles' Troubador, kicking off a seventeen-day tour.

Emerson, Lake and Palmer make their world debut at Plymouth Guild Hall, Plymouth, England.

26 The Isle of Wight Pop Festival begins in England. **Jimi Hendrix** makes his last public appearance here. **Bob Dylan, Joan Baez, Richie Havens** and **Joni Mitchell** are among those who appear. Hundreds of fans shouting "Music is free!" force their way in, joining the 250,000 already in attendance. During Joni Mitchell's set, a man jumps onstage, grabs the mike, and shouts, "This is just a hippie concentration camp!" Mitchell bursts into tears. The festival ends on August 31. ◆

WEEK ENDING AUGUST 1

U.S. #1 POP 45	"(They Long to Be) Close to You"	The Carpenters
U.S. #1 POP LP	*Blood, Sweat and Tears 3*	Blood, Sweat and Tears
U.S. #1 R&B 45	"Signed, Sealed, Delivered (I'm Yours)"	Stevie Wonder
U.K. #1 POP 45	"Lola"	The Kinks
U.K. #1 POP LP	*Let It Be*	The Beatles

WEEK ENDING AUGUST 8

U.S. #1 POP 45	"(They Long to Be) Close to You"	The Carpenters
U.S. #1 POP LP	*Blood, Sweat and Tears 3*	Blood, Sweat and Tears
U.S. #1 R&B 45	"Signed, Sealed, Delivered (I'm Yours)"	Stevie Wonder
U.K. #1 POP 45	"The Wonder of You"	Elvis Presley
U.K. #1 POP LP	*Let It Be*	The Beatles

WEEK ENDING AUGUST 15

U.S. #1 POP 45	"(They Long to Be) Close to You"	The Carpenters
U.S. #1 POP LP	*Blood, Sweat and Tears 3*	Blood, Sweat and Tears
U.S. #1 R&B 45	"Signed, Sealed, Delivered (I'm Yours)"	Stevie Wonder
U.K. #1 POP 45	"The Wonder of You"	Elvis Presley
U.K. #1 POP LP	*Let It Be*	The Beatles

WEEK ENDING AUGUST 22

U.S. #1 POP 45	"Make It with You"	Bread
U.S. #1 POP LP	*Cosmo's Factory*	Creedence Clearwater Revival
U.S. #1 R&B 45	"Signed, Sealed, Delivered (I'm Yours)"	Stevie Wonder
U.K. #1 POP 45	"The Wonder of You"	Elvis Presley
U.K. #1 POP LP	*Bridge over Troubled Water*	Simon and Garfunkel

WEEK ENDING AUGUST 29

U.S. #1 POP 45	"War"	Edwin Starr
U.S. #1 POP LP	*Cosmo's Factory*	Creedence Clearwater Revival
U.S. #1 R&B 45	"Signed, Sealed, Delivered (I'm Yours)"	Stevie Wonder
U.K. #1 POP 45	"Tears of a Clown"	Smokey Robinson and the Miracles
U.K. #1 POP LP	*Bridge over Troubled Water*	Simon and Garfunkel

3 *Rolling Stone* reports that the **Bob Dylan** bootleg *Great White Wonder* has sold over 350,000 copies and that the **Dave Clark Five** have broken up.

Also, at the Palermo Pop '70 Festival in Italy, **Arthur Brown** (of the Crazy World of . . . and Fire fame) has been arrested and imprisoned for four days in solitary confinement, after he'd set fire to his helmet and stripped naked during his stage performance at the festival. The audience threw shoes, food and bottles at him. While in solitary, Brown was given a note signed by over 200 locals telling him to get out of Italy and stay out.

3 Singer/guitarist **Al Wilson** of **Canned Heat** is found dead beside an empty bottle of barbiturates in fellow-bandmember **Bob Hite**'s garden in Topanga Canyon, Los Angeles. He was 27.

12 "Josie and the Pussycats," a Saturday morning cartoon about an all-girl rock band, debuts on CBS-TV. It runs through September 2, 1972.

15 Vice President **Spiro Agnew** says the youth of America are being "brainwashed into a drug culture" by rock music, movies, books and underground newspapers.

16 A *Melody Maker* poll finds that **Led Zeppelin** has replaced the **Beatles** as Great Britain's most popular group—the first time the Beatles haven't been Number One in eight years.

18 **Jimi Hendrix** dies in his London apartment. The death certificate lists the cause of death as "inhalation of vomit due to barbiturate intoxication." Later, insufficient evidence of circumstances will lead to an open verdict on his demise. Nonetheless, some contend that if Hendrix had been put in an upright sitting position rather than left lying on his back, he might not have suffocated.

FCC Commissioner **Nicholas Johnson** says that Vice President **Spiro Agnew**, instead of attacking rock music for spreading "drug culture" among the nation's youth, should worry about the political contributions of corporations that manufacture and sell drugs, cigarettes and liquor.

20 In Miami, **Jim Morrison** of the Doors is acquitted on charges of "lewd and lascivious behavior" but is found guilty of indecent exposure and profanity.

23 Vice President **Spiro Agnew** responds to FCC Commissioner **Nicholas Johnson**'s charges, accusing Johnson of "backing the kind of radical-liberal philosophy of permissiveness and self-flagellation that has encouraged so many of our youth to turn to marijuana and worse."

26 Tamla-Motown Records reveals that the **Jackson 5** have sold 10 million singles worldwide in nine months ("I Want You Back," "ABC," "The Love You Save")—an unsurpassed record for a period.

28 A unique new music show debuts on Hollywood TV station KCET, Channel 28. "Boboquivari" (a Hopi Indian word for the neck of an hourglass, "the place where time begins") presents rock, pop, folk and other performers in an informal, intimate studio setting—but with no host, no format and no lip-synching. The first shows feature **Tim Buckley**, **Ramblin' Jack Elliott**, **Roberta Flack** and **Freddie King**.

29 **Eric Burdon and War**'s "Spill the Wine" and **Dawn**'s debut single, "Candida," go gold. ♦

WEEK ENDING SEPTEMBER 5

U.S. #1 POP 45	"War"	Edwin Starr
U.S. #1 POP LP	*Cosmo's Factory*	Creedence Clearwater Revival
U.S. #1 R&B 45	"Signed, Sealed, Delivered (I'm Yours)"	Stevie Wonder
U.K. #1 POP 45	"The Tears of a Clown"	Smokey Robinson and the Miracles
U.K. #1 POP LP	*A Question of Balance*	The Moody Blues

WEEK ENDING SEPTEMBER 12

U.S. #1 POP 45	"War"	Edwin Starr
U.S. #1 POP LP	*Cosmo's Factory*	Creedence Clearwater Revival
U.S. #1 R&B 45	"Don't Play That Song"	Aretha Franklin
U.K. #1 POP 45	"The Tears of a Clown"	Smokey Robinson and the Miracles
U.K. #1 POP LP	*A Question of Balance*	The Moody Blues

WEEK ENDING SEPTEMBER 19

U.S. #1 POP 45	"Ain't No Mountain High Enough"	Diana Ross
U.S. #1 POP LP	*Cosmo's Factory*	Creedence Clearwater Revival
U.S. #1 R&B 45	"Don't Play That Song"	Aretha Franklin
U.K. #1 POP 45	"The Tears of a Clown"	Smokey Robinson and the Miracles
U.K. #1 POP LP	*A Question of Balance*	The Moody Blues

WEEK ENDING SEPTEMBER 26

U.S. #1 POP 45	"Ain't No Mountain High Enough"	Diana Ross
U.S. #1 POP LP	*Cosmo's Factory*	Creedence Clearwater Revival
U.S. #1 R&B 45	"Don't Play That Song"	Aretha Franklin
U.K. #1 POP 45	"Band of Gold"	Freda Payne
U.K. #1 POP LP	*Bridge over Troubled Water*	Simon and Garfunkel

1 **Jimi Hendrix** is buried in his hometown, Seattle, Washington.

Curtis Mayfield has left the Impressions, a soul group, to begin a solo career and to found his own label, Curtom, *Rolling Stone* reports.

2 Chicago's Aragon Ballroom permanently excludes rock & roll shows. Manager **Scott Deneen** issues this statement: "We can no longer guarantee the security and safety of people attending Aragon rock shows. . . ." A few nights before, at a concert by jazz-rock band the **Flock**, nineteen-year-old audience member Terry Galasby, under the influence of LSD, began taking off his clothes. Removed to an upstairs security office by authorities, Galasby broke free and, declaring himself to be Batman,

jumped out of the window, breaking an arm and fracturing his skull.

3 Former **Cream** bassist **Jack Bruce** joins ex-**Miles Davis** sidemen **John McLaughlin, Larry Young** and **Tony Williams** to form one of the first jazz-rock fusion groups, **Lifetime**.

4 **Janis Joplin** is found dead of an apparent heroin overdose in her room at Hollywood's Landmark Hotel. The twenty-seven-year-old singer had just finished recording her second solo album, *Pearl.*

10 The running battle between Vice President **Spiro Agnew** and FCC Commissioner **Johnson** continues: Johnson, in response to Agnew's charge that rock music drives young people to drugs, plays rock music during a speech,

saying that Agnew would do well to listen to song lyrics to understand what's happening in the country.

11 WNET, New York's public broadcasting TV station, begins "Fanfare," a series of programs on Fillmore East rock concerts.

12 *Jesus Christ Superstar* is released with a presentation at St. Peter's Lutheran Church in New York, where "rock opera" composers **Andrew Lloyd Webber** and **Tim Rice** explain their project.

Bill Graham holds an auction of rock memorabilia and artifacts at New York's Fillmore East to benefit peace candidates. Among the items on the block are a guitar bashed to bits by the Who's **Pete Townshend**, **Ian Anderson**'s flute, a multicolored bra tossed to the

Grateful Dead's **Jerry Garcia** by an audience member at the Avalon Ballroom and a spiral notebook containing the original scrawled lyrics to **Joni Mitchell**'s first album, *Songs to a Seagull.*

Two hundred students from Pretoria raid a Johannesburg, South Africa, rock festival and assault audience members, claiming they object that the festival is being held on President Kruger's Day, a national holiday.

24 President **Richard Nixon**, in a speech to a White House radio broadcasters conference, appeals for rock lyrics to be screened and those urging drug use to be banned.

Billboard predicts that "head shops"—drug paraphernalia boutiques—will replace rack jobbers as record retailers to the youth markets. The magazine also reports that Las Vegas' International Hotel now offers "contemporary rock nightly in the Crown Room . . . giving hard rock a dignified look."

28 **Baby Huey**, born **James T. Ramey** in 1954, is found dead on the bathroom floor of a South Side hotel room in Chicago. Baby Huey had a minor underground hit in 1968 with the rollicking soul anthem "Mighty Mighty Spade and Whitey," backed by his band, the **Babysitters**. Huey had also appeared on **Merv Griffin**'s television show and, after one New York performance, was asked by the **Baron de Rothschild** to play at his daughter's debutante ball in Paris. The death was ruled due to natural causes; Huey weighed over 350 pounds. He was recording an album for **Curtis Mayfield**'s Curtom label at the time of his death.

30 **Jim Morrison** is sentenced to six months in jail and fined $500 for exposing himself in Miami. ◆

WEEK ENDING OCTOBER 3

U.S. #1 POP 45	"Ain't No Mountain High Enough"	Diana Ross
U.S. #1 POP LP	*Cosmo's Factory*	Creedence Clearwater Revival
U.S. #1 R&B 45	"Ain't No Mountain High Enough"	Diana Ross
U.K. #1 POP 45	"Band of Gold"	Freda Payne
U.K. #1 POP LP	*Bridge over Troubled Water*	Simon and Garfunkel

WEEK ENDING OCTOBER 10

U.S. #1 POP 45	"Cracklin' Rosie"	Neil Diamond
U.S. #1 POP LP	*Cosmo's Factory*	Creedence Clearwater Revival
U.S. #1 R&B 45	"I'll Be There"	The Jackson 5
U.K. #1 POP 45	"Band of Gold"	Freda Payne
U.K. #1 POP LP	*Bridge over Troubled Water*	Simon and Garfunkel

WEEK ENDING OCTOBER 17

U.S. #1 POP 45	"I'll Be There"	The Jackson 5
U.S. #1 POP LP	*Cosmo's Factory*	Creedence Clearwater Revival
U.S. #1 R&B 45	"I'll Be There"	The Jackson 5
U.K. #1 POP 45	"Band of Gold"	Freda Payne
U.K. #1 POP LP	*Paranoid*	Black Sabbath

WEEK ENDING OCTOBER 24

U.S. #1 POP 45	"I'll Be There"	The Jackson 5
U.S. #1 POP LP	*Abraxas*	Santana
U.S. #1 R&B 45	"I'll Be There"	The Jackson 5
U.K. #1 POP 45	"Band of Gold"	Freda Payne
U.K. #1 POP LP	*Paranoid*	Black Sabbath

WEEK ENDING OCTOBER 31

U.S. #1 POP 45	"I'll Be There"	The Jackson 5
U.S. #1 POP LP	*Led Zeppelin III*	Led Zeppelin
U.S. #1 R&B 45	"I'll Be There"	The Jackson 5
U.K. #1 POP 45	"Black Night"	Deep Purple
U.K. #1 POP LP	*Led Zeppelin III*	Led Zeppelin

2 Gold records go to the **Rolling Stones'** *Get Yer Ya-Ya's Out!* (just a month after its release), the **Moody Blues'** *A Question of Balance*, **Neil Young's** *After the Goldrush* and **Jimi Hendrix** and **Otis Redding's** *Live at Monterey*.

4 **Jethro Tull** and **McKendree Spring** perform in a sold-out Carnegie Hall benefit for Phoenix House, a drug-rehabilitation center.

5 Midway through a **Beach Boys** show at L.A.'s Whiskey-a-Go-Go, **Brian Wilson**—making one of his very rare stage appearances—loses his balance several times and has to be helped offstage. His right ear—the better of the two—sustains "severe damage" because of the volume level onstage.

7 MGM Records President **Mike Curb** drops eighteen acts from his roster in a move to discredit musicians who "exploit and promote hard drugs through music." Among the acts dropped are such alleged "drug advocates" as **Connie Francis**, the **Cowsills** and the **Judy Garland Estate**—but *not* **Eric Burdon**. CBS Records chief **Clive Davis** calls Curb's announcement "an irresponsible grandstand play."

8 **Jim Morrison**, on this, his twenty-seventh birthday, records the poetry that the other members of the Doors would set to music after his death and issue on the 1978 album *An American Prayer*.

9 The **Moody Blues** earn a gold LP—their fifth in 1970—with *In Search of the Lost Chord*.

11 Two very different albums entitled *Plastic Ono Band*—one by **John Lennon** and the other by **Yoko Ono**—are released simultaneously on Apple in the U.S. and in the U.K. Also, today, **Bob Dylan's** book *Tarantula* is published by Bantam Books. The book is a collection of first person narratives and poems written mostly between 1965 and 1966. Although many are curious—one reviewer claims to have paid $210 for a set of galleys—the book is only warmly received.

12 The **Doors** make their last appearance as a quartet in New Orleans. **Ray Manzarek**, **Robbie Krieger** and **John Densmore** later recall watching **Jim Morrison** lose "all his energy" as the concert drags to the end.

17 An **Elton John** concert in New York City is broadcast live over WPLJ-FM and is recorded for his *11-17-70* LP.

18 **Jerry Lee Lewis** and wife **Myra Brown** are divorced in Memphis, with Brown claiming their marriage "has turned into a nightmare." The union started in controversy: she is his cousin and was just fourteen years old when they married; the resulting public outcry nearly ended his career.

19 **James Brown**, Godfather of Soul, marries **Deidre Yvonne Jenkins** on the front porch of her Barnwell, South Carolina, house.

20 For the second time this year, **Kinks** singer **Ray Davies** flies to a London studio to rerecord one word in a new Kinks single. The last time (in June) it was to change *Coca-Cola* to *cherry cola* in "Lola" in order to avoid copyright conflicts. This time, Ray must change a line from "Apeman" "The air pollution is a-foggin' up" which sounds too much like "a-fuckin'."

21 *Moon Walk*, an original rock musical for children by **Betty Jean Lifton**, opens at New York's City Center. According to its press handout, *Moon Walk* is "science set to rock music, telling what would happen if children could go to the moon to see for themselves what's up there." Music and lyrics for the show are by a group called the **Open Window**, which includes **Peter Schickele**, famous for his "P.D.Q. Bach" spoofs of baroque music.

25 Saxophonist **Albert Ayler**, a giant of the jazz avant-garde and a major influence on **Frank Zappa**, among others, is found drowned in New York's Hudson River at age thirty-four. Rumors that he was found tied to a jukebox remain unconfirmed.

27 **George Harrison** releases his solo album *All Things Must Pass*, produced by **Phil Spector** and featuring dozens of noted players, including **Eric Clapton**, **Dave Mason**, **Ringo Starr** and **Jim Gordon**. The album is on Apple. ♦

WEEK ENDING NOVEMBER 7

U.S. #1 POP 45	"I'll Be There"	The Jackson 5
U.S. #1 POP LP	*Led Zeppelin III*	Led Zeppelin
U.S. #1 R&B 45	"I'll Be There"	The Jackson 5
U.K. #1 POP 45	"Woodstock"	Matthews Southern Comfort
U.K. #1 POP LP	*Motown Chartbusters, Volume Four*	various artists

WEEK ENDING NOVEMBER 14

U.S. #1 POP 45	"I'll Be There"	The Jackson 5
U.S. #1 POP LP	*Led Zeppelin III*	Led Zeppelin
U.S. #1 R&B 45	"I'll Be There"	The Jackson 5
U.K. #1 POP 45	"Woodstock"	Matthews Southern Comfort
U.K. #1 POP LP	*Led Zeppelin III*	Led Zeppelin

WEEK ENDING NOVEMBER 21

U.S. #1 POP 45	"I Think I Love You"	The Partridge Family
U.S. #1 POP LP	*Led Zeppelin III*	Led Zeppelin
U.S. #1 R&B 45	"Super Bad (Parts One and Two)"	James Brown
U.K. #1 POP 45	"Woodstock"	Matthews Southern Comfort
U.K. #1 POP LP	*Led Zeppelin III*	Led Zeppelin

WEEK ENDING NOVEMBER 28

U.S. #1 POP 45	"I Think I Love You"	The Partridge Family
U.S. #1 POP LP	*Abraxas*	Santana
U.S. #1 R&B 45	"Super Bad (Parts One and Two)"	James Brown
U.K. #1 POP 45	"Voodoo Child"	The Jimi Hendrix Experience
U.K. #1 POP LP	*Led Zeppelin III*	Led Zeppelin

2 **Eric Burdon** is launching a CURB THE CLAP bumpersticker campaign aimed at fighting what he calls "the number-one sickness in the record business today—VD," *Rolling Stone* reports. Burdon's manager, **Steve Gold**, denies that it has anything to do with MGM Records president **Mike Curb**'s recent announcement that he was dropping eighteen acts from his roster because their music advocated drug use. "It's because Eric has the clap," says Gold. "He says from age fifteen to twenty-six he only had it once, but it's happened three or four times since. For every donation to the L.A. Free Clinic, Eric will send out a CURB THE CLAP bumpersticker. VD has more effect on this industry than any drug."

4 *Supersession*, an album that evolved out of an ad hoc studio jam session with **Mike Bloomfield**, **Al Kooper** and **Steve Stills**, is certified gold.

6 *Gimme Shelter*, **Albert and David Maysles'** documentary film about the **Rolling Stones'** 1969 tour of the U.S., premieres on the anniversary of the Altamont concert.

Nearly 200 Public Broadcasting stations around the United States air a sixty-minute show called *San Francisco Rock: Go Ride the Music*, featuring performances by and interviews with the **Jefferson Airplane**, **Jerry Garcia** of the **Grateful Dead**, **Quicksilver Messenger Service** and **David Crosby**.

12 Rock critic **John Mendelsohn**'s band, **Christopher Milk**, arouses the ire of **Doug Weston**, owner of the Troubador club in Los Angeles. At a Monday night audition there, the band's lead singer, **Mr. Twister**, wreaks havoc by pouring hot wax all over himself, biting audience members, overturning tables and spilling drinks in customer's laps.

Charges of "larceny by trick" are filed against **Little Richard** in Miami Beach, Florida, by Blacks, Inc., a black advocacy and self-help group that alleges the veteran rocker pocketed $250 he'd solicited for Blacks, Inc. Little Richard claims that all he wants is a receipt, and then he'll give them their money. A week later, the charges are dropped.

16 In one day, five singles and five albums by **Creedence Clearwater Revival** are certified gold: "Down on the Corner," "Lookin' out My Back Door," "Travelin' Band," "Bad Moon Rising," "Up around the Bend" and *Cosmo's Factory, Willy and the Poor Boys, Green River, Bayou Country* and *Creedence Clearwater Revival*.

17 The **Beach Boys** play a command performance for **Princess Margaret** at London's Royal Albert Hall.

18 **Creedence Clearwater**'s latest album, *Pendulum*, is added to their gold cache. And **Bob Dylan**'s second album, *Freewheelin'* (vintage 1963), is certified gold.

19 President **Richard Nixon** commends MGM chief **Mike Curb** for taking the initiative in ridding the music industry of drug users through his well-publicized dismissal of eighteen MGM acts who supposedly advocated drug use.

21 Three new albums are certified gold: **Traffic**'s reunion album, *John Barleycorn Must Die*, the original British studio recording of *Jesus Christ Superstar* and **Judy Collins'** *In My Life*.

23 **Joni Mitchell**, who's gained recognition as a songwriter through **Judy Collins'** recording of "Both Sides of Now," and renditions of "Woodstock" by **Matthews Southern Comfort** and **Crosby, Stills, Nash and Young**, earns her first gold disc as a performer with her third album, *Ladies of the Canyon*.

24 New York garbage analyst and Dylanologist **A. J. Weberman**, in an article for *Rolling Stone*, sheds light on a line in **Bob Dylan**'s "If Dogs Run Free" from the *New Morning* album: "The words are well-articulated and easy to understand until Bob sings, 'Oh winds which rush my tail to thee solglet me tone de.' When the last five unintelligible syllables are played backward at a slightly slower speed, one distinctly hears, 'If Mars invades us.'"

31 On the last day of the Year the **Beatles** Broke Up, **Paul McCartney** files a writ in London High Court against "The Beatles Co.," including Messrs. **John Lennon**, **George Harrison** and **Ringo Starr**, seeking the legal dissolution of the Beatles' partnership. ◆

WEEK ENDING DECEMBER 5

U.S. #1 POP 45	"I Think I Love You"	The Partridge Family
U.S. #1 POP LP	*Abraxas*	Santana
U.S. #1 R&B 45	"The Tears of a Clown"	Smokey Robinson and the Miracles
U.K. #1 POP 45	"I Hear You Knocking"	Dave Edmunds
U.K. #1 POP LP	*Led Zeppelin III*	Led Zeppelin

WEEK ENDING DECEMBER 12

U.S. #1 POP 45	"The Tears of a Clown"	Smokey Robinson and the Miracles
U.S. #1 POP LP	*Abraxas*	Santana
U.S. #1 R&B 45	"The Tears of a Clown"	Smokey Robinson and the Miracles
U.K. #1 POP 45	"I Hear You Knocking"	Dave Edmunds
U.K. #1 POP LP	*Led Zeppelin III*	Led Zeppelin

WEEK ENDING DECEMBER 19

U.S. #1 POP 45	"The Tears of a Clown"	Smokey Robinson and the Miracles
U.S. #1 POP LP	*Abraxas*	Santana
U.S. #1 R&B 45	"The Tears of a Clown"	Smokey Robinson and the Miracles
U.K. #1 POP 45	"I Hear You Knocking"	Dave Edmunds
U.K. #1 POP LP	*Motown Chartbusters, Volume Four*	various artists

WEEK ENDING DECEMBER 26

U.S. #1 POP 45	"My Sweet Lord"/"Isn't It a Pity"	George Harrison
U.S. #1 POP LP	*Abraxas*	Santana
U.S. #1 R&B 45	"Stoned Love"	The Supremes
U.K. #1 POP 45	"When I'm Dead and Gone"	McGuiness Flint
U.K. #1 POP LP	*Led Zeppelin III*	Led Zeppelin

1971

Where were we at in 1971? A quick scan of the top of the pop charts reveals the preponderance of such innocuous treacle as "Joy to the World," "One Bad Apple," "Knock Three Times" and "Admiral Halsey," with only occasional instances of "real" rock & roll like "Brown Sugar," "Me and Bobby McGee," "Power to the People" and "Won't Get Fooled Again" breaking through. One could almost have thought this was 1961, not '71, considering the impetus rock's counterculture had lost. Still, there were some instances of rock championing sociopolitical causes: George Harrison's Concerts for Bangla Desh, the Save the Seals campaign, Bob Dylan's "George Jackson" and John Lennon's benefits for John Sinclair. But just as often, it was soul music that most spectacularly, and popularly, captured the increasingly troubled tone of the times, as in Sly and the Family Stone's *There's a Riot Goin' On* and Marvin Gaye's aptly titled LP *What's Going On,* featuring such cuts as "Inner City Blues" and "Mercy Mercy Me (The Ecology)."

In March, Brewer and Shipley's "One Toke over the Line" was banned by most of America's radio stations because its title and refrain referred to marijuana smoking; it became a hit anyway. In April, Barbra Streisand smoked joints on stage in Las Vegas. In May, Grand Funk Railroad—the pet peeve of just about every rock critic—was snubbed by rock's fifth column at a meet-the-press reception in New York City; a month later, they sold out a show at Shea Stadium in less than three days and broke that venue's record for net box-office receipts, which was previously held by the Beatles. In April, New York's New School for Social Research became the first college to mark the institutionalization of rock with a course in rock & roll.

As Jim Morrison died in his Paris retreat, Marc Bolan and T. Rex launched the glitter-rock craze in Britain, which would further rock's dalliance with decadence and move rock rebellion into the shallower waters of fashion and style wars. In February, Pete Townshend of the Who tried—and failed—to make a big splash with his multimedia *Lifehouse* show, which he hoped would "completely negate anybody's desire to see rock in its present form." And at the Celebration of Life festival-fiasco in June, Guru Yogi Bahjan asked the audience for a moment of silence at the start of the show. One audience member immediately responded, "Fuck you, let's boogie!"

2 **George Harrison**'s *All Things Must Pass*— his first LP as an ex-**Beatle**—hits Number One in the U.S. Long regarded as the quiet, shy Beatle, who usually was able to get only one or two of his compositions on any Beatles album, Harrison has made an ambitious double album that also includes a bonus "jam" disc. The album contains two hits, "What Is Life" (#10) and "My Sweet Lord." Years later, the latter will cost Harrison plenty in a plagiarism lawsuit.

4 The film *Performance,* starring **Rolling Stone Mick Jagger**, premieres in London two years after it was filmed. Jagger plays a jaded, decadent rock star, and at one point shares a bathtub and a bed with actress **Anita Pallenberg**, the live-in girlfriend of bandmate **Keith Richards** and the former girlfriend of the late **Brian Jones**.

John Lennon/Plastic Ono Band release "Mother," one of Lennon's "primal scream" recordings. Apparently, America isn't ready for this cathartic work, and "Mother" stalls on the chart at #43, making it Lennon's second least successful solo single.

6 **Neil Young** returns to his homeland of Canada for his first concerts there since his pre-stardom coffeehouse days. His first Canadian performance is at Vancouver's Queen Elizabeth Theater.

9 The U.S. Jaycees present **Elvis Presley** with an award honoring him as one of the "ten outstanding young men of America." One of the other recipients is Nixon's press secretary, **Ronald Ziegler**.

Upon receiving the award, Presley makes a short speech. A recording of that speech was later made available on the soundtrack to the documentary *This Is Elvis.*

10 Making a rare public appearance, **Bob Dylan** accompanies country star **Earl Scruggs** on "East Virginia Blues" and "Nashville Skyline Rag" for a public-television documentary. The latter of the two is later released as part of an LP titled *Earl Scruggs—His Family and His Friends.*

22 The **Joe Cocker** film *Mad Dogs and Englishmen* premieres at London's Festival Palace. The movie, a documentary of Cocker's **Mad Dogs and Englishmen** tour, features performances by Cocker, **Leon Russell**, **Rita Coolidge** and others.

25 **Grace Slick** and **Paul Kantner** of the **Jefferson Airplane** become the proud parents of a baby girl, which the couple (not married) names **China**. Originally, the child was to be named "god," or at least so claimed Grace in October 1970. "No last name, no capital *G.* And he can change his name when he feels like it." China checked in weighing six and one-quarter pounds.

Charles Manson and three female members of his "family" are found guilty of one count of conspiracy to commit murder and seven counts of murder in the first degree and are sentenced to life imprisonment. The convictions stem from the August 9, 1969, murder and mutilation of Hollywood actress **Sharon Tate** and four guests at the Bel Air mansion that Tate and her husband, **Roman Polanski**, rented, and the similar deaths by stabbing of **Leno** and **Rosemary LaBianca** in their Los Angeles home. In December, Manson, a self-described "evangelist" and sometime-associate of **Beach Boy Dennis Wilson**, was arrested along with members of his cult of followers and charged with the crimes, beginning one of the most sensational murder trials in recent history. During the trial, it was learned that Manson regarded the **Beatles** as angels who communicated to him through their music, in particular "Helter Skelter," "Piggies," "Revolution 9" and other songs on "The White Album" (**The Beatles**).

♦

WEEK ENDING JANUARY 2

U.S. #1 POP 45	"My Sweet Lord"/"Isn't It a Pity"	George Harrison
U.S. #1 POP LP	*All Things Must Pass*	George Harrison
U.S. #1 R&B 45	"Groove Me"	King Floyd
U.K. #1 POP 45	"I Hear You Knocking"	Dave Edmunds
U.K. #1 POP LP	*Andy Williams' Greatest Hits*	Andy Williams

WEEK ENDING JANUARY 9

U.S. #1 POP 45	"My Sweet Lord"/"Isn't It a Pity"	George Harrison
U.S. #1 POP LP	*All Things Must Pass*	George Harrison
U.S. #1 R&B 45	"Groove Me"	King Floyd
U.K. #1 POP 45	"Granddad"	Clive Dunn
U.K. #1 POP LP	*Andy Williams' Greatest Hits*	Andy Williams

WEEK ENDING JANUARY 16

U.S. #1 POP 45	"My Sweet Lord"/"Isn't It a Pity"	George Harrison
U.S. #1 POP LP	*All Things Must Pass*	George Harrison
U.S. #1 R&B 45	"Groove Me"	King Floyd
U.K. #1 POP 45	"Granddad"	Clive Dunn
U.K. #1 POP LP	*Bridge over Troubled Water*	Simon and Garfunkel

WEEK ENDING JANUARY 23

U.S. #1 POP 45	"Knock Three Times"	Dawn
U.S. #1 POP LP	*All Things Must Pass*	George Harrison
U.S. #1 R&B 45	"If I Were Your Woman"	Gladys Knight and the Pips
U.K. #1 POP 45	"Granddad"	Clive Dunn
U.K. #1 POP LP	*Andy Williams' Greatest Hits*	Andy Williams

WEEK ENDING JANUARY 30

U.S. #1 POP 45	"Knock Three Times"	Dawn
U.S. #1 POP LP	*All Things Must Pass*	George Harrison
U.S. #1 R&B 45	"Groove Me"	King Floyd
U.K. #1 POP 45	"My Sweet Lord"	George Harrison
U.K. #1 POP LP	*All Things Must Pass*	George Harrison

4 The **Osmonds**, a vocal group of five brothers fronted by thirteen-year-old **Donny**, receives its first gold record for $1 million worth of sales of "One Bad Apple." The song, which is clearly imitative of the **Jackson 5**'s current hits, is the Osmonds' debut for **Mike Curb**'s MGM Records. The Utah family act is already well known to fans of "The Andy Williams Show," "The Jerry Lewis Show" and other television variety shows. In the decade ahead, the Osmond name will appear on gold records for the group, as well as for Donny and his sister **Marie**.

8 **Bob Dylan**'s one-hour-long documentary film, *Eat the Document*, is screened at New York's Academy of Music (later known as the Palladium). Much of the footage is from Dylan's 1966 U.K. tour with the **Band**, filmed by **D. L. Pennebaker**, who also did Dylan's *Don't Look Back*. Performances shown include "Like a Rolling Stone," "Just like Tom Thumb's Blues" and other classics. But the film is fragmentary and difficult for most in the audience to latch onto. *Eat the Document* is not shown on TV, as the reclusive star had hoped for, until ten years later.

10 According to a report from the *New York Times*, **Frank Zappa and the Mothers of Invention** are forced to cancel a concert at the Royal Albert Hall that was to include the Royal Philharmonic Orchestra and songs from the score of *200 Motels*. Officials of the hall objected to Zappa's film *200 Motels*, finding it obscene.

15 How does one top a rock opera? Not easily. The **Who**'s **Pete Townshend** tries, however, and on this date the Who play the first of a failed series of shows for *Lifehouse*, a multimedia event, which Townshend had hoped would "completely negate anybody's desire to see rock in its present form." But *Lifehouse* doesn't work on stage, and Townshend scraps the two-record set he'd been planning. Instead, many of the songs are used for the Who's next LP, *Who's Next*, considered by many to be their finest.

16 **Alan David Passaro**, the Hell's Angel who was tried and later acquitted for

the stabbing death of **Meredith Hunter** at the Altamont Speedway in 1969, sues the **Rolling Stones**, charging that because the **Maysles** brothers' film of the event, *Gimme Shelter*, showed the stabbing, he suffered an invasion of privacy.

17 **James Taylor** makes his prime-time television debut on "The Johnny Cash Show," singing "Fire and Rain" and "Carolina on My Mind."

Elton John's eponymously titled U.S. debut goes gold. His first U.K. LP, *Empty Sky*, is not issued in the States until 1975, by which time John has become a rock star of the first magnitude. John arrived in the States amid much publicity in the summer of '70, and was hailed by the *Los Angeles Times*' **Robert Hilburn** as the first superstar of the Seventies. *Elton John* hit #4.

18 **Captain Beefheart and his Magic Band** make their New York City concert debut at Ungano's in the wake of releasing *Lick My Decals Off, Baby* (their most "commercial" album to date); they're determined to find some sort of popular acceptance of their odd mixture of Delta blues, free jazz and rock & roll. Captain Beefheart, also known as **Don Van Vliet**, would rather stay at home in his trailer on the Mojave Desert.

23 **Charley Pride** collects three gold albums on one day, one each for *10th Album, Just Plain Charley* and *In Person*. The former professional baseball player is the first black to win wide acceptance as a country & western singer. He has had six C&W Number One hits since 1969.

24 **Janis Joplin**'s *Pearl* is awarded a gold record just four months after the singer's death. Highlighted by the **Kris Kristofferson**-penned "Me and Bobby McGee," the LP enjoyed a lengthy stay at Number One and the 45 also hit Number One in March. ◆

WEEK ENDING FEBRUARY 6

U.S. #1 POP 45	"Knock Three Times"	Dawn
U.S. #1 POP LP	*All Things Must Pass*	George Harrison
U.S. #1 R&B 45	"(Do the) Push and Pull (Part 1)"	Rufus Thomas
U.K. #1 POP 45	"My Sweet Lord"	George Harrison
U.K. #1 POP LP	*All Things Must Pass*	George Harrison

WEEK ENDING FEBRUARY 13

U.S. #1 POP 45	"One Bad Apple"	The Osmonds
U.S. #1 POP LP	*All Things Must Pass*	George Harrison
U.S. #1 R&B 45	"(Do the) Push and Pull (Part 1)"	Rufus Thomas
U.K. #1 POP 45	"My Sweet Lord"	George Harrison
U.K. #1 POP LP	*All Things Must Pass*	George Harrison

WEEK ENDING FEBRUARY 20

U.S. #1 POP 45	"One Bad Apple"	The Osmonds
U.S. #1 POP LP	*Jesus Christ Superstar*	various artists
U.S. #1 R&B 45	"Judy Got Your Girl and Gone"	Johnnie Taylor
U.K. #1 POP 45	"My Sweet Lord"	George Harrison
U.K. #1 POP LP	*All Things Must Pass*	George Harrison

WEEK ENDING FEBRUARY 27

U.S. #1 POP 45	"One Bad Apple"	The Osmonds
U.S. #1 POP LP	*Pearl*	Janis Joplin
U.S. #1 R&B 45	"Judy Got Your Girl and Gone"	Johnnie Taylor
U.K. #1 POP 45	"My Sweet Lord"	George Harrison
U.K. #1 POP LP	*All Things Must Pass*	George Harrison

4 On the same day that the **Rolling Stones** announce their upcoming move to France, they also begin a ten-day tour of the United Kingdom.

5 A fabulous night of soul and R&B at the Fillmore West becomes two LPs: **Aretha Franklin**, **King Curtis and the Kingpins** and the **Tower of Power** open a three-night stand that is chronicled on Franklin's *Aretha Live at the Fillmore West* and Curtis' *King Curtis and the Kingpins Live at the Fillmore West* LPs. **Ray Charles** makes a guest appearance on Franklin's set.

Badfinger, whose current hit is "No Matter What," begins its first American tour, of twenty cities, in Toledo, Ohio.

11 First it was the **Monkees**, then the **Archies**, now the **Partridge Family**. On this date, TV's fictional first family of rock receives a gold record for the song "Doesn't Somebody Want to be Wanted," the second of their five Top Twenty hits. "The Partridge Family" television sitcom aired from 1970 to 1974, and starred **David Cassidy** and his stepmother, **Shirley Jones**.

12 **John Lennon**'s increasing political awareness is reflected in his followup to "Working Class Hero," the plainly spoken "Power to the People," which he recorded with a New York band, **Elephant's Memory**. The song is released on this date, and hits #11, making it his biggest solo hit up to this point.

13 *Billboard* reports that ex-**Ronette** Ronnie **Spector** is recording her first solo album at London's Abbey Road Studios with her husband, **Phil Spector**, producing and ex-**Beatle George Harrison** contributing songs. Other musicians playing in the recording sessions include **Leon Russell** and **Klaus Voormann**. The first single, "Try Some Buy Some," will be released on the Beatles' Apple label.

The **Allman Brothers Band** records its breakthrough album, *Live at the Fillmore East*. Other selections recorded at the Fillmore will be included on future albums, like "Mountain Jam" from *Eat a Peach*, released after **Duane Allman**'s death in 1972.

16 **Bob Dylan** records "Watchin' the River Flow" with **Leon Russell** playing piano, which is released as a single and is later included on *Bob Dylan's Greatest Hits, Vol. II*.

The Thirteenth Annual Grammy Award Winners are announced and the big winners are: "Bridge over Troubled Water" by **Simon and Garfunkel** (Record of the Year, Album of the Year, Song of the Year, Best Arrangement Accompanying Vocalists, Best Engineered Record, Best Contemporary Song), the **Carpenters** (Best New Artist and Best Contemporary Vocal Performance by a Group for "Close to You"), **Aretha Franklin** (Best Rhythm & Blues Vocal Performance, Female, for "Don't Play That Song") and **B. B. King** (Best Rhythm & Blues Vocal Performance, Male, for "The Thrill Is Gone.") The **Beatles**' *Let It Be* wins for Best Original Score Written for a Motion Picture or Television Special, and **Miles Davis**' seminal album *Bitches Brew* wins for Best Jazz Performance, Large Group or Soloist with Large Group.

20 As of today, **Iron Butterfly**'s *In-a-Gadda-Da-Vida* has been on the charts for 138 weeks and sold more than 3 million copies.

21 **Don Drummond**, leader and trombonist of the seminal ska group the **Skatellites**, dies in a Jamaican insane asylum. Once considered a leading jazz trombonist as well as one of the premiere instrumentalists of Jamaican music, Drummond had been found guilty of murdering his common-law wife, and was placed in Kingston's Bellevue Asylum.

26 **Harold McNair**, reed-playing sessionman from England (**Ginger Baker's Air Force**, Donovan) dies of lung cancer.

The **Rolling Stones** tape a live performance at the Marquee Club for television. Although the program later aired in Europe, British television has no interest in it whatsoever.

Emerson, Lake and Palmer record their third album, *Pictures at an Exhibition*, live at Newcastle City Hall in Britain. Besides their interpretation of the title piece (the classical work by the Russian composer **Moussorgsky**), *Pictures* also includes a tongue-in-cheek rendering of "Nut Rocker," a pastiche of themes from **Tchaikovsky**'s "Nutcracker Suite" and a hit for **B. Bumble and the Stingers** nine years earlier, which becomes a minor hit for ELP in 1972.

27 The *New York Times* reports that New York radio station WNBC has banned the song "One Toke over the Line" by **Brewer and Shipley** because of its alleged drug references. Other stations around the country follow suit. **Tom Shipley**, composer of the song, is outraged. "In this electronic age, pulling a record because of its lyrics is like the burning of books in the Thirties." ◆

WEEK ENDING MARCH 6

U.S. #1 POP 45	"One Bad Apple"	The Osmonds
U.S. #1 POP LP	*Pearl*	Janis Joplin
U.S. #1 R&B 45	"Just My Imagination (Running Away with Me)"	The Temptations
U.K. #1 POP 45	"My Sweet Lord"	George Harrison
U.K. #1 POP LP	*All Things Must Pass*	George Harrison

WEEK ENDING MARCH 13

U.S. #1 POP 45	"One Bad Apple"	The Osmonds
U.S. #1 POP LP	*Pearl*	Janis Joplin
U.S. #1 R&B 45	"Just My Imagination (Running Away with Me)"	The Temptations
U.K. #1 POP 45	"Baby Jump"	Mungo Jerry
U.K. #1 POP LP	*All Things Must Pass*	George Harrison

WEEK ENDING MARCH 20

U.S. #1 POP 45	"Me and Bobby McGee"	Janis Joplin
U.S. #1 POP LP	*Pearl*	Janis Joplin
U.S. #1 R&B 45	"Just My Imagination (Running Away with Me)"	The Temptations
U.K. #1 POP 45	"Another Day"	Paul McCartney
U.K. #1 POP LP	*Bridge over Troubled Water*	Simon and Garfunkel

WEEK ENDING MARCH 27

U.S. #1 POP 45	"Me and Bobby McGee"	Janis Joplin
U.S. #1 POP LP	*Pearl*	Janis Joplin
U.S. #1 R&B 45	"What's Going On"	Marvin Gaye
U.K. #1 POP 45	"Hot Love"	T. Rex
U.K. #1 POP LP	*Bridge over Troubled Water*	Simon and Garfunkel

1 Six months after his death, **Jimi Hendrix**'s *The Cry of Love* goes gold. It is the last LP on which the guitarist was a willing participant, and it might have gone higher than its top spot of #3 had it not been for an LP by another deceased rock star, *Pearl*, by **Janis Joplin**.

5 As reported by the *New York Times*, the New School for Social Research in New York City is one of the first—if not the first—institution to offer a course on rock & roll music.

10 When a Minneapolis audience flocks to the Cafe Extraordinaire to see drummer **Buddy Miles**, only to find a rotund Miles imposter in his place, they initiate a small riot. Total damages: $50,000.

12 Crosby, Stills, Nash and Young's live *Four-Way Street* is certified gold even before it hits the LP chart. The double-record set—half acoustic, half electric—makes Number One, giving the quartet the distinction of two Number One albums in two tries (1970's *Déjà Vu* also went to the top). It is also the last LP the four will record together, although CS&N will reunite to record and tour in 1977 and 1982.

13 The **Rolling Stones** release "Brown Sugar," the first record on their own label, Rolling Stones Records, introducing the infamous licking-tongue-and-lips logo. On May 29, the song becomes the group's sixth U.S. Number One single.

15 Listening to This Music May Be Hazardous to Your Health: *Rolling Stone* reports that the Illinois Crime Commission has issued a list of "drug-oriented rock records." Included are: "Let's Go Get Stoned," "A Whiter Shade of Pale," "Hi-De-Ho (That Old Sweet Roll)" and "White Rabbit." Topping the list with three subversive entries are the **Beatles**: "With a Little Help from My Friends," "Yellow Submarine" and "Lucy in the Sky with Diamonds," which **John Lennon** claims was inspired by a painting by his son **Julian**. Most ironic of all: the inclusion of "Puff the Magic Dragon," which was awarded a

Grammy for Best Record for Children in 1964.

16 The **Rolling Stones** hold an informal celebration in Cannes, France, to mark the formation of their label, Rolling Stones Records.

23 Decca Records, the **Rolling Stones**' previous label, releases an LP titled *Stone Age*, comprised of old Stones catalog material like covers of **Chuck Berry**'s "Around and Around," and several **Jag**ger-**Richards** tunes. Last month, the Rolling Stones had placed an ad in the British music papers that read: "Re: The Decca LP *Stone Age*: We didn't know this record was going to be released. It is, in our opinion, below the standard we try to keep up, both in choice of content and cover design." The statement was signed by all five members of the group.

24 Bill Wyman describes the **Rolling Stones**' sixteenth LP, *Sticky Fingers*, as a move "back with the blues that made us."

28 **Barbra Streisand** gets a gold album for *Stoney End*, one of her rare forays into rock music. That album, along with 1969's *What about Today?*, featured material by such writers as **John Lennon**, **Randy Newman**, **Paul Simon** and **Carole King**. At twenty-eight, Streisand seems intent on changing her image ("The Jeaning of Barbra Streisand" is how *Rolling Stone* titles a 1971 piece on the singer), and even takes to lighting joints onstage in Las Vegas.

30 The *New York Times* reports that **Bill Graham** plans to close the Fillmore East, New York City's rock music mecca since 1968. Although the volatile Graham has issued similar declarations before, this time he's serious. The former movie theater is set to shut down in late May. ◆

WEEK ENDING APRIL 3

U.S. #1 POP 45	"Just My Imagination (Running Away with Me)"	The Temptations
U.S. #1 POP LP	*Pearl*	Janis Joplin
U.S. #1 R&B 45	"What's Going On"	Marvin Gaye
U.K. #1 POP 45	"Hot Love"	T. Rex
U.K. #1 POP LP	*Bridge over Troubled Water*	Simon and Garfunkel

WEEK ENDING APRIL 10

U.S. #1 POP 45	"Just My Imagination (Running Away with Me)"	The Temptations
U.S. #1 POP LP	*Pearl*	Janis Joplin
U.S. #1 R&B 45	"What's Going On"	Marvin Gaye
U.K. #1 POP 45	"Hot Love"	T. Rex
U.K. #1 POP LP	*Home Lovin' Man*	Andy Williams

WEEK ENDING APRIL 17

U.S. #1 POP 45	"Joy to the World"	Three Dog Night
U.S. #1 POP LP	*Pearl*	Janis Joplin
U.S. #1 R&B 45	"What's Going On"	Marvin Gaye
U.K. #1 POP 45	"Hot Love"	T. Rex
U.K. #1 POP LP	*Bridge over Troubled Water*	Simon and Garfunkel

WEEK ENDING APRIL 24

U.S. #1 POP 45	"Joy to the World"	Three Dog Night
U.S. #1 POP LP	*Pearl*	Janis Joplin
U.S. #1 R&B 45	"What's Going On"	Marvin Gaye
U.K. #1 POP 45	"Hot Love"	T. Rex
U.K. #1 POP LP	*Home Lovin' Man*	Andy Williams

3 New York City's Philharmonic Hall at Lincoln Center announces that it will begin presenting rock, pop and jazz concerts as well as its usual classical fare. Among the first nonclassical artists booked for the hall are **Carole King**, **Kris Kristofferson** and **Gordon Lightfoot**.

Grand Funk Railroad "consent" to meet the press, who have never treated this power trio with respect, despite their string of gold records. Manager **Terry Knight** has invited 150 reporters to New York's Gotham Hotel—only six show up, ensuring more strained relations with the press. Outraged, Knight calls the snubbing, "the grossest case of nonrecognition in the history of the music business."

6 **Ike and Tina Turner** receive their only gold

record, for their version of **Creedence Clearwater Revival**'s "Proud Mary." The song hit #4, the highest chart position ever for the husband-and-wife team.

12 **Mick Jagger** marries **Bianca Perez Morena de Macias** in St. Tropez, France. The guest list is a veritable who's who of rock & roll luminaries, including the other **Stones**, **Paul McCartney**, **Ringo Starr**, **Eric Clapton** and **Stephen Stills**. The reception, held at the Café des Arts, is described by one guest as "slightly seedy," and lasts until four in the morning. Ten hours after being married, Jagger is on stage, performing an impromtu set with singers **Doris Troy** and **P. P. Arnold**.

13 **Jefferson Airplane** recording sessions are halted after singer **Grace Slick**

smashes her Mercedes into a concrete wall near San Francisco's Golden Gate Bridge.

15 Two **John Lennon-Yoko Ono** films are screened at the Cannes Festival. The first, *Apotheosis*, is an eighteen-minute-long camera shot of a snowy countryside. Ono's *Fly* is the graphic exploration of a nude woman's body by a fly. The flies proved difficult to direct, so, there being no guild to complain to, the insects were stunned with carbon dioxide gas. Those who live are filmed walking on the woman's skin.

18 The **Band** launch their first European tour in Rotterdam, Holland. The tour ends June 3 at London's Royal Albert Hall.

21 **Paul McCartney** releases *Ram*, which, unlike his first solo LP, is not a

one-man show. Besides wife **Linda** on vocals, McCartney enlists sessionmen **David Spinozza** and **Hugh McCracken** on guitar and bass, and drummer **Denny Seiwell**, who will later become a member of **Wings**. *Ram* goes to #2.

22 *Sticky Fingers*, the **Rolling Stones**' sixteenth LP, goes to Number One. The LP is the first complete Stones album to feature guitarist **Mick Taylor**, who'd replaced original member **Brian Jones** two years earlier. While the music is mostly uptempo, lyrically the record is often lugubrious, full of paeans to the sex-and-drugs lifestyle that characterized the Stones' own outlaw image.

24 **Bob Dylan** turns thirty—even the *Peanuts* comic strip makes mention of it. Dylan celebrates at Jerusalem's Wailing Wall.

26 **Leslie West and Mountain** are awarded a gold record for *Nantucket Sleighride*, the biggest LP of the group's career (#16). It is also one of their last: Mountain's fortunes roll steadily downhill, and Leslie West soon abandons the group for **West, Bruce & Laing** (with former **Cream** singer/bassist **Jack Bruce**). In the Eighties, he'll reform Mountain with original drummer **Corky Laing**, but having slid so far, he'll be unable to get a record deal.

29 The **Rolling Stones** achieve the rare distinction of having both the Number One LP (*Sticky Fingers*) and Number One 45 ("Brown Sugar") in the U.S.

30 Three-dozen **Grateful Dead** fans were treated for hallucinations caused by LSD they have unwittingly ingested when the drug is used to spike an apple drink served at San Francisco's Winterland. Although members of the Dead are suspected of supplying the drink, they are not accused. ◆

WEEK ENDING MAY 1

U.S. #1 POP 45	"Joy to the World"	Three Dog Night
U.S. #1 POP LP	*Jesus Christ Superstar*	various artists
U.S. #1 R&B 45	"Never Can Say Goodbye"	The Jackson 5
U.K. #1 POP 45	"Double Barrel"	Dave and Ansel Collins
U.K. #1 POP LP	*Motown Chartbusters, Volume 5*	various artists

WEEK ENDING MAY 8

U.S. #1 POP 45	"Joy to the World"	Three Dog Night
U.S. #1 POP LP	*Jesus Christ Superstar*	various artists
U.S. #1 R&B 45	"Never Can Say Goodbye"	The Jackson 5
U.K. #1 POP 45	"Double Barrel"	Dave and Ansel Collins
U.K. #1 POP LP	*Sticky Fingers*	The Rolling Stones

WEEK ENDING MAY 15

U.S. #1 POP 45	"Joy to the World"	Three Dog Night
U.S. #1 POP LP	*Four-Way Street*	Crosby, Stills, Nash and Young
U.S. #1 R&B 45	"Never Can Say Goodbye"	The Jackson 5
U.K. #1 POP 45	"Brown Sugar"	The Rolling Stones
U.K. #1 POP LP	*Sticky Fingers*	The Rolling Stones

WEEK ENDING MAY 22

U.S. #1 POP 45	"Joy to the World"	Three Dog Night
U.S. #1 POP LP	*Sticky Fingers*	The Rolling Stones
U.S. #1 R&B 45	"Bridge over Troubled Water"	Aretha Franklin
U.K. #1 POP 45	"Knock Three Times"	Dawn
U.K. #1 POP LP	*Sticky Fingers*	The Rolling Stones

WEEK ENDING MAY 29

U.S. #1 POP 45	"Brown Sugar"	The Rolling Stones
U.S. #1 POP LP	*Sticky Fingers*	The Rolling Stones
U.S. #1 R&B 45	"Want Ads"	Honey Cone
U.K. #1 POP 45	"Knock Three Times"	Dawn
U.K. #1 POP LP	*Sticky Fingers*	The Rolling Stones

1 **Elvis Presley**'s birthplace, a two-room house in Tupelo, Mississippi, is opened to the public.

5 Tickets go on sale for **Grand Funk Railroad**'s appearance at New York's Shea Stadium, and are sold out within seventy-two hours, netting the band $306,000, which tops the **Beatles**' Shea Stadium ticket sales of $304,000 in 1966. Promoter **Sid Bernstein**, who also brought the Beatles to Shea Stadium, comments: "I would never say that anyone is more popular than the Beatles, but Grand Funk's fans have certainly responded more quickly and with a different kind of enthusiasm." Over 21,000 fans show up at the stadium the morning tickets go on sale, many of them having waited over twenty-four hours for the ticket booths to open.

6 **John Lennon** and **Yoko Ono** appear on stage for the first time since 1969, joining **Frank Zappa** for a jam at the Fillmore East. Says Lennon of the encounter: "I expected sort of a grubby maniac with naked women all over the place. The first thing I said was, 'Wow, you look so different. You look great!' " Zappa had his own preconceptions, too. The first thing he said, recounts Lennon, was, "You look clean too."

7 **Carole King**'s *Tapestry*, one of the largest selling LPs of all time, goes gold. *Tapestry* remains on the charts for more than three years and gives King her biggest selling hit, "It's Too Late," which is Number One for five weeks in the summer of 1971.

10 A **Jethro Tull** concert at Denver's Red Rock Amphitheater is marred by police, who fire off tear-gas canisters to quell disturbances among some of the 10,000 assembled. Undaunted, Tull plays anyway, even though keyboardist **John Evan** can't see his piano through the tear gas.

12 The South African Broadcasting Company decides to remove its ban on **Beatles** records, a ruling which has been in effect since 1966. The reason? **John Lennon**'s controversial statement that the group had become more popular than Jesus.

13 **Clyde McPhatter** dies of complications of heart, liver and kidney diseases at age thirty-eight in the Bronx. McPhatter was lead vocalist on some of the **Drifters**' biggest hits, including "Money Honey" and "Such a Night." After leaving the group, he began a solo career that started out promisingly, but which began to wane by the mid-Sixties. Problems with drugs and alcohol followed.

14 A gold record is awarded to **Black Sabbath**, a fire-and-brimstone quartet from Birmingham, England, who joyfully play a form of heavy metal termed "downer rock." If that sounds like a contradiction, an interview with one of the band's early fans sheds some light on its macabre appeal: "It's freaky. It makes you feel like you're in a graveyard. It makes you feel more alive."

21 The Celebration of Life festival finally gets underway—three and a half days late—in Pointe Coupe Parish, Louisiana. Advertisements for the eight-day festival boast an impressive array of rock, jazz and blues acts, including **Pink Floyd**, the **Beach Boys**, **Miles Davis** and **B. B. King**. A telltale sign of how the festival will fare is given at the very beginning, when guru **Yogi Bahjan** takes the stage and requests a minute of silence. "Fuck you, let's boogie!" responds a member of the crowd.

24 The Celebration of Life Festival is shut down by authorities after the promoters fail to provide sufficient supplies of food, and medical and sanitary facilities. During the three days of the aborted festival, three fans drowned, and one fan died of a drug overdose. The crowd was becoming increasingly unruly, because of the twenty-seven groups advertised to appear, only eight showed up, and more than 150 festival-goers were arrested.

27 It's an emotional evening as **Bill Graham** officially closes the Fillmore East after three years. The send-off is in the style of a New Orleans jazz funeral, and is highlighted by the performances of the **Allman Brothers Band**, **Mountain**, the **Beach Boys**, who turn out thirteen strong, and newcomers from **Boston**, the **J. Geils Band**. Patrons attending the final night are given commemorative posters at the door and find red roses on their seats.

30 **Paul Revere and the Raiders** receive a gold record for their only Number One hit, "Indian Reservation (The Lament of the Cherokee Reservation Indian)." It is their last Top Twenty hit.

San Francisco's famed rock theater the Fillmore West closes, in the wake of police harassment of the theater's promoter, **Bill Graham**. Police had threatened to cancel the permit for Graham's other San Francisco rock theater, Winterland, when a soft drink sold at a concert there was allegedly discovered to be spiked with LSD and passed through the audience, with people told, "Pass the drinks to your friends; they may be thirsty too." ◆

WEEK ENDING JUNE 5

U.S. #1 POP 45	"Brown Sugar"	The Rolling Stones
U.S. #1 POP LP	*Sticky Fingers*	The Rolling Stones
U.S. #1 R&B 45	"Want Ads"	Honey Cone
U.K. #1 POP 45	"Knock Three Times"	Dawn
U.K. #1 POP LP	*Sticky Fingers*	The Rolling Stones

WEEK ENDING JUNE 12

U.S. #1 POP 45	"Want Ads"	Honey Cone
U.S. #1 POP LP	*Sticky Fingers*	The Rolling Stones
U.S. #1 R&B 45	"Want Ads"	Honey Cone
U.K. #1 POP 45	"My Brother Jake"	Free
U.K. #1 POP LP	*Sticky Fingers*	The Rolling Stones

WEEK ENDING JUNE 19

U.S. #1 POP 45	"It's Too Late"/"I Feel the Earth Move"	Carole King
U.S. #1 POP LP	*Tapestry*	Carole King
U.S. #1 R&B 45	"Bridge over Troubled Water"	Aretha Franklin
U.K. #1 POP 45	"I Did What I Did for Maria"	Tony Christie
U.K. #1 POP LP	*Sticky Fingers*	The Rolling Stones

WEEK ENDING JUNE 26

U.S. #1 POP 45	"It's Too Late"/"I Feel the Earth Move"	Carole King
U.S. #1 POP LP	*Tapestry*	Carole King
U.S. #1 R&B 45	"Don't Knock My Love"	Wilson Pickett
U.K. #1 POP 45	"Chirpy Chirpy Cheep Cheep"	Middle of the Road
U.K. #1 POP LP	*Bridge over Troubled Water*	Simon and Garfunkel

1 *Aqualung,* the first U.S. Top Ten LP for **Jethro Tull**, goes gold. *Aqualung* signals a change in the group's direction, leaning more toward hard rock, with less of an emphasis on leader **Ian Anderson**'s classical and baroque influences. They go on to be one of the biggest acts of the early Seventies.

3 **Jim Morrison**, singer, songwriter and poet, dies in Paris at age twenty-seven. The **Doors**' leader had gone to France in March to write and relax. Morrison, who charged through life with a penchant for excess, was a heavy drinker, and drugs were known to be part of his lifestyle. The official cause of death is listed as a heart attack. Morrison is survived by his wife, **Pamela**.

4 **Donald McPherson**, lead singer and founder of the soul group the **Main Ingredient**, dies of leukemia at age thirty. McPherson formed the group in the Fifties, but it wasn't until 1966 that they had their first hit, "She Blew a Good Thing." The Main Ingredient will enjoy even greater success, however, with McPherson's replacement, **Cuba Gooding**, and their 1972 single "Everybody Plays the Fool" will become their biggest seller ever, going to #3.

7 British avant-jazz-rock band **Soft Machine** makes its first American appearance since opening for a **Jimi Hendrix Experience** tour three years earlier at New York City's Gaslight Club. Among those in the audience is avant-garde jazz giant **Ornette Coleman**.

9 **Jim Morrison** is buried at the Père Lachaise cemetery in Paris, and official word of his death is finally given to the press. **Doors** manager **Bill Siddons** explains why Morrison's death was kept secret for nearly a week, saying that those close to the late singer wished to avoid "the circuslike atmosphere that surrounded the deaths of **Janis Joplin** and **Jimi Hendrix**."

22 The **Doors** are awarded a gold album for *L.A. Woman* just thirteen days after the announcement of singer **Jim Morrison**'s death. The LP includes two hits, "Love Her Madly" and "Riders on the Storm," and the title track becomes an FM radio staple for years to come.

24 **T. Rex**'s "Get It On" becomes the Number One single in Britain, and helps inaugurate the glitter-rock fad. **Bolan**, born **Mark Feld**, has the look: a halo of dark, frizzy hair and a sullen pout that gives him a fashionably androgynous air. However, his success never really makes it to the other side of the Atlantic: in the U.S., "Get It On" (retitled "Bang a Gong (Get It On)") reaches #10 in 1972, his only American smash.

25 The **Beach Boys** are back. After suffering several years of snubbing, both by rock critics and the public, the Beach Boys stage a remarkable comeback beginning with the release of *Surf's Up,* an LP that weds their choral harmonies to progessive pop, and which shows youngest **Wilson** brother **Carl** stepping to the fore of the venerable outfit. The title track is especially noteworthy, a surfer's lullaby cowritten in 1967 by **Van Dyke Parks** and the reclusive **Brian Wilson**, who withheld the song for fear that it wouldn't be accepted. *Surf's Up* is welcomed with open arms and hits #29, making it their highest charting LP in four years.

27 **George Harrison** releases his statement on behalf of the starving refugees of the Bengal Nation, "Bangla Desh," on which he implores, "Now I'm asking all of you to help us save some lives." The single's release comes just four days before Harrison's Concerts for Bangla Desh in New York City, where he closes both sets with the song.

31 The second night of the **Who**'s first of two 1971 U.S. tours is marred by tragedy when a twenty-two-year-old security guard is stabbed to death at New York's Forest Hills Stadium. The guard, **George Byrington**, is killed by **Kerry Flaherty**, a twenty-one-year-old ex-convict recently released from prison, where he was serving a sentence for a 1967 knife assault.

Gimme Shelter, the **Maysles Brothers** documentary of the **Stones**' 1969 tour, has its British premiere at the Rialto Cinema in London. ◆

WEEK ENDING JULY 3

U.S. #1 POP 45	"It's Too Late"/"I Feel the Earth Move"	Carole King
U.S. #1 POP LP	*Tapestry*	Carole King
U.S. #1 R&B 45	"Mr. Big Stuff"	Jean Knight
U.K. #1 POP 45	"Chirpy Chirpy Cheep Cheep"	Middle of the Road
U.K. #1 POP LP	*Ram*	Paul McCartney

WEEK ENDING JULY 10

U.S. #1 POP 45	"It's Too Late"/"I Feel the Earth Move"	Carole King
U.S. #1 POP LP	*Tapestry*	Carole King
U.S. #1 R&B 45	"Mr. Big Stuff"	Jean Knight
U.K. #1 POP 45	"Chirpy Chirpy Cheep Cheep"	Middle of the Road
U.K. #1 POP LP	*Bridge over Troubled Water*	Simon and Garfunkel

WEEK ENDING JULY 17

U.S. #1 POP 45	"It's Too Late"/"I Feel the Earth Move"	Carole King
U.S. #1 POP LP	*Tapestry*	Carole King
U.S. #1 R&B 45	"Mr. Big Stuff"	Jean Knight
U.K. #1 POP 45	"Chirpy Chirpy Cheep Cheep"	Middle of the Road
U.K. #1 POP LP	*Bridge over Troubled Water*	Simon and Garfunkel

WEEK ENDING JULY 24

U.S. #1 POP 45	"Indian Reservation"	Paul Revere and the Raiders
U.S. #1 POP LP	*Tapestry*	Carole King
U.S. #1 R&B 45	"Mr. Big Stuff"	Jean Knight
U.K. #1 POP 45	"Get It On"	T. Rex
U.K. #1 POP LP	*Bridge over Troubled Water*	Simon and Garfunkel

WEEK ENDING JULY 31

U.S. #1 POP 45	"You've Got a Friend"	James Taylor
U.S. #1 POP LP	*Tapestry*	Carole King
U.S. #1 R&B 45	"Mr. Big Stuff"	Jean Knight
U.K. #1 POP 45	"Get It On"	T. Rex
U.K. #1 POP LP	*Bridge over Troubled Water*	Simon and Garfunkel

1 The Concerts for Bangla Desh are held at New York's Madison Square Garden. The two shows are put together by **George Harrison** out of concern for the starving people of the Bangla Desh nation, an issue brought to his attention by his mentor, master sitarist **Ravi Shankar**. Harrison assembles a star-studded band, including **Ringo Starr, Eric Clapton, Leon Russell, Billy Preston** and **Badfinger**. Highlights include Leon's frenzied "Jumpin' Jack Flash," Ringo's flubbing the words to his hit "It Don't Come Easy" and a special unannounced—but much rumored—appearance by **Bob Dylan**.

3 **Ringo Starr** receives a gold record for his first hit 45, "It Don't Come Easy," which the drummer wrote himself.

Paul McCartney announces the formation of his first post-**Beatles** band, **Wings**. The lineup (which will shift frequently over the next several years) includes his wife, **Linda**, ex-**Moody Blues** guitarist **Denny Laine** and drummer **Denny Seiwell**, who'd played on McCartney's *Ram* album.

4 **Emerson, Lake and Palmer**'s eponymously titled debut LP goes gold, heralding the progressive rock era. Each of the three has solid credentials: Emerson coming from the seminal progressive rock/classical rock group the **Nice**, Lake from **King Crimson**, and Palmer from **Atomic Rooster**. The trio enjoys success through its breakup in 1979.

6 **Procol Harum** records a concert with the Edmonton Symphony Orchestra in Edmonton, Alberta, Canada, portions of which will later be released as the

album *Live with the Edmonton Symphony Orchestra*. The orchestrated version of Procol Harum's "Conquistador" will become a surprise hit single.

7 **Frank Zappa**'s **Mothers of Invention** record *Just Another Band from L.A.* live at the University of California in Los Angeles. It is the last Zappa album to include former **Turtles** Howard Kaylan and **Mark Volman**, who will soon leave to record on their own as **Flo and Eddie**.

The **Bee Gees** attain their first of seven Number One records in America: "How Can You Mend a Broken Heart." This is one of the last songs in the "old" Bee Gees style; after three years of commercial drought (1972–1974), they will discover **Barry Gibb**'s high falsetto and a disco beat, which will rejuvenate their career and give them six Number Ones between 1975 and 1979.

13 Soul saxophonist **King Curtis** (born **Curtis Ousley**) is killed outside his New York City apartment at age thirty-seven. According to police, Curtis had been quarrel-

ing with a group of people standing on the stoop of his building, when one of them stabbed him with a six-inch dagger. Curtis' tenor sax was first widely heard on the **Coasters'** 1957 hit "Yakety Yak," and he quickly became a highly sought-after sessionman.

17 **King Curtis'** funeral is held in New York City. The **Reverend Jesse Jackson** preaches the sermon, and **Aretha Franklin, Stevie Wonder, Cissy Houston, Brook Benton** and **Arthur Prysock**, among others, sing. Others in attendance include **Delaney and Bonnie Bramlett, Duane Allman** and **Herbie Mann**.

27 **Freda Payne**, who previously has had hits with such fare as "Band of Gold," has a gold hit with "Bring the Boys Home," one of the few black anti-Vietnam War songs.

28 **James Brown**'s tenth Number One R&B song, "Make It Funky," enters the R&B chart. It will reach #22 on the pop chart next month. ◆

WEEK ENDING AUGUST 7

U.S. #1 POP 45	"How Can You Mend a Broken Heart"	The Bee Gees
U.S. #1 POP LP	*Tapestry*	Carole King
U.S. #1 R&B 45	"Hot Pants, Part 1"	James Brown
U.K. #1 POP 45	"Get It On"	T. Rex
U.K. #1 POP LP	*Every Good Boy Deserves Favour*	The Moody Blues

WEEK ENDING AUGUST 14

U.S. #1 POP 45	"How Can You Mend a Broken Heart"	The Bee Gees
U.S. #1 POP LP	*Tapestry*	Carole King
U.S. #1 R&B 45	"Mercy Mercy Me (The Ecology)"	Marvin Gaye
U.K. #1 POP 45	"Never Ending Song of Love"	The New Seekers
U.K. #1 POP LP	*Every Good Boy Deserves Favour*	The Moody Blues

WEEK ENDING AUGUST 21

U.S. #1 POP 45	"How Can You Mend a Broken Heart"	The Bee Gees
U.S. #1 POP LP	*Tapestry*	Carole King
U.S. #1 R&B 45	"Mercy Mercy Me (The Ecology)"	Marvin Gaye
U.K. #1 POP 45	"I'm Still Waiting"	Diana Ross
U.K. #1 POP LP	*Every Good Boy Deserves Favour*	The Moody Blues

WEEK ENDING AUGUST 28

U.S. #1 POP 45	"How Can You Mend a Broken Heart"	The Bee Gees
U.S. #1 POP LP	*Tapestry*	Carole King
U.S. #1 R&B 45	"Spanish Harlem"	Aretha Franklin
U.K. #1 POP 45	"I'm Still Waiting"	Diana Ross
U.K. #1 POP LP	*Every Good Boy Deserves Favour*	The Moody Blues

2 The **Grateful Dead** have finally tracked down and have had arrested **Lenny Hart**, the group's ex-manager, and father of the group's ex-drummer. The elder Hart, who claimed to be a reverend, is charged with having embezzled $70,000 from the band last year, leaving the Dead penniless. Manager **John McIntre** was surprised to discover the missing money, saying, "You wouldn't think that he'd fuck his own son."

The **Grateful Dead**'s second live LP is given the unimaginative title *Grateful Dead,* but it's not as if the group isn't concerned about such matters. *Rolling Stone* reports that lead-

er **Jerry Garcia** had originally wanted the LP titled *Starfuck.* It becomes the Dead's first Top Twenty-five album upon its late September release.

Rolling Stone reports that **Mick Jagger**, **Keith Richards**, **Bill Wyman**, **Charlie Watts** and the late **Brian Jones**' father have filed suit against former **Stones** managers **Eric Easton** and **Andrew Loog Oldham**, the latter the group's producer through 1967's *Flowers.* Among other things, the suit charges that Easton and Oldham deprived them of royalties, through a deal with the band's first label, Decca.

First it was the Polish National Home, then **Andy Warhol**'s Exploding Plastic Inevitable, then the Balloon Farm and then in 1967 the Electric Circus, one of New York City's taste-making rock & roll clubs. On this date, *Rolling Stone* reports that, according to owner **Stan Freeman**, the club is closing down because of a decrease in business ever since seventeen patrons were injured in a bomb blast in 1970.

4 A story in the *New York Times* says that **Sylves-**ter Stewart**'s West Hollywood landlord is suing the rock star for $3 million. The landlord claims that because of **Sly**, his building is inundated with "loud, noisy, boisterous persons," and wants Stewart out.

8 **Elvis Presley** receives the Bing Crosby Award. The award, which was first presented to **Bing Crosby** in 1962 by the National Academy of Recording Arts and Sciences, is bestowed to members of the recording industry who, according to the Academy, "during their lifetimes, have made creative contributions of outstanding artistic or scientific significance to the field of phonograph records." Presley becomes only the sixth artist so honored, preceded by Crosby, **Frank Sinatra**, **Duke Ellington**, **Ella Fitzgerald** and **Irving Berlin**.

11 **Donny Osmond**'s version of "Go Away Little Girl" hits Number One. The song had also been a Number One hit for **Steve Lawrence** in 1963, and it returned to the chart in 1966, peaking at #12 for the **Happenings**.

18 The unusual pairing of Hungarian jazz guitarist **Gabor Szabo** and soul singer **Bobby Womack** enters the soul chart with "Breezin'," a song written by session guitarist **Phil Upchurch** that will be a #63 pop hit in an instrumental version by jazz guitarist **George Benson** in 1976. The Szabo-Womack version of "Breezin'," however, will only hit #43 on the soul chart.

Pink Floyd, who'd toyed with classical music elements throughout their career, become the first rock group to appear at the Classical Music Festival in Montreux, Switzerland. The quartet performs its symphonic work *Atom Heart Mother.*

28 The *New York Times* reports on the growing interest among white youths in black gospel music. ◆

WEEK ENDING SEPTEMBER 4

U.S. #1 POP 45	"Uncle Albert/Admiral Halsey"	Paul and Linda McCartney
U.S. #1 POP LP	*Tapestry*	Carole King
U.S. #1 R&B 45	"Spanish Harlem"	Aretha Franklin
U.K. #1 POP 45	"I'm Still Waiting"	Diana Ross
U.K. #1 POP LP	*Every Good Boy Deserves Favour*	The Moody Blues

WEEK ENDING SEPTEMBER 11

U.S. #1 POP 45	"Go Away Little Girl"	Donny Osmond
U.S. #1 POP LP	*Tapestry*	Carole King
U.S. #1 R&B 45	"Spanish Harlem"	Aretha Franklin
U.K. #1 POP 45	"Hey Girl, Don't Bother Me"	The Tams
U.K. #1 POP LP	*Tapestry*	Carole King

WEEK ENDING SEPTEMBER 18

U.S. #1 POP 45	"Go Away Little Girl"	Donny Osmond
U.S. #1 POP LP	*Tapestry*	Carole King
U.S. #1 R&B 45	"Stick-Up"	Honey Cone
U.K. #1 POP 45	"Hey Girl, Don't Bother Me"	The Tams
U.K. #1 POP LP	*Every Picture Tells a Story*	Rod Stewart

WEEK ENDING SEPTEMBER 25

U.S. #1 POP 45	"Go Away Little Girl"	Donny Osmond
U.S. #1 POP LP	*Tapestry*	Carole King
U.S. #1 R&B 45	"Stick-Up"	Honey Cone
U.K. #1 POP 45	"Maggie Mae"	Rod Stewart
U.K. #1 POP LP	*Every Picture Tells a Story*	Rod Stewart

2 After years of singing in other stars' bands, including **Long John Baldry**'s and **Jeff Beck**'s, **Rod "the Mod" Stewart** establishes himself as a star in his own right: on this date, both his "Maggie Mae" 45 and his *Every Picture Tells a Story* LP hit Number One. While maintaining his successful solo career, Stewart is also the vocalist for the **Faces**, a tandem career he'll keep up through 1976.

12 **Gene Vincent**, the early rock & roller whose influence would continue to be felt even decades after his biggest hit, "Be-Bop-a-Lula," dies of a bleeding ulcer. Vincent, who recorded the song with his group, the **Bluecaps**, had suffered from severe leg pain ever since a motorcycle accident in 1955, and had become a heavy drinker. In a remark made less than a month before his death, Vincent said, "I'm going through hell." He was thirty-six.

14 In Los Angeles District Court, Arco Industries—a music publishing firm owning copyrights on all material released on Specialty Records—files a $500,000 suit against **Creedence Clearwater Revival**'s singer/guitarist/songwriter, **John Fogerty**. The suit, which names as codefendants Creedence's label, Fantasy Records; Fogerty's publishing company, Jondora Music; and BMI, which licenses Fogerty's songs for broadcast, charges that Fogerty's song "Travelin' Band" "contains substantial material copied from the music of the song 'Good Golly Miss Molly.'" The latter, **Little Richard**'s 1957 classic, was released on Specialty, hence Arco holds the publishing rights it feels have been violated. The

suit, however, is eventually dropped.

15 Fifties teen idol **Rick Nelson** is booed when he performs new material at a **Richard Nader**-produced oldies show at New York City's Madison Square Garden. As a result of this experience he pens "Garden Party," which will hit #6 in October 1972. Sample verse: "If memories are all I'd sing, I'd rather drive a truck."

21 **Mick and Bianca Jagger**'s only child, their daughter **Jade**, is born in the Belvedere Nursing Home in Paris.

23 *Tommy,* **Pete Townshend**'s rock opera about the deaf, dumb and blind boy cum messiah, spends its last week on the LP chart, two and a half years after its release. But Tommy isn't ready for retirement yet: He'll return in 1972 for a one-night-only London stage performance, and again in 1975 with the release of the *Tommy* movie, which will bring the **Who**'s original two-record-set opera back into the Top Fifty.

25 *The Allman Brothers Band Live at the Fillmore East* goes gold just four days before leader **Duane Allman** is killed in a motorcycle accident.

26 "Tired of Being Alone," the first of ten Top Twenty hits for soul singer **Al Green**, goes gold. Green later opts for a co-career as a preacher, and his musical interests return to gospel, which he sang professionally as a teenager.

29 In the first of a series of tragedies for the **Allman Brothers Band**, guitarist **Duane Allman** is killed in a motorcycle accident just outside the group's hometown of Macon, Georgia. Duane, twenty-four, had cofounded the Allmans with his younger brother **Gregg** in the late Sixties, and was a much sought-after sessionman whose slide playing evoked the memory of the late bluesman **Elmore James**.

30 John Lennon's *Imagine* hits Number One. It is the ex-**Beatle**'s only solo LP to sell a million copies during his lifetime and his most popular LP until *Double Fantasy*—the album he recorded with wife **Yoko Ono** after a five-year sabbatical, and which became Number One shortly after his assassination on December 8, 1980. ◆

WEEK ENDING OCTOBER 2

U.S. #1 POP 45	"Maggie Mae"	Rod Stewart
U.S. #1 POP LP	*Every Picture Tells a Story*	Rod Stewart
U.S. #1 R&B 45	"Make It Funky, Part 1"	James Brown
U.K. #1 POP 45	"Maggie Mae"	Rod Stewart
U.K. #1 POP LP	*Every Picture Tells a Story*	Rod Stewart

WEEK ENDING OCTOBER 9

U.S. #1 POP 45	"Maggie Mae"	Rod Stewart
U.S. #1 POP LP	*Every Picture Tells a Story*	Rod Stewart
U.S. #1 R&B 45	"Make It Funky, Part 1"	James Brown
U.K. #1 POP 45	"Maggie Mae"	Rod Stewart
U.K. #1 POP LP	*Every Picture Tells a Story*	Rod Stewart

WEEK ENDING OCTOBER 16

U.S. #1 POP 45	"Maggie Mae"	Rod Stewart
U.S. #1 POP LP	*Every Picture Tells a Story*	Rod Stewart
U.S. #1 R&B 45	"Thin Line between Love and Hate"	The Persuaders
U.K. #1 POP 45	"Maggie Mae"	Rod Stewart
U.K. #1 POP LP	*Every Picture Tells a Story*	Rod Stewart

WEEK ENDING OCTOBER 23

U.S. #1 POP 45	"Maggie Mae"	Rod Stewart
U.S. #1 POP LP	*Every Picture Tells a Story*	Rod Stewart
U.S. #1 R&B 45	"Thin Line between Love and Hate"	The Persuaders
U.K. #1 POP 45	"Maggie Mae"	Rod Stewart
U.K. #1 POP LP	*Every Picture Tells a Story*	Rod Stewart

WEEK ENDING OCTOBER 30

U.S. #1 POP 45	"Maggie Mae"	Rod Stewart
U.S. #1 POP LP	*Imagine*	John Lennon
U.S. #1 R&B 45	"Trapped by a Thing Called Love"	Denise LaSalle
U.K. #1 POP 45	"Maggie Mae"	Rod Stewart
U.K. #1 POP LP	*Every Picture Tells a Story*	Rod Stewart

1 Funeral services are held for **Duane Allman** at the Memorial Chapel in Macon, Georgia. Among those paying tribute are the other Allman band members, **Mac Rebennack** (**Dr. John**), **Jerry Wexler** and **Delaney Bramlett**. The **Allmans** perform "Stormy Monday," "In Memory of Elizabeth Reed" and "Statesboro Blues," which is sung mournfully by **Gregg**, his eyes hidden by dark sunglasses, tears streaming down his cheeks.

4 **Bob Dylan**, long under pressure to return to his political stance of the Sixties, records "George Jackson," a paean to the black militant killed in a California prison shootout. Dylan releases the tune in two versions, one electric and one acoustic. Among the lines: "He wouldn't take shit from no one," which guarantees limited radio play. Some applaud Dylan for his action, but others regard "George Jackson" suspiciously; Dylan sounds more like he's buckling under to left-wing pressure than as if he's actually committed.

8 **Sly and the Family Stone** have huge hits with "Family Affair" and *There's a Riot Goin' On* (Number One and gold). The album's title could well describe some of Sly's concerts during this time, for, much to his fans' dismay, he is a frequent no-show: of eighty concerts booked in 1970, he canceled twenty-six, and he has ducked out of twelve of forty shows in 1971.

11 According to a *Rolling Stone* report, the promoters of the disastrous Celebration of Life Festival have been indicted by a Pointe Coupe Parish, Louisiana, grand jury on charges of theft, obscenity and contributing to the delinquency of juveniles. **Steve Kapelow** and **Ken Lind**'s much ballyhooed festival, held last June, was closed by authorities after just four days.

13 The group **Slade** capture their first of six British Number One singles, "Coz I Luv You." The group is notable for its platform footwear (which resemble small buildings), its crushing volume, the siren voice of singer **Noddy Holder** and, most of all, its song titles, which are spelled out phonetically ("Mama Weer All Crazzee Now").

15 **Grand Funk Railroad** release their sixth album, *E Pluribus Funk*, whose cover is sure to further infuriate critics who criticize what they perceive as the group's exaggerated sense of self-importance. The silver package is shaped like a coin, with the likenesses of **Mark**, **Don** and **Mel** stamped on it in relief. The overall effect is that of Mount Rushmore. Regardless, the LP goes to #5.

16 **Led Zeppelin**'s debut, actually released in early 1969, finally goes gold. By this time the group is readying its fourth album, titled *Led Zeppelin IV*, which contains the all-time FM radio classic "Stairway to Heaven."

17 **Rod Stewart and the Faces** release *A Nod Is as Good as a Wink to a Blind Horse*, their third LP together. It is one of the few Faces albums to adequately capture their boozy, wonderfully sloppy live sound. The group scores its biggest hit, the taunting come-on, "Stay

with Me," which hits #17. The LP goes to Top Ten.

18 Blues harmonica player and singer **Herman "Junior" Parker** dies at age thirty-nine in Blue Island, Illinois, after a series of brain operations. His most famous songs included "Blue Shadows Falling," "How Long Can This Go On" and "Stand by Me."

19 Blues guitar giant **B. B. King** marks his twenty-fifth year in show biz by starting a European tour in London.

20 "Inner City Blues (Make Me Wanna Holler)" becomes the third R&B Number One single from **Marvin Gaye**'s *What's Going On* album; the others are the title song (also pop #2) and "Mercy Mercy Me (The Ecology)." The album represents the first time a major Motown artist has taken a public stand on controversial social issues.

23 The **Chi-Lites**' first R&B Number One, "Have You Seen Her," enters the R&B chart. The song goes to #3 on the Top 100 in December.

25 The three surviving **Doors**—keyboardist **Ray Manzarek**, guitarist **Robbie Krieger** and drummer **John Densmore**—tell *Rolling Stone* that they are determined to carry on despite singer **Jim Morrison**'s death in July, with Manzarek assuming the role as vocalist. Their two LPs, *Other Voices* and *Full Circle*, will sell only marginally, however, and the Doors will disband officially in 1973.

26 Tickets are so in demand for the **Faces'** Madison Square Garden performance that the group breaks **Led Zeppelin**'s sellout record for the New York arena. ◆

WEEK ENDING NOVEMBER 6

U.S. #1 POP 45	"Gypsys, Tramps and Thieves"	Cher
U.S. #1 POP LP	"Shaft"	Isaac Hayes
U.S. #1 R&B 45	"Inner City Blues"	Marvin Gaye
U.K. #1 POP 45	"Coz I Luv You"	Slade
U.K. #1 POP LP	*Every Picture Tells a Story*	Rod Stewart

WEEK ENDING NOVEMBER 13

U.S. #1 POP 45	"Gypsys, Tramps and Thieves"	Cher
U.S. #1 POP LP	*Santana*	Santana
U.S. #1 R&B 45	"Inner City Blues"	Marvin Gaye
U.K. #1 POP 45	"Coz I Luv You"	Slade
U.K. #1 POP LP	*Every Picture Tells a Story*	Rod Stewart

WEEK ENDING NOVEMBER 20

U.S. #1 POP 45	"Theme from *Shaft*"	Isaac Hayes
U.S. #1 POP LP	*Santana*	Santana
U.S. #1 R&B 45	"Have You Seen Her?"	The Chi-Lites
U.K. #1 POP 45	"Coz I Luv You"	Slade
U.K. #1 POP LP	*Imagine*	John Lennon

WEEK ENDING NOVEMBER 27

U.S. #1 POP 45	"Theme from *Shaft*"	Isaac Hayes
U.S. #1 POP LP	*Santana*	Santana
U.S. #1 R&B 45	"Have You Seen Her?"	The Chi-Lites
U.K. #1 POP 45	"Ernie"	Benny Hill
U.K. #1 POP LP	*Imagine*	John Lennon

2 Contemporary bluesman **Taj Mahal** plays for the men on death row at Wilmington State Penitentiary.

3 The Montreux Casino burns to the ground during a show by **Frank Zappa and the Mothers of Invention**. The incident is immortalized by opening act **Deep Purple** in their song "Smoke on the Water," which will become a major U.S. hit (#4) in 1973.

4 **Sly and the Family Stone**'s "Family Affair" begins a three-week reign in the Number One spot atop the pop chart. It is their third and last Number One record, and their last to make the Top Ten. They will have two more minor hits in 1972, "Runnin' Away," which will reach #23, and "Smilin'," which will reach #42. "Family Affair," like the album from which it came, *There's a Riot Goin' On*, stood in stark, dark contrast to the optimistic racial-unity themes of the band's earlier work. Fittingly, it was around this time that Sly's behavior would become increasingly erratic, precipitating the imminent departure of the band's original bassist, **Larry Graham**, and original drummer, **Greg Errico**, in 1972. For now, though, "Family Affair" is also Number One on the soul singles chart, and *There's a Riot Goin' On* is the #2 soul LP and #2 on the Top 100 LPs chart. In two weeks, it will reach Number One on both charts.

4 The Russian Ministry of Culture, according to a *Billboard* cover story, has formed its own Department of Amusement Games, through which the Soviets hope to develop their own jukeboxes. Two months earlier, the U.S.S.R. had held its first international jukebox and coin-machine fair, Attraktzion '71, in Moscow, a showcase of entirely non-domestic machines that had attracted widespread Russian interest. *Billboard* reports that the Russians want to permanently install jukeboxes and game machines in cafes and resorts, but they are having trouble installing, operating and maintaining the machines, simply because they are so new to the Russians. There has also been trouble in finding cafes and resorts where owners will allow the machines. But the overall outlook is best expressed by the Soviet daily *Izvestia*, which recently wrote: "A new challenge has appeared in our country—to develop a real amusement industry of our own. We need our own Russian-made jukeboxes, coin-machines and outdoor amusement installations."

Island Records releases **Traffic**'s album *The Low Spark of High Heeled Boys*. The twelve-minute-long title track will become a big favorite of FM radio, and will help make the album one of the group's best sellers.

9 **Ten Years After** has a gold album with *A Space in Time*, the last big LP for the blues-rock quartet. "I'd Love to Change the World" becomes TYA's only U.S. Top Forty hit.

11 Godfather of Soul **James Brown** has his thirty-second album released this week. *Revolution of the Mind*, subtitled *Live at the Apollo, Volume 3* and released by Polydor Records, opens with a song whose title only James Brown could have come up with: "It's a Brand New Day So Open Up the Door and Let a Man Come In to Do the Popcorn."

Blood, Sweat and Tears lead singer **David Clayton-Thomas** is among the performers making public service announcements and press statements in support of the Canadian "Save the Seals" campaign, which will try to prevent the annual slaughter of baby seals in the Gulf of St. Lawrence in the spring of 1972. Other performers contributing to "Save the Seals" include Canadian blues-rock band **Crowbar**, and Canadian folk-singers **Murray McLauchlan** and **Luke Gibson**.

John Lennon and **Yoko Ono** perform at a benefit in Ann Arbor, Michigan, for left-wing activist **John Sinclair**, ex-manager of Detroit's legendary guerrilla-rock band the **MC5**, who was arrested for possession of marijuana in 1969 and sentenced to ten years in prison. After being told about Sinclair's plight by radical politico **Jerry Rubin**, Lennon composed "John Sinclair."

18 Dial Records, a subsidiary of Mercury, releases **Joe Tex**' bawdy funk disc "I Gotcha." In late January of 1972 the song will reach #2 on the pop chart, becoming Tex's biggest hit since his 1964 #5 hit "Hold What You've Got." A big factor in the success of "I Gotcha" is Tex' slurred delivery of the line "Told you not to play with my affection," which causes millions of teenage girls to mistake the last word for *erection*.

25 Critics aren't the only music-industry people who hate **Grand Funk Railroad**. In today's *Billboard*, Grand Funk's manager, **Terry Knight**, claims that "we are virtually devoid of radio play in major markets. Our only airplay comes from the ordinary stations that the major markets snicker at." This, Knight adds, despite the band's string of gold records and sell-out tours and a recent platinum LP, *E Pluribus Funk*.

28 **Keith Moon** emcees a concert for one of his favorite acts, Fifties revivalists **Sha Na Na**. ◆

WEEK ENDING DECEMBER 4

U.S. #1 POP 45	"Family Affair"	Sly and the Family Stone
U.S. #1 POP LP	*Santana*	Santana
U.S. #1 R&B 45	"Family Affair"	Sly and the Family Stone
U.K. #1 POP 45	"Ernie"	Benny Hill
U.K. #1 POP LP	*Imagine*	John Lennon

WEEK ENDING DECEMBER 11

U.S. #1 POP 45	"Family Affair"	Sly and the Family Stone
U.S. #1 POP LP	*Santana*	Santana
U.S. #1 R&B 45	"Family Affair"	Sly and the Family Stone
U.K. #1 POP 45	"Ernie"	Benny Hill
U.K. #1 POP LP	*Led Zeppelin IV*	Led Zeppelin

WEEK ENDING DECEMBER 18

U.S. #1 POP 45	"Family Affair"	Sly and the Family Stone
U.S. #1 POP LP	*There's a Riot Goin' On*	Sly and the Family Stone
U.S. #1 R&B 45	"Family Affair"	Sly and the Family Stone
U.K. #1 POP 45	"Ernie"	Benny Hill
U.K. #1 POP LP	*Led Zeppelin IV*	Led Zeppelin

WEEK ENDING DECEMBER 25

U.S. #1 POP 45	"Brand New Key"	Melanie
U.S. #1 POP LP	*There's a Riot Goin' On*	Sly and the Family Stone
U.S. #1 R&B 45	"Family Affair"	Sly and the Family Stone
U.K. #1 POP 45	"Ernie"	Benny Hill
U.K. #1 POP LP	*Led Zeppelin IV*	Led Zeppelin

1972

By now, it seemed a foregone conclusion to most of rock's mass audience that rock as a serious political weapon was dead and buried. Not that they minded: with the apathy that set in as an inevitable after-effect of the souped-up Sixties, the Seventies audience demanded escape through entertainment and got it from a wide variety of those semipopular subgenres of the music that established a commercial stronghold this year. Progressive rock dazzled with its technical virtuosity and prolix cosmic visions. Heavy metal pummeled its all-too-willing minions with numbing volume levels and plodding tempos. For those who needed something outrageous for diversion, there was glitter rock. And there was country rock and L.A. singer/songwriter studio pop to be worn as badges of attitude by whomever it appealed to. Pick your style, reflect your outlook and be separated from all the other styles and outlooks in the process.

And yet, there were still instances of rock music connecting with politics and efforts to effect social change. Paul McCartney's "Give Ireland Back to the Irish" was banned by British radio, and John Lennon and Yoko Ono's "Woman Is the Nigger of the World" was banned by American radio. The U.S. Council for World Affairs adopted the Who's "Join Together" as its theme song. There were also the pop-star-studded benefits for presidential candidate George McGovern, but later in the year, Richard Nixon's trouncing of McGovern at the polls would seem to vindicate that portion of the rock audience that looked upon such musical-political campaigning as nostalgic, wishful thinking.

Probably the most satisfying rock anthem of the year, though, came from—of all people— Alice Cooper, the heavy-metal, glitter-rock freak-show ringmaster who never made any claims to profundity, but whose hit single "School's Out" proved to be a cathartic, near-anarchic postscript to Chuck Berry's 1957 hit "School Day." What made it a great rock anthem was that it expressed no special political view other than the perennial adolescent alienation from adult institutions. And yet Alice, with his lurid regurgitations of America's surreal pop culture, was actually closer to the adult institution of spectacularly sleazy entertainment than anything else.

Meanwhile, the ghost of the Sixties kept rearing its head. There were still big rock and pop festivals, and most were washouts, failures or catastrophes; ironically, the most successful one was the Ann Arbor Blues and Jazz Festival organized by John Sinclair, who was just out of prison, where he'd served part of a ten-year sentence for the possession of two joints of marijuana. And the comedy team of Cheech and Chong hit big with a form of Sixties sex-and-drugs humor. The collective rush the nation's youth had felt only a few years ago during the "Summer of Love" had been reduced to a tired, sick joke—but it was a *successful* joke. So, it now seemed, was most of what was passing for rock & roll.

8 **Melanie Safka**, better known simply as **Melanie**, enjoys the biggest hit of her career with "Brand New Key," which remains at Number One for the third consecutive week on this date. The daughter of a one-time jazz singer, Melanie, whose folky compositions ooze with sincerity—first gained attention with 1970's "Lay Down (Candles in the Rain)." But her career takes a sharp turn downward after the success of "Brand New Key."

16 **Ross Bagdasarian**, who had a string of novelty hits in the Fifties "sung" by TV cartoon characters the **Chipmunks**, dies at age fifty-two. Once a raisin farmer and a bit actor, Bagdasarian did the voices for **Alvin**, **Simon** and **Theodore**. Under the name **David Seville**, he recorded the Number One hit "Witch Doc-

tor" in 1957, and the following year he sold more than 4 million records with the "Chipmunk Song." Bagdasarian also cowrote the **Rosemary Clooney** hit "Come On-a My House."

22 One of the least conspicuous success stories in rock is that of **Rare Earth**, who on this date rack up their fifth—and last—Top Twenty hit, "Hey Big Brother."

The group, a white band whose Rare Earth label was a subsidiary of Motown, had its biggest hit in 1970 with a cover of the **Temptation**'s 1966 hit "Get Ready."

23 **Maybelle Smith**, also known as **Big Maybelle**, dies at age forty-seven in Cleveland. Born in Jackson, Tennessee, Smith hit her peak as a jazz singer in the late Forties and early Fifties, and accumulated several million-selling records, including "Candy," "96 Tear Drops" and "Ain't Nothin' but a Hound Dog."

27 The **New Seekers** receive a gold record for "I'd Like to Teach the World to Sing," a song that probably will be better remembered as the music for Coca-Cola commercials.

Mahalia Jackson once remarked that she sang "because I

was lonely," but she became one of America's best-loved vocalists. The sixty-year-old gospel singer, who'd been in failing health ever since a heart attack in 1964, dies in Chicago. Born in New Orleans, she earned her first recording contract in 1935 after a talent scout from Decca Records heard her sing at a funeral. "You had all those people crying in there," he said. Though Jackson was profoundly affected by the records of **Bessie Smith**, she never sang the blues, only gospel music.

31 More than 40,000 mourners file past **Mahalia Jackson**'s open coffin in Chicago's Greater Salem Baptist Church. Funeral services are held the next day; in attendance are **Coretta King**, **Mayor Richard Daley** and **Sammy Davis, Jr.**, who reads a telegram from **President Nixon**. At the end of the services, **Aretha Franklin** sings "Precious Lord, Take My Hand," moving many to tears.

Joan Baez claims a gold record for her album *Any Day Now*, which was comprised solely of songs by **Bob Dylan**. The LP went gold three years after its release. ◆

WEEK ENDING JANUARY 1

U.S. #1 POP 45	"Brand New Key"	Melanie
U.S. #1 POP LP	*Music*	Carole King
U.S. #1 R&B 45	"Family Affair"	Sly and the Family Stone
U.K. #1 POP 45	"I'd Like to Teach the World to Sing"	The New Seekers
U.K. #1 POP LP	*Electric Warrior*	T. Rex

WEEK ENDING JANUARY 8

U.S. #1 POP 45	"Brand New Key"	Melanie
U.S. #1 POP LP	*Music*	Carole King
U.S. #1 R&B 45	"Let's Stay Together"	Al Green
U.K. #1 POP 45	"I'd Like to Teach the World to Sing"	The New Seekers
U.K. #1 POP LP	*Electric Warrior*	T. Rex

WEEK ENDING JANUARY 15

U.S. #1 POP 45	"American Pie"	Don McLean
U.S. #1 POP LP	*Music*	Carole King
U.S. #1 R&B 45	"Let's Stay Together"	Al Green
U.K. #1 POP 45	"I'd Like to Teach the World to Sing"	The New Seekers
U.K. #1 POP LP	*Teaser and the Firecat*	Cat Stevens

WEEK ENDING JANUARY 22

U.S. #1 POP 45	"American Pie"	Don McLean
U.S. #1 POP LP	*American Pie*	Don McLean
U.S. #1 R&B 45	"Let's Stay Together"	Al Green
U.K. #1 POP 45	"I'd Like to Teach the World to Sing"	The New Seekers
U.K. #1 POP LP	*Teaser and the Firecat*	Cat Stevens

WEEK ENDING JANUARY 29

U.S. #1 POP 45	"American Pie"	Don McLean
U.S. #1 POP LP	*American Pie*	Don McLean
U.S. #1 R&B 45	"Let's Stay Together"	Al Green
U.K. #1 POP 45	"A Horse with No Name"	America
U.K. #1 POP LP	*Teaser and the Firecat*	Cat Stevens

5 **Paul Simon** releases his first new song minus **Art Garfunkel**, "Mother and Child Reunion," which becomes a Top Five hit. The *Paul Simon* album, issued concurrently, also reaches #4, and shows Simon further expanding his musical horizons, incorporating Latin and other influences. The LP's second hit, "Me and Julio down by the Schoolyard," is one of the quirkiest songs of the year.

9 **Paul McCartney and Wings** go mobile, traveling about England in a bus and playing unannounced in clubs and halls. On this date they perform a ninety-minute set at the University of Nottingham. The group now includes guitarist **Henry McCullough**, formerly of the **Grease Band**.

14 **John** and **Yoko** begin a week-long stint as co-hosts on "The Mike Douglas Show," a talk show for housewives, and not exactly known for its radical leanings. Highlights include an appearance by **Chuck Berry**, who is greeted with a shout of "My hero!" by John; the spectacle of **Jerry Rubin** onstage beating a conga drum, and a mind-boggling mixture of guests, from Black Panther **Bobby Seale** and **Ralph Nader** to **Louis Nye** and the Surgeon General of the United States.

With America swept by Fifties notalgia, *Grease* opens on Broadway, where it will run for the next decade. The comedy takes an irreverent look at Fifties fashion, morals and music, which it gently mocks with its own selection of original numbers like "Look at Me, I'm Sandra Dee." It will be turned into a smash movie six years later.

Los Angeles mayor **Sam Yorty** declares "**Steppenwolf** Day" in honor of the band's "retirement." (They will *un*retire just a few years later.) At a press conference to announce the group's disbanding, leader **John Kay** explains that the members were tired of being "locked into a style of music" and their leather-clad image.

15 The Anti-Bootlegging Bill, Public Law 92-140, which provides federal copyright protection for sound recordings and grants to owners of such copyrights the same legal remedies against unauthorized reproduction that owners of other copyrights have had since 1909, goes into effect. Musicians and singers had been asking for similar legislation since the mid-Fifties.

17 **Jonathan Edwards** is awarded a gold record for "Sunshine," the lone hit for this Virginia folkie. Edwards handles his brief fame in typically laid-back fashion. Instead of buying himself a Porsche, Edwards' manager says with a chuckle, "He got himself a fancy truck."

Pink Floyd begin a four-night stand at London's Rainbow Theater during which they premiere *The Dark Side of the Moon* a full year before its release as an album.

18 **Neil Young** receives a gold record for *Harvest*, the only Number One record of his lengthy career. The album includes the Number One single "Heart of Gold."

19 **Led Zeppelin** achieve their second biggest 45, "Black Dog," which hits #15 and goes on to become an FM radio staple.

Paul McCartney releases "Give Ireland Back to the Irish," his commentary about the Britain-Ireland conflict, and it's immediately banned by the BBC because of a law that prohibits public figures from making statements about public events that are under a Crown Investigation. The notoriety the song receives from the banning only increases its popularity in England, where it goes Top Twenty.

Jazz trumpeter **Lee Morgan** is shot to death in Slug's, a jazz club on New York City's Lower East Side. Morgan was killed by his girlfriend **Helen More** while he was relaxing at the bar after a late-night set by his quintet. He was thirty-three.

23 *Rockin' the Fillmore*, **Humble Pie**'s breakthrough album, and their last with guitarist **Peter Frampton**, goes gold. The two-record set was recorded at the Fillmore East in 1971 and included the Pie's nine-minute version of "I Don't Need No Doctor."

28 A *New York* magazine article written by **Peter McCabe** accuses **Allen Klein** and his ABKCO. Industries, Inc. of skimming $1.14 off the profits from each *Bangla Desh* album. Klein then sues the publication for $150 million, citing damages "for injuries to ABKCO.'s credit and reputation."

29 **John Lennon**'s U.S. immigration visa expires. Thus begins the ex-Beatle's three-and-a-half-year fight to remain in the country. Meanwhile, officials ponder whether or not Lennon is deserving of the special status of "outstanding artists whose presence would be of cultural advantage to the U.S." Lennon's problems supposedly stem from a 1968 conviction for possession of marijuana. ◆

WEEK ENDING FEBRUARY 5

U.S. #1 POP 45	"American Pie"	Don McLean
U.S. #1 POP LP	*American Pie*	Don McLean
U.S. #1 R&B 45	"Let's Stay Together"	Al Green
U.K. #1 POP 45	"Telegram Sam"	T. Rex
U.K. #1 POP LP	*Teaser and the Firecat*	Cat Stevens

WEEK ENDING FEBRUARY 12

U.S. #1 POP 45	"Let's Stay Together"	Al Green
U.S. #1 POP LP	*American Pie*	Don McLean
U.S. #1 R&B 45	"Let's Stay Together"	Al Green
U.K. #1 POP 45	"Son of My Father"	Chicory Tip
U.K. #1 POP LP	*Teaser and the Firecat*	Cat Stevens

WEEK ENDING FEBRUARY 19

U.S. #1 POP 45	"Without You"	Nilsson
U.S. #1 POP LP	*American Pie*	Don McLean
U.S. #1 R&B 45	"Let's Stay Together"	Al Green
U.K. #1 POP 45	"Son of My Father"	Chicory Tip
U.K. #1 POP LP	*Neil Reid*	Neil Reid

WEEK ENDING FEBRUARY 26

U.S. #1 POP 45	"Without You"	Nilsson
U.S. #1 POP LP	*American Pie*	Don McLean
U.S. #1 R&B 45	"Let's Stay Together"	Al Green
U.K. #1 POP 45	"American Pie"	Don McLean
U.K. #1 POP LP	*Paul Simon*	Paul Simon

3 **Paul Gadd**, a.k.a. **Gary Glitter**, has the first of his three Number One U.K. hits, "Rock and Roll—Part 2." A previously unsuccessful pop singer, Glitter found a successful formula that he would milk through the mid-Seventies: football-chant-like vocals, distorted guitar chords and predominant, primitive percussion. "Rock and Roll—Part 2" makes #7 in the U.S. later in the year.

Harry Nilsson receives a gold record for *Nilsson Schmilsson,* the best-selling album of his career. The LP contains three hits: "Without You," "Jump into the Fire" and "Coconut."

4 It's a good week for **Badfinger**, who receive a gold record for "Day after Day" one day after **Harry Nilsson** gets a gold disc for his cover of their song "Without You."

6 **John Lennon**'s visa extension is canceled by the New York Office of the Immigration Department, five days after it was granted.

9 In what will become a trend for the rest of the Seventies, pop artists unite to perform for a presidential candidate: **Carole King, James Taylor** and **Barbra Streisand**, among others, play a benefit show for Democratic hopeful **George McGovern** at L.A.'s Forum.

Allen Klein, already accused of laundering money from UNICEF, which was to receive the royalties from *Bangla Desh*'s sales, turns over just one-tenth the money due the organization, $1.2 million.

10 The group **America**, army brats who grew up in England, receive a gold record for their eponymously titled debut album. Two weeks later the 45 "A Horse with No Name" also goes gold. The group evokes memories of **Neil Young**, especially on "Horse," and in fact replaces Young at Number One on both the single and the LP charts in April.

15 Singer **Robert John** scores with a remake of the **Tokens**' Number One hit "The Lion Sleeps Tonight."

John's version goes Top Fifteen and earns him a gold record.

Radio station KHJ is raided by L.A. police after calls from listeners who feared there'd been a revolution at the station: from 6:00 to 7:30 in the morning, DJ **Robert W. Morgan** had played **Donny Osmond**'s "Puppy Love" over and over. The police, no doubt confused, left without making any arrests.

17 The Irish group **Horslips** turn pro on—appropriately enough—St. Patrick's Day. They will attract a large following in Ireland and Great Britain, but will never really crack the U.S. market.

18 **Ringo Starr** begins work on his documentary on **Marc Bolan**, *Born to Boogie,* by filming **T. Rex**'s concert at Wembley, England.

20 **Ringo Starr** releases the second of his seven Top Ten singles, "Back Off, Boogaloo," produced by **George Harrison**.

22 **Joe Tex** gets a gold record for "I Gotcha," his biggest single success (#2). It's his first hit in four years.

24 Twelve years after it was first a #2 hit for teen idol **Paul Anka**, "Puppy Love," by **Donny Osmond**, makes #3 and goes gold. The song also inspires numerous wisecracks about young Osmond.

26 **Mott the Hoople** prematurely decide to pack it in after four albums. But **David Bowie** comes to their rescue, bearing a song called "All the Young Dudes." Hoople record it, Bowie produces it; "Dudes" becomes a U.K. smash, goes Top Forty in the U.S. and revives their career.

27 **Elvis Presley** records what will be his last major hit, "Burning Love," which reaches #2 in October. The song was originally recorded by blues singer **Arthur Alexander**.

Terry Knight, self-envisioned Svengali of **Grand Funk Railroad**, is fired by the group, instigating a series of multimillion dollar lawsuits between ex-manager and group. At a press conference in New York, Knight says, "I don't know if they're acting of their own free will." They are. A settlement eventually will be reached, but the legal hassles impede GFR's momentum for most of 1972. ◆

WEEK ENDING MARCH 4

U.S. #1 POP 45	"Without You"	Nilsson
U.S. #1 POP LP	*American Pie*	Don McLean
U.S. #1 R&B 45	"Let's Stay Together"	Al Green
U.K. #1 POP 45	"Without You"	Nilsson
U.K. #1 POP LP	*Paul Simon*	Paul Simon

WEEK ENDING MARCH 11

U.S. #1 POP 45	"Without You"	Nilsson
U.S. #1 POP LP	*Harvest*	Neil Young
U.S. #1 R&B 45	"Talking Loud and Saying Nothing"	James Brown
U.K. #1 POP 45	"Without You"	Nilsson
U.K. #1 POP LP	*Paul Simon*	Paul Simon

WEEK ENDING MARCH 18

U.S. #1 POP 45	"Heart of Gold"	Neil Young
U.S. #1 POP LP	*Harvest*	Neil Young
U.S. #1 R&B 45	"I Gotcha"	Joe Tex
U.K. #1 POP 45	"Without You"	Nilsson
U.K. #1 POP LP	*Paul Simon*	Paul Simon

WEEK ENDING MARCH 25

U.S. #1 POP 45	"A Horse with No Name"	America
U.S. #1 POP LP	*America*	America
U.S. #1 R&B 45	"In the Rain"	The Dramatics
U.K. #1 POP 45	"Without You"	Nilsson
U.K. #1 POP LP	*Paul Simon*	Paul Simon

1 The three-day Mar y Sol (sea and sun) festival opens in Vega Baja, attracting 30,000 people. Promoter **Alex Cooley** gathered together such acts as the **Allman Brothers**, **Emerson, Lake and Palmer**, **B. B. King**, the **J. Geils Band** and **Black Sabbath**. The festival goes on despite efforts by Puerto Rico's Secretary of Health to prevent it. The secretary fears there will be a plague of drug abuse.

3 The Mar y Sol festival ends. The final box score: four persons dead (including one sixteen-year-old boy who was hacked to death while lying in his sleeping bag); a general lack of sufficient food supplies; a general abundance of brutal Puerto Rican sun; and even after the festival, a major snafu in which hundreds of Americans are stranded at the San Juan airport. Promoter **Cooley** calls the festival a success, but **Richard Kimball** of KMET-FM in L.A. sums it up this way: "It was a fucking drag."

14 **David Bowie** releases the first single from his conceptual *The Rise and Fall of Ziggy Stardust and the Spiders from Mars*—"Starman" backed with "Suffragette City." *Ziggy* will remain on the LP chart for more than a year, and will finally break Bowie in the U.S.

16 The **Electric Light Orchestra**, born of the **Move**, play their first live gig. The group at this time includes **Jeff Lynne**, **Bev Bevan** and **Roy Wood**, who will shortly leave for a solo career. Most of ELO's early shows are disastrous: Wood attempts to play so many instruments that he frequently trips over cords and wires just trying to get to them.

19 **Roberta Flack** is awarded a gold record for "The First Time Ever I Saw Your Face," the Number One 45 for six weeks in the spring. The former schoolteacher from North Carolina will continue to have a string of hits, several of them recorded with singer **Donny Hathaway**.

24 One of **John Lennon's** most controversial singles, "Woman Is the Nigger of the World," is released. The song goes to #57, despite the fact that virtually every radio station in the country refuses to play it.

A half-dozen teenage girls faint and several other youths sustain cuts in a stampede that occurs prior to a concert by **Jethro Tull**. An estimated 2,500 young persons press into the lobby of Long Island's Nassau Coliseum to purchase tickets, resulting in the summoning of 100 police, as well as a box-office window being smashed.

27 **Phil King**, who acted as frontman for an early version **Blue Oyster Cult** and was a sometime promoter, is shot to death after a gambling incident in Farmingdale, New York. According to police, King, twenty-five, was killed by a gambling associate who owed him money; the suspect is arrested the next day.

29 **John** and **Yoko** receive support from New York City mayor **John Lindsay** in their fight to remain in the U.S. Lindsay asks the federal government to halt deportation proceedings against the two, citing the fact that if the Lennons are deported they will lose custody of Yoko's missing daughter from a previous marriage, **Kyoko**. Lindsay calls the action "a grave injustice in light of [John and Yoko's] unique contributions in the fields of music and art." ♦

WEEK ENDING APRIL 1

U.S. #1 POP 45	"A Horse with No Name"	America
U.S. #1 POP LP	*America*	America
U.S. #1 R&B 45	"In the Rain"	The Dramatics
U.K. #1 POP 45	"Without You"	Nilsson
U.K. #1 POP LP	*Fog on the Tyne*	Lindisfarne

WEEK ENDING APRIL 8

U.S. #1 POP 45	"A Horse with No Name"	America
U.S. #1 POP LP	*America*	America
U.S. #1 R&B 45	"In the Rain"	The Dramatics
U.K. #1 POP 45	"Without You"	Nilsson
U.K. #1 POP LP	*Harvest*	Neil Young

WEEK ENDING APRIL 15

U.S. #1 POP 45	"The First Time Ever I Saw Your Face"	Roberta Flack
U.S. #1 POP LP	*America*	America
U.S. #1 R&B 45	"In the Rain"	The Dramatics
U.K. #1 POP 45	"Amazing Grace"	Royal Scots Dragoon Guards, Pipes, Drums and Band
U.K. #1 POP LP	*Harvest*	Neil Young

WEEK ENDING APRIL 22

U.S. #1 POP 45	"The First Time Ever I Saw Your Face"	Roberta Flack
U.S. #1 POP LP	*America*	America
U.S. #1 R&B 45	"Day Dreaming"	Aretha Franklin
U.K. #1 POP 45	"Amazing Grace"	Royal Scots Dragoon Guards, Pipes, Drums and Band
U.K. #1 POP LP	*Harvest*	Neil Young

WEEK ENDING APRIL 29

U.S. #1 POP 45	"The First Time Ever I Saw Your Face"	Roberta Flack
U.S. #1 POP LP	*First Take*	Roberta Flack
U.S. #1 R&B 45	"Day Dreaming"	Aretha Franklin
U.K. #1 POP 45	"Amazing Grace"	Royal Scots Dragoon Guards, Pipes, Drums and Band
U.K. #1 POP LP	*Machine Head*	Deep Purple

3 **Stone the Crows** lead guitarist **Les Harvey** is electrocuted on stage at a show in Swansea, Wales. Harvey, twenty-five, was thrown into the air after touching a poorly connected microphone. He was given mouth-to-mouth resuscitation, but died in a local hospital a few hours later. Also hospitalized is the band's singer, **Maggie Bell**, who collapsed after the accident; she had been Harvey's longtime girlfriend.

5 Ragtime blues and gospel performer the **Reverend Gary Davis** dies of a heart attack in Hammonton, New Jersey, at age seventy-six. The blind guitarist grew up on a sharecropper's farm in South Carolina, and spent most of his years as a street singer. He didn't receive national recognition for his syncopated guitar style until a performance at Newport in 1964. Artists such as **Peter, Paul and Mary** later recorded some of his songs, giving him enough royalties money to enable him to move to New York, his residence up until his death.

Thirty artists, brought together by actor **Warren Beatty**, have agreed to perform at a series of twelve benefits for the **George McGovern** presidential campaign. Included are **Judy Collins**, **Mama Cass Elliot**, **Michelle Phillips**, **Goldie Hawn** and **Jack Nicholson**. "I didn't want to do it at first," admits Collins, "but then the bombing build-ups in Vietnam started; that woke me up."

7 The **Rolling Stones** release the second album on their own label, *Exile on Main Street.* The double-record set contains two hits, "Tumbling Dice" and "Happy" (sung by **Keith Richards**), and at least a side-full of throwaway tracks with titles like "Turd on the Run." But given time, *Exile* will become regarded as perhaps the Stones' finest album.

8 Keyboardist and singer **Billy Preston** becomes the first rock performer to headline at Radio City Music Hall. Others to soon follow will include **David Bowie** and **Mountain**.

11 **John Lennon** tells **Dick Cavett** during an appearance on his show that he believes he has been followed

and has had his phone tapped over the previous months. In the meantime, a National Committee for John and Yoko continues its drive for letters and petitions opposing the U.S. government's attempt to deport the couple.

15 The **Rolling Stones'** 1972 U.S. tour encounters its first problem three weeks before it even commences. A computer designed to handle the distribution of tickets for the group's San Francisco shows overloads, leaving thousands in the lurch. "It was a madhouse," says a salesperson at Sears, one of fifty-four Ticketron outlets handling the concerts. Because of the foul-up, it took twelve minutes to process each order.

16 *Fillmore,* the film documentary of the Fillmore West's last days, premieres in New York City. The movie had been given an R rating because of Fillmore owner **Bill Graham**'s salty language, and Graham was livid when when he heard about the rating. "There is no dope, no sex, no pornography, no killing," he says about the film. Graham declares that he'll fight the Motion Picture Association of America—the film-rating body—for a PG rating.

18 The *New York Times* carries a report that the former **Beatles** have agreed to end their feuding. In addition, **Paul McCartney** claims that the four have decided to split the fortune resulting from their partnership. The four ex-Beatles came to this solution, he explains, to free $17 million now frozen in litigation.

29 Long accused of possessing a knack for schmaltz, **Paul McCartney** gives his critics further ammunition by releasing "Mary Had a Little Lamb," based on the nursery rhyme. The single is among his least successful, just barely cracking the Top Thirty. ◆

WEEK ENDING MAY 6

U.S. #1 POP 45	"The First Time Ever I Saw Your Face"	Roberta Flack
U.S. #1 POP LP	*First Take*	Roberta Flack
U.S. #1 R&B 45	"I'll Take You There"	The Staple Singers
U.K. #1 POP 45	"Amazing Grace"	Royal Scots Dragoon Guards, Pipes, Drums and Band
U.K. #1 POP LP	*Machine Head*	Deep Purple

WEEK ENDING MAY 13

U.S. #1 POP 45	"The First Time Ever I Saw Your Face"	Roberta Flack
U.S. #1 POP LP	*First Take*	Roberta Flack
U.S. #1 R&B 45	"I'll Take You There"	The Staple Singers
U.K. #1 POP 45	"Metal Guru"	T. Rex
U.K. #1 POP LP	*Fog on the Tyne*	Lindisfarne

WEEK ENDING MAY 20

U.S. #1 POP 45	"The First Time Ever I Saw Your Face"	Roberta Flack
U.S. #1 POP LP	*First Take*	Roberta Flack
U.S. #1 R&B 45	"I'll Take You There"	The Staple Singers
U.K. #1 POP 45	"Metal Guru"	T. Rex
U.K. #1 POP LP	*Bolan Boogie*	T. Rex

WEEK ENDING MAY 27

U.S. #1 POP 45	"Oh Girl"	The Chi-Lites
U.S. #1 POP LP	*First Take*	Roberta Flack
U.S. #1 R&B 45	"I'll Take You There"	The Staple Singers
U.K. #1 POP 45	"Metal Guru"	T. Rex
U.K. #1 POP LP	*Bolan Boogie*	T. Rex

2 **Dion and the Belmonts** reunite for one show at Madison Square Garden. The event is recorded and released as *Reunion* the following year.

3 The **Rolling Stones** begin their first North American tour since 1969 in Vancouver, with *Exile on Main Street* approaching Number One. The eight-week tour is the happening of the year, and tickets sell out in all of the thirty cities the Stones will play. The first show is more like a dress rehearsal in which the band gets to audition its material in front of 17,000 fans. **Keith Richards** blows out two guitars during the tepidly received one-hour-and-forty-minute set. Opening for the Stones is **Stevie Wonder**.

7 *Grease* opens at the Broadhurst Theatre on Broadway, after a four-month run off Broadway. It runs continuously until April 13, 1980, and its 3,388 performances break *Fiddler on the Roof*'s longest-running-show-on-Broadway record.

8 **Jimmy Rushing**, who rose to fame in the Thirties as the blues singer with the **Count Basie Band**, dies at age sixty-eight after a short illness. Rushing's voice was once described by novelist **Ralph Ellison** as "steel bright in its upper range and, at its best, silky smooth." Rushing remained with Basie until 1950, and later led his own band. He was still singing on weekends at New York's Half Note club up until his death.

9 **John Hammond** of Columbia Records signs a singer/songwriter from an undiscovered bastion of rock & roll—Asbury Park, New Jersey. The new recording artist is a veteran of the Jersey shore scene. His name: **Bruce Springsteen**.

12 **John Lennon** and **Yoko Ono** release *Some Time in New York City,* a two-record set full of self-conscious politicism that even Lennon himself will later regret. Two sides of the four-record set consist of the Lennons' live jam with **Frank Zappa** at the Fillmore East in 1971. The LP comes packaged as a news-paper, another self-conscious reminder of the songs' contemporary bent. Song titles include: "Sisters, O Sisters," "John Sinclair," "Attica State" and "Angela," a song written for black activist **Angela Davis**. The album only makes it to #48.

Creedence Clearwater Revival, pared down to a trio after the departure of Tom Fogerty in 1971, receive a gold album for *Mardi Gras,* the final LP of their recording career. Most CCR LPs were packed with hits, but *Mardi Gras* contains only one, "Someday Never Comes," the last of their thirteen Top Twenty-five hits. Later this year, Creedence will announce that they are splitting up.

14 The fifth show organized by actor **Warren Beatty** for presidential candidate **George McGovern** is held at Madison Square Garden. Beatty coaxes several defunct acts to reunite: **Simon and Garfunkel**, **Peter, Paul and Mary** and the comedy duo of **Mike Nichols and Elaine May**. A crowd of 18,000 attends, raising several hundred thousand dollars for the McGovern campaign.

Tucson, Arizona, police are forced to use tear gas to disperse a crowd of 200 to 300 youths who attempt to crash a **Rolling Stones** concert.

20 The Tallahatchie Bridge, immortalized in **Bobbie Gentry**'s 1967 hit "Ode to Billy Joe," collapses.

21 **Janis Joplin**'s *Joplin in Concert,* released posthumously, is awarded a gold record. The two-record set includes material that Joplin recorded as far back as 1968 with **Big Brother and the Holding Company** and as late as the summer of 1970 with the **Full-Tilt Boogie Band**. The LP makes it to #4.

Billy Preston has his first gold hit with "Out-a-Space," the first of his three hit instrumentals. Preston first achieved recognition for his keyboard work with the **Beatles** on "Let It Be." He will go on to tour and to record with the **Rolling Stones**. ◆

WEEK ENDING JUNE 3

U.S. #1 POP 45	"I'll Take You There"	The Staple Singers
U.S. #1 POP LP	*Thick as a Brick*	Jethro Tull
U.S. #1 R&B 45	"Oh Girl"	The Chi-Lites
U.K. #1 POP 45	"Metal Guru"	T. Rex
U.K. #1 POP LP	*Bolan Boogie*	T. Rex

WEEK ENDING JUNE 10

U.S. #1 POP 45	"The Candy Man"	Sammy Davis, Jr.
U.S. #1 POP LP	*Thick as a Brick*	Jethro Tull
U.S. #1 R&B 45	"Oh Girl"	The Chi-Lites
U.K. #1 POP 45	"Vincent"	Don McLean
U.K. #1 POP LP	*Exile on Main Street*	The Rolling Stones

WEEK ENDING JUNE 17

U.S. #1 POP 45	"The Candy Man"	Sammy Davis, Jr.
U.S. #1 POP LP	*Exile on Main Street*	The Rolling Stones
U.S. #1 R&B 45	"Woman's Gotta Have It"	Bobby Womack
U.K. #1 POP 45	"Vincent"	Don McLean
U.K. #1 POP LP	*Exile on Main Street*	The Rolling Stones

WEEK ENDING JUNE 24

U.S. #1 POP 45	"The Candy Man"	Sammy Davis, Jr.
U.S. #1 POP LP	*Exile on Main Street*	The Rolling Stones
U.S. #1 R&B 45	"Lean on Me"	Bill Withers
U.K. #1 POP 45	"Vincent"	Don McLean
U.K. #1 POP LP	*American Pie*	Don McLean

1 After 1,729 performances, *Hair,* Broadway's romanticized portrayal of the counterculture, closes. Not only did the play enjoy a four-year run, but it spawned a trio of soundtrack hits: "Aquarius/Let the Sunshine In," a Number One hit for the **Fifth Dimension**; "Hair," a #2 hit for the **Cowsills**; and "Good Morning Starshine," a #3 hit for **Oliver**—all in 1969.

8 An estimated 200,000 youths pack the Pocono International Raceway in upstate New York for what will be the largest rock festival since Woodstock. The festival is called Concert 10, and promises ten hours of music for an eleven-dollar admission fee. But a third of the crowd leaves after a downpour. **Emerson, Lake and Palmer**, **Humble Pie**, the **Faces**, the **J. Geils Band** and others perform, but twelve of the advertised acts fail to appear, and the two-day festival is generally considered—like the weather—a washout.

9 Traveling aboard their double-decker London bus (with psychedelic interior), **Paul McCartney and Wings** open a twenty-six-stop European tour with a date in France. The tour is McCartney's first since the **Beatles** retired from the stage in 1966, but the thirty-year-old-bassist is in fine form. Afterward, however, he says of his still-new group: "We have to get worked in before doing any big shows in Britain or America."

16 **Smokey Robinson and the Miracles** give their "farewell" concert in Washington, D.C., after a six-month long swan-song tour. But in reality, Robinson is only quitting as a member of the group. He intends to continue as a solo artist, producer, composer and vice-president for the Motown label. Smokey and the Miracles (**Bobby Rogers**, **Ronnie White** and **Pete Moore**) released their first song back in 1959. Robinson tells reporters that most of all he'll miss "the fellows. Just being with them, man. We've had a gas of a time."

17 A bomb placed under a ramp at the Montreal Forum blows out the cones of thirty speakers stored inside one of the **Rolling Stones'** equipment trucks. Montreal radio stations later receive no less than fifty calls from would-be bombers claiming responsibility, but it's never determined just who planted the dynamite, or why. Comments **Mick Jagger**: "Why didn't that cat leave a note?" The show goes on as scheduled.

19 Five members of the **Rolling Stones** entourage, including **Mick Jagger** and **Keith Richards**, are arrested in Warwick, Rhode Island, on charges of assault and obstructing police after an altercation involving a newspaper photographer. All plead guilty and are released, but the delay forces the Stones to go on stage four hours late in Boston.

21 **Rod Stewart** releases *Never a Dull Moment,* which just misses repeating the Number One status of 1971's *Every Picture Tells a Story.* The album goes to #2 and includes two Top Forty hits, "You Wear It Well" and Rod's version of **Jimi Hendrix'** "Angel."

24 "Walking in the Rain with the One I Love" becomes a gold smash for **Love Unlimited**, a soul trio that includes **Glodean James**, the wife of producer **Barry White**. White has a cameo role in the song, which he delivers in his patented basso-profundo whisper rap. The song peaks at #14.

29 "Screaming" Lord Sutch is arrested after a London publicity stunt in which he leaps from a bus on Downing Street to alert the prime minister of his upcoming concert. With Sutch are four nude women, and so he is hauled into court on charges of "insulting behavior." Charges are later dismissed.

31 **Chicago** receive a gold record for their first Number One album, *Chicago V,* titled numerically like its four predecessors. The LP features the standard Chicago mix of horn-embellished rock and cocktail-lounge jazz, and contains one of their finest singles, the beatific "Saturday in the Park," a #3 hit by September. ◆

WEEK ENDING JULY 1

U.S. #1 POP 45	"Song Sung Blue"	Neil Diamond
U.S. #1 POP LP	*Exile on Main Street*	The Rolling Stones
U.S. #1 R&B 45	"Outa-Space"	Billy Preston
U.K. #1 POP 45	"Take Me Bak 'Ome"	Slade
U.K. #1 POP LP	*American Pie*	Don McLean

WEEK ENDING JULY 8

U.S. #1 POP 45	"Lean on Me"	Bill Withers
U.S. #1 POP LP	*Exile on Main Street*	The Rolling Stones
U.S. #1 R&B 45	"(If Loving You Is Wrong) I Don't Want to Be Right."	Luther Ingram
U.K. #1 POP 45	"Puppy Love"	Donny Osmond
U.K. #1 POP LP	*Twenty Dynamic Hits*	various artists

WEEK ENDING JULY 15

U.S. #1 POP 45	"Lean on Me"	Bill Withers
U.S. #1 POP LP	*Honky Chateau*	Elton John
U.S. #1 R&B 45	"(If Loving You Is Wrong) I Don't Want to Be Right"	Luther Ingram
U.K. #1 POP 45	"Puppy Love"	Donny Osmond
U.K. #1 POP LP	*American Pie*	Don McLean

WEEK ENDING JULY 22

U.S. #1 POP 45	"Lean on Me"	Bill Withers
U.S. #1 POP LP	*Honky Chateau*	Elton John
U.S. #1 R&B 45	"(If Loving You Is Wrong) I Don't Want to Be Right"	Luther Ingram
U.K. #1 POP 45	"Puppy Love"	Donny Osmond
U.K. #1 POP LP	*Simon and Garfunkel's Greatest Hits*	Simon and Garfunkel

WEEK ENDING JULY 29

U.S. #1 POP 45	"Alone Again (Naturally)"	Gilbert O'Sullivan
U.S. #1 POP LP	*Honky Chateau*	Elton John
U.S. #1 R&B 45	"(If Loving You Is Wrong) I Don't Want to Be Right"	Luther Ingram
U.K. #1 POP 45	"Puppy Love"	Donny Osmond
U.K. #1 POP LP	*Simon and Garfunkel's Greatest Hits*	Simon and Garfunkel

2 **Brian Cole**, an original member of the **Association**, dies apparently of a heroin overdose. Cole played bass for the pop group known especially for their choral-like harmonies and for such hits as "Windy," "Cherish" and "Never My Love."

5 The London Rock Festival—which was originally intended to be an old-time rock extravaganza—turns out to be a dismal failure when most of the authentic Fifties acts fail to appear. Instead, the crowd of 50,000, largely made up of vintage Teds and Rockers, see sets by the **MC5**, **Gary Glitter** and revivalist **Roy Wood**, who, according to one disgusted Ted, looks like a "bloody fairy," despite Wood's creditable rendition of "The Girl Can't Help It." How bad is it? Even **Little Richard** gets booed.

9 **Gilbert O' Sullivan** is awarded a gold record for "Alone Again (Naturally)," a Number One record for six weeks in the summer. The tune relates an engaging tale of how the narrator was left at the altar and subsequently contemplates suicide. O'Sullivan is a singer/songwriter from Ireland via England who wears Depression-era clothing. He will fade from sight within two years, but not before racking up two more Top Ten hits, "Clair" and "Get Down."

10 **Paul and Linda McCartney** are arrested for drug possession following a concert before 3,600 enthusiastic fans in Gothenburg, Sweden. Paul is fined $1,000, Linda, $200, and drummer **Denny Seiwell**, $600. But the ex-**Beatle** is unperturbed. "This will make good publicity for our concert tonight," he says with a smile.

11 A city desperate for heroes: San Antonio declares **Cheech and Chong** Day, and even sends two delegations to the airport to meet the comedy duo. Apparently unaware of the comedians' notoriety for their profanity and sex-and-drugs routines, a mayoral rep beams: "It's a pleasure to have Cheech and Chong in our fair city. . . ."

12 The Festival of Hope, the first rock festival

used to raise funds for an established charity, gets underway at Roosevelt Raceway in Garden City, New York. The concerts are sponsored by the Nassau Society of Crippled Children and Adults, and features appearances by many rock and soul acts, including the **Jefferson Airplane**, **Stephen Stills**, **James Brown**, **Sha Na Na** and many others.

13 Festival organizers are disappointed when only 20,000 of an expected 40,000 attend the second day of the Festival of Hope. The fans react lackadaisically to the acts, even though the event proceeds with a smoothness uncommon to rock festivals. That's precisely what's wrong with the festival, claim some observers—something is lost because of the lack of adversity. When receipts are counted, it's learned that while the festival has raised $300,000, it has incurred expenses of $400,000.

21 **Grace Slick** gets Maced in the face, and **Paul Kantner** gets his head slammed to the floor after a chaotic show in Akron, Ohio. The trouble starts with a phoned-in bomb threat to the Rubber Bowl, putting the police on edge. When some fans toss rocks at squad cars, the police respond with tear gas, and when **Jack Casady** objects from the stage, he's arrested and hustled off to a basement area. Slick and Kantner go downstairs to inquire about his status, which is when the melee with the cops ensues.

28 **David Bowie and the Spiders from Mars** debut at Carnegie Hall, the third stop on his maiden U.S. tour. But Bowie contracts the flu and performs a limp, going-through-the-motions set in front of a crowd studded with some of the Big Apple's flashiest queens. Most in attendance agree: The crowd beats Bowie hands down for pure entertainment.

British art rockers **Procol Harum** have a gold LP: *Live in Concert with the Edmonton Symphony Orchestra*, one of the few successful attempts to combine a rock group with an orchestra. The record includes the Top Twenty hit "Conquistador," a reworked song from Procol's 1967 debut album.

30 **John Lennon** and **Yoko Ono** play their first "official" American solo concert, called "One-to-One," a benefit for New York's Willowbrook Hospital held at Madison Square Garden. Lennon is featured on a bill with acts like **Stevie Wonder** and **Sha Na Na**. Backed by the **Elephant's Memory** band and looking very relaxed, he performs an eighteen-song set that includes the **Beatles'** "Come Together" and four songs sung by Yoko. The show ends with a rollicking "Hound Dog" and a prayerlike "Give Peace a Chance." ◆

WEEK ENDING AUGUST 5

U.S. #1 POP 45	"Alone Again (Naturally)"	Gilbert O'Sullivan
U.S. #1 POP LP	*Honky Chateau*	Elton John
U.S. #1 R&B 45	"Where Is the Love"	Roberta Flack and Donny Hathaway
U.K. #1 POP 45	"School's Out"	Alice Cooper
U.K. #1 POP LP	*Simon and Garfunkel's Greatest Hits*	Simon and Garfunkel

WEEK ENDING AUGUST 12

U.S. #1 POP 45	"Alone Again (Naturally)"	Gilbert O'Sullivan
U.S. #1 POP LP	*Honky Chateau*	Elton John
U.S. #1 R&B 45	"I'm Still in Love with You"	Al Green
U.K. #1 POP 45	"School's Out"	Alice Cooper
U.K. #1 POP LP	*Never a Dull Moment*	Rod Stewart

WEEK ENDING AUGUST 19

U.S. #1 POP 45	"Alone Again (Naturally)"	Gilbert O'Sullivan
U.S. #1 POP LP	*Chicago V*	Chicago
U.S. #1 R&B 45	"I'm Still in Love with You"	Al Green
U.K. #1 POP 45	"School's Out"	Alice Cooper
U.K. #1 POP LP	*Never a Dull Moment*	Rod Stewart

WEEK ENDING AUGUST 26

U.S. #1 POP 45	"Brandy (You're a Fine Girl)"	The Looking Glass
U.S. #1 POP LP	*Chicago V*	Chicago
U.S. #1 R&B 45	"Power of Love"	Joe Simon
U.K. #1 POP 45	"You Wear It Well"	Rod Stewart
U.K. #1 POP LP	*Never a Dull Moment*	Rod Stewart

1 The **O'Jays** receive a gold record for their first hit single, after fourteen years together. "Back Stabbers" goes all the way up to #3 on the pop chart.

David Bowie releases "John, I'm Only Dancing" in the U.K., but presumably because of the song's supposedly gay lyrics, it isn't released in the U.S. until 1976 on the greatest-hits LP *ChangesOneBowie*. And in 1979, a six-minute disco-dance version of the song is released.

2 Roads are jammed throughout the area as rock fans flock to Indiana for a rock festival on Bull Island in the Wabash River. Indiana State Police Lieutenant N. Burnsworth estimates that 100,000 rock fans already are on the island, with another 30,000 or 40,000 on the way. By the next day, attendance figures will reach 200,000, and despite widespread and flagrant drug abuse, the crowd is described as well-behaved. Appearing at the festival are **Canned Heat, Pure Prairie League, Black Oak Arkansas** and **Brownsville Station**, among others.

4 Another rock concert tragedy occurs when concessionaire **Francisco Caruso** is killed at a Texas **Wishbone Ash** show because he refuses to give a patron a free sandwich.

5 The London Art Spectrum, held at the Alexandria Palace, is the showcase for five of **John Lennon** and **Yoko Ono**'s avant-garde films: *Cold Turkey, The Ballad of John and Yoko, Give Peace a Chance, Instant Karma* and *Up Your Leg*.

7 **Curtis Mayfield**'s *Super Fly* goes gold and later becomes the country's Number One album. The soundtrack LP also includes "Freddie's Dead (Theme from *Superfly*)," a #4 hit in October.

8 A son, **Zeke**, is born to **Neil Young** and actress **Carrie Snodgress** at Young's ranch near San Francisco.

John Sinclair organizes the Ann Arbor Jazz and Blues Festival. What makes this festival different from all others, boasts the noted political activist, is that "it's gonna be a real people's festival—produced by freaks and for the community." And he actually pulls it off, with a bill including **Dr. John, Muddy Waters, Howlin' Wolf, Bonnie Raitt, Sun Ra, Junior Walker, Freddie King, Otis Rush,** **Luther Allison** and **Bobby "Blue" Bland**.

9 The ever-changing **Miles Davis** premieres his new nine-piece band at Lincoln Center's Philharmonic Hall in New York. Unlike some of Davis' other outfits, which were made up of such stalwart players as **Tony Williams, Wayne Shorter** and **Joe Zawinul**, this one is comprised of eight "largely unknown musicians."

England's BBC-TV premieres "The Old Grey Whistle Test," a rock & roll program that will serve as a showcase for rock talent.

12 The **Faces** headline Madison Square Garden. Although the show is described as lackluster, the group does show some imagination in selecting its opening acts: a Dixieland band, a group of Charleston dancers and a Scottish bagpiper, who, some later claim, turns in the best performance of the evening.

27 **Rory Storme**, the leader of one of Liverpool's earliest beat groups, kills himself in what is presumed to be a suicide pact with his mother. **Rory Storme and the Hurricanes** are probably best remembered as the group **Ringo Starr** left, in 1962, for the Beatles. But they were also one of the era's best. Friends interviewed after his death say that Storme couldn't accept that he never enjoyed the same success as many of his peers from the early-Sixties Liverpool scene.

29 **Cat Stevens** opens his new tour before a sold-out crowd of 6,500 at L.A.'s Shrine Auditorium. Sharing the bill with Stevens are **Ramblin' Jack Elliott** and Cat's own cartoon short, *Teaser and the Firecat*. Stevens is backed by an eleven-piece orchestra for the thirty-one-date tour, scheduled to end in Toronto.

30 Columbia Records, which signed expensive deals with several artists in 1972, announces that it is closing down its four Hollywood studios, meaning unemployment for twenty-eight engineers and other staff members. ◆

WEEK ENDING SEPTEMBER 2

U.S. #1 POP 45	"Brandy (You're a Fine Girl)"	The Looking Glass
U.S. #1 POP LP	*Chicago V*	Chicago
U.S. #1 R&B 45	"Power of Love"	Joe Simon
U.K. #1 POP 45	"You Wear It Well"	Rod Stewart
U.K. #1 POP LP	*Never a Dull Moment*	Rod Stewart

WEEK ENDING SEPTEMBER 9

U.S. #1 POP 45	"Alone Again (Naturally)"	Gilbert O'Sullivan
U.S. #1 POP LP	*Chicago V*	Chicago
U.S. #1 R&B 45	"Back Stabbers"	The O'Jays
U.K. #1 POP 45	"Mama Weer All Crazee Now"	Slade
U.K. #1 POP LP	*Never a Dull Moment*	Rod Stewart

WEEK ENDING SEPTEMBER 16

U.S. #1 POP 45	"Black and White"	Three Dog Night
U.S. #1 POP LP	*Chicago V*	Chicago
U.S. #1 R&B 45	"Get on the Good Foot"	James Brown
U.K. #1 POP 45	"Mama Weer All Crazee Now"	Slade
U.K. #1 POP LP	*Simon and Garfunkel's Greatest Hits*	Simon and Garfunkel

WEEK ENDING SEPTEMBER 23

U.S. #1 POP 45	"Baby, Don't Get Hooked on Me"	Mac Davis
U.S. #1 POP LP	*Chicago V*	Chicago
U.S. #1 R&B 45	"Get on the Good Foot"	James Brown
U.K. #1 POP 45	"Children of the Revolution"	T. Rex
U.K. #1 POP LP	*Never a Dull Moment*	Rod Stewart

WEEK ENDING SEPTEMBER 30

U.S. #1 POP 45	"Baby, Don't Get Hooked on Me"	Mac Davis
U.S. #1 POP LP	*Chicago V*	Chicago
U.S. #1 R&B 45	"Get on the Good Foot"	James Brown
U.K. #1 POP 45	"How Can I Be Sure?"	David Cassidy
U.K. #1 POP LP	*Never a Dull Moment*	Rod Stewart

1 **Jon Mark**, guitarist for the **Mark/Almond Band**, loses the ring finger of his left hand in a fall while in Hawaii on tour. He is expected to recover and to play again, but the remainder of the Mark/Almond Band's tour is canceled.

14 **Joe Cocker** is arrested along with six band members in Adelaide, Australia. In the after-the-show raid, police claim to have confiscated marijuana, heroin and hypodermic syringes. Cocker is released on bail immediately, and faces penalties ranging from a $2,000 fine and two years in prison to a mere four-hour notice to leave the country.

"Ben," **Michael Jackson**'s theme song from the movie of the same name, reaches Number One on the pop chart. It is the third solo hit in a year for the thirteen-year-old lead singer of the **Jackson 5** (the other two being "Got to Be There" and "Rockin' Robin"). While it may prove that Michael can go it alone without his older brothers, he will continue to record and to tour with the other four Jacksons, in addition to making solo records.

The **Spinners** have their first R&B Number One single: "I'll Be Around" backed with "How Could I Let You Get Away." It is the first of three consecutive R&B Number Ones—followed by "Could It Be I'm Falling in Love" and "One of a Kind (Love Affair)"—for this soul vocal group formed by songwriter, singer and producer **Harvey Fuqua** in 1957.

14 **Harold Melvin and the Blue Notes** enter the soul chart with "If You Don't Know Me by Now," which in 16 weeks on the chart will peak at Number One for two weeks starting November 18. The song

will enter the pop chart in December, and will reach #3 there.

16 **Creedence Clearwater Revival** issue a press statement announcing the group's breakup. In typically ambiguous public-relations prose, the release more or less states: "We don't regard this as breaking up. We look at it as an expansion of our activities. We

will devote our time to individual rather than group projects." Translation, please: CCR are splitting.

21 Seventeen years after writing and recording the first of his many rock & roll classics ("Maybellene," followed by "Roll Over Beethoven," "School Day," "Rock and Roll Music," "Sweet Little Sixteen," "Johnny B. Goode," "Carol," "Almost Grown," "Little Queenie," "Back in the U.S.A." and so on), **Chuck Berry** gets his first American Number One pop hit with "My Ding-a-Ling," a singalong novelty song derived from grade-school-level private-parts jokes.

28 Philadelphia pop-soul balladeer **Billy Paul** enters the soul chart with the biggest hit of his career, "Me and Mrs. Jones," which will hit Number One for four weeks starting December 9; it will also hit Number One on the pop chart for three weeks starting December 16.

The United States Council for World Affairs announces that it is adopting the **Who** song "Join Together" as its official theme.

30 **Elton John** gives a command performance for Queen Elizabeth II, making him the first rock & roller to be asked to appear in a royal variety performance since the **Beatles** in November 1963. ◆

WEEK ENDING OCTOBER 7

U.S. #1 POP 45	"Baby, Don't Get Hooked on Me"	Mac Davis
U.S. #1 POP LP	*Chicago V*	Chicago
U.S. #1 R&B 45	"Get on the Good Foot"	James Brown
U.K. #1 POP 45	"Mouldy Old Dough"	Lieutenant Pigeon
U.K. #1 POP LP	*Never a Dull Moment*	Rod Stewart

WEEK ENDING OCTOBER 14

U.S. #1 POP 45	"Ben"	Michael Jackson
U.S. #1 POP LP	*Chicago V*	Chicago
U.S. #1 R&B 45	"I'll Be Around"	The Spinners
U.K. #1 POP 45	"Mouldy Old Dough"	Lieutenant Pigeon
U.K. #1 POP LP	*Simon and Garfunkel's Greatest Hits*	Simon and Garfunkel

WEEK ENDING OCTOBER 21

U.S. #1 POP 45	"My Ding-a-Ling"	Chuck Berry
U.S. #1 POP LP	*Superfly*	Curtis Mayfield (soundtrack)
U.S. #1 R&B 45	"I'll Be Around"	The Spinners
U.K. #1 POP 45	"Mouldy Old Dough"	Lieutenant Pigeon
U.K. #1 POP LP	*Simon and Garfunkel's Greatest Hits*	Simon and Garfunkel

WEEK ENDING OCTOBER 28

U.S. #1 POP 45	"My Ding-a-Ling"	Chuck Berry
U.S. #1 POP LP	*Superfly*	Curtis Mayfield (soundtrack)
U.S. #1 R&B 45	"I'll Be Around"	The Spinners
U.K. #1 POP 45	"Mouldy Old Dough"	Lieutenant Pigeon
U.K. #1 POP LP	*Simon and Garfunkel's Greatest Hits*	Simon and Garfunkel

3 Singers **James Taylor** and **Carly Simon** are married by a judge in Simon's Manhattan apartment, in front of just the bride's and the groom's mothers. Later that night, Taylor announces the news of the wedding at his Radio City Music Hall concert and confides: "I don't know whether to be more nervous about the concert or the marriage." Carly takes a bow onstage with her new hubby after the encore.

4 London gets its first permanent rock & roll theater, the 3,000-plus capacity Rainbow Theatre. With its art-deco decor, the forty-one-year-old building (originally called the Finsbury Park Astoria) becomes one of England's most popular venues. The **Who** are the inaugural act, playing for three consecutive nights.

5 **Miss Christine**, one of **Frank Zappa**'s GTOs (Girls Together Outrageously), dies in Massachusetts of a heroin overdose. Christine had been hospitalized the previous year for back troubles, spending six months in a plaster cast. At the time of her death, she was hoping to become a model, and had assembled a portfolio.

6 **Billy Murcia**, twenty-one-year-old drummer for the **New York Dolls**, dies from accidental suffocation. The freak accident occurs following a performance at London's Imperial College. According to band manager **Marty Thau**, Murcia had met a young woman at a London club and had gone back to her flat, where he apparently began to nod out. The girl panicked and poured coffee down his throat, causing suffocation. Chelsea police claimed it was also "brought on by exhaustion."

11 **Allman Brothers** bassist **Berry Oakley** is killed in a motorcycle accident, just three blocks from the site where **Duane Allman** was killed little more than one year ago. Oakley slammed into a Macon, Georgia, city bus and was thrown twenty yards. At first he appeared unhurt, but died—apparently of a brain concussion—twenty minutes after being admitted to a hospital. Oakley was twenty-four years old, the same age as Allman when he was killed.

15 Singer/songwriter **Harry Chapin** and his wife have their first son, **Joshua Burke**, born in New York.

18 **Danny Whitten**, former singer/songwriter for **Neil Young**'s **Crazy Horse**, dies in Los Angeles of a heroin overdose. Friends of the twenty-nine-year-old Whitten are saddened but not surprised; his heroin habit had been acute for some time, and was the main reason he had to leave Crazy Horse in 1971. "He had a death-wish trip," says manager **Ron Stone**. Whitten is later memorialized in Neil Young's lugubrious antidrug album, *Tonight's the Night,* released in 1975.

Two **Who** solo LPs enter the U.S. chart: **Pete Townshend**'s *Who Came First,* which makes only #69, and **John Entwistle**'s *Whistle Rhymes,* which doesn't even break the Top 100.

23 According to *Rolling Stone,* **Mick Jagger** has been named to *Women's Wear Daily's* "Cat Pack" list; also included is **Henry Kissinger, Lord Snowden, Truman Capote** and **Aristotle and Jackie Onassis.**

24 ABC-TV premieres its late-night rock show "In Concert," produced by the man who gave you the **Monkees, Don Kirshner.** The first show, taped earlier at Long Island's Hofstra University, stars **Alice Cooper, Chuck Berry, Blood, Sweat and Tears, Poco** and the **Allmans** (then with the late **Berry Oakley**). Kirshner will later leave "In Concert" and begin his own "Don Kirshner's Rock Concert."

25 *Pink Floyd Live at Pompei,* a film scheduled for a special premiere at London's Rainbow Theater, is canceled at the last minute by the theater's owner. No explanation for the decision is offered.

According to *Rolling Stone,* **Hollies** lead singer **Allan Clarke** has announced plans to leave the group. However, his departure, as it turns out, will be short-lived.

KROQ's radio spots for its rock show at the 100,000-seat L.A. Coliseum have been blasting the airwaves with bombastic boasts: "First there was Monterey, then there was Woodstock, and now KROQ presents the ultimate rock concert festival." The bill is indeed impressive: **Sly Stone, Stevie Wonder, Mott the Hoople,** the **Eagles,** the **Bee Gees,** plus others. So many acts, in fact, that they almost outnumber the audience. The "ultimate" festival draws a mere 32,000 spectators.

30 **Wings** releases "Hi, Hi, Hi," which is banned from the BBC because of its "unsuitable lyrics." Nevertheless, the song is a sizable hit, making #5 in Britain and #10 in the U.S. in early 1973.   ◆

WEEK ENDING NOVEMBER 4

U.S. #1 POP 45	"I Can See Clearly Now"	Johnny Nash
U.S. #1 POP LP	*Superfly*	Curtis Mayfield (soundtrack)
U.S. #1 R&B 45	"I'll Be Around"	The Spinners
U.K. #1 POP 45	"Clair"	Gilbert O'Sullivan
U.K. #1 POP LP	*Simon and Garfunkel's Greatest Hits*	Simon and Garfunkel

WEEK ENDING NOVEMBER 11

U.S. #1 POP 45	"I Can See Clearly Now"	Johnny Nash
U.S. #1 POP LP	*Superfly*	Curtis Mayfield (soundtrack)
U.S. #1 R&B 45	"I'll Be Around"	The Spinners
U.K. #1 POP 45	"Clair"	Gilbert O'Sullivan
U.K. #1 POP LP	*Simon and Garfunkel's Greatest Hits*	Simon and Garfunkel

WEEK ENDING NOVEMBER 18

U.S. #1 POP 45	"I Can See Clearly Now"	Johnny Nash
U.S. #1 POP LP	*Catch Bull at Four*	Cat Stevens
U.S. #1 R&B 45	"If You Don't Know Me by Now"	Harold Melvin and the Blue Notes
U.K. #1 POP 45	"My Ding-a-Ling"	Chuck Berry
U.K. #1 POP LP	*Back to Front*	Gilbert O'Sullivan

WEEK ENDING NOVEMBER 25

U.S. #1 POP 45	"I Can See Clearly Now"	Johnny Nash
U.S. #1 POP LP	*Catch Bull at Four*	Cat Stevens
U.S. #1 R&B 45	"If You Don't Know Me by Now"	Harold Melvin and the Blue Notes
U.K. #1 POP 45	"My Ding-a-Ling"	Chuck Berry
U.K. #1 POP LP	*Simon and Garfunkel's Greatest Hits*	Simon and Garfunkel

8 An advertisement placed in *Variety* magazine claims that **Frank Zappa** will give private instruction in craps, roulette, keno and blackjack—**Frank Zappa Sr.**, that is, who teaches how to win through mathematics, your place or his.

9 The all-star orchestral stage version of *Tommy* plays a one-night-only performance at London's Rainbow Theatre, and is unanimously panned. Of all the performers (including **Peter Sellers**, **Merry Clayton** and **Richie Havens**), only **Roger Daltrey** and **Steve Winwood** acquit themselves in their respective roles as Tommy and Tommy's father. According to observers, narrator **Pete Townshend** appears inebriated. The presentation is recorded and re-

leased, charting as high as #5 in early 1973.

Capitol Records has its first Number One hit in more than four years: **Helen Reddy**'s anthemic "I Am Woman." The last Capitol act (besides the **Beatles**) to do as well was also a woman, **Bobbie Gentry**, whose Number One hit was "Ode to Billie Joe," in 1967.

The **Moody Blues** attain their first U.S. Number One record, *Seventh Sojourn*. It will be their last album of new material for more than five years, as the group's members go off to record and to tour as solo artists.

10 **Roberta Flack** and two members of her backup band are injured while driving into Manhattan. Bassist **Jerry Jemon** lost control of Flack's new Citroen, totaling the car.

He suffers a broken nose and a dislocated shoulder, while guitarist **Cornell Dupree** has bone fractures and requires plastic surgery. Flack needs surgery on her lip, but is otherwise unhurt, and plans to keep her scheduled European tour, beginning in January.

11 **James Brown** is arrested after a show in Knoxville, Tennessee, and charged with "disorderly conduct." Brown and two members of his entourage were talking to fans about narcotics use when a white man told police that the singer was trying to incite a riot (Brown being the same man who so ardently urged blacks to keep the peace after **Martin Luther King**'s assassination in 1968). But after Brown threatens to sue the city for $1 million, the incident is written off by authorities as a "misunderstanding."

Art rockers **Genesis** play their first date in the U.S. at Brandeis University in Massachusetts. The group, which has yet to place an LP in the Top 200, consists of **Peter Gabriel**, **Phil Collins**, **Steve Hackett**, **Mike Rutherford** and **Tony Banks**.

14 Alexander's department store in New York stays open especially late so that **Alice Cooper**—wearing silver pants and a "PAUL LIVES" button—can do his Christmas shopping.

Ringo Starr's film about U.K. rocker **Marc Bolan**, *Born to Boogie*, premieres in London.

21 *Rolling Stone* announces the death of Memphis guitarist **Ray Jackson**, 31, composer of the hits "Who's Makin' Love" and "(If Loving You Is Wrong) I Don't Want to Be Right." Jackson died in his home last month from burns suffered in a freak fire. He was a long-time sessionman for Stax Records, playing behind artists like **Isaac Hayes**, the **Emotions**, **Carla Thomas** and **Mel and Tim**.

23 Former **Grand Funk Railroad** manager **Terry Knight** shows up at a benefit show staged by the group, armed with two deputy sheriffs and a twenty-foot moving van. Knight carries a court order that gives him the right to seize and hold $1 million in money or assets pending settlement of several lawsuits between the two parties. But because the show for the Phoenix House drug rehabilitation center can't go on without the equipment, Knight is told by lawmen not to touch the amps or drums until after the concert.

24 A concert by **Manfred Mann and His Earth Band** is cut short by Miami police, sparking a two-hour riot by students at the University of Miami. Because nearby residents had complained about the group's volume, the power to the P.A. is cut during the encore. As the battle rages, Mann and his men hide in a dressing room. ◆

WEEK ENDING DECEMBER 2

U.S. #1 POP 45	"Papa Was a Rollin' Stone"	The Temptations
U.S. #1 POP LP	*Catch Bull at Four*	Cat Stevens
U.S. #1 R&B 45	"You Ought to Be with Me"	Al Green
U.K. #1 POP 45	"My Ding-a-Ling"	Chuck Berry
U.K. #1 POP LP	*Back to Front*	Gilbert O'Sullivan

WEEK ENDING DECEMBER 9

U.S. #1 POP 45	"I Am Woman"	Helen Reddy
U.S. #1 POP LP	*Seventh Sojourn*	The Moody Blues
U.S. #1 R&B 45	"Me and Mrs. Jones"	Billy Paul
U.K. #1 POP 45	"Gudbuy T' Jane"	Slade
U.K. #1 POP LP	*Back to Front*	Gilbert O'Sullivan

WEEK ENDING DECEMBER 16

U.S. #1 POP 45	"Me and Mrs. Jones"	Billy Paul
U.S. #1 POP LP	*Seventh Sojourn*	The Moody Blues
U.S. #1 R&B 45	"Me and Mrs. Jones"	Billy Paul
U.K. #1 POP 45	"Long Haired Lover from Liverpool"	Little Jimmy Osmond
U.K. #1 POP LP	*Back to Front*	Gilbert O'Sullivan

WEEK ENDING DECEMBER 23

U.S. #1 POP 45	"Me and Mrs. Jones"	Billy Paul
U.S. #1 POP LP	*Seventh Sojourn*	The Moody Blues
U.S. #1 R&B 45	"Me and Mrs. Jones"	Billy Paul
U.K. #1 POP 45	"Long Haired Lover from Liverpool"	Little Jimmy Osmond
U.K. #1 POP LP	*Slayed*	Slade

WEEK ENDING DECEMBER 30

U.S. #1 POP 45	"Me and Mrs. Jones"	Billy Paul
U.S. #1 POP LP	*Seventh Sojourn*	The Moody Blues
U.S. #1 R&B 45	"Me and Mrs. Jones"	Billy Paul
U.K. #1 POP 45	"Long Haired Lover from Liverpool"	Little Jimmy Osmond
U.K. #1 POP LP	*Slayed*	Slade

1973

As the rock audience continued to grow, the music and the audience continued to fragment, and groups as disparate as, say, Steely Dan and Yes could earn gold records on the same day for recently released albums. Fittingly, the news of peace in Vietnam came early in a year that decisively marked the end of a general revolutionary or political commitment in rock—unless the Rolling Stones' benefit show for earthquake-torn Nicaragua counts as politics, and unless the Who and the Faces destroying hotel rooms counts as revolutionary action.

There had already been a collective assumption that the ideals and attitudes of the Sixties were at least passé, but just how dead that decade was didn't become totally clear until June of this year, when there was a British Invasion "revival" show at Madison Square Garden. The number of rock festivals held this year dropped off significantly from 1972, and what festivals were held usually provoked some kind of unseemly trouble; the mammoth Watkins Glen gathering was the exception to the rule. Even the holdover cause of black consciousness suffered from bad karma: there was fighting between Ike and Tina Turner and entourage and the Black Panthers at an Oakland show in July, and Black Expo '73 in August was a fiasco.

The charts were, for the most part, sodden with more pop pap like "Tie a Yellow Ribbon" and "The Night the Lights Went Out in Georgia." Once again, soul music provided the most arresting and distinctive sounds of the year: early on, there was Timmy Thomas' stark, hypnotic, ultraminimal (organ, rhythm box and voice, that's all) "Why Can't We Live Together"; at the end of the year, there was Stevie Wonder's "Livin' for the City," arguably the only genuine rock & roll to top the charts all year; in between, there were Marvin Gaye's "Let's Get It On," Harold Melvin and the Blue Notes' "The Love I Lost" and such prefigurements of disco as the JBs' "Doin' It to Death" and Barry White's "I'm Gonna Love You Just a Little Bit More, Baby."

If rock seemed to have run out of things to *say,* it still had a lot to *show*—that is, showbiz and image began to dominate, and in the case of lesser talents, eclipse, content. Elton John followed David Bowie's androgynous example and metamorphosed from a merely talented singer/songwriter into a talented singer/songwriter/fashion plate. And even if Bowie did announce his "retirement" from rock in July (it would prove to be a premature announcement, of course), the glitter ball was off and rolling; within days of Bowie's "final show," Queen released their debut single.

Otherwise, it was big business as usual. Since they had already proven their sales potential, progressive rockers like Yes could go on recording double- and triple-album epics to continued public acceptance and critical revilement: progressive FM radio began to rigidify—to limit the number of tracks and type of music it played—and soon it would become AOR radio. This year, two big progressive-FM outlets were dropped in Ann Arbor, Michigan, and San Francisco.

But amid all the indulgent pretension and contrived images, there were two significant rock & roll events. Pink Floyd released *The Dark Side of the Moon,* a slick, melodic ode to psychic dissolution that went gold within a month of release and entered the album chart for a decade-long stay. And as if in answer to such a yawning chasm of despair, this year saw the release of the first two albums by Bruce Springsteen, a singer/songwriter whose exuberant spirit, roots-rock revisionism and street poetry would make him perhaps the decade's greatest figure in rock.

4 *Rolling Stone* carries the announcement made by the **Allman Brothers Band** that **Lamar Williams** has been named to replace the late **Berry Oakley** on bass. The Mississippi-born Williams is a friend of Allman drummer **Jai Johanny Johanson** and has eight years' experience playing in Southern bands.

7 Former singer **Sandy Denny** rejoins **Fairport Convention** for a show in Aucklund, New Zealand. The reason, says Denny, who left Fairport for the group Fotheringay and then opted for a solo career, was simply "for old time's sake."

8 Yoko Ono releases *Approximately Infinite Universe* as a two-record set because, she says, "I figured if **George Harrison** can put out a triple album, then I can put out a double album." Although the record doesn't sell especially well, it is generally better accepted than her earlier avant-garde work.

9 Mick Jagger is refused a Japanese visa on account of a 1969 drug bust, halting the Stones' plans to tour the Orient. The band seems genuinely depressed about the cancellation, although Jagger shrugs it off as a "minor frustration." Asked by a reporter about his personal drug use, Jagger replies, "I don't take drugs. I don't approve of drugs, and I don't approve of people taking drugs, unless they're very careful."

13 **Eric Clapton**, the reluctant guitar hero who'd spent the last few years troubled by drug addiction, makes a triumphant comeback at London's Rainbow Theatre, where he sells out two shows. Clapton, prodded to return to the stage by **Pete Townshend**, is accompanied by a stellar band including Townshend, **Ron Wood**, **Steve Winwood**, **Rick Grech**, **"Reebop" Kwaku Baah** and **Jimmy Karstein**. The set opens and closes with "Layla," and afterward Clapton tells a reporter, "I was very nervous, felt sick, the whole bit." But, he adds, referring to the enthusiastic audience, "they don't know how much it helped me."

14 **Elvis Presley** draws the largest world-wide TV audience ever with a live concert, "Elvis: Aloha from Hawaii," telecast from the Honolulu International Center. The event is later released as a two-record set and is one of the singer's best-selling LPs of the Seventies, hitting Number One in 1973.

15 The **Rolling Stones** officially announce that they'll put on a benefit concert for the people of Managua, Nicaragua, which had been shattered by an earthquake on December 23, 1972. Nicaragua is the home of Jagger's wife, **Bianca**.

16 Famed gospel singer **Clara Ward** dies after suffering her second stroke within several weeks. She was forty-eight. Ward, who **Aretha Franklin** once called "my inspiration," was born in Philadelphia and first gained recognition at the 1957 Newport Jazz Festival. After that, she appeared at Carnegie Hall, was twice called upon to perform before **President Lyndon Johnson** and became a regular act at—of all places—the New Frontier Hotel Lounge in Las Vegas.

18 The **Rolling Stones'** benefit concert for Nicaraguan earthquake victims is a huge success, raising over $400,000. The show's a musical success, too, with sets turned in by **Santana**, **Cheech and Chong** and then the Stones, who perform an almost two-hour set before a crowd of nearly 19,000.

20 **Jerry Lee Lewis** makes his debut at the Grand Ole Opry. By this time, stories of Lewis' drinking and numerous arrests were well enough known that Opry officials had allowed him to perform only if he agreed to keep his repertoire to country and abstain from using obscenities. All starts off well enough, but by the end of the half-hour set, Lewis has played "Great Balls of Fire," "Whole Lotta Shakin' Goin' On" and "Good Golly Miss Molly" and proclaimed "I am a rock & rollin', country & western, rhythm & blues singin' motherfucker."

23 Jazz trombonist **Edward "Kid" Ory** dies in Honolulu of pneumonia and heart failure at age 93. Ory was the composer of such jazz classics as "Muskrat Ramble" and "Savoy Blues," and was a highly influential horn player.

Philadelphia radio station WMMR-FM celebrates the cease-fire in Vietnam by broadcasting the ringing of bells at 7:00 a.m. for twelve minutes—one minute for each year of the war.

Neil Young interrupts a New York concert to read a message handed to him. "Peace has come," he announces, sending the audience into a joyful ten-minute fit of hugging and kissing. Young and the **Stray Gators** then launched into a powerful version of "Southern Man."

30 **Kiss** play their first show, at the Conventry Club in Queens. The group's makeup at this early stage is slightly different from the look audiences eventually will know them for. **Paul Stanley** later recalls that it's more of a "New York Dolls look." ◆

WEEK ENDING JANUARY 6

U.S. #1 POP 45	"You're So Vain"	Carly Simon
U.S. #1 POP LP	*Seventh Sojourn*	The Moody Blues
U.S. #1 R&B 45	"Superstition"	Stevie Wonder
U.K. #1 POP 45	"Long Haired Lover from Liverpool"	Little Jimmy Osmond
U.K. #1 POP LP	*Slayed*	Slade

WEEK ENDING JANUARY 13

U.S. #1 POP 45	"You're So Vain"	Carly Simon
U.S. #1 POP LP	*No Secrets*	Carly Simon
U.S. #1 R&B 45	"Superstition"	Stevie Wonder
U.K. #1 POP 45	"The Jean Genie"	David Bowie
U.K. #1 POP LP	*Slayed*	Slade

WEEK ENDING JANUARY 20

U.S. #1 POP 45	"You're So Vain"	Carly Simon
U.S. #1 POP LP	*No Secrets*	Carly Simon
U.S. #1 R&B 45	Superstition	Stevie Wonder
U.K. #1 POP 45	"The Jean Genie"	David Bowie
U.K. #1 POP LP	*Slayed*	Slade

WEEK ENDING JANUARY 27

U.S. #1 POP 45	"Superstition"	Stevie Wonder
U.S. #1 POP LP	*No Secrets*	Carly Simon
U.S. #1 R&B 45	"Why Can't We Live Together"	Timmy Thomas
U.K. #1 POP 45	"Blockbuster"	Sweet
U.K. #1 POP LP	*Slayed*	Slade

1 Less than a year after they "retired," **Steppenwolf** resurrect themselves, with leader **John Kay** returning, although he promises to continue recording as a solo artist as well.

Rolling Stone reports on *The Trials of Oz,* a controversial play that opens in New York. Based on the actual transcripts from the 1971 *Oz* magazine obscenity trial, the show includes songs written by **Mick Jagger**, **John Lennon** and **Yoko Ono**. But this satire lasts only two weeks—one-third the run of the trial itself, the longest case in the history of British jurisprudence. *New York Times* critic **Clive Barnes** made his feelings known even before he returned to his desk to compose his negative review: he fell asleep early in the performance.

Island Records' **Chris Blackwell** announces to *Rolling Stone* that he is founding Mango Records, a label dedicated to molding reggae artists. "I think that reggae has a chance of breaking in America," Blackwell predicts, although he adds that he sees its audience being "musicians and professional people more than kids, who won't quite understand."

2 NBC-TV debuts its entry into the rock TV-shows sweepstakes, "Midnight Special." The program is more middle-of-the-road than ABC's "In Concert" and is hosted by **Helen Reddy**.

8 **Carly Simon** is awarded a gold record for her single "You're So Vain," the only Number One of her career. For months, fans speculate as to the identity of the song's subject—a self-possessed jet-set dandy. Many assume that it's **Mick Jagger**, whose voice can clearly be heard singing behind Carly on the chorus, making for a perfectly wonderful irony (after all, the key line is "You're so vain, you probably think this song is about you"). However, it turns out that the subject is actor **Warren Beatty**.

Max Yasgur, the upstate New York dairy farmer who rented 600 acres of land to the promoters of the Woodstock Festival in 1969, dies in Florida at age fifty-three. About 60,000 people had been expected for the

three-day event—nearly 500,000 showed up. Yasgur became an instant celebrity, making a short but memorable speech near the festival's end. His voice breaking, he told the crowd: "I don't know how to speak to twenty people, much less all of you . . . . You have proven to the world that half a million kids can get together for fun and music, and have nothing but fun and music."

10 The historic Liverpool club the Cavern is given a three-month reprieve by British Rail, who are constructing an underground railroad, necessitating the demolition of the club. Should the club have to move, says owner **Roy Adams**, he could at least preserve the original cellar room where the **Beatles** performed 292 times back in the early Sixties.

11 Jazz drummer **Elvin Jones** plays a pair of benefits in Sacramento, California, to raise funds to help rebuild Hanoi's Bach Mai Hospital, which had been destroyed by U.S. bombers last Christmas.

14 **David Bowie** collapses at the end of his Valentine's Day show at New York's Radio City Music Hall. "It was total exhaustion," promoter **Ron Delsener** later tells the press. That, and also the fact that an overzealous male fan had tried to grab and plant a wet kiss on the singer, knocking the wind out of him. The two-hour show opens with Bowie descending to the stage in a glass-domed space object, looking like **Katharine Hepburn**, in a white dress. Bowie is accompanied by the **Spiders from Mars**, as well as several additional musicians.

22 **Roberta Flack** receives a gold record for "Killing Me Softly with His Song," which is Number One for five weeks, beginning in March. It is rumored that the quietly murdering artist in question is folkie **Don McLean**. ◆

WEEK ENDING FEBRUARY 3

U.S. #1 POP 45	"Crocodile Rock"	Elton John
U.S. #1 POP LP	*No Secrets*	Carly Simon
U.S. #1 R&B 45	"Why Can't We Live Together"	Timmy Thomas
U.K. #1 POP 45	"Blockbuster"	Sweet
U.K. #1 POP LP	*Slayed*	Slade

WEEK ENDING FEBRUARY 10

U.S. #1 POP 45	"Crocodile Rock"	Elton John
U.S. #1 POP LP	*No Secrets*	Carly Simon
U.S. #1 R&B 45	"Could It Be I'm Falling in Love"	The Spinners
U.K. #1 POP 45	"Blockbuster"	Sweet
U.K. #1 POP LP	*Don't Shoot Me, I'm Only the Piano Player*	Elton John

WEEK ENDING FEBRUARY 17

U.S. #1 POP 45	"Crocodile Rock"	Elton John
U.S. #1 POP LP	*The World Is a Ghetto*	War
U.S. #1 R&B 45	"Love Train"	The O'Jays
U.K. #1 POP 45	"Blockbuster"	Sweet
U.K. #1 POP LP	*Don't Shoot Me, I'm Only the Piano Player*	Elton John

WEEK ENDING FEBRUARY 24

U.S. #1 POP 45	"Killing Me Softly with His Song"	Roberta Flack
U.S. #1 POP LP	*The World Is a Ghetto*	War
U.S. #1 R&B 45	"Love Train"	The O'Jays
U.K. #1 POP 45	"Part of the Union"	The Strawbs
U.K. #1 POP LP	*Don't Shoot Me, I'm Only the Piano Player*	Elton John

1 Woodies, surfboards and—ballet shoes? New York's Joffrey Ballet gives its first performance of its "Deuce Coupe Ballet," which is set entirely to **Beach Boys** music.

3 The Grammy Awards for 1972 are announced. Among the winners are "The First Time Ever I Saw Your Face" by **Roberta Flack**, Song of the Year and Record of the Year; *The Concert for Bangla Desh,* album of the Year; and **America**, Best New Artist. **Helen Reddy's** "I Am Woman" is voted the Best Pop Vocal Performance, Female, and **Harry Nilsson's** "Without You" is the Best Pop Vocal Performance, Male.

4 **Pink Floyd**, promoting their new album, *The Dark Side of the Moon,* begin a three-week tour of the U.S., in Madison, Wisconsin.

5 **Jimi Hendrix's** personal manager, **Michael Jeffrey**, dies in a plane crash. Later, there will be many to attest that he wasn't on the plane, and had been sighted several times after the crash occurred. Jeffrey was on an Iberia flight from Majorca to England, where he owned a nightclub. All passengers on board the plane were killed.

6 The group **War**, out from under the shadow of former leader **Eric Burdon**, receive their second gold single of the week, for "Cisco Kid," four days after "The World Is a Ghetto" did likewise.

7 **Traffic** have a gold LP with *Shootout at the Fantasy Factory,* their final LP with the extended group, which for this album included **Roger Hawkins**, **David Hood**, **Reebop** and founders **Steve Winwood**, **Chris Wood** and **Jim Capaldi**.

One of the rare instrumentals to go gold in the Seventies is "Dueling Banjos," performed by **Eric Weissberg** and **Steve Mandel**. The banjo-guitar raveup is taken from the soundtrack to the film *Deliverance.*

John Hammond, director of talent acquisition at Columbia Records, suffers a heart attack following a show by one of his biggest and most recent discoveries, **Bruce Springsteen**. It is Hammond's third heart attack, and he attributes it to overworking. Not so, says his doctor, who insists it happened because Hammond had been so enthusiastic during Springsteen's set at New York's Max's Kansas City.

8 **Paul McCartney** pleads guilty to charges of growing marijuana outside his Scottish countryside farm, and is fined $240. McCartney claims that the seeds were given to him by some fans, and that he didn't know what they would grow. According to Paul's lawyer, the ex-**Beatle** has an active interest in horticulture.

Ronald Charles McKernan—better known as **Pigpen**, organist for the **Grateful Dead**—dies in his Madera, California, apartment at age twenty-seven. A heavy drinker, McKernan had been under a doctor's care for cirrhosis, and had been unable to tour with the Dead for some time. McKernan formed **Mother McCree's Uptown Jug Champions** in 1964 with **Bob Weir** and a young guitarist and banjoist name **Jerry Garcia**; the three of them formed the **Warlocks** the following year, and later the nucleus of the Dead.

23 *Derek and the Dominos in Concert,* the two-record set released well over a year after the short-lived group's breakup, goes gold. It will be the only other document of **Eric Clapton's** group besides *Layla;* a second LP, supposedly taped and in the can, is never released.

24 **Lou Reed** is bitten on his posterior—by a fan at a Buffalo, New York, concert. The display of affection occurs while Reed is about to perform "Waitin' for the Man." Screaming "leather!" the fan leaps past the guards and assaults Reed. He is ejected. Comments Reed after the show: America "seems to breed real animals."

29 **Dr. Hook and the Medicine Show** get their wish, as their smiling faces adorn the cover of *Rolling Stone* magazine, just as the group had hoped for in its Top Ten hit "The Cover of the *Rolling Stone,"* which goes gold six days later. ◆

WEEK ENDING MARCH 3

U.S. #1 POP 45	"Killing Me Softly with His Song"	Roberta Flack
U.S. #1 POP LP	*Don't Shoot Me, I'm Only the Piano Player*	Elton John
U.S. #1 R&B 45	"Love Train"	The O'Jays
U.K. #1 POP 45	"Part of the Union"	The Strawbs
U.K. #1 POP LP	*Don't Shoot Me, I'm Only the Piano Player*	Elton John

WEEK ENDING MARCH 10

U.S. #1 POP 45	"Killing Me Softly with His Song"	Roberta Flack
U.S. #1 POP LP	*Don't Shoot Me, I'm Only the Piano Player*	Elton John
U.S. #1 R&B 45	"Love Train"	The O'Jays
U.K. #1 POP 45	"Cum On, Feel the Noize"	Slade
U.K. #1 POP LP	*Don't Shoot Me, I'm Only the Piano Player*	Elton John

WEEK ENDING MARCH 17

U.S. #1 POP 45	"Killing Me Softly with His Song"	Roberta Flack
U.S. #1 POP LP	*Dueling Banjos*	Eric Weissberg and Steve Mandel
U.S. #1 R&B 45	"Neither One of Us"	Gladys Knight and the Pips
U.K. #1 POP 45	"Cum On, Feel the Noize"	Slade
U.K. #1 POP LP	*Don't Shoot Me, I'm Only the Piano Player*	Elton John

WEEK ENDING MARCH 24

U.S. #1 POP 45	"Love Train"	The O'Jays
U.S. #1 POP LP	*Dueling Banjos*	Eric Weissberg and Steve Mandel
U.S. #1 R&B 45	"Neither One of Us"	Gladys Knight and the Pips
U.K. #1 POP 45	"The Twelfth of Never"	Donny Osmond
U.K. #1 POP LP	*Billion Dollar Babies*	Alice Cooper

WEEK ENDING MARCH 31

U.S. #1 POP 45	"Love Train"	The O'Jays
U.S. #1 POP LP	*Dueling Banjos*	Eric Weissberg and Steve Mandel
U.S. #1 R&B 45	"Neither One of Us"	Gladys Knight and the Pips
U.K. #1 POP 45	"The Twelfth of Never"	Donny Osmond
U.K. #1 POP LP	*The Dark Side of the Moon*	Pink Floyd

2 **John Lennon** and **Yoko Ono** hold a news conference in New York to discuss their appeal of the Immigration Department's decision to deport John. Another question raised is that of a **Beatles** reunion, which *Newsweek* magazine had earlier reported was "on." The reunion, Lennon stresses, "is not in the cards."

3 To combat the plethora of **Beatles** bootlegs, the group's label, Capitol, issues *The Beatles/1962–1966* and *The Beatles/1967–1970,* both two-record greatest hits packages. They make #3 and Number One on the album chart.

8 **Neil Young**'s docu-autobiography, *Journey through the Past,* premieres at the US Film Festival in Dallas. Young is typically ambiguous when describing the film, a jumbled mélange of scenes and images from throughout his career: "It's a collection of thoughts. Every scene meant something to me—although with some of them I can't say what."

9 **Paul McCartney** releases "My Love," a ballad that will be the biggest hit of his solo career to date, going Number One for four weeks. McCartney follows three weeks later with the *Red Rose Speedway* album, which also hits Number One.

10 **Led Zeppelin** get a gold record for *Houses of the Holy,* the first of their five LPs not eponymously titled.

12 *Rolling Stone* reports that a **Buffalo Springfield** reunion may be in the works. Says original member **Richie Furay,** now with **Poco,** "It's all up to **Neil [Young]** right now." **Stephen Stills** has already given his consent to the reunion, which would include the above-mentioned three plus original bassist **Bruce Palmer** and original drummer **Dewey Martin.** As it will turn out, the reunion never takes place.

13 When the **J. Geils Band** appear on ABC-TV's "In Concert" to sing their hit "Give It to Me," they're censored because of the tune's line "Get it up." The same thing happens to **Curtis Mayfield** on "Soul Train": when he performs "Pusherman," all references to drugs are clipped, including half the song's first line.

The **Who**'s **Roger Daltrey** releases his first solo album. It's a marked departure from the music of the **Who,** which is exactly the point, says Daltrey. "If it sounded anything like the Who, even one percent like the Who, I wouldn't bother." The material is composed by songwriters **Leo Sayer** and **David Courtney** and is produced by British rock idol-turned-movie star **Adam Faith.** *Daltrey* makes #45.

15 The **Divine Miss M**— **Bette Midler**—receives a gold album for her recording debut. One of the year's hottest entertainers, Midler combines borscht-belt shtick with a frenetic musical style that incorporates elements of the Forties, the Fifties and the Sixties. Midler traces her extroverted persona to a childhood made unhappy by a zoftig figure.

16 **Paul McCartney** stars in his first TV special, "James Paul McCartney," which features his wife, **Linda,** and **Wings.** Highlights include a

rendition of "Yesterday" and footage from several concerts.

17 **Pink Floyd** receive a gold album for *The Dark Side of the Moon,* one of rock's landmark albums. The LP will remain on the charts for more than a decade and become the longest charting rock record of all time.

26 According to *Rolling Stone,* **David LaFlamme,** founding member of **It's a Beautiful Day,** has been asked to leave his own group. The other members felt that the violinist was reaping an unfair share of the profits. LaFlamme has been replaced by **Graig Bloch,** grandnephew of master violinist **Jascha Heifetz.**

27 The **Diamonds,** who had nine Top Twenty hits in the Fifties, reunite for the first time in fourteen years for a "Midnight Special" show that features other golden oldie acts like **Ed ("Kookie") Byrnes, Little Richard,** the **Penguins, Little Anthony, Chubby Checker** and host **Jerry Lee Lewis.**

29 More than 15,000 persons attending a rock concert by **Elvin Bishop, Canned Heat, Buddy Miles** and **Fleetwood Mac** are routed from a baseball stadium in Stockton, California, by police firing tear-gas canisters. More than eighty people, including twenty-eight police, are injured, and fifty arrests are made. ◆

WEEK ENDING APRIL 7

U.S. #1 POP 45	"The Night the Lights Went Out in Georgia"	Vicki Lawrence
U.S. #1 POP LP	*Lady Sings the Blues*	Diana Ross
U.S. #1 R&B 45	"Neither One of Us"	Gladys Knight and the Pips
U.K. #1 POP 45	"The Twelfth of Never"	Donny Osmond
U.K. #1 POP LP	*The Dark Side of the Moon*	Pink Floyd

WEEK ENDING APRIL 14

U.S. #1 POP 45	"The Night the Lights Went Out in Georgia"	Vicki Lawrence
U.S. #1 POP LP	*Lady Sings the Blues*	Diana Ross
U.S. #1 R&B 45	"Masterpiece"	The Temptations
U.K. #1 POP 45	"Get Down"	Gilbert O'Sullivan
U.K. #1 POP LP	*Don't Shoot Me, I'm Only the Piano Player*	Elton John

WEEK ENDING APRIL 21

U.S. #1 POP 45	"Tie a Yellow Ribbon 'round the Ole Oak Tree"	Dawn
U.S. #1 POP LP	*Billion Dollar Babies*	Alice Cooper
U.S. #1 R&B 45	"Masterpiece"	The Temptations
U.K. #1 POP 45	"Tie a Yellow Ribbon 'round the Ole Oak Tree"	Dawn
U.K. #1 POP LP	*Houses of the Holy*	Led Zeppelin

WEEK ENDING APRIL 28

U.S. #1 POP 45	"Tie a Yellow Ribbon 'round the Ole Oak Tree"	Dawn
U.S. #1 POP LP	*The Dark Side of the Moon*	Pink Floyd
U.S. #1 R&B 45	"Pillow Talk"	Sylvia
U.K. #1 POP 45	"Tie a Yellow Ribbon 'round the Ole Oak Tree"	Dawn
U.K. #1 POP LP	*Ooh La La*	The Faces

1 **Bachman-Turner Overdrive**, featuring former **Guess Who** guitarist **Randy Bachman**, releases its first LP. Public reaction to this Canadian quartet is slow to come: It takes the album six months to even chart, and it's a year before the first single, "Let It Ride," will become a Top Twenty-five hit.

4 **Led Zeppelin** open their 1973 U.S. tour, which is billed in pretour publicity as the "biggest and most profitable rock & roll tour in the history of the United States." Group spokesmen predict that the tour will gross over $3 million. The first of the thirty-four dates is in Atlanta.

6 **Paul Simon** begins his first tour without **Art Garfunkel**, at Boston's Music Hall. For most of his set, he performs unaccompanied, but later is joined by **Urubamba**, a Latin American quartet, and the **Jesse Dixon Singers**, a gospel group Simon heard at the 1972 Newport Festival. It is this tour that is recorded for the 1974 album *Live Rhymin'*.

7 **George Harrison** releases "Give Me Love (Give Me Peace on Earth)," which will become his second Number One single. It's the first release from *Living in the Material World*, Harrison's second Number One LP.

9 **Mick Jagger** adds $150,000 of his own money to the $350,000 raised by the **Rolling Stones'** January concert for the benefit of Nicaraguan earthquake victims.

14 **Kenny Loggins** and **Jim Messina's** first LP, titled *Sittin' In*, goes gold. The successful duo actually got together by accident. Messina, recently out of the duo **Poco**, had been tabbed to produce a Loggins solo effort, but the two developed such a rapport that Messina was persuaded to return to performing. The partnership will last five years.

17 **Yes** receive gold records for both *Yessongs*, their triple-record live set (recorded in 1972), and *The Yes Album*, recorded in 1970 with a lineup that was two-fifths different. *Yessongs* makes #12;

The Yes Album made #40 in 1971.

21 **Sylvia** (*nom de record* for **Sylvia Robinson**) has a novelty smash with "Pillow Talk," a 45 with suggestive lyrics. Robinson was once of the duo **Mickey and Sylvia** ("Love Is Strange," 1957) and later will form her own label, Sugarhill Records. "Pillow Talk" hits #3 and goes gold.

23 **Clive Davis** is fired as president of Columbia Records, for allegedly using company money for personal use, such as $53,700 for alterations on his apartment and approximately $20,000 to pay for his son's bar mitzvah. Davis, who successfully led CBS through the Sixties rock years, will reemerge just a few years later as head of Arista Records.

25 **Carole King** gives back "a little something" to her favorite city, New York: a free concert in Central Park before an estimated 100,000 fans. Although King can be seen only by a small portion of the crowd, she is able to be clearly heard, as sound man **Chip Monck** uses six times the amount of equipment carried on the **Rolling Stones'** 1972 U.S. tour.

28 **Ronnie Lane**, a charter member of the **Small Faces** (now just **Faces**), quits the band for his own group, **Slim Chance**. His replacement is Japanese bassist **Tetsu Yamauchi**. The Faces recently released their fourth album, *Ooh La La*.

29 **Roger McGuinn** makes his solo debut at New York's Academy of Music just prior to the release of his first album. McGuinn also confirms rumors that the **Byrds** have been grounded—unless, that is, he can coax the rest of the original Byrds to reunite.

31 **Steely Dan**, an eclectic outfit fronted by keyboardist **Donald Fagen** and bassist **Walter Becker**, have a gold LP the first time out with *Can't Buy a Thrill*. The album includes the hits "Do It Again" and "Reeling in the Years." ◆

WEEK ENDING MAY 5

U.S. #1 POP 45	"Tie a Yellow Ribbon 'round the Ole Oak Tree"	Dawn
U.S. #1 POP LP	*Aloha from Hawaii Via Satellite*	Elvis Presley
U.S. #1 R&B 45	"Pillow Talk"	Sylvia
U.K. #1 POP 45	"Tie a Yellow Ribbon 'round the Ole Oak Tree"	Dawn
U.K. #1 POP LP	*Aladdin Sane*	David Bowie

WEEK ENDING MAY 12

U.S. #1 POP 45	"Tie a Yellow Ribbon 'round the Ole Oak Tree"	Dawn
U.S. #1 POP LP	*Houses of the Holy*	Led Zeppelin
U.S. #1 R&B 45	"Funky Worm"	The Ohio Players
U.K. #1 POP 45	"Tie a Yellow Ribbon 'round the Ole Oak Tree"	Dawn
U.K. #1 POP LP	*Aladdin Sane*	David Bowie

WEEK ENDING MAY 19

U.S. #1 POP 45	"You Are the Sunshine of My Life"	Stevie Wonder
U.S. #1 POP LP	*Houses of the Holy*	Led Zeppelin
U.S. #1 R&B 45	"Leaving Me"	The Independents
U.K. #1 POP 45	"Tie a Yellow Ribbon 'round the Ole Oak Tree"	Dawn
U.K. #1 POP LP	*The Beatles/1967–1970*	The Beatles

WEEK ENDING MAY 26

U.S. #1 POP 45	"Frankenstein"	The Edgar Winter Group
U.S. #1 POP LP	*The Beatles/1967–1970*	The Beatles
U.S. #1 R&B 45	"I'm Gonna Love You Just a Little More, Baby"	Barry White
U.K. #1 POP 45	"See My Baby Jive"	Wizzard
U.K. #1 POP LP	*Aladdin Sane*	David Bowie

1 Former **Soft Machine** drummer **Robert Wyatt** is seriously injured in England when he attempts to leave a party by climbing down a drainpipe and falls three stories, breaking his spine. Although Wyatt is permanently crippled, confined to a wheelchair and unable to drum, he will continue making music as a solo artist.

4 **Murray Wilson**, father of **Beach Boys Brian**, **Carl** and **Dennis**, and the group's original manager-producer, dies of a heart attack in Whittier, California, at age fifty-five. The Wilson brothers often spoke of their father as a stern disciplinarian. The elder Wilson also loved music, and in fact had released his own instrumental record in 1967, *The Many Moods of Murray Wilson*.

7 *Rolling Stone* reports—a bit prematurely—that **John David Souther**, **Chris Hillman** and **Richie Furay** are about to form a sort of country-rock supergroup. Only problem is, **Furay** hasn't yet told the members of his band, **Poco**, and denies the story (which eventually turns out to be true).

17 **Joe Salyers**, 40, business manager for **Three Dog Night**, **Steppenwolf** and **Black Oak Arkansas**, is shot in the arm after a confrontation with two strangers in his West Hollywood apartment building. Cause of the attack is unknown.

18 **Wings** enjoy yet another Top Ten hit, "Live and Let Die," the title theme song to the most recent James Bond film.

20 **Dick Clark**'s "American Bandstand" celebrates its twentieth anniversary with a TV special that features **Little Richard**, **Paul Revere and the Raiders**, the comedy team of **Cheech and Chong**, and **Three Dog Night**. The ninety-minute special also includes film clips of Fifties favorites **Fabian**, **Annette Funicello**, **Johnny Mathis** and **Conway Twitty**.

21 Soft-rockers **Bread** play their final show at the Salt Palace in Salt Lake City before a sell-out crowd of 13,075. Earlier in the day, the band's equipment truck blew a tire and overturned near Flagstaff, Arizona, destroying $30,000 worth of equipment, and forcing Bread to play their last concert with borrowed guitars, amps and drums.

24 The original **Blues Project**—**Al Kooper**, **Steve Katz**, **Danny Kalb**, **Roy Blumenfeld** and **Andy Kulberg**— reunite for the first time since 1967, in Central Park. The Project, who recorded three albums of progressive blues during 1966 and 1967, were one of the first acts to build its commercial game plan around albums, rather than hit singles. The concert is recorded and released later in the year.

26 **Mick Jagger** is named in a London paternity suit by **Marsha Hunt**, who claims that Mick is the father of her two-year-old daughter. Jagger will take a blood test when he returns to England. Hunt is a model who once was cast in the show *Hair*, and also sang with a group called **White Trash**. Says she of Jagger, "He was just a friend." The suit will prove unsuccessful.

Leon Russell's *Leon Live* goes gold. It is the last major hit for the enigmatic Russell, who, in the next decade, will release a series of tongue-in-cheek experimental country & western and jazz albums, but will never regain his huge following.

28 You know you're getting old when golden oldie shows are no longer confined to the Fifties: **Herman's Hermits** headline a bill of British Invasion acts at Madison Square Garden. Thirteen thousand paying customers turn out for an evening of blasts from the none-too-distant past by **Wayne Fontana**, **Gerry and the Pacemakers**, the **Searchers** (who inexplicably perform an extended version of **Neil Young**'s "Southern Man") and the Hermits, who run through a medley of their twenty-one gold singles in addition to a full version of "I'm into Something Good."

29 **Deep Purple** play their last show with singer **Ian Gillan** and bassist **Roger Glover**, in Japan. Gillan is replaced by **David Coverdale**, Glover by **Glenn Hughes**. Both cite exhaustion as their reason for leaving the group. ◆

WEEK ENDING JUNE 2

U.S. #1 POP 45	"My Love"	Paul McCartney and Wings
U.S. #1 POP LP	*Red Rose Speedway*	Paul McCartney and Wings
U.S. #1 R&B 45	"I'm Gonna Love You Just a Little More, Baby"	Barry White
U.K. #1 POP 45	"See My Baby Jive"	Wizzard
U.K. #1 POP LP	*Aladdin Sane*	David Bowie

WEEK ENDING JUNE 9

U.S. #1 POP 45	"My Love"	Paul McCartney and Wings
U.S. #1 POP LP	*Red Rose Speedway*	Paul McCartney and Wings
U.S. #1 R&B 45	"One of a Kind (Love Affair)"	The Spinners
U.K. #1 POP 45	"Can the Can"	Suzi Quatro
U.K. #1 POP LP	*The Beatles/1962–1966*	The Beatles

WEEK ENDING JUNE 16

U.S. #1 POP 45	"My Love"	Paul McCartney and Wings
U.S. #1 POP LP	*Red Rose Speedway*	Paul McCartney and Wings
U.S. #1 R&B 45	"One of a Kind (Love Affair)"	The Spinners
U.K. #1 POP 45	"Can the Can"	Suzi Quatro
U.K. #1 POP LP	*Aladdin Sane*	David Bowie

WEEK ENDING JUNE 23

U.S. #1 POP 45	"My Love"	Paul McCartney and Wings
U.S. #1 POP LP	*Living in the Material World*	George Harrison
U.S. #1 R&B 45	"One of a Kind (Love Affair)"	The Spinners
U.K. #1 POP 45	"Rubber Bullets"	10cc
U.K. #1 POP LP	*Aladdin Sane*	David Bowie

WEEK ENDING JUNE 30

U.S. #1 POP 45	"Give Me Love (Give Me Peace on Earth)"	George Harrison
U.S. #1 POP LP	*Living in the Material World*	George Harrison
U.S. #1 R&B 45	"One of a Kind (Love Affair)"	The Spinners
U.K. #1 POP 45	"Skweeze Me, Pleeze Me"	Slade
U.K. #1 POP LP	*Aladdin Sane*	David Bowie

3 **David Bowie** caps a grueling 60-date tour with a show at the Hammersmith Odeon. Just before the encore, he shocks his fans with an announcement: "This night shall always be special in my memory. Not only is it the last show of my British tour … but it is the last show I will ever do." As fans gasp in disbelief and girls scream, "No, David, no!" Bowie brings down the curtain with "Rock 'N' Roll Suicide." The "retirement" lasts only until the following June.

5 **Dobie Gray**, who popularized "The 'In' Crowd" in 1965, has the biggest hit of his career and earns a gold record for **Mentor Williams'** soulful "Drift Away."

6 A new British flash n' metal outfit called **Queen** release its first single, "Keep Yourself Alive," with its first LP scheduled for release one week later.

14 The **Everly Brothers**, who had their first hit, "Bye Bye Love," back in 1957, have called it quits. **Don Everly** announced his decision to leave the duo the previous evening, and on this night the Everlys play their last show together at Knott's Berry Farm—although it's hardly a graceful exit. The show is stopped by entertainment director **Bill Hollingshead** because of what he felt was a poor performance by Don, causing sibling **Phil** to smash his guitar on the floor and stalk off stage.

15 **Ray Davies** announces from the stage of the White City Festival that he is leaving the **Kinks**. "I just wanted to say goodbye and thank you for all you've done," he tells the crowd. Davies' abrupt decision to quit was brought on by exhaustion—his wife had recently left him, and the Kinks' leader hadn't eaten or slept properly for days. He returns to the group within the week.

16 **Bob Dylan** releases the soundtrack to *Pat Garrett and Billy the Kid*. Dylan appears in the movie along with **Kris Kristofferson**. The most notable track is "Knocking on Heaven's Door," which reaches #12. The soundtrack goes to #16.

19 **Clarence White** of the **Byrds** is buried in California, several days after being struck by a car. White was leaving a Palmdale nightclub when he was hit by the car, whose driver was arrested on suspicion of drunk driving and manslaughter. Born in Lewiston, Maine, White joined the Byrds in 1968 and remained with them until their official breakup early this year. He was twenty-nine.

20 **T. Rex**, whose British popularity has already been eclipsed by **David Bowie**'s, begins a six-week tour in an attempt to convert the States. **Marc Bolan**'s band consists of conga player **Mickey Finn**, bassist **Steve Curry**, drummer **Bill Legend** and guitarist **Jack Green**, plus backup singers **Gloria Jones** and **Patricia Hall**.

27 **Jethro Tull**'s *A Passion Play* turns gold, but overall is considered a disappointment. Tull leader **Ian Anderson**, who succeeded so wonderfully with Tull's previous two concept LPs, *Aqualung* and *Thick as a Brick*, appears to have missed the mark this time, and *APP* is critically panned across the boards. An angry Anderson later will whisk his group off the road in response.

28 The largest rock festival of all time is held at the Watkins Glen raceway, drawing 600,000, more than three times the number predicted by the festival's promoters. Although there is just one day of music—by the **Grateful Dead**, the **Band** and the **Allman Brothers**—a crowd of 80,000 already had converged at the site by the 26th, and with twelve hours yet to go, traffic toward the area is being affected over 100 miles away. Except for a drenching rain, the festival comes off without a hitch, with adequate toilet and water supplies.

29 **Led Zeppelin**, in the middle of a highly successful U.S. tour, are the victims of one of the largest cash thefts ever pulled off in New York City, as $180,000 is pilfered from the group's deposit box at the Drake Hotel. The money mostly represents cash receipts from the first two of three Madison Square Garden shows. Police have dusted for fingerprints and are investigating the crime.

30 At a press conference called by New York senator **James Buckley**, ex-**Papa John Phillips** accuses his former label, ABC-Dunhill, with "the systematic, cold-blooded theft of perhaps up to $60 million, stolen from each and every artist who recorded for the company during a seven-year period." Phillips and the other three members of the defunct **Mamas and the Papas** are planning to file a $9-million civil suit against the company, which claims that Phillips' charges have been made "without foundation."   ◆

WEEK ENDING JULY 7

U.S. #1 POP 45	"Will It Go Round in Circles"	Billy Preston
U.S. #1 POP LP	*Living in the Material World*	George Harrison
U.S. #1 R&B 45	"Doing It to Death"	Fred Wesley and the J.B.s
U.K. #1 POP 45	"Skweeze Me, Pleeze Me"	Slade
U.K. #1 POP LP	*Aladdin Sane*	David Bowie

WEEK ENDING JULY 14

U.S. #1 POP 45	"Will It Go Round in Circles"	Billy Preston
U.S. #1 POP LP	*Living in the Material World*	George Harrison
U.S. #1 R&B 45	"Doing It to Death"	Fred Wesley and the J.B.s
U.K. #1 POP 45	"Welcome Home"	Peters and Lee
U.K. #1 POP LP	*We Can Make It*	Peters and Lee

WEEK ENDING JULY 21

U.S. #1 POP 45	"Bad, Bad LeRoy Brown"	Jim Croce
U.S. #1 POP LP	*Living in the Material World*	George Harrison
U.S. #1 R&B 45	"I Believe in You (You Believe in Me)"	Johnnie Taylor
U.K. #1 POP 45	"Welcome Home"	Peters and Lee
U.K. #1 POP LP	*Aladdin Sane*	David Bowie

WEEK ENDING JULY 28

U.S. #1 POP 45	"Bad, Bad LeRoy Brown"	Jim Croce
U.S. #1 POP LP	*Chicago VI*	Chicago
U.S. #1 R&B 45	"I Believe in You (You Believe in Me)"	Johnnie Taylor
U.K. #1 POP 45	"I'm the Leader of the Gang"	Gary Glitter
U.K. #1 POP LP	*We Can Make It*	Peters and Lee

1 **Jerry Garcia** celebrates his thirty-first birthday by playing a concert at Roosevelt Stadium with the **Grateful Dead**. As a surprise, a cake is wheeled out onto the stage, and out pops a naked girl. Garcia, in his own words, is "embarrassed."

2 Who is **Jobriath**? According to *Rolling Stone*, impresario **Jerry Brandt** has announced that bids to sign his new artist must *start* at $1 million. Just what does Jobriath do? Sings and plays piano, for starters, but he's also designed his own stage act, which includes a replica of the Empire State Building that turns into a penis as the star sheds his King Kong suit and slips into something more comfortable. Jobriath also plans to be filmed playing piano in the Mohave Desert during an upcoming solar eclipse.

4 Guitarist **Eddie Condon**, one of the important jazz guitarists in the Thirties and Forties, dies of a lingering bone disease. He was sixty-seven. Condon led a number of small groups, from which emerged such players as **Gene Krupa**, **Johnny Mercer** and **Earl Hines**.

6 **Memphis Minnie** (**Lizzie Douglas**), a leading blueswoman for many years, dies in Memphis. She had been crippled for several years by a stroke that rendered her unable to speak or sing intelligibly. Once a street singer, Minnie went on to record at least several hundred sides, reaching her height in the Thirties when, recalled one of her blues colleagues, "You couldn't listen to a radio for more than an hour without hearing Memphis Minnie."

Stevie Wonder suffers head injuries when a car in which he is riding collides with a logging truck near Salisbury, North Carolina. The singer is taken unconscious to a hospital and placed in intensive care; he'll remain there for four days because of a coma induced by a brain contusion. According to Wonder's physicians, because he is blind, the impact of the accident was magnified three times. Wonder is expected to make a full recovery, and in fact, the only permanent damage he suffers is loss of his sense of smell.

8 **Steve Perron**, lead singer for a Texas band called the **Children**, dies at age twenty-eight. An autopsy shows that he choked on his own vomit during his sleep. Perron recently had written the hit "Francene" for **ZZ Top**.

9 Writer **Lillian Roxon** dies at age forty-one after suffering a severe asthma attack. Roxon is probably best known as the author of the *Rock Encyclopedia*, originally published in 1969. In addition, she was a music columnist for several newspapers, and wrote a women's sex column for *Mademoiselle* magazine.

17 **Paul Williams**, one of the original **Temptations**, is found dead by police, who later rule his death a suicide. Williams is clad only in a pair of swimming trunks, and is slumped over the wheel of his car, a gun in his hand, when discovered. He had shot one bullet through his forehead. Williams, the group's strong baritone, had left the Temps in 1971, but continued to draw a salary as an adviser and as a supervisor of the Temps' choreography. He was thirty-four.

Walter C. "Buddy" Clewis, manager of the Mobile, Alabama, Municipal Auditorium, is indicted for allegedly blackmailing bands appearing at the auditorium. Shows that have been "touched" by the blackmail ring include those by the **Jackson 5**, **James Brown**, the **Moments**, **Al Green**, **Joe Simon**, the **Staple Singers**, **Curtis Mayfield** and **Isaac Hayes**.

19 **Rita Coolidge** and **Kris Kristofferson** are married in Malibu, with the groom's minister-father presiding. Rita wears white, and the best man is **Bobby Neuwirth**.

23 The annual Reading Festival is held in Britain. The lineup includes **Traffic**, **Focus**, **Eric Burdon** and others.

25 The **Faces** play what they claim may be their last U.K. date, before a crowd of 30,000 in Reading, England. The reason for the startling announcement is that Faces bassist **Tetsu Yamauchi** has been refused a work permit by the Musicians Union, outraging the group, particularly **Rod Stewart**, who calls the decision "a disgrace." However, the group will stay together, and in fact Stewart says he will now devote all his time to the Faces and that his next solo LP will be his last.

28 **Bobby ("Boris") Pickett's** ghoulish novelty disc "Monster Mash" charts for the third time, hitting #10 eleven years after it made Number One in 1962. (The song appeared again in 1970, when it reached #91.) By this time, Pickett is retired from music and drives a cab.

30 After two marginally successful LPs, the post-**Jim Morrison Doors** have broken up, *Rolling Stone* reports. **Ray Manzarek** is already back in Los Angeles putting a new band together. ◆

WEEK ENDING AUGUST 4

U.S. #1 POP 45	"The Morning After"	Maureen McGovern
U.S. #1 POP LP	*Chicago VI*	Chicago
U.S. #1 R&B 45	"Angel"	Aretha Franklin
U.K. #1 POP 45	"I'm the Leader of the Gang"	Gary Glitter
U.K. #1 POP LP	*We Can Make It*	Peters and Lee

WEEK ENDING AUGUST 11

U.S. #1 POP 45	"The Morning After"	Maureen McGovern
U.S. #1 POP LP	*Chicago VI*	Chicago
U.S. #1 R&B 45	"Angel"	Aretha Franklin
U.K. #1 POP 45	"I'm the Leader of the Gang"	Gary Glitter
U.K. #1 POP LP	*We Can Make It*	Peters and Lee

WEEK ENDING AUGUST 18

U.S. #1 POP 45	"Touch Me in the Morning"	Diana Ross
U.S. #1 POP LP	*A Passion Play*	Jethro Tull
U.S. #1 R&B 45	"Let's Get It On"	Marvin Gaye
U.K. #1 POP 45	"I'm the Leader of the Gang"	Gary Glitter
U.K. #1 POP LP	*Now and Then*	The Carpenters

WEEK ENDING AUGUST 25

U.S. #1 POP 45	"Brother Louie"	Stories
U.S. #1 POP LP	*Chicago VI*	Chicago
U.S. #1 R&B 45	"Let's Get It On"	Marvin Gaye
U.K. #1 POP 45	"Young Love"	Donny Osmond
U.K. #1 POP LP	*Now and Then*	The Carpenters

1 The **Rolling Stones** open their first European tour since 1971 at Vienna's Stadthalle, the first stop of the twenty-city tour. The Stones had been hoping to play behind the Iron Curtain, but were denied permission.

7 "Here he is, the *biggest, largest, most gigantic* and *fantastic* man, the costar of my next movie . . . **Elton John!**" That's how E. J. is introduced at the Hollywood Bowl. The show's emcee: none other than porn star **Linda Lovelace**.

Mike Curb, president of slumping MGM Records since 1969, quits. Curb, twenty-eight, made a reputation for himself as a purveyor of middle-of-the-road music, who once purged eighteen acts from his label because they were allegedly "drug oriented." Curb leaves claiming he wants to move on "to bigger and better things." Lieutenant governor of California proves to be one of them.

———

The second Ann Arbor Blues and Jazz Festival is held, offering attendees five concerts over three days. Once again, activist **John Sinclair** is the festival's creative director, and he assembles more than 160 musicians, including **Ray Charles**, **Otis Rush** and **One-String Sam**, an obscure sixty-seven-year-old bluesman who sings, and plays a board strung with a single piece of wire.

9 **Todd Rundgren** keeps his promise and records 1,000 voices in San Francisco's Golden Gate Park for the left track of his song "Sons of 1984"; he had recorded over 5,000 fans in New York's Central Park on the right track. But the open-air recording session ends in a rumble, as police move in to arrest a twenty-one-year-old man for allegedly peddling cannabis, and a melee erupts. Eleven persons are arrested.

10 BBC Radio bans the **Rolling Stones'** "Star Star" because of its chorus, which contains the word *star-fucker* repeated a dozen times.

19 **Gram Parsons**, once of the **Byrds** and the **Flying Burrito Brothers**, dies under mysterious circumstances in Joshua Tree, California. The twenty-six-year-old singer/songwriter's death is attributed to heart failure due to natural causes, but later will be officially announced as due to a drug overdose. Parsons' coffin is stolen by two of his associates and is taken to Joshua Tree, where it is set afire. Police later arrest Parsons' road manager, **Phil Kaufman**, and **Michael Martin**, a former **Byrds** roadie.

20 **Neil Young** and **Crazy Horse** play the opening show at the Roxy, L.A.'s newest rock & roll nightclub.

Singer/songwriter **Jim Croce** is killed in a plane crash. Croce, 30, was en route to a concert in Sherman, Texas, when the single-engine plane carrying four others plus the pilot hits a tree on takeoff. All are killed. After years of being in and out of music, Croce had first gained fame in 1972, and his folksy, storytelling style marked him a rising star.

25 Even though bassist **Bill Wyman** had candidly admitted, "It's not my favorite album," and **Mick Jagger** had huffed, "Some people won't like it; too bad," the **Rolling Stones'** *Goat's Head Soup* turns gold. The album also goes to Number One and contains a Number One single, "Angie."

26 The Dutch instrumental group **Focus** receive a gold record for *Focus 3,* which comes on the heels of their lone hit, "Hocus Pocus." The song is notable for its lead "vocals," which are yodeled rather than sung by **Thijs Van Leer**.

27 *Rolling Stone* reports that **Carlos Santana**, now a disciple of **Sri Chinmoy**, has a new name: **Devadip**, which means "The Lamp of the Light of the Supreme." The band's name, however, will remain as Santana.

28 The **Rolling Stones** appear on U.S. television for the first time since 1967, on the new "Don Kirshner Rock Concert." The group performs, on film, three songs from its recently released *Goat's Head Soup:* "Angie," "Silver Train" and "Dancing with Mr. D." ◆

WEEK ENDING SEPTEMBER 1

U.S. #1 POP 45	"Brother Louie"	Stories
U.S. #1 POP LP	*Brothers and Sisters*	The Allman Brothers Band
U.S. #1 R&B 45	"Let's Get It On"	Marvin Gaye
U.K. #1 POP 45	"Young Love"	Donny Osmond
U.K. #1 POP LP	*Sing It Again, Rod*	Rod Stewart

WEEK ENDING SEPTEMBER 8

U.S. #1 POP 45	"Let's Get It On"	Marvin Gaye
U.S. #1 POP LP	*Brothers and Sisters*	The Allman Brothers Band
U.S. #1 R&B 45	"Let's Get It On"	Marvin Gaye
U.K. #1 POP 45	"Angel Fingers"	Wizzard
U.K. #1 POP LP	*Sing It Again, Rod*	Rod Stewart

WEEK ENDING SEPTEMBER 15

U.S. #1 POP 45	"Delta Dawn"	Helen Reddy
U.S. #1 POP LP	*Brothers and Sisters*	The Allman Brothers Band
U.S. #1 R&B 45	"Let's Get It On"	Marvin Gaye
U.K. #1 POP 45	"Rock On"	David Essex
U.K. #1 POP LP	*Sing It Again, Rod*	Rod Stewart

WEEK ENDING SEPTEMBER 22

U.S. #1 POP 45	"Delta Dawn"	Helen Reddy
U.S. #1 POP LP	*Brothers and Sisters*	The Allman Brothers Band
U.S. #1 R&B 45	"Let's Get It On"	Marvin Gaye
U.K. #1 POP 45	"Ballroom Blitz"	Sweet
U.K. #1 POP LP	*Goat's Head Soup*	The Rolling Stones

WEEK ENDING SEPTEMBER 29

U.S. #1 POP 45	"We're an American Band"	Grand Funk Railroad
U.S. #1 POP LP	*Brothers and Sisters*	The Allman Brothers Band
U.S. #1 R&B 45	"Higher Ground"	Stevie Wonder
U.K. #1 POP 45	"Eye Level"	Simm Park Orchestra
U.K. #1 POP LP	*Goat's Head Soup*	The Rolling Stones

2 The cream of the Bay Area's rock talent gets together for a performance to benefit a "friend" named **Badger**. Promoter **Bill Graham** is upset, because Badger turns out to be a member of the **Hell's Angels** who needs some legal aid. Graham is well known to be no fan of the outlaw motorcycle gang.

4 **Crosby, Stills, Nash and Young** perform together for the first time in two years—unofficially. The concert, held at San Francisco's Winterland ballroom, is actually a **Stephen Stills and Manassas** show, but first **Graham Nash** and **David Crosby** walk on stage, and then later are joined by **Neil Young** for a fifty-minute set.

9 **Elvis** and **Priscilla Presley** divorce after six years of marriage. She is awarded a sizable amount of property; $725,000 and an additional $4,200 a month for the support of their five-year-old daughter; half the proceeds from the planned sale of an L.A. home; and five percent of the total outstanding stock in two publishing companies. The couple emerge from a Santa Monica, California, courthouse arm in arm, kiss and depart separately.

11 "Hello, Hello"—again: *Rolling Stone* reports that the **Sopwith Camel**, one of Frisco's good-vibes bands of the mid-Sixties, have re-formed. The group's already recorded an LP: *The Miraculous Hump Returns from the Moon.* The Camel's lineup is unchanged, except for the addition of a keyboardist.

12 **Elton John** gets a gold record for his ambitious two-record *Goodbye Yellow Brick Road,* his third consecutive Number One LP. The album holds at the top spot for two months.

15 The Supreme Court decides, by a 7–2 vote, to refuse to review a 1971 Federal Communications directive that broadcasters, in effect, censor from the airwaves songs with drug-oriented lyrics. The two dissenting votes are cast by Justices **William J. Brennan** and **William O. Douglas**, who says, "The government cannot, consistent with the First Amendment, require a broadcaster to censor its music."

19 **David Bowie** releases *Pin Ups,* a collection of mid-Sixties cover versions including the **Easybeats'** "Friday on My Mind," the **Merseybeats'** "Sorrow" and two numbers by the **Who**. Posing next to Bowie on the cover is model **Twiggy**.

20 The **Rolling Stones** have their first Number One ballad, "Angie," a song that sparks rumors that it's a love song from Jagger to **David Bowie**'s wife, **Angela**.

21 Three hundred Louisiana state troopers are dispatched to the Day in the Sun rock concert at Southland Dragway, where they make over 100 arrests, most for alleged possession of cannabis. According to Sheriff **Charlton P. Rozards**, gunfire at the fringe of the crowd of about 7,500 and a rock-and-bottle throwing incident led to the early closing of the concert. He blames the disturbance on "a group of bad eggs from out of town on drugs."

24 The world's most famous backup singer,

Art Garfunkel, receives a gold album for his first solo effort, *Angel Clare,* which contains the biggest hit of his career, **Jimmy Webb**'s "All I Know."

Keith Richards is fined $500 and is given conditional discharges on four drug charges and three firearms offenses following trial in Marlborough Street Magistrate Court. Actress **Anita Pallenberg**, arrested with Richards back on June 26 when police raided their Chelsea home, is given a conditional discharge for possession of twenty-five Mandrax tablets. Just ten days earlier, both were fined $1,000 in France for possession of controlled substances, that also from an earlier bust.

25 **John Lennon** sues the U.S. government, maintaining that wiretaps and surveillance were employed against him and his attorney, **Leon Wildes**. The suit claims that as a result, his appeal applications in his fight against deportation were prejudged by U.S. officials.

29 The **Who**'s latest masterwork, *Quadrophenia,* goes gold. More cohesive than the more celebrated *Tommy, Quadrophenia* tells the story of this four-sided band, using the mod era of England as a backdrop, and with each band member being given his own musical theme, which is reprised at points throughout. *Quadrophenia* will later be turned into a film.

31 **John Lennon** releases the *Mind Games* LP and the title track as a single. Both become his most popular records in quite some time, the album reaching #9, the single, #18. The same day, **Ringo Starr**'s *Ringo* is released. ◆

WEEK ENDING OCTOBER 6

U.S. #1 POP 45	"Half-Breed"	Cher
U.S. #1 POP LP	*Brothers and Sisters*	The Allman Brothers Band
U.S. #1 R&B 45	"Keep On Truckin'"	Eddie Kendricks
U.K. #1 POP 45	"Eye Level"	Simon Park Orchestra
U.K. #1 POP LP	*Sladest*	Slade

WEEK ENDING OCTOBER 13

U.S. #1 POP 45	"Half-Breed"	Cher
U.S. #1 POP LP	*Goat's Head Soup*	The Rolling Stones
U.S. #1 R&B 45	"Keep On Truckin'"	Eddie Kendricks
U.K. #1 POP 45	"Eye Level"	Simon Park Orchestra
U.K. #1 POP LP	*Sladest*	Slade

WEEK ENDING OCTOBER 20

U.S. #1 POP 45	"Angie"	The Rolling Stones
U.S. #1 POP LP	*Goat's Head Soup*	The Rolling Stones
U.S. #1 R&B 45	"Midnight Train to Georgia"	Gladys Knight and the Pips
U.K. #1 POP 45	"Eye Level"	Simon Park Orchestra
U.K. #1 POP LP	*Hello*	Status Quo

WEEK ENDING OCTOBER 27

U.S. #1 POP 45	"Midnight Train to Georgia"	Gladys Knight and the Pips
U.S. #1 POP LP	*Goat's Head Soup*	The Rolling Stones
U.S. #1 R&B 45	"Midnight Train to Georgia"	Gladys Knight and the Pips
U.K. #1 POP 45	"Puppy Song"/"Day Dreamer"	David Cassidy
U.K. #1 POP LP	*Pin Ups*	David Bowie

4 A benefit concert is held for **Robert Wyatt** by his former band, **Soft Machine**, and **Pink Floyd** at London's Rainbow Theater. Wyatt had been paralyzed in a fall earlier in the year.

5 Performing *Quadrophenia* has proved problematic for the **Who** during their current tour, and on this night in Newcastle, England, it all falls apart. Much of the lengthy work is performed to taped sections, and when one of the pieces comes in fifteen seconds out of step with drummer **Keith Moon**, **Pete Townshend** explodes, berating sound engineer **Bobby Pridden** and storming off stage. Townshend returns a half hour later, but the Who abandon *Quadrophenia* for the night and perform old hits instead.

6 **Phil Kaufman** and **Michael Martin**, charged with the theft of a coffin containing **Gram Parsons**, are fined $300 each after they plead to a misdemeanor charge. West Los Angeles municipal judge **Leo Freund** also orders them to pay $708 to the Yucca Valley

funeral home for the cost of the destroyed coffin. Deputy district attorney **Anthony White** says police had found evidence that the two men merely were carrying out Parsons' wishes to be cremated in the desert.

9 **Cat Stevens** makes his national TV "debut" on ABC's "In Concert." Stevens' ninety-minute special is taped live at the Hollywood Bowl and includes some of Stevens' animated cartoons.

After years of struggling as a member of two New York–area bands, the **Hassles** and **Attila**, and as a bar piano player, **Billy Joel** releases what will ultimately be his breakthrough album, *Piano Man.* The title song will be released as a single and become a Top Twenty-five hit in early 1974.

11 Thirty stations across the country broadcast what is billed as a "live" **Mott the Hoople** show. In reality, it's nothing more than Hoople studio tracks with dubbed-in applause.

13 **Jerry Lee Lewis, Jr.**, is killed in a highway acci-

dent near Hernando, Mississippi. Just several days earlier, the nineteen-year-old had appeared on TV's "Midnight Special" as a drummer in his father's band. In 1962, the elder Lewis' only other son, Steven Allen, drowned in the family swimming pool.

16 **David Bowie** stars in his first TV special, "1980 Floor Show," broadcast here on NBC's "Midnight Special." The special had been taped a month earlier at London's Marquee Club, always a favorite of Bowie's, who used to play there with his first band, **David Jones and the Lower Third**. It was one of the few clubs that would book him, he recalls fondly, because "we were considered a very freaky band." Bowie's guests include **Marianne Faithfull**, the **Troggs** and Spanish rock group **Carmen**.

20 **Allan Sherman**, the comedian/songwriter whose album *My Son, the Folksinger* sold well over a million copies in the early Sixties, dies at the age of forty-eight. Sherman collapsed at his Hollywood apartment, and death is attri-

buted to respiratory ailments. Sherman had recently completed a book, *The Rape of the Ape*, which charted the sexual revolution since the end of World War II.

Keith Moon collapses twice during the first date of the **Who**'s U.S. tour, in San Francisco. First, the manic drummer falls over his kit during "Won't Get Fooled Again." Then, after being administered to backstage, Moon plays for another ten minutes before he's carried off again, allegedly due to jet lag. So **Pete Townshend** asks for a volunteer from the crowd to replace Moonie. He gets one: nineteen-year-old **Scott Halpin** from Muscatine, Iowa, who finishes the set with the band. Says Halpin after the set: "I really admire their stamina; I only played three numbers, and I was dead."

26 **John Rostill**, former guitarist for England's immensely popular **Shadows**, is electrocuted in his home recording studio. Here's the headline from the *International Herald-Tribune*: POP MUSICIAN DIES, GUITAR APPARENT CAUSE.

27 **Jimmy Widener**, 55, lead guitarist for ten years behind country star **Hank Snow**, is shot and killed, his body dumped in an alley. Also murdered is his companion, **Mildred Hazlewood**, wife of performer/composer **Eddie Hazlewood**. ◆

WEEK ENDING NOVEMBER 3

U.S. #1 POP 45	"Midnight Train to Georgia"	Gladys Knight and the Pips
U.S. #1 POP LP	*Goat's Head Soup*	The Rolling Stones
U.S. #1 R&B 45	"Midnight Train to Georgia"	Gladys Knight and the Pips
U.K. #1 POP 45	"Puppy Song"/"Day Dreamer"	David Cassidy
U.K. #1 POP LP	*Pin Ups*	David Bowie

WEEK ENDING NOVEMBER 10

U.S. #1 POP 45	"Keep On Truckin'"	Eddie Kendricks
U.S. #1 POP LP	*Goodbye Yellow Brick Road*	Elton John
U.S. #1 R&B 45	"Midnight Train to Georgia"	Gladys Knight and the Pips
U.K. #1 POP 45	"Puppy Song"/"Day Dreamer"	David Cassidy
U.K. #1 POP LP	*Pin Ups*	David Bowie

WEEK ENDING NOVEMBER 17

U.S. #1 POP 45	"Keep On Truckin'"	Eddie Kendricks
U.S. #1 POP LP	*Goodbye Yellow Brick Road*	Elton John
U.S. #1 R&B 45	"Space Race"	Billy Preston
U.K. #1 POP 45	"I Love You Love Me Love"	Gary Glitter
U.K. #1 POP LP	*Pin Ups*	David Bowie

WEEK ENDING NOVEMBER 24

U.S. #1 POP 45	"Photograph"	Ringo Starr
U.S. #1 POP LP	*Goodbye Yellow Brick Road*	Elton John
U.S. #1 R&B 45	"The Love I Lost"	Harold Melvin and the Bluenotes
U.K. #1 POP 45	"I Love You Love Me Love"	Gary Glitter
U.K. #1 POP LP	*Pin Ups*	David Bowie

2 After a show at the Montreal Forum, the **Who** and some companions are jailed overnight for $6,000 worth of hotel destruction. The incident is later chronicled in the **John Entwistle** song "Cell Block Number Seven."

This is D-day for millions of **Bob Dylan** fans; it's their first opportunity to mail in ticket requests for his upcoming tour. In San Francisco, traffic is backed up five blocks from one post office, and in other cities, ticket requests are stamped "Return to Sender," simply because there are far too many of them than can be handled. All the concerts sell out, which means 658,000 tickets sold.

3 **Ringo Starr** releases what will become his second consecutive Number One single, "You're Sixteen," which had been a hit for **Johnny Burnette** in 1960. Both "You're Sixteen" and the previous chart topper, "Photograph," are off Starr's *Ringo* LP.

6 **Steve Miller**, who'd been laying low for most of 1972 and 1973, gets a gold record for *The Joker*, his most successful LP to date. The title track becomes Miller's first chart-topping hit and gives cameo roles to some of his pre-

vious in-song personas, like "Maurice" and "The Gangster of Love."

George Jones and **Tammy Wynette** have reconciled, reports *Rolling Stone*, which had carried the announcement of their impending divorce just a few weeks earlier. The couple's new single, titled "We're Gonna Hold On," already is high on the country singles chart.

7 A year of trouble begins for **Fleetwood Mac**. Their manager, **Clifford Davis**, claims ownership of the band's name and assembles a bogus Fleetwood Mac, which he puts out on tour.

20 **Bobby Darin**, one of the few teen idols of the Fifties to survive the Sixties and the early Seventies, dies at age thirty-seven. Cause of death is heart failure, which occurs dur-

ing Darin's second open-heart surgery in two years. Darin never became quite the legend he once said he hoped to be, but he had an impressive string of hits: fourteen Top Twenty singles between 1958 and 1966. The song most often associated with him is "Mack the Knife," which was Number One for nine weeks in 1959.

24 **Tom Johnston** of the **Doobie Brothers** is arrested in Visalia, California, on charges of marijuana possession. He must go to court on January 10 for a hearing, right about the time the group's new album is released. Its title? *What Were Once Vices Are Now Habits*.

30 **John McLaughlin**'s original **Mahavishnu Orchestra** (comprised of McLaughlin, **Billy Cobham**, **Jan Hammer**, **Rick Laird** and **Jerry Goodman**) appear for the last time together, in Detroit's Masonic Auditorium. According to Laird, the personal relationships within the group had so deteriorated that after the show the musicians didn't even say goodbye to one another.   ◆

WEEK ENDING DECEMBER 1

U.S. #1 POP 45	"Top of the World"	The Carpenters
U.S. #1 POP LP	*Goodbye Yellow Brick Road*	Elton John
U.S. #1 R&B 45	"The Love I Lost"	Harold Melvin and the Bluenotes
U.K. #1 POP 45	"I Love You Love Me Love"	Gary Glitter
U.K. #1 POP LP	*Pin Ups*	David Bowie

WEEK ENDING DECEMBER 8

U.S. #1 POP 45	"Top of the World"	The Carpenters
U.S. #1 POP LP	*Goodbye Yellow Brick Road*	Elton John
U.S. #1 R&B 45	"If You're Ready (Come Go with Me)"	The Staple Singers
U.K. #1 POP 45	"I Love You Love Me Love"	Gary Glitter
U.K. #1 POP LP	*Pin Ups*	David Bowie

WEEK ENDING DECEMBER 15

U.S. #1 POP 45	"The Most Beautiful Girl"	Charlie Rich
U.S. #1 POP LP	*Goodbye Yellow Brick Road*	Elton John
U.S. #1 R&B 45	"If You're Ready (Come Go with Me)"	The Staple Singers
U.K. #1 POP 45	"Merry Christmas, Everybody"	Slade
U.K. #1 POP LP	*Brain Salad Surgery*	Emerson, Lake and Palmer

WEEK ENDING DECEMBER 22

U.S. #1 POP 45	"The Most Beautiful Girl"	Charlie Rich
U.S. #1 POP LP	*Goodbye Yellow Brick Road*	Elton John
U.S. #1 R&B 45	"If You're Ready (Come Go with Me)"	The Staple Singers
U.K. #1 POP 45	"Merry Christmas, Everybody"	Slade
U.K. #1 POP LP	*Brain Salad Surgery*	Emerson, Lake and Palmer

WEEK ENDING DECEMBER 29

U.S. #1 POP 45	"Time in a Bottle"	Jim Croce
U.S. #1 POP LP	*Goodbye Yellow Brick Road*	Elton John
U.S. #1 R&B 45	"Living in the City"	Stevie Wonder
U.K. #1 POP 45	"Merry Christmas, Everybody"	Slade
U.K. #1 POP LP	*Brain Salad Surgery*	Emerson, Lake and Palmer

1974

The sluggish, static Seventies ground on. This year, the pop charts continued to be ruled by an unending stream of middle-of-the-road fluff and inane novelties: "Seasons in the Sun," "The Streak," "The Night Chicago Died," "Billy, Don't Be a Hero," "Kung Fu Fighting" and "(You're) Having My Baby." A heavyweight progressive-rock band like Yes could sell out New York's Madison Square Garden in a few days without advertising. And as a true sign of the times, the Jefferson Airplane—one of the most fearlessly committed counter-culture bands of the late Sixties—mirrored the cultural evolution toward high-tech futurism by changing their name from Jefferson *Airplane* to Jefferson *Starship,* dropping politics and spacey obscurantism from their repertoire and streamlining their sound into the now-prevalent so-called corporate-rock mold. They soon began a new phase of their career even more successful than the first.

There were more rendezvous between rock stars and politicians: Jimmy Carter invited Bob Dylan to his Georgia governor's mansion in January; President Ford met George Harrison at the White House in December. There were more good-cause benefits, such as those for Chilean political prisoners in May and for the United Farm Workers and Save the Whales in December. There was one giant-size rock festival, the California Jam, that went off without a hitch, but there were riots and violent incidents at other such shows.

In the good-news department, Bob Dylan returned to form with his rip-roaring tour with the Band, the tour's live album *Before the Flood* and his best solo album in years, *Blood on the Tracks.* Rock criticism finally intersected with mass attitudes as critic Jon Landau penned his "I have seen the future of rock & roll . . ." item about Bruce Springsteen, who slowly but surely was building a nationwide grassroots following that would explode into superstardom next year.

Meanwhile, two musical movements that would soon polarize the mass-music audience began getting off the ground. In this, the same year that prepunk avatars the New York Dolls broke up, the world's first punk-rock band, the Ramones, made their debut at CBGB, the Manhattan club that would soon become the American punk movement's epicenter. And there were the first real incipient signs of disco with Barry White's four gold records in February, the success of protodisco band Kool and the Gang and the summertime smashes "Rock Your Baby" by George McCrae and "Rock the Boat" by the Hues Corporation. How ironic that those latter two hits, which would lay the foundation for a musical revolution that would turn the white-rock audience into a raving mass of parochial racists with the "Disco sucks!" battle cry, used the word *rock* in their titles and—as Pete Townshend of the Who had once said rock & roll music should do—made their audience dance to forget their troubles. Finally, things were beginning to change in a big way again.

3 **Bob Dylan** and the **Band** commence their six-week tour, at Chicago Stadium. The Band, once Dylan's backup group, are accorded their own room in the set, and they excel. Dylan is in fine form, performing both solo, on acoustic guitar, and with the Band; their electric versions of Dylan classics inspires Dylan to sing with a gutsiness rarely before heard. One especially ironic moment: his rendition of "It's Alright Ma," which contains the line "even the president of the United States sometimes must have to stand naked." The crowd of 18,500 explodes.

Jim Croce's "Time in a Bottle" goes gold, the second of three posthumous hits for the late singer/songwriter. "I Got a Name" went Top Ten just one month after Croce was killed in a plane crash, and "Time" reached Number One in December. Yet another song, "I'll Have to Say I Love You in a Song," goes Top Ten in spring 1974.

---

5 The **Carpenters'** greatest-hits collection, *The Singles 1969–1973*, hits

#1. The brother-and-sister duo of **Karen** and **Richard Carpenter** had, by this year, charted eight Top Ten hits, including a pair of Number Ones, "(They Long to Be) Close to You" (1970) and "Top of the World" (1973). By the time their career ended with Karen's death in 1983, the Carpenters had become one of the most successful duos in pop.

7 **James Taylor** and **Carly Simon** have their second child, **Sarah Martin**, in New York.

8 **Kiss** give a special dress rehearsal after being signed to Casablanca Records. The group, a *Rolling Stone* correspondent reports, "play very heavy, loud and ultimately monotonous rock in the **Black Sabbath** tradition. . . . A sure crowd pleaser. The crowds of kiddies, that is."

The Early Beatles turns gold nine years after its release, and nearly four years since the group's disbanding.

15 **Brownsville Station**, described by leader **Cub Koda** as "Chuck Berry

1973 filtered through three madmen," earn themselves a gold record for their only hit single, "Smokin' in the Boys' Room." "It was written," Koda says straight-faced, "by two guys deep into toilet slavery."

---

17 **Dino Martin**, singer and son of **Dean Martin**, is arrested on suspicion of possession and sale of two machine guns. The arrest is made at Martin's home in Beverly Hills, where Martin allegedly attempts to sell an AK-47 machine gun to an undercover

agent. Martin, who was one-third of **Dino, Desi and Billy**, the celebrity-sons group who had several mid-Sixties hits, is arraigned and released the next day on $5,000 bail. He now faces indictment by a federal grand jury.

19 Two **Bob Dylan**-the-**Band** shows cause a nine-mile-long traffic jam in Miami that keeps many ticketholders from entering the Sportatorium until the show is half over. A few demonstrators are on hand for the concerts, clutching signs that read: "$9.50—A Ripoff" and "Dylan: Master of War," a reference to recent rumors that the singer has become a Zionist.

21 At the insistence of his son **Chip**, thengovernor of Georgia **Jimmy Carter** invites **Bob Dylan** to a postconcert party at his mansion. Says Carter of Dylan: "He never initiates conversation, but he'll answer a question if you ask him."

22 **Carly Simon** receives a gold record for *Hotcakes*, her Top Five album highlighted by her duet with husband **James Taylor** on "Mockingbird," also a Top Five hit.

Bob Dylan's *Planet Waves* goes gold while the troubador is in the middle of his first tour since 1965. The LP, released on Asylum Records, not Dylan's original label, or Columbia Records, later goes to Number One, the first Dylan LP to top the charts. ♦

WEEK ENDING JANUARY 5

U.S. #1 POP 45	"Time in a Bottle"	Jim Croce
U.S. #1 POP LP	*The Singles 1969–1973*	The Carpenters
U.S. #1 R&B 45	"Superstition"	Stevie Wonder
U.K. #1 POP 45	"Merry Christmas, Everybody"	Slade
U.K. #1 POP LP	*Brain Salad Surgery*	Emerson, Lake and Palmer

WEEK ENDING JANUARY 12

U.S. #1 POP 45	"The Joker"	The Steve Miller Band
U.S. #1 POP LP	*You Don't Mess Around with Jim*	Jim Croce
U.S. #1 R&B 45	"Until You Come Back to Me"	Aretha Franklin
U.K. #1 POP 45	"You Won't Find Another Fool Like Me"	The New Seekers
U.K. #1 POP LP	*Brain Salad Surgery*	Emerson, Lake and Palmer

WEEK ENDING JANUARY 19

U.S. #1 POP 45	"Show and Tell"	Al Wilson
U.S. #1 POP LP	*You Don't Mess Around with Jim*	Jim Croce
U.S. #1 R&B 45	"I've Got to Use My Imagination"	Gladys Knight and the Pips
U.K. #1 POP 45	"Teenage Rampage"	Sweet
U.K. #1 POP LP	*Brain Salad Surgery*	Emerson, Lake and Palmer

WEEK ENDING JANUARY 26

U.S. #1 POP 45	"You're Sixteen"	Ringo Starr
U.S. #1 POP LP	*You Don't Mess Around with Jim*	Jim Croce
U.S. #1 R&B 45	"Livin' for You"	Al Green
U.K. #1 POP 45	"Tiger Feet"	Mud
U.K. #1 POP LP	*The Singles 1969–1973*	The Carpenters

2 **Keith Emerson** injures his hands when a rigged piano explodes prematurely during a concert in San Francisco. Emerson suffers various cuts and a broken fingernail.

7 Soul artist **Barry White** receives four gold records on this date: for the singles "Never, Never Gonna Give Ya Up" (#7), "Love's Theme" (Number One, by the **Love Unlimited Orchestra**, conducted by White), and the albums *Under the Influence of Love Unlimited* (#3) and *Stone Gon'* (#20).

Ex-Hot Licks **John Girton** and **Maryanne Price** are married at the home of a judge in Zephyr Cove, Nevada. Price is due shortly to fly to England to record and tour with the **Kinks**.

10 Legendary producer **Phil Spector** is injured in a serious accident, but details are, for unknown reasons, kept secret. The accident takes place somewhere between L.A. and Phoenix, and according to a statement released by Spector's office, he suffered multiple head and body injuries. Even some of Spector's closest friends know nothing more about the crash and Spector's condition.

14 *Rolling Stone* reports that **David Bowie** has turned down a Gay Liberation group who asked him to compose "the world's first Gay National Anthem."

Albert Grossman, manager of the late **Janis Joplin**, has filed suit in New York against Associated Indemnity Corporation of San Francisco, in an effort to collect a $200,000 life insurance policy, $47,500 interest and $50,000 in attorney's fees. Grossman claims the company has not honored the policy, taken out about a year before the singer's death. The company contends that Joplin's death was a suicide, thus nullifying the claim.

After thirty-nine shows in twenty-one cities, the **Bob Dylan**-the **Band** tour comes to an end in Los Angeles at the Forum. Many celebrities turn out for the final performance, including **Ringo Starr**, **Carole King**, **Neil Young**, **Jack Nicholson** and **Warren Beatty**. "It was bloody

fantastic," enthuses Ringo after the two-and-a-half-hour set, "the best concert I've ever been to."

15 The Bottom Line, a new rock club, opens in New York. Attending the opening of the 500-seat club are **Mick Jagger**, **Johnny Winter**, **Stevie Wonder**, **James Taylor** and **Carly Simon** and many other music-biz luminaries.

18 **Yes** play the first of two nights at Madison Square Garden. What's remarkable about the engagement is that the first date sold out without the benefit of a single advertisement. Fans learned of the show from listings at ticket outlets and bought out the house within a few days.

Kiss, a New York heavy-metal pseudoglitter group, release their debut album, *Kiss*. It will take the band three more albums to establish itself; *Kiss* barely cracks the Top 100.

Ringo Starr releases the third hit single from his *Ringo* LP, "Oh My My," which hits #5 in April.

19 In response to the Grammy Awards, **Dick Clark** stages his own awards show, the "American Music Awards." The program is held just days before the Grammy Awards are announced, and its purpose, as explained by Clark, is: "I kind of like the idea of asking the guy on the street who listens to radio and maybe buys an album. He has no vested interest, no label allegiance." NARAS officials have no comment about Clark's show.

27 **Joni Mitchell** has her biggest album with *Court and Spark* (#2), which turns gold on this date. *Court and Spark* features Mitchell in more of a band situation, with **Tom Scott and the L.A. Express**; the sound is slick but successful, and includes Mitchell's two highest charting singles, "Help Me" (#7) and "Free Man in Paris" (#22).

28 **Bobby Bloom**, whose "Montego Bay" made the pop Top Ten in 1970 and "Heavy Makes You Happy" took the **Staple Singers** to the Top Thirty in 1971, shoots himself to death in West Hollywood. He was twenty-eight. ◆

WEEK ENDING FEBRUARY 2

U.S. #1 POP 45	"The Way We Were"	Barbra Streisand
U.S. #1 POP LP	*You Don't Mess Around with Jim*	Jim Croce
U.S. #1 R&B 45	"Let Your Hair Down"	The Temptations
U.K. #1 POP 45	"Tiger Feet"	Mud
U.K. #1 POP LP	*The Singles 1969–1973*	The Carpenters

WEEK ENDING FEBRUARY 9

U.S. #1 POP 45	"Love's Theme"	Love Unlimited Orchestra
U.S. #1 POP LP	*You Don't Mess Around with Jim*	Jim Croce
U.S. #1 R&B 45	"Boogie Down"	Eddie Kendricks
U.K. #1 POP 45	"Tiger Feet"	Mud
U.K. #1 POP LP	*The Singles 1969–1973*	The Carpenters

WEEK ENDING FEBRUARY 16

U.S. #1 POP 45	"The Way We Were"	Barbra Streisand
U.S. #1 POP LP	*Planet Waves*	Bob Dylan
U.S. #1 R&B 45	"Boogie Down"	Eddie Kendricks
U.K. #1 POP 45	"Devil Gate Drive"	Suzi Quatro
U.K. #1 POP LP	*The Singles 1969–1973*	The Carpenters

WEEK ENDING FEBRUARY 23

U.S. #1 POP 45	"The Way We Were"	Barbra Streisand
U.S. #1 POP LP	*Planet Waves*	Bob Dylan
U.S. #1 R&B 45	"Boogie Down"	Eddie Kendricks
U.K. #1 POP 45	"Devil Gate Drive"	Suzi Quatro
U.K. #1 POP LP	*The Singles 1969–1973*	The Carpenters

2 **Stevie Wonder** wins five Grammy Awards, in Los Angeles. The singer takes the honors for Album of the Year *(Innervisions),* Best Pop Vocal Performance ("You Are the Sunshine of My Life"), Best R&B Song ("Superstition") Best R&B Vocal Performance ("Superstition"), and Best Engineered Recording *(Innervisions).* Says Wonder on his five trips to the podium that night: "I would like to thank you all for making this the sunshine of my life tonight."

5 **Gregg Allman**'s first solo album, *Laid Back,* attains gold status, and sets off rumors that the Allman Brothers are breaking up. Guitarist **Dickey Betts** will release his own solo album later in the year.

12 **John Lennon** is involved in an altercation with a photographer outside the Troubador club in Los Angeles. Lennon and **Harry Nilsson** had been heckling comedian **Tommy Smothers,** and were ejected from the club.

16 The Grand Ole Opry moves from the old Ryman Auditorium to the new $28-million Opryland complex, where it resumes regular broadcasts and telecasts.

19 The **Jefferson Airplane** begin their first tour under the name **Jefferson Starship**. Included in the lineup is **Paul Kantner, Grace Slick,** drummer **Johnny Barbata, David Freiberg, Peter Kaukonen, Papa John Creach** and **Craig Chaquico.**

26 **David Essex,** England's **David Cassidy,** enjoys his one and only successful U.S. single, "Rock On," which turns

gold on this date. Essex's overseas popularity mostly stems from his film roles, which include playing Jesus in *Godspell,* and the lead roles in *That'll Be the Day* and *Stardust.* Comparisons are made to the late **James Dean,** of which Essex says, "I really loved James Dean, but being David Essex is enough for me right now."

Mike Oldfield's *Tubular Bells* turns gold. Part of the work by the British teenage prodigy is used as the score for the film *The Exorcist.*

28 The **Raspberries** have split in two. *Rolling Stone* reports that the rhythm section of **Jim Bonfanti** and **Dave Smalley** have left and have formed a band called **Dynamite.** Original members **Eric Carmen** and **Wally Bryson,** meanwhile, plan to continue, and have added drummer **Mike McBride** and bassist **Scott McCarl.**

Arthur "Big Boy" Crudup dies at the age of sixty-nine from a stroke. Crudup, born in Mississippi, was the composer of "That's All Right (Mama)," which Elvis Presley heard on a jukebox and cut in 1954 as his first record for Sun, eight years after Crudup's own recording of the song. Unfortunately, Crudup was victimized by shady deals through his career and died in poverty. "Credit is all I ever got," he once said.

"Hooked on a Feeling" by **Blue Swede** turns gold. The group's novel version of the **B. J. Thomas** 1968 hit is best remembered for its "ooga-chugga, ooga-chugga" background chant. It hits Number One in April. ◆

WEEK ENDING MARCH 2

U.S. #1 POP 45	"Seasons in the Sun"	Terry Jacks
U.S. #1 POP LP	*Planet Waves*	Bob Dylan
U.S. #1 R&B 45	"Mighty Love"	The Spinners
U.K. #1 POP 45	"Jealous Mind"	Alvin Stardust
U.K. #1 POP LP	*The Singles 1969–1973*	The Carpenters

WEEK ENDING MARCH 9

U.S. #1 POP 45	"Seasons in the Sun"	Terry Jacks
U.S. #1 POP LP	*Planet Waves*	Bob Dylan
U.S. #1 R&B 45	"Mighty Love"	The Spinners
U.K. #1 POP 45	"Jealous Mind"	Alvin Stardust
U.K. #1 POP LP	*The Singles 1969–1973*	The Carpenters

WEEK ENDING MARCH 16

U.S. #1 POP 45	"Seasons in the Sun"	Terry Jacks
U.S. #1 POP LP	*The Way We Were*	Barbra Streisand
U.S. #1 R&B 45	"Lookin' for a Love"	Bobby Womack
U.K. #1 POP 45	"Billy, Don't Be a Hero"	Paper Lace
U.K. #1 POP LP	*The Singles 1969–1973*	The Carpenters

WEEK ENDING MARCH 23

U.S. #1 POP 45	"Dark Lady"	Cher
U.S. #1 POP LP	*The Way We Were*	Barbra Streisand
U.S. #1 R&B 45	"Lookin' for a Love"	Bobby Womack
U.K. #1 POP 45	"Billy, Don't Be a Hero"	Paper Lace
U.K. #1 POP LP	*The Singles 1969–1973*	The Carpenters

WEEK ENDING MARCH 30

U.S. #1 POP 45	"Sunshine on My Shoulders"	John Denver
U.S. #1 POP LP	*John Denver's Greatest Hits*	John Denver
U.S. #1 R&B 45	"Lookin' for a Love"	Bobby Womack
U.K. #1 POP 45	"Billy, Don't Be a Hero"	Paper Lace
U.K. #1 POP LP	*The Singles 1969–1973*	The Carpenters

6 *Ladies and Gentlemen: the Rolling Stones* opens at New York City's Ziegfeld Theatre. The premiere is turned into an event: a forty-foot-high **Rolling Stones** winged tongue that rises in the air, 2,000 white doves are released and a sixty-five-foot-long dragon is flown in from San Francisco.

The California Jam rock festival pulls in 200,000 people to see such acts as **Emerson, Lake and Palmer, Black Sabbath,** the **Eagles, Deep Purple** and **Black Oak Arkansas.** The festival runs smoothly; in fact, it starts fifteen minutes *early,* but is classified by many as relatively dull. The show is taped and is

later broadcast on network television.

8 "Bennie and the Jets" turns gold, no doubt pleasing **Elton John.** But what makes John even happier is that the tune becomes a major hit on the R&B chart as well.

14 **Pete Townshend** appears for the first time as a soloist, at a concert at London's Roundhouse. The leader of the **Who** performs at the benefit, accompanied only by his homemade tapes.

17 **Vinnie Taylor,** guitarist for **Sha Na Na,** dies of a drug overdose at the age of twenty-five. Taylor, born **Chris Donald,** is found dead in his room at the Charlottesville, Virginia, Holiday Inn.

24 **Grand Funk Railroad** receive a gold record for their update of Little Eva's "The Loco-motion," the biggest hit of their career (Number One).

Ray Stevens, who throughout his career variates between novelty tunes and more serious

pop material, enjoys his biggest hit with "The Streak," a well-timed whimsical look at the current craze among teenagers. The song hits Number One in May.

David Bowie, clearly out of retirement, releases *Diamond Dogs,* whose cover is drawn by Dutch artist **Guy** (*Rock Dreams*) **Peellaert** and depicts Bowie as a mongrel, with genitalia in full view. RCA Records opts to cover the offending body parts with a sticker. *Diamond Dogs* reaches #5.

25 According to *Rolling Stone,* streakers have struck at concerts by **Yes, Gregg Allman** (one of the offenders was promoter **Bill Graham**) and the **Beach Boys,** who were victimized by two of their very own, **Mike Love** and **Dennis Wilson.**

Gregg Allman plays the last date of his solo tour, in Cincinnati. "I want to squealch a few rumors right here and now," he tells the audience before bringing on the rest of the **Allman Brothers Band** for an hour-and-a-half encore.

Jim Morrison's widow, **Pam Morrison,** dies in her Hollywood apartment of a suspected heroin overdose. She was twenty-seven. Police speculate that she had been using heroin for about one year.

27 A four-hour battle with police rages after the Cherry Blossom Music Festival in Richmond, Virginia. The concert, held outdoors in Richmond's City Stadium and billed as "a day or two of fun and music," features the **Steve Miller Band, Boz Scaggs, Stories** and several other groups. But the music soon takes a back seat to the rioting that begins after police start busting people for possession; seventy-six people are arrested, and scores are treated for injuries.

29 **Carole King** and husband **Charles Larkey** have their first son and fourth child, **Levi.** King had finished recording her new LP just five days before the baby's birth. ◆

WEEK ENDING APRIL 6		
U.S. #1 POP 45	"Hooked on a Feeling"	Blue Swede
U.S. #1 POP LP	*John Denver's Greatest Hits*	John Denver
U.S. #1 R&B 45	"Best Thing That Ever Happened to Me"	Gladys Knight and the Pips
U.K. #1 POP 45	"Seasons in the Sun"	Terry Jacks
U.K. #1 POP LP	*The Singles 1969–1973*	The Carpenters

WEEK ENDING APRIL 13		
U.S. #1 POP 45	"Bennie and the Jets"	Elton John
U.S. #1 POP LP	*Band on the Run*	Paul McCartney and Wings
U.S. #1 R&B 45	"Best Thing That Ever Happened to Me"	Gladys Knight and the Pips
U.K. #1 POP 45	"Seasons in the Sun"	Terry Jacks
U.K. #1 POP LP	*The Singles 1969–1973*	The Carpenters

WEEK ENDING APRIL 20		
U.S. #1 POP 45	"TSOP (The Sound of Philadelphia)"	MFSB featuring the Three Degrees
U.S. #1 POP LP	*Band on the Run*	Paul McCartney and Wings
U.S. #1 R&B 45	"TSOP (The Sound of Philadelphia)"	MFSB featuring the Three Degrees
U.K. #1 POP 45	"The Cat Crept In"	Mud
U.K. #1 POP LP	*The Singles 1969–1973*	The Carpenters

WEEK ENDING APRIL 27		
U.S. #1 POP 45	"TSOP (The Sound of Philadelphia)"	MFSB featuring the Three Degrees
U.S. #1 POP LP	*Chicago VII*	Chicago
U.S. #1 R&B 45	"The Payback"	James Brown
U.K. #1 POP 45	"Waterloo"	Abba
U.K. #1 POP LP	*The Singles 1969–1973*	The Carpenters

8 **Graham Bond**, one of British rock's key figures, is found dead under a stationary train in a London subway station. Bond's early-Sixties group, the **Graham Bond Organisation**, included such notables of U.K. rock as **Jack Bruce**, **Ginger Baker** and **John McLaughlin**. Bond had just recently quit heroin, and had been hospitalized for a month for treatment of a nervous breakdown. It is not clear whether Bond has committed suicide, died accidentally or was a victim of foul play.

9 **Bruce Springsteen** delivers a performance at Boston's Harvard Square Theatre that inspires *Rolling Stone* editor/critic **John Landau** to exult, "I have seen rock & roll's future, and his name is Bruce Springsteen." Landau will eventually go on to become the Boss' manager/producer.

Bob Dylan, **Phil Ochs**, **Pete Seeger**, **Arlo Guthrie**, **Melanie** and other concerned musicians participate in a "Friends of Chile" benefit at New York's Felt Forum. The show's purpose is to raise legal-aid funds for Chilean refugees and political prisoners. "You are not here to see Bob Dylan," Ochs informs the audience of 4,600 early on. The concert nets $30,000.

10 New Jersey funk band **Kool and the Gang**'s *Wild and Peaceful* album, their seventh in five years, goes gold. The album features three top-selling singles: "Jungle Boogie" (#4 on the pop chart), "Hollywood Swinging" (#6) and "Funky Stuff" (#29). Originally a jazz-oriented band, Kool and the Gang began moving toward R&B in the early Seventies, and by the time of *Wild and Peaceful* had perfected a protodisco style in which "party" vocal chants and staccato horn fills sparred over a stark, heavy, metronomic funk rhythm.

13 More than fifty persons are hurt when youths start hurling bottles outside a **Jackson 5** concert at RFK Stadium in Washington, D.C. Forty-three are arrested.

14 **Three Dog Night**'s "The Show Must Go On" becomes the hugely successful Top Forty vocal trio's last gold record. The song, which reaches #4 on the pop chart, is also their last Top Twenty single. The group had a total of eleven gold records, three of which—"Joy to the World," "Mama Told Me Not to Come" and "Black and White"—hit Number One on the pop chart.

15 **Bill Wyman**, the so-called "quiet" **Rolling Stone**, releases his first solo LP, *Monkey Grip*. It is the first solo disc by a member of the group.

Frank Zappa and his wife announce the birth of their third child, a boy named **Ahmet Rodan**, after the Japanese movie monster who lived on a steady diet of 707s.

21 One year after his firing from Columbia Records, **Clive Davis** is hired by Bell Records as a consultant.

22 The **Stylistics** have the biggest hit of their career with "You Make Me Feel Brand New," an achingly tender ballad that hits #2. The disc goes gold.

23 According to *Rolling Stone*, two would-be promoters, **George T. McGinis** and **Archie McIntosh**, are indicted on federal mail-fraud charges in connection with a mail-order ticket offering for an "Elten John" concert, to be held June 8. That's Elten with an *e*, mind you, not an *o*, as the real Elton spells it. Authorities confiscate about $11,000 in checks and money orders as evidence.

26 A teenage girl dies, three others are hospitalized and more than 1,000 persons are treated by ambulance orderlies after a **David Cassidy** concert at London's White City athletic stadium. The head of the British Safety Council labels the show the "suicide concert"—four of six girls taken to a hospital are admitted, and one of them suffers from uncontrolled hysteria. **Bernadette Wheelen**, 14, suffers cardiac arrest and dies four days later. "I do feel responsible," says Cassidy.   ◆

WEEK ENDING MAY 4

U.S. #1 POP 45	"The Loco-motion"	Grand Funk Railroad
U.S. #1 POP LP	*The Sting*	Marvin Hamlisch (soundtrack)
U.S. #1 R&B 45	"The Payback"	James Brown
U.K. #1 POP 45	"Waterloo"	Abba
U.K. #1 POP LP	*The Singles 1969–1973*	The Carpenters

WEEK ENDING MAY 11

U.S. #1 POP 45	"The Loco-motion"	Grand Funk Railroad
U.S. #1 POP LP	*The Sting*	Marvin Hamlisch (soundtrack)
U.S. #1 R&B 45	"Dancing Machine"	The Jackson 5
U.K. #1 POP 45	"Sugar Baby Love"	The Rubettes
U.K. #1 POP LP	*The Singles 1969–1973*	The Carpenters

WEEK ENDING MAY 18

U.S. #1 POP 45	"The Streak"	Ray Stevens
U.S. #1 POP LP	*The Sting*	Marvin Hamlisch (soundtrack)
U.S. #1 R&B 45	"I'm in Love"	Aretha Franklin
U.K. #1 POP 45	"Sugar Baby Love"	The Rubettes
U.K. #1 POP LP	*The Singles 1969–1973*	The Carpenters

WEEK ENDING MAY 25

U.S. #1 POP 45	"The Streak"	Ray Stevens
U.S. #1 POP LP	*The Sting*	Marvin Hamlisch (soundtrack)
U.S. #1 R&B 45	"I'm in Love"	Aretha Franklin
U.K. #1 POP 45	"Sugar Baby Love"	The Rubettes
U.K. #1 POP LP	*The Singles 1969–1973*	The Carpenters

1 **Kevin Ayers** is joined on stage at London's Rainbow Theater by **John Cale, Nico** and **Brian Eno,** resulting in the album *A.C.N.E.* The four were put together by their label, Island Records, for the one-shot concert, which Eno describes as "only a passing thing. I can't see anything permanent coming out of it."

5 The **Eagles'** third album, *On the Border,* goes gold. The album yielded minor hit singles in "Already Gone" (#32 on the pop chart) and "James Dean" (#77), two of this slick Los Angeles country-rock band's hardest-rocking songs. But one of the album's ballads, "Best of My Love," would become one of their biggest hits, reaching Number One in early 1975.

Sly Stone, 30, is married to **Kathy Silva,** 21, on the stage of Madison Square Garden. A horde of celebrities turns out for the gala affair, which includes a postceremony set by **Sly and the Family Stone. Don Cornelius** of TV's "Soul Train" is the master of ceremonies, **Eddie Kendricks** is the opening act and the ceremony is performed by **Bishop B. R. Stewart** of San Francisco's Pentecostal Temple Church of God in Christ, the church Sly attended as a child. One fitting note: Sly is late to his own wedding—although by only two minutes.

In a year beset by an unusually large number of novelty hits and pop fluff ("Seasons in the Sun," "Hooked on a Feeling," "The Streak," "The Night Chicago Died"), add **Bo Donaldson and the Heywoods** to the list, with their Number One single, "Billy, Don't Be a Hero."

8 **Rick Wakeman** splits from **Yes.** "I gave my week's notice and left them plenty of time to pull it together," he later says. The crux of the decision is his recent solo success, but also his dislike of the group's *Tales of Topographic Oceans.* "It was embarrassing to me when people would ask me questions about *Topographic,* and I didn't understand."

10 The **Who** begin a four-day stint at Madison Square Garden. Tickets for the shows had sold out in just sixty hours, a full two months before the concert dates.

12 Philadelphia soul vocal group the **O'Jays** earn their fourth gold record, "For the Love of Money." Together since the mid-Sixties, the O'Jays are one of the most successful acts in the stable of Philadelphia International Records' renowned production team of **Kenny Gamble** and **Leon Huff.**

15 After several drummerless months, **Paul McCartney and Wings** announce the addition of drummer **Geoff Britton,** who replaces **Denny Seiwell.**

18 According to *Rolling Stone,* **Peter Hoorelbeke,** drummer for **Rare Earth,** is arrested after tossing his sticks into the crowd. Later, he tells police he had done it to get audience reaction. "If you had been trying to get crowds to see you for ten years, you'd do it too. Here I am, almost thirty years old and still doing this shit."

Ninety-six people are arrested at a concert at Atlanta's Omni. About thirty of the arrests are made inside the concert hall, where 7,500 fans have come to hear **Robin Trower** (who canceled) and **Edgar Winter.** Promoter **Howard Stein** bitterly claims that Atlanta has "reverted back to the Southern redneck-sheriff image of the early Sixties."

24 The **Hues Corporation** have a gold hit with "Rock the Boat," an early example of what will later be called disco. It's a Number One hit in July.

28 The **Ohio Players**—originators of the **Sly Stone**-influenced Dayton, Ohio, school of hard funk that would also produce **Slave**—earn a gold record for *Skin Tight,* which would yield the hit singles "Skin Tight" (#13) and "Jive Turkey" (#47).

30 The **Modern Jazz Quartet** bids farewell to the U.S. with a concert in San Francisco. The group—**Milt Jackson, John Lewis, Percy Heath** and **Connie Kay**—will end its twenty-two-year career after a tour of Australia. ♦

WEEK ENDING JUNE 1

U.S. #1 POP 45	"The Streak"	Ray Stevens
U.S. #1 POP LP	*The Sting*	Marvin Hamlisch (soundtrack)
U.S. #1 R&B 45	"Be Thankful for What You Got"	William DeVaughn
U.K. #1 POP 45	"Sugar Baby Love"	The Rubettes
U.K. #1 POP LP	*The Singles 1969–1973*	The Carpenters

WEEK ENDING JUNE 8

U.S. #1 POP 45	"Band on the Run"	Paul McCartney and Wings
U.S. #1 POP LP	*The Sting*	Marvin Hamlisch (soundtrack)
U.S. #1 R&B 45	"Hollywood Swinging"	Kool and the Gang
U.K. #1 POP 45	"The Streak"	Ray Stevens
U.K. #1 POP LP	*Diamond Dogs*	David Bowie

WEEK ENDING JUNE 15

U.S. #1 POP 45	"Billy, Don't Be a Hero"	Bo Donaldson and the Heywoods
U.S. #1 POP LP	*The Sting*	Marvin Hamlisch (soundtrack)
U.S. #1 R&B 45	"Sideshow"	Blue Magic
U.K. #1 POP 45	"The Streak"	Ray Stevens
U.K. #1 POP LP	*Diamond Dogs*	David Bowie

WEEK ENDING JUNE 22

U.S. #1 POP 45	"Billy, Don't Be a Hero"	Bo Donaldson and the Heywoods
U.S. #1 POP LP	*Sundown*	Gordon Lightfoot
U.S. #1 R&B 45	"Finally Got Myself Together (I'm a Changed Man)"	The Impressions
U.K. #1 POP 45	"Always Yours"	Gary Glitter
U.K. #1 POP LP	*Diamond Dogs*	David Bowie

WEEK ENDING JUNE 29

U.S. #1 POP 45	"Sundown"	Gordon Lightfoot
U.S. #1 POP LP	*Sundown*	Gordon Lightfoot
U.S. #1 R&B 45	"Finally Got Myself Together (I'm a Changed Man)"	The Impressions
U.K. #1 POP 45	"She"	Charles Aznavour
U.K. #1 POP LP	*Diamond Dogs*	David Bowie

7 The third Newport Jazz Festival/New York ends its ten-day run a healthy $150,000 in the red; this, in contrast to the previous year when an overextended festival incurred a hefty deficit. The 1974 festival sells out more than half of its thirty-six events. Highlights include sets by **McCoy Tyner**, **Keith Jarrett**, **Bill Evans** and the festival's headliner, **Diana Ross**.

8 **Bob Dylan** and the **Band**'s *Before the Flood* turns gold, just several months after their tour. This live set from that tour makes #3.

9 **Crosby, Stills, Nash and Young** begin their reunion tour in Seattle. The group performs a four-hour set (which leaves **David Crosby** practically without a voice for the next few shows), including both CSN&Y and solo material. A crowd of 15,000 attends.

10 **David Bowie**, in the midst of a highly successful tour, records his two-night stand at Philadelphia's Tower Theater. Released later in the year, *David Live* goes Top Ten.

11 The **Grateful Dead** receive two gold records for discs they released back in 1970, *Workingman's Dead* and *American Beauty*. Both were considered landmark albums for the Dead, who showed off their sweet, acoustic side and their love for vintage American blues.

13 **Ronnie Wood** of the **Faces** plays a two-night solo stand in London, for which he's joined by **Keith Richards** of the **Rolling Stones**. Both Richards and **Mick Jagger** play on Wood's soon-to-be-released solo debut, *I've Got My Own Album to Do*.

18 The Justice Department announces that it has ordered **John Lennon** to leave the country by September 10, after the Immigration Service denies the ex-**Beatle** an extension of his nonimmigrant visa because of his guilty plea in England to a 1968 marijuana possession charge. Even the *New York Post* comes to Lennon's defense, proclaiming in an editorial, "The crime for which

John Lennon was convicted in London in 1968 would not even land him in a New York jail."

19 After performing in twenty-eight cities, **David Bowie**'s *Diamond Dogs* tour ends with a show at Madison Square Garden. Bowie had enlisted a ten-piece band for the tour, as well as designer **Mark Ravitz**, who came up with a three-dimensional city landscape set. Bowie made it clear on the tour that Ziggy Stardust is dead, no doubt disappointing many of his earlier fans, who came out to the show bedecked in glitter and makeup.

26 **John Denver** receives a gold record for his all-time biggest hit, "Annie's Song." The former member of the

Chad Mitchell Trio has been enjoying a highly lucrative career singing earnest, "sensitive" songs about love and nature ("Take Me Home, Country Roads," "Rocky Mountain High," "Sunshine on My Shoulders") since 1971. "Annie's Song" was written about Mrs. Denver, who later divorced him.

27 **Lightnin' Slim**, often described as "the greatest living swamp bluesman," dies in Detroit of stomach cancer. Born **Otis Hicks** in St. Louis, he was in his thirties and had moved to Louisiana when he began to seriously sing the blues. Some of his most popular records were "Bad Luck," "Hoo-Doo Blues," "My Starter Won't Work" and "Rooster Blues." He was sixty-one.

29 **Mama Cass Elliot** dies at age thirty-two, in London. A postmortem the next day shows that she died as a result of choking on a sandwich while in bed and from inhaling her own vomit. It will later be revealed that she suffered a heart attack. Elliot, born Ellen Naomi Cohen in Alexandria, Virginia, made her name as a member of the **Mamas and the Papas**, who had numerous hits from 1965 to 1968. She tried a solo career after that, which was fairly successful, and by the early Seventies was playing nightclubs and appearing on TV talk shows and "Hollywood Squares." ◆

WEEK ENDING JULY 6

U.S. #1 POP 45	"Rock the Boat"	The Hues Corporation
U.S. #1 POP LP	*Sundown*	Gordon Lightfoot
U.S. #1 R&B 45	"Rock Your Baby"	George McCrae
U.K. #1 POP 45	"She"	Charles Aznavour
U.K. #1 POP LP	*Band on the Run*	Paul McCartney and Wings

WEEK ENDING JULY 13

U.S. #1 POP 45	"Rock Your Baby"	George McCrae
U.S. #1 POP LP	*Caribou*	Elton John
U.S. #1 R&B 45	"Rock Your Baby"	George McCrae
U.K. #1 POP 45	"She"	Charles Aznavour
U.K. #1 POP LP	*Band on the Run*	Paul McCartney and Wings

WEEK ENDING JULY 20

U.S. #1 POP 45	"Rock Your Baby"	George McCrae
U.S. #1 POP LP	*Caribou*	Elton John
U.S. #1 R&B 45	"My Thing"	James Brown
U.K. #1 POP 45	"Rock Your Baby"	George McCrae
U.K. #1 POP LP	*Band on the Run*	Paul McCartney and Wings

WEEK ENDING JULY 27

U.S. #1 POP 45	"Annie's Song"	John Denver
U.S. #1 POP LP	*Caribou*	Elton John
U.S. #1 R&B 45	"My Thing"	James Brown
U.K. #1 POP 45	"Rock Your Baby"	George McCrae
U.K. #1 POP LP	*Band on the Run*	Paul McCartney and Wings

1 Pete Townshend and Keith Moon join Eric Clapton at Atlanta's Omni, Townshend jamming on "Layla" and Moon singing along on "Little Queenie." Townshend later performs a modified Who finish by smashing a plastic ukelele over Clapton's head.

2 Dozens of celebrities turn out for funeral services for Cass Elliot. Among those in attendance at the Hollywood Memorial Cemetery are John and Michelle Phillips, Sonny Bono, Lou Adler and Peter Lawford. Elliot's body is cremated, and her ashes buried at Hebrew Cemetery in Woodlawn, Maryland.

3 Drummer Jim Hodder and guitarist Jeff Baxter leave Steely Dan. Baxter will go on to relative fame as lead player for the Doobie Brothers and as a producer. Hodder's defection leaves the Dan with one drummer, Jeff Porcaro, later of Toto.

5 Tickets go on sale in Los Angeles for three Elton John concerts two months away, and sell out so fast that a fourth show is added. Persons who stood on line for two days and nights say even they couldn't score good tickets.

6 Gene "Jug" Ammons, one of contemporary jazz's greatest saxophonists, dies in Chicago at age fortynine. After fading from public view in the Sixties, Ammons seemed to be making a comeback. He is probably best known for his work with the Billy Eckstine orchestra and Woody Herman, as well as his own solo groups. Several of his records were substantial hits in the soul-jazz market; one, "Canadian Sunset," was awarded a gold record.

7 Peter Wolf of the J. Geils Band and actress Faye Dunaway are married in a Beverly Hills courtroom.

8 Eric Clapton receives a gold record for *461 Ocean Boulevard,* his comeback LP. The album contains Clapton's sole Number One song, his version of Bob Marley's "I Shot the Sheriff." Clapton assembles a band for the LP and subsequent tour including George Terry, Yvonne Elliman, Carl Radle, Jamie Oldaker and Dick Sims. *461* reaches Number One, another first for Clapton.

9 Trumpeter Bill Chase and three members of his group (Walter Clark, John Emma and Wallace Yohn) are killed in an airplane crash in Jackson, Minnesota. Also killed is the plane's pilot. Chase, 39, was a veteran of Woody Herman's band, and formed Chase in 1971. The group had been touring behind its third album, *Pure Music,* at the time of the crash.

10 After recording two albums for Elektra/Asylum Records (*Planet Waves* and *Before the Flood*), Bob Dylan returns to his longtime label, Columbia.

14 Paul Anka's "(You're) Having My Baby" turns gold, despite the fact that the song is denounced by feminists. The basic objection to the song is its use of the word *my—my* baby, not *our* baby. But in the summer of 1974, it reaches Number One.

16 The Ramones play their first show at CBGB, New York City's punk mecca on the Bowery.

17 Patrick Moraz replaces Rick Wakeman in Yes, who are already finishing work on an album called *Relayer.* Moraz had once been understudy to Keith Emerson in the Nice, and later joined the group's Lee Jackson and Brian Davidson in a prog-rock band called Refugee.

23 The thirteenth annual Philadelphia Folk Festival gets under way in Schwenksville, Pennsylvania. The three-day festival features David Bromberg, John Prine, Steve Goodman, Arlo Guthrie and Bruce Cockburn, and includes both performances and workshops.

31 In Federal Court, John Lennon testifies that the Nixon administration tried to have him deported because of his involvement with antiwar demonstrations at the 1972 Republican convention in Miami. ◆

WEEK ENDING AUGUST 3

U.S. #1 POP 45	"Annie's Song"	John Denver
U.S. #1 POP LP	*Caribou*	Elton John
U.S. #1 R&B 45	"Feel Like Makin' Love"	Roberta Flack
U.K. #1 POP 45	"Rock Your Baby"	George McCrae
U.K. #1 POP LP	*Band on the Run*	Paul McCartney and Wings

WEEK ENDING AUGUST 10

U.S. #1 POP 45	"Feel Like Makin' Love"	Roberta Flack
U.S. #1 POP LP	*Back Home Again*	John Denver
U.S. #1 R&B 45	"Feel Like Makin' Love"	Roberta Flack
U.K. #1 POP 45	"When Will I See You Again"	The Three Degrees
U.K. #1 POP LP	*Band on the Run*	Paul McCartney and Wings

WEEK ENDING AUGUST 17

U.S. #1 POP 45	"The Night Chicago Died"	Paper Lace
U.S. #1 POP LP	*461 Ocean Boulevard*	Eric Clapton
U.S. #1 R&B 45	"Feel Like Makin' Love"	Roberta Flack
U.K. #1 POP 45	"When Will I See You Again"	The Three Degrees
U.K. #1 POP LP	*Band on the Run*	Paul McCartney and Wings

WEEK ENDING AUGUST 24

U.S. #1 POP 45	"(You're) Having My Baby"	Paul Anka
U.S. #1 POP LP	*461 Ocean Boulevard*	Eric Clapton
U.S. #1 R&B 45	"Feel Like Makin' Love"	Roberta Flack
U.K. #1 POP 45	"When Will I See You Again"	The Three Degrees
U.K. #1 POP LP	*Band on the Run*	Paul McCartney and Wings

WEEK ENDING AUGUST 31

U.S. #1 POP 45	"(You're) Having My Baby"	Paul Anka
U.S. #1 POP LP	*461 Ocean Boulevard*	Eric Clapton
U.S. #1 R&B 45	"Feel Like Makin' Love"	Roberta Flack
U.K. #1 POP 45	"Love Me for a Reason"	The Osmonds
U.K. #1 POP LP	*Band on the Run*	Paul McCartney and Wings

6 **George Harrison** inaugurates his new Dark Horse label, with the release of *The Place I Love* by a group called **Splinter**. Harrison produced the album.

7 **Joe Strummer**'s pre-**Clash** outfit, the **101ers**, named after the number on the torture room in **George Orwell**'s novel *1984*, play their first show, at the Briton Telegraph Club.

10 The **New York Dolls** split up after just two albums. Their career is best summed up in one of their LP titles: *Too Much Too Soon.*

11 **Crosby, Stills, Nash and Young**, the **Band** and **Joni Mitchell** play the 80,000-plus-seat Wembley Stadium in London.

13 **Stevie Wonder** begins his first tour since his near-fatal car accident, at the Nassau Coliseum on Long Island. The night before, a party is held for Wonder at New York's Delmonico's Hotel. Among the

well-wishers were **Mick Jagger**, **Andy Warhol**, **Dudley Moore** and **Roberta Flack**.

15 **Uriah Heep** bassist **Gary Thain** receives a severe electrical shock during the group's Dallas concert. He is expected to be fully recovered by mid-October, but the band is forced to cancel the three remaining shows on the tour.

18 *Antonia—a Portrait of the Woman*, a film by **Judy Collins**, premieres at New York's Whitney Museum. The fifty-eight-minute film explores the career of **Antonia Brico**, Collins' piano teacher for eleven years, when Collins lived in Denver. Brico is one of the world's few female symphony conductors.

19 *Bad Company* turns gold and goes on to give the new group its first hit, the Top Five "Can't Get Enough." The British band is comprised of former **Free** members **Paul Rodgers** and **Simon Kirke**, **Mick Ralphs**, late of **Mott the Hoople**, and **Boz Burrell**, who once played with **King Crim-**

son. Their debut is one of the few to hit Number One.

20 **Golden Earring**, a Dutch group that has been in existence since 1962, receives a gold record for *Moontan*, which contains the hit "Radar Love." It is the first U.S. success after many years for the band; it will be nine years before they have another American smash.

21 **Ariel Bender** quits **Mott the Hoople** after just one year. His place is taken by former **David Bowie** sideman **Mick Ronson**.

23 **Robbie McIntosh**, drummer for the Scottish group the **Average White**

Band, dies in his North Hollywood hotel room of a heroin overdose. McIntosh was at a party hosted by one **Ken Moss** when he inhaled a white powder thought to be cocaine, but which turned out to be pure heroin. McIntosh was twenty-four.

Although the first effort by the **Souther-Hillman-Furay Band**—country rock's supergroup—turns gold, the group's fortunes already appear to be on the wane. They will release one more album before disbanding, less than two years after their much ballyhooed formation.

24 The three-day Zaire '74 music festival ends after thirty-one groups—seventeen from Zaire, fourteen from the U.S.—participate. The purpose of the festival was to present African and black American music. **Lloyd Price**, festival coproducer, and **Don King**, boxing promoter of the postponed **Muhammad Ali-George Foreman** fight (to take place in Zaire) agree that the three-day event was a "tremendous success."

25 **Robert Fripp** announces that he is temporarily disbanding **King Crimson** after five years and seven albums, the most recent being *Red*.

26 **John Lennon** releases what will be his last album of new material for nearly six years, *Walls and Bridges*. The album becomes Number One.

30 A clash occurs between **Lynyrd Skynyrd** roadies and a sound technician during a Skynyrd-**Blue Oyster Cult** concert at the Louisville Convention Center. The Skynyrd road crew claims that **Jay Sloatman** of Tycobrahe Sound deliberately turned off the sound during the band's set and then attacked them when he was asked to leave the stage. No arrests are made. ♦

WEEK ENDING SEPTEMBER 7

U.S. #1 POP 45	"(You're) Having My Baby"	Paul Anka
U.S. #1 POP LP	*461 Ocean Boulevard*	Eric Clapton
U.S. #1 R&B 45	"Can't Get Enough of Your Love, Baby"	Barry White
U.K. #1 POP 45	"Love Me for a Reason"	The Osmonds
U.K. #1 POP LP	*Band on the Run*	Paul McCartney and Wings

WEEK ENDING SEPTEMBER 14

U.S. #1 POP 45	"I Shot the Sheriff"	Eric Clapton
U.S. #1 POP LP	*Fulfillingness' First Finale*	Stevie Wonder
U.S. #1 R&B 45	"Can't Get Enough of Your Love, Baby"	Barry White
U.K. #1 POP 45	"Kung Fu Fighting"	Carl Douglas
U.K. #1 POP LP	*Hergest Ridge*	Mike Oldfield

WEEK ENDING SEPTEMBER 21

U.S. #1 POP 45	"Can't Get Enough of Your Love, Baby"	Barry White
U.S. #1 POP LP	*Fulfillingness' First Finale*	Stevie Wonder
U.S. #1 R&B 45	"Can't Get Enough of Your Love, Baby"	Barry White
U.K. #1 POP 45	"Kung Fu Fighting"	Carl Douglas
U.K. #1 POP LP	*Hergest Ridge*	Mike Oldfield

WEEK ENDING SEPTEMBER 28

U.S. #1 POP 45	"Rock Me Gently"	Andy Kim
U.S. #1 POP LP	*Bad Company*	Bad Company
U.S. #1 R&B 45	"You Haven't Done Nothin"	Stevie Wonder
U.K. #1 POP 45	"Kung Fu Fighting"	Carl Douglas
U.K. #1 POP LP	*Tubular Bells*	Mike Oldfield

3 **Mountain** play Radio City Music Hall and dress up for the occasion, wearing grand white suits. They also inject a little theater into the proceedings: **Corky Laing**'s drum sticks are set alight, followed by his tom-tom rims while a fireworks display explodes on the big screen behind him, and at the show's end, the stage is lowered from sight.

4 Irish rockers **Thin Lizzy** play their first date with the twin-guitar lineup of **Scott Gorham** and **Brian Robertson**, in Aberystwyth, Wales.

5 **Randy Newman** performs at the Atlanta Symphony Hall, accompanied by an eighty-seven-piece symphony orchestra. Conducting the orchestra is Randy's uncle **Emil Newman**.

7 French pop singer **Veronique Sanson** plays her first show in Paris in two years. Her backup band includes **Joe Lala**, **Denny Seiwell**, **Donnie Dacus**, **Alan Savati**, a sixteen-piece string ensemble, four horns and husband **Stephen Stills** on bass. Asked if the two might become the new **Sonny and Cher**, Stills exclaims, "Good God, no!"

8 **Dionne Warwick**, one of the biggest hitmakers of the Sixties, has a dry spell for several years before making a comeback with a Number One hit, "Then Came You," recorded with the **Spinners**. It becomes the first Number One of her career.

9 **Olivia Newton-John**, destined to become one of the most popular singers of her day, earns her third gold

record for "I Honestly Love You," which reached Number One on the pop chart four days ago, and will remain atop the chart for two weeks. Her first two gold records were "If You Love Me (Let Me Know)" and "Let Me Be There," which reached #5 and #6 respectively, earlier this year.

———

Jazz-funk composer, arranger and producer **Quincy Jones**, who has already won several Grammy Awards, earns his first gold record for *Body Heat*, which includes the hit single "If I Ever Lose This Heaven," sung by **Minnie Riperton**.

15 *Alice Cooper's Greatest Hits* turns gold, but Alice already is in the process of dumping the band for a solo career.

18 **Mary Woodson**, purported to be **Al Green**'s girlfriend, shoots herself to death in the singer's home just north of Memphis. The shooting, which is later ruled a suicide, comes after the woman had thrown a pot of boiling grits on Green as he was

getting out of his bathtub. Green is taken to a local hospital with first- and second-degree burns on his back, neck and arms.

20 Ex-**Animal Eric Burdon** and his wife, **Rose**, have a baby girl in Palm Springs, California, and name her **Mirage**.

25 **Nick Drake**, the eccentric, obsessively private English singer/songwriter, is found dead in his bed at his parents' Birmingham, England, home. The coroner's report attributes the death to an overdose of a strong antidepressant and rules it an apparent suicide.

30 Less than six months after her marriage to **Sylvester Stewart** in Madison Square Garden, **Kathy Silva Stewart** files for divorce and is awarded custody of their fourteen-month-old son, **Sylvester Bubb Ali Stewart**. The boy and his father (leader of **Sly and the Family Stone**) are missing, and are believed to be hiding.

31 The **Rolling Stones'** *It's Only Rock n' Roll*, their last album with guitarist **Mick Taylor**, turns gold. It is their fourth consecutive Number One LP. ◆

WEEK ENDING OCTOBER 5

U.S. #1 POP 45	"I Honestly Love You"	Olivia Newton-John
U.S. #1 POP LP	*Endless Summer*	The Beach Boys
U.S. #1 R&B 45	"You Haven't Done Nothin'"	Stevie Wonder
U.K. #1 POP 45	"Kung Fu Fighting"	Carl Douglas
U.K. #1 POP LP	*Tubular Bells*	Mike Oldfield

WEEK ENDING OCTOBER 12

U.S. #1 POP 45	"I Honestly Love You"	Olivia Newton-John
U.S. #1 POP LP	*If You Love Me, Let Me Know*	Olivia Newton-John
U.S. #1 R&B 45	"Papa Don't Take No Mess"	James Brown
U.K. #1 POP 45	"Gee Baby"	Peter Shelley
U.K. #1 POP LP	*Back Home Again*	John Denver

WEEK ENDING OCTOBER 19

U.S. #1 POP 45	"Nothing from Nothing"	Billy Preston
U.S. #1 POP LP	*Not Fragile*	Bachman-Turner Overdrive
U.S. #1 R&B 45	"Do It ('Til You're Satisfied)"	B.T. Express
U.K. #1 POP 45	"Everything I Own"	Ken Boothe
U.K. #1 POP LP	*Smiler*	Rod Stewart

WEEK ENDING OCTOBER 26

U.S. #1 POP 45	"Then Came You"	Dionne Warwick and the Spinners
U.S. #1 POP LP	*Can't Get Enough*	Barry White
U.S. #1 R&B 45	"Higher Plane"	Kool and the Gang
U.K. #1 POP 45	"Everything I Own"	Ken Boothe
U.K. #1 POP LP	*Smiler*	Rod Stewart

NOVEMBER 1974

1 **Queen** have their largest success to date with their third album, *Sheer Heart Attack*, which contains their first U.S. hit "Killer Queen" (#12). The LP goes to #17.

2 **George Harrison** begins his first tour in eight years and makes his first onstage appearance since the Bangla Desh concerts three years earlier, in Vancouver, Washington. It will be a troublesome tour for Harrison, whose voice is ravaged throughout, after LP sessions and tour rehearsals. Accompanying him are **Billy Preston, Tom Scott, Chuck Findley, Jim Horn, Robben Ford, Andy Newmark, Willie Weeks** and **Emil Richards**.

4 **Paul McCartney and Wings** release "Junior's Farm," which becomes their fourth Top Ten hit of the past year. The song goes to #3.

5 **Traffic** receive a gold record for what ultimately will be their last album together, *When the Eagle Flies*. The band's lineup is significantly pared down at this late stage in its career, including **Steve Winwood, Chris Wood, Jim Capaldi** and **Rosko Gee**.

7 *Rolling Stone* reports that **Ted Nugent** has won the National Squirrel-Shooting Archery Contest by picking off a squirrel at 150 yards. Nugent also wiped out twenty-seven more of the small mammals with a handgun during the three-day event.

8 **Ivory Joe Hunter**, one of the first R&B singers to cross over to pop and country music, dies in Memphis at age sixty-three. Just a few weeks prior to his death, a benefit concert was held for him at the Grand Ole Opry, featuring such performers as **Tammy Wynette, George Jones** and **Isaac Hayes**. Hunter, born in Texas, wrote some 7,000 songs during his career, some of which were hit singles for **Elvis Presley** ("Ain't That Loving You Baby," "My Wish Came True").

13 An imposter posing as **Deep Purple** guitarist **Ritchie Blackmore** smashes up a borrowed Porsche in Iowa City—the real Ritchie Blackmore was playing a concert in San Francisco. The imposter had been able to con several townspeople into giving him shelter and companionship; he is charged with misrepresentation, a felony.

15 The **Faces** release what will be their last single, "You Can Make Me Dance, Sing or Anything." Two years later, **Rod Stewart** will leave them permanently to pursue his solo career.

16 Director **Tom O'Horgan**, who scored off and on Broadway with *Hair* and *Jesus Christ Superstar*, tries again with an adaptation of the **Beatles'** *Sgt. Pepper's Lonely Hearts Club Band*, which he calls "not a play" but a "spectacle on the road." *Rolling Stone* calls it "the sort of show that thirtyish liberals who were weaned on the Beatles will want to see." And the plot? "Flimsy."

John Lennon enjoys his first Number One hit with "Whatever Gets You thru the Night." Aiding Lennon on the tune is **Elton John**, on piano and vocals.

21 After years of vowing not to, **Marty Balin** joins the **Jefferson Starship** onstage at the Winterland in San Francisco. He will later be coaxed back into rejoining as a permanent member. "These guys are great," he gushes after the show. "The energy is back."

23 **Gary Wright** quits **Spooky Tooth** to go solo. Next year he will have two consecutive hits, "Dream Weaver" and "Love Is Alive."

27 Yet another novelty song becomes a Number One hit in 1974—**Carl Douglas'** "Kung Fu Fighting," which turns gold on this date. Douglas tries a followup with "Dance the Kung Fu"; some accuse him of lacking imagination.

28 **Elton John** had made **John Lennon** promise that if his "Whatever Gets You thru the Night" hit Number One, he would join Elton on stage for a Madison Square Garden appearance. "Whatever" did and Lennon does, accompanying Elton on "Whatever Gets You thru the Night," "Lucy in the Sky with Diamonds" and "I Saw Her Standing There" (which Lennon introduces as "an old Beatles song we never did on stage"). Backstage, after the show, Lennon has a brief reunion with **Yoko Ono**, from whom he'd been separated for over a year. ◆

WEEK ENDING NOVEMBER 2

U.S. #1 POP 45	"You Haven't Done Nothin'"	Stevie Wonder
U.S. #1 POP LP	*So Far*	Crosby, Stills, Nash and Young
U.S. #1 R&B 45	"Let's Straighten It Out"	Latimore
U.K. #1 POP 45	"Gonna Make You a Star"	David Essex
U.K. #1 POP LP	*Rollin'*	The Bay City Rollers

WEEK ENDING NOVEMBER 9

U.S. #1 POP 45	"You Ain't Seen Nothing Yet"	Bachman-Turner Overdrive
U.S. #1 POP LP	*Wrap Around Joy*	Carole King
U.S. #1 R&B 45	"Let's Straighten It Out"	Latimore
U.K. #1 POP 45	"Gonna Make You a Star"	David Essex
U.K. #1 POP LP	*Rollin'*	The Bay City Rollers

WEEK ENDING NOVEMBER 16

U.S. #1 POP 45	"Whatever Gets You thru the Night"	John Lennon
U.S. #1 POP LP	*Walls and Bridges*	John Lennon
U.S. #1 R&B 45	"Woman to Woman"	Shirley Brown
U.K. #1 POP 45	"Gonna Make You a Star"	David Essex
U.K. #1 POP LP	*David Essex*	David Essex

WEEK ENDING NOVEMBER 23

U.S. #1 POP 45	"I Can Help"	Billy Swan
U.S. #1 POP LP	*It's Only Rock 'n Roll*	The Rolling Stones
U.S. #1 R&B 45	"Woman to Woman"	Shirley Brown
U.K. #1 POP 45	"Gonna Make You a Star"	David Essex
U.K. #1 POP LP	*Elton John—Greatest Hits*	Elton John

WEEK ENDING NOVEMBER 30

U.S. #1 POP 45	"I Can Help"	Billy Swan
U.S. #1 POP LP	*Elton John—Greatest Hits*	Elton John
U.S. #1 R&B 45	"I Feel a Song (in My Heart)"	Gladys Knight and the Pips
U.K. #1 POP 45	"Gonna Make You a Star"	David Essex
U.K. #1 POP LP	*Elton John—Greatest Hits*	Elton John

2 **Ravi Shankar**, cobilled on the **George Harrison** tour, is hospitalized in Chicago after suffering chest pains. He will remain there for a week before rejoining the tour in Boston.

9 The **Who** receive a gold record for *Odds and Sods*, a highly intriguing package put together by bassist **John Entwistle**. It's a collection of assorted oddities culled from the Who tape archives. Of special interest is the band's version of "Pure and Easy" (which appeared on Pete Townshend's first solo record); "Naked Eye," whose instrumental section has long been a staple of Who concerts, and "Glow Girl."

George Harrison releases his first album on his Dark Horse label, titled *Dark Horse*, which makes #4.

12 The **Rolling Stones** begin sessions in Munich for what will become *Black and Blue*, their 1976 release. The LP is recorded with several guitarists, including **Wayne Perkins**, **Harvey Mandel** and **Ron Wood**.

The **Rolling Stones** also announce the departure of guitarist **Mick Taylor**, who replaced **Brian Jones** five years earlier. Taylor's immediate plans are to join a band being formed by **Jack Bruce**. Says **Mick Jagger** of Taylor's leaving, "While we are most sorry that he's going after five and a half years, we wish him every success and happiness." As for a replacement, he quips, "No doubt we can find a brilliant six-foot-three blond guitarist who can do his own makeup."

13 **George Harrison** meets **President Gerald Ford** at the White House. The President's son **Jack** had seen the Harrison tour in Salt Lake City, went backstage and invited George to Washington. Harrison and company came for lunch. Ford searches around for a WIN button to pin on the ex-**Beatle** guitarist, but he can't find one.

14 **David Crosby** and **Graham Nash** perform together in San Francisco at a benefit concert for the United Farm Workers and Project Jonah, a whale protection media project.

16 **Mott the Hoople** split. **Ian Hunter** had recently been hospitalized for a collapse due to nervous exhaustion, and there had been some resentment over new guitarist **Mick Ronson** by the older band members. Bassist **Overend Watts**, drummer **Dale Griffin** and keyboardist **Morgan Fisher** continue under the name **Mott**.

18 Singer/songwriter **Kris Kristofferson** earns his second gold record, for *Me and Bobby McGee*, four years after the album's release. The album's title song, of course, was a million-selling hit for **Janis Joplin** in 1971. It was also

covered by **Roger Miller** and the **Grateful Dead**, among others.

23 Just as **John Lennon** had done three years earlier, **George Harrison** releases a holiday single, "Ding Dong, Ding Dong." The song only reaches #36.

24 **James Taylor**, **Carly Simon**, **Linda Ronstadt** and **Joni Mitchell** are spotted singing Christmas carols around the streets of Los Angeles.

31 **Harry Chapin** has a gold Number One hit with a song that hits close to home, "Cat's in the Cradle." The lyrics come from a poem composed by his wife, **Sandy**, all about a neglectful father who's away far too much and busy far too often to watch his child grow. The lyrics apparently ring true all over the country, leading Chapin to speculate, "This one is scaring fathers from coast to coast; I suspect wives are buying it as zingers for their husbands." ◆

WEEK ENDING DECEMBER 7

U.S. #1 POP 45	"Kung Fu Fighting"	Carl Douglas
U.S. #1 POP LP	*Elton John—Greatest Hits*	Elton John
U.S. #1 R&B 45	"I Feel a Song (in My Heart)"	Gladys Knight and the Pips
U.K. #1 POP 45	"The First, The Last, My Everything"	Barry White
U.K. #1 POP LP	*Elton John's Greatest Hits*	Elton John

WEEK ENDING DECEMBER 14

U.S. #1 POP 45	"Kung Fu Fighting"	Carl Douglas
U.S. #1 POP LP	*Elton John—Greatest Hits*	Elton John
U.S. #1 R&B 45	"You Got the Love"	Rufus featuring Chaka Khan
U.K. #1 POP 45	"Lonely This Christmas"	Mud
U.K. #1 POP LP	*Elton John's Greatest Hits*	Elton John

WEEK ENDING DECEMBER 21

U.S. #1 POP 45	"Cat's in the Cradle"	Harry Chapin
U.S. #1 POP LP	*Elton John—Greatest Hits*	Elton John
U.S. #1 R&B 45	"She's Gone"	Tavares
U.K. #1 POP 45	"Lonely This Christmas"	Mud
U.K. #1 POP LP	*Elton John—Greatest Hits*	Elton John

WEEK ENDING DECEMBER 28

U.S. #1 POP 45	"Angie Baby"	Helen Reddy
U.S. #1 POP LP	*Elton John—Greatest Hits*	Elton John
U.S. #1 R&B 45	"Boogie On, Reggae Woman"	Stevie Wonder
U.K. #1 POP 45	"Lonely This Christmas"	Mud
U.K. #1 POP LP	*Elton John—Greatest Hits*	Elton John

1975

*T*his was the year that disco broke big: there were Shirley (and Company)'s "Shame, Shame, Shame," Labelle's "Lady Marmalade," Donna Summer's "Love to Love You Baby," Van McCoy's "The Hustle," Silver Convention's "Fly, Robin, Fly," KC and the Sunshine Band's "Get Down Tonight" and "That's the Way I Like It," and much more. Rock acts like the Bee Gees ("Jive Talkin' " and "Nights on Broadway"), David Bowie ("Young Americans" and "Fame") and Elton John ("Philadelphia Freedom") successfully rode the disco bandwagon. For the first time since the mid-Sixties heyday of Motown, a black-music sound was consistently topping both the pop and R&B charts; in fact, disco did better with black audiences than Motown ever did.

Disco was perhaps the first upwardly mobile musical revolution of the contemporary era. Its sound was all chintz, glitter and glamour atop a relentless, metronomic big beat signified by the 4/4 swish-thump of hi-hat and bass drum. Its ethos was hedonistic, but in an urbane style that was completely at odds with the pastoral, "organic" hedonism of the Sixties. Its dances were carefully orchestrated, romantic and decidedly nonspontaneous.

No wonder the rock audience would have none of it. Disco had banks of strings instead of guitar heroics; disco songs were lyrically simple and light-hearted compared to the portentious cosmic-symphonic epics of progressive rock; the rock audience did not learn the complicated steps of, say, the Hustle, preferring instead to keep up that formless sort of shuffling-in-place known as boogieing. And to a rock audience partial to the martial, often misogynistic macho bluster of heavy metal and its ilk, disco's revivification of *touch* dancing and its popularity among gays made it something to be feared. And on top of all that, rock was white, and disco was black.

By the middle of this year, however, disco had already proven successful with the pop audience as well. Rock and its audience had lost their hegemony—or at least part of it. By now, the so-called rock audience was big enough to support and to maintain hard rock even though it rarely dented the charts. Hard-core rockers could still take their solace: they helped Led Zeppelin sell out three Madison Square Garden shows in a record *four hours* in January. In May, Styx, a new white rock group, earned its first gold record, helping inaugurate the AOR/corporate-rock genre—equal parts heavy metal, progressive-rock symphonics, technical virtuosity and the kind of high-harmony vocals that Yes took from Crosby, Stills and Nash.

And then in August came the Springsteen explosion, with his landmark Bottom Line shows in New York followed by the release of *Born to Run*. Within two months, Springsteen had won hordes of ardent admirers and, with his unprecedented appearance on the covers of both *Time* and *Newsweek* in the same week, had fallen victim to accusations of being a "hype." Still, Springsteen was decidedly a genuine rocker. Meanwhile, over in England, pub rock was having its day with the likes of Dr. Feelgood and Ducks Deluxe. And in November, the Sex Pistols made their first public appearance.

2 U.S. District Court Judge **Richard Owen** rules in New York City that **John Lennon** and his lawyers will have access to Department of Immigration files pertaining to his deportation case. The move allows the former Beatle to look into whether or not the government's case against him stems solely from his 1968 British drug conviction or from his antiestablishment comments during the years of the Nixon administration.

5 *The Wiz*, a souled-out resetting of *The Wizard of Oz*, opens at Broadway's Majestic Theater in New York City.

6 Three thousand **Led Zeppelin** fans, waiting overnight inside the lobby of the Boston Garden for tickets to the band's February 4 concert to go on sale, cause an estimated $30,000 damage to the premises when they riot, breaking seats and doors. Boston Mayor **Kevin White** promptly cancels the show.

8 Three **Led Zeppelin** concerts at New York City's Madison Square Garden—a total of 60,000 tickets—sell out in a record four hours. The Garden box office must call on other ticket outlets to help handle the extraordinary demand.

9 British heavy-metal band **Deep Purple** wins a gold record for its eleventh album, *Stormbringer*. It is their fourth gold record; the others were for the albums *Made in Japan* (1972) and *Who Do We Think We Are!* (1973) and the single "Smoke on the Water" (1973).

10 Memphis soul singer **Al Green** earns his twelfth gold record for the album *Al Green Explores Your Mind*; twelve days later, he will earn his thirteenth gold record for the album's hit single, "Sha-La-La (Make Me Happy)." Green's other gold records were for the singles "Tired of Being Alone" (1971), "Let's Stay Together" (1972), "I'm Still in Love with You" (1972), "You Ought to Be with Me" (1972), "Call Me (Come Back Home)" and "Here I Am (Come and Take Me)" (1973), as well as the albums *Tired of Being Alone* (1971), *Let's Stay Together* (1972), *I'm Still in Love with You* (1972), *Call Me* (1973) and *Livin' for You* (1974).

11 **Shirley and Company**'s "Shame, Shame, Shame" enters both the pop and R&B charts. After sixteen weeks on the pop chart, it will reach #12, and after seven weeks on the R&B chart, it will hit Number One on March 1. The Shirley of Shirley and Company is **Shirley Goodman**, who, as half of the New Orleans duo **Shirley and Lee**, scored such hits as "Let the Good Times Roll" in the late Fifties. Shirley and Company will have only one more hit, "Cry Cry Cry," which will reach #91 in the summer of 1975.

12 A nine-city, eighteen-show tour of Europe starts for Warner Brothers acts **Little Feat**, **Tower of Power**, the **Doobie Brothers**, **Bonaroo**, **Montrose** and **Graham Central Station**. The Warner Brothers Music Show goes over well with European audiences, especially Little Feat, which establishes an adoring cult audience during the month-long tour.

14 Pop vocal trio **Three Dog Night** earn their sixteenth, and last, gold record for the album *Joy to the World—Their Greatest Hits*. Their other gold records were for the singles "One" (1969), "Mama Told Me (Not to Come)" (1970), "Joy to the World" and "Just an Old Fashioned Love Song" (1971), "Shambala" (1973) and "The Show Must Go On" (1974), plus the albums *Three Dog Night* and *Suitable for Framing* (1969), *Captured Live at the Forum* and *It Ain't Easy* (1970), *Naturally* and *Harmony* (1971), *Seven Separate Fools* (1972), *Around the World with Three Dog Night* (1973) and *Hard Labor* (1974).

Joe Walsh earns a gold record for his third solo album, *So What*. Walsh, former singer/guitarist with the **James Gang**, will go on to join Los Angeles country-rock band the **Eagles** in 1976.

16 Years of missed performances and sliding creativity finally catch up with **Sly and the Family Stone** when they begin an eight-show, six-night stand at Radio City Music Hall and bomb at the box office. Attendance averages 2,000 persons per show each, far below the hall's 6,000-plus seating capacity. Said a Radio City employee: "Sly has no credibility left."

Paul McCartney and Wings arrive in New Orleans to begin sessions for the album that becomes *Venus and Mars*. The band records with **Allen Toussaint** at his Sea-Saint Studio; the LP will be released four months later.

25 **B.T. Express** enters the R&B chart with what will become its second consecutive Number One R&B hit, "(Here Comes) The Express," which will also reach #5 on the pop chart. Its prior Number One R&B hit was 1974's "Do It (till You're Satisfied)," which went gold. ◆

WEEK ENDING JANUARY 4

U.S. #1 POP 45	"Lucy in the Sky with Diamonds"	Elton John
U.S. #1 POP LP	*Elton John—Greatest Hits*	Elton John
U.S. #1 R&B 45	"Boogie On, Reggae Woman"	Stevie Wonder
U.K. #1 POP 45	"Streets of London"	Ralph McTell
U.K. #1 POP LP	*Elton John—Greatest Hits*	Elton John

WEEK ENDING JANUARY 11

U.S. #1 POP 45	"Lucy in the Sky with Diamonds"	Elton John
U.S. #1 POP LP	*Elton John—Greatest Hits*	Elton John
U.S. #1 R&B 45	"Kung Fu Fighting"	Carl Douglas
U.K. #1 POP 45	"Streets of London"	Ralph McTell
U.K. #1 POP LP	*Elton John—Greatest Hits*	Elton John

WEEK ENDING JANUARY 18

U.S. #1 POP 45	"Mandy"	Barry Manilow
U.S. #1 POP LP	*Elton John—Greatest Hits*	Elton John
U.S. #1 R&B 45	"You're the First, the Last, My Everything"	Barry White
U.K. #1 POP 45	"Down Down"	Status Quo
U.K. #1 POP LP	*Elton John—Greatest Hits*	Elton John

WEEK ENDING JANUARY 25

U.S. #1 POP 45	"Please Mr. Postman"	The Carpenters
U.S. #1 POP LP	*Elton John—Greatest Hits*	Elton John
U.S. #1 R&B 45	"Fire"	The Ohio Players
U.K. #1 POP 45	"Ms. Grace"	The Tymes
U.K. #1 POP LP	*Elton John—Greatest Hits*	Elton John

4 Alto saxophonist **Louis Jordon** dies in Los Angeles at the age of sixty-six. The Arkansas-born Jordan had a string of rhythm & blues and pop hits throughout the Forties and early Fifties, and he and his band, the **Tympany Five**, influenced rockers from **Chuck Berry** to **Joe Jackson** with their numerous jump blues and novelty sides.

8 *Down by the Jetty*, **Dr. Feelgood**'s first record, is put out by United Artists in England. The band, headlining in England over **Kokomo** and **Chilli Willi** on the Naughty Rhythms tour, is perhaps the missing link between pub rock and punk; its hard-edged, almost brutal R&B sound and throwback stance presages much of what emerges in England over the next two years.

12 **Bob Dylan**'s *Blood on the Tracks* earns a gold record. The LP marks not only Dylan's return to Columbia Records from Asylum, but also a return to form on vinyl; the album is deemed to be of such significance that *Rolling Stone*

devotes its entire review section to a study of it by various writers. Interestingly, the liner notes by **Pete Hamill** are awarded a Grammy in 1976, despite being withdrawn from the back cover after the initial pressing.

Chad Mitchell, former leader of a folk trio named after him, is sentenced to five years in prison by a U.S. District Court judge in San Antonio for possession of marijuana. The original charges of smuggling, conspiracy with intent to distribute and possession were made after Mitchell was caught driving a truck carrying 400 pounds of grass across the border from Mexico into Texas in October 1973.

17 **John Lennon** releases *Rock 'N' Roll*, his final record before a self-imposed five-year exile from the music business. The album of oldies—with some songs coproduced by **Phil Spector** and the others rushed out at New York's Record Plant in November 1974 when Lennon's deportation seemed imminent—fails to capture much public or critical favor, reaching #6 on the chart

before plummeting rapidly. The idea for an oldies album originally came from Roulette Records President **Morris Levy**, who (claiming a verbal agreement with Lennon) later uses mail-order television ads to market *Roots*, a record culled from roughly mixed session tapes. Lennon sues to withdraw the product and wins his case in a New York courtroom a year later.

19 *Dragon Fly*, the first album by **Jefferson Starship**, a re-formed and re-vamped version of Sixties San Francisco protest and acid-rock band **Jefferson Airplane**, wins a gold record. The album, which includes "Ride the Tiger," "That's for Sure" and "Caroline," is actually the second to be released under the Jefferson Starship aegis; the first, 1970's *Blows against the Empire*, was recorded before Jefferson Airplane officially became Jefferson Starship, and Airplane-Starship singer/guitarist/songwriter **Paul Kantner** insists there is no connection between the two.

21 **John Entwistle** begins the only solo tour by a **Who** member in Sacramento, California. The quiet bassist and his band, **Ox** (after his own nickname), play for five weeks in the States, with mixed results: Entwistle later complains the tour cost him a fortune and that he hates guitarist **Robert Johnson**. It is his last public solo endeavor for over six years.

David Bowie's "Young Americans" is released, and although it climbs to only #28 on the charts, three months later, it continues the new "white soul" image projected by Bowie since his 1974 U.S. tour and *David Live* album. His second studio effort in that direction proves far more successful: "Fame," issued from his *Young Americans* LP, in March, eventually rises to Number One.

22 The second single from **John Lennon**'s *Walls and Bridges* album, "#9 Dream," peaks at—of course— #9 on the charts. ◆

WEEK ENDING FEBRUARY 1

U.S. #1 POP 45	"Laughter in the Rain"	Neil Sedaka
U.S. #1 POP LP	*Elton John—Greatest Hits*	Elton John
U.S. #1 R&B 45	"Fire"	The Ohio Players
U.K. #1 POP 45	"January"	Pilot
U.K. #1 POP LP	*Elton John—Greatest Hits*	Elton John

WEEK ENDING FEBRUARY 8

U.S. #1 POP 45	"Fire"	The Ohio Players
U.S. #1 POP LP	*Fire*	The Ohio Players
U.S. #1 R&B 45	"Happy People"	The Temptations
U.K. #1 POP 45	"January"	Pilot
U.K. #1 POP LP	*Englebert Humperdinck's Greatest Hits*	Engelbert Humperdinck

WEEK ENDING FEBRUARY 15

U.S. #1 POP 45	"You're No Good"	Linda Ronstadt
U.S. #1 POP LP	*Heart like a Wheel*	Linda Ronstadt
U.S. #1 R&B 45	"I Belong to You"	Love Unlimited
U.K. #1 POP 45	"Please Mr. Postman"	The Carpenters
U.K. #1 POP LP	*Englebert Humperdinck's Greatest Hits*	Englebert Humperdinck

WEEK ENDING FEBRUARY 22

U.S. #1 POP 45	"Pick Up the Pieces"	The Average White Band
U.S. #1 POP LP	*Average White Band*	The Average White Band
U.S. #1 R&B 45	"Lady Marmalade"	Labelle
U.K. #1 POP 45	"Make Me Smile"	Steve Harley and Cockney Rebel
U.K. #1 POP LP	*Elton John—Greatest Hits*	Elton John

1 Winners of the seventeenth annual Grammy Awards for 1974 are announced. Record of the Year is **Olivia Newton-John**'s "I Honestly Love You" (which also wins Newton-John an award for Best Female Pop Vocal Performance). Album of the Year is **Stevie Wonder**'s *Fulfillingness' First Finale* (he wins Best Male Pop Vocal Performance). Song of the Year is "The Way We Were," the theme song from the movie of the same title. **Paul McCartney and Wings** win two awards, one for Best Engineered Nonclassical Recording (*Band on the Run*) and the other for Best Pop Vocal Group Performance ("Band on the Run"). **Thom Bell** of Philadelphia International Records wins Best Producer of the Year; one of his productions, **MFSB**'s "TSOP (the Sound of Philadelphia)," wins Best Rhythm &

Blues Instrumental Performance. Best R&B Female Vocal Performance is **Aretha Franklin**'s "Ain't Nothing like the Real Thing"; Best R&B Male Vocal Performance is Stevie Wonder's "Boogie On, Reggae Woman"; and Best R&B Song is Stevie Wonder's "Living for the City." **Elvis Presley**'s "How Great Thou Art" wins Best Inspirational Performance. Best Instrumental Composition is **Mike Oldfield**'s "Tubular Bells." **Joni Mitchell** and **Tom Scott** win Best Arrangement Accompanying Vocalists for Mitchell's "Down to You."

2 After pulling over a late-model Lincoln Continental for allegedly running a red light, Los Angeles police detect the smell of marijuana and arrest **Linda McCartney** for having six to eight ounces of the drug in her pocketbook. Hus-

band **Paul**, behind the wheel, is not charged with personal possession, as Linda later is.

6 The **Average White Band**—all-white Scots playing black-sounding funk music—earns its first gold record for the instrumental "Pick Up the Pieces," which hit Number One in the pop chart in February.

10 Twenty-eight hundred fans get the opportunity to hear the world premiere playback of *Blue Jays*, the first post-**Moody Blues** project released by once and future members of the then-defunct group **Justin Hayward** and **John Lodge**. The zenith of the so-called event, held at Carnegie Hall, is reached during a standing ovation for the presentation of a huge mock-up of the album's cover.

16 Legendary blues guitarist **Aaron "T-Bone" Walker** dies of pneumonia in Los Angeles at age sixty-four. Walker, who began recording in 1929, is generally credited with developing the modern-day style of electric-guitar blues playing favored by **B. B. King** and others.

London's Rainbow, which operated since November 1971 as the British capital's answer to the Fillmores, closes down with a concert billed as Over the Rainbow, featuring **Procol Harum**, **John Martyn** and **Kevin Coyne**.

23 San Francisco's Kezar Stadium is the site for a **Bill-Graham**-run benefit show entitled SNACK (Students Need Athletics, Culture and Kicks). The show features the **Grateful Dead**, **Tower of Power**, **Jefferson Starship**, **Graham Central Station**, **Joan Baez**, **Neil Young** and "surprise guest" **Bob Dylan** appearing in an effort to add money to the drained coffers of the San Francisco school system, which recently canceled most sports and after-hours activities because of a $3-million budget deficit. The affair raises nearly $200,000, but it's no longer really needed, because the day before the event, an announcement is made that, through a financial adjustment, $2.1 million has been "found."

29 Labelle's "Lady Marmalade," already a Number One R&B hit, reaches Number One on the pop chart, where it will stay for one week. The disco anthem features the French chorus that will become a catch phrase of the disco era: "*Voulez-vous couchez avec moi ce soir?*" (literally, "Do you want to sleep with me tonight?")

Led Zeppelin registers all six of its albums on the charts simultaneously, a feat never before accomplished in pop history. For the record, coming after its chart-topping current release, *Physical Graffiti*, are: *Led Zeppelin IV* at #83; *Houses of the Holy* at #92; *Led Zeppelin II* at #104; *Led Zeppelin* at #116; and *Led Zeppelin III* at #124. ◆

WEEK ENDING MARCH 1

U.S. #1 POP 45	"Best of My Love"	The Eagles
U.S. #1 POP LP	*Blood on the Tracks*	Bob Dylan
U.S. #1 R&B 45	"Shame, Shame, Shame"	Shirley and Company
U.K. #1 POP 45	"If"	Telly Savalas
U.K. #1 POP LP	*On the Level*	Status Quo

WEEK ENDING MARCH 8

U.S. #1 POP 45	"Have You Never Been Mellow"	Olivia Newton-John
U.S. #1 POP LP	*Blood on the Tracks*	Bob Dylan
U.S. #1 R&B 45	"Express"	B.T. Express
U.K. #1 POP 45	"If"	Telly Savalas
U.K. #1 POP LP	*On the Level*	Status Quo

WEEK ENDING MARCH 15

U.S. #1 POP 45	"Black Water"	The Doobie Brothers
U.S. #1 POP LP	*Have You Never Been Mellow*	Olivia Newton-John
U.S. #1 R&B 45	"Supernatural Thing, Part One"	Ben E. King
U.K. #1 POP 45	"Bye, Bye, Baby"	The Bay City Rollers
U.K. #1 POP LP	*On the Level*	Status Quo

WEEK ENDING MARCH 22

U.S. #1 POP 45	"My Eyes Adored You"	Frankie Valli
U.S. #1 POP LP	*Physical Graffiti*	Led Zeppelin
U.S. #1 R&B 45	"Shining Star"	Earth, Wind and Fire
U.K. #1 POP 45	"Bye, Bye, Baby"	The Bay City Rollers
U.K. #1 POP LP	*Physical Graffiti*	Led Zeppelin

WEEK ENDING MARCH 29

U.S. #1 POP 45	"Lady Marmalade"	Labelle
U.S. #1 POP LP	*Physical Graffiti*	Led Zeppelin
U.S. #1 R&B 45	"Shining Star"	Earth, Wind and Fire
U.K. #1 POP 45	"Bye, Bye, Baby"	The Bay City Rollers
U.K. #1 POP LP	*Physical Graffiti*	Led Zeppelin

3 **Steve Miller** is charged with setting fire to the clothes and personal effects of a friend, **Bernita DiOrio**. When police arrive at the musician's house after receiving a call from DiOrio, he is busy putting out the fire, now out of control. In the late night confusion, Miller tussles with some of the policemen and is also charged with resisting arrest. The incident is quickly forgotten; the next day DiOrio asks that the charges be dropped, and Miller jokes with reporters that the publicity might "rekindle" his career.

7 **Ritchie Blackmore**, lead guitarist with **Deep Purple** since its inception in 1968, splits from the quintet, following the lead of vocalist **Ian Gillan** and bassist **Roger Glover**, who departed two years before. The band attempts to carry on, with **Tommy Bolin** replacing Blackmore in October, but calls it a day in 1976 after making one more record, *Come Taste the Band*; Blackmore forms **Rainbow**, enlisting members of the upstate New York bar band **Elf**.

8 **Minnie Riperton** receives her only gold record, for "Lovin' You," her recent Number One pop single. Riperton's five-octave voice has been impressing listeners for over a decade, first when she studied opera, later when she sang with **Rotary Connection** in the late Sixties and with **Stevie Wonder's Wonderlove** in the early Seventies. Appropriately, "Lovin' You" (produced by Wonder) is a virtuoso exercise in upper-register trills, accompanied by bird songs.

9 **Phoebe Snow** receives a gold record for her eponymous debut album. Applying her jazz-trained voice to her contemporary songwriter's point of view, Snow has attracted mainstream interest with "Poetry Man," a single from the album, that reached #5 on the pop chart.

12 With the release of **Ken Russell**'s cinematic interpretation of *Tommy,* all three versions of **Pete Townshend**'s rock opera—the **Who's** original recording, the "classical" rendition by the London Symphony Orchestra and an all-star cast, and the movie's soundtrack (which features some new songs written especially for the film)—are on the chart simultaneously.

14 Having already received two gold discs for their albums *The Captain and Me* and *What Once Were Vices Are Now Habits,* the **Doobie Brothers** pick up their first gold single for their country-flavored "Black Water."

19 "The Hustle," by **Van McCoy** and the **Soul City Symphony**, enters the pop and R&B charts; it will later top both. McCoy has been a distinguished songwriter and producer since the mid-Sixties and has worked with such singers as **Aretha Franklin** and **Gladys Knight and the Pips**. With "The Hustle," an instrumental inspired by the dance of that name, he becomes one of the first industry figures to get in step with the gathering beat of disco music.

23 **Peter Ham**, the twenty-seven-year-old guitarist and songwriter for **Badfinger**, hangs himself in his London garage. Ham is reported to have been deeply depressed by his recent departure from the band, as well as by managerial and financial woes that caused guitarist **Joey Molland** to leave after an American tour the previous fall and that caused Warner Bros. to halt the sale of the group's latest LP, *Wish You Were Here.*

27 As of this last show in a five-night engagement by **Pink Floyd** at Los Angeles' Sports Arena, 511 fans have been arrested for various offenses, mostly possession of marijuana. The exceedingly high count is looked upon as harassment by the promotion agency of Wolf and Rissmiller, which vows not to bring any more concerts to the rarely used auditorium. L.A. Police Chief **Ed Davis** is quoted during a Rotary Club speech on the third night as saying, "Tonight at the Sports Arena they have a dope festival. It's called a rock concert or something."

28 **Tom Donahue**, the man responsible for starting progressive radio in the Bay Area with station KMPX in 1967, dies in San Francisco. The forty-six-year-old Donahue was to sign a contract that day to mark his return as general manager to KMPX, after its acquisition by filmmaker **Francis Ford Coppola**. He had left the station in 1968 after a bitter labor dispute, moving on to the powerful KSAN station.

29 RSO Records releases the **Bee Gees'** *Main Course,* the album that will change the Brothers Gibb's course. *Main Course,* recorded under the aegis of veteran R&B producer **Arif Mardin**, contains two future Top Ten singles (the Bee Gees' first in four years)—"Jive Talkin'" (which will hit Number One on the pop chart in August) and "Nights on Broadway"—and indicates the end of the trio's infatuation with the **Beatles** and the beginning of a love affair with soul music. ◆

WEEK ENDING APRIL 5

U.S. #1 POP 45	"Lovin' You"	Minnie Riperton
U.S. #1 POP LP	*Physical Graffiti*	Led Zeppelin
U.S. #1 R&B 45	"Shoeshine Boy"	Eddie Kendricks
U.K. #1 POP 45	"Bye, Bye, Baby"	The Bay City Rollers
U.K. #1 POP LP	*Physical Graffiti*	Led Zeppelin

WEEK ENDING APRIL 12

U.S. #1 POP 45	"Philadelphia Freedom"	Elton John
U.S. #1 POP LP	*Physical Graffiti*	Led Zeppelin
U.S. #1 R&B 45	"L-O-V-E (Love)"	Al Green
U.K. #1 POP 45	"Bye, Bye, Baby"	The Bay City Rollers
U.K. #1 POP LP	*Young Americans*	David Bowie

WEEK ENDING APRIL 19

U.S. #1 POP 45	"Philadelphia Freedom"	Elton John
U.S. #1 POP LP	*Physical Graffiti*	Led Zeppelin
U.S. #1 R&B 45	"L-O-V-E (Love)"	Al Green
U.K. #1 POP 45	"Bye, Bye, Baby"	The Bay City Rollers
U.K. #1 POP LP	*Once upon a Star*	The Bay City Rollers

WEEK ENDING APRIL 26

U.S. #1 POP 45	"Another Somebody Done Somebody Wrong Song"	B. J. Thomas
U.S. #1 POP LP	*Physical Graffiti*	Led Zeppelin
U.S. #1 R&B 45	"Shakey Ground"	The Temptations
U.K. #1 POP 45	"Honey"	Bobby Goldsboro
U.K. #1 POP LP	*Once upon a Star*	The Bay City Rollers

1 With their first big hit single, "Lady," still on the chart, the Chicago-based rock band **Styx** earns its first gold record, for the 1973 album *Styx II.* Along with such bands as **Journey, REO Speedwagon, Rush** and **Kansas,** Styx will become one of the foremost exponents of the brand of commercially successful arena-rock dismissed by critics as "pomp rock"—a streamlined, merger of British art-rock technique, high-harmony vocals derived from Crosby, Stills and Nash and British art-rockers Yes (who derived their high-harmonies from CSN), as well as heavy metal. Such "pomp rock" will become the staple fare of mid-Seventies album-oriented radio.

The **Rolling Stones** announce their Tour of the Americas '75 in New York City, first by way of an incomprehensible monologue by comedian **Professor Irwin Corey,** and then by playing "Brown Sugar" with new but not yet permanent replacement **Ron Wood** on the back of a flatbed truck moving down Fifth Avenue.

8 *Straight Shooter,* the second album by British hard-rock band **Bad Company**—which features ex-**Free** vocalist **Paul Rodgers** and ex-**Mott the Hoople** guitarist **Mick Ralphs**—goes gold, as its predecessor, the band's eponymous debut album, did the year before.

10 **Stevie Wonder** plays before 125,000 people at the Washington Monument as part of Human Kindness Day, for which he is the honoree. Despite initial reservations as to whether the focus of his involvement might detract from the event's impact, Wonder and his group, **Wonderlove,** perform for over an hour.

12 The **Jefferson Starship** give a concert in New York's Central Park for 60,000 fans. The band flies into town specifically for the performance, which is free, but only for the audience. The Starship and concert sponsor WNEW-FM pick up a $14,000 tab for cleanup and damage done to the park.

American pop group **Steely Dan**—one of the few "critics' favorites" to also achieve popular success—earn their third gold record for the album *Katy Lied,* which contained the minor hit singles "Black Friday" and "Dr. Wu." Their previous gold records went to their debut album *Can't Buy a Thrill,* and their third album, *Pretzel Logic.*

13 **Bob Wills,** the King of Western Swing, dies in Kent Nursing Home in Fort Worth, Texas. He was 70 and had been suffering from heart problems and a stroke for several years. With his group, the **Texas Playboys,** Wills had popularized Western Swing, a goodtime mix of country, blues, jazz and swing.

17 Just two weeks prior to the start of the **Rolling Stones'** lengthy Tour of the Americas '75, **Mick Jagger** puts his right hand through a window at Gosman's restaurant in Montauk, on Long Island. The wound requires twenty stitches; fortunately, no real damage is done, and tour plans proceed accordingly.

19 Who leader **Pete Townshend** turns thirty years old. Excessive hours spent working on the film *Tommy* and his own uncertainty about his role in rock lead him to give an acerbic interview this month to friend and *New Musical Express* journalist **Roy Carr.** Who vocalist **Roger Daltrey** responds in the *NME* in August, and rumors fly—aided by the October release of *The Who by Numbers* LP—that the group is finally about to break up.

22 **Pure Prairie League, Rufus, Earl Scruggs** and **Joe Cocker** entertain 17,000 troops and their families at the army base in Fort Campbell, Kentucky. The concert, known as Music—You're My Mother, fails to break even at the box office, and base officials cancel another show planned for June 14th, the 200th anniversary of the army.

24 For the second show in a row, the **Beach Boys,** on tour with **Chicago,** literally have the joint jumping. The second level at the Oakland Coliseum is noticeably shaking in footage taken by a local news crew; the previous day's concert at Anaheim Stadium caused the mezzanine to vibrate as much as eighteen inches. ♦

WEEK ENDING MAY 3

U.S. #1 POP 45	"He Don't Love You (like I Love You)"	Tony Orlando and Dawn
U.S. #1 POP LP	*Chicago VIII*	Chicago
U.S. #1 R&B 45	"What Am I Gonna Do with You"	Barry White
U.K. #1 POP 45	"Lovin' You"	Minnie Riperton
U.K. #1 POP LP	*Once upon a Star*	The Bay City Rollers

WEEK ENDING MAY 10

U.S. #1 POP 45	"He Don't Love You (like I Love You)"	Tony Orlando and Dawn
U.S. #1 POP LP	*Chicago VIII*	Chicago
U.S. #1 R&B 45	"Get Down, Get Down (Get on the Floor)"	Joe Simon
U.K. #1 POP 45	"Stand by Your Man"	Tammy Wynette
U.K. #1 POP LP	*Once upon a Star*	The Bay City Rollers

WEEK ENDING MAY 17

U.S. #1 POP 45	"He Don't Love You (like I Love You)"	Tony Orlando and Dawn
U.S. #1 POP LP	*That's the Way of the World*	Earth, Wind and Fire
U.S. #1 R&B 45	"Get Down, Get Down (Get on the Floor)"	Joe Simon
U.K. #1 POP 45	"Stand by Your Man"	Tammy Wynette
U.K. #1 POP LP	*Once upon a Star*	The Bay City Rollers

WEEK ENDING MAY 24

U.S. #1 POP 45	"Shining Star"	Earth, Wind and Fire
U.S. #1 POP LP	*That's the Way of the World*	Earth Wind and Fire
U.S. #1 R&B 45	"Baby That's Backatcha"	Smokey Robinson
U.K. #1 POP 45	"Stand by Your Man"	Tammy Wynette
U.K. #1 POP LP	*Once upon a Star*	The Bay City Rollers

WEEK ENDING MAY 31

U.S. #1 POP 45	"Before the Next Teardrop Falls"	Freddy Fender
U.S. #1 POP LP	*That's the Way of the World*	Earth, Wind and Fire
U.S. #1 R&B 45	"Spirit of the Boogie"	Kool and the Gang
U.K. #1 POP 45	"Whispering Grass"	Windsor Davies and Don Estell
U.K. #1 POP LP	*Once upon a Star*	The Bay City Rollers

7 Elton John's album *Captain Fantastic and the Brown Dirt Cowboy,* which had gone gold on May 21, two weeks before its release, enters the U.S. album chart at Number One.

12 Doug Weston, owner of longtime Los Angeles showcase club the Troubadour, closes his establishment for "restructuring" because of some recent financial setbacks. The bistro doesn't remain shuttered for long, however; **Kinky Friedman and His Texas Jewboys** reopen the Troub on July 8.

Philadelphia soul vocal trio **The O'Jays** earn their fifth gold record, for the album *Survival.* Their previous gold citations were for "Backstabbers" (1972), "Love Train" and *Ship Ahoy* (1973), and "For the Love of Money" and "I Love Music" (1974).

Almost five years after her death, **Janis Joplin**'s *Greatest Hits,* released in 1973, goes gold.

16 In the continuing saga of **John Lennon**'s fight against deportation, the former Beatle sues government officials, including Nixon Administration attorney general **John Mitchell** and **Richard Kleindienst**. The action, filed in the Federal Court in Manhattan, asserts that Lennon is the victim of selective prosecution, based more on his radical political stance than on the merits of his case.

21 **Elton John** headlines a bill at Wembley Stadium in London that also features the **Eagles**, the **Beach Boys, Rufus** and **Joe Walsh** before a crowd of 120,000. The determined John plays the songs from his newest record, *Captain Fantastic and the Brown Dirt Cowboy,* straight through despite the audience's unfamiliarity with the tunes and the gig being his first public appearance with his new band. His thunder is stolen by the **Beach Boys**, who catch a wave of good cheer from the British fans and ride it for a joyous ninety-minute set.

22 On the first night of a record six-perform- ance engagement at Madison Square Garden, the **Rolling Stones** run into problems when **Ron Wood**'s and **Keith Richards**' amplifiers pick up radio and television broadcast signals. Although that trouble is corrected, the notoriously sound-swallowing Garden is still not really tamed; the only highlight of the evening comes when **Eric Clapton** joins the group onstage for an encore.

23 The potential danger in performing rock at big arenas is realized by **Vincent Furnier** (a.k.a. **Alice Cooper**), who falls off the set of his Welcome to My Nightmare tour in Vancouver and breaks six ribs, forcing the cancellation of a few subsequent dates.

The **Jefferson Starship**'s *Red Octopus* is released on the band's RCA subsidiary label, Grunt Records. The album will hit Number One on the LP chart four different times this year and later will be certified platinum. It marks the fulltime return to the band of onetime **Jefferson Airplane** (the band that became the Starship in 1974) singer/songwriter **Marty Balin**, who had written and sung on the band's minor hit "Caroline," from its previous album, *Dragon Fly.* Balin's "Miracles" will become *Red Octopus*' biggest hit single, reaching #3 later this year. The album will also yield a hit single in "Play on Love."

24 The U.S. attorney in Newark, New Jersey, hands down indictments to nineteen music-industry executives after two years of investigation into the record industry. Counts of income-tax evasion and charges of payola are leveled at, among others: **Clive Davis,** former president of Columbia Records, now head of the newly formed Arista company; **Kenneth Gamble** and **Leon Huff,** architects of the Seventies Sound of Philadelphia; and seven top-level execs at Brunswick Records.

26 Veteran R&B composer/arranger/producer **Van McCoy** earns his first gold record for the disco anthem "The Hustle," the biggest dance-craze disc of the Seventies.

27 Southern rockers **Lynyrd Skynyrd** receive their third gold album, for their third LP, *Nuthin' Fancy.* Their previous two gold albums were *Pronounced Leh-Nerd Skinnerd* and *Second Helping.*

Texas heavy-metal blues trio **ZZ Top** earn their second gold record, for their fourth album, *Fandango,* which contains their Top Twenty hit single "Tush." Their previous gold award was for their third album, *Tres Hombres.*

29 Twenty-eight-year-old **Tim Buckley** dies in a Santa Monica hospital of an overdose of heroin and morphine. The singer, whose move from Sixties folk-rock into jazz-tinged areas of music during the early Seventies cost him his commercial reputation, allegedly ingested the fatal substances at a friend's home, thinking it was cocaine.

Elton John shows up at an Oakland Coliseum concert starring the **Eagles** and the **Doobie Brothers** and sings with both bands: "Listen to the Music" with the Doobies (whose **Jeff "Skunk" Baxter** played with Elton in London in May) and the **Chuck Berry** classic "Oh, Carol" with the Eagles. ◆

WEEK ENDING JUNE 7

U.S. #1 POP 45	"Thank God I'm a Country Boy"	John Denver
U.S. #1 POP LP	*Captain Fantastic and the Brown Dirt Cowboy*	Elton John
U.S. #1 R&B 45	"Love Won't Let Me Wait"	Major Harris
U.K. #1 POP 45	"Three Steps to Heaven"	Showaddywaddy
U.K. #1 POP LP	*Captain Fantastic and the Brown Dirt Cowboy*	Elton John

WEEK ENDING JUNE 14

U.S. #1 POP 45	"Sister Golden Hair"	America
U.S. #1 POP LP	*Captain Fantastic and the Brown Dirt Cowboy*	Elton John
U.S. #1 R&B 45	"Rockin' Chair"	Gwen McCrae
U.K. #1 POP 45	"Whispering Grass"	Windsor Davies and Don Estelle
U.K. #1 POP LP	*Captain Fantastic and the Brown Dirt Cowboy*	Elton John

WEEK ENDING JUNE 21

U.S. #1 POP 45	"Love Will Keep Us Together"	The Captain and Tennille
U.S. #1 POP LP	*Captain Fantastic and the Brown Dirt Cowboy*	Elton John
U.S. #1 R&B 45	"Give the People What They Want"	The O'Jays
U.K. #1 POP 45	"I'm Not in Love"	10cc
U.K. #1 POP LP	*Captain Fantastic and the Brown Dirt Cowboy*	Elton John

WEEK ENDING JUNE 28

U.S. #1 POP 45	"Love Will Keep Us Together"	The Captain and Tennille
U.S. #1 POP LP	*Captain Fantastic and the Brown Dirt Cowboy*	Elton John
U.S. #1 R&B 45	"Look at Me (I'm in Love)"	The Moments
U.K. #1 POP 45	"I'm Not in Love"	10cc
U.K. #1 POP LP	*Venus and Mars*	Wings

1 Influential British pub-rock band **Ducks Deluxe** play their last show, at London's 100 Club. The band becomes more famous for its alumni than for its two-LP, three-year career: guitarist **Martin Belmont** joins **Graham Parker**'s **Rumour**, guitarist **Nick Garvey** and keyboardist **Andy McMasters** form the **Motors**, and leader **Sean Tyla** starts his own **Tyla Gang**.

The **Captain and Tennille** net their first gold record with "Love Will Keep Us Together." The husband-and-wife duo, known individually as **Daryl Dragon** and **Toni Tennille**, met in 1971 and soon after musicians toured as in the **Beach Boys**' band. They produced their own debut single, "The Way I Want to Touch You," before signing with A&M Records and releasing "Love Will Keep Us Together," which will eventually sell 2.5 million copies and win a Grammy for Record of the Year.

2 **David Bowie** earns his fourth gold record, for *Young Americans,* which contains two of his biggest hit singles, "Fame" (which will reach Number One later this year) and the title tune (which has already peaked at #28). *Young Americans* marks the culmination of Bowie's soul phase, which began with his previous gold album, 1974's *David Live.* His other prior gold albums include *The Rise and Fall of Ziggy Stardust and the Spiders from Mars* (released in 1972, went gold in 1974) and *Diamond Dogs* (released in 1974, went gold the same year). "Fame" will also go gold by the end of this year.

3 **Chuck Negron**, lead singer for **Three Dog Night**, is arrested at his Louisville hotel room on the opening night of the band's tour and is charged with possession of cocaine. The charge is dropped in October in a Kentucky courtroom when it's determined that the warrant used for the bust had been granted on the basis of "unfounded" information.

5 Police in Fordyce, Arkansas, pull a rented Chevrolet over after the driver swerved on the roadway. Found inside: two **Rolling Stones**, **Keith Richards** and Ron

Wood, with two friends, on their way from a show in Memphis on Independence Day to the tour's next stop, Dallas. Keith is charged on counts of reckless driving and carrying a concealed weapon (supposedly a sheathed hunting knife); he posts bail of $163.50, and the foursome leaves town in a chartered plane.

12 **K. C. and the Sunshine Band** make their pop chart debut with "Get Down Tonight." Led by Miami studio engineer **H. W. Casey** and bassist **Richard Finch**—who together wrote and backed 1974's smash hit "Rock Your Baby" for **George McCrae**—K. C. and the Sunshine Band have enjoyed considerable popularity in Europe and more recently have caught on in inner-city discos. "Get Down Tonight" will be the first of four singles by this band to hit Number One, followed by "That's the Way (I Like It)," "(Shake, Shake, Shake) Shake Your Booty" and "I'm Your Boogie Man."

20 "Miami" **Steve Van Zandt** plays his first official gig with **Bruce Springsteen and the E Street Band** at Providence, Rhode Island's Palace Theatre. Van Zandt, added as rhythm guitarist during recording sessions for *Born to Run,* has been playing with **Southside Johnny** and the still-embryonic **Asbury Jukes**, for whom he will eventually write songs and produce three albums for Epic.

26 **Natalie Cole**, daughter of **Nat "King" Cole**, makes her chart debut with "This Will Be." Hitting Number One R&B and pop #6, "This Will Be" will encourage the hope that the sort of elegant, sophisticated pop music made by her famous father is returning to vogue. Cole *fille* will find commercial and critical success with records like "I've Got Love on My Mind" and "Our Love" but never attract the widespread and long-term popularity of Cole *père.*

30 The **Charlie Daniels Band**, one of America's most popular exponents of Southern-style boogie rock, earns its first gold record for the album *Fire on the Mountain,* which yielded minor hits in "The South's Gonna Do It" and "Long Haired Country Boy." ♦

WEEK ENDING JULY 5

U.S. #1 POP 45	"Love Will Keep Us Together"	The Captain and Tennille
U.S. #1 POP LP	*Captain Fantastic and the Brown Dirt Cowboy*	Elton John
U.S. #1 R&B 45	"Slippery When Wet"	The Commodores
U.K. #1 POP 45	"Tears on My Pillow"	Johnny Nash
U.K. #1 POP LP	*Venus and Mars*	Wings

WEEK ENDING JULY 12

U.S. #1 POP 45	"Love Will Keep Us Together"	The Captain and Tennille
U.S. #1 POP LP	*Captain Fantastic and the Brown Dirt Cowboy*	Elton John
U.S. #1 R&B 45	"The Hustle"	Van McCoy and the Soul City Symphony
U.K. #1 POP 45	"Tears on My Pillow"	Johnny Nash
U.K. #1 POP LP	*Venus and Mars*	Wings

WEEK ENDING JULY 19

U.S. #1 POP 45	"Listen to What the Man Said"	Wings
U.S. #1 POP LP	*Venus and Mars*	Wings
U.S. #1 R&B 45	"Fight the Power, Part One"	The Isley Brothers
U.K. #1 POP 45	"Give a Little Love"	The Bay City Rollers
U.K. #1 POP LP	*Venus and Mars*	Wings

WEEK ENDING JULY 26

U.S. #1 POP 45	"The Hustle"	Van McCoy and the Soul City Symphony
U.S. #1 POP LP	*One of These Nights*	The Eagles
U.S. #1 R&B 45	"Fight the Power, Part One"	The Isley Brothers
U.K. #1 POP 45	"Barbados"	Typically Tropical
U.K. #1 POP LP	*Venus and Mars*	Wings

4 **Led Zeppelin**'s frontman, vocalist **Robert Plant**, and his family suffer extensive injuries in a car crash that occurs during their vacation on the Mediterranean island of Rhodes. Wife **Maureen**, daughter **Carmen**, son **Karac** and Plant all suffer fractured bones and assorted bruises; Plant's injuries force a postponement of a scheduled autumn Zeppelin American tour, and it will be a full two years before the supergroup plays in the United States again.

5 **Stevie Wonder** renews his contract with Motown Records for an estimated $13 million, or so it is assumed after a Los Angeles press conference called by the two parties. The announcement is actually a bit premature; Motown and Wonder don't actually come to terms until the following April.

8 **Robert Altman**'s cinematic interpretation of country music, *Nashville,* opens in the town it's named for and encounters a decidedly mixed reaction from the residents of the Music City. While **Minnie Pearl** admits to laughing "so hard it sometimes hurt," an alternative opinion is offered by producer **Billy Sherrill**, who claims his favorite moment in the movie comes "when they shot that miserable excuse for a country singer."

9 The Santa Monica Civic Auditorium is the site of the first annual Rock Music Award Show. The **Don Kirshner**-produced broadcast over CBS proves to be an alternative of sorts to the Grammys: **Bad Company**, the **Eagles**,

Stevie Wonder, **Roger Daltrey** and **Joan Baez** capture awards, even though the presenters include such nonrock personalities as **Olivia Newton-John** and **Mike Douglas**.

13 **Bruce Springsteen and the E Street Band** begin a five-night, two-shows-per-evening stand at New York's showcase club the Bottom Line. The performances, just prior to the release of *Born to Run,* are instrumental in spreading the gospel of rock's purported "future" (and, some would later say, furthering the "hype" associated with the Boss' imminent ascent to stardom; Columbia Records, his label, supposedly papers half the house each night with influential industry people). The early show on the fifteenth is broadcast live over New York's WNEW-FM.

16 Vocalist and songwriter **Peter Gabriel** delivers a statement to the British press announcing his departure from **Genesis**. His decision to leave was made the previous December, but he stayed on until contracted tours were finished in May. Gabriel's reasons: a desire to be with his family and because, "As an artist, I need to absorb a wide variety of experiences. It's difficult to respond to intuition and impulse within the long-term planning the band needed."

23 Former **Free** guitarist **Paul Kossoff**'s heart stops beating for thirty-five minutes at London's Northwick Park Hospital. A blood clot in his leg had reached the heart, putting him in a coma; the following day, his kidneys shut down. Somehow, Kossoff survives and returns to his band, **Back Street Crawler**, but physical problems eventually catch up to him: he will die in his sleep on a transatlantic flight the following March.

25 **Elton John** plays two sets on the first of three nights at Los Angeles' Troubadour to raise money for UCLA's Jules Stein Eye Institute. The benefit shows, with tickets priced from $25 to $250, raise over $150,000 for the clinic, named for the licensed opthamologist who runs it (and who, not so coincidentally, is head of MCA, John's label). His return to the Troub carries special weight for Elton: Five years ago to the day, he began a weeklong stint there that helped establish his superstar status in America. ◆

WEEK ENDING AUGUST 2

U.S. #1 POP 45	"One of These Nights"	The Eagles
U.S. #1 POP LP	*One of These Nights*	The Eagles
U.S. #1 R&B 45	"Fight the Power, Part One"	The Isley Brothers
U.K. #1 POP 45	"I Can't Give You Anything (but Love)"	The Stylistics
U.K. #1 POP LP	*Venus and Mars*	Wings

WEEK ENDING AUGUST 9

U.S. #1 POP 45	"Jive Talkin'"	The Bee Gees
U.S. #1 POP LP	*One of These Nights*	The Eagles
U.S. #1 R&B 45	"Hope That We Can Be Together Soon"	Sharon Paige and Harold Melvin and the Blue Notes
U.K. #1 POP 45	"I Can't Give You Anything (but Love)"	The Stylistics
U.K. #1 POP LP	*The Best of the Stylistics*	The Stylistics

WEEK ENDING AUGUST 16

U.S. #1 POP 45	"Jive Talkin'"	The Bee Gees
U.S. #1 POP LP	*One of These Nights*	The Eagles
U.S. #1 R&B 45	"Dream Merchant"	New Birth
U.K. #1 POP 45	"I Can't Give You Anything (but Love)"	The Stylistics
U.K. #1 POP LP	*The Best of the Stylistics*	The Stylistics

WEEK ENDING AUGUST 23

U.S. #1 POP 45	"Fallin' in Love"	Hamilton, Joe Frank and Reynolds
U.S. #1 POP LP	*One of These Nights*	The Eagles
U.S. #1 R&B 45	"Get Down Tonight"	K. C. and the Sunshine Band
U.K. #1 POP 45	"Sailing"	Rod Stewart
U.K. #1 POP LP	*The Best of the Stylistics*	The Stylistics

WEEK ENDING AUGUST 30

U.S. #1 POP 45	"Get Down Tonight"	K. C. and the Sunshine Band
U.S. #1 POP LP	*One of These Nights*	The Eagles
U.S. #1 R&B 45	"Your Love"	Graham Central Station
U.K. #1 POP 45	"Sailing"	Rod Stewart
U.K. #1 POP LP	*Atlantic Crossing*	Rod Stewart

2 The summer ends on a less-than-peaceful note in Syracuse, New York. A so-called Great American Music Fair featuring the **Jefferson Starship**, **Doobie Brothers**, **New Riders of the Purple Sage** and others is marred when a crowd of five hundred attempts to storm the gate, armed with rocks and bottles, in an effort to make the fest a free show. Police and state troopers retaliate, and sixty are arrested in the melee that follows.

10 A special about legendary Columbia Records executive **John Hammond** is taped in Chicago for NET (National Educational Television). **Marion Wilson**, **Benny Goodman**, **Sonny Terry** and **John Hammond Jr.** all perform for the man who signed up **Bessie Smith**, **Billie Holiday**, **Count Basie** and **Bruce Springsteen**. But it's the man once dubbed "Hammond's Folly" who ends the proceedings. **Bob Dylan**, playing with what becomes the **Rolling Thunder Revue**'s rhythm section—bassist **Rob Stoner** and drummer **Howie Wyeth**—and the tour's violinist, **Scarlet Rivera**, run through "Oh Sister," "Simple Twist of Fate" and two blistering versions of "Hurricane," his as-yet unreleased, stirring defense of former boxer and convicted (some say unjustly) murderer **Rubin "Hurricane" Carter**.

11 Folk-pop singer/songwriter **Janis Ian** earns her first gold record for the album *Between the Lines*. The album contains her single, "At 17," which is climbing the pop chart, where it will peak at #3. *Between the Lines* will eventually go platinum. "At Seventeen" is Ian's first hit since 1967's controversial "Society's Child," a protest-love song about an interracial relationship that reached #14 on the pop chart.

12 Hard rock band **Slade**'s attempt at rock moviemaking, *Flame*, opens in St. Louis. The band, as popular in its native U.K. as it is overlooked in the U.S., stars as a prepackaged Sixties band. But despite the concurrent release of *Flame*, the book, and *Flame*, the soundtrack, the venture falls far short of capturing the American interest.

17 British progressive-rock band **Pink Floyd** earn their third gold record, for the album *Wish You Were Here*, a thinly veiled tribute to **Syd Barrett**, the band's original guiding light in its early psychedelic days. One of their previous gold citations was for *The Dark Side of the Moon*, which also went platinum.

18 Veteran Detroit soul vocal group the **Spinners** earn another of their many gold records, for the album *Pick of the Litter*, which contains their current hit, "They Just Can't Stop It (the Games People Play)," which is on its way to #5 on the pop chart. Among their other gold singles are "I'll Be Around" (1972), "Could It Be I'm Falling in Love" (1973) and the 1974 Number One hit with **Dionne Warwick**, "Then Came You." They will go on to earn another gold record in 1976 for the #2 pop hit "The Rubberband Man."

19 Dickie Goodman, master of the novelty "break-in" record—where excerpts from current hits are used to flesh out what, in Goodman's case, is inevitably some sort of parody of current events or fads—earns his only gold record, for "Mr. Jaws," currently on its way to #4 on the pop chart. Goodman had many other such hits, including "The Touchables" (1961), "Ben Crazy" (1962), "Batman and His Grandmother" (1966), "On Campus" and "Luna Trip" (1969), "Watergate" (1973), "Energy Crisis '74" and "Mr. President" (1974). Before going solo, Goodman had scored several other "break-in" novelty hits as half of a duo with **Bill Buchanan**. The first of their duo hits, 1956's "Flying Saucer," was also the first "break-in" record and sparked controversy among the composers and publishers whose songs had been excerpted; Buchanan and Goodman capitalized on this publicity in their follow-up hit, "Buchanan and Goodman on Trial," and had one more hit in 1957 with "Santa and the Satellite."

20 The **Bay City Rollers** appear live on the premiere of **Howard Cosell**'s Saturday night ABC variety show in an obvious attempt to break the band (and Cosell's soon-to-be-canceled program) in the manner of the **Beatles**' appearance on "The Ed Sullivan Show" eleven years earlier.

25 Soul singer **Jackie Wilson** ("Higher and Higher") suffers a heart attack while performing at the Latin Casino in Cherry Hill, New Jersey. He suffers brain damage and lapses into a coma. Ironically, Wilson was in the middle of singing one of his biggest hits, "Lonely Teardrops," and was two words into the line "My heart is crying" when he collapsed. He is forty-one years old.

28 Fifty thousand people watch the **Jefferson Starship** and **Jerry Garcia and Friends** for free in San Francisco's Lindley Park. Garcia's "friends" turn out to be the reunited **Grateful Dead** making their first public appearance in over a year. ◆

WEEK ENDING SEPTEMBER 6

U.S. #1 POP 45	"Rhinestone Cowboy"	Glen Campbell
U.S. #1 POP LP	*Red Octopus*	The Jefferson Starship
U.S. #1 R&B 45	"How Long (Betcha' Got a Chick on the Side)"	The Pointer Sisters
U.K. #1 POP 45	"Sailing"	Rod Stewart
U.K. #1 POP LP	*Atlantic Crossing*	Rod Stewart

WEEK ENDING SEPTEMBER 13

U.S. #1 POP 45	"Rhinestone Cowboy"	Glen Campbell
U.S. #1 POP LP	*The Heat Is On*	The Isley Brothers
U.S. #1 R&B 45	"How Long (Betcha' Got a Chick on the Side)"	The Pointer Sisters
U.K. #1 POP 45	"Sailing"	Rod Stewart
U.K. #1 POP LP	*Atlantic Crossing*	Rod Stewart

WEEK ENDING SEPTEMBER 20

U.S. #1 POP 45	"Fame"	David Bowie
U.S. #1 POP LP	*Between the Lines*	Janis Ian
U.S. #1 R&B 45	"It Only Takes a Minute"	Tavares
U.K. #1 POP 45	"Moonlighting"	Leo Sayer
U.K. #1 POP LP	*Atlantic Crossing*	Rod Stewart

WEEK ENDING SEPTEMBER 27

U.S. #1 POP 45	"I'm Sorry"	John Denver
U.S. #1 POP LP	*Between the Lines*	Janis Ian
U.S. #1 R&B 45	"Do It Any Way You Wanna"	Peoples Choice
U.K. #1 POP 45	"Hold Me Close"	David Essex
U.K. #1 POP LP	*Atlantic Crossing*	Rod Stewart

1 Thirty-nine-year-old drummer **Al Jackson** is shot to death in his Memphis home. His solid reputation was achieved as the drummer for the MGs, the legendary Stax Records house band that backed **Otis Redding**, **Sam and Dave**, **Wilson Pickett** and so many others in addition to having tremendous success on its own, fronted by keyboardist **Booker T. Washington**. The influential soul group had met just weeks earlier to straighten out difficulties and was clearing the way for a reunion. Jackson's wife is questioned in connection with the murder; she had been arrested in July for shooting her husband in the chest.

2 After a bomb scare clears out Milwaukee's Uptown Theatre where **Bruce Springsteen** is performing, he returns to the Hotel Pfister to wait before the gig's rescheduled midnight commencement. Availing himself of the establishment's bar, the usually teetotaler Springsteen gets—in his own words, "a little loose"—and proceeds to give a wild performance. The comment of a British writer accompanying Spring-steen when, on the way back to the hall, the New Jersey rocker rides on top of the car: "I have seen the future of rock & roll, and he is on my windshield."

7 **John Lennon** wins his lengthy fight to stay in America, when the three-judge U.S. Court of Appeals in New York City rules that his 1968 arrest in Britain for possession of marijuana—the reason given by the U.S. Immigration Department in trying to deport Lennon—was contrary to U.S. ideas of due process and is therefore invalid as a means of banishing the former Beatle from America. The court writes: "Lennon's four-year battle to remain in our country is a testimony to his faith in this American dream."

9 **John Lennon**'s great week continues. After the immigration ruling in his favor only two days before, he and wife **Yoko** celebrate his thirty-fifth birthday with the birth of their only child, **Sean Ono Lennon**.

11 "Saturday Night Live" is broadcast for the first time, with **George Carlin** as guest host. The show really takes off the following week, when it's highlighted by the reunion of host **Paul Simon** with his former partner, **Art Garfunkel**.

12 **Rod Stewart and the Faces** play their last show together, at Long Island's Nassau Coliseum. The split between Stewart and the group, brought on mainly as a result of the former's enormous solo success (and latter's lack of same), has been brewing for years and is made official in December when Rod the Mod outlines the lineup of his new band at a London press conference. Face guitarist **Ron Wood** soon finds employment with the Rolling Stones, who accept him as a full-time member; **Ian McLagan** and **Kenney Jones** float for a few years before reviving the original **Small Faces** with **Steve Marriott**.

13 **Neil Young** is operated on at a Los Angeles hospital; an "object" is scraped from his vocal cords, which have been bothering him for a year. Although he quickly returns to the studio, Young is hampered by the setback and will bow out midway during his 1976 tour with **Stephen Stills** because of the strain on his voice.

24 Long Island's Nassau Coliseum is the site of the First Planetary Celebration, held to coincide with United Nations Day. **James Taylor**, **Pete Seeger** and **John McLaughlin** star at the event, designed to promote awareness of man's global responsibilities. Unfortunately, only 4,500 turn out to the 16,000-seat arena to hear the message.

26 Playing for the second day in a row at Los Angeles' Dodger Stadium, **Elton John** (the first rocker to play the ballpark since the **Beatles** in 1966) finishes up yet another SRO American tour. The bespectacled John takes the stage decked out in a sequined Dodgers uniform.

27 **Bruce Springsteen** simultaneously makes the covers of *Time* and *Newsweek*, a move that reportedly embarrasses the two news-weeklies and contributes to growing charges of hype associated with the singer's breakthrough.

29 Bob Dylan's **Rolling Thunder Revue** gets under way in the 1,800-seat Memorial Auditorium in Plymouth, Massachusetts. The tour, with an all-star rock and folk cast including **Ramblin' Jack Elliott**, **Roger McGuinn**, **Bob Neuwirth**, and **Joan Baez**, sticks mainly to small clubs and halls, with dates often unannounced until hours beforehand. The troupe's name comes when Dylan, waiting for inspiration, hears thunder roll across the sky one evening.

31 The **Marshall Tucker Band** performs at Atlanta's Fox Theater in a benefit show for presidential candidate and former Georgia Governor **Jimmy Carter**. **Phil Walden**, a president himself (of Capricorn Records, the group's label), sponsors this concern and, ultimately, many more with his other acts, including the **Allman Brothers**. ◆

WEEK ENDING OCTOBER 4

U.S. #1 POP 45	"Fame"	David Bowie
U.S. #1 POP LP	*Wish You Were Here*	Pink Floyd
U.S. #1 R&B 45	"This Will Be"	Natalie Cole
U.K. #1 POP 45	"Hold Me Close"	David Essex
U.K. #1 POP LP	*Atlantic Crossing*	Rod Stewart

WEEK ENDING OCTOBER 11

U.S. #1 POP 45	"Bad Blood"	Neil Sedaka
U.S. #1 POP LP	*Wish You Were Here*	Pink Floyd
U.S. #1 R&B 45	"This Will Be"	Natalie Cole
U.K. #1 POP 45	"Hold Me Close"	David Essex
U.K. #1 POP LP	*Atlantic Crossing*	Rod Stewart

WEEK ENDING OCTOBER 18

U.S. #1 POP 45	"Bad Blood"	Neil Sedaka
U.S. #1 POP LP	*Windsong*	John Denver
U.S. #1 R&B 45	"They Just Can't Stop It (the Games People Play)"	The Spinners
U.K. #1 POP 45	"I Only Have Eyes for You"	Art Garfunkel
U.K. #1 POP LP	*Wish You Were Here*	Pink Floyd

WEEK ENDING OCTOBER 25

U.S. #1 POP 45	"Bad Blood"	Neil Sedaka
U.S. #1 POP LP	*Windsong*	John Denver
U.S. #1 R&B 45	"To Each Its Own"	Faith, Hope and Charity
U.K. #1 POP 45	"I Only Have Eyes for You"	Art Garfunkel
U.K. #1 POP LP	*Atlantic Crossing*	Rod Stewart

2 **Bob Dylan** and **Allen Ginsberg** detour from the Rolling Thunder Revue to Lowell, Massachusetts, to visit the grave site of Beat writer **Jack Kerouac**. While sitting on the grave, Dylan strums his guitar, face covered with white greasepaint, and Ginsberg improvises some poetry. Their tribute, like much of the tour, is filmed and later used in Dylan's film *Renaldo and Clara*.

6 The **Sex Pistols** play their first gig, at Saint Martin's College of Art in London. The band—**Glen Matlock**, **Paul Cook**, **Steve Jones** and **Johnny Rotten** (né **Lydon**)—will later spearhead the British punk movement.

9 **David Bowie** appears on **Cher**'s CBS television show and, in addition to singing his recent Number One hit, "Fame," performs a duet with the hostess on a medley of "Young Americans," "Song Sung Blue," "One," "Da Doo Ron Ron," "Wedding Bell Blues," "Maybe," "Daytripper," "Ain't No Sunshine" and "Youngblood."

18 The pressures of instantaneous stardom get to **Bruce Springsteen** when, on unfamiliar turf in London, he reacts to the hype that's preceded him across the ocean. At his European debut in London's Hammersmith Odeon, Springsteen tears down lobby posters reading, "Finally, the world is ready for Bruce Springsteen." Fed up with the trappings of newly found fame, the Jersey musician puts on a lackluster performance; his return to the same hall, five nights later, is considerably sharper.

Rock & roll and prime-time television meet again, under the usual inane circumstances, when **Commander Cody and His Lost Planet Airmen** appear on an episode of "Police Woman." The band, playing a rock group named the Chromium Skateboard, and the Commander deliver twenty-two speaking lines. The best line actually comes from an assistant director, who outlines some professional camera behavior for the group: "Please, try not to stare at Angie's [Dickinson, the show's star] tits."

19 The **J. Geils Band** finish recording their live *Blow Your Face Out* set at Detroit's Cobo Arena. A show four nights before, at the Boston Garden, was also taped for the two-record package that will be released in 1976.

20 The **Who** kick off a month-long American tour in Houston at the Summit. The show, closely monitored by the press following the apocalyptic tone of the band's latest LP, *The Who by Numbers,* is judged less than a triumph but certainly no disaster. At a party afterward, **John Entwistle**—and not head mischief-maker **Keith Moon**—is arrested for disorderly conduct and spends a few hours in jail.

22 British soul singer and critic **Pete Wingfield**'s only U.S. chart entry, "Eighteen with a Bullet," reaches—inevitably—#18 on the chart, with a bullet.

26 The **Reverend Charles Boykin** of Tallahassee, Florida's Lakeswood Baptist Church and some of the younger members of his congregation burn approximately $2,000 worth of rock & roll records. The reverend, attempting to revive the image of rock as the "devil's music," cites a particularly damning (and hopelessly untraceable) statistic: 984 out of 1,000 unwed mothers became pregnant while rock music was playing in the background. ◆

WEEK ENDING NOVEMBER 1

U.S. #1 POP 45	"Island Girl"	Elton John
U.S. #1 POP LP	*Windsong*	John Denver
U.S. #1 R&B 45	"Sweet Sticky Thing"	The Ohio Players
U.K. #1 POP 45	"Space Oddity"	David Bowie
U.K. #1 POP LP	*Forty Golden Greats*	Jim Reeves

WEEK ENDING NOVEMBER 8

U.S. #1 POP 45	"Island Girl"	Elton John
U.S. #1 POP LP	*Rock of the Westies*	Elton John
U.S. #1 R&B 45	"Low Rider"	War
U.K. #1 POP 45	"Space Oddity"	David Bowie
U.K. #1 POP LP	*Forty Golden Greats*	Jim Reeves

WEEK ENDING NOVEMBER 15

U.S. #1 POP 45	"Island Girl"	Elton John
U.S. #1 POP LP	*Rock of the Westies*	Elton John
U.S. #1 R&B 45	"Fly, Robin, Fly"	Silver Convention
U.K. #1 POP 45	"D.I.V.O.R.C.E."	Billy Connolly
U.K. #1 POP LP	*Forty Golden Greats*	Jim Reeves

WEEK ENDING NOVEMBER 22

U.S. #1 POP 45	"That's the Way (I Like It)"	K. C. and the Sunshine Band
U.S. #1 POP LP	*Rock of the Westies*	Elton John
U.S. #1 R&B 45	"Let's Do It Again"	The Staple Singers
U.K. #1 POP 45	"You Sexy Thing"	Hot Chocolate
U.K. #1 POP LP	*Forty Golden Greats*	Jim Reeves

WEEK ENDING NOVEMBER 29

U.S. #1 POP 45	"Fly, Robin, Fly"	Silver Convention
U.S. #1 POP LP	*Rock of the Westies*	Elton John
U.S. #1 R&B 45	"That's The Way (I Like It)"	K. C. and the Sunshine Band
U.K. #1 POP 45	"Bohemian Rhapsody"	Queen
U.K. #1 POP LP	*Forty Golden Greats*	Jim Reeves

2 Disco group **Silver Convention** earn a gold record for "Fly, Robin, Fly," which hit Number One on the pop chart for three weeks starting November 29. Along with **Donna Summer**'s "Love to Love You Baby," a big hit earlier in the year, "Fly, Robin, Fly" is the first in a series of disco triumphs by producers/arrangers **Giorgio Moroder** and **Pete Bellotte**, better known as "The Munich Machine," because they work in Munich, Germany, and because their productions invariably revolve around metronomic, machinelike pulses played on electronic sequencers and rhythm machines.

4 *Alive!*, the fifth album by what has by now become America's most popular rock band—those comic-book crazies of heavy-metal glitter rock, **Kiss**—goes gold, as has every one of the band's other albums.

5 **Fleetwood Mac**'s eponymously titled tenth album goes gold and is on its way to a platinum citation as well. This is the first album by the reconstituted band—including founders **Mick Fleetwood** and **John McVie**, veteran **Christine McVie** and newcomers **Stevie Nicks** and **Lindsey Buckingham**—that, having started as blues rockers, now purveys a slick brand of California pop. This album contains the hit singles "Rhiannon," "Say You Love Me" and "Over My Head," and initiates a remarkably consistent hitmaking streak that will establish the band as one of the most popular and successful in the world.

Gratitude, a double album by funk-fusion band **Earth, Wind and Fire** (half of the album is live, the other half studio), becomes their fifth album to go gold.

6 Soul singer **Tyrone Davis** (of "If I Could Turn Back the Hands of Time" fame) enters the R&B chart with "Turning Point," which—though it will never enter the pop chart—will hit Number One in early 1976.

8 A Night of the Hurricane benefit show at Madison Square Garden brings the Rolling Thunder Revue to a climax. In addition to **Bob Dylan** and his comrades, **Muhammad Ali**, **Roberta Flack**, **Coretta King** and assorted celebrities all show up. The highlight of the evening comes when a phone call from "Hurricane" Carter reaches the Garden stage. The show raises $100,000 toward legal fees for Carter and alleged accomplice **John Artis**.

10 *The Who by Numbers*, which contains minor hit singles in "Squeeze Box" and "Slip Kid," earns the **Who** another gold record.

16 British teen idols the **Bay City Rollers** garner their first U.S. gold record for their first U.S. hit single, "Saturday Night," which will reach Number One on the pop chart in early 1976. On December 31, the album *Bay City Rollers* will also go gold. They will go on to have five more Top Forty hits in the U.S.—nothing to sneeze at, but no match for their string of British hits.

17 Chicago bluesman **Theodore "Hound Dog" Taylor**, 59, dies in Chicago's Cook County Hospital, of

lung cancer. Hound Dog, who remained spry until near the time of his death, enjoyed fame only recently with his group, the **Houserockers**, whose specialty was the type of bar-band blues boogie that dominated the city's South Side scene.

19 **C. W. McCall** earns a gold record for his novelty hit "Convoy," which will hit Number One on the pop chart in early 1976. The song, a saga of interstate truck drivers and their run-ins with the law, makes extensive use of—and helps popularize—the vernacular of citizens' band radio.

20 Guitarist **Joe Walsh** joins forces with the **Eagles**, replacing original member **Bernie Leadon**, who leaves for a solo career.

28 **Ted Nugent**, known for gun-toting hunting forays in his native Michigan, ends up looking at the wrong end of the barrel at a show in Spokane, Washington. Twenty-five-year-old **David Gelfer** points a .44 magnum at the Motor City musician but is wrestled to the ground by members of the audience and security guards. He is charged later with "intimidating with a weapon." ◆

WEEK ENDING DECEMBER 6

U.S. #1 POP 45	"That's the Way (I Like It)"	K. C. and the Sunshine Band
U.S. #1 POP LP	*Still Crazy after All These Years*	Paul Simon
U.S. #1 R&B 45	"I Love Music (Part One)"	The O'Jays
U.K. #1 POP 45	"Bohemian Rhapsody"	Queen
U.K. #1 POP LP	*Forty Golden Greats*	Jim Reeves

WEEK ENDING DECEMBER 13

U.S. #1 POP 45	"Fly, Robin, Fly"	Silver Convention
U.S. #1 POP LP	*Chicago IX—Chicago's Greatest Hits*	Chicago
U.S. #1 R&B 45	"I Love Music (Part One)"	The O'Jays
U.K. #1 POP 45	"Bohemian Rhapsody"	Queen
U.K. #1 POP LP	*Forty Golden Greats*	Jim Reeves

WEEK ENDING DECEMBER 20

U.S. #1 POP 45	"Fly, Robin, Fly"	Silver Convention
U.S. #1 POP LP	*Chicago IX—Chicago's Greatest Hits*	Chicago
U.S. #1 R&B 45	"Full of Fire"	Al Green
U.K. #1 POP 45	"Bohemian Rhapsody"	Queen
U.K. #1 POP LP	*Forty Golden Greats*	Jim Reeves

WEEK ENDING DECEMBER 27

U.S. #1 POP 45	"Let's Do It Again"	The Staple Singers
U.S. #1 POP LP	*Chicago IX—Chicago's Greatest Hits*	Chicago
U.S. #1 R&B 45	"Love Rollercoaster"	The Ohio Players
U.K. #1 POP 45	"Bohemian Rhapsody"	Queen
U.K. #1 POP LP	*A Night at the Opera*	Queen

1976

By this year, the audience for popular music had grown so vast that the Recording Industry Association of America was forced to update its standards of citation for top-selling records by inaugurating the platinum disc. Gold records were no longer indicative of the multimillion-unit sales of truly popular records.

But the pop-music audience was still as fragmented as it was vast, ranging from disco dancers to heavy-metal head bangers, from peaceful easy-listening country-rockers to virtuosity-conscious jazz-rock fusion buffs, with all kinds of sub-groups in between. Thus, the first platinum album went to the Eagles' *Greatest Hits* album in February (slick country-pop-rock), and in April the first platinum single went to Johnnie Taylor for the self-descriptive "Disco Lady."

Disco may have had more hits than any other subgenre this year—there were the Andrea True Connection's "More More More (How Do You Like It?)," K C and the Sunshine Band's "Shake Your Booty," Walter Murphy and the Big Apple Band's "A Fifth of Beethoven," Abba's "Dancing Queen" and a host of others. But just about every other commercially viable subgenre had its share of success, too. Heavy metal still sold well to its audience: Kiss were now big enough stars to implant their platform-boot prints on Hollywood's "Walk of Fame" outside Grauman's Chinese Theater.

But it was disco that most consistently ruled the top of the pop heap. By this time it was so bankable that even such an out-and-out inane novelty as "Disco Duck" by Rick Dees and His Cast of Idiots could go platinum. The title alone of Wild Cherry's Number One disco smash, "Play That Funky Music," served notice that, no matter what conservative white-rock traditionalists may have thought, disco's appeal went far beyond the inner-city ethnic audience. Disco also wielded considerable influence on a number of popular subgenres—mainly those related to jazz and its audience's fascination with instrumental virtuosity. Respected veteran jazz guitarist George Benson embarked on a whole new career by wedding jazzy balladry to a muted disco backbeat on *Breezin',* which went on to become one of the best-selling "jazz" albums in history. Jazz-rock fusion now became jazz-funk fusion, as disco-inflected rhythms supported the genre's technically involved solos and high-speed riffs. Even a noted veteran hard-rock guitarist like Jeff Beck rode the funk-fusion groove with his gold LP *Wired* (which was in the same funky instrumental vein as his *Blow by Blow,* a success of a few years before). That jazziest of pop-rock bands, Steely Dan, went gold with *The Royal Scam,* arguably their most funk-inflected album to date. There was even a *rapprochement* of sorts between disco slickness and California pop-rock slickness in Boz Scaggs' enormously successful *Silk Degrees.* The game was obvious: take any kind of reasonably popular style, inflect it with disco and/or funk rhythms and trappings (like, say, the slick strings, horns and female backup singers of *Silk Degrees*) and chances were it'd be even *more* successful.

At any rate, this year another ethnically rooted dance-music mutation began to seep its way more strongly into the consciousness of the pop audience—reggae. Bob Marley and the Wailers had their first American hit with "Roots Rock Reggae," and the Rolling Stones included an old reggae song, "Cherry-O Baby," on their *Black and Blue* LP. While the Ramones released their debut album to a small but devoted U.S. cult, punk rock began to take off seriously in England, with the Damned, the Clash and others following rapidly in the wake of the Sex Pistols, who made their first well-attended public appearance this summer. Punk poet Patti Smith toured the U.K. as well, helping inspire such future British punk girl groups as the Slits. Soon, the political and adversarial bonds between punk and reggae would become apparent; as always in postrock pop music, a vital underdog response was being fomented in reaction to what was currently established and successful. Whether or not it would effect a successful revolution remained to be seen.

4 **Mal Evans**, former roadie and bodyguard of the **Beatles**, is shot to death by police at his Los Angeles apartment. His girlfriend, Fran Hughes, had found him upset, despondent and crying. After two friends were unable to take an unloaded rifle from Evans, they called the police. When officers arrived at the apartment, Evans had the rifle in his hand. Instructed to put the weapon down, Evans then supposedly pointed it at the policemen; they opened fire and killed him with four shots. At the time of his death, Evans had been finishing up, *Living the Beatles Legend,* a memoir dealing with his Beatles days. He was forty.

7 **Kenneth Moss**, former record company executive who had already pleaded guilty to involuntary man-slaughter in the 1974 drug-induced death of **Average White Band** drummer **Robbie McIntosh**, is sentenced to 120 days in the Los Angeles County Jail and four years probation for the crime.

10 **Chester Arthur Burnett**, better known by his performing name, **Howlin' Wolf**, dies at age sixty-five after brain surgery in a veteran's hospital near Chicago, the city where he made his greatest recordings for Chess Records. The Wolf's enormous size and over-whelming vocal style command-ed the greatest respect from other blues musicians, especial-ly Britons like guitarist **Eric Clapton** and the **Rolling Stones**, who accompanied him on one of the few successful collaborations between the gen-erations, 1971's *The London Howlin' Wolf Sessions.*

13 The trial of seven Brunswick Records and Dakar Records employees on charges of bilking artists out of more than $184,000 in royalties begins in Newark, New Jersey. The charges had been brought during a federal investigation of the record industry for possible instances of payola.

16 The two-record live set *Frampton Comes Alive!* is released and exceeds all sales expectations, going gold in five weeks and platinum in less than three months, while topping the charts for over two months. The unexpected boost to the former Face of 1968's career proved to be his greatest moment, as he never again came close to the acclaim accorded him for the album.

19 Promoter **Bill Sargent** makes his first offer to the **Beatles** to reunite, offering them $30 million if they would play together again. He guaran-tees the four that sum against a percentage of the gross, which he estimates at $300 million.

25 **Bob Dylan and his Rolling Thunder Re-vue**, **Isacc Hayes** and **Stevie Wonder** entertain 40,000 peo-ple at the Night of the Hurricane II, a benefit show given for **Hurricane Carter**. Surprise guests include **Ringo Starr**, **Stephen Stills** and **Carlos San-tana**; the latter two fought out a guitar duel during "Black Queen." But despite the $12.50 tickets, confusion over the show's intent and the costs in-curred when the show was shifted from New Orleans to Houston just a week before, the Hurricane defense fund re-ceived no money except a $10,000 donation directly from the Astrodome.

27 A $2-million suit is brought against attor-ney **Michael Lippman** by his former client **David Bowie**. Bowie charges that Lippman took a fifteen percent agent's fee instead of the customary ten percent, and that he withheld $475,000 after being dismissed by Bowie.

30 Texas "songster" **Mance Lipscomb** dies of natural causes at age eighty in his Navasota, Texas, home. Popularly thought of as a coun-try bluesman, Lipscomb used the term *songster* to describe himself and to differentiate him-self from bluesmen, and with good reason: he was more of a minstrel than anything else, and played not only blues but bal-lads, reels, jigs, breakdowns, drags, shouts, jubilees, spirituals and more. In fact, perhaps no other single performer em-bodied as many aspects of the Afro-American folk-music tradi-tion as Lipscomb. He performed locally in Texas all his life, but did not record until 1960, when he was discovered by **Chris Strachwitz** of the Arhoolie label, for whom he recorded several well-received albums. ◆

WEEK ENDING JANUARY 3

U.S. #1 POP 45	"Saturday Night"	The Bay City Rollers
U.S. #1 POP LP	*Chicago IX—Chicago's Greatest Hits*	Chicago
U.S. #1 R&B 45	"Walk Away from Love"	David Ruffin
U.K. #1 POP 45	"Bohemian Rhapsody"	Queen
U.K. #1 POP LP	*A Night at the Opera*	Queen

WEEK ENDING JANUARY 10

U.S. #1 POP 45	"Convoy"	C.W. McCall
U.S. #1 POP LP	*Chicago IX—Chicago's Greatest Hits*	Chicago
U.S. #1 R&B 45	"Sing a Song"	Earth, Wind and Fire
U.K. #1 POP 45	"Bohemian Rhapsody"	Queen
U.K. #1 POP LP	*A Night at the Opera*	Queen

WEEK ENDING JANUARY 17

U.S. #1 POP 45	"I Write the Songs"	Barry Manilow
U.S. #1 POP LP	*Gratitude*	Earth, Wind and Fire
U.S. #1 R&B 45	"Wake Up Everybody (Part 1)"	Harold Melvin and the Blue Notes
U.K. #1 POP 45	"Bohemian Rhapsody"	Queen
U.K. #1 POP LP	*A Night at the Opera*	Queen

WEEK ENDING JANUARY 24

U.S. #1 POP 45	"Mahogany (Do You Know Where You're Going To)"	Diana Ross
U.S. #1 POP LP	*Gratitude*	Earth, Wind and Fire
U.S. #1 R&B 45	"Wake Up Everybody (Part 1)"	Harold Melvin and the Blue Notes
U.K. #1 POP 45	"Glass of Champagne"	Sailor
U.K. #1 POP LP	*A Night at the Opera*	Queen

WEEK ENDING JANUARY 31

U.S. #1 POP 45	"Love Rollercoaster"	The Ohio Players
U.S. #1 POP LP	*Gratitude*	Earth, Wind and Fire
U.S. #1 R&B 45	"Wake Up Everybody (Part 1)"	Harold Melvin and the Blue Notes
U.K. #1 POP 45	"Mama Mia"	Abba
U.K. #1 POP LP	*A Night at the Opera*	Queen

3 **David Bowie** begins his first U.S tour in over a year in Seattle, Washington. Guitarist **Earl Slick** has replaced **Mick Ronson**, and Bowie has shelved the white soul persona for a character he calls the Thin White Duke.

7 *Wanted! The Outlaws* enters the charts. By the end of the year, the album, which features such nontraditional country, or "outlaw," performers as **Waylon Jennings**, **Willie Nelson**, **Tompall Glaser** and **Jessi Colter**, will hit #10 on the pop chart, Number One on the country, and be certified platinum. In addition, the stars, especially Jennings and Nelson, will emerge as the leaders of the latest and, as it turns out, an enduring, country style.

14 "More More More (Part 1)" by the **Andrea True Connection** enters the pop chart. The disco smash, sung by ex-porno film star **Andrea True**, will go on to reach #4 on the pop chart and will be certified gold in September. True will go on to score some more minor hits over the next two years, all in the same

sexy-disco vein, the biggest being "N.Y., You Got Me Dancing," which will hit #27 in April 1977.

17 Harvard University's Hasty Pudding theatrical society gives its annual "Woman of the Year" award to flash-and-trash chanteuse **Bette Midler**. Upon accepting, the divine Miss M comments: "This award characterizes what the American male wants in a woman—brains, talent and gorgeous tits."

19 **Donna Summer**'s first disco hit, "Love to Love You Baby," which reached #2 on the pop chart earlier this year, is certified gold. The song—which featured Summer not only cooing the title phrase, but moaning her way through what most listeners agreed sounded like seven noisy orgasms—was the first of a long string of disco and rock hits for Summer that would continue into the Eighties.

One-time lead singer for **Tower of Power**, **Rich Stevens**, is arrested and charged in the murders the night before of three men in the San Jose, Cali-

fornia, area. Police hint that drug dealings were the motivation in the slayings. Stevens and an accomplice are found guilty on two counts of murder in November; a third defendant is acquitted.

20 **Kiss**' arrival at the pinnacle of their American stardom is noted with the placing of their footprints on the sidewalk outside Hollywood's Grauman's Chinese Theater.

New York District Court Judge **Thomas Griesa** rules that a verbal agreement between **John Lennon** and **Roulette Records** president **Morris Levy** to put out an album of Lennon-performed rock & roll

oldies was invalid because of Lennon's previous commitment to Capitol Records. Levy had sued Lennon for $42 million after being forced to halt production of the TV-marketed record called *Roots,* consisting of rough takes of some of Lennon's studio work, much of which ended up on the 1975 *Rock 'N' Roll* LP.

22 Former **Supreme Florence Ballard** dies of coronary thrombosis in Detroit at age thirty-two. Despite being an original member of the premiere female vocal trio (they had ten Number One pop hits in the Sixties), she had lived on welfare for the few years preceding her death after losing an $8.7-million suit for back royalties against Motown Records in 1971.

24 *The Eagles—Their Greatest Hits* becomes the first album in history to be certified platinum by the R.I.A.A. This new certification represents sales of at least 1 million copies for albums and 2 million copies for singles. The platinum award was conceived because early-Seventies record sales were so high that most popular recordings surpassed the gold mark (500,000 copies for LPs, 1 million copies for singles) in a short period of time. As a result, the gold record award was considered, if not meaningless, then certainly not the accomplishment it had been years before. Platinum certifications would rise and peak by the late Seventies and drop slightly as record sales declined in the early Eighties. ◆

WEEK ENDING FEBRUARY 7

U.S. #1 POP 45	"50 Ways to Leave Your Lover"	Paul Simon
U.S. #1 POP LP	*Desire*	Bob Dylan
U.S. #1 R&B 45	"Turning Point"	Tyrone Davis
U.K. #1 POP 45	"Mama Mia"	Abba
U.K. #1 POP LP	*How Dare You*	10cc

WEEK ENDING FEBRUARY 14

U.S. #1 POP 45	"50 Ways to Leave Your Lover"	Paul Simon
U.S. #1 POP LP	*Desire*	Bob Dylan
U.S. #1 R&B 45	"Inseparable"	Natalie Cole
U.K. #1 POP 45	"Forever and Ever"	Slik
U.K. #1 POP LP	*Desire*	Bob Dylan

WEEK ENDING FEBRUARY 21

U.S. #1 POP 45	"50 Ways to Leave Your Lover"	Paul Simon
U.S. #1 POP LP	*Desire*	Bob Dylan
U.S. #1 R&B 45	"Sweet Thing"	Rufus featuring Chaka Khan
U.K. #1 POP 45	"December, 1963 (Oh, What a Night)"	The Four Seasons
U.K. #1 POP LP	*Desire*	Bob Dylan

WEEK ENDING FEBRUARY 28

U.S. #1 POP 45	"Theme from S.W.A.T."	Rhythm Heritage
U.S. #1 POP LP	*Desire*	Bob Dylan
U.S. #1 R&B 45	"Sweet Thing"	Rufus featuring Chaka Khan
U.K. #1 POP 45	"December, 1963 (Oh, What a Night)"	The Four Seasons
U.K. #1 POP LP	*Desire*	Bob Dylan

6 Britain's EMI Records rereleases all twenty-two British **Beatles** singles and adds a bonus when it also puts out "Yesterday," never before a 45 in the U.K. All twenty-three records hit the chart at the same time.

7 A likeness of **Elton John** is put on display at London's Madame Tussaud's Wax Museum. He is the first rock figure so accorded the honor since the **Beatles** were first immortalized in wax in March of 1964.

9 British heavy-metal/glitter-rock band **Queen**'s breakthrough album, *A Night at the Opera,* is certified gold. Long popular in Britain, the group's three previous albums had made little impact in the U.S. But *Opera* broke big, thanks mainly to its surprise hit single, the six-minute-long "Bohemian Rhapsody."

The start of the second leg of the **Who**'s U.S. tour following their *By Numbers* album is delayed when **Keith Moon** collapses onstage at the Boston Garden ten minutes into the show. The performance is immediately rescheduled for April, and the following night's show at New York's Madison Square Garden is pushed back an extra day.

13 Philadelphia soul vocal trio the **O'Jays** enter the charts with the double-sided hit "Livin' for the Weekend" backed with "Stairway to Heaven" (*not* to be confused with the **Led Zeppelin** classic), which will go on to become one of the three R&B Number One hits for the group this year. The other two are "Message in Our Music" and "Darlin' Darlin' Baby."

Singer/songwriter **Laura Nyro**'s seventh album, *Smile,* enters the chart. Although it will only go as high as #60, the album generates a great deal of interest and some critical acclaim. It is Nyro's first LP since her collaboration with **Labelle**, *Gonna Take a Miracle,* in 1972.

14 Jazz singer **Flora Purim** begins her first tour since being released from jail in December 1975, having served sixteen months for pos-session of cocaine. She chooses to make her first performance at the Long Beach, California, Terminal Island prison where she had served her sentence.

19 Former **Free** guitarist and **Back Street Crawler** leader **Paul Kossoff** dies on a London-to-New York plane flight, of unknown causes. The twenty-six-year-old Briton's death was not wholly unexpected; in August of the previous year his heart had stopped beating for thirty-five minutes during surgery, and he had been plagued by heart disease most of his life.

20 **Boz Scaggs**' biggest album of his career, *Silk Degrees,* debuts on the chart. Although it is Scaggs' seventh solo LP, it will be the first to go platinum, largely on the strength of the #3 pop and #5 R&B smash single "Low Down." In the next four months, Scaggs' second solo album, *Boz Scaggs,* which was produced in 1969 by *Rolling Stone* publisher **Jann Wenner**, will also return to the chart. Several of the musicians on *Silk Degrees* will also appear on Scaggs' followup, *Down Two Then Left,* before coming into their own as **Toto**.

22 Presidential candidate **Jimmy Carter** tells the audience at the National Association of Record Merchandisers' Scholarship Foundation Dinner that **Bob Dylan**, the **Grateful Dead**, **Led Zeppelin** and other bands had inspired him while working late nights when he was governor of Georgia. To prove that he would never lie to them, he quoted lines from the **Beatles**' "Yesterday" and **Dylan**'s "Blowin' in the Wind."

24 The charge of assault filed by the **Dictators**' lead singer **Handsome Dick Manitoba** against transvestite rocker **Wayne County** is reduced to a misdemeanor by a New York court. The case stems from an incident at CBGB a few weeks earlier, when County responds to Manitoba's epithets by smashing him with a mike stand, fracturing his collarbone.

26 **Wings** guitarist **Jimmy McCulloch** breaks a finger after slipping in his hotel bathroom after the last show of the band's European tour, in Paris. The injury pushed back by three weeks the start of **Paul McCartney**'s first shows in the United States in a decade.

28 **Genesis** begins its first North American tour since **Peter Gabriel** left the previous year, in Buffalo, New York. Drummer **Phil Collins** has taken the lead singing chores, while still handling some drumming duties along with veteran **Bill Bruford**, recruited especially for the tour.

29 "December, 1963 (Oh, What a Night)," the Four Seasons' first Number One hit since "Rag Doll" in 1964, is certified gold.

30 The seminal British punk group the **Sex Pistols** play their first show at London's 100 Club, attracting only a reported fifty people to the venue where they would begin a weekly residency in June. ◆

WEEK ENDING MARCH 6

U.S. #1 POP 45	"Love Machine (Part 1)"	The Miracles
U.S. #1 POP LP	*Desire*	Bob Dylan
U.S. #1 R&B 45	"Boogie Fever"	The Sylvers
U.K. #1 POP 45	"I Love to Love"	Tina Charles
U.K. #1 POP LP	*The Very Best of Slim Whitman*	Slim Whitman

WEEK ENDING MARCH 13

U.S. #1 POP 45	"December, 1963 (Oh, What a Night)"	The Four Seasons
U.S. #1 POP LP	*Their Greatest Hits 1971–1975*	The Eagles
U.S. #1 R&B 45	"Disco Lady"	Johnnie Taylor
U.K. #1 POP 45	"I Love to Love"	Tina Charles
U.K. #1 POP LP	*The Very Best of Slim Whitman*	Slim Whitman

WEEK ENDING MARCH 20

U.S. #1 POP 45	"December, 1963 (Oh, What a Night)"	The Four Seasons
U.S. #1 POP LP	*Their Greatest Hits 1971–1975*	The Eagles
U.S. #1 R&B 45	"Disco Lady"	Johnnie Taylor
U.K. #1 POP 45	"I Love to Love"	Tina Charles
U.K. #1 POP LP	*Desire*	Bob Dylan

WEEK ENDING MARCH 27

U.S. #1 POP 45	"December, 1963 (Oh What a Night)"	The Four Seasons
U.S. #1 POP LP	*Their Greatest Hits 1971–1975*	The Eagles
U.S. #1 R&B 45	"Disco Lady"	Johnnie Taylor
U.K. #1 POP 45	"Save All Your Kisses for Me"	Brotherhood of Man
U.K. #1 POP LP	*Blue for You*	Status Quo

1 Paul McCartney and Wings' "Silly Love Songs" is released from the *Wings at the Speed of Sound* album. Coming out just prior to the band's first U.S. tour, the single is as welcomed by the record-buying public as it is reviled by critics.

9 Thirty-five-year-old Phil Ochs hangs himself at his sister's home in the New York borough of Queens. The Texas-born folk singer, who had stuck to protest in the mid-Sixties while Bob Dylan turned toward rock & roll, reportedly had been despondent for some time; recent attempts to regain the edge of his early music had failed. His last appearance with the old coterie of folk stars was at the October 1975 birthday celebration for Mike Porco, owner of the Greenwich Village club Folk City. Among Ochs' best known songs are "I Ain't Marchin'," "Draft Dodger Rag," "There but for Fortune," "Outside of a Small Circle of Friends" and "The Party." Among the last songs he released was entitled "Here's to the State of Richard Nixon."

14 Motown Records and Stevie Wonder hold a joint press conference to announce that he has signed a "$13 million-plus" contract with the label, which many of its acts have abandoned in recent years. This is the first time that Wonder, still mixing his *Songs in the Key of Life* LP, has confirmed having put his name on the agreement, which Motown had first announced the previous August.

Bay City Rollers singer Eric Faulkner almost dies after swallowing Seconal and Valium tablets at manager Tam Paton's house in Edinburgh, Scotland. The twenty-one-year-old Roller, after recovering, admitted to being very tired from the group's grueling schedule.

16 Boz Scaggs is cold-cocked by two bouncers outside the Austin, Texas, blues club Antone's, after attempting to go backstage to see headliner Bobby "Blue" Bland. The altercation began when Scaggs was refused admittance to the dressing room, despite claiming an in-

vitation from a member of Bland's retinue.

17 Veteran jazz guitarist George Benson's album *Breezin'* enters the album chart. It will go on to become one of the best-selling jazz albums of all time, thanks largely to its million-selling title track, which will reach #63 on the pop chart later this year. The album will go gold on June 4 and platinum on August 10.

Jailbreak, Irish rockers Thin Lizzy's most successful American release, enters the chart. It will later peak at #18 on the strength of their #12 gold single "The Boys Are Back in Town."

20 The Rolling Stones' *Black and Blue* album is released and, despite luke-warm critical reaction and feminist protest of an ad campaign that featured a photograph of a bound and bruised model reaches Number One and goes platinum within two months.

21 Ex-Raspberries lead singer Eric Carmen enters the pop chart with what will become his first and biggest solo hit, "All by Myself," which will peak at #2. Over the next two years, Carmen will have three more Top Thirty singles: "Never Gonna Fall in Love Again," later this year; "She Did It," in 1977; and "Change of Heart," in 1978.

22 Bob Dylan and his Rolling Thunder Revue tape a show at the Belleview Biltmore Hotel in Clearwater, Florida, to be shown on television in the fall. The program, directed by "Midnight Special" producer Stan Harris, was auctioned off to NBC after being offered to all three networks, but Dylan then scrapped the footage anyway in favor of a later show, taped in Fort Collins, Colorado, and titled *Hard Rain.*

Soul singer Johnnie Taylor's "Disco Lady" becomes the first single ever to be certified platinum, signifying sales of over two million copies. Taylor is known for another risqué hit, 1968's "Who's Makin' Love."

28 The Rolling Stones begin a two-month European tour at the Festhalle in Frankfurt, Germany. The concert marks their first appearance on the Continent in three years.

29 After playing in Memphis during a Southern tour, Bruce Springsteen jumps the fence at Graceland in an attempt to see his idol Elvis Presley. Rebuffed by security guards, the Boss vainly tries to gain entrance by mentioning his simultaneous appearances on the covers of both *Time* and *Newsweek*. They are not impressed; Springsteen is escorted off the grounds. ◆

WEEK ENDING APRIL 3

U.S. #1 POP 45	"Disco Lady"	Johnnie Taylor
U.S. #1 POP LP	*Their Greatest Hits 1971–1975*	The Eagles
U.S. #1 R&B 45	"Disco Lady"	Johnnie Taylor
U.K. #1 POP 45	"Save All Your Kisses for Me"	Brotherhood of Man
U.K. #1 POP LP	*Blue for You*	Status Quo

WEEK ENDING APRIL 10

U.S. #1 POP 45	"Disco Lady"	Johnnie Taylor
U.S. #1 POP LP	*Frampton Comes Alive!*	Peter Frampton
U.S. #1 R&B 45	"Disco Lady"	Johnnie Taylor
U.K. #1 POP 45	"Save All Your Kisses for Me"	Brotherhood of Man
U.K. #1 POP LP	*Their Greatest Hits 1971–1975*	The Eagles

WEEK ENDING APRIL 17

U.S. #1 POP 45	"Disco Lady"	Johnnie Taylor
U.S. #1 POP LP	*Their Greatest Hits 1971–1975*	The Eagles
U.S. #1 R&B 45	"Disco Lady"	Johnnie Taylor
U.K. #1 POP 45	"Save All Your Kisses for Me"	Brotherhood of Man
U.K. #1 POP LP	*Rock Follies*	soundtrack

WEEK ENDING APRIL 24

U.S. #1 POP 45	"Disco Lady"	Johnnie Taylor
U.S. #1 POP LP	*Wings at the Speed of Sound*	Wings
U.S. #1 R&B 45	"Livin' for the Weekend"	The O'Jays
U.K. #1 POP 45	"Save All Your Kisses for Me"	Brotherhood of Man
U.K. #1 POP LP	*Rock Follies*	soundtrack

MAY 1976

3 **Paul McCartney** makes his first concert appearance in America in almost ten years as he and **Wings** commence their Wings over America tour in Fort Worth, Texas, three weeks after its scheduled start. A hand injury to guitarist **Jimmy McCulloch** on the last date of their March European tour had forced the postponement of the earlier shows.

Paul Simon organizes a benefit show at Madison Square Garden for the financially troubled New York Public Library. **Phoebe Snow**, **Jimmy Cliff** and the **Brecker Brothers** pitch in for the concert, which nets over $30,000 for the institution.

8 **Bob Dylan** and entourage return to Houston, the city where the less than triumphant Benefit II for Rubin

"Hurricane" Carter had been held just five months earlier. For the show, Dylan requests that **Willie Nelson** and company join him, and the two sing "Will the Circle Be Unbroken." Backstage, Nelson is slapped with a subpoena for an upcoming grand jury investigation centering on drug trafficking.

12 *Look Out for #1*, the **Brothers** (George and Louis) **Johnson**'s debut LP, is certified gold. The album features two Top Ten soul hits—"I'll Be Good to You" and "Get the Funk out of My Face"—and is produced by **Quincy Jones**. Three months later, the album will go platinum.

13 *Bitches Brew*, jazz trumpeter **Miles Davis**' 1969 jazz-fusion landmark LP, is certified gold. Among the musicians appearing on the double album are **Chick Corea**, **Larry Young**, **John McLaughlin**, **Wayne Shorter**, **Lenny White**, **Joe Zawinul** and **Jack De Johnette**. The recording sessions, which were held with neither rehearsals nor charts, set the tenor for the use of electrified instruments and free-form improvisation utilizing rock rhythms in jazz.

14 Former **Yardbirds** lead singer and co-founder of **Renaissance Keith Relf** is electrocuted in his West London home. The thirty-three-year-old musician, working again with his sister Jane and hopeful of some summer touring, was found alongside a plugged-in electric guitar by his eight-year-old son and was pronounced dead on arrival at a local hospital.

16 A New York company known as AB&D Productions takes out an ad in the *New York Times* to announce a spectacular four-day Bicentennial event at Philadelphia's 100,000-seat JFK Stadium. Acts scheduled to play include the **Band**, **Chicago**, the **Ohio Players**, **Ike and Tina Turner**, the **Beach Boys**, **Lynyrd Skynyrd**, **Maxine Nightingale**, **Elvin Bishop** and **Rufus**. The planned gala event never takes place, as within two weeks all acts cancel or maintain that no contracts had ever been signed.

19 **Rolling Stone Keith Richards** crashes his Bentley into a highway divider in Newton Pagnell, a town fifty miles north of London. Police confiscate various substances from his car, and Richards is charged in August with possession of cocaine and marijuana.

21 **Aerosmith** receives a gold LP for *Rocks*. The album will eventually go to #3 on the album chart and will prove to be their last big hit. By the time their next LP, *Draw the Line*, is released, the group that was once touted as America's answer to the **Rolling Stones** will have fallen from popular favor.

The **Rolling Stones** open a six-night stand at London's Earl's Court Theatre. The seeming indifference of the Stones' performances results in their being among the first bands targeted as "dinosaurs" by the burgeoning British punk movement.

24 Arista Records president **Clive Davis** pleads guilty in New York to a charge of failing to report $8,800 of income in 1972. The money had been given to him for nonbusiness vacations by CBS Records during his tenure as president there. A greater charge of not reporting sums totalling $90,000 over three years was dismissed upon entering the plea. Davis is fined $10,000 in September for the offense.

31 The **Who** headline a bill at the Charlton Athletic Grounds in England and put their name into the *Guiness Book of World Records* as the loudest rock band ever, when their set measures at 120 decibels. ♦

WEEK ENDING MAY 1

U.S. #1 POP 45	"Let Your Love Flow"	The Bellamy Brothers
U.S. #1 POP LP	*Presence*	Led Zeppelin
U.S. #1 R&B 45	"Livin' for the Weekend"	The O'Jays
U.K. #1 POP 45	"Fernando"	Abba
U.K. #1 POP LP	*Rock Follies*	soundtrack

WEEK ENDING MAY 8

U.S. #1 POP 45	"Welcome Back"	John Sebastian
U.S. #1 POP LP	*Presence*	Led Zeppelin
U.S. #1 R&B 45	"Movin'"	Brass Construction
U.K. #1 POP 45	"Fernando"	Abba
U.K. #1 POP LP	*Rock Follies*	soundtrack

WEEK ENDING MAY 15

U.S. #1 POP 45	"Boogie Fever"	The Sylvers
U.S. #1 POP LP	*Black and Blue*	The Rolling Stones
U.S. #1 R&B 45	"Love Hangover"	Diana Ross
U.K. #1 POP 45	"Fernando"	Abba
U.K. #1 POP LP	*Abba's Greatest Hits*	Abba

WEEK ENDING MAY 22

U.S. #1 POP 45	"Silly Love Songs"	Wings
U.S. #1 POP LP	*Black and Blue*	The Rolling Stones
U.S. #1 R&B 45	"Kiss and Say Goodbye"	The Manhattans
U.K. #1 POP 45	"Fernando"	Abba
U.K. #1 POP LP	*Abba's Greatest Hits*	Abba

WEEK ENDING MAY 29

U.S. #1 POP 45	"Love Hangover"	Diana Ross
U.S. #1 POP LP	*Wings at the Speed of Sound*	Wings
U.S. #1 R&B 45	"I Want You"	Marvin Gaye
U.K. #1 POP 45	"Fernando"	Abba
U.K. #1 POP LP	*Abba's Greatest Hits*	Abba

5 The eponymous debut album by New York punk pioneers the **Ramones** enters the album chart. Like all their albums, it will be a bigger success with critics than record-buyers. Their British tour later this year will be a key catalyst of British punk rock.

7 Capitol does its best to revive Beatlemania by issuing some of the Fab Four's rockers in a package named *Rock 'N' Roll Music* (timed to fit in after the **Wings** U.S. tour and the expiration of all agreements between Capitol and Apple Records earlier in the year). Despite a dubious selection process and jacket art so garish and misleading that it draws public condemnation from **Ringo Starr**, the album reaches #2.

Funk band the **Ohio Players'** twelfth album, *Contradiction*, goes gold. It includes their most recent hits, "Fopp" (#30, a month ago) and "Rattlesnake" (#90, two months ago).

11 San Francisco Latin-rock-fusion band **Santana**'s ninth album, *Amigos*, which includes their current, albeit minor, hit "Let It Shine" (which peaked at #77 on the pop chart a few weeks ago), goes gold.

14 Some six years after their breakup, the **Beatles** garner another gold album for the *Rock 'N' Roll Music* anthology.

18 After thirteen years of watching many of his contemporaries prosper, **Phil May**, last original member left in the **Pretty Things**, quits the band. Despite starting out alongside the **Rolling Stones** and gaining a reputation in the earlier days for their raw energy and later for conceiving the first rock opera, *S. F. Sorrow*, he and the Things had never made it in the States.

Six years after its release, the album *Twelve Dreams of Dr. Sardonicus*, by California rock band **Spirit**, goes gold.

Olé ELO, a greatest-hits collection by British chamber-pop band **Electric Light Orchestra**—who mate pop-rock to the cello-driven Beatles sound of tunes like "I Am the Walrus" and "Eleanor Rigby"—goes gold. Up to this time, the band has had six Top 100 hits, the biggest being "Can't Get It Out of My Head" (#9, 1975), "Evil Woman" (#10, early 1976), "Strange Magic (#14, this month) and their version of **Chuck Berry**'s "Roll Over Beethoven" (#42, 1973). The group is led by ex-**Move** singer/guitarist **Jeff Lynne**.

19 Reggae stars **Bob Marley and the Wailers** enter the pop chart with what will become their first U.S. hit, "Roots Rock Reggae," which will peak at #37.

REO Speedwagon's sixth album, *R.E.O.*, enters the album chart. Though it will barely scrape the bottom of the chart in its brief time there, it marks the return of original vocalist **Kevin Cronin**, who will help lead the working-class pop-rock band to their first gold record with their next release, *Live: You Get What You Play for*. But it will be four more years until the band's most successful LP, *Hi-Infidelity*, becomes the biggest-selling album of 1980, taking the anonymous, hard-

working band to the platinum echelon.

Heavy-metal band **Blue Oyster Cult** enters the album chart with what will become its commercial breakthrough LP, *Agents of Fortune*, which will reach #29 on the LP chart and go gold on October 26, 1976, largely due to its hit single—the band's only chart entry so far—"(Don't Fear) the Reaper," which will reach #12 later in the year.

21 Horn-dominated rock band **Chicago**, formerly known as the **Chicago Transit Authority**, earn another gold record for the album *Chicago X*, which contains their two latest hits, "If You Leave Me Now" (their biggest hit, it will reach Number One in October and will be on the pop chart for a total of twenty weeks) and "Another Rainy Day in New York City" (which will peak at #32 later this year).

29 Disco diva **Donna Summer**, whose biggest hit to date was "Love to Love You Baby" (#2, earlier this year), earns a gold album for *Love Trilogy*.

30 Police, supposedly responding to a report of burglars on the premises of **Neil Diamond**'s Holmby Hills, California, estate, enter the singer's house with a search warrant. A three-hour inspection yields a grand total of less than one ounce of marijuana; so low-key is the bust that Diamond gives several officers copies of his latest LP, *Beautiful Noise*. Diamond's debut the following evening at the new Alladin Theater for the Performing Arts in Las Vegas goes on as scheduled. ◆

WEEK ENDING JUNE 5

U.S. #1 POP 45	"Love Hangover"	Diana Ross
U.S. #1 POP LP	*Black and Blue*	The Rolling Stones
U.S. #1 R&B 45	"Young Hearts Run Free"	Candi Staton
U.K. #1 POP 45	"Fernando"	Abba
U.K. #1 POP LP	*Abba's Greatest Hits*	Abba

WEEK ENDING JUNE 12

U.S. #1 POP 45	"Silly Love Songs"	Wings
U.S. #1 POP LP	*Black and Blue*	The Rolling Stones
U.S. #1 R&B 45	"I'll Be Good to You"	The Brothers Johnson
U.K. #1 POP 45	"No Charge"	J. J. Barrie
U.K. #1 POP LP	*Abba's Greatest Hits*	Abba

WEEK ENDING JUNE 19

U.S. #1 POP 45	"Silly Love Songs"	Wings
U.S. #1 POP LP	*Wings at the Speed of Sound*	Wings
U.S. #1 R&B 45	"Sophisticated Lady"	Natalie Cole
U.K. #1 POP 45	"Silly Love Songs"	Wings
U.K. #1 POP LP	*Abba's Greatest Hits*	Abba

WEEK ENDING JUNE 26

U.S. #1 POP 45	"Silly Love Songs"	Wings
U.S. #1 POP LP	*Wings at the Speed of Sound*	Wings
U.S. #1 R&B 45	"Something He Can Feel"	Aretha Franklin
U.K. #1 POP 45	"You to Me Are Everything"	The Real Thing
U.K. #1 POP LP	*Abba's Greatest Hits*	Abba

2 For the first time in twelve years, **Brian Wilson** joins the **Beach Boys** onstage during a performance, at the Oakland Stadium. Although he sits virtually motionless at his piano throughout the show, Wilson does handle the lead vocal (sotto voce) on his "In My Room." Proving it to be no fluke, he returns the following night as well, and television cameras record the whole thing for a Beach Boys special due to air in August on NBC.

3 Veteran soul vocal group the **Manhattans** enter the pop chart with their biggest hit, "Kiss and Say Goodbye," which will quickly climb to Number One later this month and will stay on the pop chart for twenty-six weeks. It had reached Number One on the R&B chart in May.

4 Two American rock & roll bands celebrate the Bicentennial on foreign shores. The **Ramones** and the **Flamin' Groovies** play at London's Roundhouse and move Britain's nascent punk scene along by amply demonstrating the two styles, Sixties and Seventies, that predominate over the next two years in England.

6 The **Damned** warm up for the **Sex Pistols** at the latter's regular stint at London's 100 Club. It was the Damned's first real public appearance; both groups are destined to release punk's first singles by the end of the year.

Aretha Franklin's thirty-sixth album, *Sparkle,* earns her another gold record. It contains her two current hits, "Something He Can Feel" (which will

peak at #28) and "Jump" (which will hit #72).

17 The **Beach Boys**' *15 Big Ones* enters the album chart, where it will rise to #8 and will be certified gold in September.

26 Detroit's heavy-metal guitar hero **Ted Nugent** receives a gold record for his sixth, self-titled solo album, which includes the singles

"Hey Baby" (#72, two months ago) and "Dog Eat Dog" (#91, later this year). Nugent's rock career began in the late Sixties with Detroit psychedelic garage-rockers the **Amboy Dukes**.

27 **Bruce Springsteen** sues manager **Mike Appel** in Manhattan's U.S. District Court for fraud and breach of trust in his dealings with the New Jersey musician. The lawsuit, initiated when Springsteen realizes, after *Born to Run's* success, how little artistic and financial freedom he has in his contract with Appel's Laurel Canyon management company, is countered two days later by Appel, who brings suit in New York Supreme Court. The litigation drags on for a year, temporarily halting Springsteen's rock & roll career.

John Lennon receives his green card, the certification granting him permanent residency status in the United States, at the New York offices of the Federal Immigration and Naturalization Service. Lennon's fight to obtain the card had begun four years earlier, when the government first tried to deport him on the basis of his 1968 British conviction for possession of marijuana.

28 The **Steve Miller Band**'s *Fly like an Eagle* goes gold, on its way to platinum certification. The album features such massive hit singles as the title track (which will hit #2 early next year), "Rock'n Me" (which will hit Number One later this year), "Jet Airliner" (#8, next year) and "Take the Money and Run" (#11, this month). *Fly like an Eagle* stands as a textbook example of perfect Seventies radio pop; most of the album can be heard daily on both AM and FM stations around the country.

29 **Eric Clapton** begins his first tour of Britain in five years, a three-week affair, at Hempstead's Pavillion Theatre. The guitarist's only other official appearance in his native country occurred at the London's Rainbow Theatre "comeback" shows masterminded by **Pete Townshend** in January of 1973, despite Clapton's having mounted lengthy tours of America in the previous two years. ◆

WEEK ENDING JULY 3

U.S. #1 POP 45	"Silly Love Songs"	Wings
U.S. #1 POP LP	*Wings at the Speed of Sound*	Wings
U.S. #1 R&B 45	"Something He Can Feel"	Aretha Franklin
U.K. #1 POP 45	"You to Me Are Everything"	The Real Thing
U.K. #1 POP LP	*Abba's Greatest Hits*	Abba

WEEK ENDING JULY 10

U.S. #1 POP 45	"Afternoon Delight"	Starland Vocal Band
U.S. #1 POP LP	*Wings at the Speed of Sound*	Wings
U.S. #1 R&B 45	"Something He Can Feel"	Aretha Franklin
U.K. #1 POP 45	"Young Hearts Run Free"	Candi Staton
U.K. #1 POP LP	*A Night on the Town*	Rod Stewart

WEEK ENDING JULY 17

U.S. #1 POP 45	"Afternoon Delight"	Starland Vocal Band
U.S. #1 POP LP	*Wings at the Speed of Sound*	Wings
U.S. #1 R&B 45	"Something He Can Feel"	Aretha Franklin
U.K. #1 POP 45	"The Roussos Phenomenon"	Demis Roussos
U.K. #1 POP LP	*A Night on the Town*	Rod Stewart

WEEK ENDING JULY 24

U.S. #1 POP 45	"Kiss and Say Goodbye"	The Manhattans
U.S. #1 POP LP	*Frampton Comes Alive!*	Peter Frampton
U.S. #1 R&B 45	"You'll Never Find Another Love like Mine"	Lou Rawls
U.K. #1 POP 45	"Don't Go Breaking My Heart"	Elton John and Kiki Dee
U.K. #1 POP LP	*20 Golden Greats*	The Beach Boys

WEEK ENDING JULY 31

U.S. #1 POP 45	"Kiss and Say Goodbye"	The Manhattans
U.S. #1 POP LP	*Breezin'*	George Benson
U.S. #1 R&B 45	"You'll Never Find Another Love like Mine"	Lou Rawls
U.K. #1 POP 45	"Don't Go Breaking My Heart"	Elton John and Kiki Dee
U.K. #1 POP LP	*20 Golden Greats*	The Beach Boys

10 Elton John rocks Madison Square Garden on the opening night of a seven-show stand, a stay that breaks the house record set the previous summer by the Rolling Stones. The concert marks the end of a two-month U.S. tour for John, and also represents the absolute peak of his staggering popularity.

13 The Clash give a private show at a rehearsal hall in the Chalk Farm suburb of London, revealing themselves both to the invited press and to the world at large. Lead singer Joe Strummer had just joined up with the group, which included current members Mick Jones on guitar and Paul Simonon on bass, drummer Tory Crimes (a.k.a. Terry Chimes, who left in 1977 but filled in for *his* replacement, Topper Headon, in 1982) and future PiL guitarist Keith Levene, who had left his previous band, the 101'ers, after being inspired by the Sex Pistols when they opened at a club date for them a few months earlier.

16 Cliff Richard begins an SRO, twenty-date tour of the Soviet Union at Leningrad's Hall of the October. The enthusiasm of the crowd to his performance horrifies Russian officials, who ask Richard if he wants barriers to be erected between himself and the audience at later shows. Britain's eternal pop idol declines the offer.

18 *Sniffin' Glue*, the outrageous punk fanzine that becomes a photocopy Bible for Britain's blank generation, publishes its first issue. Publisher Mark P later extends the do-it-yourself mentality to the point of forming the band Alternative TV, who release a few albums on the independent Deptford Fun City label (later the place of Squeeze's vinyl debut).

19 Democratic Presidential candidate Jimmy Carter spends his afternoon at Capricorn Records' annual picnic in Macon, Georgia. Phil Walden, president of the Southern label, escorts Carter around Lakeside Park, but the future First Citizen leaves before checking out a set delivered by Sea Level.

21 The Rolling Stones top the bill over Todd Rundgren, Lynyrd Skynyrd, Hot Tuna, 10cc and others at England's annual Knebworth Festival. The concert, held in front of an estimated 200,000 spectators (paying and otherwise), is played up as the last Stones show ever to be held in Britain. It isn't.

The self-titled debut album by the all-girl heavy-metal/punk-rock band the Runaways enters the LP chart. The band—consisting of vocalist Cherie Currie, guitarists Lita Ford and Joan Jett, bassist Jackie Fox and drummer Sandy West—is the brainchild of L.A. producer, enterpreneur and trend-hopper Kim Fowley, who conceived the group as a "female Ramones." The album will fail to sell very well, and throughout their four-year existence, the band will bear the brunt of critical abuse and will complain of not being taken seriously. Joan Jett will go on to have a highly successful solo career; Cherie Currie will go on to release an album with her twin sister in 1980, and to co-star with Jody Foster in the film

Foxes the same year; Lita Ford will release a solo album in 1983.

The self-titled debut album by New York disco-sophisticates Dr. Buzzard's Original Savannah Band enters the LP chart. The album features their only hit singles, "I'll Play the Fool" (which will reach #80 in late 1976) and "Cherchez La Femme" (which will hit #27 early in 1977). The group will become a great favorite of critics enamored of their cosmopolitan blend of disco, pop, Latin and big-band swing (what the band members themselves term "mulatto music"). But they will never be very commercially successful, and will disband after two more albums, though they will occasionally reunite in the early Eighties for New York City concerts. Savannah Band members August Darnell and "Sugar Coated" Andy Hernandez will later go on to form Kid Creole and the Coconuts, a more tropical version of the Savannah Band that will find more commercial success than the Dr. Buzzard unit. Hernandez will then leave Kid Creole to go solo as the rap act Coati Mundi.

29 Jimmy Reed, the "Big Boss Man" of the blues, and a major influence on the Rolling Stones, Pete Townshend and others, dies at age fifty in San Francisco the night after completing a three-night engagement at the Bay Area club the Savoy. His death cuts short a comeback effort made after alcoholism halted his career for most of the Sixties and early Seventies.

At a reunion concert of the original Spirit in Santa Monica, California, Neil Young joins the band onstage at bassist Mark Andes' request during their encore rendition of Dylan's "Like a Rolling Stone." Guitarist Randy California objects to Young's presence, however, and pushes him away; the song is finally completed when the misunderstanding is cleared up. ◆

WEEK ENDING AUGUST 7

U.S. #1 POP 45	"Don't Go Breaking My Heart"	Elton John and Kiki Dee
U.S. #1 POP LP	*Breezin'*	George Benson
U.S. #1 R&B 45	"Getaway"	Earth, Wind and Fire
U.K. #1 POP 45	"Don't Go Breaking My Heart"	Elton John and Kiki Dee
U.K. #1 POP LP	*20 Golden Greats*	The Beach Boys

WEEK ENDING AUGUST 14

U.S. #1 POP 45	"Don't Go Breaking My Heart"	Elton John and Kiki Dee
U.S. #1 POP LP	*Frampton Comes Alive!*	Peter Frampton
U.S. #1 R&B 45	"Getaway"	Earth, Wind and Fire
U.K. #1 POP 45	"Don't Go Breaking My Heart"	Elton John and Kiki Dee
U.K. #1 POP LP	*20 Golden Greats*	The Beach Boys

WEEK ENDING AUGUST 21

U.S. #1 POP 45	"Don't Go Breaking My Heart"	Elton John and Kiki Dee
U.S. #1 POP LP	*Frampton Comes Alive!*	Peter Frampton
U.S. #1 R&B 45	"Who'd She Coo"	The Ohio Players
U.K. #1 POP 45	"Don't Go Breaking My Heart"	Elton John and Kiki Dee
U.K. #1 POP LP	*20 Golden Greats*	The Beach Boys

WEEK ENDING AUGUST 28

U.S. #1 POP 45	"Don't Go Breaking My Heart"	Elton John and Kiki Dee
U.S. #1 POP LP	*Frampton Comes Alive!*	Peter Frampton
U.S. #1 R&B 45	"(Shake, Shake, Shake) Shake Your Booty"	K.C. and the Sunshine Band
U.K. #1 POP 45	"Don't Go Breaking My Heart"	Elton John and Kiki Dee
U.K. #1 POP LP	*20 Golden Greats*	The Beach Boys

1 Ode Records president **Lou Adler** and employee **Neil Silver** are kidnapped at the former's house in Malibu. The two are released eight hours later after paying out $25,000 in hundred dollar bills. A week later, a California couple—their motivation seemingly only the money—are charged with the crime, while a search continues for another accomplice in the scheme.

8 Rock and election-year politics mix strangely again when **Steven Ford**, the president's son, invites Briton **Peter Frampton**, his girlfriend **Penny McCall** and manager **Dee Anthony** to the White House. Frampton and company receive a grand tour of the place, and the day concludes with a visit to the First Family's living quarters, mostly spent watching television with the president.

Disco band **Wild Cherry**'s self-titled debut album, which features their Number One hit single "Play That Funky Music," goes gold.

The debut album by Vancouver-based rock band **Heart**, *Dreamboat Annie*, goes gold. The album features their hit singles "Magic Man" (which will hit #9 on the pop chart next month) and "Crazy on You" (which hit #35 two months ago).

13 Ex-**Humble Pie** singer/guitarist **Peter Frampton**'s fourth solo album, *Frampton*, goes gold. It is his commercial breakthrough album, containing the hit singles "Show Me the Way" (#6, a few months ago) and "Baby, I Love Your Way" (#12, this month).

14 *Wired*, the second jazz-rock-fusion album by British guitar hero **Jeff Beck** (after 1975's *Blow by Blow*), goes gold.

15 **Steely Dan**'s fifth album, *The Royal Scam*, goes gold. It contains the hit singles "The Fez" (which will reach #59 next month) and "Kid Charlemagne" (#82, in July), while many of the album's other songs, including the title track and "Haitian Divorce," are very popular on FM radio.

18 The second annual **Don Kirshner**-

produced Rock Music Awards program broadcasts on CBS-TV. Winners in the program, generously labeled a fiasco by critics for both its spirit and presentation, include **Fleetwood Mac** for Best Group and Best Album, and **Peter Frampton** as Rock Personality of the Year. **Bill Graham**, nominated a year earlier for a special Public Service award, continues his criticism of the event this year by likening it to "a soup that's out there for three weeks and you open it and these maggots come out."

19 Promoter **Sid Bernstein**, the man responsible for handling the **Beatles**' 1965 and 1966 Shea Stadium shows, takes out a full-page advertisement in the *New York Times* extending his hopes of reuniting the Beatles for a concert. While labeling the would-be event a "symbol of hope" that would offer solace to a world "so hopelessly divided," he takes care to point out that revenues could reach $230 million.

21 The **Bee Gees**' twentieth album, *Children of the World*, goes gold. It contains their two latest hit singles, "You Should Be Dancing" (Number One, two weeks ago) and "Love So Right" (which will hit #3 in two months).

22 **Bob Dylan**'s album *Hard Rain*, a live document of his 1976 tour with the **Rolling Thunder Revue**, goes gold.

25 **Wings** play a benefit and raise $50,000 for the restoration of water-damaged art treasures in Venice's St. Mark's Square. A reported 25,000 people attend the performance and unknowingly set back the cause of the Italian town's reclamation from water when their combined weight loosens some paving stones and allows water to seep through into the Square.

The eponymous debut album by the band **Boston** enters the album chart. It will eventually reach #3 and become the fastest-selling debut album in history. The album, which features the hit single "More Than a Feeling" (which will reach #5 early in 1977), actually consists of demo tapes produced by the band's guitarist **Tom Scholz**, a senior production manager for Polaroid Corporation. It will be certified platinum on November 22, 1976, and will go on to sell over 7.5 million copies world-wide. It will be two-and-a-half years before the band's next album, *Don't Look Back*.

29 **Jerry Lee Lewis**, attempting to shoot a soda bottle somewhere in the distance with a .357 magnum, hits his bass player **Norman "Butch" Owens** twice in the chest. Lewis is charged with shooting a firearm within the city limits. ◆

WEEK ENDING SEPTEMBER 4

U.S. #1 POP 45	"You Should Be Dancing"	The Bee Gees
U.S. #1 POP LP	*Fleetwood Mac*	Fleetwood Mac
U.S. #1 R&B 45	"Play That Funky Music"	Wild Cherry
U.K. #1 POP 45	"Dancing Queen"	Abba
U.K. #1 POP LP	*20 Golden Greats*	The Beach Boys

WEEK ENDING SEPTEMBER 11

U.S. #1 POP 45	"(Shake, Shake, Shake) Shake Your Booty"	KC and the Sunshine Band
U.S. #1 POP LP	*Frampton Comes Alive!*	Peter Frampton
U.S. #1 R&B 45	"Play That Funky Music"	Wild Cherry
U.K. #1 POP 45	"Dancing Queen"	Abba
U.K. #1 POP LP	*20 Golden Greats*	The Beach Boys

WEEK ENDING SEPTEMBER 18

U.S. #1 POP 45	"Play That Funky Music"	Wild Cherry
U.S. #1 POP LP	*Frampton Comes Alive!*	Peter Frampton
U.S. #1 R&B 45	"Play That Funky Music"	Wild Cherry
U.K. #1 POP 45	"Dancing Queen"	Abba
U.K. #1 POP LP	*20 Golden Greats*	The Beach Boys

WEEK ENDING SEPTEMBER 25

U.S. #1 POP 45	"Play That Funky Music"	Wild Cherry
U.S. #1 POP LP	*Frampton Comes Alive!*	Peter Frampton
U.S. #1 R&B 45	"Play That Funky Music"	Wild Cherry
U.K. #1 POP 45	"Dancing Queen"	Abba
U.K. #1 POP LP	*A Night on the Town*	Rod Stewart

2 **John Belushi** comes out during the second verse of **Joe Cocker**'s rendition of "Feeling Alright" on "Saturday Night Live" and performs his exaggeratedly spastic imitation of the British singer. The duet brings down the house, and Cocker, already familiar with Belushi's "tribute" to him, claims that since "(my) band likes it, I'm as happy as a pig in shit."

3 Blues singer **Victoria Spivey** dies at age seventy in a Brooklyn hospital. Spivey, a prolific songwriter and the owner of her own successful recording label, is also remembered for giving **Bob Dylan** one of his first New York City gigs, accompanying her and **Big Joe Williams** on harmonica during a session in 1961.

5 **Hall and Oates'** second album, *Abandoned Luncheonette*—which contained their original hit version of Tavares' #1 R&B hit "She's Gone"—is certified gold three years after its release.

6 **Rick Dees and His Cast of Idiots** receive a gold record for one of the more bizarre novelty hits of the decade, "Disco Duck," which will hit Number One on the pop chart in ten days. On December 13, it will become the fourth single ever to be certified platinum.

10 The **Who** and the **Grateful Dead** play the second of two back-to-back shows at Oakland Stadium for **Bill Graham**'s Days on the Green series. The unique pairing of the two stylistically divergent acts seems to split the potential audience for the shows, however, as, surprisingly, neither of the shows sell out.

Much to the horror of the giant British record corporation's more staid executives, EMI signs up the **Sex Pistols**, the seminal punk band, outbidding Polydor with a contract worth forty thousand pounds (about $75,000).

12 Veteran soul vocal group the **Spinners** earn another gold record, for their sixth album, *Happiness Is Being with the Spinners*, which features their big hit single "The Rubberband Man" (#2 on the pop chart later this year, as well as Number One on the R&B chart).

16 **Stevie Wonder**'s *Songs in the Key of Life* enters the pop album chart, where it will remain into 1978. It is Wonder's first release since signing his $13-million contract with Motown. The three-record set

will become a platinum seller, yielding hit singles with "Sir Duke," "Isn't She Lovely," "Another Star" and "I Wish."

19 **Parliament**, half of **George Clinton**'s Parliamant-Funkadelic empire, earns a gold record for *The Clones of Dr. Funkenstein*, another in Clinton's long series of bizarre concept-message albums.

20 **Led Zeppelin**'s film *The Song Remains the Same*, a mixture of concert footage and fantasy sequences, premieres in London.

"Devil Woman," the first Top Ten U.S. hit for veteran British teen-idol **Cliff Richard** (who is by now a born-again Christian), enters the pop chart. "Devil Woman" will remain on the chart for twenty-two weeks, peaking at #6. Richard will go on to score minor hits in the U.S. with "I Can't Ask for Any More Than You" (#80, late 1976), "Don't Turn the Light Out" (#57 in the summer of 1977) and "We Don't Talk Anymore" (#7 in 1979).

22 **Keith Moon** plays his last North American show with the **Who** as he and the band conclude an extensive year of touring at Toronto's Maple Leaf Gardens.

26 **Walter Murphy**'s Big Apple Band earns a gold record for its debut album, *A Fifth of Beethoven*, which features the title single, a disco treatment of Beethoven's Fifth Symphony that hit Number One. The band's only other hit, also drawn from this album, will be "Flight '76," a discofied "Flight of the Bumblebee" (#44, in early 1977). ◆

WEEK ENDING OCTOBER 2

U.S. #1 POP 45	"Play That Funky Music"	Wild Cherry
U.S. #1 POP LP	*Frampton Comes Alive!*	Peter Frampton
U.S. #1 R&B 45	"Play That Funky Music"	Wild Cherry
U.K. #1 POP 45	"Dancing Queen"	Abba
U.K. #1 POP LP	*Abba's Greatest Hits*	Abba

WEEK ENDING OCTOBER 9

U.S. #1 POP 45	"A Fifth of Beethoven"	Walter Murphy and the Big Apple Band
U.S. #1 POP LP	*Frampton Comes Alive!*	Peter Frampton
U.S. #1 R&B 45	"Just to Be Close to You"	The Commodores
U.K. #1 POP 45	"Dancing Queen"	Abba
U.K. #1 POP LP	*Abba's Greatest Hits*	Abba

WEEK ENDING OCTOBER 16

U.S. #1 POP 45	"Disco Duck (Part 1)"	Rick Dees and His Cast of Idiots
U.S. #1 POP LP	*Songs in the Key of Life*	Stevie Wonder
U.S. #1 R&B 45	"Just to Be Close to You"	The Commodores
U.K. #1 POP 45	"Mississippi"	Pussycat
U.K. #1 POP LP	*A Night on the Town*	Rod Stewart

WEEK ENDING OCTOBER 23

U.S. #1 POP 45	"If You Leave Me Now"	Chicago
U.S. #1 POP LP	*Songs in the Key of Life*	Stevie Wonder
U.S. #1 R&B 45	"The Rubberband Man"	The Spinners
U.K. #1 POP 45	"Mississippi"	Pussycat
U.K. #1 POP LP	*Abba's Greatest Hits*	Abba

WEEK ENDING OCTOBER 30

U.S. #1 POP 45	"If You Leave Me Now"	Chicago
U.S. #1 POP LP	*Songs in the Key of Life*	Stevie Wonder
U.S. #1 R&B 45	"Message in Our Music"	The O'Jays
U.K. #1 POP 45	"Mississippi"	Pussycat
U.K. #1 POP LP	*The Who Story*	The Who

3 Country-rock band **Firefall** earn a gold record for their self-titled debut album, which includes the hit singles "You Are the Woman" (#9, later this year) and "Livin' Ain't Livin'" (#42, earlier this year). The band's members include former **Flying Burrito Brother Rick Roberts** and ex-**Spirit** member **Mark Andes**.

4 **Bruce Springsteen and the E Street Band**, completing a two-month tour with a six-night stand at New York City's Palladium Theater, backed up by **Ronnie Spector** and the **Asbury Jukes' Miami Horns** section, have their final show interrupted by a phoned-in bomb threat. After a quick check shows the hall to be clear of danger, Springsteen quips that the caller might just be one **Mike Appel**, his former manager and then-current litigant in an extensive lawsuit.

New York City Mayor **Abraham Beame** hosts a luncheon for the **Bee Gees** at mayoral residence Gracie Mansion. The affair is in honor of the group's announced intentions to donate their profits from an upcoming Madison Square Garden concert to the city's Police Athletic League Organization. Upon being handed a platinum record of the Gibbs' *Children of the World*, the perhaps less than altogether hip His Honor says, "I look forward to taking it out of the frame and playing it."

Daryl Hall and John Oates' fifth album, *Bigger than Both of Us*, goes gold. It features their biggest hit single to date, "Rich Girl," which will eventually hit Number One on the pop chart in early 1977.

9 In the wake of the re-formed **Fleetwood Mac**'s phenomenal success with their latest, self-titled album, one of the band's earlier albums, *Mystery to Me*, goes gold. The band's personnel at the time of the 1973 *Mystery to Me* included **Bob Welch**, **Bob Weston**, **Martin Birch** and the only three members currently with the band—**Christine McVie**, **John McVie** and **Mick Fleetwood**.

Frank Zappa and the Mothers of Invention earn a gold record for the 1973 album *Overnite Sensation*, which includes such dirty-humor Zappaphile favorites and FM-radio staples as "Montana" and "Dinah Mo Hum."

11 **Kiss**, the cartoonish heavy-metal/glitter-rock band the critics love to hate, earn another gold record, for the album *Rock and Roll Over*, which will yield the hit single "Calling Dr. Love" (#14, in the summer of 1977).

15 California singer/song-writer **Jackson Browne**'s critically acclaimed fourth album, *The Pretender* (produced by rock critic **Jon Landau**, who has also worked with **Bruce Springsteen**), is certified gold. Browne had completed work on the album in the wake of the suicide of his wife, **Phyllis Major**, on March 25, 1976. His debut album, *Jackson Browne*, released in 1972, goes gold the next day.

19 **Van Morrison**'s album *Moondance*, released in 1970, goes gold. The album had brought Morrison two minor hits: the title track and "Into the Mystic." The latter song became a somewhat bigger hit for **Johnny Rivers**, reaching #51 in 1970.

20 **John Sebastian** and **Fred Neil** lead a show in Sacramento's Memorial Auditorium at the request of Governor **Jerry Brown**, climaxing the state's California Celebrates the Whales Day. Also appearing at the show aimed at raising public consciousness about the plight of the internationally hunted mammals are the **Paul Winter Consort**, **Country Joe McDonald** and **Joni Mitchell**.

23 Police arrest **Jerry Lee Lewis** outside the gates of Graceland after he shows up for the second time that evening and makes a scene, shouting, waving a pistol and demanding to see **Elvis Presley**. After security guards call police, Lewis is found at his car with a .38 Derringer in hand; authorities charge him on counts of public intoxication and possession of a weapon.

25 The **Band** play their "Last Waltz" Thanksgiving night before **Martin Scorsese**'s cameras and a packed house at San Francisco's Winterland. **Bill Graham** convinces the group to turn the originally scheduled show into a grand affair, complete with buffet, chandeliers, dancing to an orchestra and a twenty-five dollar ticket. Musicians and friends who help the Band celebrate their final show together include **Bob Dylan**, **Ronnie Hawkins**, **Joni Mitchell**, **Van Morrison**, **Neil Young**, **Paul Butterfield**, **Bobby Charles**, **Neil Diamond**, **Dr. John**, **Muddy Waters**, **Eric Clapton**, **Stephen Stills**, **Ron Wood** and **Ringo Starr**. A Graham aide neatly sums up the special sense of occasion that prevails throughout the evening when he sighs: "Yeah, and tomorrow night, **Ted Nugent**." ◆

WEEK ENDING NOVEMBER 6

U.S. #1 POP 45	"Rock'n Me"	The Steve Miller Band
U.S. #1 POP LP	*Songs in the Key of Life*	Stevie Wonder
U.S. #1 R&B 45	"Love Ballad"	L.T.D.
U.K. #1 POP 45	"If You Leave Me Now"	Chicago
U.K. #1 POP LP	*Songs in the Key of Life*	Stevie Wonder

WEEK ENDING NOVEMBER 13

U.S. #1 POP 45	"Tonight's the Night (Gonna Be Alright)"	Rod Stewart
U.S. #1 POP LP	*Songs in the Key of Life*	Stevie Wonder
U.S. #1 R&B 45	"Love Ballad"	L.T.D.
U.K. #1 POP 45	"If You Leave Me Now"	Chicago
U.K. #1 POP LP	*Songs in the Key of Life*	Stevie Wonder

WEEK ENDING NOVEMBER 20

U.S. #1 POP 45	"Tonight's the Night (Gonna Be Alright)"	Rod Stewart
U.S. #1 POP LP	*Songs in the Key of Life*	Stevie Wonder
U.S. #1 R&B 45	"You Don't Have to Be a Star (To Be in My Show)"	Marilyn McCoo and Billy Davis, Jr.
U.K. #1 POP 45	"If You Leave Me Now"	Chicago
U.K. #1 POP LP	*Songs in the Key of Life*	Stevie Wonder

WEEK ENDING NOVEMBER 27

U.S. #1 POP 45	"Tonight's the Night (Gonna Be Alright)"	Rod Stewart
U.S. #1 POP LP	*Songs in the Key of Life*	Stevie Wonder
U.S. #1 R&B 45	"Dazz"	Brick
U.K. #1 POP 45	"If You Leave Me Now"	Chicago
U.K. #1 POP LP	*20 Golden Greats*	Glen Campbell

1 The **Sex Pistols**, who have just released their first single, "Anarchy in the U.K.," appear on British TV's "Today Show" as a last-minute replacement for **Queen**. Interviewer **Bill Grundy**, taunting them about their "nasty" reputation, provokes bassist **Glen Matlock** to say "fuck" on the air. In the resulting nationwide uproar, the Sex Pistols will be banned from appearing in all but five cities on the itinerary of their first U.K. tour. By January, no club or concert hall in Great Britain will book the group.

3 A forty-foot-long inflatable pig being photographed for the cover of **Pink Floyd**'s *Animals* breaks loose from its guide wires and takes off from the Battersea Power Station outside of London. It heads east and eventually attains a height of 18,000 feet before landing in Kent.

Seven gunmen spray bullets into **Bob Marley**'s house in Kingston, Jamaica, where he and the **Wailers** are rehearsing for an upcoming "Smile Jamaica" festival. The shots strike Marley, his wife, **Rita**, a friend, and Wailer manager **Don Taylor**, who, standing in front of Marley, bears the brunt of the attack (none are severely hurt). The would-be assassins get away and, despite great apprehension, Marley and company go through with their performance two nights later.

4 **Tommy Bolin** overdoses on heroin, cocaine and other substances at the Newport Hotel in Miami. The guitarist, formerly with the **James Gang** and also **Ritchie Blackmore**'s replacement in **Deep Purple**, has been working with his own band for the previous year. At his funeral two days later, one-time girlfriend **Karen Ulibarri** places on his finger the ring Deep Purple's manager gave him. It had been worn by **Jimi Hendrix** the day he died.

10 A three-record set of live performances from the U.S. **Wings** tour, *Wings over America*, accurately summarizing **Paul McCartney**'s post-**Beatles** career with its thirty-song selection, is released. As expected, the compilation, which includes "Magneto and Titanium Man," "My Love," "Silly Love Songs" and "Maybe I'm Amazed," reaches Number One.

13 Ex-**Procol Harum** guitarist **Robin Trower**'s fifth solo album, *Long Misty Days*, goes gold. His third solo LP, *For Earth Below*, had gone gold earlier in the year.

Three days after its release, *Wings over America*, the live album by **Paul McCartney and Wings**, goes gold.

14 The eponymous debut album by New York sophisto-disco-fusion group **Dr. Buzzard's Original Savannah Band** goes gold.

22 **Bob Seger** begins his overdue breakthrough to stardom, as his *Live Bullet* album goes gold. Next year, with the release of *Night Moves*, Seger will consolidate this success with three hit singles off the album (the title tune, "Mainstreet" and "Rock and Roll Never Forgets"). *Live Bullet* features in-concert versions of such earlier Seger classics as "Ramblin' Gamblin' Man," "Beautiful Loser," "Travelin' Man," "Katmandu," "Nutbush City Limits" and "Get Out of Denver."

James Taylor's *Greatest Hits* album goes gold shortly after its release. Among the hits it contains are "You've Got a Friend," "Fire and Rain," "Mockingbird" (with his wife **Carly Simon**), Taylor's version of **Marvin Gaye**'s "How Sweet It Is (to Be Loved by You)," "Don't Let Me Be Lonely Tonight," "Country Road" and "Mexico."

23 **Joni Mitchell**'s album *Hejira* goes gold not long after its release. This proves that Mitchell still has her legions of devoted fans, even though most critics have by now grown weary of Mitchell's recent spate of abstract, experimental works.

25 The **Eagles**' sixth album, *Hotel California*—their first with ex-**James Gang** guitarist **Joe Walsh**—goes platinum. It features the title song, a Number One hit single for the California country-rock band in May 1977.

28 Blues guitar giant **Freddie King** (no relation to those other blues guitar giants, **Albert** and **B. B. King**) dies of hepatitis at age forty-two in Dallas, Texas. King's fleet-fingered guitar work on such songs as "Hideaway" was highly influential on **Eric Clapton**, among many others, and King recorded two albums, *Burglar* and *Freddie King (1934–1976)*, with British sessionmen.

30 Swedish pop group **Abba**, the world's most successful singing group this decade, garner a U.S. gold record award for their *Greatest Hits* album. Though people in general still tend to think that Abba are vastly more popular in Europe than in America (and, in truth, they are), the band has already had several Top Forty hits in the U.S. Among those hits included on this album are "Waterloo," "SOS," "I Do, I Do, I Do, I Do, I Do" and "Honey Honey." ◆

WEEK ENDING DECEMBER 4

U.S. #1 POP 45	"Tonight's the Night (Gonna Be Alright)"	Rod Stewart
U.S. #1 POP LP	*Songs in the Key of Life*	Stevie Wonder
U.S. #1 R&B 45	"Dazz"	Brick
U.K. #1 POP 45	"Under the Moon of Love"	Showaddywaddy
U.K. #1 POP LP	*20 Golden Greats*	Glen Campbell

WEEK ENDING DECEMBER 11

U.S. #1 POP 45	"Tonight's the Night (Gonna Be Alright)"	Rod Stewart
U.S. #1 POP LP	*Songs in the Key of Life*	Stevie Wonder
U.S. #1 R&B 45	"Dazz"	Brick
U.K. #1 POP 45	"Under the Moon of Love"	Showaddywaddy
U.K. #1 POP LP	*20 Golden Greats*	Glen Campbell

WEEK ENDING DECEMBER 18

U.S. #1 POP 45	"Tonight's the Night (Gonna Be Alright)"	Rod Stewart
U.S. #1 POP LP	*Songs in the Key of Life*	Stevie Wonder
U.S. #1 R&B 45	"Dazz"	Brick
U.K. #1 POP 45	"Under the Moon of Love"	Showaddywaddy
U.K. #1 POP LP	*20 Golden Greats*	Glen Campbell

WEEK ENDING DECEMBER 25

U.S. #1 POP 45	"Tonight's the Night (Gonna Be Alright)"	Rod Stewart
U.S. #1 POP LP	*Songs in the Key of Life*	Stevie Wonder
U.S. #1 R&B 45	"Car Wash"	Rose Royce
U.K. #1 POP 45	"When a Child Is Born"	Johnny Mathis
U.K. #1 POP LP	*Arrival*	Abba

1977

Disco kept on growing, assimilating everything into its lifeless-yet-sexy, campy-yet-populist ethos—from Shalamar's "Uptown Festival" (a medley of Sixties Motown hits that predated subsequent disco-medley hits like the Stars on 45 efforts), to a discofied "Pipeline" (yes, the early Sixties surf instrumental) by none other than Beach Boy Bruce Johnston, to Kraftwerk's all-electronic, hypnorobotic "Trans-Europe Express." And the rock audience continued to reject it. Not only could disco soak up anything and everything, but it was a faceless, assembly-line music whose lack of star performers (Donna Summer and very few others excepted) mirrored the everybody/nobody-is-a-star equality-in-communality of its dance-floor audience. Most important, disco sold records by the millions. The rock audience's reaction was conservative; in fact, they responded to disco in much the same way their grandparents had to Elvis Presley in 1956.

In England, though, rock was trying its damnedest to effect some sort of serious revolution. In January, London's Roxy Club converted from a gay disco—ironically, in the U.S. disco had arisen out of the gay subculture—to the city's premier punk-rock club with an opening show by the Clash. A few days later, the Sex Pistols, whose "Anarchy in the U.K." had only recently been released, were booted off their label, EMI. Two months later, with Sid Vicious replacing their original bassist, Glen Matlock, they were signed to and, within nine more days, kicked off A&M Records. Two months after *that,* now on Virgin Records, they released another scurrilous, revved-up rock cataclysm, "God Save the Queen," timed to coincide with Her Majesty's Silver Jubilee. Like "Anarchy," it was banned from broadcast for its "treasonous sentiments," but hit the top of the charts anyway. By then, England had seen the birth of a whole wave of punk bands, from the first all-girl punk band, the Slits, to punk's most outspokenly political faction the Clash, to its only valid romantic-pop practitioners the Buzzcocks.

But for the most part, the American rock audience rejected hard-core punk rock as they had disco. Punk was too specifically grounded in the British scene: it sprang from a mass of angry, disadvantaged kids who were disillusioned with both society and a corpulent corporate-rock establishment. There was no comparable audience in America, at least not among white kids. The only correlative was inner-city ethnic minorities, whose current music of choice was disco. Besides, the punks—with their self-conscious, selective affectation and perversion of various Fifties and Sixties styles, and their deliberately ugly, abused, torn-and-safety-pinned look and attitude—were just too weird to be taken as anything more than a sick joke or fodder for television news documentaries.

So, while America's rock audience succored itself with ever-growing album-oriented hard pop (this was a big year for Foreigner, Journey, Kansas, Rush, et cetera), there was the inevitable arrival of new wave—an essentially meaningless term that came to connote a kind of acceptable face of punk. In March, Stiff Records released the debut single by Elvis Costello, as good a place as any to mark new wave's birth out of pub rock's roots-revisionism and the punk style—energy and attitude shorn of *outré* edges of extreme perversity, negativity and nihilism. A true paradigm of the displacement of punk by new wave in America occurred in December when the Sex Pistols, scheduled to appear on "Saturday Night Live," were refused U.S. visas; in their place was Elvis Costello, who performed "Radio Radio"—a snarling, punk-paced attack on America's demographically rigidified broadcasting industry—despite being told not to. By then, an increasing number of New York bands—Blondie, Talking Heads, Television and others—released their own debut albums and launched America's version of new wave.

1 The **Clash** headline the gala opening of the Roxy. The former gay disco in London's Covent Garden fills the vacancy left by the widespread London club ban on punk groups, and immediately the Roxy becomes the central venue of the punk movement. Its stage is graced by the **Buzzcocks**, the **Slits**, **X-Ray Spex**, **Siouxsie and the Banshees** and other pioneering punk groups.

6 Three months after signing the **Sex Pistols** for 40,000 pounds, EMI terminates the contract after releasing only one single, "Anarchy in the U.K.," which is promptly taken out of circulation. No reason is given, but an EMI office memorandum alludes to the Sex Pistols' "disgraceful . . . aggressive behavior" and EMI's responsibility to "encourage restraint."

12 **Keith Richards** is fined 750 pounds for possession of cocaine in his wrecked car on May 19, 1976, and charged an additional 250 pounds for court costs. At the same English court appearance, he is found not guilty of possession of LSD.

Long May You Run, an LP by the (**Stephen**) **Stills**-(**Neil**) **Young** Band, is certified gold. The LP and a 1976 tour (cut short because of Young's throat problems) are Young's last professional collaborations with any of his ex-bandmates, although the other three, Stills, **David Crosby** and **Graham Nash**, will reunite several times in the years to come.

15 RCA Records releases **David Bowie**'s *Low,* the album that marks Bowie's transformation into the Man Machine of *"Heroes."* Recorded in Berlin, the album is heavily influenced by such German synthesizer bands as **Kraftwerk** and by "ambient music" maker **Brian Eno**, Bowie's collaborator in the studio. The first side includes the minor hit single "Sound and Vision"; the second side is totally instrumental.

19 **Aretha Franklin, Linda Ronstadt** and **Loretta Lynn** are among the performers at a special televised Inaugural Concert held at Washington, D.C.'s Kennedy Center on the eve of **Jimmy Carter**'s inauguration as President of the United States. In the audience with Jimmy and **Roslynn Carter** are **John Lennon** and **Yoko Ono**, **Paul Simon** and **Gregg Allman**. At the Inaugural Ball the next evening, celebrants will dance to the **Marshall Tucker Band** and the **Charlie Daniels Band.**

26 Opening a concert for **Bob Seger** in Tampa, Florida, **Patti Smith** falls off the stage and must be rushed to the hospital for twenty-two stitches to close head lacerations. "I look like an asshole," says Smith from the hospital, where she will remain in a neck brace for several weeks. Her injuries will necessitate temporary retirement from the stage, during which time she will write her fifth book of poetry, *Babel.*

Fleetwood Mac's first lead guitarist, **Peter Green**, is committed to a mental hospital in England after firing a pistol in the general direction of a delivery boy who was attempting to deliver to Green a check for royalties on Fleetwood Mac's records sales. Green had left the band in May 1970 to live a life of religious seclusion.

29 United Artists releases the **Stranglers**' first single, "(Get a) Grip (on Yourself)" backed with "London Lady," in Britain. Formed as a London pub-rock band in 1975, the Stranglers have more recently won the allegiance of the punk movement; their vinyl debut, therefore, is considered one of the earliest punk records. ◆

WEEK ENDING JANUARY 1

U.S. #1 POP 45	"Tonight's the Night (Gonna Be Alright)"	Rod Stewart
U.S. #1 POP LP	*Songs in the Key of Life*	Stevie Wonder
U.S. #1 R&B 45	"Car Wash"	Rose Royce
U.K. #1 POP 45	"When a Child Is Born"	Johnny Mathis
U.K. #1 POP LP	*Arrival*	Abba

WEEK ENDING JANUARY 8

U.S. #1 POP 45	"You Don't Have to Be a Star (To Be in My Show)"	Marilyn McCoo and Billy Davis, Jr.
U.S. #1 POP LP	*Songs in the Key of Life*	Stevie Wonder
U.S. #1 R&B 45	"Darlin' Darlin' Baby (Sweet, Tender, Love)"	The O'Jays
U.K. #1 POP 45	"When a Child Is Born"	Johnny Mathis
U.K. #1 POP LP	*Arrival*	Abba

WEEK ENDING JANUARY 15

U.S. #1 POP 45	"You Make Me Feel Like Dancing"	Leo Sayer
U.S. #1 POP LP	*Hotel California*	The Eagles
U.S. #1 R&B 45	"I Wish"	Stevie Wonder
U.K. #1 POP 45	"Don't Give Up on Us"	David Soul
U.K. #1 POP LP	*Arrival*	Abba

WEEK ENDING JANUARY 22

U.S. #1 POP 45	"I Wish"	Stevie Wonder
U.S. #1 POP LP	*Wings over America*	Paul McCartney and Wings
U.S. #1 R&B 45	"I Wish"	Stevie Wonder
U.K. #1 POP 45	"Don't Give Up on Us"	David Soul
U.K. #1 POP LP	*Red River Valley*	Slim Whitman

WEEK ENDING JANUARY 29

U.S. #1 POP 45	"Car Wash"	Rose Royce
U.S. #1 POP LP	*Hotel California*	The Eagles
U.S. #1 R&B 45	"I Wish"	Stevie Wonder
U.K. #1 POP 45	"Don't Cry for Me Argentina"	Julie Covington
U.K. #1 POP LP	*Red River Valley*	Slim Whitman

2 **Led Zeppelin**'s latest tour of North America must, at the last moment, be postponed indefinitely because of vocalist **Robert Plant**'s bout with tonsillitis. The tour (which, as it turns out, will be Led Zeppelin's last visit to North America), will finally get under way in late June.

4 "American Bandstand" celebrates its twenty-fifth anniversary with an ABC-TV special hosted by **Dick Clark**. An "all-star band," including **Chuck Berry**, **Gregg Allman**, **Seals and Crofts**, **Johnny Rivers**, three quarters of **Booker T. and the MGs**, **Jr. Walker**, **Charlie Daniels**, the **Pointer Sisters**, **Doc Severenson**, **Donald Byrd**, **Les McCann** and **Chuck Mangione**, joins together for a rendition of "Roll Over Beethoven."

15 **Glen Matlock**, the **Sex Pistols**' original bassist, leaves the controversial punk group, explaining that "there was no working relationship" between himself and Pistol vocalist **Johnny Rotten**. Rotten's explanation is that Matlock was kicked out of the group be-

cause "he wanted to make us fun, like the **Beatles**." Matlock will soon form his own group, the **Rich Kids**. His replacement in the Sex Pistols will be **Sid Vicious**, late of the **Flowers of Romance**, with whom he sang.

19 **Warner Bros.** releases **Fleetwood Mac**'s *Rumours*. Recorded in Los Angeles as the Anglo-American band's two couples—**John** and **Christine McVie**, and **Lindsey Buckingham** and **Stevie Nicks**—were breaking up, the album captures the emotions that clash when former lovers must continue to work closely together—a situation that evidently makes for inspired music. Containing four Top Ten hits ("Go Your Own Way," "Dreams," "Don't Stop" and "You Make Loving Fun"), *Rumours* will be the Number One pop album for thirty-one weeks and will sell over 10 million copies.

Winners of the nineteenth annual Grammy Awards (for 1976) are announced. Record of the Year is **George Benson**'s "This Masquerade"; he also wins Best Engineered Nonclassical Recording for *Breezin'*, Best

Pop Instrumental Performance for *Breezin'* and Best R&B Instrumental for "Theme from *Good King Bad.*" Album of the Year is **Stevie Wonder**'s *Songs in the Key of Life*, which also wins Best Male Pop Vocal Performance. Wonder's "I Wish" is Best Male R&B Vocal, and he is also named Best Producer of the Year. Song of the Year is Beach Boy **Bruce Johnston**'s "I Write the Songs," a big hit for **Barry Manilow**. Best New Artist of the Year is the **Starland Vocal Band** (who sang "Afternoon Delight"). Best Album is **Chicago**'s *Chicago X*. Best Female Pop Vocal Performance is **Linda Ronstadt** for *Hasten Down the Wind*. Best Pop Vocal Group Performance is Chicago's "If You Leave Me Now." Best R&B Female Vocal Performance is **Natalie Cole**'s "Sophisticated Lady." Best R&B Duo/Blues/Chorus Vocal Performance is **Billy Davis, Jr.** and **Marilyn McCoo**'s "You Don't Have to Be a Star (to Be in My Show)." Best R&B Song is **Boz Scaggs**' "Lowdown." Best Soul Gospel Performance is **Mahalia Jackson**'s *How I Got Over*. **Emmylou Harris** wins Best Country Female Vocal Performance for *Elite Hotel*.

25 Polydor Records signs the **Jam**, an English trio (guitarist **Paul Weller**, bassist **Bruce Foxton** and drummer **Rick Buckler**) popular with London punks for their energetic re-creations of bygone soul songs.

26 Seminal Delta bluesman **Bukka White** dies in City of Memphis Hospital of complications arising from a stroke. Newspaper reports list White's age variously between sixty-seven and eighty-nine. Born Booker T. Washington White in Houston, Mississippi, Bukka began wandering the Delta country as a youngster, and was one of the first and best Delta slide-guitarists and vocalists. In 1937 he recorded his biggest hit, "Shake 'Em On Down," which subsequently became a blues standard. White, however, was concurrently sentenced to Mississippi's Parchman Farm Prison on a manslaughter charge; his fortunes improved in 1939 when a Library of Congress field unit recorded him in prison (the session yielded another of his classics, "Parchman Farm Blues"), thus helping him get parole. Upon his release White found that changes in post-war music relegated him to relative obscurity until the Sixties when White was recorded by **John Fahey**'s Takoma label and blues archivist **Chris Strachwitz**'s Arhoolie label.

27 Royal Canadian Mounted Police raid **Keith Richards**' Toronto hotel suite while Richards is asleep and seize twenty-two grams of heroin, five grams of cocaine and narcotics paraphenalia. Richards is arrested, charged with possession of heroin with intent to traffic (a crime that carries a sentence of life imprisonment) and possession of cocaine, and released on $25,000 bail. His trial is set for October. After Richards' numerous previous arrests for various offenses, fans and associates of the **Rolling Stones** fear that this is the one that will bring down the fifteen-year-old band.   ◆

WEEK ENDING FEBRUARY 5

U.S. #1 POP 45	"Torn between Two Lovers"	Mary MacGregor
U.S. #1 POP LP	*Hotel California*	The Eagles
U.S. #1 R&B 45	"I Wish"	Stevie Wonder
U.K. #1 POP 45	"Don't Give Up on Us"	David Soul
U.K. #1 POP LP	*Red River Valley*	Slim Whitman

WEEK ENDING FEBRUARY 12

U.S. #1 POP 45	"Torn between Two Lovers"	Mary MacGregor
U.S. #1 POP LP	*A Star Is Born*	Barbra Streisand and Kris Kristofferson (soundtrack)
U.S. #1 R&B 45	"I Wish"	Stevie Wonder
U.K. #1 POP 45	"Don't Cry for Me Argentina"	Julie Covington
U.K. #1 POP LP	*Red River Valley*	Slim Whitman

WEEK ENDING FEBRUARY 19

U.S. #1 POP 45	"Blinded by the Light"	Manfred Mann's Earth Band
U.S. #1 POP LP	*A Star Is Born*	Barbra Streisand and Kris Kristofferson (soundtrack)
U.S. #1 R&B 45	"Don't Leave Me This Way"	Thelma Houston
U.K. #1 POP 45	"Don't Cry for Me Argentina"	Julie Convington
U.K. #1 POP LP	*Evita*	various artists

WEEK ENDING FEBRUARY 26

U.S. #1 POP 45	"New Kid in Town"	The Eagles
U.S. #1 POP LP	*A Star Is Born*	Barbra Streisand and Kris Kristofferson (soundtrack)
U.S. #1 R&B 45	"I've Got Love on My Mind"	Natalie Cole
U.K. #1 POP 45	"When I Need You"	Leo Sayer
U.K. #1 POP LP	*The Shadows' 20 Golden Greats*	The Shadows

1 In Santa Monica, California, **Sara Lowndes Dylan**—the subject of such songs as "Sad-Eyed Lady of the Lowlands," "Lay, Lady, Lay" and "Sara"—files for divorce from **Bob Dylan**, her husband of eleven years. The divorce will be granted in June, with Sara retaining legal custody of their children, **Maria**, **Jesse**, **Anna**, **Samuel** and **Jakob**, and possession of their million-dollar home in Santa Monica.

Manfred Mann gets his first gold record, for "Blinded by the Light," one of the several **Bruce Springsteen** songs covered by Mann and his group. "Blinded" hit Number One in February, thirteen years after the keyboardist's first Number One song, "Do Wah Diddy Diddy." Other Springsteen tunes interpreted by Manfred Mann's **Earth Band** include "Spirit in the Night" and "For You."

---

4 The **Rolling Stones** play the first of two concerts at El Mocambo, a small club in Toronto, Canada. While most of the attention at the time focuses on **Keith Richards**' recent arrest by Canadian authorities and the presence in the small audience of **Margaret Trudeau**, the wife of the Canadian prime minister, the real significance of the concerts will become apparent in September when *Love You Live* is released, with one side comprising the vintage R&B—**Chuck Berry**'s "Around and Around," **Willie Dixon**'s "Little Red Rooster," **Bo Diddley**'s "Crackin' Up" and **Muddy Waters**' "Mannish Boy"—recorded here.

9 **Fleetwood Mac**'s *Rumours* becomes their second album to go platinum since the addition of **Stevie Nicks** and **Lindsey Buckingham**.

10 Two months after EMI nulled its contract with the **Sex Pistols**, A&M Records, in a ceremony in front of Buckingham Palace, signs the English punk group that has been banned from airplay and from virtually every concert venue in Britain. Nine days later, without having released any Sex Pistols records, A&M will follow EMI's suit and terminate its association with the group, reportedly because of the reputation for attracting violence with which

the national news media have saddled the Sex Pistols, but more probably because of the obscenities members of the group have been hurling at A&M executives at business meetings.

Pink Floyd's *Animals*—only their second LP since 1973's landmark *The Dark Side of the Moon*—goes platinum. The album is a typical **Roger Waters**-and-company effort: moody, entrancing and lyrically conceptual. It hits #3.

11 The **Slits** make their stage debut, opening for the **Clash** at the Roxy in London. The first all-female punk group, the Slits will have to bear the double curse of their sex and their style, which takes the concept of enlightened amateurism to an extreme. Accompanying the Clash on their White Riot tour of the U.K. after having played only three gigs, the Slits will respond to charges of incompetence by inviting members of the audience on stage to play while the four women take to the floor to dance.

18 British CBS releases the **Clash**'s debut single, "White Riot" backed with "1977." In what will fast become typical of the Clash, "White Riot" sparks heated controversy. Many listeners interpret the song to advocate racial violence, when in fact it calls for a united black-and-white assault on society's powermongers.

25 After a decade of being rock's "Beautiful Loser," **Bob Seger** gets his big break, at age thirty three: *Night Moves,* his tenth LP, goes platinum, aided by three Top Forty singles: "Night Moves," "Mainstreet" and "Rock & Roll Never Forgets."

26 Stiff Records—a newly formed, London-based, small, independent company—releases "Less Than Zero" backed by "Radio Sweetheart," the first single by a former computer programmer named **Declan McManus**, whom his manager, **Jake Riviera**, has renamed **Elvis Costello**. The single is produced by **Nick Lowe** and is recorded with a California band named **Clover**; its release announces the emergence of new wave rock's sharpest songwriter.

29 Sweden's **Abba**, no strangers to the Top Ten, receive a gold record for their only U.S Number One, "Dancing Queen," a song perfectly timed for the raging disco movement. ◆

WEEK ENDING MARCH 5

U.S. #1 POP 45	"Evergreen"	Barbra Streisand
U.S. #1 POP LP	*A Star Is Born*	Barbra Streisand and Kris Kristofferson (soundtrack)
U.S. #1 R&B 45	"I've Got Love on My Mind"	Natalie Cole
U.K. #1 POP 45	"When I Need You"	Leo Sayer
U.K. #1 POP LP	*The Shadows 20 Golden Greats*	The Shadows

WEEK ENDING MARCH 12

U.S. #1 POP 45	"Evergreen"	Barbra Streisand
U.S. #1 POP LP	*A Star Is Born*	Barbra Streisand and Kris Kristofferson (soundtrack)
U.S. #1 R&B 45	"I've Got Love on My Mind"	Natalie Cole
U.K. #1 POP 45	"Chanson d'Amour"	Manhattan Transfer
U.K. #1 POP LP	*The Shadows 20 Golden Greats*	The Shadows

WEEK ENDING MARCH 19

U.S. #1 POP 45	"Evergreen"	Barbra Streisand
U.S. #1 POP LP	*A Star Is Born*	Barbra Streisand and Kris Kristofferson (soundtrack)
U.S. #1 R&B 45	"I've Got Love on My Mind"	Natalie Cole
U.K. #1 POP 45	"Chanson d'Amour"	Manhattan Transfer
U.K. #1 POP LP	*The Shadows 20 Golden Greats*	The Shadows

WEEK ENDING MARCH 26

U.S. #1 POP 45	"Rich Girl"	Hall and Oates
U.S. #1 POP LP	*Hotel California*	The Eagles
U.S. #1 R&B 45	"I've Got Love on My Mind"	Natalie Cole
U.K. #1 POP 45	"Knowing Me Knowing You"	Abba
U.K. #1 POP LP	*The Shadows 20 Golden Greats*	The Shadows

4 British CBS releases the **Clash**'s eponymous first album, a fourteen-song aural firebomb that contains such punk battle cries as "White Riot," "Police and Thieves" and "London's Burning." Claiming that the album is too harsh for American ears, American CBS will refuse to release it until 1979, and even then will delete some of the more virulent songs from the selection. In the meantime, Americans with tough ears will buy 100,000 imported copies of *The Clash*, making it one of the biggest-selling import records of all time.

5 At a three-day rally billed Japan Celebrates the Whale and Dolphin in Tokyo, **Jackson Browne**, **Richie Havens**, **John Sebastian**, **Country Joe McDonald** and **J. D. Souther** help to raise $150,000 for the effort to save whales and dolphins from the nets of the international fishing industry.

8 The **Damned**'s performance at New York City's CBGB marks the first appearance of a British punk group in America.

11 After performing for an audience of 40,000 in Sydney, Australia (the largest concert crowd in the country's history to date), **Alice Cooper** is placed under house arrest at his hotel until he posts a bond for $59,632—the sum which a local promoter, H. G. M. Attractions, claims to have paid Cooper for a 1975 Australian tour he never made. Cooper and H. G. M. will arrive at a court settlement that divides the money between the two parties when it is found that H. G. M. did not fulfill its part of the 1975 agreement either.

15 **Ronnie Van Zant** and **Gary Rossington** of **Lynyrd Skynyrd** present a gold disc awarded them for *One More from the Road* to Mayor **Maynard Jackson** of Atlanta, Georgia, in appreciation of their Atlanta fans. Another gold disc is awarded to representatives of Atlanta's Fox Theater, where the album was recorded live. In the afternoon, members of Lynyrd Skynyrd, along with **James Brown** and other prominent Georgians, are honored at a ceremony before the Atlanta Braves' opening home baseball game.

16 **Stevie Wonder** enters the soul chart with what will become another of his many Number One smash hits, "Sir Duke," a rollicking tribute to **Duke Ellington** that will top the chart in May.

24 **Joan Baez** and **Santana**, among others, perform a free concert for inmates of California's Soledad Prison. The concert was arranged and sponsored by Bread and Roses, a charitable foundation set up in 1974 by Baez' sister **Mimi Fariña**.

25 At a concert at the Saginaw, Michigan, Civic Center, **Elvis Presley** makes what will be the last recordings of his life. Three songs from the show will appear, in heavily overdubbed mixes, on the posthumously released Presley album *Moody Blue*.

26 Studio 54, destined to be the world's most famous disco during the height of the disco phenomenon, opens its carefully guarded doors for the first time. A converted television studio on New York City's West Fifty-fourth Street, the club is done up in the height of glittering chic: metallic-black walls, mirrored ceilings, neon-light sculptures, spotlit dance floors for those who want to be seen, shadowy alcoves furnished with plump couches for those involved in more private pursuits. But the décor and even the nonstop dance music take second billing to the rich, the beautiful, the famous and the infamous who annoint Studio 54 as the place for celebrities to spend those feverish hours between midnight and dawn; it is they who attract the throngs outside who wait for hours, hoping that the doormen will like their looks or their promises enough to let them past the velvet ropes and into Studio 54.

30 **Aretha Franklin**, enters the soul chart yet again, with "Break It to Me Gently," which in its fourteen weeks on the chart will peak at Number One for one week on June 18. It is her second soul Top Ten hit of the year—the first was the #10 "Look into Your Heart"—and will later be followed by one more big hit, the #16 "When I Think about You." ◆

WEEK ENDING APRIL 2		
U.S. #1 POP 45	"Rich Girl"	Hall and Oates
U.S. #1 POP LP	*Rumours*	Fleetwood Mac
U.S. #1 R&B 45	"Tryin' to Love Two"	William Bell
U.K. #1 POP 45	"Knowing Me Knowing You"	Abba
U.K. #1 POP LP	*The Shadows 20 Golden Greats*	The Shadows

WEEK ENDING APRIL 9		
U.S. #1 POP 45	"Dancing Queen"	Abba
U.S. #1 POP LP	*Rumours*	Fleetwood Mac
U.S. #1 R&B 45	"At Midnight (My Love Will Lift You Up)"	Rufus, featuring Chaka Khan
U.K. #1 POP 45	"Knowing Me Knowing You"	Abba
U.K. #1 POP LP	*Portrait of Sinatra*	Frank Sinatra

WEEK ENDING APRIL 16		
U.S. #1 POP 45	"Don't Give Up on Us"	David Soul
U.S. #1 POP LP	*Hotel California*	The Eagles
U.S. #1 R&B 45	"At Midnight (My Love Will Lift You Up)"	Rufus, featuring Chaka Khan
U.K. #1 POP 45	"Knowing Me Knowing You"	Abba
U.K. #1 POP LP	*Arrival*	Abba

WEEK ENDING APRIL 23		
U.S. #1 POP 45	"Don't Leave Me This Way"	Thelma Houston
U.S. #1 POP LP	*Hotel California*	The Eagles
U.S. #1 R&B 45	"The Pride (Part 1)"	The Isley Brothers
U.K. #1 POP 45	"Knowing Me Knowing You"	Abba
U.K. #1 POP LP	*Arrival*	Abba

WEEK ENDING APRIL 30		
U.S. #1 POP 45	"Southern Nights"	Glen Campbell
U.S. #1 POP LP	*Hotel California*	The Eagles
U.S. #1 R&B 45	"Got to Give It Up (Part 1)"	Marvin Gaye
U.K. #1 POP 45	"Knowing Me Knowing You"	Abba
U.K. #1 POP LP	*Arrival*	Abba

1 The **Clash** kick off their first tour of the U.K. with a May Day celebration at the Roxy in London. The forty-date White Riot tour—on which the Clash will be accompanied by the **Buzzcocks**, the **Slits**, the **Subway Sect** and (on some dates) the **Jam**—will spread "the scourge of punk" (as one provincial reporter will put it) outside of London before bringing it home for a concert at London's Rainbow Theatre. At that event, fans will rip out seats bolted to the floor to make room for dancing; the news media will see that as a fullfillment of the tour's billing and will describe it as a "riot."

2 More than three years after its release, **Bruce Springsteen**'s *The Wild, the Innocent and the E Street Shuffle* goes gold.

6 Attracting 76,229 fans to the Silverdome in Pontiac, Michigan, **Led Zeppelin** break their own world record for largest audience at a single-act concert.

8 **Olivia Newton-John** makes her New York City debut with a concert at the Metropolitan Opera House.

13 EMI in Britain and Capitol in the U.S. release *The Beatles at the Hollywood Bowl*, an album culled from live recordings made during the **Beatles**' American tours of 1964 and 1965. The album proves that, under the ear-splitting din of thousands of screaming Beatlemaniacs, the Beatles could perform on stage as well as they did in the studio. In the meantime, the Beatles are losing their court effort to prevent Lingasong Records from releasing *Live! At the Star Club, Hamburg, Germany, 1962*, an album recorded by **Ted "Kingsize" Taylor**, whose signed affidavit states that the Beatles agreed to let him tape a Hamburg gig with the words "It's okay by us, Ted, but you get the beer in."

Dolly Parton makes her New York City debut with a concert at the Bottom Line.

Linda Ronstadt denies reports that she has agreed to be photographed nude for the centerfold of *Hustler* magazine for a fee of $1 million. *Hustler* publisher **Larry Flynt** offered that sum to ten famous women, none of whom accepted. "I got the offer in the mail," said Ronstadt. "I laughed at it, and then threw it in the wastebasket."

16 No one paid much notice when ex-**Spooky Tooth** veteran **Mick Jones** and ex-**King Crimson Ian McDonald** joined together to form a band in 1976. The half-English, half-American sextet, called **Foreigner**, quietly released a debut LP in early 1977 and watched it soar to #4. On this date, it goes gold.

20 **Blondie** makes its U.K. stage debut with an appearance at the London Roundhouse the night before setting off on a tour of Britain with fellow New Yorkers **Television**.

26 **William Powell** of the **O'Jays** dies at age thirty-five in Canton, Ohio, after a long bout with cancer. Powell was an original member of the O'Jays (formed in 1958 as the **Mascots**) and sang with them until he was forced to quit the group in 1976 because of his health.

27 Two weeks after signing the **Sex Pistols**, Virgin Records releases "God Save the Queen" to coincide with **Queen Elizabeth**'s Silver Jubilee celebration in June. The song, which begins, "God save the Queen, she ain't no human being," will forthwith be banned from British airplay because of its "treasonous sentiments." Nonetheless, it will hit Number One on the British chart, listed in some reports with a blank line where the title should be.

28 **Bruce Springsteen** and his former manager, **Mike Appel**, reach an out-of-court settlement on Springsteen's July 1976 suit and Appel's countersuit, which have prevented the New Jersey rock & roller from recording for almost a year. The settlement grants Springsteen rights to his songs, the privilege of choosing his own producer, and the power to renegotiate his contract with Columbia Records. Appel, whose ties with Springsteen are severed, will receive a cash payment reported to be close to a million dollars.

29 **Goddard Lieberson**, an executive of Columbia Records for over thirty-five years, dies in New York City at age sixty-six. Lieberson oversaw Columbia's rise to prominence in the pop music field in the Sixties by opening the company to talent brought in by his associates, **John Hammond** and **Clive Davis**.

Elvis Presley walks off stage in the middle of a concert in Baltimore, Maryland—the first time in his twenty-three-year career he has done so except in the case of illness.

31 **Emerson, Lake and Palmer**, having recently finished recording their ambitious *Works, Volume One*, begin a tour of the United States accompanied by a seventy-piece orchestra. ◆

WEEK ENDING MAY 7

U.S. #1 POP 45	"Hotel California"	The Eagles
U.S. #1 POP LP	*Hotel California*	The Eagles
U.S. #1 R&B 45	"Got to Give It Up, Part 1"	Marvin Gaye
U.K. #1 POP 45	"Free"	Deniece Williams
U.K. #1 POP LP	*Arrival*	Abba

WEEK ENDING MAY 14

U.S. #1 POP 45	"When I Need You"	Leo Sayer
U.S. #1 POP LP	*Hotel California*	The Eagles
U.S. #1 R&B 45	"Got to Give It Up, Part 1"	Marvin Gaye
U.K. #1 POP 45	"Free"	Deniece Williams
U.K. #1 POP LP	*Arrival*	Abba

WEEK ENDING MAY 21

U.S. #1 POP 45	"Sir Duke"	Stevie Wonder
U.S. #1 POP LP	*Rumours*	Fleetwood Mac
U.S. #1 R&B 45	"Whodunit"	Tavares
U.K. #1 POP 45	"Free"	Deniece Williams
U.K. #1 POP LP	*Arrival*	Abba

WEEK ENDING MAY 28

U.S. #1 POP 45	"Sir Duke"	Stevie Wonder
U.S. #1 POP LP	*Rumours*	Fleetwood Mac
U.S. #1 R&B 45	"Sir Duke"	Stevie Wonder
U.K. #1 POP 45	"I Don't Want to Talk"/"The First Cut Is Deepest"	Rod Stewart
U.K. #1 POP LP	*Hotel California*	The Eagles

5 "Sleepy" John Estes dies at age seventy-seven after suffering a stroke in a Brownsville, Tennessee, hospital. Estes was one of the authentic country blues singers and guitarists "rediscovered" by young blues and folk-music enthusiasts in the early Sixties. In the Seventies, he recorded with **Ry Cooder** and **Mike Bloomfield**, and the **Joy of Cooking** had a minor hit with his "Going to Brownsville."

Alice Cooper, preparing for his first American concert appearance in two years (kicking off on June 19 in Anaheim, California), suffers a setback when his boa constrictor—for many years a feature of his stage act—is mortally bitten by the live rat it was fed for breakfast ("Like being hit on by your Wheaties," mourns Cooper). A public audition for a new performing snake is scheduled for June 13 at the ABC Entertainment Center in Century City, California, where a panel of judges consisting of Cooper, **Jaye P. Morgan**, **Howard Kaylan** and **Mark Volman** (**Flo and Eddie**) will choose a boa named **Angel** from a field of forty slithering herpetoids.

6 **Stevie Wonder** delivers an unannounced lecture to a UCLA class studying the record industry. (The *Billboard*-sponsored course is titled "Number One with a Star.") Wonder discusses his up-and-down relationship with Motown Records and then performs a brief set—his first in the U.S. in a year and a half.

10 **Joe Strummer** and **Topper Headon** of the **Clash** are arrested for painting their band's name on a London wall.

16 *Beatlemania*, a musical revue based on songs by **John Lennon** and **Paul McCartney** and starring four **Beatle** lookalikes, opens at the Winter Garden Theatre on New York City's Broadway. The show will run for 1,006 performances, moving later to Broadway's Lunt Theatre and then the Palace Theatre before closing in 1980.

17 **Michael Schenker**, the German lead guitarist of the English heavy-metal band **UFO**, disappears after a concert in Leeds, England, and is feared to be sick, dead or absconded by Moonies. He will turn up in Germany six months later, explaining that he wanted to quit UFO but didn't know how to say so in English, so he simply left without a word. Schenker will, however, continue to play on and off with UFO until 1980, when he forms the Michael Schenker Group.

18 Knife-wielding hoodlums, offended by the **Sex Pistols'** antimonarchist stance in their hit single "God Save the Queen," attack the group's **Johnny Rotten** on a London street, slashing his face and hands. The following day, Sex Pistol **Paul Cook** will be jumped by another gang of royalists and beaten with an iron pipe.

20 Island Records releases **Steve Winwood's** eponymous first solo album and first record under any name since **Traffic's** *When the Eagle Flies* three years earlier. *Steve Winwood* will reach #22 on the American LP chart.

24 Harvest/EMI Records releases the first punk compilation album, *Live at the Roxy*. The set includes concert numbers by the **Buzzcocks**, **Eater**, **Johnny Moped**, **X-Ray Spex**, the **Adverts**, **Slaughter and the Dogs**, the **Unwanted** and **Wire**, recorded at London's preeminent punk club.

25 The **Emotions'** "Best of My Love" hits Number One on the R&B chart; two months later, it will do the same on the pop chart. The female vocal trio was formed in 1968 by the three **Hutchinson** sisters, **Wanda**, **Sheila** and **Jeanette**, who had been singing gospel music professionally since the beginning of the decade. "Best of My Love," recorded after touring with **Earth, Wind and Fire**, was written and produced by Earth, Wind and Fire's **Maurice White**. In 1979, the Emotions will team up with Earth, Wind and Fire for "Boogie Wonderland"—a hit which, like "Best of My Love," sets gospel-style singing to a disco beat—but "Best of My Love" will remain the Emotions' biggest commercial success.

The **Floaters'** first single, "Float On," enters the R&B chart, where it will reach Number One in August. Peaking at #2 on the pop chart, it will be this Detroit vocal quartet's biggest hit.

26 **Elvis Presley** makes what will be his last public appearance with a concert at the Market Square Arena in Indianapolis, Indiana.

30 Marvel Comics, the publishing company that introduced such superheroes of American pop culture as Spider Man, issues the first of two comic books based on the costumed and masked stage characters of the members of **Kiss**. The red ink for the initial printing was reportedly mixed with small amounts of blood from each member of the group. ◆

WEEK ENDING JUNE 4

U.S. #1 POP 45	"Sir Duke"	Stevie Wonder
U.S. #1 POP LP	*Rumours*	Fleetwood Mac
U.S. #1 R&B 45	"Got to Give It Up, Part 1"	Marvin Gaye
U.K. #1 POP 45	"I Don't Want to Talk"/"The First Cut Is Deepest"	Rod Stewart
U.K. #1 POP LP	*Hotel California*	The Eagles

WEEK ENDING JUNE 11

U.S. #1 POP 45	"I'm Your Boogie Man"	K.C. and the Sunshine Band
U.S. #1 POP LP	*Rumours*	Fleetwood Mac
U.S. #1 R&B 45	"Got to Give It Up, Part 1"	Marvin Gaye
U.K. #1 POP 45	"I Don't Want to Talk"/"The First Cut Is Deepest"	Rod Stewart
U.K. #1 POP LP	*Arrival*	Abba

WEEK ENDING JUNE 18

U.S. #1 POP 45	"Dreams"	Fleetwood Mac
U.S. #1 POP LP	*Rumours*	Fleetwood Mac
U.S. #1 R&B 45	"Break It to Me Gently"	Aretha Franklin
U.K. #1 POP 45	"God Save the Queen"	The Sex Pistols
U.K. #1 POP LP	*Arrival*	Abba

WEEK ENDING JUNE 25

U.S. #1 POP 45	"Got to Give It Up, Part 1"	Marvin Gaye
U.S. #1 POP LP	*Rumours*	Fleetwood Mac
U.S. #1 R&B 45	"Best of My Love"	The Emotions
U.K. #1 POP 45	"Show You the Way to Go"	The Jacksons
U.K. #1 POP LP	*Beatles at the Hollywood Bowl*	The Beatles

4 Original **Blondie** bassist and cowriter of "Touched by Your Presence, Dear," **Gary Valentine**, leaves the band.

9 **Bernard Brook-Partridge** of the Greater London Council explains to the *New Musical Express* the G.L.C.'s intentions regarding the ban against public appearances in Greater London by the **Sex Pistols**: "I think the Sex Pistols are absolutely bloody revolting. There are two members of this authority, Mr. **John Branagan** of the Labour Party and myself, who would do anything they could within the law to stop them from ever appearing in London again. I'd be quite unscrupulous in the way I lobbied my colleagues. No way do we want them back here."

13 A city-wide power outage in New York City

brings **Boz Scaggs'** Avery Fisher Hall concert to a premature end. But at the Bottom Line, **NRBQ**, taping flashlights to their microphone stands, transform their concert into an acoustic set.

14 British television has either forgotten or forgiven the **Sex Pistols'** scatological utterances on their first TV appearance in December 1976, for the BBC has brought them back for an appearance on "Top of the Pops" to perform "Pretty Vacant."

16 The **Commodores** attain their second R&B Number One with "Easy." It is a considerably different kind of song from their first Number One, "Just to Be Close to You" in 1976, which was a conventional soul harmony ballad. "Easy" is a country & western song, and it shows the Commodores—

Motown's most successful act in the second half of the Seventies—diversifying beyond the mix of soul ballads and funky dance songs for which they are known.

20 **Gary Kellgren**, operator and part owner of two of the most popular recording studios on the West Coast—the Los Angeles Record Plant and the Sausalito Record Plant—drowns in a Hollywood

swimming pool. He had engineered or produced albums by **Jimi Hendrix**, **Rod Stewart**, **Sly and the Family Stone**, **John Lennon**, **George Harrison**, **Ringo Starr** and **Barbra Streisand**. He was thirty-eight.

22 Stiff Records releases **Elvis Costello**'s first album, *My Aim Is True*, in Britain. The **Nick Lowe**-produced album includes "Less Than Zero," "Mystery Dance," "Watching the Detectives," "Miracle Man," "Alison" and other songs about "guilt and revenge," as Costello will describe them. The album will be released in the U.S. by Columbia on October 15.

23 **Led Zeppelin**'s drummer, **John Bonham**, manager, **Peter Grant**, and two security guards are arrested backstage at the Oakland Coliseum in Oakland, California, and charged with battery after allegedly beating up three employees of **Bill Graham**, who served as promoter for Led Zeppelin's Oakland concert. After pleading guilty to misdemeanors, the Zep four will settle out of court a $2 million suit filed by the Graham three.

26 **Led Zeppelin**'s American tour, which got off to an uncertain start because of illness in the band, ends abruptly with seven dates remaining when vocalist **Robert Plant**'s six-year-old son **Karac** dies unexpectedly of a respiratory ailment in England.

30 **Slave** reaches Number One on the R&B chart with its first single, "Slide." This twelve-man funk and rock band from Dayton, Ohio, led by vocalist **Steve Arrington**, will go on to issue such hits as "Just a Touch of Love," "Watching You," "Snap Shot" and "Funkentown." ◆

WEEK ENDING JULY 2

U.S. #1 POP 45	"Gonna Fly Now (Theme from *Rocky*)"	Bill Conti
U.S. #1 POP LP	*Rumours*	Fleetwood Mac
U.S. #1 R&B 45	"Best of My Love"	The Emotions
U.K. #1 POP 45	"Show You the Way to Go"	The Jacksons
U.K. #1 POP LP	*The Muppet Show*	The Muppets

WEEK ENDING JULY 9

U.S. #1 POP 45	"Undercover Angel"	Alan O'Day
U.S. #1 POP LP	*Rumours*	Fleetwood Mac
U.S. #1 R&B 45	"Best of My Love"	The Emotions
U.K. #1 POP 45	"So You Win Again"	Hot Chocolate
U.K. #1 POP LP	*A Star Is Born*	Barbra Streisand and Kris Kristofferson (soundtrack)

WEEK ENDING JULY 16

U.S. #1 POP 45	"Da Doo Ron Ron"	Shaun Cassidy
U.S. #1 POP LP	*Live*	Barry Manilow
U.S. #1 R&B 45	"Easy"	The Commodores
U.K. #1 POP 45	"Ma Baker"	Boney M
U.K. #1 POP LP	*A Star Is Born*	Barbra Streisand and Kris Kristofferson (soundtrack)

WEEK ENDING JULY 23

U.S. #1 POP 45	"Looks Like We Made It"	Barry Manilow
U.S. #1 POP LP	*Rumours*	Fleetwood Mac
U.S. #1 R&B 45	"Best of My Love"	The Emotions
U.K. #1 POP 45	"I Feel Love"	Donna Summer
U.K. #1 POP LP	*The Johnny Mathis Collection*	Johnny Mathis

WEEK ENDING JULY 30

U.S. #1 POP 45	"I Just Want to Be Your Everything"	Andy Gibb
U.S. #1 POP LP	*Rumours*	Fleetwood Mac
U.S. #1 R&B 45	"Slide"	Slave
U.K. #1 POP 45	"I Feel Love"	Donna Summer
U.K. #1 POP LP	*The Johnny Mathis Collection*	Johnny Mathis

1 *Elvis: What Happened?*, a sensationalistic account of **Elvis Presley**'s personal life and his drug problems, is published by Ballantine. Written by ex-bodyguards **Red** and **Sonny West** and **Dave Hebler**, with *The National Star*'s entertainment editor, **Steve Dunleavy**, *What Happened?* presented Presley as an overweight recluse obsessed with religion and the supernatural (according to the authors, Presley believed he possessed the power to heal), who attempted to have **Mike Stone**, the karate instructor with whom his ex-wife, **Priscilla**, was involved, killed. Within a few weeks, the authors will call a press conference to state that their reason for writing the book was not to make money but to save Presley from himself. The book will sell over three million copies.

9 The **Tom Robinson Band** is signed to EMI. Robinson, an avowed homosexual activist, is one of the most politically minded songwriters of the British new wave, but TRB's biggest U.K. hit, "2-4-6-8 Motorway" (#5), will be in the rock & roll tradition of driving songs like "Little Deuce Coupe," "Route 66" and "Hot Rod Lincoln."

13 The **Bachman-Turner Overdrive** disbands. Formed in 1970 by **Randy Bachman**, an original member of the **Guess Who**, with his brothers **Robbie** and **Tim** in addition to **C. F. Turner**, the Canadian group recorded two albums for Warner Bros. under the name **Brave Belt** before signing with Mercury and releasing their first gold album, *BTO*. A second gold album, *BTO II*, and gold singles "Takin' Care of Business" and "You Ain't Seen Nothing Yet," followed. 1974's *Not Fragile* and *Four Wheel Drive* were platinum albums, and the musically *and* physiologically heavy band commanded huge concert audiences. BTO calls it quits just as their popularity is beginning to wane.

16 The King is dead. **Elvis Presley** dies in his Memphis mansion, Graceland, at age forty-two. According to Presley's girlfriend **Ginger Alden**, she had awakened in the afternoon, and, noticing he was not in bed, went into the master bedroom's bathroom, where she discovered him lying on the floor. Efforts to resuscitate Presley were unsuccessful, and at 3:30 p.m. today, he is pronounced dead at Memphis' Baptist Memorial Hospital. According to reports, the death resulted from coronary arrhythmia. Within the next several hours, Presley's death becomes one of the biggest media events in the past twenty years. Though Presley was the King of Rock & Roll, by the time of his death he had amassed an equally great and no less fervent following as a Las Vegas-style entertainer. Within hours, thousands of fans are en route to Memphis to pay their respects.

17 The day after **Elvis Presley**'s death, **President Jimmy Carter** issues the following statement: "Elvis Presley's death deprives our country of a part of itself. He was unique and irreplaceable. More than twenty years ago, he burst upon the scene with an impact that was unprecedented and will probably never be equaled. His music and his personality, fusing the styles of white country and black rhythm and blues, permanently changed the face of American popular culture. His following was immense, and he was a symbol to people the world over, of the vitality, rebelliousness and good humor of his country." Or, as **James Brown** had once put it, "He taught white America to get down."

Florists' Transworld Delivery (FTD) reports that in one day the number of orders for flowers to be delivered to Graceland, the late **Elvis Presley**'s earthly paradise, has surpassed the number for any other event in the company's history.

18 Funeral services for **Elvis Presley** are held at Graceland. Outside are over 75,000 mourners. Inside are 150, including his ex-wife, **Priscilla**, daughter **Lisa**, father, **Vernon**, **Ann-Margaret**, **George Hamilton** and **Colonel Tom Parker** (in shirt sleeves and a baseball cap). Presley was entombed in a white marble mausoleum at Forest Hill Cemetery in Memphis near the grave of his mother, **Gladys**.

26 Stiff Records releases **Ian Dury**'s first solo single, "Sex and Drugs and Rock and Roll." Dury, a former member of **Kilburn and the High Roads** (a favorite act on the British pub circuit) recorded the song with **High Roaders Chaz Jankel** and **Davey Payne**, with whom he will soon form the **Blockheads**. Ian Dury and the Blockheads' "Hit Me with Your Rhythm Stick" will be a million-selling international hit in 1979.

27 A picnic at **Levon Helm**'s home in Woodstock, New York, provides the occasion for the formation of the **RCO All-Stars**, with drummer **Helm**, pianist **Mac "Dr. John" Rebennack**, guitarist **Steve Cropper**, bassist **Donald Dunn** and harmonica player **Paul Butterfield**. Helm's former colleague in the Band, **Robbie Robertson**, is also at the picnic, but declines to join the group, which will set off on its first tour in the fall. ◆

WEEK ENDING AUGUST 6

U.S. #1 POP 45	"I Just Want to Be Your Everything"	Andy Gibb
U.S. #1 POP LP	*Rumours*	Fleetwood Mac
U.S. #1 R&B 45	"Strawberry Letter 23"	The Brothers Johnson
U.K. #1 POP 45	"I Feel Love"	Donna Summer
U.K. #1 POP LP	*The Johnny Mathis Collection*	Johnny Mathis

WEEK ENDING AUGUST 13

U.S. #1 POP 45	"I Just Want to Be Your Everything"	Andy Gibb
U.S. #1 POP LP	*Rumours*	Fleetwood Mac
U.S. #1 R&B 45	"Float On"	The Floaters
U.K. #1 POP 45	"I Feel Love"	Donna Summer
U.K. #1 POP LP	*The Johnny Mathis Collection*	Johnny Mathis

WEEK ENDING AUGUST 20

U.S. #1 POP 45	"Best of My Love"	The Emotions
U.S. #1 POP LP	*Rumours*	Fleetwood Mac
U.S. #1 R&B 45	"Float On"	The Floaters
U.K. #1 POP 45	"I Feel Love"	Donna Summer
U.K. #1 POP LP	*Going for the One*	Yes

WEEK ENDING AUGUST 27

U.S. #1 POP 45	"Best of My Love"	The Emotions
U.S. #1 POP LP	*Rumours*	Fleetwood Mac
U.S. #1 R&B 45	"Float On"	The Floaters
U.K. #1 POP 45	"Angelo"	The Brotherhood of Man
U.K. #1 POP LP	*Going for the One*	Yes

1 **Ethel Waters**, one of the most popular American entertainers of the century, dies in Chatsworth, California, at age eighty-one. A singer whose repertoire covered the blues, jazz, music hall and pop, and an actress of the stage and screen who was equally adept at vaudeville comedy and high drama, she is best remembered for her recordings of "St. Louis Blues," "Am I Blue?" and "Stormy Weather" and her appearances in such films as *Cabin in the Sky, Stage Door Canteen* and *Member of the Wedding*.

Blondie signs its first major record company contract, with Chrysalis. The New York City new wave band led by guitarist **Chris Stein** and fronted by his girlfriend, vocalist **Deborah Harry**, has already released records on the small, independent Private Stock label, attracting cult followings in New York City, Los Angeles and London but failing to sell many records. Such Chrysalis albums as *Parallel Lines, Eat to the Beat* and *Autoamerican,* however, will sell many millions.

3 One hundred ten thousand music fans descend on Old Bridge, New Jersey, for an eleven-hour concert by the **Grateful Dead**, the **New Riders of the Purple Sage** and the **Marshall Tucker Band**.

4 After 527 performances at Broadway's Broadhurst Theater and 2,118 performances at the off-Broadway Cherry Lane Theater, the curtains are lowered on *Godspell* for good. The **Stephen Schwartz** rock musical based on the Gospel according to Matthew spawned a Top Fifteen hit, "Day by Day," in 1972.

8 Guitarist **Jimmy McCulloch** quits **Paul McCartney and Wings** to join a re-formed lineup of the **Small Faces**. McCulloch, who had previously played with **Thunderclap Newman** and **Stone the Crows**, joined Wings in 1975, played on three of their most successful albums and accompanied them on the Wings over America tour of 1976. His stint with the Small Faces will last only the duration of a September tour of the British Isles, after which he'll be off to form his own group, the **Dukes**.

11 **Bernie Taupin**, **Elton John**'s lyricist, makes his television acting debut on ABC's "The Hardy Boys and Nancy Drew Meet Dracula." He plays the leader of a band called **Circus**.

16 **Marc Bolan** is killed when the car he is riding (driven by his girlfriend, American singer **Gloria Jones**) crashes into a tree on the outskirts of London. He was twenty-nine. Bolan (born **Mark Feld**) first appeared on the London pop scene as a model for Mod fashions in the early Sixties. He made his first record in 1966 and was a member of **John's Children** before he formed **Tyrannosaurus Rex** in 1968. T. Rex, originally an acoustic duo, became one of the most popular acts of the "glam rock" movement of the early Seventies, a period in which the group had eleven British Top Ten singles. T. Rex never managed to attract that sort of popularity in America, where only "Bang a Gong (Get It On)" made the Top Ten. By mid-decade, the records stopped hitting in Britain too, but Bolan could still draw crowds to his concerts, and he recently began work on his own weekly television show.

The **Rolling Stones** release their third live album, *Love You Live*. The two-record set on the Rolling Stones label was recorded in Paris in 1976 and in Toronto in March of this year. It's all ho-hum stuff by now, but the package shoots to #5 on the American album chart.

23 British CBS releases the **Clash**'s "Complete Control" backed with "City of the Dead." The single was recorded this summer in Kingston, Jamaica, with **Lee "Scratch" Perry**, the legendary reggae producer, at the board. Perry had introduced himself to the Clash after hearing their version of "Police and Thieves," a song he had written and produced for **Junior Murvin**. This meeting of punk and reggae will be the inspiration for Perry's next collaboration with **Bob Marley**: "Punky Reggae Party," which will be a British Top Ten single for **Bob Marley and the Wailers** in December.

28 **David Bowie** accepts **Bing Crosby**'s invitation to appear as a special guest on Der Bingle's annual Christmas television special. Bowie and Bing duet on "Little Drummer Boy" and "Peace on Earth."

29 **James Brown**'s band, complaining that the Hardest-Working Man in Show Business has been underpaying them, walk out on him in Hallendale, Florida.

30 British blues band **Foghat** plays a benefit concert at New York City's Palladium to fund the purchase and preservation of rare blues records by the Rodgers and Hammerstein Archives of Recorded Sound of the New York Public Library at Lincoln Center. ◆

WEEK ENDING SEPTEMBER 3

U.S. #1 POP 45	"Best of My Love"	The Emotions
U.S. #1 POP LP	*Rumours*	Fleetwood Mac
U.S. #1 R&B 45	"Float On"	The Floaters
U.K. #1 POP 45	"Way Down"	Elvis Presley
U.K. #1 POP LP	*Moody Blue*	Elvis Presley

WEEK ENDING SEPTEMBER 10

U.S. #1 POP 45	"Best of My Love"	The Emotions
U.S. #1 POP LP	*Rumours*	Fleetwood Mac
U.S. #1 R&B 45	"Float On"	The Floaters
U.K. #1 POP 45	"Magic Fly"	Space
U.K. #1 POP LP	*Oxygene*	Jean-Michel Jarre

WEEK ENDING SEPTEMBER 17

U.S. #1 POP 45	"Best of My Love"	The Emotions
U.S. #1 POP LP	*Rumours*	Fleetwood Mac
U.S. #1 R&B 45	"Float On"	The Floaters
U.K. #1 POP 45	"Magic Fly"	Space
U.K. #1 POP LP	*Oxygene*	Jean-Michel Jarre

WEEK ENDING SEPTEMBER 24

U.S. #1 POP 45	"Best of My Love"	The Emotions
U.S. #1 POP LP	*Rumours*	Fleetwood Mac
U.S. #1 R&B 45	"Keep It Comin' Love"	K.C. and the Sunshine Band
U.K. #1 POP 45	"Magic Fly"	Space
U.K. #1 POP LP	*20 Golden Greats*	Diana Ross and the Supremes

1 **Elton John** becomes the first rock & roller to be honored in New York City's Madison Square Garden Hall of Fame.

2 Over a month following what appeared to be an attempt to steal **Elvis Presley**'s body from Forest Hill Cemetery, both Presley's and his mother **Gladys**' bodies are moved to Graceland. There they are buried behind the mansion in the Meditation Garden.

3 Stiff Records puts together an old-fashioned package tour to promote its small, eclectic roster, with **Elvis Costello**, **Nick Lowe**, **Ian Dury and the Blockheads** and **Wreckless Eric** among them. The low-budget Live Stiffs tour of the British Isles kicks off in London.

7 After seven years with **Genesis** and a 1975 solo album to his credit, guitarist **Steve Hackett** leaves the group to concentrate on a solo career. Genesis will carry on as a trio (drummer and vocalist **Phil Collins**, keyboardist **Tony Banks** and bassist **Michael Rutherford**), titling their next album *And Then There Were Three . . .* Hackett's first album after leaving the group, *Please Don't Touch*, will be out within a year.

RCA releases **David Bowie**'s *"Heroes,"* his second album recorded in Berlin and produced by **Brian Eno**. Bowie will soon release German and French versions of the title track in addition to the original English recording.

14 At the request of the Los Angeles Dodgers, **Linda Ronstadt** sings the national anthem at Dodgers Stadium to open the third game of the World Series. The New York Yankees go on to win the game.

19 One of the most popular black rock & roll acts in 1977 is the **Brothers Johnson** (**George** and **Louis**). Their "Strawberry Letter 23" is certified gold on this date, having recently hit Number One on the R&B chart and #5 on the pop chart. The song was written by **Shuggie Otis** and produced by **Quincy Jones**.

20 Three days after the release of **Lynyrd Skynyrd**'s *Street Survivors*, an album whose cover depicts the band standing amid flames, Lynyrd Skynyrd vocalist **Ronnie Van Zant**, guitarist **Steve Gaines** and **Cassie Gaines**, Steve's sister and a freelance singer touring with the band, are killed when their rented single-engine plane crashes in the swamps of Gillsburg, Mississippi. The musicians were en route to Baton Rouge, Louisiana. Van Zant was an original member of the band, formed in Jacksonville, Florida, in the late Sixties; Gaines had joined little over a year ago. The deaths will mean the end of Lynyrd Skynyrd, whose "Free Bird" and "Sweet Home Alabama" were pop Top Twenty singles, although all of the survivors, except for **Artimus Pyle**, will go on to form the **Rossington-Collins Band**.

28 Warner Bros. releases the **Sex Pistols**' first album, *Never Mind the Bollocks, Here's the Sex Pistols*, in the U.S., jumping the gun of Virgin Records, which releases the album in the U.K. four days later. With "Anarchy in the U.K.," "God Save the Queen," "Pretty Vacant" and "Holidays in the Sun"—all British hit singles (and all included on the album)—the Sex Pistols have already created a big noise in their homeland. In America, however, the seminal punk group will be scarcely noticed (the album will peak at #106 on the chart) until they make their first appearances in person in January 1978.

29 Disco music gets a refreshing shot of wit and sophistication when **Chic**'s debut single, "Dance, Dance, Dance (Yowsah, Yowsah, Yowsah)," enters the R&B chart. The New York City quartet is led by bassist **Bernard Edwards** and guitarist **Nile Rodgers**, who will soon become the most influential figures in dance music of the late Seventies and early Eighties, working as songwriters, musicians and producers with **Sister Sledge**, **Diana Ross**, **Debbie Harry**, **David Bowie** and others. Their springy rhythms and stripped-down arrangements are introduced on "Dance, Dance, Dance," a record that will sell over 1 million copies, reaching #6 on both the R&B and pop charts. ◆

WEEK ENDING OCTOBER 1

U.S. #1 POP 45	"Stars Wars Theme/Cantina Band"	Meco
U.S. #1 POP LP	*Rumours*	Fleetwood Mac
U.S. #1 R&B 45	"It's Ecstasy When You Lay Down Next to Me"	Barry White
U.K. #1 POP 45	"Way Down"	Elvis Presley
U.K. #1 POP LP	*20 Golden Greats*	Diana Ross and the Supremes

WEEK ENDING OCTOBER 8

U.S. #1 POP 45	"Stars Wars Theme/Cantina Band"	Meco
U.S. #1 POP LP	*Rumours*	Fleetwood Mac
U.S. #1 R&B 45	"It's Ecstasy When You Lay Down Next to Me"	Barry White
U.K. #1 POP 45	"Way Down"	Elvis Presley
U.K. #1 POP LP	*20 Golden Greats*	Diana Ross and the Supremes

WEEK ENDING OCTOBER 15

U.S. #1 POP 45	"You Light Up My Life"	Debby Boone
U.S. #1 POP LP	*Rumours*	Fleetwood Mac
U.S. #1 R&B 45	"It's Ecstasy When You Lay Down Next to Me"	Barry White
U.K. #1 POP 45	"Silver Lady"	David Soul
U.K. #1 POP LP	*20 Golden Greats*	Diana Ross and the Supremes

WEEK ENDING OCTOBER 22

U.S. #1 POP 45	"You Light Up My Life"	Debby Boone
U.S. #1 POP LP	*Rumours*	Fleetwood Mac
U.S. #1 R&B 45	"It's Ecstasy When You Lay Down Next to Me"	Barry White
U.K. #1 POP 45	"Yes Sir I Can Boogie"	Baccara
U.K. #1 POP LP	*20 Golden Greats*	Diana Ross and the Supremes

WEEK ENDING OCTOBER 29

U.S. #1 POP 45	"You Light Up My Life"	Debby Boone
U.S. #1 POP LP	*Rumours*	Fleetwood Mac
U.S. #1 R&B 45	"It's Ecstasy When You Lay Down Next to Me"	Barry White
U.K. #1 POP 45	"You're in My Heart (The Final Acclaim)"	Rod Stewart
U.K. #1 POP LP	*20 Golden Greats*	Diana Ross and the Supremes

3 During a concert at the Empire Pool in London, **Elton John** announces that he is retiring from live performances. John will be good to his word for fifteen months. On February 3, 1979, he will resume touring with a concert in Sweden.

4 *The Last Waltz*, **Martin Scorsese**'s documentary about the **Band**'s Thanksgiving 1976 farewell concert, premieres in New York City. The film features performances by such long-term Band associates as **Bob Dylan** and **Ronnie Hawkins**, as well as offstage vignettes of the group and scenes with the **Staple Singers** and **Emmylou Harris** filmed on an MGM soundstage in Hollywood.

9 **Donna Summer** is awarded a gold record for "I Feel Love," a haunting, erotic recording that turns on the electronic ticker-tape sounds of a sequencer. The song is her second Top Ten hit, and though not as successful as her first hit, "Love to Love You Baby," (which was a #2 pop and a #3 R&B in 1976, whereas "I Feel Love" will peak at #6 pop

and #9 R&B within ten days), "I Feel Love" will nonetheless prove to be the more influential on future dance music. Its mesmerizing mechanical percussion and synthesizer-sequencer riffs foreshadow later "technopop" and "Euro-disco" hits by **Gary Numan**, **Wazmo Nariz**, **Human League** and countless others.

16 The Canadian trio **Rush** receive three gold records, for *2112, All the World's a Stage* and their most recent, *A Farewell to Kings*. The group, which started out as a **Led Zeppelin**-inspired power trio, opted for a more experimental, progressive direction on those LPs and found itself a sizable audience.

19 **Natalie Cole** caps off a big year as her single "Our Love" enters the soul chart, where in its twenty-four weeks on the chart it will hit Number One for two weeks starting January 21, 1979. Earlier this year, her "I've Got Love on My Mind" was Number One for five weeks starting February 26, and her "Party Lights" hit #9 in August.

22 Weddings and bar mitzvahs are never the same

K.C. and the Sunshine Band, the most successful of Miami's T.K. stable of disco-soul acts, enter the soul singles chart for the third and last time this year with "Wrap Your Arms around Me," which will peak at #24 in its thirteen weeks on the chart. Their other hits this year included the #3 "I'm Your Boogie Man" and "Keep It Comin' Love," Number One for one week starting September 24.

again after **Debby Boone** has a Number One hit with "You Light Up My Life." The song, from the **Joe Brooks** film of the same name, quickly becomes an easy-listening classic, something which no doubt makes papa **Pat Boone** quite proud. The record goes platinum on this date.

26 French "Euro-disco" unit **Le Pamplemousse** enter the soul singles chart with "Le Spank," a glossy, mechanized reworking of a classic **James Brown** riff, which will peak at #13 in its nineteen weeks on the chart.

29 **Kansas**, riding the crest of popularity forged by the 1976 hit "Carry On Wayward Son," enjoy their biggest album to date, *Point of Know Return*, which goes platinum. Earlier in the year, their *Leftoverture* turned gold.

With the advent of punk and so-called corporate rock, and a general lack of interest in the blues, **John Mayall**'s career is hardly thriving by 1977. But his 1970 album *The Turning Point* goes gold on this date. ◆

WEEK ENDING NOVEMBER 5

U.S. #1 POP 45	"You Light Up My Life"	Debby Boone
U.S. #1 POP LP	*Rumours*	Fleetwood Mac
U.S. #1 R&B 45	"(Every Time I Turn Around) Back in Love Again"	L.T.D.
U.K. #1 POP 45	"Yes Sir I Can Boogies"	Baccara
U.K. #1 POP LP	*20 Golden Greats*	Diana Ross and the Supremes

WEEK ENDING NOVEMBER 12

U.S. #1 POP 45	"You Light Up My Life"	Debby Boone
U.S. #1 POP LP	*Rumours*	Fleetwood Mac
U.S. #1 R&B 45	"(Every Time I Turn Around) Back in Love Again"	L.T.D.
U.K. #1 POP 45	"Name of the Game"	Abba
U.K. #1 POP LP	*Sound of Bread*	Bread

WEEK ENDING NOVEMBER 19

U.S. #1 POP 45	"You Light Up My Life"	Debby Boone
U.S. #1 POP LP	*Rumours*	Fleetwood Mac
U.S. #1 R&B 45	"Serpentine Fire"	Earth, Wind and Fire
U.K. #1 POP 45	"Name of the Game"	Abba
U.K. #1 POP LP	*Sound of Bread*	Bread

WEEK ENDING NOVEMBER 26

U.S. #1 POP 45	"You Light Up My Life"	Debby Boone
U.S. #1 POP LP	*Rumours*	Fleetwood Mac
U.S. #1 R&B 45	"Serpentine Fire"	Earth, Wind and Fire
U.K. #1 POP 45	"Rockin' All Over the World"	Status Quo
U.K. #1 POP LP	*Sound of Bread*	Bread

1 **Billy Joel**'s career seemed to have cracked wide open after the success of *Piano Man,* but his two follow-up albums enjoyed less than spectacular success. The singer/songwriter's fifth LP, *The Stranger,* becomes Joel's vehicle to stardom, reaching #2 and spawning the hits "Just the Way You Are," "She's Always a Woman," "Movin' Out (Anthony's Song)" and "Only the Good Die Young."

3 **Paul McCartney and Wings**' "Mull of Kintyre" reaches the top of the British singles chart, where it will remain for nine weeks. Wings' recording of this Irish folk song will become the best-selling single in British records history.

14 *Saturday Night Fever* premieres in New York

City. Based on **Nik Cohn**'s story about a young Brooklyn disco stud (portrayed by **John Travolta**), the movie will be instrumental in spreading the disco craze throughout the country. The soundtrack, packed full of recent and soon-to-be dance hits by the **Bee Gees**, the **Trammps**, **Kool and the Gang**, **Tavares**, **MFSB**, **K.C. and the Sunshine Band** and **Yvonne Elliman**, will be made into one of the biggest-selling albums of all time.

15 The **Who** perform a secret concert for long-standing fan club members and **Jeff Stein**'s movie cameras at London's Shepperton Studios. The film footage will appear in Stein's *The Kids Are Alright,* his feature-length documentary about the Who. It is the first of two concerts filmed especially for *The Kids.*

Two days before they are due to appear on American television (NBC's "Saturday Night Live") and to begin their first American tour, the **Sex Pistols** are denied visas to enter the U.S. American government officials cite various sections of the U.S. Immigration Act in way of justification: **John Lydon** (alias **Johnny Rotten**) is denied entry because of an indictment for possession of one illegal amphetamine; **Paul Cook** and **John Ritchie** (alias **Sid Vicious**) on the grounds of "moral turpitude," and **Steven Jones** because of lack of information on his criminal record.

16 The **Bee Gees** receive a gold record for "How Deep Is Your Love," the fourth of their seven Number One singles. The song will become the subject of a copyright infringement suit five years later, when an amateur songwriter claims the brothers **Gibb** lifted the melody from a composition he'd written.

17 **Elvis Costello and the Attractions** appear on NBC-TV's "Saturday Night Live" in place of the **Sex Pistols**, who have been unable to secure visas to enter the U.S. "Saturday Night Live" producer **Lorne Michaels** refuses to allow Costello to perform his "Radio, Radio" (presumably because of the song's caustic criticisms of the broadcasting industry), but a few measures into the agreed-upon "Less Than Zero," Costello halts his band and swerves into an even more caustic than usual "Radio, Radio." He will never be invited back to appear on the show.

31 **Paul Ackerman**, editor of *Billboard* for thirty years, dies of a heart attack at age sixty-nine in New York City. The man who coined the terms "rhythm & blues" and "country & western," Ackerman was one of the first record industry figures to recognize and to champion the mainstream popularity of those kinds of music. He gave **Elvis Presley** his first national reviews in 1954. ♦

WEEK ENDING DECEMBER 3

U.S. #1 POP 45	"You Light Up My Life"	Debby Boone
U.S. #1 POP LP	*Simple Dreams*	Linda Ronstadt
U.S. #1 R&B 45	"Serpentine Fire"	Earth, Wind and Fire
U.K. #1 POP 45	"Mull of Kintyre"	Wings
U.K. #1 POP LP	*Sound of Bread*	Bread

WEEK ENDING DECEMBER 10

U.S. #1 POP 45	"You Light Up My Life"	Debby Boone
U.S. #1 POP LP	*Simple Dreams*	Linda Ronstadt
U.S. #1 R&B 45	"Serpentine Fire"	Earth, Wind and Fire
U.K. #1 POP 45	"Mull of Kintyre"	Wings
U.K. #1 POP LP	*Sound of Bread*	Bread

WEEK ENDING DECEMBER 17

U.S. #1 POP 45	"You Light Up My Life"	Debby Boone
U.S. #1 POP LP	*Simple Dreams*	Linda Ronstadt
U.S. #1 R&B 45	"Serpentine Fire"	Earth, Wind and Fire
U.K. #1 POP 45	"Mull of Kintyre"	Wings
U.K. #1 POP LP	*Disco Fever*	various artists

WEEK ENDING DECEMBER 24

U.S. #1 POP 45	"How Deep Is Your Love"	The Bee Gees
U.S. #1 POP LP	*Simple Dreams*	Linda Ronstadt
U.S. #1 R&B 45	"Serpentine Fire"	Earth, Wind and Fire
U.K. #1 POP 45	"Mull of Kintyre"	Wings
U.K. #1 POP LP	*Disco Fever*	various artists

WEEK ENDING DECEMBER 31

U.S. #1 POP 45	"How Deep Is Your Love"	The Bee Gees
U.S. #1 POP LP	*Simple Dreams*	Linda Ronstadt
U.S. #1 R&B 45	"Serpentine Fire"	Earth, Wind and Fire
U.K. #1 POP 45	"Mull of Kintyre"	Wings
U.K. #1 POP LP	*Disco Fever*	various artists

1978

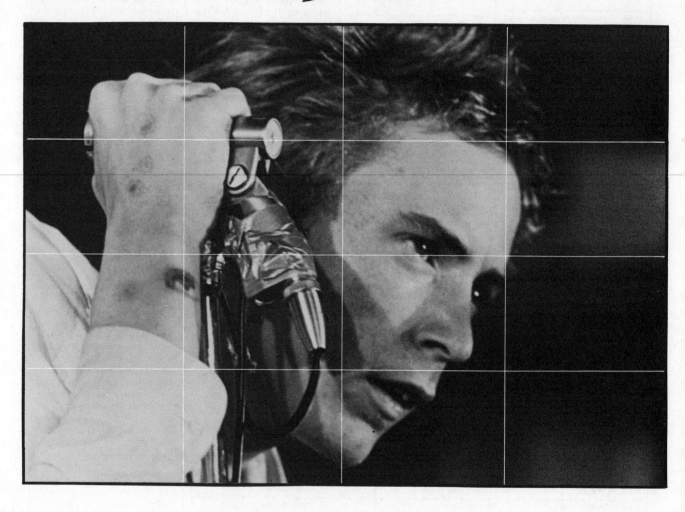

The year started off with the soundtrack album of the hit film *Saturday Night Fever* beginning its long dominance of the charts on both sides of the Atlantic, and with the arrival and self-destruction of the Sex Pistols. Perhaps self-destruction was the logical destiny for the Pistols. Why else would they have flown in the face of both music-biz conventional wisdom—and the obvious fact that nobody outside of big-city media centers had even *heard* of punk—by touring Middle America's small towns, where they could expect to be seen only as some sort of vile freak show?

Still, in England the punks kept coming, and in America the new wave bands kept popping up. New wave even gained a commercial foothold via the successes of the Cars (whose debut album was the first new wave disc to really break through AOR-FM radio) and Talking Heads (whose cover of Al Green's "Take Me to the River" was both an AM and FM hit), and through the legitimacy Bruce Springsteen lent it when he cowrote the hit "Because the Night" with punk poet Patti Smith. And since new wave was becoming acceptable, it began to sprout semipopular subgenres, from power pop (updates of Sixties Merseybeat and related strains of romantic pop with sweet harmony vocals and jangly guitars, *à la* Tom Petty and the Heartbreakers) to Kraftwerk-related electronic rock (*à la* conceptual roboticists Devo, who made their first big waves this year with an updated version of the Rolling Stones' "Satisfaction" that sounded like automaton disco).

But just as new wave was proving to be a surprisingly viable commercial proposition in the U.S., punk was having its finest moment in England: hard-line political punks the Clash, gay activist Tom Robinson, and X-Ray Spex (a punk band fronted by a pudgy, pubescent black girl with braces called Poly Styrene) performed at a massive outdoor benefit concert in London for Rock Against Racism.

Meanwhile, in the realm of black music, as disco continued to hold sway, a reaction against it was fomented by veteran bandleader George Clinton, whose Parliament-Funkadelic empire vowed, according to Clinton, to subvert disco and "rescue dance music from the blahs." And they succeeded with a phenomenally successful year capped by the Number One status of their antidisco, pro-dance-music anthem "One Nation under a Groove" and the LP of the same name. Clinton championed *funk*, which, unlike disco, heavily syncopated its backbeat and sounded altogether more aggressive and alive than disco. Funk soon inflected new wave in the form of Ian Dury's worldwide smash "Hit Me with Your Rhythm Stick."

And then there was always reggae, which had been lurking around the pop fringe for years but had recently been championed by English punks because of its political-adversarial lyrical slants.

5 One week after finally being granted visas to enter the U.S., the **Sex Pistols** begin their first and last tour of America with a concert in Atlanta, Georgia. For the most part, the tour perversely avoids the cities—such as New York and Los Angeles—where the punk group's fans can be found in the greatest numbers, in favor of southern and midwestern cities where **Johnny Rotten, Sid Vicious** and Company will usually be met by reactions ranging from bemused bafflement to violent hostility. Regardless, the news media coverage is intense.

7 The soundtrack album of the hit disco movie *Saturday Night Fever,* featuring the **Bee Gees,** the **Trammps, Tavares, K.C. and the Sunshine Band, Kool and the Gang, MFSB** and others, enters the soul album chart. It will peak at Number One for six weeks beginning February 18 in its thirty-nine weeks on the chart.

Veteran Memphis soul band the **Bar-Kays,** who in an earlier incarnation backed the late, great soul singer **Otis Redding**, enter the soul chart with "Let's Have Some Fun," which will peak at #11 in its thirteen weeks on the chart.

Stevie Wonder's twenty-seventh album, *Looking Back,* enters the soul album chart, where in nine weeks it will peak at #15.

The accomplished pop-soul songstress **Roberta Flack** enters the soul LP chart with *Blue Lights in the Basement,* which in twenty-nine weeks on the chart will peak at #5.

13 Elvis Presley's version of **Paul Anka**'s "My Way" goes gold five months after the King's death. Earlier, it had become one of Presley's 78 Top Twenty-five hits.

18 Ending the last show of the Sex Pistols' American tour, **Johnny Rotten** sneers at his San Francisco audience, "How does it feel to be swindled?" At a press conference the next morning, he will announce that the Sex Pistols are no more, blaming manager **Malcolm McLaren** for "sensationalizing" everything about

the group. Later that day, as the touring party prepares to return to London, **Sid Vicious** will be taken unconscious off the plane at Kennedy Airport in New York and rushed by ambulance to a nearby hospital, where he will be treated for an overdose of barbiturates and alcohol.

23 **Terry Kath,** guitarist and vocalist with horn-dominated pop band **Chicago,** dies after accidentally shooting himself in the head with a pistol he reportedly didn't know was loaded. Kath was thirty-two.

24 Composer/singer **Randy Newman** receives a gold record and angers those under 5'5" with his song "Short People." The tune's chorus contains the line "Short people got no reason to live." Although Newman claims it's actually a subtle poke at prejudice, shorter America protests.

26 Workers at EMI's record-pressing plant in Britain refuse to press copies of punk band the **Buzzcocks**' "Oh Shit," the flip side of their single "What Do I Get?" The single eventually does get pressed, and "What Do I Get?" goes on to become a British hit single.

28 Veteran soul vocal group the **Manhattans** enter the soul chart with "Am I Losing You," which in seventeen weeks on the chart will go as high as #6.

31 Blood, Sweat and Tears saxophonist **Greg Herbert** dies of an accidental drug overdose at age thirty in Amsterdam, during the band's European tour. ◆

WEEK ENDING JANUARY 7

U.S. #1 POP 45	"How Deep Is Your Love"	The Bee Gees
U.S. #1 POP LP	*Rumours*	Fleetwood Mac
U.S. #1 R&B 45	"Ffun"	Con Funk Shun
U.K. #1 POP 45	"Mull of Kintyre"	Wings
U.K. #1 POP LP	*Disco Fever*	various artists

WEEK ENDING JANUARY 14

U.S. #1 POP 45	"Baby Come Back"	Player
U.S. #1 POP LP	*Saturday Night Fever*	(soundtrack)
U.S. #1 R&B 45	"Ffun"	Con Funk Shun
U.K. #1 POP 45	"Mull of Kintyre"	Wings
U.K. #1 POP LP	*Disco Fever*	various artists

WEEK ENDING JANUARY 21

U.S. #1 POP 45	"Baby Come Back"	Player
U.S. #1 POP LP	*Saturday Night Fever*	soundtrack
U.S. #1 R&B 45	"Our Love"	Natalie Cole
U.K. #1 POP 45	"Mull of Kintyre"	Wings
U.K. #1 POP LP	*Rumours*	Fleetwood Mac

WEEK ENDING JANUARY 28

U.S. #1 POP 45	"Baby Come Back"	Player
U.S. #1 POP LP	*Saturday Night Fever*	soundtrack
U.S. #1 R&B 45	"Our Love"	Natalie Cole
U.K. #1 POP 45	"Mull of Kintyre"	Wings
U.K. #1 POP LP	*Rumours*	Fleetwood Mac

1 **Bob Dylan**'s film *Renaldo and Clara*, a documentary of the **Rolling Thunder Revue** tour mixed with surrealistic fantasy sequences, premieres in Los Angeles. Originally running at 232 minutes, it will be cut down to a 112-minute length after the poor initial reception. The film features most of the members of the 1975 Rolling Thunder Revue, including **Ronnie Hawkins**, **David Blue**, **Roger McGuinn**, **Ronee Blakley**, **Mick Ronson**, **Arlo Guthrie**, **Joan Baez**, **Ramblin' Jack Elliott** and **Allen Ginsberg**, as well as Dylan himself. But even after being shortened, the cryptic film will continue to baffle and try the patience of audiences in New York and other cities during its very short run.

3 This is the nineteenth anniversary of **Buddy Holly**'s death. It is also, ironically, the day on which Buddy Holly's birthplace in Lubbock, Texas, has been scheduled for demolition by the Lubbock Building Department, which, unaware that the house had any association with Lubbock's most famous son, had con-

demned the house to be razed the previous fall. Just a few days ago, however, a man bought the house, moved it, intact, outside the city limits, and renovated it so he could move his family into it. The man who saved Buddy Holly's birthplace didn't know of the house's significance, either.

"Dead Man's Curve," a made-for-TV-movie about surf-rock singing stars **Jan and Dean**, airs on ABC-TV.

11 The debut single by British band **Magazine**, "Shot by Both Sides," enters the British pop chart. The song was cowritten by Magazine vocalist **Howard Devoto** and **Buzzcocks** guitarist/vocalist **Pete Shelley**. Devoto had recently left the Buzzcocks to form Magazine. The Buzzcocks will shortly record Shelley's song "Lipstick," which is musically identical to "Shot by Both Sides" and is also credited to Devoto-Shelley.

18 Britain's first punk fan magazine, or "fanzine," *Sniffin' Glue*, ceases publication.

22 Ex-**Sex Pistol** bassist **Sid Vicious** and his girlfriend **Nancy Spungen** are arrested by police in their room at New York's Chelsea Hotel and charged with drug possession.

23 *Rolling Stone* reports on the breakup of the **Sex Pistols**, quoting **Johnny Rotten**'s explanation of their abrupt demise following the conclusion of their American tour in San Francisco: "We had gone as far as we could go. Everyone was trying to turn us into a big group, and I hated that."

Winners of the twentieth annual Grammy Awards for 1977 are announced. The **Eagles** win Best Record of the Year for "Hotel California" and Best Arrangement for Voices for "New Kid in Town." **Fleetwood Mac** win Album of the Year for *Rumours*. Song of the Year is a tie between "Love Theme from *A Star Is Born* (Evergreen)," by **Paul Williams** and **Barbra Streisand**, and **Joe Brooks**' "You Light Up My Life." Best Engineered Nonclassical Recording goes to **Steely Dan**'s *Aja*.

Best Album Package is **Linda Ronstadt**'s *Simple Dreams*. Best Male Pop Vocal Performance is **James Taylor**'s version of **Jimmy Jones**' 1960 "Handyman" (also a hit for **Del Shannon** in 1964). Best Producer of the Year is Linda Ronstadt's producer, **Peter Asher**. Best Pop Vocal Group Performance is the **Bee Gees**' "How Deep Is Your Love." Best R&B Group Vocal Performance is the **Emotions**' "Best of My Love." Best R&B Instrumental Performance is the **Brothers Johnson**'s "Q." Best R&B Song is **Leo Sayer** and **Vinny Poncia**'s "You Make Me Feel Like Dancing." Best Contemporary Soul Gospel Performance is the **Edwin Hawkins Singers**' *Wonderful!* Best Traditional Soul Gospel Performance is the Reverend **James Cleveland**'s *Live at Carnegie Hall*. Best Female Country Vocal Performance is **Crystal Gayle**'s "Don't It Make My Brown Eyes Blue." Best Male Country Vocal Performance is **Kenny Rogers**' "Lucille." Best Ethnic or Traditional Recording is **Muddy Waters**' critically acclaimed "comeback" album, *Hard Again*, recorded with bluesman **Johnny Winter**.

25 **Jefferson Starship** declares "Earth Day" for the release of its new album *Earth*, which is premiered nationally on many radio stations. Two days later, the album ships gold.

28 British punk rockers the **Damned** announce their breakup. Their farewell gig will be played April 8 in London. The band will subsequently reform and break up several times.

Bob Dylan's album *Live at Budokan* is recorded in Japan.

♦

WEEK ENDING FEBRUARY 4

U.S. #1 POP 45	"Stayin' Alive"	The Bee Gees
U.S. #1 POP LP	*Saturday Night Fever*	soundtrack
U.S. #1 R&B 45	"Theme Song from *Which Way Is Up?*"	Stargard
U.K. #1 POP 45	"Uptown Top Ranking"	Althia and Donna
U.K. #1 POP LP	*Rumours*	Fleetwood Mac

WEEK ENDING FEBRUARY 11

U.S. #1 POP 45	"Stayin' Alive"	The Bee Gees
U.S. #1 POP LP	*Saturday Night Fever*	soundtrack
U.S. #1 R&B 45	"Theme Song from *Which Way Is Up?*"	Stargard
U.K. #1 POP 45	"Uptown Top Ranking"	Althia and Donna
U.K. #1 POP LP	*Abba the Album*	Abba

WEEK ENDING FEBRUARY 18

U.S. #1 POP 45	"Stayin' Alive"	The Bee Gees
U.S. #1 POP LP	*Saturday Night Fever*	soundtrack
U.S. #1 R&B 45	"Too Hot Ta Trot"	The Commodores
U.K. #1 POP 45	"Take a Chance on Me"	Abba
U.K. #1 POP LP	*Abba the Album*	Abba

WEEK ENDING FEBRUARY 25

U.S. #1 POP 45	"Stayin' Alive"	The Bee Gees
U.S. #1 POP LP	*Saturday Night Fever*	soundtrack
U.S. #1 R&B 45	"It's You That I Need"	Enchantment
U.K. #1 POP 45	"Take a Chance on Me"	Abba
U.K. #1 POP LP	*Abba the Album*	Abba

4 "Too Much, Too Little, Too Late," by veteran pop singer **Johnny Mathis** and new soul-pop singer **Deniece Williams**, enters the soul chart, where it will hit Number One for four weeks on April 15.

The **Bee Gees** enter the soul singles chart with another hit from the *Saturday Night Fever* soundtrack, "Night Fever," which in fourteen weeks on the chart will hit #8.

8 **Steely Dan**'s sixth album, *Aja*, becomes their first album to be certified platinum. Two weeks later, their second album, *Countdown to Ecstasy,* will be certified gold, five years after its release.

11 Jazz guitarist **George Benson**'s crossover to soul-pop continues successfully, as his cover version of the old **Drifters** classic "On Broadway" enters the soul singles chart, where it will rise to #2.

15 *American Hot Wax,* **Floyd Mutrux**' film about a week in the life of pioneer rock & roll disc jockey

Alan Freed, premieres in New York City to respectable critical acclaim. It stars **Tim McIntire** as Freed and **Laraine Newman** of "Saturday Night Live" as his sidekick (though some observers feel Newman's character is closer to **Carole King** in her Brill Building songwriting days). **Chuck Berry**, **Jerry Lee Lewis** and **Screamin' Jay Hawkins** appear in specially staged concert sequences. The soundtrack features **Jackie Wilson**, **Buddy Holly**, the **Drifters**, the **Moonglows**, the **Cadillacs**, the **Spaniels**, the **Zodiacs** and others.

16 British punk band the **Stranglers** begin their first U.S. tour, and the **Jam** begin their second U.S. tour.

17 **Elvis Costello**'s second album, *This Year's Model,* is released in the U.K.

18 The rock festival California Jam II is held in Ontario, California, with 250,000 in attendance to see performances by **Santana**, **Dave Mason**, **Bob Welch**, **Ted Nugent**, **Aerosmith**, **Heart**, **Mahogany Rush** and **Rubicon**. Portions of the festival are

broadcast nationwide on ABC-TV.

22 The **Rutles'** *All You Need Is Cash,* an affectionate satire of the **Beatles**, airs on NBC-TV. The Rutles are played by **Eric Idle**, of British comedy troupe **Monty Python's Flying Circus**; ex-**Beach Boy** **Ricky Fataar**; ex-**Bonzo Dog Band** member **Neil Innes**; and real-life British rock drummer **John Halsey** (who's worked with **Roy Harper** and **Patto**, among others). **Paul Simon** and **Mick Jagger** make cameo appearances as themselves. **George Harrison** appears as an interviewer. Among the songs featured: "Cheese and Onions," "Ouch!" and "I Must Be in Love."

Win Anderson, who has been promoting a benefit concert for environmentalist group Friends of the Earth, holds a press conference in New York City substantiating rumors of a **Beatles** reunion.

23 *Rolling Stone* reports that **Fleetwood Mac** is working out final arrangements to perform at Moscow's 3,000-seat Russian Concert Hall on July 8, 9 and 10. The band's legal adviser, **Michael Shapiro**, admits: "Everything, of course, depends on world peace."

24 British courts grant British record companies the rights to seize bootleg and pirate recordings.

29 **Genesis** begin a world tour in the U.S.; they will go on to Europe May 15, then to Japan in November.

David Bowie's first tour in two years begins in San Diego, California.

30 In London, two members of the **Clash**—bassist **Paul Simonon** and drummer **Topper Headon**—are arrested for shooting pigeons from the roof of a rehearsal hall. ◆

WEEK ENDING MARCH 4

U.S. #1 POP 45	"(Love Is) Thicker Than Water"	Andy Gibb
U.S. #1 POP LP	*Saturday Night Fever*	soundtrack
U.S. #1 R&B 45	"Flashlight"	Parliament
U.K. #1 POP 45	"Take a Chance on Me"	Abba
U.K. #1 POP LP	*Abba the Album*	Abba

WEEK ENDING MARCH 11

U.S. #1 POP 45	"(Love Is) Thicker Than Water"	Andy Gibb
U.S. #1 POP LP	*Saturday Night Fever*	soundtrack
U.S. #1 R&B 45	"Flashlight"	Parliament
U.K. #1 POP 45	"Wuthering Heights"	Kate Bush
U.K. #1 POP LP	*Abba the Album*	Abba

WEEK ENDING MARCH 18

U.S. #1 POP 45	"Night Fever"	The Bee Gees
U.S. #1 POP LP	*Saturday Night Fever*	soundtrack
U.S. #1 R&B 45	"Flashlight"	Parliament
U.K. #1 POP 45	"Wuthering Heights"	Kate Bush
U.K. #1 POP LP	*Abba the Album*	Abba

WEEK ENDING MARCH 25

U.S. #1 POP 45	"Night Fever"	The Bee Gees
U.S. #1 POP LP	*Saturday Night Fever*	soundtrack
U.S. #1 R&B 45	"Bootzilla"	Bootsy's Rubber Band
U.K. #1 POP 45	"Wuthering Heights"	Kate Bush
U.K. #1 POP LP	*Abba the Album*	Abba

1 **Paul Simon** and **Peter Frampton** go to Philadelphia to see the Philadelphia Fury—the North American Soccer League team of which they and **Yes** keyboardist **Rick Wakeman** own parts—open its season against the Washington Diplomats.

Blondie's "Denis," a remake of **Randy and the Rainbows'** 1963 hit "Denise," tops the *New Musical Express* British pop chart.

---

3 Blues guitar giant **B. B. King** joins famed defense lawyer **F. Lee Bailey** for a rap session and concert for inmates at Norfolk Prison in Boston, Massachusetts, as part of their ongoing duties as co-chairmen of FAIRR (Foundation for the Advancement of Inmate Rehabilitation and Recreation). Portions of the Norfolk concert

are shot by ABC-TV for inclusion on a subsequent episode of "Good Morning America."

---

19 Arista Records releases the **Patti Smith Group**'s single "Because the Night," coauthored by Smith and **Bruce Springsteen.** The song will become Smith's only charting single, reaching #13 later this year, and will also be covered by Springsteen in concerts.

Over forty rock & roll performers petition **President Carter** to end America's commitment to nuclear power. Some of the performers—including **Bruce Springsteen, Jackson Browne, James Taylor, Carly Simon,** the **Doobie Brothers, Gil Scott-Heron, Tom Petty and the Heartbreakers** and others—will later get together for antinuclear benefit concerts

that will be recorded for the *No Nukes* album.

Outside of New York City punk-rock club CBGB, **Dead Boys** drummer **Johnny Blitz** is nearly killed when he is stabbed during a streetfight. A week-long benefit will be held for Blitz at CBGB shortly, featuring many of New York's top punk performers, including the **Ramones, Blondie** (with special guest **Robert Fripp,** one-time leader of **King Crimson**) and others.

---

21 Ex-**Fairport Convention** singer **Sandy Denny** dies at age thirty-seven from a cerebral hemorrhage suffered in a fall down a flight of stairs in her London home.

---

22 **Bob Marley and the Wailers** perform at the One Love Peace Concert at the National Arena outside Kingston, Jamaica, making their first

public appearance in their homeland since the attempt on Marley's life in December 1976. The concert was organized by youth leaders of Jamaica's feuding political parties in an effort to end the violence of the past five years. Also appearing at the concert are **Culture, Dennis Brown, Big Youth, Jacob Miller, Trinity** and **Peter Tosh,** who lights up a spliff onstage and lectures the government officials in the audience on the wisdom of legalizing marijuana. But the climax of the event comes at the end of Marley's performance, when he calls **Prime Minister Michael Manley** and Opposition leader **Edward Seaga** onstage and raises their clasped hands in a gesture of friendship and unity.

---

23 Ex-**Sex Pistol** bassist **Sid Vicious** films his rendition of **Paul Anka**'s pop standard "My Way" for the Sex Pistols' film *The Great Rock n' Roll Swindle.*

---

25 London's 100 Club, birthplace of punk rock, closes its doors to punk music following a performance by the band **Alternative TV,** which features **Mark Perry,** editor of the now-defunct punk fanzine *Sniffin' Glue.*

---

26 **Ringo Starr**'s TV special, "Ringo," a musical update of *The Prince and the Pauper,* airs on American TV. **George Harrison** narrates. It garners very low ratings, finishing fifty-third out of sixty-five shows.

---

30 The **Clash,** the **Tom Robinson Band** and **X-Ray Spexs** perform at a Rock Against Racism rally in London. ◆

WEEK ENDING APRIL 1

U.S. #1 POP 45	"Night Fever"	The Bee Gees
U.S. #1 POP LP	*Saturday Night Fever*	soundtrack
U.S. #1 R&B 45	"The Closer I Get to You"	Roberta Flack with Donny Hathaway
U.K. #1 POP 45	"Denis"	Blondie
U.K. #1 POP LP	*The Kick Inside*	Kate Bush

WEEK ENDING APRIL 8

U.S. #1 POP 45	"Night Fever"	The Bee Gees
U.S. #1 POP LP	*Saturday Night Fever*	soundtrack
U.S. #1 R&B 45	"The Closer I Get to You"	Roberta Flack with Donny Hathaway
U.K. #1 POP 45	"Denis"	Blondie
U.K. #1 POP LP	*The Kick Inside*	Kate Bush

WEEK ENDING APRIL 15

U.S. #1 POP 45	"Night Fever"	The Bee Gees
U.S. #1 POP LP	*Saturday Night Fever*	soundtrack
U.S. #1 R&B 45	"Too Much, Too Little, Too Late"	Johnny Mathis and Deniece Williams
U.K. #1 POP 45	"I Wonder Why"	Showaddywaddy
U.K. #1 POP LP	*20 Golden Greats*	Nat "King" Cole

WEEK ENDING APRIL 22

U.S. #1 POP 45	"Night Fever"	The Bee Gees
U.S. #1 POP LP	*Saturday Night Fever*	soundtrack
U.S. #1 R&B 45	"Too Much, Too Little, Too Late"	Johnny Mathis and Deniece Williams
U.K. #1 POP 45	"Night Fever"	The Bee Gees
U.K. #1 POP LP	*20 Golden Greats*	Nat "King" Cole

WEEK ENDING APRIL 29

U.S. #1 POP 45	"Night Fever"	The Bee Gees
U.S. #1 POP LP	*Saturday Night Fever*	soundtrack
U.S. #1 R&B 45	"Too Much, Too Little, Too Late"	Johnny Mathis and Deniece Williams
U.K. #1 POP 45	"Night Fever"	The Bee Gees
U.K. #1 POP LP	*Saturday Night Fever*	soundtrack

2 The **Bee Gees** receive their second platinum single awarded in less than two months, for "Night Fever," which was preceded by "Stayin' Alive." Both are from the best-selling soundtrack *Saturday Night Fever.*

3 *FM,* a film about the battle between progressives and regressives at a radio station, premieres in Los Angeles. It stars comedian **Martin Mull, Eileen Brennan** and **Cleavon Little,** with appearances by **Linda Ronstadt, Jimmy Buffett, REO Speedwagon** and **Tom Petty.** The soundtrack also features **Steely Dan, Neil Young,** the **Eagles, Billy Joel, Warren Zevon, Steve Miller** and **B. B. King.** More people buy the soundtrack album than see the film.

4 **Jefferson Starship** receive a platinum record for what will be their last LP with **Grace Slick** *and* **Marty Balin.** Just a few weeks later, both will be gone, and leader **Paul Kantner** will be forced to revamp the entire band, eventually taking on singer **Mickey Thomas** and drummer **Aynsley Dunbar.**

6 At a joint news conference at United Nations headquarters in New York with TV talk-show host **David Frost** and RSO Records chief **Robert Stigwood,** the **Bee Gees** announce the launching of a unique concept: Music for UNICEF benefit concerts by major rock and pop music stars.

7 The 90,000 tickets on sale for **Bob Dylan**'s upcoming concerts at London's Wembley Empire Pool sell out in less than eight hours.

9 Lead singer **Fee Waybill** of the **Tubes** falls off the stage during a concert in England and breaks his leg.

17 **Lou Reed** begins a week-long series of concerts at the Bottom Line club in New York City, portions of which are recorded for his forthcoming live album, *Take No Prisoners.* The highlight of the album is an extended verbal rap in which Reed castigates rock critics like **Robert Christgau** of the *Village Voice* and **John Rockwell** of the *New York Times.*

Thank God It's Friday, the cinematic celebration of disco that is Casablanca Records chief **Neil Bogart**'s response to *Saturday Night Fever,* premieres in Los Angeles. Directed by **Robert Klane** and set in a "typical" Hollywood disco on a "typical" Friday night, the film stars **Donna Summer** as a singer looking for her big break, and introduces her hit song "The Last Dance," which goes on to top the pop chart and wins the 1978 Academy Award for Best Song. The film also stars **Paul Jabara** and the **Commodores,** and its soundtrack features **Diana Ross,** the **Village People** and others. Despite all this, the film will be a resounding flop.

18 *The Buddy Holly Story,* a film directed by **Steve Rash** and starring **Gary Busey** as Holly, has its world premiere in Dallas, Texas. The film will be a critical and commercial success, with Busey—who sings such Holly classics as "That'll Be the Day," "Maybe Baby," "Peggy Sue," "Rave On" and "It's So Easy"—being nominated for an Academy Award for Best Actor.

20 *The Buddy Holly Story* premieres in Holly's home town of Lubbock, Texas.

24 Heavy metal is dead and buried—or so they say. In blacklit basements everywhere, though, copies of **Black Sabbath**'s *Paranoid* are still spun at wall-shattering volume. **Van Halen,** a young bar band-cum-heavy-rock group from Pasadena, score their first time out with *Van Halen.* But the band differs from early Seventies hard-rock groups; its songs offer a surprising degree of melody, topped with **Hollies-**like harmonies. And then there's **Eddie Van Halen,** whom lead vocalist **David Lee Roth** calls "the first guitar hero of the Eighties." Many agree. The album goes gold on this date.

25 The **Who** perform a second "secret" concert in London to be filmed for their documentary movie on the band's career, *The Kids Are Alright.* This is Keith Moon's last performance with the band before his death.

30 Swan Song Records announces that **Led Zeppelin** have entered a recording studio for the first time since the death of **Robert Plant**'s son in July 1977. The sessions will result in the band's final album, 1979's *In through the Out Door.*

31 One of the biggest disco hits of the year belongs to the **Trammps:** "Disco Inferno" (#11). Their *Disco Inferno* LP does just as well, turning gold on this date. ◆

WEEK ENDING MAY 6

U.S. #1 POP 45	"Night Fever"	The Bee Gees
U.S. #1 POP LP	*Saturday Night Fever*	soundtrack
U.S. #1 R&B 45	"Too Much, Too Little, Too Late"	Johnny Mathis and Deniece Williams
U.K. #1 POP 45	"Night Fever"	The Bee Gees
U.K. #1 POP LP	*Saturday Night Fever*	soundtrack

WEEK ENDING MAY 13

U.S. #1 POP 45	"If I Can't Have You"	Yvonne Elliman
U.S. #1 POP LP	*Saturday Night Fever*	soundtrack
U.S. #1 R&B 45	"Take Me to the Next Phase (Part 1)"	The Isley Brothers
U.K. #1 POP 45	"Night Fever"	The Bee Gees
U.K. #1 POP LP	*Saturday Night Fever*	soundtrack

WEEK ENDING MAY 20

U.S. #1 POP 45	"With a Little Luck"	Paul McCartney and Wings
U.S. #1 POP LP	*Saturday Night Fever*	soundtrack
U.S. #1 R&B 45	"Take Me to the Next Phase (Part 1)"	The Isley Brothers
U.K. #1 POP 45	"Rivers of Babylon"	Boney M
U.K. #1 POP LP	*Saturday Night Fever*	soundtrack

WEEK ENDING MAY 27

U.S. #1 POP 45	"With a Little Luck"	Paul McCartney and Wings
U.S. #1 POP LP	*Saturday Night Fever*	soundtrack
U.S. #1 R&B 45	"Use ta Be My Girl"	The O'Jays
U.K. #1 POP 45	"Rivers of Babylon"	Boney M
U.K. #1 POP LP	*Saturday Night Fever*	soundtrack

11 Rolling Stones Records releases the band's latest album, *Some Girls,* the title tune of which will once again stir up controversy around rock's baddest boys—the outcry stemming from the song's lyric "Black girls just like to fuck all night."

15 Bob Dylan begins his first British tour in several years at London's Wembley Empire Pool before a capacity throng.

16 The Clash's reggae-inflected single "White Man in Hammersmith Palais" is released in the U.K. on CBS Records.

Ex-**Pistol Sid Vicious**' version of "My Way" is released on an EP titled *The Biggest Blow* on Virgin Records in England. The EP's flip side is "The Biggest Blow—a Punk Prayer," by fugitive great train robber **Ronnie Biggs**, backed by ex-Pistols **Steve Jones** and **Paul Cook**. Vicious' "My Way" will later appear on the Virgin LP *Sid Sings* (featuring Vicious recorded live at club Max's Kansas City in New York) and the Barclay EP *Sid Vicious' Heritage.*

The film *Grease,* directed by **Randall Kleiser** and starring **Olivia Newton-John** and **John Travolta**, opens in theaters across America. This Hollywoodized look at Fifties adolescents will be a critical bombshell and a box-office smash.

17 At the Lorely Festival in St. Goarhausen, Germany, the **Jefferson Starship** fail to appear as scheduled because singer **Grace Slick**, currently in the midst of a long bout with alcoholism, is unable to go onstage. Fans riot, causing over $1 million worth of damage. Two days later, Slick will leave the band. On June 24, **Marty Balin** will assume lead vocal duties in her place at Britain's Knebworth Festival, following which the band will cancel the rest of its European tour.

The **Rolling Stones** begin another U.S. tour, in Philadelphia. The tour will end July 20 in Albuquerque, New Mexico, amid rumors that lead singer **Mick Jagger** will leave the band to embark on an acting career.

21 *The Punk Rock Movie*—consisting of 8mm film clips of London's early punk days at the Roxy Club, shot by guerrilla filmmaker **Don Letts**—premieres in London. It features the **Sex Pistols,** the **Clash,** the **Slits,** **Siouxsie and the Banshees, X-Ray Spexs, Generation X, Slaughter and the Dogs, Subway Sect, Shane, Wayne County, Eater, Alternative TV** and **Johnny Thunders and the Heartbreakers**. It will have a very brief run in New York City later this year.

22 Were the **Rolling Stones** challenged into creating their finest LP in years, *Some Girls?* That's the theory of many, who see the LP as a response to the taunts of Britain's punks. Besides inspired bar band thrashing, there's the misunderstood country parody "Girl with the Faraway Eyes" and the jagged dance hit "Miss You," which makes Number One. The record turns platinum on this date.

27 Ex-**Genesis** vocalist **Peter Gabriel**'s second eponymous solo album is released on Atlantic Records. Produced by ex-**King Crimson** guitarist **Robert Fripp**, it will yield a minor hit single for Gab-

riel in "D.I.Y. (Do It Yourself)."

Bonnie Tyler's "It's a Heartache" is one of the most talked-about songs of the spring: Is that **Rod Stewart** singing? Tyler's gravelly voice is almost identical to Stewart's, and the resulting notoriety turns the single into a hit and the LP into gold.

Bruce Springsteen's career had been thought to be damaged by the legal difficulties that prevented him from releasing a followup to *Born to Run,* but *Darkness on the Edge of Town* dispels those fears, going to #5. It's a dark, haunting album, and almost a lyrical sequel to *Born to Run.* Springsteen is awarded a platinum album on this date.

28 Pseudoclassical rock band **Kansas** are named Deputy Ambassadors of Goodwill by UNICEF.

29 Pop-rock singer/songwriter **Peter Frampton** is injured in a car crash in the Bahamas. ◆

WEEK ENDING JUNE 3

U.S. #1 POP 45	"Too Much, Too Little, Too Late"	Johnny Mathis and Deniece Williams
U.S. #1 POP LP	*Saturday Night Fever*	soundtrack
U.S. #1 R&B 45	"Use ta Be My Girl"	The O'Jays
U.K. #1 POP 45	"Rivers of Babylon"	Boney M
U.K. #1 POP LP	*Saturday Night Fever*	soundtrack

WEEK ENDING JUNE 10

U.S. #1 POP 45	"You're the One That I Want"	John Travolta and Olivia Newton-John
U.S. #1 POP LP	*Saturday Night Fever*	soundtrack
U.S. #1 R&B 45	"Use ta Be My Girl"	The O'Jays
U.K. #1 POP 45	"Rivers of Babylon"	Boney M
U.K. #1 POP LP	*Saturday Night Fever*	soundtrack

WEEK ENDING JUNE 17

U.S. #1 POP 45	"Shadow Dancing"	Andy Gibb
U.S. #1 POP LP	*Saturday Night Fever*	soundtrack
U.S. #1 R&B 45	"Use ta Be My Girl"	The O'Jays
U.K. #1 POP 45	"You're the One That I Want"	John Travolta and Olivia Newton-John
U.K. #1 POP LP	*Black and White*	The Stranglers

WEEK ENDING JUNE 24

U.S. #1 POP 45	"Shadow Dancing"	Andy Gibb
U.S. #1 POP LP	*Saturday Night Fever*	soundtrack
U.S. #1 R&B 45	"Use ta Be My Girl"	The O'Jays
U.K. #1 POP 45	"You're the One That I Want"	John Travolta and Olivia Newton-John
U.K. #1 POP LP	*Saturday Night Fever*	soundtrack

1 Disco-funk band **Con Funk Shun** enter the soul chart with "Shake and Dance with Me," which will peak at #5 in its seventeen weeks on the chart.

Michael Henderson, who had won critical praise for his bass playing in **Miles Davis'** electric-fusion units recently, enters the soul charts with "Take Me I'm Yours." Henderson's disco move will prove successful: the single will stay on the chart for twenty weeks, peaking at #3.

5 The EMI Record pressing plant in Britain stops printing the album cover for the **Rolling Stones'** *Some Girls* after some celebrities (including **Lucille Ball**) depicted in the cover's mock-wig advertisement complain.

6 New Yorker **Eddie Mahoney**, who once aspired to be a policeman, moves to the West Coast and changes his last name to **Money**—it's a fitting moniker: his debut, *Eddie Money,* goes gold and gives him two big hits, "Two Tickets to Paradise" and "Baby Hold on to Me."

8 Singer/guitarist **Joe Strummer** and bassist **Paul Simonon** of the **Clash** are arrested in Glasgow, Scotland, for drunk and disorderly behavior.

With his three older brothers, the **Bee Gees**, reaping benefits from the disco movement, **Andy Gibb** gets into the act with his album *Shadow Dancing,* which will peak at #18 in its twelve weeks on the chart. The album's title single had reached Number One earlier in the year.

15 Over 200,000 fans gather at Britain's Blackbush Airport to see **Bob Dylan** and his band off after the completion of Dylan's British tour.

Two veteran soul acts enter the soul chart this day: **Tyrone Davis** with "Can't Help but Say," which will peak at #65 in eight weeks on the chart; and the **Dells** with "Super Woman," which in thirteen weeks on the chart will go as high as #24.

Disco band **L.T.D.** enters the soul chart with "Holding On (When Love Is Gone)," which in its seventeen weeks on the chart will peak at Number One for two weeks starting September 9.

18 John Travolta, the box-office sensation of 1978 (*Saturday Night Fever* and *Grease*), enjoys his first Number One with "You're the One That I Want," sung with his *Grease*

costar, **Olivia Newton-John.** The tune is awarded a platinum single on this date.

Gerry Rafferty, once a member of **Stealer's Wheel**, scores a gold record for "Baker Street," one of the summer songs of 1978 (#2 for six weeks).

24 The **Robert Stigwood**-produced film version of *Sgt. Pepper's Lonely Hearts Club Band* opens in New York City. The film, which stars the **Bee Gees** and **Peter Frampton**, is a critical disaster and a box-office bomb.

29 Funk-fusion group **Earth, Wind and Fire** enter the soul chart with their cover version of the **Beatles'** "Got to Get You into My Life," from the soundtrack of the film *Sgt. Pepper's Lonely Hearts Club Band.* The single will peak at Number One for one week on September 23.

Funk-rock fusionist **Prince**, at this time a virtually unknown tyro out of Minneapolis, enters the soul chart for the first time, with a song the title of which will become rather typical of his sexually explicit *oeuvre*: "Soft and Wet." It will reach #12 in its twenty weeks on the chart.

30 Glen Goins, former vocalist and guitarist with **George Clinton's Parliament-Funkadelic**, dies at age twenty-four in New Jersey of complications relating to Hodgkins' Disease. Goins sang lead on their hit single "Bop Gun," as well as such tracks as "Funkin' for Fun," "Handcuff" and "Do That Stuff." ◆

WEEK ENDING JULY 1

U.S. #1 POP 45	"Shadow Dancing"	Andy Gibb
U.S. #1 POP LP	*Saturday Night Fever*	soundtrack
U.S. #1 R&B 45	"Stuff Like That"	Quincy Jones
U.K. #1 POP 45	"You're the One That I Want"	John Travolta and Olivia Newton-John
U.K. #1 POP LP	*Saturday Night Fever*	soundtrack

WEEK ENDING JULY 8

U.S. #1 POP 45	"Shadow Dancing"	Andy Gibb
U.S. #1 POP LP	*City to City*	Gerry Rafferty
U.S. #1 R&B 45	"Close the Door"	Teddy Pendergrass
U.K. #1 POP 45	"You're the One That I Want"	John Travolta and Olivia Newton-John
U.K. #1 POP LP	*Saturday Night Fever*	soundtrack

WEEK ENDING JULY 15

U.S. #1 POP 45	"Shadow Dancing"	Andy Gibb
U.S. #1 POP LP	*Some Girls*	The Rolling Stones
U.S. #1 R&B 45	"Close the Door"	Teddy Pendergrass
U.K. #1 POP 45	"You're the One That I Want"	John Travolta and Olivia Newton-John
U.K. #1 POP LP	*Saturday Night Fever*	soundtrack

WEEK ENDING JULY 22

U.S. #1 POP 45	"Shadow Dancing"	Andy Gibb
U.S. #1 POP LP	*Some Girls*	The Rolling Stones
U.S. #1 R&B 45	"You and I"	Rick James
U.K. #1 POP 45	"You're the One That I Want"	John Travolta and Olivia Newton-John
U.K. #1 POP LP	*Saturday Night Fever*	soundtrack

WEEK ENDING JULY 29

U.S. #1 POP 45	"Shadow Dancing"	Andy Gibb
U.S. #1 POP LP	*Grease*	soundtrack
U.S. #1 R&B 45	"You and I"	Rick James
U.K. #1 POP 45	"You're the One That I Want"	John Travolta and Olivia Newton-John
U.K. #1 POP LP	*Saturday Night Fever*	soundtrack

5 The **Rolling Stones'** disco-inflected single "Miss You," from their album *Some Girls,* tops the U.S. pop chart. The album's other single, "Beast of Burden," will hit #8 later this year.

Former **Stevie Wonder** drummer **Hamilton Bohannon** enters the soul chart with the disco smash "Let's Start the Dance," which will peak at #9 in its nineteen weeks on the chart. The single is from Bohannon's hit album *Summertime Groove,* which will peak at #14 on the soul LP chart.

9 Blues legend **Muddy Waters** performs at a White House picnic for **President Jimmy Carter.**

12 Pete Meaden, who had been the **Who's** publicist and manager in their **High Numbers** days, commits suicide in London by ingesting an overdose of barbiturates. Meaden, who helped the group refine their Mod image, was managing **Steve Gibbons** at the time of his death. He was thirty-five.

Disco-funk band **Atlantic Starr** enter the soul chart for the first time with "Stand Up," which will peak at #16. One week later, their eponymous debut album will enter the soul LP chart, where it will peak at #21.

The **Brothers Johnson** enter the soul LP chart with *Blam!!,* which in its twenty-six weeks on the chart will peak at Number One for seven weeks starting on September 2. The album yields two hit singles in "Ride-o-Rocket" and "Ain't We Funkin' Now," both of which will reach #45 on the soul chart later this year.

Donny Hathaway enters the soul chart with "You Were Meant for Me," which will peak at #17 in its fifteen weeks on the chart. It will be his last chart entry during his lifetime.

13 Be-Bop Deluxe, the British progressive rock group, disband. Leader and guitarist **Bill Nelson** goes on to form **Red Noise.**

19 Influential Dayton, Ohio, funk band **Slave** enter the soul LP chart with

The Concept, which will peak at #11 in its eleven weeks on the chart.

Subversive protest-funkateer **George Clinton's Funkadelic** have their biggest hit ever on their hands, as the anthemic "One Nation under a Groove" begins the first of twenty-five weeks on the soul chart, where it will peak at Number One on September 30, holding the top position for six weeks. Funkadelic's album of the same name will also be on the soul LP chart for twenty-five weeks and will reach Number One on October 28, where it will stay for four weeks.

Alicia Bridges enters the soul chart with "I Love the Nightlife (Disco Round)." Though the **Phoebe Snow** soundalike's single will only reach as high as #31 in its seventeen weeks on the chart, the song's title will become a disco-era catchphrase.

22 One of the rising young black stars of 1978 is **Rick James,** a dreadlocked punk-funkster from Buffalo, New York, who once played in a Toronto group called the

Mynah Birds with **Neil Young,** of all people. James' *Come Get It* turns gold, and he has two other hit LPs in 1978, *Bustin' Out of L Seven* and *Fire It Up.*

25 The **Tom Robinson Band, Patti Smith, John Otway, Sham 69** and others appear at the Reading Rock Festival in England.

Jackson Browne's *Running on Empty* turns platinum. The album, his fifth, is a cleverly constructed diary of the road that includes performances recorded on stage and even in hotel rooms. Browne garners two Top Twenty hits, the title track and "Stay/The Load Out."

26 Over 80,000 fans attend the first Canada Jam rock festival in Ontario, promoted by **Lennie Stosel** and **Sandy Feldman,** who worked on the California Jam concerts. Featured at Canada Jam I are the **Doobie Brothers,** the **Atlanta Rhythm Section, Dave Mason, Kansas,** the **Village People** and the **Commodores.** The show will gross $2 million.

Ashford and Simpson's "It Seems to Hang On" enters the soul chart, where it will peak at #2—their biggest hit in a year that sees them enter the soul chart four times.

27 Joe Galkin, the Southern rock & roll and R&B promoter who discovered and gave the initial push to R&B great **Otis Redding,** dies at age seventy-six.

28 Television, one of the most highly regarded and influential of New York's punk new wave rock bands, disbands. Leader, guitarist and songwriter **Tom Verlaine** will go on to a solo career, in which he will frequently be backed by Television bassist **Fred Smith.** Guitarist **Richard Lloyd** will also embark on a sporadic solo career. Drummer **Billy Ficca** will play with several bands around New York before joining the **Waitresses.** ◆

WEEK ENDING AUGUST 5

U.S. #1 POP 45	"Miss You"	The Rolling Stones
U.S. #1 POP LP	*Grease*	soundtrack
U.S. #1 R&B 45	"Boogie Oogie Oogie"	Taste of Honey
U.K. #1 POP 45	"You're the One That I Want"	John Travolta and Olivia Newton-John
U.K. #1 POP LP	*Saturday Night Fever*	soundtrack

WEEK ENDING AUGUST 12

U.S. #1 POP 45	"Three Times a Lady"	The Commodores
U.S. #1 POP LP	*Grease*	soundtrack
U.S. #1 R&B 45	"Three Times a Lady"	The Commodores
U.K. #1 POP 45	"You're the One That I Want"	John Travolta and Olivia Newton-John
U.K. #1 POP LP	*Saturday Night Fever*	soundtrack

WEEK ENDING AUGUST 19

U.S. #1 POP 45	"Three Times a Lady"	The Commodores
U.S. #1 POP LP	*Grease*	soundtrack
U.S. #1 R&B 45	"Three Times a Lady"	The Commodores
U.K. #1 POP 45	"You're the One That I Want"	John Travolta and Olivia Newton-John
U.K. #1 POP LP	*Saturday Night Fever*	soundtrack

WEEK ENDING AUGUST 26

U.S. #1 POP 45	"Grease"	Frankie Valli
U.S. #1 POP LP	*Grease*	soundtrack
U.S. #1 R&B 45	"Get Off"	Foxy
U.K. #1 POP 45	"Three Times a Lady"	The Commodores
U.K. #1 POP LP	*Saturday Night Fever*	soundtrack

2 The **Jacksons**, formerly known as the **Jackson 5**, enter the soul chart yet again with "Blame It on the Boogie," which will peak at #3.

Ex-**Blue Notes** lead vocalist **Teddy Pendergrass** performs at a "For Women Only" concert at New York City's Avery Fisher Hall. Women arriving for the concert are given white chocolate lollipops in the shape of a Teddy Bear.

4 Some 66,000 **Dead Heads** attend the **Grateful Dead**'s Labor Day concert at Giants Stadium in New Jersey. The **New Riders of the Purple Sage** open the show.

7 Ex-**Sex Pistol** bassist **Sid Vicious** performs at Max's Kansas City, New York City punk club, backed by ex-**New York Dolls Jerry Nolan** (drums), **Arthur "Killer" Kane** (bass) and the **Clash**'s **Mick Jones** (guitar).

Who drummer **Keith Moon** dies at age thirty-one in London after overdosing on Hemenephrin, a prescription drug that was supposed to have helped him withdraw from alcohol. Though Moon always earned his reputation as an incorrigible wild man, he was also highly respected by musicians—including noted modern jazz drummer **Elvin Jones**— for his unique, wide-open, crashingly polyrhythmic approach. In fact, Moon's technique of attacking the tom-toms and crash cymbals and ignoring the hi-hat and ride cymbals predated similar percussive innovations in the late Seventies and early Eighties by **Phil Collins** with **Peter Gabriel**, **Dave Bar-**

barossa with **Bow Wow Wow**, and **Bill Bruford** with **King Crimson**. Though it seems that Moon's untimely death will surely mean the end of the **Who**, he will eventually be replaced by ex-**Faces** drummer **Kenney Jones**.

8 **Public Image Ltd.**— the band formed by ex-**Sex Pistol John Lydon** (known as **Johnny Rotten** with the Pistols) and ex-**Clash** (before they ever recorded) guitarist **Keith Levene**—releases its first single, "Public Image," which will become a big underground hit in America's new wave dance clubs and on American college and underground radio stations.

15 **Bob Dylan** begins his longest American concert tour ever, in Augusta, Maine. He will play sixty-five dates in sixty-two cities in three months.

16 The **Grateful Dead** perform a concert before the pyramids of Egypt. The concert is recorded, but as of 1983 has yet to be released on record.

19 **Linda Ronstadt**'s latest album, *Living in the U.S.A.,* is released with an initial shipment of 2 million units; or, as music industry parlance would have it, the album "ships double platinum."

23 Veteran Memphis gospel-soul singer **Solomon Burke** makes a rare disco-era entry into the soul chart with "Please Don't Say Goodbye to Me," which will be on the chart for only four weeks, peaking at #91.

30 **Rick James**' second big hit of the year, "Mary Jane," a thinly veiled celebration of the herb enters the soul chart, where it will peak at #3. James's previous hit this year, "You and I," had hit Number One for two weeks on July 22. Both hits are from James' breakthrough album, *Come and Get It!*

The **Brides of Funkenstein**—yet another offshoot of **George Clinton's Parliament-Funkadelic** empire— enter the soul chart for the first time with "Disco to Go," which will peak at #7. It is taken from their debut LP, *Funk or Walk,* which will later reach #17 on the soul LP chart. ◆

WEEK ENDING SEPTEMBER 2

U.S. #1 POP 45	"Grease"	Frankie Valli
U.S. #1 POP LP	*Grease*	soundtrack
U.S. #1 R&B 45	"Get Off"	Foxy
U.K. #1 POP 45	"Three Times a Lady"	The Commodores
U.K. #1 POP LP	*Saturday Night Fever*	soundtrack

WEEK ENDING SEPTEMBER 9

U.S. #1 POP 45	"Boogie Oogie Oogie"	Taste of Honey
U.S. #1 POP LP	*Grease*	soundtrack
U.S. #1 R&B 45	"Holding On (When Love Is Gone)"	L.T.D.
U.K. #1 POP 45	"Three Times a Lady"	The Commodores
U.K. #1 POP LP	*Night Flight to Venus*	Boney M

WEEK ENDING SEPTEMBER 16

U.S. #1 POP 45	"Boogie Oogie Oogie"	Taste of Honey
U.S. #1 POP LP	*Don't Look Back*	Boston
U.S. #1 R&B 45	"Holding On (When Love Is Gone)"	L.T.D.
U.K. #1 POP 45	"Three Times a Lady"	The Commodores
U.K. #1 POP LP	*Night Flight to Venus*	Boney M

WEEK ENDING SEPTEMBER 23

U.S. #1 POP 45	"Boogie Oogie Oogie"	Taste of Honey
U.S. #1 POP LP	*Don't Look Back*	Boston
U.S. #1 R&B 45	"Got to Get You into My Life"	Earth, Wind and Fire
U.K. #1 POP 45	"Dreadlock Holiday"	10cc
U.K. #1 POP LP	*Night Flight to Venus*	Boney M

WEEK ENDING SEPTEMBER 30

U.S. #1 POP 45	"Kiss You All Over"	Exile
U.S. #1 POP LP	*Grease*	soundtrack
U.S. #1 R&B 45	"One Nation under a Groove (Part 1)"	Funkadelic
U.K. #1 POP 45	"Dreadlock Holiday"	10cc
U.K. #1 POP LP	*Grease*	soundtrack

2 **Gene Simmons, Kiss** bassist with the serpentlike tongue, receives a platinum record for his eponymously titled solo LP, one of four released concurrently by the members of Kiss. Simmons' charts the highest, to #22, guitarist **Paul Stanley**'s also goes platinum, but the biggest hit from the quartet comes from lead axeman **Ace Frehley**, whose "New York Groove" reaches #13.

9 RCA Records releases **David Bowie**'s double album *Stage,* a document of Bowie's U.S. tour earlier this year featuring both his early pop, rock and soul material and his more recent, experimental music.

10 The Be Stiff tour opens at Bristol University in England, featuring such Stiff Records acts as **Lene Lovich, Wreckless Eric, Mickey Jupp, Jona Lewie** and **Rachel Sweet**. The package tour will later come to America, where it will be moderately successful.

Singer **Steve Tyler** and guitarist

Joe Perry of **Aerosmith** are injured in Philadelphia by a cherry bomb thrown on stage by an audience member. Thereafter, the group performs from behind a cyclone fence.

After three uneven albums of Sixties influenced jams and often structureless compositions, San Francisco group **Journey** gets a new lead singer, **Steve Perry**, who can write songs. Not surprisingly, *Infinity* is their most successful album to date, and puts them on a course that will eventually make them one of the biggest commercial successes of the Eighties. The LP turns platinum on this date.

13 Ex-**Sex Pistol Sid Vicious**' girlfriend **Nancy Spungen** is found dead of abdominal knife wounds in their room at the Chelsea Hotel in New York. Vicious, who is nearly unconscious due to the effects of several different drugs, including heroin, barbiturates and alcohol, is charged with her murder, jailed and then released. Months later, Vicious will die of a heroin overdose before the case ever comes to trial.

17 1978 is the year of the movie soundtrack, and **Frankie Valli** has a Number One platinum hit with the title song from *Grease.* It is the biggest hit of his solo career and eventually sells seven million copies.

18 The film *Rockers,* produced and directed by Greek **Theodoras Bafoloukos**, premieres in Kingston, Jamaica. This reggae feature, with a plot similar to the well-known reggae cult film *The Harder They Come* with **Jimmy Cliff**, stars reggae session drummer **Leroy "Horsemouth" Wallace**; he plays himself, taking on a crime syndicate that threatens the welfare and lifestyle of Kingston's reggae musicians. The film also features such reggae stars as **Winston "Burning Spear" Rodney, Jacob "Killer" Miller, Gregory Isaacs, the Mighty Diamonds, Big Youth, Robbie Shakespeare, Dillinger, Jack Ruby, Richard "Dirty Harry" Hall**, and **Ras Michael and the Sons of Negus** as themselves. The film's soundtrack also features the music of **Prince Hammer, Peter Tosh**, the Hep-

tones and others. It will not be shown in the U.S. until 1980, when it will enjoy a brief but well-received run.

21 The **Clash** end their business relationship with their manager, **Bernie Rhodes**—the same Bernie Rhodes who will be disparagingly referred to in the line "Bernie Rhodes knows, don't argue!" in the **Specials**' hit "Gangsters."

22 Funk-fusion band **Earth, Wind and Fire** kick off a seventy-five-date American tour in Louisville, Kentucky.

23 **Sid Vicious** attempts suicide while imprisoned in the Riker's Island Detention Center in New York following the death of his girlfriend **Nancy Spungen**, with whose murder he's been charged.

CBS Records becomes the first major American label to announce a price hike to $8.98 list price for albums.

30 The made-for-TV-animated cartoon movie *Kiss Meets the Phantom of the Park,* starring comicbook, heavy-metal, glitter rockers **Kiss** as the heroes trying to foil a mad scientist operating in an amusement park, airs on NBC-TV. ◆

WEEK ENDING OCTOBER 7

U.S. #1 POP 45	"Kiss You All Over"	Exile
U.S. #1 POP LP	*Grease*	soundtrack
U.S. #1 R&B 45	"One Nation under a Groove (Part 1)"	Funkadelic
U.K. #1 POP 45	"Summer Nights"	John Travolta and Olivia Newton-John
U.K. #1 POP LP	*Grease*	soundtrack

WEEK ENDING OCTOBER 14

U.S. #1 POP 45	"Kiss You All Over"	Exile
U.S. #1 POP LP	*Grease*	soundtrack
U.S. #1 R&B 45	"One Nation under a Groove (Part 1)"	Funkadelic
U.K. #1 POP 45	"Summer Nights"	John Travolta and Olivia Newton-John
U.K. #1 POP LP	*Grease*	soundtrack

WEEK ENDING OCTOBER 21

U.S. #1 POP 45	"Kiss You All Over"	Exile
U.S. #1 POP LP	*Grease*	soundtrack
U.S. #1 R&B 45	"One Nation under a Groove (Part 1)"	Funkadelic
U.K. #1 POP 45	"Summer Nights"	John Travolta and Olivia Newton-John
U.K. #1 POP LP	*Grease*	soundtrack

WEEK ENDING OCTOBER 28

U.S. #1 POP 45	"Hot Child in the City"	Nick Gilder
U.S. #1 POP LP	*Grease*	soundtrack
U.S. #1 R&B 45	"One Nation under a Groove (Part 1)"	Funkadelic
U.K. #1 POP 45	"Summer Nights"	John Travolta and Olivia Newton-John
U.K. #1 POP LP	*Grease*	soundtrack

3 The **Cars** roll into Europe for a mini-tour that will include Germany, France, Belgium and Britain.

4 Music-business vet **General (Norman) Johnson**—whose roots go all the way back to the **Showmen**'s 1961 hit ode to rock & roll, "It Will Stand," and who also sang the scatting, stuttering, **Billy Stewart**-influenced lead on **Chairmen of the Board**'s 1970 hit "Give Me Just a Little More Time"—enters the soul chart with "Can't Nobody Love Me Like You Do," which will peak at #79.

Greg Reeves, former bassist with **Crosby, Stills, Nash and Young**, sues Crosby, Stills, Nash and Young for $1 million in unpaid back royalties.

Boston, the rock band from the city of the same name, play their hometown for the first time since becoming a huge national act, opening a two-night sold-out stand at the Boston Garden.

10 The **Clash**'s second album, *Give 'Em Enough Rope*, is released in England on CBS Records. It will soon become their first American album release, on Epic Records.

11 Memphis' long-serving soul singer, songwriter, arranger and producer **Isaac Hayes** enters the soul LP chart with *For the Sake of Love*, which will peak at #15.

On the same day that ex-**Rufus** lead singer Chaka Khan's "I'm Every Woman" hits Number One on the soul chart, the album from which it came, *Chaka*, enters the soul LP chart, where it will peak at #2.

15 **Chic** (main members, **Nile Rodgers** and **Bernard Edwards**) are awarded their second gold record of 1978, for "Le Freak," which will hit Number One in January 1979. The group had earlier received a gold disc for "Dance, Dance, Dance."

16 **Queen** play at Madison Square Garden in New York City, with several semi-nude women bicycling on stage for their hit "Fat Bottomed Girls."

17 **Linda Ronstadt**'s anthology album *A Retrospective* becomes her eighth gold album.

18 The **Boomtown Rats**' "Rat Trap" reaches Number One on the U.K. charts.

Critically acclaimed British funk-pop band **Hot Chocolate** make one of their rare entries into the U.S. soul chart with "Every 1's a Winner," which in its eighteen weeks on the chart will peak at #7.

25 New York new wave band **Talking Heads** hit #29 on the LP chart with their second album, *More Songs about Buildings and Food*—

the highest position on any U.S. chart so far for a new wave act.

Several veteran soul acts make rather rare disco-era soul-chart entries this day: former **Impressions** lead singer **Jerry Butler** with *Nothing Says I Love You Like "I Love You,"* which in twelve weeks on the soul LP chart will peak at #42; former "Duke of Earl" **Gene Chandler** with *Get Down*, which will peak at #12 in eighteen weeks on the soul LP chart, and the title single of which is currently climbing the soul chart to #3; **Gladys Knight**, with a solo single, "I'm Coming Home Again," that will peak at #54 in nine weeks, and a solo album, *Miss Gladys Knight*, that will peak at #57 in five weeks; **Joe Simon** with "Love Vibration," which will peak at #15 in fifteen weeks on the chart; and the **Temptations** with "Ever Ready Love," which will climb to #31 on the chart, from the #46 hit soul LP *Bare Back*.

29 **Neil Young**'s thirteenth solo album, *Comes a Time*, goes gold. The mainly acoustic album features such FM radio hits as "Goin' Back" and "Look Out for My Love," as well as "Human Highway"—also the title of a film, directed by and starring Young with **Devo**, which is slated for 1983 release. ◆

W E E K   E N D I N G   N O V E M B E R   4

U.S. #1 POP 45	"You Needed Me"	Anne Murray
U.S. #1 POP LP	*Living in the U.S.A.*	Linda Ronstadt
U.S. #1 R&B 45	"One Nation under a Groove (Part 1)"	Funkadelic
U.K. #1 POP 45	"Summer Nights"	John Travolta and Olivia Newton-John
U.K. #1 POP LP	*Grease*	soundtrack

W E E K   E N D I N G   N O V E M B E R   1 1

U.S. #1 POP 45	"MacArthur Park"	Donna Summer
U.S. #1 POP LP	*Live and More*	Donna Summer
U.S. #1 R&B 45	"I'm Every Woman"	Chaka Khan
U.K. #1 POP 45	"Summer Nights"	John Travolta and Olivia Newton-John
U.K. #1 POP LP	*Grease*	soundtrack

W E E K   E N D I N G   N O V E M B E R   1 8

U.S. #1 POP 45	"MacArthur Park"	Donna Summer
U.S. #1 POP LP	*52nd Street*	Billy Joel
U.S. #1 R&B 45	"I'm Every Woman"	Chaka Khan
U.K. #1 POP 45	"Rat Trap"	The Boomtown Rats
U.K. #1 POP LP	*Grease*	soundtrack

W E E K   E N D I N G   N O V E M B E R   2 5

U.S. #1 POP 45	"MacArthur Park"	Donna Summer
U.S. #1 POP LP	*52nd Street*	Billy Joel
U.S. #1 R&B 45	"I'm Every Woman"	Chaka Khan
U.K. #1 POP 45	"Rat Trap"	The Boomtown Rats
U.K. #1 POP LP	*Grease*	soundtrack

DECEMBER 1978

1 British new wave music-hall rocker **Ian Dury** releases his biggest hit single, "Hit Me with Your Rhythm Stick." It will reach Number One in the U.K. and sell 2 million copies worldwide without entering the U.S. chart.

6 **Sid Vicious**, out on bail from Riker's Island Detention Center in New York after being charged with the murder of his girlfriend **Nancy Spungen**, smashes glass in the face of **Patti Smith**'s brother **Todd** during an altercation at New York rock club Hurrah.

16 **Parliament**, part of **George Clinton**'s subversive-message funk empire, enters the soul LP chart with *Motor-Booty Affair*. The album, which yields the hit single "Aqua Boogie (A Psychoalphadiscobetabioaquadoloop),"

Number One for four weeks starting January 20, 1979, will rise to #2 on the chart. It caps off a highly successful year for Clinton, who has already had two Number One singles with Parliament's "Flashlight" (Number One for three weeks starting March 4) and **Funkadelic**'s "One Nation under a Groove" (Number One for six weeks starting September 30), and a Number One soul LP in Funkadelic's *One Nation under a Groove* (Number One for four weeks starting October 28).

Patrice Rushen, a jazz-fusion keyboardist, starts a successful pop-funk crossover, as her single "Hang It Up" enters the soul singles chart. It will rise to #16.

Bob Dylan ends his three-month U.S. tour in Miami, Florida.

James Brown makes his third

and last soul singles chart entry of the year with the title cut of his latest album, "For Goodness Sake, Take a Look at Those Cakes." The bawdy ode to one variety of girl-watching will

peak at #52.

17 Stiff Record's "Be Stiff Route 78" tour opens its American run at New York's Bottom Line club. The lineup includes **Lene Lovich**, **Rachel Sweet**, **Jona Lewie**, **Wreckless Eric** and **Mickey Jupp**.

25 **Public Image Ltd.**, the band featuring ex-**Sex Pistol John Lydon** and ex-**Clash** member **Keith Levene**, plays its first concert, at London's Rainbow Theater.

27 **Chris Bell**, a founding member of Memphis-based pop-rock band **Big Star**, is killed at age twenty-seven in an auto accident. Big Star, which formed in 1971, performed and recorded a rock & roll style that later became known as power pop. Ironically, the group disbanded in 1975, only a few years before later power pop groups like the Knack would be successful.

The most auspicious debut in years is made by the **Cars**, a Boston-based band formerly known as Cap'n Swing. Their first LP is the first new wave record to gain acceptance on FM-AOR radio, which is still enamored of arena bands like **Boston** and **Kansas**. *The Cars* turns platinum on this date.

31 **Bill Graham** closes Winterland Theater in San Francisco to rock concerts following a swan-song by the **Grateful Dead** and the **Blues Brothers**. ♦

WEEK ENDING DECEMBER 2

U.S. #1 POP 45	"You Don't Bring Me Flowers"	Barbra Streisand and Neil Diamond
U.S. #1 POP LP	*52nd Street*	Billy Joel
U.S. #1 R&B 45	"Le Freak"	Chic
U.K. #1 POP 45	"Rat Trap"	The Boomtown Rats
U.K. #1 POP LP	*Grease*	soundtrack

WEEK ENDING DECEMBER 9

U.S. #1 POP 45	"Le Freak"	Chic
U.S. #1 POP LP	*52nd Street*	Billy Joel
U.S. #1 R&B 45	"Le Freak"	Chic
U.K. #1 POP 45	"Da Ya Think I'm Sexy"	Rod Stewart
U.K. #1 POP LP	*Neil Diamond's 20 Golden Greats*	Neil Diamond

WEEK ENDING DECEMBER 16

U.S. #1 POP 45	"Le Freak"	Chic
U.S. #1 POP LP	*52nd Street*	Billy Joel
U.S. #1 R&B 45	"Le Freak"	Chic
U.K. #1 POP 45	"Mary's Boy Child"	Boney M
U.K. #1 POP LP	*Neil Diamond's 20 Golden Greats*	Neil Diamond

WEEK ENDING DECEMBER 23

U.S. #1 POP 45	"Le Freak"	Chic
U.S. #1 POP LP	*52nd Street*	Billy Joel
U.S. #1 R&B 45	"Le Freak"	Chic
U.K. #1 POP 45	"Mary's Boy Child"	Boney M
U.K. #1 POP LP	*Grease*	soundtrack

WEEK ENDING DECEMBER 30

U.S. #1 POP 45	"Le Freak"	Chic
U.S. #1 POP LP	*52nd Street*	Billy Joel
U.S. #1 R&B 45	"Le Freak"	Chic
U.K. #1 POP 45	"Mary's Boy Child"	Boney M
U.K. #1 POP LP	*Grease*	soundtrack

1979

With both disco and new wave more or less established as commercially viable pop genres, the inevitable began to happen: they merged into the pop mainstream and began affecting each other directly. Disco diva Donna Summer went rock with her platinum hits "Hot Stuff" and "Bad Girls," and Blondie scored the first new wave-disco crossover hit with "Heart of Glass"; Rod Stewart ("Da Ya Think I'm Sexy") and even Kiss ("I Was Made for Lovin' You") had major hits with disco songs; Queen imitated Chic's disco smash "Good Times" for their own smash, "Another One Bites the Dust" (a particularly telling title considering the mass-market assimilation such a move indicated); Gary Numan's "Cars" and M's "Pop Muzik" introduced disco and funk-inflected electropop to the top of the charts. By the end of the year, Donna Summer had made the final disco-pop crossover with her hit duet with Barbra Streisand, "No More Tears (Enough Is Enough)."

The continued flourishing of disco, despite some media speculation on its impending demise, finally prompted the white rock audience's reactionary response with the birth over the summer of the "Disco Sucks" movement. The less said about this example of wrong-headed ultraconservatism, the better.

Speaking of wrong-headed, there was also white arena rock's great tragedy this year with the horror of the Cincinnati Who concert, where the calloussness of big-business rock promotion resulted in a stampede for unreserved "festival" seats in which 11 innocent Who fans were trampled to death. Ultimately, this was a further verification of what punk rock had been asserting: that the rock-as-entertainment industry was just too big to really *care* about its audience. Perhaps, with its own self-destructive imploding nihilism, punk somehow knew that such an industry was also too big for punk to really be able to do anything about it.

The continued flourishing of new wave—the Cars earned their second platinum LP in a row with *Candy-O;* Elvis Costello was included along with Elvis Presley, Chuck Berry, Buddy Holly, the Beatles, Bob Dylan and Bruce Springsteen in ABC-TV's "Heroes of Rock & Roll"; the first new wave rock festival was held in Minnesota in September—resulted in the first inevitable case of a corporate, prefabricated new wave act, the Knack. Despite their blatant Beatles allusions and rank misogyny, this L.A. pop quartet had a legitimately great radio hit with "My Sharona."

While Bob Marley continued to draw great critical acclaim and modest but steady commercial success in the U.S., prompting hopes that reggae would at last have its day in the sun, the assimilation of Jamaican musical styles into the post-new wave mainstream soon saw that mainstream predictably eclipsing hard-core roots reggae. The Police became pop superstars with the international smash "Message in a Bottle." The Specials, Madness, the English Beat and others kicked off Britain's "two-tone" ska-rock movement, which in some ways was the most promising movement in a while. It was willfully political and full of acute social protest, yet its insistence on racial integration—demonstrated through the "two-tone" black-and-white membership of most of its bands—bespoke a pragmatic hopefulness, a more down-to-earth echo of Sixties utopianism. Musically, however, two-tone was too often seen as retrograde (by many rock critics) or just too jumpy and exotic (by most mainstream rock fans), and the subgenre would end up leaving little more than the fashion statement of black-and-white-check patterns as its legacy.

1 Following a New Year's Eve concert featuring the **Blues Brothers**, the **New Riders of the Purple Sage** and the **Grateful Dead**, Bill Graham closes San Francisco's Winterland Theater. The Dead had performed there a record forty-eight times.

At a New Year's Eve concert in Cleveland, **Bruce Springsteen**'s cheek is ripped open by a fire-cracker thrown onstage from the audience.

2 The trial of ex-**Sex Pistol Sid Vicious** for the October 1978 murder of his girlfriend **Nancy Spungen** opens in New York City. Vicious will not live to hear a verdict, but will die shortly of a heroin overdose.

4 One of the giants of modern jazz music, bassist/pianist/composer/arranger **Charles Mingus** dies in Cuernavaca, Mexico, at age fifty-six of a heart attack brought on by his long battle with the so-called Lou Gehrig's Disease—amyotrophic lateral sclerosis. Among Mingus' best-known composi-

tions are "Goodbye Pork Pie Hat," "Wednesday Night Prayer Meeting," "Haitian Fight Song," "Better Git It in Your Soul," "Fables of Faubus," "Pithecanthropus Erectus," "Lord Don't You Drop That Atom Bomb on Me" and "The Shoes of the Fisherman's Wife Are Just a Pair of Jive-Ass Slippers." His final project was a collaboration with **Joni Mitchell**, still in progress at the time of his death, which would be realized on her album *Mingus*. It would include a version of "Goodbye Pork Pie Hat" (also covered by rock guitarist **Jeff Beck**).

With Beatlemania continuing unabated around the world, the Star Club in Hamburg, Germany, where the **Beatles** gained a lot of early experience in the early Sixties, reopens.

5 The Blues Brothers—actually TV comedians **John Belushi** and **Dan Aykroyd**—come under some fire for their tongue-in-cheek renderings of vintage soul tunes, but some of their biggest supporters are the covered artists themselves. *Briefcase Full of Blues* goes to Number One and goes platinum on this

date, and gives the **Sam and Dave** classic "Soul Man" a new life. Interestingly, the duo approves of Belushi and Aykroyd, and why not? Their own career is temporarily revived.

8 Canadian rock band **Rush** are named the country's official "Ambassadors of Music" by the Canadian government.

9 A benefit concert titled A Gift of Song—the Music for UNICEF Concert is held at the United Nations General Assembly in New York. It is taped by NBC-TV for broadcast the following night. Such acts as **Olivia Newton-John**, the **Bee Gees**, **Rod Stewart**, **Abba**, **Donna Summer**, **John Denver**, **Kris Kristofferson and Rita Coolidge** and **Earth, Wind and Fire** raise about half a million dollars for the world-hunger organization.

13 Soul-pop singer **Donny Hathaway**, perhaps best known for such duets with **Roberta Flack** as "Where Is the Love?," dies at age thirty-four after jumping (or falling—police could not reach a conclusive decision) from a fifteenth floor

hotel room in New York City. He was working on the album *Roberta Flack Featuring Donny Hathaway* at the time. For the past few years, according to his record-company (Atlantic) spokesman, Hathaway had been having psychological problems and hadn't done much in the way of music; his most recent hit, with Flack, was 1978's #2 gold hit "The Closer I Get to You." Hathaway had been a total of four solo albums. He had also recently been working as a house producer and songwriter for Atlantic, a function he'd also fulfilled earlier on a freelance basis for such labels as Chess, Kapp, Uni and Stax. Hathaway also scored the film *Come Back Charleston Blue* and sang the theme song of the TV show "Maude."

17 Linda Ronstadt, **Emmylou Harris** and **Dolly Parton** jointly announce that, after spending a week together talking, they will record an album together. Parton describes their decision-making period as "a week-long slumber party." Although a number of tracks are recorded, as of 1983 none had been released.

24 The **Clash**'s first American single, their version of the **Bobby Fuller Four**'s "I Fought the Law," is released in the U.S. on Epic Records. Though it will garner lots of play in new wave dance-rock clubs and on college radio stations, it will not be a hit on the pop chart.

25 The **Cars** win the *Rolling Stone* annual readers' poll as best new band of the year.

Rolling Stone quotes soul singer **Al Green** on **Talking Heads**' success with their cover version of Green's "Take Me to the River": "I think it's fantastic. And I'm looking forward to covering some Talking Heads material."

29 San Diego teenager **Brenda Spencer** makes national headlines when she suddenly begins shooting at people with a gun at school. She kills two, and when later asked why she did it, answers, "I don't like Mondays." That line will subsequently become the title of a hit single by Irish band the **Boomtown Rats**. ◆

WEEK ENDING JANUARY 6

U.S. #1 POP 45	"Too Much Heaven"	The Bee Gees
U.S. #1 POP LP	*Greatest Hits, Volume 2*	Barbra Streisand
U.S. #1 R&B 45	"Got to Be Real"	Cheryl Lynn
U.K. #1 POP 45	"Y.M.C.A."	The Village People
U.K. #1 POP LP	*Showaddywaddy's Greatest Hits 1976–1978*	Showaddywaddy

WEEK ENDING JANUARY 13

U.S. #1 POP 45	"Too Much Heaven"	The Bee Gees
U.S. #1 POP LP	*Greatest Hits, Volume 2*	Barbra Streisand
U.S. #1 R&B 45	"September"	Earth, Wind and Fire
U.K. #1 POP 45	"Y.M.C.A."	The Village People
U.K. #1 POP LP	*Showaddywaddy's Greatest Hits 1976–1978*	Showaddywaddy

WEEK ENDING JANUARY 20

U.S. #1 POP 45	"Le Freak"	Chic
U.S. #1 POP LP	*Greatest Hits, Volume 2*	Barbra Streisand
U.S. #1 R&B 45	"Aqua Boogie"	Parliament
U.K. #1 POP 45	"Y.M.C.A."	The Village People
U.K. #1 POP LP	*Showaddywaddy's Greatest Hits 1976–1978*	Showaddywaddy

WEEK ENDING JANUARY 27

U.S. #1 POP 45	"Le Freak"	Chic
U.S. #1 POP LP	*52nd Street*	Billy Joel
U.S. #1 R&B 45	"Aqua Boogie"	Parliament
U.K. #1 POP 45	"Hit Me with Your Rhythm Stick"	Ian Dury and the Blockheads
U.K. #1 POP LP	*Don't Walk, Boogie*	various artists

2 Ex-Sex Pistol bassist **Sid Vicious** dies at age twenty-one of heroin overdose in the apartment of his present girlfriend, **Michelle Robinson**, in New York City's Greenwich Village. Since being charged with the murder of his then girlfriend **Nancy Spungen** in 1978—Vicious' death leaves the case unresolved—Vicious had been in and out of jail and detention centers, being detoxified from heroin addiction all the while. Apparently, he had detoxed himself well enough that when, the night before his death, he took a strong shot of heroin at his girlfriend's house party, it was too much for him. The death is ruled accidental.

3 A sold-out crowd packs into the Surf Ballroom in Clear Lake, Iowa, for a concert commemorating the twentieth anniversary of the plane crash that killed **Buddy Holly**, **Ritchie Valens** and the **Big Bopper** after their performance at the Surf. **Wolfman Jack** hosts the show, which features **Del Shannon**, **Jimmy Clanton** and the **Drifters**. One-time **Cricket** guitarist **Niki Sullivan** attends.

5 The **Pointer Sisters'** version of **Bruce Springsteen**'s "Fire" turns gold the same month as it reaches #2. The tune also is covered by New York singer **Robert Gordon**.

7 **Stephen Stills** becomes the first rock performer to record on digital equipment in Los Angeles' Record Plant Studio. However, his digital material is never released, and **Ry Cooder** will become the first rock performer to release a digitally recorded record.

11 **Stiff Little Fingers**, a punk band from Ulster, Northern Ireland, release their debut album, *Inflammable Material*, which contains their punk anthem "Alternative Ulster" and will go on to become the first independently released punk LP to enter the U.K. LP chart.

13 **Aretha Franklin** opens a stand at Harrah's resort in Lake Tahoe, Nevada.

15 The Grammy Award winners for 1978 are announced. The *Saturday Night Fever* soundtrack album wins Album of the Year and garners the **Bee Gees** Best Pop Group Vocal and Best Arrangement for Voices for the hit "Stayin' Alive." **Billy Joel**'s "Just the Way You Are" wins Record and Song of the Year. **Donna Summer**'s "Last Dance" wins Best R&B Female Vocal and Best R&B Song. **Earth, Wind and Fire** win Best R&B Group Vocal for *All 'n' All,* Best R&B Instrumental for "Runnin'," and Best Arrangement Accompanying Vocalists for their version of the **Beatles**' "Got to Get You into My Life." Best New Artist is female disco duo "A Taste of Honey." Best Ethnic or Traditional Recording is **Muddy Waters**' *I'm Ready.*

RCA records begins distributing A&M Records releases, ending A&M's long reign as the country's largest independent label.

16 **Elvis Costello**, heretofore considered one of the most arrogant of punkish performers, reveals his country roots at an unannounced solo acoustic performance at Hollywood country music club the Palomino, where Costello performs a bunch of songs by country great **George Jones**, and his own "Stranger in the House," which Jones will later cover.

17 The **Clash**, kicking off their first American tour—dubbed Pearl Harbor '79—make their first U.S. stage appearance at New York's Palladium. **Bo Diddley** opens for them. Fittingly, the first song the Clash play in America is "I'm So Bored with the U.S.A."

22 In a *Rolling Stone* article titled "Advertising Creeps into Rock," it is reported that rock band **Journey** has developed an advertising relationship with Budweiser beer. Such business ventures will become commonplace over the next few years, with the most visible example being the **Who**'s shilling for Schlitz beer.

23 **Elvis Costello**'s *Armed Forces* turns gold, the first of his albums to do so. It is a much more textured album than his first two, dominated largely by keyboards, and shows Costello to be one of the finest—and most prolific—songwriters in contemporary rock.

24 The soundtrack album of the **Sex Pistols** film *The Great Rock N' Roll Swindle* is released, though the film itself—a series of "lessons" in rock subversion by Pistols manager **Malcolm McLaren**, featuring cartoons, staged sequences and actual concert footage—has yet to find any distribution anywhere due to legal wrangles. The soundtrack features **Sid Vicious**' version of "My Way" and a hilarious disco sendup of the Sex Pistols' three biggest singles, "Anarchy in the U.K.," "God Save the Queen" and "Pretty Vacant."

26 In London, the **Sex Pistols** court case, in which they and their manager **Malcolm McLaren** try to divvy up the band's earnings, it is revealed that only £30,000 are left of the band's £800,000 gross. ◆

WEEK ENDING FEBRUARY 3

U.S. #1 POP 45	"Le Freak"	Chic
U.S. #1 POP LP	*Briefcase Full of Blues*	The Blues Brothers
U.S. #1 R&B 45	"Aqua Boogie"	Parliament
U.K. #1 POP 45	"Hit Me with Your Rhythm Stick"	Ian Dury and the Blockheads
U.K. #1 POP LP	*Don't Walk, Boogie*	various artists

WEEK ENDING FEBRUARY 10

U.S. #1 POP 45	"Da Ya Think I'm Sexy?"	Rod Stewart
U.S. #1 POP LP	*Blondes Have More Fun*	Rod Stewart
U.S. #1 R&B 45	"Aqua Boogie"	Parliament
U.K. #1 POP 45	"Heart of Glass"	Blondie
U.K. #1 POP LP	*Parallel Lines*	Blondie

WEEK ENDING FEBRUARY 17

U.S. #1 POP 45	"Da Ya Think I'm Sexy?"	Rod Stewart
U.S. #1 POP LP	*Blondes Have More Fun*	Rod Stewart
U.S. #1 R&B 45	"Bustin' Loose"	Chuck Brown and the Soul Searchers
U.K. #1 POP 45	"Chiquitita"	Abba
U.K. #1 POP LP	*Parallel Lines*	Blondie

WEEK ENDING FEBRUARY 24

U.S. #1 POP 45	"Da Ya Think I'm Sexy?"	Rod Stewart
U.S. #1 POP LP	*Blondes Have More Fun*	Rod Stewart
U.S. #1 R&B 45	"Bustin' Loose"	Chuck Brown and the Soul Searchers
U.K. #1 POP 45	"Heart of Glass"	Blondie
U.K. #1 POP LP	*Parallel Lines*	Blondie

2 Havana Jam, the first jointly sponsored U.S.-Cuban music event in twenty years, begins three days of performances today. Featured artists include **Billy Joel**, **Stephen Stills**, **Kris Kristofferson** and **Rita Coolidge**, and **Tom Scott and the L.A. Express**. CBS Records will later release an album documenting the festival.

3 British blues rock singer **Mike Patto**, who had led the bands **Patto** and **Boxer** (both bigger hits with critics than record buyers), dies of throat cancer in London at age thirty-six.

5 A little over a month after buying it for a reported $20 million, MCA Records dissolves ABC Records.

8 In one of the first public acknowledgements of the hard times that are beginning to befall the record industry, *Rolling Stone* reports that due to the "skyrocketing costs of producing, promoting and supporting a new album, now put at between $350,000 and $500,000," labels such as Warner Bros. and other majors will begin limiting their new releases.

9 ABC-TV shows the rock documentary "Heroes of Rock & Roll," narrated by **Jeff Bridges** and featuring clips of **Buddy Holly**, **Elvis Presley**, **Chuck Berry**, **Bob Dylan**, the **Beatles**, the **Rolling Stones**, **Elvis Costello** and other rock greats, as well as the first film ever seen of **Bruce Springsteen** in performance (an excerpt from "Rosalita").

16 **Twisted Sister**, a Long Island bar band formed in 1973, is the first act to headline and sell out New York City's three thousand-seat Palladium without the benefit of a record, a recording contract or radio play. It will be another three years before Twisted Sister signs its first contract, with Secret, a British label, and four years before it lands an American deal with Atlantic Records.

At a Holiday Inn in Columbus, Ohio, **Elvis Costello** and his band and members of **Stephen Stills'** touring entourage (both Costello and Stills had played concerts in Columbus earlier in the evening) get into an argument that starts when Costello makes some typically nasty and disparaging remarks about America. When **Bonnie Bramlett**, one of Stills' backup singers, points out the connections between Costello's music and American R&B, Costello angrily calls **Ray Charles** "a blind, ignorant nigger" and **James Brown** "another dumb nigger." Bramlett then punches Costello and a full-scale brawl nearly erupts. Bramlett, who, in the later Sixties performed with her husband **Delaney** and their all-star **Friends**, immediately reports the incident to the press. Costello will soon hold a New York City press conference to explain his remarks as "just a way to bring a silly argument to a quick end by saying the most outrageous thing possible. And it worked, too."

17 **Zenon de Fleur Heirowski**, guitarist with British punk band the **Count Bishops**, dies at age twenty-eight of a heart attack following an auto accident in London.

22 The day before her own birthday, soul singer **Chaka Khan** gives birth to a son, **Damien Milton Patrick Holland**.

27 Amid all the **Sex Pistols** imitators comes **Dire Straits**, whose captivating single "Sultans of Swing" quietly sneaks its way up the chart to #4. The band is led by one **Mark Knopfler**, an Englishman who sings in a voice like **Dylan**'s and plays a Stratocaster with the understated emotion of a young **Eric Clapton**. The debut album turns platinum.

29 **David Bowie** begins his first U.S. tour since 1978 in San Diego. It will end May 8 at Madison Square Garden in New York City. Bowie has just recently finished filming on *Just a Gigolo*, which will be a commercial and critical flop. ♦

WEEK ENDING MARCH 3

U.S. #1 POP 45	"Da Ya Think I'm Sexy?"	Rod Stewart
U.S. #1 POP LP	*Spirits Having Flown*	The Bee Gees
U.S. #1 R&B 45	"Bustin' Loose"	Chuck Brown and the Soul Searchers
U.K. #1 POP 45	"Heart of Glass"	Blondie
U.K. #1 POP LP	*Parallel Lines*	Blondie

WEEK ENDING MARCH 10

U.S. #1 POP 45	"I Will Survive"	Gloria Gaynor
U.S. #1 POP LP	*Spirits Having Flown*	The Bee Gees
U.S. #1 R&B 45	"Bustin' Loose"	Chuck Brown and the Soul Searchers
U.K. #1 POP 45	"Tragedy"	The Bee Gees
U.K. #1 POP LP	*Parallel Lines*	Blondie

WEEK ENDING MARCH 17

U.S. #1 POP 45	"I Will Survive"	Gloria Gaynor
U.S. #1 POP LP	*Spirits Having Flown*	The Bee Gees
U.S. #1 R&B 45	"I Got My Mind Made Up (You Can Get It Girl)"	Instant Funk
U.K. #1 POP 45	"Oliver's Army"	Elvis Costello
U.K. #1 POP LP	*Parallel Lines*	Blondie

WEEK ENDING MARCH 24

U.S. #1 POP 45	"Tragedy"	The Bee Gees
U.S. #1 POP LP	*Spirits Having Flown*	The Bee Gees
U.S. #1 R&B 45	"I Got My Mind Made Up (You Can Get It Girl)"	Instant Funk
U.K. #1 POP 45	"I Will Survive"	Gloria Gaynor
U.K. #1 POP LP	*Spirits Having Flown*	The Bee Gees

WEEK ENDING MARCH 31

U.S. #1 POP 45	"Tragedy"	The Bee Gees
U.S. #1 POP LP	*Spirits Having Flown*	The Bee Gees
U.S. #1 R&B 45	"He's the Greatest Dancer"	Sister Sledge
U.K. #1 POP 45	"I Will Survive"	Gloria Gaynor
U.K. #1 POP LP	*C'est Chic*	Chic

3 Van Halen's *Van Halen II* goes gold just five days before the band takes off on a triumphant ten-month tour. The long trip is the antithesis of the way Van Halen record: for their second LP, they took a mere six days in the studio, one-third the time required for their first album.

6 The punk-cum-new wave group **Blondie** has its first major U.S. hit with "Heart of Glass," a disco number the band originally called "The Disco Song." Naturally, they're hit with cries of "sellout." In any case, "Heart of Glass" goes platinum on this date, two months after it made Number One.

Rod Stewart marries actor **George Hamilton**'s ex-wife **Alana Hamilton** in Beverly Hills.

7 The two-day California Music Festival at the Los Angeles Memorial Coliseum opens. It will draw 110,000 people and make $1.2 million, but will still be a financial loss for the promoters. Among the acts featured there are **Ted Nugent**, **Aerosmith**, **Cheap Trick**, **Van Halen** and the **Boomtown Rats**.

8 Van Halen commence their second world tour. It will last ten months. The group carries twenty-two tons of sound equipment and ten tons of lights.

10 A Boogie 'N' Blues Concert at New York City's Carnegie Hall features performances by such giants of those forms as **John Lee Hooker**, **Lightnin' Hopkins**, **Clifton Chenier** and **Honeyboy Edwards**. **Willie Mae "Big Mama" Thornton** makes an unannounced special appearance.

12 Mickey Thomas, former vocalist with **Elvin Bishop**, replaces **Marty Balin** as lead singer with **Jefferson Starship**.

After so many years of being the Next Big Thing, only to watch other country-rock outfits enjoy much greater success, **Poco** receive a gold record for *Legend*, their twelfth LP. The only original member left by

this point is pedal steel guitar player **Rusty Young**, who, fittingly, wrote and sang the LP's first hit, "Crazy Love."

13 Five days into Van Halen's latest tour, **David Lee Roth** collapses from exhaustion onstage in Spokane, Washington.

16 Gloria Gaynor is awarded a platinum 45 for "I Will Survive," the biggest hit of her career and a Number One record for three weeks in March.

22 As part of his sentence for his 1977 Canadian drug arrest, **Rolling Stone Keith Richards** performs a benefit concert in Ottawa for the Canadian National Institute for the Blind. Richards' band, making its debut, is the **New Barbarians**, consisting of Richards, Rolling Stone guitarist **Ron Wood**, funk-fusion bassist **Stanley Clarke**, ex-**Faces** keyboardist **Ian McLagan** and ex-**Meters** drummer **Ziggy Modeliste**. The New Barbarians will shortly embark on a brief U.S. tour, but will never record.

25 The film *Rock n' Roll High School*, directed by **Alan Arkush** and starring **P. J. Soles**, **Mary Woronov**, **Vince Van Patten**, **Paul Bartel** and the **Ramones**, premieres in Los Angeles. A satire of Fifties teen-rock films set in Vince Lombardi High School, the film's soundtrack features the Ramones performing the title song, as well as **Devo** ("Come Back Jonee"), **Chuck Berry** ("School Day"), the **Velvet Underground** ("Rock and Roll"), **Wings** ("Did We Meet Somewhere Before") and **Bobby Freeman** ("Do You Wanna Dance?"). The movie does well both at the box office and with critics.

Blues giant **B. B. King** concludes a month-long, thirty-date tour of the U.S.S.R. "It reminded me of the many reformatories we've played," says King of the experience. "We go in, we play and we leave. It's sad, because we know the audience can't leave with us."

27 Stevie Wonder makes a surprise appearance at a **Duke Ellington** tribute concert at UCLA's Royce Hall. He performs "Sir Duke" and Ellington's "C-Jam Blues." ◆

WEEK ENDING APRIL 7

U.S. #1 POP 45	"I Will Survive"	Gloria Gaynor
U.S. #1 POP LP	*Minute by Minute*	The Doobie Brothers
U.S. #1 R&B 45	"I Got My Mind Made Up (You Can Get It Girl)"	Instant Funk
U.K. #1 POP 45	"In the Navy"	The Village People
U.K. #1 POP LP	*Greatest Hits, Volume 2*	Barbra Streisand

WEEK ENDING APRIL 14

U.S. #1 POP 45	"What a Fool Believes"	The Doobie Brothers
U.S. #1 POP LP	*Minute by Minute*	The Doobie Brothers
U.S. #1 R&B 45	"Disco Nights (Rock Freak)"	G.Q.
U.K. #1 POP 45	"Bright Eyes"	Art Garfunkel
U.K. #1 POP LP	*Greatest Hits, Volume 2*	Barbra Streisand

WEEK ENDING APRIL 21

U.S. #1 POP 45	"Knock on Wood"	Amii Stewart
U.S. #1 POP LP	*Spirits Having Flown*	The Bee Gees
U.S. #1 R&B 45	"Disco Nights (Rock Freak)"	G.Q.
U.K. #1 POP 45	"Bright Eyes"	Art Garfunkel
U.K. #1 POP LP	*Greatest Hits, Volume 2*	Barbra Streisand

WEEK ENDING APRIL 28

U.S. #1 POP 45	"Heart of Glass"	Blondie
U.S. #1 POP LP	*Minute by Minute*	The Doobie Brothers
U.S. #1 R&B 45	"Reunited"	Peaches and Herb
U.K. #1 POP 45	"Bright Eyes"	Art Garfunkel
U.K. #1 POP LP	*The Very Best of Leo Sayer*	Leo Sayer

1 **Elton John** becomes the first pop music star to perform in Israel. In three weeks he will become the first Western solo pop performer to tour Russia.

2 The film *Quadrophenia*, directed by **Franc Roddam** and starring **Phil Daniels** and **Sting** of the **Police**, premieres in London. The film, based on the **Who's** album of the same name, is a period piece depicting the ever-increasing alienation of one young Mod in the mid-Sixties. It will not exactly bomb at the box office, but will be a bigger hit with critics than audiences. Its soundtrack features not only the Who, doing both early songs and songs from *Quadrophenia*, but oldies by **James Brown**, the **Kingsmen**, **Booker T. and the MGs**, the **Ronettes**, the **Crystals** and the **Cascades**.

The **Who** perform their first concert after the death of **Keith Moon** with new drummer **Kenney Jones**, formerly of the **Faces**.

5 The **Boomtown Rats** end their first U.S. tour at New York's Palladium. In testament to the growing commercial power of postpunk new wave rock, they headlined the tour despite the fact that they haven't yet had a hit single in the U.S. (a situation soon to change with the release of the topical "I Don't Like Mondays").

8 **Supertramp** may not be one of contemporary music's more prolific bands, but they are one of its more successful ones. *Breakfast in America*, their first studio LP in two years, turns platinum and goes to Number One. And the group enjoys three Top Fifteen singles: "The Logical Song," "Goodbye Stranger" and "Take the Long Way Home."

11 **Eric Clapton**, **Charlie Watts** and British blues-rock veteran **Georgie Fame** perform at a reception for the wedding of noted British rock producer/engineer **Glyn Johns** (who's worked extensively with the **Who**, among others) and his wife, **Vivienne**.

Peaches and Herb, the sweet-singing soul duo, receive a platinum record for "Reunited," a Number One hit for four weeks. Singing with Herb Fame is the third "Peaches," **Linda Greene**.

12 At a free concert in San Francisco's Golden Gate Park, the new **Jefferson Starship** lineup, featuring lead vocalist **Mickey Thomas**, makes its performing debut.

Peter Gabriel, **Kate Bush** and **Steve Harley** (of **Cockney Rebel**) play a benefit concert in London's Hammersmith Odeon for the family of their lighting director, **Bill Duffy**, who died in an accident at a Bush concert April 20. The highlight of the show is Gabriel's rendition of the **Beatles'** "Let It Be."

19 **Paul McCartney**, **George Harrison** and **Ringo Starr** perform with **Eric Clapton**, **Denny Laine** and **Mick Jagger** at a wedding reception for Clapton and the former Mrs. Harrison, **Patti Boyd**. The three ex-Beatles jam with **Mick Jagger**, **Lonnie Donegan**, **Ginger Baker** and others.

21 **Elton John** begins a series of Russian concerts. The concerts will be videotaped for a cable-TV spe-

cial and a videodisc, both titled *To Russia with Elton*.

22 **Cheap Trick's** *Live at Budokan* goes platinum; not bad for an LP that wasn't supposed to be released. The group was counting on its *Dream Police* to be its fourth LP, but an import did so well that Epic Records had no choice but to release it stateside, and on this date *Live at Budokan* hits sales of 1 million.

23 *The Kids Are Alright*, **Jeff Stein's** documentary compilation of film clips detailing the history of the **Who**, premieres in New York.

Tom Petty of the **Heartbreakers**, trying to negotiate a new recording contract since his label, ABC Records, went out of business and was bought by MCA, files for bankruptcy. Perhaps his recent hit single "Breakdown" was prophetic?

Sister Sledge's *We Are Family* goes platinum. The LP's title tracker, a #2 hit in April, is later the rallying cry for baseball's Pittsburgh Pirates, who will go on to win the 1979 World Series.

31 The restored Radio City Music Hall is given a gala reopening. In coming years, acts like **Diana Ross**, **Roxy Music**, **Linda Ronstadt**, the **Grateful Dead**, **Cheap Trick** and the **Talking Heads** play Radio City. ◆

WEEK ENDING MAY 5

U.S. #1 POP 45	"Reunited"	Peaches and Herb
U.S. #1 POP LP	*Minute by Minute*	The Doobie Brothers
U.S. #1 R&B 45	"Reunited"	Peaches and Herb
U.K. #1 POP 45	"Bright Eyes"	Art Garfunkel
U.K. #1 POP LP	*The Very Best of Leo Sayer*	Leo Sayer

WEEK ENDING MAY 12

U.S. #1 POP 45	"Reunited"	Peaches and Herb
U.S. #1 POP LP	*Minute by Minute*	The Doobie Brothers
U.S. #1 R&B 45	"Reunited"	Peaches and Herb
U.K. #1 POP 45	"Bright Eyes"	Art Garfunkel
U.K. #1 POP LP	*The Very Best of Leo Sayer*	Leo Sayer

WEEK ENDING MAY 19

U.S. #1 POP 45	"Reunited"	Peaches and Herb
U.S. #1 POP LP	*Breakfast in America*	Supertramp
U.S. #1 R&B 45	"Reunited"	Peaches and Herb
U.K. #1 POP 45	"Pop Muzik"	M
U.K. #1 POP LP	*The Very Best of Leo Sayer*	Leo Sayer

WEEK ENDING MAY 26

U.S. #1 POP 45	"Reunited"	Peaches and Herb
U.S. #1 POP LP	*Breakfast in America*	Supertramp
U.S. #1 R&B 45	"I Wanna Be with You (Part I)"	The Isley Brothers
U.K. #1 POP 45	"Bright Eyes"	Art Garfunkel
U.K. #1 POP LP	*Voulez Vous*	Abba

2 Legendary Cleveland DJ **Kid Leo** is married in Cleveland. **Southside Johnny and the Asbury Jukes** perform at the reception.

3 At a wedding reception for his lighting director, **Mark Brickman**, **Bruce Springsteen and the E Street Band** are joined onstage at Los Angeles' Whisky club by **Rickie Lee Jones** and **Boz Scaggs** for a three-hour jam session.

5 Blues giant **Muddy Waters**, age sixty-four, marries **Marva Jean Brooks** on her twenty-fifth birthday. **Eric Clapton** is present at the ceremony.

7 One week before he is scheduled to appear in court on income-tax evasion charges, **Chuck Berry** performs on the White House lawn at the Black Music Association gala—and changes the chorus of his classic "Carol" to "Oh, Amy" (for the president's daughter).

14 *Rolling Stone* reports that after ten years, **Little Feat** have broken up. Long a favorite of critics and a dedicated cult of fans, Little Feat never really achieved great commercial success, though two of their songs, "Willin'" and "All That You Dream," were hits in cover versions by **Linda Ronstadt**. In exactly two weeks, Little Feat leader, guitarist, singer and songwriter **Lowell George** will die of a heart attack.

21 Guitarist **Mick Taylor** releases his first solo album, *Mick Taylor*, four-and-a-half years after leaving the **Rolling Stones**.

23 New York disco sophisticates **Chic** enter the soul chart with what will prove to be their most influential hit: "Good Times," which will stay on the chart for eighteen weeks, will peak at Number One for five weeks and will serve as the instrumental basis for the first big commercial rap hit, the **Sugar Hill Gang**'s "Rapper's Delight." "Good Times" will also serve as a musical backdrop for such other, lesser rap hits as **Count Coolout**'s "Rhythm Rap Rock" and Trickeration's "Rap, Bounce, Skate, Roll," and will subsequently serve as a major influence on the early Eighties school of New York street-funk. "Good Times" will also inspire a soundalike hit for **Queen**— "Another One Bites the Dust."

26 **Elvis Presley**'s father, **Vernon**, dies at age sixty-three of a heart ailment in Tupelo, Mississippi.

28 Ex-**Mott the Hoople** leader, singer, songwriter, guitarist and pianist **Ian Hunter** makes his first New York stage appearance in four years at the Palladium with a band featuring guitarist **Mick Ronson** (formerly with **David Bowie**'s **Spiders from Mars**) and singer **Ellen Foley** (who sang with **Meat Loaf** on the latter's hit "Paradise by the Dashboard Light").

Rolling Stone reports on the planned re-formation of two legendary psychedelic bands of the Sixties: **Blue Cheer** and **Love**.

29 Singer, songwriter and guitarist **Lowell George**, ex-**Mother of Invention** and a leader of funk-rock band **Little Feat**, dies at age thirty-four of a heart attack related to drug problems and obesity in Los Angeles. George, who had been putting on weight steadily over the past few years, weighed well over 200 pounds at the time of his death, though he had been performing recently. Among his best know compositions were "Willin'" (covered by **Linda Ronstadt**), "Dixie Chicken," "Tripe Face Boogie," "Long Distance Love," "Rock & Roll Doctor," "Cold Cold Cold" and "Spanish Moon."

30 **Gary Numan and the Tubeway Army** hit Number One in the U.K. with "Are 'Friends' Electric?" Numan is one of the first in a wave of synth-wielding performers to give birth to what critics term the "electropop" movement, and he will go on to have a massive American hit with "Cars." ♦

WEEK ENDING JUNE 2

U.S. #1 POP 45	"Hot Stuff"	Donna Summer
U.S. #1 POP LP	*Breakfast in America*	Supertramp
U.S. #1 R&B 45	"Ain't No Stoppin' Us Now"	McFadden and Whitehead
U.K. #1 POP 45	"Sunday Girl"	Blondie
U.K. #1 POP LP	*Voulez Vous*	Abba

WEEK ENDING JUNE 9

U.S. #1 POP 45	"Love You Inside and Out"	The Bee Gees
U.S. #1 POP LP	*Breakfast in America*	Supertramp
U.S. #1 R&B 45	"We Are Family"	Sister Sledge
U.K. #1 POP 45	"Dance Away"	Roxy Music
U.K. #1 POP LP	*Voulez Vous*	Abba

WEEK ENDING JUNE 16

U.S. #1 POP 45	"Hot Stuff"	Donna Summer
U.S. #1 POP LP	*Bad Girls*	Donna Summer
U.S. #1 R&B 45	"Ring My Bell"	Anita Ward
U.K. #1 POP 45	"Ring My Bell"	Anita Ward
U.K. #1 POP LP	*Voulez Vous*	Abba

WEEK ENDING JUNE 23

U.S. #1 POP 45	"Hot Stuff"	Donna Summer
U.S. #1 POP LP	*Breakfast in America*	Supertramp
U.S. #1 R&B 45	"Ring My Bell"	Anita Ward
U.K. #1 POP 45	"Ring My Bell"	Anita Ward
U.K. #1 POP LP	*Discovery*	Electric Light Orchestra

WEEK ENDING JUNE 30

U.S. #1 POP 45	"Ring My Bell"	Anita Ward
U.S. #1 POP LP	*Breakfast in America*	Supertramp
U.S. #1 R&B 45	"Ring My Bell"	Anita Ward
U.K. #1 POP 45	"Are 'Friends' Electric?"	Gary Numan and Tubeway Army
U.K. #1 POP LP	*Discovery*	Electric Light Orchestra

1 Filming is completed on *Carny,* the first theatrical film **Robbie Robertson** of the **Band** has been involved with since the Band broke up. He produced and cowrote the script, and co-starred with **Gary Busey** and **Jody Foster.**

6 Composer/arranger/ producer **Van McCoy** dies of a heart attack at age thirty-eight. A music industry veteran, he worked with such artists as **Aretha Franklin, Gladys Knight and the Pips, Barbara Lewis, Peaches and Herb, Chad and Jeremy, Jackie Wilson** and **Brenda and the Tabulations,** from the early Sixties through the Seventies. In 1975, McCoy broke through on his own with the predominantly instrumental disco smash "The Hustle," the biggest dance-craze record of the Seventies, featured on his best-selling instrumental album *Disco Baby.* His "Getting Mighty Crowded" was covered by **Elvis Costello.**

10 **Chuck Berry** is sentenced to a four-month prison term for income-tax evasion; he'd short-changed the U.S. government $200,000 on his 1973 return.

11 **Neil Young's** concert film *Rust Never Sleeps* (the title, a line in Young's song "Out of the Blue, Into the Black," is taken from an advertising slogan penned for an Akron antirust product manufacturer by **Devo's Jerry Casale** and **Mark Mothersbaugh**) premieres at the Bruin Theater in Westwood, California. Its East Coast premiere will be July 18 at New York's Palladium. The movie is a documentary of his last U.S. tour.

12 Pop-soul vocalist **Minnie Riperton** dies at age thirty-one of cancer in Los Angeles. Her one big hit was the

1975 Number One single "Lovin' You" (written and produced by **Stevie Wonder**), which amply demonstrated her incredible multi-octave range.

Chicago disc jockey **Steve Dahl** kicks off the "disco sucks" movement by burning a pile of disco records between games at a Chicago White Sox double-header in Comiskey Park. The antidisco revellers get so carried away that the second White Sox game has to be called off.

20 Seventeen-year-old **Scott Cantrell,** who'd been staying with **Keith Richards'** common-law wife **Anita Pallenberg,** shoots himself to death in the bedroom of Pallenberg's home in South Salem in Westchester County, New York.

22 At a revival meeting in North Richmond, California, **Little Richard**—now known as the **Reverend Richard Penniman**—warns the congregation about the evils of rock & roll music, and declares, "If God can save an old homosexual like me, he can save anybody."

26 Two years after its British release, the **Clash's** eponymous debut album is released, in slightly revised form, in the U.S. on Epic Records.

A *Rolling Stone* article cites promotional videotapes as "the newest selling tool in rock," and mentions **David Bowie's** "Boys Keep Swinging" and **Queen's** "Bohemian Rhapsody" as examples.

27 An Indian art store in Scottsdale, Arizona, owned by schlock-horror rocker **Alice Cooper** is hit by a fire-bomb thrown through a rear window by an unknown vandal. Over $200,000 worth of Native American artifacts are destroyed, as are some of Cooper's gold records, stored in the rear of the emporium. Cooper calls the biggest loss that of $75,000 worth of Hopi Indian dolls, and tries to explain the attack by saying, "Maybe it was some disco-music freak. I've been making some positive antidisco remarks lately."

(Gene) McFadden and **(John) Whitehead** have a platinum hit with "Ain't No Stoppin' Us Now," which reaches #13.

28 **Ted Nugent, Aerosmith, Journey** and **Thin Lizzy** headline the World Series of Rock at Cleveland Stadium.

31 **James Taylor** plays a free concert in New York's Central Park to help publicize the city's campaign to restore the park's Sheep Meadow. ◆

WEEK ENDING JULY 7

U.S. #1 POP 45	"Ring My Bell"	Anita Ward
U.S. #1 POP LP	*Bad Girls*	Donna Summer
U.S. #1 R&B 45	"Ring My Bell"	Anita Ward
U.K. #1 POP 45	"Are 'Friends' Electric?"	Gary Numan and Tubeway Army
U.K. #1 POP LP	*Discovery*	Electric Light Orchestra

WEEK ENDING JULY 14

U.S. #1 POP 45	"Bad Girls"	Donna Summer
U.S. #1 POP LP	*Bad Girls*	Donna Summer
U.S. #1 R&B 45	"Ring My Bell"	Anita Ward
U.K. #1 POP 45	"Are 'Friends' Electric?"	Gary Numan and Tubeway Army
U.K. #1 POP LP	*Parallel Lines*	Blondie

WEEK ENDING JULY 21

U.S. #1 POP 45	"Bad Girls"	Donna Summer
U.S. #1 POP LP	*Bad Girls*	Donna Summer
U.S. #1 R&B 45	"Bad Girls"	Donna Summer
U.K. #1 POP 45	"Silly Games"	Janet Kay
U.K. #1 POP LP	*Replicas*	Gary Numan and Tubeway Army

WEEK ENDING JULY 28

U.S. #1 POP 45	"Bad Girls"	Donna Summer
U.S. #1 POP LP	*Bad Girls*	Donna Summer
U.S. #1 R&B 45	"Bad Girls"	Donna Summer
U.K. #1 POP 45	"Are 'Friends' Electric?"	Gary Numan and Tubeway Army
U.K. #1 POP LP	*Replicas*	Gary Numan and Tubeway Army

4 A benefit for the widow and children of late Little Feat singer/guitarist **Lowell George** draws 20,000 people to the L.A. Forum, grossing over $230,000. **Jackson Browne, Linda Ronstadt, Bonnie Raitt, Emmylou Harris, Michael McDonald, Nicolette Larson** and the remaining members of **Little Feat**—**Paul Barrère, Billy Payne, Kenny Gradney, Sam Clayton** and **Richie Hayward**—all perform.

Led Zeppelin play their first U.K. concert date in four years to a capacity throng of 120,000 at the annual Knebworth Festival in Knebworth Park, Hertfordshire, England.

6 The **Cars** ignore all "sophomore jinx" predictions and go two-for-two: *Candy-O* is their second consecutive album to go platinum. The LP's cover is especially interesting: an auto-erotic drawing of a willowy redhead draped seductively over one of Detroit's finest, drawn by famed illustrator **Vargas**.

7 One of the most unlikely successes of 1979 is that of **Rickie Lee Jones**, considered by many to be the female equivalent of **Tom Waits**. Jones is all bop and cool—highly uncommercial—and yet her debut goes platinum and spawns a Top Five hit, "Chuck E's in Love."

13 **Cheap Trick** have the biggest hit of their career, "I Want You to Want Me." The song originally appeared on the group's second album, *In Color,* released in 1977, but becomes a hit on the basis of its inclusion on the *Live at Budokan* LP, reaching #7. It goes gold on this date.

14 **John Hall** and his songwriting partner and wife, Johanna (who together wrote **Janis Joplin**'s "Half Moon"), have a daughter, **Lilian**.

15 *Americathon,* a film directed by **Neil Israel** and starring **Harvey Korman, John Ritter** and rock singer **Meat Loaf**, premieres in Los Angeles. A futuristic satire, its soundtrack features **Elvis Costello, Eddie Money, Nick Lowe,** the **Beach Boys** and **Meat Loaf**. The film's success at the box office will far exceed its reviews.

16 Hardcore **Kiss** fans are apalled to hear "I Was Made for Lovin' You," a song with a disco rhythm. Still, the tune goes to #11 and turns gold on this date.

The biggest summer single of 1979, "My Sharona," belongs to L.A. rookies the **Knack**, who are awarded a gold record on this date. The group's brief success is based on the same gimmicks that leads to its eventual failure—its **Beatle**-esque posturing is said by the group to be tongue-in-cheek, but nobody gets the joke, and the Knack will disband less than two years later.

18 British rocker **Nick Lowe** and American rock singer **Carlene Carter,** step-daughter of **Johnny Cash,** are wed in Los Angeles. Portions of the ceremony are shot for what will become Lowe's "Cruel to Be Kind" promotional video.

19 Bassist **Dorsey Burnette,** a member of seminal rockabilly band the **Rock 'n' Roll Trio** with his brother **Johnny** in the Fifties, dies of a heart attack at age forty-six in Canoga Park, California. Burnette moved with his brother Johnny to Los Angeles from Memphis in the late Fifties, and together they cowrote country-rock hits like "Tall Oak Tree" and "Hey Little One" in 1960. He was an active mainstream country artist until his death, by which time his son **Billy Burnette** had made a well-received recording debut in the rockabilly vein.

23 Brooklyn declares this "Peter Tosh" Day," awarding the reggae star an honorary citation as he tours the borough's Jamaican neighborhoods.

24 The **Cars** perform at New York's Central Park for an audience of a half a million people.

25 Modern jazz bandleader, composer and arranger **Stan Kenton** dies at age sixty-seven after a long illness in Hollywood's Midway Hospital. Kenton's "neophonic" arranging style made bombastic use of unusual harmonies and self-consciously "difficult" charts, hence he was reviled by jazz purists, whom he reviled in turn. Never afraid of controversy and always convinced of the absolute rightness of his beliefs, Kenton's most recent spate of adverse publicity centered on his recent announcement that country music was "backward, stupid" and "an insult to anyone's intelligence." The only influence Kenton had on rock music can be heard in the horn charts used by the band **Chicago**.

28 Nineteen-seventy-nine is one of the biggest years of his career for **Neil Young**: coming off the Top Five success of last year's *Comes a Time,* Young scores two gold albums: *Decade,* an earlier triple album best-of set, and *Rust Never Sleeps.* ◆

WEEK ENDING AUGUST 4

U.S. #1 POP 45	"Bad Girls"	Donna Summer
U.S. #1 POP LP	*Bad Girls*	Donna Summer
U.S. #1 R&B 45	"Good Times"	Chic
U.K. #1 POP 45	"I Don't Like Mondays"	The Boomtown Rats
U.K. #1 POP LP	*The Best Disco Album in the World*	various artists

WEEK ENDING AUGUST 11

U.S. #1 POP 45	"Bad Girls"	Donna Summer
U.S. #1 POP LP	*Get the Knack*	The Knack
U.S. #1 R&B 45	"Good Times"	Chic
U.K. #1 POP 45	"I Don't Like Mondays"	The Boomtown Rats
U.K. #1 POP LP	*The Best Disco Album in the World*	various artists

WEEK ENDING AUGUST 18

U.S. #1 POP 45	"Good Times"	Chic
U.S. #1 POP LP	*Get the Knack*	The Knack
U.S. #1 R&B 45	"Good Times"	Chic
U.K. #1 POP 45	"I Don't Like Mondays"	The Boomtown Rats
U.K. #1 POP LP	*The Best Disco Album in the World*	various artists

WEEK ENDING AUGUST 25

U.S. #1 POP 45	"My Sharona"	The Knack
U.S. #1 POP LP	*Get the Knack*	The Knack
U.S. #1 R&B 45	"Good Times"	Chic
U.K. #1 POP 45	"I Don't Like Mondays"	The Boomtown Rats
U.K. #1 POP LP	*Discovery*	Electric Light Orchestra

8 The Second Annual Tribal Stomp—a two-day rock festival held on the site of the 1967 Monterey Pop Festival—begins, with the **Clash**, **Robert Fripp**, **Country Joe McDonald**, **Peter Tosh**, **Canned Heat** and other bands performing before small crowds.

9 Concert promoter **Sid Bernstein**, who first brought the **Beatles** to New York in 1964, places a full-page, $20,000 advertisement in the *New York Times*. The ad is an "Appeal to John, Paul, George and Ringo"—are last names necessary?—to play a benefit concert for the Kampuchean boat people.

11 The **Who** make their first American concert performance since the death of **Keith Moon**, at the Capitol Theater in Passaic, New Jersey, with new drummer **Kenney Jones**, formerly with the **Faces**.

12 Britain's independent Two Tone label releases its first record—"Gangsters" by the **Specials**. They run the label, which will later release records by other such ska-rock bands as the **Beat**, the **Selecter** and the **Bodysnatchers**.

15 Swedish pop stars **Abba** play their first concert in what has to be the only continent in the civilized world where they aren't yet big stars—North America. The show takes place in Vancouver, British Columbia.

16 Rap, the New York City ghetto music in which the performers chant rhymed and rhythmical verses over prerecorded instrumental dance tracks, makes it onto vinyl with the release of the **Sugar Hill Gang**'s "Rapper's Delight." Former singing star **Sylvia Robinson** (she was half of **Mickey and Sylvia**, whose "Love Is Strange" was a hit in 1957; as a soloist she had a hit with "Pillow Talk" in 1973) first heard rap at a party in Harlem and decided to form a company, Sugar Hill, to produce rap records, in spite of industry warnings that rap was merely an amateur's sport with no commercial appeal. Grouping three teenagers from around New York City, she formed the Sugar Hill Gang and recorded "Rapper's Delight" over the instrumental break from **Chic**'s "Good Times." The twelve-inch single will become a disco smash, selling 2 million copies in America, paving the way for other rappers like **Kurtis Blow**, the **Funky Four Plus One**, the **Furious Five** and **Spoonie Gee**.

19 The first of a five-night series of MUSE (Musicians United for Safe Energy) concerts takes place at Madison Square Garden in New York. The shows, recorded for the *No Nukes* album, feature such performers as the **Doobie Brothers**, **Jackson Browne**, **Bonnie Raitt**, **Bruce Springsteen**, **James Taylor**, **Carly Simon** and **John Hall**.

21 The *New York Post* runs a front-page headline reading THE BEATLES ARE BACK! and reports that a rumored reunion benefit for the Kampuchean boat people has been officially set. One source quotes **Paul McCartney** as saying that "if the Beatles ever did re-form, we'd have to rehearse for six months." The reunion never does take place.

22 The first New/No/Now Wave Festival draws over 5,000 to the dirt-floored Field House at the University of Minnesota to witness performances by such bands as the **dB's**, **Richard Lloyd**, the **Records**, the **Monochrome Set**, the **Fleshtones** and **Devo**—who perform in leisure-suits as "Dove." In all, twenty-two bands perform, many of them unsigned.

27 Moments after beginning the song "Better Off Dead," **Elton John** collapses onstage at Hollywood's Universal Ampitheater, suffering from exhaustion brought on by the flu. After a ten-minute intermission, John returns to finish a concert lasting nearly three hours.

28 **Jimmy McCulloch**, guitarist with **Thunderclap Newman**, **Stone the Crows** and **Paul McCartney's Wings**, is found dead in London of undetermined causes at age twenty-six. ◆

WEEK ENDING SEPTEMBER 1

U.S. #1 POP 45	"My Sharona"	The Knack
U.S. #1 POP LP	*Get the Knack*	The Knack
U.S. #1 R&B 45	"Good Times"	Chic
U.K. #1 POP 45	"We Don't Talk Anymore"	Cliff Richard
U.K. #1 POP LP	*The Best Disco Album in the World*	various artists

WEEK ENDING SEPTEMBER 8

U.S. #1 POP 45	"My Sharona"	The Knack
U.S. #1 POP LP	*Get the Knack*	The Knack
U.S. #1 R&B 45	"Don't Stop 'til You Get Enough"	Michael Jackson
U.K. #1 POP 45	"We Don't Talk Anymore"	Cliff Richard
U.K. #1 POP LP	*Discovery*	Electric Light Orchestra

WEEK ENDING SEPTEMBER 15

U.S. #1 POP 45	"My Sharona"	The Knack
U.S. #1 POP LP	*In through the Out Door*	Led Zeppelin
U.S. #1 R&B 45	"Don't Stop 'til You Get Enough"	Michael Jackson
U.K. #1 POP 45	"We Don't Talk Anymore"	Cliff Richard
U.K. #1 POP LP	*Discovery*	Electric Light Orchestra

WEEK ENDING SEPTEMBER 22

U.S. #1 POP 45	"My Sharona"	The Knack
U.S. #1 POP LP	*In through the Out Door*	Led Zeppelin
U.S. #1 R&B 45	"Don't Stop 'til You Get Enough"	Michael Jackson
U.K. #1 POP 45	"Cars"	Gary Numan
U.K. #1 POP LP	*Discovery*	Electric Light Orchestra

WEEK ENDING SEPTEMBER 29

U.S. #1 POP 45	"My Sharona"	The Knack
U.S. #1 POP LP	*In through the Out Door*	Led Zeppelin
U.S. #1 R&B 45	"Don't Stop 'til You Get Enough"	Michael Jackson
U.K. #1 POP 45	"Cars"	Gary Numan
U.K. #1 POP LP	*Rock 'n' Roll Juvenile*	Cliff Richard

1 **Elton John** performs the first of eight consecutive shows at New York's Madison Square Garden.

5 The soundtrack to the **Who**'s *The Kids Are Alright*—a loving history of the band—turns platinum, a little more than a year after the death of drummer **Keith Moon**.

6 Funk band **Fatback** enter the soul chart with "King Tim III (Personality Jock)," which will peak at #26 in its eleven weeks on the chart, and which will later be seen by many observers as a seminal pre-rap song.

10 *The Rose*, starring **Bette Midler** as a rock singer transparently based on **Janis Joplin**, premieres in Los Angeles. The film also stars **Frederick Forrest** and **Alan Bates**, and will be moderately successful.

The city of Los Angeles declares this "Fleetwood Mac Day," giving the superstar rock band its own star on Hollywood Boulevard's Walk of Fame—right in front of legendary lingerie emporium Frederick's of Hollywood.

12 At a Madison Square Garden concert in New York, **Ian Anderson** of **Jethro Tull** suffers a minor eye injury when a fan throws a rose at him and one of its thorns pierces his eye. Two shows have to be canceled before Tull resumes its tour.

13 **Chaka Khan and Rufus** enter the soul chart on the way to another Number One soul hit, with "Do You Love What You Feel," which will top the soul chart for two weeks starting December 15.

14 Postpunk rocker **Tom Robinson** performs solo at the National March on Washington for Lesbian and Gay Rights.

17 Fleetwood Mac's two-record set *Tusk*, a highly experimental album that cost the band nearly $1 million to record, is released on Warner Bros. Records. Its title track will become a minor hit single, and

Tusk will take just a little longer than usual to earn another gold disc, though it will fail to go platinum.

18 Fifteen black youths are arrested at an **Earth, Wind and Fire** concert at Madison Square Garden in New York City and are charged with having beaten and robbed patrons on their way into the concert.

19 **Journey** continue on the course begun by 1978's *Infinity* with the release of *Evolution*. This second record with singer **Steve Perry** does even better, surpassing sales of 1 million on this date.

20 George Clinton's **Funkadelic** enter the soul LP chart with *Uncle Jam Wants You*, which in its nineteen weeks on the chart will rise to #2. The album also yields the group's Number One soul hit "(not just) Knee Deep"—which hit the top of the soul chart one week ago and will stay there for two more weeks.

Bob Dylan introduces his born-again gospel-rock to the nation as he performs "Serve Somebody" on NBC-TV's "Saturday Night Live."

22 In a preliminary court hearing, actress **Carrie Snodgress** claims that veteran keyboardist and arranger **Jack Nitzsche** did not rape her with a pistol, as previously reported, but did "threaten to destroy that part of me." Faced with charges of assault with intent to commit murder, assault with a deadly weapon, and false imprisonment, Nitzsche says of Snodgress, "I still feel friendly toward her."

27 Funk band **Cameo** enter the soul chart with their second soul Top Ten hit this year, "Sparkle," which in twenty weeks on the chart will peak at #10. Their other hit this year was "I Just Want to Be," which hit #3 in August. ◆

WEEK ENDING OCTOBER 6

U.S. #1 POP 45	"Sad Eyes"	Robert John
U.S. #1 POP LP	*In through the Out Door*	Led Zeppelin
U.S. #1 R&B 45	"Don't Stop 'til You Get Enough"	Michael Jackson
U.K. #1 POP 45	"Message in a Bottle"	The Police
U.K. #1 POP LP	*The Pleasure Principle*	Gary Numan

WEEK ENDING OCTOBER 13

U.S. #1 POP 45	"Don't Stop 'til You Get Enough"	Michael Jackson
U.S. #1 POP LP	*In through the Out Door*	Led Zeppelin
U.S. #1 R&B 45	"(not just) Knee Deep"	Funkadelic
U.K. #1 POP 45	"Message in a Bottle"	The Police
U.K. #1 POP LP	*Pleasure Principle*	Gary Numan

WEEK ENDING OCTOBER 20

U.S. #1 POP 45	"Rise"	Herb Alpert
U.S. #1 POP LP	*In through the Out Door*	Led Zeppelin
U.S. #1 R&B 45	"(not just) Knee Deep"	Funkadelic
U.K. #1 POP 45	"Video Killed the Radio Star"	The Buggles
U.K. #1 POP LP	*Regatta de Blanc*	The Police

WEEK ENDING OCTOBER 27

U.S. #1 POP 45	"Rise"	Herb Alpert
U.S. #1 POP LP	*In through the Out Door*	Led Zeppelin
U.S. #1 R&B 45	"(not just) Knee Deep"	Funkadelic
U.K. #1 POP 45	"Video Killed the Radio Star"	The Buggles
U.K. #1 POP LP	*Regatta de Blanc*	The Police

1 A *Rolling Stone* article reports that "the disco boom may be over," noting a sharp recent decrease in the sale of disco LPs.

At the opening show of his Slow Train Coming tour in San Francisco's Warfield Theater, born-again Christian **Bob Dylan** is booed by the audience.

3 Guyana-born British reggae-funk-rocker **Eddy Grant** enters the U.S. soul chart for the only time this decade with "Walking on Sunshine," which will only reach #86 in just three weeks on the chart. The song will later be an international funk hit in a 1982 cover version by Brooklyn-based **Rockers Revenge**. Grant himself—a former member of late-Sixties interracial British teenybopper band the **Equals**—will reemerge triumphant in 1983 with the hit singles "Electric Avenue" and "I Don't Wanna Dance" and the hit album *Killer on the Rampage*.

The debut albums by two-tone ska-rock bands the **Specials** and **Madness** enter the U.K. album chart at #4 and #16 respectively.

6 The **English Beat**, another two-tone ska-rock band, release their debut single, a cover of **Smokey Robinson and the Miracles'** "The Tears of a Clown" backed with "Ranking Full Stop," on the Specials' Two-Tone label.

10 "The Genius," **Ray Charles**, enters the soul singles chart for the only time this year with "Just Because," which will peak at #69 in five weeks on the chart. His only other soul chart entry this year will be with the LP *Ain't It So*, which will enter the soul LP chart in two weeks, remaining there for four weeks and peaking at #59.

12 **Jefferson Starship** singer **Marty Balin's** rock opera *Rock Justice* opens a four-day run at San Francisco's Old Waldorf night club. Balin stars in and codirects the musical, about a rock star who dreams he's on trial for not having a hit record. It will also be made into a videotape.

16 Young turk record executive **Ron Alexenberg's** Infinity label goes out of business. Infinity's parent company, MCA Records, takes on Infinity's roster of talent, which includes **Spryo Gyra** (whose gold *Morning Dance* LP was Infinity's only big seller), **Hot Chocolate**, **Orleans** and **Rupert Holmes**. Infinity's much-ballyhooed acquisition of an album of songs by **Pope John Paul II** turned out to be a commercial flop. MCA president **Sidney Sheinberg** cited "present-day economic realities" as the reason for closing the label. In response, Alexenberg—a former senior vice-president for promotion at Epic Records—files a $2-million suit alleging breach of contract against MCA.

17 Former Jethro Tull bassist **John Glascock** dies of a heart attack at age twenty-six in London. Though he recorded with Jethro Tull, Glascock's long battle with heart disease kept him from ever touring with the band.

19 **Chuck Berry** is released from Lompoc Prison farm in California after serving two months of his four-month sentence for tax evasion.

23 **Marianne Faithfull**, currently embarking on her second solo singing career, is arrested at Oslo Airport in Norway for possession of marijuana.

24 **Peabo Bryson**, who broke through to stardom in 1978, enters the soul chart with his biggest hit of the year, "Gimme Some Time," a duet with **Natalie Cole** that will peak at #8 in its fourteen weeks on the chart.

26 **Fleetwood Mac's** first tour in two years begins in Pocatello, Idaho, just over a month after the release of the band's latest album, *Tusk*.

29 **Anita Pallenberg**, **Keith Richards'** common-law wife, is cleared of murder charges in the shooting death of her young male companion, whose body had been found in her New York state home.

Michael Jackson receives a gold record for "Don't Stop 'til You Get Enough," the first of four Top Ten hits from his album *Off the Wall*. Both "Don't Stop..." and the album's "Rock with You" will hit Number One on the soul and pop charts, and *Off the Wall* will become a Number One pop and soul LP.

Paul Simon, in an attempt to leave his record label, CBS, files two lawsuits against the company in New York State Supreme Court.   ◆

WEEK ENDING NOVEMBER 3

U.S. #1 POP 45	"Pop Muzik"	M
U.S. #1 POP LP	*In through the Out Door*	Led Zeppelin
U.S. #1 R&B 45	"(not just) Knee Deep"	Funkadelic
U.K. #1 POP 45	"One Day at a Time"	Lena Martell
U.K. #1 POP LP	*Regatta de Blanc*	The Police

WEEK ENDING NOVEMBER 10

U.S. #1 POP 45	"Heartache Tonight"	The Eagles
U.S. #1 POP LP	*The Long Run*	The Eagles
U.S. #1 R&B 45	"Ladies Night"	Kool and the Gang
U.K. #1 POP 45	"When You're in Love"	Dr. Hook
U.K. #1 POP LP	*Regatta de Blanc*	The Police

WEEK ENDING NOVEMBER 17

U.S. #1 POP 45	"Still"	The Commodores
U.S. #1 POP LP	*The Long Run*	The Eagles
U.S. #1 R&B 45	"Ladies Night"	Kool and the Gang
U.K. #1 POP 45	"When You're in Love"	Dr. Hook
U.K. #1 POP LP	*Regatta de Blanc*	The Police

WEEK ENDING NOVEMBER 24

U.S. #1 POP 45	"No More Tears (Enough Is Enough)"	Barbra Streisand and Donna Summer
U.S. #1 POP LP	*The Long Run*	The Eagles
U.S. #1 R&B 45	"Off the Wall"	Michael Jackson
U.K. #1 POP 45	"When You're in Love"	Dr. Hook
U.K. #1 POP LP	*Greatest Hits*	Rod Stewart

2 **Stevie Wonder** performs at New York's Metropolitan Opera House, performing material from his recent *Journey through the Secret Life of Plants* LP, accompanied by the **National Afro-American Philharmonic Orchestra**. The remainder of the three-hour concert features Wonder's more conventional recent hits.

3 Eleven **Who** fans are trampled to death in the rush to gain admittance for general or festival (unreserved) seating to the Who's concert this evening at Cincinnati's Riverfront Coliseum. As is typical in festival-seating concerts, thousands of fans had arrived early for the show, all hoping to get into the Coliseum as quickly as possible to get the best seats they could. Since they could be admitted through only two doors, a crushing human bottleneck formed; the eleven people died when the doors were finally opened and the mob stampeded for the doors. Coroner's reports ruled that the eleven died from "suffocation by asphyxiation due to compression" and "suffocation due to accidental mob stampede." The mayor of Providence, Rhode Island, will cancel the Who's concert scheduled there in two days. Multiple suits will be filed by the families of the deceased against the city of Cincinnati, Riverfront Coliseum, the Who and the Cincinnati concert's promoters, Electric Factory (run by **Larry Magid**, who in the late Sixties ran one of the first East Coast rock ballrooms, Philadelphia's Electric Factory). Festival seating itself will be almost universally blamed for the tragedy (except by **Walter Cronkite**, who on tonight's "CBS Evening News" blames it on "a drug-crazed mob of kids"), but festival seating will continue to be used in concerts around the country.

5 "Pop Muzik" by **M** (**Robin Scott**) turns gold. The Number One disc epitomizes the Euro-pop sound, with its dance rhythm and high-tech gloss.

6 **AC/DC**'s big breakthrough comes with its fifth U.S. album, *Highway to Hell,* which turns gold. It is the last LP recorded with original vocalist **Bon Scott**, who dies just two months later.

10 **Michael Jackson**'s *Off the Wall*—containing four Top Ten singles—goes platinum.

Kool and the Gang receive a gold record for "Ladies Night," the third Top Ten hit of their career.

15 **Pink Floyd**'s "Another Brick in the Wall" hits Number One on the U.K. pop chart before subsequently finding similar success in the U.S.

21 The **Eagles**, **Chicago** and **Linda Ronstadt** perform at a benefit show for the presidential campaign of California governor **Jerry Brown**, who also happens to be Ronstadt's boyfriend. The show, at the San Diego Sports Arena, is followed by a similar benefit at the Aladdin Theater in Las Vegas. The two shows raise over $450,000.

22 The first of three concerts for the people of Kampuchea are held at London's Hammersmith Odeon. The shows feature **Paul McCartney**, the **Clash**, **Elvis Costello**, the **Who**, **Rockpile** and many other rock stars.

27 **Ian Dury** and the **Clash** headline the second of four concerts for the people of Kampuchea, in London.

28 The **Who**, the **Pretenders**, the **Specials** and others perform at the third of four concerts for the people of Kampuchea.

29 At the last of four benefit concerts for the people of Kampuchea performers include **Paul McCartney and Wings**, **Elvis Costello**, **Rockpile** with special guest **Robert Plant** of Led Zeppelin, and an all-star "Rockestra."

30 **Emerson, Lake and Palmer**, the art-rock supergroup beloved by millions of fans and hated by most rock critics, announce their breakup.

31 The **Jefferson Starship**'s New Year's Eve concert at X's night club in San Francisco is broadcast over radio to much of the Western world. ◆

WEEK ENDING DECEMBER 1

U.S. #1 POP 45	"No More Tears (Enough Is Enough)"	Barbra Streisand and Donna Summer
U.S. #1 POP LP	*The Long Run*	The Eagles
U.S. #1 R&B 45	"I Wanna Be Your Lover"	Prince
U.K. #1 POP 45	"When You're in Love"	Dr. Hook
U.K. #1 POP LP	*Greatest Hits, Vol. 2*	Abba

WEEK ENDING DECEMBER 8

U.S. #1 POP 45	"Babe"	Styx
U.S. #1 POP LP	*The Long Run*	The Eagles
U.S. #1 R&B 45	"I Wanna Be Your Love"	Prince
U.K. #1 POP 45	"Walking on the Moon"	The Police
U.K. #1 POP LP	*Greatest Hits, Vol. 2*	Abba

WEEK ENDING DECEMBER 15

U.S. #1 POP 45	"Babe"	Styx
U.S. #1 POP LP	*The Long Run*	The Eagles
U.S. #1 R&B 45	"Do You Love What You Feel"	Rufus and Chaka
U.K. #1 POP 45	"Another Brick in the Wall"	Pink Floyd
U.K. #1 POP LP	*Greatest Hits, Vol. 2*	Abba

WEEK ENDING DECEMBER 22

U.S. #1 POP 45	"Escape"	Rupert Holmes
U.S. #1 POP LP	*The Long Run*	The Eagles
U.S. #1 R&B 45	"Do You Love What You Feel"	Rufus and Chaka
U.K. #1 POP 45	"Another Brick in the Wall"	Pink Floyd
U.K. #1 POP LP	*Greatest Hits, Vol. 2*	Abba

WEEK ENDING DECEMBER 29

U.S. #1 POP 45	"Escape"	Rupert Holmes
U.S. #1 POP LP	*The Long Run*	The Eagles
U.S. #1 R&B 45	"Rock with You"	Michael Jackson
U.K. #1 POP 45	"Another Brick in the Wall"	Pink Floyd
U.K. #1 POP LP	*Greatest Hits, Vol. 2*	Abba

1980

As the new decade dawned, Studio 54 closed, signaling the beginning of the end of the disco era. And just in time, a vital new black-music phenomenon arose—rap music, which set the slangy, streetwise, rhythmic-rhyme talk-singing of Harlem and South Bronx house-party emcees to lean, strutting funk. Rap was radical because of both its vocal and musical approaches: the colloquial, conversational jive of the rappers was so *un*assimilated into the mainstream; rap's musical backings were not only a tough, minimal reaction to disco's glitzy excess, but in many cases, they were already-available funk hits used as found ready-mades. Thus, Chic's "Good Times" became the ultimate rap backing track; it was the basis of the Sugar Hill Gang's "Rapper's Delight," one of the first of this year's crossover rap hits to go gold. The other big rap hit was Kurtis Blow's "The Breaks"—the exception to the ready-made rule, as its musical track was especially composed and recorded for the record.

Meanwhile, among the white rock audience, the old style of extended suite-length classical rock was falling away, due to the continued dominance of the heavy-metal-inflected AOR rock that classical rock had helped spawn in the first place. Last year, classical-rock supergroup Emerson, Lake and Palmer had tried the AOR-ish shorter-song format before calling it quits; this year, another progressive-rock dinosaur, Yes, would try to change with the times by incorporating new wavers the Buggles into its lineup. Soon, Yes would disband, too. The AOR rockers whom Yes and ELP had helped spawn—Styx, Kansas, Rush, Journey—continued to rack up platinum-level sales despite the record industry's much-publicized sales slump and home-taping crisis. Heavy metal saw a big sales resurgence through such bands as AC/DC. And by the end of the year, the AOR hard-rock genre had its new queen, New York cabaret pop singer Pat Benatar, who adopted the hard-rock sound and took on a vaguely punkish image.

But by far the biggest rock event of the year was one of the most horrible rock-related tragedies of all time: the senseless murder of John Lennon by Mark David Chapman, a young drifter and self-professed Beatlemaniac. The murder occurred just as Lennon was returning home from remixing Yoko Ono's "Walking on Thin Ice." After five years in seclusion, Lennon seemed to be ready to take pop music by storm again. But such timeliness was hardly needed to magnify the tragedy. As the news of the murder spread, the proof of what Lennon meant to several generations came swift and sure, with continuous, days-long tributes and vigils the world over. It was like an instant, compacted reprise of all that had happened in pop, rock, and the world at large since the early Sixties—since the Beatles; it echoed the similar tragedies of the Sixties and the ugly deranged "Beatlemania" of Charles Manson, and brought the diffused negativity and alienation of the Seventies to a head. The scope and intensity of the world's reaction to the murder recalled the unifying belief in love and hope that Lennon, as much as any one person, had articulated for generation-spanning multitudes. His death was more than the loss of musical genius, more even than the end of an era—it was the negation of a spirit and life force that embodied just about all of what was great and important about rock music, about life. The one question a shocked and anguished world kept asking itself was "Why?" And though there seemed to be no answer, the way everyone came together in the days following December 8, 1980, was more than a remembrance and tribute—it *was* an answer to the senselessness; it was the completion and confirmation of Lennon's brilliant body of work. Even in death, Lennon inspired and united people around the world.

1 **Cliff Richard**, acceding to the title held by the **Beatles** and **Elton John** alone among pop musicians, is awarded the MBE by **Queen Elizabeth II** for services to the British Empire. Born **Harry Rodger Webb** in India of British parents, Richard began his career in 1957 after seeing **Bill Haley** in concert. In the next five years—an era in which he was called "the English Elvis"—he had twenty-two U.K. Top Ten singles, including seven Number Ones. He remained popular, expanding his career into movies and television, even after the Beatles had overshadowed him. While he had failed to attract much of an American following during the height of his British career, he arrived in the American Top Ten with "Devil Woman" in 1976 and "We Don't Talk Anymore" in 1979. Even so, Richard remains quintessentially a British star—a fact that the MBE recognizes.

2 **Larry Williams**, a rock singer of the late Fifties who had such hits as "Dizzy Miss Lizzy," "Short Fat Fanny" and "Bony Maronie," is found dead in his Los Angeles home at age forty-five of a gunshot wound to the head. Whether his death was murder or suicide is never resolved.

3 R&B pianist and singer **Amos Milburn**, a star of the late Forties and early Fifties who influenced the likes of **Fats Domino**, among others, dies in Houston, Texas, at age fifty-two. His biggest hits included "One Scotch, One Bourbon, One Beer," "Walkin' Blues" and "Chicken Shack Boogie."

6 **Georgeanna Tillman Gordon**, a singer with Motown girl group the **Marvelettes**, dies in Inkster, Michigan, at age forty-six after a long illness.

7 Singer/guitarist **Hugh Cornwell** of British punk rockers the **Stranglers** is sentenced to two months in a London jail for possession of heroin, cocaine and marijuana.

Carl White, one of the four singers who made up the novelty group the **Rivingtons**, dies at age forty-eight in his Los Angeles home. The Rivingtons had a #48 hit in 1962 with the crazed, nonsensical "Papa-Oom-Mow-Mow," and in 1963 hit #52 with the equally strange "The Bird's the Word." The latter song was remade in a surf-rock version in 1964 by the **Trashmen**, who based their brief career on the Rivingtons' sound, and hit #4 with "Surfin' Bird," which would later be covered by punk rockers the **Ramones**.

Led Zeppelin's *In through the Out Door* turns platinum. It is the last album issued before the September 25, 1980, death of drummer **John Bonham**.

Foreigner's *Head Games* goes gold, but group leader **Mick Jones** is more troubled than excited. The LP was a disappointment even to the band, and Jones is forced to reconsider the current lineup—a major shakeup will occur later in the year.

13 The **Grateful Dead**, the **Jefferson Starship** and the **Beach Boys** are the featured acts at a benefit concert for the people of Kampuchea, held at Oakland Alameda Coliseum in California.

16 **Paul McCartney** is jailed in Tokyo for possession of a half pound of marijuana. He will spend ten days in jail before being extradicted by Japanese authorities. His tour is canceled.

18 **Steve Rubell** and **Ian Schrager**, owners of New York's trendiest, most star-studded disco, Studio 54, are each sentenced to three-and-a-half years in prison and $20,000 in fines for income tax evasion. Studio 54's quick fall from grace as New York's hottest hot spot will serve as an indication that the disco age is coming to a close.

Capricorn Records, the Macon, Georgia, based home of such Southern-rock boogie acts as the **Allman Brothers Band**, files for bankruptcy.

25 **Paul McCartney** is released from a Tokyo jail, where he'd been imprisoned for ten days after trying to carry a half pound of marijuana through customs at the Tokyo airport.

The day after his birthday, comedian **John Belushi** of "Saturday Night Live" and **Blues Brothers** fame jams with punk rockers the **Dead Boys** at L.A.'s Whisky. Says Dead Boys lead singer **Stiv Bators** after the show: "Belushi? He's a good drummer."

British two-tone ska rockers the **Specials** play the first date of their first U.S. tour at New York's new wave rock club Hurrah.

30 New Orleans piano giant **Professor Longhair**, whose mixture of blues, boogie-woogie, ragtime, stride and barrelhouse styles was a protean influence on **Fats Domino** and rock & roll music in general, dies at age sixty-two. Born **Roy Byrd**, his best-known tunes include "In the Night," "Ball the Wall," "Mardi Gras in New Orleans," "Tipitina" and "Bald Head." ◆

WEEK ENDING JANUARY 5

U.S. #1 POP 45	"Please Don't Go"	K.C. and the Sunshine Band
U.S. #1 POP LP	*On the Radio—Greatest Hits*	Donna Summer
U.S. #1 R&B 45	"Rock with You"	Michael Jackson
U.K. #1 POP 45	"Another Brick in the Wall (Part II)"	Pink Floyd
U.K. #1 POP LP	*Greatest Hits—Vol. 2*	Abba

WEEK ENDING JANUARY 12

U.S. #1 POP 45	"Rock with You"	Michael Jackson
U.S. #1 POP LP	*Bee Gees Greatest*	The Bee Gees
U.S. #1 R&B 45	"Rock with You"	Michael Jackson
U.K. #1 POP 45	"Another Brick in the Wall (Part II)"	Pink Floyd
U.K. #1 POP LP	*Greatest Hits*	Rod Stewart

WEEK ENDING JANUARY 19

U.S. #1 POP 45	"Rock with You"	Michael Jackson
U.S. #1 POP LP	*The Wall*	Pink Floyd
U.S. #1 R&B 45	"Rock with You"	Michael Jackson
U.K. #1 POP 45	"Brass in Pocket"	The Pretenders
U.K. #1 POP LP	*Abba's Greatest Hits—Volume 2*	Abba

WEEK ENDING JANUARY 26

U.S. #1 POP 45	"Rock with You"	Michael Jackson
U.S. #1 POP LP	*The Wall*	Pink Floyd
U.S. #1 R&B 45	"Rock with You"	Michael Jackson
U.K. #1 POP 45	"Brass in Pocket"	The Pretenders
U.K. #1 POP LP	*Regatta de Blanc*	The Police

2 In honor of the first anniversary of the death of ex-**Sex Pistols**-bassist **Sid Vicious**, 1,000 punks march from London's Chelsea section to Hyde Park. Vicious' mother, forty-eight-year-old **Ann Beverly**, was to have been at the head of the procession, but the night before, she was hospitalized for a drug overdose.

7 **Pink Floyd** begin one of the more unusual coast-to-coast tours in rock history, playing only fourteen shows in just two cities. This day marks the first of seven shows at the Los Angeles Sports Arena; they will go on to play seven more shows at the Nassau Coliseum in New York starting February 23. As in their London shows earlier this year, the stage show for this tour, in support of the band's latest album, *The Wall*, features a 120-by-60-foot wall made of hundreds of five-pound Styrofoam blocks, which gradually envelops the band as the show progresses.

8 In London, **David Bowie** and his wife, **Angie** (the former **Angela Bar-**nett), are divorced after nearly ten years of marriage. David retains custody of their nine-year-old son, **Zowie**.

13 British police raid **Public Image Ltd.** singer **John Lydon**'s London home for the second time in one month, smashing in his front door with an axe. Lydon meets them at the top of the stairs, wielding a ceremonial sword. Police find nothing illegal in Lydon's home except a tear-gas cannister he keeps to discourage attackers.

14 **Lou Reed** marries **Sylvia Morales** at his Christopher Street apartment in New York City's Greenwich Village. Among those in attendance are **Garland Jeffreys**. The marriage will be one of the main themes of his acclaimed 1982 album *The Blue Mask*.

15 **Bob Dylan** returns to Muscle Shoals Studios in Muscle Shoals, Alabama, to record his second gospel-rock album, *Saved*.

19 **Bon Scott**, born **Ronald Belford Scott**, lead singer of Scottish heavy-metal band **AC/DC**, dies in Lon-don while on tour at age thirty-four, when he chokes on his own vomit after an all-night drinking binge.

20 Director **Nicolas Roeg**'s third film to feature a pop performer in the starring role, *Bad Timing/A Sensual Obsession*, premieres in New York City, with **Art Garfunkel** and **Theresa Russell** starring. Roeg had starred **David Bowie** in *The Man Who Fell to Earth* and **Mick Jagger** in *Performance* (which he codirected with **Donald Cammell**).

21 Reggae singer **Jacob "Killer" Miller**, the rotund, robust lead singer with Jamaican reggae band **Inner Circle**, is killed in a motorcycle accident in Jamaica. Among his hits with the group were "Each One Teach One," "We a Rockers" and "Tenement Yard" (the last two are included on the soundtrack album of the reggae film *Rockers*, in which Miller played a buffoonish over-eater).

22 Former **Sex Pistols** manager **Malcolm McLaren** kicks **Stuart "Adam" Goddard** out of his new band, **Adam and the Ants**. Goddard will go on to form a group of his own, retaining the Adam and the Ants *nom de disque*. McLaren will take the remaining Ants musicians—guitarist **Matthew Ashman**, bassist **Leroy Gorman** and drummer **Dave Barbarossa**—and turn them into **Bow Wow Wow** with the addition of fourteen-year-old Burmese singer **Annabella Lwin** (who, for a time, is backed up vocally by singer **George O'Dowd**—later known as **Boy George** of **Culture Club**.)

27 The Twenty-second Annual Grammy Award winners (for 1979) are named. The **Doobie Brothers**' "What a Fool Believes" wins both Record of the Year and Song of the Year. **Billy Joel**'s *52nd Street* wins both Album of the Year and Best Male Pop Vocal Performance. **Rickie Lee Jones** wins Best New Artist of the Year. Best Female Pop Vocal Performance is **Dionne Warwick**'s "I'll Never Love This Way Again." Best Female Rock Vocal Performance is **Donna Summer**'s "Hot Stuff." Best Male Rock Vocal Performance is the **Eagles**' "Heartache Tonight." Warwick wins again for Best Female R&B Vocal Performance, with "Déjà Vu." **Michael Jackson**'s "Don't Stop 'til You Get Enough" wins Best Male R&B Vocal Performance. **Gloria Gaynor**'s "I Will Survive" wins Best Disco Recording. **Emmylou Harris**' *Blue Kentucky Girl* wins Best Female Country & Western Vocal Performance. **Muddy Waters** wins Best Ethnic or Traditional Recording for *Muddy "Mississippi" Waters Live*.

29 **Buddy Holly**'s glasses and the **Big Bopper**'s wristwatch—the ones each was wearing when their plane crashed on February 3, 1959—are discovered in old police files by the sheriff of Mason City, Iowa. ◆

WEEK ENDING FEBRUARY 2

U.S. #1 POP 45	"Rock with You"	Michael Jackson
U.S. #1 POP LP	*The Wall*	Pink Floyd
U.S. #1 R&B 45	"Rock with You"	Michael Jackson
U.K. #1 POP 45	"My Girl"	Madness
U.K. #1 POP LP	*The Pretenders*	The Pretenders

WEEK ENDING FEBRUARY 9

U.S. #1 POP 45	"Rock with You"	Michael Jackson
U.S. #1 POP LP	*The Wall*	Pink Floyd
U.S. #1 R&B 45	"Rock with You"	Michael Jackson
U.K. #1 POP 45	"Too Much Too Young"	The Specials
U.K. #1 POP LP	*The Pretenders*	The Pretenders

WEEK ENDING FEBRUARY 16

U.S. #1 POP 45	"Do That to Me One More Time"	The Captain and Tennille
U.S. #1 POP LP	*The Wall*	Pink Floyd
U.S. #1 R&B 45	"The Second Time Around"	Shalamar
U.K. #1 POP 45	"Coward of the County"	Kenny Rogers
U.K. #1 POP LP	*The Pretenders*	The Pretenders

WEEK ENDING FEBRUARY 23

U.S. #1 POP 45	"Crazy Little Thing Called Love"	Queen
U.S. #1 POP LP	*The Wall*	Pink Floyd
U.S. #1 R&B 45	"Special Lady"	Ray, Goodman and Brown
U.K. #1 POP 45	"Coward of the County"	Kenny Rogers
U.K. #1 POP LP	*Last Dance*	various artists

1 New York rock poet and singer **Patti Smith** marries veteran Detroit underground rocker and one-time **MC5** member **Fred "Sonic" Smith** in Detroit. As of 1983, neither had produced any music since the marriage.

3 Renowned auction house Sotheby Park-Bernet in London auctions off a Riviera Hotel, Las Vegas, paper napkin signed by **Elvis Presley**, for £500. Also auctioned are four American dollar bills signed by the **Beatles**, for £220, and a batch of **Rolling Stones** letters and autographs, also for £220.

13 **Pink Floyd**'s *The Wall* turns platinum a few weeks into its fifteen-week reign at Number One. The two-record conceptual work is largely the brainchild of bassist **Roger Waters**, who emerges more than ever as the group's creative head.

15 The film *Rude Boy,* featuring British punk rockers the **Clash**, premieres in London. The semidocumentary movie details the misadventures of a regular London street kid, played by **Ray Gange**, who tries to befriend and work as a roadie for the Clash. It also features plenty of concert footage of the Clash and some shots of life backstage and on the road with the band.

19 **Bob Seger**'s American tour for his new album, *Against the Wind,* kicks off in Fayetteville, North Carolina.

Elvis Presley's autopsy is subpoened in the "Dr. Nick" drug case—"Dr. Nick" being **Dr. George Nichopoulous,** Presley's personal physician, who will soon be found guilty of overprescribing drugs to Presley and other of his clients, including **Jerry Lee Lewis**.

20 **Joseph Riviera,** a twenty-eight-year-old truck driver from Texas, walks into the New York offices of Elektra/Asylum Records, draws a gun and takes the office manager hostage, demanding to see either **Jackson Browne** or the **Eagles**, from whom he wants money to finance his trucking operation. Eventually, Riviera surrenders to police without having hurt anyone.

21 British punk rockers the **Jam** enter the U.K. singles chart at Number One with "Going Underground"—the first single to enter the singles chart there at Number One since **Gary Glitter**'s "I Love You Love Me Love" in 1973.

26 Seven years after its release, **Pink Floyd**'s *The Dark Side of the Moon* album breaks the record for the longest-charting pop album, previously held by **Carole King**'s *Tapestry. Tapestry* had been on the album chart for 302 weeks, from April 1971 to January 1977; *The Dark Side of the Moon* has, to date, been on the chart for 303 weeks.

British reggae rockers the **Police** perform to a massive crowd in Bombay, India—the first rock band to perform there since British sci-fi rockers **Hawkwind** in 1970.

29 **Ronald Selle**, a Chicago antique dealer and part-time musician and songwriter, files suit in Chicago against the **Bee Gees**, Paramount Pictures and PolyGram Records. Selle alleges that the Bee Gees' "How Deep Is Your Love," a big hit single for them in 1978 and included in the massive hit film *Saturday Night Fever,* plagiarized two sections of "Let It End," a song Selle wrote and sent to fourteen record companies in 1975. On February 23, 1983, Selle will win his case, thanks mainly to the testimony of Northwestern University music theorist **Dr. Arrand Parsons**. The Bee Gees, who will maintain that they never copied Selle's song, never *heard* Selle's song, and that the whole thing is just a coincidence, will have to determine how much money they actually made from the success of "How Deep Is Your Love?" before Selle's settlement—which could reach $25 million—could be determined. The Bee Gees will successfully appeal the decision in mid-1983.

Genesis begin a world tour in Vancouver, British Columbia, Canada. After covering North America, the tour will take them across the Atlantic to Europe, and will finish in Japan in November. ◆

WEEK ENDING MARCH 1

U.S. #1 POP 45	"Crazy Little Thing Called Love"	Queen
U.S. #1 POP LP	*The Wall*	Pink Floyd
U.S. #1 R&B 45	"And The Beat Goes On"	The Whispers
U.K. #1 POP 45	"Atomic"	Blondie
U.K. #1 POP LP	*Last Dance*	various artists

WEEK ENDING MARCH 8

U.S. #1 POP 45	"Crazy Little Thing Called Love"	Queen
U.S. #1 POP LP	*The Wall*	Pink Floyd
U.S. #1 R&B 45	"And the Beat Goes On"	The Whispers
U.K. #1 POP 45	"Atomic"	Blondie
U.K. #1 POP LP	*Last Dance*	various artists

WEEK ENDING MARCH 15

U.S. #1 POP 45	"Crazy Little Thing Called Love"	Queen
U.S. #1 POP LP	*The Wall*	Pink Floyd
U.S. #1 R&B 45	"And the Beat Goes On"	The Whispers
U.K. #1 POP 45	"Atomic"	Blondie
U.K. #1 POP LP	*String of Hits*	The Shadows

WEEK ENDING MARCH 22

U.S. #1 POP 45	"Another Brick in the Wall (Part II)"	Pink Floyd
U.S. #1 POP LP	*The Wall*	Pink Floyd
U.S. #1 R&B 45	"And the Beat Goes On"	The Whispers
U.K. #1 POP 45	"Together We Are Beautiful"	Fern Kinney
U.K. #1 POP LP	*Tears and Laughter*	Johnny Mathis

WEEK ENDING MARCH 29

U.S. #1 POP 45	"Another Brick in the Wall (Part II)"	Pink Floyd
U.S. #1 POP LP	*The Wall*	Pink Floyd
U.S. #1 R&B 45	"And the Beat Goes On"	The Whispers
U.K. #1 POP 45	"Going Underground"	The Jam
U.K. #1 POP LP	*Tears and Laughter*	Johnny Mathis

5 EMI Records announce a £28 million loss for the second half of 1979. The company had seen a £18 million profit for the same period in 1978. These statistics are indicative of the hard times the record industry is currently experiencing.

11 In the Night, a benefit concert for the bankrupt family of New Orleans piano giant **Professor Longhair**, draws only 900 people to the New Orleans Municipal Auditorium, despite the presence onstage of such performers as **Allen Toussaint**, the **Neville Brothers**, the **Wild Magnolias**, **Lee Dorsey**, **Snooks Eaglin** and other New Orleans legends.

13 The Broadway Fifties musical *Grease* finally closes its run of 3,883 performances—which made it the longest-running show on Broadway and earned it a gross of over $8 million.

14 A New Jersey State assemblyman introduces a resolution to make **Bruce Springsteen**'s "Born to Run" the official state song.

A forty-five-minute concert video recording by **Gary Numan**, *The Touring Principle*, becomes the first commercially available home rock videocassette when it's released on the market today by Warner Home Video. Blondie's *Eat to the Beat* will become the second, several weeks later.

The **Knack** release their second album just seven months after *Get the Knack*. Titled "*. . . but the little girls understand*," it could have been recorded from the very same sessions as the first, yet it meets with less acceptance. Although Knack leader **Doug Fieger** claims that anything the band released would have been anticlimactic, it's apparent that the group is in trouble.

17 Reggae star **Bob Marley**, who in 1979 had recorded the anthemic "Zimbabwe" on the **Wailers** album *Survival*, is an official guest of state at Independence Day ceremonies for the new African nation of Zimbabwe, formerly known as Rhodesia. After the new nation's first premier, **Robert Mugabe**, is sworn in, Marley and the Wailers play a concert. Marley later calls the occasion "the greatest honor of my life."

18 New Jersey-based avant-punk drone-rock band the **Feelies** perform at the Electric Ballroom in Camden Town, London, on the first date of their first U.K. tour.

19 The *New Musical Express* reports that **Brian Johnson**, late of the band **Geordie**, has replaced the late **Bon Scott** as lead vocalist with Australian heavy-metal band **AC/DC**.

22 J. Geils begins its great comeback with *Love Stinks*, its second album on its new label, EMI America. After several successful years in the mid-Seventies, Geils had fallen on hard times and was nearly bankrupt when it left Atlantic for EMI, began producing itself and turning its fortunes around. *Love Stinks*, produced by keyboardist **Seth Justman**, goes as high as #18 and turns gold.

25 Singer/guitarist **Hugh Cornwell** of British

punk rockers the **Stranglers** is released from a London prison after serving six weeks for possession of drugs.

26 Three years to the day from its opening, Studio 54 shuts down amidst charges of New York State Liquor License violations and allegations that owners **Steve Rubell** and **Ian Schrager** have been supplying habitués of the fashionable New York City disco with cocaine. In September 1981, after a year of operating "underground," Studio 54 will reopen under new management.

British two-tone ska-rock band the **Beat** release the first digitally recorded British single, "Mirror in the Bathroom," on their own Go-Feet label.

28 Marshall Tucker Band bassist **Tommy Caldwell** dies of injuries sustained in a car accident in his hometown of Spartanburg, South Carolina.

29 Bob Seger's *Against the Wind* turns gold. It's Seger's second album since the breakthrough success of *Night Moves* and his first in a year and a half. The album spawns four Top Forty singles and presents a less raucous, more thoughtful Seger in songs like the title track and the evocative "Fire Lake."

30 *McVicar*, a film based on the true adventures of famous British recidivist **John McVicar** and starring **Who** vocalist **Roger Daltrey** and veteran British rock singer **Adam Faith**, premieres in London. The film is produced by the Who, and its soundtrack features Daltrey singing songs (including the hit single "Free Me") written by **Jon Lind**, **Billy Nichols** and ex-Argent **Russ Ballard**. ◆

WEEK ENDING APRIL 5

U.S. #1 POP 45	"Another Brick in the Wall (Part II)"	Pink Floyd
U.S. #1 POP LP	*The Wall*	Pink Floyd
U.S. #1 R&B 45	"Stomp!"	The Brothers Johnson
U.K. #1 POP 45	"Going Underground"	The Jam
U.K. #1 POP LP	*Greatest Hits*	Rose Royce

WEEK ENDING APRIL 12

U.S. #1 POP 45	"Another Brick in the Wall (Part II)"	Pink Floyd
U.S. #1 POP LP	*The Wall*	Pink Floyd
U.S. #1 R&B 45	"Stomp!"	The Brothers Johnson
U.K. #1 POP 45	"Dance Yourself Dizzy"	Liquid Gold
U.K. #1 POP LP	*Duke*	Genesis

WEEK ENDING APRIL 19

U.S. #1 POP 45	"Call Me"	Blondie
U.S. #1 POP LP	*The Wall*	Pink Floyd
U.S. #1 R&B 45	"Don't Say Goodnight (It's Time for Love)"	The Isley Brothers
U.K. #1 POP 45	"Call Me"	Blondie
U.K. #1 POP LP	*Greatest Hits*	Rose Royce

WEEK ENDING APRIL 26

U.S. #1 POP 45	"Call Me"	Blondie
U.S. #1 POP LP	*The Wall*	Pink Floyd
U.S. #1 R&B 45	"Don't Say Goodnight (It's Time for Love)"	The Isley Brothers
U.K. #1 POP 45	"Call Me"	Blondie
U.K. #1 POP LP	*Greatest Hits*	Rose Royce

2 **Pink Floyd**'s hit single "Another Brick in the Wall (Part II)"—with its chorus of children chanting "We don't need no education"—is banned by the South African goverment after black children, boycotting schools in protest against inferior education, adopted the song as their anthem. South African authorities declare the song "prejudicial to the safety of the state."

12 **Linda Ronstadt** receives a gold album for *Mad Love*, her new wave experiment that includes three **Elvis Costello** songs and backing from L.A.'s **Cretones**. Costello is less than happy about Ronstadt's interpretations of his material, although, she scoffs in return, he didn't *not* like them enough to refuse the royalties. . . .

16 **Dr. George C. Nichopoulous** is indicated in Memphis on fourteen counts of overprescribing drugs to **Elvis Presley**, **Jerry Lee Lewis** and nine other of his patients.

17 **Kiss** drummer **Peter Criss**—the one who wore the catlike makeup—leaves the cartoonish heavy-metal quartet for a solo career.

18 **Trevor Horn** and **Geoff Downes**, vocalist and keyboardist of new wave pop band the **Buggles** (who had a hit with **Bruce Wooley**'s "Video Killed the Radio Star") join veteran British progressive-rock band **Yes**, replacing departing vocalist **Jon Anderson** and keyboardist **Rick Wakeman**. Horn and Downes will stay with Yes for one album *(Drama)* and one world tour before the band calls it quits.

Downes will then join **Asia** (with **Steve Howe** and **John Wetton** and **Carl Palmer** completing the band), while Horn would go on to become a successful British pop producer with such Eighties pop bands as **Dollar** and, especially, **ABC**.

———

Ian Curtis, lead singer with British postpunk band **Joy Division**, is found dead in his Manchester home, having apparently hung himself. Many observers found Curtis' apparent suicide eerily logical, given his extremely *angst*-ridden lyrics, which seemed mostly to be about paranoia, loss of self, and death. Still, wedded to the band's **Velvet Underground**-derived drone rock, Joy Division made compelling, critically admired music, and had some new wave underground hits with "She's Lost Control," "Transmission" and "Love Will Tear Us Apart." After Curtis'

death, the other three members of Joy Division would re-form as **New Order** and would have some new wave hits of their own with "Everything's Gone Green" in 1981 and "Temptation" in 1982.

21 Singer/guitarist **Joe Strummer** of the British punk group the **Clash** is arrested in Hamburg, Germany, following a concert in which a fracas erupted between the Clash and the audience, Strummer hitting one young fan on the head with his guitar.

22 An unknown thief breaks into Electric Lady Studios in New York City—the recording complex built by **Jimi Hendrix**—and steals five Hendrix gold records, for the albums *Are You Experienced?*, *Axis: Bold as Love*, *Cry of Love*, *Rainbow Bridge* and *Live at Monterey.*

24 **Phil Collins**, **Mike Rutherford** and **Tony Banks** of **Genesis** surprise their fans by showing up in person at the box office of Los Angeles club the Roxy to sell tickets to their benefit for local hospitals the following night.

30 **Carl Radle**, bassist for **Derek and the Dominos**, **Delaney and Bonnie Bramlett** and **Leon Russell**, dies of a chronic kidney ailment at age thirty-seven in a hospital near his Tulsa, Oklahoma, home.

———

Although many music industry observers claim that disco is deader than a doormouse, *Mickey Mouse Disco* turns platinum. ◆

WEEK ENDING MAY 3

U.S. #1 POP 45	"Call Me"	Blondie
U.S. #1 POP LP	*Against the Wind*	Bob Seger and the Silver Bullet Band
U.S. #1 R&B 45	"Don't Say Goodnight (It's Time for Love)"	The Isley Brothers
U.K. #1 POP 45	"Geno"	Dexy's Midnight Runners
U.K. #1 POP LP	*Sky 2*	Sky

WEEK ENDING MAY 10

U.S. #1 POP 45	"Call Me"	Blondie
U.S. #1 POP LP	*Against the Wind*	Bob Seger and the Silver Bullet Band
U.S. #1 R&B 45	"Don't Say Goodnight (It's Time for Love)"	The Isley Brothers
U.K. #1 POP 45	"Geno"	Dexy's Midnight Runners
U.K. #1 POP LP	*Sky 2*	Sky

WEEK ENDING MAY 17

U.S. #1 POP 45	"Call Me"	Blondie
U.S. #1 POP LP	*Against the Wind*	Bob Seger and the Silver Bullet Band
U.S. #1 R&B 45	"Let's Get Serious"	Jermaine Jackson
U.K. #1 POP 45	"What's Another Year"	Johnny Logan
U.K. #1 POP LP	*The Magic of Boney M*	Boney M

WEEK ENDING MAY 24

U.S. #1 POP 45	"Call Me"	Blondie
U.S. #1 POP LP	*Against the Wind*	Bob Seger and the Silver Bullet Band
U.S. #1 R&B 45	"Let's Get Serious"	Jermaine Jackson
U.K. #1 POP 45	"What's Another Year"	Johnny Logan
U.K. #1 POP LP	*The Magic of Boney M*	Boney M

WEEK ENDING MAY 31

U.S. #1 POP 45	"Funkytown"	Lipps, Inc.
U.S. #1 POP LP	*Against the Wind*	Bob Seger and the Silver Bullet Band
U.S. #1 R&B 45	"Let's Get Serious"	Jermaine Jackson
U.K. #1 POP 45	"Theme from M*A*S*H"	The Mash
U.K. #1 POP LP	*McCartney II*	Paul McCartney

5 The **Grateful Dead** play their "Fifteenth Anniversary Celebration" concert at Compton Terrace in Phoenix, Arizona.

12 Motown Records releases **Diana Ross'** *Diana,* her new album produced by the reigning princes of dance music, **Bernard Edwards** and **Nile Rodgers** of **Chic**. After a decade of ballads, movie theme songs and prima donna material, Ross returns to the kind of music that made her famous when she led the **Supremes** in the Sixties: dance music. The album contains "Upside Down" (which will be her first pop and R&B Number One in four years) and "I'm Coming Out"—both songs written by Edwards and Rodgers—and will hit Number One on the R&B LP chart and #2 on the pop LP chart.

13 *Roadie,* a rock-comedy film about the trials and tribulations of a typical rock band equipment handler (a roadie), opens in theaters across America. It stars **Meat Loaf,** and features appearances by **Blondie, Alice Cooper,**

Roy Orbison and **Hank Williams, Jr.** It will be a critical and commercial dud.

Pat Benatar opens a home game for the Philadelphia Phillies baseball team by playing a brief set on a makeshift stage set up in the infield and dancing with the Phillies' mascot, a large green duck.

14 Having already sold an estimated 300,000 copies in New York City alone, **Kurtis Blow's** twelve-inch single "The Breaks" enters the national R&B chart, where it will peak at #4. Blow (born **Kurt Walter**) began his career four years ago as a disc jockey at a Harlem disco, where he de-

veloped his rap style with turntable-spinner **Grandmaster Flash**. His "Christmas Rappin'" of 1979 was one of the first rap hits to catch on outside of New York. "The Breaks," which features spinner **Davy D** (born **David Reeves**), will become the first rap single to be certified gold.

17 **Led Zeppelin** begin a three-week European tour, their first on the Continent since 1973, and their first public appearances since Britain's Knebworth Festival in 1979. It will be the group's last tour anywhere.

18 The film *The Blues Brothers,* a musical caper-comedy starring John Belushi and Dan Aykroyd of "Saturday Night Live" as the scuffling, enigmatic, R&B fanatics **Jake** and **Elwood Blues,** premieres in New York City. The film gives cameos to such performers as **Aretha Franklin, Ray Charles, James Brown** and **John Lee Hooker,** and supporting roles to Thirties bandleader **Cab Calloway** and two members of the **Blues Brothers** band, **Steve Cropper** and **Donald "Duck" Dunn**

(both formerly with **Booker T. and the MGs**), and blues guitarist **Matt Murphy**.

19 **Donna Summer** becomes the first artist to sign with veteran label chief **David Geffen's** own new label, Geffen Records, which will go on to add **John Lennon** and **Yoko Ono, Elton John, Neil Young** and others to its roster.

21 British punk rockers the **Stranglers** are arrested for allegedly starting a riot at a concert at Nice University in France.

26 Rolling Stones **Keith Richards, Ron Wood** and **Mick Jagger** go to New York City nightclub Trax to check out a show by Rolling Stones Records artist **Jim Carroll**. Richards jams with Carroll's band on Carroll's minor FM hit "People Who Died."

27 **John Lydon** and **Keith Levene** make an extremely sullen and near-belligerent appearance on NBC-TV's late-night talk show "Tomorrow," hosted by **Tom Snyder.** ◆

WEEK ENDING JUNE 7		
U.S. #1 POP 45	"Funkytown"	Lipps, Inc.
U.S. #1 POP LP	*Against the Wind*	Bob Seger and the Silver Bullet Band
U.S. #1 R&B 45	"Let's Get Serious"	Jermaine Jackson
U.K. #1 POP 45	"Theme from M*A*S*H"	The Mash
U.K. #1 POP LP	*McCartney II*	Paul McCartney

WEEK ENDING JUNE 14		
U.S. #1 POP 45	"Funkytown"	Lipps, Inc.
U.S. #1 POP LP	*Glass Houses*	Billy Joel
U.S. #1 R&B 45	"Let's Get Serious"	Jermaine Jackson
U.K. #1 POP 45	"Theme from M*A*S*H"	The Mash
U.K. #1 POP LP	*McCartney II*	Paul McCartney

WEEK ENDING JUNE 21		
U.S. #1 POP 45	"Funkytown"	Lipps, Inc.
U.S. #1 POP LP	*Glass Houses*	Billy Joel
U.S. #1 R&B 45	"Let's Get Serious"	Jermaine Jackson
U.K. #1 POP 45	"Funkytown"	Lipps, Inc.
U.K. #1 POP LP	*Flesh and Blood*	Roxy Music

WEEK ENDING JUNE 28		
U.S. #1 POP 45	"Coming Up (Live at Glasgow)"	Paul McCartney and Wings
U.S. #1 POP LP	*Glass Houses*	Billy Joel
U.S. #1 R&B 45	"Take Your Time (Do It Right)"	S.O.S. Band
U.K. #1 POP 45	"Crying"	Don McLean
U.K. #1 POP LP	*Peter Gabriel*	Peter Gabriel

2 **Grateful Dead** members **Bob Weir** and **Mickey Hart** and manager **Danny Rifkin** are arrested for suspicion of inciting a riot at the San Diego Sports Arena after they tried to interfere in a drug-related arrest.

4 Los Angeles punk band **X** perform at Dingwalls club in London with ex-Door and X producer **Ray Manzarek** sitting in on keyboards.

10 **Bob Marley and the Wailers** begin what will be Marley's last tour of the British Isles, in Dublin, Ireland.

12 **Elvis Costello** performs at the Montreux Jazz Festival in Switzerland.

14 Singer **Malcolm Owen** of British punk rockers the **Ruts** overdoses on heroin in London and dies in his bathtub. The band will change its name to **Ruts DC** and continue without him for two years. Their one minor underground hit, recorded before Owen's death, is "Babylon's Burning."

Former **Beatles** and **Rolling Stones** manager **Allen Klein** surrenders to authorities at New York's Metropolitan Correction Center to begin serving a two-month sentence for filing a false federal income-tax return.

15 **Linda Ronstadt** makes her dramatic debut in the part of Mabel in the **Gilbert and Sullivan** operetta *The Pirates of Penzance,* opening at the Delacorte Theatre in New York City's Central Park. Her leading man is another pop singer, **Rex** ("You Take My Breath Away") **Smith**. Ronstadt, Smith and the whole New York Shakespeare Festival production will win very enthusiastic

reviews and will move to Broadway in January 1981. The century-old musical comedy will eventually be made into a movie starring Ronstadt, Smith and other original cast members **Kevin Kline**, **George Rose** and **Tony Azito**.

16 *No Nukes,* a film documentary of the MUSE antinuclear benefit concerts, premieres in New York City. Performers featured in the film include the **Doobie Brothers, Gil Scott-Heron, Crosby, Stills and Nash, Jackson Browne, Jesse Colin Young, James Taylor, Carly Simon, Bruce Springsteen, John Hall, Bonnie Raitt** and **Nicolette Larson**.

19 **David Bowie** makes his theatrical debut playing the title role in **Bernard Pomerance**'s long-running play *The Elephant Man* in its Denver production. Bowie will shortly take over the lead role in the New York production on Broadway, to generally favorable critical reaction.

21 **Genesis'** first album in over two years, *Duke,* goes gold. The LP reflects the growing influence of drummer/vocalist **Phil Collins**, and contains more elements of R&B and fewer traces of the group's patented progressive-rock sound. *Duke* goes to #11 and gives Genesis their first major hit, "Turn It On Again."

22 **Clive Davis** announces that his record label, Arista, has signed the **Allman Brothers Band**, whose previous label, Capricorn, recently declared bankruptcy.

23 Keyboardist **Keith Godchaux**, formerly of the **Grateful Dead**, dies at age thirty-two of injuries sustained in a car accident in Marin County, California.

25 **Kiss** introduce their new drummer, **Eric Carr**—who wears fox makeup, whereas his predecessor, **Peter Criss**, was made up as a cat—at a concert at the Palladium in New York City.

31 **John Phillips** is arrested on drug charges at his summer home in Water Mill, Long Island, New York. He is charged with, and later convicted of, conspiracy to distribute narcotics. ◆

WEEK ENDING JULY 5

U.S. #1 POP 45	"Coming Up (Live at Glasgow)"	Paul McCartney and Wings
U.S. #1 POP LP	*Glass Houses*	Billy Joel
U.S. #1 R&B 45	"Take Your Time (Do It Right)"	S.O.S. Band
U.K. #1 POP 45	"Crying"	Don McLean
U.K. #1 POP LP	*Flesh and Blood*	Roxy Music

WEEK ENDING JULY 12

U.S. #1 POP 45	"Coming Up (Live at Glasgow)"	Paul McCartney and Wings
U.S. #1 POP LP	*Glass Houses*	Billy Joel
U.S. #1 R&B 45	"Take Your Time (Do It Right)"	S.O.S. Band
U.K. #1 POP 45	"Xanadu"	Olivia Newton-John
U.K. #1 POP LP	*Flesh and Blood*	Roxy Music

WEEK ENDING JULY 19

U.S. #1 POP 45	"It's Still Rock and Roll to Me"	Billy Joel
U.S. #1 POP LP	*Glass Houses*	Billy Joel
U.S. #1 R&B 45	"Take Your Time (Do It Right)"	S.O.S. Band
U.K. #1 POP 45	"Xanadu"	Olivia Newton-John
U.K. #1 POP LP	*Emotional Rescue*	The Rolling Stones

WEEK ENDING JULY 26

U.S. #1 POP 45	"It's Still Rock and Roll to Me"	Billy Joel
U.S. #1 POP LP	*Emotional Rescue*	The Rolling Stones
U.S. #1 R&B 45	"Take Your Time (Do It Right)"	S.O.S. Band
U.K. #1 POP 45	"Xanadu"	Olivia Newton-John
U.K. #1 POP LP	*The Game*	Queen

4 **John Lennon** and **Yoko Ono** begin recording their album *Double Fantasy* at New York's Hit Factory Studio with producer **Jack Douglas.**

8 The Greater London Council orders a halt to the plans of American heavy-metal, punk-destructo band the **Plasmatics** to blow up a car on-stage tonight at their Hammersmith Odeon concert, the group's U.K. performing debut.

9 **George Landry,** "Big Chief Jolly" of New Orleans Mardi Gras funk clan the **Wild Tchoupitoulas,** dies in New Orleans at age sixty-three.

13 Four masked men break into **Todd Rundgren**'s home in Woodstock, New York, binding and gagging Rundgren, his girlfriend and three houseguests. The masked men then strip the house of valuable stereo equipment, tapestries and other art objects. Reportedly, one of the thieves hummed Rundgren's "I Saw the Light" throughout the heist.

15 Beatle George Harrison's book *I Me Mine* is published in London at £148 a copy.

The first *Urgh!* two-day festival of local national and international punk and new wave rock bands is held at the Santa Monica Civic Auditorium in Santa Monica, California. Performers include **X, Pere Ubu,** the **Dead Boys** and the **Dead Kennedys.** This and subsequent *Urgh!* festivals around the country will be filmed for the movie *Urgh! A Musical War.*

16 According to published reports, several bands have lost members: bassist **Jah Wobble** leaves **Public Image, Ltd.** (he will later form a power trio, the **Human Condition**); drummer **Bill Ward** leaves **Black Sabbath;** keyboardist **Jools Holland** leaves **Squeeze** (he will later form his own group, the **Millionaires**); and drummer **Cozy Powell** leaves **Ritchie Blackmore's Rainbow.**

19 Who is **Christopher Cross,** and why is his debut album one of the biggest hits of the year? Cross, from Austin, Texas, has three Top Fifteen hits, including the Number One "Sailing." His album goes platinum on this date, and Cross will go on to win a record five Grammy Awards the following February.

Four of the surviving members of **Lynyrd Skynyrd** return as the **Rossington Collins Band** with *Anytime, Anyplace, Anywhere,* which goes gold on this date. In place of the late **Ronnie Van Zant,** the group makes a wise choice by taking on a female singer, **Dale Krantz.** In concert, RCB play no Skynyrd material except their closer, an instrumental version of "Freebird."

21 The film *Breaking Glass,* starring British rock singer **Hazel O'Connor** in the story of a punk band's rise and fall, premieres in London.

23 Heatwave, a one-day festival of new wave rock music, is held outside Toronto, Ontario, Canada. Though the festival does not end up making any money, over 50,000 people show up to see **Elvis Costello and the Attractions,** the **Pretenders,** the **B-52's, Rockpile,** and **Talking Heads**—who unveil their new nine-piece Afro-funk lineup here—and others.

26 **Cheap Trick** bassist **Tom Petersson** quits the band, due to the inevitable "personal and musical differences." He will be replaced by Italian-born **Pete Comita.**

27 **Talking Heads** make their first U.S. stage appearance in a new nine-piece lineup at Wollman Rink in New York's Central Park. In addition to original members **David Byrne, Tina Weymouth, Chris Frantz** and **Jerry Harrison,** the band now includes ex-**Frank Zappa** and **David Bowie** guitarist **Adrian Belew,** ex-**Funkadelic** keyboardist **Bernie Worell,** bassist **Busta Cherry Jones,** percussionist **Steven Scales** and vocalist **Dolette McDonald.** The new lineup, playing an expansively orchestrated, African-derived polyrhythmic funk-rock, is ecstatically received by both audience and critics.

30 **Cher** makes an unannounced appearance as lead singer with **Black Rose,** the band led by her lover, guitarist **Les Dudek,** at a show in New York's Central Park. The audience responds favorably; the critics don't. ◆

WEEK ENDING AUGUST 2

U.S. #1 POP 45	"Magic"	Olivia Newton-John
U.S. #1 POP LP	*Emotional Rescue*	The Rolling Stones
U.S. #1 R&B 45	"One in a Million You"	Larry Graham
U.K. #1 POP 45	"Use It Up and Wear It Out"	Odyssey
U.K. #1 POP LP	*Xanadu*	soundtrack

WEEK ENDING AUGUST 9

U.S. #1 POP 45	"Magic"	Olivia Newton-John
U.S. #1 POP LP	*Emotional Rescue*	The Rolling Stones
U.S. #1 R&B 45	"One in a Million You"	Larry Graham
U.K. #1 POP 45	"Upside Down"	Diana Ross
U.K. #1 POP LP	*Xanadu*	soundtrack

WEEK ENDING AUGUST 16

U.S. #1 POP 45	"Magic"	Olivia Newton-John
U.S. #1 POP LP	*Emotional Rescue*	The Rolling Stones
U.S. #1 R&B 45	"Upside Down"	Diana Ross
U.K. #1 POP 45	"Winner Takes It All"	Abba
U.K. #1 POP LP	*Flesh and Blood*	Roxy Music

WEEK ENDING AUGUST 23

U.S. #1 POP 45	"Magic"	Olivia Newton-John
U.S. #1 POP LP	*Emotional Rescue*	The Rolling Stones
U.S. #1 R&B 45	"Upside Down"	Diana Ross
U.K. #1 POP 45	"Winner Takes It All"	Abba
U.K. #1 POP LP	*Flesh and Blood*	Roxy Music

WEEK ENDING AUGUST 30

U.S. #1 POP 45	"Sailing"	Christopher Cross
U.S. #1 POP LP	*Emotional Rescue*	The Rolling Stones
U.S. #1 R&B 45	"Upside Down"	Diana Ross
U.K. #1 POP 45	"Ashes to Ashes"	David Bowie
U.K. #1 POP LP	*Give Me the Night*	George Benson

1 **Fleetwood Mac** end a nine-month tour with a performance at the Hollywood Bowl, as **Lindsey Buckingham** announces from the stage, "This is our last show for a long time."

6 *Melody Maker* reports that keyboardist songwriter **Ken Hensley** has left British heavy-metal art rockers **Uriah Heep** after ten years.

12 British blues-rock drummer **Keef Hartley**, one-time **John Mayall** drummer, as well as leader of his own bands **Dog Soldier** and the **Keef Hartley Group**, opens his own nightclub, the Riviera, in Maidenhead, Berkshire, England.

13 *Melody Maker* reports that guitarist **Dave Knopfler**, brother of **Dire Straits** lead guitarist and singer **Mark Knopfler**, has left Dire Straits.

Jackson Browne has the first Number One album of his career with the platinum *Hold Out*, his first LP in well over two years.

17 **Bette Midler's** *Divine Madness*, a film of a 1979 concert in Pasadena, California, premieres in Los Angeles.

18 The two-day Festival for **Jimi Hendrix** commences at the Paradise Club in Amsterdam. Over 1,100 people will show up each night to see Hendrix films and performances by the **Noel Redding Band**, with whom fellow **Experience** member **Mitch Mitchell** makes a guest appearance. The memorial show is sponsored by Amsterdam's Hendrix Information Center.

British political-avant-punk-funk band **Gang of Four** play at London's Rainbow Theater in a show that is filmed for the movie *Urgh! A Music War*.

21 The **Michael Schenker Group**, led by Schenker, a former heavy-metal guitarist with **UFO** and the **Scorpions**, starts its first U.K. tour with a show at Bristol's Colston Hall.

Elton John signs a long-term, exclusive, worldwide recording contract with Geffen Records, the new label that recently signed **Donna Summer**. This marks the first time that Elton's records will be released on the same label around the world.

23 **David Bowie** replaces **Philip Anglim** in the title role of the hit Broadway play *The Elephant Man*, in New York City.

24 The Son of Stiff Tour—the third British package tour by British new wave independent label Stiff Records—begins in London, featuring **Joe "King" Carrasco and the Crowns**, **Tenpole Tudor**, the **Equators**, **Any Trouble** and **Dirty Looks**.

25 **Led Zeppelin** drummer **John "Bonzo" Bonham** dies of asphyxiation on his own vomit after drinking forty measures of vodka on the eve of the band's U.S. tour. He was thirty-two. Led Zeppelin eventually decides that Bonham cannot be replaced and disbands.

26 With their career established as more than a fluke after two years of rock dance-club hits, the **B-52's** return to their home turf of Atlanta, Georgia (they originally came from the neighboring suburb of Athens) to play a sold-out concert at the Agora Ballroom.

29 The **Stray Cats**—an American rockabilly-revival band who have moved to England in search of more receptive audiences, and who are still two years away from their big commercial breakthrough—open the show for **Elvis Costello and the Attractions** at London's Rainbow Theater.

In an interview with *Newsweek* magazine, **John Lennon** gives details about the soon-to-be-released album he's making with **Yoko Ono**, *Double Fantasy*. ◆

WEEK ENDING SEPTEMBER 6

U.S. #1 POP 45	"Upside Down"	Diana Ross
U.S. #1 POP LP	*Emotional Rescue*	The Rolling Stones
U.S. #1 R&B 45	"Upside Down"	Diana Ross
U.K. #1 POP 45	"Ashes to Ashes"	David Bowie
U.K. #1 POP LP	*Give Me the Night*	George Benson

WEEK ENDING SEPTEMBER 13

U.S. #1 POP 45	"Upside Down"	Diana Ross
U.S. #1 POP LP	*Hold Out*	Jackson Browne
U.S. #1 R&B 45	"Give Me the Night"	George Benson
U.K. #1 POP 45	"Start"	The Jam
U.K. #1 POP LP	*Flesh and Blood*	Roxy Music

WEEK ENDING SEPTEMBER 20

U.S. #1 POP 45	"Upside Down"	Diana Ross
U.S. #1 POP LP	*The Game*	Queen
U.S. #1 R&B 45	"Give Me the Night"	George Benson
U.K. #1 POP 45	"One Day I'll Fly Away"	Randy Crawford
U.K. #1 POP LP	*Signing Off*	UB40

WEEK ENDING SEPTEMBER 27

U.S. #1 POP 45	"Upside Down"	Diana Ross
U.S. #1 POP LP	*The Game*	Queen
U.S. #1 R&B 45	"Give Me the Night"	George Benson
U.K. #1 POP 45	"One Day I'll Fly Away"	Randy Crawford
U.K. #1 POP LP	*Telekon*	Gary Numan

1 **Paul Simon**'s semi-autobiographical film *One Trick Pony* premieres in New York City. Aside from Simon, those appearing in the film include **Lou Reed** as a record producer, and **Sam and Dave**, the **B-52's**, and the **Lovin' Spoonful** as themselves.

Queen receive a platinum record for their most successful album to date, *The Game*, which also becomes their first Number One, a position it holds for five weeks. The group backs its recorded success with a lavish U.S. tour and enjoys its second consecutive Number One single, "Another One Bites the Dust," the first release since 1979's rockabilly-style hit "Crazy Little Thing Called Love."

2 Tenor singer **Leaveil Degree** of the soul group the **Whispers** begins serving a two-year prison term in Boron, California, for his part in a 1979 gem heist. At the time, the Whispers' self-titled album is in the soul Top Ten LPs chart.

3 **Bob Seger** joins **Bruce Springsteen** onstage at the first date of the latter's U.S. tour in Ann Arbor, Michigan. Seger lends his vocals to Springsteen's "Thunder Road."

Five years after forming, British band **Rockpile** releases its first—and so far only—album, *Seconds of Pleasure*, on Columbia Records. The band—led by veteran British rockers **Dave Edmunds** and ex-**Brinsley Schwarz** member Nick Lowe, and also featuring **Billy Bremner** and **Terry Williams**—is an occasional, friendly project that tends to get together only when Edmunds and Lowe aren't busy producing their own or someone else's records. As with almost everything Edmunds and Lowe do, Rockpile is a great critical success but doesn't fare quite so well commercially, since its no-nonsense, roots-rock approach always seems just a bit too much out of fashion with the times.

4 **Carly Simon** collapses onstage at Pittsburgh's Stanley Theater from nervous exhaustion. The rest of her tour is canceled.

Mick Fleetwood, Lindsey Buckingham and **Stevie Nicks** of **Fleetwood Mac** join the University of Southern California **Trojan Marching Band** for a halftime show at a USC football game. As half-time ends, the Trojans are presented with a platinum record for their contribution to the song.

6 The **Bee Gees** sue their manager, **Robert Stigwood**, and their record label, PolyGram, for $200 million, charging misrepresentation, fraud and unfair enrichment at their expense.

John Lydon of **Public Image, Ltd.** is arrested in Dublin, Ireland, following a barroom brawl and is sentenced to three months in jail for disorderly conduct. He will be released on bail and later will be acquitted by an appeals court.

7 British pop singer **Dusty Springfield** makes her first New York stage appearance in eight years at the Grand Finale club.

8 Reggae giant **Bob Marley** collapses onstage during a **Wailers** concert in Pittsburgh—the last concert he will ever perform. He is flown directly to Sloan-Kettering Hospital in New York City, where spokesmen will deny that Marley is dying of a brain tumor or cancer. Marley will then fly to Ethiopia to rest and will later turn up at a German disease-treatment center. Marley will die of a brain tumor in May 1981, enroute to Jamaica.

9 **John Lennon** celebrates his fortieth birthday by releasing "(Just Like) Starting Over," his first record in five years, on Geffen Records. The song is a joyful ode to domestic contentment. His wife, **Yoko Ono**, commissions a sky writer to etch him a "Happy Birthday" message over New York City's skyline.

13 **AC/DC** position themselves as the heirs to **Led Zeppelin** with *Back in Black*, which turns platinum on this date. The album's title makes reference to the late **Bon Scott**, AC/DC's original vocalist, who died in February. His replacement is **Brian Johnson**, a burly ex-roofer from Newcastle who possesses a similarly shrill, piercing voice. *Back in Black* places as high as #4.

15 The **Cars** rack up their third consecutive platinum album with *Panorama*. Although the LP goes to #5, it's considered something of a let-down after the back-to-back smashes of *The Cars* and *Candy-O*. "Touch and Go" from the album reaches #11.

24 **Paul McCartney** receives a rhodium-plated (rhodium is a metal related to platinum) disc from the *Guinness Book of World Records* for being history's all-time best-selling songwriter and recording artist.

27 Percussionist **Steve Peregrine Took** dies at age thirty-one in London. In the late Sixties, he was co-founder with **Marc Bolan** of British flower-power-folk band **Tyrannosaurus Rex**; in 1970 Took left to be replaced by **Mickey Finn**, and the band went electric to become **T. Rex**, idols of glitter-era British teens. ◆

WEEK ENDING OCTOBER 4

U.S. #1 POP 45	"Another One Bites the Dust"	Queen
U.S. #1 POP LP	*The Game*	Queen
U.S. #1 R&B 45	"Funkin' for Jamaica (New York)"	Tom Browne
U.K. #1 POP 45	"Don't Stand So Close to Me"	The Police
U.K. #1 POP LP	*Never Forever*	Kate Bush

WEEK ENDING OCTOBER 11

U.S. #1 POP 45	"Another One Bites the Dust"	Queen
U.S. #1 POP LP	*The Game*	Queen
U.S. #1 R&B 45	"Funkin' for Jamaica (New York)"	Tom Browne
U.K. #1 POP 45	"Don't Stand So Close to Me"	The Police
U.K. #1 POP LP	*Scary Monsters*	David Bowie

WEEK ENDING OCTOBER 18

U.S. #1 POP 45	"Another One Bites the Dust"	Queen
U.S. #1 POP LP	*The Game*	Queen
U.S. #1 R&B 45	"Funkin' for Jamaica (New York)"	Tom Browne
U.K. #1 POP 45	"Don't Stand So Close to Me"	The Police
U.K. #1 POP LP	*Zenyatta Mondatta*	The Police

WEEK ENDING OCTOBER 25

U.S. #1 POP 45	"Woman in Love"	Barbra Streisand
U.S. #1 POP LP	*Guilty*	Barbra Streisand
U.S. #1 R&B 45	"Funkin' for Jamaica (New York)"	Tom Browne
U.K. #1 POP 45	"Don't Stand So Close to Me"	The Police
U.K. #1 POP LP	*Zenyatta Mondatta*	The Police

1 Singer **Graham Bonnet** leaves **Ritchie Blackmore's Rainbow** after just a year-and-a-half to resume his solo career. His departure comes just weeks after drummer **Cozy Powell** left. Their replacements, singer **Joe Lynn Turner** and drummer **Bob Rondinelli**, will be the fifteenth and sixteenth musicians in Blackmore's five-year-old heavy-metal band.

6 **Paul Simon** plays his first British concert in five years, accompanied by studio-funk band **Stuff**, at London's Hammersmith Odeon.

7 British soul-rock band **Dexy's Midnight Runners**, who had scored a British hit with the single "Dance Stance" (it also found some success in America's new

wave dance-rock clubs), split up. The majority of the band continues in the Dexy's Stax/Volt vein as the **Bureau**; leader **Kevin Rowland**, a controversially polemical soul purist, will resurface three years later as leader of a new Dexy's Midnight Runners, integrating traditional Celtic music into the soul-rock revivalism for the smash hit "Come On, Eileen."

8 *Melody Maker* reports that British electropop experimentalists **Human League** are splitting up into two factions. Keyboardist **Ian Marsh** and **Martyn Ware** are forming the British Electrical Foundation, an umbrella production company that will go on to record electropop and synth-funk discs under its own name (on the various-artists sampler *Music of Quality and Distinction*, featuring **Tina Turner**, **Gary Glitter**, **Sandie**

Shaw and others, and the made-for-Walkman-tape-only *Music for Stowaways*) and as **Heaven 17** (with the critically acclaimed single "We Don't Need This Fascist Groove Thang" and album *Penthouse and Pavement*). Keyboardist **Adrian Wright** and singer **Phil Oakey** will stay together as the Human League. With the addition of more musicians, including two female singers, they will go on to achieve massive pop success in 1982 with the single

"Don't You Want Me."

13 Cashing in on the resurgence of his old tribal-stomp sound (revived by **Joan Jett** in "Do You Wanna Touch?"), glitter-era rock star **Gary Glitter** launches a comeback tour of Britain in Norwich's Cromwell's Club. The next day he releases his first record in several years, "What Your Momma Don't See (Your Momma Don't Know)."

18 The **B-52's** self-titled debut goes gold. The Athens, Georgia, group's quirky compositions are highlighted by **Fred Schneider**'s deadpan recitation of the lyrics and **Kate Pierson**'s and **Cindy Wilson**'s vocal acrobatics, which recall the earlier work of **Yoko Ono**. In fact, the band is indirectly responsible for the Lennon's return to music later in the year: when **John Lennon** hears the B-52's, he realizes the time is right.

21 **Eagles** drummer/vocalist **Don Henley** is arrested in Los Angeles after paramedics treat a nude sixteen-year-old girl suffering from drug intoxication at this home. Henley is charged with unlawful possession of marijuana, cocaine and Quaaludes, and contributing to the delinquency of a minor.

A one-hour documentary film, *Van Morrison in Ireland,* featuring shots of the singer onstage in Belfast and Dublin as well as offstage, is premiered at London's National Film Theater. It was produced by **Rex Pyle**.

30 At the Top Rank club in Swansea, Wales, **Elvis Costello** and **Squeeze** perform a benefit concert for the family of the late Welsh boxer **Johnny Owen**, killed recently by head injuries sustained in an American match. ◆

WEEK ENDING NOVEMBER 1

U.S. #1 POP 45	"Woman in Love"	Barbra Streisand
U.S. #1 POP LP	*Guilty*	Barbra Streisand
U.S. #1 R&B 45	"Master Blaster (Jammin')"	Stevie Wonder
U.K. #1 POP 45	"Woman in Love"	Barbra Streisand
U.K. #1 POP LP	*Zenyatta Mondatta*	The Police

WEEK ENDING NOVEMBER 8

U.S. #1 POP 45	"Woman in Love"	Barbra Streisand
U.S. #1 POP LP	*The River*	Bruce Springsteen
U.S. #1 R&B 45	"Master Blaster (Jammin')"	Stevie Wonder
U.K. #1 POP 45	"Woman in Love"	Barbra Streisand
U.K. #1 POP LP	*Zenyatta Mondatta*	The Police

WEEK ENDING NOVEMBER 15

U.S. #1 POP 45	"Lady"	Kenny Rogers
U.S. #1 POP LP	*The River*	Bruce Springsteen
U.S. #1 R&B 45	"Master Blaster (Jammin')"	Stevie Wonder
U.K. #1 POP 45	"Woman in Love"	Barbra Streisand
U.K. #1 POP LP	*Hotter Than July*	Stevie Wonder

WEEK ENDING NOVEMBER 22

U.S. #1 POP 45	"Lady"	Kenny Rogers
U.S. #1 POP LP	*The River*	Bruce Springsteen
U.S. #1 R&B 45	"Master Blaster (Jammin')"	Stevie Wonder
U.K. #1 POP 45	"The Tide Is High"	Blondie
U.K. #1 POP LP	*Hotter Than July*	Stevie Wonder

WEEK ENDING NOVEMBER 29

U.S. #1 POP 45	"Lady"	Kenny Rogers
U.S. #1 POP LP	*The River*	Bruce Springsteen
U.S. #1 R&B 45	"Master Blaster (Jammin')"	Stevie Wonder
U.K. #1 POP 45	"The Tide Is High"	Blondie
U.K. #1 POP LP	*Super Trouper*	Abba

1 The newly expanded nine-piece **Talking Heads** start a brief U.K. tour at London's Hammersmith Palais. A new Irish band that will go on to achieve great success in America within the next two years, **U2**, opens the show.

2 **Joni Mitchell**'s concert video special "Shadows and Light" is broadcast on nationwide cable TV network Showtime. It will later be released as a home videocassette.

3 Popular British folk-rock band **Steeleye Span** re-form for an album, *Sails of Silver,* and a tour that starts this day in Brighton at the Dome. Members **Maddy Prior** (vocals) and **Rick Kemp** (bass) are now married.

4 **Jimmy Page, Robert Plant** and **John Paul Jones** make public their decision *not* to re-form **Led Zeppelin** in the wake of the death of drummer **John "Bonzo" Bonham.**

8 **John Lennon** is assassinated by **Mark David Chapman** as he walks through the gate of his New York City apartment building, the Dakota, after returning with his wife, **Yoko Ono**, from a recording session. Having suffered gunshot wounds in his chest, back and left arm, Lennon is pronounced dead within thirty minutes. Chapman, a twenty-five-year-old itinerant **Beatles** fan and would-be suicide from Hawaii—described by police as "some kind of wacko" —had been hanging around in front of the Dakota for three days. Earlier this day, on his way to his last recording session, Lennon had autographed an album for Chapman. The news of Lennon's death spreads rapidly through New York City, and within an hour, hundreds of fans have gathered outside the Dakota, chanting "Give Peace a Chance." Announcer **Howard Cosell** informs the nation of Lennon's shooting—but not his death—during a broadcast of ABC-TV's "Monday Night Football." Within the next few days, memorials and candlelight vigils will be held in cities all over the world. Three days later, two people will have killed themselves, unable to cope with the loss of Lennon: a sixteen-year-old Florida girl who overdoses on sleeping pills, and a thirty-year-old Utah man who shoots himself.

———

Pat Benatar receives a platinum record for her debut album, *In the Heat of the Night,* capping a year in which she goes from unknown to renown, and is rivaled only by the **Pretenders' Chrissie Hynde** and **Fleetwood Mac's Stevie Nicks** for most popular female singer honors. Benatar, a former waitress and bank teller from Lindenhurst, New York, was discovered late one night at Catch a Rising Star club in New York City by manager **Rick Newman**. *Heat* reached the Top Ten, and the followup, *Crimes of Passion,* #2.

12 **Devo**'s "Whip It" turns gold. The song is misinterpreted to be an ode to masturbation, but not so, insists the group. "We were writing a can-do, self-help song," says **Jerry Casale**. "Whip it—as in whip it into shape."

14 At **Yoko Ono**'s request, at two p.m. Eastern Standard Time today, **John Lennon**'s fans around the world mourn him with ten minutes of silent prayer. In New York, where hundreds still keep a round-the-clock vigil outside the Dakota, the entrance of which is now festooned with wreaths, flowers, pictures of Lennon and gifts to Yoko Ono and her son, **Sean**, from fans—over 100,000 people converge on Central Park, where the bandshell is empty but for wreaths and a large photo of Lennon, and the speakers play such songs as "In My Life," "You've Got to Hide Your Love Away," "Norwegian Wood," "All You Need Is Love," "Give Peace a Chance," and "Imagine" before the 10-minute silence. In Liverpool, a crowd of over 30,000 gathers outside St. George's Hall on Lime Street. Other such gatherings are held formally and informally all over the world.

20 British folk-rock band **Lindisfarne** celebrate their tenth year together with ten special Christmas shows at Newcastle City Hall in their hometown.

27 Nearly three weeks to the day after **John Lennon**'s murder in New York, Lennon and **Yoko Ono**'s "(Just Like) Starting Over" hits Number One in the U.S. and the U.K. simultaneously.

29 Folksinger/songwriter **Tim Hardin** dies at age forty of a heroin overdose in his Hollywood apartment. Hardin's best-known songs included "If I Were a Carpenter" (an international hit for **Bobby Darin** in 1966 and the **Four Tops** in 1968) and "Reason to Believe" (a hit for **Rod Stewart** in 1971).

31 Louisiana Delta bluesman **Robert Pete Williams** dies at age sixty-six in Rosedale, Louisiana. His best-known songs include "Angola Penitentiary Blues" (he served four years in Angola State Penitentiary in Louisiana in the late Fifties on a manslaughter charge) and "Ugly," covered by **Captain Beefheart and his Magic Band** on *Safe as Milk* as "Grown So Ugly." Williams had recently been rediscovered by acoustic guitar master **John Fahey**, who recorded Williams for his Takoma label in the late Seventies. ◆

WEEK ENDING DECEMBER 6

U.S. #1 POP 45	"Lady"	Kenny Rogers
U.S. #1 POP LP	*Guilty*	Barbra Streisand
U.S. #1 R&B 45	"Master Blaster (Jammin')"	Stevie Wonder
U.K. #1 POP 45	"Super Trouper"	Abba
U.K. #1 POP LP	*Super Trouper*	Abba

WEEK ENDING DECEMBER 13

U.S. #1 POP 45	"Lady"	Kenny Rogers
U.S. #1 POP LP	*Greatest Hits*	Kenny Rogers
U.S. #1 R&B 45	"Master Blaster (Jammin')"	Stevie Wonder
U.K. #1 POP 45	"Super Trouper"	Abba
U.K. #1 POP LP	*Super Trouper*	Abba

WEEK ENDING DECEMBER 20

U.S. #1 POP 45	"Lady"	Kenny Rogers
U.S. #1 POP LP	*Greatest Hits*	Kenny Rogers
U.S. #1 R&B 45	"Celebration"	Kool and the Gang
U.K. #1 POP 45	"Stop the Cavalry"	Jona Lewie
U.K. #1 POP LP	*Super Trouper*	Abba

WEEK ENDING DECEMBER 27

U.S. #1 POP 45	"(Just Like) Starting Over"	John Lennon
U.S. #1 POP LP	*Double Fantasy*	John Lennon and Yoko Ono
U.S. #1 R&B 45	"Celebration"	Kool and the Gang
U.K. #1 POP 45	"Stop the Cavalry"	Jona Lewie
U.K. #1 POP LP	*Super Trouper*	Abba

1981

This year the record industry really began to crow about its sales slump, homing in on the phenomenon of home taping—whereby potential record buyers tape their favorite tunes off the radio or off a friend's album, thus saving money on albums tagged with ever-escalating list prices. Whether or not home taping has been as widespread and destructive (certainly it does infringe on artists' royalties) as the record companies claimed has never been conclusively determined; at any rate, there were still plenty of big-selling records. Platinum-level stars like REO Speedwagon and Rick James came into their own this year, commercially speaking. And with a whole new generation of young record buyers who'd been born too late to experience the Sixties, record companies could now capitalize on the unlikely revival in popularity of such bands as the Doors, who, a full decade after the death of Jim Morrison, were one of the biggest sellers of the year with their *Greatest Hits* anthology. It went platinum even as Simon and Garfunkel were reuniting before huge crowds in New York.

Speaking of recycling the past, there was more money-making nostalgia this year in the form of the various "Stars on . . ." disco medleys, which set Beatles tunes, Sixties pop hits or Seventies disco hits to a relentless, metronomic disco beat. And despite the supposed decline of disco, that beat still sold records in a big way. Soon there would be "Hooked on . . ." albums in the "Stars on . . ." mold, with the same disco beat backing quick excerpts from swing standards *(Hooked on Swing)* or famous classical-music themes *(Hooked on Classics)* or Broadway show tunes *(Turned-on Broadway)*. And they, too, would sell.

Meanwhile, rap music continued to evolve. Blondie lent it a more accessible, pop veneer with "Rapture" in March. Rap as a genre had already become self-conscious enough that there was the release of a battle-of-the-rap-stars disc, "Showdown," by "The Furious Five Meets the Sugar Hill Gang." Shortly thereafter, Grandmaster Flash of the Furious Five took rap to the level of postmodern avant-garde art with his "Adventures on the Wheels of Steel" twelve-inch single. The disc took rap's use of ready-made musical backing tracks to a logical extreme, and dispensed with spontaneous raps altogether, as Flash instead worked out what one critic called "turntable jazz"—the manual manipulation of two or more turntables and the rap and/or funk hits they were spinning to effect a stunning, surreal patchwork of intentional scratches, skips and stuck grooves, all done in perfect "on the one" rhythm.

"Adventures on the Wheels of Steel" was far and away the most revolutionary disc of the year; yet, in another indication of where things stood overall, shortly after its release Grandmaster Flash and the Furious Five opened for the Clash at their two-week series of concerts in New York City and were booed off the stage by the crowd. By this time, the Clash had become virtually the sole commercial survivors of British punk. They now had a mass audience, and that audience came mainly from the heavy-metal hordes, heavy metal being the one form of popular music to which the Clash's guitar-army sound was closest. It's no wonder that a mass of impatient and crowded heavy-metal fans would have none of the Furious Five's unabashedly inner-city grooving. Only an hour or so after pelting the Furious Five with debris, however, the crowd reacted favorably to the Clash's own rap-style "The Magnificent Seven."

Such a phenomenon had been building for some time, due mainly to radio's demographically enforced segregation of black music from white. There were scattered exceptions to this rule, but in general, the situation was such that critics began to champion Minneapolis funk-rock phenom Prince as the Great Black/White Hope.

Then, on August 1, the music took another segregational turn with the debut of the first national twenty-four-hour, all-rock-video cable-TV channel, Warner-Amex's MTV. In the current sales slump, record companies had turned to cost-effective promotional videos as never before, and while this would go on to have a sizable effect on the way music was made and consumed as well as promoted, for the time being MTV failed to live up to what its initials stood for—music television. MTV was white-rock TV, and it would be well over a year before it would put black artists into its rigid, AOR-FM-style playlist. Until then, MTV would be screening the same old song.

7 The *Eagles Live* album goes platinum. The two-record set will turn out to be the final **Eagles** album; the group will dissolve a year later.

9 Keyboardist **Jerry Dammers** and singer **Terry Hall** of the **Specials** are fined in London for inciting violence at a concert in the fall of 1980.

10 **John Lennon** and **Yoko Ono**'s *Double Fantasy* goes platinum, a little more than a month after Lennon's assassination. The album is Number One for eight weeks.

The Pirates of Penzance, **Gilbert and Sullivan**'s century-old comic operetta, opens at Broadway's Uris Theatre, starring pop singers **Linda Ronstadt** and **Rex Smith**. The New York Shakespeare Festival production has already enjoyed a successful summer at Central Park's Delacorte Theatre, where Ronstadt and Smith made their dramatic debuts. After winning favorable reviews in the part of Mabel, Ronstadt will be replaced by other pop singers, first **Karla DeVito** (who has toured with **Meat Loaf**) and then **Maureen McGovern** (who had a Number One hit with "The Morning After" in 1973). Smith, in the part of Frederick, will be replaced in turn by actor **Robbie Benson** (he and DeVito will be married before their Broadway engagement is through) and by former **Herman's Hermit Peter Noone**. The show will move from the Uris to the Minskoff Theatre to complete a run of 772 performances, then be made into a movie starring Ronstadt and Smith.

12 Among the rock albums donated to the Library of Congress by the Recording Industry Association of America are **Bob Dylan**'s *Blonde on Blonde*, **Kiss'** *Alive!* and *Never Mind the Bollocks, Here's the Sex Pistols*.

17 **Prince**, the funk-rock fusion phenom from Minneapolis, enters the soul chart for the fourth time since September 1979 with "Dirty Mind," which will peak at #65 in its six weeks on the chart. At this time, Prince is still more of a favorite with critics than audiences, although "I Wanna Be Your Lover" hit Number One R&B in 1979. That will change later this year, though, when Prince breaks big with the album *Controversy* and its title single.

18 Vocalist **Wendy O. Williams** of the de-

structo heavy-metal band the **Plasmatics** is arrested during a Milwaukee concert for "simulating masturbation with a sledgehammer in front of an audience." Williams is pinned to the stage by police and, in the ensuing fracas, suffers a cut over one eye that requires twelve stitches.

24 **Tom Browne**, who in 1980 broke through with the soul Number One "Funkin' for Jamaica (NY)" (as in Jamaica, Queens, New York, Browne's hometown), enters the soul chart with "Thighs High (Grip Your Hips and Move)," which in eighteen weeks on the chart will peak at #4. Like "Funkin' for Jamaica," it will never enter the pop chart—just one of many examples of the increasing demographic fragmentation and segregation of musical genres and their audiences in America. "Thighs High" is from Browne's #5 soul LP *Magic*.

26 **Blondie**'s *Autoamerican* turns platinum. The album leaves their progressive pop sound behind, but reaches the Top Five nonetheless. Two of its singles, the reggae song "The Tide Is High" and the rap vamp "Rapture," reach #1, and the band is responsible (if unheralded) for introducing different ethnic musical styles to the largely white, hard-rock Top 100.

31 Female disco duo **A Taste of Honey** enter the soul chart with a disco remake of **Kyu Sakamoto**'s 1963 novelty pop Number One hit "Sukiyaki." Taste of Honey's version will peak at Number One on the soul chart for one week starting May 9, and will be on the soul chart a total of twenty-four weeks. It will enter the pop chart in March, and will peak at #3 pop. ◆

WEEK ENDING JANUARY 3

U.S. #1 POP 45	"(Just Like) Starting Over"	John Lennon
U.S. #1 POP LP	*Double Fantasy*	John Lennon and Yoko Ono
U.S. #1 R&B 45	"Celebration"	Kool and the Gang
U.K. #1 POP 45	"(Just Like) Starting Over"	John Lennon
U.K. #1 POP LP	*Double Fantasy*	John Lennon and Yoko Ono

WEEK ENDING JANUARY 10

U.S. #1 POP 45	"(Just Like) Starting Over"	John Lennon
U.S. #1 POP LP	*Double Fantasy*	John Lennon and Yoko Ono
U.S. #1 R&B 45	"Celebration"	Kool and the Gang
U.K. #1 POP 45	"Imagine"	John Lennon
U.K. #1 POP LP	*Double Fantasy*	John Lennon and Yoko Ono

WEEK ENDING JANUARY 17

U.S. #1 POP 45	"(Just Like) Starting Over"	John Lennon
U.S. #1 POP LP	*Double Fantasy*	John Lennon and Yoko Ono
U.S. #1 R&B 45	"Celebration"	Kool and the Gang
U.K. #1 POP 45	"Imagine"	John Lennon
U.K. #1 POP LP	*Super Trouper*	Abba

WEEK ENDING JANUARY 24

U.S. #1 POP 45	"(Just Like) Starting Over"	John Lennon
U.S. #1 POP LP	*Double Fantasy*	John Lennon and Yoko Ono
U.S. #1 R&B 45	"Celebration"	Kool and the Gang
U.K. #1 POP 45	"Imagine"	John Lennon
U.K. #1 POP LP	*Double Fantasy*	John Lennon and Yoko Ono

WEEK ENDING JANUARY 31

U.S. #1 POP 45	"The Tide Is High"	Blondie
U.S. #1 POP LP	*Double Fantasy*	John Lennon and Yoko Ono
U.S. #1 R&B 45	"Fantastic Voyage"	Lakeside
U.K. #1 POP 45	"Imagine"	John Lennon
U.K. #1 POP LP	*Kings of the Wild Frontier*	Adam and the Ants

2 **REO Speedwagon**, the journeyman band that almost found itself out of a deal by the mid-Seventies, have the biggest LP of 1981 with *Hi-Infidelity*, which goes platinum on this date. The LP quickly surpasses the success of the rest of their catalogue, reaching Number One for a number of weeks and selling 7 million copies by the end of the year. "We were counting on 750,000 to a million," says Epic Records' director of merchandising, **Larry Stessel**. Of the avalanche of sales, he says, laughing, "We sit here and go, 'What happened?' "

6 A *New York Post* headline reads SURVIVING BEATLES PLAN NEW ALBUM AS LENNON TRIBUTE. In fact, **Ringo Starr** was in Montserrat working with **Paul McCartney** on his *Tug of War* LP. **George Harrison** was nowhere in sight. The resulting LP, however, did contain McCartney's elegy to his late partner **John Lennon**, "Here Today."

9 **Bill Haley** dies of natural causes in Harlingen, Texas, at age fifty-six. One of the first white performers to play rhythm & blues, Haley and his band the **Saddlemen** began sowing the seeds of rock & roll in the early Fifties with a string of singles that fused R&B with country & western over a steady beat and used adolescent colloquialisms as titles and catch phrases—such as "Crazy Man Crazy" in 1953, the first rock & roll record to enter the U.S. pop chart. In 1954, Haley, with the **Comets**, released what would become his most famous song, "Rock around the Clock," which was a commercial failure. The followup, a version of **Big Joe Turner**'s "Shake, Rattle and Roll," however, made the Top Twenty on the U.S. pop chart. Later in 1954, "Rock around the Clock" was used as the theme song of the hit film *Blackboard Jungle*. Due to the success of the film, the song was re-released and became a worldwide hit, reaching Number One in the U.S. Haley went on to star in the film *Rock around the Clock* (the film caused youth riots in America and especially in Britain) and recorded several more successful singles, such as "See You Later Alligator" and "Don't Knock the Rock," before fading into obscurity. Haley did not reemerge until the mid-Seventies, when he took part in **Richard Nader**'s "Rock & Roll Revival" tours. His last years were apparently painful ones: reportedly, Haley could often be found wandering the streets of Harlingen, drunk and cursing the moon or bragging to whomever he bumped into that he was *the* Bill Haley.

12 **Deborah Harry**, **Blondie**'s vocalist and sex symbol, confirms that she will be making a solo album—her first—with **Bernard Edwards** and **Nile Rodgers** of **Chic**.

13 With the recording industry up in arms over the home-taping of albums, **Chris Blackwell** of Island Records inflames the situation while "trying to meet it head-on" by introducing "One Plus One" cassettes. They contain a full album of music on one side of the tape, with the other side blank.

15 **Mike Bloomfield** is found dead in his car in San Francisco at age thirty-nine. An autopsy reveals that he died of a drug overdose. Bloomfield had emerged in the mid-Sixties with the **Paul Butterfield Blues Band** and was immediately acclaimed as one of the best white blues guitarists in rock. He went on to play electric guitar with **Bob Dylan** when the latter first "went electric"; he formed the **Electric Flag**, recorded some "super session" jams with **Al Kooper** and **Stephen Stills** and then retreated into an erratic solo career.

19 **Judge Richard Owen** of the New York State Supreme Court rules that **George Harrison** "subconsciously plagiarized" "He's So Fine," the **Chiffons**' 1963 hit written by their manager, **Ronald Mack**, in his 1970 hit "My Sweet Lord." Harrison is ordered to pay $587,000 to ABKCO Music, a company owned, ironically, by Harrison's former business manager (when he was one of the **Beatles**), **Allen Klein**.

22 **Kermit Chandler**, a guitarist and songwriter with Sixties soul-vocal group the **Sheppards**—who last year reentered the critical limelight with an eponymous reissue album on San Francisco independent label Solid Smoke—dies at age thirty-eight in Chicago after a long illness.

25 **Christopher Cross** wins four Grammy Awards as the 1980 citations are announced: he is Best New Artist, "Sailing" is Song of the Year and Record of the Year, and his eponymous debut album is Album of the Year. Best Rock Vocals go to **Pat Benatar**'s *Crimes of Passion*, **Billy Joel**'s *Glass Houses* and **Bob Seger and the Silver Bullet Band**'s *Against the Wind*. Best Rock Instrumental is the **Police**'s "Regatta de Blanc."

27 The **Police** receive a gold record for *Zenyatta Mondatta*, their third LP—and their most blatantly commercial. Even more blatant: the LP's first hit, "Da Doo Doo Doo, Da Da Da Da." ◆

WEEK ENDING FEBRUARY 7

U.S. #1 POP 45	"Celebration"	Kool and the Gang
U.S. #1 POP LP	*Double Fantasy*	John Lennon and Yoko Ono
U.S. #1 R&B 45	"Fantastic Voyage"	Lakeside
U.K. #1 POP 45	"In the Air Tonight"	Phil Collins
U.K. #1 POP LP	*Kings of the Wild Frontier*	Adam and the Ants

WEEK ENDING FEBRUARY 14

U.S. #1 POP 45	"Celebration"	Kool and the Gang
U.S. #i POP LP	*Double Fantasy*	John Lennon and Yoko Ono
U.S. #1 R&B 45	"Burn Rubber on Me (Why You Wanna Hurt Me)"	The Gap Band
U.K. #1 POP 45	"In the Air Tonight"	Phil Collins
U.K. #1 POP LP	*Double Fantasy*	John Lennon and Yoko Ono

WEEK ENDING FEBRUARY 21

U.S. #1 POP 45	"9 to 5"	Dolly Parton
U.S. #1 POP LP	*Hi Infidelity*	REO Speedwagon
U.S. #1 R&B 45	"Burn Rubber on Me (Why You Wanna Hurt Me)"	The Gap Band
U.K. #1 POP 45	"Vienna"	Ultravox
U.K. #1 POP LP	*Kings of the Wild Frontier*	Adam and the Ants

WEEK ENDING FEBRUARY 28

U.S. #1 POP 45	"I Love a Rainy Night"	Eddie Rabbitt
U.S. #1 POP LP	*Hi Infidelity*	REO Speedwagon
U.S. #1 R&B 45	"Don't Stop the Music"	Yarbrough and Peoples
U.K. #1 POP 45	"Shaddup You Face"	Joe Dolce
U.K. #1 POP LP	*Double Fantasy*	John Lennon and Yoko Ono

7 Memphis-based soul singer **Peabo Bryson** continues his hitmaking ways: his new album, *Turn the Hands of Time,* enters the soul LPs chart, where in nineteen weeks it will peak at #23. It will also yield a #61 soul single in the title tune. In three weeks, Bryson will again enter the chart with a duet with **Roberta Flack**, "Love Is a Waiting Game," which in six weeks will peak at #45. Last month, Bryson's duet with pop songstress **Melissa Manchester**, "Lovers after All," entered the pop and soul charts, where it rose to #54 and #34, respectively.

If imitation is the sincerest form of flattery, then what does **Parliament-Funkadelic** leader **George Clinton** think of this? A band calling itself Funkadelic—which is *not* the real Clinton-led Funkadelic but a group of dissatisfied former Clinton sidemen—enters the soul chart with "Connections and Disconnections," which in twelve weeks will peak at #68. Three weeks later, the band's album of the same name will enter the soul LPs chart, where in five

weeks it will peak at #41. A few weeks after that, the *real* Funkadelic will enter both soul charts with its new LP, *The Electric Spanking of War Babies* (#41 in five weeks), featuring **Sly Stone**, and the album's title single (#60 in six weeks).

14 **Eric Clapton** is admitted to United Hospital in St. Paul, Minnesota, after a serious attack of bleeding ulcers. Clapton is forced to cancel a sixty-date U.S. tour.

British-American reggae popsters the **Police** receive one of the highest compliments the world of black dance music can pay any white group: black New York "street-funk" band **Com-**

mon Sense's faithful cover version of "Voices inside My Head"—an album cut from the Police's *Zenyatta Mondatta* that, though never released as a single, has received much attention on the dance-club and rap-DJ circuits—enters the soul singles chart, where in seven weeks it will peak at #58.

17 The **Blues Project** reunites for a once-only concert at Bond's in New York City, bringing together original members **Al Kooper**, **Steve Katz**, **Danny Kalb**, **Andy Kulberg** and **Roy Blumenfeld**. The group was formed in 1965 by some of the prominent musicians on the Greenwich Village folk scene and soon became a pioneering force in rock experiments with jazz, blues and electronic music—experiments

that Kooper and Katz later advanced in **Blood, Sweat and Tears**.

19 **Styx**' *Paradise Theatre* goes platinum. The album is a conceptual work, a path the group will take for its next LP as well. *Paradise* makes Number One and gives the group two Top Ten hits, "The Best of Times" and "Too Much Time on My Hands."

21 New wave pop rockers **Blondie** enter the soul LPs chart with *Autoamerican,* which will peak at #7 in its twenty-five weeks on the chart; it has already risen to #7 on the pop chart. The album yields one of the first big crossover rap hits, "Rapture" (#33 R&B, Number One pop for two weeks starting March 28), and a hit cover version of the old **Paragons** reggae tune "The Tide Is High" (which hit Number One on the pop chart for one week on January 31, but which never entered the R&B singles chart).

28 Buffalo-based self-styled "punk-funk" singer/bassist **Rick James** and his **Stone City Band** enter the soul singles chart with "Give It to Me Baby," which in its twenty-five weeks on the chart will peak at Number One for five weeks starting June 13; it will also hit #40 on the pop chart. The song is from James' smash hit album *Street Songs,* which has already entered the soul LPs chart, where it will stay for fifty-seven weeks, peaking at Number One for a remarkable twenty weeks starting June 3. The album will also be on the pop LPs chart for fifty-four weeks, peaking at #3, and will give James another massive hit single in "Super Freak," which will hit #3 on the soul chart and #16 on the pop chart. ◆

WEEK ENDING MARCH 7		
U.S. #1 POP 45	"I Love a Rainy Night"	Eddie Rabbitt
U.S. #1 POP LP	*Hi Infidelity*	REO Speedwagon
U.S. #1 R&B 45	"Don't Stop the Music"	Yarbrough and Peoples
U.K. #1 POP 45	"Shaddup You Face"	Joe Dolce
U.K. #1 POP LP	*Face Value*	Phil Collins

WEEK ENDING MARCH 14		
U.S. #1 POP 45	"9 to 5"	Dolly Parton
U.S. #1 POP LP	*Hi Infidelity*	REO Speedwagon
U.S. #1 R&B 45	"Don't Stop the Music"	Yarbrough and Peoples
U.K. #1 POP 45	"Jealous Guy"	Roxy Music
U.K. #1 POP LP	*Kings of the Wild Frontier*	Adam and the Ants

WEEK ENDING MARCH 21		
U.S. #1 POP 45	"Keep On Loving You"	REO Speedwagon
U.S. #1 POP LP	*Hi Infidelity*	REO Speedwagon
U.S. #1 R&B 45	"Don't Stop the Music"	Yarbrough and Peoples
U.K. #1 POP 45	"Jealous Guy"	Roxy Music
U.K. #1 POP LP	*Kings of the Wild Frontier*	Adam and the Ants

WEEK ENDING MARCH 28		
U.S. #1 POP 45	"Rapture"	Blondie
U.S. #1 POP LP	*Hi Infidelity*	REO Speedwagon
U.S. #1 R&B 45	"Don't Stop the Music"	Yarbrough and Peoples
U.K. #1 POP 45	"This Ole House"	Shakin' Stevens
U.K. #1 POP LP	*Kings of the Wild Frontier*	Adam and the Ants

1 John Lennon's "Woman," from *Double Fantasy*, turns gold, The 45 is the third Top Ten hit from the LP.

2 Long a sensation in Canada, **April Wine** finally receive their first U.S. gold album, for their tenth LP, *The Nature of the Beast*. The LP's success is spurred by the hit single "Just between You and Me," a surprisingly soft ballad. Says **Myles Goodwyn**, leader of the hard-rocking quintet, "The beast has its gentler side too, you know."

5 Canned Heat vocalist **Bob "the Bear" Hite** dies of a heart attack in Venice, California, at the age of thirty-six. Hite had been a record-store manager before meeting **Al Wilson** in Los Angeles in the mid-Sixties and forming an embryonic, jug-band version of what would soon become one of America's hardiest blues-rock "boogie" bands. Despite near-constant personnel changes, Hite stayed with Canned Heat through their last album, 1974's *One More River to Cross*.

7 Early **Who** manager **Kit Lambert** dies after falling down a flight of stairs in his mother's London home. With his partner **Chris Stamp**, Lambert managed the Who from 1964 through 1967 and produced several of their albums, including *The Who Sell Out* and *Tommy*.

10 **Pretenders** guitarist **James Honeyman-Scott** marries **Peggy Sue Fender** in London.

11 **Van Halen** lead guitarist **Eddie Van Halen** weds actress **Valerie Bertinelli**, costar of television's "One Day at a Time," in Los Angeles.

18 British progressive-rock band **Yes** announces its breakup. During its thirteen-year career, the band became one of the world's most popular exponents of intricate, mystical, symphonic rock, despite the fact that they had only one real hit single, "Roundabout," which reached #13 on the pop chart in early 1972. But Yes truly belonged to the age of the album and side-

long, convoluted suites. Following the breakup, singer **Trevor Horn** will go on to become a successful pop producer in England with bands like **Dollar** and **ABC**; guitarist **Steve Howe** and keyboardist **Geoff Downes** will cofound progressive-rock supergroup **Asia**; and bassist **Chris Squire** and drummer **Alan White** have yet to do anything to date, though for a time there will be rumors that either White will replace the late **John Bonham** in a new version of **Led Zeppelin**, or that Squire, White and Led Zeppelin's **Jimmy Page** will form a power trio to be called **XYZ**.

20 One-time member of the **Mamas and the Papas John Phillips**, who had

been arrested for possession of cocaine by federal narcotics agents on July 30, 1980, is imprisoned in Los Angeles after pleading guilty in court to drug-possession charges. His five-year sentence will be suspended after thirty days in exchange for 250 hours worth of community service.

22 After being released from St. Paul's Hospital in Minnesota on April 17, following a month-long treatment for bleeding ulcers, **Eric Clapton** is hospitalized again in Seattle, Washington, following an auto accident in which he lacerates a shin and bruises some ribs.

23 **Johnny Cash**, **Carl Perkins** and **Jerry Lee Lewis** reunite in Stuttgart, Germany, and record what is later released in 1982 as *The Survivors*.

25 With the departure of singer/guitarist **Denny Laine** (a one-time member of the **Moody Blues** in their early days), **Paul McCartney**'s backing group, **Wings**, disbands.

27 **Ringo Starr** weds actress **Barbara Bach**, his costar in the movie *Caveman*, in London. Both **Paul McCartney** and **George Harrison** attend the ceremony. Though the *New York Post* later reported that the trio "sounded as if they'd never been apart," the three ex-**Beatles** did *not* play together. ◆

WEEK ENDING APRIL 4

U.S. #1 POP 45	"Rapture"	Blondie
U.S. #1 POP LP	*Paradise Theatre*	Styx
U.S. #1 R&B 45	"Being with You"	Smokey Robinson
U.K. #1 POP 45	"This Ole House"	Shakin' Stevens
U.K. #1 POP LP	*Kings of the Wild Frontier*	Adam and the Ants

WEEK ENDING APRIL 11

U.S. #1 POP 45	"Kiss on My List"	Daryl Hall and John Oates
U.S. #1 POP LP	*Paradise Theatre*	Styx
U.S. #1 R&B 45	"Being with You"	Smokey Robinson
U.K. #1 POP 45	"This Ole House"	Shakin' Stevens
U.K. #1 POP LP	*Kings of the Wild Frontier*	Adam and the Ants

WEEK ENDING APRIL 18

U.S. #1 POP 45	"Kiss on My List"	Daryl Hall and John Oates
U.S. #1 POP LP	*Hi-Infidelity*	REO Speedwagon
U.S. #1 R&B 45	"Being with You"	Smokey Robinson
U.K. #1 POP 45	"Making Your Mind Up"	Bucks Fizz
U.K. #1 POP LP	*Kings of the Wild Frontier*	Adam and the Ants

WEEK ENDING APRIL 25

U.S. #1 POP 45	"Kiss on My List"	Daryl Hall and John Oates
U.S. #1 POP LP	*Hi-Infidelity*	REO Speedwagon
U.S. #1 R&B 45	"Being with You"	Smokey Robinson
U.K. #1 POP 45	"Making Your Mind Up"	Bucks Fizz
U.K. #1 POP LP	*Kings of the Wild Frontier*	Adam and the Ants

8 **Loverboy**, a quintet from Vancouver that sounds an awful lot like such successful hard-rock bands as **Journey** and **Foreigner**, have a gold album with their debut. Leader **Paul Dean** is a veteran of some fourteen Canadian bands—at age thirty-five he's finally struck gold.

———

Sheena Easton, a singer from Scotland, hits gold the first time out, with "Morning Train (Nine to Five)," a Number One smash. Easton has three more before 1981 is out.

———

11 In Miami's Cedars of Lebanon Hospital, reggae star **Bob Marley** dies at age thirty-six, succumbing to a brain tumor that had ended his career in October 1980. He was in Miami to see his mother en route from Germany, where he had been undergoing cancer therapy, to his native Jamaica, where he was to receive the Order of Merit from **Prime Minister Edward Seaga**. Marley recorded his first record in 1962 and formed the **Wailers** with **Peter Tosh** and **Bunny Livingston** the following year. Through such songs as "Stir It Up," "I Shot the Sheriff," "Get Up, Stand Up," "No Woman, No Cry," "Rastaman Vibration," "Jamming" and "Could You Be Loved," Bob Marley and the Wailers probably did more than any other musicians to popularize reggae around the world. In addition, because of the strong commitment to political and social causes expressed in his music, Marley was regarded as a hero both in Jamaica and abroad. He will be given a state funeral and buried near his birthplace in St. Ann's Parish, Jamaica.

12 The **Who**'s first album without **Keith Moon**, *Face Dances,* goes gold, but is considered a disappointment, even to the band itself. The record reaches #4, but offers just one hit, "You Better You Bet" (#18).

15 **Public Image, Ltd.,** substituting for **Bow Wow Wow**, play the Ritz and incite a near riot. The group— leader **John Lydon** (a. k. a. **Rotten**), guitarist **Keith Levene** and a hired drummer—performed from behind a video screen. The 1,500 in attendance booed and threw bottles at the stage, and Lydon got angry and yelled, "You're not throwing enough!" The audience threw more, and then Levene said, "You're a silly fucking audience." Only after a dozen fans had been injured did the fifty-minute "set" come to a close. Lydon and Levene consider the show a success. A scheduled performance for the following evening is canceled.

16 **Pretenders** drummer **Martin Chambers** marries **Tracy Atkinson** in a London ceremony.

22 **Hall and Oates**' "Kiss on My List" goes gold. The song also reaches Number One, the first of three Number Ones the duo will amass in the following twelve months.

25 R&B singer **Roy Brown**, who in 1948 wrote and recorded the original version of "Good Rockin' Tonight" (later a hit for **Elvis Presley**), dies of heart failure at age fifty-five in Los Angeles. Brown had other minor R&B hits in the Fifties with "Boogie at Midnight" and "Hard Luck Blues." Such blues giants as **B. B. King** and **Bobby "Blue" Bland** have cited Brown as an influence on their singing styles. Brown was still playing frequent West Coast club dates at the time of his death.

———

Motown Records announces plans for a year-long silver-anniversary salute, starting in 1982, to mark the twenty-fifth year of association between Motown chief **Berry Gordy** and one of his label's most successful, distinguished and respected artists—**William "Smokey" Robinson**, who is currently a vice-president at the label. ◆

WEEK ENDING MAY 2

U.S. #1 POP 45	"Morning Train (Nine to Five)"	Sheena Easton
U.S. #1 POP LP	*Hi-Infidelity*	REO Speedwagon
U.S. #1 R&B 45	"Being with You"	Smokey Robinson
U.K. #1 POP 45	"Theme from *Lloyd George*"	Ennio Morricone
U.K. #1 POP LP	*Kings of the Wild Frontier*	Adam and the Ants

WEEK ENDING MAY 9

U.S. #1 POP 45	"Morning Train (Nine to Five)"	Sheena Easton
U.S. #1 POP LP	*Paradise Theatre*	Styx
U.S. #1 R&B 45	"Sukiyaki"	A Taste of Honey
U.K. #1 POP 45	"Stars on 45"	Starsound
U.K. #1 POP LP	*Kings of the Wild Frontier*	Adam and the Ants

WEEK ENDING MAY 16

U.S. #1 POP 45	"Bette Davis Eyes"	Kim Carnes
U.S. #1 POP LP	*Hi-Infidelity*	REO Speedwagon
U.S. #1 R&B 45	"A Woman Needs Love"	Ray Parker, Jr. and Raydio
U.K. #1 POP 45	"Stand and Deliver"	Adam and the Ants
U.K. #1 POP LP	*Kings of the Wild Frontier*	Adam and the Ants

WEEK ENDING MAY 23

U.S. #1 POP 45	"Bette Davis Eyes"	Kim Carnes
U.S. #1 POP LP	*Hi-Infidelity*	REO Speedwagon
U.S. #1 R&B 45	"A Woman Needs Love"	Ray Parker, Jr. and Raydio
U.K. #1 POP 45	"Stand and Deliver"	Adam and the Ants
U.K. #1 POP LP	*Kings of the Wild Frontier*	Adam and the Ants

WEEK ENDING MAY 30

U.S. #1 POP 45	"Bette Davis Eyes"	Kim Carnes
U.S. #1 POP LP	*Hi-Infidelity*	REO Speedwagon
U.S. #1 R&B 45	"What Cha' Gonna Do for Me"	Chaka Khan
U.K. #1 POP 45	"Stand and Deliver"	Adam and the Ants
U.K. #1 POP LP	*Kings of the Wild Frontier*	Adam and the Ants

3 **Phil Collins** of **Genesis** establishes himself as a major artist with *Face Value*, his first solo album. Collins enjoys two solo hits as well: "In the Air Tonight" and "I Missed Again," both of which go Top Twenty.

AC/DC have a Top Five platinum album with *Dirty Deeds Done Dirt Cheap*, even though the album was originally released in Australia in 1977 and features the late **Bon Scott**.

5 **James Brown**, **B. B. King**, **Lionel Hampton**, **Little Milton** and **Tyrone Davis** join the governor of Mississippi, other state and federal government dignitaries, and civil-rights activists **Dick Gregory** and **James Baldwin** in commemorating the death of civil-rights leader **Medgar Evers** at a three-day festival in Fayette, Mississippi, hosted by **Charles Evers, Jr.**, brother of the slain leader and mayor of Fayette. Medgar Evers was shot dead as he led a protest march in Mississippi in 1963.

12 Long regarded as just another Southern rock band, **.38 Special** finally achieves a gold album with *Wild-Eyed Southern Boys*, an album notable for its very north-of-the-border sounding music. The LP reaches #18. The group's leader is **Donnie Van Zant**, the late **Ronnie Van Zant**'s younger brother.

14 **Bruce Springsteen** headlines a No-Nukes benefit concert at the Hollywood Bowl in Los Angeles. Among the other stars performing for 17,845 fans **Jackson Browne**, **Gary "U.S." Bonds**, **Bonnie Raitt**, **Graham Nash**, **Stephen Stills**, **Nicolette Larson**, **Peter Yarrow**, **Timothy B. Schmit** and others.

20 Funk band **Cameo** enters the soul LPs chart with *Knights of the Sound Table*, which will peak at #2. It yields the #3 soul hit "Freaky Dancin'" and the #25 soul hit "I Like It."

21 **Donald Fagen** and **Walter Becker** announce the breakup of **Steely Dan**. The news is received with some bemusement in the music industry, as Steely Dan had long since ceased being an actual band; rather, for the past several years, it was simply Fagen and Becker going into a studio with some sessionmen. This bemusement, however, is generally overshadowed by disappointment that one of rock's most intelligent and sophisticated bands—and one which nevertheless remained popular—has called it a day. Fagen will go on to release a critically acclaimed solo album, *The Nightfly*, in 1982, which would yield a hit single in "I.G.Y."

26 **Steve Winwood**'s *Arc of a Diver* is awarded a platinum record. It marks quite a comeback for the ex-**Traffic** vocalist/keyboardist, who hadn't released an LP since

1977. *Arc* hits #3 and a single, "While You See a Chance," #7.

27 Veteran soul vocal group the **Commodores** retain their hit making knack, as their "Lady (You Bring Me Up)" enters the soul chart, where it will peak at #5; the song had entered the pop chart one week ago, where it would rise to #8. It is one of two smash hits from the **Commodores**' #4 R&B, #13 pop LP *In the Pocket*, which also yields the #5 R&B, #4 pop hit "Oh No."

"Showdown," a rap extravaganza twelve-inch single billed as "The **Furious Five** Meets the **Sugar Hill Gang**," enters the R&B chart, where in ten weeks it will peak at #49.

Veteran soul-funk bassist-singer **Larry Graham**—who, with **Sly and the Family Stone** and his own band **Graham Central Station** pioneered the "thumb-thwack" school of funk bass playing popularized by the likes of **Bootsy Collins** with **Funkadelic**—enters the soul chart with the title ballad of his new LP, "Just Be My Lady." In its nineteen weeks on the chart it will peak at #4. The LP will rise to #8 on the soul LPs chart.

30 **Jerry Lee Lewis**, age forty-five, is rushed to Memphis' Methodist Hospital South for an operation to patch up a two-centimeter hole in his stomach. Ten days later, he will undergo a five-hour operation for internal bleeding. Doctors will announce that Lewis has less than a fifty-percent chance of surviving the operation; **Johnny Cash** will join Lewis in a moment of silent prayer at the latter's bedside. After a few more weeks, "The Killer" will leave the hospital in fine fettle. ◆

WEEK ENDING JUNE 6

U.S. #1 POP 45	"Bette Davis Eyes"	Kim Carnes
U.S. #1 POP LP	*Hi-Infidelity*	REO Speedwagon
U.S. #1 R&B 45	"What' Cha Gonna Do for Me"	Chaka Khan
U.K. #1 POP 45	"Stand and Deliver"	Adam and the Ants
U.K. #1 POP LP	*Kings of the Wild Frontier*	Adam and the Ants

WEEK ENDING JUNE 13

U.S. #1 POP 45	"Bette Davis Eyes"	Kim Carnes
U.S. #1 POP LP	*Hi-Infidelity*	REO Speedwagon
U.S. #1 R&B 45	"Give It to Me Baby"	Rick James
U.K. #1 POP 45	"Being with You"	Smokey Robinson
U.K. #1 POP LP	*Anthem*	Toyah

WEEK ENDING JUNE 20

U.S. #1 POP 45	"Stars on 45 Medley"	Stars on 45
U.S. #1 POP LP	*Hi-Infidelity*	REO Speedwagon
U.S. #1 R&B 45	"Give It to Me Baby"	Rick James
U.K. #1 POP 45	"Being with You"	Smokey Robinson
U.K. #1 POP LP	*Present Arms*	UB40

WEEK ENDING JUNE 27

U.S. #1 POP 45	"Stars on 45 Medley"	Stars on 45
U.S. #1 POP LP	*Mistaken Identity*	Kim Carnes
U.S. #1 R&B 45	"Give It to Me Baby"	Rick James
U.K. #1 POP 45	"One Day in Your Life"	Michael Jackson
U.K. #1 POP LP	*Stars on 45*	Starsound

2 One of the strangest phenomenons of the year is the medley single, the most popular of which is "Stars on 45" by a group of Dutch studio musicians and singers. The medley contains strung-together sound-alike versions of hits like "Sugar Sugar," "Venus" and several **Beatles** songs. Because the song actually hits Number One and goes gold, other medley singles are rushed out.

Bruce Springsteen plays the first shows ever at the 21,000-seat Meadowlands Brendan Byrne Arena in New Jersey. The six shows sold out in one day. The audience was so loud that Springsteen later said: "When we got onstage, I couldn't hear the band. We felt like the **Beatles**."

3 Race riots break out in Southall, England, following a concert there by the band the **4 Skins**, sparking a week of battles between police and disaffected youth, both black and white.

On the tenth anniversary of **Jim Morrison**'s death, the three surviving members of the Doors—**Robbie Krieger**, **Ray Manzarek** and **John Densmore**—lead fans in a graveside tribute in the Paris cemetery where Morrison is buried.

4 **Willie Nelson** hosts his annual Fourth of July picnic not in Dripping Springs, Texas, where the annual bash has been held since 1973, but at Caesar's Palace in Las Vegas. And you thought he left Nashville to get away from show business.

9 The **Jacksons** kick off a thirty-six-city tour. The group grosses $5.5 million, $100,000 of which is donated to the Atlanta Children's Foundation after a show at the Omni in Atlanta, Georgia. Later in the year, Epic will release *The Jacksons Live*.

16 **Jefferson Starship** have a gold record with *Modern Times*. Although **Grace Slick** is back on board, she only makes a few vocal appearances on the record, which had been nearly finished by the time she rejoined the group. *Modern Times* goes to #26.

Folk-pop singer/songwriter **Harry Chapin** dies at age thirty-nine in a car crash in Jericho, New York. Always more popular with audiences than with critics, Chapin had hit singles with "Taxi," "W.O.L.D." and "Cat's in the Cradle." But he was also perhaps the most politically active and committed of all contemporary pop performers. It is estimated that Chapin's benefit concerts alone raised over $5 million for such organizations and charities as the Presidential Commission on World Hunger, Ralph Nader's Public Interest Research Group and Congresswatch, Consumer Action Now and the Cambodia Action Crisis Committee, of which Chapin was a member. He was also an active member in several local civic and cultural organizations near his Long Island, New York, home, and campaigned on behalf of such U.S. senators as **Patrick Leahy**, **Morris Udall**, **Frank Church**, **Gary Hart** and **Alan Cranston**. At a memorial service in one week, New York state representatives **Tom Downey** and **Ben Gilman** (a member of the Commission on World Hunger) will give eulogies, as will Vermont senator Leahy; the first Democratic Senator ever elected in Vermont, he attributed his narrow 1980 victory to Chapin's campaigning on his behalf. In Congress, nine senators and thirty congressmen paid tribute to Chapin. At the Brooklyn memorial service, it will be announced that a Harry Chapin Memorial Fund has been established, with an initial $10,000 contribution from Chapin's label, Elektra Records. There will also be a benefit concert for the fund August 17 at the Nassau Coliseum on Long Island, to be headlined by **Kenny Rogers**.

21 British unemployment, which has been on a steady rise for a few years, reaches an all-time high of 11.8 percent. This long and relentless rise in unemployment gave birth to punk rock, and is now resulting not only in more harsh, angry youth music, but also in frequent rioting, with white youths battling blacks, and both battling police. The bleak desperation of Britain's situation is mirrored in the song that moved into the Number One spot on the U.K. pop chart just three days ago: "Ghost Town" by the **Specials**.

23 **Billy Squier** receives his first gold album, at age thirty-one. A veteran of several Boston and New York bands (**Sidewinders**, **Piper**), he has a major hit with his second solo LP, *Don't Say No*.

25 Confirming the growing stature of rap music, British group the **Evasions** enter the U.S. soul chart with "Wikka Wrap"—a comic rap disc in which the rapper mimics the arch inflections of popular British TV talk-show host **Paul Wikka**. ◆

WEEK ENDING JULY 4

U.S. #1 POP 45	"Stars on 45 Medley"	Stars on 45
U.S. #1 POP LP	*Mistaken Identity*	Kim Carnes
U.S. #1 R&B 45	"Give It to Me Baby"	Rick James
U.K. #1 POP 45	"One Day in Your Life"	Michael Jackson
U.K. #1 POP LP	*Present Arms*	UB40

WEEK ENDING JULY 11

U.S. #1 POP 45	"Stars on 45 Medley"	Stars on 45
U.S. #1 POP LP	*Mistaken Identity*	Kim Carnes
U.S. #1 R&B 45	"Give It to Me Baby"	Rick James
U.K. #1 POP 45	"One Day in Your Life"	Michael Jackson
U.K. #1 POP LP	*No Sleep Till Hammersmith*	Motorhead

WEEK ENDING JULY 18

U.S. #1 POP 45	"Stars on 45 Medley"	Stars on 45
U.S. #1 POP LP	*Mistaken Identity*	Kim Carnes
U.S. #1 R&B 45	"Double Dutch Bus"	Frankie Smith
U.K. #1 POP 45	"Ghost Town"	The Specials
U.K. #1 POP LP	*No Sleep Till Hammersmith*	Motorhead

WEEK ENDING JULY 25

U.S. #1 POP 45	"The One That You Love"	Air Supply
U.S. #1 POP LP	*Long Distance Voyager*	The Moody Blues
U.S. #1 R&B 45	"Double Dutch Bus"	Frankie Smith
U.K. #1 POP 45	"Ghost Town"	The Specials
U.K. #1 POP LP	*Love Songs*	Cliff Richard

6 The Fourth International Reggae Sunsplash Festival draws 20,000 reggae fans from around the world to Jarrett Park in Montego Bay, Jamaica. The four-day event was billed as a tribute to the late **Bob Marley**, and features performances by Marley's band, the **Wailers**, fronted by his wife, **Rita**, and his four children, whose group is called the **Melody Makers**. The Wailers also play behind one of Jamaica's newest stars, **Eek-a-Mouse**. Other Reggae Sunsplash acts include **Jimmy Cliff**, **Steel Pulse**, **Gregory Isaacs** and **Third World**. Stevie Wonder makes an unannounced appearance onstage during Third World's set, bringing on **Rita Marley** to sing with him.

8 British rock band the **Pretenders**, led by transplanted Akron, Ohio, native **Chrissie Hynde**, start their second U.S. tour, an eleven-week stint, in Fort Pierce, Florida. The tour is in support of their new album, *Pretenders II*, which, in direct opposition to their smash debut LP, has been critically blasted as a weak followup.

"Don't Stop the Music," an extended reggae-funk twelve-inch single by **Bits and Pieces**—which is actually a Jamaican studio aggregate produced and arranged by legendary reggae rhythm team **Sly Dunbar** and **Robbie Shakespeare**—enters the soul chart, where it will peak at #45.

Luther Vandross—an experienced and respected soul-pop backup singer/songwriter who's worked with **Quincy Jones**, **Roberta Flack**, **David Bowie** and others in the past—kicks off his own solo career with a bang. His "Never Too Much," the title cut of his first solo album, enters the soul chart, where it will peak at Number One for two weeks starting October 24; it will also hit #33 on the pop chart. The album will hit #19 on the pop chart and will be in the soul LPs chart for thirty-seven weeks, peaking at Number One for one week starting November 14.

15 **Stevie Wonder**, **Evelyn King**, **Grover Washington, Jr.**, **Third World** and other performers draw a crowd of over 50,000 to the Rose Bowl in Pasadena, California, for the Black Family Fair, an outdoor festival of contemporary black music. Wonder presents one of his gold records to **Tami Rogoway**, whose boyfriend, **Randy Burrell**, had been slain on December 12, 1980, following a Wonder concert in Los Angeles.

"Get It Up," the debut single by the **Time**, enters the soul chart, where in nineteen weeks, it will peak at #6. If the Time's lead singer **Morris Day** looks a bit like **Prince**, and if the band's music sounds a lot like Prince's, it's for good reason: the Time, like Prince, are a part of the new Minneapolis funk-rock-fusion wave, and they will go on to open many of Prince's concerts. In fact, music-industry rumors will have it that Prince has done uncredited songwriting arranging and producing work for the Time.

18 The **Moody Blues** reconvened to record their ninth album, *Long Distance Voyager,* and have a gold hit. It is their first since 1978's *Octave,* and only their second since *Seventh Sojourn* in 1972. The band embarks on a major tour, its first in years.

20 **Bruce Springsteen and the E Street Band** perform a benefit concert for Vietnam veterans at the Los Angeles Sports Arena.

24 **John Lennon**'s killer, **Mark David Chapman**, is sentenced to a prison term of twenty years to life in a New York courtroom. Over the next few months, Chapman would claim on several occasions to have been beaten by fellow inmates, some of whom allegedly tried to kill him with items like scissors.

26 **Lee Hays**, a cofounder of seminal folk vocal group the **Weavers**, dies of a heart attack at age sixty-seven in his upstate New York home after a long battle with diabetes. Hays was bass vocalist with the Weavers and cowrote one of their biggest hits, the classic "If I Had a Hammer," with fellow Weaver **Pete Seeger**. A documentary film on the Weavers, *Wasn't That a Time!,* filmed at a 1980 Weavers reunion concert at Carnegie Hall in New York City, was released to great critical acclaim shortly before Hays' death. ♦

WEEK ENDING AUGUST 1

U.S. #1 POP 45	"Jessie's Girl"	Rick Springfield
U.S. #1 POP LP	*Long Distance Voyager*	The Moody Blues
U.S. #1 R&B 45	"Double Dutch Bus"	Frankie Smith
U.K. #1 POP 45	"Chant No. 1"	Spandau Ballet
U.K. #1 POP LP	*Love Songs*	Cliff Richard

WEEK ENDING AUGUST 8

U.S. #1 POP 45	"Jessie's Girl"	Rick Springfield
U.S. #1 POP LP	*Long Distance Voyager*	The Moody Blues
U.S. #1 R&B 45	"Double Dutch Bus"	Frankie Smith
U.K. #1 POP 45	"Green Door"	Shakin' Stevens
U.K. #1 POP LP	*Love Songs*	Cliff Richard

WEEK ENDING AUGUST 15

U.S. #1 POP 45	"Endless Love"	Diana Ross and Lionel Richie
U.S. #1 POP LP	*Precious Time*	Pat Benatar
U.S. #1 R&B 45	"I'm in Love"	Evelyn King
U.K. #1 POP 45	"Happy Birthday"	Stevie Wonder
U.K. #1 POP LP	*Love Songs*	Cliff Richard

WEEK ENDING AUGUST 22

U.S. #1 POP 45	"Endless Love"	Diana Ross and Lionel Richie
U.S. #1 POP LP	*4*	Foreigner
U.S. #1 R&B 45	"Endless Love"	Diana Ross and Lionel Richie
U.K. #1 POP 45	"Green Door"	Shakin' Stevens
U.K. #1 POP LP	*Time*	Electric Light Orchestra

WEEK ENDING AUGUST 29

U.S. #1 POP 45	"Endless Love"	Diana Ross and Lionel Richie
U.S. #1 POP LP	*4*	Foreigner
U.S. #1 R&B 45	"Endless Love"	Diana Ross and Lionel Richie
U.K. #1 POP 45	"Green Door"	Shakin' Stevens
U.K. #1 POP LP	*Time*	Electric Light Orchestra

12 Long-serving Motown soul vocal group the **Four Tops**—now recording for Casablanca Records—enter the soul LPs chart with *Tonight!*, which in twenty-three weeks on the chart will peak at #5; it also enters the pop LPs chart, where it will reach #37. It yields a smash hit single in "When She Was My Girl," which hits #11 pop and Number One soul for two weeks October 10.

14 Bluesman **Furry Lewis** dies of natural causes at age eighty-eight in his Memphis home. Immortalized in **Joni Mitchell**'s song "Furry Sings the Blues" (for which Lewis cantankerously blasted Mitchell as a lying, know-nothing charlatan), the singer, guitarist and harmonica player was born **Walter Lewis** in Greenwood, Mississippi, but spent most of his life in Memphis, working as a street sweeper by day (though he had lost one leg in a 1917 railroad accident) and a blues singer by night. He was made an honorary colonel of the state of Tennessee in 1973, and had recently appeared in two films, *W. W. and the Dixie Dance Kings* and *This Is Elvis*. One of

the first bluesmen to play slide or bottleneck guitar, Lewis was a seminal, influential figure on all of Delta blues. Among his most famous songs are "Furry's Worried Blues," "A Chicken Ain't Nothin' but a Bird," "I'm Black," "Good Looking Girl Blues" and "Billy Lyons and Stock O'Lee"—arguably the original version of the song "Stagger Lee," which was redone several times; the best-known version was Lloyd Price's.

15 Under the new ownership of **Mark Fleischmann** and **Stanley Tate**, Studio 54 reopens in New York City after sixteen dark months following the tax-evasion arrests of former owners **Steve Rubell** and **Ian Schrager**. In order to compete with Manhattan's new breed of rock-disco dance clubs, Studio 54 will offer live concerts by the likes of **James Brown**, **Bow Wow Wow** and others in upcoming months, in addition to all-night record spinning. But it will fail to regain its former status as New York's most fashionable nightspot.

18 More than ten years after the death of **Jim Morrison**, **Doors**-mania is

greater than ever. *Greatest Hits* goes platinum on this date.

19 **Paul Simon** and **Art Garfunkel** perform before 400,000 fans in New York's Central Park. The twenty-two song set, which opened with "Mrs. Robinson," was recorded and released as *The Concert in Central Park* and filmed as a Home Box Office cable television special.

22 *The Catherine Wheel*, an hour-long ballet choreographed by **Twyla Tharp** to the music of **David Byrne**, premieres at Broadway's Broadhurst Theater in New York City. Tharp's repertoire already includes shorter dances set to songs by **Chuck**

Berry, the **Beach Boys**, **Bruce Springsteen** and **Supertramp**, and she was the choreographer of the dance sequences in **Milos Foreman**'s movie version of the rock musical *Hair*. But this is the first time she has commissioned a pop musician to write music specifically for her. She offered Byrne the commission after a year of using records by Byrne's group, **Talking Heads**, as exercise music for her dance company. After a month on Broadway and performances around North America and in Europe, *The Catherine Wheel* will be presented on television by PBS in March of 1983.

25 The **Rolling Stones** embark on another U.S. tour, performing in Philadelphia. This tour will be filmed by director **Hal Ashby** for the 1983 concert documentary *Let's Spend the Night Together,* and one show in Hampton, Virginia, will be simulcast live via pay-per-view cable transmission.

26 **Prince** finally finds as much success with audiences as with critics, as the title cut of his new LP, *Controversy* (in which he acknowledges and takes on all those who wonder if, as he sings, "I'm black or white, straight or gay," and turns in a bawdy version of the Lord's Prayer on the fade), enters the soul chart. It will peak there at #3, and the album will exactly duplicate the single's chart performance. The single and album will hit #70 and #21 on the pop charts, respectively. ◆

WEEK ENDING SEPTEMBER 5

U.S. #1 POP 45	"Endless Love"	Diana Ross and Lionel Richie
U.S. #1 POP LP	*Bella Donna*	Stevie Nicks
U.S. #1 R&B 45	"Endless Love"	Diana Ross and Lionel Richie
U.K. #1 POP 45	"Japanese Boy"	Aneka
U.K. #1 POP LP	*Time*	Electric Light Orchestra

WEEK ENDING SEPTEMBER 12

U.S. #1 POP 45	"Endless Love"	Diana Ross and Lionel Richie
U.S. #1 POP LP	*Escape*	Journey
U.S. #1 R&B 45	"Endless Love"	Diana Ross and Lionel Richie
U.K. #1 POP 45	"Tainted Love"	Soft Cell
U.K. #1 POP LP	*Time*	Electric Light Orchestra

WEEK ENDING SEPTEMBER 19

U.S. #1 POP 45	"Endless Love"	Diana Ross and Lionel Richie
U.S. #1 POP LP	*Tattoo You*	The Rolling Stones
U.S. #1 R&B 45	"Endless Love"	Diana Ross and Lionel Richie
U.K. #1 POP 45	"Prince Charming"	Adam and the Ants
U.K. #1 POP LP	*Dead Ringer*	Meat Loaf

WEEK ENDING SEPTEMBER 26

U.S. #1 POP 45	"Endless Love"	Diana Ross and Lionel Richie
U.S. #1 POP LP	*Tattoo You*	The Rolling Stones
U.S. #1 R&B 45	"Endless Love"	Diana Ross and Lionel Richie
U.K. #1 POP 45	"Prince Charming"	Adam and the Ants
U.K. #1 POP LP	*Dead Ringer*	Meat Loaf

1 After playing about three-quarters of their scheduled eleven-week U.S. tour, the **Pretenders** are forced to cancel the remainder of their American dates today after drummer **Martin Chambers**

severs tendons and arteries in his hand while trying to open, and breaking, a window, following a Philadelphia concert.

2 The fifth annual Bread and Roses Festival begins its three-day run at the Greek Theater in Berkeley, California, featuring performances by **Paul Simon**, **Joan Baez**, **Ann** and **Nancy Wilson** of **Heart** and one-time **Incredible String Band** leader **Robin Williamson**. The shows fail to sell out and produce no profits to be given to the Bread and Roses prisoners-aid group, which is run by Baez' sister **Mimi Fariña**.

3 **Kool and the Gang** enter the soul chart with "Take My Heart," which will peak at Number One for one week on November 21; it will also hit #17 pop. The song is from their album *Something Special*, which in two weeks will enter the soul and pop LPs charts; it will become a #12 pop LP, and in thirty-two weeks on the soul LPs chart, will peak at Number One for one week on November 21.

10 **Earth, Wind and Fire**'s "Let's Groove" enters the soul chart, where it will stay for twenty-two weeks, peaking at Number One for eleven weeks starting November 28. The album from which it comes, *Raise!*, will enter the soul LPs chart next month, and will hit Number One for ten weeks starting November 28. "Let's Groove," which last week entered the pop chart, will become a pop #3, and *Raise!* will become a #5 pop LP.

14 British funk band **Central Line** enters the U.S. soul chart with "Walking into Sunshine" (not to be confused with British reggae-funkster **Eddy Grant**'s "Walking on Sunshine"), which in twenty weeks will peak at #14.

16 **Bob Dylan** begins his Shot of Love tour with

a concert at the Milwaukee Auditorium. After generating mostly negative reactions to his Christian proselytizing on his last American tour in 1979, this time Dylan restricts his preaching to his songs—a mix of pre-rebirth and post-rebirth material.

19 Though it yielded only one minor hit single in "Backfired," *Koo Koo*—the solo album by **Blondie**'s **Deborah Harry**, produced and cowritten by **Chic**'s **Nile Rodgers** and **Bernard Edwards**—goes gold today.

24 **Booker T.**—the same **Booker T. Jones** who led the immortal Memphis soul-instrumental combo the **MG's** in the Sixties—begins a comeback, as his first record since the early Seventies, "I Want You," enters the soul chart. In fourteen weeks there, it will peak at #35. One month later, his LP of the same name will enter the soul LPs chart, where in seven weeks it will peak at #49.

30 **Fun Boy Three**—consisting of ex-**Specials** **Terry Hall**, **Neville Staples** and **Lynval Golding**—release their first record, the single "The Lunatics Have Taken Over the Asylum." It will become a chart hit in Britain, but in the U.S., will find success only in rock-dance clubs and on college radio stations.

31 **Peabo Bryson**'s "Let the Feeling Flow" enters the soul chart, where in its twenty chart weeks, it will peak at #6. ◆

WEEK ENDING OCTOBER 3

U.S. #1 POP 45	"Endless Love"	Diana Ross and Lionel Richie
U.S. #1 POP LP	*Tattoo You*	The Rolling Stones
U.S. #1 R&B 45	"Endless Love"	Diana Ross and Lionel Richie
U.K. #1 POP 45	"Prince Charming"	Adam and the Ants
U.K. #1 POP LP	*Abacab*	Genesis

WEEK ENDING OCTOBER 10

U.S. #1 POP 45	"Endless Love"	Diana Ross and Lionel Richie
U.S. #1 POP LP	*Tattoo You*	The Rolling Stones
U.S. #1 R&B 45	"When She Was My Girl"	The Four Tops
U.K. #1 POP 45	"Prince Charming"	Adam and the Ants
U.K. #1 POP LP	*Dead Ringer*	Meat Loaf

WEEK ENDING OCTOBER 17

U.S. #1 POP 45	"Arthur's Theme (Best That You Can Do)"	Christopher Cross
U.S. #1 POP LP	*Tattoo You*	The Rolling Stones
U.S. #1 R&B 45	"When She Was My Girl"	The Four Tops
U.K. #1 POP 45	"Prince Charming"	Adam and the Ants
U.K. #1 POP LP	*Ghost in the Machine*	The Police

WEEK ENDING OCTOBER 24

U.S. #1 POP 45	"Arthur's Theme (Best That You Can Do)"	Christopher Cross
U.S. #1 POP LP	*Tattoo You*	The Rolling Stones
U.S. #1 R&B 45	"Never Too Much"	Luther Vandross
U.K. #1 POP 45	"It's My Party"	D. Stewart and B. Gaskin
U.K. #1 POP LP	*Ghost in the Machine*	The Police

WEEK ENDING OCTOBER 31

U.S. #1 POP 45	"Arthur's Theme (Best That You Can Do)"	Christopher Cross
U.S. #1 POP LP	*Tattoo You*	The Rolling Stones
U.S. #1 R&B 45	"Never Too Much"	Luther Vandross
U.K. #1 POP 45	"It's My Party"	D. Stewart and B. Gaskin
U.K. #1 POP LP	*Ghost in the Machine*	The Police

2 British ska rock band the **Specials** split up, citing the inevitable musical differences. In their few years of existence, the racially integrated, politically conscious band had had minor hit singles with "Gangsters," "A Message to You Rudy" and the band's funereal swan song, "Ghost Town." The Specials also became a favorite of rock critics. Following the breakup, singers **Terry Hall** and **Neville Staples** and guitarist **Lynval Golding** will form **Fun Boy Three**, who will release *FB3* in 1982 and *Waiting* in 1983 and who will have a minor hit single in a cover version of the swing-era standard "It Ain't What You Do (It's the Way That You Do It)" in 1982; and guitarist **Roddy Radiation** will form the **Tearjerkers**, from whom nothing has yet been heard.

4 **Daryl Hall and John Oates'** *Private Eyes* is certified both gold and platinum. The album, now peaking at #5 on the pop LPs chart, contains two Number One pop singles, "Private Eyes" (which will top the pop chart for two weeks starting in three days)

and "I Can't Go for That (No Can Do)," which will hit Number One on both the pop and soul charts—a rare achievement for white artists these days—early in 1982.

Bob Seger and the Silver Bullet Band earn another gold record—and a platinum one—for *Nine Tonight,* on its way to peaking at #3 on the pop LPs chart. It contains two hit singles: the #5 "Tryin' to Live My Life without You" and the #48 "Feel Like a Number."

7 In an unusual example of black-white cross-cultural exchange in an age of rampant musical fragmentation and audience segmentation, German robotic-synthesizer band **Kraftwerk** enter the soul chart with "Numbers," which will peak at #22 in fifteen charting weeks—and will never enter the pop chart. It is from their album *Computer World,* which has already risen to #32 on the soul LPs chart—and which will also fail to make the pop LPs chart. Kraftwerk's computerized, rhythm-machine-dominated sound will prove to be enormously influential on an

important school of post-rap, techno-funk music, the best example of which will be the 1982 hit "Planet Rock" by Bronx-based rap crew **Afrika Bambaataa and the Soul Sonic Force.** In fact, Bambaataa actually uses some rhythm patterns and synthesizer melodies from earlier Kraftwerk songs like "Trans-Europe Express" in "Planet Rock."

11 **Rod Stewart** kicks off his first North American tour in three years in Greensboro, North Carolina. Billed "Le Grand Tour of America and Canada—Worth Leaving Home For," the tour promotes his latest album, *Tonight I'm Yours,* and builds on the album's effort to present Stew-

art as a rock & roller again after six or seven years as a Hollywood celeb.

18 Heavy-metal heroes **Van Halen** earn a platinum disc for *Fair Warning,* which despite its lack of hit singles rose to #5 on the pop LPs chart.

20 The LP *The Many Facets of Roger* by **Roger Troutman,** critically acclaimed leader of funk band **Zapp,** is certified gold. The album, on the soul chart for thirty-two weeks, hit Number One for one week on November 7, and contains Troutman's Number One soul hit "I Heard It through the Grapevine (Part I)" (Number One soul for two weeks starting November 7; it also hit #79 pop) and the #24 soul "Do It Roger."

22 **Rolling Stones Mick Jagger, Keith Richards** and **Ronnie Wood** jam with blues giants **Muddy Waters** (whose "Rollin' Stone" gave the Stones their name) and **Buddy Guy** at Chicago's Checker Board Lounge. The jam session is filmed, though the footage has yet to be released in any form.

27 The British Phonographic Industry—with the endorsement of rock stars like **Elton John, Gary Numan, Cliff Richard, 10cc** and the **Boomtown Rats**—places advertisements in the British press claiming that "Home taping is wiping out music."

The times, they appear to be a-changin': a Thanksgiving concert by the **Grateful Dead** and the **Allman Brothers Band** scheduled at the Tangerine Bowl in Orlando, Florida, is canceled today because only 10,000 of 60,000 tickets have been sold; when the same two bands played together eight years ago at Watkins Glen, New York, they drew over 600,000. ◆

WEEK ENDING NOVEMBER 7

U.S. #1 POP 45	"Private Eyes"	Daryl Hall and John Oates
U.S. #1 POP LP	*Tattoo You*	The Rolling Stones
U.S. #1 R&B 45	"I Heard It through the Grapevine (Part I)"	Roger
U.K. #1 POP 45	"Happy Birthday"	Altered Images
U.K. #1 POP LP	*Dare*	The Human League

WEEK ENDING NOVEMBER 14

U.S. #1 POP 45	"Private Eyes"	Daryl Hall and John Oates
U.S. #1 POP LP	*Tattoo You*	The Rolling Stones
U.S. #1 R&B 45	"I Heard It through the Grapevine (Part I)"	Roger
U.K. #1 POP 45	"Every Little Thing She Does Is Magic"	The Police
U.K. #1 POP LP	*Dare*	The Human League

WEEK ENDING NOVEMBER 21

U.S. #1 POP 45	"Physical"	Olivia Newton-John
U.S. #1 POP LP	*4*	Foreigner
U.S. #1 R&B 45	"Take My Heart"	Kool and the Gang
U.K. #1 POP 45	"Every Little Thing She Does Is Magic"	The Police
U.K. #1 POP LP	*Prince Charming*	Adam and the Ants

WEEK ENDING NOVEMBER 28

U.S. #1 POP 45	"Physical"	Olivia Newton-John
U.S. #1 POP LP	*4*	Foreigner
U.S. #1 R&B 45	"Let's Groove"	Earth, Wind and Fire
U.K. #1 POP 45	"Under Pressure"	Queen and David Bowie
U.K. #1 POP LP	*Prince Charming*	Adam and the Ants

8 A letter carrying this post date is printed on the last page of *Rolling Stone*'s January 21, 1982 issue. The date is, of course, the first anniversary of the murder of **John Lennon**. The letter, signed "Love, **Yoko**," begins: "I think of John's death as a war casualty—it is the war between the sane and the insane." It goes on to ask for contributions to John and Yoko's Spirit Foundation, and details where past Spirit Foundation contributions have gone.

9 **Sonny Til**, lead singer of the **Orioles**, dies of a heart attack at age fifty-six in Washington, D.C. Born **Earlington Tilghman**, he formed a vocal quartet named the **Vibra-Naires** in Baltimore after World War II. After an appearance on **Arthur Godfrey**'s "Talent Show" in 1947, the Vibra-Naires were signed to Natural Records (later Jubilee), changing their name to the Orioles. On Jubilee, the group issued a half-dozen R&B Top Ten singles—mostly sentimental love songs—culminating in "Crying in the Chapel" in 1953. Til continued to lead the Orioles through changing lineups into the mid-Seventies.

18 An estimated 35 million people around the world watch **Rod Stewart**'s satellite-televised concert at the Los Angeles Forum. The concert features guest appearances by **Kim Carnes**, who sings "Tonight's the Night" with Stewart, and **Tina Turner**, who duets on "Hot Legs," "Stay with Me" and "Get Back." The broadcast is the first of its kind since **Elvis Presley**'s 1973 satellite-televised "Aloha from Hawaii," and is directed by **Steve Binder**, who also directed Presley's 1968 television special.

19 The **Rolling Stones** play the last show of their 1981 U.S. tour in Hampton, Virginia. This show was

televised via closed-circuit cable and seen by thousands across the country.

22 Sotheby's in London holds a rock & roll auction. Although the majority of items are eventually sold for far more than was expected—an enameled Abbey Road street sign, $600; an autographed program from the **Beatles**' Royal Command Performance, $2,000; a small self-portrait by **John Lennon**, $15,000; a 1956 letter from **Buddy Holly**, $1,850—other items prove disappointing. A jacket that once was worn by **Tom Jones** only fetches $12.

25 The **J. Geils Band** play a Christmas concert for the inmates of Norfolk Correctional Center near Boston, Massachusetts—the Geils Band's hometown. At the end of the show, Geils lead singer **Peter Wolf** tells the audience, "We wanna be the first to buy you all a free drink on the outside!"

27 **Hoagland Howard "Hoagy" Carmichael**, pianist, vocalist and songwriter, as well as a great raconteur of the early days of jazz and Tin

Pan Alley, dies of natural causes at age eighty-two in his Rancho Mirage, California, home. Carmichael wrote such immortal standards as "Stardust," "Lazy River," "Rocking Chair" and "Georgia on My Mind"—the latter became **Ray Charles**' first Number One hit single in 1960.

28 Warner/Elektra/Asylum, following the lead set by RCA on November 7, raises its list price for 45 rpm discs to $1.99.

30 The **J. Geils Band** enjoy the biggest LP of their career with *Freeze-Frame*, which turns gold on this date. The LP will go on to Number One early in 1982.

31 **Elvis Costello and the Attractions** play the first concert of their three-city mini tour at New York City's Palladium. The first half of the concert is devoted to the material from Costello's country music album, *Almost Blue*; after an intermission, Costello (wearing a tuxedo) and his band return to play older songs, concluding the concert after three and a half hours onstage. His pleasant manner, outgoing stage delivery and lengthy show indicate that Britain's angriest young man is not angry anymore. From New York, the tour will travel to Nashville and Los Angeles. ◆

WEEK ENDING DECEMBER 5

U.S. #1 POP 45	"Physical"	Olivia Newton-John
U.S. #1 POP LP	4	Foreigner
U.S. #1 R&B 45	"Let's Groove"	Earth, Wind and Fire
U.K. #1 POP 45	"Under Pressure"	Queen and David Bowie
U.K. #1 POP LP	Queen Greatest Hits	Queen

WEEK ENDING DECEMBER 12

U.S. #1 POP 45	"Physical"	Olivia Newton-John
U.S. #1 POP LP	4	Foreigner
U.S. #1 R&B 45	"Let's Groove"	Earth, Wind and Fire
U.K. #1 POP 45	"Begin the Beguine"	Julio Iglesias
U.K. #1 POP LP	Chart Hits '81	various artists

WEEK ENDING DECEMBER 19

U.S. #1 POP 45	"Physical"	Olivia Newton-John
U.S. #1 POP LP	4	Foreigner
U.S. #1 R&B 45	"Let's Groove"	Earth, Wind and Fire
U.K. #1 POP 45	"Don't You Want Me"	The Human League
U.K. #1 POP LP	Dare	The Human League

WEEK ENDING DECEMBER 26

U.S. #1 POP 45	"Physical"	Olivia Newton-John
U.S. #1 POP LP	For Those about to Rock, We Salute You	AC/DC
U.S. #1 R&B 45	"Let's Groove"	Earth, Wind and Fire
U.K. #1 POP 45	"Don't You Want Me"	The Human League
U.K. #1 POP LP	Dare	The Human League

1982

*I*n many ways, 1982 was a year of fruition—a year in which some things long a-brewing finally bubbled to the surface of the pop world.

There was electropop, or synth-rock, or whatever one might call it, which became so big in England that the London Musicians Union even proposed banning synthesizers and rhythm machines from recording sessions. Early in the year, there was the resounding success of British synth-duo Soft Cell with "Tainted Love"; as the year progressed, there came the Human League with an even bigger smash, "Don't You Want Me," Depeche Mode with "I Just Can't Get Enough" and Yaz with "Situation." Even Pete Shelley, one-time leader of defunct punk-pop band the Buzzcocks, became a one-man electronic band with his rock-dance-club hit "Homosapien."

Just as intriguing was the effect of computer circuitry on black music—remember Kraftwerk's unlikely success in the black charts last year? This year, Bronx rapping crew Afrika Bambaattaa and the Soul Sonic Force reworked and rapped over some Kraftwerkian synth and rhythm-machine riffs for one of the most influential hits of the year, "Planet Rock," which went gold. The new electronic style even affected established, slick black pop; witness Marvin Gaye's comeback late in the year with the hit album *Midnight Love* and the single "Sexual Healing," which Gaye played almost entirely himself on synths and sequencers.

The synth approach also inflected Grandmaster Flash and the Furious Five's hit "The Message"—an epochal disc, as it was the first record to give rap, which had previously been all about exhortations to party, a hard-hitting social conscience. In related news, the Clash—rock's most politically conscientious band, according to most observers—finally aligned themselves with rap and its subculture, recording *Combat Rock* and touring with Bronx graffiti artist Futura 2000. The album's single "Rock the Casbah" was a street-funk-style seriocomic protest against the regime of Iran's Ayatollah Khomeini. It did surprisingly well on the pop chart, but its harder-funk disco remix, "Mustapha Dance," did even better, bulleting up the black chart and getting heavy play in rock-dance clubs. Its success helped make *Combat Rock* the Clash's first platinum LP. Political-protest-with-a-beat was back in style and back on top.

Then there was the continued rise of rock video. There were MTV, USA Cable Network's weekend "Night Flight" shows and a spate of other more localized programs around the country devoted to televised exposure of rock and related music—not to mention most rock dance clubs and many concert clubs being outfitted with video screens. But the big news was MTV, which "broke" such acts as Men at Work and the Stray Cats—phenomenally commercial acts that were getting regular MTV exposure long before they were being played on the radio all the time. Rock video was beginning to make dollars and sense to the industry. It had arrived.

Meanwhile, the emergence and immediate popularity of Asia—four British progressive-rock stars forming the first Eighties supergroup—conclusively indicated that classic classical rock had given up and joined forces with the tighter strictures and structures of the AOR pomp rock that progressive rock had helped spawn. Musicians who a decade before had been heroes to the white rock audience and villains to the rock critics were playing out the same roles again in a different style, for a new audience. However sterile and prefabricated Asia's music may have sounded, Asia had adapted to the times. And by this time, that—as much as, if not more so than, putting protest-with-a-beat on top—was what rock was all about.

Finally, in the wake of pan-African infusions over the past few years by the likes of Talking Heads, Bow Wow Wow, Adam and the Ants, Peter Gabriel and others, 1982 saw the unexpected emergence of genuine African pop, as Island Records' Mango subsidiary released the first American album by Nigerian juju-music star King Sunny Adé. Predictably, the album was lionized by critics but had only moderate sales. But when, in early 1983, it would be followed by a successful American tour for Adé and his eighteen-strong African Beats, it would not only seem an encouraging harbinger of further cross-cultural pollination, but would revive the hopes that some had buried last year with the untimely death of reggae champion Bob Marley. That is, the hope that music could be international in both sound and view.

6 Ex-**Specials** guitarist **Lynval Golding** is attacked and stabbed in Coventry, England, by a group of white racists. He sustains neck wounds—one just a fraction of an inch from his jugular vein. The year before, Golding was the victim of a similar attack in London, after which he wrote "Why" for the Specials' *Ghost Town* EP.

7 *Hooked on Classics*, using the extended-medley format made popular by "Stars on 45," sets popular classical-music themes from the eighteenth, nineteenth and early twentieth centuries to a relentless disco beat and garners a platinum disc for **Britain's Royal Philharmonic Orchestra**. Over the next year, more volumes of *Hooked on Classics*, as well as related offspring like *Hooked on Broadway* and *Hooked on Swing*, will be released.

16 The **Tom Tom Club**, an informal studio group led by **Chris Frantz** and **Tina Weymouth**—**Talking Heads**' husband-and-wife rhythm section—hits Number One on the disco chart with "Genius of Love," which will soon reach #2 on the R&B chart, giving the Tom Tom Club a bigger hit than any single by the Talking Heads. The impact made by this single will become more apparent when its synthesizer riff is used as a basis for a number of rap songs, most notably **Grandmaster Flash and the Furious Five**'s "It's Nasty (Genius of Love)."

Earth, Wind and Fire's "Let's Groove" becomes the longest-running R&B Number One single in the past ten years, having held that position now for eight weeks. **Al Green**'s "Let's Stay Together" was Number One for nine weeks in 1972, then tying a record set by the Four Tops' "I Can't Help Myself" in 1965. The only other singles to log eight weeks at the top of the R&B chart were **James Brown**'s "Papa's Got a Brand New Bag" in 1965, the **Temptations**' "Ain't Too Proud to Beg" in 1966 and **Aretha Franklin**'s hit cover of **Otis Redding**'s "Respect" in 1967.

17 **Tommy Tucker**, author of "Hi Heel Sneakers" and other R&B hits, dies in New York City of carbon tetrachloride poisoning sustained while he was finishing floors in his home. He was forty-eight years old.

18 Los Angeles mayor **Tom Bradley** declares today "Bob and Doug McKenzie Day" in honor of the Canadian characters from the television comedy program "SCTV." Back-bacon sandwiches and Molson Ale are served at the celebration.

21 Blues guitar giant **B. B. King** donates his entire record collection—including some 7,000 rare and critically acclaimed blues records that King spun on the air when he was a Mississippi and Tennessee disc jockey in the Forties—to the University of Mississippi's Center for the Study of Southern Culture.

25 **Johnny Cash**'s country-rock singing daughter **Rosanne** and her country-rock singer/songwriter husband **Rodney Crowell** have a daughter, Chelsea Jane.

28 **Jackson Browne** and his second wife, **Lynne Sweeney**, have their first child, **Ryan Daniel Browne**.

30 **Hall and Oates**' "I Can't Go for That (No Can Do)" hits Number One on the pop chart and the R&B chart simultaneously, one week after hitting Number One on the disco chart. It is the fourth single by a white act to reach the top of the R&B chart since 1965.

Texas blues giant **Sam "Lightnin'" Hopkins** dies at age seventy in Centerville, Texas, of cancer. One of the last great exponents of Texas blues, Hopkins was very influential as both an acoustic and electric guitarist, modernizing the legacy of seminal Texas bluesman **Blind Lemon Jefferson**. **Jimi Hendrix** cited Hopkins' influence, and Hopkins' talking-blues vocal style influenced **Bob Dylan**, among others. His best-known songs include "Big Mama Jump," "Bald Headed Woman," "Blues Is a Feeling" and "Short Haired Woman." In the summer of 1981, he had undergone surgery for cancer of the esophagus. He gave his last performance at Trax in New York City on November 9, 1981. ◆

WEEK ENDING JANUARY 2

U.S. #1 POP 45	"Physical"	Olivia Newton-John
U.S. #1 POP LP	*For Those about to Rock, We Salute You*	AC/DC
U.S. #1 R&B 45	"Let's Groove"	Earth, Wind and Fire
U.K. #1 POP 45	"One of Us"	Abba
U.K. #1 POP LP	*The Visitors*	Abba

WEEK ENDING JANUARY 9

U.S. #1 POP 45	"Physical"	Olivia Newton-John
U.S. #1 POP LP	*For Those about to Rock, We Salute You*	AC/DC
U.S. #1 R&B 45	"Let's Groove"	Earth, Wind and Fire
U.K. #1 POP 45	"Don't You Want Me"	The Human League
U.K. #1 POP LP	*Dare*	The Human League

WEEK ENDING JANUARY 16

U.S. #1 POP 45	"Physical"	Olivia Newton-John
U.S. #1 POP LP	*4*	Foreigner
U.S. #1 R&B 45	"Let's Groove"	Earth, Wind and Fire
U.K. #1 POP 45	"Land of Make Believe"	Bucks Fizz
U.K. #1 POP LP	*Dare*	The Human League

WEEK ENDING JANUARY 23

U.S. #1 POP 45	"Physical"	Olivia Newton-John
U.S. #1 POP LP	*4*	Foreigner
U.S. #1 R&B 45	"Turn Your Love Around"	George Benson
U.K. #1 POP 45	"Land of Make Believe"	Bucks Fizz
U.K. #1 POP LP	*Dare*	The Human League

WEEK ENDING JANUARY 30

U.S. #1 POP 45	"I Can't Go for That (No Can Do)"	Daryl Hall and John Oates
U.S. #1 POP LP	*4*	Foreigner
U.S. #1 R&B 45	"I Can't Go for That (No Can Do)"	Daryl Hall and John Oates
U.K. #1 POP 45	"The Model/Computer Love"	Kraftwerk
U.K. #1 POP LP	*Dare*	The Human League

3 The City of Memphis declares this day **Bar-Kays** Day in honor of the band that began as **Otis Redding**'s backing band, survived the plane crash that killed Redding and three members of the band, and went on to make such hits as "Soul Finger," "Shake Your Rump to the Funk," "Too Hot to Stop," "Move Your Boogie Body" and "Boogie Body Land."

4 **Alex Harvey**, Scottish-born leader of mid-Seventies cult band **Sensational Alex Harvey Band** (whose best-known records include *Vambo Rools* and *Tomorrow Belongs to Me*) dies of a heart attack at age forty-six in Belgium. His brother, **Stone the Crows** guitarist **Les Harvey**, had been electrocuted to death onstage in 1972.

6 **Van Halen**'s remake of **Roy Orbison**'s 1964 chart topper, "Oh, Pretty Woman," enters the Hot 100, where it will peak at #12, making it the California heavy-metal band's biggest hit single to date.

Joan Jett's "I Love Rock 'n' Roll" enters the pop chart at #63.

Produced by former bubble-gum producers **Ritchie Cordell** and Jett's current manager, **Kenny Laguna**, the song will catapult the ex-**Runaway** to the top of the chart by late March.

13 On this day, **Pink Floyd**'s *The Dark Side of the Moon* becomes the longest-running rock LP on the *Billboard* chart, finishing up its 402nd week. The two LPs that have charted longer are **Johnny Mathis**' *Greatest Hits* (490 weeks) and the *My Fair Lady* original cast recording (480 weeks).

A 300-pound marble slab bearing an inscription by **Charlie Daniels** is stolen from the grave site of late **Lynyrd Skynyrd** singer **Ronnie Van Zant** in an Orange Park, Florida, cemetery. Police will find the slab two weeks later in a nearly dried-up river bed.

17 Jazz great **Thelonious Sphere Monk**, one of the most eccentric, original, innovative and influential pianists the music has ever produced, dies after a long illness at age

sixty-four in Englewood, New Jersey. Among Monk's most famous compositions are "Epistrophy," "Round Midnight," "Well You Needn't," "Brilliant Corners," "Criss Cross" and "Straight, No Chaser."

Today—the twenty-ninth anniversary of talk show "The Joe Franklin Show" being on the air in New York City—the **J. Geils Band** make an appearance on Franklin's show to celebrate their Number One single "Centerfold" and Number One LP *Freeze-Frame*. During the course of the show, the band build a human pyramid and splash each other with paint—as they had done in the promotional video for "Freeze-Frame."

20 The **Jam**'s "A Town Called Malice" enters the U.K. singles chart at Number One. Like many of the group's big British hits, it will not even appear on the U.S. chart despite heavy promotion of the song's video on MTV.

Nine years after **Gram Parson**'s death, Warner Bros. announces it will be releasing two singles—"Return of the Grievous Angel" and "Hearts on Fire"—from his 1973 album (his last) *Grievous Angel*.

Hard-rock chanteuse **Pat Benatar** and her guitarist, **Neil Geraldo**, are married on the Hawaiian island of Maui. It is Benatar's second marriage.

21 Legendary rock & roll disc jockey **Murray "The K" Kaufman**, known as "The Fifth Beatle" in the mid-Sixties, dies in Los Angeles at age sixty of cancer. With WMCA and WNEW in New York, Kaufman was one of the first and best-known of the "personality" disc jockeys.

24 The 1981 Grammy Award winners are announced. **Kim Carnes** wins Record of the Year and Song of the Year with "Bette Davis Eyes," while **John Lennon** and **Yoko Ono** win Album of the Year with *Double Fantasy*. **Sheena Easton** is named Best New Artist and **Quincy Jones** Producer of the Year. **Michael Nesmith** is the first recipient of the new award for Video of the Year, won with his "Michael Nesmith in Elephant Parts." Other Grammy Awards go to **Lena Horne**, **Al Jarreau**, the **Manhattan Transfer**, **Pat Benatar**, **Rick Springfield**, the **Police**, **Aretha Franklin**, **James Ingram**, **David Sanborn**, **Grover Washington, Jr.**, **Dolly Parton**, **Ronnie Milsap**, the **Oak Ridge Boys**, **Chet Atkins**, **André Crouch**, **Al Green**, **B. J. Thomas**, **B. B. King** and **Richard Pryor**. ♦

WEEK ENDING FEBRUARY 6

U.S. #1 POP 45	"Centerfold"	The J. Geils Band
U.S. #1 POP LP	*Freeze-Frame*	The J. Geils Band
U.S. #1 R&B 45	"Call Me"	Skyy
U.K. #1 POP 45	"The Model/Computer Love"	Kraftwerk
U.K. #1 POP LP	*Love Songs*	Barbra Streisand

WEEK ENDING FEBRUARY 13

U.S. #1 POP 45	"Centerfold"	The J. Geils Band
U.S. #1 POP LP	*Freeze-Frame*	The J. Geils Band
U.S. #1 R&B 45	"Call Me"	Skyy
U.K. #1 POP 45	"The Model/Computer Love"	Kraftwerk
U.K. #1 POP LP	*Dare*	The Human League

WEEK ENDING FEBRUARY 20

U.S. #1 POP 45	"Centerfold"	The J. Geils Band
U.S. #1 POP LP	*Freeze-Frame*	The J. Geils Band
U.S. #1 R&B 45	"That Girl"	Stevie Wonder
U.K. #1 POP 45	"A Town Called Malice"	The Jam
U.K. #1 POP LP	*Dare*	The Human League

WEEK ENDING FEBRUARY 27

U.S. #1 POP 45	"Centerfold"	The J. Geils Band
U.S. #1 POP LP	*Freeze-Frame*	The J. Geils Band
U.S. #1 R&B 45	"That Girl"	Stevie Wonder
U.K. #1 POP 45	"A Town Called Malice"	The Jam
U.K. #1 POP LP	*Love Songs*	Barbra Streisand

1 Swan Song Records releases the soundtrack album of the film *Death Wish II*, written and produced by **Jimmy Page** of **Led Zeppelin**. It is Page's first solo LP.

3 The re-formed **Mamas and the Papas**—with original members **John Phillips** and **Denny Doherty** joined by Phillips' actress daughter **MacKenzie** and **Spanky McFarlane** of Sixties folk-pop group **Spanky and Our Gang** ("Sunday Morning," "I'd Like to Get to Know You")—play the first show of their brief reunion tour at New York's Other End club. Though original Mama **Cass Elliot** has been dead for nearly ten years, they do *not* change the lyric to their old hit "Creeque Alley" that goes, "No one's getting fat except Mama Cass."

4 *Rolling Stone* reports that **Frank Zappa**'s son **Dweezil** and daughter **Moon Unit** (who will soon have a big hit with "Valley Girl") have formed a band called **Fred Zeppelin**. Their first single will be called "My Mother Is a Space Cadet." No word on the doings of Zappa's other children, **Ahmet Rodin** and **Diva**.

5 Comedian and **Blues Brother John Belushi** dies of a drug overdose at age thirty-three in the Chateau Marmont Hotel, Los Angeles, where he was working on a new movie with longtime cohort, friend and fellow ex-"Saturday Night Live" star and Blues Brother **Dan Aykroyd**. Belushi's vulgar, dangerous and physical sense of humor brought comedy closer to rock & roll than perhaps any other comedian ever had.

6 An item in *Billboard* mentions that **Dick Clark** has donated the podium he stood behind on the original "American Bandstand" to the national museum at the Smithsonian.

The **Go-Go's** debut LP, *Beauty and the Beast*, released in July 1981, begins its seven week run at Number One.

Willie Nelson's "Always on My Mind" enters the pop chart at #88. Originally recorded by **Elvis Presley** in 1972, Nelson's

version will later reach Number One on the country chart and will win a Grammy for Song of the Year.

8 **Elton John**'s first tour in two years kicks off in New Zealand.

17 **Samuel George, Jr.,** lead singer of Sixties band the **Capitols**, dies in Detroit at age thirty-nine after being stabbed with a knife in a family argument. The Capitols were best-known for their 1966 pop and R&B Top Ten hit "Cool Jerk," recently covered by the **Go-Go's**.

18 Disco-soul singing star **Teddy Pendergrass**, formerly with **Harold Melvin and the Blue Notes**, is severely injured in a car accident in Philadelphia. He emerges from the crash paralyzed from the waist down.

19 **Randy Rhoads**, twenty-five-year-old lead guitarist for heavy-metal hero **Ozzy Osbourne**, is killed in a freak accident in Leesburg, Florida, when the plane in which he's riding buzzes Osbourne's tour bus—which is carrying Osbourne and the rest of the band—and crashes into a house. The plane's pilot also dies, as does a female passenger. Rhoads had won a *Guitar Player* magazine award for Best New Talent of 1981.

22 **Diana Ross'** first solo album for RCA, *Why Do Fools Fall in Love*, goes platinum less than three months after its release.

28 **David Crosby** of **Crosby, Stills and Nash** is arrested for possession of Quaaludes and drug paraphernalia, driving under the influence of cocaine, and carrying a concealed .45-caliber pistol, in Los Angeles.

31 The **Doobie Brothers** announce their breakup. The band had started in the '70s as country rockers with the #11 hit "Listen to the Music," but following their 1975 Number One "Black Water," they began drifting toward a slick, L.A. pop-soul direction, that year thanks mainly to the addition of ex-**Steely Dan** singer/keyboardist **Michael McDonald**, who sang such massive Doobie hits as "Takin' It to the Streets," "Little Darling (I Need You)," "What a Fool Believes" and "It Keeps You Runnin'." ◆

WEEK ENDING MARCH 6

U.S. #1 POP 45	"Centerfold"	The J. Geils Band
U.S. #1 POP LP	*Beauty and the Beat*	The Go-Go's
U.S. #1 R&B 45	"That Girl"	Stevie Wonder
U.K. #1 POP 45	"A Town Called Malice"	The Jam
U.K. #1 POP LP	*Love Songs*	Barbra Streisand

WEEK ENDING MARCH 13

U.S. #1 POP 45	"Centerfold"	The J. Geils Band
U.S. #1 POP LP	*Beauty and the Beat*	The Go-Go's
U.S. #1 R&B 45	"That Girl"	Stevie Wonder
U.K. #1 POP 45	"The Lion Sleeps Tonight"	Tight Fit
U.K. #1 POP LP	*Love Songs*	Barbra Streisand

WEEK ENDING MARCH 20

U.S. #1 POP 45	"I Love Rock 'n' Roll"	Joan Jett and the Blackhearts
U.S. #1 POP LP	*Beauty and the Beat*	The Go-Go's
U.S. #1 R&B 45	"That Girl"	Stevie Wonder
U.K. #1 POP 45	"The Lion Sleeps Tonight"	Tight Fit
U.K. #1 POP LP	*Pelican West*	Haircut 100

WEEK ENDING MARCH 27

U.S. #1 POP 45	"I Love Rock 'n' Roll"	Joan Jett and the Blackhearts
U.S. #1 POP LP	*Beauty and the Beat*	The Go-Go's
U.S. #1 R&B 45	"That Girl"	Stevie Wonder
U.K. #1 POP 45	"The Lion Sleeps Tonight"	Tight Fit
U.K. #1 POP LP	*The Gift*	The Jam

10 "Ebony and Ivory," a duet by **Paul McCartney** and **Stevie Wonder**, debuts on the U.S. chart at #29. It will eventually go to Number One on both sides of the Atlantic, thus becoming Wonder's first British Number One.

Only a year and one week after opening the Savoy music club at the cost of $1.5 million in an elegant old Broadway theater off New York's Times Square, concert promoter **Ron Delsener** is forced to close the 1000-seat venue he had hoped to make New York's classiest concert club. Classy it was, as well as acoustically fine, but the Savoy's eclectic range of acts—**Cliff Richard**, **James Brown**, **Angela Bofill**, **Miles Davis**, **King Crimson**, **Burning Spear**, **Barbara Cook** and the **Soul Clan** (**Wilson Pickett**, **Solomon Burke**, **Don Covay** and **Joe Tex**) gave some of the more notable shows—kept it from acquiring a steady clientele. Also, its tiny dance floor discouraged audiences from arriving early and staying late, as they had done and still do at New York's many flourishing dance-rock clubs.

15 **Billy Joel** is injured in a motorcycle accident on Long Island, New York, and enters the hospital, where he will stay for over a month undergoing therapy for his injured hand.

Rolling Stone reports on the growing trend towards EPs, or "Mini-Albums," which have been successfully released recently by **Devo**, the **Pretenders** and the **B-52's**, among others.

Island Records chief **Chris Blackwell** severs Island's distribution deal with Warner Bros. Records, leaving Island one of the world's biggest independent labels once again. He later signs with Atlantic.

---

17 **Iron Maiden**'s third album, *The Number of the Beast,* enters the U.K. LP chart at Number One. The British heavy-metal group reports that the making of the album, which contains references to Satanism, was haunted by mysterious happenings—amplifiers blowing out for no apparent reason and tapes losing recorded tracks and picking up

strange voices. But the best story is about a car accident their producer was involved in soon after the album's title song was recorded: his auto repair bill came to 666 pounds, the Number of the Beast.

Toto, a group of veteran Los Angeles studio sessionmen, enter the pop chart again with "Roseanna" at #81. It will later peak at Number One and will be named Record of the Year at the Grammy Awards ceremony in 1983.

24 **John Cougar**—who in his several years in the music industry has had little success as a performer but has seen his composition "I Need a Lover" become a big hit for **Pat**

Benatar, but not for him—kicks off a rise to massive pop success this year as his "Hurts So Good" enters the pop chart at #82. It will eventually hit #2. "Jack and Diane" and the LP from which they came, *American Fool,* will both hit #1 later this year. The album will yield another hit in "Everyone Needs a Hand to Hold Onto."

---

26 On his way to the **Clash**'s West London rehearsal studio, lead singer **Joe Strummer** hops a train for the English coast and from there takes a ferry across the channel to France. His disappearance forces the Clash to cancel their May tour of the U.K. and jeopardizes their June tour of the U.S. He will show up in London on May 18, explaining that exhaustion and doubts about his career drove him to Paris, where he spent the three weeks "living like a bum." Two days after his return, the Clash will surprise the audience at an outdoor festival in Holland with an unscheduled concert.

---

30 Rock critic **Lester Bangs** dies of a heart attack at age thirty-three in his apartment in New York City. In his writings for such periodicals as *Rolling Stone, Creem* and the *Village Voice,* and his book *Blondie—an Unauthorized Biography,* Bangs proved not only to be acutely perceptive, funny and opinionated, but demonstrated an inimitable post-New Journalism style that, in its directness and vitality and refusal to stand for shallow shams, trends and fads, was closer to the esthetic of rock & roll music than anyone else's prose ever was. Bangs also recorded an album, *Jook Savages of the Brazos,* in 1981, and previous to that had a band called Birdland. ◆

WEEK ENDING APRIL 3

U.S. #1 POP 45	"I Love Rock 'n' Roll"	Joan Jett and the Blackhearts
U.S. #1 POP LP	*Beauty and the Beat*	The Go-Go's
U.S. #1 R&B 45	"That Girl"	Stevie Wonder
U.K. #1 POP 45	"Seven Tears"	Goombay Dance Band
U.K. #1 POP LP	*The Gift*	The Jam

WEEK ENDING APRIL 10

U.S. #1 POP 45	"I Love Rock 'n' Roll"	Joan Jett and the Blackhearts
U.S. #1 POP LP	*Beauty and the Beat*	The Go-Go's
U.S. #1 R&B 45	"That Girl"	Stevie Wonder
U.K. #1 POP 45	"Seven Tears"	Goombay Dance Band
U.K. #1 POP LP	*Pelican West*	Haircut 100

WEEK ENDING APRIL 17

U.S. #1 POP 45	"I Love Rock 'n' Roll"	Joan Jett and the Blackhearts
U.S. #1 POP LP	*Chariots of Fire*	Vangelis
U.S. #1 R&B 45	"That Girl"	Stevie Wonder
U.K. #1 POP 45	"My Camera Never Lies"	Bucks Fizz
U.K. #1 POP LP	*The Number of the Beast*	Iron Maiden

WEEK ENDING APRIL 24

U.S. #1 POP 45	"I Love Rock 'n' Roll"	Joan Jett and the Blackhearts
U.S. #1 POP LP	*Chariots of Fire*	Vangelis
U.S. #1 R&B 45	"If It Ain't One Thing, It's Another"	Richard "Dimples" Fields
U.K. #1 POP 45	"My Camera Never Lies"	Bucks Fizz
U.K. #1 POP LP	*Love Songs*	Barbra Streisand

2 **Adam and the Ants** disband when Adam (born **Stuart Goddard**) opts for a solo career rather than troubling to find replacements for drummer **Terry Lee Miall** and bassist **Gary Tibbs**, who left the popular New Romantic group in January. As the lone Adam Ant, Goddard will have more success in the U.S. than he ever had with the Ants. His first solo single, "Goody Two Shoes," will hit Number One in the U.K. and the Top Fifteen in the U.S.

6 A court in Edinburgh, Scotland, sentences **Tam Paton**, the forty-three-year-old former manager of the **Bay City Rollers**—a group of young male teen idols—to three years in jail when he pleads guilty to charges of conducting himself "in a shamelessly indecent manner" with ten teenage boys.

8 Veteran record executive **Neil Bogart**—current chairman of Boardwalk Entertainment Co. and prime mover of the disco era with his Casablanca Records—dies of cancer at age thirty-nine in Los Angeles. Born Neil Bogatz in Brooklyn, New York, Bogart started as a recording artist, under the name **Neil Scott**, with a minor hit called "Bobby" in the early Sixties. He went on to a brief acting career, using the name **Wayne Roberts**. Then, as **Neil Stewart**, he wrote want-ads for a New York employment agency before going to work for music-business trade magazine *Cashbox* as Neil Bogart. In the late Sixties, Bogart went to Kama Sutra Records, where he produced thirty "bubblegum" hits in three years. Almost a decade later, Bogart did it all over again with disco on Casablanca Records and with the hard-rock band **Kiss**. Kiss, along with **Donna Summer**, helped with their success to bring Bogart and Casablanca back to the heights after a flop LP of excerpts from "The Tonight Show" with **Johnny Carson** forced Bogart to the brink of bankruptcy. More recently, Bogart had found massive success with ex-**Runaway Joan Jett** on Boardwalk Records.

14 **Motorhead** guitarist **Fast Eddie Clark** quits the British heavy-metal group in the middle of their American tour. **Brian Robertson**, formerly of **Thin Lizzy** and the **Wild Horses**, jets across the Atlantic to replace him.

22 The original cast album of the hit Broadway musical *Dream Girls*—a pop operatic account of the rise and fall of a **Supremes**-type female soul singing group—enters the pop LPs chart. One song from the show, "And I'm Telling You I'm Not Going," sung by **Jennifer Holliday**, will become a Grammy-winning Top Forty hit.

23 The Central London chapter of the British Musicians Union moves a resolution to band synthesizers and rhythm machines from all recording sessions and live engagements. The resolution will be defeated.

24 Less than a week after **Joe Strummer** rejoined the **Clash**, drummer **Topper Headon** leaves, ostensibly because of "political differences." Headon, who joined the Clash in 1977, has recently written "Rock the Casbah," which will become the Clash's biggest American hit to date. He will be replaced by **Terry Chimes**, the Clash's first drummer, but Chimes' stint is officially termed "temporary," indicating that Headon might return to the group when he has kicked his drug habit.

28 A benefit concert for the Vietnam Veterans Project is held in San Francisco's Moscone Center, where the **Jefferson Starship**, the **Grateful Dead**, **Boz Scaggs** and **Country Joe McDonald** appear, raising about $175,000.

29 Epic Records releases the **Clash**'s *Combat Rock*, produced by **Glyn Johns** and featuring Beat poet **Allen Ginsberg** and New York City graffiti artist **Futura 2000**. *Combat Rock* will be the first of the Clash's five U.S. LPs to be certified platinum.

31 The **Rolling Stones** play an unannounced show at the 100 Club in London, where the **Sex Pistols** started the punk-rock movement some six years before. ♦

WEEK ENDING MAY 1

U.S. #1 POP 45	"I Love Rock 'n' Roll"	Joan Jett and the Blackhearts
U.S. #1 POP LP	*Chariots of Fire*	Vangelis
U.S. #1 R&B 45	"If It Ain't One Thing, It's Another"	Richard "Dimples" Fields
U.K. #1 POP 45	"Ebony and Ivory"	Paul McCartney and Stevie Wonder
U.K. #1 POP LP	*Pelican West*	Haircut 100

WEEK ENDING MAY 8

U.S. #1 POP 45	"Chariots of Fire"	Vangelis
U.S. #1 POP LP	*Chariots of Fire*	Vangelis
U.S. #1 R&B 45	"If It Ain't One Thing, It's Another"	Richard "Dimples" Fields
U.K. #1 POP 45	"Ebony and Ivory"	Paul McCartney and Stevie Wonder
U.K. #1 POP LP	*Live in Britain*	Barry Manilow

WEEK ENDING MAY 15

U.S. #1 POP 45	"Ebony and Ivory"	Paul McCartney and Stevie Wonder
U.S. #1 POP LP	*Asia*	Asia
U.S. #1 R&B 45	"It's Gonna Take a Miracle"	Deniece Williams
U.K. #1 POP 45	"I Won't Let You Down"	Ph.D
U.K. #1 POP LP	*Tug of War*	Paul McCartney

WEEK ENDING MAY 22

U.S. #1 POP 45	"Ebony and Ivory"	Paul McCartney and Stevie Wonder
U.S. #1 POP LP	*Asia*	Asia
U.S. #1 R&B 45	"It's Gonna Take a Miracle"	Deniece Williams
U.K. #1 POP 45	"A Little Peace"	Nicole
U.K. #1 POP LP	*Complete Madness*	Madness

WEEK ENDING MAY 29

U.S. #1 POP 45	"Ebony and Ivory"	Paul McCartney and Stevie Wonder
U.S. #1 POP LP	*Tug of War*	Paul McCartney
U.S. #1 R&B 45	"Let It Whip"	The Dazz Band
U.K. #1 POP 45	"Goody Two Shoes"	Adam Ant
U.K. #1 POP LP	*Complete Madness*	Madness

6 Over 85,000 people gather at the Rose Bowl in Pasadena, California, for Peace Sunday: We Have a Dream. Among those performing at this antinuclear rally are **Joan Baez** and **Bob Dylan**, **Jackson Browne**, **Crosby, Stills and Nash**, **Linda Ronstadt**, **Stevie Wonder**, **Dan Fogelberg**, **Bonnie Raitt**, **Stevie Nicks**, **Tom Petty** and **Gary "U.S." Bonds**. The event kicks off a Peace Week of benefits and rallies across the country.

8 Folk-pop duo **Simon and Garfunkel**, together again, embark on a nine-date European tour beginning today at the Hippodrome d'Auteuil in Paris and ending on June 19 in London.

9 **James Taylor**, **Linda Ronstadt** and **Jackson Browne** appear at another Peace Week benefit, at the Nassau Coliseum on Long Island, New York.

10 **Micki Harris**, a singer with Sixties girl group the **Shirelles**, dies at age forty-two after a heart attack suffered following a Los Angeles concert. Harris, along with **Shirley**

Owens, **Doris Coley** and **Beverly Lee**, formed the Shirelles in Passaic, New Jersey, in 1958. In the next six years, the group hit the Top Ten in both the pop and R&B charts with "Will You Love Me Tomorrow," "Dedicated to the One I Love," "Mama Said," "Baby It's You," "Soldier Boy" and "Foolish Little Girl." Though their hits stopped with the British Invasion in 1964, the Shirelles continued to perform frequently on revival bills and on their own, on the strength of their reputation as queens of the girl groups, through 1983 when they celebrated their twenty-fifth anniversary.

12 Approximately 1 million people participate in a Peace Walk rally in New York's Central Park to witness performances by **Jackson Browne** (joined by surprise guest **Bruce Springsteen**), **Gary "U.S." Bonds**, **James Taylor**, **Linda Ronstadt**, **Rita Marley** and **Joan Baez**.

16 **Pretenders** guitarist **James Honeyman-Scott** dies in his sleep of a drug overdose in London at age twenty-five. Apparently, the re-

markably talented, versatile and already much-respected Honeyman-Scott had been detoxifying himself from cocaine addiction, but at a party, he took some cocaine that was just too strong for him. The day before Honeyman-Scott's untimely death, Pretenders bassist **Pete Farndon** had left the band. Farndon would also die an untimely death due to a drug overdose, on April 15, 1983.

19 The eponymously titled debut album by **Asia** hits Number One, beginning a nine-week run atop the pop LPs chart. Asia is a supergroup consisting of British progressive-rock veterans **Steve Howe** (guitar, ex-Yes), **John Wetton** (bass, ex-King

Crimson, Roxy Music, Uriah Heep and U.K.), **Carl Palmer** (drums of **Emerson, Lake and Palmer**), and ex-**Buggles** and latter-day **Yes** keyboardist **Geoff Downes**.

Steve Miller begins his first tour in three years in Lake Tahoe, Nevada, to support his current hit album, *Abracadabra*, and its his title single.

25 The **Rolling Stones** make their first British concert appearance in six years, playing the first of two dates at London's Wembley Stadium for a crowd of 140,000.

26 **Roxy Music** singer and songwriter **Bryan Ferry** breaks the hearts of women the world over by marrying **Lucy Helmore** in Sussex, England.

27 Virgin Music Publishing Company reaches an out-of-court settlement with **Police** bassist and vocalist **Sting** on the contract between the two parties signed in 1977, when Sting was an unknown jazz singer. A statement issued jointly by both parties describes each side as "grimly satisfied." ◆

WEEK ENDING JUNE 5

U.S. #1 POP 45	"Ebony and Ivory"	Paul McCartney and Stevie Wonder
U.S. #1 POP LP	*Tug of War*	Paul McCartney
U.S. #1 R&B 45	"Let It Whip"	The Dazz Band
U.K. #1 POP 45	"House of Fun"	Madness
U.K. #1 POP LP	*Complete Madness*	Madness

WEEK ENDING JUNE 12

U.S. #1 POP 45	"Ebony and Ivory"	Paul McCartney and Stevie Wonder
U.S. #1 POP LP	*Tug of War*	Paul McCartney
U.S. #1 R&B 45	"Let It Whip"	The Dazz Band
U.K. #1 POP 45	"House of Fun"	Madness
U.K. #1 POP LP	*Complete Madness*	Madness

WEEK ENDING JUNE 19

U.S. #1 POP 45	"Ebony and Ivory"	Paul McCartney and Stevie Wonder
U.S. #1 POP LP	*Asia*	Asia
U.S. #1 R&B 45	"Let It Whip"	The Dazz Band
U.K. #1 POP 45	"Goody Two Shoes"	Adam Ant
U.K. #1 POP LP	*Avalon*	Roxy Music

WEEK ENDING JUNE 26

U.S. #1 POP 45	"Ebony and Ivory"	Paul McCartney and Stevie Wonder
U.S. #1 POP LP	*Asia*	Asia
U.S. #1 R&B 45	"Early in the Morning"	The Gap Band
U.K. #1 POP 45	"Goody Two Shoes"	Adam Ant
U.K. #1 POP LP	*Avalon*	Roxy Music

1 WABC-AM of New York City, Arbitron's nationally top-rated music station during the glory years of AM radio in the Fifties and Sixties, changes its format from Top Forty and golden oldies to an all-talk-show format.

2 The **Rolling Stones** begin their summer tour of Europe in Rotterdam, Holland.

3 The **Stray Cats'** *Built for Speed* and **Men at Work's** *Business as Usual* both enter the pop LPs chart on their way to becoming two of the biggest-selling albums of the year. The Stray Cats are a trio of American rockabilly revivalists who went to England to hit it big. With the singles "Rock This Town" and "Stray Cat Strut" and heavy exposure on Warner-Amex's new nation-wide satellite-cable twenty-four-hour rock-video network, MTV, Music Television, they'll hit big at home, too. Men at Work are an Australian band with a reggae-pop sound heavily influenced by the **Police**; they, too, will benefit from heavy MTV exposure of songs like "Who Can It Be Now?" and "Down Under," and will end up winning a Grammy while *Business as Usual* passes the quadruple-platinum mark.

4 **Diana Ross** kicks off her first world solo tour with a concert at Giants Stadium in the Meadowlands, New Jersey. Jazz trumpet great **Miles Davis** opens the show with his new electric sextet.

5 **Bill Justis**, whose "Raunchy" was a ground-breaking hit in instrumental rock & roll, dies of undisclosed causes at age fifty-five in his Nashville home. Justis began his career as a jazz alto saxophonist after World War II. In 1957, he became a session musician and arranger at Sun Studios in Memphis and, in that capacity, worked with **Jerry Lee Lewis**, **Johnny Cash** and **Charlie Rich**. In the meantime, he recorded his own material—always instrumental—for Phillips International; "Raunchy," his biggest hit, reached #3 on the R&B chart and #6 on the C&W chart in 1957. In the Sixties and Seventies, he worked as a recording artist, arranger and producer in Nashville.

17 "Valley Girl," the novelty hit by **Frank Zappa** and his fourteen-year-old daughter **Moon Unit**, enters the pop chart at #75. Frank Zappa, a veteran pop-culture satirist, had wanted to record a parody of the wealthy, spoiled, conspicuously consuming offspring of movie and television executives who live in California's San Fernando Valley, particularly the city of Encino. So, after he and the **Mothers of Invention** had recorded a danceable funk-rock backing track one night, Zappa called Moon Unit into the studio at midnight, and she spontaneously declaimed—in a style analogous to rap singing—in the eccentric dialect of the Valley Girl. As a result of the disc's phenomenal success (which will bring Moon Unit several appearances on nationwide TV), such Valley Girl terms as "grody to the max," "barf out!," "bag your face," "fer sure, fer sure" and "gag me with a spoon" will find their way into the popular lexicon; Valley Girl-type characters will turn up in TV commercials, on such TV shows as the CBS situation comedy "Square Pegs" and in such teen-oriented films as *Fast Times at Ridgemont High* and *Valley Girl*; and Valley Girl clothing, jewelry, handbooks, posters and calendars will sell by the thousands.

24 With the success of the television series "Fame," **Irene Cara's** title theme song from the original movie hits the top of the U.K. singles chart. A week later, the original soundtrack album will take the same position on the U.K. album chart. In the U.S., Cara's "Fame" reached #4 on the pop singles chart in 1980, while the movie soundtrack album went to #7.

With the release of **Sylvester Stallone's** *Rocky III*, **Survivor's** "Eye of the Tiger"—the movie's theme song—hits Number One on the U.S. pop chart, soon to reach the same position on the U.K. chart. It is the first hit for this Chicago band led by **Jim Peterik**, formerly of the **Ides of March**, whose "Vehicle" reached #2 on the American pop chart in 1970. ◆

WEEK ENDING JULY 3

U.S. #1 POP 45	"Don't You Want Me"	The Human League
U.S. #1 POP LP	*Asia*	Asia
U.S. #1 R&B 45	"Let It Whip"	The Dazz Band
U.K. #1 POP 45	"I've Never Been to Me"	Charlene
U.K. #1 POP LP	*Avalon*	Roxy Music

WEEK ENDING JULY 10

U.S. #1 POP 45	"Don't You Want Me"	The Human League
U.S. #1 POP LP	*Asia*	Asia
U.S. #1 R&B 45	"Early in the Morning"	The Gap Band
U.K. #1 POP 45	"Happy Talk"	Captain Sensible
U.K. #1 POP LP	*Avalon*	Roxy Music

WEEK ENDING JULY 17

U.S. #1 POP 45	"Don't You Want Me"	The Human League
U.S. #1 POP LP	*Asia*	Asia
U.S. #1 R&B 45	"Early in the Morning"	The Gap Band
U.K. #1 POP 45	"Abracadabra"	The Steve Miller Band
U.K. #1 POP LP	*The Lexicon of Love*	ABC

WEEK ENDING JULY 24

U.S. #1 POP 45	"Eye of the Tiger"	Survivor
U.S. #1 POP LP	*Asia*	Asia
U.S. #1 R&B 45	"And I'm Telling You I'm Not Going"	Jennifer Holliday
U.K. #1 POP 45	"Fame"	Irene Cara
U.K. #1 POP LP	*The Lexicon of Love*	ABC

WEEK ENDING JULY 31

U.S. #1 POP 45	"Eye of the Tiger"	Survivor
U.S. #1 POP LP	*Asia*	Asia
U.S. #1 R&B 45	"And I'm Telling You I'm Not Going"	Jennifer Holliday
U.K. #1 POP 45	"Fame"	Irene Cara
U.K. #1 POP LP	*The Lexicon of Love*	ABC

2 Veteran Latin folk-pop singer **Jose Feliciáno** marries **Susan Omillian** in California.

6 *Pink Floyd the Wall,* a two-hour, $10 million film version of **Pink Floyd's** best-selling double-album *The Wall,* has its U.S. premiere in New York City. Directed by British filmmaker **Alan Parker** (*Fame, Shoot the Moon, Midnight Express*), written by Pink Floyd bassist/vocalist **Roger Waters,** featuring the grotesque animations of **Gerald Scarfe** and starring **Boomtown Rats** lead singer **Bob Geldof** as Pink, a near-catatonic rock star, the film has virtually no dialogue and no plot. It is instead a series of surreal episodes equating rock & roll with fascism, women and sex with pain and death, and life in general with an inescapable, nihilistic madness. Though it will be roundly lambasted by critics for its perceived misanthropy, misogyny and rampant negativity, it will do fairly well at the box office.

8 **Jefferson Starship** singer **Mickey Thom-** as marries **Sara Kendrick** in San Francisco.

9 **Survivor's** *Eye of the Tiger,* which contains the hit title single that is also the theme song of the hit movie *Rocky III,* goes gold. In one more week, the soundtrack album of *Rocky III* will also go gold; another week after that, "Eye of the Tiger" will be certified platinum.

10 **Southside Johnny Lyon,** leader of the **Asbury Jukes,** marries **Jill Glasner** in—where else?—Asbury Park, New Jersey. The Jukes and **Bruce Springsteen** perform at the wedding.

11 The eponymous debut album by Anglo-American pop-rock band the **Pretenders** is certified platinum some three years after its release. The album contained two hit singles, "Brass in Pocket" and "Kid," and a batch of tunes that received heavy FM radio play, including "Precious," "Up the Neck," "Tattooed Love Boys," "Private Life" (later covered by **Grace Jones**) and "Mystery Achievement."

Amanda Grace Sudano is born to **Donna Summer** and her husband, **Bruce Sudano.**

13 R&B-soul singer **Joe Tex** dies at age forty-nine of a heart attack in Navasota, Texas. Born in Baytown, Texas, Tex became one of the leading soul singers of the Sixties with such hits as "Hold What You Got" (#5, 1965), "Skinny Legs and All" (#10, 1967), "I Want To (Do Everything for You)" (#23, 1965) and "A Sweet Woman Like You" (#29, 1966). Most of them featured Tex's humorous, tongue-in-cheek versions of homespun, secular-gospel philosophy. Highly influenced by **James Brown,** Tex had a frenetically athletic stage act that, at one point in the mid-Sixties, led him to start billing himself as "Soul Brother Number One" until an onstage confrontation with JB himself ended that. In the late Sixties, Tex briefly retired to devote himself to the church before returning to recording with his biggest chart hit, "I Gotcha," which reached #2 in 1972. Tex' last chart entry, "Ain't Gonna Bump No More (with No Big Fat Woman)," reached #12 in 1977. Just prior to his death, Tex had been appearing at certain cities in America with the "Soul Clan Revue," also featuring **Solomon Burke, Don Convay** and **Wilson Pickett.**

17 **Benjamin Ashburn,** manager of soul vocal group the **Commodores** since 1969, dies of a heart attack at age fifty-four in Englewood, New Jersey.

25 **Fleetwood Mac** rack up another platinum disc for the album *Mirage,* which yields hit singles in "Hold Me" and "Gypsy."

27 **Crosby, Stills and Nash's** *Daylight Again,* the folk-pop trio's first album since the 1977 *CSN,* is certified gold, several months after its release. The album features the current Top Twenty hit "Wasted on the Way."

Led Zeppelin lead vocalist **Robert Plant's** solo album *Pictures at Eleven,* his first recorded work since Led Zeppelin broke up in the wake of the death of drummer **John "Bonzo" Bonham,** is certified gold. The LP is currently in it seventh week on the Top LPs chart, and its fifth consecutive week in the Top Ten. ◆

WEEK ENDING AUGUST 7

U.S. #1 POP 45	"Eye of the Tiger"	Survivor
U.S. #1 POP LP	*Mirage*	Fleetwood Mac
U.S. #1 R&B 45	"And I'm Telling You I'm Not Going"	Jennifer Holliday
U.K. #1 POP 45	"Come On, Eileen"	Dexy's Midnight Runners
U.K. #1 POP LP	*The Kids from Fame*	various artists

WEEK ENDING AUGUST 14

U.S. #1 POP 45	"Eye of the Tiger"	Survivor
U.S. #1 POP LP	*Mirage*	Fleetwood Mac
U.S. #1 R&B 45	"And I'm Telling You I'm Not Going"	Jennifer Holliday
U.K. #1 POP 45	"Come On, Eileen"	Dexy's Midnight Runners
U.K. #1 POP LP	*The Kids from Fame*	various artists

WEEK ENDING AUGUST 21

U.S. #1 POP 45	"Eye of the Tiger"	Survivor
U.S. #1 POP LP	*Mirage*	Fleetwood Mac
U.S. #1 R&B 45	"Dance Floor"	Zapp
U.K. #1 POP 45	"Come On, Eileen"	Dexy's Midnight Runners
U.K. #1 POP LP	*Too-Rye-Ay*	Dexy's Midnight Runners

WEEK ENDING AUGUST 28

U.S. #1 POP 45	"Eye of the Tiger"	Survivor
U.S. #1 POP LP	*Mirage*	Fleetwood Mac
U.S. #1 R&B 45	"Dance Floor"	Zapp
U.K. #1 POP 45	"Come On, Eileen"	Dexy's Midnight Runners
U.K. #1 POP LP	*Too-Rye-Ay*	Dexy's Midnight Runners

3 The three-day US Festival gets under way in San Bernardino, California, with over 400,000 people present to see performances by **Fleetwood Mac**, **Tom Petty**, the **Police**, **Jackson Browne**, **Pat Benatar**, the **Cars**, **Talking Heads**, the **Grateful Dead**, the **Kinks**, the **B-52's**, **Dave Edmunds**, **Santana**, **Eddie Money**, **Gang of Four**, the **Ramones**, the **English Beat** and **Jerry Jeff Walker**. Financed by **Steven Wozniak**, founder of the Apple Computer Company, the US Festival cost a considerable amount of money, and it was technically one of the best-presented rock festivals ever, featuring enormous video-screen images of performers for the benefit of the many fans who were far from the stage.

9 **Al Green** and **Patti LaBelle** make their Broadway debuts in **Vinnette Carroll**'s gospel-inspired stage musical, *Your Arm's Too Short to Box with God*, opening at the Alvin Theatre in New York City. Green brings a special authenticity to his portrayal of a preacher: he is, in fact, an ordained minister; his appear-

ance at the Alvin marks the first time the former pop star has performed outside a church since his ordination in 1979. "What I'm doing every night here on Broadway," he tells reporters, "I do every Sunday morning at my church in Memphis: preach the gospel." LaBelle also draws on real life to play her role, a choir mistress: since disbanding her pop group, **Labelle**, in 1976, she has sung gospel, in addition to disco and R&B music. Both Green and LaBelle will win raves from critics and audiences, and the limited engagement of thirty performances will be expanded to eighty performances.

11 **John Cougar** becomes the first artist in over a

year and a half to have the Number One LP (*American Fool*) and two singles in the Top Ten ("Jack and Diane" and "Hurts So Good") in the same week. This feat had been previously accomplished by **Michael Jackson** in 1980 with the album *Off the Wall* and the singles "Don't Stop 'Til You Get Enough" and "Rock with You."

13 RCA Records announces that **David Bowie** has left for the South Seas, where he will begin filming *Merry Christmas, Mr. Lawrence*, a World War II drama directed by noted Japanese director **Nagisa Oshima**, whose *In the Realm of the Senses* provoked controversy in

the U.S. over its unflinching depictions of sexual perversities.

16 **Afrika Bambaataa and the Soul Sonic Force**'s "Planet Rock" is certified gold. Bambaataa, a prominent New York City disco DJ, originally created this synthesizer-dominated dance-floor favorite spontaneously on the job by mixing sections of **Kraftwerk**'s "Trans-Europe Express" with electronic rhythm tracks and cueing in his MCs—the Soul Sonic Force—to rap to the beat. "Planet Rock" is exemplary of the recent fusion of highly technological electronic music and ghetto-streets dance rhythms.

20 **Joan Jett and the Blackhearts**' "I Love Rock 'n' Roll" is certified a platinum single. "I Love Rock 'n' Roll," a remake of the B side of a 1974 British hit by the **Arrows**, has brought Jett her first measure of respect and extensive acclaim since she began her career as a sixteen-year-old guitarist in the all-girl band the **Runaways** in 1975. Five years with the Runaways brought some notoriety, but Jett left the group and its reputation for foxy poses and musical incompetence to form her own group in 1979. "I Love Rock 'n' Roll" is the title track from her second album with the Blackhearts. Earlier this month, the success of both the single and the album summoned her first album, *Bad Reputation*, to the chart for the second time.

25 Boston-based heavy-metal band **Aerosmith** return to the chart for the first time since 1980's *Greatest Hits* album with the LP *Rock in a Hard Place*, their first release of new material since lead guitarist **Joe Perry** left the band in 1979. Although the album enters the chart at #53, it will never reach the Top Twenty. ◆

WEEK ENDING SEPTEMBER 4

U.S. #1 POP 45	"Abracadabra"	The Steve Miller Band
U.S. #1 POP LP	*Mirage*	Fleetwood Mac
U.S. #1 R&B 45	"Jump to It"	Aretha Franklin
U.K. #1 POP 45	"Eye of the Tiger"	Survivor
U.K. #1 POP LP	*The Kids from Fame*	various artists

WEEK ENDING SEPTEMBER 11

U.S. #1 POP 45	"Hard to Say I'm Sorry"	Chicago
U.S. #1 POP LP	*American Fool*	John Cougar
U.S. #1 R&B 45	"Jump to It"	Aretha Franklin
U.K. #1 POP 45	"Eye of the Tiger"	Survivor
U.K. #1 POP LP	*Upstairs at Eric's*	Yaz

WEEK ENDING SEPTEMBER 18

U.S. #1 POP 45	"Hard to Say I'm Sorry"	Chicago
U.S. #1 POP LP	*American Fool*	John Cougar
U.S. #1 R&B 45	"Jump to It"	Aretha Franklin
U.K. #1 POP 45	"Eye of the Tiger"	Survivor
U.K. #1 POP LP	*The Kids from Fame*	various artists

WEEK ENDING SEPTEMBER 25

U.S. #1 POP 45	"Abracadabra"	The Steve Miller Band
U.S. #1 POP LP	*American Fool*	John Cougar
U.S. #1 R&B 45	"Jump to It"	Aretha Franklin
U.K. #1 POP 45	"Private Investigations"	Dire Straits
U.K. #1 POP LP	*The Kids from Fame*	various artists

2 Bruce Springsteen's *Nebraska* enters the rock albums chart at #24. Though the album, which consists mainly of morose, solo-acoustic songs, will receive virtually no radio play, it will remain on the best-seller charts for several months.

The Clash's "Rock the Casbah" enters the Hot 100 at #90. It will eventually hit the pop Top Ten, and its funk-dub remix, "Mustapha Dance," will make the disco singles Top Ten, helping the band's latest album, *Combat Rock,* become its first gold and platinum LP.

Diana Ross' "Muscles," written and produced for her by **Michael Jackson,** enters the Hot 100 at #61 and the black singles chart at #33. It will eventually hit the Top Ten on both charts.

9 Toni Basil's "Mickey," now hovering at #39 in the Hot 100, enters the dance-disco Top Eighty chart at #54. The success of the tune—which sets cheerleading vocals to a backing track that merges Eighties funk with Sixties garage-rock—in discos and on black radio will spur it on to greater pop success, and it will eventually hit the Top Ten.

12 The **Clash** open for the **Who** at Shea Stadium for the first of two New York City shows on what the Who call their "Farewell Tour."

15 Marvin Gaye's "Sexual Healing" enters the black singles chart at #25. Within a month, it will rocket to the Number One spot on the chart, and will later win a Grammy as Best R&B Male Vocal Performance of the Year.

Lionel Richie of veteran soul-pop vocal group the **Commodores** again fuels rumors that he'll be leaving that group, as his solo single "Truly" enters the R&B singles chart at #28. It will eventually rise to the Top Ten on both the R&B singles and pop singles charts, nearly matching the phenomenal success of Richie's earlier duet with **Diana Ross,** "Endless Love."

Despite all this—and Richie's acquisition of a personal manager in the wake of the recent death of Commodores manager **Ben Ashburn**—Richie will continue to deny allegations that he is leaving the group.

16 RCA Records releases **Daryl Hall** and **John Oates'** *H₂0,* which will match the phenomenal performance of their last LP, *Private Eyes,* by going to Top Five on the pop LPs chart and yielding two singles that will go Top Five on both the pop and R&B charts: "Maneater" and "One on One."

22 Worcester, Massachusetts mayor Sara Robertson declares today **Van Halen** Day after local fans collect 25,000 signatures on a petition requesting that the band add another show to their tour.

30 Paul Weller of the Jam tells the *New Musical Express* that the Jam is disbanding after six years at the vanguard of the British new wave. "It really dawned on me," says Weller, "how secure the situation was, the fact that we could go on for the next ten years, making records, getting hit records, getting bigger and bigger and all the rest of it. That frightened me because I realized we were going to end up the same like the rest of them." Weller has been an outspoken critic of such "obsolete" bands as the **Rolling Stones** and the **Who,** bands which have "overstayed their welcome." ◆

WEEK ENDING OCTOBER 2		
U.S. #1 POP 45	"Jack and Diane"	John Cougar
U.S. #1 POP LP	*American Fool*	John Cougar
U.S. #1 R&B 45	"Love Come Down"	Evelyn King
U.K. #1 POP 45	"The Bitterest Pill"	The Jam
U.K. #1 POP LP	*The Kids from Fame*	various artists

WEEK ENDING OCTOBER 9		
U.S. #1 POP 45	"Jack and Diane"	John Cougar
U.S. #1 POP LP	*American Fool*	John Cougar
U.S. #1 R&B 45	"Love Come Down"	Evelyn King
U.K. #1 POP 45	"Pass the Dutchie"	Musical Youth
U.K. #1 POP LP	*Love over Gold*	Dire Straits

WEEK ENDING OCTOBER 16		
U.S. #1 POP 45	"Jack and Diane"	John Cougar
U.S. #1 POP LP	*American Fool*	John Cougar
U.S. #1 R&B 45	"Love Come Down"	Evelyn King
U.K. #1 POP 45	"Pass the Dutchie"	Musical Youth
U.K. #1 POP LP	*Love over Gold*	Dire Straits

WEEK ENDING OCTOBER 23		
U.S. #1 POP 45	"Jack and Diane"	John Cougar
U.S. #1 POP LP	*American Fool*	John Cougar
U.S. #1 R&B 45	"Love Come Down"	Evelyn King
U.K. #1 POP 45	"Do You Really Want to Hurt Me?"	Culture Club
U.K. #1 POP LP	*Love over Gold*	Dire Straits

WEEK ENDING OCTOBER 30		
U.S. #1 POP 45	"Who Can It Be Now?"	Men at Work
U.S. #1 POP LP	*American Fool*	John Cougar
U.S. #1 R&B 45	"Love Come Down"	Evelyn King
U.K. #1 POP 45	"Do You Really Want to Hurt Me?"	Culture Club
U.K. #1 POP LP	*The Kids from Fame*	various artists

3 Kicking off a U.S. tour in Minneapolis, **Devo** prove that they're still in the vanguard of the rock-video interface by presenting the first "video-synchronized" rock concert: for the first half of the show, featuring material from the band's latest album, *Oh No! It's Devo*, the members of Devo perform live in front of a fifty-foot-diagonal, rear-projection video screen that shows song lyrics, computer-graphic and animated images, and pretaped live-action scenes featuring characters with whom the live band interacts both verbally and physically. For instance, in the new album's single "Peek-a-Boo!" a pirate on the video screen "kicks" the band members over, in a scene also included in the promotional video for the song currently showing on MTV. The flow of music and video is kept in perfect synchronization by a taped electronic sequencer pulse that serves as both a musical metronome and the basis of the video's soundtrack. Another show later in this tour, in Los Angeles, will be simulcast via satellite-cable TV to dozens of college campuses across America.

4 **Talking Heads'** husband-and-wife rhythm section, **Chris Frantz** and **Tina Weymouth**, have a baby—**Robert Weymouth**—in Nassau, Bahamas, where they are recording at Compass Point Studios.

6 **John Cougar**'s *American Fool* enters its ninth consecutive week at the top of the pop LPs chart, tying with the eponymous debut album by corporate-rock supergroup **Asia** for most weeks at Number One of any pop LP this year; it's also the longest time an album by a male artist has held the top spot since **Stevie Wonder**'s fourteen-consecutive-weeks run in 1976 with *Songs in the Key of Life.* Meanwhile, "Hand to Hold Onto," Cougar's third hit single from *American Fool* after "Hurts So Good" and "Jack and Diane," enters the Hot 100 at #72.

With "Sexual Healing," **Marvin Gaye** reaches Number One on the R&B chart for the thirteenth time in seventeen years and the first time since "Got to Give It Up" in 1977. "Sexual Healing" will also become—in January

1983—Gaye's fourth pop Number One. All told, "Sexual Healing" will be the biggest hit of Gaye's long and erratic career, reviving him after a rather lackluster five (some would say ten) years. The song will win Gaye a Grammy Award for Best Male R&B Performance and its instrumental flip side will net the Grammy for Best R&B Instrumental.

Joe Cocker caps a remarkable comeback as he goes to the top of the pop chart with his duet with **Jennifer Warnes**, "Up Where We Belong," the theme song of the popular film *An Officer and a Gentleman.* Cocker's last hit was "You Are So Beautiful" in 1975. "Up Where We Belong," written by **Jack Nitzsche, Buffy Sainte-Marie** and **Waylon Jennings**, will win an Oscar for Best Original Theme Song.

21 **Joni Mitchell** marries her bassist, **Larry Klein**, at the Malibu, California, home of her manager, **Elliot Roberts**.

24 Following the phenomenal success in Bri-

tain of **Musical Youth**'s "Pass the Dutchie" (the group's debut record, it went to Number One), MCA Records releases the twelve-inch single and the group's first album, *Youth of Today,* in the U.S., where "Pass the Dutchie" will reach #8 on the pop chart, and will do well on both the R&B and disco charts, making it the most successful reggae song in America since **Johnny Nash**'s "I Can See Clearly Now" in 1972. Musical Youth is made up of five boys between the ages of eleven and fifteen who write their own songs (with the exception of "Pass the Dutchie," which was written by **Jackie Mitoo** and the **Mighty Diamonds**), play their own instruments and do their own arrangements.

25 The three-day Jamaica World Music Festival draws 45,000 people to the **Bob Marley** Performing Center located near Montego Bay to hear and see the **Clash**, the **Grateful Dead**, **Rick James**, **Rita Marley**, **Aretha Franklin**, the **English Beat**, **Joe Jackson**, the **B-52's**, **Squeeze**, **Black Uhuru**, **Yellowman**, **Gladys Knight**, **Bobby and the Midnites** (featuring the Grateful Dead's **Bob Weir**) and **Peter Tosh**. Squeeze perform what will be their last concert together here—ironically, just as they have reached a commercial peak in the U.S. with the hit single "Tempted," hit albums *East Side Story* and *Sweets from a Stranger* and sold-out, ecstatically received shows at Madison Square Garden in New York. Squeeze guitarist, singer, and songwriter **Chris Difford** will later explain, "We didn't plan on making our last show one like this. It blew in on the wind. Like our career."

26 Jazz trumpet giant **Miles Davis** is married, for the third time, in New York City to actress **Cicely Tyson**. Comedian **Bill Cosby** is the best man. ◆

WEEK ENDING NOVEMBER 6

U.S. #1 POP 45	"Up Where We Belong"	Joe Cocker and Jennifer Warnes
U.S. #1 POP LP	*American Fool*	John Cougar
U.S. #1 R&B 45	"Sexual Healing"	Marvin Gaye
U.K. #1 POP 45	"Do You Really Want to Hurt Me?"	Culture Club
U.K. #1 POP LP	*Love over Gold*	Dire Straits

WEEK ENDING NOVEMBER 13

U.S. #1 POP 45	"Up Where We Belong"	Joe Cocker and Jennifer Warnes
U.S. #1 POP LP	*Business as Usual*	Men at Work
U.S. #1 R&B 45	"Sexual Healing"	Marvin Gaye
U.K. #1 POP 45	"I Don't Want to Dance"	Eddy Grant
U.K. #1 POP LP	*The Kids from Fame*	various artists

WEEK ENDING NOVEMBER 20

U.S. #1 POP 45	"Up Where We Belong"	Joe Cocker and Jennifer Warnes
U.S. #1 POP LP	*Business as Usual*	Men at Work
U.S. #1 R&B 45	"Sexual Healing"	Marvin Gaye
U.K. #1 POP 45	"I Don't Want to Dance"	Eddy Grant
U.K. #1 POP LP	*The Kids from Fame*	various artists

WEEK ENDING NOVEMBER 27

U.S. #1 POP 45	"Truly"	Lionel Richie
U.S. #1 POP LP	*Business as Usual*	Men at Work
U.S. #1 R&B 45	"Sexual Healing"	Marvin Gaye
U.K. #1 POP 45	"Heartbreaker"	Dionne Warwick
U.K. #1 POP LP	*Heartbreaker*	Dionne Warwick

1 Epic Records releases *Thriller,* **Michael Jackson**'s first solo album in three years and his second produced by **Quincy Jones**. Like its predecessor, *Off the Wall, Thriller* will yield four smash hit singles: "The Girl Is Mine" (a duet with **Paul McCartney**), "Wanna Be Startin' Somethin'," "Billie Jean" and "Beat It." The album features guest performances by **Eddie Van Halen**, the members of **Toto** and actor **Vincent Price** (on the title track).

2 Folksinger and songwriter **David Blue** (born **Cohen**) suffers a fatal heart attack while jogging around New York City's Washington Square Park. He was forty-one. Blue was an active member of the Greenwich Village folk scene in the early Sixties and was closely associated with **Eric Andersen**, **Leonard Cohen**, **Joni Mitchell**, the **Eagles** and **Bob Dylan** (he toured with Dylan's **Rolling Thunder Revue** in 1975 and 1976, and appeared in Dylan's film *Renaldo and Clara*). Although he recorded eight albums, he never achieved the widespread recognition accorded his peers.

7 Veteran R&B studio bassist **Tom Cogbill** dies of a stroke at age fifty in Nashville. He produced such records as **Neil Diamond**'s "Holly Holy" (#6, 1969) and **Merrilee Rush**'s "Angel of the Morning" (#7, 1968).

8 Blues-harmonica giant **Walter "Shakey" Horton**—also known as **"Big Walter"** to differentiate him from Chicago blues-harmonica great **Little Walter Jacobs**—dies of a heart attack in Chicago at age sixty-five. In his long career, which began in the late Twenties, he performed with such greats as the **Memphis Jug Band**, **Ma Rainey**, **Honeyboy Edwards**, **Homesick James**, **Muddy Waters**, **Johnny Shines**, **Sonny Boy Williamson** and **Howlin' Wolf**. His best-known songs include "Blues in the Morning," "Hard Hearted Woman," "I Got the Blues," "I Need Your Love," "Tell Me Baby" and "Walter's Blues."

Country singer/songwriter **Marty Robbins**, who won a 1959 Grammy for his Number One hit "El Paso," dies in Nashville at age fifty-seven after a long battle with heart disease. In 1954, Robbins' version of **Arthur "Big Boy" Crudup**'s blues song "That's All Right" outsold **Elvis Presley**'s; in 1957, Robbins reached his pop peak with the Top Three smash "A White Sport Coat (and a Pink Carnation)," which was later affectionately parodied by **Jimmy Buffett** with his LP *A White Sport Coat and a Pink Crustacean.* From the late Fifties on, Robbins alternated a series of Western story songs like "El Paso" with heavily sentimental country numbers that earned him the nickname "Mr. Teardrop." More recently, Robbins had some country chart hits, but little in the way of pop success.

17 Blues giant **Big Joe Williams** dies of natural causes at age seventy-nine in Macon, Mississippi. His best-known songs include "Baby Please Don't Go" (covered by many blues-rock bands, including Detroit's Sixties psychedelic garage rockers the **Amboy Dukes**), "Big Fat Mama," "I Want to Know What My Baby's Putting Down," "President Roosevelt," "Sugar Hill" and "Vitamin A Blues."

The **Who** play what is the "last concert of our farewell tour" at Toronto's Maple Leaf Gardens. The concert is simulcast around America on pay-per-view satellite-cable TV to closed-circuit arena outlets; video rights for the concert are sold to Home Box Office, America's largest pay-cable network; and home videocassettes of the event will later be sold.

29 Jamaica issues a **Bob Marley** commemorative stamp in honor of the late reggae giant. Jamaica's **High Commissioner Herman Walker** explains: "His music spread all over the world, and he put his country firmly on the map."

31 **Miami Steve Van Zandt**, guitarist with **Bruce Springsteen's E Street Band**, marries **Maureen Santora** in Asbury Park, New Jersey (of course). **Bruce Springsteen** is best man, and at the reception, **Percy Sledge** and preacher **Richard Penniman**—formerly known as **Little Richard**—sing Sledge's hit "When a Man Loves a Woman."

One of New York City's longest-running rock clubs, Max's Kansas City, closes. Recently a haven of punk rock bands, Max's had been the watering hole for **Andy Warhol**'s coterie, including the **Velvet Underground**, in the late Sixties. Here, the Velvets, the **New York Dolls** and many other important rock bands made their reputations. **Devo** made its first sensational New York stage debut, introduced by David Bowie, at Max's in 1976. And it was at Max's that the young, unknown **Bruce Springsteen** played solo acoustic sets in the early Seventies, opening for **Bob Marley and the Wailers**. In May of 1983, **Mickey Ruskin**, who owned Max's and several other New York City clubs, died. ◆

WEEK ENDING DECEMBER 4

U.S. #1 POP 45	"Truly"	Lionel Richie
U.S. #1 POP LP	*Business as Usual*	Men at Work
U.S. #1 R&B 45	"Sexual Healing"	Marvin Gaye
U.K. #1 POP 45	"Mirror Man"	The Human League
U.K. #1 POP LP	*The Singles—the First Ten Years*	Abba

WEEK ENDING DECEMBER 11

U.S. #1 POP 45	"Mickey"	Toni Basil
U.S. #1 POP LP	*Business as Usual*	Men at Work
U.S. #1 R&B 45	"Sexual Healing"	Marvin Gaye
U.K. #1 POP 45	"The Beat Surrender"	The Jam
U.K. #1 POP LP	*The Singles—the First Ten Years*	Abba

WEEK ENDING DECEMBER 18

U.S. #1 POP 45	"Maneater"	Daryl Hall and John Oates
U.S. #1 POP LP	*Business as Usual*	Men at Work
U.S. #1 R&B 45	"Sexual Healing"	Marvin Gaye
U.K. #1 POP 45	"The Beat Surrender"	The Jam
U.K. #1 POP LP	*The Singles—the First Ten Years*	Abba

WEEK ENDING DECEMBER 25

U.S. #1 POP 45	"Maneater"	Daryl Hall and John Oates
U.S. #1 POP LP	*Business as Usual*	Men at Work
U.S. #1 R&B 45	"Sexual Healing"	Marvin Gaye
U.K. #1 POP 45	"Time (Clock of the Heart)"	Culture Club
U.K. #1 POP LP	*The John Lennon Collection*	John Lennon

KENNY AARONSON
Apr. 14, 1952

MICK ABRAHAMS
Apr. 7, 1943

JOHNNY ACE
Jun. 29, 1929–Dec. 24, 1954

DAVID ACKLES
Feb. 20, 1937

BARBARA ACKLIN
Feb. 28, 1943

ROY ACUFF
Sep. 15, 1903

CLIFF ADAMS
Oct. 8, 1952

JULIAN "CANNONBALL"
ADDERLEY
Sep. 15, 1928–Aug. 8, 1975

JAN AKKERMAN
Dec. 24, 1946

SKIP ALAN
Jun. 6, 1944

PETER ALBIN
Jun. 11, 1944

GEORGE ALEXANDER
May 18, 1946

JIM ALEXANDER
Dec. 17, 1948

BARBARA ALLBUT
Sep. 24, 1940

FRANK ALLEN
Dec. 14, 1943

LEE ALLEN
Jul. 2, 1925

PETER ALLEN
Feb. 10, 1944

RICK ALLEN
Jan. 28, 1946

VERDEN ALLEN
May 26, 1944

JERRY ALLISON
Aug. 31, 1939

LUTHER ALLISON
Aug. 17, 1939

MOSE ALLISON
Nov. 11, 1927

GREGG ALLMAN
Dec. 8, 1947

DUANE ALLMAN
Nov. 20, 1946–Oct. 29, 1971

GERALD ALSTON
Nov. 8, 1942

SHIRLEY ALSTON
Jun. 10, 1941

MIKE ALLSUP
Mar. 8, 1947

HERB ALPERT
Mar. 31, 1937

ERIC ANDERSEN
Feb. 14, 1943

ALFA ANDERSON
Sep. 7, 1946

IAN ANDERSON
Aug. 10, 1947

JON ANDERSON
Oct. 25, 1944

RICK ANDERSON
Aug. 1, 1947

ANNA-FRID ANDERSSON
Nov. 15, 1945

BENNY ANDERSSON
Dec. 16, 1946

MARK ANDES
Feb. 19, 1948

BOB ANDREWS
Jun. 20, 1949

SAM ANDREWS
Dec. 18, 1941

PAUL ANKA
Jul. 30, 1941

ADAM ANT (STUART GOD-
DARD)
Nov. 3, 1954

MICHAEL ANTHONY
Jan. 20. 1955

CARMINE APPICE
Dec. 15, 1946

ROD ARGENT
Jun. 14, 1945

JOAN ARMATRADING
Dec. 9, 1950

DESI ARNAZ, JR.
Jan. 19, 1953

PETER ASHER
Jun. 22, 1944

NICKOLAS ASHFORD
May 4, 1943

ROSALIND ASHFORD
Sep. 2, 1943

TONY ASHTON
Mar. 1, 1946

CHET ATKINS
Jun. 20, 1924

MARTIN ATKINS
Aug. 3, 1959

PAUL ATKINSON
Mar. 19, 1946

BRIAN AUGER
Jul. 18, 1939

FRANKIE AVALON
Sep. 18, 1939 or 1940

MICK AVORY
Feb. 15, 1944

HOYT AXTON
Mar. 25, 1938

KEVIN AYERS
Aug. 16, 1945

ROY AYERS
Sep. 10, 1940

BURT BACHARACH
May 12, 1929

RANDY BACHMAN
Sep. 27, 1943

ROBBIE BACHMAN
Feb. 18, 1953

JOAN BAEZ
Jan. 9, 1941

BARRY BAILEY
Jun. 12, 1948

PHILIP BAILEY
May 8, 1951

GINGER BAKER
Aug. 19, 1940

LAVERNE BAKER
Nov. 11, 1929

LENNY BAKER
Apr. 18, 1946

MICKEY BAKER
Oct. 15, 1925

LONG JOHN BALDRY
Jan. 12, 1941

MARTY BALIN
Jan. 30, 1942

DAVE BALL
Mar. 30, 1950

ROGER BALL
Jun. 4, 1944

FLORENCE BALLARD
Jun. 30, 1943–Feb. 22, 1976

HANK BALLARD
Nov. 18, 1936

RUSS BALLARD
Oct. 31, 1947

TONY BANKS
Mar. 27, 1951

NICOEL BARCLAY
Apr. 21, 1951

BARRIEMORE BARLOW
Sep. 10, 1949

MARTIN BARRE
Nov. 17, 1946

ASTON BARRETT
Nov. 22, 1946

CARLTON BARRETT
Dec. 17, 1950

SYD BARRETT
Jan. 6, 1946

JEFF BARRY
Apr. 3, 1938

LEN BARRY
Dec. 6, 1942

DAVE BARTHOLOMEW
Dec. 24, 1920

FONTELLA BASS
Jul. 3, 1949

SHIRLEY BASSEY
Jan. 8, 1937

SKIP BATTIN
Feb. 2, 1934

JOSEPH BAUER
Sep. 26, 1941

JOHN "BOWSER" BAUMAN
Sep. 14, 1947

JEFF "SKUNK" BAXTER
Dec. 13, 1948

JEFF BECK
Jun. 24, 1944

GERRY BECKLEY
Sep. 12, 1952

CAPTAIN BEEFHEART
Jan. 15, 1941

ARCHIE BELL
Sep. 1, 1944

CHRIS BELL
Jan. 12, 1951–Dec. 27, 1978

MAGGIE BELL
Jan. 12, 1945

ROBERT "KOOL" BELL
Oct. 8, 1950

RONALD BELL
Nov. 1, 1951

GEORGE BELLAMY
Oct. 8, 1941

JESSE BELVIN
Dec. 15, 1933–Feb. 6, 1960

DWIGHT BEMENT
Dec. 28, 1945

BRIAN BENNETT
Feb. 9, 1940

ESTELLE BENNETT
Jul. 22, 1944

PATRICIA BENNETT
Apr. 7, 1947

GEORGE BENSON
Mar. 22, 1943

RAY BENSON
Mar. 16, 1951

JOHN BENTLEY
Apr. 16, 1951

BROOK BENTON
Sep. 19, 1931

AL BERGER
Nov. 8, 1949

BYRON BERLINE
Jul. 6, 1944

CHUCK BERRY
Oct. 18, 1926 or 1931

JAN BERRY
Apr. 3, 1941

DICKEY BETTS
Dec. 12, 1943

BEV BEVAN
Nov. 25, 1946

THE BIG BOPPER (J. P.
RICHARDSON)
Oct. 24, 1930 or Oct. 29, 1932–
Feb. 3, 1959

CINDY BIRDSONG
Dec. 15, 1939

PETE BIRRELL
May 9, 1941

ELVIN BISHOP
Oct. 21, 1942

EDWARD "SONNY" BIVINS
Jan. 15, 1942

BILL BLACK
Sep, 17. 1926–Oct. 21, 1965

CILLA BLACK
May 27, 1943

JAY BLACK
Nov. 2, 1941

RITCHIE BLACKMORE
Apr. 14, 1945

STEPHEN JO BLADD
Jul. 13, 1942

BOBBY "BLUE" BLAND
Jan. 17, 1930

CARLA BLEY
May 11, 1938

MIKE BLOOMFIELD
Jul. 28, 1944–Feb. 15, 1981

DAVID (COHEN) BLUE
Feb. 18, 1941–Dec. 2, 1982

COLIN BLUNSTONE
Jun. 24, 1945

TIM BOGERT
Aug. 14, 1944

TOM BOGGS
Jul. 16, 1947

BOB BOGLE
Jan. 16, 1937

MARC BOLAN
Sep. 30, 1947–Sep. 16, 1977

TOMMY BOLIN
1951–Dec. 4, 1976

GARY "U.S." BONDS
Jun. 6, 1939

GRAHAM BOND
c. 1937–May 8, 1974

JIM BONFANTI
Dec. 17, 1948

JOHN "BONZO" BONHAM
May 31, 1948–Sep. 25, 1980

SONNY BONO
Feb. 16, 1935

JAMES BOOKER
Dec. 17, 1939

DEBBY BOONE
Sep. 22, 1956

PAT BOONE
Jun. 1, 1934

STEVE BOONE
Sep. 23, 1943

EARL BOSTIC
Apr. 25, 1913–1965

DAVID BOWIE
Jan. 8, 1947

MICK BOX
Jun. 8, 1947

EDDIE BOYD
Nov. 25, 1914

LES BRAID
Sep. 15, 1941

BONNIE BRAMLETT
Nov. 8, 1944

DELANEY BRAMLETT
Jul. 1, 1939

BARRY BRANDT
Nov. 14, 1951

CREED BRATTON
Feb. 8, 1943

ERIK BRAUNN
Aug. 11, 1950

MICHAEL BRECKER
Mar. 29, 1949

RANDY BRECKER
Nov. 27, 1945

DON BREWER
Sep. 3, 1943

EDDIE BRIGATI
Oct. 22, 1946

VIC BRIGGS
Feb. 14, 1945

RONNIE BRIGHT
Oct. 18, 1938

CHRIS BRITTON
Jun. 21, 1945

TONY BROCK
Mar. 31, 1954

DAVID BROMBERG
Sep. 19, 1945

STAN BRONSTEIN
Jul. 17, 1938

GARY BROOKER
May 29, 1945

DANNY BROOKS
Apr. 1, 1942

ELKIE BROOKS
Feb. 25, 1945

EDGAR BROUGHTON
Oct. 24, 1947

ARTHUR BROWN
Jun. 24, 1944

CLARENCE "GATEMOUTH"
BROWN
Apr. 18, 1924

GEORGE BROWN
Jan. 5, 1949

HAROLD BROWN
Mar. 17, 1946

MICHAEL BROWN
Apr. 25, 1949

PETER BROWN
Dec. 25, 1940

ROY BROWN
Sep. 10, 1925–May 25, 1981

RUTH BROWN
Jan. 30, 1928

TONI BROWN
Nov. 16, 1938

WILLIAM BROWN
Jun. 30, 1946

JACKSON BROWNE
Oct. 9, 1948

JACK BRUCE
May 14, 1943

MICHAEL BRUCE
Mar. 16, 1948

BILL BRUFORD
May 17, 1948

AB BRYANT
Nov. 15, 1954

BOUDLEAUX BRYANT
Feb. 13, 1920

FELICE BRYANT
Aug. 7, 1925

PEABO BRYSON
Apr. 13, 1951

WALLY CARTER BRYSON
Jul. 18, 1949

ROY BUCHANAN
Sep. 23, 1939

LINDSEY BUCKINGHAM
Oct. 3, 1947

TIM BUCKLEY
Feb. 14, 1947–Jun. 29, 1975

JIMMY BUFFETT
Dec. 25, 1946

CORNELIUS BUMPUS
Jan. 13, 1952

DEWEY BUNNELL
Jan. 19, 1952

CLIVE BUNKER
Dec. 12, 1946

ERIC BURDON
May 11, 1941

PAT BURKE
Oct. 9, 1937

BILLY BURNETTE
May 8, 1953

DORSEY BURNETTE
Dec. 28, 1932–Aug. 19, 1979

JOHNNY BURNETTE
Mar. 25, 1934–Aug. 1, 1964

ROCKY BURNETTE
Jun. 12, 1953

HEINZ BURT
Jul. 24, 1942

TREVOR BURTON
Mar. 9, 1944

KATE BUSH
Jul. 30, 1958

RON BUSHY
Sep. 23, 1945

GEEZER BUTLER
Jul. 17, 1949

FLOYD BUTLER
Jun. 5, 1941

JERRY BUTLER
Dec. 8, 1939

JOE BUTLER
Jan. 19, 1943

PAUL BUTTERFIELD
Dec. 17, 1942

DAVID BYRON
Jan. 29, 1947

LARRY BYRON
Dec. 27, 1948

DAVID BYRNE
May 14, 1952

FRAN BYRNE
Mar. 17, 1948

ALAN CADDY
Feb. 2, 1940

CHARLOTTE CAFFEY
Oct. 21, 1953

RANDY CAIN
May 2, 1945

J. J. CALE
Dec. 5, 1938

JOHN CALE
Dec. 3, 1940

JOE CALLIS
May 2, 1955

RANDY CALIFORNIA
Feb. 20, 1951

BERNARD CALVERT
Sep. 16, 1943

GLEN CAMPBELL
Apr. 22, 1938

FREDDIE CANNON
Dec. 4, 1940

JIM CAPALDI
Aug. 24, 1944

BELINDA CARLISLE
Aug. 17, 1958

ERIC CARMEN
Aug. 11, 1949

KAREN CARPENTER
Mar. 2, 1950–Feb. 4, 1983

RICHARD CARPENTER
Oct. 15, 1946

PAUL CARRACK
Apr. 21, 1951

EARL "SPEEDOO" CARROLL
Nov. 2, 1937

ALVIN PLEASANT (A. P.)
CARTER
Apr. 15, 1891–Nov. 7, 1960

MAYBELLE ADDINGTON
CARTER
May 10, 1909–Oct. 23, 1978

SARA DOUGHERTY CARTER
Jul. 21, 1898–Jan. 9, 1979

ALAN CARTWRIGHT
Oct. 10, 1945

JACK CASADY
Apr. 13, 1944

HARRY WAYNE CASEY
Jan. 31, 1951

FRED CASH
Oct. 8, 1940

JOHNNY CASH
Feb. 26, 1932

ROSANNE CASH
May 24, 1955

DAVID CASSIDY
Apr. 12, 1950

ED CASSIDY
May 4, 1931

SHAUN CASSIDY
Sep. 27, 1958

JIMMY CASTOR
Jun. 22, 1943

PEPPY CASTRO
Jun. 16, 1949

JOANNE CATHERALL
Sep. 18, 1963

CLEM CATTINI
Aug. 28, 1939

FELIX CAVALIERE
Nov. 29, 1944

PETE CETERA
Sep. 13, 1944

JOHN CHADWICK
May 11, 1943

GERALD CHAMBERLAIN
Jan. 31, 1942

GEORGE CHAMBERS
Sep. 26, 1931

JOE CHAMBERS
Aug. 24, 1942

LESTER CHAMBERS
Apr. 13, 1940

WILLIE CHAMBERS
Mar. 3, 1938

BRYAN "CHAS" CHANDLER
Dec. 18, 1948

GENE CHANDLER
Jul. 6, 1940

BRUCE CHANNEL
Nov. 28, 1940

HARRY CHAPIN
Dec. 7, 1942–Jul. 16, 1981

MARSHALL CHAPMAN
Jan. 7, 1949

MICHAEL CHAPMAN
Jan. 24, 1948

ROGER CHAPMAN
Apr. 8, 1944

RAY CHARLES
Sep. 23, 1930

KERRY CHATER
Aug. 7, 1945

CHUBBY CHECKER (ERNEST EVANS)
Oct. 3, 1941

CLIFTON CHENIER
Jun. 25, 1925

CHER
May 20, 1946

ALEX CHILTON
Dec. 28, 1950

LOU CHRISTIE
Feb. 19, 1943

CHICK CHURCHILL
Jan. 2, 1949

AL CINER
May 14, 1947

JOHN CIPOLLINA
Aug. 24, 1943

RAOUL CITA
Feb. 11, 1928

ERIC CLAPTON
Mar. 30, 1945

DAVE CLARK
Dec. 15, 1942

DICK CLARK
Nov. 30, 1929

GENE CLARK
Nov. 17, 1941

PETULA CLARK
Nov. 15, 1932

ALLAN CLARKE
Apr. 15, 1942

MARK CLARKE
Jul. 25, 1950

MICHAEL CLARKE
Jun. 3, 1944

MIKE CLARKE
Jul. 25, 1950

STANLEY CLARKE
Jun. 30, 1951

ADAM CLAYTON
Mar. 13, 1960

MERRY CLAYTON
Dec. 25, 1948

DAVID CLAYTON-THOMAS
Sep. 13, 1941

JESSICA CLEAVES
Dec. 10, 1943

ROD CLEMENTS
Nov. 17, 1947

ZAL CLEMINSON
May 4, 1949

DAVID "CLEM" CLEMPSON
Sep. 5, 1949

REV. JAMES CLEVELAND
Dec. 23, 1932

DOUG "COSMO" CLIFFORD
Apr. 24, 1945

PATSY CLINE
Sep. 8, 1932–Mar. 5, 1963

GEORGE CLINTON
Jul. 22, 1940

JEREMY CLYDE
Mar. 22, c. 1945

J. R. COBB
Feb. 5, 1944

RICK COBB
Nov. 5, 1948

BILLY COBHAM
May 16, 1944

EDDIE COCHRAN
Oct. 3, 1938–Apr. 17, 1960

JOE COCKER
May 20, 1944

CHARLIE COE
Nov. 19, 1944

DAVID ALLAN COE
Sep. 6, 1939

LEONARD COHEN
Sep. 21, 1934

CHARLES COLBERT
Aug. 30, 1944

NATALIE COLE
Feb. 6, 1950

ORNETTE COLEMAN
Mar. 19, 1930

JOHN FORD COLEY
Oct. 31, 1951

ALBERT COLLINS
Oct. 1, 1932

BOOTSY COLLINS
Oct. 26, 1951

JUDY COLLINS
May 1, 1939

CLARENCE COLLINS
Mar. 17, 1941

PHIL COLLINS
Jan. 31, 1951

BOBBY COLOMBY
Dec. 20, 1944

TONY COLTON
Feb. 11, 1942

TERRY COMER
Feb. 23, 1949

ARTHUR CONLEY
Apr. 1, 1946

BRIAN CONNOLLY
Oct. 5, 1948

RY COODER
Mar. 15, 1947

JEFF COOK
Aug. 27, 1949

STU COOK
Apr. 25, 1945

SAM COOKE
Jan. 22, 1935–Dec. 11, 1964

RITA COOLIDGE
May 1, 1944

RICKY COONCE
Aug. 1, 1947

ALICE COOPER (VINCENT FURNIER)
Dec. 25, 1945

COLIN COOPER
Oct. 7, 1939

RALPH COOPER
Apr. 6, 1951

STEWART COPELAND
Jul. 16, 1952

CHRIS COPPING
Aug. 29, 1945

MIKE CORBY
Jul. 3, 1955

CHICK COREA
Jun. 12, 1941

GLENN CORNICK
Apr. 24, 1947

GENE CORNISH
May 14, 1945

JOE CORRERO
Nov. 19, 1946

DAVID COSTELL
Mar. 15, 1944

LARRY CORYELL
Apr. 2, 1943

MICHAEL COTTEN
Jan. 25, 1950

JAMES COTTON
Jul. 1, 1935

PAUL COTTON
Feb. 26, 1943

JOHN COUGAR
Oct. 7, 1951

DON COVAY
Mar. 1938

DAVID COVERDALE
Sep. 22, 1949

GARY COVEYOU
Nov. 25, 1958

DENNIS COWAN
May 6, 1947

HOWARD COWART
Jun. 12, 1944

SIMON COWE
Apr. 1, 1948

BARRY COWSILL
Sep. 14, 1954

BILL COWSILL
Jan. 9, 1948

BOB COWSILL
Aug. 26, 1950

DICK COWSILL
Aug. 26, 1950

JOHN COWSILL
Mar. 2, 1956

PAUL COWSILL
Nov. 11, 1952

SUE COWSILL
May 20, 1960

KEVIN COYNE
Jan. 27, 1944

ANDY COX
Jan. 25, 1956

FLOYD CRAMER
Nov. 27, 1933

LOL CREME
Sep. 19, 1947

ROY CREWSDON
May 29, 1941

PETER CRISS (PETER CRISS-COULA)
Dec. 20, 1947

JIM CROCE
Jan. 10, 1943–Sep. 20, 1973

DASH CROFTS
Aug. 14, 1940

KEVIN CRONIN
Oct. 6, 1951

STEVE CROPPER
Oct. 21, 1941

DAVID CROSBY
Aug. 14, 1941

RODNEY CROWELL
Aug. 7, 1950

BURTON CUMMINGS
Dec. 31, 1947

GEORGE CUMMINGS
Jul. 28, 1938

BILL CUNNINGHAM
Jan. 23, 1950

MIKE CURB
Dec. 24, 1944

CHRIS CURTIS
Aug. 26, 1942

CLEM CURTIS
Nov. 28, 1940

SONNY CURTIS
May 9, 1937

MICHAEL D'ABO
Mar. 1, 1944

GEOFF DAKING
Dec. 8, 1947

ANGELO D'ALEO
Feb. 3, 1940

ROGER DALTREY
Mar. 1, 1944

DENNIS DALZIEL
Oct. 10, 1943

DINO DANELLI
Jul. 23, 1945

JEFFREY DANIELS
Aug. 24, 1957

RICK DANKO
Dec. 9, 1943

DON DANNEMANN
May 9, 1944

RON DANTE
Aug. 22, 1945

MIGUEL VICENS DANUS
Jun. 21, 1944

BOBBY DARIN
May 14, 1936–Dec. 20, 1973

SARAH DASH
May 24, 1942

PAT DAUGHERTY
Nov. 11, 1947

DEAN DAUGHTRY
Sep. 8, 1946

JOHNNY "JAY" DAVID
Aug. 8, 1942

LENNY DAVIDSON
May 30, 1944

DAVE DAVIES
Feb. 3, 1947

RAY DAVIES
Jun. 21, 1944

RICHARD DAVIES
Jul. 22, 1944

BILLY DAVIS, JR.
Jun. 26, 1940

REV. GARY DAVIS
Apr. 30, 1896–May 5, 1972

MILES DAVIS
May 25, 1926

SPENCER DAVIS
Jul. 17, 1942

TERESA DAVIS
Aug. 22, 1950

BRIAN "BLINKY" DAVISON
May 25, 1942

TOM DAWES
Jul. 25, 1944

CORY DAYE
Apr. 25, 1952

JOHN DEACON
Aug. 19, 1951

SANDY DEANE
Jan. 30, 1943

JOEY DEE
Jun. 11, 1940

TOMMY DEE
Nov. 3, 1946

DESMOND DEKKER
Jul. 16, 1942

BRAD DELP
Jun. 12, 1951

BENNY DEFRANCO
Jul. 11, 1954

MARISA DEFRANCO
Jul. 23, 1955

MERLINA DEFRANCO
Jul. 20, 1957

NINO DEFRANCO
Oct. 19, 1956

TONY DEFRANCO
Aug. 31, 1959

KEITH DENUNZIO
Apr. 27, 1958

VINNY DENUNZIO
Aug. 15, 1956

MIKE DENNIS
Jun. 3, 1943

SANDY DENNY
Jan. 6, 1941–Apr. 21, 1978

JOHN DENSMORE
Dec. 1, 1945

JOHN DENVER
Dec. 31, 1943

JACKIE DESHANNON
Aug. 21, 1944

WILLY DEVILLE
Aug. 27, 1953

TOMMY DEVITO
Jun. 19, 1936

NEIL DIAMOND
Jan. 24, 1941

DICK DIAMONDE
Dec. 28, 1947

MAGIC DICK (DICK SALWITZ)
May 13, 1945

B. B. DICKERSON
Aug. 3, 1949

BO DIDDLEY
Dec. 30, 1928

CHRIS DIFFORD
Apr. 11, 1954

DOUG DILLARD
Mar. 6, 1937

RODNEY DILLARD
May 18, 1942

FRANK DIMINO
Oct. 15, 1951

DION DIMUCCI
Jul. 18, 1939

WILLIE DIXON
Jul. 1, 1915

BILL DOGGETT
Feb. 6, 1916

DENNIS DOHERTY
Nov. 29, 1941

MICKEY DOLENZ
Mar. 8, 1945

FATS DOMINO
May 10, 1929

JERRY DONAHUE
Sep. 24, 1946

ROBERT "BO" DONALDSON
Jun. 13, 1954

LONNIE DONEGAN
Apr. 29, 1931

RAL DONNER
Feb. 10, 1943

DONOVAN
May 10, 1946

LEE DORMAN
Sep. 19, 1945

RAY DORSET
Mar. 21, 1946

LEE DORSEY
Dec. 24, 1924

LAMONT DOZIER
Jun. 16, 1941

DARYL DRAGON
Aug. 27, 1942

NICK DRAKE
Jun. 18, 1948–Nov. 25, 1974

CHRIS DREJA
Nov. 11, 1946

DANTE DROWTY
Sep. 8, 1941

SPENCER DRYDEN
Apr. 7, 1943

DENNIS DUNAWAY
Dec. 9, 1948

SLY DUNBAR
May 10, 1952

CLEVELAND DUNCAN
Jul. 23, 1935

GARY DUNCAN
Sep. 4, 1946

MALCOLM DUNCAN
Aug. 24, 1945

DONALD "DUCK" DUNN
Nov. 24, 1941

LARRY DUNN
Jun. 19, 1953

IAN DURY
May 12, 1942

BERNIE DWYER
Sep. 11, 1940

RON DYKE
Feb. 13, 1945

BOB DYLAN
May 24, 1941

COLIN EARL
May 6, 1942

SHEENA EASTON
Apr. 27, 1959

DUANE EDDY
Apr. 26, 1938

GRAEME EDGE
Mar. 30, 1942

JERRY EDMONTON
Oct. 24, 1946

DAVE EDMUNDS
Apr. 15, 1944

BERNARD EDWARDS
Oct. 31, 1952

DENNIS EDWARDS
Feb. 3, 1943

GORDON EDWARDS
Dec. 26, 1946

JONATHAN EDWARDS
Jul. 28, 1946

CASS ELLIOT
Sep. 19, 1943–Jul. 29, 1974

MIKE ELLIOT
Aug. 6, 1929

BOBBY ELLIOTT
Dec. 8, 1943

RAMBLIN' JACK ELLIOTT
Aug. 1, 1931

RON ELLIOTT
Oct. 21, 1943

BARBARA LAINE ELLIS
Feb. 20, 1940

RALPH ELLIS
Mar. 8, 1942

GREG ELMORE
Sep. 4, 1946

HARRY ELSTON
Nov. 4, 1938

RICHARD ELSWIT
Jul. 6, 1945

KEITH EMERSON
Nov. 2, 1944

SCOTT ENGEL
Jan. 9, 1944

RALPH ELLIS
Mar. 8, 1942

RAY ENNIS
May 26, 1942

BRIAN ENO
May 15, 1948

JOHN ENTWISTLE
Oct. 9, 1944

GREG ERRICO
Sep. 1, 1946

PETER ERSKINE
May 5, 1954

DAVID ESSEX
Jul. 23, 1947

"SLEEPY" JOHN ESTES
Jan. 25, 1903–Jun. 5, 1977

JOHN EVAN
Mar. 28, 1948

DAVE "THE EDGE" EVANS
Aug. 18, 1961

TOM EVANS
Jun. 21, 1947

DON EVERLY
Feb. 1, 1937

PHIL EVERLY
Jan. 19, 1939

FABIAN (FORTE)
Feb. 6, 1943

TOMMY "BUBBA" FACENDA
Nov. 10, 1939

JIMMIE FADDEN
Mar. 9, 1948

ADAM FAITH (JERRY
NELHAMS)
Jun. 23, 1940

AGNETHA "ANNA" FÄLTSKOG
Apr. 5, 1950

GEORGIE FAME
Jun. 26, 1943

MIMI FARIÑA
Apr. 30, 1945

RICHARD FARIÑA
1937–Apr. 30, 1966

CHRIS FARLOWE
Oct. 13, 1940

PETE FARNDON
1953–Apr. 14, 1983

MARK FARNER
Sep. 29, 1948

ERIC FAULKNER
Oct. 21, 1955

JOSE FELICIANO
Sep. 10, 1945

LEO FENDER
Aug. 10, 1909

JAY FERGUSON
May 10, 1947

MANUEL FERNANDEZ
Sep. 29, 1943

STEVE FERRONE
Apr. 25, 1950

BRYAN FERRY
Sep. 26, 1945

JIM FIELDER
Oct. 4, 1947

RICHARD FINCH
Jan. 25, 1954

MATHEW FISHER
Mar. 7, 1946

ROBERTA FLACK
Feb. 10, 1939

GORDON FLEET
Aug. 16, 1945

MICK FLEETWOOD
Jun. 24, 1942

HUGHIE FLINT
Mar. 15, 1942

EDDIE FLOYD
Jun. 25, 1935

DAN FOGELBERG
Aug. 13, 1951

JOHN FOGERTY
May 28, 1945

TOM FOGERTY
Nov. 9, 1941

WAYNE FONTANA
Oct. 28, 1945

FRANKIE FORD
Aug. 4, 1940

KIM FOWLEY
Jul. 21, 1942

CHARLIE FOXX
Oct. 23, 1939

INEZ FOXX
Sep. 9, 1942

PETER FRAMPTON
Apr. 22, 1950

CONNIE FRANCIS
Dec. 12, 1938

MICHAEL FRANCIS
Jun. 25, 1951

WILLIAM FRANCIS
Jan. 16, 1942

RICK FRANK
Feb. 12, 1942

ARETHA FRANKLIN
Mar. 25, 1942

MELVIN FRANKLIN
Oct. 12, 1942

MICHAEL FRANKS
Sep. 18, 1944

CHRIS FRANTZ
May 8, 1951

ANDY FRASER
Aug. 7, 1952

JOHN FRED
May 8, 1941

ALAN FREED
Dec. 15, 1922–Jan. 20, 1965

BOBBY FREEMAN
Jun. 13, 1940

ACE FREHLEY (PAUL
FREHLEY)
Apr. 22, 1951

DAVID FREIBERG
Aug. 24, 1938

GLENN FREY
Nov. 6, 1948

KINKY FRIEDMAN
Oct. 31, 1944

CRAIG FROST
Apr. 20, 1948

VAL FUENTES
Nov. 25, 1947

BOBBY FULLER
Oct. 22, 1943–Jul. 18, 1966

JESSE "LONE CAT" FULLER
Mar. 12, 1896–Jan. 29, 1976

RAYMOND "TIKI" FULWOOD
May 23, 1944

HARVEY FUQUA
Jul. 27, 1929

RICHIE FURAY
May 9, 1944

BILLY FURY
Apr. 17, 1941–Jan. 28, 1983

PETER GABRIEL
May 3, 1950

MELVYN GALE
Jan. 15, 1952

RORY GALLAGHER
Mar. 2, 1949

JERRY GARCIA
Aug. 1, 1942

CARL GARDNER
Apr. 29, 1928

KIM GARDNER
Jan. 27, 1946

ART GARFUNKEL
Nov. 5, 1942

LEIF GARRETT
Nov. 8, 1961

FREDDIE GARRITY
Nov. 14, 1940

TERRY GARTHWAITE
Jul. 11, 1938

BRUCE GARY
Apr. 7, 1952

LUIS GASCA
Mar. 23, 1940

DAVID GATES
Dec. 11, 1940

BOB GAUDIO
Nov. 17, 1942

PETE GAVIN
Sep. 9, 1946

MARVIN GAYE
Apr. 2, 1939

GLORIA GAYNOR
Sep. 7, 1949

RICKEY GAZDA
Jun. 18, 1952

J. GEILS (JEROME GEILS)
Feb. 20, 1946

BOB GELDOF
Oct. 5, 1954

BOBBIE GENTRY
Jul. 27, 1944

TEDDY GENTRY
Jan. 22, 1952

RINUS GERRITSEN
Aug. 9, 1946

ANDY GIBB
Mar. 5, 1958

BARRY GIBB
Sep. 1, 1947

ROBIN GIBB
Dec. 22, 1949

MAURICE GIBB
Dec. 22, 1949

MICHAEL GIBBONS
Dec. 29, 1953

RUSS GIGUERE
Oct. 18, 1943

GREG GIUFFRIA
Jul. 28, 1951

RONNIE GILBERT
Apr. 25, 1946

IAN GILLAN
Aug. 19, 1945

GARY GLITTER
May 8, 1944

ROGER GLOVER
Nov. 30, 1945

DONNA GODCHAUX
Aug. 22, 1947

KEITH GODCHAUX
Jul. 14, 1948–Jul. 23, 1980

PAUL GODDARD
Jun. 23, 1945

KEVIN GODLEY
Oct. 7, 1945

REX GOH
May 5, 1951

ANDREW GOLD
Aug. 2, 1951

BOBBY GOLDSBORO
Jan. 18, 1941

PABLO GOMEZ
Nov. 5, 1943

TONY GOMEZ
Dec. 13, 1938

IAN GOMM
Mar. 17, 1947

SAM GOODEN
Sep. 2, 1939

CUBA GOODING
Apr. 27, 1944

AL GOODMAN
Mar. 31, 1947

STEVE GOODMAN
Jul. 25, 1948

RONNIE GOODSON
Feb. 2, 1945

MYLES GOODWYN
Jun. 23, 1948

DERVIN GORDON
Jun. 19, 1948

FLORENCE LARUE GORDON
Feb. 4, 1944

LINCOLN GORDON
Jun. 29, 1948

BERRY GORDY, JR.
Nov. 28, 1929

LESLEY GORE
May 2, 1946

SCOTT GORHAM
Mar. 17, 1951

ALAN GORRIE
Jul. 19, 1946

GRAHAM GOULDMAN
May 10, 1946

ANTHONY GOURDINE
(LITTLE ANTHONY)
Jan. 8, 1941

BARRY GOUDREAU
Mar. 29, 1951

JOHNNY GRAHAM
Aug. 3, 1951

LARRY GRAHAM
Aug. 14, 1946

EDDY GRANT
Mar. 5, 1948

GEORGE GRANTHAM
Nov. 20, 1947

ALAN GRATZNER
Nov. 9, 1948

EDDIE GRAY
Feb. 27, 1948

LEE GRAZIANO
Nov. 9, 1943

RICK GRECH
Nov. 1, 1946

AL GREEN
Apr. 13, 1946

DAVID GREEN
Oct. 30, 1949

GARY GREEN
Nov. 20, 1950

JACK GREEN
Mar. 12, 1951

PETER GREEN
Oct. 29, 1946

NORMAN GREENBAUM
Nov. 20, 1942

FREDERICK DENNIS GREENE
Jan. 11, 1949

KARL GREENE
Jul. 31, 1947

DAVE GREENSLADE
Jan. 18, 1943

JIMMY GREENSPOON
Feb. 7, 1948

BRIAN GREENWAY
Oct. 1, 1951

ELLIE GREENWICH
Oct. 23, 1940

DALE "BUFFIN" GRIFFIN
Oct. 24, 1948

ROB GRILL
Nov. 5, 1944

DON GROLNICK
Sep. 23, 1947

LUTHER GROSVENOR
Dec. 23, 1949

KELLY GROUCUTT
Sep. 8, 1945

EDDIE GRUNDY
Mar. 10, 1948

HUGH GRUNDY
Mar. 6, 1945

DAVE GUARD
Nov. 19, 1934

WILLIAM GUEST
Jun. 2, 1941

GUITAR SLIM (EDDIE JONES)
Dec. 10, 1926–Feb. 7, 1959

ARLO GUTHRIE
Jul. 10, 1947

WOODY GUTHRIE (WOOD-
ROW WILSON GUTHRIE)
Jul. 14, 1912–Oct. 3, 1967

BILLY GUY
Jun. 20, 1936

STEVE HACKETT
Feb. 12, 1950

SAMMY HAGAR
Oct. 13, 1949

MERLE HAGGARD
Apr. 6, 1937

MALCOLM HALE
May 17, 1941–1968

BILL HALEY
Jul. 6, 1925–Feb. 9, 1981

BRUCE HALL
May 3, 1953

DARYL HALL
Oct. 11, 1949

JOHN HALL
Oct. 25, 1947

WILLIE HALL
Aug. 8, 1950

JOHNNY HALLIDAY
Jun. 15, 1943

DICK HALLIGAN
Aug. 29, 1943

PETE HAM
Apr. 27, 1947–Apr. 23, 1975

ROY HAMILTON
Apr. 16, 1929–Jul. 20, 1969

TOM HAMILTON
Dec. 31, 1951

JAN HAMMER
Apr. 17, 1948

PETE HAMMILL
Nov. 5, 1948

JEFFREY HAMMOND-
HAMMOND
Jul. 30, 1946

JOHN HAMMOND, SR.
Dec. 10, 1910

JOHN PAUL HAMMOND, JR.
Nov. 13, 1943

HERBIE HANCOCK
Apr. 12, 1940

JEFF HANNA
Jul. 1947

GLEN HARDIN
Apr. 18, 1939

TIM HARDIN
Dec. 23, 1941–Dec. 29, 1980

BRENDAN HARKIN
Dec. 10, 1948

STEVE HARLEY
Feb. 27, 1951

ROY HARPER
June 12, 1941

SLIM HARPO (JAMES MOORE)
Jan. 11, 1924–Jan. 31, 1970

BARBARA HARRIS
Aug. 18, 1949

DAMON HARRIS
Jul. 3, 1950

JET HARRIS
Jul. 6, 1939

DON "SUGARCANE" HARRIS
Jun. 13, 1939

PHILLIP HARRIS
Jul. 17, 1948

TIM HARRIS
Jan. 14, 1948

WYNONIE HARRIS
Aug. 24, 1915–Jun. 14, 1969

BOBBY HARRISON
Jun. 28, 1943

GEORGE HARRISON
Feb. 25, 1943

JERRY HARRISON
Feb. 21, 1949

MIKE HARRISON
Sep. 3, 1945

WILBERT HARRISON
Jan. 6, 1929

DEBORAH HARRY
Jul. 1, 1945

WILBERT HART
Oct. 19, 1947

WILLIAM HART
Jan. 17, 1945

JOHN HARTFORD
Dec. 30, 1937

ALEX HARVEY
Feb. 5, 1935–Feb. 1982

LES HARVEY
1947–May 3, 1972

JOHN HARTMAN
Mar. 18, 1950

SID HASHIAN
Aug. 17, 1949

DONNIE HATHAWAY
Oct. 1, 1945–Jan. 13, 1979

BOBBY HATFIELD
Aug. 10, 1940

RICHIE HAVENS
Jan. 21, 1941

DALE HAWKINS
Aug. 22, 1938

RONNIE HAWKINS
Jan. 10, 1935

SCREAMIN' JAY HAWKINS
Jul. 18, 1929

BARRY HAY
Aug. 16, 1948

PETER HAYCOCK
Apr. 4, 1952

JIMMY HAYES
Nov. 12, 1943

ISAAC HAYES
Aug. 6, 1938

LEE HAZELWOOD
Jul. 9, 1929

EDDIE HAZEL
Apr. 10, 1950

BOBBY HEBB
Jul. 26, 1941

DICK HECKSTALL-SMITH
Sep. 26, 1934

RICHARD HELL (RICHARD
MEYERS)
Oct. 2, 1949

LEVON HELM
May 26, 1942

BILL HENDERSON
Nov. 6, 1944

JIMMY HENDERSON
May 20, 1954

JIMI HENDRIX
Nov. 27, 1942–Sep. 18, 1970

NONA HENDRYX
Aug. 18, 1945

DON HENLEY
Jul. 22, 1947

ROBERT HENRIT
May 2, 1945

KEN HENSLEY
Aug. 24, 1945

CLARENCE "FROGMAN"
HENRY
Mar. 19, 1937

MARK HERNDON
May 11, 1955

MIKE HERON
Dec. 12, 1942

HEWETT
Oct. 1, 1957

ANTHONY HICKS
Dec. 16, 1943

DAN HICKS
Dec. 9, 1941

DAVE HILL
Apr. 4, 1952

JESSIE HILL
Dec. 9, 1932

STEVE HILL
Mar. 13, 1950

CHRIS HILLMAN
Dec. 4, 1942

BILLY HINSCHE
Jun. 29, 1953

JON HISEMAN
Jun. 21, 1944

RUSSELL HITCHCOCK
Jun. 15, 1949

BOB "BEAR" HITE
Feb. 26, 1945–Apr. 5, 1981

GENE HOLDER
Jul. 10, 1954

NODDY HOLDER
Jun. 15, 1950

CHAS HODGES
Nov. 11, 1943

BRIAN HOLLAND
Feb. 15, 1941

BUDDY HOLLY
Sep. 7, 1938–Feb. 3, 1959

EDDIE HOLLAND
Oct. 30, 1939

LES HOLROYD
Mar. 12, 1948

PETER HOLSAPPLE
Feb. 19, 1956

DEREK HOLT
Jan. 26, 1949

ISAAC HOLT
May 16, 1932

JAMES HONEYMAN-SCOTT
Nov. 4, 1957–Jun. 16, 1982

JOHN LEE HOOKER
Aug. 22, 1917

LIGHTNIN' HOPKINS (SAM HOPKINS)
Mar. 15, 1912–Jan. 30, 1982

MARY HOPKIN
May 3, 1950

NICKY HOPKINS
Feb. 24, 1944

KEITH HOPWOOD
Oct. 26, 1946

JOHNNY HORTON
Apr. 30, 1927–Nov. 5, 1960

WALTER HORTON (AKA "SHAKEY")
Apr. 6, 1910–Dec. 8, 1982

MICHAEL HOSSACK
Sep. 18, 1950

SON HOUSE (EDDIE HOUSE)
Mar. 21, 1902

STEVE HOWE
Apr. 8, 1947

HOWLIN' WOLF (CHESTER ARTHUR BURNETT)
Jun. 10, 1910–Jan. 10, 1976

GARTH HUDSON
Aug. 2, c. 1943

MIKE HUGG
Aug. 11, 1942

LEON HUGHES
Jun. 20, 1936

ALAN HULL
Feb. 20, 1945

ANDY HUMMELL
Jan. 26, 1951

ALBERTA HUNTER
Apr. 1, 1895

IAN HUNTER
Jun. 3, 1946

IVORY JOE HUNTER
Oct. 10, 1914–Nov. 8, 1974

MISSISSIPPI JOHN HURT
Jul. 3, 1893–Nov. 2, 1966

SHEILA HUTCHINSON
Jan. 17, 1953

WANDA HUTCHISON
Dec. 17, 1951

DANNY HUTTON
Sep. 10, 1946

RICK HUXLEY
Aug. 5, 1942

BRIAN HYLAND
Nov. 12, 1943

JERRY HYMAN
May 19, 1947

CHRISSIE HYNDE
Sep. 7, 1952

JANIS IAN
May 7, 1951

DOUG INGLE
Sep. 9, 1946

NEIL INNES
Dec. 9, 1944

TONY IOMMI
Feb. 19, 1948

O'KELLY ISLEY
Dec. 25, 1937

RONALD ISLEY
May 21, 1941

RUDOLPH ISLEY
Apr. 1, 1939

AL JACKSON
Nov. 27, 1935–Oct. 1, 1975

CHUCK JACKSON
Jul. 22, 1937

JERMAINE LAJAUNE JACKSON
Dec. 11, 1954

JOE JACKSON
Aug. 11, 1955

MAHALIA JACKSON
Oct. 26, 1911–Jan. 27, 1972

MARLON JACKSON
Mar. 12, 1957

MICHAEL JACKSON
Aug. 29, 1958

RAY JACKSON
Dec. 12, 1948

SIGMUND ESCO (JACKIE) JACKSON
May 4, 1951

TONY JACKSON
Jul. 16, 1940

TORIANO ADARYLL (TITO) JACKSON
Oct. 15, 1953

STEVEN RANDALL (RANDY) JACKSON
Oct. 29, 1961

WANDA JACKSON
Oct. 20, 1937

MICK JAGGER
Jul. 26, 1943

ELMORE JAMES
Jan. 27, 1918–May 24, 1963

RICK JAMES
Feb. 1, 1952

TOMMY JAMES
Apr. 29, 1947

BERT JANSCH
Nov. 3, 1943

AL JARDINE
Sep. 3, 1942

"BLIND" LEMON JEFFERSON
Jul. 1897–Dec. 1930

BARRY JENKINS
Dec. 22, 1944

WAYLON JENNINGS
Jun. 15, 1937

JOAN JETT
Sep. 22, 1960

EDDIE JOBSON
Apr. 28, 1955

BILLY JOEL
May 9, 1949

JAI JOHANNY JOHANSON
Jul. 8, 1944

DAVID JOHANSEN
Jan. 9, 1950

ELTON JOHN
Mar. 25, 1947

LITTLE WILLIE JOHN (WILLIAM J. WOODS)
Nov. 15, 1937–May 27, 1968

ALPHONSE JOHNSON
Feb. 2, 1951

GEORGE JOHNSON
May 17, 1953

GENERAL NORMAN JOHNSON
May 23, 1943

LOUIS JOHNSON
Apr. 13, 1955

RALPH JOHNSON
Jul. 4, 1951

ROBERT JOHNSON
May 8, 1911–Aug. 16, 1938

ROBERT JOHNSON
Mar. 21, 1953

BRUCE JOHNSTON
Jun. 24, 1944

BOOKER T. JONES
Dec. 11, 1944

BRIAN JONES
Feb. 28, 1942–Jul 3, 1969

DAVY JONES
Dec. 30, 1945

EDDIE "GUITAR SLIM" JONES
Dec. 10, 1926

GRACE JONES
May 19, 1952

JOHN PAUL JONES (JOHN BALDWIN)
Jun. 3, 1946

KENNEY JONES
Sep. 16, 1948

MICK JONES
Jun. 26, 1956

MICKEY JONES
Dec. 17, 1952

PETE JONES
Sep. 22, 1957

PHALIN JONES
1949–Dec. 10, 1967

QUINCY JONES
Mar. 14, 1933

RAYMOND JONES
Oct. 20, 1939

RICKIE LEE JONES
Nov. 8, 1954

SANDRA "PUMA" JONES
Oct. 5, 1953

TOM JONES
Jun. 7, 1940

JANIS JOPLIN
Jan. 19, 1943–Oct. 4, 1970

LONNIE LEROY JORDAN
Nov. 21, 1948

SETH JUSTMAN
Jan. 27, 1951

HARVEY KAGAN
Apr. 18, 1946

ERNIE K–DOE (ERNEST KADOR, JR.)
Feb. 22, 1936

JIM KALE
Aug. 11, 1943

MIKE KAMINSKY
Sep. 2, 1951

HOWIE KANE
Jun. 6, 1942

PAUL KANTNER
Mar. 12, 1942

TERRY KATH
Jan. 31, 1946–Jan. 23, 1978

STEVE KATZ
May 9, 1945

JORMA KAUKONEN
Dec. 23, 1940

KEVIN KAVANAUGH
Aug. 27, 1951

JOHN KAY
Apr. 12, 1944

HOWARD KAYLAN
Jun. 22, 1945

KENNETH KELLEY
Jan. 9, 1943

MIKE KELLIE
Mar. 24, 1947

H. ANN KELLY
Apr. 24, 1947

BETTY KELLY
Sep. 16, 1944

SCOTT "TOP TEN" KEMPNER
Feb. 6, 1954

EDDIE KENDRICKS

CHRIS KENNER
Dec. 25, 1929

RIK KENTON
Oct. 3, 1945

RICHARD KERMODE
Oct. 5, 1946

DOUG KERSHAW
Jan. 24, 1936

CHAKA KHAN
Mar. 23, 1953

JOHNNY KIDD (FREDERICK HEATH)
Dec. 23, 1939–Oct. 7, 1966

KING CURTIS (CURTIS OUSLEY)
Feb. 7, 1934–Aug. 13, 1971

KING FLOYD
Feb. 13, 1945

ALAN "BAM" KING
Sep. 18, 1946

ALBERT KING
Apr. 25, 1923

B. B. KING
Sep. 16, 1925

BEN E. KING (BENJAMIN EARL SOLOMAN HENDERSON)
Sep. 28, 1938

CAROLE KING
Feb. 9, 1942

EARL KING (SOLOMON JOHNSON)
Feb. 7, 1934

FREDDIE KING
Sep. 3, 1934–Dec. 28, 1976

JONATHAN KING (KENNETH KING)
Dec. 6, 1948

PAUL KING
Jan. 9, 1948

SIMON KIRKE
Jul. 28, 1948

DANNY KIRWAN
May 13, 1950

DANNY KLEIN
May 13, 1946

GLADYS KNIGHT
May 28, 1944

MERALD "BUBBA" KNIGHT
Sep. 4, 1942

STAN KNIGHT
Feb. 12, 1949

TERRY KNIGHT
Apr. 9, 1943

DAVE KNIGHTS
Jun. 28, 1945

MARK KNOPFLER
Aug. 12, 1949

KEN KNOX
Dec. 15, 1951

KEITH KNUDSEN
Oct. 18, 1952

CUB KODA
Oct. 1, 1948

MICHAEL KOGEL
Apr. 25, 1945

AL KOOPER
Feb. 5, 1944

GEORGE KOOYMANS
Mar. 11, 1948

ALEXIS KORNER
Apr. 19, 1928

PAUL KOSSOFF
Sep. 14, 1950–Mar. 19, 1976

LEO KOTTKE
Sep. 11, 1945

BILLY J. KRAMER (WILLIAM HOWARD ASHTON)
Aug. 19, 1943

JOEY KRAMER
Jun. 21, 1950

PHIL KRAMER
Jul. 12, 1952

WAYNE KRAMER
Apr. 30, 1948

BILL KREUTZMANN
Apr. 7, 1946

ROBBIE KRIEGER
Jan. 8, 1946

KRIS KRISTOFFERSON
Jun. 22, 1937

NORMAN KUHLKE
Jun. 12, 1942

PATTIE LABELLE
Oct. 4, 1944

DAVID LAFLAMME
Apr. 5, 1941

RAY LAIDLAW
May 28, 1948

DENNY LAINE
Oct. 29, 1944

RICK LAIRD
Feb. 5, 1941

GREG LAKE
Nov. 10, 1948

ROBERT LAMM
Oct. 13, 1944

ALAN LANCASTER
Feb. 7, 1949

MAJOR LANCE
Apr. 4, 1941

BOB LANG
Jan. 10, 1946

RONNIE LANE
Apr. 1, 1948

STEVE LANG
Mar. 24, 1949

ANNE LANTREE
Aug. 28, 1943

JOHN LANTREE
Aug. 20, 1940

STACY LATTISAW
Nov. 25, 1966

JERRY LAWSON
Jan. 23, 1944

LEADBELLY (HUDDIE LEDBETTER)
Jan. 20, 1889–Dec. 6, 1949

JIMMY LEA
Jun. 14, 1952

BERNIE LEADON
Jul. 19, 1947

SIMON LEBON
Oct. 27, 1958

DEREK LECKENBY
May 14, 1945

ALBERT LEE
Dec. 21, 1943

ALVIN LEE
Dec. 19, 1944

BARBARA LEE
May 16, 1947

BEVERLY LEE
Aug. 3, 1941

BRENDA LEE
Dec. 11, 1944

CLAIR LEE
Apr. 24, 1944

CURTIS LEE
Oct. 28, 1941

DICKEY LEE (DICK LIPSCOMB)
Sep. 21, 1943

GEDDY LEE
Jul. 29, 1953

LEONARD LEE
Jun. 29, 1935

RIC LEE
Oct. 20, 1945

GARY LEEDS
Sep. 3, 1944

THIJS VAN LEER
Mar. 31, 1948

JOHN LEES
Jan. 13, 1948

JERRY LEIBER
Apr. 25, 1933

JOHN LENNON
Oct. 9, 1940–Dec. 8, 1980

PHIL LESH
Mar. 15, 1940

GREG LESKIW
Aug. 5, 1947

EDDIE LEVERT
Jun. 16, 1942

BARBARA LEWIS
Feb. 9, 1944

BOBBY LEWIS
Feb. 17, 1933

FURRY LEWIS (WALTER LEWIS)
Mar. 6, 1893–Sep. 14, 1981

GARY LEWIS (GARY LEVITCH)
Jul. 31, 1946

JERRY LEE LEWIS
Sep. 29, 1935

RAMSEY LEWIS
May 27, 1935

SMILEY LEWIS (OVERTON AMOS LEMONS)
Jul. 5, 1920–Oct. 7, 1966

ALEX LIFESON
Aug. 27, 1953

GORDON LIGHTFOOT
Nov. 17, 1938

EARL "WIRE" LINDO
Jan. 7, 1953

ARTO LINDSAY
May 28, 1953

MARK LINDSAY
Mar. 9, 1942

LARRY LINGLE
Apr. 4, 1949

MANCE LIPSCOMB
Apr. 9, 1895–Jan. 30, 1976

FRED LIPSIUS
Nov. 19, 1943

JIMMY LITHERLAND
Sep. 6, 1949

LITTLE EVA (EVA NARCISSUS
BOYD)
Jun. 29, 1945

LITTLE MILTON (MILTON
CAMPBELL)
Sep. 17, 1934

LITTLE RICHARD (RICHARD
PENNIMAN)
Dec. 25, 1932

LITTLE WALTER (MARION
WALTER JACOBS)
May 1, 1930–Feb. 15, 1968

BUNNY LIVINGSTON
Apr. 10, 1947

PAT LLOYD
Mar. 17, 1948

JOHN LOCKE
Sep. 25, 1943

DENNIS LOCORRIERE
Jun. 13, 1949

KENNY LOGGINS
Jan. 7, 1948

GARY LOIZZO
Aug. 16, 1945

JACKIE LOMAX
May 10, 1944

ROY LONEY
Apr. 13, 1946

ALAN LONGMUIR
Jun. 20, 1953

DEREK LONGMUIR
Mar. 19, 1955

JON LORD
Jun. 9, 1941

JOHN LOUDERMILK
Mar. 31, 1934

BARBARA LOVE
Jul. 24, 1941

MIKE LOVE
Mar. 15, 1941

WINFRED "BLUE" LOVETT
Nov. 16, 1943

NICK LOWE
Mar. 25, 1949

TREVOR LUCAS
Dec. 25, 1943

PETER LUCIA
Feb. 2, 1947

LULU
Nov. 3, 1948

JOHN LYDON (JOHNNY
ROTTEN)
Jan. 31, 1956

FRANKIE LYMON
Sep. 30, 1942–Feb. 28, 1968

TIM LYNCH
Jul. 18, 1946

LORETTA LYNN
Apr. 14, 1935

LEO LYONS
Nov. 30, 1944

SOUTHSIDE JOHNNY LYON
Dec. 4, 1948

TIM LYNCH
Jul. 18, 1946

PHILIP LYNOTT
Aug. 20, 1951

BARBARA LYNN
Jan. 16, 1942

JEFF LYNNE
Dec. 30, 1947

PETER MACBETH
Feb. 2, 1943

ROBIN MACDONALD
Jul. 18, 1943

ANDY MACKAY
Jul. 23, 1946

BRIAN MACLEOD
Jun. 25, 1952

JOHNNY MAESTRO
May 7, 1939

WESLEY MAGOOGAN
Oct. 11, 1951

TAJ MAHAL
May 17, 1942

MELISSA MANCHESTER
Feb. 15, 1951

CHUCK MANGIONE
Nov. 29, 1940

JIM DANDY MANGRUM
Mar. 30, 1948

BARRY MANILOW
Jun. 17, 1946

HANDSOME DICK MANITOBA
Jan. 29, 1954

BARRY MANN
Feb. 9, 1939

MANFRED MANN
Oct. 21, 1940

TONY MANSFIELD
May 28, 1943

RICHARD MANUEL
Apr. 3, 1945

PHIL MANZANARA
Jan. 31, 1951

RAY MANZAREK
Feb. 12, 1935

JOHN "JOCKO" MARCELLINO
May 13, 1950

MITCHEL MARGO
May 25, 1947

FRANK MARINO
Aug. 22, 1954

BOB MARLEY
Apr. 6, 1945–May 11, 1981

STEVE MARRIOTT
Jan. 30, 1947

GERRY MARSDEN
Sep. 24, 1942

FREDDIE MARSDEN
Nov. 23, 1940

VINCENT MARTELL
Nov. 11, 1945

DEWEY MARTIN
Sep. 30, 1942

DINO MARTIN, JR.
Nov. 17, 1953

LUCI MARTIN
Jan. 10, 1955

JERRY MARTINI
Oct. 1, 1943

HANK B. MARVIN
Oct. 28, 1941

DAVE MASON
May 10, 1947

NICK MASON
Jan. 27, 1945

NICK MASSI
Sep. 19, 1935

CARLO MASTANGELO
Oct. 5, 1938

JOHNNY MATHIS
Sep. 30, 1935

DAVE MATTACKS
Mar. 1948

JOHN MAUS
Nov. 12, 1943

HARRY JACK MAX
Sep. 6, 1942

BRIAN MAY
Jul. 19, 1947

PHIL MAY
Nov. 9, 1944

JOHN MAYALL
Nov. 29, 1943

CURTIS MAYFIELD
Jun. 3, 1942

PAUL MCCANDLESS
Mar. 24, 1947

JIMMY MCCARTY
Jul. 25, 1943

PAUL MCCARTNEY
Jun. 18, 1942

DELBERT MCCLINTON
Nov. 4, 1940

MARILYN MCCOO
Sep. 30, 1943

VAN MCCOY
Jan. 6, 1944–Jul. 6, 1979

CHET MCCRACKEN
Jul. 17, 1952

JIMMY MCCULLOCH
Aug. 13, 1953–Sep. 27, 1979

DAVID MCCULLOUGH
Jul. 18, 1945

COUNTRY JOE MCDONALD
Jan. 1, 1942

ROBIN MCDONALD
Jul. 18, 1943

HUGH MCDOWELL
Jul. 31, 1953

MISSISSIPPI FRED MCDOWELL
Jan. 12, 1904–Jul. 3, 1972

ELAINE "SPANKY" MCFAR-
LANE
Jun. 19, 1942

JOHN MCFEE
Nov. 18, 1953

PEGGY SANTIGLIA
MCGANNON
May 4, 1944

MIKE MCGEAR
Jan. 7, 1944

PAT MCGLYNN
Mar. 31, 1958

BROWNIE MCGHEE
Nov. 30, 1915

ROGER MCGUINN
Jul. 13, 1942

BARRY MCGUIRE
Oct. 15, 1937

ELLEN MCILWAINE
Oct. 1, 1948

ROBBIE MCINTOSH
1950–Sep. 23, 1974

ONNIE MCINTYRE
Sep. 25, 1945

GOLDY MCJOHN
May 1, 1945

AL MCKAY
Feb. 2, 1948

LESLIE MCKEOWN
Nov. 12, 1955

RON "PIGPEN" MCKERNAN
Sep. 8, 1945–Mar. 8, 1973

IAN MCLAGAN
May 12, 1946

JOHN MCLAUGHLIN
Jan. 4, 1942

DON MCLEAN
Oct. 2, 1945

LAMONTE MCLEMORE
Sep. 17, 1940

JOHN MCNALLY
Aug. 3, 1941

BIG JAY MCNEELY
Apr. 29, 1928

CLYDE MCPHATTER
Nov. 15, 1933–Jun. 13, 1972

T. S. "TONY" MCPHEE
Mar. 22, 1944

DON MCPHERSON
Jul. 9, 1941–Jul. 4, 1971

CHRISTINE PERFECT MCVIE
Jul. 12, 1943

JOHN MCVIE
Nov. 26, 1945

PUNKY MEADOWS
Feb. 6, 1950

RON MEAGHER
Oct. 2, 1941

MEAT LOAF (MARTIN ADAY)
Sep. 27, 1947

ROGER MEADOWS
Jul. 26, 1949

BILL MEDLEY
Sep. 19, 1940

HANK MEDRESS
Nov. 19, 1938

TONY MEEHAN
Mar. 2, 1942

RANDY MEISNER
Mar. 8, 1946

PHYLLIS "JIGGS" ALLBUT
MEISTER
Sep. 24, 1942

MELANIE (SAFKA)
Feb. 3, 1947

JERRY MERCER
Apr. 27, 1939

FREDDIE MERCURY
Sep. 5, 1946

MERRICK
Mar. 3, 1954

JIM MESSINA
Dec. 5, 1947

AUGIE MEYER
May 31, 1941

TERRY LEE MIALL
Nov. 8, 1958

JOE MICELLI
Jul. 9, 1946

LEE MICHAELS
Nov. 24, 1945

"MICHAL"
Apr. 20, 1949

BETTE MIDLER
Dec. 1, 1945

FRED MILANO
Aug. 22, 1939

AMOS MILBURN
Apr. 1, 1927–Jan. 3, 1980

BUDDY MILES
Sep. 5, 1946

CHARLES WILLIAM MILLER
Jun. 2, 1939

JERRY MILLER
Jul. 10, 1943

STEVE MILLER
Oct. 5, 1943

KENNY MINNEAR
Apr. 2, 1948

GARNETT MIMMS
Nov. 26, 1937

IAN MITCHELL
Aug. 22, 1958

JONI MITCHELL
Nov. 7, 1943

GARY MOFFET
Jun. 22, 1949

JOEY MOLLAND
Jun. 21, 1948

MICHAEL MONARCH
Jul. 5, 1950

JUNE MONTIERO
Jul. 1, 1946

KEITH MOON
Aug. 23, 1947–Sep. 7, 1978

TONY MOON
Sep. 21, 1941

THOM MOONEY
Jan. 5, 1948

GLENN MOORE
Oct. 28, 1941

PETE MOORE
Nov. 19, 1939

SAM MOORE
Oct. 12, 1935

PATRICK MORAZ
Jun. 24, 1948

IKUE ILE MORI
Dec. 17, 1953

JIM MORRISON
Dec. 8, 1943–Jul. 3, 1971

VAN MORRISON
Aug. 31, 1945

STEVE MORSE
Jul. 28, 1954

EVERETT MORTON
Apr. 5, 1951

BOB MOSLEY
Dec. 4, 1942

ALPHONSE MOUZON
Nov. 21, 1948

DAVID MOYSE
Nov. 5, 1957

MARIA MULDAUR
Sep. 12, 1943

DAVID MUNDEN
Dec. 2, 1943

ELLIOTT MURPHY
Mar. 16, 1949

WALLY MURPHY
Aug. 26, 1954

MARTIN MURRAY
Oct. 7, 1941

MOON MULLICAN
Mar. 29, 1909–Jan. 1, 1967

GRAHAM NASH
Feb. 2, 1942

JOHNNY NASH
Aug. 19, 1940

JERRY NAYLOR
Mar. 6, 1939

CHUCK NEGRON
Jun. 8, 1942

JOE NEGRONI
Sep. 9, 1940–1977

RICK NELSON
May 8, 1940

SANDY NELSON
Dec. 1, 1938

WILLIE NELSON
Apr. 30, 1933

MICHAEL NESMITH
Dec. 30, 1942

RANDY NEWMAN
Nov. 28, 1944

GEORGE NEWSOME
Aug. 14, 1947

OLIVIA NEWTON-JOHN
Sep. 26, 1948

STEVIE NICKS
May 26, 1948

HARRY NILSSON
Jun. 15, 1941

PETER NOONE
Nov. 5, 1947

CARLO NOVI
Aug. 7, 1949

TED NUGENT
Dec. 13, 1948

GARY NUMAN
Mar. 1958

PHILIP OAKEY
Oct. 2, 1955

RAYMOND BERRY OAKLEY
Apr. 4, 1948–Nov. 11, 1972

JOHN OATES
Apr. 7, 1949

PHIL OCHS
Dec. 19, 1940–Apr. 9, 1976

CHRIS O'CONNELL
Mar. 21, 1952

ODETTA
Dec. 31, 1930

MIKE OLDFIELD
May 15, 1953

OLIVER
Feb. 22, 1945

YOKO ONO
Feb. 18, 1935

ROY ORBISON
Apr. 23, 1936

JIMMY O'ROURKE
Mar. 14, 1947

OZZY OSBOURNE
Dec. 3, 1948

LEE OSKAR
Mar. 24, 1948

ALAN OSMOND
Jun. 22, 1949

DONNY OSMOND
Dec. 9, 1957

JAY OSMOND
Mar. 22, 1955

JIMMY OSMOND
Apr. 16, 1963

MARIE OSMOND
Oct. 13, 1959

MERRILL OSMOND
Apr. 30, 1953

WAYNE OSMOND
Aug. 28, 1951

GILBERT O'SULLIVAN
Dec. 1, 1946

JOHNNY OTIS
Dec. 8, 1921

SHUGGIE OTIS
Nov. 30, 1953

JOHN OTWAY
Oct. 2, c. 1952

RANDY OWEN
Dec. 13, 1949

WALTER "CLYDE" OWEN
Dec. 13, 1949

JIMMY PAGE
Jan. 9, 1944

IAN PAICE
Jun. 29, 1948

CARL PALMER
Mar. 20, 1951

JOHN "POLI" PALMER
May 25, 1943

ROBERT PALMER
Jan. 19, 1949

JAMES PANKOW
Aug. 20, 1947

FELIX PAPPALARDI
1939–Apr. 17, 1983

WALTER PARAZAIDER
Mar. 14, 1945

RICHARD PARFITT
Oct. 12, 1948

FRED PARRIS
Mar. 26, 1936

BARBARA PARRITT
Oct. 1, 1944

JUNIOR PARKER
Mar. 3, 1927–Nov. 18, 1971

VAN DYKE PARKS
Jan. 3, 1941

GRAM PARSONS
Nov. 5, 1946–Sep. 19, 1973

DOLLY PARTON
Jan. 19, 1946

JACO PASTORIUS
Dec. 1, 1951

EDWARD PATTEN
Aug. 2, 1939

BILLY PAUL
Dec. 1, 1934

LES PAUL
Jan. 9, 1915

TOM PAXTON
Oct. 31, 1937

FREDA PAYNE
Sep. 19, 1945

SHERRI PAYNE
Nov. 14, 1944

DENNIS PAYTON
Aug. 11, 1943

NEIL PEART
Sep. 12, 1952

DAVE PEGG
Nov. 2, 1947

ANN PEEBLES
Apr. 27, 1947

MIKE PENDER
Mar. 3, 1942

MICHAEL PENDERGAST
Mar. 3, 1942

CARL PERKINS
Apr. 9, 1932

JOE PERRY
Sep. 10, 1950

GARRY PETERSON
May 26, 1945

JOHN PETERSON
Jan. 8, 1945

RAY PETERSON
Apr. 23, 1939

SYLVIA PETERSON
Sep. 30, 1946

ESTHER PHILLIPS
Dec. 23, 1935

JOHN PHILLIPS
Aug. 30, 1935

MICHELLE PHILLIPS
Apr. 6, 1944

SAM PHILLIPS
Jan. 5, 1923

NIGEL PICKERING
Jun. 15, 1929

BOBBY "BORIS" PICKETT
Feb. 11, 1940

ROBERT PICKETT
Dec. 11, 1945

WILSON PICKETT
Mar. 18, 1941

MIKE PINDER
Dec. 12, 1942

MIKE PINERA
Sep. 29, 1948

BILLY PINKNEY
Aug. 15, 1925

MARCO PIRRONI
Apr. 27, 1959

GENE PITNEY
Feb. 17, 1941

ROBERT PLANT
Aug. 20, 1948

JEROME "DOC" POMUS
Jun. 27, 1925

JEAN-LUC PONTY
Sep. 29, 1942

BRIAN POOLE
Nov. 3, 1941

CHARLES M. PORTZ
Mar. 28, 1945

JOHN POVEY
Aug. 20, 1944

DON POWELL
Sep. 10, 1950

DAVID PRATER
May 9, 1937

ELVIS PRESLEY
Jan. 8, 1935–Aug. 16, 1977

REG PRESLEY
Jun. 12, 1943

BILLY PRESTON
Sep. 9, 1946

JOHNNY PRESTON
Aug. 18, 1930

ALAN PRICE
Apr. 19, 1942

LLOYD PRICE
Mar. 9, 1934

STEVE PRIEST
Feb. 23, 1950

PRINCE
Jun. 7, 1960

PRAIRIE PRINCE
May 7, 1950

MELVYN JOHN PRITCHARD
Jan. 20, 1948

P. J. PROBY
Nov. 6, 1938

PROFESSOR LONGHAIR
Dec. 10, 1918–Jan. 30, 1980

GARY PUCKETT
Oct. 17, 1942

BOBBY PURIFY
Sep. 2, 1939

JAMES PURIFY
May 12, 1944

PETE QUAIFE
Dec. 27, 1943

SUZI QUATRO
Jun. 3, 1950

ROBERT QUINE
Dec. 30, 1942

DEREK QUINN
May 24, 1942

EDDIE RABBITT
Nov. 27, 1944

BONNIE RAITT
Nov. 8, 1949

MICK RALPHS
Mar. 31, 1948

DEE DEE RAMONE
Sep. 18, 1952

JOEY RAMONE
May 19, 1952

AL RAMSEY
Jul. 27, 1943

TEDDY RANDAZZO
May 20, 1937

JIMMY RANDELL
Feb. 14, 1949

RICHIE RANNO
Jan. 21, 1950

DANNY RAPP
May 10, 1941–Apr. 1983

LOU RAWLS
Dec. 1, 1935

HARRY RAY
Dec. 15, 1946

JOHNNIE RAY
Jan. 10, 1927

MICHAEL RAY
Dec. 24, 1962

ROBERT RAYMOND
Mar. 4, 1946

OTIS REDDING
Sep. 9, 1941–Dec. 10, 1967

HELEN REDDY
Oct. 4, 1942

JERRY REED
Mar. 20, 1937

JIMMY REED
Sep. 6, 1925–Aug. 29, 1976

LOU REED
Mar. 2, 1944

TERRY REED
Mar. 20, 1937

MARTHA REEVES
Jul. 18, 1941

TONY REEVES
Apr. 18, 1943

TERRY REID
Nov. 13, 1949

LARRY REINHARDT
Jul. 7, 1948

KEITH RELF
Mar. 22, 1943–May 14, 1976

NICK REYNOLDS
Jul 27, 1933

RICKY REYNOLDS
Oct. 29, 1948

HARRIS RHOAD
Oct. 1, 1944

RANDY RHOADS
1956–Mar. 19, 1982

NICK RHODES
Jun. 8, 1962

CLIFF RICHARD
Oct. 14, 1940

KEITH RICHARDS
Dec. 18, 1943

GARY RICHRATH
Oct. 18, 1949

GREG RIDLEY
Oct. 23, 1947

WILL RIGBY
Mar. 17, 1956

JEANNIE C. RILEY
Oct. 19, 1945

MINNIE RIPERTON
Nov. 8, 1947–Jul 12, 1979

JOHNNY RIVERS
Nov. 7, 1942

ROBBIE ROBERTSON
Jul. 5, 1944

CYNTHIA ROBINSON
Jan. 12, 1946

WILLIAM SMOKEY ROBINSON
Feb. 19, 1940

SYLVIA ROBINSON
May 6, 1936

MAGGIE ROCHE
Oct. 26, 1951

SUZZY ROCHE
Sep. 29, 1956

TERRE ROCHE
Apr. 10, 1953

JIM RODFORD
Jul. 7, 1945

JIMMIE RODGERS
Sep. 8, 1897–May 26, 1933

NILE RODGERS
Sep. 19, 1952

PAUL RODGERS
Dec. 12, 1949

TOMMY ROE
May 9, 1942

RANKING ROGER
Feb. 21, 1961

BOBBY ROGERS
Feb. 19, 1940

KENNY ROGERS
Aug. 21, 1941

LINDA RONSTADT
Jul. 15, 1946

DUANE ROLAND
Dec. 3, 1952

FRANK ROSENTHAL
Nov. 12, 1941

ROSS THE BOSS
Jan. 3, 1954

DIANA ROSS
Mar. 26, 1944

MICHAEL ROSE
Jul. 11, 1957

FRANK ROSENTHAL
Nov. 12, 1941

RONALD ROSMAN
Feb. 28, 1945

FRANCIS ROSSI
Apr. 29, 1949

JOHN ROSTILL
Jun. 16, 1942–Nov. 26, 1973

DAVID LEE ROTH
Oct. 10, 1955

RICK ROTHWELL
Mar. 11, 1944

DAVE ROWBERRY
Dec. 27, 1943

RAY ROYER
Oct. 8, 1945

PHILLIP RUDD
May 19, 1946

DAVID RUFFIN
Jan. 18, 1941

BERT RUITER
Nov. 26, 1946

TODD RUNDGREN
Jun. 22, 1948

BILLY RUSH
Aug. 26, 1952

TOM RUSH
Feb. 8, 1941

JIMMY RUSHING
Aug. 26, 1903–Jun. 8, 1972

GRAHAM RUSSELL
Jun. 1, 1950

JOSEPH "JESSE" RUSSELL
Sep. 25, 1939

KARL RUSSELL
Apr. 10, 1947

LEON RUSSELL
Apr. 2, 1941

MICHAEL RUTHERFORD
Oct. 2, 1950

BOBBY RYDELL
Apr. 26, 1942

DOUG SAHM
Nov. 6, 1941

BUFFY SAINTE-MARIE
Feb. 20, 1941

CRISPIAN ST. PETERS
Apr. 5, 1944

PAUL SAMWELL-SMITH
May 8, 1943

MARTY SANDERS
Feb. 28, 1941

SAMANTHA SANG
Aug. 5, 1953

CARLOS SANTANA
Jul. 20, 1947

JORGE SANTANA
Jun. 13, 1954

HERMAN SANTIAGO
Feb. 18, 1941

TONY SANTINI
Aug. 3, 1948

PATTIE SANTOS
Nov. 16, 1949

ARNIE SATIN
May 11, 1943

RAY SAWYER
Feb. 1, 1937

LEO SAYER
May 21, 1948

BOZ SCAGGS
Jun. 8, 1944

RALPH SCALA
Dec. 12, 1947

MEL SCHACHER
Apr. 3, 1951

TIMOTHY SCHMIT
Oct. 30, 1947

GINA SCHOCK
Aug. 31, 1957

TOM SCHOLZ
Mar. 10, 1947

DICK SCOPPETTONE
Jul. 5, 1945

ANDY SCOTT
Jul. 30, 1949

BON SCOTT
Jul. 9, 1946–Feb. 19, 1980

HOWARD E. SCOTT
Mar. 15, 1946

TOM SCOTT
May 19, 1948

JIMMY SEALS
Oct. 17, 1941

JOHN SEBASTIAN
Mar. 17, 1944

NEIL SEDAKA
Mar. 13, 1939

PETE SEEGER
May 3, 1919

BOB SEGER
May 6, 1945

JAY SEIGEL
Oct. 20, 1939

DANNY SERAPHINE
Aug. 28, 1948

ROBBIE SHAKESPEARE
Sep. 27, 1953

BOB SHANE
Feb. 1, 1934

DEL SHANNON
Dec. 30, 1939

SANDIE SHAW
Feb. 26, 1947

FRAN SHEEHAN
Mar. 26, 1949

BOBBY SHERMAN
Jul. 22, 1945

ADNY SHERNOFF
Apr. 19, 1952

JERRY SHIRLEY
Feb. 4, 1952

WAYNE SHORTER
Aug. 25, 1933

DEREK SHULMAN
Feb. 2, 1947

PHIL SHULMAN
Aug. 27, 1937

RAY SHULMAN
Dec. 8, 1949

MORT SHUMAN
Nov. 12, 1936

PATRICK SIMMONS
Jan. 23, 1950

CARLY SIMON
June 25, 1945

PAUL SIMON
Oct. 13, 1942

SCOTT SIMON
Dec. 9, 1948

NINA SIMONE
Feb. 21, 1933

DERRICK "DUCKIE" SIMPSON
June 24, 1950

VALERIE SIMPSON
Aug. 26, 1948

NANCY SINATRA
Jun. 8, 1940

RODNEY DESBOROUGH
SLATER
Nov. 8, 1944

GRACE SLICK
Oct. 30, 1939

DAVE BRUCE SMALLEY
Jul. 10, 1949

HUEY "PIANO" SMITH
Jan. 26, 1934

JEROME SMITH
Jun. 18, 1953

"LEGS" LARRY SMITH
Jan. 18, 1944

MICHAEL LEE SMITH
Oct. 9, 1951

MIKE SMITH
Dec. 6, 1943

NEAL SMITH
Sep. 23, 1947

O. C. SMITH
Jun. 21, 1936

PATTI SMITH
Dec. 31, 1946

RAY SMITH
Jul. 9, 1943

SAMMI SMITH
Aug. 5, 1943

WARREN SMITH
May 14, 1934

FLOYD SNEED
Nov. 22, 1943

PHOEBE SNOW
Jul. 17, 1952

LEW SOLOFF
Feb. 20, 1944

JOE SOUTH
Feb. 28, 1942

ROGER RUSKIN SPEAR
Jun. 29, 1943

PHIL SPECTOR
Dec. 25, 1940

RONNIE BENNETT SPECTOR
Aug. 10, 1943

CHRIS SPEDDING
Jun. 17, 1944

SKIP SPENCE
Apr. 18, 1946

JEREMY SPENCER
Jul. 4, 1948

CHARLIE SPINOZA
Dec. 29, 1948

DUSTY SPRINGFIELD
Apr. 16, 1939

RICK SPRINGFIELD
Aug. 23, 1949

BRUCE SPRINGSTEEN
Sep. 23, 1949

BILLY SQUIER
May 12, 1950

CHRIS SQUIRE
Mar. 4, 1948

CHRIS STAMEY
Dec. 6, 1954

PETER STAMPFEL
Oct. 29, 1930

VIVIAN STANSHALL
Mar. 21, 1943

ROEBUCK "POPS" STAPLES
Dec. 2, 1915

EDWIN STARR
Jan. 21, 1942

RINGO STARR (RICHARD
STARKEY)
Jul. 7, 1940

JOHN STEEL
Feb. 4, 1941

DAVID STEELE
Sep. 8, 1960

TOMMY STEELE
Dec. 17, 1936

ROGER STEEN
Nov. 13, 1949

CHRIS STEIN
Jan. 5, 1950

MARK STEIN
Mar. 11, 1947

JODY STEPHENS
Oct. 4, 1952

CAT STEVENS
Jul. 21, 1947 or 1948

TONY STEVENS
Sep. 12, 1949

AL STEWART
Sep. 5, 1945

ERIC STEWART
Jan. 20. 1945

JOHN STEWART
Sep. 5, 1939

ROD STEWART
Jan. 10. 1945

STEWKEY (ROBERT ANTONI)
Nov. 17, 1947

STEPHEN STILLS
Jan. 3, 1945

STING (GORDON SUMNER)
Oct. 2, 1951

WALLY STOCKER
Mar. 17, 1954

MIKE STOLLER
Mar. 13, 1933

FREDDIE STONE
Jun. 5, 1946

ROSIE STONE
Mar. 21, 1945

SLY STONE
Mar. 15, 1944

PAUL STOOKEY
Nov. 30, 1937

RICHARD STREET
Oct. 5, 1942

KEITH STRICKLAND
Oct. 26, 1953

BARRETT STRONG
Feb. 5, 1941

HAMISH STUART
Oct. 8, 1949

RE STYLES
Mar. 3, 1950

DONNA SUMMER
Dec. 31, 1948

ANDY SUMMERS
Dec. 31, 1942

JERRY SUMMERS
Dec. 29, 1942

RICHARD SUSSMAN
Mar. 28, 1946

BILLY SWAN
May 12, 1944

DAVE SWARBRICK
Apr. 5, 1947

PETER SWEVEL
Apr. 13, 1948

CHARMAINE ELAINE SYLVERS
Mar. 9, 1954

EDMUND THEODORE SYL-
VERS
Jan. 25, 1957

FOSTER EMERSON SYLVERS
Feb. 25, 1962

JAMES JONATHAN SYLVERS
Jun. 8, 1955

JOSEPH RICHARD SYLVERS
Oct. 13, 1958

LEON FRANK SYLVERS
Mar. 7, 1943

OLYMPIA-ANN SYLVERS
Oct. 13, 1951

TERRY SYLVESTER
Jan. 8, 1945

GARY TALLEY
Aug. 17, 1947

NEDRA TALLEY
Jan, 27, 1946

RICHARD TANDY
Mar. 26, 1948

BERNIE TAUPIN
May 22, 1950

ALDER TAYLOR
Sep. 10, 1951

ANDY TAYLOR
Feb. 16, 1961

JAMES TAYLOR
Aug. 16, 1953

JAMES TAYLOR
Mar. 12, 1948

JOHN TAYLOR
Jun. 20, 1960

JOHNNIE TAYLOR
May 5, 1958

KATE TAYLOR
Aug. 15, 1949

KOKO TAYLOR
Sep. 28, 1935

LARRY TAYLOR
Jun. 26, 1942

LIVINGSTON TAYLOR
Nov. 21, 1950

MICK TAYLOR
Jan. 17, 1948

ROGER TAYLOR
Jul. 26, 1949

ANTONE "CHUBBY" TAVARES
Jun. 2, 1950

ARTHUR "POOCH" TAVARES
Nov. 12, 1949

FELICIANO "BUTCH" TAVARES
May 18, 1953

PERRY LEE "TINY" TAVARES
Oct. 24, 1954

RALPH TAVARES
Dec. 10, 1948

RITCHIE TEETER
Mar. 16, 1951

TED TEMPLEMAN
Oct. 24, 1944

TONI TENNILLE
May 8, 1943

JOE TERRANOVA
Jan. 30, 1941

"SONNY" TERRY
Oct. 24, 1911

TAMMY TERRELL
1946–Mar. 16, 1970

JOE TEX
Aug. 8, 1933–Aug. 12, 1982

B. J. THOMAS
Aug. 27, 1942

DENNIS THOMAS
Feb. 9, 1951

RAY THOMAS
Dec. 29, 1942

RUFUS THOMAS
Mar. 26, 1917

PAUL THOMPSON
May 13, 1951

RICHARD THOMPSON
Apr. 3, 1949

BIG MAMA THORNTON
Dec. 11, 1926

BLAIR THORNTON
Jul. 23, 1950

GARY TIBBS
Jan. 25, 1958

SONNY TIL
Aug. 18, 1925–Dec. 9, 1981

GLENN TILLBROOK
Aug. 31, 1957

JOHNNY TILLOTSON
Apr. 20, 1939

TINY TIM
Apr. 12, 1925

PETER TOLSON
Sep. 10, 1951

STEVEN PEREGRINE TOOK
Jul. 28, 1949–Oct. 27, 1980

PETER TORK
Feb. 13, 1944

DEAN TORRENCE
Mar. 10, 1941

PETER TOSH
Oct. 19, 1944

RALPH TOWNER
Mar. 1, 1940

ROB TOWNSEND
Jul. 7, 1947

PETE TOWNSHEND
May 19, 1945

RON TOWNSON
Jan. 20, 1941

MARY TRAVERS
Nov. 7, 1937

ROBIN TROWER
Mar. 9, 1945

GARY TROXEL
Nov. 28, 1939

JAMES RAY TUCKER
Oct. 17, 1946

MICK TUCKER
Jul. 17, 1948

TANYA TUCKER
Oct. 10, 1958

FRED TURNER
Oct. 16, 1943

IKE TURNER
Nov. 4, 1931

JOE TURNER
May 18, 1911

TINA TURNER
Nov. 26, 1938

MARY TRAVERS
Nov. 7, 1937

DWIGHT TWILLEY
Jun. 6, c. 1952

STEVEN TYLER
Mar. 26, 1948

IAN TYSON
Sep. 25, 1933

SYLVIA TYSON
Sep. 19, 1940

BJÖRN ULVAEUS
Apr. 25, 1945

DINO VALENTI
Nov. 7, 1943

HILTON VALENTINE
May 21, 1943

KATHY VALENTINE
Jan. 7, 1959

SAL VALENTINO
Sep. 8, 1942

RITCHIE VALENS
May 13, 1941–Feb. 3, 1959

FRANKIE VALLI
May 3, 1937

ROSS VALORY
Mar. 22, 1942

KENNY VANCE
Dec. 9, 1943

HARRY VANDA
Mar. 22, 1947

PIERRE VAN DER LINDEN
Feb. 19, 1946

ALEX VAN HALEN
May 8, 1955

EDWARD VAN HALEN
Jan. 26, 1957

THIJS VAN LEER
Mar. 31, 1948

CARSON VAN OSTEN
Sep. 24, 1946

DAVE VAN RONK
Jun. 30, 1936

BOBBY VEE
Apr. 30, 1943

BILLY VERA
May 28, 1944

HENRY VESTINE
Dec. 24, 1944

MICHAEL VICKERS
Apr. 18, 1941

GENE VINCENT
Feb. 11, 1943–Oct. 12, 1971

MIROSLAV VITOUS
Dec. 6, 1947

MARK VOLMAN
Apr. 19, 1944

KLAUS VOORMANN
Apr. 29, 1942

BONO VOX
May 10, 1960

BUNNY WAILER
Apr. 10, 1947

LOUDON WAINRIGHT III
Sep. 5, 1946

JOHN WAITE
Jul. 4, 1955

TOM WAITS
Dec. 7, 1949

DAVE WAKELING
Feb. 19, 1956

RICK WAKEMAN
May 18, 1949

JERRY JEFF WALKER
Mar. 16, 1942

T-BONE WALKER
May 28, 1910–Mar. 16, 1975

BILL WALLACE
May 18, 1949

GORDON WALLER
Jun. 4, 1945

JOE WALSH
Nov. 20, 1947

ALAN WARD
Dec. 12, 1945

ALAN WARNER
Apr. 21, 1947

CLINT WARWICK
Jun. 25, 1949

DIONNE WARWICK
Dec. 12, 1941

DINAH WASHINGTON
Aug. 29, 1924–Dec. 14, 1963

GROVER WASHINGTON, JR.
Dec. 12, 1943

JAYOTIS WASHINGTON
May 12, 1945

ROGER WATERS
Sep. 6, 1944

MUDDY WATERS
Apr. 4, 1915–Apr. 30, 1983

JODY WATLEY
Jan. 30, 1961

JOHNNY "GUITAR" WATSON
Feb. 3, 1935

CHARLIE WATTS
Jun. 2, 1941

OVEREND PETE WAITS
May 13, 1947

FEE WAYBILL
Sep. 17, 1950

CARL WAYNE
Aug. 18, 1944

JIMMY WEBB
Aug. 15, 1946

JOHNNY WEIDER
Apr. 21, 1947

BOB WEIR
Oct. 16, 1947

JERRY WEISS
May 1, 1946

BOB WELCH
Jul. 31, 1946

BRUCE WELCH
Nov. 2, 1941

CORY WELLS
Feb. 5, 1944

JUNIOR WELLS
Dec. 9, 1934

MARY WELLS
May 13, 1943

LESLIE WEST
Oct. 22, 1945

RICKY WESTWOOD
May 7, 1943

JOHN WETTON
Jul. 12, 1949

JERRY WEXLER
Jan. 10, 1917

TINA WEYMOUTH
Nov. 22, 1950

PAUL WHEATBREAD
Feb. 8, 1946

IAN WHITCOMB
Jul. 10, 1941

ALAN WHITE
Jun. 14, 1949

BARRY WHITE
Sep. 12, 1944

BUKKA WHITE
Nov. 12, 1906–Feb. 26, 1977

CARL WHITE
1932–Jan. 7, 1980

CHRISTOPHER TAYLOR
WHITE
Mar. 7, 1943

CLARENCE WHITE
Jun. 6, 1944–Jul. 1973

FREDDIE WHITE
Jan. 13, 1955

MAURICE WHITE
Dec. 19, 1941

RONNIE WHITE
Apr. 5, 1939

TONY JOE WHITE
Jul. 23, 1943

VERDINE WHITE
Jul. 25, 1951

BRAD WHITFORD
Feb. 23, 1952

CHARLIE WHITNEY
Jun. 4, 1944

CLIFF WILLIAMS
Dec. 14, 1949

CURTIS WILLIAMS
Dec. 11, 1962

HANK WILLIAMS
Sept. 17, 1923–Jan. 1, 1953

HANK WILLIAMS, JR.
May 26, 1949

LARRY WILLIAMS
May 10, 1935–Jan. 2, 1980

MASON WILLIAMS
Aug. 24, 1938

MAURICE WILLIAMS
Apr. 26, 1938

OTIS WILLIAMS
Oct. 23, 1949

TONY WILLIAMS
Dec. 12, 1945

PAUL WILLIAMS
Sep. 19, 1940–Aug. 17, 1973

WALTER WILLIAMS
Aug. 25, 1942

ROBIN WILLIAMSON
Nov. 24, 1943

SONNY BOY WILLIAMSON
(JOHN LEE)
Mar. 30, 1914–Jun. 1, 1948

SONNY BOY WILLIAMSON
(ALECK MILLER)
Dec. 5, 1899–May 25, 1965

CHUCK WILLIS
Jan. 31, 1928–April 10, 1958

AL WILSON
Jun. 19, 1939

ALAN WILSON
Jul. 4, 1943–Sep. 3, 1970

ANN WILSON
Jun. 19, 1951

B. J. WILSON
Mar. 18, 1947

BRIAN WILSON
Jun. 20, 1942

CARL WILSON
Dec. 21, 1946

CINDY WILSON
Feb. 28, 1957

DENNIS WILSON
Dec. 4, 1944

DON WILSON
Feb. 10, 1937

JACKIE WILSON
Jun. 9, 1934

MARY WILSON
Mar. 6, 1944

NANCY WILSON
Mar. 16, 1954

RON WILSON
Feb. 5, 1933

JESSE WINCHESTER
May 17, 1944

CHUCK WINFIELD
Feb. 5, 1943

WILLIAM WINFIELD
Aug. 24, 1929

EDGAR WINTER
Dec. 28, 1946

JOHNNY WINTER
Feb. 23, 1944

KURT WINTER
Apr. 2, 1946

DAVE WINTHROP
Nov. 27, 1948

MUFF WINWOOD
Jun. 14, 1943

STEVE WINWOOD
May 12, 1948

BILL WITHERS
Jul. 4, 1938

PETER WOLF
Mar. 7, 1946

STEWART "WOOLY" WOL-
STENHOLME
Apr. 15, 1947

BOBBY WOMACK
Mar. 4, 1944

STEVIE WONDER
May 13, 1950

CHRIS WOOD
Jun. 24, 1944–Jul. 12, 1983

RON WOOD
Jun. 1, 1947

ROY WOOD
Nov. 8, 1946

DANNY WOODS
Apr. 10, 1944

ANDREW WOOLFOLK
Oct. 11, 1950

BERNIE WORRELL
Apr. 19, 1944

BETTY WRIGHT
Dec. 21, 1953

EARNEST WRIGHT, JR.
Aug. 24, 1941

GARY WRIGHT
Apr. 26, 1943

NORMAN WRIGHT
Oct. 21, 1937

O. V. WRIGHT
Oct. 9, 1939

RICHARD WRIGHT
Jul. 28, 1945

STEVIE WRIGHT
Dec. 20, 1948

BILL WYMAN
Oct. 24, 1941

ZAL YANOVSKY
Dec. 19, 1944

PETER YARROW
May 31, 1938

ROY YEAGER
Feb. 4, 1946

PETE YORK
Aug. 15, 1942

BILL YOUNG
May 25, 1942

GEORGE YOUNG
Nov. 6, 1947

JESSE COLIN YOUNG
Nov. 11, 1944

MALCOLM YOUNG
Jan. 6, 1953

NEIL YOUNG
Nov. 12, 1945

RUSTY YOUNG
Feb. 23, 1946

ROBIN ZANDER
Jan. 23, 1952

FRANK ZAPPA
Dec. 21, 1940

JOSEF ZAWINUL
Jul. 7, 1932

DAVE ZELMON
Nov. 15, 1951

WARREN ZEVON
Jan. 24, 1947

1954 Fats Domino (2); Muddy Waters, Guitar Slim (4); Bill Haley, Joe Turner (5); The Chords, Johnny Otis (6); Ruth Brown, The Crew-Cuts (7); LaVern Baker (8); The Drifters (9)

1955 Alan Freed (10); Etta James (12); The Penguins (13); The Nutmegs, Bo Diddley (14); Pat Boone (15); Les Paul and Mary Ford, Johnnie Ray (16); The Cadillacs (17)

1956 Elvis Presley (18); Little Richard (20); Carl Perkins (21); The Everly Brothers (22); Elvis Presley (23); Elvis Presley, Gene Vincent (24); Elvis Presley, Maurice Williams and the Zodiacs (25)

1957 Buddy Holly (26); Elvis Presley (28); The Diamonds, Frankie Lymon (29); Isley Brothers (30); Dick Clark (31); Buddy Holly (32); Ricky Nelson (33)

1958 Chuck Berry (34); Buddy Holly (36); Dion and the Belmonts (37); Jerry Lee Lewis, The Platters (38); Ray Charles (39); The Big Bopper, The Teddy Bears (40); Sam Cooke, Eddie Cochran (41)

1959 The Everly Brothers (42); Frankie Avalon (44); The Coasters, Clyde McPhatter (45); Fabian (46); Cliff Richard, Bobby Darin (47); Paul Anka, Neil Sedaka (48); Jan and Dean (49)

1960 Connie Francis (50); Jesse Belvin (52); Elvis Presley, Lonnie Donegan (53); Joan Baez, The Kingston Trio (54); Duane Eddy, Ike and Tina Turner (55); The Flamingos, Maurice Williams and the Zodiacs (56); Mary Wells, The Drifters (57)

1961 Bob Dylan (58); Carla Thomas, The Miracles (60); Chris Kenner (61); Chuck Berry, Patsy Cline (62); The Marvelettes, Chubby Checker (63); Dion (64); The Tokens (65)

1962 Smokey Robinson and the Miracles (66); Jackie Wilson, Dee Dee Sharp (68); Gary "U.S." Bonds (69); Cliff Richard, Dusty Springfield (70); The Four Seasons, Little Eva (71); Stevie Wonder, Marvin Gaye (72); The Tornadoes (73)

1963 Stevie Wonder, Lesley Gore (74); Ruby and the Romantics (76); Bobby "Blue" Bland (77); Jackie Wilson (78); Jan and Dean (79); Cilla Black (80); Bobby Vee (81)

1964 The Beatles (82); Phil Spector (84); Phil Ochs (85); Cassius Clay, Mary Wells (86); The Impressions (87); The Dave Clark 5 (89); The Animals (90); Petula Clark, Sam Cooke (95)

1965 The Rolling Stones (96); The Kinks (98); Screaming Jay Hawkins (99); Freddie and the Dreamers (100); The Temptations, Gerry and the Pacemakers (101); The Beatles, Sonny and Cher (104); The Small Faces (105); The Who, Len Barry (106); Joe Tex (107); Bob Dylan (108)

1966 The Supremes (110); Wilson Pickett (115); The Lovin' Spoonful (119); The Beatles (120); Paul Revere and the Raiders (122)

1967 The Doors (124); Pete Townshend, The Bee Gees (127); Traffic (128); Beatles (131); Jerry Lee Lewis (133); Cass Elliot (136)

1968 The Jefferson Airplane (138); Jimi Hendrix (140); Otis Redding (142); Cream (144); Traffic (145); Tiny Tim (148); The MC5 (149)

1969 The Who (152); Steppenwolf, Tyrannosaurus Rex (155); Tina Turner (157)

1970 Simon and Garfunkel (166); The Who (169); The Faces, Tammi Terrell and Marvin Gaye (170); Crosby, Stills and Nash (172); Derek and the Dominos (173); Stevie Wonder, Jim Morrison (176); Ray Davies (178); Joni Mitchell (179)

1971 Marvin Gaye (180); Mick Jagger (182); Donny Osmond (183); Three Dog Night (185); George Harrison, Freda Payne (189); Pink Floyd, Carole King (190); Rick Nelson (191); Issac Hayes (192)

1972 Marc Bolan (194); Melanie, Don McLean (196); Joe Tex (198); Harry Nilsson (199); Roberta Flack (200); Bobby Gentry (201); Procol Harum (203); The Spinners, Joe Cocker (205)

1973 David Bowie (208); Slade (211); Roger Daltrey (213); Loggins and Messina (214); Gladys Knight (219); Cat Stevens (220); Gary Glitter, Jim Croce (221)

1974 Eric Clapton (222); Gene Simmons (224); Barry White (225); Eric Carmen (226); The Eagles, David Bowie (227); Frank Zappa (228); John Lennon (230); King Crimson (232); Quincy Jones, Sly Stone (233); Harry Chapin, Mott the Hoople (235)

1975 The Eagles (236); Linda Ronstadt (239); Graham Parker and the Rumour (244); Bad Company (245); Queen (248); Donna Summer (249)

1976 Peter Frampton (250); Willie Nelson (253); Bruce Springsteen (255); Abba (257); Steve Miller (258); Steely Dan (260); The Commodores (261)

1977 The Bee Gees (264); Rod Stewart (266); Daryl Hall and John Oates (268); The Sex Pistols (272); Debby Boone (276); Billy Joel (277)

1978 Johnny Rotten (278); Stevie Wonder (280); The Rutles (282); Patti Smith (283); Lou Reed (284); Bruce Springsteen (285); Eddie Money (286); John Travolta and Olivia Newton-John (288); Peter Tosh (289); The Cars (290); Parliament-Funkadelic (291)

1979 The Knack (292); Twisted Sister (296); B. B. King (297); Rick Nielsen of Cheap Trick (298); Ian Hunter (299); Minnie Riperton, Ted Nugent (300); Led Zeppelin (303); Marianne Faithfull (304)

1980 The Police (306); Blondie (311); Meat Loaf, The Grateful Dead (313); Linda Ronstadt, David Bowie (314); Diana Ross (316); Devo (318)

1981 The Jacksons (320); Prince (322); The Police, REO Speedwagon (324); The Clash (325); Daryl Hall and John Oates (326); AC/DC (327); Bruce Springsteen (328); Simon and Garfunkel (330); The Pretenders, Adam Ant (331); George Benson (332); Human League, Elvis Costello (333)

1982 Men at Work (334); The J. Geils Band (337); Elton John (338); The Go-Go's (339); Roxy Music (341); Pink Floyd (343); The Cars, Chicago (344); Dave Edmunds, John Cougar (345)

ABOUT THE CONTRIBUTORS

Philip Bashe was formerly managing editor of *Good Times* and *Focus,* publisher of *Foxtrot,* a staff writer for the *Buffalo Evening News* and a progressive FM radio announcer. He has contributed to *Trouser Press* and *On Your Own,* and is currently senior editor at *Circus.*

Ken Braun has written biographies of musicians for the *Rolling Stone Encyclopedia of Rock & Roll* and the *Annual Obituary.* He currently contributes to the *Record.*

Wayne King is assistant editor of the *Record.* He was formerly a staff member at *Trouser Press* and contributed to the *Rolling Stone Encyclopedia of Rock & Roll* and the *Rolling Stone Record Guide.*

Michael Shore, a former editor of *SoHo News* and *Home Video,* has written about music, video and related matters for the *Village Voice, Omni, Musician, Music Sound Output, ARTnews* and *Popular Computing.* He also contributed to the *Rolling Stone Encyclopedia of Rock & Roll.*